CRITICAL REALISM

Since the publication of Roy Bhaskar's *A Realist Theory of Science* in 1975, critical realism has emerged as one of the most powerful new directions in the philosophy of science and social science, offering a real alternative to both positivism and post modernism. This reader is designed to make accessible in one volume, to lay person and academic, student and teacher alike, key readings to stimulate debate about and within critical realism.

The four parts of the reader correspond to four parts of the writings of Roy Bhaskar:

- part one explores the transcendental realist philosophy of science elaborated in *A Realist Theory of Science*
- the second section examines Bhaskar's critical naturalist philosophy of social science
- part three is devoted to the theory of explanatory critique, which is central to critical realism
- the final part is devoted to the theme of dialectic, which is central to Bhaskar's most recent writings

The volume includes extracts from Bhaskar's most important books, as well as selections from all of the other most important contributors to the critical realist programme. The volume also includes both a general introduction and original introductions to each section.

CRITICAL REALISM

Essential Readings

Edited by Margaret Archer, Roy Bhaskar, Andrew Collier, Tony Lawson and Alan Norrie

London and New York

First published 1998
by Routledge
11 New Fetter Lane, London EC4P 4EE

Simultaneously published in the USA and Canada
by Routledge
29 West 35th Street, New York, NY 10001

© 1998 Selection and editorial matter Margaret Archer, Roy Bhaskar,
Andrew Collier, Tony Lawson and Alan Norrie

Typeset in Garamond by RefineCatch Limited, Bungay, Suffolk
Printed and bound in Great Britain by
TJ International Ltd, Padstow, Cornwall

All rights reserved. No part of this book may be reprinted or reproduced or utilized in any form or by any electronic, mechanical, or other means, now known or hereafter invented, including photocopying and recording, or in any information storage or retrieval system, without permission in writing from the publishers.

British Library Cataloguing in Publication Data
A catalogue record for this book is available from the British Library

Library of Congress Cataloguing in Publication Data
A catalogue record for this book has been requested

ISBN 0–415–19631–0 (hbk)
ISBN 0–415–19632–9 (pbk)

CONTENTS

GENERAL INTRODUCTION

Critical realism is a movement in philosophy and the human sciences and cognate practices most closely associated with – in the sense of identified with or emanating from – though by no means restricted to – the work of Roy Bhaskar. This movement is now fully international and multidisciplinary and arguably in the quarter century since the initial publication of *A Realist Theory of Science* (1975) has transformed the intellectual scene. At least, at the turn of the millennium it presents an intellectual challenge to other philosophies that they can scarcely refuse. This reader is designed to make accessible, in one volume, to layperson and academic, student and teacher alike, key readings to stimulate debate about and within critical realism.[1]

The four parts of the reader correspond to four parts of the writings of Roy Bhaskar: section one to his *transcendental realist* philosophy of science, elaborated in RTS (1975, 1978) and subsequently augmented and refined; section two to his *critical naturalist* philosophy of social science, first systematically presented in PON (1979, 1989, 1998) and likewise developed; section three to the theory of *explanatory critique* implicit in PON, elaborated in a number of articles published in the early 1980s (see e.g. RR Chapter 6) and most fully in SRHE (1986); and section four to the theme of *dialectic* on which Bhaskar had published since the early 1980s but only fully developed in DPF (1993) (and PE (1994)). Extracts from all four canonical books are included below. These theories did not appear in an intellectual vacuum and this introduction will say something about the context in which they arose as well as their principal features.

The term 'critical realism' arose by elision of the phrases 'transcendental realism' and 'critical naturalism', but Bhaskar and others in this movement have accepted it since 'critical', like 'transcendental', suggested affinities with Kant's philosophy, while 'realism' indicated the differences from it. It should be noted that the principal themes of each section both presuppose and develop the themes of the sections preceding it, so that there is a definite ordination to 'critical realism'. Thus Bhaskar refers to the philosophy espoused in DPF and PE as 'dialectical critical realism' and this does radically refine and rework the theories of science, social science and ethics presented earlier; as he has indicated they will be further recast in his turn to the third (totalizing) and fourth (reflexive or transformatively practical) moments of his dialectical philosophy. Something will now be said about the context and content of the theories of transcendental realism, critical naturalism, explanatory critique and dialectic sequentially by way of general introduction to the readings excerpted below.

Transcendental realism

Transcendental realism was born in the context of vigorous critical activity oriented against the positivist conception of science that had dominated the first two-thirds of the twentieth century. This was based squarely on Humean empiricism, epitomized in the claim of Mach[2] that 'natural laws were nothing but the mimetic reproduction of facts in thought, the object of which is to replace and save the trouble of new experience'. It is perhaps most familiar to us retrospectively in the guise of the logical positivism of the Vienna circle of the 1920s and 1930s which married the epistemological empiricism and reductionism of Mach, Pearson and Duhem with the logical innovations of Frege, Russell and Wittgenstein. The positivist vision of science pivoted on a *monistic* theory of scientific development and a *deductivist* theory of scientific structure. The attack on the former came from three main sources. First, from Popper and (ex-) Popperians like Lakatos and Feyerabend who argued that it was falsifiability, not verifiability, that was the hallmark of science and that it was precisely in revolutionary breakthroughs such as those associated with Galileo or Einstein that its epistemological significance lay. Second, from Kuhn and other historians and sociologists of science who drew scrupulous attention to the real social processes involved in the reproduction and transformation of scientific knowledge in what critical realism called the transitive (epistemological and geo-historical-social) dimension of science. Finally, from Wittgensteinians such as Hanson, Toulmin and Sellars who latched on to the non-atomistic or theory-dependent and mutable character of facts in science.

A problem for all these trends was to sustain a clear concept of the continued independent *reality* of *being* – of the intransitive or ontological dimension – in the face of the *relativity* of our *knowledge* – in the transitive or epistemological dimension. This arose particularly acutely in the debate about the possibility and, according to Kuhn and Feyerabend, the actuality of meaning variance as well as inconsistency in scientific change. Kuhn and Feyerabend suggested that it may come to pass that no meaning was shared in common between a theory and its successor. This seemed to render problematic the idea of a rational choice between such 'incommensurable' theories and even encouraged (superidealist) scepticism about the existence of a theory-independent world. However, if the relation between the theories is one of conflict rather than merely difference, this presupposes that they are alternative accounts of the *same* world, and if one theory can explain more significant phenomena in terms of its descriptions than the other can in terms of *its*, then there is a rational criterion for theory choice, and *a fortiori* a positive sense to the idea of scientific development over time (cf. RTS, p. 248). In this sort of way critical realism claims to be able to combine and reconcile *ontological realism*, *epistemological relativism* and *judgmental rationality*.

The deductivist theory of structure initially came under fire from, among others, Michael Scriven, Mary Hesse and Rom Harré for the lack of *sufficiency* of Humean criteria for causality and law, Hempelian criteria for explanation and Nagelian criteria for the reduction of one science to another more basic one. This critique was then generalized by Roy Bhaskar to incorporate the lack of *necessity* for them also. Bhaskar argued that positivism could sustain neither the necessity nor the universality – and in particular the transfactuality (in open and closed systems alike) – of laws; and for an ontology (1) that was irreducible to epistemology; (2) that did not identify the domains of the real, the actual and the empirical; and (3) that was both stratified, allowing emergence, and differentiated. That is, in effect for three kinds of *ontological depth* which may be summarized by the concepts of *intransitivity*, *transfactuality* and *stratification.*

The lynchpin of deductivism was the Popper-Hempel theory of explanation, according to which explanation proceeded by deductive subsumption under universal laws (interpreted as empirical regularities). Its critics pointed out, however, that deductive subsumption typically does not explain but merely generalizes the problem (for instance, from 'why does x θ?' to 'why do all x's θ?'). Instead what is required for a genuine explanation is, as Whewell had inveighed against Mill in the 1850s and Campbell against Mill's latter-day successors in the 1920s, the introduction of *new* concepts not already contained in the explanandum, models, picturing plausible generative mechanisms, and the like. But the new realism broke with Campbell's Kantianism by allowing that, under some conditions, these concepts or models could describe newly identified and deeper or subtler or otherwise more recondite levels of reality. Theoretical entities and processes, initially imaginatively posited as plausible explanations of observed phenomena, could come to be established as real, through the construction either of sense-extending equipment or of instruments capable of detecting the effects of the phenomena. (In the latter case we invoke a *causal* criterion for attributing reality: *esse* no longer *est percipi*.) All this strongly suggests a *vertical* or theoretical realism. Science could now be seen as a continuing and reiterated process of movement from manifest phenomena, through creative modelling and experimentation or other empirical controls, to the identification of their generative causes, which now become the new phenomena to be explained. The stratification of nature imposes a certain dynamic logic to scientific discovery, in which progressively deeper knowledge of natural *necessity a posteriori* is uncovered.

However critical or transcendental realism argued that a *horizontal* or transfactual realism was additionally necessary to sustain the *universality* (within their range) of the workings of generative mechanisms or laws. Thus it is a condition of the intelligibility of experimentation that the laws which science identifies under experimental or analogously closed conditions continue to hold (but transfactually, not as empirical regularities) extra-experimentally. And this provides the rationale or ground for practical and applied explanatory, diagnostic, exploratory, scientific work too. Indeed the whole point of an experiment is to identify a universal (within its range) law, which, by virtue of the necessity for the experiment, is not actually, or even less empirically, so. Laws, then, and the workings of nature have to be analysed dispositionally as the powers, or more precisely tendencies, of underlying generative mechanisms which may on the one hand – the horizontal aspect – be possessed unexercised, exercised unactualized, and actualized undetected or unperceived; and on the other – the vertical aspect – be discovered in an ongoing irreducibly empirical open-ended process of scientific development.

A transcendental argument from the conditions of the possibility of experimentation in science thus establishes at once the irreducibility of ontology, of the theory of being, to epistemology and a novel non-empiricist but non-rationalist, non-actualist, stratified and differentiated ontology, that is characterized by the prevalence of structures as well as events (stratification) and open systems as well as closed (differentiation).

Thus let us revert to the three kinds of depth in transcendental realism:

(1) *Intransitivity*. The Western philosophical tradition has mistakenly and anthropocentrically reduced the question of what is to the question of what we can know. This is the '*epistemic fallacy*' (cf. RTS, p. 36), epitomized by concepts like the 'empirical world'. Science is a social product, but the mechanisms it identifies operate prior to and independently of their discovery (existential intransitivity). Transitive and intransitive dimensions must be distinguished. Failure to do so results in the reification of the fallible social products of science. Of course being contains, but it is irreducible to, knowledge, experience or any other human attribute or product. The domain of the real is distinct from and greater than the domain of the empirical.

(2) *Transfactuality*. The laws of nature operate independently of the closure or otherwise of the systems in which they occur, and the domain of the real is distinct from and greater than the domain of the actual (and hence the empirical too). Failure to appreciate this results in the fallacy of *actualism*, collapsing and homogenizing reality. Once the ubiquity of open systems and the necessity for experimentation or analogous procedures are appreciated, then laws must be analysed as transfactual, as universal (within their range) but neither actual nor empirical. Constant conjunctions are produced not

found. Laws operate independently of both the conditions for and their identification. *Theoretical explanations* for their part explain laws in terms of the structures which account for or perhaps merely ground them, while they are applied transfactually in the *practical* explanation of the phenomena they co-produce in open systems.

(3) There is *stratification* both in nature, and reflecting it in science, and both (a) within a single science or subject matter and (b) between a series of them.

(a) Recognition of the stratification of nature and the isolation of a concept of natural necessity discernible *a posteriori* allows the resolution of a whole host of philosophical problems, most notoriously the problem of induction, the untheorized or tacit condition of possibility of which is actualism. Thus if there is a real reason, located in its molecular or atomic constitution, why water boils rather than freezes when it is heated, then it *must* do so (cf. RTS, chapter 3.5–3.6).

(b) The real multiplicity of natural mechanisms grounds a real plurality of sciences which study them. Even though one kind of mechanism may be explained or grounded in terms of another, it cannot necessarily be reduced to or explained away in terms of it. Such grounding is consistent with its *emergence* so that the course of nature is different than it would have been if the more basic stratum alone operated; so that, to invoke our causal criterion for reality, the higher-order structure is real and worthy of scientific investigation in its own right.

This takes us neatly to the domain of the social sciences, where what Outhwaite has called the 'law-explanation' orthodoxy[3] was never even remotely plausible.[4]

Critical naturalism

For most of its recognized history, the philosophy of the human sciences has been dominated by dichotomies and dualisms. It was the aim of *The Possibility of Naturalism* to transcend them. (1) The overriding dichotomy or split was between a *hyper-naturalistic positivism* and an *anti-naturalistic hermeneutics*, resolved in the generation of a *qualified critical naturalism*. I discuss this in detail immediately below. (2) Then there was the split between individualism and collectivism (or holism), which critical naturalism would resolve by seeing society *relationally* and as *emergent*. (3) A connected split, upon which the debate about structure and agency was joined, was between the *voluntarism* associated with the Weberian tradition and the *reification* associated with the Durkheimian one. This critical naturalism would transcend in its *transformational model of social activity*. (4) Then there was the dichotomy between facts and values, most sharply expressed in Hume's law (discussed in the next section), which critical naturalism would refute in its theory of *explanatory critiques*. (5) Then, fuelling the positivism/hermeneutics debate, was the dichotomy between *reasons* and *causes*, which critical naturalism would resolve by showing how, once one rejected Humean causality, reasons could be causes *sui generis* on a critical realist conception of causality. (6) Finally underpinning many of these dichotomies was the dualism between *mind* and *body* (or, more macroscopically, between society and nature), which critical naturalism would overcome, by seeing mind as an emergent power of matter in its *synchronic emergent powers materialism*.

The Possibility of Naturalism, first published in 1979, was oriented primarily to the first of these questions, which was whether society, and human phenomena generally, could be studied in the same way as nature, i.e., 'scientifically'. There were two leading positions. (1) A more or less unqualified naturalism, which asserted that they could, which normally took the form of *positivism*, dominant in the philosophy and practice of the social sciences. Its immediate philosophical antecedents lay in the work of Hume, Mill, Mach and the Vienna Circle, providing the spine of the orthodox conception of science which it transplanted to the social world. (2) An anti-naturalism, based on a distinctive conception of the uniqueness of the social realm, that is as pre-interpreted, conceptualized or linguistic in character – *hermeneutics*, the official opposition to positivism. Its philosophical ancestry came from Dilthey, Simmel, Rickert and Weber who fused Hegelian and Kantian dichotomies to produce a contrast between the phenomenal world of nature and the intelligible world of freedom so as to ground dichotomies between causal explanation and interpretive understanding, the nomothetic and ideographic, the repeatable and the unique, the realms of physics and of history. If positivism found expression in the Durkheimian sociological tradition and in behaviourism, structuralism and functionalism, hermeneutics did so in aspects of the Weberian tradition and in phenomenological, ethnomethodological and interpretive studies. A discrimination must be made within the second camp between those who sought to synthesize or combine positivist and hermeneutical principles such as Weber and Habermas, and those dualists, such as Gadamer or Winch, who denied positivism any purchase in the human sphere. (It should be noted in passing that it is less easy to characterize the work of post-structuralist or, more generally, post-modernist thinkers. For the most part they adopt a Nietzschean epistemological perspectivism on a Humean or positivist ontological base.)

Now both positivist and hermeneuticist views, that is the standard naturalist and anti-naturalist positions, shared an essentially positivist account of natural science. If this is, as critical realists argue, *false*, then the possibility arises of a third position: (3) a qualified, *critical* and non-reductionist, *naturalism*, based upon a transcendental realist account of science and, as such, necessarily respecting (indeed grounded in) the specificity and emergent properties of the social realm. Moreover if the positivist account of natural science is false, then positivists have to make out a special case as to why positivism should be uniquely (and most implausibly) applicable to the human realm; and hermeneuticists, for their part, have to reassess their contrasts. Thus both of Winch's two main arguments in his very influential *The Idea of a Social Science* (1959) are parasitic on a positivist ontology. Constant conjunctions of events are neither necessary nor sufficient either for natural or for social scientific understanding: both alike are concerned with the discovery of intelligible connections in their subject matter. Nor do the conceptual and the empirical jointly exhaust the real. Critical realism can allow that conceptuality is distinctive, without supposing that it is exhaustive, of social life.

Let me elaborate on this. The social world is characterized by the complete absence of laws and explanations conforming to the positivist canon. In response to this positivists plead that the social world is much more complex than the natural world or that the laws that govern it can only be identified at some more basic, e.g. neurophysiological, level. But positivists are wrong to expect the social sciences to find constant conjunctions in the human world, for they are scarce enough in the natural; while hermeneuticists are wrong to conclude from the absence of such conjunctions that the human sciences are radically unlike the natural sciences. Closed systems cannot be artificially established in the human sciences. But, as Tony Lawson has shown in his contributions to Part I, this does not mean that the identification of epistemically significant non-random patterns or results cannot provide the empirical controls and contrasts that experimentation plays in physics and chemistry. Moreover the fact that social life is pre-interpreted provides a ready-made starting point for the social sciences. But there are no grounds for treating these data as exhaustive of the subject matter of social science, as incorrigible or their operation as non-causal. Thus rejecting Humean causality and acknowledging emergence allows us to see reasons as causes, but causes which may, for instance, be rationalizations.

Thus the hermeneutical position is often buttressed by the argument that the human sciences are concerned with the reasons for agents' behaviour and that such reasons cannot be analysed as causes. For, first, reasons are not logically independent of the behaviour they explain. Moreover, second, they operate at a different language level (Waismann) or belong to a different language-game (Wittgenstein) from causes. But natural events can likewise be redescribed in terms of their causes (for instance, toast as burnt). Furthermore, unless reasons were causally efficacious in producing one rather than another sequence of bodily movements, sounds or marks, it is difficult to see how there can be grounds for preferring one reason explanation to another, and indeed eventually the whole practice of giving reason explanations must come to appear as without rationale.

The positive case for critical naturalism turns on the extent to which an independent analysis of the objects of social and psychological knowledge is consistent with the transcendental realist theory of science. Thus whereas on the Weberian tradition social objects are seen as a result of, or constituted by intentional or meaningful human behaviour, tending to voluntarism, and on the Durkheimian tradition social objects are seen as possessing a life of their own, external to and coercing the individual, tending to reification, the critical realist conception stresses that society is both (a) a pre-existing and (transcendentally and causally) necessary condition for intentional agency (Durkheim's insight) but equally (b) as existing and persisting only in virtue of it. On this conception, then, society is both the condition and outcome of human agency and human agency both reproduces and transforms society. However there is an important asymmetry here: at any moment of time society is pre-given for the individuals who never create it, but merely reproduce or transform it. The social world is always pre-structured. This is a major difference between Bhaskar's transformational model of social activity and Giddens's theory of structuration which Margaret Archer highlights in Part 2. It means that agents are always acting in a world of structural constraints and possibilities that they did not produce. Social structure, then, is both the ever-present condition and the continually reproduced outcome of intentional human agency. Thus people do not marry to reproduce the nuclear family or work to sustain the capitalist economy. Yet it is the unintended consequence (and inexorable result) of, as it is the necessary condition for, their activity.

On this conception, in contrast to the hermeneutical perspective, then, actors' accounts are both corrigible and limited by the existence of unacknowledged conditions, unintended consequences, tacit skills and unconscious motivations; but in opposition to the positivist view, actors' accounts form the indispensable starting point of social enquiry. The transformational model of social activity entails that social life possesses a recursive and non-teleological character, as agents reproduce and transform the very structures which they utilize (and are constrained by) in their substantive activities. It also indicates a relational conception of the subject matter of social science, in contrast to the methodological individualist and collectivist conceptions characteristic of the utilitarian (and Weberian) and Durkheimian traditions of social thought. Related to this is the controversy about ideal types. For critical realists the grounds for abstraction lie in the real stratification (and ontological depth) of nature and society. They are not subjective classifications of an undifferentiated empirical reality, but attempts to grasp (for example, in real definitions of forms of social life already understood in a pre-scientific way) precisely the generative mechanisms and causal structures which account in all their complex and multiple determinations for the concrete phenomena of human history. Closely connected with this is a reassessment of Marx as, at least in *Capital*, a scientific realist – contrary to pre-existing marxist and non-marxist interpretations. In its wake too is a reassessment of other founding figures in the social sciences (such as Durkheim and Weber) as combining aspects of a realist and some or other non-realist method and ontology.

Certain emergent features of social systems which, on the invocation of a causal criterion for ascribing reality, can be regarded as *ontological* limits on naturalism, are immediately derivable from the transformational model of social activity. These may be summarized as the concept-dependence, activity-dependence and greater space–time specificity of social structures. The causal interdependency between social science and its subject matter specifies a *relational* limit; while the condition that social systems are intrinsically open – the most important *epistemological* limit – accounts for the absence of crucial or decisive test situations in principle, necessitating reliance on exclusively explanatory (not predictive) criteria for the rational assessment of theories. (A fourth *critical* limit will be discussed in the next section.) However subject to (and, arguably, just in virtue of) these qualifications both the characteristic modalities of theoretical and applied explanation which critical realists specify appear possible in the social, just as in the natural sphere. Thus theoretical explanation proceeds by *d*escription of significant features, *r*etroduction to possible causes, *e*limination of alternatives and *i*dentification of the generative mechanism or causal structure at work (which now becomes a new phenomenon to explain) (DREI); applied explanation by *r*esolution of a complex event (etc.) into its components, theoretical *r*edescription of these components, *r*etrodiction to possible antecedents of the components and *e*limination of alternative causes (RRRE).

On critical naturalism, then, the social sciences can be 'sciences' in exactly the same sense as natural ones, but in ways which are as different (and specific) as their objects. If the hermeneutical starting point of social science, in some pre-conceptualized social practice, lends to them a closer affinity with the transcendental and dialectical methods characteristic of philosophy, any slight on a *critical* naturalism is dissolved by reflection on the fact that these forms of argument are merely a species of the wider genus of retroductive ones familiar to all the sciences.

Explanatory critiques

The Possibility of Naturalism had identified a fourth *critical* difference between the social and natural sciences, necessitated by the consideration that the subject matter of social science includes not just social objects but beliefs about those social objects (or put another way that social objects include beliefs about themselves), making possible an *explanatory critique* of consciousness (and being), entailing judgements of value and action without parallel in the domain of the natural sciences, so vindicating a modified form of a substantive *ethical naturalism*, i.e., the absence of an unbridgeable logical gap between statements of facts and values of the kind maintained by Hume, Weber and Moore. And the theory of explanatory critique is most economically presented as a refutation of the philosophical orthodoxy known as 'Hume's law' that the transition from factual to evaluative statements, although frequently made (and perhaps even psychologically necessary), is logically inadmissible.

It need not be denied by the advocate of Hume's law that causal relations exist between factual and evaluative statements such that they motivate, predispose or *causally influence* each other, but it is asserted to be the case that facts do not *logically entail* values. Doubt is immediately cast upon this by the value-impregnated character of much social scientific discourse. This seems closely bound up with the value-impregnated character of the social reality that the social sciences are seeking to describe and explain, which is such that the best (most precise or accurate or complete) description of a social situation will almost inevitably be evaluative, i.e., possess value implications. However the defender of Hume's law can still argue that one is free to reject the value, so to speak, in the social reality which necessitates such a description. It is for these sort of reasons that the arguments, prevalent in the mid- and late-1960s of Searle from institutional facts, Prior, Philippa Foot and others from functional facts and Anscombe's generalization of their arguments through to the notion of flourishing are less than logically compelling. For one can always dispute that promising, good watches, knives or guns or the flourishing of some particular species are themselves good things.

The critique of Hume's law really gets off the ground when we refuse to detotalize or extrude (e.g. by hypostatization) social beliefs from the societies in which they are found, i.e., which include or contain them and in which they are in some manner formed. Such beliefs may patently be logically contradictory, as Edgley and Archer note, or in some other way, be false to the subject matter they are *about*. And it is clearly within the remit of factual social science, which includes in its subject matter not just social objects but, as social objects, beliefs about those objects, to show this. If and when it has done so we can pass immediately to a negative evaluation of them and of action based on them, and, *ceteris paribus*, to a positive evaluation of their rejection.

The second step is taken when we reject the idea that beliefs cannot be causally explained. If we have a true account of the causes of such false beliefs then we may pass immediately to a negative evaluation of those causes, and thence to any condition, structure or state of affairs found to be necessary for them, and thence, *ceteris paribus*, to a positive evaluation of action directed at removing or transforming those causes and their conditions. In a nutshell, as Collier points out, the theory of explanatory critique opens up the exciting possibility that we may be able to *discover* values, where beliefs prove to be *incompatible* with their own true explanation.

Let us now consider some possible rejoinders. First, it might be objected that this refutation depends upon our acceptance of the value that truth is a good and falsity is an ill. But that this is so is a condition of factual discourse (an aspect, as it were, of the logical geography of the concept of a belief), and so it does not involve anything other than considerations intrinsic to facts to legitimate the deduction of values, as is denied by Hume's law.

Second it is not an objection to point out that truth is not the only social good or falsity the only social ill, so that the inference schemes of explanatory critique may be overridden by other considerations. Science is only one among other social institutions, and truth among a number of values. But this does not gainsay the fact that other things being equal truth is good and falsity is ill. Third, it is the case that the inference from the negative evaluation of a structure or state of affairs accounting for the falsity of a belief to a positive evaluation of action rationally directed at transforming it is contingent upon (i) substantive theory and (ii) concrete practical judgements. *That* something should be done *ceteris paribus* is undeniable; *what* should be done is a different matter. It is perhaps this consideration that motivates Lacey's emphasis on the importance of insider, shared, tacit, 'movement-based' knowledge as distinct from 'grand theory'.

Finally all these inference schemes only hold *ceteris paribus*, other things being equal. But this has an exact parallel in scientific discourse *simpliciter*. To invoke a causal law is not to say what will happen but what tends to happen or what would happen *ceteris paribus*. The *ceteris paribus* clause is a condition for moving from fact to fact in the open-systemic world to which the laws of nature transfactually apply as much as it is to moving from fact to value in the practical social world of belief, judgement and action. Where philosophical orthodoxy poses radical dichotomies, critical realism finds instead exact parallels. It is difficult not to feel that the theory of explanatory critiques has definitively refuted Hume's law.

Dialectic

The dialectical phase of critical realism was initiated by the publication of DPF in 1993 (the principal themes of which were resumed in PE (1994)). This had three main objectives: (1) the dialectical enrichment of critical realism; (2) the development of a general theory of dialectic, of which Hegelian dialectic could be shown to be a special, limiting, case; (3) the generation of the rudiments of a totalizing critique of Western philosophy. DPF argued that *determinate absence* was the void at the heart of the Western philosophical tradition; that it was this concept that was crucial to dialectic, a concept which in the end Hegel could not sustain. It essayed a real definition of dialectic as the *absenting of constraints* (which could be viewed as *absences*) on *absenting absences or ills*, applicable quite generally, whether in the epistemic, ethical or ontological domains; and it adumbrated a system – of dialectical critical realism (DCR), the terms of which were themselves related dialectically. This system was composed of a *first moment* (1M) – of *non-identity* – corresponding roughly to transcendental realism; a *second* dialectical *edge* (2E), pivoting on the notion of absence and other concepts of *negativity*; a *third level* (3L), revolving around notions of *totality*, holistic causality and the like and a *fourth dimension* (4D), turning on *transformative praxis*, the unity of theory and practice in practice and so on. It should be noted that even though the triadic Hegelian dialectic – of identity, negativity and totality – shared two of these terms in common, their content in the critical realist dialectic is radically different. Thus DPF argued that Hegel ultimately could not sustain real negativity and that his totalities were all essentially closed rather than open. The upshot of DPF is that the moral good, more specifically a vision of a freely flourishing society, is implicit in every expressively veracious action or remark. Moral realism is here now combined with ethical naturalism; and the theory of explanatory critique is conjoined with a very radical emancipatory axiology turning on the theoretico-practical duality of every judgement and act. There is objective good, but it cannot necessarily or normally be identified with the actually existing morality of any particular society.

The introduction to Part IV outlines some of the main themes of DPF. Here it will be sufficient to contextualize it and say a little about its structure and its relation to pre-dialectical critical realism. I have already noticed that critical realists tended to (and were in part motivated by) a reassessment of Marx as a scientific realist, at least in *Capital*. There he maintains that explanatory structures (or, in his favoured terminology, essential relations) are (a) distinct from (b) often, and even normally, out of phase with (i.e., disjoint from) and (c) perhaps in opposition to the phenomena (or phenomenal forms) they generate. But, Marx never satisfactorily theorized his scientific, as distinct from material object, realism. This, together with four other imbalances or asymmetries in his intellectual formation – *viz.* the underdevelopment of (i) his critique of empiricism in comparison with his critique of idealism, (ii) of the theme of (α) objectivity as distinct from (β) labour (i.e., of the intransitive in contrast with the transitive dimension), (iii) and of normativity in relation to geo-historicity (i.e., of the intrinsic – judgementally rational – within the extrinsic – epistemically relative – aspect of the transitive dimension) and (iv) of the research programme of geo-historical materialism in comparison with the critique of political economy, helped to account for all of (1) Marx' mature return to Hegel, (2) the Hegelian residues in Marxist thought, (3) the ambivalences and contradictory tendencies within his writings and (4) the tendency for Marxist epistemology to fluctuate between a sophisticated idealism (roughly β without α) and a crude materialism (roughly α without β). Be that as it may, this inevitably led to the reopening of the question of the nature of the Marxian dialectic and of Marx's relation to Hegel.

There is a remarkable consistency in Marx's criticisms of Hegel from 1843 to 1873. These turn, formally, on Hegel's subject–predicate inversions (including the critique of his idealistic sociology which confounds alienation and objectification, thus implicating Hegel in a metaphysical closure and betraying the presence of what Bhaskar calls '*ontological monovalence*', i.e., the generation of a purely positive account of being, the absenting of absence which is the cardinal mistake of Western philosophy), his principle of identity (involving the reduction of being to thought, i.e., the epistemic fallacy) and his logical mysticism (including the reduction of science to philosophy, i.e., the 'speculative illusion'); and, substantively on his failure to sustain the autonomy or intransitivity of nature and the geo-historicity, i.e., the non-monovalent character, of social forms. Notoriously, Marx never realized his wish to make accessible to the ordinary human intelligence, in two or three printer's sheets, what is *rational* in the *method* which Hegel discovered and at the same time mystified. This sets the agenda for Bhaskar's project in DPF which is conceived as an essentially preservative generalization and enrichment of critical realism but a non-preservative sublation of Hegelian dialectic. Before I turn to the rational kernel and the mystical shell in the Hegelian dialectic it is worth sketching a plausible critical realist reconstruction of Marx's dialectic.

Thus: Marx understood his dialectic as *scientific*, because it set out to explain the contradictions in thought and the crises of socio-economic life in terms of the particularly contradictory essential relations generating them; as *historical*, because it was both rooted in, and (conditionally) an agent of the changes in the very relationships and circumstances it described; as *critical*, because it demonstrated the historical conditions of validity and limits of adequacy of the categories, doctrines and practices it explained; and as *systematic*, because it sought to trace the various historical tendencies and contradictions of capitalism back to certain existentially constitutive features of its mode of production. The most important of these were the contradictions between the use-value and value of the commodity, and between the concrete useful and abstract social aspects of the labour it embodies. These contradictions, together with the other structural and historical contradictions they ground, are both (a) *real inclusive oppositions* in that the terms or poles of the contradictions existentially presuppose each other, and (b) *internally related* to a mystifying form of appearance. Such dialectical contradictions do not violate the principle of non-contradiction, for they may be *consistently described*. Nor are they scientifically absurd, for the notion of a real inverted – or otherwise mystifying – misrepresentation of a real object, generated by the object concerned is readily accommodatable within a non-empiricist, *stratified* ontology in which thought is included within reality, not hypostatized.

What of the rational kernel and the mystical shell? The rational kernel of the Hegelian dialectic is essentially an epistemological learning process, in which inconsistencies are progressively remedied by resort to greater depth and/or (more generally) totality. Thus the Hegelian dialectic functions in one or other of two basic modes: (1) by bringing out what is implicit, but not explicitly articulated, in some notion; or (2) by repairing some want, lack or inadequacy in it. In either case some *absence* or *incompleteness* in the pre-existing conceptual field comes to be experienced as an *inconsistency* which is remedied by resort to a greater *totality*. This is essentially the epistemological dialectic called 'the logic of scientific discovery' presented in RTS Chapter 3 and revisited as a dialectic of truth in DPF Chapter 3.2. The mystical shell of Hegelian dialectics is ontological monovalence, manifest *inter alia* in the absence of the concept of determinate absence, and with it of uncancelled contradiction, open totality and ongoing transformative praxis.

For DCR, dialectic is essentially the positive identification and elimination of *absences*, whether then conceived as argument, change or the augmentation of (or aspiration to) freedom. For these depend upon the positive identification and elimination of mistakes, states of affairs and constraints, all of which can be seen as involving or depending upon absences. Indeed absence is ontologically prior to, and the condition for, presence or positive being. It includes processes as well as states (products) and states-in-process as well as process-in-states. Moreover it opens up, in what DCR styles the dialectic of dialectical and analytical reasoning (in which dialectical reasoning overreaches but contains analytical reasoning), the critique of the fixity of the subject, in the traditional subject–predicate form. Most characteristically in the 'identity thinking' of the 'analytical problematic'. Indeed it is the absence of the concept of absence in ontological monovalence that underpins the failures of traditional philosophy even at 1M.

The moments of the system of DCR will now be briefly rehearsed. 1M is characterized by non-identity relations such as those involved in the critique of the epistemic and anthropic fallacies, of identity theory and actualism. Unified by the concept of alterity, it emphasizes scientific intransitivity, referential detachment (the process whereby we detach the referent (and referential act) from that to which it refers), the reality principle and ontology which it necessitates. More concretely, 1M fastens on to the transcendentally necessary stratification and differentiation of the world, entailing concepts of causal powers and generative mechanisms, alethic truth and transfactuality, natural necessity and natural kinds. *Alethic truth* is the truth of, or real reason(s) for, or dialectical ground of, *things* as distinct from *propositions*. This is possible in virtue of the ontological stratification of the world and attainable in virtue of the dynamic character of science, social science, explanatory critique and emancipatory axiology. It is the concept of alethic truth that is the ground for the transcendental realist resolution of problems such as those of induction which arise from actualizing, destratifying nature (and then science) and for the explanatory critical refutation of Hume's law.

2E is unified by the category of absence, from which as I shall shortly show the whole circle of 1M–4D links and relations can be derived. Its critical cutting edge is aimed at the Parmenidean doctrine of ontological monovalence, the Platonic analysis of negation in terms of difference and the Kantian analysis of negative into positive predicates. It spans the gamut of categories of negativity, contradiction and critique. It emphasizes the tri-unity of causality, space and time in tensed 'rhythmic' spatializing process, thematizing the presence of the past and existentially constitutive process. Contradictions, which fall under 2E, include internal and external, formal logical and dialectical ones. Dialectical contradictions are mutually exclusive internally related oppositions, conveying tendencies to change. If the dialectics of 1M are most characteristically of stratification and ground, those of 2E are typically of process, transition, frontier and node; but also generally of opposition including reversal.

3L is unified by the category of totality. It pinpoints the error of ontological extensionalism, including the hypostatization of thought. It encompasses such categories and themes as reflexivity, emergence, transcendence, constellationality, holistic causality, concrete universality and singularity, internal relationality and intra-activity, but also detotalization, alienation, split and split off, 'TINA formation', illicit fusion and fissure. Its dialectics are of centre and periphery, form and content, figure and ground, generative separation and dealienation, retotalization in a unity-in-diversity.

4D is unified by the category of transformative praxis or agency. In the human sphere it is implicit in the other three moments. There is a special affinity with 2E, since agency is (intentional) causality, which is absenting. Agency is sustained philosophically – in opposition to dualistic disembodiment and reductionist reification – by an emergent powers materialist orientation and substantively by the concept of four-planar social being. On this generalization of critical naturalism, social life *qua* totality is constituted by four dialectically interdependent planes: of material transactions with nature, interpersonal relations, social structures and the stratification of the personality. And the moral evolution of the species, like the future generally, is conceived as open. Its dialectics are the site of ideological and material struggles, but also of absolute reason (the unity of theory and practice in practice) and it incorporates DCR's dialectic of desire to freedom.

Let me give, by way of conclusion, an indication of how dialectical critical realism can be dialectically presented. We may start with the concept of absence, say as manifest in desire. This immediately gives us the concepts of referential detachment, existential intransitivity and thence ontology. Whence we proceed to classification and causality. With the first glimpse of ontological structure we have alethic truth and the transfactual efficacy it affords. But to cause is to negate and all negation is in space–time and so we have the entire range of 2E categories from constraint to dialectical contradiction to rhythmic spatio-temporal efficacy. The contradictions within and between entities yield emergence, and thence it is a short route to the 3L categories of totality, holistic causality and concrete universal = singular. Totality is inwardized as, *inter alia*, the reflexivity shown in judgement and the monitoring of practice. Now in the realm of 4D, in virtue of the transcendental necessity of social structure for practice, we can derive from the sole premiss of the activity-dependence of social structure, the transformational model of social activity, the relational social paradigm and the epistemological, ontological, relational and critical limits on naturalism, including the derivation of values from facts. In virtue of our intentional embodied agency, to act is to absent, and in desire or the solidarity implicit in the fiduciariness of the judgement form, the object of our absenting agency is constraint. Then, by the logic of dialectical universalizability, we are driven to absent all dialectically similar constraints, and then to absent constraints as such in virtue of their being dialectically similar; and finally to engage, on the basis of the progressive generalization of the concept of freedom to incorporate flourishing and potentialities for development, and the negative generalization of constraint to include ills and remediable absences generally, in the totalizing depth praxis that would usher in the eudaemonistic or good society, which in this way can be shown to be already implicit in the most elemental desire.

R.B.

Notes

1 Its publication coincides with the second Annual Conference of the Centre for Critical Realism (CCR) which is a registered educational charity designed to promote and network for critical realism; and the establishment of the International Association for Critical Realism (IACR), a democratically constituted membership body affiliated to the CCR.
2 *Popular Scientific Lectures*, 1894, p.192
3 *New Philosophy of the Social Sciences*, London, 1987.
4 Cf. A. Donegan, 'The Popper-Hempel Theory Reconsidered', *Philosophical Analysis and History*, ed. W. Dray, New York, 1966.
All references in the text refer to the original books.

Acknowledgements

I would like to take this opportunity to thank my fellow Trustees of the Centre for Critical Realism (CCR), namely Margaret Archer, Andrew Collier, Tony Lawson, Alan Norrie and Sean Vertigan, and all those, including Mike Jellicoe, Roberta Keenan and Maria Perna, who have helped in its establishment and that of the International Association for Critical Realism (IACR). I am enormously indebted to Alan Jarvis of Routledge for organising and supervising the launch of the *Critical Realism: Interventions* Series and for the publication with exemplary efficiency and rapidity of *Critical Realism: Essential Readings* and the new edition of *The Possibility of Naturalism*. Thanks are also due to Steven Jarman, Belinda Dearbergh and everyone else at Routledge concerned with the production of these two initial books in what looks like becoming an extremely valuable series.

R.B.
May 1998

Part I

TRANSCENDENTAL REALISM AND SCIENCE

1

INTRODUCTION

Basic texts and developments

Roy Bhaskar and Tony Lawson

Roy Bhaskar's *A Realist Theory of Science* emerged into the intellectual scene at a time of vigorous critical activity in western philosophy of science. Central to the latter was a sustained challenge to the then dominant positivist conception of science. Two fundamental elements of the positivist world view undergoing particular scrutiny and criticism were the assumptions that science is monistic in its development and deductive in its structure. Even so support for the positivist conception was far from giving way entirely. And a significant reason for its continuing survival was the inability of its opponents to sustain in a sufficiently coherent manner, precisely those features – scientific change and the non-deductive aspects of theory – that had been found to be fundamental to the anti-positivist critique. A major achievement of Bhaskar's *A Realist Theory of Science* is that it explained and contributed significantly to resolving this situation. Specifically, Bhaskar demonstrated how the preservation of the rational insights of both the anti-monistic and anti-deductivist tendencies in the philosophy of science necessitated the construction of a new ontology – and of a corresponding account of (natural) science. It necessitated, in fact, a reorientation of philosophy towards a non-anthropomorphic conception of the place of humanity in nature. This was a shift in philosophy, referred to by some as a Copernican Revolution, that culminated in a new *realist* philosophy of science.

It is conceivable that most scientists would subscribe to being scientific realists in the sense that they accept that the theoretical terms they employ possess real referents independently of their theorising. It is important to recognise, however, that Bhaskar's support for a realist conception of science does not depend upon any empirical assessment that scientists (implicitly or explicitly) so subscribe. Rather Bhaskar sustains a metaphysical realism by way of elaborating an account of what the world 'must' be like for those scientific practices accepted *ex posteriori* as successful, to have been possible. In this manner a realist perspective is obtained which neither presupposes nor justifies a realistic interpretation of any substantive scientific theory, and which preserves the possibility of criticising specific practices of scientists.

In establishing such a metaphysical realism Bhaskar confirms the feasibility of a (revelatory) philosophy of science, as well as, within philosophy, of an ontology. Philosophy is distinguished from science *not* according to its subject field, nor even in virtue of the questions asked, and certainly not because of any supposed investigation of some autonomous order of being. Rather philosophy is distinguished by its method and more generally by the sorts of arguments it deploys, which are transcendental in the sense of Kant.

Specifically, the general form of a philosophical investigation accepted by Bhaskar, the transcendental argument, turns upon elaborating necessary conditions of certain human (in the case of *A Realist Theory of Science*, scientific) activities. Now Kant employed the transcendental procedure (in elaborating his transcendental idealism) in an individualist and idealist mode. However, Bhaskar demonstrates that there is little need to be so restrictive. In particular the social activities described in the premises which initiate the argument may be both historically transient and also dependent upon the powers of human beings as material objects or causal agents rather than merely thinkers or perceivers. Similarly, philosophical conceptions of scientific activities may also be historically transient, just as the results of philosophical analysis may constitute transcendental realist, not idealist, and epistemically relativist, rather than absolutist, conclusions. Philosophical argument so interpreted can be seen to be dependent upon the form of scientific practices but irreducible to the content of scientific beliefs. In applying the transcendental procedure in this less-restrictive manner Bhaskar develops and sustains his account of *transcendental realism.*

But how is it possible for premises of transcendental arguments to be selected without implying an invalid commitment to the epistemic significance of the activities described? Why, in particular, should opponents of any transcendental realist conception be convinced by Bhaskar's choice of premises for his argument? Avoidance of arbitrariness can be achieved only by focusing upon accounts of activities that are acceptable to both (or all) sides to a dispute. If possible, indeed, it is best to find premises that opponents have regarded as fundamental. Where this is achieved the aim is to demonstrate not only that the transcendental realist account can accommodate the activities in question, but also that opponent positions sponsoring the activities cannot so accommodate them consistently, i.e., without generating metaphysical absurdity or some such.

Such a demonstration is precisely what Bhaskar achieves in his classic analysis of experimental activity, an analysis which forms the centrepiece of chapter 1 of *A Realist Theory of Science* reprinted below. By so considering experimentation, sponsored by both empiricists and Kantians (as well as conceptual transformations sponsored by super idealists) Bhaskar demonstrates how, in the end, it is only a realist analysis that can sustain the intelligibility of such practices. Moreover the resulting realist theory, Bhaskar's transcendental realism, provides an alternative to positivism which allows us both to recognise the cumulative character of scientific knowledge without collapsing this into a monism, and also to acknowledge a surplus component in scientific theory without sliding into subjectivism.

In the course of his analysis, Bhaskar grounds the insight that causal laws are ontologically distinct from the pattern of events. Specifically Bhaskar shows how the intelligibility of experiments presupposes that reality is constituted not only by experiences and the course of actual events, but also by structures, powers, mechanisms and tendencies – by aspects of reality that underpin, generate or facilitate the actual phenomena that we may (or may not) experience, but are typically out of phase with them. Bhaskar also establishes that reality in general is both multi-dimensional and stratified and also open and differentiated (in the sense that closed systemic situations in which event regularities occur are highly restricted).

From this transcendental realist ontology of structures and differences an account of rational scientific development is quickly determined. This Bhaskar sets out in chapter 3 of *A Realist Theory of Science*, the relevant parts of which are also reproduced below. Briefly put, explanatory science, according to the perspective supported, seeks to account for some phenomenon of interest – typically an experimentally produced event pattern – in terms of a (set) of mechanism(s) most directly responsible. Producing this explanation will involve drawing upon existing cognitive material, and operating under the control of something like a logic of analogy and metaphor, to construct a theory of a mechanism that, if it were to work in the postulated way, could account for the phenomenon in question. The reality of the mechanism so retroduced is subsequently subjected to empirical scrutiny, and the empirical adequacy of the hypothesis maintained compared to that of competing explanations. Following this any explanation that is (tentatively) accepted must itself be explained, and so forth, a move which, in itself, presupposes a certain stratification of reality. On the transcendental realist view of science, then, its essence lies in the *movement* at any one level from knowledge of manifest phenomena to knowledge, produced by means of antecedent knowledge, of the structures that generate them.

So among the distinctive features of Bhaskar's original account of transcendental realism are:

(i) A revindication of ontology, of the theory of being, as distinct from (ultimately containing) epistemology, the theory of knowledge, and a critique of the 'epistemic fallacy' which denies this;
(ii) A distinction between the domain of the real, the actual and the empirical and a critique of the reduction of the real to the actual in 'actualism' and then to the empirical in 'empirical realism', together with a conception of the transfactual, non-empirical universality of laws as the causal

powers, or more specifically tendencies, of *generative mechanisms* which may be possessed, unexercised, exercised, unactualised and actualised independently of human perception or detection;

(iii) A conception of the stratification, differentiation and openness of both nature and sciences, and of the distinction between pure and applied sciences and explanations;

(iv) Isolation of a general dynamic of scientific discovery and development involving the identification of different levels of natural necessity, which in turn is understood as radically non-anthropomorphic. And thence:

(v) The associated resolution of a whole series of philosophical problems to which orthodox accounts of science had given rise, most notoriously the problem of induction (cf. *Realist Theory of Science*, 3.5/3.6, reprinted below).

It is easy enough to see how philosophy of science has the potential to provide a directional input into the practices of science. For although Bhaskar's analysis suggests that when scientists are practising science they are implicitly acting upon something like transcendental realism, it does not follow that transcendental realism, or any other philosophy, is always or consistently acted upon, or dominant, or even acknowledged. It is for this reason that in his subsequent *Possibility of Naturalism*, Bhaskar is able to conclude that 'one is . . . *qua* philosopher of science, at perfect liberty to criticise the practice of any science' (p. 16). Nothing in the foregoing should be taken to imply that philosophy can do the actual work of science for it. If the elaboration of a transcendental realist perspective provides grounds for supposing that science can successfully uncover structures and mechanisms that govern some identified phenomenon of interest, philosophy cannot do the work of uncovering. This is the task of science. Philosophy, however, is able to make a difference to science in the manner noted: by, amongst other things, affecting the questions put to reality, and the manner in which this is done.

If *A Realist Theory of Science* demonstrates that an adequate account of scientific development requires the concepts of a stratified and differentiated reality, it is clearly a further requirement that knowledge cannot be equated with direct experience. Nor is it intelligible that knowledge is created out of nothing. Rather knowledge can only be a produced means of production, as revised understandings are achieved via the transformation of existing insights, hypotheses, guesses and anomalies, etc. Bhaskar's own contribution, of course, is itself a transformation of prior claims and understandings, and the work of Rom Harré figures prominently amongst those whose contributions significantly influenced *A Realist Theory of Science.* One such influential contribution by Harré – chapter 1 of *Causal Powers*, written jointly with E.H. Madden – is reprinted below, albeit a contribution that only appeared in this published form at the same time as *A Realist Theory of Science* was also appearing in print.

In line with much philosophy of science of the period, the starting point for Harré and Madden is a conviction that positivism, specifically the Humean conception of causality and its linear descendent, the 'regularity theory', is not sustainable. Indeed, for Harré and Madden it is essential to explain why the Humean point of view continued over many centuries to attract so many adherents. In providing their explanation Harré and Madden identify two widely held, but questionable, assumptions, which lead inexorably to the Humean position. The first assumption presupposes, amongst other things, an exclusive dichotomy between the formal and the psychological. Specifically, it is a belief maintained by empiricist philosophers, that the philosophical analysis of non-empirical concepts must be wholly in terms of formal logic, and that any residual features not so susceptible to philosophical analysis, must be capable of analysis in terms of its psychological origins. Against this Harré and Madden argue that adequate accounts of the most important metaphysical concepts with which philosophy deals, like cause, theory, explanation, natural necessity, can be neither purely formal nor psychological but require attention to what they term 'the content of knowledge', content which usually goes beyond reports of immediate experience. These authors argue that such concepts can be successfully differentiated, the rationality of science defended, and the possibility of an independent reality sustained only by way of considering certain general features of the 'content' of relevant propositions by which they can ultimately be distinguished as possessing a conceptual necessity, irreducible to either logical necessity or psychological illusion.

The second Humean assumption questioned by Harré and Madden is that the ontology of science is restricted to the world of events. This conception, of course, is encouraged by Hume's opening comments in both the *Treatise* and the *Enquiry*, in which he quickly moves from a theory that experience comes in atomistic impressions, to a conception of the experienced world whereby this too is atomistic, comprising atomistic events. The supposed independence of successive events, and of coexisting properties, is a related and also fundamental aspect of this Humean view. Against this standpoint Harré and Madden draw upon the psychology of perception to demonstrate the untenability of Hume's doctrine of atomist impressions. And against the conception that the experienced world can be adequately conceived as a sequence of atomistic and independent events, the authors defend an ontology of ultimate and derived things whose interactions produce the flux of events. Specifically, through developing concepts of powers, natures and generative mechanisms, Harré and Madden, like Bhaskar, are able to demonstrate that a variety of rational constraints upon logical possibility can be determined so as to limit expectations as to the patterns of events likely to be identified and what ensembles of properties the things and materials of the world are likely to manifest. From these constraints Harré and Madden develop a theory of natural necessity. The upshot is a conception of the natural world as a interacting system of powerful particulars, giving rise to a patterning of events and a manifestation of properties, bearing upon the multitudinous phenomena of the world we experience.

In the chapter of *Causal Powers* reproduced below, Harré and Madden indicate how natural necessity in the world is reflected in discourse about the world. In particular, they argue that causal hypotheses invariably involve conceptual necessity, and that this necessity is not merely stipulative or conventional in character but expresses something about the nature of physical systems. Fundamental here are the categories of 'power' and 'ability' possessed by something in virtue of its 'nature'. Specifically they defend the position that it is the 'ineliminable but non-mysterious powers and abilities of particular things . . . [that] are the ontological "ties that bind" causes and effects together and are what the conceptual necessity of causal statements reflects' (p. 11).

A further insight defended in this chapter is that conceptual and natural necessity are also reflected in descriptions of substances. The transformations, etc., that particulars or substances are liable to undergo as well as what they are able to do are explained by reference to the thing in itself. As Harré and Madden summarise 'the relation between what a thing is and what it is capable of doing and undergoing is naturally necessary. It is this natural necessity that the conceptual necessity of the ensemble of powers and liabilities ascribed by the use of a term like "copper" reflects' (p. 14).

These authors further argue that it is essential that an account of natural sciences sustain a distinction between two ranges of essential properties. First, there are the nominal essences, those properties whose manifestations, according to Harré and Madden, are essential to a thing or sample or substance being of a certain kind. Although acknowledging that meanings have histories, Harré and Madden hold that nominal essences are fixed, and can be known *a priori.* And second, science is also concerned with real essences, with the natures of things or substances. These are *ex posteriori* discoveries, and serve to explain manifest properties. Harré and Madden argue that it is only through considering the empirical status of the predicates involved in any investigation, as opposed merely to looking at the logical structure of definitions, that it is possible to distinguish adequately between the kinds of definitions that appear in the natural sciences.

Now when discoveries of real essences justify our holding that certain properties are its nominal essence, then a diachronic process of meaning development creates a genuine conceptual necessity. In particular, where the co-presence of an *ensemble* of manifest properties is explained in terms of the real definition of a substance, the more the corresponding predicates are used as part of the meaning of the term for the thing or substance. And when discoveries about the means of causal production make clear the role of the appropriate powerful particular in that production, and the nature of that particular allows us to claim the necessity of just such an outcome of the productive process, then the concept of that particular can legitimately be allowed to come to include the power to produce those effects. This is the theoretical account, formulated by Harré and Madden, of the origin of necessary connections between empirical concepts, an account which, in the chapter excerpted below, is shown to make sense of the conceptual development of the substance concept 'copper'.

The realist theory of science supported by the contributions by Bhaskar and by Harré and Madden is taken up by Andrew Sayer in the next essay included below. Sayer's purpose is to use the realist theory to clarify the relations between the *theoretical* and the *empirical*, and between the *abstract* and the *concrete*. Sayer's starting point is the problematic history of these terms within Marxist writings – although, of course, the history of their usage is no less problematic in social theory more widely conceived (see, for example, Lawson's discussion of how abstraction is conceived in modern mainstream economics in the final essay reproduced below). According to Sayer, the possibility of sustaining a basis for distinguishing theoretical research (or critique or reflection) and empirical research, necessitates a prior consideration of the related, but distinct, contrast between the abstract and the concrete. And in order to proceed, it is also necessary to explicate Marx's insights that abstractions may or may not be useful or adequate ones. In Marx's terminology the result may be 'rational abstractions' or 'chaotic conceptions'. It is in making sense of these categories that Sayer first draws upon realist insights and argument.

As Bhaskar and Harré and Madden indicate, realist analysis undermines the Humean predilection for atomism. And in the realist theory causation is bound up with natural necessity: things have powers and dispositions to act in certain ways in virtue of their intrinsic structures or natures or real essences. Things possess powers in virtue of their intrinsic structures, powers that may or may not be exercised. If they are triggered they can be in play as mechanisms, whose effects may or may not be actualised, depending upon the play of countervailing mechanisms. In transcendental and critical realism it is, as we can see, the notion of a tendency which denotes characteristic ways of acting or effects of mechanisms which may or may not be actualised.

Accepting this perspective Sayer underlines the insight that scientific 'laws', or its fundamental results, are not about universal empirical regularities but expressive of structures, powers, mechanisms and tendencies. The essential characteristic of law-likeness is not (empirical) universality but (natural) necessity. Given this insight Sayer feels able to present a clarification of the relationship between both the abstract and the concrete and also between good and bad abstraction. Good or 'rational' abstractions are interpreted as those which isolate necessary relationships. The concrete, being a unity of diverse determinations, is a combination of several necessary relationships. However, because the form of the combination is contingent, it is only determinable though empirical research. As such, insists Sayer, 'its form cannot be assumed to have already been "taken up" into the theoretical framework in the same way that the nature of the abstraction can' (p. 9). A bad abstraction or 'chaotic conception' is one which is based upon a non-necessary relationship, or which divides the indivisible by failing to recognise a necessary relationship. The same distinctions are drawn when considering external and internal relations. Specifically, a rational abstraction – unlike a chaotic conception – takes due account of structures of internal relations.

With these distinctions established it is possible to clarify the relationship between the 'theoretical' and 'empirical'. The theoretical, according to Sayer, makes its strongest claims about necessary relations in the world, and does so by 'anchoring itself' upon abstract concepts. The latter may be sufficient to indicate something about the tendencies in play in a given context. But in an open world such claims are inevitably non-committal about contingent relations occurring in concrete configurations. The latter, concludes Sayer, requires empirical analysis. Finally Sayer points to both the positive implications of recognising these distinctions as well as the analytical complications, limitations or regressions that follow from a failure so to do.

It is clear that the switch of emphasis in the philosophy of science engendered by the contributions of Bhaskar, Harré and others is away from epistemology towards ontology. Even so any philosophical position, even an ontologically oriented one, ultimately bears epistemological implications. Tony Lawson's *Economics and Reality* considers the epistemological consequences of critical realism at length. It is true, as has already been indicated, that Bhaskar gives a broad outline of theory development in his 'The Logic of Scientific Discovery', included as chapter 3 of *A Realist Theory of Science*, reproduced below. But it is arguable that his epistemological elaborations do not go very far. They are informative about primary objectives, e.g. to uncover natural necessity in an irreducibly *a posteriori* process of discovery, but less specific about *how* these are to be achieved. Mostly, in section 1 of chapter 3, Bhaskar distinguishes transcendental realism from 1) empiricism in seeing the initial patterning of events as signalling an invariance of a *result* rather than of a regularity; and from 2) idealism in interpreting constructed hypotheses of generative mechanisms as something that may be real rather than *merely* imaginary, stimulating a project on continuous empirical assessment. However little is said about how explanatory projects might proceed in conditions where the experimental production of event regularities is not feasible, and where, as in the social realm, few of any interest seem to occur spontaneously.

One of the features of *A Realist Theory of Science* is that it constituted an immanent critique of orthodox – mainly empirical realist – philosophies of science. As such it focused on the experimental sciences of nature, such as physics and chemistry, of which these philosophies derived their *prima facie* plausibility and ideological power. However Lawson cautions against viewing the fact of openness of the social realm as an 'epistemological limit on naturalism', a move that risks encouraging the inference that the natural sciences can be reduced to the experimental natural sciences or astronomy. Amongst other things this may limit the possibility of inferring insights from the successful non-experimental natural sciences, such as geology, seismology and so forth. Thus, although Lawson himself is expressly addressing the possibilities for social science, in the relevant chapters reproduced below he is discussing the wider issue of the possibilities for explanatory conduct in non-experimental contexts. As such his considerations are just as relevant to many natural sciences, with the well-controlled experiment being seen to be a special case. Hence his chapters are included here in Part 1.

Despite emphasising the open, dynamic and highly internally related nature of much of reality including the social world, Lawson is confident – contrary to the views of some other critical realists such as Andrew Collier – that it *is* possible to identify causal mechanisms of interest, and even possible to say something about general strategies for doing so. Central to Lawson's assessment are the concepts of *contrastives, demi-regs* and *relative explanatory power.* Now if reality, including the social realm, is open and complexly structured, with a shifting mix of mechanisms lying behind the surface phenomena of direct experience, how can we begin even to detect the separate effects of (relatively distinct) mechanisms? In motivating his answer, Lawson emphasises that controlled experiments do not *all* take the form of insulating single stable mechanisms in 'repeated trials' with the intention of generating event regularities. An alternative scenario, illustrated for example by plant-breeding experiments, involves the use of control groups to help identify the effects of specific mechanisms of interest. Where, for example, crops are grown in the open there can be no expectation that all the causal factors affecting the yields are stable, reproducible or even identifiable. Yet progress in understanding can be achieved: through ensuring that two sets of crops receive broadly similar conditions except for one factor that is systematically applied to one set but not to the other. In this case any systematic differences in average yields of the two sets of crops can with reason be attributed to the factor in question.

In other words, experimental control frequently takes the form of comparing two different groups or populations with common or similar (if complex, irreversible and unpredictable) histories and shared (if non-constant) conditions, excepting that one group is 'treated' in some definite way that the second, control, group is not. Or, more typically, when various (similar but non-uniform) background factors such as soil composition and light are not directly controllable, it may be possible to divide the relevant land into a set of plots and then attempt to assign certain quantities of fertiliser to the various plots in a random way, with some plots receiving no fertiliser at all. Under such conditions the difference between the mean yield of the unfertilised plots is contrasted with that of fertilised plots to see if there is a systematic and significant difference – which can be attributed to the fertiliser.

In the plant breeding scenario just described, of course, the aim is to experiment with some compound that is already suspected of possessing yield-increasing causal powers. Lawson's primary concern, however, is with detecting the effects of hitherto unknown or unrecognised mechanisms. But it is easy enough to appreciate that the logic of the argument carries over to the latter conditions. Consider, for example, a situation wherein, say, it was expected *a priori* that the yield would be roughly the same for a given crop in all parts of the field but is discovered *ex posteriori* to be systematically higher at one end. In this case an experimentalist has *not* actively treated the relevant end of the field. But it seems *prima facie* that there is an additional causal factor in operation here, even if we are as yet unaware of its identity.

The general situation Lawson is identifying as being relevant for social scientific explanation in open systems, then, is one in which there are two or more comparable populations involved, wherein our background knowledge leads us to expect a specific relation between outcomes of these populations (frequently a relationship of similarity but not always), but wherein we are *ex posteriori* surprised by the relation we actually discover. Under such conditions it is *prima facie* plausible that there is a previously unknown and identifiable causal mechanism at work.

An important methodological category here is that of *contrastives.* Contrastives are descriptive statements taking the form 'this rather than that'. And contrastive explanation is concerned with addressing such questions as 'why this rather than that in these conditions?', or 'why P rather than Q in S?'. Contrastive explanation, clearly, is concerned not so much with such questions as 'why is the average crop yield x?' but 'why is the average crop yield in that end of this field significantly higher than that achieved elsewhere?' Explaining this is much less demanding than explaining the total yield. While the latter requires an exhaustive list of all the causal factors bearing upon the yield, the contrastive question requires that we identify only the causes responsible for the difference. But the import of contrastives here lies not so much (or just) in the fact that the task delineated is less demanding, but more in the fact that contrastives alert us to the situation that there is something to be explained at all.

Lawson is suggesting, then, that the effects of causal mechanisms can be identified through formulating interesting contrastives. This, to repeat, means identifying differences (or surprising relations) between outcomes of two groups whose causal histories are such that the outcomes in question might reasonably have been expected to be broadly the same, or at least to stand in some definite anticipated or plausible relationship which is systematically at odds with what we observe. We do not and could not explain the complete causal conditions of any social or other phenomenon. To do so would presumably mean accounting for everything back to the 'big bang' and beyond. Rather we aim to identify single sets of causal mechanisms and structures. And these are indicated where outcomes or features of different groups are such that, given the respective causal histories and conditions of these groups, their observed relation is other than might have been expected or at least imagined as a real possibility.

But if contrastives are vital for explanatory purposes in non-experimental situations, they are not sufficient for it. The possibility of a useful science depends upon being able to identify relatively enduring mechanisms or processes of the world. Now this requires that at some stage it is possible to detect any such mechanisms and to get some indication of their endurability. According to Lawson, it is frequently the case that in order to detect their effects all that is required is for partial, or rough and ready, regularities to appear. *Ex posteriori* these are frequently found to be the result of underlying mechanisms shining through. In other words, it is not the case that the surface manifestations of our world need divide into just two scenarios: either i) closed systems supporting strict regularities (whether strictly deterministic or those covered by well-behaved probability laws); or ii) a totally unsystematic random flux. A range of real possibilities lies between these polar extremes. Lawson recognises that it could have turned out that the possibility of reasonably stable mechanisms putting in an appearance in the form of rough but detectable patterns was never actualised; that it remained only a possibility. But *ex posteriori* this has not been the case: rough and ready regularities are everywhere in evidence. Women usually (but not always) get worse jobs than men; a car journey from Cambridge to London is usually (but not always) quicker late at night than during the day; football teams from the UK premier division normally do better than teams from lower divisions in cup competitions; over the 100 years until 1980, measured productivity growth in the UK was frequently less than most otherwise comparable continental industrial countries, and so forth.

Lawson refers to such partial regularities as *demi-regularities* or *demi-regs* for short, and suggests they be categorised as (the objects of) *demi-laws.* This characterisation turns upon both of the common interpretations of the term 'demi' – as either half-way or as false. Certainly any regularity observed can be expected to be partial or incomplete. But equally, although such partial regularities may be about real phenomena and capturing associations, they are not real laws at all, but epiphenomena. Even so, these are nevertheless epiphenomena of potential significance. A demi-reg is precisely a partial event regularity which *prima facie* indicates the occasional, but less than universal, actualisation of a mechanism or tendency, over a definite region of time–space. The patterning observed will not be strict if countervailing factors sometimes dominate or frequently co-determine the outcomes in a variable manner. But where demi-regs are observed there is *prima facie* evidence of relatively enduring and identifiable tendencies in play. Of course, as with the examples detailed above, the demi-regs in evidence will usually capture *relations* between actual phenomena – such as the productivity of UK firms compared with the productivity performances of otherwise comparable firms elsewhere. In short, a basic feature to be expected of explanatory work in science is an initial focus upon *contrastive demi-regs* considered to be of interest.

If one hypothesis of a mechanism capable of explaining a given contrastive demi-reg of interest is produced, experience suggests that there will usually be many such hypotheses in contention. These can be selected amongst on the basis of relative explanatory power, that is we can (provisionally) accept that theory which can accommodate the largest range of phenomena (typically expressed as contrastive demi-regs) upon which it bears. This remains a context-dependent affair, but entirely feasible. And Lawson suggests that skills of ordinary people in successfully negotiating their daily affairs indicates that this feasibility is regularly actualised. The task is to bring this causalist approach back into the academy. It may not satisfy the mathematical drives, preferences or ideals of the deductivist project of mainstream economists against which Lawson is mainly orienting himself, but it can facilitate an explanatory successful non-experimental science all the same.

How does Lawson's account fit into the schema outlined by Roy Bhaskar in *A Realist Theory of Science*? Contrastives, including contrastive demi-regs, along with the protolaws focussed upon by Bhaskar in *A Realist Theory of Science* (chapter 3.3) are all members of the class of potentially epistemically significant non-random patterns or results in nature (including in the laboratory). The crucial scientific transition is from a member of this class into a generative mechanism or structure which explains it and would ground a law, i.e., a transfactually efficacious tendency, understood as universal (within its range) but non-empirical, necessary but discovered *a posteriori*. Now we are only justified in inferring from the existence of a contrastive demi-reg to the causal efficacy of the mechanism which explains it (rather to the existence of a single mechanism, or set of mechanisms, which would explain it), if this is the *only relevant difference within contrast*, i.e., the intrinsic and extrinsic conditions and principles of organisation are constant (cf. RTS, p. 76) *or* their differences and changes and geo-histories, etc., are otherwise causally irrelevant; that is to say, that for epistemic purposes other things are equal, i.e., a *de facto* ontic or epistemically significant closure has been obtained. In this case the tendency will be actualised and the demi-reg, when explained, will be a law. The experimental situation is contrasted but this broader-contrasted case presupposes a *de facto* epistemically significant closure, i.e., quality (constancy or causal irrelevance or insignificance or accountability) or other things: that *ceteris* are *paribus*.

Notice, incidentally, that Lawson's marrying of realist theory and contrastive explanation facilitates a conception of science that preserves many of the recent insights of feminist philosophy without thereby going into the characteristic postmodernist judgemental-relativist overdrive. That is, Lawson's account naturally accommodates the insight that the sort of issues that are addressed in science will reflect the situations, perspectives and personal-social histories, and so forth, of the scientist without supposing thereby that all knowledge is *merely* a social construct, immune to rational critical assessment. It is clear, for example, that in the process of choosing a primary phenomenon for explanatory analysis, scientific (and other) interests necessarily come to bear. But once we accept the contrastive nature of social scientific explanation it is equally apparent that the interests of the researcher determine which causal mechanism is pursued as well. For when phenomena in an open system are determined by a multiplicity of causes, the particular one singled out for attention depends upon the contrastive identified as puzzling, surprising, unusual, undesirable or otherwise of interest. It may be that it is only the interested farmer that can recognise that his or her animals are behaving strangely, only the parent that perceives that all is not well with the child, and only the marginalised group that appreciates the nature or extent/effects of certain inequalities, and so forth. Clearly, the inescapably interested and practically conditioned nature of all scientific explanatory endeavour is a fundamental feature of the perspective Lawson defends.

Notice, finally that contrastive explanation along the lines defended by Lawson does indeed generalise the modes of inference already seen to be employed in specific contexts. The significance of the well-controlled experimental situation is precisely that *under such conditions but not others* certain triggering conditions are frequently found to be systematically associated with definite predictable effects, that an even regularity is produced. It is this contrast that renders the experimental setup so significant in science. And, of course, Bhaskar's transcendental argument in support of transcendental realism itself turns upon this more general contrastive assessment, that outside astronomy, event regularities of interest to science are mostly confined to experimental setups. As Lawson summarises the directionality involved: 'Particular differentiations of the world to hypotheses about specific mechanisms; generalised differentiations to philosophical ontologies' (p. 212). Given the *ex posteriori* pervasiveness of contrastive demi-regs, the fact of open systems is seen to be debilitating neither for science nor for philosophy.

R.B.
T. L.
February 1998

2

PHILOSOPHY AND SCIENTIFIC REALISM

Roy Bhaskar

1. Two sides of 'knowledge'

Any adequate philosophy of science must find a way of grappling with this central paradox of science: that men in their social activity produce knowledge which is a social product much like any other, which is no more independent of its production and the men who produce it than motor cars, armchairs or books, which has its own craftsmen, technicians, publicists, standards and skills and which is no less subject to change than any other commodity. This is one side of 'knowledge'. The other is that knowledge is '*of*' things which are not produced by men at all: the specific gravity of mercury, the process of electrolysis, the mechanism of light propagation. None of these 'objects of knowledge' depend upon human activity. If men ceased to exist sound would continue to travel and heavy bodies fall to the earth in exactly the same way, though ex hypothesi there would be no-one to know it. Let us call these, in an unavoidable technical neologism, the *intransitive objects of knowledge.* The *transitive* objects of knowledge are Aristotelian material causes.[1] They are the raw materials of science – the artificial objects fashioned into items of knowledge by the science of the day.[2] They include the antecedently established facts and theories, paradigms and models, methods and techniques of inquiry available to a particular scientific school or worker. The material cause, in this sense, of Darwin's theory of natural selection consisted of the ingredients out of which he fashioned his theory. Among these were the facts of natural variation, the theory of domestic selection and Malthus' theory of population.[3] Darwin worked these into a knowledge of a process, too slow and complex to be perceived, which had been going on for millions of years before him. But he could not, at least if his theory is correct, have produced the process he described, the

Source: A Realist Theory of Science, London: Verso, 1997, chap. 1, pp. 21–62.

intransitive object of the knowledge he had produced: the mechanism of natural selection.

We can easily imagine a world similar to ours, containing the same intransitive objects of scientific knowledge, but without any science to produce knowledge of them. In such a world, which has occurred and may come again, reality would be unspoken for and yet things would not cease to act and interact in all kinds of ways. In such a world the causal laws that science has now, as a matter of fact, discovered would presumably still prevail, and the kinds of things that science has identified endure. The tides would still turn and metals conduct electricity in the way that they do, without a Newton or a Drude to produce our knowledge of them. The Wiedemann-Franz law would continue to hold although there would be no-one to formulate, experimentally establish or deduce it. Two atoms of hydrogen would continue to combine with one atom of oxygen and in favourable circumstances osmosis would continue to occur. In short, the intransitive objects of knowledge are in general invariant to our knowledge of them: they are the real things and structures, mechanisms and processes, events and possibilities of the world; and for the most part they are quite independent of us. They are not unknowable, because as a matter of fact quite a bit is known about them. (Remember they were introduced as objects of scientific knowledge.) But neither are they in any way dependent upon our knowledge, let alone perception, of them. They are the intransitive, science-independent, objects of scientific discovery and investigation.

If we can imagine a world of intransitive objects without science, we cannot imagine a science without transitive objects, i.e. without scientific or pre-scientific antecedents. That is, we cannot imagine the production of knowledge save from, and by means of, knowledge-like materials. Knowledge depends upon knowledge-like antecedents. Harvey thought of blood circulation in terms of a hydraulic model. Spencer, less successfully perhaps, used an organic metaphor to express his idea of society. W. Thomson (Lord Kelvin) declared in 1884 that it seemed to him that 'the test of "do we understand a particular topic in physics [e.g. heat, magnetism]?" is "can we make a mechanical model of it?".'[4] And as is well known this was the guiding maxim of physical research until the gradual disintegration of the Newtonian world-view in the first decades of this century. Similarly economists sought explanations of phenomena which would conform to the paradigm of a decision-making unit maximizing an objective function with given resources until marginalism became discredited in the 1930's. No doubt at the back of economists' minds during the period of the paradigm's hegemony was the cosy picture of a housewife doing her weekly shopping subject to a budget constraint; just as Rutherford disarmingly confessed in 1934, long after the paradigm was hopelessly out of date, to a predilection for corpuscularian models of atoms and fundamental particles as 'little hard billiard balls, preferably red or black'.[5] Von Helmont's concept of an arche was the intellectual ancestor of the concept of a bacterium, which furnished the model for the concept of a virus. The biochemical structure of genes, which were initially introduced as the unknown bearers of acquired characteristics, has been explored under the metaphor of a linguistic code. In this way social products, antecedently established knowledges capable of functioning as the transitive objects of new knowledges, are used to explore the unknown (but knowable) intransitive structure of the world. Knowledge of B is produced by means of knowledge of A, but both items of knowledge exist only in thought.

If we cannot imagine a science without transitive objects, can we imagine a science without intransitive ones? If the answer to this question is 'no', then a philosophical study of the intransitive objects of science becomes possible. The answer to the transcendental question 'what must the world be like for science to be possible?' deserves the name of ontology. And in showing that the objects of science are intransitive (in this sense) and of a certain kind, viz. structures not events, it is my intention to furnish the new philosophy of science with an ontology. The parallel question 'what must science be like to give us knowledge of intransitive objects (of this kind)?' is not a petitio principii of the ontological question, because the intelligibility of the scientific activities of perception and experimentation already entails the intransitivity of the objects to which, in the course of these activities, access is obtained. That is to say, the philosophical position developed in this study does not depend upon an arbitrary definition of science, but rather upon the intelligibility of certain universally recognized, if inadequately analysed, scientific activities. In this respect I am taking it to be the function of philosophy to analyse concepts which are 'already given' but 'as confused'.[6]

Any adequate philosophy of science must be capable of sustaining and reconciling both aspects of science; that is, of showing how science which is a transitive process, dependent upon antecedent knowledge and the efficient activity of men, has intransitive objects which depend upon neither. That is, it must be capable of sustaining both (1) the social character of science and (2) the independence from science of the objects of scientific thought. More specifically, it must satisfy both:

(1)′ a criterion of the non-spontaneous production of knowledge, viz. the production of knowledge from and by means of knowledge (in the transitive dimension), and

(2)′ a criterion of structural and essential realism, viz. the independent existence and activity of causal structures and things (in the intransitive dimension).

For science, I will argue, is a social activity whose aim is the production of the knowledge of the kinds and ways of acting of independently existing and active things.

2. Three traditions in the philosophy of science

Viewed historically, three broad positions in the philosophy of science may be distinguished. According to the first, that of *classical empiricism*, represented by Hume and his heirs, the ultimate objects of knowledge are atomistic events. Such events constitute given facts and their conjunctions exhaust the objective content of our idea of natural necessity. Knowledge and the world may be viewed as surfaces whose points are in isomorphic correspondence or, in the case of phenomenalism, actually fused. On this conception, science is conceived as a kind of automatic or behavioural response to the stimulus of given facts and their conjunctions. Even if, as in logical empiricism, such a behaviourism is rejected as an account of the genesis of scientific knowledge, its valid content can still in principle be reduced to such facts and their conjunctions. Thus science becomes a kind of epiphenomenon of nature.

The second position received its classical though static formulation in Kant's *transcendental idealism*, but it is susceptible of updated and dynamized variations. According to it, the objects of scientific knowledge are models, ideals of natural order etc. Such objects are artificial constructs and though they may be independent of particular men, they are not independent of men or human activity in general. On this conception, a constant conjunction of events is insufficient, though it is still necessary, for the attribution of natural necessity. Knowledge is seen as a structure rather than a surface. But the natural world becomes a construction of the human mind or, in its modern versions, of the scientific community.

The third position, which is advanced here, may be characterized as *transcendental realism.* It regards the objects of knowledge as the structures and mechanisms that generate phenomena; and the knowledge as produced in the social activity of science. These objects are neither phenomena (empiricism) nor human constructs imposed upon the phenomena (idealism), but real structures which endure and operate independently of our knowledge, our experience and the conditions which allow us access to them. Against empiricism, the objects of knowledge are structures, not events; against idealism, they are intransitive (in the sense defined). On this conception, a constant conjunction of events is no more a necessary than it is a sufficient condition for the assumption of the operation of a causal law. According to this view, both knowledge and the world are structured, both are differentiated and changing; the latter exists independently of the former (though not our knowledge of this fact); and experiences and the things and causal laws to which it affords us access are normally out of phase with one another. On this view, science is not an epiphenomenon of nature, nor is nature a product of man.

A word of caution is necessary here. In outlining these positions, I am not offering them as a complete typology, but only as one which will be of some significance in illuminating current issues in the philosophy of science. Thus I am not concerned with rationalism as such, or absolute idealism. Moreover, few, if any, modern philosophers of science could be unambiguously located under one of these banners. Nagel for example stands somewhere along the continuum between Humean empiricism and neo-Kantianism; Sellars nearer the position characterized here as transcendental realist; and so on. One could say of such philosophers that they combine, and when successful in an original way synthesize, aspects of those philosophical limits whose study we are undertaking. It is my intention here, in working out the implications of a full and consistent realism, to describe such a limit; in rather the way Hume did. As an intellectual exercise alone this would be rewarding, but I believe, and hope to show, that it is also the only position that can do justice to science.

Transcendental realism must be distinguished from, and is in direct opposition to, *empirical realism.* This is a doctrine to which both classical empiricism and transcendental idealism subscribe. My reasons for rejecting it will be elaborated in a moment. 'Realism' is normally associated by philosophers with positions in the theory of perception or the theory of universals. In the former case the real entity concerned is some particular object of perception; in the latter case some general feature or property of the world. The 'real entities' the transcendental realist is concerned with are the objects of scientific discovery and investigation, such as causal laws. Realism about such entities will be seen to entail particular realist positions in the theory of perception and universals, but not to be reducible to them.

Only transcendental realism, I will argue, can sustain the idea of a law-governed world independent of man; and it is this concept, I will argue, that is necessary to understand science.

Classical empiricism can sustain neither transitive nor intransitive dimensions; so that it fails both the criteria of adequacy (1)′ and (2)′ advanced on page 18 above. Moreover in its most consistent forms it involves both solipsism and phenomenalism; so that neither (1) nor (2) can be upheld. In particular not even the idea of the independence of the event from the experience that grounds it, i.e. the intransitivity of events, can be sustained; and, in the last instance, events must be analysed as sensations or in terms of what is epistemologically equivalent, viz. human operations.

Transcendental idealism attempts to uphold the objectivity (intersubjectivity) of facts, i.e. (1). And, if given a dynamic gloss, it can allow a transitive dimension and satisfy criterion (1)′; so that, in this respect, it is an improvement on empiricism. According to such a dynamized transcendental idealism knowledge is given structure by a sequence of models, rather than a fixed set of a priori rules. However in neither its static nor its dynamic form can it sustain the intransitive dimension. For in both cases the objects of which knowledge is obtained do not exist independently of human activity in general. And if there are things which do (things-in-themselves), no scientific knowledge of them can be obtained.

Both transcendental realism and transcendental idealism reject the empiricist account of science, according to which its valid content is exhausted by atomistic facts and their conjunctions. Both agree that there could be no knowledge without the social activity of science. They disagree over whether in this case there would be no nature also. Transcendental realism argues that it is necessary to assume for the intelligibility of science that the order discovered in nature exists independently of men, i.e. of human activity in general. Transcendental idealism maintains that this order is actually imposed by men in their cognitive activity. Their differences should thus be clear. According to transcendental realism, if there were no science there would still be a nature, and it is this nature which is investigated by science. Whatever is discovered in nature must be expressed in thought, but the structures and constitutions and causal laws discovered in nature do not depend upon thought. Moreover, the transcendental realist argues, this is not just a dogmatic metaphysical belief; but rather a philosophical position presupposed by key aspects of the social activity of science, whose intelligibility the transcendental idealist cannot thus, anymore than the empiricist, sustain.

Neither classical empiricism nor transcendental idealism can sustain the idea of the independent existence and action of the causal structures and things investigated and discovered by science. It is in their shared ontology that the source of this common incapacity lies. For although transcendental idealism rejects the empiricist account of science, it tacitly takes over the empiricist account of being. This ontological legacy is expressed most succintly in its commitment to empirical realism, and thus to the concept of the '*empirical world*'. For the transcendental realist this concept embodies a sequence of related philosophical mistakes. The first consists in the use of the category of experience to define the world. This involves giving what is in effect a particular epistemological concept a general ontological function. The second consists in the view that its being experienced or experienciable is an essential property of the world; whereas it is more correctly conceived as an accidental property of some things, albeit one which can, in special circumstances, be of great significance for science. The third thus consists in the neglect of the (socially produced) circumstances under which experience is in fact epistemically significant in science.

If the bounds of the real and the empirical are co-extensive then of course any 'surplus-element' which the transcendental idealist finds in the analysis of law-like statements cannot reflect a real difference between necessary and accidental sequences of events. It merely reflects a difference in men's attitude to them. Saying that light travels in straight lines ceases then to express a proposition about the world; it expresses instead a proposition about the way men understand it. Structure becomes a function of human needs; it is denied a place in the world of things. But just because of this, I shall argue, the transcendental idealist cannot adequately describe the principles according to which our theories are constructed and empirically tested; so that the *rationality* of the transitive process of science, in which our knowledge of the world is continually extended and corrected, cannot be sustained.

To say that the weaknesses of both the empiricist and idealist traditions lie in their commitment to empirical realism is of course to commit oneself to the impossibility of ontological neutrality in an account of science; and thus to the impossibility of avoiding ontological questions in the philosophy of science. The sense in which every account of science presupposes an ontology is the sense in which it presupposes a schematic answer to the question of what the world must be like for science to be possible. Thus suppose a philosopher holds, as both empiricists and transcendental idealists do, that a constant conjunction of events apprehended in sense-experience is at least a necessary condition for the ascription of a causal law and that it is an essential part of the job of science to discover them. Such a philosopher is then committed to the belief that, given that science occurs, there are such conjunctions. As Mill put it, that 'there are such things in nature as parallel cases; that what happens once will, under a sufficient degree of similarity of circumstance, happen again'.[7]

There are two important points to register about such ontological beliefs and commitments. The first is that they should only be interpreted hypothetically, viz. as entailing what must be the case for science to be possible; on which interpretation it is a contingent fact that the world is such that science can occur. It is only in this relative or conditional sense that an account of science presupposes an ontology. The status of propositions in ontology may thus be described by the following formula: It is not necessary that science occurs. But given that it does, it is necessary that the world is a certain way. It is contingent that the world is such that science is possible. And, given that it is possible, it is contingent upon the satisfaction of certain social conditions that science in fact occurs. But given that science does or could occur, the world *must* be a certain way. Thus, the transcendental realist asserts, that the world is structured and differentiated can be established by philosophical argument; though the particular structures it contains and the ways in which it is differentiated are matters for substantive scientific investigation. The necessity for categorical distinctions between structures and events and between open systems and closed are indices of the stratification and differentiation of the world, i.e. of the transcendental realist philosophical ontology. These distinctions are presupposed, it will be shown, by the intelligibility of experimental activity. Whenever there is any danger of confusion between an 'ontology' in the sense of the kind of world presupposed by a philosophical account of science and in the sense of the particular entities and processes postulated by some substantive scientific theory I shall explicitly distinguish between a philosophical and a scientific ontology.

The second point to stress is that propositions in ontology cannot be established independently of an account of science. On the contrary, they can only be established by reference to such an account, or at least to an account of certain scientific activities. However, it will be contended that this essential order of analysis, viz. science → being, *reverses* the real nature of dependency (or, we could say, the real burden of contingency). For it is not the fact that science occurs that gives the world a structure such that it can be known by men. Rather, it is the fact that the world has such a structure that makes science, whether or not it actually occurs, possible. That is to say, it is not the character of science that imposes a determinate pattern or order on the world; but the order of the world that, under certain determinate conditions, makes possible the cluster of activities we call 'science'. It does not follow from the fact that the nature of the world can only be *known* from (a study of) science, that its nature is *determined* by (the structure of) science. Propositions in ontology, i.e. about being, can only be established by reference to science. But this does not mean that they are disguised, veiled or otherwise elliptical propositions about science. What I shall characterize in a moment as the '*epistemic fallacy*' consists in assuming that, or arguing as if, they are.

3. The transcendental analysis of experience

The empiricist ontology is constituted by the category of experience. What transcendental arguments can be produced to show its inadequacy to science; and, on the other hand, to demonstrate the intransitivity and structured character of the objects of scientific knowledge? Now the occurrence of experience in science would be agreed upon by all three combatants. Moreover, it is generally assumed that, whatever its other inadequacies, empiricism can at least do justice to the role of experience in science. Now I want to argue that the intelligibility of experience in science itself presupposes the intransitive and structured character of the objects to which, in scientific experience, 'access' is obtained. This establishes the inadequacy, in its most favoured case, of the empiricist ontology. Further I want to argue that, in virtue of their shared ontological commitment, neither empiricism nor transcendental idealism can reveal the true significance of experience in science.

Scientifically significant experience normally depends upon experimental activity as well as sense-perception; that is, upon the role of men as causal agents as well as perceivers. I will consider the two independently.

A. The analysis of perception

The intelligibility of sense-perception presupposes the intransitivity of the object perceived. For it is in the independent occurrence or existence of such objects that the meaning of 'perception', and the epistemic significance of perception, lies. Among such objects are events, which must thus be categorically independent of experiences. Many arguments have been and could be deployed to demonstrate this, which there is no space here to rehearse. For our purposes, it is sufficient merely to note that both the possibility of scientific change (or criticism) and the necessity for a scientific training presuppose the intransitivity of some real objects; which, for the empirical realist at least, can only be objects of perception. If changing experience of objects is to be possible, objects must have a distinct being in space and time from the experiences of which they are the objects. For Kepler to see the rim of the earth drop away, while Tycho Brahe watches the sun rise, we must suppose that there is something that they both see (in different ways).[8] Similarly when modern sailors refer to what ancient mariners called a sea-serpent as a school of porpoises, we must suppose that there is something which they are describing in different ways.[9] The intelligibility of scientific change (and criticism) and scientific education thus presupposes the ontological independence of the objects of experience from the objects of which they are the experiences. Events and momentary states do not of course exhaust the objects of perception. Indeed, I do not think they are even the primary objects of perception, which are probably processes and things, from which events and states are then 'reconstructed'.[10] However I do not wish to argue the point here – as it depends upon a prior resolution of the problems of causality and induction, upon which their status as objects of experience must, at least for the empiricist, depend.[11]

Events then are categorically independent of experiences. There could be a world of events without experiences. Such events would constitute *actualities* unperceived and, in the absence of men, unperceivable. There is no reason why, given the possibility of a world without perceptions, which is presupposed by the intelligibility of actual scientific perceptions, there should not be events in a world containing perceptions which are unperceived and, given our current or permanent capacities, unperceivable. And of such events theoretical knowledge may or may not be possessed, and may or may not be achievable. Clearly if at some particular time I have no knowledge of an unperceived or unperceivable event, I cannot say that such an event occurred (as a putative piece of substantive knowledge). But that in itself is no reason for saying that such an occurrence is impossible or that its supposition is meaningless (as a piece of philosophy). To do so would be to argue quite illicitly from the current state of knowledge to a philosophical conception of the world. Indeed, we know from the history of science that at any moment of time there are types of events never imagined, of which theoretical, and sometimes empirical, knowledge is eventually achieved. For in the transitive process of science the possibilities of perception, and of theoretical knowledge, are continually being extended. Thus unless it is dogmatically postulated that our present knowledge is complete or these possibilities exhausted, there are good grounds for holding that the class of unknowable events is non-empty, and unperceivable ones non-emptier; and no grounds for supposing that this will ever not be so.

Later, I will show how the domain of actualities, whose categorical independence from experiences is presupposed by the intelligibility of sense-perception, may be extended to include things as well as events.

B. *The analysis of experimental activity*

The intelligibility of experimental activity presupposes not just the intransitivity but the structured character of the objects investigated under experimental conditions. Let me once again focus on the empiricist's favourite case, viz. causal laws, leaving aside for the moment such other objects of investigation as structures and atomic constitutions. A causal law is analysed in empiricist ontology as a constant conjunction of events perceived (or perceptions). Now an experiment is necessary precisely to the extent that the pattern of events forthcoming under experimental conditions would not be forthcoming without it. Thus in an experiment we are a causal agent of the sequence of events, but not of the causal law which the sequence of events, because it has been produced under experimental conditions, enables us to identify.

Two consequences flow from this. First, the real basis of causal laws cannot be sequences of events; there must be an ontological distinction between them. Secondly, experimental activity can only be given a satisfactory rationale if the causal law it enables us to identify is held to prevail outside the contexts under which the sequence of events is generated. In short, the intelligibility of experimental activity presupposes that a constant conjunction is no more a necessary than a sufficient condition for a causal law. And it implies that causal laws endure and continue to operate in their normal way under conditions, which may be characterized as '*open*', where no constant conjunction or regular sequence of events is forthcoming. It is worth noting that in general, outside astronomy, *closed systems*, viz. systems in which constant conjunctions occur, must be experimentally established.

Both Anscombe and von Wright have recently made the point that our active *interference* in nature is normally a condition of empirical regularities.[12] But neither have seen that it follows from this that there must be an *ontological* distinction between the empirical regularity we produce and the causal law it enables us to identify. Although it has yet to be given an adequate philosophical rationale, the distinction between causal laws and patterns of events is consistent with our intuitions. Thus supposing a nuclear explosion were to destroy our planet no-one would hold that it violated, rather than exemplified, Newton's laws of motion;[13] just as if something were to affect Mercury's perihelion it would not be regarded as falsifying Einstein's theory of relativity. Similarly it lies within the power of every reasonably intelligent schoolboy or moderately clumsy research worker to upset the results of even the best designed experiment,[14] but we do not thereby suppose they have the power to overturn the laws of nature. I can quite easily affect any sequence of events designed to test say Coulomb's or Guy-Lussac's law; but I have no more power over the relationships the laws describe than the men who discovered them had. In short, laws *cannot* be the regularities that constitute their empirical grounds.

Thus the intelligibility of experimental activity presupposes the categorical independence of the causal laws discovered from the patterns of events produced. For, to repeat, in an experiment we produce a pattern of events to identify a causal law, but we do not produce the causal law identified. Once the categorical independence of causal laws and patterns of events is established, then we may readily allow that laws continue to operate in open systems, where no constant conjunctions of events prevail. And the rational explanation of phenomena occurring in such systems becomes possible.

In a world without men there would be no experiences and few, if any, constant conjunctions of events, i.e. had they been experienced Humean 'causal laws'. For both experiences and invariances (constant conjunctions of events) depend, in general, upon human activity. But causal laws do not. Thus in a world without men the causal laws that science has now as a matter of fact discovered would continue to prevail, though there would be few sequences of events and no experiences with which they were in correspondence. Thus, we can begin to see how the empiricist ontology in fact depends upon a concealed *anthropocentricity.*

The concept of causal laws being or depending upon empirical regularities involves thus a double identification: of events and experiences; and of constant conjunctions (or regular sequences) of events and causal laws. This double identification involves two category mistakes, expressed most succinctly in the concepts of the empirical world and the actuality of causal laws. The latter presupposes the ubiquity of closed systems. Both concepts, I shall argue, are profoundly mistaken and have no place in any philosophy of science. This double identification prevents the empirical realist from examining the important question of the conditions under which experience is in fact significant in science. In general this requires both that the perceiver be theoretically informed[15] and that the system in which the events occur be closed.[16] Only under such conditions can the experimental scientist come to have access to those underlying causal structures which are the objects of his theory. And not until the categorical independence of causal laws, patterns of events and experiences has been philosophically established and the possibility of their disjuncture thereby posed can we appreciate the enormous effort – in experimental design and scientific training – that is required to make experience epistemically significant in science.

The intelligibility of experimental activity presupposes then the intransitive and structured character of the objects of scientific knowledge, at least in so far as these are causal laws. And this presupposes in turn the possibility of a non-human world, i.e. causal laws *without* invariances and experiences, and in particular of a non-empirical world, i.e. causal laws and events without experiences; and the possibility of *open systems*, i.e. causal laws *out of phase* with patterns of events and experiences, and more generally of epistemically insignificant experiences, i.e. experiences out of phase with events and/or causal laws.

In saying that the objects of scientific discovery and investigation are 'intransitive' I mean to indicate therefore that they exist independently of all human activity; and in saying that they are 'structured' that they are distinct from the patterns of events that occur. The causal laws of nature are not empirical statements, i.e. statements about experiences; nor are they statements about events; nor are they synthetic a priori statements. For the moment I merely style them negatively as 'structured intransitive', postponing a positive analysis of them until §5.

4. The status of ontology and its dissolution in classical philosophy

This analysis of experimental episodes enables us to isolate a series of metaphysical, epistemological and methodological mistakes within the tradition of empirical realism. For if the intelligibility of experimental activity entails that the objects of scientific understanding are intransitive and structured then we can establish at one stroke: (i) that a philosophical ontology is possible; (ii) some propositions in it (causal laws are distinct from patterns of events, and events from experiences); and (iii) the possibility of a philosophy which is consistent with (and has some relevance for), i.e. which is itself 'in phase with', the realist practice of science. Ontology, it should be stressed, does not have as its subject matter a world apart from that investigated by science. Rather, its subject matter just is that world, considered from the point of view of what can be established about it by philosophical argument. The idea of ontology as treating of a mysterious underlying physical realm, which owes a lot to Locke and some of his rationalist contemporaries (particularly Leibniz), has done much to discredit it; and to prevent metaphysics from becoming what it ought to be, viz. a conceptual science. Philosophical ontology asks what the world must be like for science to be possible; and its premises are generally recognized scientific activities. Its method is transcendental; its premise science; its conclusion the object of our present investigation.

The metaphysical mistake the argument of the previous section allows us to pinpoint may be called the 'epistemic fallacy'. This consists in the view that statements about being can be reduced to or analysed in terms of statements about knowledge; i.e. that ontological questions can always be transposed into epistemological terms. The idea that being can always be analysed in terms of our knowledge of being, that it is sufficient for philosophy to 'treat only of the network, and not what the network describes',[17] results in the systematic dissolution of the idea of a world (which I shall here metaphorically characterize as an ontological realm) independent of but investigated by science. And it is manifest in the prohibition on any transcendent entities. It might be usefully compared with the naturalistic fallacy in moral philosophy. For just as the naturalistic fallacy prevents us from saying what is good about e.g. maximizing utility in society, so the epistemic one prevents us from saying what is epistemically significant about e.g. experience in science. To show that it is a fallacy and to trace its effects are two of the principal objectives of this study. In showing that the intelligibility of experimental activity entails that the objects of scientific knowledge, in so far as they are causal laws, are intransitive I have already succeeded in the first of these aims. For this means that a statement of a causal law cannot now be reduced to or analysed in terms of a statement about anyone's knowledge of it or knowledge in general. On the contrary, its assertion now entails that a causal law would operate even if unknown, and even if there were no-one to know it. So that knowledge ceases to be, as it were, an essential predicate of things.

The epistemic fallacy is most marked, perhaps, in the concept of the empirical world. But it is manifest in the criteria of significance and even the problems associated with the tradition of empirical realism. Kant committed it in arguing that the categories 'allow only of empirical employment and have no meaning whatsoever when not applied to objects of possible experience; that is to the world of sense.'[18] (For us on the other hand if the Kantian categories were adequate to the objects of scientific thought then they would continue to apply in a world without sense, and have a meaning in relation to that possibility.) Similarly, the logical positivists committed it when arguing, in the spirit of Hume, that if a proposition was not empirically verifiable (or falsifiable) or a tautology, it was meaningless.[19] Verificationism indeed may be regarded as a particular form of the epistemic fallacy, in which the meaning of a proposition about reality (which cannot be designated 'empirical') is confused with our grounds, which may or may not be empirical, for holding it. Once this doctrine is rejected there is no need to identify the necessary and the *a priori*, and the contingent and the *a posteriori*; or, to put it another way, one can distinguish between natural and logical necessity, and between natural and epistemic possibility. Further there is no need to assume that the order of dependence of being must be the same as the order of dependence of our knowledge of being. Thus we can allow that experience is in the last instance epistemically decisive, without supposing that its objects are ontologically ultimate, in the sense that their existence depends upon nothing else. Indeed if science is regarded as a continuing process of discovery of ever finer and in an explanatory sense more basic causal structures, then it is rational to assume that what is at any moment of time least certain epistemically speaking is most basic from the ontological point of view.[20] More generally, the epistemic fallacy is manifest in a persistent tendency to read the conditions of a particular concept of knowledge into an implicit concept of the world. Thus the problem of induction is a consequence of the atomicity of the events conjoined, which is a function of the necessity for an epistemically certain base.

Although the epistemic fallacy is of most interest to us as it is manifest in the tradition of empirical realism, it is worth mentioning that a philosopher who rejected empirical realism might still commit the epistemic fallacy, i.e. analyse being in terms of knowledge, if, as in some varieties of Platonism and rationalism, he were to define the world in terms of the possibility of non-empirical knowledge of it. For the transcendental realist it is not a necessary condition for the existence of the world that science occurs. But it is a necessary condition for the occurrence of science that the world exists and is of a certain type. Thus the possibility of our knowing it is not an essential property, and so cannot be a defining characteristic, of the world. Rather on a cosmic scale, it is an historical accident; though it is only because of this accident that we can establish in science the way the world is, and in philosophy the way it must be for science to be possible.

The view that statements about being can be reduced to or analysed in terms of statements about knowledge might be defended in the following way: ontology is dependent upon epistemology since what we can know to exist is merely a part of what we can know.[21] But this defence trades upon a tacit conflation of philosophical and scientific ontologies. For if 'what we can know to exist' refers to a possible content of a scientific theory than that it is merely a part of what we can know is an uninteresting truism. But a philosophical ontology is developed by reflection upon what must be the case for science to be possible; and this is independent of any actual scientific knowledge. Moreover, it is not true, even from the point of view of the immanent logic of a science, that what we can know to exist is just a part of what we can know. For a law may exist and be known to exist without our knowing the law. Much scientific research has in fact the same logical character as detection. In a piece of criminal detection, the detective knows that a crime has been committed and some facts about it but he does not know, or at least cannot yet prove, the identity of the criminal.

To be is *not* to be the value of a variable;[22] though it is plausible (if, I would argue, incorrect) to suppose that things can only be *known* as such. For if to be were just to be the value of a variable we could never make sense of the complex processes of identification and measurement by means of which we can sometimes represent some things as such. Knowledge follows existence, in logic and in time; and any philosophical position which explicitly or implicitly denies this has got things upside down.

The metaphysical mistake the analysis of experimental episodes pinpoints, viz. the epistemic fallacy, involves the denial of the possibility of a philosophical ontology. But if transcendental realism is correct, and ontology cannot in fact be reduced to epistemology, then denying the possibility of an ontology merely results in the generation of an *implicit ontology* and an *implicit realism*. In the empirical realist tradition the epistemic fallacy thus covers or disguises an ontology based on the category of experience, and a realism based on the presumed characteristics of the objects of experiences, viz. atomistic events, and their relations, viz. constant conjunctions. (Such presumptions can, I think, only be explained in terms of the needs of a justificationist epistemology, e.g. for incorrigible foundations of knowledge.) This in turn leads to the generation of a methodology which is either consistent with epistemology but of no relevance to science; or relevant to science but more or less radically inconsistent with epistemology. So that, in short, philosophy itself is 'out of phase' with science. Let us see how this happens.

First, the general line of Hume's critique of the possibility of any philosophical ontology or account of being, and in particular his denial that we can philosophically establish the independent existence of things or operation of natural necessities, is accepted. Now it is important to see what Hume has in fact done. He has not really succeeded in banishing ontology from his account of science. Rather he has replaced the Lockean ontology of real essences, powers and atomic constitutions with his own ontology of impressions. To say that every account of science, or every philosophy in as much as it is concerned with 'science', presupposes an ontology is to say that the philosophy of science abhors an ontological vacuum. The empiricist fills the vacuum he creates with his concept of experience. In this way an implicit ontology, crystallized in the concept of the empirical world, is generated. And it is this ontology which subsequent philosophers of science have uncritically taken over. For whether they have agreed with Hume's epistemology or not, they have accepted his critique of ontology, which contains its own implicit ontology, as valid.

Let us examine the generation of this implicit ontology in greater detail. In Hume's positive analysis of perception and causality experiences constituting atomistic events and their conjunctions are seen as exhausting our knowledge of nature. Now, adopting a realist meta-perspective this means that such events and their conjunctions must occur in nature, if science is to be possible. But from Hume onwards the sole question in the philosophy of science is whether our knowledge is exhausted by our knowledge of such events and their conjunctions; it is never questioned whether they in fact occur. That is, philosophy's concern is with whether our knowledge of the world can be reduced to sense-experience as so conceived or whether it must include an a priori or theoretical component as well; not with whether experience can adequately constitute the world.

But in Humean empiricism two things are done. First, knowledge is reduced to that of atomistic events apprehended in sense-experience. Secondly, these events are then identified as the particulars of the world. In this way our knowledge of reality is literally identified, or at best taken to be in isomorphic correspondence, with the reality known by science. From Hume onwards philosophers have thus allowed, for the sake of avoiding ontology, a particular concept of our knowledge of reality, which they may wish to explicitly reject, to inform and implicitly define their concept of the reality known by science. The result has been a continuing *'ontological tension'* induced by the conflict between the rational intuitions of philosophers about science and the constraints imposed upon their development by their inherited ontology. This has led to a nexus of interminably insoluble problems, such as how we can reason from one experience to another, and to a displacement of these rational intuitions whereby, for example, the locus of necessity is shifted from the objective necessity of the natural world to the subjective necessity of causally-determined or the inter-subjective necessity of rule-governed minds.

Now if transcendental realism is true, and scientists act as if the objects of their investigation are intransitive and structured, then any adequate methodology must be consistent with the realist practice of science, and so inconsistent with the epistemology of empirical realism. It is instructive to look at Hume here. One finds in the *Treatise* an eminently sensible realist methodology in almost total dislocation from, and certainly lacking any foundation in, his radical epistemology. Thus one might be forgiven for wondering what has become of his phenomenalism and the doctrine of impressions when Hume allows that the 'understanding corrects the appearances of the senses'.[23] Or what has happened to the idea of the contingency of the causal connection and the problem of induction when he argues that scientists, when faced with exceptions to established generalizations, quite properly search for the 'secret operation of contrary causes' rather than postulate an upset in the uniformity of nature.[24] This is typical. There is a similar dislocation between Kant's *Critique of Pure Reason* and his *Metaphysical Foundations of Natural Science.*

It might be argued in defence of Hume that he is concerned to show that our realist intuitions cannot be justified; that his point is precisely that there is a dislocation between what can be shown and what must be believed (that 'there is a direct and total opposition twixt our reason and our senses');[25] and that he leaves the latter intact. But the matter is not so simple as this. Humean empiricism is not neutral in its consequences for scientific practice. Taken consistently, it does generate a methodology; not indeed Hume's (or Newton's), but Mach's. For in the absence of the concept of an ontological realm, the implicit realism generated implies that whatever is experienced in sense-experience is an event and whatever constant conjunctions are experienced are causal laws. In this way, our current knowledge fills the vacuum left by the dissolution of the ontological realm; and in so doing it squeezes out, metaphorically speaking, the possibility of any substantive scientific criticism. In the methodology of Humean empiricism facts, which are social products, usurp the place of the particulars of the world; and their conjunctions, which are doubly social products (once qua fact, once qua event-conjunction), the place of causal laws. The result is the generation of a conservative ideology which serves to rationalize the practice of what

Kuhn has called 'normal science'.[26] Descriptivist, instrumentalist and fictionalist interpretations of theory do not do away with e.g. scientific laws, but by reducing their ontological import to a given self-certifying experience, they serve to exempt our current claims to knowledge of them from criticism.

It is thus quite incorrect to suppose that realist as opposed to non-realist interpretations of scientific theory have consequences for science which are in practice more dogmatic;[27] or to suppose that the concept of natural necessity is a kind of survival from the bad old days of scientific certainty.[28] On the contrary, the converse is the case. For it is only if the working scientist possesses the concept of an ontological realm, distinct from his current claims to knowledge of it, that he can philosophically think out the possibility of a rational criticism of these claims. To be a fallibilist about knowledge, it is necessary to be a realist about things. Conversely, to be a sceptic about things is to be a dogmatist about knowledge.

Now it is not only the doctrine of empirical realism, and philosophers' uncritical acceptance of it, that accounts for the ontological tension within philosophy and the dislocation of epistemology from methodology, of philosophy from science. It must be accounted for in part by the conditions of science, as well as philosophy. For the period in which Humean ontology became embedded in philosophy (1750–1900) was, at least in physics, a period of scientific consolidation rather than change. The role of philosophy was seen more and more to be that of showing how our knowledge is justified as distinct from showing how it was produced, can be criticized and may come to be changed. Thus whereas transcendental realism asks explicitly what the world must be like for science to be possible, classical philosophy asked merely what science would have to be like for the knowledge it yielded to be justified. It was presumed that our knowledge was justified; science was not viewed as a process in motion; and doing away with ontology left philosophy without any critical purchase on science. The transcendental realist, on the other hand, allows a limited critical role for philosophy. For by restoring the idea of an ontological realm distinct from science, he makes it possible for us to say that in a particular field, say social psychology, science is not being done, although as a philosopher he cannot say dogmatically whether or not a science of social psychology is possible.[29] (An ontological dimension is in this way necessary not only to render intelligible scientific criticism, but to make possible philosophical criticism of the practice of a science.) Increasingly then it was the logical structure of justificatory argument that defined philosophy's concept of science; and the philosophy of science itself became a kind of battleground for internecine warfare between opposed concepts of justified belief. Moreover, when the idea of scientific certainty eventually collapsed, the absence of an ontological dimension discouraged anything other than a purely voluntaristic reaction – in which it was supposed that because our beliefs about the world were not causally determined by the world then they must be completely 'free creations of our own minds, the result of an almost poetic intuition'.[30]

Behind this state of affairs there ran a stong *anthropocentric* current in classical and subsequent philosophy,[31] which sought to rephrase questions about the world as questions about the nature or behaviour of men. One aspect of this is the view, which I have characterized as the epistemic fallacy, that ontological questions can always be rephrased as epistemological ones. The anthropocentric and epistemic biases of classical philosophy led to the dissolution of the concept of the ontological realm, which we need to render intelligible the transitive process of science. In this way the world, which ought to be viewed as a multi-dimensional structure independent of man, came to be squashed into a flat surface whose characteristics, such as being constituted by atomistic facts, were determined by the needs of a particular concept of knowledge. This led to a barrage of problems and an impossible account of science. For from now on any structure, if it was allowed at all, had to be located in the human mind or the scientific community. Thus the world was literally turned inside out in an attempt to confine it within sentience. An inevitable 'involution' in the philosophy of science occurred. Without a concept of a reality unknown, but at least in part knowable, philosophy could not display the creative and critical activity of science, and ceased to be of any practical relevance for it. This was the price paid for the dissolution of ontology. A philosophy for science depends upon its reconstitution.

5. Ontology vindicated and the real basis of causal laws

In §3 I argued that only if causal laws are not the patterns of events that enable us to identify them can the intelligibility of experimental activity be sustained. But causal laws are, or have seemed to philosophers to be, pretty mysterious entities. What can it mean to say that they have a real basis independent of events? The answer to this question will be seen to necessitate the development of a non-anthropocentric ontology of structures, generative mechanisms and active things.

The ontological status of causal laws can best be approached by considering the divergent responses of transcendental realism and idealism to the problem of distinguishing a necessary from a purely accidental sequence of events. Both may agree, in their modern versions, that without some conception of a generative mechanism at work no attribution of necessity is justified. For the transcendental idealist, however, this necessity is imposed by men on the pattern of events; the generative mechanism is an irreducible figment of the imagination. For the transcendental realist, on the other hand, the generative mechanism may come to be established as real in the course of the ongoing activity of science. Indeed he will argue that it is only if existential questions can be raised about the objects of scientific theory that the rationality of theory construction can be sustained. For without them science would remain, as in empiricism, a purely internal process – with the familiarity of image replacing the reinforcement of sensation, still lacking a rational dynamic of change.

Now once it is granted that mechanisms and structures may be said to be real, we can provide an interpretation of the independence of causal laws from the patterns of events, and a fortiori of the rationale of experimental activity. For the real basis of this independence lies in the independence of the generative mechanisms of nature from the events they generate. Such mechanisms endure even when not acting; and act in their normal way even when the consequents of the law-like statements they ground are, owing to the operation of intervening mechanisms or countervailing causes, unrealized. It is the role of the experimental scientist to exclude such interventions, which are usual; and to trigger the mechanism so that it is active. The activity of the mechanism may then be studied without interference. And it is this characteristic pattern of activity or mode of operation that is described in the statement of a causal law. It is only under closed conditions that there will be a one-to-one relationship between the causal law and the sequence of events. And it is normally only in the laboratory that these enduring mechanisms of nature, whose operations are described in the statements of causal laws, become actually manifest and empirically accessible to men. But because they endure and continue to act, when stimulated, in their normal way outside those conditions, their use to explain phenomena and resistance to pseudo-falsification in open systems can be rationally justified.

Only if causal laws persist through, which means they must be irreducible to, the flux of conditions can the idea of the universality of a *known* law be sustained. And only if they have a reality distinct from that of events can the assumption of a *natural* necessity be justified. On this view laws are not empirical statements, but statements about the forms of activity characteristic of the things of the world. And their necessity is that of a natural connection, not that of a human rule. There is a distinction between the *real* structures and mechanisms of the world and the *actual* patterns of events that they generate. And this distinction in turn justifies the more familiar one between *necessary* and *accidental* sequences. For a necessary sequence is simply one which corresponds to, or is in phase with, a real connection; that is, it is a real connection actually manifest in the sequence of events that occurs.

The world consists of mechanisms not events. Such mechanisms combine to generate the flux of phenomena that constitute the actual states and happenings of the world. They may be said to be real, though it is rarely that they are actually manifest and rarer still that they are empirically identified by men. They are the intransitive objects of scientific theory. They are quite independent of men – as thinkers, causal agents and perceivers. They are not unknowable, although knowledge of them depends upon a rare blending of intellectual, practico-technical and perceptual skills. They are not artificial constructs. But neither are they Platonic forms. For they can become manifest to men in experience. Thus we are not imprisoned in caves, either of our own or of nature's making. We are not doomed to ignorance. But neither are we spontaneously free. This is the arduous task of science: the production of the knowledge of those enduring and continually active mechanisms of nature that produce the phenomena of our world.

Objections may be made to my proposed reconstitution of an ontological realm, which question in turn the intransitivity and the structured character of the postulated objects of scientific inquiry, i.e. the ideas of their categorical independence from men and events respectively. I will consider the two kinds of objections in turn.

Thus, it might be objected that the very idea of a world without men is unintelligible because the conditions under which it is true would make its being conceived impossible. But I can think of a world without men; and I can think of a world without myself. No-one can truly say 'I do not exist' but that does not mean that 'I do not exist' is unintelligible; or that it cannot be meaningfully, just because it cannot be truly said. It is no objection to the intelligibility of a statement that it is counter-factual. Indeed it is only because it is intelligible that we can say that it is counter-factual.

Someone might hold that to think of a world without men is not so much unintelligible as impossible; that we must picture ourselves in any picture. Now it is a fact about human beings that we can do this. But we do not have to do it, any more than an artist must initial his work. The idea may be perhaps that a thought must always contain, or at least be accompanied by, a thought of the thinker of the thought thinking the thought. Clearly if this were so, an infinite regress would be impossible to avoid. However, to be aware of the fact that I am thinking of a particular topic x, it is not necessary for me to be thinking of that fact. Such awareness may be expressed in thought, but when it is the topic is no longer x but my thought of x. It is possible for A to think ε and to be aware of thinking ε without thinking about thinking ε; and unless this were so no-one could ever intelligently think. Moreover it is possible for A to think about thinking ε without thinking about his (A's) thinking ε. Thinking about thinking about a particular topic must be distinguished from thinking about the thinker of the topic.[32]

There is no absurdity in the supposition of a world without men. Rather it is a possibility presupposed by the social activity of science. It is important to establish this fact. For we are too liable to underestimate the power of the pictures, often unconscious, which underpin philosophical theories. Such pictures indeed often hold our philosophical imagination 'captive'.[33] Our philosophy of science is heavily anthropocentric, which is why it is important to consider what it would be possible to say about our world if there were no men, given that we know that our world is one in which science is as a matter of fact possible. For example things would still act, be subject to laws and preserve their identity through certain changes.

A second kind of objection might focus on the structured character of the postulated objects of scientific inquiry, questioning not so much the idea itself but the interpretation I have given to it; and in particular the explanatory value of the particular ontology proposed. Thus it might be objected that, while the transcendental argument from experimental activity in §3 establishing the distinctiveness of causal laws and patterns of events, is sound, the introduction of the concept of generative mechanisms to provide a real basis for causal laws is gratuitous.

What does it mean to say that a generative mechanism endures and acts in its characteristic way? It does not *mean,* we have seen, that a regular sequence of events occurs or is experienced; though the occurrence of such a sequence may, in special circumstances, provide empirical *grounds* for the hypothesis of the existence of the mechanism. For the intelligibility of experimental activity entails that the particular mechanism endures and at least some mechanisms act through the flux of conditions that determine whether they are active and co-determine the manifest outcome of their activity. That is to say, it entails that generative mechanisms endure even when inactive and act even where, as in open systems, there is no one-to-one relationship between the causal law representing the characteristic mode of operation of the mechanism and the particular sequence of events that occurs. In particular, it entails that mechanisms act in their normal way outside the closed conditions that enable us to experimentally identify them and whether or not we do so; i.e. whether or not the results of their operations are modified, and whether or not these results are perceived by men. (In the former case we could talk of a disjuncture between the domains of the real and the actual; in the latter case of a disjuncture between the domains of the real and the empirical.)

Now the reason why the concept of a causal law cannot itself be taken as ontologically basic is because its analysis presupposes a 'real something' over and above and independent of patterns of events; and it is for the status of this real something that the concept of a generative mechanism is groomed. But then does to say that a generative mechanism endures and acts in its characteristic way mean anything more than to say that a thing goes on acting in a certain way? As stated the reformulation is ambiguous. For the continuance of a form or pattern of activity can be interpreted in an empirical or a non-empirical way. The intelligibility of experimental activity requires the latter non-empirical interpretation. For it entails, as we have seen, that causal laws persist and are efficacious in open systems, i.e. outside the conditions that enable us to empirically identify them. Now accepting this non-empirical interpretation means that reference to causal laws involves centrally reference to *causal agents*; that is, to things endowed with causal powers. On this interpretation then the generative mechanisms of nature exist as the causal powers of things. We now have a perfectly acceptable ontological basis for causal laws. For if it is wrong to reify causal laws, and it is wrong to reify generative mechanisms, it cannot be wrong to reify things! However, the fact that the transcendental analysis of experimental activity showed that generative mechanisms must go on acting (i.e. that causal laws must be efficacious) outside the closed conditions that permit their identification means that causal laws cannot be simply analysed as powers. Rather they must be analysed as tendencies. For whereas powers are potentialities which may or may not be exercised, tendencies are potentialities which may be exercised or as it were 'in play' without being realized or manifest in any particular outcome. They are therefore just right for the analysis of causal laws.[34]

If the analysis of causal laws (and generative mechanisms) is to be given by the concept of things and not events (a possibility which I have already rejected by demonstrating in §3 their categorical independence from events), the consideration that they not only persist but are efficacious in open systems, which is presupposed by the intelligibility of experimental activity, entails that causal laws must be analysed as tendencies. For tendencies are powers which may be exercised without being fulfilled or actualized (as well as being fulfilled or actualized unperceived by men). It is by reference not just to the enduring powers but the unrealized activities or unmanifest (or incompletely manifest) actions of things that the phenomena of the world are explained. It is the idea of continuing activity as distinct from that of enduring power that the concept of tendency is designed to capture. In the concept of tendency, the concept of power is thus literally dynamized or set in motion.

In the full analysis of law-like statements we are thus concerned with a new kind of conditional: which specifies the exercise of possibilities which need not be manifest in any particular outcome. Such conditionals are *normic*,[35] rather than subjunctive. They do not say what would happen, but what is happening in a perhaps unmanifest way. Whereas a powers statement says A would ψ, in appropriate circumstances, a normic statement says that A really is ψ'ing, whether or not its actual (or perceivable) effects are counteracted. They are not counter-factuals, but *transfactuals*; they take us to a level at which things are really going on irrespective of the actual outcome. To invoke a causal law is to invoke a normic conditional. A full analysis of normic and tendency statements will be provided later. For the moment, it should be noted that normic statements provide the correct analysis of the normic indicative form. A normic statement is a transfactual statement, with actual instances in the laboratory that constitute its empirical grounds.

The world consists of things, not events. Most things are complex objects, in virtue of which they possess an ensemble of tendencies, liabilities and powers. It is by reference to the exercise of their tendencies, liabilities and powers that the phenomena of the world are explained. Such continuing activity is in turn referred back for explanation to the essential nature of things. On this conception of science it is concerned essentially with what kinds of things they are and with what they tend to do; it is only derivatively concerned with predicting what is actually going to happen. It is only rarely, and normally under conditions which are artificially produced and controlled, that scientists can do the latter. And, when they do, its significance lies precisely in the light that it casts on the enduring natures and ways of acting of independently existing and transfactually active things.

There is nothing esoteric or mysterious about the concept of the generative mechanisms of nature, which provide the real basis of causal laws. For a generative mechanism is nothing other than a way of acting of a thing. It endures, and under appropriate circumstances is exercised, as long as the properties that account for it persist. Laws then are neither empirical statements (statements about experiences) nor statements about events. Rather they are statements about the ways of acting of independently existing and transfactually active things.

It is now possible to give a positive interpretation of our characterization in §3 of the objects of scientific investigation, at least in so far as they are causal laws, as 'structured intransitive'. 'Structured' in so far as it is the activities of mechanisms and causal structures, not the occurrence of events, that are designated in statements of causal law. 'Intransitive' in so far as the mechanisms and causal structures, whose activity is designated, endure and act quite independently of men. To discover the independently existing and transfactually active machinery of nature is not, it should be stressed, the aim of an independent inquiry of metaphysics. Rather, it is the end to which all the empirical efforts of science are directed. Ontology has been vindicated not as providing a set of necessary truths about a mysterious underlying physical realm, but as providing a set of conditionally necessary truths about our ordinary world as investigated by science. It is important to be clear about what philosophical argument can achieve. Thus as a piece of philosophy we can say (given that science occurs) that some real things and generative mechanisms must exist (and act). But philosophical argument cannot establish which ones actually do; or, to put it the other way round, what the real mechanisms are. That is up to science to discover. That generative mechanisms must exist and sometimes act independently of men and that they must be irreducible to the patterns of events they generate is presupposed by the intelligibility of experimental activity. But is up to actual experiments to tell us what the mechanisms of nature are. Here, as elsewhere, it is the task of philosophy to analyse notions which in their substantive employment have only a syncategorematic use. Thus whenever a scientist refers to a thing or event, structure or law, or says that something exists or acts in a certain way he must refer to it under some particular description; he is using the notion of thing, law, existence, etc. But it is the task of the philosopher to analyse the concept as such. To argue that this task is both legitimate and necessary is not to populate the world with (or to suppose that there is a world of) things without names or events-in-general.

I am now in a position to tidy up my analysis of experimental activity. The experimental scientist must perform two essential functions in an experiment. First, he must trigger the mechanism under study to ensure that it is active; and secondly, he must prevent any interference with the operation of the mechanism. These activities could be designated 'experimental production' and 'experimental control'. The former is necessary to ensure the satisfaction of the antecedent (or stimulus) conditions, the latter to ensure the realization of the consequent, i.e. that a closure has been obtained. But both involve changing or being prepared to change the 'course of nature', i.e. the sequence of events that would otherwise have occurred.[36] In a simple electrical experiment designed to illustrate say Ohm's Law, the wiring of an electric circuit and the generation of an electric current would constitute 'experimental production'; maintaining the appropriate resistance levels, ensuring that no new magnetic field is suddenly placed in the neighbourhood of the circuit, etc. would then constitute 'experimental control'.

Only if the mechanism is active and the system in which it operates is closed can scientists in general record a unique relationship between the antecedent and consequent of a law-like statement. The aim of an experiment is to get a single mechanism going in isolation and record its effects. Outside a closed system these will normally be affected by the operations of other mechanisms, either of the same or of different kinds, too, so that no unique relationship between the variables or precise description of the mode of operation of the mechanism will be possible. In general, experimental activity requires a degree of plasticity of the antecedent (stimulus) and circumambient conditions to human manipulation and control. Such plasticity is not easily won. 'Experimental design' is a substantial theoretical labour in itself.

It has often been said, metaphorically speaking, that in an experiment we put a question to nature. But it has not been said that the question we put is a practical one – with our hands, so to speak. The weakness of previous analyses of experimental activity is that they have not appreciated the significance of the fact that conjunctions of phenomena have to be worked for practically (as well as in thought); that conjunctions are not given to, but *made by* us. In an important study, von Wright has seen this. But he has not drawn the correct conclusion from it: which is that, just because the experimenter is a causal agent of the sequence of events, there must be an ontological distinction between the sequence he generates and the causal law it enables him to identify. Any other conclusion renders experimental activity pointless. (Why generate that sequence?) The reason for von Wright's failure to see this stems from his unfortunate initial assumption of (as he puts it) a 'Tractatus-world', i.e. a world of logically independent atomistic states of affairs (which astonishingly he seems to regard as a harmless simplification);[37] which precludes him from seeing laws as anything other than conditional statements about atomistic states of affairs. It is of course something of a scandal that empiricists who invoke experience as the sole ground of knowledge and scientific knowledge as their paradigm should not have undertaken an analysis of the conditions under which experience is significant in science. It should be stressed that the result that there is an ontological distinction between causal laws and patterns of events depends upon only two premises: (i) that men are causal agents capable of interfering with the course of nature and (ii) that experimental activity, the planned disruption of the course of nature, is a significant feature of science.

In stressing the practical component of experimental activity, it is important not to forget the theoretical side. In an experiment men put a question to nature. But they must put it in a language that nature understands, as well as in a form that makes possible an unambiguous reply. It is difficult to overestimate the importance for modern science of the development of instruments such as clocks and telescopes, which may be seen as devices designed to decipher the vocabulary of nature. Both the construction and the interpretation of such instruments depended upon theory. Hooke's law, for example, is literally built into the construction of spring balances.[38] Experimental confirmation of Galilean dynamics was delayed for a long time by the difficulty of measuring 'the most fundamental magnitude of dynamics', i.e. time. But when the Huyghens eventually succeeded in building such a clock in 1659 it was only by basing it on the new dynamics (the very dynamics it was designed to vindicate) and in particular the theory of the isochronous curve of the pendulum.[39] Similarly it has been convincingly argued that the development of cosmology in the early 17th century was held up by the absence of an adequate theory of telescopic vision.[40] In short, experimental activity depends crucially upon the adequacy of the theories (sometimes referred to as 'auxiliary') according to which the experimental equipment is constructed and its results interpreted.

Two problems are raised by my analysis of experimental activity. First, we know that much science, of what might be called a fundamental kind, has proceeded by way of 'thought' rather than by actual experiment. As Dijksterhuis has put it: 'In general one has to take stories about experiments by Galileo, as well as his opponents with some reserve. As a rule they were performed mentally, or they are merely described as possibilities.'[41] It seems that Einstein too was not averse to the occasional 'Gedankexperimente'.[42] This raises the question of whether, and if so how, pure thought can anticipate a law? And the problem of how, if it can, we then avoid the rationalist conclusion that provided only our axiom base is strong enough we could deduce all the laws of nature without recourse to experience. Secondly, we know that in many fields, most notably history and the human sciences and in the biological sciences in aspects of their work, experimental activity is impossible. This raises the question of whether there are, or it is possible to devise for them, surrogates of the experimental establishment of closed systems in physics and chemistry? And here again there lurks an unacceptable rationalist implication. Both pose prima facie problems for transcendental realism, which I hope to be able to resolve at a later stage in this study.

6. A sketch of a critique of empirical realism

I have argued that the causal structures and generative mechanisms of nature must exist and act independently of the conditions that allow men access to them, so that they must be assumed to be structured and intransitive, i.e. relatively independent of the patterns of events and the actions of men alike. Similarly I have argued that events must occur independently of the experiences in which they are apprehended. Structures and mechanisms then are real and distinct from the patterns of events that they generate; just as events are real and distinct from the experiences in which they are apprehended. Mechanisms, events and experiences thus constitute three overlapping domains of reality, viz. the domains of the *real*, the *actual* and the *empirical*. This is represented in Table 1 below. The crux of my objection to the doctrine of empirical realism should now be clear. By constituting an ontology based on the category of experience, as expressed in the concept of the empirical world and mediated by the ideas of the actuality of the causal laws and the ubiquity of constant conjunctions, three domains of reality are collapsed into one. This prevents the question of the conditions under which experience is in fact significant in science from being posed; and the ways in which these three levels are brought into harmony or phase with one another from being described.

Table 1

	Domain of Real	*Domain of Actual*	*Domain of Empirical*
Mechanisms	√		
Events	√	√	
Experiences	√	√	√

Note. For transcendental realism $d_r \geqslant d_a \geqslant d_e$ . . . (i) where d_r, d_a, and d_e are the domains of the real, the actual and the empirical respectively.

For empirical realism $d_r = d_a = d_e$ . . . (ii).

Comment: (ii) is a special case of (i), which depends in general upon antecedent social activity, and in which

(a) for $d_a = d_e$ the events are known under epistemically significant descriptions, which depends upon skilled perception (and thus a skilled perceiver);
(b) for $d_r = d_a$ an antecedent closure has been obtained, which depends upon skilled experimentation (and thus the planned disruption of nature).

Now these three levels of reality are not naturally or normally in phase. It is the social activity of science which makes them so. Experiences, and the facts they ground, are social products; and the conjunctions of events, that, when apprehended in experience, provide the empirical grounds for causal laws, are, as we have seen, social products too. It can thus be seen that underlying and necessary for the implicit ontology of empirical realism is an *implicit sociology* in which facts and their conjunctions are seen as given by nature or spontaneously (voluntaristically) produced by men. In this chapter I have outlined an answer to the question 'what must the world be like for science to be possible?'. In Chapter 3 I will ask 'what must society be like for science to be possible?'; i.e. I shall attempt a transcendental deduction of certain basic sociological categories from an investigation of the conditions for the possibility of science. The answer to these two questions will constitute the interwoven themes of this work. It is impossible to overemphasize how closely they are connected. For once, for example, we reject the doctrine that there are everywhere in nature such things as spontaneously occurring parallel cases and see rather that in general they have to be assiduously worked for and artificially produced in the social activity of science, we are forced to constitute an ontology of structures distinct from events.

For us, for the moment, it is sufficient merely to note that the most important feature of science neglected by the doctrine of empirical realism is that it is *work*; and hard work at that. Work consists, paradigmatically, in the transformation of given products. Scientific change is an integral feature of science, in which what is transformed is a part of the formally accredited stock of scientific knowledge. In a scientific training the object transformed is not knowledge but man himself. But in both cases what is transformed is itself already a social product. The peculiar significance of experimental activity is that man qua material object (rather than simply thinker or perceiver) exercises his causal powers to transform the natural world itself, of which he is also a part. Now corresponding to the dissolution of ontology in philosophy, there has been a parallel denegation of the social character of science. In Chapter 3 I will set out to vindicate sociology in an attempt to render intelligible scientific change. This will enable me to reconstitute a transitive dimension, as complementary to the intransitive one established here.

The concept of the empirical world is anthropocentric. The world is what men can experience. But the couple of this concept, and from a realist metaperspective necessary to sustain it, is the absence of the concept of the antecedent social activity necessary to make experience significant in science. And this has the objectionable ideological consequence (from the point of view of the practice of science) that whatever men currently experience is unquestionably the world. Now it is central to the argument of this study that the concepts 'empirical' and 'sense-experience' belong quite unequivocally to the social world of science. Experiences are a part, and when set in the context of the social activity of science an epistemically critical part, of the world. But just because they are a part of the world they cannot be used to define it. An experience to be significant in science must normally be the result of a social process of production; in this sense it is the end, not the beginning of a journey. But only transcendental realism can explain why scientists are correct in regarding experience as in the last instance the test of theory. For it is by means of it that, under conditions which are artificially produced and controlled, skilled men can come to have access to those enduring and active structures, normally hidden or present to men only in distorted form, that generate the actual phenomena of our world. Empirical realism depends upon a reduction of the real to the actual and of the actual to the empirical. It thus presupposes the spontaneity of conjunctions and of facts. And in doing so presupposes a closed world and a completed science.

It is important to stress that I am not saying that experiences are *less* real than events, or events less real than structures. This is the kind of mistake that is encouraged by the way in which Eddington formulated his problem of the relationship between the familiar and the scientific worlds; in which he described the situation as one in which there were 'duplicates' of every object: two tables, two chairs, two pens, etc.[43] Since then the problem has always seemed to be that of saying *which* object is real. For the ordinary language instrumentalist the scientific object is an artificial construct;[44] for the scientistic super-realist the familiar object a mere illusion.[45] For the transcendental realist however this formulation of the problem is bogus. For if there is a relationship between the worlds it is one of natural generation, not an interpretation of man. The relationship is not between a real and an imaginary object, but between two kinds of real object, one of which is very small. The relationship between electrons and tables has to be understood in terms of causal connections, not correspondence rules. Consequents are not less real, or the statements describing them less true, in virtue of their being effects; any more than causes, in virtue of being recondite, must be imaginary. In particular, the fact that the properties of everyday objects, at what has been picturesquely described as the zone of the middle dimensions,[46] can be explained in terms of the very small (or the very large) does not render them less real than the entities that account for them; anymore than zinc and sulphuric acid cease to react in a certain way when we explain their reaction in terms of their atomic structure.

For the transcendental realist laws, though not our knowledge of them, are categorically independent of men – as thinkers, causal agents and perceivers. Transcendental realism can thus accommodate both Locke's view that there are (or may be) laws which are unknowable;[47] and Kneale's suggestion that there are (or may be) laws whose instances are unperceivable.[48] But it allows in addition the possibility of known laws, whose instances are perceivable, but which, when not instanced in closed systems, remain unmanifest to men. However, my interpretation of these possibilities is different from Locke's (and Kneale's). For the transcendental realist, our knowledge, perceptual skills and causal powers are set in the context of the ongoing social activity of science; and in the course of it they are continually being extended, to which process there can be no a priori limits. Thus though it may be necessary, to the extent that science is always incomplete, that at any moment of time some laws are unknowable; it is not necessary that any particular laws are.

Locke's mistake in failing to appreciate the possibility that the 'sad experience' of chemists who 'sometimes in vain, search for the same qualities in one parcel of sulphur, antimony or vitriol, which they have found in others'[49] might come to be transformed in the course of the development of science into a knowledge of the 'constitution of their insensible parts, from which flow those sensible qualities, which serve us to distinguish one from another'[50] was not a scientific mistake. It did not consist in his failure to foresee the development of the theory of atomic number and valency or to predict Mendeleyeev's predictions. His scepticism over the possibility of a scientific knowledge of real essences was a philosophical mistake, rooted in his theory of ideas. For if all our knowledge is acquired in perception and perception constitutes the world, there can be no place for an antecedent cause of knowledge (or of perception). But as only what is seen as socially produced can be seen as putatively socially transformable, this leads inevitably to an a-historical view of science.

Locke's error was not therefore based on an inadequate knowledge of chemistry. But on an inadequate concept of the transitive dimension of science, which prevented him from seeing the current state of chemistry as what it was, viz. the *current* state of a science; and which thus allowed him to be influenced by it into propounding a general philosophical thesis about knowledge – and in particular of course about the impossibility of a certain kind of knowledge, viz. of real essences. Locke's case has a general moral. For without a concept of science as a process-in-motion and of knowledge as possessing (in the sense indicated in §1 above) a material cause, it is easy to argue from the current state of a science to a philosophical thesis about knowledge. Consider, for example, the Copenhagen interpretation of Quantum theory. More important perhaps, the influence of Newtonian mechanics on 18th century philosophy led to a kind of stasis in thought from which the philosophy of science has still to recover. Action-by-contact as a paradigm of causality, the celestial closure as a model of knowledge, gravity as the template of our ignorance all had a disastrous effect. The underdevelopment of the sciences of substance in comparison with the science of motion (of the time), and the form that the latter took, thus had, at a decisive moment in the history of philosophy, through the generation of a static philosophical conception of knowledge, a permanent effect on all subsequent 'philosophy of science'. It is in this sense that in philosophy we are still prisoners of the scientific thought of the past.

The anthropocentric and epistemic biases of classical philosophy have resulted in the dominance, in philosophy, of what might be styled 'idols' of a Baconian kind. These are false conceptions which cause men to see, in philosophy, everything in relation to themselves (cf. the concept of the empirical world) and their present knowledge. Six hundred years ago, Copernicus argued that the universe does not revolve around man. And yet in philosophy we still represent things as if it did. In the philosophy of science there must be two Copernican Revolutions. The first establishing a transitive dimension in which our knowledge is seen to be socially produced, and as such neither an epiphenomenon of nature nor a convention of man. The second establishing an intransitive dimension, based on the reconstitution of a philosophical ontology, in which the world of which, in the social activity of science, knowledge is obtained is seen to be in general quite independent of man. These Copernican Revolutions must be given a Copernican interpretation (for Philosophy has its Osianders too); which is why we need the metaphysics of transcendental realism, which will be vindicated by its capacity to render intelligible the underanalysed phenomenon of science.

Corresponding to the two criteria advanced on page 24 above two acid tests for a philosophy of science may be developed:

(1) is knowledge regarded as socially produced, i.e. as having a material cause of its own kind? or is it read straight onto the natural world or out of the human mind?
(2) are the objects of knowledge regarded as existing and acting independently of men? or do they depend implicitly or explicitly upon men for their existence and/or activity?

Scientists try to discover the reasons for things and events, patterns and processes, sequences and structures. To understand how they do so one needs both a concept of the transitive process of knowledge-production and a concept of the intransitive objects of the knowledge they produce: the real mechanisms that generate the actual phenomena of the world, including as a special case our perceptions of them.

Notes

1 See Aristotle, *Metaphysics*, 1.3.
2 See J. R. Ravetz, *Scientific Knowledge and its Social Problems*, pp. 116–19.
3 Cf. R. Harré, *Philosophies of Science*, pp. 176–7.
4 W. Thomson, *Notes of Lectures on Molecular Dynamics*, p. 132.
5 See A. S. Eve, *Rutherford.*
6 Cf. I. Kant, *On the Distinctiveness of the Principles of Natural Theology and Morals.*
7 J. S. Mill, *A System of Logic*, Bk. III, Chap. 3, Sect. 1.
8 Cf. N. R. Hanson, *Patterns of Discovery*, Chap. 1.
9 Cf. J. J. C. Smart, *Philosophy and Scientific Realism*, pp. 38–9.

10 Cf. J. J. Gibson, *The Senses Considered as Perceptual Systems.*
11 Cf. M. Hollis, 'Reason and Reality', *P.A.S. Vol. LXVIII* (1967–8), p. 279.
12 G. E. M. Anscombe, *Causality and Determination*, p. 22; and G. H. von Wright, *Explanation and Understanding*, pp. 60–4.
13 Cf. G. E. M. Anscombe, *op. cit.*, p. 21.
14 Cf. Ravetz's '4th law of thermo-dynamics': no experiment goes properly the first time. See J. R. Ravetz, *op. cit.*, p. 76.
15 Cf. F. Dretske, *Seeing and Knowing*, Chap. 3.
16 Cf. G. H. von Wright, *op cit.*, Chap. 2.
17 L. Wittgenstein, *Tractatus Logico-Philosophicus*, 6.35.
18 I. Kant, *Critique of Pure Reason*, B.724.
19 See e.g. A. J. Ayer, *Language, Truth and Logic*, pp. 31–41.
20 A recent book, A. Quinton's *Nature of Things*, is vitiated by a failure to distinguish these two questions. From the outset Quinton tends to identify the problem of fundamental entities with that of the foundations of knowledge (p. 5). This leads him to argue that 'if all possible evidence for the existence of theoretical entities is provided by common observables it follows . . . that the logically indispensable evidence, and thus the sense, of assertions about theoretical entities must be capable of being expressed in terms of those common observables and thus that theoretical entities can have only a derived and dependent existence' (p. 285).
21 D. H. Mellor, 'Physics and Furniture', *American Philosophical Quarterly, Studies in the Philosophy of Science*, p. 184.
22 See W. V. O. Quine, 'Designation and Existence', *Readings in Philosophical Analysis*, ed. H. Feigl and W. Sellars, p. 50; *Methods of Logic*, p. 224; and *From a Logical Point of View*, Chap. 1 and passim.
23 D. Hume, *Treatise on Human Nature*, p. 632.
24 D. Hume, *op. cit.*, p. 132. Cf. Newton's 4th rule of reasoning in philosophy: 'propositions inferred by general induction from phenomena [are to be regarded as] true . . . till such time as other phenomena occur by which they may either be made more accurate or liable to exceptions', I. Newton, *Principia Mathematica*, Bk. III.
25 D. Hume, *op. cit.*, p. 231.
26 T. S. Kuhn, *The Structure of Scientific Revolutions*, Chaps. II–IV.
27 See e.g. M. Hesse, *In Defence of Objectivity*, p. 14.
28 See e.g. G. Buchdahl, *op. cit.*, p. 31.
29 The structure of such a critique would be as follows: If the subject matter of social psychology is such that a science of social psychology is possible and social psychologists are to have knowledge of it, then social psychologists should do φ, ψ, etc. rather than x, ω, etc. The transcendental realist could thus not accept the notorious definition of economics as what economists do. For him, whether or not they actually do economics is at least in part a contingent question. Notice that the formula I have used leaves the question of whether a science of social psychology is possible open. This is important because for the transcendental realist it is the nature of the object that determines the possibility of a science. Thus he can allow, without paradox, that there may be no humanly intelligible pattern to be discovered in the stars or politically intelligible pattern in voting behaviour. So that no science of astrology or psephology is possible, no matter now scrupulously 'scientific method' is adhered to.
30 K. R. Popper, *Conjectures and Refutations*, p. 192.
31 Cf. J. J. C. Smart, *op. cit.*, pp. 149–51.
32 In fact men have the capacity to be self-conscious in two ways: first, in being

conscious of what they are doing; and secondly, in being conscious of their doing it. That these two are not equivalent is shown by the fact that in some contexts a person may know what he has done but not that he has done it and vice-versa.

33 L. Wittgenstein, *Philosophical Investigation*, 115.

34 A recent antecedent of the view that causal laws should be analysed as tendencies is contained in P. T. Geach, 'Aquinas', *Three Philosophers*, G. E. M. Anscombe and P. T. Geach, pp. 101ff. Important works in the recent development of the concept of powers are W. D. Joske, *Material Objects*, Chaps. 4 and 5; M. R. Ayers, *The Refutation of Determinism*, Chaps. 3–5; and R. Harré, *Principles of Scientific Thinking*, esp. Chap. 10.

35 I owe this term to M. Scriven, 'Truisms as the Grounds for Historical Explanation', *Theories of History*, ed. P. Gardiner, pp. 464ff. Scriven uses it to refer to generalizations grounding historical explanations which contain modifiers such as 'normally', 'tendency', 'usually', etc. My use of the term is substantially different. But it is the nearest thing to an antecedent for the kind of conditional I am concerned with.

36 Formally we could say that in experimental production by doing φ we change α to a so altering the state that would otherwise have prevailed; and in experimental production by doing or being prepared to do ψ we exclude the intervention of elements $\beta_I \ldots \beta_n$ so allowing the mechanism M set in motion by a to generate b. The sequence a.b thus appears as a consequence of the results of our actions. It is in this sense that a closure is normally a human product.

37 See G. H. von Wright, *op. cit.*, pp. 43–45.

38 Cf. N. R. Hanson, *Observation and Explanation*, p. 56.

39 See e.g. A. Koyré, *Metaphysics and Measurement*, Chap. 4.

40 V. Ronchi, 'Complexities, advances and misconceptions in the development of the science of vision: what is being discovered?', *Scientific Change*, ed. A. Crombie, pp. 542–61.

41 E. J. Dijksterhuis, *The Mechanisation of the World Picture*, p. 338.

42 See K. R. Popper, *The Logic of Scientific Discovery*, App. XI.

43 A. S. Eddington, *The Nature of the Physical World*, p. xi. Stebbing substituted the idea of 'counterparts' for that of 'duplicates' in her rendering of the problem. See L. S. Stebbing, *Philosophy and The Physicists*, p. 60.

44 See e.g. L. S. Stebbing, *op. cit.*, p. 66; and G. Ryle, *Dilemmas*, p. 80.

45 See e.g. W. Sellars, 'The Language of Theories', *Current Issues in the Philosophy of Science*, ed. H. Feigl and G. Maxwell, p. 76; and P. K. Feyerabend, 'Explanation, Reduction and Empiricism', *Minnesota Studies in the Philosophy of Science*, Vol. III, ed. H. Feigl and G. Maxwell, p. 83.

46 M. Čapek, *The Philosophical Impact of Contemporary Physics*, p. 294.

47 J. Locke, *Essay Concerning Human Understanding*, esp. Bk. IV, Chap. III.

48 W. Kneale, *Probability and Induction*, pp. 97–103. Kneale's point could be strengthened by an argument to show that in the case of physical theories the basic entities must be unperceivable. For if they were perceivable it would seem possible to ask what caused them to manifest themselves to us as perceivable; in which case they could not be basic. This is a general argument in favour of a field-theoretic interpretation of basic entities in physics. Cf. Dingle's comment that if photons could be seen they would get in the way (J. J. C. Smart, *op. cit.*, p. 38).

49 J. Locke, *op. cit.*, Bk. III, Chap. 6.9.

50 J. Locke, *op. cit.*, Bk. IV, Chap. 3.7.

3

THE LOGIC OF SCIENTIFIC DISCOVERY

Roy Bhaskar

1. Introduction: on the contingency of the causal connection

In Chapter 2 I assumed the existence of a body of knowledge and asked how it could be applicable to the world. My particular concern was to establish its universality (transfactuality). I now want to turn to the question of how such knowledge, given that it is transfactually applicable to the world, comes to be produced; and in particular to the question of how law-like statements come to be established as necessary. My concern shifts here then from the synchronic to the diachronic aspects of science, and in particular to the question of how, in the social activity of science, natural necessity comes to be ascribed. In the course of this chapter I will consider to what universality and necessity is properly ascribed, and what must be the case for these ascriptions to be possible.

In order to show how the concept of natural necessity is possible I will need to turn from a critique of the ontology of closed systems to a critique of the ontology of atomistic events that implies it; and hence from a critique of the idea of the actuality of the causal connection to a critique of the idea of its contingency. In Chapter 4 I will ask what accounts for the assumption of the atomicity of the events conjoined that entails a closed system and generates, in its wake, a host of philosophical problems.

The connection between my concerns in this and the preceding chapter is clear. For once an ontology of atomistic events is constituted, it follows that, for general knowledge to be possible, events must be always conjoined (under appropriate descriptions) and never connected.[1] That is, order in the world must consist of an unfailing or invariant order of the co-existence of events in space and their succession in time. Conversely once it is appreciated that events, though caused (and consisting in transformations), are very rarely

Source: *A Realist Theory of Science*, London: Verso, 1997, chap. 3, sections 3.1–3.3, pp. 143–84, and sections 3.5 and 3.6, pp. 199–228.

conjoined, it can be seen why order in the world must be pitched at a level categorically distinct from events. Now I have argued in effect that we produce conjunctions to discover connections and apply connections in a world of non-conjunctions; so that events, though rarely conjoined, are sometimes connected. In this chapter I want to consider the nature of the connection that holds between events (when it does) and the nature of the necessity implicit in the concept of law. I will thus be shifting my attention from the differentiation of the world as such to the nature of the stratification that, if we are to render intelligible the experimental establishment and practical application of our knowledge, it implies. Science attempts, I will argue, in its essential movement, to capture the stratification of the world. In order to describe this movement I will need to reconstitute the other dimension of the Copernican Revolution in the philosophy of science, viz. the transitive (or sociological) dimension in which men come, in their social activity, to acquire knowledge of the enduring and transfactually acting mechanisms of nature, in virtue of which some but not other sequences of events are necessarily connected and some but not other statements are universally applicable. The idea that there are no necessary connections between matters of fact occupies an analogous position in underpinning the doctrine of the contingency of the causal connection, as the idea that there are always descriptions for events such that the formula 'whenever this, then that' applies does in underpinning the doctrine of its actuality. And I will argue that just as for science to be possible the world must be open; so there must be necessary connections between matters of fact, if science is to be possible.

In Chapters 1 and 2 I have shown how the intelligibility of the activities of the experimental establishment and the practical application of our knowledge presupposes the categorical independence of causal laws from the patterns of events, and how causal laws must be given an ontological basis in the enduring and transfactually active mechanisms of nature. Modern transcendental idealist philosophies of science, which are perhaps more influenced by Wittgenstein than Kant, stop at what is in effect the second stage of a dialectic or process of discovery in science, by refusing to allow (or inadequately interpreting) the possibility of a realist interpretation of theory.

Thus there is in science a characteristic kind of dialectic in which a regularity is identified, a plausible explanation for it is invented and the reality of the entities and processes postulated in the explanation is then checked. This is the logic of scientific discovery, illustrated in Diagram 1 below. If the classical empiricist tradition stops at the first step, the neo-Kantian tradition sees the need for the second. But it either denies the possibility, or does not draw the full (transcendental realist) implications of the third step. If and only if the third step is taken can there be an adequate rationale for the use of laws to explain phenomena in open systems (where no constant conjunctions prevail) or for the experimental establishment of that knowledge in the first place.

Just as transcendental realism differentiates itself from empiricism by

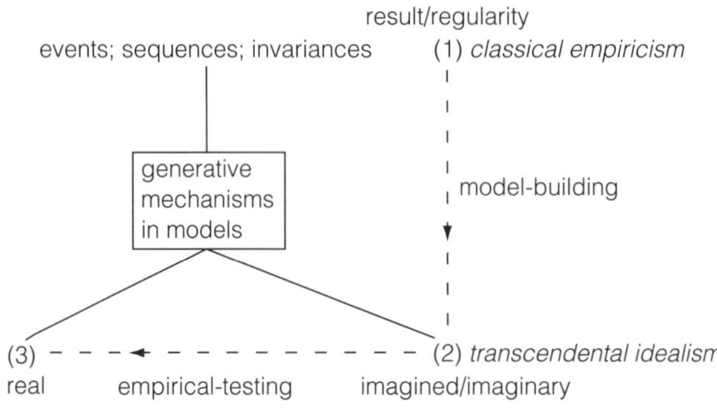

Diagram 1 The logic of scientific discovery

interpreting the first stage of the dialectic as the invariance of a *result* rather than that of a *regularity*, so it differentiates itself from transcendental idealism in its interpretation of the second stage. Both transcendental realism and idealism see the move from (1) to (2) as involving creative model-building, in which plausible generative mechanisms are *imagined* to produce the phenomena in question. But whereas for transcendental idealism the imagined mechanism is *imaginary*, for realism it may be *real*, and come to be established as such. What is imagined may be real; but what is imaginary cannot. 'Imaginary/real' marks an ontological watershed; 'imagined/known to be real' an epistemic one. Now what is imagined at t_1 may come at t_2 to be known to be real. And for transcendental realism the move from (2) to (3) involves experimental production and control, in which the reality of the mechanisms postulated in the model are subjected to empirical scrutiny. For transcendental realism that some real things and generative mechanisms *must* exist can be established by philosophical argument (their existence, and transfactual activity, is a condition of the possibility of science). But it is contingent and the job of substantive science to discover which ones actually do. That is, it is the task of science to discover which hypothetical or imagined mechanisms are not imaginary but real; or, to put it the other way round, to discover what the real mechanisms are, i.e. to produce an adequate account of them.

Science is a process-in-motion. It involves three distinct stages, which cannot be omitted or collapsed into one another without doing tremendous violence to our understanding of science. But these stages cannot be identified with moments of chronological time; they are phases of science. It should be noted that the move from (1) to (2) just because it involves the postulation of novel entities and processes cannot be given a deductive interpretation. But given this it can only be justified in a non-pragmatic way if we hold out the possibility of a realist interpretation of some of the hypothetical entities etc. invoked to explain the behaviour. Such an interpretation can in turn only be justified empirically if it is set in the context of the ongoing social activity of science. Thus it is in the planning of future experiences rather than in the ordering of present ones or the memory of past ones that our rational and empirical 'faculties', 'whose unkind and ill-starred divorce' Bacon saw as responsible for all the confusion in 'the affairs of the human family',[2] are most productively combined.

It is only, I shall argue, if we allow the possibility of the move from (2) to (3) that we can, in the end, uphold the legitimacy of the move from (1) to (2). Moreover it is only if we begin to see science in terms of *moves* and are not mesmerized by terminals that we can give an adequate account of science. In this respect much philosophy is still in the same position as a Martian trying to discover what trams are but able only to observe them in open-air museums with children scrambling over them. It is the task of the philosophy of science to capture science's essential movement, not to guess its eventual destination.

Recent work in the philosophy of science has established (i) the fact of scientific change and (ii) the poverty of a purely deductivist analysis of explanation. In this way it has done much towards the establishment of a conception of science as a critical social activity. The case for transcendental realism can, however, be strengthened by considering the limitations of this work. For unless these two insights are taken together and a new ingredient is added to the existing philosophical mix they are, I think, vulnerable to positivist counter-attack. This new ingredient must be in the field of ontology. The argument of Chapter 1 enables us to see why this is so. For the logical empiricism against which recent philosophy of science has reacted contained not only an account of science, but (implicitly) an account of reality, of the world known by science. And it is in this unacknowledged ontological legacy that the weaknesses of both developments lie. My aim in this chapter and the next is to pinpoint these weaknesses. And to show in particular why and how an adequate non-empiricist account of science, capable of accommodating the facts of scientific change and structure, requires an ontology of the kind outlined in Chapter 1 and elaborated in Chapter 2. Indeed, recent philosophy of science illustrates very well the kind of 'ontological tension' that can occur when a fundamental objection is made to a philosophical theory without simultaneously questioning that theory's ontology. The general difference between recent philosophy of science and transcendental realism could be summed up by saying that whereas recent philosophy has asked merely what are the conditions of the possibility of individual experience and found an answer in the intersubjective world of science, transcendental realism asks in addition for the conditions of the possibility of the social activity of science, finding an answer in the intransitive world of things.

I will need in this chapter not only to show the necessity for the philosophical ontology of transcendental realism, but also to begin the development of the philosophical sociology that I argued in 1.6 is presupposed by any theory of science. Scientific development, I have argued so far, consists in the transformation of social products, antecedently established items of knowledge, which may be regarded as Aristotelian material causes. Certain implications flow from this conception. First, that men never construct their knowledge from scratch. It stands to them always as a given product, a social transmit;[3] which they must themselves reproduce or partially transform. The Copernican Revolution in the transitive dimension of the philosophy of science thus has the profound implication that man never *creates*, but only *changes*, his knowledge, with the cognitive tools at his disposal. Secondly, what is to be changed, has first to be acquired. And what is acquired consists always of an *ensemble* of theoretical and empirical ideas, so that knowledge can never be analysed out as a function of individual sense-experience. Once this is grasped the grounds for the atomistic ontology that generates the idea of the contingency of the causal connection collapse.

Science then is an ongoing social activity which pre-exists any particular generation of scientists and any particular moment of consciousness. Its aim is the production of the knowledge of the independently existing and transfactually active mechanisms of nature. Corresponding to the criterion developed in the intransitive dimension of the philosophy of science, viz. the conceivability of a world without men, we thus have a criterion in the transitive dimension, namely the inconceivability of knowledge without antecedents.

2. The surplus-element in the analysis of law-like statements: a critique of the theory of models

It has often been held that a constant conjunction of events is not a sufficient condition for a causal law. This may be because it is regarded as incapable of sustaining the intuitively obvious and important difference between necessary and accidental sequences or in Johnson's time-honoured terminology between 'universals of law' and 'universals of fact'.[4] Or it may be because it is regarded as incapable of licensing what it is intuitively felt causal laws do licence, namely counter-factual conditionals.[5] It is never seriously denied that we feel, and scientists act as if, some but not other sequences of events are 'necessarily connected'; so that we must possess the concept. What the radical empiricist, in the form of Hume, denies is: (a) that there is any objective basis for this distinction, i.e. that it corresponds to any real difference between the two sequences of events; and (b) that there is any justification, apart from habit or custom, for our ascriptions of natural necessity and accident.[6] Most philosophers since Hume have attempted to show how he was wrong in (b) without objecting to (a). I want to argue that Hume was wrong in (a); and that it is only if we can establish this that we can show why he was wrong in (b) also.

The radical empiricist challenge to philosophers then is to provide an alternative account of the 'surplus-element'[7] in the analysis of law-like statements; that is, that element over and above the (presumed) constant conjunction that explains our ascriptions of necessity; and which will show how, and the conditions under which, a distinction between necessary and accidental sequences and the assertion of counter-factuals can be rationally justified. The usual response to this challenge consists in the attempt to locate the surplus-element in the statement's 'explanation', and more particularly in the 'theory' which explains it. However the terms 'explanation' and 'theory' cover a gamut of philosophical positions, which must now be considered.

The deducibility of a law-like statement from a set of higher order statements is often regarded as a criterion of 'explanation'.[8] However if deducibility is the only criterion for explanation and the source of the surplus-element is its explanation there will be an infinite number of surplus-elements for *any* statement. Hence any statement can be said to be law-like on an infinite number of grounds![9] Deducibility alone cannot explicate the distinction between necessary and accidental or nomic and non-nomic universals. Moreover additional criteria such as simplicity can only reduce the number of possible explanations for a statement which has already been identified as law-like. But they cannot be used to say which statements are law-like and so possess the surplus-element. For even if there were a simplest explanation for every statement, there are no absolutely simple explanations. Thus such criteria can at best be used to explain why we choose one explanation rather than another, but not why one statement rather than another is regarded as law-like.[10]

Of course it might be objected that when everything is explained all factual statements will be law-like. But what would count as an explanation then? Could it be anything other than an inexplicable constant conjunction of events, as in the case of Mill's unconditional laws?[11] If it could not, we are back with Hume, and have done nothing to allay the sting of the radical empiricist challenge. If it could, some alternative non-Humean analysis of the ultimate or highest-order laws must be given which will show how they, as uniquely qualified 'explainers', do possess a genuine surplus-element. We are thus faced with the following dilemma: either explanation is achieved by subsumption under higher-order laws in which case the problem is merely shifted, for a surplus-element must be found for them if they are to qualify as 'laws'; or an alternative analysis of 'explanation' must be given, which does not identify the explanans with a further set of laws, and so provides room for the location of a surplus-element in the analysis of laws, within the context of their explanation, at any one level.

It might be thought that it is in the capacity of the law-like statement to yield successful predictions that the source of the surplus-element lies. But this will not do without an analysis of the 'capacity' or 'power'. For the

Humean it is the past and actual successes of the statement that count, not its potential ones. And these can at best explain, not justify, the surplus-element. It is the surplus-element that must provide our inductive warrant, if we have one; rather than the other way round. Moreover even an accidental generalization is capable of yielding correct predictions, viz. as long as the conditions that account for it persist. This suggests that, even if we were to possess some general inductive warrant, predictive success alone could not differentiate necessary from accidental sequences or license the assertion of counterfactuals.

It seems clear that if we are to get any further in our search for the surplus-element the idea of purely formal differentiae must be abandoned. Inductive considerations prove no better than deductive ones. For accidental generalizations may be inductively confirmed, just as they may be deductively explained. In practice then the non-radical empiricist, if he is not to concede the game, is forced to re-examine the account of science that seems to render any non-Humean conclusion impossible. The fundamental fact about science that has been missing from the discussion so far is the existence at any moment of time of an antecedently established body of theory. And it is here that the non-radical empiricist attempts to locate the surplus-element. But can 'theory' do what experience and deducibility fail to do, i.e. provide a rational ground for our ascriptions of natural necessity? The answer clearly depends upon the extent to which the former contains components irreducible to the latter. And the onus is on the philosopher who attempts to locate the surplus-element in the systematic organization of our knowledge or the capacity of a theory to explain many different laws[12] or to predict novel kinds of facts[13] to show how their concept of theory escapes Humean analysis. Goodman's notion of entrenchment,[14] for example, functions in exactly the same way as Hume's notion of custom and can no more justify our attributions of necessity than the latter could.

In short, unless theory contains elements irreducible to experience and truth-functional operations on it there is no basis for a non-Humean theory of natural necessity.[15] Thus the possibility of the latter depends upon some terms of the theory not being explicitly defined in terms of experience and/or some statements of the theory not being deductively connected and/or some ideas of the theory being non-propositional in logical (or non-sentential in linguistic) form. These establish the possibilities of intensional relationships between predicates, non-deductive (e.g. analogical) relationships between ideas and non-propositional (e.g. iconic) ideas respectively as potential sources of necessity. It is the second of these that has been most thoroughly explored; and it is to Campbell's initial formulation of the theory of models that I now turn.

On Campbell's view a theory must contain not only a 'dictionary' correlating some, but not all, of the theoretical concepts with empirical terms but a 'model' for the hypotheses or theoretical statements of a theory, by means of which its hypothetical subject matter may be imagined to be like in some, but not all, respects the real empirical subject matter of some field which is already known.[16] On this view the surplus-element just is the model. Thus what distinguishes Boyle's law from a merely accidental generalization is, according to Campbell, the corpuscularian model informing the kinetic theory of gases. By means of this model gas molecules are imagined to be, in certain respects, like billiard balls bouncing off each other and exchanging their momentum by impact. And it is in our prior understanding of this that the necessity of the gas laws ultimately lies. Notice that for Campbell it is not the mere availability of a theory or even the organization that the theory makes possible (e.g. the fact that Boyle's law, Charles' law and Graham's law are all deductive consequences of the kinetic theory) but the interpretation of the theory in a model that accounts for the necessity of the law the theory explains.[17]

As a critique of the deductivist view of the structure of scientific theories, as typified by Mill, Duhem and Hempel, Campbell's case is a strong one. The deductivist, he says, merely exhibits 'the dry bones of science from which all the spirit has departed'.[18] His project is to revitalize it. He sees the driving force of science as the exploitation of analogies in the conquests of new fields, without which neither theory nor the range of facts could grow or the language in which to state them develop.[19] But is his case unanswerable? How does it fare when faced with the challenge of radical empiricism? Is it capable of providing an adequate account of the surplus-element in the analysis of law-like statements? To answer these questions we must look more closely at the terms of the modelling relationship which is intended to provide the basis for a non-Humean theory of natural necessity.

Now essential to Campbell's correction of the deductivist view of explanation is the idea that for the explanation of a range of phenomena say E_a to have occurred the relationship between the theory T_a which explains the phenomena and from which the latter is deducible must be supplemented and informed by another relationship. This is a relationship of analogy not deduction; and it is by means of it that we render T_a intelligible to ourselves. See Diagram 2 below. According to Campbell the entities and processes

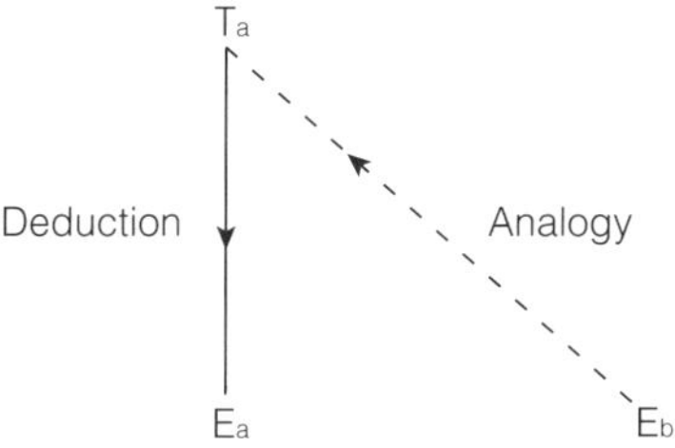

Diagram 2 Campbell's 'theory'

postulated at T_a are unknowable; i.e. they do not constitute part of the phenomenal world described by science. Although we cannot know what produces E_a we can imagine it to be like something we do know. Such an act of imaginative daring need not be totally arbitrary. For it is possible to conceive of principles of analogical, just as there are principles of deductive or inductive reasoning. Only when we have constructed a model can we be said to have achieved scientific understanding. That is, not just saved the facts, preferably with elegance and economy, but explained them. Using the analogy provided by E_b a real or empirical phenomena can thus 'enliven' the abstract theoretical relationships from which E_a is deduced. And E_b does this by standing in for or representing (in the sense of the German 'darstellung') the unknown causes of E_a. Explanation thus involves, centrally, the substitution in our imagination of a real or empirical relationship for an unreal or theoretical one.[20] This is Campbell's debt to empiricist ontology: a debt that it summed up by his tacit acceptance of the concept of the empirical world. For on his theory T_a cannot be, or come to be known as, real; though it is at any moment of time, and perhaps forever, unperceivable to us. For him theoretical entities, such as molecules, can only be said to be 'real' by analogy with material objects.

Campbell does not deny that deducibility is necessary for explanation, merely that it is sufficient. His theory may thus be regarded as providing an alternative shave to Occam's razor. Tyndall formulated the criterion for the selection of explanations implicit in Campbell's theory as follows: 'ask yourself whether your imagination will accept it'.[21] Now such a criterion is clearly capable of selecting a theory within a given metaphysical schema, such as that provided by the classical mechanical world-view. But it is not capable of judging between different schemas, when it is precisely the nature or the limits of the imagination that is in question. To take an obvious example: Aristotelian and Galilean dynamics are in conflict over whether when a stone falls to the earth, the earth should be conceived as fixed (Aristotle, Ptolemy and Tycho Brahe) or as moving (Copernicus, Giordano Bruno, Kepler and Galileo). Now, try as you may, there is no neutral way of conceiving the falling of the stone.[22] Our imagination, although not fixed, is either Aristotelian or Galilean. Tyndall's criterion cannot help us to decide between the competing frameworks, because what is in question is the nature of the concept in terms of which any motion has to be understood.

There is a similar break involved in the transition from Newtonian to Einsteinian dynamics. Part of the trouble with current micro-physics is that our imagination cannot accept it, and in particular find an adequate pictorial representation for it, and yet we have every reason to believe it to be true. If Tyndall's criterion were acted upon it could have effects on scientific practice as conservative and dogmatic as the consistency and meaning-invariance conditions of classical empiricism. A new scientific ontology or a fundamental change in scientific concepts may transform our conception of what is plausible. At such times in the history of science it becomes necessary for the scientist to stand Tyndall's criterion on its head, and dizzily ask himself whether he can continue to accept his imagination.

Although its inadequacy to deal with fundamental scientific change is most evident, Tyndall's criterion is no less inadequate to deal with the continuing processes of conceptual micro-adjustment, in which our imagination is continually modified and extended, that are a part and parcel of the process of 'normal science'. More generally, it is always legitimate for scientists to ask and sometimes possible for them to answer, questions about whether gases are really composed of molecules or whether the earth really moves. Such questions cannot be rephrased as questions about the plausibility of our conceptions. This would be, in terms of Diagram 1, to reduce phase (1) to phase (2). Rather the normal procedure in science is if we have a plausible conception to go on to ask whether it is true, which is to ask whether the entities and processes it postulates are real, or only fictional. Plausibility is a prima facie criterion for a theoretical explanation. But it is neither sufficient, nor in the last instance necessary.

How does Campbell's theory fare as a response to the challenge of radical empiricism? According to it, the surplus-element in the analysis of law-like statements is the model at the heart of the theory that explains it. But for Campbell the model cannot prompt questions about the reality of the abstract entities and processes postulated in the theory. For theoretical entities are by definition unperceivable and hence, given the fundamental equation of empiricist ontology, viz. real = empirical, cannot exist. Models function then not as knowledge-extending but as essentially pragmatic devices, servicing the needs of the understanding. Theory involves a journey from one set of experiences E_b to another E_a. Because of this it is always possible for the radical empiricist to ask whether the journey is really necessary. Moreover, even if a way could be found of showing that *some* model is necessary, there would seem to be no way of justifying the choice of any particular one (given that the idea that its necessity could be demonstrated a priori is rejected as being inconsistent with the fact of scientific change).

To this it may be contended that models are necessary not only as conceptual crutches for the tender-minded and as heuristic devices for the young (which the radical empiricist may graciously concede) but for a theory's growth and development, and in particular (so as not to beg the issue by positing non-empiricist criteria of development) for the generation of facts empirically relevant for the theory but which would not have been forthcoming without it.[23] But this only pushes the argument back a stage further. In a completed science models would be dispensable. For, as Duhem has put it, 'to explain is to strip reality of the appearances in which it is wrapped as in veils in order to see this reality naked and face to face'.[24] When we have done this, what more can there be to do? The objection that 'explanations are practical context-bound affairs'[25] either is covered by the heuristic role allowed to models or depends upon the incompleteness of science, in which case their nemesis is merely (if perhaps indefinitely) postponed.

We are thus forced inexorably back to a particular conception of reality, the only 'world' that Campbell's account of science contains: the world of Mach and Hume. In such a world causality is bare and invariant conjunction; and scientific knowledge consists, for its part, in 'description, that is the mimetic reproduction of facts in thought, the object of which is to replace and save the trouble of new experience'.[26]

Suppose now that arguments are advanced to show that no science can ever be complete in the requisite sense. Science still remains, on the Campbellian conception, a purely internal process, locked in a closed circle of thought. Science is still a creature of custom and habit, the only difference being that the habit is now one of the imagination, rather than sensation. In virtue of their shared ontology Campbell is closer to Mach and Tyndall to Occam than one might think.[27] In neither case can the possibility of major conceptual revisions be accommodated or the mechanism of scientific discovery be displayed.

Let us apply to Campbell's theory the litmus test for the adequacy of an account of science developed in Chapter 1. Can it sustain the idea of the applicability of the concept in question, viz. that of necessary connection, in a world without men? The answer is obvious. In the case of Campbell, as of Hume, there is still no difference, *independent of men*, between a necessary and an accidental sequence of events. The Campbellian can at best talk of a nomically necessary statement; he cannot talk of a nomically necessary sequence. The attempt to locate the surplus-element in the analysis of law-like statements in the imagination of men is a failure.

For transcendental realism the surplus-element distinguishing a law-like from a non law-like statement is the concept of the generative mechanism at work producing the effect in question. Such mechanisms exist and act independently of men; so that the necessity can be properly ascribed to the sequence. Moreover as the world is open not all events will be connected by a generative mechanism; so that the transcendental realist can sustain a concept of natural accident.

Only a real difference between necessary and accidental sequences can justify our distinguishing law-like from non-law-like statements. Hence one cannot deny Humean conclusion (b) (on page 52 above) without objecting to Humean conclusion (a), and thus to the ontology that implies it.

Nowhere is the anthropocentricity of post-Humean philosophy more evident than in the notion that natural necessity must be sought in the behaviour or nature of men. And nowhere is the displacement of rational intuitions more obvious than the attempt to locate structure in the imagination of men. 'Connection' is, as Chisholm has remarked, an 'ontological category and a source of embarrassment to empiricism'.[28] But it is not an irreducible one. For its basis lies in the generative mechanisms of nature which connect events as cause and effect and which exist as the powers of things. Thus to assert a counterfactual is not to make a meta-statement[29] (which would be to make a statement about its grounds), but to make a statement about the way some thing would have behaved (exercised its tendencies, liabilities or powers) had the conditions in fact been different. Theory is not an elliptical way of referring to experience,[30] but a way of referring to hypothesized inner structures of the world, which experience can (in ways to be explored in §3 below) confirm or falsify. We are not locked in a closed circle of thought; because there are activities, viz. perception and experimentation, by means of which under conditions which are deliberately generated and carefully controlled, relatively independent cross-bearings on the intransitive objects of thought can be obtained. Such activities are not independent of thought, but their results are not implied by them either.

Campbell's achievement is to have seen that scientific theory cannot be identified with a deductive system erected on the basis of a single set of experiences. But he made two mistakes. He too, like the empiricists, missed the essential point that science is essentially developing; so that the hypothetical mechanisms of yesterday may become today's candidates for reality and tomorrow's phenomena. But behind this failure also lay an inadequate intransitive dimension, and in particular the absence of the concept of objects apart from our changing knowledge and possibilities of perception of them. Campbell's theory has been extended in two ways. Some have rectified his first mistake but not his second, and viewed science as a sequence of models, an unfolding process of shifts in intellectual fashion. Others have developed his theory in a realist way. Harré, for example, has drawn attention to the role of the existential questions prompted by the creative use of analogies in the development of science.[31] By way of concluding my discussion of Campbell's theory I want to sketch out such a dynamized realist version of it.

In Diagram 3 below the dotted lines now stand for relationships of deduction and the continuous lines for relationships of analogy (to indicate their reversed relative importance). T_a has come to be established as real, and in this case also is perceivable. In the course of this process facts E_a have been corrected and now become facts E'_a. T_a now provides one of the sources for a new model designed to explain phenomena E_α. And the process of checking its reality (which will almost certainly modify our conception of it) has begun. Needless to say there will in general be more than one model for E_α. The state of chemistry c.1930 provides an illustration of the model. T_a is Prout's hypothesis and T_α the theory of sub-atomic structure. $E_a \rightarrow E'_a$ consists in the elimination of the impurities that dogged the verification of Prout's hypothesis for over a century. And the new model might be the Bohr-Rutherford model of atomic structure; which conceived as a hypothesis about the internal structure of atoms is, we now know, false. The source of such models may lie either in some general conceptual scheme (such as atomism in chemistry) or some other science or proto-science (such as the wave

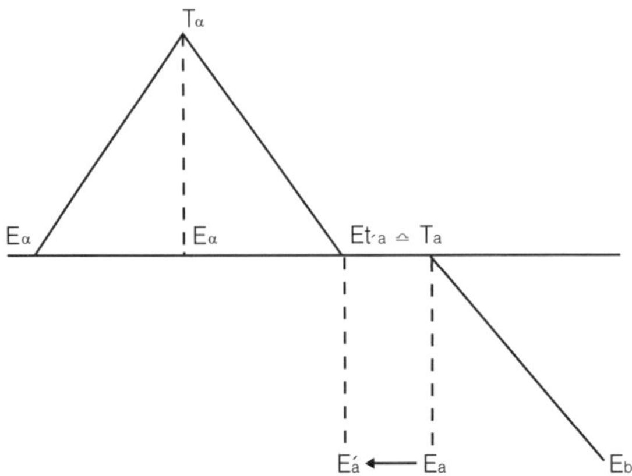

Diagram 3 A dynamic realist development of Campbell's theory

models of light and sound in particle physics). The subject of such models is the unknown but knowable intransitive structure of the world. It is by means of the experimental testing of the hypotheses suggested by already existing knowledge that new knowledge comes to be produced.

The problem of the surplus-element, and Hume's challenge, has another aspect. This turns on the question of what warrant we have for distinguishing between cases of genuine and pseudo-falsification, and hence for invoking the CP clause in defence of generalizations in the former case. This calls into question the necessity of deducibility, not just its sufficiency in the explanation of laws.

Science needs a concept of pseudo-falsification for three reasons, two of which are epistemic and one of which is ontological. Firstly, because a theory may not be at present sufficiently refined or developed to cope with anomalous counter-instances; that is to say, every theory needs a 'protective-belt' for its development.[32] Secondly, because the 'facts' may be wrong: either in the simple sense that they are misrepresentations of the phenomena or more profoundly because they depend upon false or inadequate observational theories.[33] As is well known, every new theory is faced with innumerable anomalies and counter-instances of these kinds. They form in a sense the staple diet of normal science. A successful theory is one which, like Newton's, though it never resolves them all and generates new ones in the process of their resolution, 'turns each new difficulty into a victory for its programme'.[34] Thirdly, science needs a concept of pseudo-falsification because a countervailing cause or interfering agent may be at work generating the 'counter-instance'. It is only under closed conditions, as we have seen, that a theory can be given a fair test or that a crucial experiment – Bacon's 'instance of the fingerpost'[35] – becomes possible.

The problems of the necessity and universality of law are indeed inextricably linked, but not in the way Hume thought. For if the surplus element in the analysis of law-like statements is the concept of a generative mechanism at work and this concept is irreducible to that of a sequence of events then it is quite rational to uphold an ontological distinction between cases of genuine and pseudo-falsification (in which, as exemplified by the case of Prout's hypothesis referred to above, our epistemic distinctions too may be grounded). For we may readily allow that the generative mechanism in virtue of which natural necessity is ascribed is not undermined by the instability of the conditions under which it operates. So that if a law has been confirmed under closed conditions and there is no reason to suppose that the generative mechanism at work in those instances has ceased to operate, the law that the concept of the mechanism grounds may be supposed to continue to apply outside the conditions under which it was confirmed, whether or not the consequent of the statement happens to be realized.

By now it would, I think, be generally agreed that models play some cognitive role in science and that there is a feature about such models which renders them irreducible to the experiences that they are in some way intended to embroider or explain. (This feature is, I have argued, typically an idea of a mechanism which would, if it were real, generate the phenomena in question.) But the representatives of the three traditions in the philosophy of science differ radically in their interpretations of the status and role of such models, and of the irreducible concept that constitutes its essential core.

The classical positivist view is that it is merely a heuristic device (Duhem, Hempel and Brodbeck). This is liable to encourage the view that the rationale for distinguishing necessary from accidental sequences is solely pragmatic; that it is, as it were, a question of our greater attachment to the former (Quine),[36] or of the deeper entrenchment of their predicates in our conceptual system (Goodman). Similarly it encourages the idea of the CP clause as a device that can be relaxed or invoked, switched off or on, according to whether or not we are prepared to forego the falsified law-like statement. This view carries the implication of course that the use of the CP clause is bound to be more or less arbitrary or dogmatic.[37] And this in turn creates the Kuhn-Popper problem of the functions of dogma.

The concept of the generative mechanism may be given a firmer status, and the distinctions it grounds a better rationale, by seeing its function as concerned essentially with the development of science. Protection from pseudo-falsification then becomes protection from too easy or too early falsification; that is, before the full potentialities of the theory have been developed (Lakatos and Feyerabend). This view allows that our knowledge is structured – that it contains, as it were, layers of different age. The conditions of knowing are here explicitly distinguished from the conditions of being. But positivism still provides the underlying account of the world. And because of this the rationale of the concept of the generative mechanism, which forms the heart or essential core of the theory, is still more or less pragmatic, still science- or knowledge- or man-dependent.

The third position consists in coming to see not just our knowledge but the world itself as structured and differentiated. According to this conception, which is that of transcendental realism, science is concerned neither with the incessant accumulation of confirming facts (or the incessant search for falsifying ones), nor even with its own growth and development, but rather with the understanding of the different mechanisms of the production of phenomena in nature. Thus it allows that under certain conditions the concept of the generative mechanism at work may be given a realist interpretation as a representation in thought of the transfactually active causal structures of the world. The possibility of such an interpretation supplements internal consistency and contextual plausibility as a constraint on the possible forms of theoretical advance; and it constitutes the ultimate goal of all theory construction.

Now empirical realism generates the following dilemma: Either theoretical entities refer ultimately to experience, in which case they can be eliminated. Or theoretical entities constitute experience (in whole or in part), in which case they cannot be eliminated, but must, given the equation of empirical realism, constitute the world (in whole or in part). Now as long as an ontology based on the category of experience is retained there can be no grounds independent of man for ascribing necessity to some but not other statements. On the first horn this generates the problem of what justifies our belief that the future will resemble the past, or the unobserved the observed, i.e. the problem of the induction. But on the second horn it generates the problem of what justifies the assumption of intellectual conformity. And, on this horn, scientific change, or even dissent, actually constitutes (in whole or in part) a breakdown in the uniformity of nature!

3. Natural necessity and natural kinds: the stratification of nature and the stratification of science

In the process of the establishment of a law of nature three questions may be asked:

(i) is there an empirical regularity which constitutes a prima facie candidate for a law?
(ii) is there some reason, other than the regularity, why the predicates instantiated in the law-like statement should be conjoined?
(iii) is this reason located in the enduring powers of things and the transfactually active mechanisms of nature?

If the answer to (i) is yes we have what might be called a 'protolaw'.[38] If the answer to (ii) is yes we have strong grounds for a law. If the answer to (iii) is

Table 1 Status of constant conjunction of events

	Necessary	*Sufficient*	*for Law*
classical empiricism	√	√	
transcendental idealism	√	×	
transcendental realism	×	×	

yes we have a law. Typically of course the reason in question in (ii) will be provided by a model of the connection between antecedent and consequent, putative cause and putative effect. The transition from (ii) to (iii) typically occurs when a realist interpretation of the mechanism posited in the model becomes acceptable.

The answers to (i)–(iii) correspond of course to three levels of criteria for law, viz. those specified by the classical empiricist, transcendental idealist and transcendental realist philosophies of science. At the Humean level laws just are empirical regularities. At the Kantian level both (i) and (ii) must be satisfied. Here we have what might be called the dual criterion theory of law.[39] I have already noted its vulnerability to Humean counter-attack. At the level of transcendental realism, a distinction is drawn between the empirical identifiability and the universal (transfactual) applicability of laws; and the latter is seen to be a condition of the possibility of the former. As the application of laws in open systems is justified, and presupposed by the intelligibility of experimental activity, the existence of an empirical regularity or a constant conjunction of events is now not even necessary for the ascription of a law (see Table 1 above). I have argued that it is only at this level that a distinction between necessary and accidental sequences can be sustained. A sequence $E_a.E_b$ is necessary if there is a generative mechanism M such that whenever E_a, E_b tends to be produced; a sequence is accidental if this is not the case. Their difference is represented in Diagram 4 below. Most events

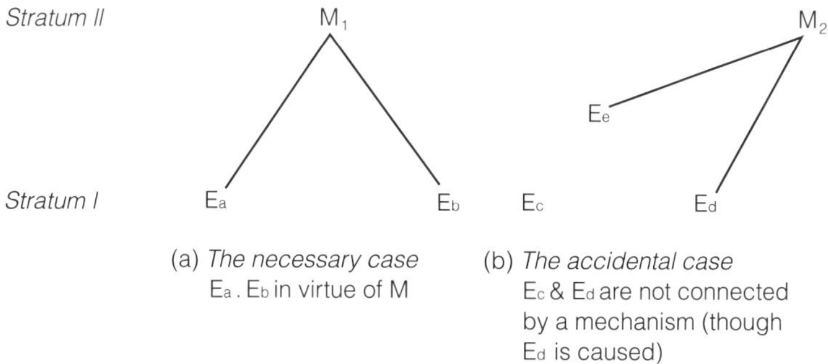

Diagram 4

occur in open systems and must be conceived, as argued in 2.6 above, as 'conjunctures'. This is illustrated in Diagram 5 below. Necessity as such, like universality, is thus ascribed essentially to the activity of the mechanism; and only derivatively to some particular event sequence. For the result of the activity of the mechanism will in general be co-determined by the activity of other mechanisms too.[40]

Now these three levels of criteria generate and are generated by different views of science. Thus whereas the classical empiricist will ask merely:

(i)* is there a regularity such that whenever C then E? The transcendental idealist will ask in addition:

(ii)* given a regularity, is there an explanation such that we can render it intelligible to ourselves that whenever C then E? The transcendental realist will however, after making an essential correction, go one step further and ask:

(iii) out of the plausible explanations for this regularity, is there one which correctly describes the mechanism by means of which, upon the occurrence or obtaining of C, E tends to be produced?

That is to say, the transcendental realist will demand that models be tested not just for plausibility but for truth; i.e. for their adequacy in correctly describing the real generative mechanism at work (if the connection between C and E is necessary) such that when C occurs, E tends to be produced (is produced in the absence of interfering causes or the transformation of M). That real things and generative mechanisms must exist can be established by philosophical argument. It is the job of the scientist to discover which ones actually do. Given the identification of some prima facie non-random pattern in nature or protolaw the scientist thus builds up ideas of various plausible hypothetical mechanisms by the creative employment of his imagination (cf. Diagram 6) and subjects these ideas to rigorous theoretical criticism and

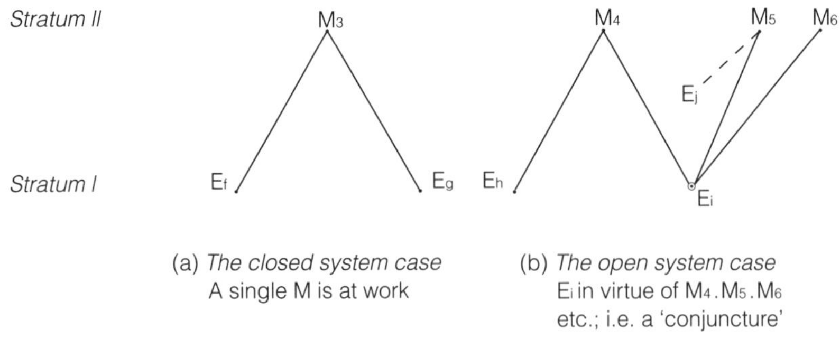

(a) *The closed system case*
A single M is at work

(b) *The open system case*
E_i in virtue of $M_4.M_5.M_6$ etc.; i.e. a 'conjuncture'

Diagram 5

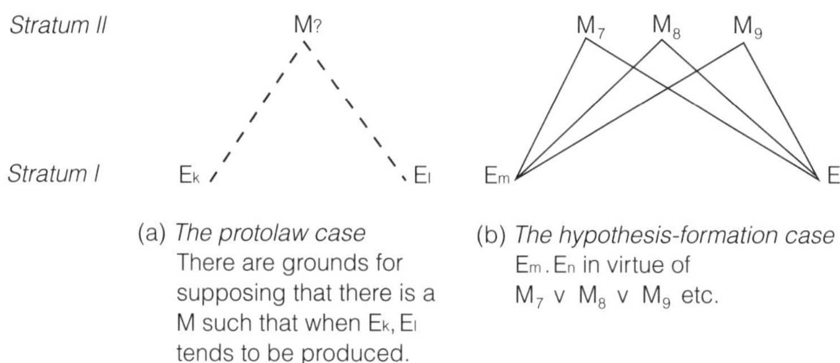
Stratum II
M?
Stratum I
Ek
El
M7 M8 M9
Em
En
(a) The protolaw case
There are grounds for supposing that there is a M such that when Ek, El tends to be produced.
(b) The hypothesis-formation case
Em . En in virtue of
M7 v M8 v M9 etc.

Diagram 6

empirical test. These three phases of science are of course those represented in Diagram 1 on page 114.

For the transcendental realist then a model has a relationship with its subject as well as with its source. And it is within the nexus formed by this double articulation that new knowledge is produced. For new knowledge is doubly articulated, articulated in two dimensions (transitive and intransitive): it is a socially produced knowledge of a natural (man-independent) thing. It is this bipolarity that a model expresses in standing in two sorts of relationship: a relationship of *analogy* with its source; and a relationship of *adequacy* (when it is) with its subject matter.

Many philosophical problems arise from a misunderstanding of the second relationship. It is not a relationship of correspondence; the terms of the relationship are not necessarily like each other, though pictures and iconic models may play an important role in scientific thought.[41] Moreover there are no general philosophical criteria for such judgements of adequacy; they are necessarily intrinsic to the particular science concerned. Analogy is one of the possible relationships that models may have with respect to their source. The existence of the first type of relationship (in the transitive dimension) is important in establishing both a constraint on the number of possible explanations[42] and an indispensable means of their production. It cannot be described at all adequately as one of coherence; and here again no general philosophical criteria can be laid down for it. Science is work that requires creative intelligence, and there can be no mechanical surrogate for that. The idea of an automatic science is a will-o'-the-wisp that the philosophy of science has pursued, with damaging consequences, since Bacon's search for a 'sure and certain method' that would eliminate the need for human thought, which of course inevitably entails the possibility of human error.

Most science proceeds by way of a two-tiered method designed to identify invariances in nature, normally under conditions which are experimentally produced and controlled, and to explain them by reference to enduring mechanisms.[43] It is in the movement from the identification of an invariance to the mechanisms and structures that account for it that the logic of scientific discovery must be found. Thus the observable reactions of chemistry, which are represented in textbooks by formula such as $2Na + 2HCl = 2NaCl + H_2$, are explained by reference to the atomic hypothesis and the theory of valency and chemical bonding. The patterns which constitute the explananda of the theory of valency are needless to say by no means superficially obvious or readily available. Both the concepts and the substances and conditions had and have to be worked for, produced in the social activity of science. The theory itself sets out to describe the causal mechanisms responsible for the overt behaviour of the substances. Once its reality has been established (which justifies our assuming that chemical bonding occurs and the laws of chemistry hold outside the laboratory) and the consequences of the theory have been fully explored, the next task consists in the discovery of the mechanisms responsible for chemical bonding and valency. This has been explained in terms of the electronic theory of atomic structure. Once the reality of this explanation has been established, science moves on to the discovery of the mechanisms responsible for what happens in the sub-atomic microcosm of electrons, protons, and neutrons; and we now have various theories of sub-atomic structure. The historical development of chemistry may thus be represented by the following schema:

Stratum I	$2Na + 2HCl = 2NaCl + H_2$	
	explained by	
Stratum II	theory of atomic number and valency	Mechanism 1
	explained by	
Stratum III	theory of electrons and atomic structure	Mechanism 2
	explained by	
Stratum IV	[competing theories of sub-atomic structure]	[Mechanism 3]

It should be noted that the historical order of the development of our knowledge of strata is opposite to the causal order of their dependence in being. No end to this process of the successive discovery and description of new and ever deeper, and explanatorily more basic, strata can be envisaged. Other sciences reveal a similar open-ended stratification. Geometrical optics is explained in terms of Young and Fresnel's wave optics; which is explained in terms of the electromagnetic theory of light; which can be explained in terms of the quantum theory of radiation.[44]

A general pattern of scientific activity emerges from this. When a stratum of reality has been adequately described the next step consists in the discovery of the mechanisms responsible for behaviour at that level. The key move in this involves the postulation of hypothetical entities and mechanisms, whose reality can then be ascertained. Such entities need not be smaller in size,[45] though in physics and chemistry this has normally proved to be the case. The species of explanation here identified itself falls under a wider genus: in which the behaviour of individuals is explained by reference to their natures and the conditions under which they act and are acted upon (see 2.3 above).

Now for the transcendental realist the stratification this form of explanation imposes upon our knowledge reflects a real stratification in the world. Without the concept of real strata apart from our knowledge of strata we could not make sense of what the scientist, striving to move from knowledge of one stratum to knowledge of the next, is trying to do: viz. to discover the reasons why the individuals which he has identified (at a particular level of reality) and whose behaviour he has described tend to behave the way they do. Without this concept the stratification of science must appear as a kind of historical accident, lacking any internal rationale in the practice of science (if indeed it is not denied altogether in a reductionist and ultimately phenomenalist account of science).

As it is clear that the hypothetical entities and generative mechanisms imagined for the purposes of theory-construction must initially derive at least part of their meaning from some other source (if they are to be capable of functioning as possible explanations at all) theories *must* be already understood before correspondence rules for them are laid down.[46] Equally this means that the descriptive terms must have initially possessed a meaning independent of them. This enables us to see how meaning-change is possible, and indeed if the independence of predicates is denied, inevitable in the transitive process of science. Similarly we can see how knowledge of newly discovered strata may correct knowledge of less fundamental strata, as concepts and measurement techniques are refined. Now if changing knowledge of strata is to be possible the strata must not change with our knowledge of them. Thus the concept of real strata apart from our knowledge of them is necessary if both the ideas of scientific structure and scientific change, which are central to recent critical philosophy of science, are to be intelligibly sustained. More generally, acknowledgement of the real stratification of the world allows us to reconcile scientific discovery (of new strata) with scientific change (of knowledge of strata).

Now the stratification of the world must be assumed by the scientist, working in any field, to be in principle unbounded. For it will always be possible for him that there are reasons, located at a deeper level, for the phenomena he has hitherto identified and described. But his knowledge may be in practice bounded by semi-permanent technical or conceptual problems or by the domain assumptions of his particular science; or by the fact that reality is itself bounded at the level knowledge of which he has attained. However, if the stratification of the world has an end, i.e. if there are 'entities' which are truly ultimate – and I can see no reason for supposing this must be so – and the scientist has achieved knowledge at that level, he can never know *that* the level is ultimate. For it will still remain possible for him that there are reasons, located at a still deeper level, for the causes of the phenomena he has succeeded in identifying and describing. I will return to this point below.

Now the only kind of necessity that holds between events is connection by a generative mechanism. But there are two other concepts of necessity applicable to the objective world order: there is the necessity implicit in the concept of a law, i.e. in the activity of a generative mechanism as such or the exercise of a thing's tendencies irrespective of their realization; and the necessity implicit in the concept of a thing's real essence, i.e. those properties or powers, which are most basic in an explanatory sense, without which it would not be the kind of thing it is, i.e. which constitute its identity or fix it in its kind. The first concept of 'natural necessity' is clearly derivative from the second, dependent upon the contingent feature of the system in which the thing's behaviour occurs, viz. that it be closed (see 2.4 above). I am therefore going to refer to the second as the concept of natural necessity, and the third as the concept of natural kinds. Knowledge of natural necessity is expressed in statements of causal laws; knowledge of natural kinds in real definitions. But natural kinds exist and naturally necessary behaviour occurs independently of our definitions and statements of causal laws.

Now in the transition from knowledge of any one stratum to knowledge of the next, knowledge of three levels of the objective world order is progressively obtained: of relations between events, of causal laws and of natural kinds. I am going to refer to these three levels as the Humean, Lockean and Leibnizian levels respectively. The transcendental idealist, as well as the classical empiricist, is, in virtue of his ontological commitment, restricted to the first level of knowledge of the objective world order. I shall argue that even at the Leibnizian level science remains empirical, so that the transcendental argument of Chapter 1 remains valid; and that even at that level the deductively justified prediction of events is impossible, so that the critique of philosophy of science contained in Chapter 2 continues to apply with undiminished force. Moreover I shall argue that the concepts, such as that of natural powers, that we need to render intelligible the transition to the Leibnizian level remain categorically valid even at that level.

At the *Humean* level a pattern is identified or an invariance is produced. (This, we know, empirical realism cannot sustain.) We thus have a protolaw (at let us say Stratum I). This is to be explained by reference to the circumstances and nature of the thing whose behaviour is described. The scientist never doubts for a moment that something is generating the effect in question. His problem is: what is? That is, why does x behave the way it does, viz. B, in conditions $C_1 \ldots C_n$?

The first step in the scientific explanation of B is to ascribe a power (or liability) of x to B, i.e. to do (or suffer) φ. This is to say, very roughly, that x does φ in virtue of its nature N.[47] The next step is thus to investigate N (defining Stratum II). This involves inter alia creative model-building and rigorous empirical-testing (cf. Diagram 3). As a result of this investigation we may say x comes to do φ in virtue of its having a certain constitution or intrinsic structure, e.g. genetic constitution, atomic structure or electric charge. Now it is contingent that x has the nature (e.g. constitution or structure) that it has. But given that it has, it is necessary that it behaves the way it does. One criterion of this is our capacity to deduce the tendency to B from N. This is the *Lockean* level of knowledge. Note that at this level it is still contingent that the thing has the structure that it has.

Now at the third *Leibnizian* level possession of that structure or constitution comes to be regarded as defining the kind of thing that x is. Now it is necessary that x has the structure it has if it is to be the kind of thing it is. It is no longer contingent that hydrogen is a gas with a particular atomic structure; rather anything possessing that structure is hydrogen. That is, the criterion for the application of the concept 'hydrogen' ceases to be the lightest gas and becomes instead possession of that structure. At this level the only contingent questions are whether and where things of a given kind exist.[48] But note contingency still lies in the flux of the circumstances in which things act, so that events are still not deductively predictable. That is, the 'contingency' of events deriving from open systems applies even at the Leibnizian level, so that laws must still be formulated as tendencies (whatever their scope of application). Moreover it is important to see that knowledge at the Leibnizian level is, or may be, attained empirically. We may discover, quite empirically, that the most important explanatory property or real essence of hydrogen, identified as the lightest gas, is its atomic structure; and then attempt to express this discovery in a real definition of hydrogen. Once more the importance of viewing science as a process in motion is clear. For if we stay at any one level, phase or moment of science the idea that a definition may be arrived at empirically will appear absurd. If it is accepted, however, the reason why the laws of nature cannot be deduced a priori from self-evident axioms becomes clear. For the axiomatic base of a science at any moment of time, at any stratum of reality, is something that has had to be worked for, produced, as part of the irreducibly empirical process of science.

Scientists attempt to discover what kinds of things there are, as well as how the things there are behave; to capture the real essences of things in real definitions and to describe the ways they act in statements of causal laws. The real essences of things are their intrinsic structures, atomic constitutions and so on which constitute the real basis of their natural tendencies and causal powers. Thus there is no conflict between explanatory and taxonomic knowledge. Rather, at the limit, they meet in the notion of the real essences of the natural kinds, whose tendencies are described in statements of causal laws.

At the Leibnizian level statements of law are substitution instances of necessary truths about the individuals to which they refer. For any individual which did not behave in that way would not be an individual of that kind.

They may thus be regarded as analytic truths. But they are arrived at in the transitive process of science a posteriori, by empirical means. Thus a fully dynamic philosophy of science must take seriously the question 'how is analytic knowledge arrived at *a posteriori* possible?' To this question I will return in §5 below.

The situation at the Humean level is rather like that faced by the citizens of Königsberg who knew, from experience, that there was no way of crossing each of the town's seven bridges just once.[49] See Figure 1 below. At the Lockean level this fact is deducible from the topology of Königsberg, given Euler's theorem. At the Leibnizian level, there is a necessary truth about a certain physical set-up, whether or not there is a town called 'Königsberg' or any town at all to which it applies. At the Leibnizian level, Mendeleyeev was able to deduce from his Periodic Table, interpreted as dealing with atomic number and valency, the properties of several new elements. But it remained contingent whether, and if so where, there were elements in the world to which his predictions applied. Certain chess games have only one possible solution. But it remains contingent whether they are ever played.

The concept of powers has played a key role in our analysis of science's transition from knowledge of one stratum to knowledge of the next. To ascribe a power is to say that a thing will do (or suffer) something, under the appropriate conditions, in virtue of its nature. This is not, as is so often claimed, a pseudo-explanation[50] or a purely verbal formula.[51] Rather it is an indication of work to be done. Molière's doctors in *Le Malade Imaginaire* have often been ridiculed for speaking of opium as possessing a 'dormitive virtue'. But in doing so they left open the possibility of an investigation, at some future date, into the nature of opium without committing themselves to what would doubtless have been, for them, a rash conjecture at the time. Moreover it is far preferable to the Humean alternative, viz. that whenever men smoke opium they fall asleep. For in the first place, the latter is untrue. Secondly, it is less informative. It might be a complete accident that everyone in the den is asleep: the powers formula rules this out. It says that there is something about opium in virtue of which when men smoke it they tend to fall asleep. The connection is necessary. But it is only a tendency. Thirdly, the Humean formula is regulatively useless. The powers statement is by contrast quite suggestive. For it indicates the need for an investigation into the chemical properties of opium and the way they induce sleep in men.[52] In

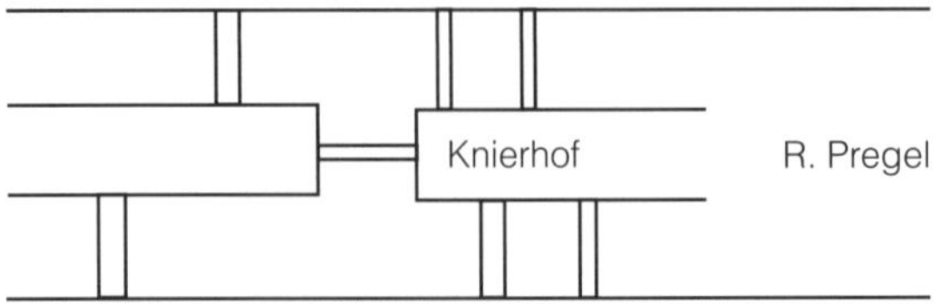

Figure 1 The seven bridges of Königsberg

context, it constitutes an open admission of ignorance. The Humean, on the other hand, must pretend that once he has his generalization there is nothing more to be known. And if he should stumble upon a higher-order generalization this can be, for him, only accidentally related to the original one: there is no inner logic connecting the two, or rationale by which science moves from the first to the second.

To this it might be objected that the concept of powers does not figure in the discourse of science. This is true. And the reason for it is of course that the scientist, unlike Molière's doctors, is never just content to ascribe a power but moves immediately to the construction of possible explanations for it with the paradigms and other instruments of thought at his disposal. That is his job. (Sometimes, however, when we are completely at a loss we do just ascribe a power.) The concept of powers is introduced precisely to describe this normally instantaneous (or simultaneous) and unselfconscious response of the scientist to the identification of protolaws; it represents, if you like, an attempt to reconstruct the internal rationality of the inter-strata move. The concept of powers is not intended to figure in the discourse of science, but in the discourse of the philosophy of science (which is the former's rational reconstruction).

It should perhaps be stressed here that the stages of my rational reconstruction of the process of scientific discovery represent phases of scientific activity; they cannot be identified with moments of chronological time. Thus most scientific work must occur, for reasons I will bring out in §4, in the context of a research programme designed to show that on the supposition of the mechanism M the field of phenomena can be rendered intelligible. Thus the identification of a protolaw normally depends upon the prior existence of a conjecture or a hypothesis of a mechanism intended to function as a possible explanation for the presumed protolaw.[53]

To ascribe a power is to say that there is something about the thing, which may be unknown, in virtue of which it behaves the way it does. The grounds for the ascription of a power must thus be stronger than the mere occurrence of a regularity. For we must possess some reason to suppose the connection necessary (though in the limiting case this may just be the invariance of an experimentally produced result). It is because it indicates the power-ascriber's belief in the existence of a reason, located at the next highest level of inquiry (in the nature of the thing), whether or not the reason is currently known, that the concept of powers, in pinpointing an essential moment in the transition from knowledge of one stratum to knowledge of the next, plays such a key developmental or strata-bridging role. In this way, a powers statement is a promissory note cashed in the development of science, a schematic explanation filled out in the growth of our knowledge.[54]

It is worth noting that the structure of a powers ascription is well adjusted to accommodate both falsification (obviously, as the hypothesized reasons may be subjected to independent tests) and meaning-change (less obviously).

If meaning change is to be possible, some elements of meaning must remain constant through the change. Now if 'x does B' is analysed as 'x is of such a nature N {defining Stratum II} that it will do φ in conditions $C_1 \ldots C_n$ {defining Stratum I}' we may allow that the meaning of 'φ' remains constant while the meaning of the N component changes between theories (and vice-versa). This applies even in the case of simple descriptive observational predicates such as 'blue'. For 'x is blue' may be analysed as 'x looks blue {defining Stratum I} in virtue of its reflecting light of a certain wavelength {Stratum II}'. The simple theory that things look blue because they are blue may then be replaced by the scientific theory that they tend to look blue in normal circumstances because they reflect light of wavelength 4400Å. Subsequently we may allow the latter to define the scientific use of 'blue'; in which case of course it is no longer contingent that blue surfaces reflect light of that wavelength.

Now although the concept of powers serves this essential developmental function, it cannot be reduced to it. For when we have climbed up to Stratum II, we cannot throw away the ladder, so to speak. To pursue the analogy, the ladder is a rope, not a wooden one. For to make a powers statement is to make a categorical statement about the nature of the thing situated at the level to which we have climbed. It is to make a statement about possibilities which are possessed by the thing quite categorically, whether they are known (or actualized) or not. Dogs do not lose their power to bark when we understand how they do so, just as glass does not cease to be brittle when we know its molecular structure.

The ontological bases of powers just are the properties that account for them; i.e. the natures in virtue of which they are ascribed. Now in the transitive process of science such natures may come to be qualitatively described. When this happens it will of course initiate a search for the higher-order entities and mechanisms that account for them. But how does it happen?

In general, at any one level, individuals must be identified and their normic behaviour described. Now for a qualitative description of a thing or a dispositional account of its behaviour it must be present to the scientist's senses and he must be able to describe it correctly, i.e. as being of the kind or type that it is. This will normally depend upon two kinds of work: practical (experimental and technical) work, in which the scientist's causal and perceptual powers are augmented (the latter with the aid of the construction of sense-extending equipment, such as microscopes); and theoretical work, in which the scientist's conceptual and descriptive powers are augmented. It is the aim of the former to produce the object, i.e. to render the thing or behaviour directly accessible to the scientist's senses (so that it becomes the possible object of an act of immediate demonstrative reference). And it is the aim of the latter to produce the concept of the object, so that the scientist is capable of an adequate description of it. Both are necessary for a qualitative description.

It should be noted that the two kinds of criteria, viz. demonstrative and recognitive, are distinct. For my incapacity to identify the chromosome structure by peering down an electron-microscope does not mean that it is not a possible object of an act of demonstrative reference. It is present to my senses, whether I recognize it or not. Conversely to render it accessible to my senses is an independent labour (itself only possible if some concept of it is possessed), requiring great ingenuity, just as experimental production and control does, when we are concerned with the description of the law-like behaviour of some thing already identified. The production of the object and the production of its concept are thus independent tasks, each essential to a qualitative description of a thing or account of its behaviour. The thing must be there and I must know what kind of thing it is, i.e. how to describe it; in general this will involve a theoretical redescription of it.

Now it is important to realize that though the production of the object and the production of its concept are distinct, the judgement that the object has been produced itself depends upon a tacit theory of vision and the instruments according to which its range is extended. The case of the electron-microscope illustrates this very well. In general it is the function of such background or auxiliary theories to specify the conditions under which an object of the appropriate type may be said to be present to the senses. In this sense they constitute, as it were, the criteriology of empirical science.

It is clearly essential to the theory of scientific development proposed here that imagined entities may come to be established as real. Now an entity may be 'theoretical' either in the sense that its existence is open to doubt (theoretical$_1$) or in the sense that it cannot be directly perceived, either unaided or with the help of sense-extending equipment (theoretical$_2$). The same distinction applies in the case of behaviour. Now an entity (or mode of behaviour) may be theoretical$_1$ at t_1 and perceived and adequately described at t_2, so that it then *ipso facto* ceases to be theoretical$_1$. The existence of bacteria, initially conceived as minute hostile micro-organisms, and molecules, initially modelled on material objects, came to be established in this way. This is typical of science and shows once more the importance of viewing it as a process in motion.

But if an entity cannot be perceived, i.e. is theoretical$_2$, does this mean that it cannot be known to exist, so that it must be theoretical$_1$? If this were the case all theoretical$_2$ entities would indeed be hypothetical, and our knowledge would be necessarily confined to the domain of observable things, even if this were now regarded as an expanding class. Fortunately this conclusion does not follow. For theoretical$_2$ entities may be known to exist indirectly, viz. through the perception of their effects. The paradigm here is the case of the detection of radio-active materials by a geiger counter, of electricity by an electroscope, of a magnetic field by a compass needle. That there is a difference between the cases of detection and perception is clear. In the case of detection the thing can be individuated only indirectly, i.e. via the spatio-temporal framework or through its effects on particular things; it cannot be the object of an act of immediate demonstrative reference. Whatever the mental imagery we use to think of a magnetic field it can be present to us only through its effects. On the other hand my incapacity to identify a bacterium under a microscope as being of a particular type, or even as being a bacterium at all, does not mean that it is not present to my senses; and so capable of functioning as the object of a possible act of immediate demonstrative reference, although ex hypothesi I am incapable of intentionally performing it.

It should be stressed that in the detection case that something does exist producing the effect is not in question. Nor is the fact that it exists and acts independently of its detection. To say 'electricity is what electricity does'[55] is to collapse powers to their exercise. Electricity is not what electricity does; but what it can do. The mode of reasoning employed in inferring the existence of causal agents through the ostension of their effects is thus perfectly proper. Hence though it is correct to say that when we cannot qualitatively describe the cause we know less about it than when we can (given that in the latter case we know the thing's causal powers as well) it is not true to say that it is less certain there is a cause. It is just that in the detection case what we can know about a thing is limited to its causal powers.

Now there are two possibilities here. One is that there is a nature, susceptible in principle to a qualitative description, as yet unknown, which is the bearer of its causal powers. The other is that the nature of the thing just is its causal powers, as in the case of physical field theories. At any moment of time a science may have to put down its ultimate entities just as powers to produce effects, e.g. to affect observers and equipment, possible observers and possible equipment, material things, in certain ways. About such entities all the scientist knows is their powers. It always remains possible that he will be able to achieve a qualitative description of them, and he must strive to do so. On the other hand, it is also possible that such entities are their powers. The scientist can never dogmatically eliminate one of these alternatives in advance. If there is a frontier to possible knowledge of the world the scientist can never know when he has reached it. But whatever is responsible for the world as manifest must possess causal powers which are continually being exercised; it must be co-extensive with space and continuous with time. It must be structured and complex; it cannot be atomistic or event-like. The concept of a field of potential seems closest to meeting these requirements.[56] However it seems to me there is no reason in principle why there should not be strata of fields (of perhaps radically different kinds), forever unknown to us. It should be noted that only the identification, not the existence, of fields depends upon the existence of material things in general. Here again the order of dependence in being is opposite to the order of dependence of our knowledge of being. The ontological order is distinct from the epistemic one.

The general thrust of my argument in Chapter 2 was against reductionism. How does this square with my emphasis on strata of knowledge? It will be remembered that I did not deny the possibility of an explanatory reduction but stressed (a) the need for a well-defined reductans (so that a reduction could not in general be a means of acquiring knowledge of a higher-order or less fundamental stratum); and (b) that a reduction left the reality of the higher-order entities intact, at least in as much as they were causal agents capable of acting back on the materials out of which they are formed (see 2.5 above). It is clear that I was there taking possession of causal powers, and hence existence in time, as the most general criterion of reality. There is an asymmetry between space and time here. For powers must be possessed and exercised in time, but they need not be localized at any point in space. Relations, for example, such as that of spin (in physics) and marriage endure through time and have causal effects. But they have no position in space. Now in general a reduction is possible because the entities in terms of which the behaviour of the thing is explained occupy a different volume of space, either larger or (more usually) smaller. Thus the possibility of a reduction implies in general that the individuals of the different kinds cannot be said to occupy the same place at the same time and one not be part of the other. This gives us a general criterion which imposes limits on regresses of strata, i.e. upon the possibility of a sequence of (explanatory) reductions. For one could define a branch of science as a series of theories within which this criterion is satisfied. On it, quantum mechanics and chemistry would belong to the same branch. But electromagnetism and mechanics, neurophysiology and psychology and (it will be argued) psychology and sociology would belong to different branches.

Changes of things are explained in terms of unchanging things. If there are ultimate entities they must be unchanging. Atoms have already been disqualified as possible ultimate entities (see 2.3 above). So ultimate entities must be powers; that is, individuals characterized solely by what they can do. For if one could describe the changing states or conditions in virtue of which their powers were exercised they could not be ultimate (unchanging). In the last instance to be is just to be able to do. But this does not rule out the possibility of a science of cosmology (which would be concerned with the distribution in space and redistribution in time of the ultimate entities) or of irreducibly historical branches of science in which the ultimate entities were Aristotelian or even Strawsonian individuals. The transformation of the principles governing such things would in general have to be conceived as conjuncturally determined open systemic events (see 2.6 above). In this way a complex thing such as a person (or a society) could come to be the cause of its own transformation.

Now it is because we are ourselves material things that our criteria for establishing the reality of things turn on the capacity of the thing whose existence is in doubt to bring about (or suffer) changes in its material constitution or the constitution of some material thing. Space, for example, might be regarded quite abstractly just as any system of relations in which objects stand to one another. And we can conceive the possession and exercise of causal powers in time in ways, and at levels, forever unknowable to men. We can never know where we stand absolutely in the chain of being. Despite this cosmic incapacity, science has succeeded in identifying strata of reality. Now a scientist never doubts for a moment that there are reasons for the behaviour he has identified and described. It is in the search for such reasons, at a deeper level of reality, at present known to him only through its effects, that the essence of scientific discovery lies. This search necessitates the construction of both new concepts and new tools. But, as what is produced must possess a material cause, the scientist stands for his essential task, in two systems of social relationships, depending necessarily on the work of others.

I have argued that the concept of natural necessity is the concept of a real generative mechanism at work, a concept which is applicable to the world quite independently of men. And it is in virtue of their connection by such a mechanism, of which knowledge may be attained in the social activity of science, that necessity is properly ascribed to some but not other sequences. In §5 I will analyse and criticize some objections to this concept of natural necessity and the related concept of natural kinds. But I want to deal here with the following basic objection to the account I have proposed: If, as I have contended, at each stratum or level of reality an entity is identified and its behaviour is described what positive advantages does this account have over the traditional empirical realist ones?

I think it has at least four substantial advantages. First, it reveals the essential movement of science. Second, it allows room for the location of a surplus-element, reflecting a difference independent of men, in the analysis of law-like statements at any one level. Third, it alone is capable of sustaining the ideas of the necessity and universality of laws, which are necessary for the rationality of theory-construction and the intelligibility of experimental activity. Finally, it alone is capable of accommodating the possibility of the existence of entities and the necessary phase of the knowledge of entities which cannot be analysed as substances with qualities, but must be conceived as powers to produce effects, powers which are possessed and may be exercised quite independently of their detection. (Needless to say, these advantages are not independent of each other.)

Science never stops still for a moment. At whatever level we look, it always involves something more than the empirical realist concedes. For example, if we consider the phase of the identification of a protolaw (which seems prima facie most susceptible to empirical realist analysis), we find the categorical clause implicit in a powers ascription, representing the scientist's instantaneous response to this situation, indicating his belief in the existence of a reason, located at the next highest level of inquiry, for the predicates being conjoined. Only the powers conceptual system is capable of giving an account of the internal rationality of science, by which it moves from knowledge of one stratum to knowledge of the next, so displaying the actual historical development of the sciences as something other than a sequence of accidents.

Now it is our knowledge of the reasons at Stratum II for the behaviour at Stratum I that warrants our designating the behaviour as necessary. But the reasons for the behaviour at Stratum II cannot be collapsed into the behaviour at Stratum I or an interpretation or model of that behaviour consistently with the intelligibility and rationality (respectively) of theory-construction or the possibility of empirical test. Nor can such reasons be glossed simply as more fundamental regularities,[57] if they are to be subject to experimental confirmation (or corroboration).

I have already shown in detail that the empirical realist account of laws, and hence the ontology that underpins it, is defective. Laws, I have argued, cannot be interpreted as conjunctions of events, but must be analysed as tendencies of things. If science is to be rendered intelligible the world must be seen as one of persisting things, of differing degrees of structure and complexity, to which powers and tendencies are ascribed; it cannot be reconstructed as a world of atomistic events apprehended in sense-experience. Briefly, to summarize my account of laws: To invoke a law I must have grounds for supposing a generative mechanism at work. These comprise: (a) independent grounds, preferably under experimentally closed conditions, for the mode of operation of the mechanism; (b) grounds for the satisfaction of the antecedent (or stimulus) conditions for the operation of the mechanism on the particular occasion in question; and (c) the absence of specific grounds for supposing a breakdown or transformation of the mechanism in that case. Generative mechanisms, I have argued, must be analysed as the ways of acting of things; and their operations must be understood in terms of the exercise of tendencies and causal powers. Tendencies may be possessed unexercised, exercised unrealized, and realized unperceived (or undetected) by men.

Finally, the empirical realist cannot deal with the case of entities which just are their powers or about which all we know are their powers. He thus rules out dogmatically, tout court the possibility of a certain kind of entity and a necessary phase of knowledge. In virtue of this he is no more able to make sense of the frontiers of knowledge, than show the mechanism by which science, if it can and when it does, will advance.

[Section 4 of Chapter 3 of *A Realist Theory of Science* omitted.]

5. Objections to the account of natural necessity proposed

Having outlined the principal advantages of my account of natural necessity and natural kinds (on pp. 183–5 above), I now want to consider some objections to it. In Chapter 4 I will consider the conditions of the plausibility of these objections.

The chief Humean counter-arguments may be put in the form of three theses:–

(i) there can be no, or at least no knowledge of, necessary connections between matters of fact;
(ii) if there were necessary corrections between matters of fact they would have to be known *a priori*; so science could not be empirical;
(iii) men are never directly aware of any causal power or agency or necessary connections between matters of fact, so these concepts cannot be justified by experience (though they may be explained by it; or are, for the neo-Kantian, imposed upon it).

The argument for thesis (i) is typically constructed as follows: there is nothing inconsistent about the supposition that the cause of a phenomenon, say putting a kettle of water on the stove and heating it, should not be accompanied by the effect in question. It is conceivable that water might freeze instead of boil when it is heated. Now thesis (i) is, as stated, highly ambiguous. It is not clear whether it is an ontological or an epistemological thesis (this ambiguity is of course explicit in the way I have formulated it); whether the 'necessity' is logical or non-logical; and whether the 'matters of fact' are events and states of affairs or the statements describing them. Before returning to the argument, we must see exactly what is at stake in it.

Now, it will be remembered, that for the transcendental realist to say that a sequence $E_a.E_b$ is necessary is to say that there is a generative mechanism at work such that when E_a occurs E_b tends to be produced (is produced in the absence of interfering causes). If there is such a mechanism the sequence is necessary; and its necessity is quite independent of any knowledge of it. To analyse the necessity of the connection in terms of our knowledge of the necessity of the connection would be to commit the epistemic fallacy (see 1.4 above). There is a real difference, quite independent of men, between the fact that when I heat the kettle of water it boils and the fact that it boils when the time is half-past two or the colour of my socks is blue. The necessary connections that bind some but not other events together (which are the enduring mechanisms of nature) are quite independent of our knowledge of them.

Statements clearly belong to the epistemic not the ontological order; and logical connections hold only between statements, not between events and states of affairs. Hence the prima facie absurdity of those who, in attempting to refute Hume, try to establish that nomic necessity is, or may be, a species of logical necessity.[58] Natural necessity is not logical necessity. Natural connections hold between things, events, states of affairs and the like; logical connections between propositions. Moreover there could be a world without propositions, in which the concept 'logical connection' had no application.

The laws of logic are not features of the world, nor are they imposed upon it. Rather, we must say: the world is such that changes in it can be consistently described.

Neither natural necessity nor knowledge of natural necessity can be identified with logical necessity. But our capacity to deduce the Wiedmann-Franz law from Drude's theory of electrical conductivity may serve as a *criterion* of our knowledge of the necessity the theory describes. I suggested in §3 above that three levels of knowledge of the objective world order can be distinguished in the development of science; so that statements can be classified as definitions, deductive consequences of true theories and simple protolaws according to the position they occupy (at any moment of time) in the development of our knowledge. Hence the deducibility of a tendency from a nature may serve as a criterion at the Lockean level for our knowledge of natural necessity, just as a correct definition may serve as a criterion at the Leibnizian level for our knowledge of natural kinds. But whether or not a sequence of events is necessary is quite independent of the logical status of the proposition used to express it; which is a function of the way it is described in the context of our knowledge; which in turn may be shown to have a certain rationale in the development of science.

Some causal statements expressing necessary connections are logically necessary and some are logically contingent.[59] For the Humean, however, logical and natural necessity are easily confused. For given the isomorphic relationship between knowledge and the world assumed in empirical realism and restricting our knowledge of nature to the protolegal phase of science (see page 172 above) he naturally comes to regard relationships between events as characterizable in the same kind of way as the statements expressing their relationships are at that phase typically, though not invariably, characterized; namely as contingent. But it is into this very same trap that defenders of the entailment view of natural necessity fall.

I shall construe thesis (i) as an epistemological claim to the effect that knowledge of necessary connections between events is impossible. And I will attempt to refute it by arguing that unless there were necessary connections between some (but not other) events, science would be impossible; and that in science the most stringent criteria for knowledge of natural necessity may be satisfied.

Unless there were necessary connections between matters of fact neither confirmation nor falsification would be possible. For without them no confirmation instance adds any probability whatever to any inductive instance.[60] On the other hand for it to be rational to reject what is falsified it must be assumed that a hypothesis which has been false in the past will not suddenly become true in the future.[61] Whether the conclusions of inductive arguments are weakened to probability judgements or it is denied that science is inductive in nature there must be necessary connections between matters of fact. Such necessary connections are provided by enduring mechanisms.

Moreover, if experimental science is to be possible, there must be necessary connections between some but not other events. This implies a dynamic principle of indifference: to the effect that mechanisms not only endure but are transfactually active. Neither their enduring nor their transfactual activity is in need of explanation.

Unless there were necessary connections between matters of fact we could have no knowledge, even particular knowledge (in as much as this depends upon inferences beyond what is immediately observed), of the world. For science to be possible then the world must consist of enduring and transfactually active mechanisms; and there must be necessary connections between some but not other matters of fact.

Natural mechanisms are of course nothing other than the powers or ways of acting of things. Thus, if science is to be possible, there must be a relationship of natural necessity between what a thing is and what a thing can do; and hence between what a thing is and what it tends to do, in appropriate conditions. The deducibility of a tendency from a nature thus constitutes a criterion for our knowledge of natural necessity. Events are necessarily connected when natural tendencies are realized.

With this in mind, let us return to a detailed examination of the argument for thesis (i). Is it conceivable that water should not boil when it is heated? Now it might be said straightaway that it is inconceivable to suppose that water might not boil when it is heated. Since anything that did not boil when it was heated could not properly be said to be 'water' at all. That is, that, in Lockean terminology, 'boiling when heated' specifies part of the nominal essence of water; or we could say with Putnam that 'water' functions as a 'law-cluster concept'.[62] Now the strength of this reply should not be under-rated. I have no doubt that we should ordinarily say something on these lines. Indeed, unless we have some criteria for the correct application of the term 'water' there is no reason why we should use it to refer to substances which as a matter of fact boil when heated rather than to say desk lamps or Saturday afternoons (which do not boil when heated). And such criteria would be at least in part dispositional; appearances, notoriously, can be misleading. Litmus paper that does not turn red when dipped into acid, a metal that does not conduct electricity, or petrol that does not explode when ignited could not be said to be 'litmus paper', 'a metal' or 'petrol' respectively; since the point of referring to the particulars concerned in those ways would be gone.[63] A magnet that could not magnetize, a fire that cannot burn or a pen that can never write would not be 'magnets', 'fires' and 'pens' at all. Things must satisfy certain criteria for them to be (correctly identified as) the kinds of things they are. By far the most important of such criteria are those that depend upon their powers to affect other bodies (a class which may be extended, analytically, to include their powers to affect observers under specified conditions in certain standard ways).

Such a reply will not however satisfy the Humean (particularly if he believes that definitions are merely matters of convention and cannot express empirically ascertained truths about kinds of things). More to the point it will not satisfy the scientist: for, accepting that 'boiling when heated' specifies part of the nominal essence of water, i.e. the criteria for the identification of a substance as 'water', he will want to know what it is about water in virtue of which it boils when it is heated. That is, he will set out to construct an explanation, in terms of the molecular and atomic structure of water, from which he can deduce its tendency to boil when it is heated. Now it is clearly inconsistent with this explanation to suppose that water might freeze, blush shyly or do anything else rather than boil when it is heated. That is, if the explanation is correct water *must* boil when it is heated.

Suppose however we came across a stuff which in all other respects looked and behaved like water but which did not boil when it was heated. Assuming standard conditions and a closed system (so as to eliminate the possibility of intervening causes) it would seem that we have the following alternatives:–

(a) our explanation was false;
(b) the fact that it was intended to explain, viz. that water boils when heated, was false;
(c) the particular concerned had been wrongly identified: it was not a sample of water after all;
(d) the particular concerned had changed; so that it had ceased to be water by the time it was heated.

Now the Humean asks us to imagine, and inductive scepticism requires that it be possible, that the cause event occurs and the effect event fails to materialize. Let me call this the critical situation. Now I want to argue that, given only that possibility (a) is ruled out, so that we have a correct explanation, the critical situation is impossible; that is, it is not possible that the cause event occurs and the effect event fails to materialize – in our example, that water is heated and does not boil.

Let me show this. If the explanation is correct water must boil rather than freeze when it is heated (though of course the converse is not the case); so possibility (b) is ruled out. Consider (c), the misidentification of the particular concerned. Now in this case it is not true to say that water did not boil when it was heated. For what did not boil was not water but only something which looked, and perhaps otherwise behaved, like it, say 'nwater'. Finally consider (d), a change in the particular concerned: what was water when it was put into the kettle at time t_1 ceased to be water by the time it froze at t_2. Here again it is not true to say that water did not boil when it was heated. For by the time it froze it had become something else, say 'retaw'. Hence given only the possibility of a realist interpretation of the entities postulated in the explanation, the conditions for inductive scepticism cannot be satisfied. If there is a real reason, located in the nature of the stuff, independent of the disposition concerned, water *must* tend to boil when it is heated (though in an open world any particular prediction may be defeated). The stratification of nature thus provides each science with its own internal inductive warrant.

Now it might be objected that I have omitted from my list of alternatives the possibility of the explanation, though correct up to time t_1, subsequently breaking down. But this possibility equally does not satisfy the requirements of the critical case. For, now at Stratum II (defining the Leibnizian level of the particular movement of science with which we are here concerned), nothing which did not possess the molecular and atomic structure that water has been discovered to possess could be said to be 'water'. So, here again, it would not be water that was freezing. A stuff remains water only so long as its nature (or real essence) remains unchanged. (Of course scientists could make a taxonomic change, but this does bear upon the argument of thesis (i).)

It is of course possible that the nature of some particular will be transformed: in which event, scientists will search both for an underlying substance or quasi-substance which preserves material continuity through change (e.g. a gene pool through species change, an atom in chemical reactions, energy in microphysics) and for the agent or mechanism which brought about the change. The principles of substance and causality are interdependent and complementary. Things persist (and continue to act in their normal way) unless acted upon; and their changes are explained in terms of the action of persisting (and transfactually active) things. If science is to be possible changes must be transformations, not replacements; and transformations must be effected by the actions of causes (causal agents). Things cannot pass clean out of existence or events happen for no reason at all. These are ideals of reason. But if science is to be possible our world must be such that they hold. This entails that it must be a world of enduring and continually acting things. It is of course true that it is impossible to prove that cases of ex nihilo production and miracles cannot ever happen. All we can say is that they cannot be known to happen. For it always remains possible for the scientist that what appears to be a case of an ex nihilo production or a miracle at time t_1 can come eventually at t_2 to be explained in terms of the transformation of real things and the action of real causes upon them.

I have argued that provided we have a correct explanation the critical situation cannot occur; that, for example, as long as the particular stuff remains water it must tend to boil when heated. But it might be urged if, as I have acknowledged, the nature of some particular may be changed does this not open the flood-gates of inductive scepticism once more? The answer is no: for there is a big difference between wondering whether some particular will be so acted upon by real causes in its environment that its nature (in this case, molecular structure) will be transformed, so that it ceases to be an individual of that kind; and wondering whether, while remaining an individual of that kind, it will cease to behave in the way that it has tended to behave in the past. The point is even clearer if we generalise it, so raising the questions of the boundaries of kinds and of the scope of application of laws. The difference is between wondering whether water will cease to exist; and wondering whether, while continuing to exist, it will stop boiling (in exactly the same circumstances) when it is heated.

It might be objected that while what I have said clearly covers case (d), viz. that of a particular changing, I have not taken the possibility of case (c), viz. that of a particular being misidentified, of nwater being mistaken for water, seriously enough. What is to prevent us continuously misidentifying particulars in just this way? Now just as particulars may be transformed, so they may be misidentified. But the situation the inductive sceptic asks us to imagine only gets off the ground if we assume that the relevant particulars have been correctly identified. The problem of induction is the problem of what guarantee we have that the unobserved will resemble the observed, or the future the past; it is not the problem of what guarantee we have that we have correctly observed the observed or correctly described the past. The suggestion that what I have here may in fact be a piece of lead piping is irrelevant to the question of what warrant I have for assuming that water will continue to boil when heated or for supposing that there is a necessary connection between water boiling and its being heated.

Nevertheless despite this irrelevance to our present concern, scepticism about particular knowledge can and should be met. It might be met in the following way: Any argument in which the case for the general misidentification of particulars is stated itself presupposes the capacity to identify certain particulars, namely words as tokens of a type and hence possessing a certain standard meaning in a given context. Hence no argument for the general misidentification of particulars can be consistently stated. If this argument does not carry conviction try to imagine a world in which we (a) systematically (b) at random misidentified (α) some particulars (β) all particulars (ᾱ) all the time (ῑ) some of the time. A world in which we systematically misidentified some given class of particulars (such as books as saucers and vice versa) would just be a world in which objects had different names. But a world in which our misidentifications were haphazard or universal is not coherently conceivable. It makes no sense to say that a particular has been misidentified unless one is prepared to say in what respect it has been misidentified. This itself presupposes the capacity to identify the particular as of a certain type. Of course our capacity to identify particulars presupposes the extended or dynamic principle of substance enunciated above, namely that things persist and continue to act unless acted upon, and hence in this way it presupposes the existence of necessary connections between matters of fact. It is up to the criteriology of empirical science to determine whether a particular has been misidentified or a perceptual report is nonveridical. The point is, however, that if science it to be an ongoing concern it cannot persistently demand and persistently return negative verdicts.

It might be objected to my refutation of thesis (i) that I have not considered the possibility that the explanation, which gives each science at any moment of time its own inductive warrant, is incorrect. Now it is of course always possible that we are mistaken in our explanation of why water must boil when heated; that our description of the mechanism in virtue of which it does so is wrong. But this is a general condition of all knowledge; it does not bear on the argument of thesis (i), which concerns the special difficulty of knowledge of necessary connections between matters of fact. I have already argued against the idea that all knowledge is conjectural on the grounds that refutations presuppose acceptances (progress requires a material cause). But whether or not my account of the transitive dimension of the philosophy of science is accepted, refutations presuppose necessary connections between matters of fact.

I have argued that scepticism about change, about our capacity to identify particulars and about the possibility of non-conjectural knowledge as such are all distinct from the special kind of scepticism involved in thesis (i), which is scepticism about the possibility of knowledge of necessary connections between matters of fact. I have shown how the second and third forms of scepticism, though irrelevant to thesis (i), may be averted. But how can Heraclitean scepticism be countered? Changes in things, I have argued, are explained in terms of unchanging things. The world is stratified. We need only worry about whether atoms will cease to exist when tables and chairs do; we need only worry about whether electrons will cease to exist when atoms do. It is contingent that the world is such that science is possible. But given that it is the dynamic principles of substance and causality that I have formulated must be true of it.

Three further forms of Heraclitean scepticism are possible in which we could be invited to imagine that our world is replaced (a) by a totally different one; (b) by one in which the principles of substance and causality no longer held; and (c) by one in which science ceased to be possible. I shall argue that the replacements envisaged in (a) and (b) are impossible, but that I am precluded by my own premises from saying anything about (c).

In (a) it is supposed that our world could be replaced by a totally different one; but to which, once it had come into being, inductive techniques could be reapplied. Now this is not an intelligible supposition, not only because scientific continuity would be lost during the replacement (so it would make little sense to talk of reapplying inductive techniques), but because there is no possible way in which such a replacement could be affected save by the action of real causes.[64] In (b) it is supposed that our world might be replaced by one to which the principles of substance and causality do not apply. Now although the existence of our world is contingent, given that it exists the supposition that *it* might be replaced in this way is not an intelligible one. Transcendental realism demands that we reason from the effect, science, to the condition of its possibility, viz. a world of enduring and transfactually active mechanisms. So we can rest assured that long after mankind has perished things will persist and continue to interact in the world that we once lived in. This leaves us with (c), about which I have said my premises preclude me from speaking. But a moment's reflection shows that (c) is devoid of interest for us. It is an empty counterfactual. For we know as a matter of fact that our world is one in which science is possible. Hence to assert the possibility of a world without science is merely to reassert the contingency of the circumstance that makes a study of the conditions of the possibility of science possible.

I have established that we can have (and that science actually possesses) knowledge of necessary connections between matters of fact. And I have shown how inductive scepticism proper, namely that arising from the assumption of the possibility of what I have called the critical situation, viz. the occurrence of the cause event and the non-occurrence of the effect, can be allayed, viz. by the provison of an adequate explanation; and how the other forms of scepticism often confused with inductive scepticism can be countered. I now turn to theses (ii) and (iii) which the Humean uses to bolster his central contention.

Thesis (ii) alleges that if there were necessary connections between matters of fact they would have to be known a priori, so that science could not be empirical. It is clear that this argument trades on a tacit conflation of logical and natural necessity and the identification of the resultant concept with that of the a priori. To refute it, I will have to show how knowledge of the natures or real essences of things, which I have argued ground our ascriptions of natural necessity, can come to be attained empirically; that is, how a posteriori knowledge of natural necessity is possible.

As there is some misunderstanding about the role of the concept of essence (and, as we shall see, the nature of definition) in science, some preliminary terminological clarification is necessary. The nominal essence of a thing or substance consists of those properties the manifestation of which are necessary for the thing to be correctly identified as one of a certain type. The real essences of things and substances are those structures or constitutions in virtue of which the thing or substance tends to behave the way it does, including manifest the properties that constitute its nominal essence. Science, I have argued, seeks to explain the properties of things identified at any one level of reality by reference to their intrinsic structures, or the structures of which they are an intrinsic part (defining the next level of inquiry). Thus the dispositional properties of say nickel, e.g. that it is magnetic, malleable, resistant to rust, melts at 1445°C and boils at 2900°C are explained, in the context of post-Daltonian atomic theory, by reference to such facts about its intrinsic structure as that its atomic number is 28, its atomic weight is 58.71 and its density is 8.90. The atomic constitution of nickel is its real essence. But it was discovered a posteriori, in the transitive process of science. And it itself constituted an explanandum of the next phase of scientific inquiry.

In general to classify a group of things together in science, to call them by the same name, presupposes that they possess a real essence or nature in common, though it does not presuppose that the real essence or nature is known. Thus we are justified in classifying alsations, terriers and spaniels together as different varieties of the same species dog because we believe that they possess a common genetic constitution which, despite their manifest sensible differences, serves to differentiate them from the members of the species cat. A chemist will classify diamonds, graphite and black carbon together because he believes that they possess a real essence in common, which may be identified as the atomic (or electronic) structure of carbon, of which these are allotropic forms. To classify a thing in a particular way in science is to commit oneself to a certain line of inquiry. Ex ante there will be as many possible lines of inquiry as manifest properties of a thing, but not all will be equally promising. Thus if one's concern is to account for the manifest properties of cucumbers it is clearly preferable to classify a 12 in. long green cucumber under the sortal universal 'cucumber' rather than under the universals 'green' or '12 in. long'. Not all general terms stand for natural kinds or taxa; because not all general features of the world have a common explanation. Carbon and dogs constitute natural kinds; but tables and chairs, red things and blue, chunks of graphite and fuzzy dogs do not. The justification of our systems of taxonomy, of the ways we classify things, of the nominal essences of things in science thus lies in our belief in their fruitfulness in leading us to explanations in terms of the generative mechanisms contained in their real essences. Not all ways of classifying things are equally promising; because not all sets of properties individuate just one and only one kind of thing.

The distinction between real and nominal essences should not be confused with that between real and nominal definitions. Real definitions are definitions of things, substances and concepts; nominal definitions are definitions of words. (Nominal essences are the properties that serve to identify things). Real definitions, in science, are fallible attempts to capture in words the real essences of things which have already been identified (and are known under their nominal essence) at any one stratum of reality. As so conceived, they may be true or false (not just – or even – more or less useful). The atomic weight of copper is 63.5. It would be wrong to claim that it was 53.4 or alternatively that 63.5 was the atomic weight of tin. Of course this fact was discovered a posteriori; but it may now be said to constitute part of the real definition of copper. If the real essence of copper consists in its atomic (or electronic) structure, its nominal essence might consist in its being a red sonorous metal, malleable and a good conductor of electricity etc. Something that did not satisfy these properties could not properly be said to be 'copper'. But conversely just because the word 'copper' in science has a history, and at any moment of time a use, the nominal essence of copper cannot suddenly be designated by the use of 'reppoc' or 'tin'. Nominal definitions in science cannot therefore be conceived as stipulative, arbitrary or matters of convention. Although there is a sense in which any other symbol could have been used to refer to copper; given this usage and that history 'copper' cannot be replaced by 'bronze' or '♀' for no reason at all.[65] Changes in the definitions of words in ongoing social activities require justification.

On the view advanced here science consists in a continuing dialectic between taxonomic and explanatory knowledge; between knowledge of what kinds of things there are and knowledge of how the things there are behave. It aims at real definitions of the things and structures of the world as well as statements of their normic behaviour. The source of the failure to see this is the ontology of empirical realism which reduces things to qualities, taxa to classes, enduring and active mechanisms to constant conjunctions of independent and atomistic qualia.[66] Now if the world consists only of qualia and qualia are independent of one another then the particular names that we give to qualia cannot matter and all qualia will appear on a par. On this conception, predicates must be independent of one another and classification is ultimately arbitrary.

Now just as it is a mistake to assume that science is concerned with any and all behaviour it is a mistake to assume that it is concerned with any and all things. Scientists do not seek to describe the behaviour of or to classify common objects like tables and chairs, though the laws of physics and the principles of scientific taxonomy (e.g. the identification of a table as an oak one) may be brought to bear on them. Now from the fact that tables have no real essence it does not follow that carbon has none. Electrons are not related in the same way as games. A resemblance theory of universals works best for the complex Strawsonian individuals of ordinary life. But the universals of interest to science are real: they are the generative mechanisms of nature which account, in their complex determination, for the phenomena of the world, including (upon analysis) the genesis and behaviour of ordinary things. The dialectic of explanatory and taxonomic knowledge must thus be formulated as follows: science is concerned with the behaviour of things only in as much as it casts light upon their reasons for acting, and hence upon what kinds of things there are; and science is only concerned with things of a particular kind, in as much as they constitute the reason for some pattern of normic behaviour and thus themselves become an appropriate object of inquiry.

The importance of taxa in science may be expressed by saying that what is non-accidentally true of a thing is true of a thing in virtue of its essential nature. A thing acts, or at least tends to act, the way it is. It should be stressed that the difference between a thing which has the power or tends to behave in a certain way and one which does not is not a difference between what they will do, since it is contingent upon the flux of conditions whether the power is ever manifested or tendency exercised. Rather, it is a difference in what they themselves are; i.e. in their intrinsic natures. A copper vase remains malleable even if it is never pressed out of shape. It is contingent whether an electric current is ever passed through a copper wire. But it is necessary, given its electronic structure, that it be a good conductor of electricity. We know how things will behave, if certain conditions materialize, if we know what the things are. But we can only know what things are a posteriori, via the empirical process of science.

This view may be contrasted with the idea that scientists are not concerned with questions such as 'what is energy?' or 'what is an atom?' but only with questions of the kind 'how can the energy of the sun be made useful?' or 'under what conditions does an atom radiate light?'[67] Popper's 'methodological nominalism' seems to be based on the idea that to suppose that things have essences is to suppose that it is possible to give explanations which are 'ultimate' in the sense that they are insusceptible in principle of further explanation (which is what he calls 'essentialism').[68] Although Locke may have held this view, is it certainly no more a necessary feature of the concept of real essence than it is a necessary feature of the concept of behaviour to suppose that because a thing can be described as behaving in a certain way the behaviour itself cannot be subject to further explanation. It is clear that to suppose that things have real essences is not to suppose that the real essences of those things cannot be explained in terms of more fundamental structures and things.

Two other arguments sometimes invoked against the concept of real essences should be mentioned. The first depends upon the assumption that differences in nature are continuous, not discrete; that 'God makes the spectrum, man makes the pigeon-holes';[69] so that 'genera, species, essences, classes and so on are human creations'.[70] I can find no possible warrant for such an assumption. Taken literally, it would imply that a chromosome count is irrelevant in determining the biological sex of an individual, that the class of the living is only conventionally divided from the class of the dead, that the chemical elements reveal a continuous gradation in their properties, that tulips merge into rhododendron bushes and solid objects fade gaseously away into empty space. The second involves the belief that to suppose that there are natural kinds is to suppose that these kinds are fixed, and is in particular to rule out the possibility of a mechanism of evolution.[71] Again, this is completely unwarranted. For natures may change; and whether, and if so the ways in which they do, are matters for substantive scientific investigation. No spectrum exists between men and apes but that does not preclude the possibility of a mechanism of evolution (involving a whole sequence of 'missing links'). What happens in such cases is that biologists posit a novel entity, a gene pool, as the underlying continuant through the species' change. The objection is only valid at the level of ultimate physical entities since necessarily if such entities exist they must be enduring.

Scientists attempt to discover the real essences of things *a posteriori*, and to express their discoveries in real definitions of the natural kinds. From a description of the nature of a thing its behavioural tendencies can be deduced. When such tendencies are realized the events describing the stimulus or releasing conditions for the exercise of the tendency and its realization may be said to be necessarily connected. Thus scientists can come to possess knowledge of necessary connections between events as a result of an a posteriori process of discovery. Scientists are not content to collect conjunctions of events. Rather they try to discover the natures of things. Given this, no problem of induction can arise. Since it is not possible for a thing to act inconsistently with its own nature and remain the kind of thing it is. That is, a thing must tend to act the way it does if it is to be the kind of thing it is. If a thing is a stick of gelignite it must explode if certain conditions materialize. Since anything that did not explode in those circumstances would not be a stick of gelignite but some other substance. Now given the satisfaction of the criteria for the identification of a substance, say water, and the recording, preferably under experimentally closed conditions, of its most significant and suggestive behavioural properties, scientists move immediately to the construction and testing of possible explanations for the protolaws identified. But *if* there is an explanation, located in the nature of the stuff or the system of which the stuff is a part, *whether or not it is known by men*, water must tend to boil when it is heated. It is the real stratification of nature that justifies induction in science. It is not we that impose uniformities upon the world, but nature that makes induction (properly circumscribed) a rational activity for men.

The third Humean counter-argument is that we are never directly aware of any necessary connection between matters of fact or causal power or agency so that these concepts cannot be justified by experience. Thesis (iii) thus completes a triangle, whose other sides are theses (ii) and (i). It could be argued that we are sometimes directly aware of necessarily connected sequences (see 2.3 above), and that we are sometimes directly aware of the exercise of causal powers (though the powers themselves can only be known, not shown, to exist; i.e. we are never directly aware of causal powers as such).[72] It seems clear that we are aware of ourselves as causal agents *in* a world of other causal agents; and that unless we were so aware we could not act intentionally, or come to know ourselves as causal agents at all. (Projective explanations of our idea of necessary connection are clearly anthropocentric.) However for the transcendental realist this is incidental. For, for him, the status of the concept of necessary connection is clear: it has been established, by philosophical argument, as applicable to some but not other sequences of events as a necessary condition of the social activity of science. (It should be stressed that this does not mean that any particular science has correctly identified, let alone adequately described, the necessary sequences: it is a condition of the *possibility* of science.) Thus the concept of natural necessity does not have to be justified in terms of or traced back to its source in sense-experience;

though there must be a scientific explanation of how we come to possess the concept.

That science has a posteriori knowledge of necessary connections between matters of fact is a proposition that can be given no further justification.

6. The problem of induction

In the concluding section of this chapter I intend to argue that traditional approaches to the problem of induction fail; to reveal a crucial ambiguity in the formulation of the problem; and to show how transcendental realism can resolve it. In doing so I will be bringing together my critiques of the ideas of the actuality and contingency of law; and I will relate my resolution of the problem of induction to the problem of universals. I shall argue that the condition of the intelligibility of the traditional problem of induction is an ontology of atomistic events and closed systems; but that in our world inductive reasoning may be shown to have a rational place.

The traditional problem of induction is the problem of what warrant we have for reasoning from particular instances to general statements (induction proper) or from observed to unobserved or past to future instances (eduction). Now it is clear that unless we (sometimes) have some such warrant nothing can be justified, shown to be mistaken or called into doubt: memory cannot be relied upon, a mistake demonstrated or grounds for a sceptical conclusion given. (Why, for instance, should the fact that my senses have deceived me in the past be a ground for believing that they will do so in the future?) Indeed complete scepticism about induction seems literally unthinkable.[73] So pervasive a feature of our social life is inductive-type reasoning that it seems patently unsatisfactory to be told that it is just a contingent fact about the world that induction is successful.[74] If inductive-type reasoning is necessary, then it seems incumbent upon us to ask what the world must be like for it to be possible; and what must have been assumed (inter alia about the world) for the problem to have remained intractable. The answer to the first question will constitute a set of synthetic a priori truths about the world; the answer to the second a set of synthetic a priori truths about received philosophy of science.

The standard responses to the traditional problem of induction are of course: (i) to deny that science is inductive in nature (e.g. Popper); (ii) to justify induction inductively (e.g. Black, Braithwaite); (iii) to strengthen the premises of inductive arguments, so that they become in effect enthymematic deductive arguments (e.g. Mill); (iv) to weaken the conclusions of inductive arguments to probability judgements (e.g. Carnap); (v) to justify induction pragmatically or vindicate it (e.g. Reichenbach, Salmon); (vi) to dissolve the problem, i.e. to claim that it is a pseudo-one (e.g. Strawson, Edwards). The objections to (ii)–(v) are well known; they all in one way or other beg the point at issue which is:

(A) the problem of what warrant we have for supposing that the course of nature will not change.

(A) must of course be distinguished from:

(B) the problem of what warrant we have for believing some proposition, statement or theory true.

For to say that the special theory of relativity refuted Newtonian mechanics is not to say that the course of nature changed: it is to say that Newtonian mechanics was (at least in one respect) wrong all along. I will leave aside considerations pertaining to question (B) and the rationale for distinguishing it from question (A) until Chapter 4.

Popper claims to have solved the problem of induction, by accepting Hume's conclusion that induction cannot be justified but denying that science is inductive in nature. According to Popper science proceeds by the refutation of bold conjectures (general statements) by their deductive consequences (singular relatively observational statements). However, for a relatively observational statement to refute a general law-like statement (or theory) it must be presupposed that the course of nature will not change so that the experimental and observational context in which the refuting observation statement is true ceases to be true. Popper would reply to this objection as follows: '. . . there is a logical asymmetry: one singular statement – say about the perihelion of Mercury – can formally falsify Kepler's laws; but these cannot be formally verified by any number of singular statements. The attempt to minimize this asymmetry can only lead to confusion'.[75] But the decision to accept the singular statement about the perihelion of Mercury as falsifying Kepler's laws presupposes that in exactly the same circumstances Mercury's perihelion would behave in exactly the same way. The asymmetry is there alright. But what warrant is there in Popper's system for supposing that nature is uniform so that its course will not change, in the way Hume and Goodman invite us to imagine, so that our best-falsified theories (astrology, Marxism, psycho-analysis, Newtonian mechanics) become true? Whatever the merits of Popper's philosophy of science, his claim to have solved the logical problem of induction is manifestly untenable and based on a confusion of problems (A) and (B).

(vi) also fails, for a number of reasons. First, it seems possible to imagine worlds in which induction would be unsuccessful – not just 'counter-inductive' worlds, in which the unexpected always happens, but *capricious* worlds, for which no kind of rule could be formulated.[76] Secondly, even a straightforwardly counter-inductive world would be incapable of sustaining scientific or social life. For the unexpected is a potentially infinite class. No inductive rule could be operationalized in a counter-inductive world. 'Expect the unexpected' can only be applied ex post, after the unexpected has actually happened. The fact that induction is (sometimes) successful places a constraint on the world in which we live. For in some conceivable worlds induction would be unsuccessful or unoperationisable. Hence it would seem reasonable, and indeed necessary, to isolate the conditions that must obtain for induction to be successful. If there are necessary conditions for the success of induction, they must constitute the missing 'justification'. Thirdly, it is clear that not all inductive arguments are equally good. To appeal to induction as an institution does not help us to decide between good and bad inductive arguments (any more than appeal to the law helps us to decide between good and bad laws). Finally, induction is not always justified. If it is not always justified there must be conditions under which it is justified, about which the approach represented by (vi) has nothing to say.

Induction, I have said, is not always justified. In general induction is only justified if we have some reason other than positive instances for the generalization concerned. Two kinds of reasons are distinguishable:–

(α) a plausible model or hypothesis of a mechanism by means of which we can render it intelligible to ourselves that when E_a then E_b.[77]
(β) knowledge of the mechanism which given E_a generates E_b.

Induction is only justified if the generalization concerned is a law of nature.[78] Of course ex ante when inductive reasoning occurs we do not know *whether* the sequence is necessary. But it is justified *if* it is necessary. And to justify it we need only have grounds for supposing *that* it is necessary. Now I have already argued that (α), though representing an important moment in the process of scientific discovery, carries too little ontological bite to justify the assumption of a law of nature (see §2 above). The generative mechanisms of nature are of course nothing other than the powers or ways of acting of things.

Now *eduction*, or inference from particular instances to other particular instances, is only justified if *in addition* the system in which the consequent event occurs is closed. The crucial ambiguity in the formulation of the problem of induction to which I referred earlier now becomes clear. It turns on the question of whether the generalization referred to (or in eduction assumed) is an empirical or a normic statement, a statement about the conjunctions or events or the tendencies of things, a statement about actualities or possibilities. Now a belief in the uniformity of nature is quite misplaced if it is a belief in the invariance of patterns of *events* (or experiences). For the non-invariance of their patterns is, I have shown in Chapter 2, a condition of the possibility of science. A belief in the uniformity of nature is only rational if it is a belief in the invariance of *structures*. The eventsequential past is an unreliable guide to the future. Instead what we require, and in small measure actually possess, is a knowledge of the invariant tendencies and natures of things (though this does not legitimate predictions).

Induction is only justified if the generalization is a law of nature and eduction is only justified if the system is closed (so that the tendency designated in the law statement must, given the occurrence of the antecedent, be realized). Induction is justified because nature is stratified. Now we do not need to know *what* the structures are to know *that* nature is stratified. (We do not need to know what the explanation is to know that there is an explanation.) We know that nature is stratified because its stratification is a condition of the possibility of science-in-general. And we know that science is possible in general because it in fact occurs. To know that induction is justified we do not need to know what any particular explanation is.

Now if we know what the correct explanation is we do not need to reason inductively. And when we need to reason inductively we do not know what the correct explanation is. Given then that our knowledge that nature is stratified is secured a priori how can we justify any particular piece of inductive reasoning? By giving grounds for supposing that there is an explanation, located in the nature of things (at the next highest rung of reality), for the generalization claimed. It is the possibility of an adequate explanation, in terms of real invariances, from which the behaviour concerned can, normically understood, be deduced that must justify any piece of inductive reasoning in science. Thus it is the possibility of the satisfaction of a deductive criterion that justifies induction in science. But we know that the world must be such that this is so. It is the structure of the world that makes induction, when it is, a rational activity for men.

I have of course already argued that the conditions for inductive scepticism only obtain if we deny the possibility of (β) above. If we allow (β), i.e. a realist interpretation of the entities postulated in scientific theory, then we do have a reason independent of the facts identified at any one level of reality as to why one but not another sequence of events must be forthcoming (if the system is closed). Now as the argument for inductive scepticism turns on the alleged impossibility of knowledge of necessary connections between matters of fact and I have demonstrated how we can (and do) come to have such knowledge a posteriori in science, it remains only for me to examine the conditions of the plausibility of the traditional problem of induction and to show how the galaxy of problems in its wake can be rationally resolved.

The problem of induction arises if we restrict the grounds for a generalization to its instances, i.e. if we accept Nicod's criterion of the evidence for a law. It is resolved in two steps: (α)* by allowing a model of a generative mechanism or structure to supply the missing reason that the coherence of scientific practice demands, and in particular to provide a crucial part of the grounds for a law; and (β)* by allowing that under certain conditions, i.e. if certain criteria are satisfied, such models held out in the scientific imagination as plausible representations of the real mechanisms of nature may come to be established as real. Mechanisms are enduring; they are nothing but the powers of things. Things, unlike events (which are changes in them), persist.

Their persistence does not need explaining. Space and time are causally inert: they possess neither liabilities nor powers. Now step (β)* involves experimentation. It is a condition of the intelligibility of experimental activity that causal structures not only persist but act independently of the patterns of events. Thus the world is open, and the laws of nature must be analysed as the tendencies of things. The dynamic realist principles of substance and causality to which I have been working may thus be stated as follows: the world consists of enduring and transfactually active things (substance) which endure and act in their normal way unless acted upon (causality). Effects presuppose both continuants and causes. They must occur in things and be brought about by things (other than position in space or moment in time). On the other hand only effects need explaining.

The condition of the intelligibility of the problem of induction is an ontology of atomistic events and closed systems. For without closed systems there is no reason for the past to resemble the future and without atomistic events there is reason why it should. The grounds for the atomistic ontology of empirical realism disappear when we realise that sense-experience is neither the only ground nor the only source of knowledge; and that it is analysable neither in purely atomistic terms[79] nor as a happening to passive men.[80] The grounds for the actualist ontology of closed systems disappear when we realise that in general, outside astronomical contexts, they need to be experimentally established. In place of the ontology of experience and atomistic events constantly conjoined, transcendental realism establishes an ontology of complex and active structures and things. In place of the contrast (and unbridgeable gulf) between our particular and our general knowledge of the world, transcendental realism allows knowledge both of things and of their powers or ways of acting. In place of the analysis of laws as constant conjunctions of events, transcendental realism analyses laws in terms of the tendencies of things which may be exercised unrealized and realized unperceived by men. Science becomes a social activity, difficult and discriminating; not an automatic, individualistic affair. Science is explanatory non-predictive.

I now want to show how the replacement of the empirical realist ontology of atomistic events and closed systems by the transcendental realist ontology of persisting and transfactually active things allows us to resolve the problems and paradoxes associated with the problem of induction. This problem, I have argued, only arises if we deny the possibility of a reason, located in the enduring nature of some thing, for the behaviour concerned. In its sharpest form it may be expressed as follows: if all predicates refer ultimately to experience and experiences are independent of each other, as they must be if they are to ground (in part or in whole) our knowledge of the world, then predicates must be independent of one another. There can then be no reason for expecting one rather than another set of experiences so that for all we know predicates may become associated in entirely new ways. Thus there is no reason why cabinet ministers should not suddenly start bearing figs or Mancunians disintegrate when exposed to the sun (the problem of induction); no reason why emeralds examined after A.D. 2000 should not turn out to be blue or blue things become green next Christmas (Goodman's paradox);[81] no reason why the sighting of a black raven should confirm the proposition that all ravens are black better than the sighting of a red herring or a white shoe (Hempel's paradox);[82] no reason to suppose that if I had gone for a walk in the rain five minutes ago I would in fact have got wet (the problem of subjunctive conditionals). Now there are two ways of meeting these absurdities. The first is to hold that the paradoxes and problems stem from the insertion of artificial predicates and fanciful conjectures into already functioning and well-connected scientific contexts, for which no positive reason can be given. The trouble with this line of response is that it is still vulnerable to the objection that there is no ground, independent of custom or convention or past practice or mob psychology, for expecting one sequence of events rather than another. And besides the nature of the 'connection' predicates are supposed to enjoy is unclear. The second is the transcendental realist line. This line holds that there are objective connections in the nature of things, which may be identified as enduring mechanisms, which bind or link some but not other events and states of affairs. I will now sketch the transcendental realist resolution of these problems.

It is physically impossible for a cabinet minister to bear figs; that is, nothing which bore figs could properly be said to be a cabinet minister at all. Desk lamps cannot fly or walk about the room, just as Mancunians do not disintegrate when exposed to the sun. A particular must tend to behave in certain ways if it is to be of the kind that it is. On an ontology of things the general problem of induction cannot arise, though there may be specific problems of identification and special reasons for expecting change. Things persist. They are natural endurers and their changes are explained in terms of unchanging things. What is the rationale for this resolution? The scientific explanation of scientifically significant behaviour is in terms of invariant principles of structure. Thus the scientist assumes that there is something about metals (their possession of free electrons, perhaps) in virtue of which it is not possible for them not to conduct electricity. Their possession of free electrons is the invariant principle of structure. There is something about cabinet ministers (their genetic constitution, perhaps) in virtue of which it is not possible for them to bear figs; just as, if Socrates is a man he must die.

On an ontology of things Goodman's paradox cannot arise. Now either 'all emeralds are green' is law-like or it is not. If it is not the Goodmanesque alternative 'all emeralds are grue' is equally admissible. For it is then ex hypothesi purely accidental that all emeralds happen to be green. On the other hand, to suppose that 'all emeralds are green' is law-like is to suppose that there is a reason, located in its crystalline structure of chemical composition, why it differentially reflects light the way it does. Now given that structure, emeralds must, to normal observers under standard conditions, look green. So anything which looked blue could not possess that structure, and hence would not be an emerald at all. Now of course occasionally we may have grounds for supposing that a particular and even a kind will cease to exist, i.e. be transformed into a different thing or kind (or even into an entirely different kind of thing or kind). Thus a genuine Goodman-type problem could arise. However it would be a specific problem, itself presupposing the existence of both a continuant and a cause. Moreover no predicate such as 'grue' could ever be admissible to science. Since the mere passage of time cannot constitute a cause. It would have to be a coincidence that emeralds examined after A.D. 2000 looked blue. Dates can be at best only proxy causes.

Hempel's paradox may be resolved quite simply once the significance of his intuition, viz. that propositions about shoes and herrings are irrelevant to the truth of propositions about ravens, is grasped. If laws are statements about things and there must be some reason other than instances for accepting them, then Hempel's paradox may be resolved as follows: If 'all ravens are black' is law-like there must be a reason, located in the nature of ravens (not in the nature of black), why ravens are black. 'All ravens are black' is a truth about ravens, not about colour. Hence the contrapositive 'all non-black-things are non-ravens' has no bearing on it. The logical subject of a law of nature is a (natural kind of) thing. Hence there is a logical asymmetry built into its structure, reflecting the site of the mechanism designated, in virtue of which its terms are not equivalent and contraposition is prohibited. To put this another way: the mechanism that, to use Strawson's term, 'collects'[83] red under herring or white under shoe is either entirely different from the mechanism that collects black under ravens or else, where as in the shoe case the 'connection' is entirely accidental, there is no mechanism involved at all.

The problem of subjunctive conditionals is easily and rationally resolved on an ontology of things. To assert a law of nature is to ascribe a possibility to a thing – a possibility which is possessed by the thing, and has a real basis in the enduring nature of the thing, whether it is exercised or not. To assert a subjunctive conditional is just to say that the possibility possessed by the thing would have been exercised, had the conditions in fact been different. I would have got wet alright, rain being what it is.

The source of these problems lies in the reduction of things to qualities and laws, which are statements about things, to conjunctions of events. This is reflected most sharply in the failure to sustain the idea of the *necessity* of law. But side by side with these well-known problems is a less well-known set (due to the tacit assumption, by almost all philosophers of science, of closed systems), which turn on the failure of the actualist ontology of empirical realism to sustain the idea of the *universality* of law. Lacking from the former set is a criterion for distinguishing necessary from accidental sequences (depending upon a concept of the stratification of the world); lacking from the latter set is a criterion for distinguishing open from closed systems (depending upon a concept of the differentiation of the world). For empirical realism all sequences are accidental and the world is closed; for transcendental realism some sequences are necessary and the world is open.

Let us briefly note these homologues of the well-known problems on the universality axis. Corresponding to the problem of induction we have the problem of what justifies the assumption that laws will continue to hold outside the laboratory. This is resolved by allowing (or rather seeing that it is a condition of the intelligibility of experimental science) that things endure and continue to act in their normal way outside as well as inside the laboratory (as they will do in the future as in the past) unless, as may sometimes happen, they are themselves transformed. Corresponding to the problem of subjunctive (and counterfactual) conditionals we have the problem of normic (and transfactual) ones. Corresponding to the paradoxes of confirmation, paradoxes of falsification. (Laws and theories are straightaway falsified by any open-systemic instance, just as they are straightaway confirmed by any contrapositive instance, if we regard laws as empirical statements.) Corresponding to the problem of justifying the use of hypothetical entities in theory construction (which Hempel has called 'the theoretician's dilemma')[84] we have the problem of justifying the use of the CP clause in theory application (which we could call 'the engineer's dilemma', or the problem of the applied scientist's excuse). All these problems can be rationally resolved by an account of science which sees it as an attempt to penetrate ever deeper into the nature of things and to describe more adequately the things of nature.

The Humean analysis of laws is a failure: it does too little and too much. The causal contingent is neither contingent nor actual, but necessary and real.

The intelligibility of perception presupposes that objects persist, in space and time, independently of our perception of them. The intelligibility of experimental activity presupposes that they act, in space and time, independently of the patterns of events they generate. Now the use of general terms in identifying these objects presupposes that they fall into natural kinds. But it is not possible to say anything in general about the number of kinds there are or about the numbers in any particular kind. Now the things posited by science in its investigations may be quite recondite and abstract with respect to our ordinary experience. It is wrong to think of them as necessarily like material objects – they may be powers, forces, fields or just complex structures or sets of relationships. Their metaphysical character, which justifies us labelling them as 'things' to mark their insusceptibility to analysis as 'events' or 'experiences', lies in their persistence and transfactual activity. This entails that they persist even when they do not act, and act in their normal way in the flux of conditions that co-determine the actual outcome of their activity. Things, as so conceived, must be complex and structured; in virtue of which possibilities may be ascribed to them which may be unexercised or exercised unactualized or actualized unperceived by men. On this account of science the actual is seen as an instance of the possible; and a normic mood is added to the hierarchy of conditionals marking the space of possibilities exercised but unactualized.

On the account of laws advanced here they cannot be identified with constant conjunctions of atomistic events or regarded as reporting correlations between either independent or equivalent variables. On the contrary, they must always be grounded in some conception of an explanatory mechanism and ascribed, as tendencies, to specific kinds of things. This is consistent with the view of ordinary things as subject to dual (and multiple) control, perhaps by principles of relatively different kinds. Laws do not describe the patterns of events. Rather, we could say, they describe the normic behaviour of novel kinds and impose constraints on familiar things. Ordinary things may be conceived, metaphysically, as *compounds.* This allows us to make sense of the *individuality* of historical particulars; just as the conception of ordinary events as 'conjunctures' (see 2.6 above) allows us to make sense of the uniqueness of historical events.

If the ordinary things of the world are compounds then it is natural that they should share nothing in common except resemblances. But just as only some events are significant in science, although all in principle may be explained by it, so with things. Ordinary things have a genesis and their changes may be rationally explained (in terms of continuants and causes) by reference to the exercise of the tendencies of things which share a common identity, i.e. which fall into a natural kind. Scientifically significant generality does not lie on the face of the world, but in the hidden essences of things.

How can this be shown? Either classification is arbitrary or it is not. If it is non-arbitrary it must be based on a relationship of resemblance (similarity) or identity. If it is only based on the assumption of a relationship of resemblance there is no rationale for the stratification of science. On the other hand if it is based on an assumed theoretical identity then we do have a rationale for the move from manifest behaviour to essential nature that we have seen lies at the heart of rational theory-construction in science. To stress, nothing can be said about the number or variety of real universals there are. But it is clear that 'table' and 'red' are not real universals; and 'gene' and 'molecule' are.

A similar trilemma may be applied to our explanatory knowledge of the world. Either explanation is arbitrary or it is not (arbitrariness is suggested by the problem of induction or any of the paradoxes discussed above). If it is non-arbitrary the ground for the explanation is either imposed by men or it exists in the world. If it is imposed by men we are left without any rationale for experimental activity, the process of testing human constructions against the world. Predicates are not independent of each other and classifications are not arbitrary in science because there are necessary connections in the world and things fall into natural kinds.

I can now return to the question I asked at the beginning of this chapter. To what, in our ascription of laws, is necessity and universality properly ascribed? The answer is to the transfactual activity of things, i.e. to enduring mechanisms at work. For these ascriptions to be possible the world must be composed of enduring mechanisms which act independently of men; science must be an ongoing social activity; and men must be (in the sense indicated in 2.5 above) free.

Now it is because we are material things, possessed of the senses of sight and touch, that we accord priority in verifying existential claims to changes in material things. But scientists posit for these changes both continuants and causes, some of which are necessarily unperceivable. It is true that 'that a flash or a bang occurs does not *entail* that anything flashes or bangs. "Let there be light" does not *mean* "let something shine"'.[85] But a scientist can never rest content with effects: he must search for causes; and causes reside in or constitute things. Charged clouds, magnetic fields and radio stars can only be detected through their effects. But this does not lead us to deny their existence, any more than we can rationally doubt the existence of society or of language as a structure irreducible to its effects. There could be a world of electrons without material objects; and there could be a world of material objects without men. It is contingent that we exist (and so know this). But given that we do, no other position is rationally defensible. It is the nature of the world that determines which aspects of reality can be possible objects of knowledge for us.[86] But it is the historical development of the various sciences that determines in what manner and to what degree these possibilities are taken up by men.

Notes

1 This is the ontological form of Hume's doctrine that events 'seem conjoined, but never connected'. See D. Hume, *An Enquiry Concerning Human Understanding*, p. 74.

2 F. Bacon, *Novum Organum.*

3 To borrow Toulmin's useful concept. See S. Toulmin, *Human Understanding, Vol. I*, p. 158 and passim.

4 W. E. Johnson, *Logic, Vol. III*, Chap. 1.

5 R. Chisholm, 'The Contrary to Fact Conditional', *Mind* 55 (1946), reprinted in *Readings in Philosophical Analysis*, eds. H. Feigl and G. Maxwell, pp. 482–97.

6 (a) and (b) correspond of course to Hume's two definitions of 'cause'. See D. Hume, *Treatise*, p. 172 and *Inquiry*, pp. 76–7.

7 I owe this term of G. Buchdahl, *op. cit.*, p. 27 and passim.

8 See e.g. R. B. Braithwaite, *op. cit.*, Chap. 8; C. G. Hempel, *op. cit.*, Chap. 12; and E. Nagel, *op. cit.*, Chap. 4.

9 The Jesuit mathematician Clavius demonstrated this fallacy in Osiander's apologetic preface to Copernicus' *De Revolutionibus.* Osiander had argued, as Galileo was later invited to before the Inquisition, that the helio-centric theory was merely a mathematically adequate representation of the facts of planetary motion that made no claim to be true. Clavius pointed out that it was never a good

argument in favour of a theory that it 'saved the appearances', as a true result could be derived from any number of absurd or false premises. (Cf. J. Losee, *An Historical Introduction to the Philosophy of Science*, pp. 44–5.) Indeed even if we exclude all premises which we know to be false or which are not explicitly defined there will still be an infinite number of sets of premises from which the facts can be deduced, provided we allow for the introduction of artificial predicates such as Hesse's 'tove' (M. B. Hesse, *Models and Analogies in Science*, p. 30), of which place- and time-dependent predicates such as Goodman's 'grue' (N. Goodman, *Fact, Fiction and Forecast*, p. 74) merely form a special class. Hence deducibility cannot provide a sufficient criterion for choosing one set of premises rather than another (the source of Goodman's paradox) or for justifying one statement rather than another as law-like.

10 This is of course a very poor best. For (i) the simplest of any small number of explanations is not necessarily the best (cf. M. Bunge, *The Myth of Simplicity*, pp. 51–134); (ii) there will still be an in principle infinite number of equally simple explanations, if we restrict ourselves to formal or syntactical criteria alone (cf. J. J. Katz, *The Problem of Induction and its Solution*, Chaps. 4 and 5).

11 J. S. Mill, *A System of Logic, Vol. I*, p. 378.

12 E. Nagel, *op. cit.*, pp. 64–5.

13 I. Lakatos, *op. cit.*, p. 116.

14 N. Goodman, *op. cit.*, pp. 92–122.

15 For, as Craig's theorem shows, if it does not the theoretical component is then completely eliminable. See W. Craig, 'The Replacement of Auxiliary Expressions', *Philosophical Review* 65 (1956), pp. 35–55.

16 N. R. Campbell, *The Foundations of Science*, esp. Chap. 6.

17 *Ibid.* pp. 126–40.

18 N. R. Campbell, *What is Science?*, p. 99.

19 N. R. Campbell, *Foundations*, pp. 132–7; and M. B. Hesse, *op. cit.*, pp. 35–43.

20 N. R. Campbell, *op. cit.*, pp. 243–56.

21 J. Tyndall, 'Scientific Uses of Imagination', *Fragments of Science for Unscientific People*, p. 131.

22 P. K. Feyerabend, 'Problems of Empiricism, Part II', *The Nature and Function of Scientific Theory*, ed. R. G. Colodny, p. 317.

23 See e.g. M. B. Hesse, *op. cit.*, pp. 35ff. Cf. also P. K. Feyerabend, 'Problems of Empiricism', *op. cit.*, pp. 173ff.

24 P. Duhem, *op. cit.*, p. 7.

25 M. Scriven, 'Truisms', p. 450.

26 'This', says Mach, 'is all that natural laws are', *op. cit.*, p. 192.

27 Indeed one might be tempted to see the difference as merely one of taste or temperament as when Duhem compared the 'rolling drums', 'pearl beads' and 'toothed wheels' of the mechanical models of English physicists such as Maxwell, Kelvin and Lodge with his own Cartesian conception of an axiomatic electricity. See *op. cit.*, pp. 70–1.

28 R. Chisholm, *op. cit.*, p. 496.

29 See e.g. E. Nagel, *op. cit.*, p. 75; or S. Toulmin, *op. cit.*, p. 185.

30 *Ibid.*, p. 185.

31 R. Harré, *op. cit.*, esp. Chaps. 2–3.

32 I. Lakatos, *op. cit.*, pp. 134–8.

33 As Feyerabend has put it: a theory may be in trouble only because of 'the backwardness of the observational ideology'. See 'Problems of Empiricism, Part II', pp. 292ff.

34 P. S. de Laplace, *The System of the World*, Bk. III, Chap. II.

35 F. Bacon, *op. cit.*, Bk. II, Aphorism XXXVI.

36 'Any statement may be held true come what may, if we make drastic enough changes elsewhere in the system', W. V. O. Quine, *From a Logical Point of View*, p. 43.

37 See e.g. K. R. Popper, *Logic of Scientific Discovery*, p. 42 and pp. 80–2; and T. W. Hutchison, *The Significance and Basic Postulates of Economic Theory*, pp. 40–6. I have of course argued (in 2.4 above) on quite distinct realist grounds that once the irrationality of pseudo-falsification is granted the CP clause becomes superfluous.

38 R. Harré, *op. cit.*, p. 132.

39 This theory is most clearly stated in R. Harré, *op. cit.*, Chap. 4. Although Harré is I think logically committed to, and may be prepared to accept, transcendental realism in the form in which it is developed here, he does not say how laws 'explain away counter-instances' and 'so achieve universality', *ibid.* p. 92.

40 It should be remembered that transcendental realism not only warrants subjunctive and counterfactual statements (where antecedents are uninstantiated) but normic and transfactual ones (where consequents may be unrealised). This is another nail in the coffin of deductivism. For at level (iii) a law may be upheld even when P is true and Q is false; which is of course the only case, according to the principle of material implication, when a conditional is false. The moral is that falsification always depends upon the non-formal requirement that the system in which the putative counter-instance occurs be closed.

41 See e.g. N. R. Hanson, 'A Picture Theory of Theory Meaning', *The Nature and Function of Scientific Theories*, ed. R. G. Colodny, pp. 233–73.

42 I have argued in §2 above that without such a constraint on the *content* of possible explanations, sorting them with respect to their plausibility, there will be an infinite number of possible explanations, even of equal simplicity. The plausibility of a possible explanation cannot be identified by purely syntactical or formal criteria alone but depends upon a complex relationship between what is so far known about the process generating the behaviour in question and established explanation patterns drawn from analogous fields. It is thus in part a function of the existing knowledge in which the predicates occurring in the possible explanations are already embedded, so that the paradoxes of confirmation, etc. that flow from the insertion of artificial predicates into already-functioning and well-connected scientific contexts cannot (at least at that point of application) arise. Cf. R. Harré, 'Surrogates for Necessity', *Mind 1973*, pp. 355–80.

43 *Ibid.* p. 366.

44 Cf. M. Bunge, *op. cit.*, p. 38.

45 Cf. G. Schlesinger, 'The Prejudice of Micro-Reduction', *B.J.P.S., Vol. 12*, pp. 215–24.

46 Cf. K. Schaffner, 'Correspondence Rules', *Philosophy of Science, Vol. 36* (1969), pp. 280–90.

47 Given that B is law-like and allowing for open systems we must say: x tends to do φ in virtue of its nature N. A discussion of the rather complex relationship between tendencies and powers must be postponed to the appendix to this chapter. For the moment they may be regarded as a class of powers whose exercise is normically qualified. But this is not a complete analysis. For a power may be exercised when the behaviour is not law-like, so that it would be wrong to attribute a tendency. The logic of power ascriptions, their role in science and the ontological status of powers will be discussed below.

48 The second question is both distinct from the first and important. Because it raises the question of the range or scope of application of the statements expressing the tendencies of the individuals concerned. It cannot be assumed that all

tendencies will be spatio-temporally universal; for individuals and kinds may be transformed in time and bounded in space. A law may of course be universal (transfactually applicable) within its range and restricted in this way.

49 Cf. M. Hollis and E. J. Nell, *Rational Economic Man*, Chap. 7.

50 See e.g. A. Flew, *An Introduction to Western Philosophy*, p. 49; or E. Nagel, *op. cit.*, p. 37.

51 See e.g. L. Kolakowski, *Positivist Philosophy*, p. 34.

52 Cf. R. Harré, *Principles of Scientific Thinking*, pp. 274–5.

53 Cf. K. R. Popper, *Conjectures and Refutations*, Chap. 5. However the protolaw itself when it finally emerges, pari passu with its explanation, after the limitations and modifications necessitated by the experimental process, may be in a form far more complex and refined than that in which it was originally conceived (cf. S. Körner, *Experience and Theory*, passim). The normal response to a (genuine) counter-instance is modification within a continuous research programme, rather than (as is implied by naïve falsificationism) the complete abandonment of the original conjecture and its replacement by a totally different one (cf. I. Lakatos, *op. cit.*).

54 Cf. R. Harré, *op. cit.*, p. 275.

55 See A. J. Ayer, *The Fundamental Questions of Philosophy.*

56 See R. Harré and E. H. Madden, 'Natural Powers and Powerful Natures', *Philosophy, Vol. 45* (1973), esp. pp. 223–30.

57 See e.g. P. Achinstein, *Law and Explanation*, pp. 13ff.

58 See e.g. A. C. Ewing, *The Fundamental Questions of Philosophy*, pp. 159–81 and B. Blanshard, *Reason and Analysis*, Chaps. 11–12. Cf. also N. Maxwell, 'Can there be necessary connections between successive events?', *B.J.P.S. Vol. 19* (1967), pp. 1–25; and M. Fisk, 'Are there Necessary Connections in Nature?' *Philosophy of Science, Vol. 37* (1969), pp. 385–404.

59 Cf. 'Tania pushed the door open' logically implies 'the door opened'. As Davidson has put it: 'the truth of a causal statement depends upon *what* events are described; its status as analytic or synthetic depends upon *how* they are described', *op. cit.*, p. 90.

60 Cf. M. Fisk, *op. cit.*, p. 390.

61 Cf. R. Harré, 'Surrogates for Necessity', p. 380.

62 H. Putnam, 'The Analytic and the Synthetic', *Minnesota Studies in the Philosophy of Science, Vol. III*, eds. H. Feigl and G. Maxwell, p. 376.

63 Cf. E. H. Madden, 'Hume and the Fiery Furnace', *Philosophy of Science 1971*, p. 66.

64 It is of course inconceivable that a fundamental entity or entities should act inconsistently with its (their) nature. Hence in the last (non-Laplacean) instance everything is as it must be.

65 For a discussion of the history of 'copper' see M. Crosland, *Historical Studies in the Language of Chemistry* and R. Harré and E. H. Madden, *Causal Powers*, Chap. 1.

66 To use Goodman's very useful term. See N. Goodman, *The Structure of Appearance*, p. 130 and passim. Goodman himself attributes the term to C. I. Lewis, *Mind and the World Order.*

67 K. R. Popper, *The Open Society and Its Enemies*, Vol. I, p. 32.

68 K. R. Popper, *Conjectures and Refutations*, Chap. 3, esp. p. 102.

69 A. Flew, *op. cit.*, p. 450.

70 *Ibid.*, p. 449.

71 S. Toulmin, *op. cit.*, pp. 135–6.

72 E. H. Madden and P. Hare do not clearly distinguish powers from their exercise in their criticism of this Humean argument in 'The Powers That Be', *Dialogue* 1971, pp. 12–31.

73 Cf. K. Campbell, 'One Form of Scepticism about Induction', *Analysis, Vol. 23*, pp. 80–3, reprinted in ed. R. Swinbourne, *The Justification of Induction*, pp. 144–8.
74 P. Strawson, *An Introduction to Logical Theory*, Chap. 9, Pt. II, esp. p. 261.
75 K. R. Popper, *op. cit.*, p. 41, n. 8.
76 M. Hollis, 'Reason and Reality', *P.A.S. 1967–8*, esp. pp. 282ff.
77 See e.g. G. Harman, 'Enumerative Induction as inference to the Best Explanation', *Journal of Philosophy 65* (1968), pp. 529–33.
78 The stringency of this requirement may be relaxed in the kind of way indicated in 2.6 above when we move from scientific contexts to the rough-and-ready generalizations of everyday life.
79 See e.g. M. Vernon, *The Psychology of Perception.*
80 See esp. J. J. Gibson, *The Senses Considered as Perceptual Systems.*
81 See N. Goodman, *Fact, Fiction and Forecast*, pp. 73–80.
82 See e.g. C. G. Hempel, *op. cit.*, Chap. 1.
83 P. Strawson, *Individuals*, pp. 167ff and passim.
84 C. G. Hempel, *op. cit.*, Chap. 8.
85 Cf. P. Strawson, *op. cit.*, p. 46 (my emphasis).
86 Cf: 'In the Newtonian world and in Newtonian science . . . the conditions of knowledge do not determine the conditions of being; quite the contrary, it is the structure of reality that determines which of our facilities of knowledge can possibly (or cannot) make it assessible to us. Or, to use an old Platonic formula: in the Newtonian world and in Newtonian science, it is not man but God who is the measure of things', A. Koyré, 'The Influence of Philosophical Trends on the Formulation of Scientific Theories', *The Validation of Scientific Theories*, ed. P. G. Frank, p. 199.

4

CONCEPTUAL AND NATURAL NECESSITY

R. Harré and E.H. Madden

II

A. Conceptual necessity in statements of causality

Our fundamental contention is that the necessity that is such a striking feature of the conceptual relation between the predicates descriptive of events, things and states of affairs as causes and the predicates descriptive of their usual effects, as it is unreflectingly understood, matches a natural necessity in the relation between the states, powers and natures of those physical systems which in fact constitute the universe. In this chapter we undertake the task of exactly locating these concepts in preparation for the detailed analyses to come.

That there is a conceptual necessity involved in statements descriptive of causal relations can be brought out fairly easily. A certain colourless fluid can come under several, logically independent descriptions. By a pair of logically independent descriptions we mean two descriptions for which there are no known principles in accordance with which propositions attributing either could imply one attributing the other. But when this fluid comes under the description 'acid', part of the meaning of that description is the dispositional predicate 'can turn logwood solution red'. This may, for example, be because we have good empirical reason for thinking that the presence of an acid in dilute solution, under suitable conditions, is sufficient to turn logwood solution red. Thus we can say the acidity of the liquid is the cause of the colour change of the indicator. In this situation the predicates 'acid' and 'can turn logwood solution red' are no longer logically independent, and the causal hypothesis 'Acid solutions turn logwood solutions red' no longer a mere empirical generalisation.

Source: *Causal Powers: A Theory of Natural Necessity*, Oxford: Basil Blackwell, 1975, chap. 1, Sections II–VI, pp. 8–26.

One must be careful to maintain the proper grammatical form of causal statements in the course of the analysis. A causal statement relates, for example, a common noun and a predicate by a verb of causal activity. Thus: 'Acid solution *turns* logwood solution red.' One would already have conceded the Humean analysis if one treated such a proposition as having the form: 'If acid is present then logwood solution turns red'. Clearly to achieve this form the transfer of the verb of causal activity from its place as a main verb, the subject of which is the powerful particular, the acid in that solution, to a passive qualification of effect has deprived it of its sense of activity, the sense it had in the original statement. The argument offered, for example by Davidson, to support the view that causal statements relate pairs of propositions, is clearly a *petitio,* since the analysis only conveys conviction provided the Humean theory, denying activity to the acid, is assumed all along, for only on that theory can the neutralisation of the active force of the main verb be justified.

The test for whether a relation of meaning has developed between two descriptions is to ask how someone, using the predicates, would react if on some specific occasion dilute acid was mixed with logwood solution and this time the mixture failed to change colour. It seems clear to us that it would never be rational to claim both that those conditions were in fact usually sufficient to produce the colour change, and that though they had been fully present on this occasion, it just happened that no effect was produced. We believe that the concept of causality is such that the rational response to the failure of the usual conditions to produce their expected outcome may take either of two forms.

1 We admit that our original ideas as to what were the true causal conditions were faulty and, in abandoning the generalisation about the effect of acid solutions on logwood, we abandon any putative conceptual necessity between 'acidity' and 'the power to change the colour of logwood solution'.
2 Alternatively we can preserve the conceptual relation between the predicates by the claim that something had gone wrong in the aberrant case.

There are three possible hypotheses as to something going wrong on a particular occasion which would account for the deviance and preserve the necessary relation of the predicates. All three involve the *nature* of the solution under test. We might have been mistaken as to the nature of the reagent added in one of three possible ways. We might have poured the reagent out of the wrong bottle, say carelessly mistaking the caustic soda bottle for that containing dilute sulphuric acid. Or we might have picked up the bottle we had used for previous demonstrations but unbeknown to us the nature of the reagent within it had changed. It had, perhaps, attacked the glass and so been neutralised. We would say that it was no longer acidic, and so, necessarily, had lost its power to change the colour of logwood solution. Or thirdly, that though there was some acid present, and no other substance than the solvent, the solution had been so diluted that the concentration of hydrogen ions was insufficient to bring about the change.[1] This case introduces the important concept of a threshold of action. All the conditions, powerful particulars and so on may be present, and of the required nature, but the level of activity can be insufficient to bring about the action. This is the case of not pushing quite hard enough to overturn the stone, or of the pan being not quite warm enough to melt the butter.

The reasoning behind this anecdote is something like this. If the solution does not turn logwood red in the conditions in which it is usually effective, it has lost the power to do so. If it now lacks the power to do so this may be either because it has changed its chemical composition in some relevant way or because the proper threshold of activity has not been reached. In short, if it does not turn logwood red, and we have no reason to believe it has been diluted beyond the minimum effective concentration, it *cannot* be an acid. The ground for this inference is the conceptual necessity of the relation that obtains between 'acidity' and 'the power to turn logwood solution red'. In a science in a fairly advanced stage of development, the conceptual necessity would be further backed up by chemical explanations of the powers of acids.

So the failure of a normally efficacious substance to produce its usual effect is, in the absence of any indication of trouble in the surrounding conditions, explained either by the substitution of a substance of a different nature, or by a change in the nature of the original substance, or by the failure of that substance to reach the threshold level of activity.

It is worth pointing out that the conditions for action are not usually intensionally related to the powerful particulars which produce the action, that is, they form no part of its meaning. So the relation between the obtaining of those conditions and the coming to be of the effect *is* Humean. This fact may be another source of the Regularity Theory, since if the central role of the powerful particular is overlooked, and the effect is considered only in relation to the conditions of its action, that relation is extensional.

So far we have seen how causal hypotheses seem naturally to involve conceptual necessity, but the question immediately arises whether this necessity is only stipulative and conventional in character or whether it mirrors something about the nature of physical systems. The latter, we shall proceed to argue, is clearly the case if we take our ordinary ways of thinking seriously.[2] We shall show that there is no compelling reason to depart from them.

B. Natural necessity in causal production

To see that the conceptual necessity involved in relations between the predicates involved in causal hypotheses reflects the natural necessity of the upshot of the activities of physical systems, consider the case of a suction pump. Let us say that the pressure of the air on the reservoir and the partial vacuum in the cylinder of the pump are the conditions the obtaining of which are jointly sufficient for raising the water up the pump and out of the spigot. Ordinarily we would say that the atmosphere has the ability or power to push the water up the cylinder, which manifests itself when there is no counteracting pressure, and that the water has the liability, or disposition, to be pushed up the cylinder in the absence of air. This power or ability of the atmosphere, in turn, would be explained by referring to the nature of the atmosphere. The atmosphere is a blanket of air around the surface of the earth. Air has weight and so exerts pressure, and the farther down in the blanket of air the greater the weight of the air above, and so the greater the pressure, etc.

While the power or ability of the atmosphere to raise water is understood by referring to its nature, such reference does not explain away the power. A Reliant Scimitar GTE has the ability (is able, has the power) to do 125 m.p.h., and this ability is explained in terms of its having six cylinders, a certain kind of fuel pump, etc.—that is, in terms of the nature of the car.[3] But such explanations in terms of the nature of the car do not lead to the elimination of the notion of 'power' in the description of the car as a potent thing, since that power is specified in terms of an effect which is not part of the description of the nature in virtue of which the power is possessed. 'Power', 'ability' and 'nature' are intimately interwoven and any effort to assign ontological priorities among them is as futile as trying to assign priorities among the concepts of particulars, properties and relations. The ineliminability of 'power' and 'ability' shows up again on the most fundamental level of explanation. At that level one can do no more than ascribe powers to individuals identified purely referentially, since there is no further level in which the nature that helps explicate that power could be found. Confining ourselves to classical physics, we would say, e.g., that the masses of the earth and the atmosphere have the power of attracting each other, but we do not know anything in the nature of the masses that explains that power.

The ineliminable but non-mysterious powers and abilities of particular things, then, are the ontological 'ties that bind' causes and effects together and are what the conceptual necessity of causal statements reflects.[4] The atmosphere *has* the power to raise the water, though it will not produce an effect unless the partial vacuum in the cylinder exists. The earth has the power of attraction which is manifested when the barn collapses, though this effect would not have occurred unless the centre beam had been removed. Furthermore, reference to the same power is equally effective in the explanation of the non-occurrence of any of certain classes of events, which the Regularity Theory must countenance as possible. It is not just a matter of fact that barns don't float off their foundations, it is, in ordinary circumstances, impossible. And that impossibility is derived from the fact that the heavy barn is in still air, within a uniform and stable gravitational field.

An important aspect of this concept of power is that it catches what might be called the strong sense of potentiality or potency, namely, 'what would happen, as a matter of course, if interfering conditions were absent or taken away'. As long as there is air in the cylinder of the pump the power of the atmosphere to raise the water is frustrated; and as long as the centre beam is intact the attraction between barn roof and earth is kept in check. But as soon as the air is removed, or the beam rots, the operation of these powers, whose constancy in the given set-up is ultimately a product of the basic structural nature of our universe, comes into play. They finally produce the effect which had been held in abeyance by interfering conditions.

For us, efficient causes comprise both the presence of stimuli which activate a quiescent individual and the absence or removal of constraint upon an individual already in a state of activity. There is an argument upon which we ourselves do not put much weight, that the latter case, if admitted as involving a genuine form of efficient causality, is itself sufficient to rebut the Humean regularity theory, since it is impossible to specify a regularity in terms of the regular absence of the antecedent condition, while the powerful particular to which one must refer in explanation of the causal action *was* present all along, with many other states of affairs than the final effect.

C. *Conceptual and natural necessity in descriptions of substances*

In the case of concepts used to refer to material substance, the conceptual necessity involved in causal hypotheses creeps in, in addition to the conceptual necessity built into any concept whose analysis into component predicates has definitional force. Take, for example, the apparently non-causal concept 'copper'.[5] For the scientist this term refers to something having the properties of malleability, fusibility, ductility, electric conductivity, density 8.92, atomic weight 63.54, and atomic number 29. All but the last of these properties are dispositional, ascribing powers and liabilities to the substance and hence already have a force over and above the attribution of manifest properties. But since the properties set out above serve to specify what a substance has to be, and to be capable of doing to be copper, if an entity lacked any of these properties it would not properly be called 'copper'. The ascription of that material identification to that sample at any given time necessarily implies the presence of a cluster of properties, each member of which is a necessary attribute of the substance. The reason for this latter necessity is clear. All the dispositional properties whose manifestations make up the nominal essence are explicable by reference to *the* atomic structure and hence, via that structure, connected with each other. Thus, if any of those dispositional properties were not manifested by some reddish metal, the whole conceptual framework implicit in the scientific concept of 'copper' would be vitiated and the ascription of the concept 'copper' would fail since the other properties of the linked cluster would have to be denied it. Again, this conceptual necessity, far from being merely the reflection of a stipulative definition, has important ontological implications, in that it is, in principle, possible that the atomic structure might be investigated independently of any one of the dispositional properties in the above 'definition'.

The passivity of the definitional dispositions in this example is of no significance. A concept such as 'malleability' refers to a capacity to undergo rather than an ability to do, while 'conductivity' refers to a disposition to react in certain ways under given conditions rather than a power to act in certain ways when the occasion arises. Yet the dispositional properties of malleability, fusibility and conductivity are just as much explained by the atomic structure of copper as the power of the atmosphere actively to raise water is explained by the nature of the atmosphere. Capacities just as much as powers, what particulars or substances are liable to undergo as well as what they are able to do, are explained by reference to what the thing is in itself.[6]

What particulars are liable to undergo and what they are able to do are determined by their natures since they are manifestations of their natures—and hence to talk about particulars remaining the same and yet lacking their usual capacities and powers is at once to assert and deny that a certain object or sample of material has a given nature. If we had compelling reason to believe that a certain entity had existed continuously for a certain time, during which it ceased to be malleable, then we could correctly conclude that since it had different capacities and powers at the end from those it had at the beginning of the period, it must have undergone a change in nature. We would be forced to conclude that it was no longer the particular copper it was before. It is physically impossible for a substance to act or react incompatibly with its own nature. It is not impossible for an object or sample to act and react differently at one time rather than another. But in general it *cannot* do so under the same circumambient conditions and be deemed to have remained the same substance. In short, the relation between what a thing is and what it is capable of doing and undergoing is naturally necessary. It is this natural necessity that the conceptual necessity of the ensemble of powers and liabilities ascribed by the use of a term like 'copper' reflects.

There seems, however, to be an immediate problem with this view, since some individuals do gain or lose certain capacities or powers but do not thereby lose their identity. They still have the same nature.[7] A drug may lose its effectiveness over a period of time, photographic paper will not make prints after a while, and a person may lose his capacity to remember names; but the drug, paper and person do not thereby lose their identities. This is only a *prima facie* problem, however, since such changes in powers and capacities occur in the ambit of theory which explains them. The overall theory provides a justification for the assumption of the invariable and hence continuously identical nature of an entity which continues constant throughout *certain* changes. Such a concept as 'same paper' refers to the cellulose backing rather than light-sensitive coating. Such an explanation of continued identity presupposes the nature of some relatively 'fundamental particulars', for example, chemical atoms, which are fundamental in the sense that their natures are taken as unchanging and explain the self-identity of those less fundamental particulars which are held to be identical through certain changes of powers and liabilities.

III. The place of necessity in explanation and the non-necessity of worlds

A. *The relative necessity of explanatory theories*

Now let us turn our attention briefly to a preliminary analysis of the nature of scientific explanation and see what implications it has for the concept of causal necessity. Recall again the example in which the power of the atmosphere is cited in explanation of the rising of water in the cylinder of a pump. The necessity that the water will rise in the cylinder is relative to the truth of gravitational theory, we say, because that theory plus information to the effect that there is a partial vacuum in the cylinder, explains why the water *rises*, rather than, say, turns purple. If anything else than the water's rising could have happened, given our account of the set-up, we would not have succeeded in explaining why it did that rather than anything else. Conversely, we have good reason for believing that gravitational theory is true because it is indirectly and independently established by the various particular events and circumscribed laws that it conceptually unites. Hence, the necessity in a body of knowledge follows from what must be the case if the most general theory of causal efficacy in that body of knowledge is true, and we have good reason in this case for believing that gravitational theory is true.

B. *A fundamental theory defines a world*

It does not follow, however, that a general theory which explains all sorts of particular cases of causal efficacy, such as gravitational theory, is necessarily true in the sense that its meaning entails its truth. Gravitational theory is not necessarily true in that sense though its necessity in *this world* derives from the fact that it is sufficiently fundamental to be in part definitive of the nature of this world. But a world defined by our contemporary fundamental theories is not the only possible physical framework. Rather the point is that given some general theory specifying the fundamental causal powers and thereby laying down the general lineaments of a world, the necessity of certain effects can be inferred. Such effects are 'hypothetically necessary' in the sense that, given the specification of the causal powers of the things and substances of the world, the denial of statements describing these effects of those powers, when the environment allows them to be exercised, would be inconsistent with the natures of those things ascribed to them on the basis of the theory.

C. That the world as we conceive it, our world, is contingent

Even though this universe is not the only possible one, the unification of disparate phenomena brought about by a theory which is general enough to be taken as a specification of a universe suggests the hypothesis that that universe *is* the actual one, though, that the necessary character of the world so specified describes our world must be found out *a posteriori.* The adequacy of the theory in the sense of its power to unify disparate phenomena can be taken to mean that it reflects the nature of *this* universe. In so far as such a theory is adequate, it has the kind of conceptual necessity that reflects physical or natural necessity, since a change in the physical universe would involve a change in the nature of the particulars of that universe. Supposing such a change to occur, there would be a new universe with a new nature, described in a new adequate theory, etc. So there is a necessity corresponding to the nature of the actual, though this necessity does not imply that the actual is itself necessary in the sense that the denial of its existence would be self-contradictory.

Thus we depend upon just the same formal framework as the most ardent logicist for identifying the presence of necessitation by the appearance of an inconsistency. But we claim that what we have thus identified is a conceptual relation which is a reflection of a real relation of necessitation between a particular thing endowed with the power to produce an effect in virtue of its nature, in the absence of constraint and when properly stimulated.

IV. The scientific use of the distinction between real and nominal essence

A distinction between two ranges of essential properties is required by any theory purporting to give an account of natural science which preserves its main outlines. There are those properties the manifestation of which are necessary to a thing or sample of substance being of a certain kind. We follow Locke in calling this the nominal essence of a thing or substance. We hold that nominal essences are fixed, and can be known *a priori* by an examination of the meaning given to general sortal terms in a natural science, though we acknowledge that that meaning has a history, a fact to which we shall pay considerable attention. The only empirical question relevant to nominal essences, *at some moment in time,* is whether there are any things or samples of substances falling under them. Populations change, and nominal essences cease to be exemplified in anything real. Of course, which nominal essences we think worth espousing is a product of a diachronic process of conceptual construction, guided by what properties we observe to go together, and which of these can usefully serve the practical requirements of criteria for the identification of sorts and kinds.

But the task of natural science is to investigate the nature of a thing or substance, and to test hypotheses as to the constitution of that thing or substance. The result of such investigations are *a posteriori* discoveries that, for example, the real essence or chemical nature of diamond is a tetrahedral crystal of carbon atoms. That this is the nature of diamond explains its manifest properties, and *provides the ground for the choice of criteria of individuation and identity of diamonds.* A substance continues to be diamond only while it has that nature; just as a population only continues to be rabbits while each member has just so many chromosomes, and just such a genetic inheritance. A more widely known example of the operation of the distinction between real and nominal essence in practical life is the substitution of chromosome counts for anatomical examination in determining the sex of an athlete.

Natural science still uses the distinction just as Locke set it out: 'For it is the real constitution of its insensible parts, on which depend all those properties of colour, weight, fusibility, fixedness, etc. which makes it to be gold, or gives it a right to that name, which is therefore its nominal essence.'[8] Yet, if we wish to preserve the distinction between real and nominal essence, we must note that definitions of nominal essence are very different in kind from definitions of real essence, despite a common logical form. It is clear that a statement which asserts that a substance or thing must manifest certain properties in order to be identified as a thing or substance of that sort can be laid down *a priori.* In short, that copper has the properties by which we recognise it as such is clearly an *a priori* truth, though 'copper' has an etymology, and a conceptual history. But once we have abandoned the idea that knowledge of the natural world is confined wholly to the surface appearances of things, their manifest properties and the flux of such ontologically simple things as events, changes in their manifest properties, we are obliged to conceive of another kind of definition, namely that of the real essence of things. Science, it is plain, is concerned with real essences, at least as much as it is concerned with nominal. It is part of the scientific investigation of copper to try to discover in what way it differs as a structure of subatomic 'particles' from other chemical elements. It turns out that there are structural differences in terms of which the various chemical elements can be differentiated and the differentia which appear in the nominal essence explained.

If this is the case, and it plainly is in chemistry, then the definitions which express the real essences of substances are to be discovered *a posteriori* and cannot be laid down *a priori.* We have to discover by experimental technique, under our general theory of the nature of materials, what is the real essence of a particular metal or of any other chemical element. In a similar way, we can distinguish between the phenotypical specification of a natural species, in which anatomical and physiological features are used to differentiate members of that species from categories of other living creatures, from the real essences or genotype of the species which can be discovered only *a posteriori.*

It is plain that the epistemological distinction between our knowledge of each kind of essence rests upon an indisputable and rather simple historical fact, that is, that we can learn to differentiate one subject from another, successfully, without knowing at that time the underlying structure or nature of the entity which will explain the regular appearance of the differentia which we use, as it were, in the natural state. Chemistry and genetics provide the necessary underpinning to our assumptions about the viability as differentia of what predicates appear in nominal essences.

Now none of this can be found in the logical structure of definitions. From a logical point of view all definitions look exactly alike, that is, they contain a logical subject and a set of predicates which are attributed of necessity to that subject. Only by paying attention to the differing empirical status of the several predicates involved can we distinguish adequately between the kinds of definitions that appear in the natural sciences. The more adequately the co-presence of an ensemble of manifest properties is explained in terms of the nature of a thing or substance, the more inclined are we to treat the corresponding predicates as part of the meaning of the term we use for the thing or substance. Thus there is a diachronic process by which relations of meaning between predicates are established, and change.

It is worth noticing that one of the effects of making the distinctions we have made in this section is that the concepts of necessity and contingency are detached from those of the *a priori* and the *a posteriori.* It is our contention that such simple examples as the history of the study of the chemical elements shows that we are required to employ the notion of an *a posteriori* discovery of necessary relations both between properties and correspondingly between predicates in order to make sense of that history. Whether there can be *a priori* knowledge of contingent matters of fact is a matter upon which we have no opinion. We do not make any use of that notion in the course of this book.

V. The modes of necessity

In the system we are constructing we recognise four modes of necessity, two conceptual and two natural. We believe that the concept of necessity is univocal, that its sense is always the same but that the contexts of and grounds for its application are very various. In each major context there are appropriate grounds for attributions of necessity. We recognise the differentiated grounds and univocal sense of the concept by speaking of 'modes' of necessity.

A. The meaning of an attribution of necessity

To attribute necessity to items as various as a condition, an outcome or effect, the truth of a statement, a conclusion, is, we contend, to indicate that within the relevant context no alternative to that condition, outcome, truth-value or conclusion is possible. In each context, there are certain appropriate grounds upon which such a judgement is made. For instance, in the case of the outcome of a physical process, the grounds are our knowledge of the natures of the powerful particulars which are the productive agents of the effect and of the conditions within which they are then operating. In the case of the truth-value of a statement, the grounds are our knowledge of the logical form of that statement.

'Possibility' we define by reference to the range of states, truth-values etc. expressed in the consequent clauses of the conditionals, assertoric or counter-factual, true of some system of particulars, in virtue of the natures of those particulars. Thus, from the chemical nature of dynamite we infer 'If detonated it will explode'. Exploding then, is a possibility for dynamite. If our knowledge of its nature and the conditions of a particular sample shows that that is the only possibility, then if the antecedent is realised, it *must* explode. (If the wall is a sheer face ten metres high and there is only one break in its circumference, then an invading army without ladders or cannon, *must* enter the city there.)

B. *The distinctions between modes of necessity*

Modes of necessity attributable a priori

When the logical form of a statement is offered as the grounds for the judgement that it cannot but be true we have logical necessity. When the conditions for a rational being having knowledge of the nature of a world are offered as the grounds for the judgement that such a world must have certain characteristics, we have transcendental necessity. These modes of necessity have some colour of universality about them, though we believe transcendental necessity to be a more stringent concept than logical necessity since it is not the case that a rational being could have knowledge, or even exist, in all possible worlds. For a strict Humean, logical possibility and the possibility of experience are in perfect match. Both these modes of necessity can be attributed *a priori*, since the grounds for an attribution of logical necessity are the logical forms of statements, and the grounds for the attribution of transcendental necessity are the meanings of such concepts as 'experience', 'rational being', 'world', and the like.

Modes of necessity attributable a posteriori

When the natures of the operative powerful particulars, the constraining or stimulating effect of conditions and so on are offered as the grounds for the judgement that a certain effect cannot but happen, or cannot but fail to happen, we have natural necessity. When the probability of its happening falls within a certain range, we have the natural necessity of a range or function of probabilities. This is clearly attributable to the outcomes of the action of a system of particulars only *a posteriori.*

When the discovery of natural necessity is used as the basis for the inclusion or exclusion of the appropriate predicate in the meaning of a concept of a kind of particular, then that that kind of particular has the property or power to produce the effect so attributed is conceptually necessary. The development of the meaning of a concept is a diachronic process, absorbing or excluding predicates in response to discoveries about the natures of things and substances and the conditions for their activity or inactivity. Thus the mode of necessity for a component of meaning cannot be decided by the fact that it is revealed by a synchronic conceptual analysis, since reference to the history of the concept is necessary to determine how far it has developed its meaning in response to empirical discovery. We are unable to offer a clear cut boundary condition to differentiate some cases of transcendental necessity from some cases of conceptual necessity. For example, we do not think one can decide at all readily how far the concept of time reflects the temporal experience of mankind and how far its form and content are transcendentally necessary to a world capable of being understood by any rational being.

In each mode we recognise, we have attributed necessity to an entity, state or property; to a statement, outcome, nature of a world or thing, and so on. But philosophers speak too of certain relations being necessary, particularly entailment, a relation between propositions. We are convinced that this use of the apodeictic modality is appropriate only in the case of logical necessity where it is the statement of the entailment that cannot but be true. Notoriously, the conclusion of most splendid entailments are only too often themselves false. But in the other modes, it is, for example, the inherence (presence within) of a property that is necessary, not the relation between that property and the thing, whatever that might be, though, of course, the proposition which states that the object has that property is, or may be, conceptually necessary.

C. The inter-relations of the modes

What of the relations between these modes of necessity? Clearly, whatever is logically necessary must be reflected in a corresponding transcendental necessity. But there are a great range of transcendental necessities which are not reflected in any logical necessity. For example, that no thing may be in two places at once clearly depends upon current relations between the concepts of thing, space and time, and is certainly not a property of all logically possible worlds.

Though our discovery of the natural necessity of the production of some effect by a system of powerful particulars is a common ground for the incorporation of the power to produce that effect in the concept of those particulars, we may hold to conceptual necessities which are groundless in reality, and there are certainly many natural necessities which, being so far unknown, could not be reflected in meanings. And since our knowledge of natural necessities is *a posteriori,* we may be mistaken about them and have incorporated meanings into our conceptual system in response to wholly or partly mistaken ideas about some natural process. For example, in its original meaning, the word 'malaria' reflected a mistaken view as to the nature of the productive process of the disease.

VI. The true history of 'copper'

We have argued that in the two contexts of natural necessity, the inherence of essential properties in a thing or substance and causal production, *a posteriori* discoveries about the natures of things and the means of causal production are in certain conditions reflected in the establishment of meaning relations between the corresponding predicates. The conditions under which this occurs relate the two contexts. When discoveries about the nature of a thing or substance explain and justify our holding that certain properties are its nominal essence, that is, are the set of properties by which we recognise it as a thing of a certain kind, then the diachronic process of meaning development creates a genuine conceptual necessity. And when the discoveries about the means of causal production make clear the role of the appropriate powerful particular in that production, and the nature of that particular enables us to claim the necessity of just such an outcome of the productive process, then the concept of that particular can legitimately be allowed to come to include the power to produce just those effects.

However convincing this account may be as a possible theoretical account of the origin of necessary connections between empirical concepts, in order to establish it we must show that it makes sense of an actual case of conceptual development. So we turn to an account of the actual history of a substance concept, 'copper'.

As Crosland points out,[9] the metals seem to have been first distinguished by their sensible qualities, and their 'names' were little more than succinct expressions of their nominal essences, there being no theory according to which hypotheses as to real essences could be devised. 'One of the Aryan words for copper, "roudhos" is said to mean red.' Even sonority could be used as a distinguishing quality as in Geber's use of the term *plumbum stridens* for tin, which creaks when bent.

The first clear case of a theory about the nature of metals affecting metal terms appears 'in medieval alchemy where the relationship between the metals and the planets was so intimate that the names of the planets were used as synonyms for the names of metals. . . . Occasionally the names of metals were entirely replaced by the names of planets.'[10] Thus in the works of Origen, copper appears as 'Mars'. The later, more common name 'Venus' for the metal seems to derive from the guardianship which that goddess was supposed to exercise over Cyprus, the island from which copper, 'aes cyprium' gets its English name. It is perhaps entertaining to note that Boerhaave, mistakenly supposing that natural necessity followed from conceptual necessity, and not, as we insist, the other way round, took the occurrence of O, the symbol for gold, in ♀ the Venus symbol, to show that copper contained gold.

One of the clearest statements of a hypothesis as to the real essence of copper is to be found in the works of Paracelsus, where he says:

> Copper is generated of a purple sulphur, a redish salt, and a yellow mercury. These three colours if they be mingled among themselves, then Copper is produced. But Copper doth contain in itself its female, that is its dross or refuse; which is separated by Art, and the body reduced, then the male doth appear. But this is the nature of them both, that the male doth not suffer itself again to be destroyed, and the female doth not any more send forth dross or scorias, and they are different in their fusion and malleability, as Iron and Steel differ. And also if this separation be used, either of them being severed into its nature, there do arise two Metals, different one from another in essence, species, kind and propriety. And further saith, that though commonly the male and female go together, yet they ought to be separated.[11]

Webster, writing in 1671, and quoting Paracelsus, offers the following account of copper, which gives first its nominal essence and then a brief description of its real essence in Paracelsian terms, together with the empirical evidence in favour of that hypothesis.

> Aes or Copper (which was so called from the Isle of Cyprus, where it was first gotten in great plenty) is a metallick body, participating of a fuscous or darkish redness, being ignible, and fusible, and is as the mean betwixt Gold and Silver; and is generated of *Argent vive,* impure, not fixt, earthy, burning, red, not clear, and of such a sulphur, it wants fixation, purity, and weight.
>
> And *Casalpinus* tells us that it differs from both Gold and Silver because it does not bear the trial of fires as they do, but is universally burnt; from whence it is noted to contain much of combustible exhalation, for above the metals it yieldeth a sulphurous smell and flame.[12]

Wilson's description of 1709 is on identical lines. '*Venus* or *Copper* is a metalline Body, Foul, Imperfect, and Generated of an Impure *Mercury*; Its Sulphur is Earthy, Combustible, and of an obscure Red, it wants Fixation, Purity and Weight, but if handled by an Expert Artist, is of great use both for Internal and External Medecines.'[13]

But by 1796, confidence in the chemical theories that had allowed the development of hypotheses about real essences had all but evaporated. Nicholson's definition is of the nominal essence only. 'Copper,' he says, 'is a metal of a peculiar reddish brown colour; hard, sonorous, very malleable, and ductile, of considerable tenacity, and of moderate specific gravity.'[14] And in the first half of the nineteenth century, the situation remained substantially the same, Dalton's atoms being generally taken non-realistically. Thomson's immensely influential *System of Chemistry* of 1817, after providing a general classification of the elements into Simple Supporters of Combustion, Simple Incombustibles, and Simple Combustibles, on the basis of a rather feeble caloric theory, slid back into a nominal essence account:

> 1 This metal is of a fine red colour, and has a great deal of brilliancy. Its taste is styptic and nauseous, and the hands, when rubbed for some time on it, acquire a peculiar and disagreeable odour.
> 2 It is harder than silver . . .
> 3 Its malleability is great . . .
> 4 When heated to . . . 1450°F. it melts . . .
> 5 Copper is not altered by water . . .[15]

Even in 1855, still four years before Cannizaro's memoir, purely nominal essence accounts are given:

> Copper possesses several excellent properties, which have rendered it an exceedingly useful metal.
> a It is ductile . . . *strong* and *tenacious* . . .
> b It *fuses with difficulty* . . .
> c When exposed to air, it *suffers from rust much less* than iron . . .
> d It is tolerably hard . . .
> e With zinc, tin and nickel, it forms very useful *alloys* . . .
> f It is precipitated from its solutions by the galvanic current . . .
> g It yields with oxygen and several acids . . . a beautiful green and blue colour, of various application in painting.[16]

But by 1872, with the atomic theory thoroughly established in chemistry, a brusque but adequate reference to real essence appears:[17]

COPPER

	symbol	weight		
Atom	Cu	63.5	/	Density = 8.9

coupled with a traditional outline of the nominal essence of the metal: 'Copper is the only metal of a red colour. It is highly malleable and ductile, and an excellent conductor of heat and electricity,' since at that time, the causal relations between the two essences were unknown.

In 1972, so fully articulated is the corpus of theory and observation, including both real and nominal essences and all the chemical and physical reactions of the metal, that Cotton and Wilkinson content themselves with a purely real essence exegesis of the concept of copper: 'Copper,' they say, 'has a single electron outside the filled 4d shell but cannot be classed in Group I, since it has little in common with the alkalis.'[18]

There are thus a multiplicity of explications of the concept 'copper': as a red, easily worked metal; a mixture of sulphur, mercury and salt; a collection of atoms each sixty-three and a half times the weight of a hydrogen atom; and finally a collection of atoms each with a definite and identical internal structure. It is our view that these explications disclose substantially different meanings of the concept, limited by a core of identity in the nominal essence, and the changes so disclosed are the product of *a posteriori* discoveries as to the nature of copper.[19]

Notes

1 Our attention was drawn to this case by S. L. Godlovitch.
2 Cf. Sterling Lamprecht, *The Metaphysics of Naturalism*, Appleton-Century-Crofts, New York, 1967, 129–45.
3 M. R. Ayers, *The Refutation of Determinism*, Methuen, London, 1968, 84 ff.
4 Lamprecht, *op. cit.*, 141.
5 Professor Ducasse's favourite example.
6 For an analysis similar to ours, of power, capacity and liability statements, see D. M. Armstrong, *A Materialist Theory of the Mind*, Routledge and Kegan Paul, London, 1968, 86.
7 M. R. Ayers, *op. cit.*, 84–9.
8 J. Locke, *Essay Concerning Human Understanding*, III, 3, 18.
9 M. Crosland, *Historical Studies in the Language of Chemistry*, Heinemann, London, 1962, 68.
10 *Ibid.*, 80.
11 Paracelsus, *De Mineralibus*, I, 349.
12 J. Webster, *An History of Metals*, London, 1671, 235.
13 G. Wilson, *A Compleat Course of Chymistry*, London, 1709, 64.
14 W. Nicholson, *The First Principles of Chemistry*, London, 1796, 217.
15 Thomas Thomson, *A System of Chemistry*, London, 1817, 442.
16 J. A. Stöckhardt, *The Principles of Chemistry*, London, 1855, 296–7.
17 G. Wilson, *Inorganic Chemistry*, London and Edinburgh, 1872, 399.
18 F. A. Cotton and G. Wilkinson, *Advanced Inorganic Chemistry*, Wiley, New York, 1972, 903–4.
19 This point has been greatly clarified by W. I. Matson, 'How Things Are What They Are', *The Monist*, 56 (1972), 234–49. An early version of this theory is due to Whewell, *The Philosophy of the Inductive Sciences* (1847), Johnson Reprints, London and New York, 1967, vol.1, ch. 2, sect. 4.

5

ABSTRACTION

A realist interpretation

Andrew Sayer

The relations between the theoretical and the empirical, the abstract and the concrete, have always been problematic in marxism. Marx's disdain for knowledge based upon mere appearances has meant that few marxists have accepted the empiricist doctrine of the theory-neutrality of observation. But while, in a negative way, there is a consensus about the rejection of this doctrine among marxists, and while we often quite readily talk of '*essence* and appearance' and 'underlying' structures and causes, there is little agreement about an alternative view of the status of marxist concepts and of the relations between the theoretical and the empirical. The radical undermining of empiricist views on this relation in the philosophy of science has been similarly unsettling, producing shifts towards idealism, particularly in the form of conventionalism. The abandonment of the dangerous innocence of certainty in knowledge based on experience has given way to possibly more dangerous views in which knowledge is believed not to be subject to any extra-discursive checks.

This crisis at the philosophical level has surely made its impact on substantive marxist research. A major characteristic of recent marxist study has been a withdrawal from empirical research and a turning inwards towards a continual reconstitution of abstract theoretical concepts (even where new objects of study – such as the state – are concerned), or else a kind of 'pseudo-concrete' analysis where the specificities of the concrete are reduced to an abstract category. It is not too much to say that for some the recognition of the impossibility of theory-neutral observation has induced a fear that any empirical research would inevitably be tainted by empiri*cism*.

An early opponent of this anti-empirical or 'pseudo-concrete' tendency was Sartre:

Source: *Radical Philosophy*, 1981, Summer, pp. 6–15.

> 'There is no longer any question of studying facts within the general perspective of Marxism so as to enrich our understanding and to clarify action. Analysis consists solely in getting rid of detail and forcing the significance of events'[1]

and, more strongly:

> 'Marxism possesses theoretical bases, it embraces all human activity; but it no longer *knows* anything. Its concepts are dictates: its goal is no longer to increase what it knows but to be itself constituted a priori as an absolute knowledge'.[2]

A strikingly similar kind of criticism is made in many of Raymond Williams' writings. For example, in *Marxism and Literature*, he attacks the kind of marxism in which:

> '. . . the analytic categories, as so often in idealist thought, have, almost unnoticed, become substantive descriptions, which then take habitual priority over the whole social process to which, as analytic categories, they are attempting to speak.'[3]

And again, in less sober style but with similar intention, E. P. Thompson has polemicised against a condition which he aptly terms 'intellectual agoraphobia'[4] epitomised by those for whom the concept 'mode of production'

> '. . . has become like a base camp in the Arctic of Theory which the explorers may not depart from for more than a hundred yards for fear of being lost in an ideological blizzard.'[5]

This kind of reductionism is common to many areas of marxist analysis, whether economic, political or cultural. It is politically damaging because the failure to grasp the specificities of the concrete inevitably weakens attempts to inform practice. Practice always takes place in the muddy waters of the concrete: it cannot be usefully informed by a theory which does no more than reduce the concrete to the abstract.

But all this is no more than a statement of the problem. To solve it, it is at least necessary to clarify concepts such as 'theoretical', 'empirical', 'abstract', and 'concrete'. This paper attempts this by drawing upon arguments from the realist theory of science, especially as it has been recently developed by Bhaskar and Harré.[6] In so doing, I shall try to shift debate about these concepts outside the crippling polarity of empiricism and rationalism which characterises the present crisis of epistemology.

Theory and observation: preliminary points

It is now widely recognised that observation is not theory-neutral but theory-laden, and that theory does not merely 'order facts' but makes claims about the nature of its object. So, in evaluating observations we are also assessing particular theoretical concepts and existential claims. A common response to this shattering of innocent beliefs in the certainty and neutrality of observation has been the development of idealist (especially conventionalist and rationalist) philosophies which assume that if observation is theory-*laden*, it must necessarily be theory-*determined*, such that it is no longer possible to speak of criteria of 'truth' or 'objectivity' which are not entirely internal to 'theoretical discourse'. However, this is a non-sequitur for at least two reasons. First, theory-laden observation need not be theory-determined. Even the arch-conventionalist Feyerabend (1970) acknowledges that 'it is possible to refute a theory by an experience that is entirely interpreted within its own terms'.[7] If I ask how many leaves there are on a tree, my empirical observation will be controlled by concepts regarding the nature of trees, leaves and the operation of counting, but to give an answer I'd still have to go and look! In arguing that there are no extra-discursive criteria of truth, recent idealists such as Hindess and Hirst echo Wittgenstein's identification of the limits of our world with the limits of language, and share the confusion of questions of What exists? with What can be known to exist? The truism that extra-discursive controls on knowledge can only be referred to in discourse does not mean that what is referred *to* is purely internal to discourse.[8] Secondly, and more simply, it does not follow from the fact that all knowledge is fallible, that it is all *equally* fallible.

While recognition of the theory-laden nature of observation suggests that any rigid distinction between description and explanation should be abandoned, we presumably would wish to retain a distinction between theoretical research (or critique or reflection) and empirical research. Certainly empirical research can never be a-theoretical, but it would seem to be a different activity from theoretical debate.

Abstract and concrete

To try to provide a sound basis for the distinction: theoretical/empirical it is necessary to consider a related, but not identical, distinction that is fundamental to marxist method: that between the abstract and the concrete.

Marx's own definition of the concrete from the *1857 Introduction* has been trotted out in scores of recent marxist writings but is worth examining to see how it differs from the more familiar concept of the 'empirical'.

> 'The concrete concept is concrete because it is a synthesis of many definitions, thus representing the unity of diverse aspects.'[9]

By 'concrete' we mean something real, but not something which is reducible to the empirical: we mean far more than just 'factual'. The concrete object is concrete not simply because it exists, but because it is a combination of many diverse forces or processes. In contrast, an abstract concept represents a one-sided or partial aspect of an object. For example, if we conceptualise an object such as a factory simply in terms of its outward appearance, the concept will be abstract in the sense of one-sided even though it refers to something which can be empirically observed. To make this a concrete concept we would have to specify all the relationships in which the factory is involved: with its workforce; its suppliers and buyers; its creditors and competitors, etc. These diverse determinations are not simply listed and 'added up', but are synthesised; that is, their combination qualitatively modifies each constituent element. However, in order to understand this combination, we normally have to isolate each element in thought first, even though they do not and sometimes could not exist in isolation in reality. It's important to note that whether the concrete is observable (and hence an empirical object for us) is contingent (i.e. neither necessary nor impossible). *The concepts 'concrete' and 'empirical'* are *not* equivalent.

What is then awkward is that Marx also sometimes uses the term 'abstraction' pejoratively. Again, in the *1857 Introduction*, he discusses various ways of studying the political economy of a country.[10] The possibility of beginning with the population is dismissed as an abstraction unless it is broken down into its constituent classes, for in concealing these, it would be a 'chaotic conception'. So evidently there are good (rational) and bad ('chaotic') abstractions. It would take quite a long discussion of marxist theory to demonstrate why it is essential to deal with classes rather than population or, for that matter, any other aspect of the population. Without such a defence, Marx's criticism is liable to appear to the non-marxist as simply a dogmatic assertion. What is required here is surely a general epistemological distinction for discerning misleading abstraction from enlightening or rational abstraction: the abstract-concrete distinction is not enough on its own. Moreover, as we shall see, it doesn't help us distinguish between what can be known from theoretical analysis and what must be learned from (theoretically-informed) empirical study. To try to solve these problems, I shall draw upon some recent work in the realist philosophy of science.

One of the most direct challenges realism makes is on the question of Hume's problems of causation and induction. Starting from an ontology of discretely-distinct, atomistic events and objects, Hume insisted that there could be no necessary connexions between these. We might observe regularities in patterns and sequences of events, but any attributions of causal connexion could only be of psychological origin, for knowledge that C has always been followed by E in past experience does not logically guarantee that it will always do so. Even if we could establish that constant conjunctions were universal, they would still be contingent. Causation is therefore equated with regular succession, and so cannot be distinguished from correlation or accidental succession.

This counterintuitive, but logically sound argument concerning the problem of induction has come to be known as the 'scandal of philosophy', for it would seem that we are perfectly capable of distinguishing between the causal processes that make the hands of a clock move, and the accidental relationships that might arise between the Swiss bank rate and the Australian divorce rate. If we take the 'scandal' seriously, then *(pace* Popper) neither verification nor falsification can be of any use, for without any necessity in nature, what is confirmed today may be falsified tomorrow – *and vice versa*![11]

Realists have argued that, although it is logically possible that the world itself may suddenly change completely (the 'big' problem of induction), this does not mean that everything in our present world is contingently related.[12] If all objects or events are independent, then their pattern or succession is certainly accidental, but precisely because some changes are changes *in* things, not all changes are independent or accidental.[13] In other words, an atomistic ontology makes it impossible to distinguish between the concepts of a change in the nature of a thing and successive replacements of the thing, with the consequence that regularities have to be treated as accidental persistences of events for which there is no rational explanation.[14]

Realists dispense with the Humean metaphysical predilection for atomism, and causation is understood instead as the necessary ways-of-acting of an object which exist in virtue of its nature. That is, causation is not conceptualised in terms of a relationship between separate events 'C' and 'E', but in terms of the changes in each of 'C' and 'E'. Gunpowder has the 'causal power' to explode in virtue of its unstable chemical structure. Copper can conduct electricity because of the presence of free ions in its chemical structure. Whether either of these causal powers are ever 'realised' or 'activated' depends upon *contingently* related conditions, such as the presence of oxygen, low humidity and a spark in the first case, and an electric current in the second. Because the conditions are independent of the causal powers, the succession of events cannot be known just on the basis of knowledge of the causal powers. So it is contingent that gunpowder ever explodes, but in certain conditions it will do so *necessarily.*

Scientific 'laws' are therefore not understood as well-corroborated, universal empirical regularities in patterns of events, but as statements about *mechanisms.*

> 'The citation of a law presupposes a claim about the activity of some mechanism but not about the conditions under which the mechanism operates and hence not about the results of its activity i.e. the actual outcome on any particular occasion.'[15]

The essential characteristic of law-likeness is not universality but *necessity*. This necessity has nothing to do with the logical necessity which may hold in the relationships between statements, for what happens in the natural world has nothing to do with the statements we use to describe it. Rather, it is natural necessity. By this we mean that a particular substance or object could not be what it is unless it had that particular power, that way-of-acting. If a substance cannot conduct electricity, it certainly cannot be copper. It is logically possible that the world – including copper – may suddenly change into something different, but while the substance is still copper it must have these causal powers and a specific nature. That this is not simply a matter of tautology will be explained later.

The realist account of scientific laws is compatible with the marxian notion of laws as *tendencies*. The law of value does not refer to an empirical regularity, nor a generalisation, nor a trend, but a mechanism which operates in virtue of the competitive nature of capitalist commodity production. The effects produced by it at the empirical level depend upon contingently related conditions, including those produced by other mechanisms which are sometimes called 'counteracting tendencies'. In the case of many of the tendencies of marxist theory, surplus empirical information has to be gained in order to know how the mechanism itself is operating. For example, it is necessary that, given capitalist relations of production, the law of value will produce a lowering of the value of commodities over time. But the rate of this lowering for different commodities is affected by use-value considerations – in particular the kind of use-values demanded and the kind of technologies available to produce them – and considerations of class struggle in terms of value as a social relation.

On this realist account, there is no presumption that real relations are structured like conceptual relations and so epistemological legislations founded upon logical relationships are considered to be unhelpful. Nevertheless, it is argued that it is possible that relations between concepts can be made to map real ones.[16] Although the real object is quite separate from the thought object, this does not rule out the possibility that some sort of 'correspondence', or relation of 'practical adequacy', can be achieved between the two.[17] In other words realism neither assumes an epistemologically privileged observation language which guarantees correspondence to the real object nor falsely assumes that the lack of a theory-neutral observation language means that observation is completely theory-determined such that there can be no correspondence whatsoever.

Take the example used by Harré and Madden (1975) of the definition of the term 'father'. It is true by definition that a father (in the biological sense) is a man who has or has had a child. However, the conceptual necessity here is used to denote an empirically-discovered natural necessity in the relationships between males and procreation. Apparently, certain aborigine peoples are not aware that the male has any role in procreation and so do not have any equivalent in their language for the word 'father'. When we discover such natural necessities we frequently make what were previously understood as contingently related elements part of the definition of objects; indeed, one might say that progress in science, in terms of reduction of the burden of facts, depends on this.[18] That a father is a man who has or has had children is not *just* a tautology, for if it were, science could develop simply by inventing tautologies freely at will. But it is always an empirical question whether any real object is like our definitions. In this way, natural necessities can be 'taken up' into the language in the form of conceptual necessities.

> 'Should the relation between the nature of an entity and its powers be naturally necessary, we hold this to be an *a posteriori* truth about the entity, and so it must be the case that in that world such an entity is capable of an alternative, earlier and more naive description, under which its nature thus described is merely contingently related to those of its powers and liabilities which are later discovered to be necessary consequences of its real nature.'[19]

Not all natural necessities that we discover are 'taken up' into the language in the form of conceptual necessities, for some can be described by contingently related statements.[20] It is necessary that we eat and satisfy certain physical requirements if we are to survive, but this natural necessity has not been 'taken up' into the definition of human beings, probably for the good reason that it would not differentiate us from animals. It might also seem possible that a capitalist could stop purchasing labour-power, stop accumulating capital and therefore break the necessary relationship between these actions and being a capitalist, but in acting this way s/he would be becoming a non-capitalist. In marxism, these necessary relationships are 'taken up' into the definition of capital,[21] but there are other claims about natural necessities which have a simpler description, but which are implicit in the theory nonetheless.

As Harré and Madden suggest, relationships which were once considered to be independent may later come to be recognised as necessary. Yet as some recent trends in marxist theory have shown, progress has, in some instances, consisted in showing that certain (sets of) relationships which were formerly seen as *necessarily* linked are now known to be only contingently related or capable of a wider range of forms of combination than was previously realised. This is true of historicist, stage-theory notions of development.

Also, as Banaji shows, the concept of modes of production can be inadequate both as an abstract or a concrete concept because it is now realised that modes of production are not nearly as limited in terms of possible forms of interlocking combinations of relations and forces of production as was originally thought.[22] It seems, therefore, that the concept 'modes of production' can be given a less crucial *summarising* role. It is more important to establish the actual combinations of forces and relations of production that exist and work out how they cohere and function. Trying to force aberrant facts into simple categorisations of feudal or capitalist or even into 'articulations' of several modes of production (each of whose form can be known in advance from theory) by arguing that the facts must have been theorised incorrectly is neither useful nor necessary. Banaji shows that restricted, idealised views of modes of production have inhibited the development of marxist theory of the transition between feudalism and capitalism and Third World social formations. The consequences of relegating the concept to a lesser theoretical role need not be damaging (surprising though it may seem) for the essential notions of a relatively enduring interlocking of relations between people, and between people and nature can be retained using lower-order concepts or at least less restrictive formulations of 'mode of production' than is found in much marxist writing.

We can now clarify the relationship between the abstract and the concrete, and also the distinction between good and bad abstraction. Good or 'rational' abstractions should isolate necessary relationships. The concrete, as a unity of diverse determinations, is a combination of several necessary relationships, but the form of the combination is contingent, and *therefore only determinable through empirical research. As such, its form cannot be assumed to have already been 'taken up' into the theoretical framework in the same way that the nature of the abstract can.*

A bad abstraction or 'chaotic conception' is one which is based upon a non-necessary relationship, or which divides the indivisible by failing to recognise a necessary relationship. The same point can be made in a different way by using the distinction between external and internal relations. The relation between a person and a lump of earth is *external* and contingent in the sense that each object can exist without the other. On the other hand the relations between landlord and tenant, master and slave are *internal* and necessary in that what each part of the relation is depends upon its relation to the other. Sometimes internal relations may be asymmetric as in the case of state and council housing, money and banking system in which the former object in each pair can exist without the latter, but not vice versa.[23] A rational abstraction – unlike a chaotic conception – takes due account of structures of internal and external relations.

Theories make their strongest claims at the abstract level, about necessary and internal relations, about causal powers which exist in virtue of the nature of particular things. They quite properly remain more agnostic towards the form of external relations. Physics quite rightly makes a strong claim about copper's power to conduct electricity, but does not commit itself on whether any particular piece of copper ever will be in a position to do so. And similarly with marxism; given that capital cannot exist as such without wage-labour, we should not develop abstractions which treat them as independent. If General Motors could function in its present form with serf labour, the theory really would be in trouble, but it quite properly does not commit itself on the contingent matter of whether that labour is American, British or Turkish. We may make *theoretical* claims about the former and agree that confirmations or falsifications are epistemically significant, but the testing of *empirical* claims made about *contingently* related processes need not affect our confidence in the theoretical claims. It may be important to establish what proportion of General Motors' labour force is American, but if we get it wrong, this is unlikely to warrant a challenge to basic theory.

This is not of course to say that concrete objects are unimportant – far from it; but what theory provides us with is an understanding of the concrete by means of abstract concepts denoting its *determinations*. In this context, the primary position of the concept of 'commodity' in Capital is rightly noted in making the point that, although abstract concepts have to be used to explain the concrete, we have to start with what we have to explain. But the major theoretical issues are not about a *simple* category of the commodity, as it might be instantiated in, say, a car, but about the *abstraction* of use-value and exchange-value as its essential determinations.

In Bhaskar's terms rational abstractions concern the level of the '*real*' – causal powers or generative mechanisms; concrete concepts concern the level of the '*actual*' – the effects, operation and activation of mechanisms, it then being contingent whether these are possible *empirical* objects for us.[24]

Figure 1 sums up the hierarchy of types of concepts in marxism ranging from the most basic abstract concepts which refer to transhistorical necessities, through historically-specific abstract concepts, through the 'tendencies' which are the equivalents of 'mechanisms' in realist philosophy of science, to the more concrete 'level'. As we have seen, because of the historical nature of society, *which* historically-specific abstractions must be used depends upon the kind of basic necessary relationships which obtain at any point in time. In natural science, natural necessities are empirically discovered too, but in general, they do not change. And this is why marxism (indeed, *any* social theory) cannot take its more basic concepts for granted to the extent that natural sciences can: the concepts must change with the reality they depict, or of which they are constitutive.

Although we can say that certain necessary relationships in capitalism have been 'taken up' into marxist theory in such a way that we can 'know in advance' that wherever there is capital, there must also be value-producing wage-labour, it must be stressed that this knowledge is ultimately grounded *a posteriori*. In like manner, given the existence of a child, we can 'know in advance' of the existence of a father, but even this knowledge is, as we have seen, an *a posteriori* discovery of a necessary connexion. So even the most basic theoretical claims at the top of the diagram are in principle revisable; they are not to be taken on faith. Necessary relationships may exist in reality but it is contingent whether we know them.[25]

In moving down the diagram towards the concrete, knowledge of

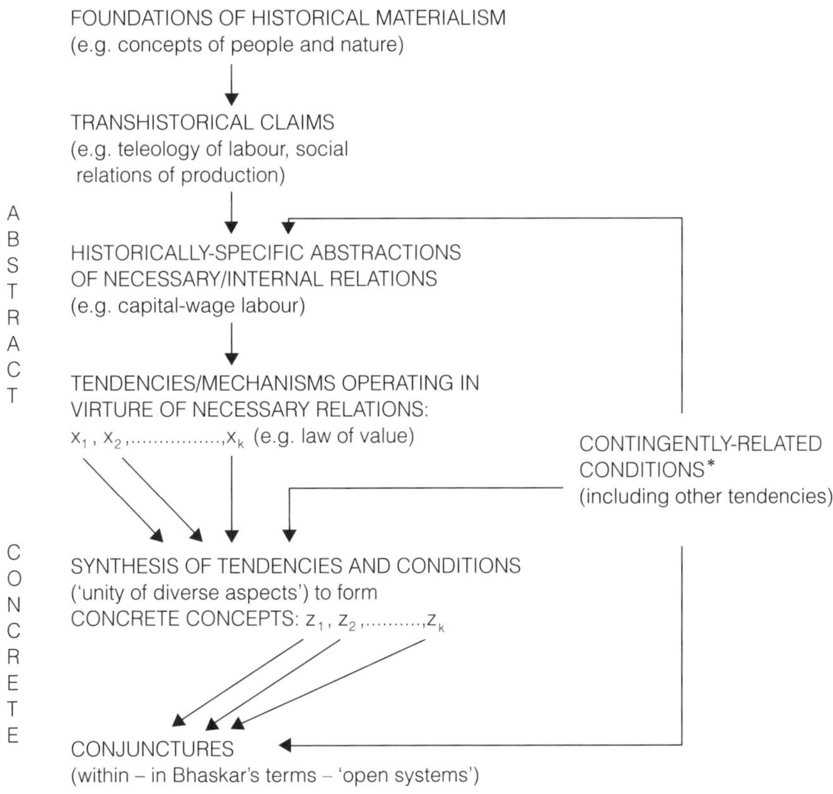

Figure 1 The relation of abstract and concrete

contingently related phenomena must be combined with knowledge of abstract necessities. These contingent relations are affected by: (a) class struggle – which can also change the structures in virtue of which mechanisms or tendencies operate; (b) theory itself, as in praxis; and (c) future knowledge, which, for the reasons given by Popper, is unknowable now. Some of these conditions may be satisfactorily theorised outside marxism, others may need re-theorising. And of course, as the example of the critical insights on marxism generated by feminism show, the direction of conceptual change need not be one-way. So, for example, although we can say from basic theoretical propositions about capitalism that the law of value forces a continual restructuring of capital upon firms, we cannot know in advance what form that will take because it depends, among other things, upon the nature of technology, which in turn depends on the growth of knowledge; we simply have to go and find out through theoretically-informed empirical research.

Marx's own position on this movement down the diagram from the abstract to the concrete is ambiguous in terms of whether he overlooked this essential element of contingency. What Marx considered to be

> '. . . obviously the correct scientific method . . . [led] . . . from abstract definitions by way of reasoning to the reproduction of the concrete situation.' [26]

'By way of reasoning . . .' suggests a movement which is purely internal to thought, which cannot or need not ask empirical questions.[27] However, elsewhere in the Introduction, Marx says that the '"concrete in thought" is a product of the working-up of observation and conception into concepts'.[28] The latter interpretation is the only one which can make sense of his concrete historical studies. So, movement between the levels of the diagram does not generally involve moves of deductive logic. To move from trans-historical theoretical claims (e.g. 'All production is carried out under social relations') to historically-specific claims ('capitalist production requires a propertyless class of workers'), we have to add historical information which is not implicit in the premises of the trans-historical claims.[29]

There is also a more general reason why these things cannot be known in advance, and again it depends upon a distinction between necessary and contingent relations between things.

> 'It is because things cannot be reduced to the conditions of their formation that events are not determined before they are caused to happen. This fact accounts for both the temporal asymmetry of causes and effects and the irreversibility of causal processes in time.'[30]

So, while everything is 'determined', things are not *pre*-determined except where, as in experiments, conditions are controlled. The chemical structure of gunpowder 'determines' its explosive causal powers, but whether it ever does explode is not thereby *pre*-determined.

Although the 'knowledge' represented in the diagram centres on marxism, it should not be seen as self-contained but as extending horizontally and vertically into knowledges with different domains such as the natural sciences and psychology. These 'discourses' are neither reducible to a single discourse nor are they discrete. Often discourses which compete in the same domain share an agreement or indifference towards certain concepts which they both use. Non-marxists may accept some of the most basic claims of historical materialism e.g. about trans-historical necessities or about some limited aspects of very specific concrete concepts, but the 'penumbra of meaning' of these concepts will vary according to the other elements of their discourse.

Marxists, qua marxists, are unlikely to question the technical knowledge of an engineer although they may have different interpretations of the social context of engineering. In neither case need there be incommensurability between the two discourses, and in the first case there may be mutual agreement and/or indifference. In both cases marxists may have to draw upon this non-marxist knowledge, to understand their own concerns (e.g. restructuring of capital) when moving from the abstract to the concrete.

The knowledge represented in the diagram also reflects a 'stratification' of the real.[31] What marxism may take as 'a given' (e.g. human anatomy) may be the prime object of study for another subject working upon a different stratum. The existence of this stratification need not mean that every event in society can only be explained through a regress which goes back through these strata to some first cause, because each stratum is, despite being constituted through processes at another stratum, irreducible: it has emergent powers. Just as water has powers irreducible to those of hydrogen and oxygen; just as human beings as organisms have powers irreducible to the chemical processes which constitute them, so certain combinations of material and social relations produce social structures which have emergent powers.[32] And it's in virtue of these emergent powers that 'higher stratum objects' intentionally or unintentionally react back upon lower strata, not by 'breaking' natural necessities, but by exploiting contingency at the lower levels.

(Although it is far beyond the scope of this paper and its author to outline an aetiology of society which would substantively specify this stratification, a word of caution is needed to guard against any unexamined over-hasty reinterpretation of (Althusserian) 'levels' of the 'economic' 'political' and 'ideological' as distinct strata, for they may possibly be more accurately seen as different parts of the same stratum.)

It should also be noted that there is no necessary correspondence between the abstractness (or 'onesidedness') of a concept or the 'height' of the stratum to which it refers, and its social significance. It is only because we usually forget the abstract nature of many *commonplaces* that we tend to associate abstractness with 'theoretical significance'. Adorno provides a convenient illustration:

> 'The category "societies with a division of labour" is of a higher and more general order than the category "capitalist society"; but it is a less, not a more essential one, with less to say about the lives of human beings and what threatens them – without this implying that a lower order category such as "urbanism" has more to say on the subject. The degree of abstraction of sociological categories varies neither directly nor inversely with their contribution to the understanding of society.'[33]

On this view of theory, the conceptualisation of necessary relationships is absolutely critical. The identification of mechanisms depends upon careful description of the objects and relationships in virtue of which they act. In contrast, description of entities is treated as an unimportant preliminary to theorising in empiricism. 'Facts' are assumed to be capable of simple, atomistic description, and theoretical issues are seen as problems of ordering these facts. In this way, many necessary relationships are overlooked or distorted; usually by tearing objects from the context upon which they are dependent and ignoring their historically-specific character.

One of the most striking things about Marx's work is the thoroughness of this basic description. Exchange-value is examined in terms of what it 'presupposes' – private property, division of labour, production of commodities etc. The passage in the *1857 Introduction* documenting the ways in which production, distribution, exchange and consumption interpenetrate and presuppose one another is a particularly good example; in noting that distribution was first and foremost a distribution of the means of production, and hence a relation within production, Marx demonstrated the existence of an *internal* relation.[34]

From the standpoint of modern bourgeois social science, this kind of analysis has an unfamiliar aspect. For example, consider the following:

> 'All production is appropriation of nature on the part of an individual within and through a specific form of society. But it is altogether ridiculous to leap from that to a specific form of property e.g. private property.'[35]
>
> '. . . that there can be no production and hence no society where some form of property does not exist is a tautology. . . .'[36]
>
> 'The obvious, trite notion: in production the members appropriate (create, shape) the products of nature in accord with human needs: . . .'[37]

Marx clearly regarded such statements as an essential foundation, but also as unexceptional, 'obvious', 'trite'. And yet so much of liberal social science appears not to know of these 'trite' notions. Entire social theories have been constructed in which society is 'organised' but somehow not dependent on the appropriation of nature for its existence; and the treatment of production and distribution as simply externally related is still common.

On first encounter, much of this repetitive, painstaking – even ponderous – description of basic entities and relations does seem 'trite' as Marx admitted: do we really need to be told that exchange-value presupposes a division of labour; or that language cannot exist for an individual? But it is these foundations that provide a means of distinguishing rational abstractions from the chaotic conceptions which characterise 'sciences' which adopt a casual attitude towards initial conceptualisation, or at worst, as in much of neo-classical economics, reduce it to a matter of defining mathematical notation – ' "K" is capital and capital is "K", and let's get on with the model'.

Yet if we refer back to the quotations from the *Grundrisse* and the passages in which they occur, an ambiguity in Marx's discussion can be seen. By referring to the relationships as 'tautologies' in which 'categories' 'presuppose' one another, it appears that they are *conceptual* necessities and nothing more. The theory has the appearance of what Marx himself called an *a priori* construction. Nevertheless, consideration of instances of these conceptual connexions shows, as we have seen, that they are based on real, necessary connexions.[38] And indeed, many theories appear to be largely *a priori* constructions. This is not unusual, and it need not be a cause for concern unless, like Humeans, we render natural necessity unintelligible by adopting an atomistic ontology and hence make it impossible to recognise that some conceptual necessities have a real basis.[39] The important question is *How*, if at all, are they grounded in necessary relationships?; How are the latter 'taken up' into the theoretical concepts?[40] Provided that those relationships between objects which are genuinely independent are not treated as necessary connexions, so that empirical questions are prejudged in an *a priori* manner, the generally *a priori* character of a theory need not be a problem.

Some of the most basic elements of Marx's critique of political economy concern his corrections of confusions about the real which arise from the misleading logical structure of discourse. Interpreted in commonsense fashion the concepts 'production' and 'distribution' do not mutually presuppose one another: their relation is not analytic but synthetic. It is only when each of these concepts is 'unpacked' and their objects examined in their material contexts that it becomes clear that they denote necessarily or internally related objects.

We can now go back and give further clarification of the proper meaning of 'empirical' and 'theoretical'.

The empirical

Implicit in the above critique of empiricist ontology and the discussion of laws of tendency was an attack upon the concept of an 'empirical world'. Interpreting 'empirical' here as 'that which is observable', the concept of 'empirical world' arises from an illegitimate reduction of an ontological question to an (empiricist) epistemological one. Now it would be extraordinary if 'the real' just happened to be exactly coextensive with the limits of our sensory powers. This solipsistic exclusion of a non-empirical real world also generates a whole range of problems, one of the most obvious of which is that of understanding how we ever come to discover anything new. Moreover, as we have seen, it also secretes a notion of an identity of thought-object and real-object, and therefore implies a *completed* science grounded in certain or absolute empirical knowledge. However, if we accept that observation is theory-laden, such that no clear distinction between what can be observed and what can be inferred on the basis of observation can be sustained, then we must acknowledge that the boundaries of 'the empirical' are both fuzzy and changeable. What is empirical depends upon our knowledge and sensory powers: what is concrete (excluding conceptual objects) does not.

Marxism's distinction of essence and appearance and its rejection of empiricist epistemology are incompatible with the 'empirical world'. Where marxists have attempted to reject this epistemology while retaining its flat, unstratified ontology, the result has been idealist contortions where the essential and the abstract are denied any reference to real objects and are reduced to heuristic devices for understanding the empirical. In the philosophy of science, the recent development of conventionalist critiques of positivism have been based on this same incompatible combination.[41]

If we do not accord real status to mechanisms and instead treat laws as statements about universal empirical regularities we run into what Bhaskar terms a dilemma of 'actualism'.[42] Faced with the conspicuous rarity of spontaneously-occurring, precise, universal empirical regularities, we can either:

(a) conclude that any contenders for the status of 'law' are thereby refuted, or
(b) conclude that laws apply *only* to ideal conditions equivalent to those of scientific experiments, *and nowhere else.*

It is only if laws are understood as referring to mechanisms, and not empirical events, that the manifestly successful applications of scientific knowledge in systems where empirical regularities are rare become intelligible. Indeed, it is only if mechanisms operate in such 'open systems' that successful lay interventions in nature in the form of labour are possible.

A second sense of 'empirical', which can be equally confusing, is 'that which might be other than it is'. Many interpretations conflate and confuse (i) questions of contingency if and where it occurs in the ontological domain (i.e. in the relations of objects and events) with (ii) questions of contingency – or better 'fallibility' – in the epistemological domain (i.e. in the relation between the world and our knowledge). (i) and (ii) are themselves only contingently related, and furthermore, within (i) there is also the common non-sequitur mentioned above in which it is assumed that because it is logically possible that the world itself may suddenly change, everything in our world is contingently related. Another source of confusion is generated where the empirical is associated with that which is referred to by logically contingent *statements* in contrast to the necessary truths of analytic statements.

On our account, both contingency and necessity characterise the real as a whole, and not just that part which happens to be empirically observable: much of the real could be 'other than it is', but there are also natural necessities. It is contingent whether we know either case, but whichever is the case has nothing to do with logical relations of statements, for, as we saw earlier, necessity in the world can be described by either logically necessary or logically contingent statements.

The theoretical

We have argued that theory makes its strongest claims about[43] necessary relations in the world and about the natures of the objects in virtue of which they obtain. It does so by 'anchoring itself' upon abstract concepts, but these, on their own, permit *less* committal statements about contingent relations occurring in common concrete configurations. The latter require 'empirical analysis'.

This interpretation had several corollaries:

(1) Given that theory makes claims about the real and is not a heuristic aid for ordering a privileged empirical knowledge, the relation between observation and theory is not to be understood in terms of correspondence rules but in terms of statements about causal connexions between real objects.

(2) With the development of conventionalist critiques of positivism and the renewed interest in the history of science by philosophers of science, it has often been noted that scientists sometimes put more faith in their theories than in observations, even where the latter appear to contradict the former. This behaviour has sometimes been rationalised as a healthy 'tenacity' which protects newly-emerging theories from premature refutation. Given our agreement with the critique of theory-neutral, certain observation, this is unobjectionable. But because this critique fails to reject empiricism's flat ontology, it fails to note that the real disjunction between mechanisms and events also gives scientists good grounds for being sceptical about the significance of their non-correspondence.

(3) As they lack a concept of natural necessity and a distinction between necessary (internal) and contingent (external) relations, these philosophies have difficulty sustaining any distinction between empirical research and theoretical reflection.

(4) Just as there are no grounds for identifying the concrete with the empirical, there are none for identifying the abstract level of causal powers and mechanisms with the *un*observable as Keat and Urry tend to do.[44]

(5) What is theoretical has nothing to do with difficulty or unfamiliarity. Commonsense or informal knowledge contains many implicit assumptions about real necessities. Commonplaces – such as the claims that 'we must eat in order to survive' or 'we are all mortal' can therefore be, in our sense, as 'theoretical' as that knowledge of natural necessities which is the product of considerable scientific labour and which is usually exclusive to a minority and unfamiliar to the masses. In saying this, I am not trying to invest commonsense with any privileged status; it is often content with ignorance about

the nature of the objects in virtue of which mechanisms operate, or else is mistaken about them, as in the characteristic error of reification of social relations and processes. I would simply wish to deny that scientific and lay knowledges are an incommensurable pair of autonomous 'discourses' about which a priori judgements can be made. Commonsense is certainly characteristically an 'unexamined discourse', but if we try examining it, we can find examples of interpenetration with scientific discourse. The adequacy of particular lay and scientific knowledges is a substantive and not a philosophical question. We cannot simply contrast an immaculately conceived 'science' or 'theory', whose privileged status is guaranteed by the conditions of its production, with 'ideology', which is similarly condemned by its conditions of production. Therefore the abstract concepts upon which we anchor our analysis may include some which are quite mundane. As we have seen, competing scientific 'discourses' at one level (e.g. social theory) may share commitment or indifference to concepts which are crucial at another. Without a recognition of the stratification of the real, such asymmetries tend to be interpreted as evidence of the autonomy and incommensurability of discourses or paradigms in relation to some flat ontology. The fiction of incommensurability arises from: (i) a flat ontology; (ii) an unawareness of the hermeneutical character of discourse; (iii) a blindness to the mundane assumptions common to several discourses produced by the reduction of a discourse to those concepts which are unique to it; (iv) the mistaken belief that discourses must be logically continuous for translation between them to occur; (v) a conception of networks of concepts composing discourse existing in a kind of equilibrium, rather than differential stress.

Critical implications

This discussion has important critical implications for the way in which analyses and explanations of the concrete are conducted. Neither empiricism nor rationalism are of any help here; the former cannot comprehend the role of theory, the latter cannot grasp how theory has any purchase on the real. We have seen that the false view that the move from abstract to concrete is deductive and purely internal and unique to marxist theory is based upon notions of observation as entirely theory-determined, and discourses as entirely discrete and incommensurable. These views legitimise a kind of reductionist or 'pseudo-concrete' analysis in which the concrete is simply reduced to the abstract and in which the extent of contingency in the systems of interest is radically underestimated. But the mediation of discourses required by concrete analysis and the non-deductive relation between abstract and the concrete need not be seen as problems. On the contrary, they prevent a blinkered imprisonment within the 'self-ratifying circles'[45] of the consecrated abstract concepts of marxism. 'Pseudo-concrete' research produces precisely that 'forcing [of] the significance of certain events' (Sartre), that 'intellectual agoraphobia' (Thompson) or that 'naming-of-parts approach' which has so often passed for analysis. This is not to deny that theoretical reconstitutions of higher-order abstract concepts are worthwhile, only that they cannot provide the sole basis for the generation of new concepts. These have to be integrated into the existing networks of concepts if they are to be meaningful and usable, and the integration usually involves meaning change in the network rather than a simple accretion of knowledge. But the integration should not take place only 'from above', in terms of Figure 1, but should also be connected to more mundane and concrete concepts. A one-sided integration has characterised much of the recent writing on the state which has shown that the hypotheses were already implicit in existing theory, and only needed a theoretical exegesis, an appropriate 'reading', to 'draw them out'.[46] It is certainly important to realise that the state has its own 'labour processes', that it is the 'condensate of class struggle' or an 'instrument of the dominant fractions of capital', or whatever, but it is also important to relate it to 'lower-order' concepts if these ideas are to inform concrete study. And if these 'lower-order' concepts refer to some of the same objects (differently understood, of course) as bourgeois analyses e.g. 'governments', 'civil service', this does not make the analysis irredeemably 'empiricist'. These 'lower-order' concepts are certainly not 'operationalisations' of 'theoretical terms' (which is how empiricists would see the matter), but different aspects of the object of study.

Reductionism in economic analysis

One of the main forms of reductionism in marxist 'economic' analysis is an interpretation of empirical patterns as simple manifestations of the abstractions developed in *Capital*. A common tendency (fortunately becoming rarer now) is the making of cavalier, unqualified assumptions about value movements on the basis of price movements of physical volumes of plant. Given that mechanisms and their effects rarely correspond spontaneously in a one-to-one fashion, this generates an actualist dilemma: *either* the abstract tendencies do not exist as such *or* else the empirical phenomena have to be distorted so that they are *made* to reflect the abstract. This dilemma is familiar in concrete studies of class but it has also characterised neo-marxist analyses of uneven development. In the latter case, at worst, ideal type representations of contingent empirical patterns of development (such as centre-periphery, metropolis-satellite forms) are assumed to be the unique expressions of capitalist development. The actualist dilemma is confronted when counter-examples of peripheral 'autonomous' capitalist development are pointed out: either the claims have to be retracted or the existence of the exceptions denied. A similar problem arises when certain novel empirical forms (e.g. runaway industries, neo-Fordism) are extrapolated and granted epochal significance as *unique* manifestations of the latest phase of capitalist development. In both cases, both the empirical 'rules' and the exceptions are quite compatible with the abstract propositions of Marx's *Capital*.

Much the same result is produced where the effects of a necessary relation forming part of an open system (i.e. one whose internal and external parameters are inconstant) are projected onto the whole of the system. For example, it is common to note the necessary contradiction of capital accumulation in 'Newly Industrialised Countries' in which the cheapness of the labour power both blocks as well as assists accumulation because it restricts the size of the market. While it is true that the low-paid cannot generate much purchasing power, it is contingent whether there may be sufficient numbers of *other* people in those countries who are affluent enough to create an internal market. The fact that the latter cannot be known in advance on the basis of knowledge of abstract necessities creates traps for pseudo-concrete research.[47]

This failure to acknowledge contingency in economic systems is not only produced by an implicit concept of an empirical world. Particularly in dependency theory it also derives from a theorisation of tendencies or mechanisms which ignores much of the marxist theory which explains how they are grounded. The tendencies float uneasily and unconvincingly between the abstract and the concrete, neither grounded in the former nor engaging with the latter.[48]

Common to these approaches is the expectation of a 'theory of uneven development' which pre-empts its concrete form, and which is as misguided as the expectation of a 'theory of ideology' which specifies, in advance, its content. Once again, abstraction can only be expected to help explain the structures or mechanisms which produce the concrete.[49]

Mandel's *Late Capitalism*[50] is certainly not in this league, for it attempts the ambitious project of explaining concrete developments in the world economy through abstraction by reference to movements in value. However, the success of this project is considerably hindered by his ambiguous usage of the term 'abstract' and by his *empirical* treatment of 'tendencies'.

> 'From the standpoint of historical materialism, "tendencies" which do not manifest themselves materially and empirically [Are these terms meant to be equivalent?] are not tendencies at all. They are products of false consciousness, or for those who dislike that phrase, of scientific errors.'[51]

Having excluded the possibility of a non-empirical real world, he is then forced to regard abstract concepts which refer to it as having no explanatory purchase on the concrete.

> 'As soon as "laws of development" come to be regarded as so abstract that they can no longer explain the actual process of concrete history, then the discovery of such tendencies ceases to be an instrument for

> the revolutionary transformation of this process. All that remains is a degenerate form of speculative socio-economic philosophy in which the "laws of development" have the same shadowy existence as Hegel's "world spirit" . . .'[52]

Here, Mandel comes face-to-face with the idealist alternative generated by the retention of an unstratified ontology of the empirical. He obviously sees its unacceptable implications, and in order to avoid retracting laws of tendency he turns a blind eye to the conspicuous absence of empirical regularities or simple empirical manifestations of laws of tendency. In other words, his response to the actualist dilemma is to ignore its existence. And in the rest of the book, 'tendencies' appear to be inferred from or read into empirical patterns exhibiting very little regularity.[53] But this is not necessarily wrong for, given the non-identity of mechanisms and their effects, empirical regularities are neither necessary nor sufficient for retroducing the existence of mechanisms.

An associated misconception about abstract/concrete and theoretical/empirical relations in marxist 'economic' theory is 'deductivism'.[54] Here theory is supposed to provide a set of propositions from which empirical forms can be logically deduced, and it is assumed that this deduction provides an explanation. From the statement 'All capitalists employ wage-labourers', we can deduce that any particular capitalist must employ wage-labourers, but this does not explain why this is so. Therefore, the point which has often been made in debates about value-theory, that prices cannot be deduced (or, which is the same thing, 'calculated') from values, does not count as a legitimate argument against its explanatory ability; it could still explain price movements (though this is not its intention), the origin of profit etc.[55] The theory could only be expected to be formulable mathematically in such a way that concrete movements were calculable if real world causal processes happened to conform to the relations of logic. However, the uneven relation of use-value and exchange-value guarantees that this cannot be so.

In theoretical discussions (e.g. of reproduction formulae) we often abstract from this unevenness by assuming a fixed relationship between use-value and exchange-value, as Marx often did,[56] but while this may be a convenient heuristic aid, it cannot possibly be used as a simplifying assumption in the study of concrete development. Capital accumulation in the face of the pressure of the law of value depends upon a *changing* relationship between use-values and exchange-values. In virtue of this:

> 'There is, then, no necessary inner relation between the value of the constant capital, nor, therefore, between the value of the total capital (= c+v) and the surplus value.'[57]

The element of contingency introduced by this unevenness is also ignored by those accounts of the tendency of the rate of profit to fall which turn the contingent empirical questions of the relation between technical composition and organic composition into a priori ones.

Deductivism's associated neglect of careful initial description and conceptualisation is a particularly common occupational hazard in mathematical analysis in marxian economics, where conceptualisation is so often made the slave of quantification. The quantities easily become little more than 'variables' and 'functions' which take on a life of their own, cut off from the theoretical setting of Marx's abstractions which exhaustively examine their contexts and determinations.[58] And the matter is made all the more complicated by the fact that exactly the same kind of 'abstraction' from real determinants actually underpins the concrete social practices which produce exchange-value.[59] In other words this misleading form of abstraction, this chaotic but 'practically-adequate' conception, is actually constitutive of marxism's object.

Monism

In all these cases, the failure to acknowledge contingent relations between the abstract and concrete generates a *monism*. If the mechanisms abstracted can in fact lead to several different concrete results, then the denial of this contingency will generate several competing monisms, each able to cite (carefully selected) 'empirical evidence'. And the reductionist character of this kind of analysis will also seriously underestimate the degree of internal differentiation and flexibility in its objects.

The political consequences of monism and reductionism are a failure to grasp the complexities of the concrete, whether they be the rigidities and diverse forms of capital, which are so important for understanding the crisis, or the web of cross-currents which constitute the concrete forms of the labour movement. For example, depending on which monism you choose, this can lead either to an unwarranted optimism about the potential of the working class or a defeatist unfounded pessimism produced by a projection of bad features of the labour movement onto the whole. And this latter kind of pessimism is in no small part reinforced by the self-justifying and self-induced political isolation of reductionist marxism.

Acknowledgements

The ideas in this paper owe much to the work of Roy Bhaskar and Rom Harré – more than can be indicated by mere references. I would like to thank Roy and also Simon Duncan, Tony Fielding, Suzanne Mackenzie, Peter Saunders, John Urry, Anthony Giddens, Roy Edgley and Scott Meikle for comments on earlier drafts. The usual disclaimers apply.

Notes

1 *Search for a Method*, 1963, Vintage, p. 27; 'studying facts' now seems unsatisfactory, but I don't think this vitiates his criticism.
2 ibid. p. 28, emphases in original. Also note the following widely-quoted passage: 'Valéry is a petit bourgeois intellectual, no doubt about it. But not every petit bourgeois intellectual is Valéry. The heuristic inadequacy of contemporary Marxism is contained in these two sentences. . . . Characterising Valéry as a petit bourgeois and his work as idealist, the Marxist will find in both alike only what he has put there.' (ibid, p. 56)
3 *Marxism and Literature*, 1977, Oxford University Press, p. 81.
4 *The Poverty of Theory*, Merlin, 1978, p. 303. A daft title, some polemical excesses, and a general failure to recognise the importance of 'structure' (cf. P. Anderson, *Arguments Within English Marxism*, NLB, 1980) should not be allowed to detract from the importance of this critique as an (albeit one-sided) corrective to some of the idealist elements within Althusserianism.
5 ibid. p. 346.
6 R. Bhaskar, 1975a, *A Realist Theory of Science*, Leeds Books; 1975b, 'Two Philosophies of Science', *New Left Review* 94; 1979, *The Possibility of Naturalism*, Harvester Press, Brighton. R. Harré, 1970, *The Principles of Scientific Thinking*, Macmillan; 1972, *The Philosophies of Science*, Oxford UP, London. R. Harré and E.H. Madden, 1975, *Causal Powers*, Blackwell, Oxford. R. Harré and P. F. Secord, 1972, *The Explanation of Social Behaviour*, Blackwell, Oxford. R. Keat and J. Urry, 1975, *Social Theory as Science*, Routledge and Kegan Paul.
7 P. K. Feyerabend, 1970, 'Consolations for the Specialist' in I. Lakatos and A. Musgrave (eds.), *Criticism and the Growth of Knowledge*, Cambridge UP.
8 Cf. A. Collier, 1979, 'In Defence of Epistemology', *Radical Philosophy* 20, pp. 8–21, and T. Skillen, 1979, 'Discourse Fever: Post-marxist modes of production', *Radical Philosophy* 20, pp. 3–8.
9 K. Marx, 1973, *Grundrisse*, Penguin, p. 101.
10 ibid. p. 100.
11 Bhaskar, 1975a, op.cit., pp. 201–02.
12 Harré and Madden, op.cit.
13 Harré, 1970, op.cit.
14 Harré and Madden, op.cit., p. 110.
15 Bhaskar, 1975a, op.cit., p. 95.
16 Collier, ibid.
17 Cf. ibid and M. Hesse, 1974, *The Structure of Scientific Inference*, Macmillan.
18 Harré and Madden, op.cit.
19 ibid. p. 80.
20 Bhaskar, 1975a, op.cit., p. 201.
21 It has often been said that the entire three volumes of *Capital* are a definition of capital.
22 J. Banaji, 1977, 'Modes of Production in a Materialist Conception of History', *Capital and Class* 3, pp. 1–44.
23 Bhaskar, 1979, op.cit., p. 54.
24 Bhaskar, 1975a, op.cit., p. 52.
25 Bhaskar, 1975a, op.cit., pp. 199–215.
26 Marx, *1857 Introduction*, in Arthur, C. (ed.) *The German Ideology*, Lawrence and Wishart, p. 141.
27 The translation in the Penguin/NLR edition of the *Grundrisse* is possibly less committal: '. . . the abstract determinations lead towards a reproduction of the

concrete by way of thought.' (Marx, 1973, op.cit., p. 101). Compare Althusser: '. . . the process that produces the concrete-knowledge takes place wholly in the theoretical practice.' (L. Althusser, 1969, *For Marx*, NLB, p. 186).

28 Marx, 1973, op.cit., p. 101.

29 D. Sayer, 1979, *Marx's Method: Ideology, Science and Critique in Capital*, Harvester Press, Brighton.

30 Bhaskar, 1975a, op.cit., p. 107. Compare Raymond Williams' distinction between determinism and determination in his 1973b 'Base and Superstructure in Marxist Cultural Theory', *New Left Review* 82, and Sartre's concept of the 'project', op.cit., pp. 91ff.

31 Bhaskar, 1975a, op.cit., pp. 163ff. and his 1979, op.cit., pp. 124ff.

32 ibid.

33 T.W. Adorno, 1976, 'Sociology and Empirical Research', p. 239 in P. Connerton (ed.), *Critical Sociology*, Penguin.

34 Marx, 1973, op.cit., p. 96.

35 ibid. p. 87.

36 ibid. p. 88.

37 ibid.

38 As Nicolaus notes, Marx was keenly aware of the limitations of a purely idealist dialectic of categories: '. . . as if the task were the dialectic balancing of concepts, and not the grasping of real relations', Marx, 1973, ibid. pp. 36 and 90.

39 Bhaskar, 1975a, p. 149.

40 See the Postface to the 2nd edition of Volume 1 *Capital* (1976, Penguin, p. 102):
'Of course the method of presentation must differ in form from that of inquiry. The latter has to appropriate the material in detail, to analyse its different forms of development and to track down their inner connection. Only after this work has been done successfully, if the life of the subject-matter is now reflected back in the ideas, then it may appear as if we have before us an *a priori* construction.'

41 Bhaskar, 1975b, op.cit.

42 Bhaskar, 1975a, op.cit., pp. 91ff.

43 Here, as in many places, we could insert the qualification – 'what are believed to be' – but given that all knowledge is fallible, there seems little point in making a special emphasis of this here.

44 R. Keat and J. Urry, op.cit.

45 'History and Theory', in *History Workshop* 6, 1978, p. 2.

46 Compare Sartre, op.cit., pp. 27–28.

47 See the criticisms of Jacobson, D., Wickham, D. and Wickham, J., 1979, review of *Die Neue Internationale Arbeitsteclung* by F. Fröbel, J. Heinricks and O.K. Rowolt, in *Capital and Class* 7, pp. 125–30, and Nayyar, D., 1978, 'Transnational Corporations and Manufactured Exports from Poor Countries', *Economic Journal*, 88, pp. 59–84.

48 I have also criticised Castells' marxist analysis of capitalist urbanization in *The Urban Question*, 1977, Arnold, and *City, Class and Power*, 1978, Macmillan, London, on these grounds in my 'Theory and Empirical Research in Urban and Regional Political Economy', 1979, *University of Sussex Urban and Regional Studies, Working Paper*, 14.

49 David Harvey develops this point in 'The Geography of Capitalist accumulation: a Reconstruction of the Marxian theory', *Antipode* 7 (2), pp. 9–21. Cf. also E.O. Wright, 'The Value Controversy and Social Research', *New Left Review* 116, 1979, which makes some points that are convergent with this.

50 E. Mandel, 1975, NLB.

51 ibid. p. 20.
52 ibid.
53 As would be expected of one caught in a dilemma, Mandel's larger argument contains several bewildering oscillations between different interpretations of the 'abstract', and these perhaps account for his curious interpretations of *Capital*, particularly the reproduction schemes of Vol. II.
54 Cf. Harré, 1970, op.cit.
55 B. Fine, 1980, *Economic Theory and Ideology*, Arnold. Cf. also S. Meikle, 'Dialectical Contradiction and Necessity', in J. Mepham and D.-H. Ruben (eds.), 1979, *Issues in Marxist Philosophy: Vol. 1, Dialectics and Method*, Harvester, Brighton.
56 'If now our spinner, by working for one hour, can convert $1\frac{2}{3}$ lbs. of cotton into $1\frac{2}{3}$ lbs. of yarn, it follows that in 6 hours he will convert 10 lb. of cotton into 10 lbs. of yarn.' Marx, 1976, *Capital*, Vol. 1, Penguin, p. 297.
57 K. Marx, 1971, *Capital*, Vol. 3, pp. 46–47, Lawrence and Wishart.
58 Cf. the important critiques of modes of abstraction in economic analysis developed by Bettelheim in his critique of Emmanuel in the latter's *Unequal Exchange*, 1972, NLB, pp. 271ff. and by Maurice Dobb in his 'The Trend of Modern Economics', 1937, reprinted in E.K. Hunt and J. Schwartz (eds.), *A Critique of Economic Theory*, Penguin, 1972.
59 A. Sohn-Rethel, *Intellectual and Manual Labour*, 1978, Macmillan.

6

ECONOMIC SCIENCE WITHOUT EXPERIMENTATION

Tony Lawson

The question I now must confront is how social scientific research can proceed in the absence of real possibilities of experimental control. How can the scientific enterprise even get under way without event regularities to account for? And how are competing theories to be assessed when the social sciences are generally denied the crucial test situation? Despite the lack of opportunities for controlled experimentation in the social sciences I remain optimistic about the social scientific prospects. In setting a context for developing my position I refer first, albeit extremely briefly, to relevant assessments of Bhaskar (1979) and Collier (1994). Each has questioned whether the potential for social scientific successes exists given the limited opportunities for meaningful experimentation in the social realm. And each has done so supporting a framework similar to that defended here. While Bhaskar sustains a degree of optimism Collier is rather pessimistic. A feature of social life that is fundamental to these opposed assessments is something which Bhaskar construes as a 'compensator' for the lack of experimental control in the social sciences. To the extent that Bhaskar is optimistic about the prospects for the social sciences this appears to turn on the existence of the suggested compensator. And it is through rejecting Bhaskar's arguments on this point that Collier concludes that any optimism concerning the possibilities of a successful social science are misplaced. I too find problems with Bhaskar's arguments, yet I do not share Collier's degree of scepticism about the consequences. I now run briefly though the various issues involved, and indicate the basis of my optimism. My reason for proceeding in this contrastive fashion is that I think it helps both to convey the central significance of the question posed at the beginning of this chapter and also to bring certain fundamental features of the argument into greater relief. These latter aspects

Source: *Economics and Reality*, London: Routledge, 1997, chaps 15 and 16, pp. 199–226 and 227–237.

include some upon which rather a lot ultimately turns but which appear not to be emphasised sufficiently by either Bhaskar or Collier.

The hermeneutic moment in science

Bhaskar's compensator for the impossibility of experimentation in the social sciences turns on the insight that 'social structures, unlike natural structures, do not exist independently of the agents' conceptions of what they are doing in their activity' (1979: 38). This observation is certainly correct. And it does bear the already noted consequences (further developed in Chapter 19) that the results of social scientific research have the potential to influence the very objects of such enquiry. This is a potential that does not usually figure in the natural scientific context. Now a recognition of this capacity for social science thus to engender changes in the social world, including the practices of science itself, may well affect the sort of research that is encouraged, financed and accorded status. But, as we have seen, it is not the case that this undermines the possibility of social science. Social objects exist intransitively at the time any social scientific analysis of them is initiated, whatever the eventual effect upon them induced by such an enquiry.

The question here, though, is whether the insight in question actually *assists* the cause of social science, and specifically whether a compensator for experimental activity is entailed. Bhaskar's argument is that because 'most of the phenomena which the social scientist has to deal with will already be identified, thanks to the concept-dependent nature of social activities under some descriptions' (Bhaskar, 1979: 49), social science is provided with a ready-made entry point for analysis. It is this that in some way *compensates* social science for its lack of experimental possibilities. Now it is certainly the case that this hermeneutic moment is fundamental for any social science. This has been acknowledged above. Indeed, without the agents' own conceptions of what they are doing, social analysis could not easily get off the ground. Moreover, it is clearly the case that the concept-dependent nature of social structures serves to distinguish them from natural ones.

But does the associated hermeneutic moment really constitute a distinct feature of the social sciences relative to the natural ones, a compensator for the impossibility of controlled experimentation? The point here is that while the concept-dependent nature of social activities under some description must be acknowledged, the concepts which people hold and act upon relate as much to natural structures as to social ones. We know a lot about *both* the social and the natural worlds by being agents within them. Activities such as cooking, farming, fishing and manufacture (of everything from baskets to boats, and shoes to shelter) have long depended upon the knowledge of the natural world that humans possess. Collier (1994) is correct to conclude that conceptualised practices such as these are informative about the natural world in exactly the same way that the 'practices of commerce and state craft, conflict and cooperation, "knowing oneself" and "knowing others" are about the human world' (1994: 247). In each case, the sources of information, the conceptions of lay agents, provide an entry point for scientific analysis, just as, in each case, the conceptions held are fallible and corrigible. If there is a difference between natural and social science with respect to the hermeneutic moment, it appears to be that the natural sciences have gone significantly beyond what the conceptions of lay agents can give (ibid.). But, however that may be (see below), it does not seem to follow that, in recognising the concept-dependent nature of social structures, a social science compensator for the lack of experimental possibilities is entailed.

For Collier, the recognition that the hermeneutic moment occurs in the natural sciences in the same way as it does in the social sciences, and that it is as reliable and informative in the former as it is in the latter, encourages a pessimism with regard to social scientific prospects. For it follows, Collier suggests, that the prominence of the hermeneutic moment in the social sciences must be interpreted as a sign that the latter really have almost *nothing more* to go on. We have seen in Chapter 13 that the subjectivist tradition in economics (incorrectly) supposes that the grasping of agents' conceptions is more or less all there is for social science to be concerned with. Although Collier rejects the subjectivist analysis (and acknowledges, of course, that the social world is structured and agents' conceptions of social structures are fallible) he concludes that the impossibility of controlled experimentation in the social realm limits the possibilities for getting much beyond the hermeneutic moment in practice. If agent conceptions are erroneous, the inability to experiment places a constraint on uncovering significantly more adequate conceptions through science:

> [The human sciences'] input from agents' conceptions is no more authoritative than such input is in regard to the natural world; but our capacity to correct, revise and add to the knowledge derived from agents' conceptions is immeasurably more advanced in those sciences where experiments are possible. The teachability even of an experimental natural science doubtless presupposes our initial familiarity with (for example) heat, light and sound, push and pull, speed and weight; but before we have gone very far, we have redefined such concepts and left our homely understanding of them far behind. The hermeneutic moment is so prominent in the social sciences not because it is a more essential stage or a more reliable or informative source than in the natural sciences, but because, in the absence of experiments, we have so little else. As a result, we are also much more likely to get things wrong and much less likely to correct them in the human than in the experimental natural sciences. . .
>
> My conclusion from what we know about the ontology of the

> human world is that it gives grounds for scepticism about the prospects of the human sciences.
>
> (Collier, 1994: 248)

The reason I do not share Collier's scepticism stems from a different assessment of what follows from the inability of the social sciences to achieve meaningful experimental control. This certainly is the crux of the issue. In fact, it seems to me that the question of how social science can manage without the possibility of experimental control is *the* central question of methodology for those social scientists alive to the general irrelevance to social explanation of the deductivist model. The remainder of this chapter is mainly concerned with laying out in detail my position on this matter. Only at the end of the chapter do I reconsider Collier's position as stated above.

Experimental and non-experimental conditions contrasted

Before giving the details of my position, however, it is useful first to recall briefly certain features of the experimental situation which the discussion of Part I has indicated to be significant. We have seen, first, that experimentation is fundamentally about *intervening* in the world. It is about manipulating aspects of reality in order that certain causal mechanisms can be (more easily) identified and/or theories about them tested. It is a process of empirically identifying and/or assessing non-empirical structures and mechanisms through human contrivance. Second, experiments give us access to relatively enduring structures and powers and transfactually active mechanisms and their tendencies. For the intelligibility of experimental activity and results indicates that (at least some) mechanisms act through the flux of conditions that determine whether they are active and co-determine any actual outcome. That is to say, powers endure even when unexercised and, when exercised as mechanisms, act even where, as in open systems, there is no one-to-one relationship between their mode of operation and the particular sequence of events that occurs. In short, mechanisms act in their characteristic manner outside the closed conditions of their experimental identification. Such endurability, indeed, is equally a precondition (and so explanation) of *ex posteriori* successes in repeated trials, whether in a single location or in different laboratories. Third, the experiment is a situation in which the scientist must usually both enable or trigger the mechanism whose existence or nature is being investigated, to ensure that it is active, and also prevent any countervailing mechanism from interfering with the experimental outcome. The aim is to get a single mechanism going and to record its effects. Only if a mechanism is active and the system so controlled can scientists reasonably expect, or base their evaluations upon, the occurrence of an empirical regularity. In short, the stimulus and enabling conditions for the mechanism must be satisfied, and the mechanism must be insulated and the flux of conditions held constant or otherwise controlled.

Now while there clearly is a difference between the conditions of the natural and social realms the dividing line can get drawn in the wrong place. Collier appears to agree with Bhaskar (1979) that the 'chief epistemological limit on naturalism', i.e. the epistemological feature of the social sciences which qualifies the manner in which the thesis of naturalism can be sustained, is that social scientific objects 'only ever manifest themselves in open systems' (1979: 45). The claim involved here is true as it stands. But I am not sure that it constitutes a limit to naturalism. At the very least something more needs to be said.

First, by interpreting the inescapable openness of the social domain as a limit to naturalism there is a risk of encouraging the inference that the natural sciences can be reduced to the *experimental* natural sciences or astronomy, a conflation, I suspect, that neither Bhaskar nor Collier would accept. We understand the causes of earthquakes, the formation of mountains, and the spread of diseases without access to, or being able to engineer, appropriate closures. Indeed, some of the more promising developments in contemporary physics collected under the heading of superstring theory focus upon a postulated domain of reality where experimentation, at least for the foreseeable future, is completely infeasible (see e.g. Witten, 1988).

Second, it remains the case that, even where controlled experimentation is possible in the natural sphere, the goal of a perfect closure, turning as it does upon system or mechanism insulation, constitutes an ideal scenario that cannot always adequately be engineered; indeed it may very rarely be. Problems of replicating the experimental results of others (or oneself), of 'false alarms', of inconclusive measurements and results, of unaccounted for disturbances, of equipment failures, of the often prohibitive costs of experimental equipment and so forth, are legion. Even at the conceptual level uncertainty will always remain as to whether the experimental design anticipates all the disturbing mechanisms that must somehow be held at bay.

Third, and perhaps most significantly, these practicalities and/or limitations of the experimental sciences must be set against an adequate conception of any particular non-experimental contrast. It is certainly reasonable to doubt that controlled experimentation will ever be particularly meaningful in economics due to the impracticality of manipulating social structures and mechanisms in order more clearly to identify them. But just as this does not entail that relatively enduring social structures and mechanisms do not occur, so it does not necessitate *a priori* that they cannot be detected. They cannot be intentionally activated, at least not by the investigative economist; so evidence of their operation must always be sought or discovered, not generated. Thus, the initiation of explanatory research is necessarily backward, not forward, looking. Nor can mechanisms of interest be insulated in the manner of experimental manipulation or the background conditions be purposefully held constant or otherwise controlled. Yet, this in itself does not rule out the possibility of mechanisms being detected.

The fundamental point, here, is that it is not the case that the only conceivable alternative to well controlled experimentation, or more generally the production of a closure, of a strict event regularity, is a totally unsystematic, incoherent, random flux. Over restricted regions of time–space certain mechanisms may come to dominate others and/or shine through: non-spurious, rough and ready, partial regularities may be observed. Although the social world is open, dynamic and changing, certain mechanisms may, over restricted regions of time–space, be reproduced continuously and come to be (occasionally) apparent in their effects at the level of actual phenomena, giving rise to rough and ready generalities or partial regularities, holding to such a degree that *prima facie* an explanation is called for. If it is conceivable that a completely non-systematic flux could have dominated, *ex posteriori* this is evidently not the case. Thus, just as autumn leaves do fall to the ground *much* of the time, so women are *concentrated* in secondary sectors of labour markets and productivity growth in the UK over the last century has *frequently* been slower than that of most other, otherwise comparable, industrial countries, and so on.

Interpreting partial event regularities

Let me refer to such partial regularities in the first instance as *demi-regularities* or *demi-laws*.[1] A demi-regularity, or *demi-reg* for short, is precisely a partial event regularity which *prima facie* indicates the occasional, but less than universal, actualization of a mechanism or tendency, over a definite region of time–space. The patterning observed will not be strict if countervailing factors sometimes dominate or frequently co-determine the outcomes in a variable manner. But where demi-regs are observed there is evidence of relatively enduring and identifiable tendencies in play.

Now, a realisation that such demi-regs do occur, and the suggestion that they are even pervasive, may, on the face of things at least, seem rather remarkable. After all we have observed that the social world is perpetually changing, being continually transformed. Even supposing that certain structures and mechanisms of interest are often reproduced over significant regions of time–space and that countervailing mechanisms are such that the primary mechanism often dominates and/or shines through them, the numerous background factors which constitute the social and natural environment nevertheless remain in play. In natural experiments any mechanism that is empirically identified is only isolated, or better insulated, in a relative sense; there are an uncountable number of factors held constant or controlled. How, then, can there be a pervasion of demi-laws or demi-regs in the intrinsically dynamic and open social world which lacks the possibility of experimental control?

Explaining the preponderance of demi-regs

To understand how demi-regs, as interpreted here, nevertheless are widely in evidence it is insightful to consider still further the typical conditions of experimental control. Not all experiments aim to hold background conditions constant. Such constancy seems essential if repeated trials are to be carried out. But, if this situation has no obvious parallel in social science, it is often, and perhaps usually, impossible in natural science too. Rather, experimental control frequently takes the form of comparing two different groups or populations with common or similar histories and shared (if non-constant) conditions, excepting that one group is 'treated' in some definite way that the second *control* group is not. Alternatively put, such experiments consist in observing two (or more) groups of 'participants' experiencing broadly similar conditions excepting (at least) one factor which is varied over the two groups in a controlled way.

Experiments in plant breeding provide obvious examples. Often two sets of plants of the same type are grown in identical conditions except for (at least) one factor, perhaps a new fertiliser, which is varied over the two sets. Or, more typically, when various (similar but non-uniform) background factors such as soil composition and light are not directly controllable, it may be possible to divide the relevant land into a set of plots and then attempt to assign certain quantities of fertiliser to the various plots in a random way, with some plots receiving no fertiliser at all. Under such conditions the difference between the mean yield of the unfertilised plots is contrasted with that of fertilised plots to see if there is a systematic and significant difference, which can be attributed to the fertiliser.

To repeat, a significant aspect of the experimental process is the existence of both a primary group and a second control group that acts as a foil. The aim is to link specific effects to a particular causal factor by having it operate in one of the two sets of situations but not the other. And it is such a relationship between aspects of a primary group and those of a relevant contrast group which appears to explain the experience, nature and significance of most *social* demi-regs. That is, most social demi-regs capture reasonably systematic differences (or more generally patterns) at the level of actual outcomes between two groups whose causal histories are such that the outcomes in question might reasonably have been expected to be broadly the same, or at least to stand in some definite anticipated or plausible relationship which is systematically at odds with what we observe. We do not and could not explain the complete causal conditions of any social or other phenomenon. To do so would presumably mean accounting for everything back to the 'big bang' and beyond. Rather we aim to identify single sets of causal mechanisms and structures. And these are indicated where outcomes or features of different groups are such that, given the respective causal histories and conditions of these groups, their observed relation is other than might have been expected or at least imagined as a real possibility.

Let me refer to empirical facts about relationships (typically differences) of this sort as *contrastives*. Although it is possible to argue that most explanation is concerned with such contrastives,[2] not all contrastives necessarily rest upon the operation of *enduring* causes. (Thus, the immediate reason why Heather went through the door before Hannah is that Hannah paused to pick up some object she dropped on approaching it.) To the extent, then, that science is concerned to identify and understand relatively enduring structures and mechanisms, the starting point will often be contrastives with at least some significant degree of space–time extension. Given that few scientifically interesting empirical contrasts involving social phenomena are likely to hold strictly or uniformly, the aim is to uncover those that at least hold to an extent that an enduring mechanism seems the likely explanation of the contrast involved. In short, the initiation of much social scientific research will inevitably depend upon the detection of *contrastive social demi-regs.*

Contrastive demi-regs

The world might have been such that partial regularities of interest were never, or perhaps only rarely, in evidence. In fact, it is clear that in the social sphere, as elsewhere, contrastive demi-regs are pervasive at all levels. For example: 'women look after children more often than men do'; 'a relatively small proportion of children from poor backgrounds in the UK continue into higher education'; 'average unemployment rates in western industrial countries are higher in the 1990s than the 1960s'; 'in the 1990s UK firms are externalising or "putting out" more parts of the production process than twenty years ago'; 'in the late nineteenth century UK firms increasingly internalised parts of the production process'; 'an increasing proportion of the world's population lives in cities'; 'women in the UK usually wear brighter colours, use more makeup, but go alone to the pub less often than men do'; 'the proportion of the UK public that reveals an intention to vote for the Conservative Party increases in run-ups to general elections'; 'government spokespersons tell more lies in war-time'; 'reported crime in the UK has increased steadily since the 1970s' ; 'Cubans currently spend more time in queues than the English, who in turn spend more time in queues than Italians'; and so on. Or, at a general level, the persistence of inflationary trends in certain economies but not others, of significant variations in rates of growth or decline of area-specific manufacturing sectors, of poverty in the midst of plenty, of production primarily for exchange rather than, as previously, for immediate use, provide examples of notable space–time patterns in economic phenomena. In each such case there is not an invariable relation but repetition of such a nature, or to such a degree, that an explanation seems required all the same. In each such case it is to be expected, or anyway is *prima facie* plausible, that there are systematic and identifiable mechanisms in play which social science can uncover.

The point I want to draw out here is that these partial regularities or contrastive demi-regs facilitate social science properly conceived, even if they are inadequate to the (misguided) objectives and needs of orthodox economists. Let me develop each part of this assessment in turn.

Contrastive demi-regs and science

The most obvious role for observable rough patterns or demi-regs is that they can serve to *direct* social scientific investigations, through providing evidence that, and where, certain relatively enduring and potentially identifiable mechanisms have been in play. And by their nature, by the fact that they are patterned at all, they reveal something in turn of the nature of the tendency in play. Notice that this role for contrastive demi-regs in the initiation or directing of research is the same in social and natural (including experimental) sciences alike. Thus, the natural sciences often take their leave from signs of some recurring animal or plant disorder, evidence of environmental deterioration, unanticipated 'side-effects' of some important experiment, and so on. In both social and natural sciences researchers can and do start from empirical facts that do not invariably hold, yet hold in a sufficiently large number of cases that an explanation appears to be required.

Of course, a recognition of the role of broad but less than strict regularities in the initiation of scientific investigation is hardly novel, even in economics. Kaldor, for example, explicitly argues the need to initiate explanatory research in this way. In detailing certain 'stylised facts' Kaldor remarks that

> we do not imply that any of these 'facts' are invariably true in every conceivable instance but that they are true in the broad majority of observed cases – in a sufficient number of cases to call for an explanation that would account for them.
>
> (Kaldor, 1985: 9)

I should add that although previously I have adopted the terminology of *stylised facts* myself, I now consider this to be strategically unwise. For I take it that usage of the term *stylised* in this context means[3] something like 'to cause to conform to a style of expression often extreme in character rather than the appearance of nature' (*Webster's Third New International Dictionary*). In other words, a supposed 'stylised fact' is intended to express a partial regularity reformulated as a strict one, in the form of a law. Kaldor, of course, saw this as a matter of mere presentation as we have seen, and always emphasised the role of such 'facts' as suggestive of a phenomenon in need of an explanation. Increasingly, however, we can see mainstream deductivist modellers attempting to legitimise their 'whenever this then that' formalisations as stylised facts interpreted as Kaldorian. In other words, the terminology, or rather its lineage, is being used to attempt to justify some fictitious set of idealisations, with the aim, in turn, of facilitating nothing more than model tractability, or some such. It is in order to avoid further encouraging this trend that I have preferred the terminology of demi-regs. It serves as a continual reminder that most empirical facts do not take the form of strict regularities, that they express phenomena to be explained, not the end-points of research or mere devices to be built into formal systems.

The detection of interesting demi-regs

It is easy enough to see how demi-regs may be identified. I have already indicated that the important category here is that of contrast or comparison and especially difference. The significance of patterns collected under the heading of demi-regs usually turns upon comparisons, and in particular upon differences: between men and women; or old and young; events or states of affairs (rates of unemployment, inflation or profits, etc.) in the UK today compared with twenty (or a hundred) years ago, or in modern Britain compared say with the continent of Europe; and so forth. In other words, we notice the effects of sets of structures through detecting relatively systematic differences in the outcomes of *prima facie* comparable types of activities (or perhaps similar outcomes of *prima facie* different activities) in different space–time locations, or differences in types of position-related activities in comparable space–time locations, and so forth.

Moments of social upheavals, crises and disruption may be especially revealing in this respect. Bhaskar (1979) explicitly remarks that moments of social transformation 'provide a partial analogue to the role played by experimentation in natural science' (p. 48). I think they do. But such moments should be recognised as particular, albeit highly significant, instances of the wide range of occasions where mechanisms or processes become visible. In the case of social upheavals the contrast is largely temporal. And, indeed, generative mechanisms become that much more accessible at any geohistorical turning point. But such situations provide insight into underlying tendencies in just the same manner as the contrasting positioned activities (and non-activities) of, say, men and women, or of immigrant or native, old and young, of people in different geographical regions or cultural contexts. In the social realm such contrastives all tend to indicate something of the positioned structures that people are acting on.

In short, any patterning, any 'standing-out', of phenomena which turns upon differences or unanticipated or surprising or implausible relationships of some kind, whether primarily social, historical or geographical, can serve to alert us to the existence or way of acting of some item previously unknown, unrecognized or perhaps known only implicitly, in some taken for granted way.

Science and scientific interests

Let me briefly make explicit certain implications of this conception. I am suggesting that scientific explanation is inherently contrastive. We have seen that in accounting for some social phenomenon the aim could not be to provide its complete causal history. Rather, we can only aim to identify one (set of) causal mechanism(s). And to this end the obvious strategy is to seek out two (or more) situations where the outcomes might have been expected to be related in some manner other than turns out to be the case, and to attempt to determine the reason(s). Typically, this will involve identifying at least one mechanism that operates, or does so in a particular fashion, in the one (set of) situation(s) only.

In consequence, we can now see even more clearly than hitherto that explanatory projects are inherently dependent on the interests of those involved. For it is now evident that the interests of the investigator influence not only the choice of phenomenon to be explained, but also, by selecting the contrast, the *particular* explanatory mechanism to be researched. For example, suppose that the primary phenomenon that we wish to explain is the average reported level of a certain crime in the UK in the mid-1990s. Then it is clear that the explanation provided, the causal factor identified, will vary according to whether the contrast, reflecting our interests, is, for example,

1 the situation that prevailed in the UK twenty years previously when the corresponding figure was significantly lower;
2 the current situation today in country x, say the US, where the corresponding figure is perceived to be significantly higher; or even
3 a desired situation of zero reported crime.

In each case, an explanation considered to be satisfactory will identify at least one systematic difference between the causal history of the primary component and that of the chosen contrast, or which would appear to be essential for the contrast if, like zero crime, it is only an imagined situation. In each case, the set of causal factors responsible is likely to be different.

Now for an explanation to be warranted it does appear that any contrast that is only imagined must be recognised as at least a real possibility (or perhaps once having been a real possibility). Perhaps few people living in modern western conditions conceive zero reported crime to be even remotely achievable. To the extent then that zero crime appears compatible with our species-being but unimaginable in practice, any explanation of the existence of crime presumably turns upon why or how certain types of societies or human relationships arose, and are reproduced, rather than others. But if this situation seems all too speculative it is easy enough to observe all sorts of quite plausible alternatives to the events and states of affairs, including persistent ones, that have actually come about. The aim then is to identify a causal factor (including perhaps an absence) which contributed to the state of affairs actually pertaining, but which would not have facilitated the imagined or expected, or did not condition an actual, alternative. Whatever else may be characteristic of the positioned social practice which is science, it is highly interest-dependent.

Inconsistency, surprise and criticism

I turn at this point to a rather significant feature of the approach I am developing, one that has been implicit throughout this chapter and is bound up with the interest-dependent nature of all scientific practice, but which, mainly for ease of exposition, I have yet to elaborate upon explicitly. I refer to the fact that enquiry will usually be initiated not just by any partial regularities and/or contrasts, but those that, along with other beliefs, occasion certain contradictions, inconsistencies, experiences of surprise and ultimately doubt. I have indicated that contrastive social demi-regs are easy enough to come by. Often, though, they will be quite uninteresting in the sense of generating little surprise from the point of current understandings.

For example, in the UK today 'on average more people go to church on a Sunday than on Tuesday'; and 'people with smaller incomes on average spend less than those with larger incomes'. While these observations, like all beliefs, are fallible, they seem unlikely to conflict with the current standpoints, and in particular the deeply held beliefs or theories, of social scientists or indeed people in general. That is, not only are these observations unlikely to pose problems of theory doubt for any individual but equally they appear unlikely to condition significantly different, competing explanations, a situation which would itself be a stimulus to further enquiry.[4] In contrast, reported observations that 'productivity growth in the UK has usually been slower than that of other major industrial countries'; or that 'children in single sex schools in the UK perform significantly better academically than children in mixed schools', have occasioned surprise in many and been met with an array of competing explanations. Consider also the attention recently given in economics (David, 1985, 1986) to studying and explaining the widespread employment of computer keyboards where the top row spells QWERTYUIOP (an example discussed further in Chapter 18). Presumably, if the letter arrangement had been something like ABCDEFGHIJ then we would not so readily identify it as something in particular need of being explained, at least in areas where the Roman alphabet is dominant. In short, theoretical explanatory enquiry is likely to be initiated or further stimulated where contrastive demi-regs occasion a sense of surprise, doubt or inconsistency, either between the observed phenomenon and a set of prior beliefs, or between competing explanations of it, and so forth.[5]

This part of my argument should not itself occasion any surprise. For an emphasis on the sort of inconsistencies in question has not only been implicit throughout this chapter but explicit throughout the book. The opening chapters were oriented to elaborating and resolving various theory/practice inconsistencies that pervade the subject; in Chapter 5 it was argued that the central role for philosophy is immanent critique (exposing internal inconsistencies in beliefs implicit in practices, or demonstrating how beliefs held cannot accommodate practices actually achieved); and in the same chapter we saw a specific form of immanent critique, namely determinate negation, wherein only a transcendental realist conception is capable of sustaining certain practices which competing philosophies of science sponsor. Science is like philosophy, then, in that both are stimulated by puzzles, contradictions and inconsistencies. And science is also like philosophy in that both are concerned fundamentally with transforming, including negating aspects of, some set of beliefs. In brief, according to the account which I am arguing for, science, like philosophy, is inherently critical. There are various reasons for the *critical* in 'critical realism'.

Causal hypotheses

The detection of contrastive social demi-regs of interest, then, can be used to initiate the investigation of causal factors. And the objective can be recognised as determining one or more factors directly responsible for any contrastive demi-reg identified, to identify factors that were operative in one set of conditions but not the other that helped produce or facilitate the contrast in question. But is there anything to be said about the process of reasoning by which causal hypotheses are obtained? We saw in Part I that the central mode of inference is neither deduction or induction. Rather it is retroduction. The aim is not to cover a phenomenon under a generalisation (this metal expands when heated because all metals do) but to identify a factor responsible for it, that helped produce, or at least facilitated, it. The goal is to posit a mechanism (typically at a different level to the phenomenon being explained) which, if it existed and acted in the postulated manner, could account for the phenomenon singled out for explanation. Not much can be said about this process of retroduction independent of context other than it is likely to operate under a logic of analogy or metaphor and to draw heavily on the investigator's perspective, beliefs and experience.

Notice, parenthetically, that this process of retroducing explanations of contrastive demi-regs is once more as significant in philosophy as in science. Bhaskar's observation that outside astronomy most event regularities of interest in science are brought about in conditions of experimental control is itself a contrastive demi-reg. It is this contrastive demi-reg which conditions Bhaskar's transcendental arguments for a structured ontology. Thus, just as substantive contrastive demi-regs as well as any experimentally confined specific regularities serve as bases for retroductive inferences to hypotheses about particular causal mechanisms, so the contrastive demi-reg of experimentally confined regularities serves as the basis for a transcendental argument to transcendental realism. Particular differentiations of the world to hypotheses about specific mechanisms; generalised differentiations to philosophical ontologies. Transcendental reasoning is thus but a special case of the retroduction.

Explanatory power

If an obvious role for contrastive demi-regs in economics, one which they also fulfil in the experimental sciences, lies in the directing of investigative research, a second role is as an aid in assessing causal hypotheses once they have been formulated. We have seen that economics and the social sciences generally are denied the crucial test situation. However, the consequences of this *for the process of theory assessment* is merely that event-predictive accuracy cannot be the criterion of theory selection. Rather the appropriate criterion outside of the controlled-experimental (or any fortuitously spontaneously closed) situation must be *explanatory power*. Theories can be assessed according to their abilities to illuminate a *wide range* of empirical phenomena. And typically this will entail accommodating precisely such contrastive demi-regs as are recorded or can be found.

Several aspects to the process of assessing a theory's explanatory power can be anticipated. The first relies on deduction. The point is to deduce from any retroduced hypotheses those consequences or effects which would follow if the hypothesis were true and the mechanism operative. The second involves checking out the various deduced consequences empirically. With a permanent possibility of countervailing factors there can be no guarantee that any such effects will be straightforwardly manifest. But the aim must be to try and identify conditions where, in the light of all that is known about the situation, the effects ought in some way to be in evidence. A third aspect to the process involves explaining the explanation. It includes identifying the conditions of any explanatory mechanism and checking they are or were operative. Let me expand upon these themes.

The possibility of empirically assessing theories in the absence of crucial test conditions is perhaps clearest in the (most common) situation where the objective is to select amongst two or more hypotheses. For in this case we are ultimately interested in the *relative* performance of hypotheses whatever the relevant selection criteria. It is thus straightforwardly reasonable to search out that theory whose consequences appear mostly born out and which illuminates the widest range of empirical phenomena including any intersection upon which all competing theories have some possible bearing. Relative explanatory power is likely to be sufficient as well as appropriate here.

Of course, whether or not the explanatory power of a theory is easily assessed necessarily depends on context. Ultimately assessments of the empirical adequacy of hypotheses always do.[6] Consider an example formulated by

Leamer (1983). Econometricians, according to Leamer, like to project themselves in the image of agricultural experimenters who, in a manner similar to that already attributed to plant breeders above, subdivide farm land into a set of plots and then assign random quantities of fertiliser to each plot, with some plots receiving no fertiliser at all. We have already noted that under these conditions it may be supposed that the difference between the mean yield of the fertilised plots and the mean yield of the unfertilised plots is a measure of the effect of fertiliser on agricultural yields. The task of the agricultural experimenter is to determine whether the difference, assuming it is positive, is large enough to suggest a real effect of the fertiliser (or so small that it could plausibly be attributed to random fluctuations).

Against this preferred scenario, one approximating the situation referred to as a stochastic closure in Chapter 7, Leamer's assessment is that the econometrician's predicament is rather different:

> This image of the applied econometrician's art is grossly misleading. I would like to suggest a more accurate one. The applied econometrician is like a farmer who notices that the yield is somewhat higher under the trees where birds roost, and he uses this as evidence that bird droppings increase yield. However, when he presents this finding at the annual meeting of the American Ecological Association, another farmer in the audience objects that he used the same data but came up with the conclusion that moderate amounts of shade increase yields. A bright chap in the back of the room then observes that these two hypotheses are indistinguishable, given the available data. He mentions the phrase 'identification problem,' which, though no one knows quite what he means, is said with such authority that it is totally convincing.
>
> (Leamer, 1983: 31)

Notice first how the imagined investigation is initiated by an observed, contrastive demi-reg of interest. Yields are higher under trees than elsewhere. The problem is that two competing explanatory conjectures both seem consistent with the evidence. The obvious response of course, albeit one that econometricians occupied with fitting a line to *given* sets of data rarely contemplate, is to add to the 'available data'. Specifically the aim must be to draw consequences for, and seek out observations on, actual phenomena which allow the causal factor responsible to be identified. If, for example, bird droppings is a relevant causal factor then we could expect higher yields wherever birds roost. Perhaps there is a telegraph wire that crosses the field which is heavily populated by roosting birds, but which provides only negligible shade in comparison (and shade which moves significantly as the earth revolves around the sun). Perhaps too there is a plot of land somewhere close to the farm house which is shaded by a protruding iron roof, but which birds avoid because of a patrolling cat. And so on. It all depends. The fact that it is not possible to state categorically at this abstract level the precise conditions under which substantive theories can be selected amongst, i.e. without knowing the contents of the theories themselves or the nature or context of the conditions upon which they bear, is an unfortunate fact of all science. Science is a messy business. It requires an abundance of ingenuity, as well as patience, along with skills that may need to be developed on the job.[7]

Problems in discriminating between theories

It must be admitted that there will be occasions when, even with a range of types of data, it still proves difficult to discriminate between competing hypotheses. But this is the experience of all the sciences. The strategy in such circumstances can only be to continue to search out conditions for which the competing hypotheses bear different implications with regard to empirical phenomena and then to check out which hypothesis proves to be the most empirically adequate in those conditions. Any such difficulties of discrimination do not imply problems for the philosophy of science perspective I am defending, of course, they merely indicate situations in which there are practical difficulties in science. If two or more hypotheses do really appear to command the same degree of empirical adequacy then, *ceteris paribus*, the correct epistemic attitude,[8] whatever the science, must be to attach the same degree of belief to each, or to suspend judgement.

Notice that the possibility of difficulties in discriminating between theories does not turn upon whether or not the hypothesised causal mechanism is observable or otherwise. Although Boylan and O'Gorman (1995) invoke Quine's under-determination thesis to suggest that there may be a multiplicity of empirically (or 'descriptively') adequate theories and explanations in terms of non-observable items, there is no reason to suppose that this applies any less (or more) to hypotheses concerning observables-in-principle.[9] Is the perpetrator of the crime always the only suspect to fit the available empirical facts, and is the guilty person always the one convicted? Perhaps Leamer's agricultural econometrician does not after all find a mid-field telegraph wire or a protruding farm house roof, while other data-consistent hypotheses come to mind: the concentration of nutritious leaf-mould near the trees, the wind-break or partial rain (or air-borne pollution) shelter provided by the trees, the proximity of the trees to a previously unconsidered brook, and so on.

More to the point, if to elaborate upon the argument of the last chapter, unobservable natural forces as well as structures of a language or rules of a game can be, and frequently are, described and known. Thus, while the unobservable wind can be known to be responsible for the flying hat or the swirling leaves, the rules of grammar facilitating the speech acts of some group, or the secret code used by children to send messages to each other, may each be quite unproblematically retroducible and/or describable. By demonstrating the empirical adequacy of theories of gravitational and magnetic fields, social rules and relations, structures of languages and so forth, these items can be known whether or not they can be directly observed.

I have been discussing a situation of competing hypotheses. But it is not just in the comparing of hypotheses that demi-regs can be used in the manner described. Even a single maintained hypothesis can be continually assessed by examining the range of phenomena it bears upon. In other words, the empirical adequacy of any hypothesis can be progressively checked-out by deducing such implications as follow, with regard to any domain for which such implications hold and can in practice be 'observed'. Where it is argued, for example, that gender relations in many societies are such that mechanisms are reproduced which serve to discriminate against women in favour of men, this assessment can be checked out against detectable patterns occurring in, for example, factories, homes, schools and universities, and any other place where the mechanism will conceivably reveal its effects.

Responses to explanatory failure

Needless to say, there can be no expectation that each stage of the proceedings will always be clear cut, even in those cases where the evidence available appears not to support a hypothesis in contention. For example, if definite mechanisms are hypothesised to be operative in certain situations where their anticipated effects do not at first sight appear to be in evidence, this outcome may warrant examining further, where possible. For, if there is reason to suppose that in such conditions a specific mechanism is nevertheless operating transfactually, it should be possible to identify offsetting countervailing factors. If, to continue the last example, it is thought that mechanisms which work to discriminate against women operate throughout the economy, yet it is discovered that in a particular factory women do not predominate in the positions regarded as secondary, further investigation may reveal that this is because the least desired jobs are given to (possibly illegal) immigrants, most of whom happen to be male, or to some other locally discriminated against group, and so forth. One obvious response to such a finding, then, is to examine situations where any such suspected countervailing tendencies are unlikely to be in operation.

Of course, this practice of examining whether (perhaps the most notable) exceptions to patterns can be explained in terms of countervailing mechanisms is not confined to social science. Recall, for example, the way in which Neptune was discovered. On recording observations of the motion of the planet Uranus, nineteenth-century scientists found that its orbit did not conform to predictions derived using Newton's theory of gravity. Instead of rejecting that theory, however, they looked for countervailing factors which could account for the noted discrepancies. Specifically, Adams in England

and Leverrier in France conjectured the existence of a previously unknown planet somewhere in the vicinity of Uranus. In response Galle turned to focus his telescope on the appropriate region of the skies and came to discover the planet we now know as Neptune. In natural and social science alike, then, exceptions to an observed pattern do not necessitate an automatic rejection of a given theory. Rather they constitute specific contrastive demi-regs which mark sites where further investigative work can fruitfully be undertaken. The ultimate outcome necessarily depends on context.

Assessing the reality of a hypothesised mechanism

A further component of the process of assessing the explanatory power of some hypothesis is checking the reality of any mechanism postulated. This may involve checking the 'triggering' conditions (if there are any) to see if the mechanism is in play. It is not enough to know that a suspect had the motive and know-how for a particular crime if he or she could not have been at the relevant scene when the crime took place. It is not good enough to argue, like Friedman (1953), that the hypothesis of mobile leaves moving about the branches of the tree searching out the light, explains the distribution of leaves on the tree, when we know the hypothesis of mobile leaves to be false. It is not good enough because, unlike Friedman, we have accepted (through argument and evidence) that the explanatory goal is to identify mechanisms, etc., really productive of any identified phenomenon of interest. Thus any hypothesis couched in terms of some mechanism known *not* to exist or to be in play cannot be said to be explanatory in the requisite sense at all. It is for this reason that the assessing of the reality of some hypothesised mechanism can be subsumed under the head of assessing that hypothesis's explanatory power.

In the social realm, however, if structures and mechanisms endure over stretches of time–space it can only be by way of human action. If then we wish to explain some *relatively enduring* contrastive demi-reg, a full understanding of the situation requires that the mode of reproduction of the identified causal mechanism be itself investigated. In other words, it is necessary that the conditions governing the reproduction (and perhaps 'initial' emergence) of any identified causal mechanisms be accounted for, that the explanation be explained. Again this may entail the explaining of a contrast: why and how certain structures or mechanisms have emerged and been continuously reproduced in one situation but not another.

When an explanation of an explanation is successfully achieved, of course, we are likely to have greater confidence in each part of the overall explanation of the original phenomena. Moreover, conceptions of the practices which led to research being undertaken in the first place may themselves require reinterpretation once an overall understanding is achieved, i.e. in the light of the broader explanatory picture. Needless to say, there will often be competing explanations of the original explanation; there may be several accounts of why or how certain mechanisms have (or have not) emerged, and, where they have, why they have been reproduced and/or transformed in particular ways. Where this is so the criterion of theory assessment, once more, can only be relative explanatory power in the sense described above.

Notice, finally, that the process of economic explanation here *is* aided by the fact that many of the relevant social phenomena in any situation are already conceptualised under some description by the agents involved. In addition, the set of activities being explained may already have been redescribed by observers and/or other interpreters. The realisation that this feature does not represent a 'compensator' for the infeasibility of experimental control does not thereby undermine its *generalised* value to science.

The requirements of orthodox economics

If contrastive demi-regs, as conceived above, are seen to be fundamental to social science properly interpreted and facilitative of likely successes, it is easy enough to see that they are nevertheless inadequate to the (misconceived) requirements of mainstream economics. The term demi-regs, we can recall, is used here to denote patterns or regularities of sorts, regularities that are recognisable as such despite being something rather less than strict.[10] Now we have seen that there are essentially two sets of reasons why a recognisable patterning of events will usually not be strict, both of which were discussed at length in Chapters 7 and 8 in connection with the theses of regularity stochasticism and regularity determinism. First, the environment in which any mechanism acts need not be sufficiently homogeneous. In the social realm, indeed, there will usually be a potentially very large number of countervailing factors acting at any one time and/or sporadically over time,[11] and possibly each with varying strength.[12] This means not only that where mechanisms 'shine through' they are unlikely to do so in a continuous, unimpeded, clear-cut fashion, but equally that operative mechanisms need not always 'shine through' in any recognisable manner at all. The implication of the latter situation, as we have also previously noted, is that the usual starting point for research into the nature of social mechanisms will invariably be conditions where the effect of mechanisms have in some way *already* been detected. We start from situations where, fortuitously, relatively stable tendencies are revealed. In this sense social scientific explanation is inherently backward looking.

The second reason for the absence of strict regularities is that the mechanisms or processes which are being identified are themselves likely to be unstable to a degree over time and space. I see no *a priori* reason to suppose that any relatively enduring, transfactually acting, social mechanism need be particularly constant in the way it operates over time and space; nor am I aware of any evidence which indicates that any are. Indeed, given the fact of the dependence of social mechanisms upon inherently transformative human agency, where human beings *choose* their courses of action (and so could always have acted otherwise), strict constancy seems a quite unlikely eventuality. Just as there is always some continuity in social change, so there is usually some (and often quite substantial) change in social continuity.

In short, if it is a special situation of the open world that certain mechanisms (whether natural or social) reveal themselves in rough and ready patterns, it is as a *special case of this special situation* that the patterns produced correspond to strict event regularities, including any consistent with well-defined probability 'laws'. The latter can really be expected only where (a set of) intrinsically constant and separable causal factors act in (relative) isolation. While such special cases of special cases are obviously of value to science where they occur or are feasible, it can now be seen that they are not essential to it if (non-spurious) demi-regs are in evidence.

But if strict event regularities are inessential to science in its endeavour to uncover causal mechanisms and to discriminate between competing hypotheses, they are essential to the requirements of orthodox economics. That is, they are essential to the preoccupation with predicting future states of the economy and/or to any hoped for deductivist 'explanation' of economic actualities, including events and states of affairs. In other words, mainstream economics models itself on, or aims to achieve, the one set of natural science possibilities which is not available to it. Lacking the opportunities for controlled experimentation yet mistakenly supposing the strict event regularities which are sought after in such set-ups to be essential to the scientific enterprise, orthodox economists react by assuming that social phenomena are after all but the results of an experiment, one that just happens to be well-controlled by 'Nature', or at least that can usefully be treated as such (see e.g. Haavelmo, 1944: 9, 14). Armed with this conception of social reality and with deductivist (predictive) goals and criteria, mainstream economists, and perhaps this group alone, conclude that such patterns as can be detected at the level of actual phenomena are never strict enough, with the result that such contrastive demi-regs as abound have far too little (or the wrong sort of) influence upon the theories that economists hold.

Pure and applied explanation

Now if contrastive demi-regs abound they too nevertheless constitute a special case of a more general situation. It is to be expected that many aspects of social events are relatively unique occurrences, being the conjoint effects of numerous mechanisms acting simultaneously. In other words, there is a possibility, already noted, of a continuum of pattern outcomes stretching from closed systems of constant conjunctions of events to an inchoate random flux, with contrastive demi-regs lying between these extremes. In consequence, the question arises as to whether it is possible to explain the *range* of pattern outcomes. For it will often be of interest to understand quite novel or unusual social phenomena, whether spectacular ones such as stock market crashes or major increases in OPEC prices, or less dramatic ones such as the demise of local markets or large changes in local prices.

In order to account for the range of actual phenomena it is necessary that economic explanation be divided into two relatively distinct movements or separate modes of activity. In fact, most of the discussion so far has implicitly concerned a mode of inference that should really be termed *pure* or *abstract* or *theoretical* explanation, the identification of underlying structures, powers, mechanisms and their tendencies. A necessary condition for this explanatory activity is that certain relatively stable and enduring mechanisms *do* at some time and place come to be reproduced, to endure, and do to some extent dominate, or shine through, others – at least to a degree that rough or partial event regularities of sorts are discernible. However, it is equally apparent that a second mode or type of inference, which is appropriately termed an *applied* or *concrete* or *practical* explanation, is also called for. For, to the extent that (relevant features of) concrete phenomena of experience are relatively unique or novel, being conjunctures of numerous countervailing tendencies, their explanation entails *drawing upon antecedently established knowledge* of relatively enduring structures and mechanisms (rather than revealing them), and investigating the manner of their joint articulation in the production of the novel event in question.[13]

Again this is a situation that holds just as much in natural science. Seismologists know the mechanism by which earthquakes are produced but can only explain particular manifestations after the event. Similarly, meteorologists do not always forecast the weather very well, yet after the event they convincingly draw on their (well grounded) knowledge of relevant physical principles to explain whatever took place.

For sake of clarity let me briefly contrast the modes of reasoning employed in theoretical and applied explanation. Clearly *neither* of the identified modes of explanation is primarily deductive or inductive in form. Rather, in each case the aim is to redescribe some phenomenon under a new scheme of concepts designating the structures, mechanisms or agents that are to some degree responsible for it. Theoretical explanations, we have seen, are characteristically *analogical* (scientists first searched, albeit unsuccessfully, for a virus responsible for 'mad cow disease' because viruses have so frequently been found to be responsible for disorders in animals previously) and *retroductive* (positing mechanisms which, if they were to exist and act in the postulated matter, would account for phenomena singled out for explanation). In short, theoretical explanations entail transforming existing cognitive resources into plausible theories of the mechanisms responsible for identified (typically less than strict) patterns of phenomena. These theories are then empirically assessed, of course, and, when found to be empirically adequate, themselves explained in turn, in the continuous unfolding of explanatory knowledge.

Applied explanations, in contrast, are characteristically *resolutive* and *retrodictive*. They entail, first of all, the resolution of conjunctions or complexes, and the redescription of their components. This is followed by the determination (retrodiction) of possible antecedents of these components, and the empirical elimination of possible causes. For example, if we attribute weather pattern x to a particular combination of (already understood) causal mechanisms y, it is necessary to determine (retrodict) the conditions for y and then to check empirically whether these conditions actually obtained.

Economics as an empirical and abstract science

If it is by now clear that the explanatory project that I am arguing for is contrastive, interest laden and critical, it should also be apparent that it necessarily contains a significant empirical component. The measuring and recording of states of affairs, the collection, tabulation, transformation and graphing of statistics about the economy, all have an essential (if usually non-straightforward) role to play. So do detailed case studies, oral reporting, including interviews, biographies, and so on. Indeed, I suggest it is precisely to such indispensable activities that the heading of *econometrics* is properly attributed.

It is the case, furthermore, that the detection of non-spurious patterns will often require a good deal of more specialised, perhaps rather technical, knowledge and understanding of relevant situations. This is likely to be so whether the contrastive demi-regs are of the more mundane sort: 'sportsperson x has not been performing well for the last n games', or of a more unfamiliar and complicated variety: 'the usual rough correspondence between the type of product market in which a firm operates and the employee conditions it sustains (itself a demi-reg) has been systematically contravened over the last n years by the conditions obtaining in firm x'.[14] Certainly, the ability to observe or detect patterns will necessitate looking at situations not only in the light of current understandings but also from different angles, at varying levels of generality, under varying space–time extensions, and so forth.

Once more, the need to discern or detect patterns which may not be immediately obvious is a requirement that does not fall on social science alone. Currently, for example, symmetry principles play a prominent role in the development of elementary particle physics principally because they have been found to reveal patterns in the properties of *prima facie* quite distinct particles. Once these patterns are observed it frequently proves possible to explain them in terms of, i.e. to identify, the underlying forces (see e.g. Green, 1988). A further, and well known, example of the use of symmetry patterns in natural science is provided by nineteenth-century chemistry, with

Mendeleyev's discovery that the chemical elements could be arranged into groups with certain properties in common, i.e. with his elaboration of the periodic table. This led to an understanding of how elements are made of atoms and how, in consequence, many dozens of elements could be grouped in the suggested manner.

It is evident, then, that there is a need for attention to be given to the processes of elaborating any such patterns. Clearly, they involve looking at phenomena in a one-sided way, focusing on some attributes to the neglect of others. I have already rejected any isolationist strategy that treats definite features as though they exist cut off from everything else. Rather, the relevant procedure here is *abstraction*. The failure to consider this procedure in any explicit fashion so far is an omission I turn to rectify in Chapter 16. Abstraction, though, is an essential feature of all cognitive enterprise; it is no more fundamental to science than any other social practice. And if the need for abstraction is more apparent when we consider seemingly complex patterns such as noted above, I must emphasise that it is nevertheless inevitably employed in all acts of apprehension, no matter how apparently simple the item involved (see, especially, Whitehead, 1926). Within science it is also fundamental to all *aspects* of the endeavour, not merely to the description of patterns in actual phenomena. Even so, one specific and important task for it lies in the delineation of such rough and ready patterns as arise, conceptions which provide, amongst other things, a marker where science might with reason, and some expectation of achieving illumination, continue its work.

The apparent failures of social research including economics

Before considering such matters explicitly, however, there is one loose end to tidy up. There remains the question of what to make of Collier's observation of the prominence of the hermeneutic moment in the social sciences and his belief that this indicates their relative failure. Now it is essential to exercise care here in interpreting any claim that the social sciences have failed to emulate the successes of natural science. Of course the naive attempts of orthodox economists to extrapolate forced correlations and to 'explain' on the basis of the deductivist model, have contributed very little to understanding the world in which we live. Nevertheless, endeavours at elucidating the nature of aspects of society and economy on the part of others (and even by mainstream academic economists when forsaking their official postures) *may* have been more fruitful than is usually imagined.

On the one hand there is always the possibility, already noted, that insights obtained will have been appropriated by lay agents and incorporated into their activities. This can have the effect that knowledge which proved to be revelatory when it was obtained, eventually takes on the appearance of the banal or of common sense. On the other hand, there are various further considerations that are relevant here arising out of the situation that social structures and mechanisms seem usually to be more highly space–time specific than natural ones. A natural scientist working on gravitational fields or the molecular structure of copper may be confident that any illumination obtained will be as relevant in, say, contemporary Cambridge as in Beijing in a hundred years time (or a hundred years ago). But an economist examining the nature of industrial relations currently in place in a Cambridge firm may not even find them in place in a second Cambridge firm along the road let alone in Beijing in a hundred years time or one hundred years past. In short social scientific knowledge, when gained, will rarely have as wide a sphere, or scope, of relevance as natural scientific findings. But this, by itself, does not entail that the processes of social study are necessarily any less revelatory or scientific in nature, or less successful in illuminating their objects of study in fact.

Perhaps this latter assessment requires further elaboration. Bhaskar, in his original contribution on the matter even argues that any acceptable version of naturalism is qualified by the fact 'that social structures, unlike natural ones, may be only relatively enduring (so that the tendencies they ground may not be universal in the sense of space–time invariant)' (Bhaskar, 1979: 38). But this statement seems incorrect in its characterisation of the objects of natural science. Certainly any social tendency in play will be dependent upon certain social structures being in place. But the operations of any natural tendencies will be conditional upon natural structures in exactly the same way. Thus, just as any inherent tendency for (capitalist) profit rates to fall will depend upon capitalist structures (or other appropriate conditions) being sustained, so the disposition for, say, water to dissolve sugar will only be exercised where water exists. Both structures are currently present on planet Earth but (apparently) absent on planet Venus.

Now it does appear to be the case that *some* natural mechanisms do not depend upon their time–space location. Newton's laws, including the inverse square law of gravity, for example, are usually interpreted in this light; the same is true of electromagnetic laws and quantum mechanics. But even these examples can appear questionable once we turn to cosmology and explorations into the origins of the universe and the way in which it developed. From this perspective it seems at least feasible that such 'laws change absolutely with time; that gravity for instance varies with time and that this inverse square law has a strength which depends on how long it is since the beginning of time' (Feynman, 1988: 206). In truth, in a (1989) postscript to his original work Bhaskar acknowledges that the suggested ontological limit to naturalism 'only marks a necessary limit in relation to standard philosophy conceptions of physics and chemistry' (Bhaskar 1979 [1989]: 175). But a fundamental objective here, and most certainly of Bhaskar's own contributions, is precisely to criticise and transcend these standard, if influential, conceptions. It is such conceptions that account for the widespread but erroneous impression that practices can be scientific only if they are concerned to uncover unconditional universalities. This insistence requires correction just as much as does the belief that scientific results necessarily take the form of constant event conjunctions. Science, it must now be recognised, is concerned to identify and understand structures and their mechanisms which govern actual events, but which themselves are only relatively enduring.

To reiterate, the claim that the natural sciences are more successful than the social sciences requires careful interpretation. Certainly, some allowance must be made for the fact that the natural sciences, by and large (but not exclusively), concern themselves with improving their theories of a relative unchanging (or only slowly changing) reality while the social sciences concern themselves with understanding, and with continually improving their understanding, of a relatively fast changing, i.e. highly space–time specific, world. To the extent that certain strands of the natural sciences also concern themselves with a relatively fast changing reality, it is perhaps with the achievements of these strands that the successes of the social sciences can most easily be compared. In any case, any contrast drawn should be a considered one. I suspect, indeed, that when this is the case it will be found that social science has not fared quite so badly after all.

However that may be, it also follows that the faster nature, or greater space–time specificity, of social structures and mechanisms is itself sufficient for the hermeneutic moment to arise more frequently in social science. It is this, I think, which mainly explains Collier's observation that the hermeneutic moment is always so prominent in social science As structures and actions are continually transformed the social scientist will frequently need to re-investigate what is going on to keep abreast of the inherently non-predictable developments regularly taking place, including the transformations of human concepts. For this reason by itself the hermeneutic moment will usually be prominent in serious social research. But if this marks a distinguishing feature of social scientific practice, it no more follows by this token alone that social science is failing than it does that the possibility of naturalism is curtailed. (It does, though, mark a specificity of social science research that contemporary orthodox approaches rooted in positivistic injunctions appear to be totally unable to comprehend.)

Now despite all such considerations, in the end it cannot be denied that, for the last fifty years or so especially, it is difficult to identify any obvious successes (explanatorily powerful, revelatory, hypotheses) of mainstream academic economics, let alone find results that can be held up to the achievements of the sciences of nature. Why then has mainstream academic economics in particular fared so badly? The explanation is precisely the mechanism that this book is attempting to counteract. That is, contemporary academic economists, for whatever reason, and no doubt under the influence of certain spectacular results of the Enlightenment, continue to labour under the apprehension that all scientific work is, or necessitates, or relates to, seeking out constant event conjunctions, that the goal just is deductivist modelling.

In other words, I do not think that the failure of mainstream economics is a consequence of an unfathomable, overly complex and dynamic social reality, nor even of the infeasibility of meaningful experimental control. Rather, the continuing failure of the discipline must be put down to the often quite irrelevant, typically formalistic, methods and techniques which economists naively and unthinkingly wield in a forlorn hope of thereby gaining illumination of a social world that they do not 'fit'.

Of course, a failure to appreciate this, coupled with the corresponding persistent failure of the project to achieve any result of interest leads, in its turn, to the development of immunising strategies, ever increasing levels of technical complexity of models, the resort to computer simulations, and so forth. It leads, in short, to any response that is consistent with the misconceived, taken for granted, yet hardly fruitful, standard conception of science being sustained. The intention here is to indicate that all such efforts are likely to be beside the point, and how, despite everything, a successful social science of economics remains a viable option. For this latter possibility to be realised, however, it is essential that economists abandon their preconceived (and upon examination clearly untenable) positivist conceptions of the structure of science and focus instead upon fashioning their methods to available insights bearing upon the nature of social reality. Through doing so, though, economists may yet find themselves explaining social phenomena in just the sense that natural scientists in fact, and successfully, explain the various phenomena of nature.

ABSTRACTION

I have outlined broad objectives and modes of explanatory reasoning that are sponsored by the theory of social ontology sketched earlier. Although in so doing I have drawn some inferences about general procedures of enquiry that are often likely to be involved, there remains one procedure to which I have hardly referred explicitly, yet which is vital to any cognitive enterprise. I refer to the method or process of *abstraction*. Despite the limited explicit attention given to it in modern social theorising (including, curiously, the contributions of Bhaskar), abstraction is an indispensable method in science. Moreover, given the often found assertion that orthodox 'economic modelling' is itself based upon abstraction, it seems vital that I indicate why the procedure to which I refer does not at all reduce to the activities of the 'modelling' project in question.

I interpret abstraction according to its traditional meaning of focusing upon certain aspects of something to the (momentary) neglect of others. It is a process of focusing on some feature(s) of some thing(s) while others remain in the background. For example, in considering the ability of copper to conduct electricity well I may focus upon its atomic structure and thereby abstract from its colour, texture, malleability, and so on. It follows that there is always something which is abstracted *from*. Indeed, if this implication were always born in mind the mis-uses of the term that abound in mainstream economics (which we encounter below) might more frequently be avoided.

That which is abstracted from is the *concrete*. The point of abstraction is to individuate one or more aspects, components, or attributes and their relationships in order to understand them better. Once this has been achieved it may be possible to combine or synthesise the various separate understandings into a unity that reconstitutes, or provides a better understanding of, the concrete. Thus, a comprehension of the various properties or aspects of copper may reveal its suitability for a particular technological application. Ultimately, the concrete can be understood as a synthesis.[15]

Abstraction and critical realism

It follows that abstraction, as interpreted here, can be both appropriately and inappropriately applied. There is nothing intrinsic to the method that determines, independently of considerations of the (type of) concrete object(s) of study, or the required focus, etc. that an abstraction is necessarily relevant or insightful. In particular, this understanding of abstraction as taking a particular focus or emphasis immediately raises the question of the appropriate *vantage point*, the *level of generality*, the space–time *extension* or scope involved. That is, the boundary setting and bringing into focus that characterises the process of abstraction simultaneously achieves a specific vantage point, a level of generality and a definite extension to any analysis. And it is important to recognise that the appropriate choice of these parameters cannot be determined independently of other considerations.

Ultimately, the context of the analysis is crucial. Some things, though, can be said about the consequences which follow on acknowledging the critical realist perspective, despite its rather abstract nature. That is, it is possible to anticipate various definite and central tasks for abstraction associated with uncovering and understanding the powers, structures and tendencies that produce the actual course of events and states of affairs of the differentiated and open, natural and social worlds. In particular, abstraction will figure fundamentally both in the initial analysis of the phenomenon to be explained and in the attempt to illuminate the mechanisms that give rise to them. If some economic phenomenon of interest is a conjunction it can be resolved into its causal components, that is resolved into the different effects of various causal mechanisms. To focus upon one or a few such components is to abstract from the original phenomenon. The autumn leaf, for example, may be viewed under its aspect of moving to the ground, or under its aspect of 'fluttering' in the breeze, or even just in terms of its reddish colour. Economic structure too can be abstracted from by focusing upon certain powers or tendencies possessed amongst others. This is particularly clear if we focus upon particular capacities of the human individual.

These claims can be expanded upon if we examine briefly how the theory of ontology systematised under the head of critical realism bears specific implications for the various aspects of determining a focus just noted, i.e. in determining an abstraction's vantage point, level of generality, and scope (or extension).

The vantage point

The selection of any specific phenomenon for explanation will necessarily reflect the *vantage point* of the enquirer not only because any individual's material and other interests depend upon the relationships in which he or she stands to others, but also in virtue of the fact that the possibility for direct experience of any individual is always highly relative. The identification of the particular phenomenon to be explained always depends upon the position, perspective and understanding of the viewer involved.

Someone not trained in medical research, for example, may, on viewing an x-ray sheet, be absorbed in explaining the lighter and darker marks in terms of the human anatomy. A person with some medical training, in contrast, may immediately observe a mark or pattern that should not be there (in the sense that most people's x-rays do not manifest this phenomenon), and as a result ponder upon the explanation. But if, say, an experienced surgeon observes the same x-ray sheet and 'mark', he or she may immediately 'recognise' the unwanted agent and wonder how it came to reside in the patient in question. For each person, the contrast, the phenomenon to be explained, and so the object of explanation, is different.[16]

To take a more familiar example: a first year economics undergraduate examining the results of running a statistical estimation programme may be mystified by all the diagnostics shown and wonder what explains them, whereas an experienced econometrician will be able to tell at a glance whether a preferred equation has performed well according to various conventional criteria.

We have also seen that it is not merely the choice of phenomenon to be explained that reflects our knowledge, understandings, values and interests; in the end the latter bear upon the *particular* set of causal factors pursued as well. Of course, we could not explain the entire causal history of any phenomenon. I observed in the previous chapter that if the universe originated with the 'big bang' then this is presumably part of the causal history of any present day social phenomenon. Hence it is part of its explanation. At the same time, contemporary social life mostly depends on, and so is also in part explained by, the action of gravitational forces. Yet few social scientists make explicit reference to any such factors when offering an account of social phenomena. And we saw in Chapter 15 that the main reason why this does not matter is that explanation is made inherently contrastive. When we look to explain phenomenon x we essentially pose the question 'why x rather than y?'. The objective is not the elaboration of the complete causal history of some phenomenon but the identification of at least one significant difference between the latter's causal history and that of the chosen contrast. This feature of causal explanation seems particularly transparent in the social realm where the question of why some agency has performed differently from another frequently arises. And while it is the nature of the contrast that determines how far back or how far afield we must look to find a satisfactory explanation, the contrast chosen reflects our interests and understandings.

The level of generality

The first part of the preceding sentence is fundamental, of course. Certainly the interests of investigators and other concerned parties are significant in the determination of which causal factors, in the event, are pursued. Thus, for example, a feminist economics *is* likely to be distinctive in facilitating an orientation towards factors hitherto unappreciated in the (predominantly male) academy (see Chapter 19). But the interests of social scientists do not usually constitute or shape those factors. Causal mechanisms that are productive of actual phenomena exist at their own level of being, independently, for the most part, of any investigation.

It follows that if the choice and conception of the phenomenon to be explained as well as that of the contrast are always dependent upon the individual investigator or a specific community of researchers, the *level of generality* of abstractions appropriate to determining an adequate explanation (given the contrast) will depend upon the nature of the structures or mechanisms that are really responsible. In other words, abstraction must be put to work in identifying and comprehending that aspect, or set of aspects, of reality that is *essential* to the phenomenon (including the contrast) that we want to explain, rather than, say, in determining that aspect which is merely the most general.

If, for example, we want to account for the phenomenon that goods are now usually produced for *exchange* in the market place rather than for immediate or eventual *use* by their producers, our explanation is *un*likely to turn on characteristics peculiar to a specific firm. Indeed, production for exchange, i.e. commodity production, appears to be a characteristic feature of the system of capitalist production. In consequence, any meaningful analysis of the mechanisms and structures which condition this phenomenon will require abstractions at a high level of generality, and specifically at the level of features common to all forms of capitalist production. If, instead, the phenomenon to be explained is of the character that a specific firm's prices are, say, 50 per cent below those of its competitors, or that its productivity growth rate is twice as high, the explanatory focus will necessarily be at a significantly lower level of generality, upon distinctive features of the local employer–employee relations, and so on. Similarly, the level of abstraction required to understand the high concentration of women in secondary sectors of employment will inevitably be higher than that required to explain how, in 1979, Margaret Thatcher became the prime minister of Britain.

Now it is important to recognise that when an abstraction at a relatively low level of generality is made, any mechanisms already identified, or the features of reality brought into focus at a higher level of abstraction, cannot thereby be disregarded as inconsequential or otherwise irrelevant. Thus, any insight into mechanisms that are fundamental to capitalist production and which are identified at a high level of abstraction will, if correct, be just as relevant to analysis and understanding at the lower level of explaining more regionally and historically specific factors and contrasts. Indeed, it is precisely because the basic process of accumulation, competition, and so on, operates throughout the capitalist world that, typically, geo-historical peculiarities, or unevenness in development, are phenomena that are considered particularly interesting and warranting of explanation. To repeat, to focus upon highly context-specific features of reality is not to treat that which is out of focus, which operates at higher (or at different) levels of generality, as something that can thereby be assumed away. Something, to repeat, is always abstracted *from.*

The scope or extension

We can note, finally, that the additional dimension to abstraction distinguished above, namely its scope or *extension*, also varies according to the vantage point determined by the investigator's knowledge and interests, as well as the level of generality. Broadly speaking, the higher the level of generality of any feature of interest the greater the extension to abstraction required to understand it. Thus, if an abstraction is to identify a set of mechanisms essential to capitalist production, its extension will inevitably encompass the space–time region over which the capitalist system of production has existed. If, instead, the focus is upon peculiarities of a particular firm's performance relative to those of others in a comparable situation, then its space–time extension is likely to be significantly circumscribed in comparison.

In the light of the theory of ontology systematised under the heading of critical realism it is especially apparent, then, that the list of features of abstraction which are *crucial* to social analysis includes not only the vantage point, but also the level of generality and the scope or extension. For if considerations bearing upon the level of generality are fundamental to identifying a mechanism operating at a different level to some phenomenon for which it is essential, considerations of extension are especially significant in the light of the now clearly recognised intrinsic-dynamism and internal-relationality of the material of the social realm. When an abstraction sets spacial boundaries to the focus taken, limits are thereby set on the interdependencies which, at any point in time, can be brought under consideration. And when the process of abstraction sets temporal boundaries to the focus taken, limits are thereby set on the histories of any particular aspects that can be comprehended, including the past development of any feature as well as what it may yet become. Significant skill is therefore required in choosing the appropriate generality and scope of an abstraction when addressing any specific question. In order to illuminate a structure responsible for the production of some phenomenon of interest it is necessary to identify connections and relations essential both to that structure's efficacy and to its existence and mode of reproduction. A comprehension of any (set of) structure(s) will entail identifying the nature of its internal relatedness as well as its particular history.[17]

Notice that this conception does not undermine the possibility of features or aspects of an internally-related set of structures or dynamic process being considered explicitly and individually at a moment in time. The implication, rather, is that such features cannot be considered as isolated momentary phenomena, like punctiform events. Each must be seen as expressing the remaining features, or whole, to which it is related, as well as (or including) its own history. When, for example, we focus upon a particular footballer or hockey player setting off down one side of the playing field with the ball just in front of him or her, we do not suppose that other players, who may be momentarily out of view, cease to exist. Indeed, we interpret the objectives or tactics of the player in view conditional upon our understandings and expectations of others, the rules of the games, the player's own ambitions, competencies, confidence and history, as well as upon our assessment of his or her understanding of the tactics and competencies of others, and so on.

Abstraction and generalisation

Let me re-emphasise that the just discussed insights on the central role for abstraction are facilitated by the understanding which critical realism provides. I do not want to imply, of course, that abstraction is other than essential, whatever the perspective on science that is provided. Different perspectives, though, do encourage competing conceptions of how abstraction is most centrally deployed. In particular, for those guided by the positivistic image of science as the elaboration of regularities between events or states of affairs, the goal of abstraction inevitably becomes that of seeking formal relations of similarity rather than uncovering the essential. As Dobb (1972 [1937]), distancing himself from this perspective, says of it, the aim is to base

> abstraction, not on any evidence of fact as to what features in a situation are essential and what are inessential, but simply on the formal procedure of combining the properties common to a heterogeneous assortment of situations and building abstraction out of analogy.
>
> (Dobb, 1972 [1937]: 40)

Of course, generality of some kind is also an objective acknowledged here – to determine non-empirical features at the 'deeper' level of necessary relations and tendencies of things. These, however, are unlikely to be uncovered just by adopting the *a priori* aim of seeking broad generalisations. As Dobb concludes, what the positivistic form of 'abstraction gains in breadth it more than loses, as it were, in depth – in relevance to the particular situations which are the focus of interest' (ibid.).

It is a characteristic of economic structures, for example, that much of what is essential to the explaining of a form of human activity is highly context-related. Thus, through a process of seeking merely wide generalisations, economic structures can easily be emptied of their context-related, but often essential, content. The employer–worker relationship may be identified as a widespread feature of human society. But this observation abstracts from the numerous variations in the nature of this relationship across time and space, and it is certainly insufficient for an understanding of the various work practices and activities that exist at a specific stage of human evolution in any particular region or place. Similarly, to note such generalities as people have preferences, or beliefs, or the ability to make choices, is to provide insufficient detail of these generative structures or causal powers for explaining any concrete form of human activity they govern.[18]

Perhaps the greatest danger of merely seeking broad generalisations, of pushing the abstractions so far that they are almost devoid of substantive content, arises from the fact that they then need to be supplemented by other propositions in order to have any analytic value; for this opens the door to the inclusion of 'highly artificial' or 'bogus abstractions', or, more accurately, convenient fictions. In other words, almost contentless abstractions can easily, if unwittingly, be manipulated or 'strengthened' in illegitimate ways to yield conceptions that really are no longer abstractions at all. In this, the strengthening additions may (correctly) be interpreted by those who formulate them as other than abstractions – typically as assumptions. But this does not render them, or the exercises conditioned by them, as thereby somehow harmless or neutral. In mainstream economics, for example, such 'assumptions', which may even creep in unnoticed, are usually designed to achieve mathematical tractability, system closure and completeness, or some such thing, rather than an understanding of the real causal mechanisms at work.

Inevitably, if the original abstractions alone possess little explanatory content, then it is the additional 'strengthening' assumptions that do all the work and determine the upshot. And a failure to appreciate this may lead either to an unthinking and erroneous belief that these assumptions can eventually be replaced with accounts of essential aspects of real generative mechanisms without the whole construction collapsing entirely, or to a misguided attempt to extract more meaning from the constructions than can possibly be legitimate. Once more this appears to be a point that Dobb has already emphasised:

> There is the danger of introducing, unnoticed, purely imaginary or even contradictory assumptions and in general of ignoring how limited a meaning the corollaries deducible from these abstract propositions must have and the qualifications which the presence of

> other concrete factors (which may be the major influences in this or that particular situation) may introduce. All too frequently the propositions which are products of this mode of abstraction have little more than formal meaning and at most tell one that an expression for such-and-such a relation must find a place in any of one's equational systems. But those who use such propositions and build corollaries upon them are seldom mindful of this limitation and in applying them as 'laws' of the real world invariably extract from them more meaning than their emptiness of real content can possibly hold.
>
> (Dobb, 1972 [1937]: 41)

Abstraction and economic 'modelling'

If those who accept the familiar positivist results inevitably set off in the wrong direction when making abstractions (seeking out merely broad generalisations rather than attempting to identify what is essential to some phenomenon of interest) there is a second greater error characteristic of contemporary economics which turns on a misunderstanding or misconstrual of what abstraction is. For in modern mainstream economics abstraction is interpreted not only, and not even mainly, as the legitimate activity of leaving momentarily out of focus something that is real. Rather, any explicit reference to the term is taken almost exclusively to denote the (typically illegitimate) activity, or result, of *excluding* something real, of assuming it away entirely. In place of abstraction as a one-sided focus upon an aspect of a concrete entity, an aspect brought momentarily into closer view, economic modelling thus interprets abstraction as a focus upon the aspect in question as though it existed in isolation – and typically as though it were free of internal instability as well.

In other words, in mainstream economics the term abstraction stands in as rhetoric for the pretence that economic phenomena are, after all, generated under conditions equivalent to those achieved through experimental control. Economies are 'modelled' as closed in the sense that the rest of the world does not exist, uncertainty is all but banished, as are becomings, and 'begoings', mortalities and (systematic) mistakes, conflicts and crises, internal relations and transformations. In the name of abstraction all features of social reality that prove inconvenient to deductivist modes of reasoning are ultimately assumed away. Those features which are not consistent with the two overriding closure conditions of the methods of contemporary modelling – that the material under discussion be viewed as atomistic-like and isolated – are, under the heading of abstraction, never allowed in the frame. It is as though when someone goes to a concert, say, and focuses momentarily upon one particular instrument, the rest of the orchestra does not exist; or that, when we focus upon the team player discussed above, the opposing players or supporting mid-fielders are no longer on the playing field. In short, the notion of abstraction is employed merely to gloss the already encountered fallacies of atomism and isolationism.

Notice that such fictionalising cannot, in general, be legitimately defended as a heuristic device, as a useful first approximation or step. In Chapter 9 we came across the 'method of successive approximation', a procedure advocated by Musgrave (1981), supported by Nowak (1980) and examined by Mäki (1992a), amongst others. This is a step-wise procedure wherein one feature of reality is first looked at as though it existed in isolation, and then, when understood on those terms, combined with a second aspect, and then a third, and so on. Now it can readily be admitted that such a procedure may be valid *if* the material under analysis is of a nature such that it can really be decomposed into atomistic, isolated, components, whose effects can be mechanically added together or otherwise combined in some predictable fashion. The problem, however, is that, contra both Mill and recently Cartwright,[19] but as Keynes clearly recognised, social material does not usually conform to this requirement at all.

It is as though, to return to our football or hockey game, the team player with the ball can be treated as if in isolation at least as a first step or approximation. Or it is as if the coach of the team in question determines the tactics of the game by starting from the assumption that the noted player will be the only one on the pitch. Even this restriction is too lax, in fact, for the player may run with the ball at the opponents' goal, or kick/hit it straight there from a distance. In other words, the player in our conception is not yet sufficiently atomistic. The intrinsic closure conditions must be shorn up, all but one of the player's possible internal states must be assumed away or closed off. As with everything else intrinsic complexity can be added back in, it must be supposed, as part of the step-wise procedure that constitutes the method of successive approximation.

Such a procedure is patently absurd as a generalised tool for social science.[20] Instead, continuing the sports example, the legitimate strategy can only be to cycle in and out of different frames of focus, sometimes 'standing back' and 'seeing' the movement on the pitch as a whole, sometimes focusing on individual aspects. On occasion, if to repeat, a player will be interpreted from the perspective of his or her relationship to the goal, sometimes from the perspective of his or her history (what are thought to be his or her skills, competencies and strengths, etc.), or from the perspective of the history of the game itself (e.g. in terms of a recognised trend for referees to penalise certain offences).

And if this cycling in and out, this continual changing of focus and perspective (depending upon which phenomenon at any point we want to understand) is the only way to comprehend a football or hockey match (and, of course, in a televised match this cycling or zooming in and out on specific aspects of the play is literally what happens with the camera) it is also the only way of gaining an understanding of society and economy. When we focus upon varying productivity performances here, conditions of work there, rising or falling unemployment rates, and so on, we do not suppose that those features we choose to emphasise exist in isolation, even as a temporary, heuristic, measure. To do so is to assume a totally different world from the one in which we live, and one that has no bearing upon it. Indeed, the fiction of atomistic, quasi-omniscient, infallible ('economically rational') agents acting in the closed, isolated conditions described in contemporary modelling, does indeed constitute such a different world, one hopelessly irrelevant for providing insight into our own. In short, there is literally a world of difference between leaving something (temporarily) out of focus and treating it as though it does not exist. The achieving of an abstraction and treating something as though it existed in isolation are not the same thing at all.

Abstraction, meaning looking at something in a 'one-sided' manner, is indispensable in science. Its object is to individuate some component or aspect of a concrete entity in order better to understand the latter. And it is essential to recognise that this entails understanding the aspect in question within the relationships in which it stands, relationships which may be essential to its existence and/or mode of activity. The purpose of abstraction is not to mask (or legitimate) a pretence that the aspect in question exists in isolation. Specifically, where – as in social science – meaningful, well controlled, experimentation appears impossible, abstraction is not usefully employed to denote (and usage of the term certainly does not render legitimate) 'modelling', which assumes that conditions analogous to those engineered through well controlled experiments have occurred after all. Indeed, the procedure of abstraction allows science to proceed in the absence of such occurrences. In particular, abstraction, when skilfully executed, can, amongst other things, enable us to access and understand a structured, dynamic and holistic reality. In other words, abstraction, though not a licence for the largely irrelevant modelling activities of mainstream economists, is a procedure that can facilitate the illumination of the open social world in which we live.

Notes

1 I think this characterisation is appropriate given both of the common interpretations of the term 'demi' (as either half-way or as false). First any regularity observed is partial or incomplete. Second although any such partial regularities may be about real phenomena and capturing associations, they are not real laws at all. As Cartwright (1989) expresses the matter:

> Nature selects the capacities that different factors shall have and sets bounds on how they can interplay. Whatever associations occur in nature arise as a consequence of the actions of these more fundamental capacities. In a sense, there are no laws of association at all. They are epiphenomena.
>
> (Cartwright, 1989: 181)

2 Though some, such as Lipton (1991) express reservations about whether this conclusion can be drawn.

3 As is its meaning in other contexts such as sculpture or pictorial art.

4 Notice, however, that there may be an inconsistency between the phenomenon reported and certain normative views of how things *ought* to be. Under such conditions we might well see a further enquiry initiated, either into ways of ameliorating the situation, or perhaps into a fuller understanding of the conditions sustaining it with a view to encouraging their transformation (see Chapter 19).

5 I take it that this orientation is essentially Peircean. According to Peirce the point of enquiry is to assuage doubt and attain a state of ('fixed') belief. For Peirce, you cannot criticise what you do not doubt. (Such doubt, though, is not that of Cartesian rationalism – indeed, just as you cannot choose whether or not to doubt something so doubt presupposes previous belief.) Such doubt then is essential to enquiry; without it, and the contradictions that give rise to it, enquiry does not ensue. He writes for example:

> The irritation of doubt causes a struggle to attain a state of belief. I shall term this struggle *enquiry*, though it must be admitted that it is sometimes not a very apt designation.
>
> The irritation of doubt is the only immediate motive for the struggle to attain belief. It is certainly best for us that our beliefs should be such as may truly guide our actions so as to satisfy our desires; and this reflection will make us reject any belief which does not seem to have been so formed as to insure this result. But it will only do so by creating a doubt in the place of that belief. With the doubt, therefore, the struggle begins, and with the cessation of doubt it ends.
>
> (Peirce, 1966: 99, 100)

Elsewhere Peirce adds:

> Every enquiry whatsoever takes its rise in the observation, in one or another of the three Universes, of some surprising phenomenon, some experience which either disappoints an expectation, or breaks in upon some habit of expectation of the *inquisiturus*; and each apparent exception to this rule only confirms it. There are obvious distinctions between the objects of surprise in different cases. . . . The enquiry begins with pondering these phenomena in all their aspects, in search of some point of view whence the wonder shall be resolved.
>
> (ibid.: 367)

6 There can be no context-independent account of what is meant by *adequacy*. The specificity of any criteria by which adequacy is determined is characteristic of *all* scientific explanation. It is once more the lingering influence of positivism, with its insistence on the generality of rules across disciplines, that misleads economists from recognising the necessarily contingent, pragmatic and field-specific nature of this aspect of explanation (see Miller, 1987: 6). A recent consequence of this mistake in the UK at least, is the tendency to direct economic graduates away from fieldwork, and case study, where skills and methods can be determined on the job, to longer 'taught masters courses', where largely irrelevant *a priori* techniques provide but a superficial semblance of an education in economics.

7 Leamer's own (largely methodological) contribution is admirable in such respects. But it aims to make life too straightforward for others. Indeed, a major

problem with contemporary economics generally is that it attempts to render science far too easy. As it currently stands, with its almost exclusive reliance on computer packages, official data, and sanctioned statistical, or other mathematical, procedures, economics can be pursued, or so it is clearly supposed, without any knowledge of, or thought to, the economy at all. No wonder, then, that so many senior posts in economics faculties are being taken by engineers and applied mathematicians without previous experience of studying features of actual economies. No wonder, too, the current disarray within contemporary economics discipline and the fast growing suspicion of its affairs by those who remain on the outside.

8 Of course there may be many pragmatic reasons for preferring one theory.

9 In a contribution which I cannot fully do justice to here (it appeared as the present one was being finished) Boylan and O'Gorman, in putting forward their 'causal holism', write:

> Our objection is to the Lawsonian realist thesis that the structured entities which possess these powers are claimed to be non-empirical. If one postulates non-empirical entities, how can economists go on to furnish theoretical descriptions of these and know that their descriptions are correct or approximately true? Quine has taught us that it is not beyond the ingenuity of economists to construct a range of incompatible economic theories such that each one is compatible with the empirical evidence. Given this pluralism, causal holists do not see any rational way of deciding which non-empirical referents they should choose nor which theoretical descriptions are true of these non-empirical entities.
>
> (1995: 212)

On the following page they add:

> Furthermore, causal holists acknowledge that the process of inference to the best explanation (Lipton, 1991) is a valuable inductive process. For instance, if we see shoe prints in the snow the best explanation is that a human being, rather than a monkey wearing shoes, passed by. However, if the scientific realist wishes to explicate the notion of abductive inference in terms of an inference to the best explanation and thereby argue that the non-empirical entities postulated by our mature, best confirmed economic theory is the best explanation of the observable economic facts and observable tendencies, the causal holist refuses to take this final step. According to causal holism, abductive inferences understood as inferences to the best explanation are limited to the domain of the observable. The principal reason for this limitation is the same as that used against the transcendental realist's use of non-empirical mechanisms. Quine teaches us that there is a multiplicity of such explanations, each compatible with the empirical evidence and hence we have no rational way of choosing between these. In other words, when the process of inference to the best explanation is extended to postulated non-empirical entities, there is no best explanation. There are many best explanations with no rational way of deciding between them. In causal holism economists can discover the hidden causal webs operating through economic systems and their transformations without recourse to the additional realist strategy of non-empirical mechanism and specific abductive inferences to these mechanisms.
>
> (ibid.: 213)

10 Under the heading of strict regularities I include 'well-behaved' i.e. tractable, probability 'laws'.

11 As Haavelmo (1944) is forced to admit in setting out the 'probability approach to econometrics' 'there is, in general, no limit to the number of . . . factors that might have a *potential* influence' on any variable of interest (1944: 24).

12 This, to repeat, is no less true of natural phenomena. As Cartwright (1989) argues:

> Nature, as it usually occurs, is a changing mix of different causes, coming and going; a stable pattern of association can emerge only when the mix is pinned down over some period or in some place. Indeed, where is it that we really do see associations that have the kind of permanence that could entitle them to be called law-like? The ancient examples are in the heavens, where the perturbing causes are rare or so small in their influence; and the modern examples are in the physics laboratory, where . . . our control is so precise that we ourselves can regulate the mix of causes at work. Otherwise, it seems to me, these vaunted laws of association are still very long-outstanding promissory notes: laws of association are in fact quite uncommon in nature, and should not be seen as fundamental to how it operates. They are only fundamental to us, for they are one of the principal tools that we can use to learn about nature's capacities; and, in fact, most of the regularities that do obtain are ones constructed by us for just that purpose.
>
> (1989: 182)

13 If I understand Boylan and O'Gorman (1995) correctly this distinction mirrors their contrast between pure and applied economics. The difference is that they construe only the latter to be an explanatory exercise (see e.g. pp. 135–41). However I am not convinced that anything very significant hangs on this contrasting use of terminology.

14 For an example of this sort see Lawson (1981). In this enquiry the phenomenon singled out as warranting an explanation is that a particular Cambridge firm over a longish period – throughout the twentieth century up until the 1960s at least (when it was taken over by a large overseas-based multi-national) – had successfully combined a primary product market structure (high and stable demand for [advance technology] products) with secondary employment conditions (low wages, limited possibilities for personal advancement), while the general pattern in the economy at large had been for product market and employment conditions to positively correspond (see e.g. Wilkinson, 1981).

15 As Marx (1973) formulates it, the

> concrete is concrete because it is the concentration of many determinations, hence unity of the diverse. It appears in the process of thinking, therefore, as a process of concentration, as a result, not a point of departure, even though it is a point of departure in reality and hence also the point of departure for observation [Anschauung] and conception.
>
> (Marx, 1973: 101)

For a useful recent discussion of the process of abstraction in Marx's method, a contribution that also has numerous parallels with the discussion set out below, see Ollman, 1993.

16 And whatever the level, to the extent that there is an inconsistency between theory and evidence then *prima facie* some kind of explanatory investigation is required.

17 See Ollman (1993) for an extremely good and extensive recent discussion of these and related issues.

18 Thus Dobb (1972 [1937]) notes that if

> all that is postulated is simply that men *'choose'*, without anything being stated even as to how they choose or what governs their choice, it would seem impossible for economics to provide us with any more than a sort of algebra of human choice, indicating certain rather obvious forms of interrelationship between choices, but telling us little as to the way in which any actual situation will behave.
>
> (Dobb, 1972 [1937]): 71)

Of course, broad generalisations as descriptions of some manifest economic phenomenon can be useful as marking sites for analysis to begin – indeed this is the rationale for the notion of stylised facts noted above. But such generalisations will typically not be useful as explanatory devices, as statements of economic causes. As Dobb again observes, if

> an economic law is a statement of what actually tends to happen and not a mere statement of a relation between certain implicitly defined variables, then such propositions [as result from such high level abstractions] can surely be precious little guide to the 'laws of motion of capitalist society' – or, indeed, to any of the other matters on which they are intended to pass an economic judgement.
>
> (ibid.: 42)

19 Specifically, this appears to be Cartwright's recent (1989) position. Although Cartwright argues for an ontology of capacities, which at one point are likened to propensities or powers (1989: 9), these capacities, or their associated causes, are nevertheless interpreted as 'atomic' (ibid.: 170, 174), and even as measurable, at least in principle, by probabilities (ibid.: 13). This metaphysical perspective, which she identifies with Mill, but recognises is explicitly rejected by Keynes (ibid.), does not, however, lead Cartwright to expect event regularities to be pervasive. Indeed, she repeatedly rejects such a scenario. For while the atomistic assumption guarantees that the *intrinsic closure condition* is automatically satisfied, Cartwright recognises that actual outcomes are generally produced by a shifting mixture of causes (ibid.: 175, 176). In other words, it is recognised that (what I am referring to as) the *extrinsic closure condition* cannot be guaranteed. Now, it is ultimately the accepted metaphysics, her belief that economic phenomena are atomic, that allows Cartwright to suppose that to conceptualise any cause quite independently of all context is a form of abstraction rather than a form of idealisation. She writes:

> Here is how I want to distinguish idealization and abstraction for the purposes of this book: in idealization we start with a concrete object and we mentally rearrange some of its inconvenient features – some of its specific properties – before we try to write down a law for it . . .
>
> By contrast, when we try to formulate Mill's laws of tendencies, we consider the causal factors out of context altogether. It is not a matter of *changing* any particular features or properties, but rather of *subtracting*, not only the concrete circumstances but even the material in which the cause is embedded and all that follows from that. This means that the law we get by abstracting functions very differently from idealized laws. For example, it is typical in talking about idealizations to say . . . the 'departure from truth' is often 'imperceptibly small', or 'if appreciably

> large' then often 'its effect on the associated model can be estimated and allowed for'. But where relevant features have been genuinely subtracted, it makes no sense to talk about the departure of the remaining law from truth, about whether this departure is small or not, or about how to calculate it. These questions, which are so important when treating of idealizations, are nonsense when it comes to abstractions.
>
> . . . When my problem of abstraction is assimilated to the problem of idealization, it is easy to think, erroneously, that one can solve the combined problem by developing some notion of approximating truth. But that does not work.
>
> (Cartwright, 1989: 187, 188)

It is also Cartwright's metaphysics that conditions her support for the method of successive approximation (at least as formulated by Nowak, 1980), and encourages her to view it, with Nowak, as probably the principal method used throughout the sciences (ibid.: 204).

20 Of course, this is equally true of natural science. As Hacking (1983) observes:

> We have the idea of numerous laws of nature adding up to a 'resultant'. That metaphor comes from mechanics. You have this force and that force, this vector and that vector, and you can draw a pretty diagram with ruler and compass to see what results. John Stuart Mill remarked long ago that this fact about mechanics does not generalise. Most science is not mechanics.
>
> (Hacking, 1983: 226)

References

Bhaskar, R. (1979) *The Possibility of Naturalism*, Hemel Hempstead: Harvester Press Ltd.

Boylan, T.A. and O'Gorman, P.F. (1995) *Beyond Rhetoric and Realism in Economics: towards a reformulation of economic methodology*, London: Routledge.

Cartwright, N. (1989) *Nature's Capacities and their Measurement*, Oxford: Clarendon Press.

Collier, A. (1994) *Critical Realism: An Introduction to Roy Bhaskar's Philosophy*, London: Verso.

David, P.A. (1985) 'Clio and the Economics of QWERTY', *American Economic Review (Papers and Proceedings)* 75(2): 332–7.

David, P.A. (1986) 'Understanding the Economics of QWERTY: The Necessity of History', in *Parker* (1986): 30–49.

Dobb, M. (1972 [1937]) 'The Trend of Modern Economics', in Hurst, E.N. and Schwartz, J.G. (eds) *A Critique of Economic Theory*, Harmondsworth: Penguin Books Ltd. Originally in *Political Economy and Capitalism*, Routledge and Kegan Paul.

Feynman, R. (1988) Chapter 9, in Davies, P.C.W. and Brown, J. (eds) *Superstrings: a theory of everything*. Cambridge: Cambridge University Press.

Friedman, M. (1953) *Essays in Positive Economics*, Chicago: University of Chicago Press.

Green, M. (1988) Chapter 4, in Davies, P.C.W. and Brown, J. (eds) *Superstrings: a theory of everything*. Cambridge: Cambridge University Press.

Haavelmo, T. (1944) 'The Probability Approach in Econometrics', *Econometrica* 12: 1–118, supplement.

Hacking, I. (1983) *Representing and Intervening: introductory topics in the philosophy of natural science*, Cambridge: Cambridge University Press.

Kaldor, N. (1985) *Economics Without Equilibrium*, Cardiff: University College Press.

Keynes, J.M. (1973) 'The Collected Writings of John Maynard Keynes: the General Theory and after: Part II defense and development', *Royal Economic Society* XIV.

Lawson, T. (1981) 'Paternalism and Labour Market Segmentation Theory', in Wilkinson, F.S. *Dynamics of Labour Market Segmentation*, Academic Press.

Leamer, E.E. (1983) 'Lets take the Con out of Econometrics', *American Economic Review*: 34–43.

Lipton, P. (1991) *Inference to the Best Explanation*. London: Routledge.

Mäki, U. (1992a) 'On the Method of Isolation in Economics', in Dilworth, C. (ed.), *Intelligibility in Science*, Poznan Studies in the Philosophy of the Sciences and the Humanities 26: 317–51.

Marx, K. (1973) *Grundrisse: foundations of a critique of political economy*, translated by Nicolaus, M., Penguin Books in association with New Left Review.

Miller, R.W. (1987) *Fact and Method: Explanation, Confirmation and Reality in the Natural and Social Sciences*, Princeton: Princeton University Press.

Musgrave, A. (1981) 'Unreal assumptions in Economic Theory: the f-twist untwisted', *Kyklos* 34: 377–87.

Nowak, L. (1980) *The Structure of Idealization, Towards a Systematic Interpretation of the Marxian Idea of Science*, Dordrecht: Reidel.

Ollman, B. (1993) *Dialectical Investigations*, New York and London: Routledge.

Peirce, C.S. (1966) 'Selected Writings: Values in a Universe of Chance', edited with an introduction and notes by Weimer, P.P., New York: Dover Publications.

Whitehead, A.N. (1926) *Science and the Modern World*. Cambridge: Cambridge University Press.

Wilkinson, F.W. (1981) *The Dynamics of Labour Market Segmentation*, London: Academic Press.

Witten, E. (1988) Chapter 9, in Davies, P.C.W. and Brown, J. (eds), *Superstrings: a theory of everything*. Cambridge: Cambridge University Press.

Part II

CRITICAL NATURALISM AND SOCIAL SCIENCE

7

INTRODUCTION

Realism in the social sciences

Margaret Archer

'But social reality is different. . . .' Whether this statement comes from the guts of popular phenomenalism (the feeling that football players are doing something quite unlike billiard balls), or from one of the long philosophical traditions accentuating society's intrinsic meaningfulness and activity-dependence (which are the main ways of upholding that social life is not self-subsistent like nature), this assertion of difference forbids us to move *directly* from Part I to Part II. The reason behind this embargo is always some conviction about the impossibility of naturalism; the ontology of the natural and social worlds being so distinct that they preclude any version of the 'unity of method' claim.

Unsurprisingly, those who first endorsed the 'unity of method' and sought to transform the study of society from speculation to 'social science' did so by nullifying ontological differences between natural and social reality. Comte was prototypical and his terminology is fully revealing: riveted by Newtonian mechanics, he conceived of its direct parallel in 'social physics'. Later to be renamed *la sociologie*, the sovereignty he accorded to this queen of the sciences derived from it over-arching all other subject-matters. The image is of an empire where the sun never sets on efforts to find equivalents to the second law of thermodynamics in every domain. From the beginning then, the 'science' of society was predicated on a mimetic process embedded in the empiricist project (which thus shackled it to observables at the level of events) and wedded to the search for constant conjunctions (which thus settled for correlations and eschewed causal mechanisms, on the Newtonian-Humean model of explanation). This simultaneously denied any notion of sociology as queen of hearts, not only because hermeneutics falls to scientism, but more fundamentally because men and women are reduced to Durkheim's 'indeterminate material'. As beings unilaterally moulded by the holistic properties of society, they become completely uninteresting, except as the site of socialisation. As 'flesh and blood', people are (phylogenetically) subjects for biologists and (ontogenetically) for anatomists and their latter-day equivalents.

Critical realism accepts the challenge of ontological difference between physical and social reality, it too resists a *direct* transition from Part I to Part II and it dissociates itself completely from the empiricism which was traditionally foundational to 'scientific sociology'. As Roy Bhaskar has often remarked, his book could just as well be entitled *The Impossibility of Naturalism* for it is *not* advocating the unity of method *if* this is taken to be synonymous with a 'unity of methodology' in the positivist tradition. The latter can be crudely represented as 'Observation + Correlation = Explanation + Prediction'. This traduces both natural and social reality as well as the differences between them. It has already been seen in Part I that a realist theory of science breaks with all above terms and equivalences. Instead, it substitutes the quest for non-observable generative mechanisms whose powers may exist unexercised or be exercised unrealised, that is with variable outcomes due to the variety of intervening contingencies which cannot be subject to laboratory closure.

In social realism it is quintessential that society is an open system: and not in the milk and water terms of those methods' textbooks warning about the difficulties of 'controlling for extraneous variables'. At best these point to the (insurmountable) problem of introducing *extrinsic* closure into the social system, or any part of it. What they neglect are the *intrinsic* sources of openness, which ontologically preclude closure. To the realist, the one factor which guarantees that social systems remain open (and even forbids thought experiments about closure) is that they are necessarily peopled. Since realism insists upon a stratified view of the social, like any other reality, then there are properties and powers particular to people which include a reflexivity towards and creativity about any social context which they confront. If, *per impossible*, we could shut the door of any social situation against the intervention of extraneous factors (thus effecting extrinsic closure) we would only have closed in those whose innovativeness enables them to design a new exit or creatively to redesign their environment (absence of intrinsic closure). There is, in short, no such thing as an enclosed order in society because it is not just the investigators but the inhabitants who can engage in thought experiments and put them into practice. This is the tip of the iceberg where the ontological differences between natural and social reality are concerned.

Social reality is so different that the 'vexatious fact of society' can be expressed as a riddle: what is it that depends upon intentional human action but which never conforms to these intentions? What is it that is reliant upon people's conceptualisations but which they never fully know? What is it that is always activity-dependent but that never exactly corresponds to the activities of even the most powerful? What is it that has no organisational form without us, yet which also forms us its makers? And what is it whose constitution never satisfies the precise designs of anyone, but because of this always motivates its attempted reconstitution? This is the riddle of 'structure and agency' and its solution ultimately precludes scientism, even for those who believe in it for science.

Instead, there have been four major solutions offered, all of which remain in currency, though subject to fluctuating valuations. (These correspond to the '*Four Concepts of Social Structure*' outlined by Porpora). In them, it is clear that society has never been short of ontologists and there are strong traditions which assert that the ultimate constituents of social reality are entirely different things. Historically, the first two contenders locate these constituents respectively in 'agency' and in 'structure'. These are represented in the old debate between individualism and collectivism, which was already well articulated in the nineteenth century. Thus to J.S. Mill, 'Men in a state of society are still men. Their actions and their passions are obedient to the laws of individual human nature. Men are not, when brought together, converted into another kind of substance with different properties.'[1] Conversely, for Comte, 'Society is no more decomposable into individuals than a geometrical surface is into lines, or a line into points'.[2]

Thus the terms of the old debate were set with Individualists advocating a reductionist programme, such that the ultimate ontological constituents of the social world were 'individual people' whose dispositions were the terminus of explanations. Every contribution in this section repudiates the individualist social ontology and the reductionism which is transmitted in a principled manner to the explanatory programme of methodological individualism. The argument can be stated at length (see my *Realist Social Theory*, chapter 2), but the root objection to reductionism is captured economically by Bhaskar's comment that 'the predicates designating properties special to persons all presuppose a social context for their employment. A tribesman implies a tribe, the cashing of a cheque a banking system. Explanation, whether by subsumption under general laws, advertion to motives and rules, or redescription (identification), always involves irreducibly social predicates'.[3]

The deficiencies of the Collectivist response, in the debate which preoccupied the 1950s and 1960s, lay basically in its ontological timidity; advocates being haunted by the spectre of reification and hamstrung by the need for empiricist demonstration. References to 'societal facts' are indeed defended, but as ineradicable 'remainders' (Mandelbaum), without which Individualist descriptions must remain incomplete. Similarly their explanations come up against 'unreduced concepts' which have to be incorporated every time that composition rules, intended to reduce 'group behaviour' to the behaviour of individuals in groups, break down, i.e. most of the time.[4]

Instead of advancing a robust ontology of 'social structure', the Collectivist plays a defensive methodological game, introducing 'structure' as a disparate collection of factors which are only adduced when individualist explanations fail. Yet when these structural factors are brought forward, then questions concerning their ontological status cannot be avoided. The fear was that to assert their reality either countenanced the existence of some new 'social substance' or designated entities produced by society itself, independently of the actions of people yet exercising superordinate force over actors. To evade these charges, the tendency was to take ontological cover under a 'heuristic' – making the claim only to be utilising a useful mental construct. This defensive manoeuvre can be seen in the pioneering work of David Lockwood and of William Buckley alike in the sixties. They wished to theorise about the causal influence of systemic properties, precisely in order to examine the interplay between the 'parts' of society and the 'people', yet both began by retreating behind heuristic devices.[5] Gellner is revealing here because he clearly doubts that structural properties and powers are properly represented as mental constructs, but they are rather, 'I am somewhat sheepishly tempted to say, "really there"'.[6]

It was not that the better class of Collectivists were unwilling to acknowledge *relational* properties as influential, nor that they were unaware that their status was that of emergent properties, the problem was that these are incapable of being known in empiricist terms, via sense data, since they are non-observables. To talk about emergent properties is simply to refer to those entities which come into being through social combination. They exist by virtue of interrelations (although not usually interpersonal ones) and not all social relations give rise to them (compare the division of labour amongst Adam Smith's pin makers, which generates the power of mass production, with the sewing bee, which does not). Now whilst the division of labour in the pin factory might just have been acceptable in accounting for the hundred fold increase in productivity (*observable* workers plus a few composition rules), we often wish to talk about the results of the results of emergent properties, that is their own combination *qua* emergents (as Adam Smith wanted to link the emergence of mass production to the Wealth of Nations and all that then stemmed from their, again relational, pecking order). Yet the reality of relational concepts cannot be secured on the perceptual criterion of empiricism; the alternative is to demonstrate their causal efficacy, that is employing a causal criterion to establish reality. Here the empiricist conception of causation, in terms of Humean constant conjunctions at the level of observable events, represented another brick wall. For 'internally related structures' may have powers remaining unexercised due to contingent interventions, ineradicable from open systems, and therefore 'emergent properties' will not necessarily or usually be demonstrable by some regular covariance in observable events and thus will almost always fail to establish a claim to reality on the empiricist criterion of causality.

Only with the demise of the empiricist hegemony and the undermining of positivist domination, did siding with neither individualism nor collectivism become a genuine option. What went wrong with sociology (standing for social theorizing in general) was basically ontological disenchantment and an increasingly torrid affair with epistemology. This cut its moorings with reality (or its analysis) in the born-again idealism of the 'discursive' and the associated devices and designs of rhetorical persuasion – the 'methodology' of the linguistic wrong turn. For there is no innocence in those committing the epistemic fallacy which is entailed in claiming that 'everything in our social life . . . can be said to have become cultural'[7] (and ontologically why should culture be regarded as plastic textualism?). Explanatory 'myths' are out, but rhetorical story-telling is very much in – especially the biggest story making for the most interesting of times, namely the superseding of that homogeneous entity called 'modernity' and the advent of the 'post-modern'. Hence the rhetorical montage of Foucauldian aspect, whose verificatory collage works by persuasion without any context of justification, yet is immune to critique. Attempt the latter and rhetoric beats a quick epistemic retreat – it is *merely* rhetorical, one image in a new world which allows a thousand images to bloom, privileging their plurality and counselling us to increase our tolerance of incommensurability. Yet this state of mind deemed possible in the West is a luxury dependent on the state of the rest. The post-modern experience is not on globally for those needing bread not circuses and seeking freedom of expression not expressive freedom. There are transcendental material requirements for the existence of the Collège de France and for the privileged practice of 'playing with the pieces'.

Ultimately any representation of 'structures' as constructs, subject only to discursive negotiation, sells out on human emancipation. Thus Rorty severs his aesthetic project of 'self-enlargement' from the structural pre-conditions of economic subsistence and freedom from political oppression, which are integral to any social definition of the good life. Yet there can be no post-modernist protesters because 'agency', like 'structure' has been shorn of 'hors textuelle' properties. In the literal anti-humanism of post-modern thought, humanity becomes the Baudrillardian 'spongy referent, that opaque but equally translucent nothingness', the Lyotardian nodal point through which multifarious cultural messages pass, or, with Foucauldian brutalism, 'Man (sic) has come to an end'. Yet transcendentally we have to ask what humankind must be like if 'social science' can possibly serve all of it, that is aspire to universalism. And the answer has to be in terms of a unicity of humanity which sees us as more than similar organic parcels with space–time co-ordinates and proper names. Unless we hold to humanity as a natural kind (meaning species-beings who are more than their biology but less than their socialization), then anything goes, but it gets nowhere beyond our campus language game.

Hence the need to struggle on with the riddle of society's constitution and to re-confront the problem of structure and agency outside the confines of empiricism, especially now that transcending the terms the 'old debate' between Individualism and Collectivism can be envisaged. The demise of positivism was also the demise of the view that all knowledge is obtained from human *experience*, for only then did 'individuals' (because alone capable of *experiencing*) lose their automatic primacy in social theorising. Simultaneously non-observable features of society could avoid the suspicion that they were reified (because incapable of being *experienced* as sense data), rather than real. This then opened the way for an ontologically robust reformulation of social science rather than calling a plague on all scientific endeavours attempting to say something about social reality and licensing the epistemological primacy (and investigative playfulness) of post-modernism. Once again realism and idealism confronted one another, but this time it was the realist alternative whose break with empiricism hinged on transcendental arguments about what made society a possible object of investigation, whilst idealism abandoned these even for categories of thought when settling for the celebration of local incommensurable language games.

Bhaskar's charter for social realism is based four square on a rejection of positivism but it is not neutral towards the variety of approaches current in social theorising. A social ontology does not dictate a specific form of practical social theory, but since it commits itself (corrigibly) to what exists, then it necessarily regulates the explanatory programme because its specification of the constituents (and non-constituents) of reality are the only ones which can appear in explanatory statements (which does not rule out *substantive* debate about the most promising contenders within the abstractly defined domain of the real). In this sense, social realism is no different from individualism, collectivism or any other developed perspective because logically there must always be a tripartite regulatory relationship governing the aetiology of theory and the division of labour within it, such that the following formula is universal: Social Ontology → Explanatory Methodology → Practical Social Theories.

In contrast, instrumentalism uncouples the last element from the other two. There is no working backwards from the empirical connections found between social problems and related properties or conditions, because the composition of the EM is merely that collection of indices which have demonstrated their workability. Such concepts, whose only common denominator is their predictive utility (i.e. the capacity to account for some variance in phenomena), prevents the distillation of a social ontology from this diverse cluster, since nothing can preclude their mutual inconsistency. On the other hand, post-modernism proceeds in the opposite direction, detaching social ontology from EM and PST. Because social reality is defined as being discursive, but discourses themselves are held to be incommensurable and untranslatable, this cannot lead to an EM. It only governs it in the sense of condemning the explanatory enterprise as such and replacing it by aesthetic appreciation. In consequence, post-modernism represents a principled refusal to 'move forward' to PST.

Realist social theory begins from three basic ontological premises about social reality. These are outlined in chapter 1 of *The Possibility of Naturalism* and summarised at the start of William Outhwaite's chapter, namely *intransitivity*, *transfactuality*, and *stratification*. Here I want to comment briefly on the role they play in the SO → EM → PST formula. First, the rejection of positivism depends on substituting an ontology of structures for one of (observable) events. In other words, the existence of *intransitive entities*, which is independent of their identification, is a condition of the possibility of social science. Without this there could be no explanatory programme. Explanation of social matters requires the generic assertion that there is a state of the matter which is what it is, regardless of how we do view it, choose to view it or are somehow manipulated into viewing it. This precludes any collapse of the ontological into the epistemological and convicts those who endorse this move of the 'epistemic fallacy', namely confusing what is with what we take it to be. Conversely the realist insists that what is the case places limitations upon how we can construe it.

However, things social are not immutable: indeed one of the defining features of society is its morphogenetic nature, its capacity to change its shape or form (and its lack of any preferred state or the cybernetic equivalent of homeostatic feedback mechanisms which supposedly ensure that chimera called social equilibrium). Yet if mutability is intrinsic to society as a natural kind, then what are the intransitive (hence durable) objects of our study? Here Bhaskar is ontologically precise and thus serves to regulate the explanatory programme of social realism: 'neither individuals nor groups satisfy the requirement of continuity . . . for the autonomy of society over discrete moments of time. In social life only relations endure.'[8] Consequently it follows for EM that realism 'will be seen to entail a *relational* conception of the subject matter of social science'.[9] In turn this means that reductionist theorising is out, for these upward or downward manoeuvres aim to eliminate the relational in order to arrive at the real – the ultimate constituent of social life. Whether this is held to be the 'individual' or the 'societal' the other element becomes epiphenomenal and thus *reflection* is substituted for interplay between the two (*relational*). Therefore explanatory programmes like realist methodological individualism or realist methodological holism are simply inconceivable. Because of its social ontology, realism must generate a form of theorising which transcends this old debate in social science.

The second core premise is that of the *transfactuality* of mechanisms (i.e. that their activities are continuous and invariant, stemming from their relatively enduring properties and powers, despite their outcomes displaying variability in open systems). This again entails both a generic assumption and also has a specific impact on the explanatory programme. Generically, transfactuality entails that although the form of society at any given time is historically contingent, this is not the same as viewing things social as pure contingency. Were the latter the case, then the notion of social science falls and there would be no history left to fall back on, since pure contingency also rules out the modest chronicler of historical Brownian motion since there is no story to tell. In any domain, if all occurrences are contingently related and everything is flux then the Popperian bold conjecture, like the historical grand narrative, is not brave but inane. Nor does the seeming humility of the *petit récit* constitute a shelter, for this too relies upon the relative durability of the local. In short, only on the metaphysical assumption that some relations are necessary and at least relatively enduring can we reasonably set out to practise science or to study society. Long traditions of social theorising have not only made this necessary commitment to determinacy, they also began from a prior commitment to *how* society was durably ordered. Instead, social realism's acknowledgement that transfactuality is only *relatively* enduring *and* quintessentially *mutable* means that its explanatory programme (EM) has no baggage of preconceptions that society's ordering (at a given time or over time) resembles any other form of reality (mechanism or organism), nor that the totality is homologous with some part of it (language), or some state of it (simple cybernetic systems). If society is only like itself, meaning that it is contingent *that* any particular social structure exists, then we are committed to providing a particular kind of explanation – an analytical history of its emergence, of why it is so and not otherwise – at S1, T1. The realist EM refuses to use analogical crutches, which produce inadequate retrodictions because they *presume* a transfactual mechanism of a particular kind, whereas the task for the realist is to find them and the tendencies emanating from them.

Finally, the realist insistence that reality is *stratified* underpinned the general rejection of a social or any other science reliant only upon surface sense data. Thus Bhaskar maintains that 'by secreting an ontology based on the category of experience, three domains of realities (the domains of the real, the actual and the empirical) are collapsed into one'.[10] This absence of ontological depth precludes crucial questions about the *conditions* under which *experience* is possible to agency (observing a cherry tree in England depends on its prior importation from China, just as experiencing educational discrimination is posterior to a given definition of achievement being institutionalised, or owing rent depends upon antecedent relationships between landlords and tenants). In terms of the explanatory programme, the stratified nature of reality introduces a necessary historicity (however short the time period involved) for instead of *horizontal* explanations relating one experience, observable or event to another, the fact that these themselves are conditional upon antecedents, requires *vertical* explanations in terms of the generative relationships indispensable for their realisation (and equally necessary to account for the systematic non-actualisation of non-events and non-experiences – such as the absence of black prime ministers in the West). Ontological depth necessarily introduces vertical causality which simultaneously entails temporality.

Andrew Collier shows that although the chain of horizontal causality can extend forever backwards ('. . . and thus the kingdom was lost; all for the want of a nail'), nevertheless, the factual production of any given event depends on the precise conjuncture of factors present in the present, which together are sufficient to produce it. However, as his analysis of ideological practices shows, their efficacy depends upon, because it is superimposed upon, relations in the vertical dimension which predate them yet which they presuppose for their effectiveness.[11] This historicity/temporality of vertical explanations is intrinsic to the fact that all legitimatory practices 'presuppose an ideological stratum that they did not create . . . religion produces the churches, not vice versa. And if we had not already acquired a certain ideology from the practice of doing the family shopping, Saatchi and Saatchi could not have presented Thatcher's cuts as "good housekeeping".'[12] Of course, such historicity is integral to the nature of the transcendental argument itself. When we ask what needs to be the case for x to be possible, we predicate any realisation of x upon the *prior* materialisation of the conditions of its possibility.

This is why Bhaskar states unambiguously that 'social forms are a necessary condition for any intentional act, (and) that their *pre-existence* establishes their *autonomy* as possible objects of scientific investigation'.[13] Some of those working in social theory have sought to evade the verticality–historicity entailment by maintaining the simultaneity of the elements constituting social reality.[14] This as will be seen is *always* the case for those who stress the affinity between Bhaskar and Giddens and we will have to examine such arguments when we come to the contributions of Manicas, Archer and Porpora.

First however, there is the broader issue to examine as to whether critical realism fosters a particular form of social theorising or if it is broadly compatible with a whole range of approaches. William Outhwaite begins by asking the basic question in this context, namely what are the implications of a realist theory of science for doing social research? Having distilled the five main ontological principles of realism, he then plays a high-powered telescope over social research, through which he sees a broad church of approaches which are compatible with realism. As with all forms of ecumenism it is important to know what prompts it: here there are two reasons.

The first turns on what Bhaskar has called 'underlabouring'. Being a philosophy of science, realism proffers a metatheory or 'philosophical ontology', rather than a 'scientific ontology' which tells us what structures, entities and mechanisms make up the (in this case, social) world. Thus Outhwaite argues that, in principle, a realist metatheory will not of itself enjoin that explanations be cast in terms of social action or social structure. However, in practice, philosophical underlabourers for social science cannot avoid addressing society, since without some reference to its constitution, how can the ontological transfer of realism be entertained let alone commended? Crucially, as Outhwaite signals, the realist philosopher must at least be assured that there exist intransitive objects with relative durability in social life. And they cannot assert this without minimally ascertaining that there are such candidates, of which 'structure' and 'agency' are the prime contenders. So 'our' problem immediately has to become 'theirs'. As it does, it becomes clear that the relations which endure cannot be captured in terms of individuals and groups (Outhwaite and Bhaskar reject individualism on identical grounds) or in terms of holistic properties which entail reification. These must be anchored in agential mediation. In other words, membership of the broad church cannot be all-inclusive and exclusion begins when both under-labourer and groundsman start inspecting 'structure' and 'agency', which is unavoidable in making statements about society including the one that realism is appropriate for its study.

The second reason for Outhwaite's ecumenism turns on the whole question of *what are* the 'intransitive objects' in the social sciences, i.e. those things which exist and act independently of our descriptions of them? Here, again, Outhwaite is very latitudinarian for he will include constructionist approaches which maintain that the elementary structures of society are nothing but (relatively enduring) sets of interpretations. In one sense this presents no difficulties for it can be maintained (as I have done in *Culture and Agency*)[15] that cultural systems have exactly the same temporal priority, relative autonomy and causal efficacy vis-à-vis socio-cultural action as do structural properties. Similarly, Bhaskar himself maintains that realism can sustain 'the intransitivity of beliefs and meanings':[16] for no single theoretical proposition can be advanced *ex nihilo*, but involves climbing on the shoulders of prior theorists and confronting the existing corpus of knowledge.

However, it seems that Outhwaite's generous inclusiveness actually hinges on his belief in the concept-dependence of social life (though not on the infallibility of our conceptions, whose incorrectness is sometimes essential to the possibility of such activities as lying). Rather he attaches particular importance to those actions which, like quarrelling, depend upon agents knowing what they are doing. Undoubtedly this category of activity exists where the dance and the dancers are nearly one: but should it be taken as paradigmatic? Here Outhwaite seems to say 'yes', given his approving citation of Harré: 'in the social sciences facts, *at the level at which we experience them*, are wholly the creation of theorising, of interpreting them'.[17] Now this seems to equate the *interpreted experience* of the agent with the *efficacy* of a fact, thus ruling out those factors which influence us, as constraints and enablements, without *any* conceptualisation of them on our part. I would always want to defend the existence of this category, for the effects of structural factors like inflation, upon spending-power, are causally influential whether we have any concept of economics or none. To maintain otherwise is either to deny their existence, or to make every unintended consequence transparent (in principle) to actors, and, more contentiously, to be without influence unless and until it has been discursively mediated. Yet pensioners are constrained to trade-off heating against eating *regardless* of their understandings of index-linked incomes. We are not disagreeing that structural factors require agential mediation in order to be influential, but whilst Outhwaite requires this process to be mental, I would stress the ways in which structure shapes the situations we confront and also the influential distribution of material and cultural resources with which we can strategically conduct this confrontation. Some things do go on behind our backs and the effects of many that go on before our faces do not require us to face up to them.

What is really at issue here is the interface between critical realism and hermeneutics. Outhwaite wants a big bridge with heavy traffic, and this he methodologically guarantees by designating common-sense knowledge as the entrée to interpretations and hence to structures. Rather than confining ourselves to this agential entrée, I prefer double doors, permitting structural access which is possible through detecting the causal efficacy of properties which do not depend upon consciousness of them. By maintaining this distinction between structure and agency (and the découpage between ontology and epistemology), this enables one *additionally* to explain the hermeneutic *struggle* to make sense of our environment, and to make nonsense of it because usually not all is revealed to consciousness and sometimes that is because it is shaped outside our conscious awareness. Revealing the latter is what makes for *critical* realism and its emancipatory potential: at times we can point to the contextual causes of epistemic fallibility. Whether these are manipulated or circumstantial, there is no warrant for confining social causes to the mental or to meanings. It is also what makes for social *realism*: we do not uncover real social structures by interviewing people in-depth about them.

'So why be a social realist?' Here Outhwaite stands outside practical activity (PST), as is fully consistent with him viewing realism as a 'philosophical ontology'. Thus, 'the most powerful reason for adopting a realist metatheory is to acquire a framework for the rational discussion of ontological questions'.[18] He wants us in the broad church to keep us talking. I am part of the messy business of practical social theorising and whilst agreeing that both Harré and Bhaskar are both attempting to get at the 'fundamental generative structures and generative mechanisms of social life',[19] since the former entertains only mentalistic contenders and the latter does not, then one of them has to be (fundamentally) wrong. As a realist sociologist, I have to judge which in order to advance any concrete explanatory proposition. By all means let us keep talking and avoid excommunicating, but as we go on *working* we cannot do so as sociological agnostics about the nature of structures or of agents.

Yet here is the crux of the matter: in what way can the realist conceptualise intransitive social properties as pertaining to society *sui generis*, *given* the vexatious fact that things social, unlike things natural, are *all* activity-dependent? If this is the case, do not structural and cultural properties (the main contenders for social intransitivity) become inseparable from agential doings, which would mean that they do not belong to society *sui generis*? This is the force of Benton's critique. Taking up Bhaskar's acceptance that one of the limits of naturalism is the fact that social structures are present only in and through the activities of human agents, Benton concludes that Bhaskar can only distinguish between the powers of agents possessed in virtue of their intrinsic natures and those possessed in virtue of their relational properties, neither of which does anything to uphold social structures as the autonomous possessors of causal powers. Thus Benton argues that the whole enterprise seems to collapse back into individualism; although he suspects his own conclusion is not watertight.

Somewhat similar arguments are deployed by Manicas when again pinpointing activity-dependence as the feature which means that a social structure does not exist in the way that a magnetic field exists. As he puts it, 'the reason would seem to be this: that society is incarnate in the practices and products of its members'.[20] From the fact that society does not exist apart from the practices of individuals, Manicas, along with many others, then sees very close affinities between Bhaskar's transformational model and Giddens's 'ontology of praxis' where 'structure enters simultaneously into the constitution of the agent and social practices, and "exists" in the generating moments of this constitution'.[21] If this case is developed, then social realism collapses into structuration theory: and the ontological status of social reality retreats into scare quotes.

On the other hand, the contributions of Porpora, Archer and Collier resist both of the above 'collapses', maintaining the distinctiveness of the critical realist approach precisely because they do believe that emergent properties can be upheld as pertaining to society *sui generis*. How then do they vindicate ontological depth and warrant 'structure' and 'agency' being treated as distinct strata of social reality *without* denying society's activity-dependence upon its agents? Basically their arguments turn upon emphasising, as Bhaskar does, 'the importance of distinguishing categorically between people and societies', because 'the properties possessed by social forms may be very different from those possessed by the individuals upon whose activity they depend'.[22] Now to Bhaskar this effect of emergent properties implies that some 'point of contact' is required between the two and that their linkage depends upon a 'mediating system' consisting of 'the *positions* (places, functions, rules, tasks, duties, rights, etc.) occupied (filled, assumed, enacted, etc.) by individuals, and of the *practices* (activities, etc.) in which, in virtue of their occupancy of these positions (and vice versa), they engage'.[23]

This distinction between positions and practices is crucial and it is by maintaining it and working on its implications that what is *sui generis* to society can be extracted. Although Manicas had argued (above) that society was incarnational in the *practices and products* of its agents, it is the exclusive attention he gives to *practices* which induces the slide towards Giddens and the affinity claimed with his 'ontology of practices'. Conversely, if *products* are given their due and *positions* are not conflated with *practices*, then the slide is arrested and social realism represents an approach which is antithetical to structuration theory. In making this case, Porpora insists that 'relationships do have [*sui generis*] independent causal properties and, moreover, that such relationships, *once established*, are analytically prior to the *subsequent* rule-following behaviour of actors'.[24] In short, *positions* must predate the *practices* they engender: although activity is necessarily ceaseless for society to be, it is discontinuous in nature because changes in society's structure then condition practices in distinctively different ways. Thus the 'causal effects of the structure on individuals are manifested in certain structured interests, resources, powers, constraints and predicaments that are built into each position by the web of relationships. These comprise the material circumstances in which people must act and which motivate them to act in certain ways.'[25] And these ways which pattern social interaction are incomprehensible without back reference to the conditional influences (which are thus prior) of the position, the resources associated with it and the interests vested in it, none of which can be captured by a seamless web of 'practices'.

Thus Porpora asks

> if we now want to analyse the interaction of the incumbents of these positions, the question is which is analytically prior, the established relationship into which they have entered or the rule-like, routinized manner of the interaction they subsequently establish. It seems clear that the relationship and the causal powers it affords the boss are what predominantly determine the character of the subsequent interaction. Much of that interaction is not even rule-like. The rules don't usually tell the subordinate that he or she has to endure the angry outbursts of the boss. . . .[26]

This argument is identical with Thompson's critique[27] of structuration theory which demonstrates that certain practices cannot even be properly *identified* without reference to the occupancy of positions, which are themselves embedded in broader structures, nor can regular patterns of action be explained as the coincidences of voluntarism, but are only explicable as being positionally conditioned.

All of this is fully congruent with my own contribution which tackles the question of activity-dependence by asking upon *whose* activities particular distributions, positions, roles and institutions themselves depend? Since the answer is that the structuring of all the above arose from the *past activities* of agents (possibly now dead), then the emergence of such properties and powers cannot be attributed to practices of *current agents*, who can maintain and transform the above, rather than creating them, but whose strategic actions are conditioned by their inherited structural and cultural context in so doing. Moreover *qua* agents they are shaped and reshaped in their sequential attempts to remould the structures they confront but did not create. Arguments about the continuity of activity must not be confused with the continuous nature of agency. A position has to exist prior to its occupancy and even if the same people become the incumbents of newly elaborated positions, the new set of internal relations into which they are then embroiled exert a *sui generis* conditional influence upon them – which is causally detectable precisely through their changed *practices* as agents and the elaboration of agency itself.

This means that structural and agential transformation are not just randomly out of synchrony (due to the exercise of their respective powers), but that we are dealing with an inherently 'tensed' phenomenon because *given* structures and *given* agents stand in temporal relations of priority and posteriority towards one another. Hence to stress the necessary continuity of activity for the existence of society is only to assert the truism 'no people: no society'. Methodologically, activity-dependence does constrain us to analytical (not philosophical) dualism, but if tense is given its proper due we can still properly distinguish cycles of 'Structural Conditioning → Social Interaction → Structural Elaboration' according to the emergent properties which interest us, within the existential flow. This is compatible not only with the Transformational Model of Social Action as outlined in *The Possibility of Naturalism* but accords with its development in Bhaskar's later writings. Thus in the *Dialectic*, Bhaskar insists that social reality 'must be differentiated into analytically discrete moments . . . as rhythmically processual and plastic to the core. This is a feature which . . . distinguishes it from structuration, or more generally any "central conflation" theory.'[28] I am suggesting that such morphogenetic cycles, based on two simple propositions, that structure necessarily predates the actions which transform it and that structural elaboration necessarily post-dates those actions, provide social realism with a *method* of explaining social structuring over time in terms of the *interplay* between structure and agency – which can be used to generate practical social theories in particular domains. Conversely, structuration theory's 'ontology of praxis' deprives it of the SO → EM → PST relationship, which restricts it to being only a 'sensitisation device'[29] rather than a research programme. The fundamental reason for the difference in practical utility is that the 'duality of structure' only permits the artificial bracketing of structural properties and strategic conduct by placing a methodological *epoché* upon each in turn. Yet since these are two sides of the same thing, the pocketed elements must thus be *co-terminous in time* (co-existence of the *epochés* confines analysis to the same *époque*) and it follows from this that the temporal interplay *between* structure and agency logically cannot be examined.

Thus following the demise of positivism and the desuetude of the old debate between Individualists and Collectivists, what has not disappeared is the enduring need to make a choice. The burden of choosing is inescapable because the 'ontology of praxis' endorses the mutual constitution of structure and agency which is neither reductionist (contra individualism) nor anti-reductionist (contra-holism) but is *a*reductionist. Because of this, what I have termed 'elisionism' becomes a distinct theoretical orientation for the following three reasons: (i) a denial of the *separability* of structure and agency, because (ii) every aspect of 'structure' is held to be activity-dependent *in the present tense* and thus equally open to transformation, and (iii) the conviction that any causal efficacy of structure is dependent upon its *instantiation* by agency.

Consequently the separability/inseparability of structure and agency represents the ontological parting of the ways between Elisionists and Realists: a necessary parting due to realism's endorsement of stratification, emergence and temporality. Hence Bhaskar stresses

> The importance of distinguishing, in the most categorical way, between human action and social structure . . . For the properties possessed by social forms may be very different from those possessed by the individuals upon whose activity they depend . . . I want to distinguish sharply then between the genesis of human actions, lying in the reasons, intentions and plans of human beings, on the one hand; and the structures governing the reproduction and transformation of social activities, on the other.[30]

The insistence upon their distinction is ontological, but also methodological because as distinct entities it is possible to examine the interplay between them, which is crucial for theorising about the vexatious fact of society, whether our preoccupation is with everyday personal dilemmas or with macroscopic social transformations. Separability is the predicate for examining the interface between structure and agency upon which practical social theorising depends. Only on that basis is it possible to talk about the stringency of structural constraints versus degrees of agential freedom. On the contrary, any theory which treats structure and agency as a mutually constitutive amalgam also implies that causation is always the joint and equal responsibility of the two and therefore that no state of affairs is ever more attributable to one than the other. The social ontology of realism warrants our speaking about 'pre-existence', 'relative autonomy' and 'causal influence' in relation to these two distinct strata by virtue of their emergent properties and powers. As such, it empowers us to analyse the processes by which structure and agency shape and re-shape one another over time and to explain variable outcomes at different times. It is the same premises which enable *critical* realism to have a cutting edge through identifying contextual constraints upon our freedoms and specifying strategic uses of our freedoms for social transformation.

M. A.
February 1998

Notes

1 J.S. Mill, *A System of Logic: Ratiocintive and Inductive*, People's Editions, London, 1884, p. 573.
2 Auguste Comte, *Système de Politique Positive*, L. Mathias, Paris, 1951, vol. II, p. 181.
3 Roy Bhaskar, *The Possibility of Naturalism*, Harvester, Hemel Hempstead, 1989, p. 28.
4 Maurice Mandelbaum, 'Societal Facts', in John O'Neill (ed.), *Modes of Individualism and Collectivism*, Heinemann, London, 1973.
5 David Lockwood, 'Social Integration and System Integration', in G.K. Zollschan and W. Hirsch (eds), *Explorations in Social Change*, Houghton Mifflin, Boston, 1964. In answering the question 'what are the "component elements" of social systems which give rise to strain, tension or contradiction?' (p. 250), Lockwood first answers that the distinction between these properties is a 'wholly artificial one' (p. 245), yet five pages later this heuristic claim gives way to the ontological and methodological claim that the social and the systemic are 'not only analytically separable, but also because of the time elements involved, factually distinguishable' (p. 250). William Buckley made the same heuristic claim in *Sociology and Modern Systems Theory*, Prentice Hall, New Jersey, 1967, that 'the "structure" is an abstract construct, not something distinct from the ongoing interactive process but rather a temporary, accommodative representation of it at any one time'. However, in the forthcoming (1998) collection of his works, *Society: A Complex Adaptive System*, he now gives a definition of the system which is uncompromisingly realist since it is defined as 'a complex of elements or components directly or indirectly related in a network of interrelationships of various kinds, such that it constitutes a dynamic whole *with emergent properties*' (p. 36, my italics).
6 Ernest Gellner, 'Holism versus individualism', in May Brodbeck (ed.), *Readings in the Philosophy of the Social Sciences*, Macmillan, New York, 1971, p. 264.
7 This phrase (from Jameson) is part of post-modernist idealism, summarised in the credo, 'il n'y a pas dehors texte'.
8 Roy Bhaskar, *The Possibility of Naturalism*, op. cit., p. 41.
9 Ibid., p. 26.
10 Ibid., p. 15.
11 Andrew Collier, *Scientific Realism and Socialist Thought*, Harvester Wheatsheaf, Hemel Hempstead, 1989, p. 56.
12 Ibid., p. 54.
13 Roy Bhaskar, *The Possibility of Naturalism*, op. cit., p. 25.
14 Derek Layder correctly takes Structuration theory to task for endorsing the 'simultaneity model'. For how 'can objectives structures be both outside and determinative of interaction, whilst at the same time being the internally generated outcome of such interactions? This is what the simultaneity model asks us to accept.' *Structure, Interaction and Social Theory*, Routledge and Kegan Paul, London, 1981, p. 3.
15 Margaret S. Archer, *Culture and Agency: The Place of Culture in Social Theory*, Cambridge University Press, 1989.
16 Roy Bhaskar, *The Possibility of Naturalism*, op. cit., p. 22.
17 William Outhwaite, *New Philosophies of Social Science*, Macmillan, London, 1987, p. 52.
18 Ibid., p. 59.
19 Ibid., p. 5.
20 Peter T. Manicas, *A History and Philosophy of the Social Sciences*, Basil Blackwell, p. 22.

21 Anthony Giddens, *Central Problems of Social Theory*, Macmillan, London, 1979, p. 5.
22 Roy Bhaskar, *The Possibility of Naturalism*, op. cit., p. 35.
23 Ibid., p. 41.
24 Douglas V. Porpora, 'Four Concepts of Social Structure', *Journal for the Theory of Social Behaviour*, 19:2, 1989, p. 206.
25 Ibid., p. 200.
26 Ibid., pp. 20–8.
27 John B. Thompson, 'The Theory of Structuration', in David Held and John B. Thompson (eds), *Social Theory in Modern Societies: Anthony Giddens and His Critics*, Cambridge University Press, 1989.
28 Roy Bhaskar, *Dialectic: The Pulse of Freedom*, Verso, London, 1993, p. 160.
29 Thus he does 'not think it useful, as some others have tried to do, to "apply" structuration theory as a whole to research projects'. Anthony Giddens, 'Structuration Theory and Sociological Analysis', in J. Clarke, C. Modgil and S. Modgil (eds), *Anthony Giddens: Consensus and Controversy*, Falmer, Basingstoke, 1990, pp. 310–11.
30 Roy Bhaskar, *Reclaiming Reality*, Verso, London, 1989, p. 9.

8

SOCIETIES

Roy Bhaskar

Introduction

What properties do societies possess that might make them possible objects of knowledge for us? My strategy in developing an answer to this question will be effectively based on a pincer movement. But in deploying the pincer I shall concentrate first on the ontological question of the properties that societies possess, before shifting to the epistemological question of how these properties make them possible objects of knowledge for us. This is not an arbitrary order of development. It reflects the condition that, for transcendental realism, it is the nature of objects that determines their cognitive possibilities for us; that, in nature, it is humanity that is contingent and knowledge, so to speak, accidental. Thus it is because sticks and stones are solid that they can be picked up and thrown, not because they can be picked up and thrown that they are solid (though that they can be handled in this sort of way may be a contingently necessary condition for our *knowledge* of their solidity).[1]

In the next section I argue that societies are irreducible to people and in the third section I sketch a model of their connection. In that and the following section I argue that social forms are a necessary condition for any intentional act, that their *pre-existence* establishes their *autonomy* as possible objects of scientific investigation and that their *causal power* establishes their *reality*. The pre-existence of social forms will be seen to entail a *transformational* model of social activity, from which a number of ontological limits on any possible naturalism can be immediately derived. In the fifth section I show how it is, just in virtue of these emergent features of societies, that social science is possible; and I relate two other types of limit on naturalism (viz. epistemological and relational ones) back to the fundamental properties of the transformational model itself. In the last section I use the results established in the previous section to generate a critique of the traditional fact/value dichotomy; and in an appendix to the chapter I illustrate the notion of social

Source: The Possibility of Naturalism, chap. 2, Harvester Wheatsheaf, Hemel Hempstead, 1989 (referred to as PON in this chapter).

science as critique in the reconstruction of an essentially Marxian concept of ideology. Now it is important to note that because the causal power of social forms is mediated through human agency, my argument can only be formally completed when the causal status of human agency is itself vindicated. This is accomplished in Chapter 3 [of PON] in the course of a parallel demonstration of the possibility of naturalism in the domain of the psychological sciences.

The transformational model of social activity developed here will be seen to entail a *relational* conception of the subject-matter of social science. On this conception 'society does not consist of individuals [or, we might add, groups], but expresses the sum of the relations within which individuals [and groups] stand'.[2] And the essential movement of scientific theory will be seen to consist in the movement from the manifest phenomena of social life, as conceptualized in the experience of the social agents concerned, to the essential relations that necessitate them. Of such relations the agents involved may or may not be aware. Now it is through the capacity of social science to illuminate such relations that it may come to be 'emancipatory'. But the emancipatory potential of social science is contingent upon, and entirely a consequence of, its contextual explanatory power.

Consider for a moment a magnet F and the effect it has on iron filings placed within its field. Consider next the thought T of that magnet and its effect. That thought is clearly the product of science, of culture, of history. Unlike the magnet it has no (discounting psycho-kinesis) appreciable effect on iron. Now every science must construct its own object (*T*) in thought. But it does not follow from the fact that its thought of its real object (*F*) must be constructed in and by (and exists only in) thought that the object of its investigations is not independently real. (Indeed it was to mark the point, and the associated ambiguity in the notion of an object of knowledge, that I distinguished in Chapter 1 [of PON] between transitive and intransitive objects.)

Now whereas few people nowadays, at least outside the ranks of professional philosophers, would hold that a magnetic field is a construction of thought, the idea that society is remains quite widely held. Of course in the case of society the grounds for this view are liable to consist in the idea that it is constituted (in some way) by the thought of social actors or participants, rather than, as in the case of the magnetic field, the thought of observers or theorists (or perhaps, moving to a more sophisticated plane, in some relationship – such as that of Schutzian 'adequacy',[3] accomplished perhaps by some process of dialogue or negotiation – between the two). And underlying that idea, though by no means logically necessary for it,[4] is more often than not the notion that society just consists (in some sense) in persons and/or their actions. Seldom does it occur to subscribers to this view that an identical train of thought logically entails their own reducibility, via the laws and principles of neurophysiology, to the status of inanimate things!

In the next section I am going to consider the claims of this naïve position, which may be dubbed *social atomism*, or rather of its epistemological manifestation in the form of *methodological individualism*,[5] to provide a framework for the explanation of social phenomena. Of course, as already mentioned in Chapter 1 [of PON], if I am to situate the possibility of a non-reductionist naturalism on transcendental realist lines, then I must establish not only the autonomy of a possible sociology, but the reality of any objects so designated. That is to say, I must show that societies are complex real objects irreducible to simpler ones, such as people. For this purpose, merely to argue against methodological individualism is insufficient. But it is necessary. For if methodological individualism were correct, we could dispense entirely with this chapter, and begin (and end) our inquiry into the human sciences with a consideration of the properties, be they rationally imputed or empirically determined, of the individual atoms themselves: that is, of the amazing (and more or less tacitly gendered) homunculus man.

Against individualism

Methodological individualism is the doctrine that facts about societies, and social phenomena generally, are to be explained solely in terms of facts about individuals. For Popper, for example, 'all social phenomena, and especially the functioning of social institutions, should be understood as resulting from the decisions etc. of human individuals . . . we should never be satisfied by explanations in terms of so-called "collectives"'.[6] Social institutions are merely 'abstract models' designed to interpret the facts of individual experiences. Jarvie has even committed himself to the linguistic thesis that '"army" is just the plural of "soldier" and all statements about the army can be reduced to statements about the particular soldiers comprising it'.[7] Watkins concedes that there may be unfinished or half-way explanations of large-scale phenomena in terms of other large-scale phenomena, such as of inflation in terms of full employment(!),[8] but contends that one will not have arrived at so-called rock-bottom (ultimate?) explanations of such phenomena until one has deduced them from statements about the dispositions, beliefs, resources and interrelations of individuals.[9] Specifically, social events are to be explained by deducing them from the principles governing the behaviour of the 'participating' individuals and descriptions of their situation.[10] In this manner, methodological individualism stipulates the *material* conditions for adequate explanation in the social sciences to complement the *formal* ones laid down by the deductive–nomological model.

Now when one considers the range of predicates applicable to individuals and individual behaviour – from those that designate properties, such as shape and texture, that people possess in common with other material things, through those that pick out states, such as hunger and pain, that they share with other higher animals, to those that designate actions that are, as far as we know, uniquely characteristic of them – the real problem appears to be not so much that of how one could give an individualistic explanation of social behaviour, but that of how one could ever give a non-social (i.e., strictly individualistic) explanation of individual, at least characteristically human, behaviour![11] For the predicates designating properties special to persons all presuppose a social context for their employment. A tribesman implies a tribe, the cashing of a cheque a banking system. Explanation, whether by subsumption under general laws, advertion to motives and rules, or redescription (identification), always involves irreducibly social predicates.

Moreover, it is not difficult to show that the arguments adduced in support of methodological individualism cannot bear the weight placed upon them. Thus comparison of the motives of a criminal with the procedures of a court indicates that facts about individuals are not necessarily either more observable or easier to understand than social facts; while comparison of the concepts of love and war shows that those applicable to individuals are not necessarily either clearer or easier to define than those that designate social phenomena.

Significantly, the qualifications and refinements proposed by methodological individualists weaken rather than strengthen their case. Thus the admission of ideal types, anonymous individuals *et al.*, into the methodological fold weakens the force of the ontological considerations in favour of it, while allowing 'half-way' and statistical explanations undercuts the epistemological ones. Moreover, the examples cited of supposedly genuinely 'holistic' behaviour, such as riots and orgies,[12] merely reveal the poverty of the implicit conception of the social. For, upon analysis of their oeuvre, it turns out that most individualists regard 'the social' as a synonym for 'the group'. The issue for them then becomes that of whether society, the whole, is greater than the sum of its constituent parts, individual people. And social behaviour then becomes explicable as the behaviour of groups of individuals (riots) or of individuals in groups (orgies).

Now I am going to argue that this definition of the social is radically misconceived. Sociology is not concerned, as such, with large-scale, mass or group behaviour (conceived as the behaviour of large numbers, masses or groups of individuals). Rather it is concerned, at least paradigmatically, with the persistent *relations* between individuals (and groups), and with the relations between these relations (and between such relations and nature and the products of such relations). In the simplest case its subject-matter may be exemplified by such relations as between capitalist and worker, MP and constituent, student and teacher, husband and wife. Such relations are general and relatively enduring, but they do not involve collective or mass behaviour as such in the way in which a strike or a demonstration does (though of course they may help to explain the latter). Mass behaviour is an interesting social-psychological phenomenon, but it is not the subject-matter of sociology.

The situation is made ironic by the fact that the more sophisticated individualists formally concede that relations may play a role in explanation.

Why then the passion? I think that it must be explained, at least in part, by their predilection for a species of substantive social explanation, which they mistakenly believe to be uniquely consonant with political liberalism. As Watkins candidly puts it 'Since Mandeville's *Fable of the Bees* was published in 1714, individualistic social science, with its emphasis on unintended consequences, has largely been a sophisticated elaboration on the simple theme that, in certain situations, selfish private motives [i.e. capitalism] may have good social consequences and good political intentions [i.e. socialism] bad social consequences'.[13] There is in fact one body of social doctrine, whose avatars include utilitarianism, liberal political theory and neo-classical economic theory, which does conform to individualistic prescriptions, on the assumption that what is in effect a generalized aggregation problem can be solved. According to this model reason is the efficient slave of the passions[14] and social behaviour can be seen as the outcome of a simple maximization problem, or its dual, a minimization one: the application of reason, the sole identifying characteristic of human beings, to desires (appetites and aversions in Hobbes) or feelings (pleasure and pain, in Hume, Bentham and Mill) that may be regarded as neurophysiologically given. Relations play no part in this model; and this model, if it applies at all, applies as much to Crusoe as to socialized humanity – with the corollary expressed by Hume that 'mankind is much the same at all times and places',[15] simultaneously revealing its ahistorical and *a priori* biases.

The limitations of this approach to social science should by now be well known. To say that people are rational does not explain *what* they do, but only at best (that is, supposing that an objective function could be reconstructed for their behaviour and empirically tested independently of it) *how* they do it. But rationality, setting out to explain everything, very easily ends up explaining nothing. To explain a human action by reference to its rationality is like explaining some natural event by reference to its being caused. Rationality then appears as an *a priori* presupposition of investigation, devoid of explanatory content and almost certainly false. As for neo-classical economic theory, the most developed form of this tendency in social thought, it may be best regarded as a normative theory of efficient action, generating a set of techniques for achieving given ends, rather than as an explanatory theory capable of casting light on actual empirical episodes: that is, as a praxiology,[16] not a sociology.

Besides its championship of a particular explanation form, individualism derives plausibility from the fact that it seems to touch on an important truth, awareness of which accounts for its apparent necessity: namely the idea that society is made up or consists of – and only of – people. In what sense is this true? In the sense that the material presence of social effects consists only in changes in people and changes brought about by people on other material things – objects of nature, such as land, and artefacts, produced by work on objects of nature. One could express this truth as follows: *the material presence of society = persons and the (material) results of their actions*. It is this truth that individualists have glimpsed, only to shroud it with their apologetic shifts.

It is evident that there is at work in methodological individualism a sociological reductionism and a psycho- (or praxio-) logical atomism, determining the content of ideal explanations in exact isomorphy with the theoretical reductionism and ontological atomism fixing their form.[17] It thus expresses particularly starkly the couple defining the method and object of investigation (viz. sociological individualism and ontological empiricism) which I earlier (in Chapter 1 [of PON]) suggested structure the practice of contemporary social science.

Now the *relational* conception of the subject-matter of sociology may be contrasted not only with the *individualist* conception, illustrated by utilitarian theory, but with what I shall call the 'collectivist' conception, best exemplified perhaps by Durkheim's work, with its heavy emphasis on the concept of the group. Durkheim's group is not of course Popper's. It is, to invoke a Sartrean analogy, more like a fused group than a series.[18] In particular, as an index of the social, it is characterized by the possession of certain emergent powers, whose justification will be considered below. Nevertheless, the key concepts of the Durkheimian corpus, such as *conscience collective*, organic v. mechanical solidarity, anomie, etc., all derive their meaning from their relationship to the concept of the collective nature of social phenomena. Thus, for Durkheim, to the extent at least that he is to remain committed to positivism, enduring relationships must be reconstructed from collective phenomena; whereas on the realist and relational view advanced here collective phenomena are seen primarily as the expressions of enduring relationships. Note that, on this conception, not only is sociology not essentially concerned with the group, it is not even essentially concerned with behaviour.

If Durkheim combined a collectivist conception of sociology with a positivist methodology, Weber combined a neo-Kantian methodology with a still essentially individualist conception of sociology. His break from utilitarianism is primarily at the level of the form of action or type of behaviour he is prepared to recognize, not at the level of the unit of study. It is significant that just as the thrust contained in Durkheim's isolation of the emergent properties of the group is checked by his continuing commitment to an empiricist epistemology, so the possibilities opened up by Weber's isolation of the ideal type are constrained by his continuing commitment to an empiricist ontology. In both cases a residual empiricism holds back, and ultimately annuls, a real scientific advance.[19] For it is as futile to attempt to sustain a concept of the social on the basis of the category of the group, as it is to attempt to sustain a concept of necessity on that of experience. Marx did, I think, make an attempt to combine a realist ontology and a relational sociology.[20] One can thus schematize four tendencies in social thought as in Table 1.

Table 1 Four tendencies in social thought

	Method	*Object*
Utilitarianism	empiricist	individualist
Weber	neo-Kantian	individualist
Durkheim	empiricist	collectivist
Marx	realist	relational

N.B. Concepts of method (social epistemology) underpinned by general ontology; concepts of object (social ontology) underpinned by general epistemology.

It should be noted that as the relations between the relations that constitute the proper subject-matter of sociology may be *internal*, only the category of *totality* can, in general, adequately express it. Some problems stemming from this will be considered below. But first I want to consider the nature of the connection between society and the conscious activity of people.

On the society/person connection

It is customary to draw a divide between two camps in sociological theory: one, represented above all by Weber, in which social objects are seen as the results of (or as constituted by) intentional or meaningful human behaviour; and the other, represented by Durkheim, in which they are seen as possessing a life of their own, external to and coercing the individual. With some stretching the various schools of social thought – phenomenology, existentialism, functionalism, structuralism, etc. – can then be seen as instances of one or other of these positions. And the varieties of Marxism can then also be neatly classified. These two stereotypes can be represented as in the diagrams below.

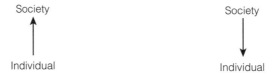

Model I The Weberian stereotype 'Voluntarism'

Model II The Durkheimian stereotype 'Reification'

Now it is tempting to try and develop a general model capable of synthesizing these conflicting perspectives, on the assumption of a dialectical interrelationship between society and people. I want to discuss a plausible variant of such a model, advocated most convincingly by Peter Berger and his associates.[21] Its weaknesses will, I think, enable us to work our way to a more adequate conception of the relationship between society and people, as well as to better display the errors of the conventional stereotypes.

According to the Berger model, which I shall call Model III, society forms the individuals who create society; society, in other words, produces the individuals, who produce society, in a continuous dialectic. Model III can be represented as below.

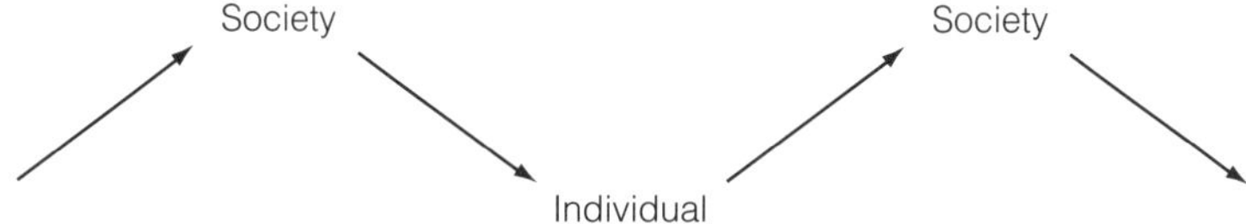

Model III The 'Dialectical' conception 'Illicit Identification'

According to the protagonists of this model 'social structure is not characterizable as a thing able to stand on its own, apart from the human activity that produced it'.[22] But equally, once created, 'it is encountered by the individual [both] as an alien facticity [and] . . . as a coercive instrumentality'.[23] 'It is *there*, impervious to his wishes . . . other than [and resistant to] himself.'[24] This scheme thus seems able to do justice both to the subjective and intentional aspects of social life and to the externality and coercive power of social facts. And thus to avoid at once any voluntaristic implications of the Weberian tradition and any reification associated with the Durkheimian one. For a categorial distinction is now drawn between natural and social facts, in that the latter, but not the former, depend essentially upon human activity.

Thus, while agreeing with Durkheim that 'the system of signs I use to express my thoughts, the system of currency I employ to pay my debts, the instruments of credit I utilize in my commercial relations, the practices followed in my profession, etc., function independently of my use of them',[25] the advocates of this model regard such systems, instruments and practices as *objectivations* that, under certain conditions, take on an alienated form. According to them, objectivation is 'the process whereby human subjectivity embodies itself in products that are available to oneself and one's fellow men as elements of a common world'[26] and alienation is 'the process whereby the unity of the producing and its product is broken'.[27] Thus languages, forms of political and economic organization, and cultural and ethical norms are all ultimately embodiments of human subjectivity. And any consciousness which does not see them as such is necessarily reified. Reification must, however, be distinguished from *objectivication*, which is defined as 'the moment in the process of objectivation in which man establishes distance from his producing and its product, such that he can take cognizance of it and make of it an object of his consciousness',[28] and is regarded as necessary to any conceivable social life.

On Model III, then, society is an objectivation or externalization of human beings. And human beings, for their part, are the internalization or reappropriation in consciousness of society. Now I think that this model is seriously misleading. For it encourages, on the one hand, a voluntaristic idealism with respect to our understanding of social structure and, on the other, a mechanistic determinism with respect to our understanding of people. In seeking to avoid the errors of both stereotypes, Model III succeeds only in combining them. People and society are not, I shall argue, related 'dialectically'. They do not constitute two moments of the same process. Rather they refer to radically different kinds of thing.

Let us consider society. Return for a moment to Durkheim. It will be recalled that, reminding us that the member of a church (or let us say, the user of a language) finds the beliefs and practices of his or her religious life (or the structure of his or her language) ready-made at birth, he argues that it is their existence *prior* to his or her own that implies their existence *outside* themselves, and from which their coercive power is ultimately derived.[29] Now if this is the case and the social structure, and the natural world in so far as it is appropriated by human beings, is always *already made*, then Model III must be corrected in a fundamental way. It is still true to say that society would not exist without human activity, so that reification remains an error. And it is still true to say that such activity would not occur unless the agents engaging in it had a conception of what they were doing (which is of course the fundamental insight of the hermeneutical tradition). But it is no longer true to say that agents *create* it. Rather one must say: they *reproduce* or *transform* it. That is, if society is always already made, then any concrete human praxis, or, if you like, act of objectivation can only modify it; and the totality of such acts sustain or change it. It is not the product of their activity (any more, I shall argue, than human action is completely determined by it). Society stands to individuals, then, as something that they never make, but that exists only in virtue of their activity.

Now if society pre-exists the individual, objectivation takes on a very different significance. For it, conscious human activity, consists in work on *given* objects and cannot be conceived as occurring in their absence. A moment's reflection shows why this must be so. For all activity presupposes the prior existence of social forms. Thus consider *saying, making* and *doing* as characteristic modalities of human agency. People cannot communicate except by utilizing existing media, produce except by applying themselves to materials which are already formed, or act save in some or other context. Speech requires language; making materials; action conditions; agency resources; activity rules. Even spontaneity has as its necessary condition the pre-existence of a social form with (or by means of) which the spontaneous act is performed. Thus if the social cannot be reduced to (and is not the product of) the individual, it is equally clear that society is a necessary condition for any intentional human act at all.

Now the necessary pre-existence of social forms suggests a radically different conception of social activity from that which typically informs discussion of the society/person connection. It suggests an essentially Aristotelian one, in which the paradigm is that of a sculptress at work, fashioning a product out of the material and with the tools available to her. I shall call this the *transformational model of social activity*. It applies to discursive as well as to non-discursive practices; to science and politics, as much as to technology and economics. Thus in science the raw materials used in the construction of new theories include established results and half-forgotten ideas, the stock of available paradigms and models, methods and techniques of inquiry, so that the scientific innovator comes to appear in retrospect as a kind of cognitive *bricoleur*.[30] To use the Aristotelian terms, then, in every process of productive activity a material as well as an efficient cause is necessary. And, following Marx, one can regard social activity as consisting, analytically, in *production*, that is in work on (and with), entailing the transformation of, those material causes. Now if, following Durkheim, one regards society as providing the material causes of human action, and following Weber, one refuses to reify it, it is easy to see that both society and human praxis must possess a *dual character*. Society is both the ever-present *condition* (material cause) and the continually reproduced *outcome* of human agency. And praxis is both work, that is, conscious *production*, and (normally unconscious) *reproduction* of the conditions of production, that is society. One could refer to the former as the *duality of structure*,[31] and the latter as the *duality of praxis.*

Let us turn now to people. Human action is characterized by the striking phenomenon of intentionality. This seems to depend upon the feature that persons are material things with a degree of neurophysiological complexity which enables them not just, like the other higher-order animals, to initiate changes in a purposeful way, to monitor and control their performances, but to monitor the monitoring of these performances and to be capable of a commentary upon them.[32] This capacity for second-order monitoring also makes possible a retrospective commentary upon actions, which gives a person's account of his or her own behaviour a special status which is acknowledged in the best practice of all the psychological sciences.

The importance of distinguishing categorically between people and societies, and correspondingly between human actions and changes in the social structure, should now be clear. For the properties possessed by social forms may be very different from those possessed by the individuals upon whose activity they depend. Thus one can allow, without paradox or strain, that purposefulness, intentionality and sometimes self-consciousness characterize human actions but not transformations in the social structure.[33] The conception I am proposing is that people, in their conscious activity, for the most part unconsciously reproduce (and occasionally transform) the structures governing their substantive activities of production. Thus people do not marry to reproduce the nuclear family or work to sustain the capitalist economy. Yet it is nevertheless the unintended consequence (and inexorable result) of, as it is also a necessary condition for, their activity. Moreover, when social forms change, the explanation will not normally lie in the desires of agents to change them that way, though as a very important theoretical and political limit it *may* do so.

I want to distinguish sharply, then, between the genesis of human actions, lying in the reasons, intentions and plans of people, on the one hand, and the structures governing the reproduction and transformation of social activities, on the other; and hence between the domains of the psychological and the social sciences. The problem of how people reproduce any particular society belongs to a linking science of 'socio-psychology'. It should be noted that engagement in a social activity is itself a conscious human action which may, in general, be described either in terms of the agent's reason for engaging in it or in terms of its social function or role. When praxis is seen under the aspect of process, human choice becomes functional necessity.

Now the autonomy of the social and the psychological is at one with our intuitions. Thus we do not suppose that the reason why garbage is collected is necessarily the garbage collector's reason for collecting it (though it depends upon the latter). And we can allow that speech is governed by the rules of grammar without supposing either that these rules exist independently of usage (reification) or that they determine what we say. The rules of grammar, like natural structures, impose *limits* on the speech acts we can perform, but they do not *determine* our performances. This conception thus preserves the status of human agency, while doing away with the myth of creation (logical or historical), which depends upon the possibility of an individualist reduction. And in so doing it allows us to see that necessity in social life operates in the last instance via the intentional activity of agents. Looked at in this way, then, one may regard it as the task of the different social sciences to lay out the structural conditions for various forms of conscious human action – for example, what economic processes must take place for Christmas shopping to be possible – but they do not describe the latter.

The model of the society/person connection I am proposing could be summarized as follows: people do not create society. For it always pre-exists them and is a necessary condition for their activity. Rather, society must be regarded as an ensemble of structures, practices and conventions which individuals reproduce or transform, but which would not exist unless they did so. Society does not exist independently of human activity (the error of reification). But it is not the product of it (the error of voluntarism). Now the processes whereby the stocks of skills, competences and habits appropriate to given social contexts, and necessary for the reproduction and/or transformation of society, are acquired and maintained could be generically referred to as *socialization*. It is important to stress that the reproduction and/or transformation of society, though for the most part unconsciously achieved, is nevertheless still an *achievement*, a skilled accomplishment of active subjects, not a mechanical consequent of antecedent conditions. This model of the society/person connection can be represented as below.

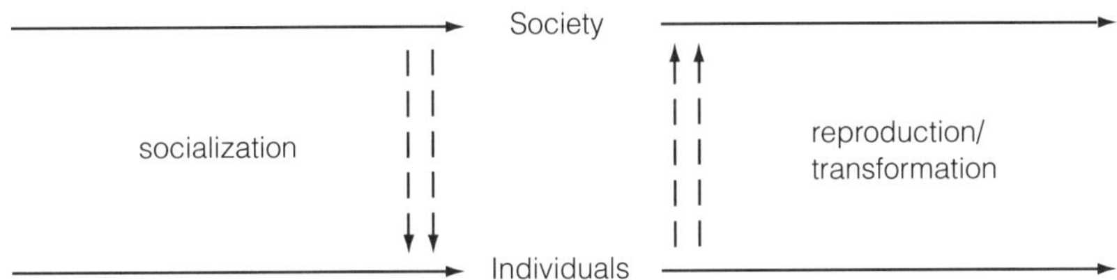

Model IV The transformational model of the society/person connection

Society, then, provides necessary conditions for intentional human action, and intentional human action is a necessary condition for it. Society is only present in human action, but human action always expresses and utilizes some or other social form. Neither can, however, be identified with, reduced to, explained in terms of, or reconstructed from the other. There is an ontological hiatus between society and people, as well as mode of connection (viz. transformation) that the other models typically ignore.

Notice that on Model I there are actions, but no conditions; on Model II conditions, but no actions; on Model III no distinction between the two. Thus in Durkheim, for example, subjectivity tends to appear only in the guise of the interiorized form of social constraint. But it should be equally clear, against voluntarism, that real subjectivity requires conditions, resources and media for the creative subject to act. Such material causes may be regarded, if one likes, as the results of prior objectivations. But they are, in *any* act, analytically irreducible and actually indispensable all the same. The 'given' component in social action can never be reduced to zero, analysed away. This conception of the society/person connection thus implies a radical transformation in our idea of a non-alienating society. For this can now no longer be conceived as the immaculate product of unconditioned ('responsible') human decisions, free from the constraints (but presumably not the opportunities) inherited from its past and imposed by its environment. Rather it must be conceived as one in which people self-consciously transform their social conditions of existence (the social structure) so as to maximize the possibilities for the development and spontaneous exercise of their natural (species) powers.

It should be noted that Model IV, as a result of its emphasis on material continuity, can sustain a genuine concept of *change*, and hence of *history*.[34] This is something that neither Model III nor the methodological stereotypes it attempts to situate as special cases can do. Thus Model III appears to involve continuous recreation, with genuine novelty, seemingly entailing incomplete social formation, something of a mystery. On the Weberian stereotype change reduces to contrast, and on the Durkheimian it can only be explained by advertion to exogenous variables. Model IV, moreover, generates a clear criterion of historically significant events: viz. those that initiate or constitute ruptures, mutations or more generally transformations in social forms (such as Dalton's training as a meteorologist or the French Revolution).

Some emergent properties of social systems

Now if social activity consists, analytically, in production, that is in work on and the transformation of given objects, and if such work constitutes an analogue of natural events, then we need an analogue for the mechanisms that generate it. If social structures constitute the appropriate mechanism-analogue, then an important difference must be immediately registered – in that, unlike natural mechanisms, they exist only in virtue of the activities they govern and cannot be empirically identified independently of them. Because of this, they must be social products themselves. Thus people in their social activity must perform a double function: they must not only make social products, but make the conditions of their making, that is reproduce (or to a greater or lesser extent transform) the structures governing their substantive activities of production. Because social structures are themselves social products, they are themselves possible objects of transformation and so may be only relatively enduring. Moreover the differentiation and development of social activities (as in the 'division of labour' and 'expanded reproduction' respectively) implies that they are interdependent; so social structures may be only relatively autonomous. Society may thus be conceived as an articulated ensemble of such relatively independent and enduring generative structures; that is, as a complex totality subject to change both in its components and their interrelations. Now, as social structures exist only in virtue of the activities they govern, they do not exist independently of the conceptions that the agents possess of what they are doing in their activity, that is, of some theory of these activities. Because such theories are themselves social products, they are themselves possible objects of transformation and so they too may be only relatively enduring (and autonomous). Finally, because social structures are themselves social products, social activity must be given a social explanation, and cannot be explained by reference to non-social parameters (though the latter may impose constraints on the possible forms of social activity).

Some ontological limitations on a possible naturalism may be immediately derived from these emergent social properties, on the assumption (to be vindicated below) that society is *sui generis* real:

1 Social structures, unlike natural structures, do not exist independently of the activities they govern.
2 Social structures, unlike natural structures, do not exist independently of the agents' conceptions of what they are doing in their activity.
3 Social structures, unlike natural structures, may be only relatively endur-

ing (so that the tendencies they ground may not be universal in the sense of space–time invariant).

These all indicate real differences in the possible objects of knowledge in the case of the natural and social sciences. (The internal complexity and interdependence of social structures do not mark a *necessary* difference from natural ones.) They are not of course unconnected, though one should be wary of drawing conclusions of the sort: 'Society exists only in virtue of human activity. Human activity is conscious. Therefore consciousness brings about change'. For (a) social changes need not be consciously intended and (b) if there are social conditions for consciousness, changes in it can in principle be socially explained. Society, then, is an articulated ensemble of tendencies and powers which, unlike natural ones, exist only as long as they (or at least some of them) are being exercised; are exercised in the last instance via the intentional activity of human beings; and are not necessarily space–time invariant.

I now want to turn to the ontological status of societies. I have argued elsewhere that living things determine the conditions of applicability of the physical laws to which they are subject, so that their properties cannot be reduced to the latter; that is, that emergence characterizes both the natural and the human worlds[35] (and that this is consistent with what may be termed a 'diachronic explanatory reduction', that is, a reconstruction of the historical processes of their formation out of 'simpler' things). Now if, as I shall show in Chapter 3, intentional action is a necessary condition for certain determinate states of the physical world, then the properties and powers that persons possess in virtue of which intentionality is correctly attributed to them are real. Similarly, if it can be shown that but for society certain physical actions would not be performed, then employing the causal criterion set out in Chapter 1 [of PON], one is justified in asserting that it is real.

Now I think that Durkheim, having established the *autonomy* of social facts using the criterion of *externality*, in effect employed just such a criterion to establish their *reality*, in invoking his other criterion of *constraint:*

> I am not obliged to speak French with my fellow-countrymen nor to use the legal currency, but I cannot possibly do otherwise. If I tried to escape this necessity, my attempt would fail miserably. As an industrialist I am free to apply the technical methods of former centuries, but by doing so I should invite certain ruin. Even when I free myself from these rules and violate them successfully, I am always compelled to struggle with them. When finally overcome, they make their constraining power felt by the resistance they offer.[36]

Durkheim is saying in effect that but for the range of social facts, particular sequences of sounds, movements of bodies, etc., would not occur. Of course, one must insist, against Durkheim, that the range of social facts depends upon (though it is irreducible to) the intentional activity of human beings. The individualist truth that people are the only moving forces in history – in the sense that nothing happens, as it were, behind their backs; that is, everything that happens, happens in and through their actions – must be retained. Moreover, social structures must be conceived as in principle *enabling*, not just coercive. Nevertheless, in employing a causal criterion to establish the reality of social facts, Durkheim observed perfectly proper scientific practice – though it must be recognized that one is here dealing with a most peculiar kind of entity: a structure irreducible to, but present only in its effects.

Although Durkheim used a causal criterion to establish the reality of social facts, on a collectivist conception of sociology, the same criterion can be employed (with more epistemological consistency) to establish their reality on a relational one. (There is no special difficulty, as for example the concept of spin in physics shows, in ascribing reality to relations on a causal criterion.) Indeed, given the openness of the world within which its phenomena occur, it is only if a non-empirical object is specified for it that sociology's theoretical autonomy can be definitely secured – a point dramatically illustrated by the pitfalls into which Weber's definition of sociology,[37] which logically includes worship (because other-orientated) but excludes prayer, plunges it.

What is the connection between the transformational model of social activity developed in the previous section and the relational conception of sociology advanced in the second section? The relational conception does not of course deny that factories and books are social forms. Nor does it insist that the rules of grammar (or the generative complexes at work in other spheres of social life) are, or must be conceived as, relations. But it maintains that their being *social*, as distinct from (or rather in addition to) material objects, and their consisting in *social* rules, as distinct from purely 'anankastic' ones[38] (which depend upon the operation of natural laws alone), depends essentially on, and indeed in a sense consists entirely in, the relationships between people and between such relationships and nature (and the products and functions of such relationships) that such objects and rules causally presuppose or entail.

It is not difficult to see why this must be so. For it follows from the argument of the previous section that social structures (a) be continually reproduced (or transformed) and (b) exist only in virtue of, and are exercised only in, human agency (in short, that they require active 'functionaries'). Combining these desiderata, it is evident that we need a system of mediating concepts, encompassing both aspects of the duality of praxis, designating the 'slots', as it were, in the social structure into which active subjects must slip in order to reproduce it; that is, a system of concepts designating the 'point of contact' between human agency and social structures. Such a point, linking action to structure, must *both* endure and be immediately occupied by individuals. It is clear that the mediating system we need is that of the *positions* (places, functions, rules, tasks, duties, rights, etc.) occupied (filled, assumed, enacted, etc.) by individuals, and of the *practices* (activities, etc.) in which, in virtue of their occupancy of these positions (and vice versa), they engage. I shall call this mediating system the position-practice system. Now such positions and practices, if they are to be individuated at all, can only be done so *relationally*.

It follows as an immediate consequence of this that the initial conditions in any concrete social explanation must always include or tacitly presuppose reference to some or other social relation (however the generative structures invoked are themselves best conceived). And it is, I suggest, in the (explanation of the) differentiation and stratification, production and reproduction, mutation and transformation, continual remoulding and incessant shifting, of the relatively enduring relations presupposed by particular social forms and structures that sociology's distinctive theoretical interest lies. Thus the transformational model implies a relational interest for sociology. And it suggests in terms of that interest a way of differentiating sociology from the other social sciences (such as linguistics, economics, etc.), which, however, logically presuppose it.

It should be noted that neither individuals nor groups satisfy the requirement of continuity derived from the reapplication of Durkheim's criterion (of externality or pre-existence) for the autonomy of society over discrete moments of time. In social life only relations endure.[39] Note also that such relations include relationships between people and nature and social products (such as machines and firms), as well as interpersonal ones. And that such relations include, but do not all consist in, 'interactions'. (Thus contrast the relationship between speaker and hearer in dialogue with the deontic relationship between citizen and state.) Finally, it is important to stress that from the standpoint of the social sciences, though not necessarily either that of the psychological sciences or of historical explanation, the relations one is concerned with here must be conceptualized as holding between the positions and practices (or better, positioned-practices), not between the individuals who occupy/engage in them.[40]

One advantage of the relational conception should be immediately apparent. It allows one to focus on a range of questions having to do with the *distribution* of the structural conditions of action, and in particular with differential allocations of: (a) productive resources (of all kinds, including for example cognitive ones) to persons (and groups) and (b) persons (and groups) to functions and roles (for example in the division of labour). In doing so, it allows one to situate the possibility of different (and antagonistic) interests, of conflicts *within* society, and hence of interest-motivated transformations in social structure. In focusing on distribution as well as exchange, the relational conception avoids the endemic weakness of (market) economics. And in allowing conflicts within society as well as between society and the individual, it remedies the chronic failing of (orthodox) sociology, preoccupied as that was (and indeed still is) with the 'Hobbesian problem of order'.[41]

Marx combined an essentially relational conception of social science and a transformational model of social activities with the additional premise – of historical materialism – that it is material production that ultimately determines the rest of social life.[42] Now, as is well known, although it can be established a priori that material production is a necessary condition for social life, it cannot be proved that it is the ultimately determining one. And so, like any other fundamental conceptual blueprint or paradigm in science, historical materialism can only be justified by its fruitfulness in generating projects encapsulating research programmes capable of generating sequences of theories, progressively richer in explanatory power. Not the least of the problems facing historical materialism is that, although considerable progress has been made in particular areas of explanation, the blueprint itself still awaits adequate articulation. (One has only to think of the problem of reconciling the thesis of the relative autonomy of the superstructures with that of their determination in the last instance by the base to be reminded of this.)[43]

It is doubtful if any topic in philosophy has been more dogged by dogma than that of internal relations. The doctrine that all relations are external is implicit in the Humean theory of causality, where it is enshrined in the notion of the contingency of the causal connection. But it has been accepted by virtually the whole orthodox (empiricist and neo-Kantian) tradition in the philosophy of science. Conversely, rationalists, absolute idealists and mistresses of the arts of Hegelian and Bergsonian dialectics have usually subscribed to the equally erroneous view that all relations are internal. Here again, a major philosophical difference cuts across the Marxist/non-Marxist divide. Colletti and Ollman[44] represent only the most recent, and particularly extreme, variants of positions already fully articulated within Marxism at least as far back as Hilferding and Dietzgen. Now it is essential to recognize that some relations are internal, and some are not. Moreover, some natural relations (such as that between a magnet and its field) are internal, and many social relations (such as that between two cyclists crossing on a hill top) are not. It is in principle an open question whether or not some particular relation, in historical time, is internal.

A relation R_{AB} may be defined as *internal* if and only if A would not be what it *essentially* is unless B is related to it in the way that it is. R_{AB} is *symmetrically internal* if the same applies also to B. ('A' and 'B' may designate universals or particulars, concepts or things, including relations.) The relation bourgeoisie–proletariat is symmetrically internal; traffic warden–state asymmetrically internal; passing motorist–policeman not (in general) internal at all. The fact that it is an epistemically contingent question as to whether or not some given relation is internal is obscured by the condition that when one knows what a thing's essential nature is, one is then often in a position to give a real definition of it; so that it will then appear to be analytic that *B* is related to it in the way that it is. But of course real definitions are not plucked a priori out of hats, spun out of thought alone. Rather they are produced a posteriori, in the irreducibly empirical process of science.[45]

It is vital to appreciate that there can be no presumption of explanatory equality between the *relata* of an internal relationship. Thus capitalist production may dominate (determine the forms of) exchange, without the latter ceasing to be essential for it. Internally related aspects may command, as it were, differential causal force. Or, to put it another way, *ontological depth* or stratification, defined causally, is consistent with *relational internality*, including symmetry, that is, existential parity. Indeed it is characteristic of the social sphere that surface structure is necessary for deep, just as *langue* is a condition of *parole* and intentionality of system.

Now most social phenomena, like most natural events, are *conjuncturally* determined and, as such, in general have to be explained in terms of a multiplicity of causes.[46] But, given the epistemic contingency of their relational character, the extent to which their explanation requires reference to a *totality* of aspects, bearing internal relations to one another, remains open. However, even a superficially external relationship, such as that between Breton fishermen and the owners of the shipwrecked tanker *Amoco Cadiz* may, given the appropriate focus of explanatory interest, permit (or necessitate) a totalization revealing, for example, the relationships between forms of economic activity and state structure. This ever-present possibility of discovering what is a (potentially new) totality in a nexus accounts for the chameleon-like and 'configurational'[47] quality of a subject-matter which is not only always changing but may (in this respect like any other) be continually redescribed. Now although *totalization* is a process in thought, totalities are *real*. Although it is contingent whether we require a phenomenon to be understood as an aspect of a totality (depending upon our cognitive interests), it is not contingent whether it *is* such an aspect or not. Social science does not create the totalities it reveals, although it may itself be an aspect of them.

It has always been the special claim of Marxism to be able to grasp social life as a totality, to display it, in Labriola's words, as 'a connection and complexus',[48] whose various moments may of course be asymmetrically weighted, primed with differential causal force. And Marxism has claimed to be able to do so in virtue of a theory of history, specifying *inter alia* the mode of articulation of the moments of that totality or instances of the social structure. The theory of history can only be judged by historical materials. But can anything be said, in the light of the foregoing analysis, about the intentions, if not the results, of this project?

Our analysis indicates a way of conceptualizing the relationship between the special social sciences (such as linguistics, economics, politics, etc.), sociology, history and a totalizing theory of society such as that ventured by Marxism. If history is above all the science of the 'past particular' and sociology is the science of social relations, the various social sciences are concerned with the structural conditions for (that is, the generative complexes at work in the production of) particular types of social activity. Of course, given the interdependence of social activities, hypostatization of the results of such particular analyses must be most assiduously avoided. Moreover, as external conditions may be internally related to the generative mechanisms at work in particular spheres of social life, the special sciences logically presuppose a totalizing one, which, on the transformational model, can only be a theory of history. If sociology is concerned with the structures governing the relationships which are necessary, in particular historical periods, for the reproduction (and transformation) of particular social forms, its *explananda* are always specific; so there can be no sociology-in-general, only the sociology of particular historically situated social forms. In this way, sociology presupposes both the special sciences and history. But the relational conception entails that the *social* conditions for the substantive activities of transformation in which agents engage can only be *relations* of various kinds. And the transformational model entails that these activities are essentially *productions*. The subject-matter of sociology is, thus, precisely: *relations of production* (of various kinds). Now if such relations are themselves internally related and subject to transformation, then sociology must either presuppose or usurp the place of just such a totalizing and historical science of society as Marxism has claimed to be. In short, to invoke a Kantian metaphor,[49] if Marxism without detailed social scientific and historical work is empty, then such work without Marxism (or some such theory) is blind.

On the limits of naturalism

In the third section I argued that the pre-existence of social forms is a necessary condition for any intentional act, and I showed how such pre-existence entails a transformational model of social activities. In the previous section I derived a number of ontological limits on naturalism, as emergent features of societies, and vindicated the notion of their *sui generis* reality. I now want to complete my argument by showing how, given that societies exist and have the properties (derived from the transformational model) that they do, they might become possible objects of knowledge for us.

It will be recalled that the major ontological limits on the possibility of naturalism turn on the activity-, concept-, and space–time-dependence of social structures (see (1) to (3) on p. 38). Before considering how social science is possible despite, or rather (as I shall attempt to show) because of, these features, differentiating its subject-matter from nature, I want to consider two other types of limit of naturalism, which may be characterized as epistemological and relational respectively.

Society, as an object of inquiry, is necessarily 'theoretical', in the sense that, like a magnetic field, it is necessarily unperceivable. As such it cannot be empirically identified independently of its effects; so that it can only be known, not shown, to exist. However, in this respect it is no different from many objects of natural scientific inquiry. What does distinguish it is that not only can society not be identified independently of its effects, it does not *exist* independently of them either. But however strange this is from an ontological point of view,[50] it raises no special epistemological difficulties.

The chief epistemological limit on naturalism is not raised by the necessarily unperceivable character of the objects of social scientific inquiry, but rather by the fact that they only ever manifest themselves in open systems; that is, in systems where invariant empirical regularities do not obtain. For social systems are not spontaneously, and cannot be experimentally, closed. Now it is as easy to exaggerate the real methodological import of this point, as it is to underestimate its critical significance for the doctrines of received philosophy of science. For, as I have shown in detail elsewhere,[51] practically all the theories of orthodox philosophy of science, and the methodological directives they secrete, presuppose closed systems. Because of this, they are totally inapplicable in the social sciences (which is not of course to say that the attempt cannot be made to apply them – to disastrous effect). Humean theories of causality and law, deductive–nomological and statistical models of explanation, inductivist theories of scientific development and criteria of confirmation, Popperian theories of scientific rationality and criteria of falsification, together with the hermeneutical contrasts parasitic upon them, must all be totally discarded. Social science need only consider them as objects of substantive explanation.

The real methodological import of the absence of closed systems is strictly limited: it is that the social sciences are denied, in principle, decisive test situations for their theories. This means that criteria for the rational development and replacement of theories in social science must be *explanatory and non-predictive*. (Particularly important here will be the capacity of a theory (or research programme) to be developed in a non-*ad hoc* way so as to situate, and preferably explain, without strain, a possibility once (and perhaps even before) it is realized, when it could never, given the openness of the social world, have predicted it.) It should be stressed that this difference has in itself no ontological significance whatsoever. It does not affect the form of laws, which in natural science too must be analysed as tendencies; only the form of our knowledge of them. Moreover, because the mode of application of laws is the same in open and closed systems alike,[52] there is no reason to suppose that the mode of application of social laws will be any different from natural ones. And although the necessity to rely exclusively on explanatory criteria *may* affect the subjective confidence with which beliefs are held, if a social scientific theory or hypothesis has been *independently* validated (on explanatory grounds) then one is in principle just as warranted in applying it transfactually as a natural scientific one. Moreover, given that the problem is typically not *whether* to apply some theory T to the world, but rather *which* out of two or more theories, T, T', to apply, the degree of our *relative* preference for one theory over another will not be affected by a restriction on the grounds with which that preference must be justified.

The fact that the subject-matter of the social sciences is both intrinsically historical and structured by relations of internal, as well as external, interdependency sets a constraint upon the kinds of permissible theory-construction. For it may, as argued in the previous section, necessitate reference in principle to conceptions of historically developing totalities. But it does not pose an additional difficulty, over and above the unavailability of closures, for the empirical testing of theories.[53] However, two significant limits on the possibility of meaningful *measurement* in the social sciences should be noted. The *irreversibility* of ontologically irreducible processes, comparable to entropy in the natural sphere, entails the necessity for concepts of qualitative rather than merely quantitative change.[54] But the *conceptual* aspect of the subject-matter of the social sciences circumscribes the possibility of measurement in an even more fundamental way.[55] For meanings cannot be measured, only understood. Hypotheses about them must be expressed in language, and confirmed in dialogue. Language here stands to the conceptual aspect of social science as geometry stands to physics. And precision in meaning now assumes the place of accuracy in measurement as the a posteriori arbiter of theory. It should be stressed that in both cases theories may continue to be justified and validly used to explain, even though *significant* measurement of the phenomena of which they treat has become impossible.

Now experimental activity in natural science not only facilitates (relatively)[56] decisive test situations, it enables *practical access*, as it were, to the otherwise latent structures of nature. And the malleability achieved in the laboratory may provide an invaluable component in the process of scientific discovery that the social sciences, in this respect, will be denied. However, our analysis of the relational and ontological limits will yield an analogue and a compensator respectively for the role of experimental practice in discovery.

The chief relational difference is that the social sciences are part of their own field of inquiry, in principle susceptible to explanation in terms of the concepts and laws of the explanatory theories they employ; so that they are *internal* with respect to their subject-matter in a way in which the natural sciences are not. This necessitates a precision in the sense in which their objects of knowledge can be said to be 'intransitive' (see Chapter 1 [of PON]). For it is possible, and indeed likely, given the internal complexity and interdependence of social activities, that these objects may be causally affected by social science, and in some cases not exist independently of it (as for example in the sociology of social science!). Conversely, one would expect social science to be affected or conditioned by developments in what it patently cannot exist independently of, viz. the rest of society. Thus, whereas, in general, in the natural world the objects of knowledge exist and act independently of the process of the production of the knowledge of which they are the objects, in the social arena this is not so. For the process of knowledge-production may be causally, and internally, related to the process of the production of the objects concerned. However, I want to distinguish such *causal interdependency*, which is a contingent feature of the processes concerned, from *existential intransitivity*, which is an a priori condition of any investigation and applies in the same way in the social, as the natural, sphere. For, although the processes of production may be interdependent, once some object O_t exists, if it exists, however it has been produced, it constitutes a possible object of scientific investigation. And its existence (or not), and properties, are quite independent of the act or process of investigation of which it is the putative object, even though such an investigation, once initiated, may radically modify it. In short, the concept of existence is univocal: 'being' means the same in the human as the natural world, even though the modes of being may radically differ. The human sciences, then, take intransitive objects like any other. But the categorial properties of such objects differ. And among the most important of these differences is the feature that they are themselves an aspect of, and causal agent in, what they seek to explain. It is vital to be clear about this point. For if it is the characteristic error of positivism to ignore (or play down) interdependency it is the characteristic error of hermeneutics to dissolve intransitivity. As will be seen, both errors function to the same effect, foreclosing the possibility of scientific critique, upon which the project of human self-emancipation depends.

So far the case for causal interdependency has turned merely on the possibility of a relatively undifferentiated society/social science link. But the case for such a link may be strengthened by noting that just as a social science without a society is impossible, so a society without some kind of scientific, proto-scientific or ideological theory of itself is inconceivable (even if it consists merely in the conceptions that the agents have of what they are doing in their activity). Now if one denotes the proto-scientific set of ideas P, then the transformational model of social activity applied to the activity of knowledge-production suggests that social scientific theory, T, requiring cognitive resources, is produced, at least in part, by the transformation of P. The hypothesis under consideration is that this transformation will be vitally affected by developments in the rest of society, S.

It might be conjectured that in periods of transition or crisis generative structures, previously opaque, become more visible to agents.[57] And that this, though it never yields quite the epistemic possibilities of a closure (even when agents are self-consciously seeking to transform the social conditions of their existence), does provide a partial analogue to the role played by experimentation in natural science. The conditions for the emergence of a new social scientific theory must of course be distinguished from the conditions for its subsequent development and from the conditions for its permeation into the *Lebenswelt* of lived experience (or incorporation into social policy), though there are evident (and reciprocal) connections between them.[58] Thus it is surely no accident that Marxism was born in the 1840s or stunted under the combined effects of Stalinism, on the one hand, and Fascism, the Cold War and the 1945–70 boom, on the other;[59] or that sociology, in the narrow sense, was the fruit of the two decades before the First World War.[60]

It should be noted that because social systems are open, historicism (in the sense of deductively justified predictability) is untenable. And because of their historical (transformational) character, qualitatively new developments will be occurring which social scientific theory cannot be expected to anticipate. Hence for ontological, as distinct from purely epistemological, reasons, social scientific (unlike natural scientific) theory is *necessarily* incomplete. Moreover as the possibilities inherent in a new social development will often only become apparent long after the development itself, and as each new development is, in a sense, a product of a previous one, we can now see why it is that history must be continually rewritten.[61] There is a relational tie between the development of knowledge and the development of the object of knowledge that any adequate theory of social science, and methodology of social scientific research programmes, must take account of. In particular, Lakatosian judgements about the progressive or degenerating nature of research programmes[62] cannot be made in isolation from judgements about developments in the rest of society conditioning work in particular programmes.

I have argued that once a hypothesis about a generative structure has been produced in social science it can be tested quite empirically, although not necessarily quantitatively, and albeit exclusively in terms of its explanatory power. But I have so far said nothing about how the hypothesis is produced, or indeed about what its status is. Now in considering theory-construction in the social sciences it should be borne in mind that the putative social scientist would, in the absence of some prior theory, be faced with an inchoate mass of (social) phenomena, which she would somehow have to sort out and define. In systems, like social ones, which are necessarily open, the problem of constituting an appropriate (that is, explanatorily significant) object of inquiry becomes particularly acute. It becomes chronic if, as in empirical realism, lacking the concepts of the stratification and differentiation of the world, one is unable to think the irreducibility of transfactually active structures to events, and the effort, which is science, needed to reveal them. Undifferentiated events then become the object of purely conventionally differentiated sciences, producing a crisis of definitions and boundaries, the existence of a merely arbitrary distinction between a theory and its applications (or the absence of any organic connection between them) and, above all, a problem of verification – or rather falsification. For when *every* theory, if interpreted *empirically*, is false, no theory can ever be falsified.[63] Goldmann's claim that 'the fundamental methodological problem of any human science . . . lies in the division [*découpage*] of the object of study . . . [for] once this division has been made and accepted, the results will be practically predictable'[64] is then not at all surprising.

How, then, given the mishmash nature of social reality, is theory-construction accomplished in social science? Fortunately most of the phenomena with which the social scientist has to deal will already be identified, thanks to the *concept-dependent* nature of social activities, under certain descriptions. In principle, the descriptions or nominal definitions of social activities that form the transitive objects of social scientific theory may be those of the agents concerned, or theoretical redescriptions of them. The first step in the transformation $P \rightarrow T$ will thus be an attempt at a real definition of a form of social life that has already been identified under a particular description. Note that in the absence of such a definition and failing a closure, any hypothesis of a causal mechanism is bound to be more or less arbitrary. Thus in social science attempts at real definitions will in general precede rather than follow successful causal hypotheses – though in both cases they can only be justified empirically, viz. by the revealed explanatory power of the hypotheses that can be deduced from them.

Our problem, then, is shifted from that of how to establish a non-arbitrary procedure for generating causal hypotheses to that of how to establish a non-arbitrary procedure for generating real definitions. And here a second differentiating feature of the subject-matter of the social sciences should be recalled – the *activity-dependent* nature of social structures, viz. that the mechanisms at work in society exist only in virtue of their effects. In this respect society is quite distinct from other objects of scientific knowledge. But note that, in this, it is analogous to the objects of philosophical knowledge. For just as the objects of philosophical knowledge do not exist apart from the objects of scientific knowledge, so social structures do not exist apart from their effects. So, I suggest that in principle as philosophical discourse stands to scientific discourse, so a discourse about society stands to a discourse about its effects. Moreover in both cases one is dealing with conceptualized activities, whose conditions of possibility or real presuppositions the second-order discourse seeks to explicate. However there are also important differences. For in social scientific discourse one is concerned not to isolate the a priori conditions of a form of knowledge as such, but the particular mechanisms and relations at work in some identified sphere of social life. Moreover its conclusions will be *historical*, not formal; and subject to empirical test, as well as various a priori controls.[65]

Now the substantive employment of an essentially apodeictic procedure should occasion us no surprise. For transcendental arguments are merely a species of which retroductive ones are the genus, distinguished by the features that their *explanandum* consists in the conceptualized activities of agents and, as becomes an arena characterized by a multiplicity of causes, that they isolate necessary not sufficient conditions for it. But in view of this homology are we not in danger of collapsing the philosophy/science distinction upon which I insisted in Chapter 1 [of PON]? No. For the syncategorematic (or, as it were, only proxy-referential) character of the nevertheless irreducible discourse of philosophy (discussed in that Chapter 1) has to be contrasted with the directly referential character of social scientific discourse. Hence, though in both cases there are two levels of discourse, in social science there are two levels of reality (social structures, and their effects), whereas in philosophy there is just one, viz. that investigated by science itself. Of course in both cases more than one set of conditions will normally be consistent with the activity concerned, so that supplementary considerations will be needed to establish the validity of the analysis. But in social science, wherever possible, such considerations will include the provision of independent empirical grounds for the existence (and postulated mode of activity) of the structural mechanisms concerned, whereas, in philosophy, in the nature of the case, this is impossible. Thus a scientific (or substantive) transcendental argument may be distinguished from a philosophical (or formal) one according to the autonomous reality (or lack of it) of the object of the second-order discourse, the way (or rather immediacy) with which reference to the world is secured, and the possibility or otherwise of a posteriori grounds for the analysis.

Our deduction of the possibility of social scientific knowledge, from the necessary pre-existence of social forms for intentional action, illustrates the formal use of a transcendental procedure. The results of such an analysis may be used both as a critical grid for the assessment of existing social scientific theories and as a template for adequate conceptualizations of social scientific *explananda*. Marx's analysis in *Capital* illustrates the substantive use of a transcendental procedure. *Capital* may most plausibly be viewed as an attempt to establish what must be the case for the experiences grasped by the phenomenal forms of capitalist life to be possible; setting out, as it were, a pure schema for the understanding of economic phenomena under capitalism, specifying the categories that must be employed in any concrete investigation. I have already suggested that for Marx to understand the essence of some particular social phenomenon is to understand the social relations that make that phenomenon possible. But the transformational model suggests that, to understand the essence of social phenomena as such and in general, such phenomena must be grasped as productions; so that the relations one is concerned with here are, above all, relations of production.

Now the minor premise of any substantive social scientific transcendental argument will be a social activity as conceptualized in experience. Such a social activity will be in principle *space–time-dependent*. And in the first instance of course it will be conceptualized in the experience of the agents concerned. It is here that the hermeneutical tradition, in highlighting what may be called the conceptual moment in social scientific work, has made a real contribution. But it typically makes two mistakes. Its continuing commitment to the ontology of empirical realism prevents it from seeing the following:

1 The *conditions* for the phenomena (namely social activities as conceptualized in experience) exist *intransitively* and may therefore exist independently of their appropriate conceptualization, and as such be subject to an unacknowledged possibility of historical transformation.
2 The *phenomena* themselves may be *false* or in an important sense inadequate (for example, superficial or systematically misleading).

Thus what has been established, by conceptual analysis, as necessary for the phenomena may consist precisely in a level (or aspect) of reality which, although not existing independently of agents' conceptions, may be inadequately conceptualized or even not conceptualized at all. Such a level may consist in a structural complex which is really generative of social life but unavailable to direct inspection by the senses or immediate intuition in the course of everyday life. It may be a tacit property of agents (such as knowledge of a grammar) utilized in their productions; or a property of the relationships in which agents stand to the conditions and means of their productions, of which they may be unaware. Now such a transcendental analysis in social science, in showing (when it does) the historical conditions under which a certain set of categories may be validly applied, *ipso facto* shows the conditions under which they may not be applied. This makes possible a second-order critique of consciousness, best exemplified perhaps by Marx's analysis of commodity fetishism.[66] Value relations, it will be remembered, are real for Marx, but they are historically specific social realities. And fetishism consists in their transformation in thought into the natural, and so ahistorical, qualities of things. An alternative type of transformation is identified by Marx in the case of idealistic (rather than naturalistic) explanations of social forms, such as money in the eighteenth century, 'ascribed a conventional origin' in 'the so-called universal consent of mankind'.[67] The homology between these two types of substantive mystification and the metatheoretical errors of reification and voluntarism should be clear.

But, as Geras has pointed out,[68] Marx employed another concept of mystification, in which he engages in what one may call a first-order critique of consciousness – in which, to put it bluntly, he identifies the phenomena themselves as false; or, more formally, shows that a certain set of categories is not properly applicable to experience at all. This is best exemplified by his treatment of the wage form, in which the value of labour power is transformed into the value of labour – an expression which Marx declares to be 'as imaginary as the value of the earth', 'as irrational as a yellow logarithm'.[69] Once more, this mystification is founded on a characteristic category mistake

– that, intrinsic to the wage–labour relation, of reducing powers to their exercise, comparable to confusing machines with their use. One can also see this categorial error as an instance of the reduction of efficient to material causes, as Marx's critique of the Gotha Programme[70] turns on the isolation of the contrary mistake.

Thus, contrary to what is implied in the hermeneutical and neo-Kantian traditions, the transformation $P \rightarrow T$ both (1) isolates real but non-empirical and not necessarily adequately conceptualized conditions and (2) consists essentially, as critique, in two modes of conceptual criticism and change. Now the appellation 'ideology' to the set of ideas *P* is only justified if their *necessity* can be demonstrated: that is, if they can be explained as well as criticized. This involves something more than just being able to say that the beliefs concerned are false or superficial, which normally entails having a better explanation for the phenomena in question. It involves, in addition, being able to give an account of the *reasons* why the false or superficial beliefs are *held* – a mode of explanation without parallel in the natural sciences. For beliefs, whether about society or nature, are clearly social objects.

Once this step is taken then conceptual criticism and change pass over into social criticism and change, as, in a possibility unique to social science,[71] the object that renders illusory (or superficial) beliefs necessary comes, at least in the absence of any overriding considerations, to be criticized in being explained; so that the point now becomes, *ceteris paribus*, to change it. Indeed in the full development of the concept of ideology, theory fuses into practice, as facts about values, mediated by theories about facts, are transformed into values about facts. The rule of value-neutrality, the last shibboleth in the philosophy of the social sciences, collapses, when we come to see that values themselves can be false.

At the beginning of this section I distinguished epistemological and relational limits on naturalism from the ontological ones immediately derived from the transformational model of social activity. But a moment's reflection shows that these limits may be derived from that model too. For the historical and interdependent character of social activities implies that the social world must be open, and the requirement that social activity be socially explained implies that social science is a part of its own subject-matter. Similarly, it is not difficult to see that the application of the transformational model to beliefs and cognitive material generally implies commitment to a principle of epistemic relativity,[72] and that this lends to moral and political argument in particular something of a necessarily transitional and open character.[73]

Our deduction of the possibility of naturalism in the social sciences is complete, although we have still to explore an important range of consequences of it. Society is not given in, but presupposed by, experience. However, it is precisely its peculiar ontological status, its transcendentally real character that makes it a possible object of knowledge for us. Such knowledge is non-natural but still scientific. The transformational model implies that social activities are historical, interdependent and interconnected. The law-like statements of the social sciences will thus typically designate historically restricted tendencies operating at a single level of the social structure only. Because they are defined for only one relatively autonomous component of the social structure, and because they act in systems that are always open, they designate tendencies (such as for the rates of profit on capitalist enterprises to be equalized) which may never be manifested, but which are nevertheless essential to the understanding (and the changing) of the different forms of social life, just because they are really productive of them. Society is not a mass of separable events and sequences. But neither is it constituted by the concepts that we attach to our physiological states. Rather it is a complex and causally efficacious whole – a totality, which is being continually transformed in practice. As an object of study it can neither be read straight off a given world nor reconstructed from our subjective experiences. But, although empirical realism cannot think it, in this respect at least it is on a par with the objects of study in the natural sciences too.

Social science as critique: facts, values and theories

The generally accepted, and in my opinion essentially correct, interpretation of Hume, is that he enunciated what has – at least since Moore's *Principia Ethica* – become an article of faith for the entire analytical tradition, namely that the transition from 'is' to 'ought', factual to value statements, indicatives to imperatives, is, although frequently made (and perhaps even, like education, psychologically necessary), logically inadmissible.[74] I want to argue that, on the contrary, it is not only acceptable but mandatory, provided only that minimal criteria for the characterization of a belief system as 'ideological' are satisfied.

For the anti-naturalist tradition in ethics, then, there is a fundamental logical gulf between statements of what *is* (has been or will be) the case and statements of what *ought* to be the case. It follows from this, first, that no factual proposition can be derived from any value judgement (or, more generally, that any factual conclusion depends upon premises containing at least (and normally more than) one factual proposition); and second, that no value judgement can be derived from any factual proposition (or, more generally, that any value conclusion depends upon premises containing at least one value judgement). Accordingly, social science is viewed as neutral in two respects: first, in that its propositions are logically independent of, and cannot be derived from, any value position; second, in that value positions are logically independent of, and cannot be derived from, any social scientific proposition. I shall write these two corollaries of 'Hume's Law' as follows:

(1) $V \not\rightarrow F$
(2) $F \not\rightarrow V$

It is important to keep (1) and (2) distinct. For it is now often conceded that the facts are in some sense tainted by, or contingent upon, our values. But whatever doubt is cast upon (1), (2) is still deemed canonical. That is, it is still held that the findings of social science are consistent with any value-position; so that even if social science cannot be value-free, social values remain effectively *science-free*. It is of course accepted that science may be used instrumentally in the pursuit of moral ideals, political goals, etc., but science cannot help to determine the latter. We remain free in the face of science to adopt any value-position. 'Keep Science out of Politics (Morality, etc.)' could be the watchword here.

My primary argument is against (2). But I reject (1) as well; that is, I accept the thesis of the value-dependency of (social) facts, and will consider it first. It will be seen, however, that without a rejection of axis (2) of the dichotomy, criticism directed at axis (1), or its implications, must remain largely ineffectual. And my aim will be to show how theory, by throwing into relief the (ever-diminishing) circle in which facts and values move, can presage its transformation into an (expanding) explanatory/emancipatory spiral.

(1) has been criticized from the standpoint of the subjectivity of both (a) the *subject* and (b) the *object* of investigation (as well as, more obliquely, in the hermeneutical, critical and dialectical traditions from the standpoint of (c) the *relationship* between the two). Thus to consider (a) first, it has been argued that the social values of the scientist (or the scientific community) determine (i) the selection of problems; (ii) the conclusions; and even (iii) the standards of inquiry (for example by Weber, Myrdal and Mannheim respectively).

(i) is often treated as uncontroversial; in fact, it embodies a serious muddle. It is most usually associated with Weber's doctrine that although social science could and must be *value-free*, it had nevertheless to be *value-relevant.*[75] Crudely summarized, Weber's position was that because of the infinite variety of empirical reality, the social scientist had to make a choice of what to study. Such a choice would necessarily be guided by his or her values, so that s/he would choose to study precisely those aspects of reality to which s/he attached cultural significance, which thereby became the basis for the construction of 'ideal-types'. Now this is doubly misleading. For, on the one hand, the natural world is similarly complex; and, on the other, aspects of the work of the natural sciences are equally motivated by practical interests. In fact, one needs to make a distinction between the pure and the applied (or practical) natural sciences. In pure science choice of the properties of an object to study is motivated by the search for explanatory mechanisms;[76] in applied science it may be motivated by the industrial, technological, medical or more generally socio-cultural significance of the properties. Thus while it is practical interests which determine which out of the infinite number of possible compounds of carbon are studied,[77] it is theoretical interests which motivate the identification of its electronic structure. Weber's neo-Kantianism misleads him into substituting the distinction *natural/social* for the distinction *pure/applied*. There is nothing in the infinite variety of the surface of the social cosmos to necessitate a difference in principle in the structure of the search for explanatory mechanisms. Nor, *pace* Habermasians, is an interest in emancipation something with which one has to *preface* that search, although, as I shall argue shortly, explanatory social science necessarily has emancipatory implications.[78] At a deeper level, any doctrine of value-relevance (or knowledge-constitutive-interests) also suffers from the defect that it leaves the *source* of the values (or interests) unexplained.

(ii) is altogether more powerful. The underlying notion at work is that social science is so inextricably 'bound up' with its subject-matter that its interest in it will affect, and (if some concept of objectivity – relational or otherwise – is retained) distort, its perception, description or interpretation of it. Examples of such affecting/distorting are readily available.[79] It is clear that (ii) rests on an epistemological premise, viz. that of the internality of social science with respect to its subject-matter, together with a psychological or sociological one, asserting the practical impossibility of making the analytical separation the positivist enjoins on the social scientist. And it posits, with respect to the claim made in (1) above, an *interference* between the subject's interests in the object and its knowledge of it.

Now it is vital to distinguish three ways in which such interference could operate. It could operate *consciously* (as in lying); it could operate *semi-consciously* (as in the wishful thinking of the incurable optimist or the special pleading of a pressure group); or it could operate *unconsciously* (whether or not it can become accessible to consciousness). It is only the third case that raises serious difficulties for (1). I want to distinguish the case where the conclusions of such an unconscious mode of 'interference' are *rationalizations* of motivation from the case where they constitute *mystifications* (or ideologies) of social structure. In either case the interference may be regarded as necessary or as contingent upon a particular set of psychic or social circumstances.

Recognition of the phenomena of rationalization and mystification as the effects of unconscious interference enables us to pinpoint the error in an influential 'solution' to the problem of 'value-bias', authorized *inter alia* by Myrdal.[80] On this solution, recognizing that value-neutrality is impossible, all the social scientist needs to do is state his or her own value assumptions fully and explicitly at the beginning of some piece of work so as to put the reader (and possibly also the writer) on their guard. It is not difficult to see that this solution begs the question. For it presupposes that *X* knows what his or her values are; that is, it presupposes that s/he has the kind of knowledge about him- or herself that *ex hypothesi*, in virtue of unconscious interference, s/he cannot have about society. Now for *X* to have such knowledge about him- or herself, s/he would have had to become fully conscious of the formerly unconscious mode of interference, in which case a statement of value assumptions is *unnecessary*, because objectivity is now possible. Conversely, if X is not conscious of the (unconscious) mode of interference, then any statement of his or her (professed) value assumptions will be *worthless*. Moreover, one cannot say in general whether any such statement will be more or less misleading. (Thus consider, for instance, what often follows professions of the kind 'I'm not prejudiced about . . .' or 'I'm a tolerant sort of person/true liberal/good democrat . . .') *Mutatis mutandis*, similar considerations apply in the case of conscious and semi-conscious modes of interference: avowals are either unnecessary or potentially misleading.

(iii) posits a relativity in the methodological norms secreted by different conceptual schemes or paradigms, together with a value-dependence of such conceptual schemes of the sort already discussed under (ii). I want to consider it *pari passu* with the general problem of relativism, of which it is just a special case. Two objections to relativism are regularly trotted out: first, that it is self-refuting; second, that it denies what we do in fact do, for example translate, make cross-cultural comparisons, etc.[81]

The argument for the self-refuting character of relativism is easily refuted. The argument asserts that if all beliefs are relative, then there can be no good grounds for relativism; hence one has no reason to accept it. Conversely, if one has reason to accept it, then at least one belief is not relative; so that relativism is false. Now this argument confuses two distinct theses (which are indeed typically confused by pro- as well as anti-relativists). The first is the correct thesis of *epistemic relativity*, which asserts that all beliefs are socially produced, so that all knowledge is transient, and neither truth-values nor criteria of rationality exist outside historical time. The other is the incorrect thesis of *judgemental relativism*, which asserts that all beliefs (statements) are equally valid, in the sense that there can be no (rational) grounds for preferring one to another. Denying the principle of epistemic relativity inevitably entails embracing some type of epistemological *absolutism* (which, by a short route, invariably results in some kind of idealism), while acceptance of judgemental relativism inevitably leads to some or other form of *irrationalism*. Epistemic relativity is entailed both by ontological realism[82] and by the transformational conception of social activity: it respects a distinction between the sense and reference of propositions, while insisting that all speech acts are made in historical time. Such a principle neither entails nor (even if any were logically possible) gives grounds for a belief in the doctrine of judgemental relativism. On the contrary, it is clear that if one is to act at all there must be grounds for preferring one belief (about some domain) to another; and that such activity in particular practices is typically codifiable in the form of systems of *rules*, implicitly or explicitly followed.

The anti-relativist argument may now be refuted. Epistemic relativism is a particular belief (about the totality of beliefs). Like any belief (including its contrary), it arises under, and is (analytically) only comprehensible, and therefore only acceptable, under definite historical conditions. Epistemic relativism is certainly comprehensible to us. And it is clear that there are in fact excellent grounds, both transcendental and empirical, for accepting it, and denying its contrary. (Of course if, on some inter-galactic voyage, we were to unearth some 'World 3' or world of timeless forms, in which it could be shown that our knowledge had been all the while participating, then we should certainly revise this judgement and accept some form of absolutism!)

Turning to the second objection to relativism, the undeniable fact that we can translate, etc., no more proves the existence of neutral languages or absolute standards than our interaction with lions proves that they can talk.[83] Whorf's hypothesis is not refuted by the existence of appropriate bilinguals (or it could never have been consistently formulated); any more than the *psychological* capacity of a physicist to understand both Newtonian and Ensteinian theory indicates that they are not *logically* incommensurable; or our ability to see a drawing as either a duck or a rabbit shows that there must be a way of seeing it as both at once. I will return to the special problems raised by the notion of our understanding other cultures and other times in Chapter 4 [of PON].

Arguments of type (b) turn not on the 'value-bias' of social science, but on the 'value-impregnation' of its subject-matter. They typically depend upon the fact that the subject-matter of social science is itself in part constituted by, or indeed just consists in, values or things to which the agents themselves attach (or have attached for them) value, that is, objects of value. Presumably no one would wish to deny this. The point only becomes a threat to (1) if it is established that the value-dependency of the subject-matter of social science makes it impossible or illegitimate to perform the required analytical separation in social scientific discourse. (For it is clear that one might be able to describe values in a value-free way.) If one represents the subject-matter of social science by S_1 and social science by S_2, as in the diagram below, the

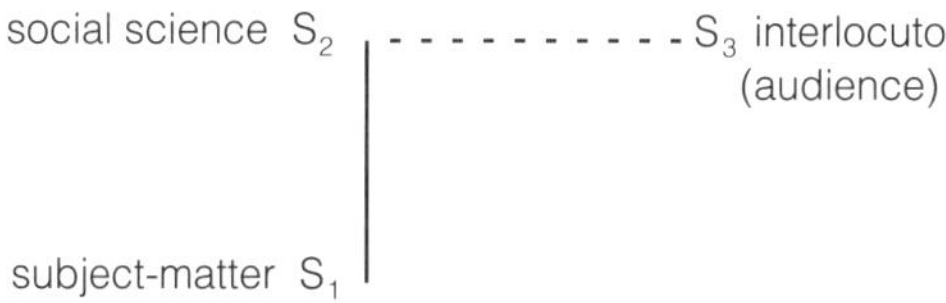

claim is that the nature of S_1 is such that, in virtue of its value-impregnation, either no description in L_2 satisfies (1), or at least the best or most adequate scientific description in L_2 does not satisfy (1). (This may be held to be a necessary, normal or occasional state of affairs.)

The significance of the fact that one is here concerned with questions of *descriptive* (and more generally scientific) *adequacy* may best be introduced by considering a famous example of Isaiah Berlin's. Thus compare the following accounts of what happened in Germany under Nazi rule: (α) 'the country was depopulated'; (β) 'millions of people died'; (γ) 'millions of people were killed'; (δ) 'millions of people were massacred'. All four statements are true. But (δ) is not only the most evaluative, it is also the best (that is, the most precise and accurate) description of what actually happened. And note that, in virtue of this, all but (δ) generate the wrong perlocutionary force. For to say of someone that he died normally carries the presumption that he was *not* killed by human agency. And to say that millions were killed does not imply that their deaths were part of a single organized campaign of brutal killing, as those under Nazi rule were. This point is important. For social science is not only *about* a subject matter, it is *for* an audience. That is, it is always in principle a party to a triadic relationship, standing to an actual or possible interlocutor (S_3) as a potential source of (mis-/dis-) information, explanation, justification, etc. Now I want to argue that, even abstracting from perlocutionary considerations, criteria for the scientific adequacy of descriptions are such that in this kind of case only the (δ) statement is acceptable.

If one denotes some social phenomenon in S_1 as 'P_1' then the most adequate description of P_1 in L_2 will be that description – let us call it D^*_2 – (with whatever evaluative components it incorporates) entailed by that theory T^* (formulated in L_2) with the *maximum explanatory power* (including of course the power, wherever possible, to explain descriptions of P_1 in S_1). In general the attainment of hermeneutic adequacy is a necessary but not a sufficient condition for generating the appropriate description D^*_2. Indeed if the hermeneutically adequate description is D°_2 and its target in L_1 is D°_1, then whether or not $D^*_2 = D^\circ_2$ is contingent. And the susceptibility of D°_1 to scientific *critique* is exactly reflected in the *process* of description, explanation and redescription that, as has been noted in Chapter 1 [of PON], characterizes scientific activity at any one level or stratum of reality. (This process is of course implicit in the transformational model, with the relevant ruptural point being the identification of the operative explanatory structure.) Such a process respects the *authenticity* of D°_1, but does not regard it as an incorrigible datum.[84] So that although the achievement of *Verstehen* is, in virtue of the concept-dependence of social structures, a condition for social science, the process of social science does not leave the initial descriptions – either in L_2 or in principle in L_1 – intact. In short, just as natural science has no foundations, there are no foundations of social knowledge – scientific or lay.

It is important to note that commitment to a principle of hermeneutic adequacy as a moment in social science is not only consistent with a subsequent critique of the *verstehende* description, it itself stands in need of supplementation by semiotic analysis. For the hermeneutic mediation of meanings (or fusion of horizons) must be complemented by consideration of the question posed by semiotics as to how such meanings (horizons, etc.) are produced. (Of course such a question must itself be expressed in a language, so that the process mediation-analysis is an iterative one.) Now if, following Saussure, one regards meanings as produced by, as it were, cutting into pre-existing systems of difference,[85] then in science our cut must be made so as to maximize total explanatory power. And another type of critique – a *metacritique* of L_1 – becomes possible if it can be shown that L_1 (or some relevant subsystem of it) is such that the adequate representation of P_1 in L_1 is impossible. This concern with the production of meaning corresponds exactly to the attentiveness shown in the natural sciences to the construction of instruments and equipment; so that one can say that if the hermeneutic moment corresponds (with respect to the conceptual aspect of social life) to observation, then the semiotic one corresponds to instrumentation in the empirical work of the natural sciences.

Now of course it does not follow that commitment to a principle of hermeneutic adequacy will automatically result in the replication in L_2 of the evaluative components in $D°_1$; nor does the production of $D°_2$ itself imply any value commitment. The question is rather whether the scientifically adequate description $D*_2$ breaks the rule of value-neutrality. Where it constitutes a critique of $D°_1$ it does so necessarily. For to show that agents are systematically deluded about the nature of their activity is (logically) impossible without passing the judgement that $D°_1$ is false; and 'D_1 is false' is not a value-neutral statement. Strictly speaking, this is sufficient for the purposes of our argument. For we require only to show that S_1 is such that in social science value-neutral descriptions are not always possible. But it is worth dwelling on the point in its more general aspect. Our problem is to utilize the powers of L_2 so as to maximize our understanding in L_2 of S_1. L_2 is the only language we can use. And the terms we use to describe human behaviour will be terms which function *inter alia* regulatively and evaluatively in S_2: these are the only terms we can, without parody or satire, use; and we cannot dislocate them from their living context without misrepresenting as lifeless the context they are employed to describe. Hence just as to define a foetus as an unborn human being is already to load the debate on abortion in a certain way, so to attempt to construct an index of fascism comparable to that of anaemia[86] is both absurd (because the elements of a fascist state are internally related) and value-laden (because it functions so as to remove from our purview, in science, precisely that range of its implications internally related to objects that we value, such as human life). In short, not to call a spade a spade, in any human society, is to misdescribe it.

Positivist dogma (1) must thus be rejected both on the grounds that it ignores the subject's interest in the object and on the grounds that the nature of the object is such that criteria for descriptive (and more generally scientific) adequacy entail at least the possibility of irreducibly evaluative descriptions. Criticism of (1) however leaves the questions of the determination, and non-instrumental justification, of values unresolved. Moreover, by making facts partially dependent upon values (and leaving value-choice undetermined) a seemingly inevitable element of arbitrariness is introduced into the scientific process. Indeed there seems no reason why, in the light of our special interests, we should not generate whatever facts we please. In order to forestall such a radical conventionalism, let us cross to the other side of the divide, viz. (2), and see if science has any implications for values; if one can break into the circle here. Before offering my own account of the matter, I want to discuss two recent attempts to break down the fact/value distinction along the axis denied in (2).

Charles Taylor, in an important article,[87] shows clearly how theories (or 'explanatory frameworks') do in fact secrete values. The structure of his argument may be represented as follows:

$$(3)\, T \leftrightarrow F \rightarrow V$$

Unfortunately, however, by failing to specify any criterion for choosing between theories, he leaves himself open to the interpretation that one should choose that theory which most satisfies our conception of what 'fulfills human needs, wants and purposes';[88] rather than that theory which, just *because it is explanatorily most adequate* and capable *inter alia* of explaining illusory beliefs about the social world, best allows us to situate the possibilities of change in the value direction that the theory indicates. He thus merely displaces, rather than transcends, the traditional fact/value dichotomy. Alternatively, one might attempt to interpret Taylor as arguing that one ought to opt for the theory that secretes the best value-position, because theories tend to be acted upon and human needs are the independent (or at least chief) variable in social explanation.[89] But this involves a dubious set of propositions, including a substantive scheme of explanation with voluntaristic implications.

Searle's attempted derivation of 'ought' from 'is', where the critical 'is' statement is a statement describing institutional facts (that is, facts constituted by systems of rules), turns on the existence of a series of connections between saying 'I promise', being under an obligation and it being the case that one ought to do what one is under an obligation to do.[90] The structure of Searle's argument may be represented as:

$$(4)\ I.F. \rightarrow V$$

It has been criticized (for example by Hare) on the grounds that the institutional facts upon which it rests merely encapsulate general moral principles, and (for example by Flew) on the grounds that the mere utterance of words does not imply the kind of commitment that alone warrants a normative conclusion. Now it is certainly the case that the mere fact that one acts within an institution in such a way that one's action would not be possible but for its constitutive rules, does not imply a moral (as distinct from a motivational, or purely instrumental) commitment to it. Otherwise it would be logically impossible to be a socialist within a capitalist society, or a libertarian within a totalitarian one. Promising is an institution within a network of institutions which one might decide, on moral grounds,[91] either to opt out of or merely 'play' (sincerely or insincerely). A society of discursive intelligences where promising is regarded rather as Americans regard cricket, is, although perhaps not very attractive, certainly conceivable – in a way in which a society not subject to norms of truth, consistency and coherence is not. To derive a morally unrevocable (*ceteris paribus*) 'ought' from an 'is' one has to move from premises which are constitutive of purely factual discourse, to ones which are transcendentally necessary.

My argument, it is important to note, does not permit a simple inference from facts to values. It turns, rather, on the capacity of a *theory* to explain false consciousness, and in particular on the capacity of a theory to allow the satisfaction of minimal criteria for the characterization of a system of beliefs as *ideological*. (Fuller criteria will be elaborated in the appendix to this chapter.) Now it will be remembered that I argued in the last section that one is only justified in characterizing a set of ideas P as 'ideological' if both (a) P is false, that is, one possesses a superior explanation for the phenomena in question; and (b) P is more or less contingently (conjuncturally) necessary, that is, one possesses an explanation of the falsity of the beliefs in question. It should be noted that the necessity one is dealing with here may only be the necessity for *some* illusion, rather than any *particular* one; and that, where (as in the case of myths about nature) *different* theories are required for the satisfaction of (a) and (b), they must at least be consistent with one another. One can write these criteria as follows:

(a) $T > P$
(b) $T \exp I(P)$

Now to criticize a belief as false is *ipso facto* not only to criticize any action or practice informed or sustained by that belief, but also anything that necessitates it. In social science this will be precisely the object that renders illusory (or superficial) beliefs, along any of the dimensions of mystification already indicated in the last section, necessary. The structure of my argument may be represented as:

(5) $T > P.\ T \exp I(P) \rightarrow -V(O \rightarrow I(P))$

Of course this only entails the imperative 'change it' if change is possible and in the absence of overriding considerations. But that is the case with *any* valuation (for example, smoking is harmful).[92]

If, then, one is in possession of a theory which explains why false consciousness is necessary, one can pass immediately, without the addition of any extraneous value judgements, to a negative evaluation of the object (generative structure, system of social relations or whatever) that makes that consciousness necessary (and, *ceteris paribus*, to a positive evaluation of action rationally directed at the removal of the sources of false consciousness). Might it not be objected, however, that the fact/value distinction only breaks down in this way because one is committed to the prior valuation that truth is a good, so that one is not deriving a value judgement from entirely factual (natural) premises? But that truth *is* a good (*ceteris paribus*) is not only a condition of moral discourse, it is a condition of any discourse at all. Commitment to truth and consistency apply to factual as much as to value discourse; and so cannot be seized upon as a concealed (value) premise to rescue the autonomy of values from factual discourse, without destroying the distinction between the two, the distinction that it is the point of the objection to uphold.

Given that clear paradigms exist of the form of explanation represented by (5), can a case be made out for supposing such an explanation-form to be transcendentally necessary? Now it is evident that there can be no action without beliefs, and no beliefs save by work on or with other beliefs, so that judgements of falsity are transcendentally necessary. Further, it is clear that it is only if an agent can *explain* a belief that s/he can set out to rationally *change* it, in the case where it is not susceptible to direct criticism. Now if beliefs are not to be given a totally voluntaristic explanation; if they are at all recalcitrant – like the rest of the social structure (as is implied by their internality to it); or if a sociology of knowledge is to be possible and necessary (and one is already implicit in lay practice); then the form of ideological explanation schematized in (5) is *a condition of every rational praxis*. Put informally, the possibility of coming to say to another or oneself 'now this is why you (*I*) erroneously believe such-and-such' is a presupposition of any rational discourse or authentic act of self-reflection at all.

Ceteris paribus, then, truth, consistency, coherence, rationality, etc., are good, and their opposites bad, precisely because commitment to them are conditions of the possibility of discourse in general. Now it is certainly the case that to say of some belief *P* that it is illusory is *ceteris paribus* (henceforth *CP*) to imply that it is detrimental to the achievement of human goals and the satisfaction of human wants. But it is not *because* of this, on the argument I have advanced, that *P* is bad. Of course science is not the only human activity, or the most important (in an explanatory sense). Further, just as the values it encapsulates may be undermined in certain kinds of societies, so they may be overridden by other values. However, such overriding cannot consistently be argued to be either necessarily or even normally warranted. Moreover it is only by reference to social scientific (and psychological) theories that an infinite regress of values can be avoided and questions of ultimate values resolved (as of course in practice they always – implicitly or explicitly – are). Different 'highest-order' explanatory theories will contain their own conception of what kinds of social organization are possible and of what human beings essentially are (or can become). The most powerful explanatory theory, by situating the greatest range of real (non-Utopian) possibilities, will increase our rational autonomy of action. But it is a mistake of the greatest magnitude to suppose that, in Laplacean fashion, it will tell us what to do. The most powerful explanatory theory in an open world is a non-deterministic one.

Aside from this, science, although it can and must illuminate them, cannot finally 'settle' questions of practical morality and action, just because there are always – and necessarily – social practices besides science, and values other than cognitive ones; because, to adapt a famous metaphor of Neurath's, while we mend the boat, we still need to catch fish in the sea. On the other hand, once we break from the contemplative standpoint of traditional epistemology and conceive human beings as engaged in practical and material activity, and not just thinking and perceiving, it becomes difficult to see how (2) could have held philosophers in thrall for so long. For we can certainly derive technical imperatives from theoretical premises alone (subject to a *CP* clause).[93] Moreover, to criticize a belief or theory is *ipso facto* to criticize any action informed, or practice sustained, by that belief or theory, so that even at level (a) of (5) we pass directly to practical imperatives. But to stop there is to halt at 'that kind of criticism which knows how to judge and condemn the present, but not how to comprehend it'.[94] To move beyond such criticism we need to reveal the object that makes false consciousness necessary, in a moment – level (b) of (5) – which I have called 'critique'. Once we have accomplished this, we have then done as much as science alone can do for society and people. And the point becomes to transform them.

Appendix

A note on the Marxist concept of ideology

It is not my intention here to provide a full treatment of the Marxist concept of ideology, but rather merely to consider two problems associated with it. The first concerns the location of ideology (and science) within the topography of historical materialism; the second concerns the criteria for the characterization of beliefs as 'ideological', and specifically for distinguishing ideology from science.

A. *Sciences and ideologies in historical materialism*

In the work of the mature Marx the concept of ideology has a double designation: on the one hand, it is assigned to the superstructure to be explained in terms of the base; and on the other, it forms part of the analysis of the base itself, most notably in the figure of commodity fetishism. Now this double designation, not to say schism, in the thematization of the concept of ideology within Marxism itself reflects a historical fact of some importance. Marx inaugurated two distinct research programmes: an economic theory, or critique, of the capitalist mode of production, elaborated above all in *Capital*; and a theory of history, historical materialism, sketched, for example, in the famous 1859 Preface and put to work in a few justly celebrated conjunctural analyses. But he never satisfactorily integrated the two. (One symptom of this is the absence, in his mature work, of any theory of capitalist *society*.) And it was left to Engels, and subsequent Marxists, following their own intuitions and Marx's clues, to try to resolve the problems engendered by this original cleavage within Marxism.

Foremost among such problems is of course that of reconciling the thesis of the relative autonomy and specific efficacy of the various superstructures (however individuated and enumerated) with that of their determination in the last instance by the base (however identified and defined) – see n. 43 below. In general terms Marxists have long recognized two errors: *idealism*, dislocation of a superstructure from the base (or the totality); and *reductionism* (or economism), reduction of a superstructure to a mechanical effect or epiphenomenon of the base (or to an expression of the totality). Now if one places science within society, as one surely must, these opposed errors can be identified in the works of Althusser in the mid-1960s (in his so-called 'theoreticist' phase) and of the early Lukács respectively. Thus for Althusser science is effectively *completely* autonomous,[95] while for Lukács it tends to be merely an *expression* of (the reification intrinsic to) capitalist society.[96] Lysenkoism, in which science is conceived as a mechanical function of the economic base, is an *economistic* variant of reductionism.[97]

This problem of simultaneously avoiding economic reductionism and theoretical idealism has a direct counterpart on the plane of ideology. For, on the one hand, there is, in *Capital*, a theory of false or superficial economic ideas, which cannot just be extrapolated (without detailed independent investigations) into a general theory of ideas-in-capitalist-society. And, on the other hand, if historical materialism is to mark any advance over empiricist sociology and historiography, it must presumably provide a framework for accounting for legal, political, cultural, religious, philosophical and scientific ideas as well as economic ones. Specifically, I want to suggest that (1) ideas cannot just be lumped together and assigned in an undifferentiated bloc to the category of superstructure; and (2) all activity, including purely economic activity, necessarily has an ideational component or aspect (as the 1st Thesis on Feuerbach implies), that is to say, it is unthinkable except in so far as the agent has a conception of what s/he is doing and why s/he is doing it (in which of course s/he may be mistaken). The critique of idealism developed in *The German Ideology* consists: firstly, in the rejection of the Hegelian notion of the autonomous existence of the ideal;[98] and secondly, in the assertion of the primacy of the material over the ideal.[99] But however precisely the latter claim is to be interpreted, Marx can hardly be plausibly committed to a materialist inversion of Hegel on the first count, viz. as asserting the autonomous existence of the material in social life. Thus the crude distinction economic base/ideological superstructure must be rejected and replaced instead by a conception of the *different ideologies* associated with the *different practices*, including both scientific practices and the practices identified, in any particular formation, as basic. Of course these ideologies will stand in various relations to one another, and sometimes reveal striking homologies and straightforward functionalities. But this way of looking at ideologies leaves open their nature and relations for substantive scientific investigation. Moreover, it allows both that the various practices may have different, and varying, degrees of autonomy from the base; and that in some cases (physics, technology, literature, warfare) the practices concerned may have relatively autonomous bases of their own.[100]

In its classical tradition, Marxism has conceived ideologies as systems of false beliefs, arising in response to the objective conditions of material existence and as playing an essential role in reproducing (and/or transforming) social relations of production. Typically, moreover, it has opposed ideology to science; and science has been conceived, at least by Marx, Engels and Lenin, as a weapon in the emancipation of the working class. Ideology is categorially false consciousness, grounded in the existence of a particular historically contingent form of (class) society and serving the interests of a system of domination (at root, class domination) intrinsic to it. Now, as Poulantzas has noted, the only fully worked out theory of ideology in Marxism is in Marx's critique of political economy; so it is to this that we must turn in considering what is involved in the Marxist notion of a critique, and the counterposition of ideology to science.

B. Science v. ideology in the critique of political economy

I suggest that a system of beliefs *I* may be characterized as 'ideological', within this conceptual lineage, if and only if three types of criteria – which I shall call critical, explanatory and categorial – are satisfied. To consider the *critical* criteria first, in order to designate *I* as 'ideological' one must be in possession of a theory (or a consistent set of theories) *T* which can do the following:

1 Explain most, or most significant, phenomena, under its own descriptions, explained by *I* (under *I*'s descriptions, where these are 'incommensurable' with those of *T*).
2 Explain in addition a significant set of phenomena not explained by *I*.

To satisfy the *explanatory* criteria for the designation of *I* as 'ideological', *T* must be able to do the following:

3 Explain the reproduction of *I* (that is, roughly, the conditions for its continued acceptance by agents) and, if possible, specify the limits of *I* and the (endogenous) conditions for its transformation (if any), specifically:
 3′. In terms of a real stratification or connection (that is, a level of structure or set of relations) described in *T* but altogether absent from or obscured in *I*.
4 Explain, or at least situate, itself within itself.

Finally, to satisfy the *categorial* criteria for the designation of *I* as 'ideological', *I* must be *unable* to satisfy either of the following:

5 A criterion of scientificity, specifying the minimum necessary conditions for the characterization of a production as scientific; or
6 A criterion of domain-adequacy, specifying the minimum necessary conditions for a theory to sustain the historical or social (or whatever) nature of its subject-matter.

And *T* must be able to satisfy both.

(1) and (2) explicate the sense in which *T* is cognitively superior to *I*.[101] But (3′) assigns to *T* a specific type of cognitive superiority. It possesses an ontological depth or totality that *I* lacks. (3) demarcates social scientific from natural scientific explanation. The condition that beliefs about phenomena, as well as phenomena, are to be explained derives from the internality of social theories with respect to their subject-matter (see p. 47). And this of course also indicates the desirability of the satisfaction of a criterion of reflexivity, viz. (4). It should perhaps be stressed that one is *only* justified in characterizing a system of beliefs as 'ideological' if one is in possession of a theory that can explain them. The categorial criteria (5) and (6) presuppose of course that *T*, or some metatheory consistent with it, specifies the appropriate conditions (as has been done here in Chapters 1 and 2 [of PON] respectively). For Marx classical political economy satisfied (5), but not properly speaking (6), in virtue of the category mistakes, such as that of fetishism, in which it was implicated. But vulgar economy did not even satisfy (5). Finally, it should be noted that, traditionally, theoretical ideologies have been distinguished from the forms of consciousness they reflect, or rationalize (or otherwise defend); so that within the analysis of any '*I*' an internal differentiation with respect to discursive level will be necessary. Now let us put this formal apparatus to work on *Capital.*

Capital is subtitled 'a critical analysis of capitalist production'. It is at one and the same time a critique of bourgeois political economy; a critique of the economic conceptions of everyday life that, according to Marx, bourgeois political economy merely reflects or rationalizes; and a critique of the mode of production that renders these conceptions necessary for the agents engaging in it. It is the structure of this triple critique that provides the key to the analysis of ideology in Marx's mature economic writings.

For Marx vulgar economy merely reflects the phenomenal forms of bourgeois life. It does not penetrate to the essential reality that produces these forms.[102] But it is not just laziness or scientific 'bad faith' that accounts for this. For the phenomenal forms that are reflected or rationalized in ideology actually mask the real relations that generate them. As Godelier has put it: 'it is not the subject who deceives himself [nor, one might add, is it any other subject – be it individual, group or class], but *reality* [that is, the structure of society] that deceives [or better, produces the deception in] him'.[103] Marx's project is thus to discover the mechanisms by which capitalist society necessarily appears to its agents as something other than it really is; that is, of its specific opacity. And inasmuch as he succeeds in this task, showing these forms to be both false *and* necessary, *Capital's* status as a triple critique is explained (and its right to its subtitle fully justified).

I noted above (p. 52) how fetishism, by *naturalizing* value, *dehistoricizes* it. Its social function is thus to conceal the historically specific class relationships that underlie the surface phenomena of circulation and exchange. Now the wage form, in confusing the value of labour and the value of labour power, reduces *powers* to their *exercise*. Its social function is thus to conceal the reality, in the process of capitalist production, of unpaid labour (the source of surplus value). And as Marx says, 'if history took a long time to get to the bottom of the mystery of wages, nothing is easier than to understand the necessity, the *raison d'être* of this phenomenon'.[104] So both the value and wage forms, on which Marx's critique of political economy turn, involve characteristic, and (within the context of Marx's theory) readily explicable, category mistakes.

Now once one accepts that phenomenal forms are necessary to the functioning of a capitalist economy (that is, once one rejects a crude materialistic inversion of the Hegelian notion of the autonomy of the ideal), one can set out the following schema, adapted from an article by John Mepham.[105]

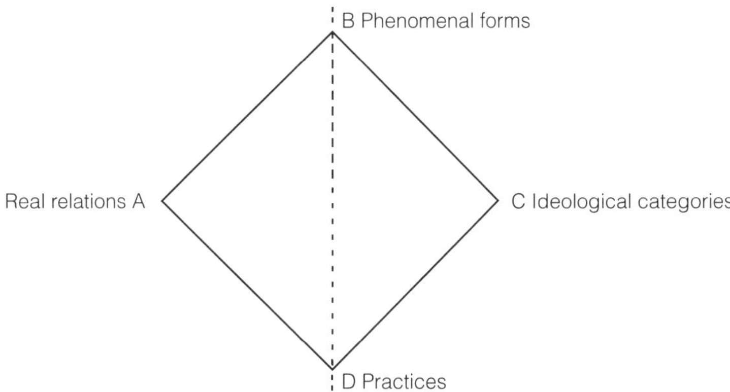

Real relations, *A*, characteristically located by Marx in the sphere of production, generate phenomenal forms, *B*, characteristic of the spheres of circulation and exchange, which in turn are reflected in the categories of ideological discourse, *C*, which sustain and underpin such ordinary commercial practices as buying and selling, wage-negotiating, etc., at *D*. These are in turn, of course, necessary for the reproduction of the real relations *A*. The dotted line through *BD* denotes, as it were, the cut of everyday life. Marx's analysis typically moves retroductively from *B* to *A*, enabling a critique of *C* and informing practice at *D*. Moreover the analysis, in isolating the conditions for the phenomenal forms in a mode of production necessitating forms which are false (as in the case of the wage form) or systematically misleading (as in the case of the value form), *ipso facto*, without the intervention of any value judgements (other than those bound up in the assessment of the cognitive adequacy of the theory and *a fortiori* its superiority over bourgeois political economy), issues in a negative valuation of that mode of production. In discovering that the source of consciousness is such that it is false, Marx automatically discredits that source, while simultaneously showing how that consciousness may yet be necessary. It follows from this also that, although a critique in Marx's sense is at once transcendentally and subversively critical, Marxist science is subversive in virtue of its cognitive power alone.

Finally, it should be noted that Marx's analysis of political economy reveals not only a gap between how an object is and how it appears to be, but a 'contradiction', which I shall call a 'Colletti contradiction',[106] between the way it presents itself in experience and the way it really is. This is not just because analysis reveals a level of structure and set of relations not manifest to experience (or bourgeois ideology), which it does (see criterion (3′) above), but which does not justify reference to a 'contradiction'. Nor is it only because the very forms in which social life presents itself to experience embody fundamental category mistakes (such as the presentation of the social as natural in fetishism or the 'interpellation' of individuals as free agents in their constitution as subjects).[107] Rather it is because, through the theorem of the necessity of phenomenal forms for social life, they are themselves internally related to (that is, constitute necessary conditions for) the essential structures that generate them. On Marx's analysis, social reality is shot through with such Colletti contradictions. Paradoxically, however, far from confirming Colletti's diagnosis of 'two Marx's'[108] it is precisely the existence of just one – the scientist – that explains this. (For were criticism to be separable from analysis there would be no problem, and no contradictions of this type.) Moreover it is important to stress that such contradictions, which involve merely the necessary co-existence in social reality of an object and a categorially false presentation of it, can be *consistently described*, as indeed can the more straightforward logical kind present in the thought of every mathematics student. Colletti's transcendental idealism misleads him into viewing the principle of non-contradiction, conceived as a regulative ideal for thought, as a constitutive principle of thinkable reality. But of course where, as in social life, thought is itself part of social reality, there are bound to exist logical contradictions in reality. And if thought does not constitute (and so completely exhaust) social reality, there are bound to exist misrepresentations of reality in reality. And among such misrepresentations will be some which are necessary for what they misrepresent. Now if such misrepresentations are themselves generated by what they misrepresent it will *seem* as if one has just moved in a circle, that one has a simple case of the identity of opposites here. But of course this is not so. For at each moment in the analysis concept and object remain distinct; and the relations involved are causal, not logical. Such a relation is still characterizable as one of 'contradiction', in virtue of the misrepresentation involved. But because one of the *relata* consists in a (misrepresented) real object, the contradiction is not internal to thought, as in the dialectics of both Plato and Hegel. And because the *relata* are necessary for each other, they do not stand in a purely contingent, external relationship to one another, as in a Newtonian conflict of forces or a Kantian *Realrepugnanz*.[109] So that if one chooses to use the term 'dialectical', in deference to custom but in opposition to history, to refer to *such* oppositions, it seems advisable to preface it, to indicate its specificity, by some such term as 'Marxian'.

Notes

1 See *A Realist Theory of Science*, 1st edn (Leeds 1975), 2nd edn (Hassocks and New Jersey 1978), esp. ch. 1 sec. 4.
2 K. Marx, *Grundrisse* (Harmondsworth 1973), p. 265.
3 See, for example, A. Schutz, 'Common-Sense and Scientific Interpretations of Human Actions', *Collected Papers* 1 (The Hague 1967), or 'Problems of Interpretative Sociology', reprinted from *The Phenomenology of the Social World* (London 1967) in A. Ryan (ed.), *The Philosophy of Social Explanation* (Oxford 1973).
4 As is evinced by the possibility of absolute idealism as the ontological ground for idealist sociologies (often, and arguably necessarily, combined with individualism – for example Weber or Dilthey – or collectivism – for example Durkheim or, say, Lévi-Strauss – in the work of a single author). See also T. Benton, *Philosophical Foundations of the Three Sociologies* (London 1977), p. 85, n. 11.
5 See the specific analogy drawn by J.W.N. Watkins between methodological individualism in social science and mechanism in physics in 'Ideal Types and Historical Explanation', *British Journal for the Philosophy of Science* 3 (1952), reprinted in A. Ryan (ed.), *op. cit.*, p. 90, and 'Historical Explanation in the Social Sciences', *British Journal for the Philosophy of Science* 8 (1957), reprinted as 'Methodological Individualism and Social Tendencies' in *Readings in the Philosophy of the Social Sciences*, M. Brodbeck (ed.) (London 1970), p. 270.
6 K. R. Popper, *The Open Society and its Enemies* 2 (London 1962), p. 98.
7 I. Jarvie, 'Reply to Taylor', *Universities and Left Review* (1959), p. 57.
8 J. W. N. Watkins, 'Methodological Individualism', p. 271.
9 *Loc. cit.*
10 J. W. N. Watkins, 'Ideal Types', p. 88.
11 See A. Danto, *Analytical Philosophy of History* (Cambridge 1965), ch. 12, and S.

Lukes, 'Methodological Individualism Reconsidered', *British Journal of Sociology* 19 (1968), reprinted in A. Ryan (ed.), *op. cit.*

12 See J. W. N. Watkins, 'Ideal Types', p. 91 and 'Methodological Individualism', p. 273.

13 *Ibid.*, p. 278.

14 D. Hume, *A Treatise on Human Nature* (Oxford 1967), p. 415.

15 D. Hume, *Essays Moral and Political* 2 (London 1875), p. 68. Although this paradigm is perhaps for the first time clearly articulated by Hume, it is significant that in his thought, unlike many who followed him, it is counterbalanced by a stress on certain intrinsically social sensibilities, most notably sympathy, and an interest in history – both characteristic of the Scottish Enlightenment generally (see, for example, G. Davie, *The Democratic Intellect* (Edinburgh 1961)). Indeed for Hume it is precisely sympathy among the 'constant and universal principles of human nature' that provides the ground for our interest in history. See, for example, *Enquiries* (Oxford 1972), p. 223.

16 See S. Kotarbinski, 'Praxiology', *Essays in Honour of O. Lange* (Warsaw 1965).

17 See, for example, J. W. N. Watkins, 'Ideal Types', p. 82, n. 1.

18 J.-P. Sartre, *Critique of Dialectical Reason* (London 1976), bk. 2, ch. 1 and bk 1, ch. 4.

19 There are of course non-, and even anti-individualist tendencies in Weber's thought – see, for example, R. Aron, *Philosophie critique de l'histoire* (Paris 1969). Similarly there are non- and (especially in *The Elementary Forms of Religious Life*) anti-positivist strains in Durkheim's thought – see, for example, S. Lukes, *Durkheim* (London 1973), and R. Horton, 'Lévy-Bruhl, Durkheim and the Scientific Revolution' in *Modes of Thought*, R. Finnegan and R. Horton (eds.) (London 1973). My concern here is only with the *dominant* aspects.

20 See, for example, R. Keat and J. Urry, *Social Theory as Science* (London 1975), ch. 5; and B. Ollman, *Alienation* (Cambridge 1971), esp. chs. 2 and 3. Of course there are positivist and individualist elements in Marx's work as well.

21 See especially P. Berger and S. Pullberg, 'Reification and the Sociological Critique of Consciousness', *New Left Review* 35 (1966) and P. Berger and T. Luckmann, *The Social Construction of Reality* (London 1967).

22 P. Berger and S. Pullberg, 'Reification', pp. 62–3.

23 *Ibid.*, p. 63.

24 *Loc. cit.*

25 E. Durkheim, *The Rules of Sociological Method* (New York 1964), p. 2.

26 P. Berger and S. Pullberg, 'Reification', p. 60.

27 *Ibid.*, p. 61.

28 *Ibid.*, p. 60.

29 E. Durkheim, *The Rules of Sociological Method*, pp. 1-2.

30 See C. Lévi-Strauss, *The Savage Mind* (London 1966), ch. 1.

31 See A. Giddens, *New Rules of Sociological Method* (London 1976), p. 121; and J. Lyons, *Chomsky* (London 1970), p. 22.

32 See R. Harré and P. Secord, *The Explanation of Social Behaviour* (Oxford 1972), esp. ch. 5.

33 Mentalistic predicates may play a legitimate role in the explanation of social changes either as a result of their literal use to refer to processes of conscious choice, deliberation, etc., or as a result of their metaphorical use to refer to the effects of teleonomic processes or homeostatic systems. See, for example, A. Giddens, 'Functionalism: après la lutte', *Studies in Social and Political Theory* (London 1977), esp. p. 116, or A. Ryan, *The Philosophy of the Social Sciences* (London 1970), pp. 182–94. But on the whole, persons make a bad model for societies (and vice versa).

34 Marx, perhaps, comes closest to articulating this conception of history:

History is nothing but the succession of the separate generations, each of which exploits the materials, the capital funds, the productive forces handed down to it by all preceding generations, and thus, on the one hand, continues the traditional activity in completely changed circumstances and, on the other, modifies the old circumstances with a completely changed activity (K. Marx and F. Engels, *The German Ideology* (London 1965), p. 65).

The epistemic distance established in Model IV between society and people also indicates, at least schematically, a way in which substance can be given to the celebrated Marxian proposition that 'people make history, but not under conditions of their choice'. The 'people' here must of course be understood not just as acting idiosyncratically, but as expressing the definite and *general* interests and needs of particular strata and classes, where these are defined in the first instance by their differential relationships (of possession, access, etc.) to the productive resources constituting structural conditions of action. These productive resources in turn must be conceptualized generically so as to include *in principle*, for example, political and cultural resources as well as purely economic ones.

35 See *A Realist Theory of Science*, p. 113. See also M. Polanyi, *The Tacit Dimension* (London 1967), ch. 2.

36 E. Durkheim, *The Rules of Sociological Method*, p. 3.

37 See M. Weber, *Economy and Society* (New York 1968), p. 4.

38 See G. H. von Wright, *Norm and Action* (London 1963), p. 10.

39 Of course populations are continuous and provide a biological basis for social existence. But their social attributes, whether analysed stochastically or not, must be explicated on either relational or collectivist lines. And so they cannot provide the required social substrate without begging the question we are concerned with here.

40 Cf. Marx:

I paint the capitalist and landlord in no sense *couleur de rose*. But here individuals are dealt with only in so far as they are personifications of economic categories, embodiments of particular class-relations and class-interests. My standpoint, from which the evolution of human society is viewed as a process of natural history, can no less than any other make the individual responsible for relations whose creature he socially remains, however much he may subjectively raise himself above them (*Capital*, 1 (London 1970), p. 10).

41 See especially T. Parsons, *The Structure of Social Action* (New York 1959), pp. 89–94 and *passim.*

42 According to Marx human beings 'begin to distinguish themselves from animals as soon as they begin to *produce* their means of subsistence' (*The German Ideology*, p. 31).

The first premiss of all human existence and therefore of all history [is] the premiss . . . that men must be in a position to live in order to be able to 'make history' . But life involves before anything else eating and drinking, a habitation, clothing and many other things. The first historical act is thus the production of the means to satisfy these needs, the production of material life itself (*ibid.*, p. 39).

The 'first historical act' must of course be understood in an analytical, not chronological, sense. Cf. also: 'In all forms of society it is a determinate production and its relations which assigns every other production and its relations their rank and influence. It is a general illumination in which all other colours are plunged and which modifies their specific tonalities. It is a special ether which defines the specific gravity of everything found within it' (*Grundrisse*, p. 107).

43 The problem for Marxism has always been to find a way of avoiding both economic (or worse technological) reductionism and historical eclecticism, so that it does actually generate some substantive historiographic propositions. It is a problem of which both Marx and Engels were aware. Thus as Engels was at pains to stress:

According to the materialist conception of history, the economy is the ultimately determining element in history. [But] if someone twists this into saying that it is the *only* determining [one], he thereby transforms that proposition into a meaningless, abstract, senseless phrase. The economic situation is the basis, but the various elements of the superstructure . . . also exercise their influence upon the course of events . . . and in many cases preponderate in determining their form. There is an interaction of all these elements in which, amid the endless host of accidents, the economic movement finally asserts itself as necessary (F. Engels, Letter to J. Bloch, 21 Sept. 1890, *Marx–Engels Selected Works* 2 (London 1968), p. 692).

But how is one to conceptualize this ultimate necessity? Marx provides a clue. Replying to an objection he concedes that 'the mode of production of material life dominates the development of social, political and intellectual life generally . . . is very true for our time, in which material interests preponderate, but not for the Middle Ages, in which Catholicism, nor for Athens or Rome, where politics, reigned supreme'. But Marx contends: 'this much [also] is clear. That the Middle Ages could not live on Catholicism, nor the Ancient World on politics [alone]. On the contrary, it is the economic conditions of the time that explain why here politics and there Catholicism played the chief part' (*Capital* 1, p. 81). Althusser has attempted to theorize this insight by saying that it is the economy that *determines* which relatively autonomous structure is the *dominant* one. See L. Althusser, *For Marx* (London 1969), especially chs. 2 and 6, and L. Althusser and E. Balibar, *Reading Capital* (London 1970).

44 See especially L. Colletti, 'Marxism and the Dialectic', *New Left Review* 93 (1975), and B. Ollman, *op. cit.*

45 See *A Realist Theory of Science*, esp. pp. 17–34. See also Marx's distinction between the 'method of presentation', which he characterizes 'as if a priori', and the (a posteriori) 'method of inquiry' in *Capital*, 1, p. 19.

46 *Ibid.*, esp. ch. 2, sec. 6.

47 See N. Elias, 'The Sciences: Towards a Theory', *Social Processes of Scientific Development*, R. Whitley (ed.) (London 1974).

48 A. Labriola, *Essays on the Materialistic Conception of History* (Chicago 1904).

49 I. Kant, *Critique of Pure Reason*, N. Kemp Smith (trans.) (London 1970), B74/A51.

50 But is the notion of a 'field' that exists only in virtue of its effects any stranger, or prima-facie more absurd, than the combination of the principles of wave and particle mechanics in elementary micro-physics, which is now reckoned a commonplace?

51 See *A Realist Theory of Science*, app. to ch. 2.

52 *Ibid.*, ch. 2, sec. 4.

53 There is no problem about the empirical testing of theories of phenomena which are internally related (although there is a problem, which can only be resolved intra-theoretically, about the appropriate specification or individuation of the different aspects or parts). For the locus of the empirical is the observable, and

discrete observable items can always be described in ways which are logically independent of one another. Hence even if social scientific theories can only be compared and tested *en bloc*, they can still be tested empirically. Thus because, say, 'capital' cannot be empirically identified and even if, as argued by Ollman (*op. cit.*), 'capital' cannot be univocally theoretically defined (or even conceptually stabilized), it does not follow that *theories* of capital cannot be empirically evaluated. The problem of the best individuation may then be resolved by considering which individuation is implied by (or necessary for) that theory which has the best causal grip on reality.

54 See, for example, N. Georgescu-Roegen, *The Entropy Law and the Economic Process* (Cambridge, Mass. 1971), esp. ch. 2.

55 See, for example, A. Cicourel, *Method and Measurement in Sociology* (New York 1964), esp. ch. 1.

56 See, for example, P. Duhem, *op. cit.*, pp. 180–90.

57 If correct, this has an analogue in the conscious technique of 'Garfinkelling' in social psychology – see, for example, H. Garfinkel, *Studies in Ethnomethodology* (New Jersey 1967) – and perhaps also in the role played by psychopathology in the development of a general psychology. See also A. Collier, *R. D. Laing: The Philosophy and Politics of Psychotherapy* (Hassocks 1977), p. 132.

58 Consider, for example, the way in which the mass unemployment of the 1930s not only provided the theoretical dynamo for the Keynesian innovation, but facilitated its ready acceptance by the relevant scientific community.

59 See P. Anderson, *Considerations on Western Marxism* (London 1976), for an extended discussion.

60 See, for example, G. Therborn, *Science, Class and Society* (London 1976), ch. 5, sec. 3.

61 See H. Lefebvre, 'What is the Historical Past?', *New Left Review* 90 (1975), esp. pp. 33–4.

62 See I. Lakatos, 'Falsification and the Methodology of Scientific Research Programmes', *Criticism and the Growth of Knowledge*, I. Lakatos and A. Musgrave (eds.) (Cambridge 1970).

63 See *A Realist Theory of Science*, p. 132. Cf. the notorious 'unfalsifiability' of economic theories. See, for example, E. Grunberg, 'The Meaning of Scope and External Boundaries of Economics', *The Structure of Economic Science*, S. Krupp (ed.) (New Jersey 1966).

64 L. Goldmann, *Marxisme et sciences humaines* (Paris 1970), p. 250. See also Gadamer's strictures on statistics: 'such an excellent means of propaganda because they let facts speak and hence simulate an objectivity that in reality depends on the legitimacy of the questions asked' (*Truth and Method*, p. 268).

65 For example, the transformational model of social activity implies that it is a necessary condition for any adequate social theory that the theory be consistent with the reproduction (and/or transformation) of its object, and preferably that it should be able to specify the conditions under which such reproduction (and transformation) occurs. See, for example, M. Hollis and E. Nell, *Rational Economic Man* (Cambridge 1975), esp. ch. 8 for a criticism of neo-classical economic theory along these lines.

66 See *Capital*, 1, ch. 1. Such a critique bears a formal analogy to Kant's *Dialectic*. See D. Sayer, 'Science as Critique: Marx vs Althusser', *Issues in Marxist Philosophy*, J. Mepham and D. Ruben (eds.) (Hassocks 1979).

67 *Capital*, 1, pp. 90–1.

68 N. Geras, 'Essence and Appearance: Aspects of Fetishism in Marx's *Capital*', *New Left Review* 65 (1971), reprinted as 'Marx and the Critique of Political Economy', *Ideology in Social Science*, R. Blackburn (ed.) (London 1972), p. 297.

69 See *Capital*, 1, p. 537 and *Capital*, 3, p. 798 respectively.
70 K. Marx, 'Critique of the Gotha Programme', *Selected Works* (London 1968), p. 319.
71 See R. Edgley, 'Reason as Dialectic', *Radical Philosophy* 15 (Autumn 1976).
72 See, for example, S. B. Barnes, *Interests and the Growth of Knowledge* (London 1977), esp. ch. 1.
73 See, for example, J. Brennan, *The Open Texture of Moral Concepts* (London 1977), esp. pt. 2.
74 *Treatise*, esp. pp. 469–70. See R. Hare, *Freedom and Reason* (Oxford 1963), p. 108.
75 See M. Weber, *The Methodology of the Social Sciences* (Chicago 1949), esp. pp. 72–6.
76 See *A Realist Theory of Science*, p. 212.
77 See, for example, J. Slack, 'Class Struggle Among the Molecules', *Counter Course*, T. Pateman (ed.) (Harmondsworth 1972).
78 See Engels to Lafargue, 11 Aug. 1884: 'Marx rejected the "political, social and economic ideal" you attribute to him. A man of science has no ideals, he elaborates scientific results, and if he is also politically committed, he struggles for them to be put into practice. But if he has ideals, he cannot be a man of science, since he would then be biased from the start'; quoted in M. Godelier, 'System, Structure and Contradiction in *Capital*', *Socialist Register* (1967), reprinted in R. Blackburn (ed.), *op. cit.*, p. 354, n. 43. Of course what Engels omitted to mention was the possibility that Marx's scientific results might *imply* a political commitment.
79 For example G. Myrdal, *The Political Element in the Development of Economic Theory* (London 1953), or N. Chomsky, 'Objectivity and Liberal Scholarship', *American Power and the New Mandarins* (London 1969).
80 See, for example, G. Myrdal, *Value in Social Theory* (London 1959), p. 120.
81 See, interestingly, K. Mannheim, *Ideology and Utopia* (London 1960), pp. 300–1.
82 See *A Realist Theory of Science*, p. 249.
83 See L. Wittgenstein, *Philosophical Investigations* (Oxford 1963), p. 223.
84 A. Giddens, in an important work, *New Rules of Sociological Method*, p. 16, p. 161 and *passim*, systematically confuses the fact that the sociologist must utilize the cognitive resources of the agents under investigation in order to generate adequate descriptions of their conduct with the idea of their incorrigibility. He thus relapses into the pre-relativistic notion of incorrigible foundations of knowledge – despite an attempt to distinguish such incorrigible data from their representations as 'commonsense' (*ibid.*, p. 158). This is akin to trying to disentangle sense-data from their physical object implications. For such cognitive resources do not exist save in the form of beliefs such as 'X is voting, praying, stealing, working, etc.', embodying factual and theoretical presuppositions about the activities under question. It is thus not surprising that Giddens only sees the relationship between S_2 and S_1 as one of 'slippage' (*ibid.*, p. 162), potentially compromising, moreover, to S_2. But the relationship $S_2 \rightarrow S_1$ is not just of slippage, but potentially one of critique; and such a critique is far from neutral in its implications. For though slaves who fully comprehend the circumstances of their own subordination do not thereby become free, such an understanding is a necessary condition for their rational self-emancipation. Conversely their master has an interest in their remaining ignorant of the circumstances of their slavery. Knowledge is asymmetrically beneficial to the parties involved in relations of domination. Moreover, quite generally, explanatory knowledge increases the range of known possibilities and so *ceteris paribus* tilts the 'ideological balance-of-forces' against conservatism and the status quo (quite apart from its other effects). It is thus quite wrong to regard social science as *equally* 'a potential instrument of

domination' as of 'the expansion of the rational autonomy of action' (*ibid.*, p. 159).

85 See, for example, R. Coward and J. Ellis, *Language and Materialism* (London 1977), p. 41.

86 According to Nagel, any threat to the value-neutrality of social science can be blocked by rigorously distinguishing between *appraising* value judgements which 'express *approval* or *disapproval* either of some moral (or social) ideal or of some action (or institution) because of commitment to such an ideal' and *characterizing* value judgements which 'express an *estimate* of the degree to which some commonly recognized (and more or less clearly defined) type of action, object or institution is embodied in a given instance' – E. Nagel, *The Structure of Science* (London 1961), p. 492. Thus the judgement that a person is anaemic on the basis of a red blood cell count is a characterizing one; while the judgement that anaemia is undesirable is an appraising one (*loc. cit.*). There are several problems with this counter. Firstly, it is unclear why Nagel calls a characterizing judgement a value judgement at all. In effect the characterizing/appraising distinction just transposes the very fact/value one in question. Secondly, Nagel treats social reality as unproblematic and social science as approximating the deductive model. He thus fails to see that while the atomic resolution of theoretically defined concepts may be plausible in the case of some externally related natural phenomena, it is totally inapplicable to the reconstruction of social phenomena comprised of internally related elements. Institutions, such as the monarchy, and systems, for example of morality, either exist (and so must be grasped) *in toto* or they do not exist at all. Of course there are fuzzy boundaries and borderline cases, and descriptions require empirical testing. However, the occurrence of qualitative changes and the conceptual aspect of social reality limit the possibility of significant quantification in social science. Moreover, to confuse the empirical checking out of our descriptions in L_2 and the properties of *that* process, with what such descriptions describe (in S_1), and the properties *they* possess, is to commit the verificationist fallacy.

87 C. Taylor, 'Neutrality in Political Science', *Philosophy, Politics and Society*, 3rd Series, P. Laslett and W. Runciman (eds.) (Oxford 1967), reprinted in A. Ryan (ed.), *op. cit.*

88 *Ibid.*, p. 161.

89 See, for example, *ibid.*, pp. 145–6, p. 148 and *passim.*

90 See J. R. Searle, 'How to Derive "Ought" from "Is"', *Philosophical Review* 73 (1964) and *Speech Acts* (Cambridge 1969), ch. 8.

91 For example if one believed that it was morally wrong to commit oneself and others to action in the future.

92 See, for example, R. Swinburne, 'The Objectivity of Morality', *Philosophy* 51 (1976).

93 See R. Edgley, *Reason in Theory and Practice* (London 1969), esp. 4.11.

94 K. Marx, *Capital*, 1, p. 505.

95 See N. Geras, 'Althusser's Marxism: An Assessment', *New Left Review* 71, reprinted in *Western Marxism: A Critical Reader*, G. Stedman Jones *et al.* (London 1977).

96 See G. Stedman Jones, 'The Marxism of the Early Lukács', *New Left Review* 70, reprinted in G. Stedman Jones *et al., op. cit.*

97 See D. Lecourt, *Proletarian Science?* (London 1977).

98 The key to Hegelian philosophy, which enables it to achieve its philosophical coup. viz. the reconciliation of the Kantian antinomies, is precisely the realization by consciousness, in the form of the absolute spirit, that its object is in the end nothing other than itself. This involves precisely the denial of the *autonomous*

existence of matter; that is, of its existence except as one moment in the development of Geist, the self-realization of the absolute idea. For Marx, in contrast, 'neither thought nor language . . . form a realm of their own, they are only *manifestations* of actual life' (*The German Ideology*, C. Arthur (ed.) (London 1974), p. 118), so that 'consciousness can never be anything else than conscious existence' (*ibid.*, p. 47).

99 This notion cannot be explicated here. But among its standard implications are the following ideas: (1) that the economic, and beneath that, the biological and ultimately the physical – see S. Timpanaro, *On Materialism* (London 1975) – set boundary conditions for the non-economic; (2) that the economic partly – and over – determines the non-economic; (3) that ideas must be explained at least in part by something other than ideas – something which need not be material but must be 'materialized' in order to exist as a social object; (4) that all social phenomena are intransitive (in the sense of p. 47); (5) that all social phenomena require a material substrate and/or possess a material referent.

100 See, for example, N. Stockman, 'Habermas, Marcuse and the *Aufhebung* of Science and Technology', *Philosophy of the Social Sciences* 8 (1978), and T. Eagleton, *Criticism and Ideology* (London 1976), on the material bases of science and literature respectively.

101 The currently fashionable rejection of the criterion of false consciousness by those who wish to define ideology solely by reference to its serving 'concealed' interests or its embodying 'unnecessary' domination presupposes that it might be possible to detect those interests or its role without a theory capable of explaining the phenomena that the ideological theory did. It thus presupposes that the conditions under which the *I*-theory holds are irrelevant to its explanation; and hence either that it is groundless or that one can study it in isolation from its grounds.

102 'The vulgar economists' way of looking at things stems . . . from the fact that it is only the direct form of manifestation of relations that is reflected in their brains and not their inner connections' (letter from Marx to Engels, 27 June 1867, *Marx–Engels Selected Correspondence* (Moscow 1956)). 'Vulgar economy actually does no more than interpret, systematize and defend in doctrinaire fashion the conceptions of agents of bourgeois production who are entrapped in bourgeois production relations' (K. Marx, *Capital*, 3, p. 817). 'In opposition to Spinoza, it believes that "ignorance is sufficient reason"' (K. Marx, *Capital*, 1, p. 307).

103 M. Godelier, 'System, Structure and Contradiction in *Capital*', *Socialist Register* (1967), reprinted in R. Blackburn (ed.), *op. cit.*, p. 337.

104 K. Marx, *Capital*, 1, p. 540. Dealing with the transformation of the value of labour power into that of labour in consciousness, Marx says 'this phenomenal form which makes the real relation invisible, and indeed shows the exact opposite of that relation, forms the basis for all the juridical notions of both labourer and capitalist, of all the mystifications of the capitalist mode of production, of all its illusions as to liberty, of all the apologetic shifts of the vulgar economists' (*loc. cit.*). Moreover, whereas 'the value of labour appears directly and spontaneously as a current mode of thought, the [value of labour power] must first be discovered by science. Classical political economy nearly touches the true relations of things, without, however, consciously formulating it. This it cannot do so long as it sticks to its bourgeois skin' (*ibid.*, p. 542).

105 J. Mepham, 'The Theory of Ideology in *Capital*', *Radical Philosophy* 2 (1972), p. 18.

106 After L. Colletti, *op. cit.*

107 See, for example, L. Althusser, 'Ideology and Ideological State Apparatuses',

Lenin and Philosophy (London 1971), pp. 160ff. It should be noted that these category mistakes are corrigible in analysis, so that Marković's paradox, viz. that an account of social reality as reified (etc.) must itself embody reified elements (see M. Marković, 'The Problem of Reification and the *Verstehen–Erklären* Controversy', *Acta Sociologica* 15 (1972)) does not vitiate Marxism.

108 L. Colletti, *op. cit.*, especially pp. 21–2.

109 See *ibid.*, p. 6.

9

STRATIFIED EXPLANATION AND MARX'S CONCEPTION OF HISTORY

Andrew Collier

Continents or strata?

In theorising the relation of revolutionary scientific advances to the philosophies to which they gave rise, Althusser uses the metaphor of theoretical *continents* 'before Marx, two continents *only* had been opened up to scientific knowledge by sustained epistemological breaks: the *continent of mathematics* with the Greeks (by Thales or those designated by that mythical name) and the *continent of physics* (by Galileo and his successors)' (*Lenin and Philosophy* [LP], p. 42). Althusser goes on to locate chemistry and biology, which achieved their 'epistemological breaks' with Lavoisier and with Darwin and Mendel, within the continent of physics. Marx is credited with opening a third continent – that of history; and it is 'probable' that Freud has discovered another. Now let us grant (for the moment at least) the unrivalled importance and novelty of the discoveries listed as continents, and also the idea of a philosophical lag. The question remains whether this metaphor of continents can be pushed any further. In fact, Althusser has already pushed it further by calling the various natural sciences *regions* of physics (loc. cit.): they presumably lie alongside of each other like Normandy and Brittany, parts of the same land mass, distinguished for historical and cultural reasons; but with no common boundaries with, or land routes to, other continents. The metaphor, so extended, suggests several questionable notions.

First, it minimises the hiatuses between 'regions'. According to Althusser, the discovery of the molecular basis of biology shows that biology is part of the continent of physics; rather as someone landing in Brittany might doubt whether it was part of the same land mass as the already familiar Normandy, and then, by making the journey, discover that it is.

Source: Scientific Realism and Socialist Thought, chap. 2, pp. 43–72.

Surely, it is not quite like that. The discovery is not of a crossable boundary, but of a *basis*: we already knew various genetic laws; now we know more about how those laws operate, because we can identify some of the entities known through that science – genes – under a description drawn from another science – DNA molecules. We can then use our knowledge of the behaviour of molecules to understand why these particular molecules behave in the ways already mapped out by the biological sciences.

Does not the metaphor of *strata* catch these features of the chemistry – biology relation better than that of regions?

One may then ask, secondly, whether the same sort of ontological relation that obtains between chemistry and biology may not also obtain between the different continents. Are not human societies, for instance, dependent for their possibility on certain facts of biology, just as living organisms are on certain chemical facts? And is there not an asymmetry between the maths/physics divide and the physics/history one? That is, in that there is surely some ontological relation between nature and society; both are aspects of the real world, awaiting empirical discovery; nature is prior, both in time and in order of ontological dependence; society can only exist because nature is such that human life and social production are possible, and so on. But the continent of mathematics surely does not appear on the same map; it is in a sense constituted by its rules, not discovered by empirical investigation.

This suggests, thirdly, that the metaphor of continents may also lead us astray in matters of epistemology and method. Althusser uses the unlikeness of methods in the natural and the mathematical sciences to lend plausibility to the idea of a similar unlikeness between the natural and social sciences. This makes it all too easy to limit experiment to the natural sciences, leaving the social scientist with much too clear an epistemological conscience.

Finally, on the one hand, this metaphor leaves it quite unclear what, if anything, can be learnt about scientific procedure on one continent from what we know about scientific procedure on another; and on the other hand, it becomes falsely obvious that whatever can be identified as on one scientific continent can be investigated according to the methods of (other regions of) that continent. Such a view gives credence to an idea which has haunted Marxist researchers since long before Althusser: the idea that Marxism has the key to all knowledge, at least so far as the 'continent of history' is concerned. This idea has licensed 'Marxist' theories of the psychological, semiological and even biological sciences, on which some of the best minds of the Left have dissipated their energies. Lenin even coined a Russian portmanteau-word for this sort of error: '*komchvanstvo*', 'communist swagger'.[1]

The direction of my remarks, I think, is clear: that what is required is an ordered hierarchy, a 'tree' of sciences, rather than the continent/region model. Oversimplifying a lot, it would presumably contain some such ordering as this:

?
psychological and semiological sciences
social sciences
biological sciences
molecular sciences
?

There are several aspects to this ordering; let us start with what might be called 'epistemological depth'. Bhaskar sees it as a common feature of the progress of the sciences that when some mechanism has been discovered which explains some event, underlying mechanisms are sought which explain the first mechanism. For example (RTS, p. 169):

Stratum I	$2Na + 2HC = 2NaCl + H_2$ explained by	
Stratum II	theory of atomic number and valency explained by	Mechanism 1
Stratum III	theory of electrons and atomic structure explained by	Mechanism 2
Stratum IV	(competing theories of sub-atomic structure)	(Mechanism 3)

This process of deepening an explanation may well involve revising and correcting the original explanation at certain points, and is also one way in which a theory can be confirmed or strengthened. Verification therefore takes place not only on the horizontal axis, by finding instances of the operation of a law, but on the vertical, showing how that law is possible. But there is no necessity that upper-stratum facts be discovered first. This is worth saying for two reasons. First, because it indicates that the depth is not just epistemological, but has an ontological basis: there is a real ordering of the strata, not just a difference in ease of access to knowledge about them. And secondly, because it illustrates the inadequacy of reductive theories of the relations between strata. According to a reductive theory, we may well discover certain laws of psychology before those of neurophysiology, or of genetics before those of biochemistry, and that is just what gives provisional legitimacy to the upper-stratum discipline: for as soon as we can translate these laws into the terms of the more basic science, the *raison d'être* of the 'upper' science disappears. But this familiar reductivist programme won't do – in the first place, because, in Roy Bhaskar's words, of 'the need for a well-defined reductans' (RTS, p. 181). In order to translate colour-concepts into light-wave concepts, linguistic concepts into descriptions of marks on a page, psychological concepts into talk of brain-states, we need to know just what we are translating, and it is this that tells us why the translation is important. This is supported by the fact that there has never been a route even from a highly developed lower-stratum science to a science with a higher-stratum object. Only when the latter is independently theorised can we begin to correlate the two, and perhaps explain the upper by the lower.[2]

This all supports the view that the epistemological stratification is not founded in contingent aspects of human cognitive capacities, but in a real ontological stratification of the object of the sciences. It is the real distinctions between the strata and their irreducibility one to another (of which more shortly), which explain the distinctions between the various sciences, the fact that 'science' does not exist except as a multiplicity of sciences. Hence Bhaskar, like Althusser, rejects what has become a popular orthodoxy about science: the idea that in itself nature is one, and the ideal science would therefore also be unitary; that the divisions between the sciences are arbitrary effects of some contingent human arrangement. There are reductive and romantic variants of this idea: the reductive one has as its project an ultimate translation of all sciences into the terms of physics; the romantic ones blame analytical reason, or industrialism, or capitalism, or some other cosmic bogey for the 'fragmentation' of our knowledge. Althusser's metaphor of continents can be seen as a protest against this prejudice, but he leaves it unclear just what is wrong with it (the stratification of the objects of the sciences could be some necessary feature of our theoretical practices, rather than a contingent feature of the world we live in), and this metaphor also allows the reductive programme to go through within each continent. But for Bhaskar, the plurality of sciences is necessary because of the irreducibly stratified character of the mechanisms at work in the real world, so that the unity of nature is that of a laminate. Perhaps a little experiment in thought will illustrate this.

Let us imagine a multiplicity of gods in Valhalla, each one of whom conforms to the popular image of an academic in that he is omniscient about his own subject, and absolutely ignorant about everything else. Thor, the physicist among the gods, will be able to predict the course of the world under a physical description, but this knowledge gives him no clues about the social realities on which Woden is the expert. Thor does not know there is a strike on. He knows only that certain arrangements of matter are not chugging away as usual, and that certain other more complex ones are sprawled on armchairs or kicking balls around fields instead of stationed in the factory. There are no gaps in his physical description of this, but in an important sense he does not know why certain of these events are occurring, and that sense is not analysable without residue in terms of the question: which descriptions are of interest to humans. A particular event which is certainly an event in the physical world and as such fully describable by Thor – let us say the chief shop steward's visit to the local lorry depot asking them to black the plant – could not have taken place just as it did (even in purely physical terms) were it not for the existence of causal mechanisms at the social level, which of all the gods only Woden understands. There are, of course, events with purely physical determinants within the whole process which may affect its outcome, e.g. the police chief being struck by lightning on his way to arrest the pickets. So Woden's knowledge is full of gaps, though he does at least know there is a strike on. In order to predict the outcome, collaboration would be necessary in Valhalla. Only when Thor and Woden get together with Frey, god of biology, and Loki, god of the unconscious, could it be learnt that the boss's daughter is going to elope with the chief shop steward, the boss is going to die of apoplexy, and the daughter inherit the firm and turn it into a workers' co-operative.

For the purposes of simplicity I have treated physics as if it were a rock-bottom science in the sense that, so long as it sticks to its own terms, it can give an account of any process without causal gaps; in fact this appears not to be the case, though it is the most basic extant science. It may be doubted that there is any rock-bottom stratum. It is no more incoherent that the chain of vertical causality should extend forever downwards than that the chain of horizontal causality should extend forever backwards. I mention this only to take my distance from the epistemic fallacy which philosophical reflections on the frontiers of physics so often commit.

In the most important of the senses in which the classical Marxist tradition has described itself as 'materialist', this theory is also materialist. That is to say, in that the lower strata explain the higher. This materialist direction of explanation operates as between *mechanisms* but not as between the concrete events governed by those mechanisms: it is the laws of chemistry which explain the laws of biology, but the presence of C_2H_5OH (alcohol) in the demijohn is explained by the life-process of the yeast. Hence there is no tendency to play down the effectivity of mechanisms belonging to the upper strata of nature (using 'nature' here to include social and mental realities).

Stratification in open systems

Several features of this ontological stratification are worth noting. Let us distinguish between the area of reality *governed* by laws at a given stratum, and that *affected* by them. The human activities of the production and exchange of goods are governed by economic laws. The colour of moths is not governed by economic, but by biological laws. However, it is affected by economic laws, as the rise and fall of industrial melanism illustrates. Indeed, granted that a given law governs *any* stratum, there is nothing which cannot be affected by it. But this does not mean that all laws govern all entities. This can be illustrated by the following diagrams:

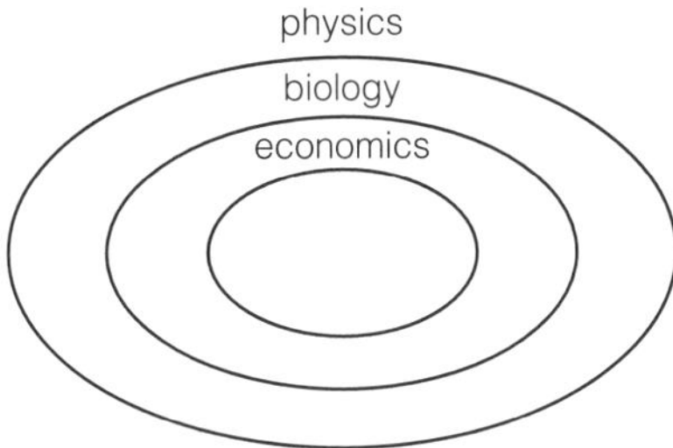

Relations between the realms consisting of entities governed by the various sciences. Asymmetrical relations of inclusion. All 'biological' entities are 'physical' but not vice versa, etc.

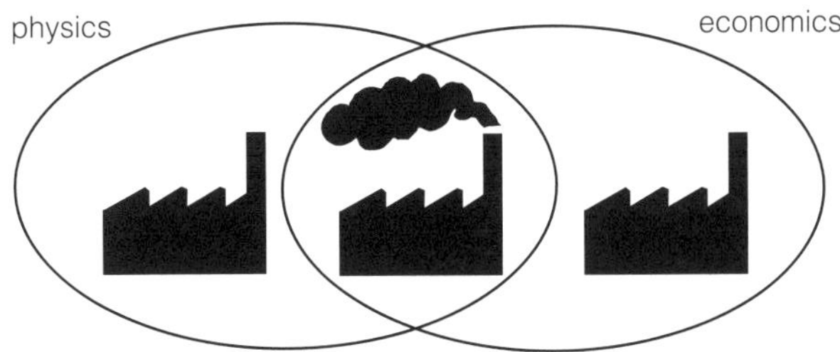

Relations between the actions of the mechanisms of the various sciences. Symmetrical relations of co-determination. The factory will work when the laws of physics and economics permit, but either a mechanical breakdown or a recession will stop it.

Having made this distinction, it can be said that the areas governed by the higher strata laws always appear later in the history of the universe and remain smaller than those governed by more basic laws. Everything is governed by the laws of physics; since a few hundred million years ago, some of those but not all have been governed by the laws of biology; for a few hundred years, some but not all of those have been governed by the laws of capitalist economics, and so on.

The above model of the relations between the strata enables us to say more about the idea of freedom-within-determinism. We have already seen that Bhaskar's theory of multiple determination enables us to combine 'ubiquity determinism' (the notion that every event has a cause) with the denial of 'regularity determinism' (which treats the universe as if it were a closed system, within which a single causal mechanism operated, such that knowledge of that mechanism and of the state of the universe would make the future perfectly predictable).

Once we have seen that the determination of events is not merely pluralistic but *stratified*, we can give an account of freedom which would, I think, lay to rest some of the fears that anti-determinists have had about ubiquity determinism, while retaining it.[3] Each emergent stratum will effect alterations in the entities governed by the stratum from which it emerged, which would not have been effected had the new stratum not emerged. This is so even before the emergence of human life. The proliferation of bright colours at a certain point in evolutionary development, due to their survival value in many plants and animals, is a case in point. Although it is possible to translate colour-concepts into physicalistic terms, it is not possible to explain physicalistically why there were a lot more brightly coloured creatures about the earth at one time than there had been at an earlier time. And this, of course, has nothing to do with the phenomenology of colours, since there were no human beings around at the time.

One feature of the stratification of nature requires mention because of its epistemological effects – both in accounting for 'epistemological depth', and in explaining the methodological problems specific to the upper-stratum sciences. There could be no laws of biological evolution if 'random' mutations of genes did not occur as a result of processes governed not by biological but only by physical laws (the randomness, of course, being relative only to concepts internal to biological theory); economic (and, more generally, social) laws could not operate if human beings did not, as a result of their biological nature, have a certain degree of adaptability in their manner of producing the means of life. It is this ontological stratification that makes 'vertical explanations' possible, but it also means that every stratum which has another one below it must reckon with events which are accidents relative to its own laws: and not just accidental accidents – that is to say, it is not a matter of operating in contingently open systems, but of the impossibility, not only in practice but in principle, of experimental closure or exact prediction. The higher the stratum, the more sources of accidents, the more distant the possibility of closure. Hence the gappiness of Woden's knowledge in my little myth: gaps not just at the level of the Actual, where every science must recognise its limits and take its place among the multiple explanations of events; but gaps inherent in the generative mechanisms of the stratum.

There is one more relation between strata which must be mentioned: the relation of structuration or composition. Entities inhabiting one stratum will be composed of entities inhabiting a lower one. Societies are composed (in part, at least) of people; living cells are composed of molecules, and so on. Bhaskar is explicit about the reality of the complexity of complex entities, whose powers are 'emergent' with respect to their components. In the Marxist context, the nature of the composition relation is crucial in the society/people instance. I shall discuss this whole question in the next chapter.

Base and superstructure

It may be useful at this stage to turn to an issue in traditional Marxist theory on which Bhaskar's conception of the stratification of nature might throw some light, although he himself has been silent about it: the model of historical materialism as a system of explanation of the 'superstructure' (politics, ideology, etc.) in terms of the 'base' (economic, or more generally 'material').

The number of 'storeys' in the base/superstructure model has always been somewhat indeterminate. Marx and Engels tended to think in terms of material (or economic) versus the rest. This fits in with what I take to be their view (and also that of Plekhanov and Lenin) that the materialist conception of history is an *application* to history of a more general materialist world outlook. Existence precedes consciousness, so social existence precedes social consciousness.[4] Plekhanov and Lenin in particular are quite explicit about the fact that this view involves the primacy of the *material*, not merely of the economic.[5] I think that this classical Marxist position is best understood if the ramifications of the superstructure on the one hand (particularly the interposition of a political level between the economic and the ideological), and the specifically economic character of the laws governing the base on the other, are taken as features of specific historical societies. These features are specifically denied to be present, for instance, in pre-class societies, though the polarity material/ideational of course applies there too.

For modern societies, however, a useful starting point is the five-level model proposed by Plekhanov (working from the base up):

1 the state of the productive forces;
2 the economic relations these forces condition;
3 the socio-political system that has developed on the given economic 'base';
4 the mentality of men living in society, a mentality which is determined in part directly by the economic conditions obtaining, and in part by the entire socio-political system that has arisen on that foundation;
5 the various ideologies that reflect the properties of that mentality.

(*Fundamental Problems of Marxism*, p. 80)

Althusser, whom I shall discuss next, generally uses a three-level model (economic, political, ideological), but all five levels in fact figure in his account. (He refers to the indeterminacy of the number of storeys in Marx's work at ESC, p. 182.)

It may be noted in passing that the relation between levels (1) and (2) is that of structuration or composition, i.e. (2) is a structure of which (1) forms the elements. This is not so with respect to the other levels.

This disanalogy between the relations between levels (1) and (2) on the one hand, and between these and the superstructure on the other, has important consequences, for the 'forces/relations' distinction can be made within the superstructural levels too. Althusser has drawn attention to this with his talk of ideology having its own materiality, and this notion has been interestingly applied to artistic production. However, the crucial application is to the materiality of the state – i.e. the armed forces – and the transformation of the modern state as a result of the technological development of the forces of production in what Marx referred to in this context as 'the human slaughter industry' (letter to Engels, 7 July 1866). The task of analysing the change in the relations of the nation-state both to possible insurgency within and to other nation-states, as a result of the development of this 'industry' is crucial, since the prospects, not only of socialism but of life on earth, are bound up with the resolution of the contradictions that have arisen at this level.

Nevertheless, when I have pointed out some inadequacies of Althusser's account, I shall argue that it is useful to see the levels as ontological strata, in the sense that Bhaskar argues that the distinctions between the sciences reflect distinctions between strata.

I have already argued that Althusser's basic error *re* the science/ideology distinction is that of attributing misplaced concreteness to the various types of practice which, for him, make up the hierarchy of social practices, and hence distinguishing them as practices, rather than as aspects of practices. It seems to me that he falls into this error, not only in drawing the science/ideology distinction, but also in his theory of the relations of the superstructural levels to the material base. And this is compounded by the fact that he writes not only of ideological practices but also of ideological apparatuses, which are alleged to produce ideology in an all-too-neatly functional manner. The 'ISA's' (ideological state apparatuses) as Althusser calls them include schools, families, media, political parties, churches, sporting and cultural institutions, and so on. He does wryly admit that one such apparatus, the family, also has non-ideological functions: 'It intervenes in the reproduction of labour power' (LP, p. 137n). He also admits that 'ideological relations are immediately present in [economic] processes' (op. cit., p. 141n). But this does not go far enough. As several commentators have pointed out, the economic apparatuses themselves are among the prime producers of ideology. Once this is seen, the idea of *specifically* ideological apparatuses begins to break down. We can then give full due to the pleasure-giving functions of the media and cultural apparatuses, the presence of science as well as ideology in the educational apparatuses, and on the other hand the ideological effects of economic production, scientific research, sexual relationships, shopping, gardening, and so on. And this returns us to the classical Marxist position: that base and superstructure can be separated only in thought.[6]

None of this is meant to deny that there are, also, specialised ideological apparatuses in modern societies – though of course these have economic (etc.) aspects too. But the important point is that they presuppose an ideological stratum of social relations that they did not create. As Poulantzas remarks, religion produces the churches, not vice versa. And if we had not already acquired a certain ideology from the practice of doing the family shopping,

Saatchi and Saatchi could not have presented Thatcher's cuts as 'good housekeeping'.

Some allusions to the various things that Marx and Engels say about ideology may help to avoid confusion here (the main source of this is *The German Ideology*, Part I, but I shall avoid tedious textual analysis).

We find at least four ways of describing the primacy of material production in Marx and Engels – ways which are not equivalent, and at first sight appear to fit badly together.

(i) There is seemingly economistic talk of material production *determining* or *conditioning* ideas, or ideas being 'sublimates of their material life-process'.
(ii) There is talk of ideas as the *form* in which struggles generated at the level of material production are fought out.
(iii) There is the assertion that the ruling ideas of any age are the ideas of the ruling class of that age.
(iv) There is the notion that ideology has no history: it is developed *by* developments in the relations of material production; but it is developed out of raw ideological materials handed down by the last generation.

Exclusive attention to any of these formulations can be misleading, as can the conflation of one with another. Let us look at each in turn:

(i) It is clear enough that in *any* society, including those before the division between manual and mental labour had occurred, ideas are involved in the production process; it is this that distinguishes 'the worst of architects from the best of bees'; and this mental aspect of labour is by no means annulled – even if it is impoverished – for the manual worker when this division of labour does take place. A worker is not an automaton. The metaphor of a 'superstructure' sounds rather odd if it is used to refer to a carpenter saying 'Pass me that hammer, Bill, will you?' – leaving the passing of the hammer and the hammering that ensued as part of the 'base'. At this level it is best to say: ideas are an *aspect* of the process of production. But it is important to see that this doesn't exhaust the account of the ideological life of mankind. It hardly even gets started.

(ii) People think and talk about their situations. They ask: Why is it so? Could it be otherwise? These thoughts are not aspects of the production process, as the request for a hammer is. For this reason already, the idea of ideology as merely an aspect (however essential) of material production is not adequate. John Ball asked: 'When Adam delved and Eve span, who was then the gentleman?', implying: the inequality of lord and peasant is sinful. The ideologists of the ruling class in turn could say: 'private property and secular power are not themselves sin, but remedies for sin' – a nice theological dispute, in the course of which the Savoy Palace got burnt, and Wat Tyler got his head cut off and displayed from London Bridge. Few would dispute that the peasants' revolt was in substance a class struggle. Yet it didn't take the simple form of the peasants saying: 'we want land' and the gentry saying 'we're hanging on to it'. And the form that it – or rather the class struggles of the Middle Ages in general – did take, was not without its effects; and not only on the form of the peasants' demands, but also on the power structure of medieval society: an essentially ideological institution, the Church, acquiring immense political and economic power. Here we are concerned with the form in which class struggles are fought out, and therefore with the need for the ruling class to dominate in ideas if it is to be secure in its privileges. This takes us then to the question of *specialised ideological apparatuses* and their role in the *reproduction* of *class relations*, not merely in the production process.[7]

(iii) In all class society there is a division of labour between mental and manual which, as Marx and Engels say, really gives a certain autonomy to ideology. Law, religion, science, art, become the work of special groups whose interests are bound up with their branch of ideological production, and are generally tied to or dominated by ruling class interests in one way or another (class affinities, patronage, the market, state control).

In analysing these ideological structures it is legitimate to ask 'functionalistic' questions about the ideological *requirements* of a given ruling class – what must occur if agents are to be fitted to the social positions assigned to them by the reproduction of existing relations of production. It is legitimate to speak of the 'ideological apparatuses' of the ruling class, and of the 'dominant ideas' of any age being the ideas of the dominant class of that age (always provided that this is not understood in a crude, conspiratorial way – kings and priests – or teachers and advertisers – deceiving the people).

But it should never be forgotten that these mechanisms of ideological production are *superimposed on*, and *presuppose for their effectiveness*, the ideological effects of the institutions of material production and reproduction. Legal fictions, consoling illusions and journalistic lies are purveyed to people whose consciousness is already moulded by their experience in their workplace and their family.

(iv) Great ideological changes take place under the impact both of normal development at the material level of society, and of great class struggles, where the rising class needs a new ideology.

The transformation of sexual ideology in the present century, for instance (both the mitigation of the anti-sensual tendencies in bourgeois culture, and the partial breakdown of traditional sex-roles and male privileges), originates not in the widespread dissemination of the ideas of Ibsen or Wedekind, Freud or Reich, Marie Stopes or Simone de Beauvoir, but rather in the availability of contraception, the increasing job opportunities for women, better social services, the increasingly 'consumeristic' nature of capitalism, which finds both sexual freedom and female independence to its advantage, and so on. All of these factors belong to the development (technical or structural) of the economic base. If this had not occurred, these cultural developments would not have been assimilated by, and hence successful in, bourgeois society.

On the other hand, great ideological revolutions can occur as a result of changes in class power. The Protestant Reformation or the secularisation accompanying the French and Russian Revolutions illustrate this. However, it is necessary to recognise the limitations placed on such transformations by the state of spontaneous ideology generated by relations at the material level. Thus, the imposition of Protestant theology and worship on people whose conditions of life remained pre-capitalist, gave rise to such phenomena as Pietism. Again, the Bolshevik attempts to eliminate religion – which despite the stated policy of the leaders, included violent persecution which could not be excused by the exigencies of civil war – were not successful. Bukharin and Preobrazhensky, in their *ABC of Communism*, put forward a hypothesis which might have explained this: that only the experience of power over their conditions of life would provide the Russian people with the material foundation for a secular world-view. This theory was neither verified nor falsified since that experience did not come to pass. And what emerged were the phenomena of Stalinist pietism – the necrolatrous vows to Lenin, the idea that faith could move mountains and fulfil five year plans in four years, the diabolization of Trotsky, the muscular atheism of the Komsomol, the naming of cities after dead bureaucrats, and even live ones, and so on. All consciously enacted 'cultural revolutions' end in such pietisms. A genuinely liberating cultural transformation could, from a Marxist point of view, only occur as a spontaneous long-term result of the reduction of the working day, the increasingly democratic control of economic and political life, increasingly needs-oriented distribution, and so on. The direction of such a transformation would be in all respects opposed to that of Stalin, Mao, Pol Pot or their Western admirers.

These considerations suggest that the Althusserian theory has overestimated the effectiveness of distinct ideological *practices* and *apparatuses*; it does not follow that he is wrong to stress the distinct effectiveness of *ideology* in the making of history. I hope to clarify this statement in what follows.

The position I have outlined may be summarised in these conclusions:

1. there is an ideological aspect to all human practices in all human societies; it may be added that that aspect always extends beyond the ideas necessarily involved in the practice in question, and includes much more general interpretations of the world, secreted by everyday practices.
2. Specialised ideological practices and agencies exist in *some* societies, but

their effectiveness depends on the spontaneous ideologies arising out of the totality of current practices.

3 The formula: 'The ruling ideas of any epoch are the ideas of the ruling class of that epoch' will not do as a general account of ideology, except in so far as it is interpreted as a tautology, related to the Darwinian tautology 'the fittest survive'. A ruling class cannot rule unless the ruling ideology enables it to do so. It is particularly important to reject the teleological account of ideologies as serving the purposes of the class in which they arise. For instance, ideologies of the oppressed often serve to keep them oppressed, and this is typically the case with all oppressed groups other than the proletariat.

'Determinance in the last instance' as vertical explanation

Althusser's conception of a hierarchy of distinct practices, and the 'functional' production of ideologies by the ISAs, does not seem an adequate way of understanding ideological phenomena. The facts he points to are real enough, but they are not the crucial ones. This is compounded by a certain indeterminacy in Althusser's formulation – perfectly correct so far as it goes – of the manner in which the economic level is basic. Those who are familiar with Popper's criticisms of Marxism will recall the idea that Marx's stress on the economic is a useful rule of thumb if left vague, but a false hypothesis if made specific. However, if a rule of thumb is useful in historical explanation, there must be some feature of real human societies by virtue of which it is useful; it ought therefore to be possible to find a more exact formulation which would be true, even if a particular attempt has come up with a false one. Indeed, the one supplied by Popper as an interpretation of Marx – that superstructural revolutions occur later in time than the corresponding economic revolutions – is one that no Marxist could accept: it would imply that socialism would precede workers' power. Another obvious candidate – the idea that economic factors are, so to speak, quantitatively predominant among the various factors that determine the course of history – has all the disadvantages: it is vague, it would itself require an explanation, and it is false.

Althusser, taking a footnote to *Capital* as his text,[8] puts forward a view that suggests that there are two kinds of causal relationship between the various levels: *dominance* and *determinance in the last instance.* Sometimes one level is dominant, sometimes another. In revolutionary periods, as Marxists have long recognised, politics is always dominant.[9] In 'theocratic' societies, ideology may be dominant. In classical capitalism, economics is dominant. But whatever is dominant, the economic structure is determinant in the last instance. This does not mean that economics will prevail in the long term: 'The last instance never comes.' It does mean (at least) that the nature of the economic structure of any society determines which level will be dominant in that society (as Marx's footnote had implied). This relation between the levels is said to be that of 'relative autonomy'. I have already shown this to be an inadequate concept for theorising the science/ideology relation. As regards the base/superstructure relations, it is not, I think, actually false to say that the superstructure is relatively autonomous, but it is rather vague. Relative to what? Or does it just mean 'somewhat autonomous'. It seems to me that Bhaskar's theory of the stratification of nature, the explicability of the mechanisms of the upper strata in terms of those of the lower, and the irreducibility of the upper to the lower strata, provides a coherent and well-exemplified general theory, of which the base/superstructure stratification can be seen as an instance.

According to Bhaskar, stratification is between generative mechanisms not between entities:

> the predicates 'natural', 'social', 'human', 'physical', 'chemical', 'aerodynamical', 'biological', 'economic', etc. ought not to be regarded as differentiating distinct kinds of *events*, but as differentiating distinct kinds of *mechanisms*. For in the generation of an open-systemic event several of these predicates may be simultaneously applicable.'
>
> (RTS, p. 119)

Applying this to society: it is generative mechanisms which are economic or political or ideological, not institutions or events or any other denizens of the Actual. This is in accordance with the classical Marxist position that these strata are separable only by abstraction, and the recognition that an institution may have aspects at all levels.

On this view, the two questions of the relations of 'dominance' and 'determinance in the last instance' could be located in two kinds of explanatory discourse: 'dominance' in what might be called *horizontal explanation* – the explanation of events in terms of various generative mechanisms operating conjointly, of which those events are the output resulting from a given input; 'determinance in the last instance' as the *vertical explanation* of some of those mechanisms (the upper storey ones) in terms of others (the lower storey ones).

In the discourse of explaining events, there is no need to claim that certain mechanisms – say, economic ones – are more effective than others – say, ideological or political ones. Their primacy is not a matter of their quantitative contribution to the process that in fact results from the conjoint operation of the various mechanisms, any more than, in a demijohn of fermenting liquor, chemical processes can be said to have contributed *more* than biological to the production of the wine. To say that chemistry is a more basic science than biology is to say that the mechanisms of chemistry explain (vertically) the mechanisms of biology; it is not to say that the act of adding 'chemicals' to the demijohn is somehow more effective in producing the wine than is the life-process of the yeast. Indeed, this use of the term 'chemicals' in this sense – as when a wholefood seller tells you there are no chemicals in their wares – is a vulgar mistake. Mechanisms, not substances, are chemical; mechanisms, not apparatuses, are ideological.

Thus at the level of horizontal causality (the production of events as a result of a prior operation upon a pre-existing complex of generative mechanisms), generative mechanisms of any stratum may play their part, and no one can say in advance what the relative weight of those various parts might be.[10] But at the level of vertical causality (the dependence of one stratum of generative mechanisms on another) it is true that the ideological and political mechanisms are what they are because the economic (and more generally, material) ones are what they are – and not at all vice versa.

Here then we have at last a fully worked-out sense for the idea of determination by the base combined with the effectivity of the superstructures. The former is the one-way explanation of upper by lower mechanisms, the latter the contribution of the upper mechanisms to the course of events. For example, one can't say in advance of concrete historical research how important the specific belief-systems of the Russian peasantry or intelligentsia were relative to the economic causes of the Russian Revolution or its subsequent degeneration; but one can explain the ideological mechanisms governing those belief-systems in terms of the economic structure of the country.

Overdetermination and multiple determination

Now if we leave aside for a few moments the issue of vertical explanation, we can describe Marx's theory of history as I have interpreted it as a theory of multiple determination. I now want to ask whether this concept does the same work – perhaps even is the same concept – as Althusser's 'overdetermination'.

One might expect that Althusser's concept, purpose-built for use in Marxist conjunctural analysis, would be more specific, more closely defined in relation to social reality; while Bhaskar's notion of multiple determination, belonging as it does to a general theory about the relations between the objects of all the various sciences, would require further specification before it could be applied to this distinctive subject-matter.

In fact, despite Althusser's commitment to the importance of rigour, clear definition, specificity of concepts, his practice has often been to water down what had been a clearly defined concept, and so to *lose* specificity. The concept of overdetermination, borrowed from Freud, is a case in point. For Freud, overdetermination does not just mean that a phenomenon has more than one cause. It does not merely mean that more than one factor has to come into play to produce the phenomenon, as more than one bale of straw has to be placed on the camel's back before it breaks. And it does not mean at all that there was more causal force than necessary to produce the effect: the 'over ' in overdetermination is not equivalent to that in the atomic warriors' expression 'overkill', i.e. when megadeaths exceed megapeople. Overdetermination in Freud's sense occurs when a phenomenon has two functions, which would otherwise have required two separate expenditures of energy to fulfil. The overdetermined phenomenon occurs rather than others because an economy of energy is thereby effected, rather as sheep farmers have cross-bred sheep to produce breeds which supply both good wool and good lambs for meat.

Althusser's use of the term is not so specific, and sometimes seems to mean no more than 'superimposition'. But if we examine the example that he uses to illustrate the concept, and the political conclusions that he draws from it, it will become clear that the concept he needs is precisely multiple determination in Bhaskar's sense.

It is by now well known that Marx envisaged the possibility that the socialist revolution would first break out in Russia, since it was ripening for a democratic and agrarian revolution at a time when the example of proletarian politics and scientific socialist theory already existed in the West. For Marx himself, it is worth remarking in passing, this was combined with the belief that Russia might conceivably 'bypass' capitalism, since there are no general developmental laws of history, as opposed to laws of specific modes of production.[11] Plekhanov, however, showed that Russia had already embarked on capitalist development. He also argued that the task of making a democratic (not yet a socialist) revolution would fall on the proletariat. This was because, of the classes confronting obsolete Tsardom, the peasants' conditions of life were not conducive to organised revolt, and the bourgeoisie was weak in two ways: it was numerically small relative to the proletariat, partly because Russia, coming to industrialisation late, acquired large-scale industry from the outset; partly because many of the exploiters of the Russian proletariat were not Russian, but Western capitalists. And secondly, the bourgeoisie was weak in political resolve, partly due to consciousness of its numerical weakness, partly because it drew its own conclusions from the class struggles of the west.

Trotsky went further and argued that the coming revolution, being vanguarded by the workers, would necessarily have a socialist character, telescoping the bourgeois-democratic-and-agrarian and the proletarian-socialist revolutions into a single process.

These theories about the 'exceptional' character of the Russian situation were all impeccably 'Marxist' in that they analysed politics in terms of classes (economically defined), their conflicts and their relative power. That is to say, the underlying mechanisms of this process are those of economic development and class struggle in the Marxist sense. The concrete possibility predicted, however – the most advanced revolution occurring in the most backward world power – might look paradoxical from the standpoint of a certain simplistic Marxism, which has occasionally existed and more often been imagined by anti-Marxists. How should we describe the error of such simplistic Marxism? Is it not precisely 'actualism', the idea that conditions of closure obtain naturally, such that causal relations manifest themselves spontaneously in constant conjunctions: Britain was the most industrialised country, so Britain would have the first workers' revolution. Compare Althusser:

> *are we not always in exceptional situations?* The failure of the 1849 Revolution in Germany was an exception, the failure in Paris in 1871 was an exception, the German Social-Democratic failure at the beginning of the twentieth century pending the chauvinist betrayal of 1914 was an exception . . . exceptions, but *with respect to what?* To nothing but the *abstract*, but comfortable and reassuring idea of a pure, simple 'dialectical' schema, which in its very simplicity seems to have retained a memory (or rediscovered the style) of the Hegelian model and its faith in the resolving 'power' of abstract contradiction as such.
>
> (FM, p. 104)

That is to say, the effects of a single contradiction (Capital v. Labour) may be predictable, other things being equal, but other things never are equal. However, as in the case of all interesting *ceteris paribus* clauses, that is not all that can be said.

> *the Capital–Labour contradiction is never simple, but is always specified by the historically concrete forms and circumstances in which it is exercised.* It is specified by the forms of the *superstructure* (the State, the dominant ideology, religion, politically organised movements, and so on); it is specified by *the internal and external historical situation* which determines it on the one hand as a function of the *national past* (completed or 'relapsed' bourgeois revolution, feudal exploitation eliminated wholly, partially or not at all, local 'customs', specific national *traditions,* even the 'etiquette' of political struggles and behaviour, etc.), and on the other as functions of the existing *world context* (what dominates it – competition of capitalist nations, or 'imperialist internationalism', or competition within imperialism, etc.), many of these phenomena deriving from the 'law of uneven development' in the Leninist sense.
>
> What can this mean but that the apparently simple contradiction is *always overdetermined?*
>
> (FM, p. 106)

What is this 'overdetermination' but 'multiple determination'? (Always with the proviso, of course, that it is *stratified* determination, that the various determinants stand in one-way relations of vertical causality.) The mechanisms of the various strata co-determine the course of events: ideological (in the case of Russia: the spread of ideas 'ahead of their time', learnt from Western experience), political (the place of Russia among the world powers, her military defeat) and from outside 'society' (e.g. geographical) as well as economic.

This theory seems to meet all the requirements, sometimes thought to be inconsistent, of a Marxist account of historical process. It is certainly 'deterministic' as against voluntarist or subjectivist theories; it retains the one-way vertical explanation of superstructure by base; and it is certainly not a fatalistic doctrine of 'historical inevitability'.

There is no necessary 'ceiling' to the stratification of nature. So it is always possible that the entities governed by the mechanisms of any given level are also affected by those of a higher level. Living beings have effects on the inorganic world, society on nature, politics on the economy, ideology on politics, science and reason generally on ideology. This is surely all that was ever needed for a theory of human freedom that would vindicate the practical effectiveness of conscious thinking, and hence refute fatalism.

A word is appropriate here about the alleged connection between fatalism and/or determinism and the *'attentisme'* of the Social Democratic parties of the Second International. The error of those parties was twofold: (i) they expected a linear growth of membership and support to lead to victory of its own inner dynamic, without the institutions of the existing order breaking down. While this view is certainly determinist in that the growth was held to be a law-governed process, what is wrong with it is the *actualism,* the reduction of historical causation to a single mechanism.

But is it *fatalist?* If fatalism is simply belief in 'prophecy' in Popper's sense, in actual processes having inevitable outcomes, then it is. But if fatalism implies the inefficacy of human activity, then it is certainly not. On the contrary, the power of the activity of the workers' movement is overestimated. So far from holding (as a fatalist might) that victory would come whatever people did, it predicts victory purely on the basis of what (it predicts) people will do, and do by way of a conscious, rational, organised political practice.

This error was compounded by the belief (ii) that the bourgeois state apparatus could simply be taken over and used by the working class to establish socialism once it had an electoral majority. Revolutionary socialists have avoided the latter error, but not usually the former. They frequently believe that once the workers were won over to their views in large enough numbers it would be possible simply to take power. Yet in reality revolutions have only ever been successful when, in addition to a revolutionary party with mass support, there is a breakdown in the old order – either a military defeat, or the isolation of a corrupt regime which cannot even command the loyalty of the ruling class. It must be recognised that in addition to the organisation and class consciousness of the workers, the transition to socialism requires something which it is not in the power even of the biggest and best organised workers' movement to supply: political breakdown in the old order.

The common confusion between the voluntarist/necessitarian debate on the one hand (a debate which need never have arisen in socialist thought since so long as it is not denied either that human actions have effects or that historical possibilities are constrained by laws, it is of purely speculative interest), and on the other hand, the practical question: what sort of action could bring about a socialist transformation under what conditions? – this confusion (starting, I think, with Gramsci) has kept debate about both issues at a consistently lower level than it reached in the theoretical literature of the Second International. Consider for instance Brecht's cryptic saying:

> The master Sa taught: Liberation comes like the eruption of a volcano. The master Lan-Kü taught: Liberation is achieved through a surprise attack. Mi-en-leh taught: Both elements are necessary – something that erupts and something that attacks.
>
> (Quoted by Timpanaro in *On Materialism*, New Left Books, London, 1975, p. 226. Timpanaro points out that Sa is Luxemburg, Lan-Kü is Blanqui, and Mi-en-leh is Lenin)

Mi-en-leh would be dead right if the eruption were taken as referring to the breakdown of the old order and the attack as referring to the political action of the workers (two events which will of course be causally related, but not so closely that one could be the necessary or sufficient condition of the other). But we are presumably intended to take the eruption to refer to the mass action of the workers, the attack to a *coup* planned by the party leadership. In either case, the views of the master Sa are seriously misinterpreted. She did not think an eruption could bring about socialism – capitalist collapse could equally well end in barbarism. And of course, she never made the careless mistake of thinking that workers erupted.

Applications: the falling rate of profit; the effectiveness of politics

Let me conclude this section with two examples to illustrate the applications of this theory. The first will clarify the place of laws in explaining the open system of history. One of the more mathematically elaborated of Marx's putative laws is the Law of the Tendency of the Rate of Profit to Fall, or more briefly, the falling rate of profit (FRP). This law-claim has been the subject of a lively ongoing debate in recent years, with different Marxist economists giving it different interpretations, and some rejecting it entirely. It would be quite out of place for me to try to pre-empt that debate by means of a purely philosophical argument. I shall merely make some points against one argument used against the FRP, Geoff Hodgdson's:[12]

> a conjunctural explanation of the crisis, based on the dynamics of class struggle and power, rests uneasily with the raw mechanistic and deterministic vision within [sic] Marx's law, of capitalism grinding down a pre-ordained path, by virtue of its inbuilt 'logic', towards an 'inevitable' demise.

He adds in a footnote:

> It must be noted that Ben Fine and Laurence Harris have a quite different conception of this law, where the counter-acting forces are just as significant as the law itself, and the 'law' does not necessarily manifest itself in any empirically observable tendency for the rate of profit to fall. The law is valid, whatever happens in the real world! Needless to say, the Fine–Harris version of the law cannot be invoked to explain the empirical decline of the rate of profit in the British economy any more than it can be used to explain a *rising* profit rate elsewhere.

Here the FRP theory is being presented with a familiar Popperian dilemma: either it is interpreted in a fatalistic sense, or it is deemed to operate even when not empirically manifested. Both interpretations are supposed to be damning, for science abhors both unconditional prophecies and statements compatible with any set of facts whatever. Of course, if these were the *only* alternatives, no sort of science would be possible. Not only the falling rate of profit, but the inverse square law would have to go. But if there is a multiplicity of generative mechanisms at work, science must necessarily *abstract from* some of them in order to formulate laws, while remembering that the concrete situation is always a *conjuncture*, i.e. a joint effect of several interacting processes. (This, of course, is precisely Marx's stated method, with his talk about the power of abstraction replacing chemical reagents, and of the concrete as a union of many determinations.)[13] As a result it is impossible to read off the result of any process outside of experimental conditions, from a conception of that process in isolation; not because it eludes determinism, but because it is multiply determined.

So to say that there is a mechanism in capitalism which necessarily generates a tendency of the rate of profit to fall, is not to say that the rate of profit will fall no matter what else happens, any more than a doctor who says a patient is out of danger is saying that that patient can safely step in front of a bus.

Of course, it is necessary to say what the other mechanisms are which co-determine events, if one wishes to explain why the rate of profit is falling here and rising there; but just such conjoint explanation is what we need and all we can hope for, unless we could reduce all economic laws to a single one, and isolate economic from non-economic processes; the former has not been done, and the latter is demonstrably impossible.

This is, of course, far from solving the real epistemological problems of disentangling the mechanisms of economics; nor does it mean that we can't forecast with some degree of confidence that capitalism will collapse: only such a forecast is not like the prediction that a billiard ball placed on an inclined plane surface at a carefully measured slope will roll down in a given direction at a given acceleration – it is more like the prediction that a drunken driver speeding along a precipitous and winding mountain road in the fog, in a car with no brakes and faulty steering, will come a cropper. And in such a case, we can have little confidence about what, if anything, will replace capitalism.

The second application is also a response to a Popperian criticism, but this time at the level of political theory rather than epistemology. One of Popper's most fantastic allegations about Marx is that he believed politics to be powerless. But we can understand how he could think this of Marx if we look at his own political prescription – 'democratic interventionism'. This theory, as I understand it, consists of two explicit principles, backed up by two implicit assumptions. The explicit principles are (1) that piecemeal social engineering (reform) is the best – most realistic and painless – way forward; (2) that violence is only ever justified to secure or defend parliamentary democracy.

The underlying assumptions are: (a) that in a parliamentary democracy, the only obstacle to the implementation of technically possible reforms, is the opinion of the majority – and conversely, of course, that all one has to do to get such a reform implemented is to persuade the majority; (b) that the sort of reforms required are agreed by all 'men of good will', so that it is possible to speak in the first person plural and assume that 'we' are agreed about what is desirable, and are prepared to take the democratic steps necessary to achieve those ends. Politics becomes a matter of rational argument and voting.

It is easy to see how Marx could, from this standpoint, seem to believe in the impotence of politics. If things are wrong with society and we have parliamentary democracy, thinks Popper, 'we' have the power to put things right. Having rejected a theory of the constraints of economic and political reality in a capitalist society, and failed to replace it by anything, leaving history as a zone free of scientific laws, Popper was perhaps bound to come to this view.

But what happens if 'we' try to carry out Popper's programme? There are many political parties dedicated to doing so, in particular 'social democratic' ones.[14] Whenever these parties come to power, they find that there are economic constraints preventing their reforms from being effective. Easy as it might seem for the more prosperous of the world's nations to provide adequate health, housing and education for all their citizens, or to bring together unemployed workers, unused resources and unsatisfied needs, the best-intentioned social democratic governments never manage to solve these problems. The obstacles are not technical; they are laws of economics and politics in a capitalist society, which trap the would-be reformers inside circles of constraint narrower than those set by the limits of the technically possible. Marxian economic theory explains the mechanisms of this constraint, and socialist politics offers a means to their abolition: it is explained how an optimum use of resources could be made, and why this is not possible under capitalism. Yet the social democrats never tire of telling their socialist critics: 'You are doctrinaire; everything you can do, we can do better by a little state intervention without altering the system', and telling the electors: 'We are sorry we can't fulfil our election pledges – the laws of the economy won't allow it.' Bryan Magee says that Popper provides the best possible grounds for 'democratic socialist' (i.e. social democratic) politics.[15] He is only too right: Popper rejects historical laws as unscientific, and substitutes voluntaristic optimism; there could be no better justification of the social democratic practice of banging one's head against a brick wall and calling people 'doctrinaire' when they try to find a way round it.

Continuing with this metaphor of 'circles of constraint', i.e. sets of laws at one level which prevent the realisation of possibilities 'permitted' by the laws of another level, it can be said that one theme of Marxist thinking is that the Popperian model just described would actually hold in a socialist society, though it does not in a capitalist one.[16] Luxemburg, for instance, sees economics as a science applicable only to capitalist society, whilst a socialist society would abolish economic laws, leaving only technical limits to the possible uses of society's resources. The idea is that it is only the emergence of market forces which gives rise to specifically economic mechanisms, dictating what is produced and the division of the product, independently of any decision-procedure. Where there is a common plan, that plan is a more or less rational decision based on the people's wants and the material and technical resources available; this collective decision replaces economic mechanisms, enlarging the area of human freedom. The idea of the withering away of the specialised state apparatuses envisages a similar dissolution of specifically political mechanisms.

There is nothing incoherent about these prospects, but we should not let these dizzying vistas of freedom blind us to the fact that history would still be a law-governed process – made, indeed, for the first time by the joint decisions of the human race, but still in conditions not of their own choosing. Not only is our power over nature necessarily limited, but we are necessarily born helpless, dependent and ignorant; every bit of consciousness, activity, knowledge and autonomy we have has to be won out of an original unconsciousness, passivity, error and dependence. Even if the economic and political strata of constraint could be removed, our descendants, like our ancestors, will still be governed by material and ideological laws.[17]

Notes

1 'Whenever any Marxist attempted to transmute the theory of Marx into a universal master key and ignore all other spheres of learning Vladimir Ilyich would rebuke him with the expressive phrase 'Komchvanstvo' ["communist swagger"]' (Trotsky, *Problems of Everyday Life*, Monad Press, New York, 1973, p. 221).
2 Bhaskar does say (RTS, p. 169), 'It should be noted that the historical order of the development of our knowledge of strata is opposite to the causal order of their dependence in being.' But his point is not that the more basic layer is never discovered first, but that vertical explanation is not possible unless the explanans is known.
3 Bhaskar's own account of the implications of multiple determination with respect to the freedom/determinism debate can he read on pp. 112–13 of RTS.
4 See for example Lenin: 'If materialism in general explains consciousness as the outcome of existence, and not conversely, then materialism as applied to the social life of mankind must explain *social* consciousness as the outcome of *social* existence' (entry on Karl Marx in *Granat Encyclopedia*, in *Marx and Engels Selected Works in Two Volumes*, Lawrence and Wishart, London, 1942, Vol. I p. 29).
5 For example: 'where have you read in the works of Marx or Engels that they necessarily spoke of economic materialism? When they described their world outlook they called it simply materialism' (Lenin, *Collected Works*, Progress Publishers, vol. I, p. 151).
6 Plekhanov is especially insistent on this, though this has been obscured by the compulsion felt by all Western Marxists to lie about him. In *Fundamental Problems of Marxism* he writes:

> A historico-social factor is an *abstraction,* and the idea of it originates as the result of a process of *abstraction.* Thanks to the process of abstraction, various *sides* of the social *complex* assume the form of separate *categories*, and the various manifestations and expressions of the activity of social man – morals, law, economic forms, etc. – are converted in our minds into separate forces which appear to give rise to and determine this activity and to be its ultimate causes.
>
> (1969, p. 108)
>
> But however legitimate and useful the theory of factors may have been in its time, today it will not stand the light of criticism. It dismembers the activity of social man and converts his various aspects and manifestations into separate forces, which are supposed to determine the historical movement of society.
>
> (p. 110)

7 The layering of these first and second strata of ideology is neatly illustrated by George Thompson's Marxist account of the origins of poetry, with sounds or words indicating the rhythm of work alternating with social comment. For example the English sea-shanty from the late eighteenth century:

> Louis was the King of France afore the Revolution,
> Away, haul away, boys, haul away together!
> Louis had his head cut off, which spoilt his constitution,
> Away, haul away, boys, haul away together!
>
> ('The Art of Poetry', in *The Prehistoric Aegean*, Lawrence and Wishart, London, 1978, pp. 435–62)

8 'The Middle Ages could not live on Catholicism, nor could the ancient world on politics. On the contrary, it is the manner in which they gained their livelihood which explains why in the one case politics, in the other case Catholicism, played the chief part' (*Capital*, Vol. I, Pelican Marx Library, London, 1976, p. 176n).

9 Cf. Lenin, 'Politics cannot but have dominance over economics. To argue otherwise is to forget the ABC of Marxism' (quoted by Alec Nove, *An Economic History of the U.S.S.R.*, Penguin, Harmondsworth, 1969, p. 7).

10 Here we may have to correct Althusser and possibly Marx, i.e. if they were claiming that economics necessarily dominated in capitalist countries, ideology in feudal or politics in ancient societies. 'Dominance' here, unlike determinance, can only be a matter of weight, of one kind of generative mechanism predominating over others, and, though Marx's statement is broadly historically accurate, we cannot be sure *a priori* that, e.g., all capitalist societies will be characterised by the predominance of economic mechanisms. Most modern capitalist societies are not.

11 Letter to the Editorial Board of 'Otechestvenniy Zapiski', November 1877 (*Selected Correspondence*, Progress Publishers, Moscow, 1968, pp. 311–13).

12 From his article 'On the Political Economy of Socialist Transformation', *New Left Review* no. 133, pp. 57–8, May–June, 1982.

13 See *Capital,* Vol. I, p. 90, and *Grundrisse*, Pelican Marx Library, London, 1973, p. 101.

14 I use this term here, not in the pre-1960 sense (one who believes in the parliamentary road to socialism), nor yet in the sense of the British SDP, which has no serious commitment to real social reforms, but to refer to those parties or tendencies within parties which have a working-class electoral base and an interventionist programme for social welfare, but which oppose any substantial changes in ownership.

15 In his book *Popper*, Fontana, London, 1973, p. 84. At the time of his writing that book, Bryan Magee was a Labour MP. He has since joined the SDP.

16 By the 'Popperian model' I mean here simply the idea that the only obstacles to reform are technical or ideological ones.

17 Cf. p. 52 above.

10

REALISM AND SOCIAL SCIENCE

William Outhwaite

What are the implications of the approach outlined in the previous chapter for the practice of social research? We can begin to answer this question by reviewing some of the realist principles which have already been mentioned. In the sphere of ontology, we have:

1 The distinction between transitive and intransitive objects of science: between our concepts, models etc. and the real entities, relations and so forth which make up the natural and the social world.
2 The further stratification of reality into the domains of the real, the actual and the empirical. The last of these is in a contingent relation to the other two; to be (either for an entity or structure or for an event) is *not* to be perceived.
3 The conception of causal relations as tendencies, grounded in the interactions of generative mechanisms; these interactions may or may not produce events which in turn may or may not be observed.
4 In addition to these three ontological claims, and related to the first one, we have the rejection of both empiricism and conventionalism above. The practical expression of this epistemological position is the concept of real definition. Real definitions, which are important for both realist and rationalist philosophies of science, are neither summaries of existing verbal usage nor stipulations that we should use a term in a particular way. Although they are of course expressed in words, they are statements about the basic nature of some entity or structure. Thus a real definition of water would be that its molecules are composed of two atoms of hydrogen and one of oxygen. This human discovery about water comes to be expressed as a definitional property of it.
5 Finally, and related to (3) above, the realist conception of explanation involves the postulation of explanatory mechanisms and the attempt to demonstrate their existence.

Source: *New Philosophies of Social Science*, chap. 3, pp. 44–60 (referred to in the text as NPSS).

In considering the implications of these principles for the social sciences, it is essential to bear in mind the distinction between a philosophical and a scientific ontology. A philosophical ontology of the kind outlined here does not tell us what the structures, entities and mechanisms which make up the world actually are; this is a matter for the individual sciences. In the case of the social sciences, for example, a realist metatheory will not, of itself, enable us to choose between a conception which confines itself to the study of individual actions and one which casts its explanations in terms of larger social structures.

What we first need to ask, then, is what account of social reality would *rule out* a realist programme of the kind outlined above. Broadly speaking, realism will be inapplicable if there are:

(a) no intransitive objects of social science, no objects susceptible of real definition and
(b) nothing capable of being explained in terms of generative mechanisms.

Let us take (a) first. Intransitivity, it will be recalled, means essentially that 'things exist and act independently of our descriptions',[1] where 'our' refers to human beings in general. It seems fairly clear that this principle needs to be modified in the case of human actions and social structures, where the agents' conceptions are not external to the facts described but make up part at least of the reality of those facts. A quarrel, for example, cannot adequately be described except with reference to the participants' perceptions of their situation as one of hostility. If they do not perceive the situation in this way, they are merely simulating a quarrel. Quarrelling, in other words, is 'concept-dependent' for the participants in a way in which the collision of two asteroids or two sub-atomic particles is not.

This concept-dependence of social phenomena does not however rule out their intransitivity. The First World War, or the Sino-Soviet rift of the late 1950s were as they were independently of anything I write about them today. What the anti-realist requires is a more radical argument which denies that there is any fact of the matter about such matters. The most plausible way to make such an argument is to say something like this:

1 Social situations do not exist independently of the way they are interpreted by those involved in them or by outside observers.
2 Such interpretations are essentially arbitrary.

This argument is not of course essentially different from a radical conventionalism about the natural world. What needs to be explained is its apparently greater plausibility as an account of the social. Let us take three assertions about 'society':

1 Society is not observable.
2 Society is theoretical.
3 Any assertion about society is as good as any other.

The first must clearly be accepted. We can of course study a national community or a group by observing what goes on, asking questions, etc., but there is no such thing as observing a society *as such.* The limits of French society are not the state frontiers of France, not only because France has territories and influence elsewhere in the world but because 'French society' is a theoretical concept, where 'theoretical' means something more than just unobservable. The best way of illustrating this is by looking at the history of the term 'society' and the different ways in which it has been used since, roughly, the eighteenth century.

In other words, to talk about a collection of people, in one or more geographical sites, with various forms of material equipment etc. as a '*society*' is to enter a particular language-game which licences some theoretical moves and not others, and in particular introduces an element of abstraction.

Now a residual element of truth in empiricism is that the use of abstract or theoretical terms has to be legitimated in a way in which a 'lower-level' vocabulary does not. The modern concept of society, for instance, had to be squeezed into some of the conceptual space occupied by the earlier and somewhat more concrete term 'state'.[2] The early resistance to its introduction was fairly obviously political: the term 'society' was seen as in some way linked with the third estate and potentially threatening to the state. In our time this political hostility to the concept of society generally takes the form of individualism: 'the individual and society'. But this ethical or political individualism is only one aspect of an approach whose sharpest theoretical tool is the reductionist thesis of 'methodological individualism'. Talk of society, or of social wholes in general, it is claimed, is only a shorthand or summary redescription of something which must ultimately be described and explained in terms of individual action. As J. S. Mill put it, 'the laws of the phenomena of society are, and can be, nothing but the actions and passions of human beings united together in the social state'.[3]

But can we in fact do without a concept of society? As we have seen, the most favoured alternative is an ontology of individual persons and their actions, where social structures are merely summary, metaphorical redescriptions of these. The advantage is that the identity criteria of people are given unproblematically by their bodies, which are almost always clearly distinct from other bodies. It turns out, however, that this does not get us very far, because the more interesting human actions are those which presuppose a network of social relations. And if these social relations are a precondition of individual actions, it seems odd to think of them as any less real than those actions.

What is true, of course, is that we are not sure how to characterise these relations and that our characterisations will be tentative, relative to particular explanatory purposes, and so forth. But this does not mean that some set of real social relations is not a necessary condition for all but the most banal human actions. I can pick my nose all by myself, but I cannot cash cheques, write books, or declare war.

What needs to be explained is why most people in our society will take on trust any confidently presented assertion about, say, the structure of DNA, but will look sceptically at an assertion about the social structure of modern Britain – and why they are right to do so. To say that biochemistry is a 'mature' science, and that sociology is not, is not very helpful. References to accuracy of measurement are also somewhat beside the point. The problem is not that we cannot make precise measurements in the social sciences but that we are not sure what purpose they serve, since the interesting explanatory structures, and even their *explananda,* seem irremediably opaque.

Considerations like these may seem to point towards a conventionalist account of the social sciences, in which all their significant terms are surrounded by scare quotes and all their assertions preceded by an implicit 'everything takes place as if'.[4] Yet this is to concede too much to the sceptics. There are some effects, such as the tendency for the social position of parents to influence the educational achievements of their children, which are as real and general as one could reasonably expect, though of course we still need to investigate the mechanisms which produce these effects. The fact that processes of interpretation underlie all these terms as well as our postulated explanations of the links between them does not rule out a realist construal of these theories. Instead, as I shall argue later in this chapter, it suggests that we should recognise that the social sciences are more closely related to common-sense thinking than are the natural sciences; they do not so much provide radically new knowledge as more adequate formulations of our intuitions about social affairs.

We have seen, then, that the question of intransitive objects of social science turns out to be essentially a question about the scope and implications of interpretation in this domain. I have sketched out an argument to the effect that even if the building-bricks of social science are 'interpreted' building-bricks in a more radical and far-reaching sense than are the component parts of natural scientific theories, and even if the structures postulated within the social sciences tend to be presented, for good reasons, in a tentative way, this does not prevent us asking questions of a realist kind about these structures. In a moment I shall look more closely at the idea that the elementary structures of society are not just interpreted, but are *nothing but interpretations.* But even if this radical interpretivist position could be sustained, it still would not follow without further argument that there were no criteria for judging interpretations.

Before directly addressing these issues, let me deal rapidly with (b) above, the question whether there is anything in the social world which can be explained in realist terms by generative mechanisms. This of course depends on (a) above, since if we cannot even specify the explananda in the social sciences there is not much point in looking for explanatory mechanisms. And depending what we admit as explananda, the types of mechanism will presumably vary too: it would be odd if system equilibrium could be explained in just the same way as individual choice.

As with (a) above, the most radical version of (b) takes the form of the recommendation that the social sciences should confine themselves to the study of individual action. It can then be argued, in either hermeneutic or rationalist terms, that the explanation of human actions in terms of the actors' reasons for acting is something distinct from causal explanation. Part of the appeal of this claim has derived from the obvious inapplicability of the empiricist analysis of causality in terms of the constant conjunction of logically independent events. My reasons for making a cup of coffee (to revive myself, to relieve my thirst, to have a break from writing, etc.) are not logically independent of my doing so. Even if my fatigue does not cause me to drink a cup of coffee, in the directly physical sense in which it might cause me to fall asleep over my manuscript, it can surely contribute to the reasons for my coffee-drinking, as part of a complex concatenation of physical and mental states. And there seems no reason why the realist concept of mechanism should not stretch over all these conditions. Even if one wants, as Rom Harré does, to deny that reasons are causes, one can still argue (as Harré and Secord do) that reason-explanations are the analogues of mechanism-explanations in the natural sciences. In other words, whatever view one adopts on the reasons/causes issue, a realist interpretation can be given of the resultant explanatory models.[5]

In my view, 'the real reason' for an action is best understood as the reason which was causally efficacious in producing that action, but the realist analysis will work, I think, equally well for a rationalist who defines 'real' in this context as something like 'rationally compelling' and, like Martin Hollis, holds that 'rational action is its own explanation'.[6]

It seems, then, that questions about the applicability of realism in the social sciences will turn essentially around the first of the questions raised in this chapter: the existence of intransitive objects of social science. I shall therefore outline (1) Roy Bhaskar's arguments for naturalism, and intransitivity; (2) Ted Benton's criticism that his position is not naturalistic enough and (3) Rom Harré's alternative, anti-naturalist conception of social being.

First, we need to get clear what is at stake in debates over naturalism. As we saw in Chapter 1 [of NPSS], the logical positivist thesis of unified science made strong claims for the unity of the laws of science or of the language of science, based on a physicalist reductionism. The contemporary debates focus instead around the weaker claim of a methodological unity of science, in the sense that the methods of the natural sciences can, in general, be applied to the social sciences or; as Bhaskar puts it, 'that it is possible to give an account of science under which the proper and more-or-less specific methods of both the natural sciences and social sciences can fall'. Naturalism in this sense 'does not deny that there are significant differences in these methods grounded in real differences in their subject matters and in the relationships in which their sciences stand to them'.[7] What it claims is that a realist interpretation can meaningfully be given to social scientific knowledge.

Bhaskar starts from the question: 'What properties do societies possess that might make them possible objects of knowledge for us?'[8] He argues, in the way summarised at the beginning of this chapter, 'that societies are irreducible to people', 'that social forms are a necessary condition for any intentional act,[9] that their *pre-existence* establishes their *autonomy* as possible objects of scientific investigation and that their *causal power* establishes their reality'. This in turn entails a 'transformational model of social activity': 'Society is both the ever-present *condition* (material cause) and the continually reproduced *outcome* of human agency.'

> The conception I am proposing is that people, in their conscious activity, for the most part unconsciously reproduce (and occasionally transform) the structures governing their substantive activities of production. Thus people do not marry to reproduce the nuclear family or to work to sustain the capitalist economy. Yet it is nevertheless the unintended consequence (an inexorable result) of, as it is also a necessary condition for, their activity.[10]

This in turn entails a relational conception of the subject matter of the social sciences, in which the practices of agents take place within a set of structurally (and hence relationally) defined positions.[11] Where these relations are part of the definition of the relata, as in buyer/seller, they will be termed internal relations; where they are contingent (e.g. shopper/traffic warden), they are external relations.

This abstract model of social reality, which of course displays strong similarities with other contemporary specifications of the relation between action and structure,[12] is clearly compatible with wide variations in the degree to which particular actions are structured. It does not take the expertise of a labour lawyer to notice that the contractual obligations of an academic are very different from those of the majority of workers. A more interesting, and less determinate area of controversy arises between those who stress the essentially voluntary character of all human actions and those who emphasise structural constraints (which may of course be enabling as well as constraining in a narrow sense). There are powerful currents in textual interpretation, for example, which would analyse this book as the more or less automatic product of a set of theoretical and ideological structures, plus a residual category of authorial desire and a few other material conditions.

It is perhaps not appropriate for me, as author, to address this hyperstructuralist conception; all that is required here is to point out that it still logically requires some notion of agency to make the structures work. Sceptical doubts about the possibility of social science take the opposite tack of questioning the reality and efficacy of social structures. Rom Harré, in his brilliant book *Social Being*, seems to flirt with this view, by confining his attention to structures-of-action as the object of social psychology, conceived in non-naturalistic terms:

> The fact that both natural and social sciences use models in the same way may suggest misleadingly that they share a common epistemology. The differences emerge when we compare the relation of fact to theory in each kind of science. In the social sciences facts, *at the level at which we experience them*, are wholly the creation of theorizing, of interpreting. Realists in social science hold, and I would share their belief, that there are global patterns in the behaviour of men in groups, though as I have argued we have no adequate inductive method of finding them out.[13]

Harré's strategy, in a nutshell, is to bracket out a noumenal realm of latent structures and to confine his research programme in social psychology to structures as they are perceived by actors. Role, he plausibly suggests, 'is experienced, not as a relational property in which the individual stands to the collectives of which he or she is a member, but rather as a systematic set of psychological and microsocial imperatives and constraints'.[14] This, I think, is true and important, but to stress the latter conception of role is not to imply that the former is in some way inaccessible, even (!) to actors. A whole series of techniques, from organisational design to transactional analysis is aimed precisely at explicating the former conception. Indeed if socialisation is to mean something more than behaviour modification it can only be the inculcation of structural conceptions of this kind. To teach a child that it should not make excessive noise is to give it a conception of an environment made up of other people who are the bearers of rights to a reasonable degree of peace and quiet. I am not sure that Harré would want to question any of this, but his discussion constantly points towards a distinction between an empirically oriented ethogenic social psychology and an inevitably speculative sociology. And the rationale for any such distinction remains unclear.

What does emerge, I think, from this discussion, is that we must look more closely at the relations between social structures and the activities they govern. Roy Bhaskar suggests three 'ontological limitations on a possible naturalism':

1 Social structures, unlike natural structures, do not exist independently of the activities they govern;

2 Social structures, unlike natural structures, do not exist independently of the agents' conceptions of what they are doing in their activity;
3 Social structures, unlike natural structures, may be only relatively enduring (so that the tendencies they ground may not be universal in the sense of space–time invariant).[15]

These qualifications are, I think, on the right lines, but they must themselves be qualified in ways suggested by some criticisms made by Ted Benton.[16] The third principle is of limited relevance and can be dealt with fairly swiftly. As Benton points out, it does not mark out a sharp dividing line between natural and social structures, since many natural structures are also only relatively enduring. All that is required for social science to be possible is that social structures be sufficiently enduring for their examination to be feasible and worthwhile. And even the most radical proponents of the view that only synchronic investigation is possible in the social sciences always allow themselves time at least to carry out their investigations. If there is a problem about social structures, it is surely not their mutability *per se* but their general messiness and fluidity.

Bhaskar's first principle of differentiation seems to require little more than a bit of tinkering to render it acceptable. First, it must be counterfactualised, such that the reference includes *possible* actions governed by the structure (e.g. a power structure). These may be negative possible actions, as in deterrence. Secondly, it must be noted that the activities which sustain a structure are not always identical with those which it governs in its functioning. A structure of gift exchange does not exist independently of the giving of gifts, but it also presupposes the possession or acquisition of potential gifts (whether or not these are possessed or acquired under that description).

Bhaskar's second principle also requires some clarification, but even when clarified it points further to the central issue which is at stake between naturalism and anti-naturalism. First, we should note that agency itself requires that the agents have *some* conception of what they are doing; sleepwalking is only a marginal case of action. Conversely, this conception need not be correct for the action to be successful, and in some cases a correct conception of the activity will render it impossible; I can mislead you deliberately or unintentionally, but not if you perceive me to be misleading you. More broadly, agents need not be conscious of their implication in structures such as that of the capitalist economy, which nevertheless govern their actions; other structures get their efficacy from their imaginary power as slogans. Ideologies will tend to contain a mixture of conscious and unconscious beliefs, and this may be an important part of their power.

It will be helpful here to refer to Bhaskar's distinction between causal interdependence (between social structures and human representations of them) on the one hand, and existential intransitivity 'which is an a priori condition of investigation and applies in the same way in the social, as the natural sphere'. Both principles are required for realist social science, as against positivism which neglects interdependence and hermeneutic theories which 'dissolve intransitivity'.[17] Hermeneutics is right however to draw attention to the central importance of meanings for the social sciences, and to the fact that they have to be understood, not simply registered or measured. To this must be added the practical difficulties of measurement and empirical testing in the social sciences: the virtual unavailability of experimentation and closure, the irreversibility of most social processes, etc.[18] Here we can see that certain consequences, such as the impossibility of prediction, do not vitiate a realist conception of social science as they would one which was positivistically conceived.

Behind all this, however, is the fundamental issue, briefly raised at the beginning of this chapter, of the relation between the social sciences and common-sense social knowledge. This issue is conceived in very different ways in different theories about the social and natural sciences,[19] but what seems to emerge fairly clearly is that the social sciences remain closer to common-sense thinking, which is anyway more pervasive and powerful in the social world. By this I mean that we have intuitions about the structure of almost all the social processes we may care to think about; these may be right or wrong, but they at least give us an *entrée* into the subject matter. In physical reality, by contrast, we have intuitions only about a restricted range of phenomena – billiard balls but not particles, chairs but not molecular structures, people and animals but not bacteria and viruses, and so on. In crude terms, the social sciences begin with a head-start over the natural sciences, but instead of running straight ahead in pursuit of new knowledge they move around in small circles and spend a lot of time re-inspecting the starting-block.[20]

One diagnosis of this situation is to say that social scientists are too ambitious in their speculations, that they try to run before they can walk. This is probably true of all science; the difference, I think, for the social sciences is that they *cannot* really walk; a better metaphor is a bicycle, which is easy to ride at 10 m.p.h. and impossible at 2. It is of course possible to replicate standardised tests *ad nauseam*, but replication makes little difference to the acceptance or rejection of the results previously obtained; these tend to be accepted or rejected on more global theoretical principles.

One has to recognise the utopianism in the nineteenth-century aspiration that the social sciences would produce 'the same kind of sensational illumination and explanatory power already yielded up by the sciences of nature'.[21] Social science is not without surprises, but the important ones are arguably not the findings which go against our expectations, but the qualitative discovery of new ways of conceiving social reality – ways which are however still in some sense continuous with common-sense perceptions.

Social science, it seems, is necessarily tentative, theoretically pluralistic, and incomplete.

The other side of this coin, however, is that common-sense descriptions of social phenomena can and must be taken as a starting-point in social scientific theorising. *Can*, because they provide the beginnings of definitions of the phenomena and thus help in the otherwise bewildering activity of object-constitution or, in Goldmann's term, *découpage*,[22] 'given the mish-mash nature of social reality'.[23] *Must*, because however imperfect they may be, to the extent that they are the perceptions of agents involved in that situation they will influence the very nature of that situation. This is the (partial) truth of W. I. Thomas's famous claim that 'If men define situations as real they are real in their consequences.'[24] The extent to which this is true, as I suggested earlier, will depend on the specific features of a given social situation.

It can now be seen that the concept-dependence and activity-dependence of social structures appears not so much as an obstacle but as a resource in social theorising. We can ask, in other words, what a given society must be like in order for people to behave within it, and to conceive it, in the ways they do. (Here, as Bhaskar notes,[25] there is a partial analogy with philosophical investigations into the transcendental presuppositions of an empirically identified activity, such as that of scientific practice.) As I shall suggest in more detail in Chapter 6 [of NPSS], a good example of this process of theorising is Marx's *Capital*, conceived simultaneously as an investigation into the mechanisms of the capitalist mode of production and a critique of its representations in common-sense conceptions and in the theories of classical political economy.[26] This mode of enquiry is not however peculiar to Marx, whose philosophical orientation is close to transcendental realism;[27] it can also be found, in a neo-Kantian framework, in much of classical sociology, e.g. in the work of Durkheim and Max Weber.[28]

It is now time to summarise this outline of a realist strategy in the social sciences, which will serve as a basis for the more detailed discussions in subsequent chapters. The notion of real definition serves as a leitmotif to the practice of social research on a realist basis. The social scientist directs his or her attention to an object of inquiry which is already defined in certain ways in the world of everyday life and ordinary language. (This is of course true of natural objects as well, but with the important difference that natural objects do not have concepts of what they are doing when they fall, collide, melt, die and so forth.) The social scientist will typically seek to redescribe this object so as to bring out its complexity, the way in which it is determined by its internal and external environment as an outcome of a multiplicity of interacting tendencies.

The conception of the object of inquiry will crucially determine the sorts of method which are appropriate to its investigation. The ethnomethodological approach of conversational analysis will not help us to understand the rate of profit in a capitalist economy, nor will the law of value explain how one can terminate a telephone conversation without embarrassment. Historical analysis may or may not be relevant to the study of a particular contemporary situation. In other words, the question of what is needed to explain an observable social phenomenon will receive a contextually specific answer.

In this redefinition of objects of social inquiry and prior to any choice of methods of investigation, are questions of social ontology. What sort of object are we trying to describe and explain? To what extent is it a product of the interpretations of human beings, and to what extent is it structured by 'deeper causes which are opaque to human consciousness'.[29] Now arguments can be made, by realists as by anyone else, about these perennial disputes within social ontology, but they are not, I think, specifically realist arguments. In other words, they concern the nature of human societies rather than the nature of social scientific theories.

Rom Harré, who has argued for an interactionist, interpretivist social psychology, and Roy Bhaskar, who has upheld a more structuralist and materialist approach in the social sciences, can both legitimately construe their proposals in realist terms. Both can claim to be propounding ways of getting at the fundamental structures and generative mechanisms of social life: where they differ is in their accounts of the constitution of social reality and of how this reality can be known.[30] Realism does not uniquely license either of these approaches. What it *does* provide, however, is a framework in which these alternative social ontologies can be rationally compared and discussed – in which they are not brushed aside, as in the positivist and conventionalist traditions, as 'mere' definitional assumptions.

Realist philosophies of science, as we have seen, abandon a number of positivist assumptions about scientific theorising. The most important of these are probably the theory-observation distinction and the covering-law model of explanation, which are replaced, respectively, by the idea of a complex network of relatively 'theoretical' and relatively 'observational' statements and by the idea of explanation as the attempt to represent the generative mechanisms which bring about the *explanandum.* A corollary of the latter principle is that explanation is not identified with prediction, the latter being possible, strictly speaking, only where the system is closed by natural or experimental means. For practical purposes in the social sciences we can forget about closures, so that any predictions we make will be necessarily tentative and will not provide decisive tests of our theories.

If, then, the criteria of theory-choice in the social sciences are purely explanatory, how are we to judge explanations? It will be remembered that the realist model of explanation involves three basic steps, the postulation of a possible mechanism, the attempt to collect evidence for or against its existence, and the elimination of possible alternatives. We shall therefore feel we have a good explanation if

1 the postulated mechanism is capable of explaining the phenomena;
2 we have good reason to believe in its existence;
3 we cannot think of any equally good alternatives.

So far so good, but this abstract model does not help in the characteristic situation in the social sciences in which we are expected to choose between several alternative theories and their associated mechanisms and where the object of inquiry is complex and over-determined. Any guidelines will be necessarily vague, but I think that the following principles are not entirely trivial. First, we should not be afraid of theoretical abstraction, since 'observational' statements have no special privilege in this framework. Entities are not to be multiplied unnecessarily, but nor are they to be excluded for being unobservable. Second, the realist emphasis on the stratification of reality should make us aware of the need to fit particular explanations within a wider context. This does not mean that the social totality needs to be invoked to explain the most microscopic social event, but it does mean, for example, that micro-economic theories should connect up with propositions about economic systems and their reproduction, and are inadequate to the extent that they do not.[31] In other words, and this may be counted as a third principle, *a priori* considerations of this kind have a part to play in the evaluation of social theories. I have already discussed some apparently *a priori* constraints on social theories of the relation between agency and social structure, although it emerged that the precise form of their interrelations was a matter for empirical determination in each case.

I do not think one can go far beyond these very general principles. Where two or more theories score equally well according to all these criteria, there seem to be no general grounds for rational preference. Simplicity is an obvious candidate, but a preference for simplicity in all cases cannot be justified once one abandons conventionalist positions for which it is pretty well the only available criterion. There is however something of importance behind discussions of simplicity: namely, the idea that choices thus governed maximise the speed of scientific advance by making theories more easily testable. I do not here want to go into the question whether the choice in all cases of the simpler theory *does* in fact have these beneficial consequences, but merely to uphold the underlying principle that theories should be adopted which on the whole maximise the chances of further intertheoretical debate within the sciences concerned. In other words, we should adopt, other things being equal, theories which are open in this way, rather than, say, reductionist theories, which close off discussion within one level even if they promise to reopen it at another.

The slogan, then, is 'keep them talking'. Once again, it might be thought that this *desideratum* would be best satisfied by conventionalist metatheories. This however seems not to be the case if we recall that the 'talking' necessarily includes the rational critique of existing theories, and it is precisely conventionalism which tends to block off theoretical criticism with its doctrine of the arbitrariness of 'definitional questions'. Once again, it needs to be stressed that the most powerful reason for adopting a realist metatheory is to acquire a framework for the rational discussion of ontological questions.

This principle of dialogue-preservation may be relevant to theory-choice in a further way. It has been suggested, by Mary Hesse and others, that in those cases, particularly frequent in the social sciences, in which there are no clear scientific grounds for the choice between two or more theories, it may be legitimate to choose on grounds of general social values.[32] And among such values, the maximisation of serious discussion might well be argued to have a special place, for the Habermasian reason that it may be a condition for consensus on central issues of truth and justice.

The realist emphasis on the legitimacy and importance of theoretical argument should not be understood to imply the depreciation of empirical research. What it does suggest, I think, is that such research cannot achieve useful results in the absence of theoretical reflection on the structuration of empirical data and a rejection of empiricism, understood as an exclusive focus on social phenomena which are empirically observable and measurable. As Bhaskar puts it,

> the *conceptual* aspect of the subject matter of the social sciences circumscribes the possibility of measurement. . . . For meanings cannot be measured, only understood. Hypotheses about them must be expressed in language, and confirmed in dialogue. Language here stands to the conceptual aspect of social science as geometry stands to physics. And precision in meaning now assumes the place of accuracy in measurement as the a posteriori arbiter of theory. It should be stressed that in both cases theories may continue to be justified and validly used to explain, even though *significant* measurement of the phenomena of which they treat has become impossible.[33]

The upshot, I think, is that a realist strategy for the social sciences needs to engage in a detailed way with the conceptions of interpretation which have been worked out within the frameworks of hermeneutics and critical theory. The following chapters are devoted to this task.

Notes

1 Bhaskar, *A Realist Theory of Science*, p. 250.
2 See Outhwaite, *Concept Formation in Social Science* (London: Routledge and Kegan Paul, 1983), chapter 5.
3 *A System of Logic*, 7th edn (London: Longmans, 1868), book 6, chapter 7, p. 466. Cf. Steven Lukes, 'Methodological Individualism Reconsidered', *British Journal of Sociology*, vol. 19, 1968. Reprinted in Lukes, *Essays in Social Theory* (London: Macmillan, 1977).

4 Pierre Bourdieu, *Outline of a Theory of Practice* (Cambridge: Cambridge University Press, 1977), p. 203, no. 49. Although Bourdieu repeatedly insists upon this principle, his metatheory seems in practice closer to the position argued for in this book.
5 Cf. M. von Cranach and R. Harré (eds) *The Analysis of Action* (Cambridge: Cambridge University Press, 1982), p. 31.
6 Hollis, *Models of Man* (Cambridge: Cambridge University Press, 1977), p. 21 and *passim.*
7 Bhaskar, *The Possibility of Naturalism*, p. 3.
8 Ibid., p. 31.
9 Trevor Pateman has pointed out that this is a gross over-statement; the wild boy of Aveyron presumably performed intentional acts before he encountered human society. It seems to me however that the statement holds, when qualified along the lines of p. 48 above.
10 Ibid., pp. 43 *f.*
11 Ibid., p. 51.
12 Cf. in particular the work of Anthony Giddens.
13 Harré, *Social Being* (Oxford: Basil Blackwell, 1979), p. 237. (Cf. p. 349: 'After all, in this work I am trying to locate the social psychological processes and not to solve the great traditional problems of sociology!')
14 Ibid., p. 94.
15 Bhaskar, *The Possibility of Naturalism*, pp. 48 f.
16 Ted Benton, 'Realism and Social Science', *Radical Philosophy*, no. 27, 1981.
17 Bhaskar, *The Possibility of Naturalism*, p. 60.
18 Ibid., p. 59.
19 See Outhwaite, *Concept Formation in Social Science*, pp. 51–67.
20 Of course the natural sciences are subject to periodic revolutions, but there usually emerges fairly rapidly a consensus on a limited number of post-revolutionary research programmes, and in general a cumulative development of knowledge, at least empirical knowledge. (Cf. Hesse, *Revolutions and Reconstructions in the Philosophy of Science* (Brighton: Harvester, 1980), pp. 176 f.).
21 A. Giddens, *New Rules of Sociological Method* (London: Hutchinson, 1976), p. 13.
22 L. Goldmann, *Marxisme et sciences humaines* (Paris: Gallimard, 1970), p. 250.
23 Bhaskar, *The Possibility of Naturalism*, p. 63.
24 W. I. and D. S. Thomas, *The Child in America* (New York: Knopf, 1982), p. 572.
25 Bhaskar, *The Possibility of Naturalism*, pp. 63 ff.
26 Cf. Karl Marx, *Capital*, vol. 1 (Harmondsworth: Penguin, 1976), pp. 173 f.
27 See, for example, Derek Sayer, *Marx's Method. Ideology, Science and Critique in Capital* (Brighton: Harvester Press, 1979), and Bhaskar's entry on 'Realism' in Tom Bottomore (ed.), *A Dictionary of Marxist Thought* (Oxford: Blackwell, 1983), pp. 407–9.
28 I discuss this further in Chapter 6 [of NPSS]. See also Gillian Rose, *Hegel Contra Sociology* (London: Athlone, 1981), p. 1. Rose argues that 'The very idea of a scientific sociology, whether Marxist or non-Marxist, is only possible as a form of neo-Kantianism.'
29 Emile Durkheim, Review of A. Labriola, *Essays on the Materialist Conception of History*, in Ken Thompson (ed.), *Readings from Emile Durkheim* (Chichester: Ellis Horwood, 1985), p. 28.
30 Compare, for example, chapter 2 of *The Possibility of Naturalism* with *Social Being*, pp. 19 ff., 139 ff., 237, 348 ff. and 356.
31 Cf. Hollis and Nell, *Rational Economic Man* (Cambridge: Cambridge University Press, 1975), chapter 8.

32 'Theory and Value in the Social Sciences', in C. Hookway and P. Pettit (eds), *Action and Interpretation* (Cambridge: Cambridge University Press, 1978). Reprinted in Mary Hesse, *Revolutions and Reconstructions in the Philosophy of Science* (Brighton: Harvester, 1980).
33 Bhaskar, *The Possibility of Naturalism*, p. 59.

11

REALISM AND SOCIAL SCIENCE

Some comments on Roy Bhaskar's 'The Possibility of Naturalism'

Ted Benton

1 Introduction

An increasing body of philosophical work[1] is now available which (a) presents a 'realist' alternative to the hitherto pre-dominant 'positivist' and 'conventionalist' currents in the philosophy of science and (b) attempts to use this realist account of science in the analysis of social scientific practice. In general the objective of this analysis has been to transcend the polar opposition, which has always characterised debate in the philosophy of the social sciences, between positivism and 'humanist', 'hermeneutic', or 'neo-Kantian' dualisms. Commonly the outcome of this work has been to sustain the explanatory procedures of historical materialism, in one reading or another, as compatible with realist philosophy. Further, elements of realist epistemology have also been attributed to Marx, Engels and other Marxists in their philosophical writings. What is remarkable, though, has been the great diversity of readings of Marxism – ranging from Critical Theory to Althusserian structuralism – which seem to be indifferently assimilable to the realist defence.

Since, though, the new 'transcendental' realism is concerned solely with the general conditions of possibility of a number of characteristic forms of scientific activity (experiment, scientific education, etc.), it is neither surprising nor worrying to discover that it is equally compatible with several different, even mutually incompatible substantive attempts at explanation within a particular science. What might be more worrying, though, is that it appears to be compatible with more than one of a number of conflicting philosophical reflections on those scientific traditions. In part, I shall argue,

Source: Radical Philosophy, 27, 1981, pp. 13–21.

this difficulty derives from the reliance of the most influential realist account of the natural sciences on consideration of a narrow and inappropriate range of these sciences. The application of the resulting model of natural scientific activity to the social sciences has been problematic in such a way as to reproduce some of the familiar characteristics of the positivist/dualist opposition.

The influential work in question is that by Roy Bhaskar. His first book, *A Realist Theory of Science* (*RTS* from now on), made an immense contribution in establishing and systematising transcendental realism as a coherent and well-articulated alternative to the established traditions in the philosophy of science. These rival accounts of science, characterised as 'empirical realism' and 'transcendental idealism', were subjected to formidable critiques, but almost wholly in relation to their accounts of the natural sciences. In *RTS* the question of the possibility of naturalistic social and psychological sciences is posed, but not systematically dealt with. Roy Bhaskar's second book, *The Possibility of Naturalism* (hereafter *PN*), takes up this challenge, arguing for:

> 'a qualified anti-positivist naturalism, based on an essentially realist view of science. Such a naturalism holds that it is possible to give an account of science under which the proper and more-or-less specific methods of both the natural and social sciences can fall. But it does not deny that there are significant differences in these methods grounded in real differences in their subject matters and in the relationships in which their sciences stand to them.'[2]

Stated in these general terms, I am in broad sympathy with Roy Bhaskar's project, but on the nature of the differences which he identifies, and their significance, I shall take issue. In particular, I propose to argue that the extent and significance of the natural science/social science asymmetries which Roy Bhaskar claims to identify would justify description of his position as a form of anti-naturalism, rather than as a 'qualified naturalism'. It would follow from this that his intended transcendence of the positivism/hermeneutics polarity is not entirely successful. The failure in this respect derives from the reproduction in Roy Bhaskar's work of the very dualist ontology of a natural/human opposition which is the basis of hermeneutic and neo-Kantian forms of anti-positivism. This ontology is, in turn, sustained by an unnecessarily restricted conception of the natural sciences. This excludes, or under-represents, the philosophical and methodological characteristics of a range of historical and life-sciences whose bearing on the social sciences, both philosophically and substantively, is direct and most pertinent to Roy Bhaskar's philosophical project.

2 The argument of *RTS*

It will be remembered that *RTS* poses in relation to a number of characteristic natural scientific practices the transcendental question, 'what are the conditions of possibility (presuppositions) of these activities (or their rationality, or intelligibility)?' The practices investigated in this way include experimentation, the application of scientific knowledge in 'open' systems, scientific perception, scientific education, and change and development in science. There are, unfortunately, some ambiguities in Roy Bhaskar's posing of these questions, however, which have implications for the status of the answers he gives. Some of these ambiguities, and possible sources of misunderstanding, are cleared up in Chapter 1 of *PN*, but some are persistent. Most significant are ambiguities surrounding the premises of the transcendental deductions.[3] Are we to take as a premise the *existence* of a scientific practice, such as experiment, or, rather, its intelligibility, or, yet again, its rationality (in the sense of 'rational justifiability')? It could well be argued, of course, that, since experiment is a symbolically meaningful cognitive practice, it could hardly be said to exist unless it were intelligible. But there remains an important difference between accepting as a premise the intelligibility of scientific experiment and accepting it as rationally justifiable. It seems to me that the strong ontological conclusions of the transcendental deduction follow only from the latter version of the premise, and not the former. In other words, it is legitimate to argue from the *intelligibility* of scientific experiment to the *presupposition* that the world has such-and-such characteristics (i.e. that scientists who conduct experiments are thereby *committed* to the existence of a world with these characteristics) but that the world *really does* possess those characteristics follows only from the premise that experimentation is rationally justified. It is, however, my view that these difficulties of articulation can be resolved, and, in any case, they are not centrally involved in this paper's concern with the application of the transcendental realist model of science to the social sciences.

In *RTS*, then, transcendental arguments are adduced to demonstrate the general characteristics which must be possessed by the world if it is to be a possible object of scientific knowledge, and by society if knowledge, as a species of social practice, is to be sustained. These 'conditions of possibility' of science can be grouped as belonging to two 'dimensions', a 'transitive' and an 'intransitive' dimension, which are characterised as follows:

> '. . . a transitive dimension, in which the object is the material cause or antecedently established knowledge which is used to generate the new knowledge, and an intransitive dimension, in which the object is the real structure or mechanism which exists and acts quite independently of men and the conditions which allow men access to it.'[4]

In the intransitive dimension, transcendental deduction yields the conclusion that the world is both structured and differentiated. That is to say, that the world (unlike the world of *empirical* realist epistemology) has ontological depth. It is constituted by mechanisms whose tendencies and powers may or may not be exercised. When exercised, the powers of real mechanisms may not be 'realised', and even when realised, the resulting event-sequences may not be detected by 'man'. The world is differentiated in the sense that mechanisms may exist and operate either in closed systems, where 'constant-conjunction' event-sequences do occur, or in open systems where the outcomes of the operation of a multiplicity of mechanisms are such that constant conjunctions do occur. Characteristically mechanisms in nature operate in open systems: usually, though not always, closure is artificial, the achievement of experimental practice. Laws are 'normic' statements concerning the tendencies or powers of things, which are manifested in the form of constant conjunctions under conditions of closure, but which must be supposed also to exist and be exercised in open systems, where no constant conjunction is manifest, because of co-determination of outcomes by other mechanisms.

In the transitive dimension, *RTS* concludes, society must be an 'ensemble of powers irreducible to, but present only in the intentional actions of men'[5] who must, in turn, be causal agents, capable of intentionally acting on the world, monitoring this activity, and second-order monitoring of this. In the transitive dimension, the 'object' is antecedently established knowledge which is transformed to produce new knowledge.

Now, it follows directly from this that, since social and psychological mechanisms and structures clearly cannot exist and act 'quite independently of men', they are not possible intransitive objects of scientific knowledge. It may be that certain of their general characteristics may be derived by transcendental deductions of the conditions of possibility of *natural* scientific practices, but here they figure as conditions, in the transitive dimension, of scientific knowledge of nature only, and as objects of *philosophical*, rather than scientific, knowledge.

Furthermore, since Roy Bhaskar's central arguments have been concerned with the implications of experimental activity, since experimental activity presupposes the possibility of closed systems, and since we are told that social and psychological mechanisms occur only in open systems, there follows a further epistemological obstacle to naturalistic social and psychological sciences: the absence of experimental practice.

Strictly speaking, then, Roy Bhaskar's position in *RTS* commits him to a radical dualism of the natural and human domains, which further commits him to an epistemological dualism with respect to the possibility of knowledge of these domains:

NATURAL	*HUMAN*
1 Person-independent mechanisms	1 Person-dependent mechanisms
2 Predictive science possible	2 Predictive science impossible
3 Experimental practice sustained	3 No experimental practice
4 Intransitive objects of scientific knowledge	4 Transitive *condition* of scientific knowledge only

The outcome of the position adopted in *RTS*, then, seems to be a dualist anti-naturalism, so far as the human sciences are concerned.

But this is not a conclusion which Roy Bhaskar is readily prepared to accept. Though apparently already ruled out by definitional fiat, the possibility of a naturalistic scientific knowledge of social and psychological mechanisms *does* get discussed in *RTS*. Roy Bhaskar recognises that so far his central argument has 'turned on the possibility of experimental activity',[6] so either some analogue of this in the human sciences must be found, or we must 'appreciate the great gulf that must separate them from the sciences of nature'.[7]

Throughout the discussion there appears to be an assumed correspondence of experimental sciences with natural sciences, on the one hand, and non-experimental with human, on the other, though this is neither explicitly stated nor defended.

Fortunately, there is an analogue of experimentation in the social sciences. It is that the theories which become embodied in social practices may come to be seen by participant social actors themselves as incapable of non-*ad hoc* explanation of significant phenomena (e.g. Neo-Classical economics and the 1930s depression). However, the characterisation of this experiment-analogue in *RTS* is very brief and sketchy. It also seems to be rather unpromising for any proponent of a naturalistic approach in the social sciences. Society itself is to be understood as a colossal self-constructed and self-interpreted experiment. There seems to be no room for social science as a distinct cognitive practice, with distinctive methods, and autonomous theory, as is the case with the natural sciences. The conception also is comparable in several respects to the Popperian notion of 'social engineering' as the social science analogue of experiment, and is susceptible to broadly similar objections.[8]

However, leaving aside the question of the adequacy of this proposed experiment-analogue, it is important to recognise that the very speculation which gives rise to it – that naturalistic social science might be possible – entails a revision in the definition of the transitive/intransitive boundary. If it is possible even to consider that there may be scientific knowledge of social and psychological mechanisms, then it follows that it must be possible to consider person-dependent mechanisms as potential intransitive objects of knowledge. Since this is ruled out by Roy Bhaskar's original definition of the intransitive dimension, then it follows that a revision of this definition is required if consistency is to be restored and the possibility of naturalism explored.

3 The argument of *PN* and some criticisms

A necessary condition of Roy Bhaskar's project in *PN*, then, is some revision of the transitive/intransitive distinction, and consequent dispersal of the natural/human opposition. Without this, the impossibility of naturalism follows directly. The first revision of the distinction comes in Chapter 1, where the mark of intransitive objects of knowledge becomes that they 'exist and act independently of the knowledge of which they are the objects'.[9] This revision does allow for the possibility that social and psychological mechanisms, processes etc., at least under some characterisations of them, might be possible intransitive objects of knowledge. It does, however, seem to rule out the possibility in the case of one class of such mechanisms and processes, namely those which *constitute* knowledge. This problem of the partial identity of subject and object of knowledge is, indeed, a general difficulty for the maintenance of the transitive/intransitive distinction in the human sciences, and Roy Bhaskar later[10] produces a further revision in the distinction to take account of it. We can distinguish between existential and causal independence: such social relationships are existentially independent of knowledge of, but causally interdependent with it. For the social and human sciences, their intransitive objects are existentially but not causally independent of the processes by which they are known.

But of course, to remove one obstacle to the consideration of the possibility of naturalism is not the same thing as to establish its possibility. It is to Roy Bhaskar's attempt to argue this that I shall now turn, focussing on his argument as it affects specifically social, as distinct from psychological sciences. The main burden of the argument with which I shall be concerned is given in Chapter 2 of *PN*. Here, the argument is that there are fundamental differences between natural and social objects of knowledge, which constitute 'limits' to naturalism in the social sciences, but that these differences are themselves conditions of possibility of social scientific knowledge, in the same *sense*, but not achieved in the same way as natural scientific knowledge.

It might seem that, in investigating the conditions of possibility, and the question of their satisfaction, of social scientific knowledge, the most obvious method would be for a transcendental realist to apply the procedures of *RTS* to this new domain. Social scientific practices would be identified, and a transcendental deduction of their conditions of possibility attempted. But, as Roy Bhaskar rightly points out, what is at issue here is precisely the question whether there *are* any social scientific practices, and, *if* there are, *which* they are. The extension of the method of *RTS* would simply beg the question in favour, not just of the possibility but the actuality, of naturalism.

But the method adopted in *PN* as an alternative isn't entirely clear. There are conflicting accounts of it, and the practice of it doesn't appear to be entirely consistent with any of these accounts. My reconstruction of the argument is, therefore, rather tentative. The argument appears to have three main phases. First, the *a priori* deduction of certain general properties of societies (and persons). Second, a comparison of these with those general properties of natural objects in virtue of which they are possible objects of natural scientific knowledge. This comparison yields a series of epistemologically significant ontological differences. Third, the attempted demonstration that scientific knowledge of social objects is possible, notwithstanding, or rather, because of, these differences.

I shall deal with each of these three phases of the argument in turn. The first phase, the *a priori* demonstration of the relevant emergent properties of societies, is problematic in several respects. Sometimes the claim is that this demonstration consists in an analysis of the necessary conditions for any form of social life,[11] whereas elsewhere it is presented as a derivation from the analysis of a number of characteristic types of human activity ('saying', 'doing', 'making').[12] The principal argument, however, seems to be one which takes the existence of intentional activity as such as its premise.[13] On all three of these characterisations the argument is a transcendental one – what *must* be the case if 'a' (activity etc.) is possible. If we take Roy Bhaskar's argument that the pre-existence of social forms is necessary for intentional action, for example, this is clearly a transcendental argument. But there seems to be nothing, except, perhaps, its greater generality, to distinguish it from other uses of transcendental argument-forms in substantive social scientific research.[14] Its status as a specifically *philosophical* argument is in doubt. Its content and plausibility rely on the acceptability of the 'transformational' model of human practice which is introduced along with it, and on a specific *characterisation* of intentional action which is subject to controversy among the different sociological research traditions.

Now, the significance of this criticism is not simply that Roy Bhaskar fails to sustain a distinction between philosophical and substantive enquiry in the social sciences. I am not sure that I would wish to place too much weight on this distinction, in any case, though *ad hominem* the argument must have some force, since Roy himself devotes considerable space and ingenuity in the attempt to preserve the distinction.[15] Rather, the significance of this criticism is that the procedure adopted in this first phase of the argument involves Roy Bhaskar, after all, in siding with certain substantive research traditions within the social sciences (specifically, Durkheimian, and Marxian, or, rather, some versions of these) against others, and not just in his conclusions, but in his very *premise*: the characterisation of intentional action. In short this procedure is question-begging just as much as would have been a direct application of the method of *RTS*. There are, indeed, systematic links between disputes over the proper characterisation of intentional action and disputes over what is and what is not a properly 'scientific' approach to social scientific investigation. Similar remarks could be made about Roy Bhaskar's use of Durkheim's conception of the 'coercive power' of society to demonstrate its *sui generis* reality.

The second phase of the argument – the comparison of the general properties of societies with those of the objects of the natural sciences with a view to their epistemological significance – is no less problematic. Of course, strictly speaking, if the first phase of the argument fails, then so does the second, but I propose to treat the comparison of natural and social object in abstraction from the methodological difficulties involved in independently establishing the epistemologically significant properties of social objects. This is partly because Roy Bhaskar's argument has a great deal of intrinsic interest, and partly because I am in broad sympathy with some of the most important features of this characterisation of social objects, despite my reservations both about his methods of demonstrating them and about his ways of representing those methods.

Having introduced a limited dispersal of the human/natural opposition (by means of the revision of the transitive/intransitive boundary) as a condition of even posing the question of the 'possibility of naturalism', Roy Bhaskar now proceeds to re-consolidate that opposition in the form of a series of ontological, epistemological and relational 'limits to naturalism'. The first ontological difference between natural and social structures, which constitutes a limit to the possibility of naturalism, is that social structures do not, whereas natural ones do, exist independently of 'the activities they govern'.[16] Now, this supposed dis-analogy is imprecisely expressed, and, moreover, does not appear to have been established in phase one of the argument. It is introduced, rather, as if self-evidently true. However, on the most obvious interpretation of 'activities they govern', it simply is not true that the existence of social structures depends on these activities. For example, the concept of a power-structure required in empirical sociological research must enable the investigator to identify power-relations where powers are not, in fact, exercised, though they continue to be possessed.[17] In such cases, the activities constituting the exercise of powers (= governed by the power-structure?) are not necessary to the existence of the power-structure (though other activities may well be). The full coercive power of the state, for example, may continue to be possessed without being exercised, though such activities as the raising of taxes, the recruiting, training, and equipping of armed personnel may well be necessary to the maintenance of that structure of power-relations. This is entirely comparable with many natural mechanisms. An organism may, for example, never engage in reproductive activity, but yet retain its reproductive system and powers. However, *some* activities of the organism (such as nutrition) would be necessary to the retention of these powers, but not the ones directly governed by the reproductive system itself.

Elsewhere, Roy Bhaskar offers, possibly as a general proposition including the above, the characterisation of social structures as not existing independently of their effects: they (social structures) are present only in and through the activities of human agents.[18] It follows from this, then, that in the social domain, all activities are activities of human agents. But, to sustain the *sui generis* character of social structures, it is necessary to distinguish between those activities of agents which are exercises of their own intrinsic powers, and those activities which are really exercises of powers which reside in social structures, but operate through the activities of human agents. Surely, though, if any person 'A' is the agent of an activity, 'a', then 'A' must be the possessor of the power of which 'a' is the exercise. If this is accepted then it follows that, at best, we can distinguish only between powers of agents possessed in virtue of their intrinsic natures, and powers of agents possessed in virtue of their relational properties. Roy's conception of social structures does not, after all, sustain them as autonomous possessors of causal powers, or, therefore, as *sui generis* realities. Roy Bhaskar is, it seems, committed to a variant form of individualism in social science.[19]

A second ontological limit to naturalism is that social structures do not, whereas natural structures do, exist independently of agents' conceptions of what they are doing. This thesis of the concept-dependence of social structures plays a large part in the argument of *PN*, as well as in other anti-naturalist works,[20] but is subject to varying interpretations which radically affect its epistemological significance. Is the thesis that, in general, social structures exist only if agents have *some* conception of what they are doing? Now, it seems to me hard to sustain the concept of an agent at all without the notion of conceptualisation of activity, so that in so far as human agents are a necessary condition for the existence of social structures (and this is hardly disputable) then the thesis is sustained. But, as it stands, it seems to me that it has little or no epistemological significance. Certainly, it suggests that, once established, scientific conceptions may be in competition with pre-existing agents' conceptions of the same activities. A series of political consequences and problems flow from this, but no special epistemological ones, vis-à-vis the natural sciences, where similar disparities between science and 'common-sense' persist.

At the opposite extreme, the thesis of concept-dependence may be to the effect that the existence of social structures depends upon agents' having the particular conception they do have of what they are doing. Some relationships are, indeed, like this (e.g. friendship). If *each* party to the relationship changes his or her conception of what the relationship is, then the relationship *ipso facto* ceases to exist. But many, perhaps most, and certainly the most sociologically significant, social relationships are not like this at all. Where society surrounds and sustains a relationship with sanctions, including coercive powers, social relationships can be, and are, sustained across great diversity of and through immense changes in participating actors' conceptions of what they are doing (employer/employee relationships, imperial domination, and marriage are three clear examples of such social structures).

Alternatively, the thesis of concept-dependence may be taken as specifying a causal relationship between actors' conceptions and the character of social structures, such that changes in actors' conceptions of what they are doing are among the causes of structural change. Such changes may or may not be in line with the intentions of the actors whose conceptions change. Again, it seems to me that this thesis is not obviously wrong. On the other hand, it hardly counts as an *a priori* demonstrable truth about society as such. Questions as to the causal relationships between social structures of various types, and actors' conceptions of them are open questions, whose answers require empirical and theoretical research. There is no reason to suppose that any answer universalisable across all types of social structure will be forthcoming. Furthermore, on this version, too, there seem to be no serious epistemological difficulties for the possibility of a social science arising from the thesis of concept-dependence.

The third supposed ontological limitation on the possibility of naturalism is that 'social structures, unlike natural structures, may be only relatively enduring (so that the tendencies they ground may not be universal in the sense of space-time invariant)'.[21] It is, of course, true that social structures may be in fact instantiated for historically limited periods of time, and within geographically restricted areas, but this is quite consistent with their tendencies and powers being universal wherever the appropriate structures are instantiated. This *is* space-time invariance in the required sense – i.e. spatio-temporal locations are not in themselves causal factors. Oddly, Roy Bhaskar himself seems to recognise this when, later on, he says that social laws may be universal within their range, though restricted in their scope.[22] But precisely the same is true of the laws and structures of the natural world. As Engels argued, the discovery of historicity in nature was a distinctively nineteenth-century achievement, culminating in Lyell's geology and Darwin's evolutionary biology.[23] Natural mechanisms, like social ones, are not eternal, but have definite conditions of existence which may or may not be present at any point in space or time. If we take into account Roy Bhaskar's later qualification of his position with respect to the space-time variance of social structure, then he is committed to a denial of historicity in nature. This would, indeed, constitute a limit to naturalism in the social sciences. Fortunately, we do not have to agree that natural mechanisms are not historical in character.

There is one respect, though, in which the historicity of the social presents dis-analogies with the historicity of natural mechanisms which might be held to have epistemological consequences. It is generally the case that the historical changes which require basic conceptual distinctions in their science (i.e. 'qualitative' changes, in some uses of this term), have a temporal periodicity which is very great in relation to the periodicity of conceptual change in science itself. In all cognitively relevant senses, then, it can be said that the world which is grasped through the categories of a science following a revolution in that science is *the same world* as was grasped, perhaps with less penetration, by the superseded categories of the science. No major new division of living organisms was, for example, emerging contemporaneously with the Darwin/Wallace production of the concept of natural selection and which itself rendered earlier theories obsolete. Now, scientific revolutions and cognitive advances generally are social processes. When they take social processes as their objects, too, their objects have a temporal periodicity of change which is of the same order as the periodicity of change in the knowledge-process itself. Now this certainly can give rise to methodological problems in the social sciences – particularly with respect to long-term historical prediction. But epistemologically speaking, the situation is quite comparable with the natural sciences. On the very much greater time-scale of biological, geological and cosmological change the comparable long-term historical prediction is equally suspect. There would be a distinctive epistemological problem for the social sciences only if there were some mechanism which ensured a necessary correspondence between cognitive and broader social change. Such a mechanism is, indeed, suggested in *RTS* and is a familiar feature of some historicist Marxisms. Such a necessary correspondence is, however, quite incompatible with a conception of science as a distinct and relatively autonomous cognitive social practice which Roy Bhaskar (most of the time) and myself, too, would wish to sustain.

Next, Roy Bhaskar presents, as an epistemological limit to naturalism, the argument familiar from *RTS*, that social mechanisms exist only in open systems and that, therefore, controlled experiment, prediction and decisive tests of theory are impossible in the social sciences. In answer to this, it is first necessary to ask whether decisive tests of theory are possible in the natural sciences either. Even with an experimental closure of the classic kind, assumptions have to be made in practice about whether a closure has, in fact, been obtained (i.e. an assumption of the non-interference of undetected extrinsic influences on the instance of the mechanism under investigation). Theoretical assumptions also have to be made concerning the characterisation of the mechanism and its activities, as well as the instrumentation employed. Of course, Roy Bhaskar is, in other contexts, well aware of this, but the sharp natural/social science contrast he draws can only be understood, I think, in terms of a residuum of the positivist conception of the experiment/prediction/testing relationship in his thinking.

Connectedly, it seems to be presupposed in Roy's argument that the constant conjunction of events associated with closure is necessary for prediction. Why should this be so? What is to rule out the calculation of the resultant effects of the joint operation of a plurality of mechanisms? Prediction is always, of course, prediction of something *under some description*. Where very complex systems of interacting mechanisms, operating under conditions and initial states which may be known only approximately, outcomes may only be predictable as falling within a certain range of possibilities. Of course, it might be argued that even assuming a wide sense of 'prediction', the outcomes of multi-mechanism ('open') systems are only predictable if it is possible to first isolate each constituent mechanism to examine its operation independently and its relations with others. This, of course, is a methodological problem of the social sciences but not, it seems to me, an epistemological one. Durkheim, for example, in his classic work on suicide,[24] uses elementary statistical comparisons in an effort to demonstrate that a definite coefficient of preservation or aggravation is associated with each of several different religious ways of life. The purpose of the statistical comparison in each case is to rule out the possibility that a given outcome (in this case, suicide rate), or given contribution to such an outcome, really is the result of religious confession, rather than the operation of some other mechanism (minority status in a society, persecution etc.). Of course, Durkheim's implementation is susceptible of criticism, but the principle is clear, and more sophisticated (though still, of course, problematic in various ways) statistical techniques have since been developed. In cases like this, the isolation of mechanisms is achieved theoretically and theory is corrected on the basis of statistical comparisons of differently constituted systems which nevertheless have one or more mechanisms in common.

Most importantly, Roy Bhaskar again seems to neglect a range of natural sciences in which experimental closure is not an available means of empirical control on theory. Historical natural sciences such as geology and evolutionary biology explain phenomena in terms of the interaction of pluralities of mechanisms in open systems. In each of these sciences techniques have been developed – many of them directly comparable to the uses of statistics in sociology – for including an element of empirical control into theory-production and theory-correction. The classic experimental closure is one technique (class of techniques) among many, which is available in some, but by no means all, natural sciences. Roy Bhaskar's critique of the empirical realist, 'constant conjunction', conception of causal laws is insufficiently radical in that it retains a certain paradigm of experimental closure and its role in the testing of theories in common with the 'constant-conjunction' account. Again, the result of this is an artificial and unnecessary natural/social contrast.

Finally, Roy Bhaskar thinks there is a 'relational' limit to naturalism. This derives from the familiar thesis of the partial identity of subject and object of social knowledge. Knowledge is itself a social practice, so that when it takes social practice as its object, maintenance of the distinction between transitive and intransitive objects of knowledge is problematic. As I have already indicated, though,[25] Roy Bhaskar distinguishes existential and causal independence of the intransitive objects of knowledge. In the social sciences, it is possible to sustain the existential independence of social structures, etc., whilst conceding that there is a causal interaction between subject and object of knowledge. But the same is true, surely, of the natural sciences. Experiment, for example, as *RTS* well argues, presupposes causal interaction between natural systems and human agents. If these points are recognised then continued commitment to a natural science/social science dualism on the basis of the 'partial identity' thesis must derive from some conception of the special or distinctive status of self-knowledge, such as would be sustained by a residual Cartesian conception of the subject. This is, for example, the metaphysical basis of Lukacs's classic formulation of this natural/social science opposition.

The result of Roy Bhaskar's comparison of social and natural objects seems, then, to be a series of concessions to anti-naturalism, such that his position would be better described as a form of anti-naturalism, rather than as a naturalism, however qualified. Nevertheless, he remains committed to the possibility of a *scientific* social science, if not a naturalistic one. But the greatest obstacle to even this – the absence of prediction and experiment in the social sciences – remains to be removed. As in *RTS*, the search is for a social-science analogue of experimentation. This time, it is the epistemological significance of social crises which seems to offer promise of a solution. If it is supposed that during periods of social crisis, the underlying generative structures of society become visible to them, then one result of crisis will be a transformation of participant actors' conceptions of their activities. These new conceptualisations may now serve as raw materials in the production of new knowledge of the social form.[26]

There are, however, some serious difficulties in the way of such a process providing even a partial analogue of scientific experiment. First, it appears to be a condition of production of new knowledge, rather than a means of empirical control or correction. Second, it seems to entail that social scientific knowledge is possible only for those societies characterised by periodic crises of the required sort (capitalist societies?), unless there are yet other experiment-analogues appropriate to other types of society. Third, Roy Bhaskar gives us no theoretical account of the visibility/invisibility of generative structures and, surely, even if he could, this would beg the epistemological question. Finally, one universal feature of social crisis which is difficult to reconcile with Roy Bhaskar's epistemological requirements is that they polarise populations ideologically and politically. If actors make sense of the newly visible generative structures in profoundly diverse and antagonistic ways, what sense is it still possible to make of metaphor of 'visibility', and how are we to solve the problem of *which* actors' conceptions are adequate raw materials for scientific transformation?

It seems, then, that Roy Bhaskar, having minimally dispersed the natural/social opposition as a condition of posing the question of the possibility of naturalism, goes on to reconstitute that opposition. The resulting philosophy of the social sciences is anti-naturalistic, and seems incapable of sustaining the possibility of even a non-naturalistic social science. The ontological opposition of the natural and human domains continues to affect the epistemological argument throughout *The Possibility of Naturalism*, determining concessions to anti-naturalism which are quite unnecessary. The ontology of the natural/human opposition is itself sustained by the unduly restricted range of sciences (mainly, though not exclusively, physics and chemistry) and, therefore, of scientific practices, which are paradigmatic for the model of science constructed in *RTS* and presupposed in *PN*. This model of the natural sciences has in common with the logical empiricism which it so effectively refutes that it under-represents historicity and development as epistemologically significant characteristics of the objects of the natural sciences. Evolutionary biology, cosmology, geology, embryology are all natural sciences for which historicity and qualitative transformation pose epistemological and methodological problems which are in many respects directly comparable with those encountered in the sciences of human history, society and psychology.

It is also a characteristic of these historical natural sciences that the explanatory models they employ designate mechanisms which are not practically isolable in experimental closures. If the impossibility of closure is an epistemological obstacle to a scientific sociology, then it must also be so for this range of natural sciences. In fact, a great diversity of non-experimental means of empirical control and correction, as well as adaptations of experimental methods themselves, have been developed in these sciences. This is true just as much of the historical social as of the historical natural sciences. If we consider, for example, the range of empirical controls involved in the production and later correction of Darwin's evolutionary biology, it is easy to see that these by no means all fit the paradigm of the classic 'experiment'. An important raw material for Darwin, which both establishes the possibility of organic transformation, and sets definite limits to the range of possible mechanisms which might be supposed to bring it about, are rule-of-thumb generalisations derived from stock-breeders and gardeners. These are forms of reflection on non-experimental human interventions in nature, which rule out certain theoretical explanatory possibilities, and set definite target-requirements for theoretical reasoning.

Another important set of empirical controls was the range of theoretically informed observations of the geographical distribution of living forms, together with palaeontological evidence of their historical succession, and the geographical distribution of 'related' forms. Again these are evidences from a non-experimental source which tell against the idea of special creation, and for the notion of common descent by gradual transformation. As to the mechanism of natural selection itself, of course, no experimental demonstration of the formation of new species by its agency is available, but the subsequent development of such adjacent sciences as genetics and ecology have both sustained and modified Darwin's conception, whilst *elements* of the process are relatively isolable, and have been examined by means of adaptations of experimental technique. For example, numerous investigators have exposed different colour-varieties of insect larvae against various backgrounds in the vicinity of the nests of insectivorous birds to discover differential rates of predation on them. These 'experiments' can be combined with statistical 'thought-experiments' to determine the effects on the gene-pool of a population through successive generations of such differential predations.

Finally, on the 'human' side of Roy Bhaskar's natural/human opposition, there is an unwillingness to conceive of forms of historical causality as really distinct from individual human agency, *despite* the prominence of the argument for the *sui generis* reality of social structures. It is this remnant of what has been called 'the problematic of the subject' which further sustains the ontological and epistemological dualism of *PN*.

At the beginning of this paper, I quoted Roy Bhaskar as advocating an anti-positivist naturalism, according to which 'it is possible to give an account of science under which the proper and more-or-less specific methods of both the natural and social sciences can fall'.[27] It seems to me that the anti-naturalist conclusions of *PN* are part of a demonstration that *RTS* failed in this respect, and that the model of science produced in that work requires revision to take into account, in particular, epistemologically significant characteristics of historical, developmental, and non-experimental natural *and* social sciences. This would involve a systematic attempt to adequately characterise and analyse the conditions of possibility of the non-experimental empirical controls which I have above sketched in relation to evolutionary biology and Durkheim's work on suicide. I remain convinced that the outcome of such investigations would be a confirmation of the broad outlines of Roy Bhaskar's realist model, if not of some of its more detailed articulation.

In case I should be misunderstood as advocating the kind of conception of a monolithic unified science which for so long characterised logical empiricist orthodoxy, it may be necessary to point out that my arguments against Roy Bhaskar's anti-naturalism are designed less to show that the social sciences are (or could be) more like the natural ones than he supposes, than to show that the natural sciences, or, at least, some of them, are more like the social than he supposes. More importantly, though, I remain committed, as he does, to the view that there are significant differences in the methods of the different sciences, which are grounded in real differences in the subject matters of those sciences and the relationships of those sciences to their subject-matters.[28] Where I differ from Roy Bhaskar and other anti-naturalists is that I think these differences to be almost always of a methodological rather than epistemological kind, and that I do not, whereas Roy Bhaskar does, align the whole range of methodological diversity along a single fault-plane, dividing the natural and the social. Methodologically, if not epistemologically, the sciences display a 'family resemblance', of cross-cutting and overlapping differences and similarities of method.

Notes

1 This includes: Roy Bhaskar, *A Realist Theory of Science*, Leeds, 1975, and Hassocks and New Jersey, 1978, 'Feyerabend and Bachelard: Two Philosophies of Science', *New Left Review* 94 (1975); 'On the Possibility of Social Scientific Knowledge and the Limits of Naturalism', in Mepham and Ruben (eds.), *Issues in Marxist Philosophy*, Vol. III, Hassocks, 1979; and *The Possibility of Naturalism*, Brighton, 1979; Russell N. Keat, 'Positivism, Naturalism and Anti-Naturalism in the Social Sciences', *Journal for the Theory of Social Behaviour*, I, pp. 3–17; Russell Keat and John Urry, *Social Theory as Science*, London, 1975; T. Benton, *Philosophical Foundations of the Three Sociologies*, London, 1977, and 'Natural Science and Cultural Struggle' in Mepham and Ruben (eds.), *op. cit.*, Vol. II; Andrew Collier, 'In Defence of Epistemology', in *Radical Philosophy* 20, Summer 1978; and David Thomas, *Naturalism and Social Science*, Cambridge, 1979.
2 Roy Bhaskar, *The Possibility of Naturalism*, op. cit., p. 3.
3 See, for example, *RTS*, pp. 30–36, where 'presuppositions' become 'conditions of possibility' on p. 36. Connectedly, we get shifts from the 'intelligibility' to the 'rationality' and 'existence' of practices such as scientific perception, as if these were equivalent.
4 *RTS*, p. 17.
5 *RTS*, p. 20.
6 *RTS*, p. 244.
7 *RTS*, p. 245.
8 See, for example, my *Philosophical Foundations*, op. cit., p. 38ff.
9 *PN*, p. 14.
10 *PN*, p. 60.
11 *PN*, p. 18.
12 *PN*, p. 43.
13 *PN*, p. 46 and p. 65.
14 See *PN*, p. 64ff.
15 See *PN*, p. 64ff.
16 *PN*, p. 48.
17 See, for example, Steven Lukes, *Power: A Radical View*, London, 1976. My paper, 'Objective Interest and the Sociology of Power' (unpublished) presents this argument at greater depth.
18 For example *PN*, p. 50.
19 I am now somewhat sceptical as to the power of this argument, but I retain it because it seems to me to have intrinsic interest. I suspect that to see where it goes wrong, assuming it does, would be illuminating.
20 Most well known of these is, perhaps, Peter Winch's *Idea of a Social Science*, London, 1959.
21 *PN*, p. 49.
22 *PN*, p. 165.
23 See my 'Natural Science and Cultural Struggle', *op. cit.* (n. 1).
24 E. Durkheim, *Suicide*, London, 1952.
25 p. 15 above.
26 *PN*, p. 61ff.
27 *PN*, p. 3.
28 *PN*, p. 3.
29 I should like to thank the organiser of the Sociology Graduate Seminar at the University of Sussex for providing the stimulus to write this paper, and the participants in that seminar for helping me to clarify and correct my ideas. I should also like to thank Andrew Sayer, whose written comments were most helpful.

12

A REALIST SOCIAL SCIENCE

Peter Manicas

Chapter 10 [of AHPSS] suggested that the differences among theoretical science, applied science, and technology were rapidly being eroded. There is now a growing critical literature which shows that our customary understanding of the distinctions between these is not as straightforward as one might have supposed (Ben-David, 1971; Kuhn, 1977; Mayr, 1982; de Solla Price, 1982). Nevertheless, it is crucial that the distinctions be acknowledged. My aim in this chapter is to defend social science as a theoretical science which, like physical science analogs, seeks to understand the world. This task must be distinguished from other familiar tasks of existing social-scientific practice, especially 'social research', the effort to develop data about society, and 'applied social science', whose ostensible task is to use knowledge to solve some of life's social and individual problems. I will have something more to say about applied social science in the next chapter [of AHPSS]. But in the interest of precluding needless confusion and misunderstanding, it may be well to add a few words on the idea of social research.

As noted in part I [of AHPSS], social research emerged with the modernizing processes of the modern state. There can be little doubt that today, governing depends heavily on information provided by social researchers – from demographic data to data about unemployment, the balance of trade, the inflation rate, crime, health, and welfare. Some of this information is reliable, some not. This is not the place, however, to attempt to discuss the problems, which range from familiar statistical problems to more serious conceptual issues, like those associated with data on unemployment or 'crime', for example (Reiman, 1984). Nothing in what follows argues against the desirability of good information and, hence, the need for good social research. Rather, what is contended is that social science ought not to be conceived *exclusively* as social research.

Source: A History and Philosophy of the Social Sciences, chap. 13, pp. 266–293 (referred to in the text as AHPSS).

No one, I think, would maintain that social science is identical with *statistical* inquiry, but it is a widely shared opinion that the methodology of social research generates an explanatory capacity and that, accordingly, 'social research', broadly construed, is identifiable with social science. This view is not restricted to so-called 'quantitative' researchers; the confusion has infected *all* mainstream social science. In the last part of this chapter, I will try to make clear how this is the case.

The main goal of the chapter is to sketch a realist conception of social science as an alternative to the mainstream view. I noted in the Introduction [of AHPSS] that the most important way in which the present study is incomplete lies in the absence of an account of the arguments regarding the nature and tasks of the social sciences since the 1930s, and especially since World War II. This last period has been an especially fertile one. But, while much work remains to be done, there are now a number of very good discussions of various aspects of it.[1] Before starting on my sketch, which draws heavily on this work, it may be useful to characterize, if briefly, a portion of the discussion, recognizing that the characterization may ultimately turn out to be a caricature.

The recent debate

The recent debate in the philosophy of the social sciences has turned on two related polarities, that between a 'subjectivist' and an 'objectivist' pole, and that concerning the relationship of agency to structure. The first has been haunted by the specter of philosophical idealism, the second by that of a world without agents. While there are some very critical differences among them, it is not impossible to include in the subjectivist approach all of the following: phenomenology (Schutz, 1962), versions of ethnomethodology (Garfinkel, 1967), the post-Wittgensteinian views of Winch (1958), and versions of hermeneutics and critical theory (Gadamer, 1960; Habermas, 1968; Ricoeur, 1970; Taylor, 1971).

The point of departure of these views is criticism of the objectivism of 'positivist' social science. Again, with differences, this criticism concerns the failure of mainstream theory even to acknowledge that the social world is constituted by agents and thus becomes intelligible only insofar as one can discover the meanings or intentions of those agents. The radical objectivist treats meaningful action as 'behavior', but even those who do not – for example, Merton – because they remain wedded to the hypothetical-deductive model of explanation, take social reality for granted and thus treat it the way they treat the natural world. The objectivists thus misconstrue 'explanation' and never address the question of how social reality is constituted and maintained (Natanson, 1963). Worse, the 'objectivity' of social science as the dispassionate and detached view of the social world is but the standpoint of the person as alienated. Society and culture, as in Talcott

Parsons, become autonomous *things* which constitute persons instead of being constituted by them (Gouldner, 1970).

According to the view presented here, these criticisms are wholly on the mark, but in saying that the specter of philosophical idealism haunts these views, I mean that, as regards the social world, these views tend to undermine an appearance/reality distinction; in Marxist terms, these views rule out the possibility of 'false consciousness'. Put simply, while it is true that the social world is constituted by agents and has meaning by virtue of this and that, accordingly, we must appeal to the cognitive resources of agents if we are to offer adequate descriptions of the social world, it may be the case that the understandings that agents have of their social world is incorrect (Gellner, 1970; MacIntyre, 1970). Social science needs to do more than give a description of the social world as seen by its members (ethnography); it needs also to ask whether members have an adequate understanding of their world and, if not, to explain, why not. 'Critical theory', with its antecedents in the Marxism of the Frankfurt school, acknowledges this, of course. Yet recent critical theory, since Habermas (1968), has taken an idealist turn (McCarthy, 1981, pp. 96ff.; Keat, 1981). The problem is to accept the 'hermeneutic circle' and, at the same time, to sustain the possibility of critique: to acknowledge that there is no neutral or transcendental standpoint, but to hold also that *explanatory* social theory, insofar as it exposes domination concealed *as* domination, is inherently emancipating (Bhaskar, 1979, 1982). This suggests, as I will argue, the need for a realist conception of social science.

The second polarity, between agency and structure, overlaps with the first, but it is most familiarly associated with French 'structuralism'. Sartre's *Critique of Dialectical Reason* of 1960, written in response to Merleau-Ponty's criticisms of the 1950s, was followed by Lévi-Strauss's *The Savage Mind* (1962), which contained a direct attack on Sartre. Lacan (1966), who like Lévi-Strauss had been influenced by Saussure's structural linguistics, brought Freud back into the debate which by then had been joined by Barthes (1967), but especially by Foucault, who, in *The Order of Things* (1970), outdid both Durkheim and Lévi-Strauss in unearthing the underlying 'code' of civilization. At the same time, and in response to Sartre, came Louis Althusser's *For Marx* and, with Balibar, *Reading Capital*, 'a counter-signature of the structuralist claim' (Anderson, 1983, p. 37). Poulantzas (1969) and Colletti (1969) enlarged the debate, and since then, we have had the polemic of E. P. Thompson (1978) against Althusser, Anderson's 1980 effort – successful in my view – to mediate this, and, of course, the influential work of the 'post-structuralists', in particular Derrida (1974). This is surely a mixed collection of figures, and no effort will be made here to clarify the many differences or issues. My brief characterization is designed only to focus what follows.

It is fair to say, I believe, that 'structuralism' was motivated mostly by a recognition that the mainstream tradition of social science is methodologically individualist and voluntarist, key features, as I have argued, of the tradition deriving from Hobbes, Locke, Adam Smith, J. S. Mill, Spencer, Pareto, and, on most contemporary readings, to Max Weber. The background of the critique of this tradition, unsurprisingly, is the French tradition of Comte and especially Durkheim and the tradition of Hegel, especially in versions of Marxist historical materialism. The problem, already noted in our accounts of Hegel and Durkheim, is the evaporation of agents who become, in effect, but manifestations or, in Althusserian terminology, 'bearers' of autonomous 'structures' which exist quite independently of them. One form of this, that found in Lévi-Strauss, involves an escape from history via a form of Platonism in which 'ethnographic analysis tries to arrive at invariants beyond the empirical diversity of human societies', and where 'the ultimate goal of the human sciences is not to constitute [persons] but to dissolve them' (Lévi-Strauss, 1966, p. 247). On the Althusserian variant, history is 'a process without a subject'. Social change is but the gradual and discontinuous 'bricolage' of structures which have no human bricoleur, structures which in complex systems of autonomy, dependence, and contradiction offer 'conjunctures' like the one in 1917 which became the Bolshevik Revolution (Kurzweil, 1980). Insofar as these views are correctives to methodological individualism and voluntarism, they are to be welcomed. On the other hand, they do not, in my view, resolve the root difficulty. This requires a form of realism in social theory, but it cannot adopt either of the historical poles which are the legacy of the nineteenth century, either 'absolute idealism' (Neoplatonism) or 'materialism'.

Post-structuralism is a descendent of structuralism. Influenced by Heidegger, as well as by Saussure and Lévi-Strauss, Anderson (1983) would seem to be correct in arguing that post-structuralism represents a dissolution of 'structures'; thus, in the battle-cry 'there is nothing outside the text', we have not merely a relativism, tolerable enough in itself, but an epistemological nihilism in which truth is an illusion. On this view, the pretense to it reflects metaphysical prejudice (the Western philosophical quest for 'presence').[2] What results, then, is 'a subjectivism without a subject' (Anderson, 1983, p. 54). Undoubtedly there are insights for the social sciences in the writings of Derrida and Foucault, including, for example, the critique of subjectivity as never transparent and the knowledge/power relations analysed by Foucault in his more specifically 'historical' writings. This is not the place, however, to review the difficult, but interesting, questions involved. Instead, I turn to what seems to me to be the most pressing problem for a viable philosophy of social science, that of formulating in a clear and adequate way the 'object' of theory in social science, what social-scientific theory is about. We need to be clear, that is, about the 'ontology' of society.

The ontology of society

It would be more than merely convenient if we could say without qualification that, just as physical theory is about theorized natural structures

– quarks, molecules, viruses, mammals, galaxies, space–time cones and so on – so social theory is about social structures; that in both cases, theory aims at knowledge of the dispositional properties (laws) of abstracted objects which together help us to explain what happens in the world; and that in both cases, the theorized 'strata' of reality are the *raison d'être* of the different explanatory 'sciences'. To be sure, we would need to notice differences in the kinds of structures theorized; but this in itself constitutes no problem. It has been presupposed right along that the various theorized 'mechanisms' of physical science are very different; accordingly, social structures need not be 'like' natural structures in all relevant respects. Moreover, despite the ease of talking about 'mechanisms', it is not intended by such talk that the very different structures theorized by the sciences are like those theorized in the classical science of mechanics; that, as the corpuscularists had it, 'matter' and mechanical causality, vectors of 'forces', give us the whole story. Plainly this will not do, not even for physical theory. Indeed, despite the continuing attractiveness of these crude ideas in some quarters, they have been defunct in science for well over a hundred years now. One need not look at quantum mechanics or classical field theory, but only to the more familiar ideas of molecular chemistry or biochemistry.

'Social structures' and causality in society need not, then, be the same as any of these. But exactly how these are to be conceptualized is a matter of contention. For example, 'racism' surely *affects* opportunities for individuals, and there are social *mechanisms* by virtue of which what occurs does occur; but what exactly does this mean? Is such talk merely metaphorical? I think not. On the contrary, and despite some fundamental differences which we will consider, this way of talking about 'social structures' is more than metaphorical or just plain convenient. After making some critical qualifications, we can continue to use the language of social structure so as to deliberately reinforce the analogy between the theoretical physical sciences and theoretical social science.

Individuals and persons surely exist. Social structures do not exist in the sense of either of these. Yet, as suggested in chapter 8 [of AHPSS], without the concept of social structure (or something like it), we cannot make sense of persons, since all the predicates which apply to individuals and mark them uniquely as persons are social. We can, for example, predicate a shape, size, color, or position of a person, just as we can of a stone or a tree. We can say that a person is hungry or in pain, just as we can say that a lower animal is hungry or in pain. But the moment we say that the person is a tribesman or a revolutionary, cashed a check, or wrote a sonnet, we are presupposing tribes (a social order), a banking system, and a literary form (Bhaskar, 1979, pp. 34f.).

If, then, methodological individualism is construed as holding that facts about society or human action are to be explained solely in terms of facts about individuals, and if facts about persons requires predicates which presuppose a social context which cannot be reduced (translated) to predicates having no reference to social context, then methodological individualism must be false.

Both historically (see chapters 2 and 3 [of AHPSS]) and in its contemporary forms (Popper, 1962; Watkins, 1963; Brodbeck, 1968), methodological individualism has an anti-metaphysical motivation. And opponents of it – Rousseau, Herder, Hegel, Marx, Durkheim, and others – are accused, often rightly, of being 'metaphysicians'. In its modern form, it was a critical part of the logical empiricist program of eliminating inferred entities in favor of logical constructions. Thus, just as 'magnetic field' was to be 'translated' into witnessable conditions and consequences and thereby incorporated into the language of science, so society was a logical construction and social predicates were to be translated into witnessable conditions and 'behaviors'. That nobody today gives credence to the possibility of such a translation is critical, for it means that, although methodological individualism has been shown to be false, we nevertheless lack a consensus on what this means.[3]

The concept of social structure

The problem, then, is just this. We need the idea of social structure, but social structure does not exist in the way that a magnetic field exists. And the reason would seem to be this: that *society is incarnate in the practices and products of its members.* It doesn't exist apart from the practices of individuals; it is not witnessable; only its activities and products are. As Giddens writes, 'structure enters simultaneously into the constitution of the agent and social practices, and "exists" in the generating moments of this constitution' (Giddens, 1979, p. 5). It is both medium and product, enabling as well as constraining.

It is 'medium' in being what one uses when one acts as a person. It is thus also that it is enabling and constraining. For example, a person has a language, and thus *can* speak. Evidently, to be understood, that person *must* conform, more or less, to the 'rules' of that language. A person has 'knowledge' and a range of skills. That person can use these only because other individuals possess particular skills, are related in particular ways, and have available to them particular 'materials', all of which at the same time constrains them.

Social structure is 'product' in the sense that speaking reproduces the language, going to work reproduces the system of capitalism, and voting reproduces electoral politics. Without people speaking English, English ceases to be 'a living language'. As with all social structures, its continuing existence requires continuing speech-practices. On the other hand, the continuing practices may be comprehended in terms of the structures. That is, structures need not be 'independent' of practices for it to be said that practices are structured in such and such a way. Thus, while they do not 'exist' in the same way that natural structures exist, they can be, as in physical science, the objects of *theory.*

Since social structures do not exist independently of activities, they are not simply reproduced but are, as Bhaskar notes, reproduced *and* transformed. Because the language is 'living', it is continually changing. If only a small minority of people were to take the trouble to vote, elections would become transformed into rituals which lack the meaning they now have (Edelman, 1964); and eventually, like the 'hearths' of the ancient *polis*, they would then probably disappear altogether.[4]

Because society is incarnate in the practices of its members, it is easy to lapse into methodological individualism, in which society disappears and only individuals exist. Of course, society has *not* disappeared, since these individuals are *persons* and their acts are *situated*, not simply in a 'natural' world but in a world constituted by past and ongoing human activity, a humanized natural and social world. Farmland and forest-land, the city streets, neighborhoods, the buildings which house machines, icons, and law-books; violins and folios of music, all both enable and constrain the members who use them. *Per impossibile*, were we to find non-socialized persons interacting with none of these 'artifacts' of humanity, we would not lapse into supposing that only individuals exist, and not society – as, of course, Rousseau and Herder saw.

Because individuals become persons only in society, it is easy to fall into the Platonizing trap of Ranke (see chapter 5) or Durkheim (see chapter 8), to suppose that society has to be something *more than* the organized social practices which embody social structures. Social structures, including language, do pre-exist for *some* individuals, but never for all. When it is said that someone appropriates language from 'society', this means that they appropriate it from existing speakers of the language, who, of course, also appropriated it from 'society', that is, from previous speakers, and so on back into pre-history.

We move in the direction of Platonism (as does recent French structuralism, for example) by supposing that the language does not simply pre-exist for some individuals, which must be the case, but that it is absolutely prior to activity. 'The language' then 'accounts for' the activity in the sense that the abstract 'forms' account for their concrete manifestations (see chapter 4). When we say that 'the language is "possessed" by speakers', we reinforce this error. 'The language' (like any other structure) is whatever the continued reproduction/transformation by speakers makes it. Elections, nurturing practices, and so on are what they are only by virtue of the activities which constitute them.[5]

To talk about *the* language or *the* structure of a language or, more generally, the structures which are the properties of some concrete society is heuristic in the sense that because activity constitutes them and not conversely, social structures can and do undergo relatively rapid change. Talk about *the* structure is a static idealization, even if indispensable. This makes for an important difference between social science and physical science. Theorizing is never finished in any science, but in the social sciences, theory is continually revisable not merely in the sense that new theories replace or amend older theories, but in the sense that *reality* is changing. The 'rules' – of language or other forms of social activity – are but normative abstractions drawn from shifting uniformities, incapable of being formulated as a closed system (Barnes, 1982; Margolis, 1984).

Accordingly, social science is *inevitably* historical. History is not merely 'the past', but *a sedimented past which, as transformed, is still present.* As Marx and Engels wrote in *The German Ideology*, 'history is nothing but the succession of separate generations, each of which exploits the materials, the capital funds, the productive resources handed down to it by all preceding generations.' By this we must understand that what is 'handed down' is not merely the legacy of material goods but also includes 'knowledge' and the 'handed down' social forms themselves. Moreover, this whole legacy is continually being exploited by each succeeding generation. It is not merely window-dressing or deference to 'context' which demands that an attempt to explain, for example, the emergence of martial law in the Philippines must engage the question of the Philippine colonial past (Lallana, 1986). On the contrary, present forms have their particular nature *by virtue of* their past, and thus present understanding requires an understanding of their genesis.

On this conception, discriminable starting-points or breaks will be signalled by events which made for what, to us, are significant ruptures or transformations in the theorized inherited forms. Periods, epochs, eras will span these. On this view, we expect continuity with change, both of which are always 'more or less'.

Because social structures are incarnate in the practices of persons, this means that they do not exist independently of the *conceptions* of the persons whose activities constitute (reproduce, transform) them. It is because persons have beliefs, interests, goals, and practical knowledge acquired in their epigenesis as members of society that they do what they do and thus sustain (transform) the structures. That is, there is no question here that persons are the ultimate causal agents as regards everything that makes society what it is; nor is it the case that individuals are 'dupes' of culture (Parsons) or structure (Althusser), that everything that happens goes on 'behind their backs'.

This does not imply a regression to methodological individualism, for two reasons. First, as noted, a person/society dichotomy is spurious; for there is a duality in the sense that society always pre-exists for individuals.[6] Second, while it is true that, as Giddens writes (in criticism of both Parsons and Althusser), all agents have practical knowledge (not necessarily cognitively available) and some degree of understanding of the real nature of social structure which their activities sustain, unintended consequences, unacknowledged conditions, and tacit rules limit the individual's understanding of his or her social world. For example, one works at Los Alamos to earn one's living; one does not work there *in order to* encourage the arms race, still less to bring the world closer to a nuclear holocaust. Nevertheless, these may well be unintended consequences of such work.[7]

Moreover, it may be that the structures which are reproduced by one's voluntary activity are rightly understood as oppressive, and thus that one becomes party to one's continued oppression – quite voluntarily. Indeed, in contrast to methodological individualisms, because social structure is both constraining *and* enabling, what one can and cannot do is determined both by existing social resources and, more particularly, by the nature of the social relations defined by the structures and by one's place in them. Had they even conceived the possibility, neither Louis XIV nor all the peasants in his kingdom could have destroyed the world. But Louis XIV could, of course, do many things that his peasant subjects could not do – from dine regularly on white bread to call for the execution of a traitor. *Versus* methodological individualism, then, 'voluntary acts' are just those done by a person *given* alternatives not chosen by that person (whose faculties are intact and who is unconstrained by force).[8]

Recognizing that social structure does not exist independently of an agent's conceptions and that persons are the causal agents of existing social reality may seem to lead to a voluntarism in which society is the creation of (rational) individuals (see chapter 3 [of AHPSS]). But such is not the case. Such 'creation' is only with materials at hand (see above); it is never *ex nihilo* and never unconditioned. Second, even if the acts of individuals are more or less 'rational', related to definite interests, and so on, their (structured) practices and the changes in them are not generally, if ever, *intended*; still less are these changes 'rational'. As historically sedimented unintended consequences of intentional activities, they appear as 'natural' (Marx), but there is *no* reason to suppose that their 'development' is telic, that change is under the governance of some grand design (see chapter 4 [of AHPSS]).

But changes in activity *do* change society. This suggests that social science is potentially *liberating*. For Marx, social science was *revolutionary*, and while he put considerable emphasis on the problem of ideology construed as 'false consciousness', he saw that this was not the whole story. On his view, capitalist organization would bring workers to understand that their own activities sustained oppressive relations and would, at the same time, make them organizationally *able* to act *collectively* to reconstitute society. This is hardly the place to evaluate Marx's views on revolutionary social change or on the changes in conditions which altered the problem of revolutionary change, changes which, after all, Marx could not have foreseen. Still, it cannot be denied that his most fundamental insights regarding history and society, insights preserved, I hope, in the foregoing, stand in distinct contrast to the prevailing practices of academic social science. Indeed, though only part of the story has been outlined in part II [of AHPSS], one must conclude that the modern social sciences have been, unwittingly or not, defenders of the *status quo.* As Veblen put it, rather than 'disturb the habitual convictions and preconceptions' on which present institutions rest, social science has 'enlarged on the commonplace' and offered 'complaisant interpretations, apologies, and projected remedies' – none of which have been dangerous to the *status quo.* Most fundamentally, this was a result of failure on the part of mainstream social scientists to acknowledge that, while social reality is real enough, it is not like unchanging nature, but is just that which is sustained by human activities, activities regarding which humans have the *only* say.

If people are causal agents, they are capable of re-fashioning society in the direction of greater humanity, freedom, and justice. To do this, of course, they must see that they have this power; they must acknowledge that present arrangements can be improved; and they must have some clarity about how they can be improved. It is a simplification to hold that only 'false consciousness' stands in the way of progressive social change, for, as noted earlier, people are not dupes of society. But even if they have some grasp of the reality of society, then, if the foregoing is correct, the solitary individual cannot make change. For change to come about, *practices* must be altered, which means that most of those engaged in reproducing the practices must together alter their activity (Manicas, 1982). This is not the place to develop an account of the causal complexities whose understanding would help us grasp why this has not happened; but I believe it is fair to say that not least of these is our structured incapacity, promoted by technocratic social science, to constitute any sort of adequate social mechanism for unconstrained social inquiry (Dewey, 1927; Mills, 1956; Poulantzas, 1969; Habermas, 1975; Manicas, 1982).

In sum, then, as Bhaskar writes, the foregoing allows us to undercut reification and voluntarism, social determinism and methodological individualism, and the connected errors of the substantive traditions of structuralism and functionalism, on the one hand, and the action-oriented and interpretative sociologies on the other. Thus:

> Society is not the unconditioned creation of human agency (voluntarism), but neither does it exist independently of it (reification). And individual action neither completely determines (individualism) nor is completely determined by (determinism) social forms. In [this conception], unintended consequences, unacknowledged conditions and tacit skills . . . limit the actor's understanding of the social world, while unacknowledged (unconscious) motivation limits one's understanding of oneself.
>
> (Bhaskar, 1982, p. 286)

Understanding society and historical explanation

The aim of social science is an understanding of society and social process, where 'understanding' does not have any special sense – for example, involving empathy or some intuition of subjectivity. To be sure, action is meaningful, and understanding society involves understanding what acts *mean* to actors, but while this is part of the story, it is not the whole of it. As Weber argued, understanding society involves *causal understanding*, an understanding of how it is what happens in society happens. On the present view, understanding society involves hermeneutic social science – having a member's knowledge of society – for otherwise one cannot know what one is explaining; but it also involves, as Marx saw, a knowledge of how definite practices are structured, the relations between structured practices, and the tendencies of such practices towards transformation or disintegration.[9]

This is not a functionalism, we should add, if by that one means that we explain when we know how what some 'institution' does contributes to 'the needs of the system' or to 'system-maintenance' (Giddens, 1979, pp. 111ff.). It is one thing to discover how an institution came to be, how it works, what it does, and what its effects are; it is quite another to import into this an unwarranted teleology, an assumption that society, like an organism, has a *telos* (see chapter 8) or that what is 'needed' will somehow get provided. Nor should one suppose that the availability of a system-hypothesis completes the social scientific task. For example, it may be that the reproduction of capitalist relations of production requires that profit be available for reinvestment, but this has not been explained until an account can be given of the particular social mechanisms constituting the causal loop (Giddens, 1979, p. 113). In this regard, of course, social science differs not at all from any of the theoretical sciences, even if we are used to thinking of the biological sciences as particularly concerned with 'systems' notions.

As noted in chapter 7 [of AHPSS], Weber employed an extremely useful distinction between the abstract and concrete sciences, conceiving of physics as 'abstract' and social science as 'concrete'. On the present view, however, any science which restricts itself to the theorizing of structure is abstract, and any science which aims at the explanation of concrete events is concrete. And since all concrete outcomes are the result of a plurality of causes, operating at different strata of reality, we can make a distinction between *understanding structure* and *explaining events*, between having a grasp of the nomic dispositions of the structures and providing an account of how particular 'mechanisms' and events came together to produce some outcome. Each of the theoretical sciences offers theories of particular strata of reality, and any of them might be involved in the explanation of an event. This is as true of social phenomena as any other.

That is, we can think of social theory as aimed at the theorization of social reality, a non-reducible stratum of reality. But the explanation of a social event, the Great Crash of 1929, the Bolshevik Revolution, the emergence of martial law in the Philippines, the election of an American president, and so on, involves knowledge of the 'social mechanisms' of existing structures and whatever else causally contributed to the particular outcome. That the scope of this effort is global was seen by Herder, Montesquieu, and Marx. It is also the grist of much sound historical writing. Indeed, it is not implausible to argue, here with our account of Weber in mind, that in the last analysis, a theoretically informed, multi-causal history is the human science which has the most significance for us.[10]

We do social theory because we want to understand what happens in society; but concrete happenings require a multi-causal account. We need to have an understanding of social structures and their tendencies, to know how they are related and their effects; and we need to relate this sometimes to geography, sometimes to a natural event, such as the eruption of Pompeii or the consequences of a long drought. Finally, if we are to provide an explanation of the event in question, we need to relate the whole business to the acts of people working with and in response to these things. To explain, for example, the Bolshevik Revolution, we need at the very least a grasp of the complicated social relations of Imperial Russia and a knowledge of the inter-state relations obtaining prior to and during World War I; we need to know how the long winter of 1916 affected what happened, and, within the nexus of these complicated structures and events, we need to grasp the particular sequence of steps taken by both individuals and groups – for example, the decision of the provisional government to pursue the war and the ride to the Finland station.

As with the broken water pipes (see chapter 12 [of AHPSS]), the event to be explained is unique, even if we have reason to believe that it could not have happened otherwise, given the particular configuration of causes. Of course, the explanation of a particular historical event, even events of less monumental historical consequence – the more typical task of social scientists – is not likely to be as satisfying as an explanation depending more fundamentally on natural scientific understanding. The reasons are clear. Not only do we have much less confidence in the social theory which gives us insight into the relevant structures but the dominating presence of human agency increases the causal complexity enormously. On the other hand, this is not sufficient reason to abandon the search for causes, or, as with Weber, to try to simplify the problem with the artificial and misleading device of 'ideal types'.

Nothing in the foregoing implies that history is an immanent process (see chapter 4 [of AHPSS]) or, accordingly, that there are *laws of history*, even if on the present view, there are social laws. But this must mean that we can discover tendencies (again, realistically understood) in the structured practices. It clearly does not commit us to the implausible idea that these are universal. Not every society was or will be 'capitalist', even if at some level of abstraction, all societies generate relations of production. However, we can say that between any two capitalist societies, there will be specific capitalist social mechanisms involved in its reproduction. But we cannot say that for this reason everything that happens in one will happen in the other. Particular contingent events, as well as the irreducible embeddedness of mechanisms in a historically sedimented social reality which has not lost its historicity or particularity, will make for differences of all sorts.

Accordingly, capitalist societies were not 'inevitable'; nor is it inevitable that capitalist societies will be replaced by this or that form of society. If there are laws of capitalism (as I believe there are), we *can* say that some forms will be *likely* and others *unlikely.* Not only do the existing social processes have tendencies, but the materials at hand, the social materials 'exploitable' by the existing generation, make some transformations of these more likely than others. Yet, as before, how agents exploit what is given and how currently unforeseen structural conjunctures will affect action in the future are unknown and at present unknowable. And, as before, this is exactly the same situation, logically, as in physical science.

As Giddens has emphasized, there is no eliminating time from social science, which means, as the foregoing has suggested, that a distinction between social science and history is an abstract distinction, which in the final analysis is not sustainable. At the same time, the interests (and abilities) of inquirers vary. Some will concentrate on 'ethnography', focusing on how members understand their social world (Geertz, Garfinkel); others will emphasize abstract structure (de Saussure, much neo-Marxism). Some will write 'sociological' history (Fustel de Coulanges, Weber, Marc Bloch, Braudel, Perry Anderson, Eric Wolf); some will write historically oriented social science (Barrington Moore, C. W. Mills, Arendt, Beer, Bendix, Galbraith, Tilly, Sahlins); and some will concentrate on historical narrative, taking for granted the underlying structural considerations or calling our attention to them only as needed (Hobsbawm, Christopher Hill, E. P. Thompson, Gordon Wood, LeFebvre, Hexter, Avrich, Genovese).

The disciplines of the social sciences

The divorce of history from social science was in some ways the most devastating development in the Americanization of social science. This and the arbitrary branching of the social sciences led to institutionalized impoverishment. The problem here is different from that in physical science, since, whereas a physical science can develop a theory of a stratum of physical reality – for example, molecular chemistry – and thereby produce genuine knowledge, it is not clear that social reality is stratified in the appropriate way. That is, because individuals are socialized into society, and not into specific, discrete, and isolable practices; because the materials for the constitution of practices – beliefs, skills, and so on – often overlap; and because society exists only as incarnate in practices, efforts to 'decompose' society into its 'parts' and then analyse these will inevitably be problematic. Indeed, although we can think of society as a 'whole' comprised of connected structured practices, it is not, for the foregoing reasons, like an organism or some complicated physical system. These metaphors, useful up to a point, simply break down. Thus, while there are different practices (even different kinds of practices) and an inevitable connectedness between them, they are not 'parts' nor 'pieces'. There are, of course, 'households', and people raise families; and there are schools and places of worship, play, and work, but it is the same people who raise families, go to work, pray, and play.

We do, of course, identify practices as 'political', 'economic', 'familial', and so on, but from the present point of view, these are but 'theoretical' distinctions, subject to critique by more refined and more powerful theory; and in any case, this fact is perfectly consistent with the foregoing. The upshot is that any division of labor as regards the attempt to theorize structures and their relations can, ultimately, be defended as no more than a convenience. Indeed, as I argued in part I [of AHPSS], the division of labor in the social sciences was not a consequence of any independent 'givenness of social reality' (even in physical science, there is no such), but of circumstances and events whose outcome had very little to do with the disinterested pursuit of 'truth'.

On the other hand, even after distinguishing between the explanatory sciences and 'sciences' with other concerns, such as 'applied science' and 'social research', there may still be a justification for some sort of division of labor *within* explanatory social science. The idea that the special interests of the inquirer and the need for special skills and training leads an inquirer to develop ideas about but one aspect (the word is chosen carefully) of a society seems plausible enough. Thus, for the purposes of construction of theory, some restricted ensemble of practices may be the focus of inquiry. One might then have, to use Poulantzas's useful terminology, 'regional theories' – for example, of the contemporary democratic state of the United States, of 'the world-economy', the health-care system of Great Britain, or the New York City school system.

But there are dangers. One is the temptation to leap to an illicit universalizing generalization and to assume that what is true of the particular practices under study is true of all such practices (Manicas, 1985). Language gets in our way. After all, schools are schools, agricultural work is agricultural work. On the present view, however, as concrete historical forms, they cannot lose their historicity and particularity. Another danger is the temptation to forget the embeddedness of practices in the ensemble, so that these become one-sidedly severed from their connections. The result is explanatory reductionism in which one causal factor pretends to explain everything.[11]

Finally, if, as Montesquieu, Marx, and Weber insisted, society is a 'totality', there still might be practices which are theorized as *primary* in the sense that they are causally fundamental. This is, of course, the locus of the Marxist concept of 'historical materialism' and the critical role of 'mode of production'. But, as I argued in chapter 6 {of AHPSS}, this will not do as a theory of history. It also has problems as a theory of society, whether in the familiar 'base/superstructure' formulation or in the more recent versions of Althusser and others. While I believe that the idea can be rescued and is important, this is not the place to attempt a defense (but see Manicas, 1985; Giddens, 1985, pp. 135f.).

The program of behavioral social science

I want to round out this chapter with a more specific comparison between the dominating mainstream paradigm and the realist alternative just sketched. This will bring into sharper focus the contrast between the definition of the task and nature of explanatory social science as conceived here and the mainstream conception. My point of departure is a recent text in behavioral research by Kerlinger (1979) and an actual study described therein.

The study is Marjoribanks's 'competent and imaginative study of influences on mental ability'. The dependent variable was 'mental development', which was measured by four subtests of a standard test, the SRA Primary Abilities Test: verbal, number, spatial, and reasoning. There were two independent variables, 'environmental press' and ethnic group membership, or 'ethnicity'. 'Environmental press' was measured in terms of eight 'environmental forces': 'press for achievement', 'press for intellectuality', and so on. Each in turn was specified by several indices. Marjoribanks's sample consisted of 37 families. From the quantified data derived therefrom, Marjoribanks did several multiple regressions, which are partially summarized in Table 1.

Table 1 Variances accounted for by environment and ethnicity, Majoribanks (1972) study[a]

Dependent variable	*Independent variable*	R^2	
Verbal ability	Environment + ethnicity (A)	0.61	
	Environment (B)	0.50	
	Ethnicity (C)	0.45	
	Effect of ethnicity alone = A − B =		0.11
	Effect of environment alone = A − C =		0.16
Reasoning ability	Environment + ethnicity (A)	0.22	
	Environment (B)	0.16	
	Ethnicity (C)	0.08	
	Effect of ethnicity alone = A − B =		0.06
	Effect of environment alone = A − C =		0.14

Note

a This table was derived from Majoribanks, tables 5 and 6. It is in a somewhat different form from his tables.

Quoting Kerlinger's conclusions regarding this study:

> Taking the values of Table 1 at face value, we can reach two or three conclusions. Both environment and ethnicity seem to have considerable 'influence' on verbal ability, especially when they 'work together' (34 per cent). Their contributions alone, while not large, are appreciable (11 per cent and 16 per cent). The 'influence' of environment independent of ethnicity appears to be larger than the 'influence' of ethnicity independent of environment (16 per cent versus 11 per cent). A similar analysis can be applied to reasoning ability. We note especially that environment and ethnicity are not nearly as strongly related to reasoning ability as verbal ability. It is not hard to understand this rather important [sic] finding. The reason is left to the reader to deduce.
>
> (p. 176)

Kerlinger is conscientious in warning his readers that, with more than two independent variables, 'analysis and interpretation become much more complex, difficult and even elusive'. Worse, like all methods of statistical analysis, this method (multiple regression) yields only estimates of the values of the R^2s (p. 177). Finally, and 'perhaps above all, researchers will be extremely cautious about making causal statements'.

> Even though we used expressions like 'accounted for' and 'effects', causal implications, while perhaps inescapable because of language connotations, were not intended. . . . When we talk about the influence of ethnicity on verbal ability, for example, we certainly intend the meaning that the ethnic group to which a child belongs influences his verbal ability – for obvious reasons. The more accurate research statement is that there are differences in verbal ability between say, Anglo-Saxon Canadians and French Canadians. But this is a functional difference in ability in the English language. We do not mean that being Anglo-Saxon, in and of itself, somehow 'causes' better verbal ability in general than being French Canadian. The safest way to reason is probably the conditional statement emphasized through this book: If *p*, then *q*, with a relative absence of causal implication.
>
> (p. 177)

The foregoing suggests a number of important points. It shows, first, that methodologists in the social sciences are aware that a host of ordinary language expressions have, as Kerlinger says, 'causal implications', that 'influences' (notice the scare quotes in the foregoing), 'effects', 'is due to', 'accounted for', and others ordinarily connote causal efficacy in exactly the realist sense that causes *bring about their* effects.

This is the second point. On the standard (Humean) view, Kerlinger should not be uncomfortable since, on this view, 'if *p*, then *q*' is sufficient for causality. And if so, then, as the Marjoribanks study shows, since 'being Anglo-Saxon' is regularly associated with superior verbal ability, we have the causal expression 'If someone is Anglo-Saxon, then there is a probability K that this person will have verbal ability superior to. . . .' As Paul Lazarsfeld, an eminent methodologist, long ago pointed out:

> If we have a relationship between 'x' and 'y' and if for any antecedent test factor the partial relationships between 'x' and 'y' do not disappear, then the original relationship should be called a causal one. It makes no difference here whether the necessary operations are actually carried through or made possible by general reasoning.
>
> (Lazarsfeld, 1955, p. 125)

Lazarsfeld, a theorist of social science, is here consistently Humean. A matter-of-fact connection warrants the imputation of causality, for that is all that causality can mean. But Kerlinger, a pedagogue of social scientists, is not a consistent Humean. While, for him, *in the ordinary sense*, 'the ethnic group to which a child belongs influences his verbal ability – for obvious reasons', the 'more accurate' research statement is that there is a measurable difference in verbal ability between Anglo-Saxon Canadians and French Canadians. What could 'influence' here mean except that there is something about *being* Anglo-Saxon or French Canadian which *brings about* this difference? And while Kerlinger is baffled by how simply 'being Anglo-Saxon' could be a cause, it is for him, nonetheless, 'obvious' that being such 'influences' verbal ability.

In terms of the foregoing account there is no mystery here, of course. 'Ethnicity' is incarnate in speakers. The causality is complicated, but the idea is clear. If one is reared in an Anglo-Saxon household, one *learns* English as one learns the styles, customs, and rules of Anglo-Saxons!

Moreover, on the standard empiricist account of explanation, law-like statements can function in explanatory and predictive contexts. The explanation (or prediction) takes the form of *modus ponens*: If *p*, then *q* (covering law); *p*, therefore *q* (event to explained or predicted). To be sure, as Kerlinger notes, 'such explanations are necessarily only partial and incomplete', and, equivalently, predictions are not certain. This is because there are many variables, and their relationships will be complex. There are 'influences' on verbal ability other than 'ethnicity', and no one pretends that they have all been identified in their exact relation to the dependent variable. Nevertheless, this is not disheartening, since it merely sets the agenda for further research. As a psychologist faced with the same problem recently pointed out: 'The only way psychologists will ever come to understand complex psychological causation is to analyse variables, one by one, sub-set by sub-set, until whole systems of variables are understood' (Stroud, 1984, p. 92). Before concluding this chapter, I want to show that this research program is futile. But first we need to see how 'theory' relates to the foregoing.

Theory and explanation

Kerlinger says, 'A *theory* . . . is a set of interrelated constructs (variables), definitions, and propositions that presents a systematic view of phenomena by specifying relations among the variables, with the purpose of explaining the phenomena' (Kerlinger, 1979, p. 64). As far as I know, no one has ever given a very clear example of a real social-scientific theory spelled out so as to fit Kerlinger's definition. Presumably, everyone has the general idea, and that is sufficient. In his book, Kerlinger 'represents' a theory (of his own contrivance) by a picture (see Figure 1).

This 'small theory' seems close to the one Marjoribanks employed in his study. It will suffice in any case. Presumably, a researcher recognizes a pattern and generates some hypotheses regarding the relationships involved. He or she then seeks to specify quantitatively the variables involved and to discover, through analytic techniques, their precise relationships. Theory will serve to 'interpret' the results.

Consider then the relation between 'intelligence' and 'school achievement'. We may guess that the correlation here will be quite high and positive. But is it merely a correlation? Consider the statements: (1) If a person

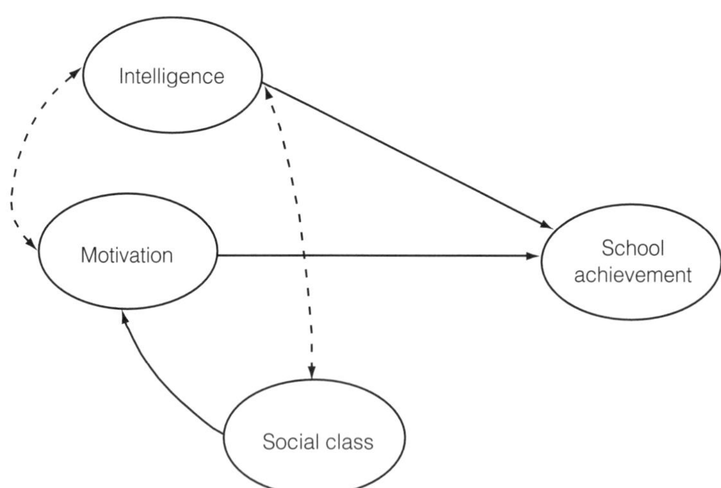

Figure 1 Kerlinger's 'small theory'

scores well on standard intelligence tests, then there is a probability *K* that he or she will be a high achiever in school, and (2) If salt is put in water, then there is a probability *K* that it will dissolve. *Formally*, these are identical. As regards the second there is surely a causal relationship. Indeed, it is an implication of a third statement, that salt is water-soluble, where 'water-soluble' refers to a causal power of salt (see chapter 12 [of AHPSS]). In this case, moreover, we have theoretical knowledge of that causal power, of why it is that salt tends to dissolve in water.

Can similar things be said about the first statement? Plainly, there is some sort of real (non-spurious) relationship between school achievement and intelligence. It is not like a high correlation, say, between the price of eggs in China and sales of the *Wall Street Journal.* But is there anything in the statement corresponding to 'water-soluble' in the third statement?

Now I do not for a moment doubt that there is, and that, therefore, one can, anti-naturalisms in the philosophy of social science notwithstanding, pursue the idea that social science searches for causes. But it will be a fundamental point of the following that the behavioral researcher, following the empiricist methodology set out by Kerlinger (and countless others!) forbids one to do exactly what is necessary in order to advance our knowledge about what it is that corresponds to 'water-soluble'.

The point involves a tangle which takes some unravelling. It takes us back to the critique of Durkheim and involves much of what was said in this chapter and the last [of AHPSS]. In a nutshell, Kerlinger grasps that understanding is what science is all about, but at the same time, his empiricist commitments to methodological individualism, Humean causality, and theory as an 'interpreted' system of axioms leads him to misconstrue 'understanding' and identify it with prediction and control.

In the preceding example, 'water-soluble' refers to a causal power of salt, made intelligible by means of a grasp of theorized natural structures and their dispositional properties, to NaCl, H_2O, and their nomic relations. A moment's reflection will lead one to see that in the first statement what corresponds to 'water-soluble' is *a social mechanism which depends on a set of structured practices*, including for example, the system of intelligence testing, the measures it employs, the nature of the tests and quizzes which are used to grade students for 'achievement', and so on. Just as a theory of the chemical properties of things gives us an understanding of the pattern 'salt tends to dissolve in water', we need a (regional) theory about schools, the structuring of their practices, and the relation of these to other causally relevant structures – those of class, the state, and so forth.

The 'small theory' represented in Kerlinger's picture (Figure 1) is not wrong so much as seriously misleading, because it *seems* to explain but in fact does not do so. It does this exactly because we take for granted exactly what is needed to do the job of explaining. We 'know', however unreliably, something about the practices of schools. This, in fact, is 'the general reasoning' referred to by Lazarsfeld in the text quoted above. Such 'general reasoning' does indeed make it plausible that sometimes relationships among 'variables' are causal. *It is the real theory in the background of such analyses*, a real, but unstated theory, which fools us into believing that the theory which is up front, the 'partial relationships' among 'dependent' and 'independent variables', is in any way explanatory.

Behavioral researchers are misled in part because they think of their equations as being on a par with the mathematical representations familiar to physical theorists, or at least with the familiar construction of them in textbooks and standard accounts in the philosophy of science. But, as was argued in the last chapter [of AHPSS], one must consider what in physics or chemistry these representations represent, what they do, and how they function.

In these physical sciences, the meanings of the key concepts, symbols, and principles are not part of the explicit representation; in marked contrast to the situation with 'theories' of behavioral research, the meanings are part of a *well-established theory into which scientists are socialized* – not as in behavioral research, *the unarticulated meanings of what is taken for granted.* The point is central, for it is precisely here that ideology enters and wreaks its damage. This, indeed, is Veblen's point about 'the vulgar commonplace convictions' – racism, sexism, nationalism, and the 'prepossessions prevalent among those well-to-do classes'.

It is easy to forget that training to be a physicist or a biologist involves learning an enormous amount which is *unspoken*, but without which the continuing practice of science is impossible. Moreover, the implications of the genuine revolution in the received view of theory, the centrality of iconic models, of non-propositional ideas, non-deductive relationships, and intentional meanings, seem not to have made an impact on behavioral researchers. 'Theory' remains for them 'a set of interrelated constructs', innocently void of a host of meanings and assumptions which never get articulated. Physical scientists acquire the 'surplus meaning' of well-established theories in learning their craft; we are all socialized into society. Hence, it would be amazing if commonsensical 'knowledge' did not play a vital role in providing the background meaning of 'hypotheses' in social science. Indeed, it is, *unavoidable.* What is avoidable, however, is the *uncritical appropriation* of this stock of ideas. Plainly this cannot be done if, as is the case, it is not even acknowledged that 'general reasoning' is playing this explanatory role. Doesn't everyone know that women are loving and non-aggressive, that Polynesians are not ambitious, and that in a free society, if you try hard enough, you will succeed?

There is also the question of the goals of science. Kerlinger wrote that 'science is an enterprise exclusively concerned with knowledge and understanding of natural phenomena. Scientists want to understand things' (1979, p. 3). If Kerlinger is talking about the ideal of what we have called 'theoretical science' (the classical ideal of science), then this formulation is exactly correct, and it is a main point of this book to defend such a conception. Science is not one thing, however; nor – and this is more important for the present point – is behavioral research as it is practiced as interested in understanding as it is in prediction and control. Kerlinger would argue, perhaps, that to say this is to cavil; that unless the word 'understanding' is being used in some special sense, as in the way that *verstehen* sociologists use it, for example, then understanding, prediction, and control are *inherently* related. As we know, on the standard covering law model of explanation, explanation and prediction are perfectly symmetrical.

It is surely true that advances in our understanding of the properties which lie behind the manifest phenomena of the world have given us a greatly increased ability to generate technologies. Examples abound, from the biochemical knowledge of growth which has yielded improved fertilizers to the physical knowledge of the atom which has yielded weapons of horrifying destructive power. And in this sense, we increasingly make 'nature' subject to our wills. Understanding is thus connected to 'control', if control is the capacity to put natural processes to use; but 'control' in this sense is not prediction.

We can, in fact, often predict very well without having the slightest understanding; and, conversely, we can understand very well and be utterly unable to predict. We can predict when we have a reliable regularity, one that exists independently of our intervention or because of it. But in neither case, do we need to understand why the pattern occurs, what its causes are, or, in the case where we bring about some effect through some act, why our action has the predictable effect it has. Humans can predict rain by observing that, in general, ominous clouds of a characteristic sort precede it. They do not need an understanding of temperature, dewpoint, the physics of condensation, and so on. Similarly, people knew how to make a fire long before they had any understanding of combustion.

On the other hand, we can understand very well the mechanisms of combustion and fail to predict a catastrophic hotel fire. This is both typical and unsurprising. As was argued in the last chapter, what happens in the world is always the result of complex causation, so that even patterns are often and easily upset. That is, radical contingency is consistent with the lawfulness of the structures of reality. Perhaps this is obvious enough. But if it is, then why does Kerlinger assert, immediately after saying that 'science is . . . exclusively concerned with knowledge and understanding', that scientists 'want to be able to say: If we do such-and-such, then so-and-so will happen' (1979, p. 17). *Understanding has suddenly collapsed into instrumental control.*

It is clear why. If 'theory' is nothing more than 'relations of variables', and variables 'must be observable or potentially measurable or manipulable' (p. 62), then understanding necessarily becomes synonymous with prediction or instrumental control. For purposes of methodological incantations, at least, there is no surplus meaning in theory, and theory does not offer a representation of the structures of reality, structures and processes which, when cognized, would give an understanding but not, by themselves, the ability to predict or control. Theoretical science has been collapsed into its twentieth-century industrialized counterpart, technocratic science.

There is an analog to theoretical physical science in current social science. To go back to our example, if one is interested in understanding differential school achievement, then one is advised to consider the writings of Paul Goodman, John Holt, Jonathan Kozol, Charles Silberman, Stephen Steinberg, and Samuel Bowles and Herbert Gintis. Their 'theories' are not 'sets of interrelated variables', and they do not look much like the mathematical models of textbook 'theories'. Nevertheless, the writers are interested in explaining the patterns which the practices of schools generate, and they see that to do this, one must have an understanding of the underlying, connected social mechanisms. That such analyses raise the hackles of the establishment would not have surprised Veblen – or Marx.

Causal analysis and the analysis of variation

Readers may not yet be persuaded that the realist alternative *is* an alternative; that, on the one hand, the works of the writers just cited seem hardly 'scientific', and on the other, that theory in behavioral research is aimed at discovering the causes of phenomena and that quantitative methods remain the best means to that end. I want now to argue that, if the search for causes is the aim of the standard research program, that program is futile. The reason for this is straightforward: causes are not additive, and all the quantitative methods in current use must assume that they are.

Let us return for a moment to Marjoribanks's study. The basic question was 'How do environmental force and ethnicity affect mental development?' (Kerlinger, 1979, p. 173). As seems clear, mental development is the causal outcome of a complex epigenetic process which begins with conception and ends with the death of the organism. A particular genome, itself the product of the conjunction of haploid sex cells is, in embryogenesis, the locus of continuous transactions both in itself and in relation to its 'environment'. It subsequently emerges from the womb and is then in continuous transaction with a human environment. Through both of these conditions, as biologist Paul Weiss says, 'the latitude for epigenetic vagaries of the component elements on all levels . . . is immense'.

Marjoribanks aims to tackle a piece of these complicated problems and to do this by discovering how each of the independent variables separately affects mental development and how they affect it in concert (1979, p. 173). It is not denied, of course, that heredity influences mental development. The aim, presumably, is to better understand the role of social factors. I earlier summarized the sources of the data. What is now needed is to calculate several regression equations. These are of the form: $Y = a + b_1X_1 + b_2X_2$, where Y is the dependent variable (for example, mental development); a is a constant which is irrelevant for present purposes; X_1 and X_2 are independent variables (for example, 'environmental force' and 'ethnicity'); and b_1 and b_2 are regression coefficients, which, as multipliers of the independent variables, weight them, as is obvious. Moreover, as is also obvious, the independent variables are taken to have additive features.

Determining the regression coefficients is not easy, but the details need not trouble us here. All that is necessary here is to emphasize that 'regression equations give the best possible prediction given sets of data. No other equation will give us as good a prediction' (p. 170). That is, the test of the adequacy of any particular equation will be its predictive success, given the set of data.

The upshot then will be the determination of R, the coefficient of multiple correlation. This is determined by correlating two sets of scores, the Ys calculated ('predicted') from the regression equations and the actual Ys, as specified by independent measures of Y. Given R, we can then calculate R^2, which expresses the variance of the dependent variable accounted for by the regression combination of the independent variables.

To recur to the study (see Table 1 above), the correlation between verbal ability, a measure of mental development, and the combination of environment and ethnicity (as measured by Marjoribanks's various measures), R, was 0.78, and thus R^2 was 0.61. This means that '61% of the variance of verbal ability was accounted for by environment and ethnicity in combination'. Separate regressions between verbal ability and environment and between verbal ability and ethnicity yielded 0.50 and 0.45, respectively. By subtracting these from 0.61 we get 'the separate effects' of environment and ethnicity; thus 16 per cent of the variance in verbal ability is 'accounted for' by environment alone.

This perhaps unduly detailed summary, unnecessary for those familiar with the technique, has at least made clear that if this is causal analysis, causes must be additive. But of course, except for mechanical causation, represented by vectors of forces, causes are not additive. In consequence, the foregoing 'analysis' is almost totally *meaningless.*

The near meaninglessness of this 'competent and imaginative study' is perhaps most convincingly demonstrated by comparing it to typical studies in biology which study the relationship of 'heredity' to 'environment'.

If we take a particular genotype – for example, seeds replicated by inbreeding or cloning (this minimizes genotypic individuality, a dominant feature of human genotypes) – and place specimens in various controlled environments, it is possible to establish rough tables of correspondence between phenotype on the one hand, and genotype-environmental combinations on the other. The results, *never predictable in advance*, give what is called 'the norm of reaction' of that genotype, its 'range of reaction' to environmental variations. Now, it is not possible to predict these norms because – and this is crucial – 'genetic' and 'environmental' factors are not additive. They are *causes in transaction*, which are not independent and which do not interact like vectors of force. That is, because 'genes' cause different outcomes in different transactions, and because the developmental process is mediated and transactional, the latitude for vagaries, as Weiss noted, is immense. Of course, it is not unlimited, and thus one can arrive empirically at norms of reaction in such cases.

Multiple regression techniques are *not* meaningless *given* that such norms *have been established experimentally.* Across a range of environments in which independent variables have been specified and controlled, one can relate the variability in outcome with changes in the independent variables. In a word, one can produce meaningful R^2s. This will not, it should be emphasized, show what proportion of the causation is attributable to what component, since causation does not suddenly become additive. One will have, however, a satisfactory analysis of the variations.

There is a parallel here to Marjoribanks's study, yet there is a gigantic difference. As regards Marjoribanks's project, there is no experimental way to establish norms of reaction. In the first place, we are limited morally. We cannot clone fetuses and establish them in strictly controlled environments. But were this permissible, there would still be no way to specify all the relevant environmental variables, precisely because they are not independent. The social world is real enough, but the mere fact that, *necessarily*, the social world is mediated by consciousness makes it impossible to say how controlled changes are related to what stays the same and how the new condition is then *experienced* by agents. Compare here a change in the amount of nitrogen in the soil as it bears on the development of a cloned seed of grain and a change in the physical environment of an infant on development. Clearly, causes are profoundly mediated in the course of an organism's development, and even the language of transaction – as opposed to interaction – is a radical oversimplication of the causal reality.

Of course, social scientists, including here psychologists, have always known this, and we may assume that this is *a* reason why prediction becomes the sole test of the adequacy of the measures and equations. We simply rework the specifications and relations, from 'predicted' to actual, until we get a good fit. But the justification in terms of 'good prediction' is profoundly reinforced by Humean assumptions about causality and by technocratic assumptions about 'explanation'

On the covering law model, explanation and prediction are symmetrical, and with this conception of explanation, it is necessary only that there is a constant relation between the independent and the dependent variable. Given the extraordinary limits on experimentation in the social sciences, it is no wonder, then, that regression techniques, path analyses, and so on are so attractive. Given all these assumptions, one can be a real scientist without having a theory and without ever doing a real experiment. All we need is data – and plenty of it!

Notes

1 Included here are books by Jay (1973), Poster (1975), Pettit (1975), Bernstein (1976), Anderson (1976, 1980, 1983), Giddens (1976, 1979), Buck-Morss (1977), Bhaskar (1979), Kurzweil (1980), McCarthy (1981), James (1984), and Skinner (1985).

2 Rorty has defended these ideas in his *Consequences of Pragmatism* (1982). In the essay 'Method, social science, social hope', he argues that the old argument between 'behaviorese' and 'hermeneutics' are differences between different 'jargons' – not to be resolved but lived with. 'There is no connection between "explanation" and "understanding" – between being able to predict and control people in a certain way and being able to sympathize and associate with them, to view them as fellow citizens' (p. 198). It is plain that Rorty believes that social science is aimed at 'prediction and control' and as such, is 'useful'. Perhaps a consequence of Rorty's dismissal of the idea that social science can and ought to aim at an understanding of how things stand and why, is his belief that 'we should be more willing than we are to celebrate bourgeois capitalist society as the best polity actualized so far, while regretting that it is irrelevant to most of the problems of most of the population of the planet' (p. 210). See also Rorty, 1986, 'From logic to language to play', *Proceedings and Addresses of the American Philosophical Association*, 59.

3 The connectedness of so many of the themes in the recent debate has tended to go unnoticed, a point to be emphasized in the next chapter [of AHPSS]. We will re-emphasize here, however, that as Margolis (1984, *Philosophy of Psychology*, Englewood Cliffs, N.J.: Prentice-Hall) has pointed out, the assumption that the language of science must be an extensional language has fuelled an immense amount of discussion in recent accounts of a proper science. Thus, the 'translation' program (reduction-sentence, operational definition, and so on) of empiricism presupposed that scientific sentences expressed in a natural language could be re-expressed in a wholly extensionalist language. A language is said to be extensional if (to quote Margolis):

1 In its sentences, the substitution of codesignative expressions does not alter the truth-value of the resultant sentence. [That is, synonomy, an intensional (meaning) relation, gives way to extensional equivalence, identity of reference] . . .

2 For its compound and complex sentences, truth-values are a function only of the truth-values of its constitutive clauses [the connectives of *Principia Mathematica* are the only ones to be employed; thus causality must be rendered as of the form $(x)(Fx \rightarrow Gx)$].

3 For those clauses, the substitution criterion is satisfied.

It is easy to show, unsurprisingly, that so-called 'intentional contexts', for example, 'Tom believes that Cicero denounced Catiline', resist this treatment; thus, it was not unexpected that behaviorist efforts at 'translations of' psychological predicates also fail. But the problem was not merely the 'intentionality' of the mental, but the fact that the problem of meaning, of the intensional, takes one to the *social.* See below for a sketch of language (as a social structure) depending upon practices, and the next chapter [of AHPSS] for the bearing of this on psychology.

4 We might keep the word, of course, and have it identify a *different* practice. Compare 'democracy' ancient and modern. See Barnes, 1982, *T.S. Kuhn and Social Science*, New York: Columbia University Press, pp. 27–35.

5 Kurzweil (1980, *The Age of Structuralism: Lévi-Strauss to Foucault*, New York: Columbia University Press) remarks that 'Foucault's archeology must reject

subjectivity. Authors, works, and language are said to be objects in search of a logic independent of grammars, vocabularies, synthetic forms, and words' (p. 207), an excellent example of the trap just noted.

6 This was a key theme in the writings of John Dewey and George Herbert Mead, especially in *Human Nature and Conduct* (1922; New York: Holt) and those writings of Mead's collected as *Mind, Self and Society* (1934, Chicago: University of Chicago Press). But strange as it may seem, the full force of these writings *never* had an impact on social science. Instead, what one got was a 'social psychology' with a pervasive misconstrual of 'the social'. See chapter 14 [of AHPSS].

7 The example is deliberately provocative. The 'may' in 'may be an unintended consequence' is all the argument needs. Such is the nature of the social reality currently sustained by *all* our activities.

8 Structure and freedom are not counterposed, as in radical existentialisms. For an emphatic individualist explication of 'the voluntary', see Nozick, 1974, *Anarchy, State and Utopia*, New York: Basic Books. This is almost a *reductio ad absurdum* of the position. On this view, involuntary acts are 'coerced', 'coercion' is physical force, and that is all that needs to be said.

9 Marx's *Capital*, despite its problems, is the best historical example of social theory as conceived here. 'Things', of course, are 'commodities' which are exchanged at the market price – everybody knows this. But we can explain why things, including labor-power, are commodities and the implications of this. Once accomplished, we can *understand* capitalism.

10 There is nothing precious in the label 'social science' as here conceived, especially since distinct alternative 'genres', particularly literature, may quite successfully offer us knowledge of persons and society. See Kenneth Burke, 1971, *The Philosophy of Literary Form*, Baton Rouge: Louisiana State University Press, and Clifford Geertz, 1973, *The Interpretation of Cultures*, New York: Basic Books. The analogue to theoretical physical science is a social science which seeks causal knowledge. But plainly, not only are there many other important things to know about persons and society, but we sometimes get causal knowledge from alternative genres.

11 An excellent recent example is world-systems theory. Wallerstein and his colleagues have done a genuine service in insisting that there is a global dynamic which has interconnected effects on 'economies'. But instead of making this one of the causally relevant factors, world-systems theory has tended to displace or reduce to marginality all other causes. See Giddens, 1985, *The Nation State and Violence*, Berkeley: University of California Press, pp. 161–70.

13

FOUR CONCEPTS OF SOCIAL STRUCTURE

Douglas V. Porpora

Social structure is one of the most central concepts in sociology. Yet there is wide disagreement about what it means. This disagreement is consequential because differences in the way sociologists conceptualize social structure lead to very different approaches to sociology. The purpose of this paper is two-fold. First, because there is so much dispute about what social structure means or should mean, in the first part of this paper I will simply present without argument four different conceptions of social structure that are prominent in the field. Although the alternative conceptions I will examine are not necessarily exhaustive, they do represent what are probably the most commonly held views. Examining them, therefore, should significantly advance our thinking on this important but elusive concept. The second objective of this paper, which I will pursue in a subsequent discussion, is to make a case in favor of one of these four alternatives, namely one that traditionally has been associated with Marx.

As far as the views that will be considered are concerned, social structure refers to one of the following:

1 Patterns of aggregate behavior that are stable over time
2 Lawlike regularities that govern the behavior of social facts
3 Systems of human relationships among social positions
4 Collective rules and resources that structure behavior

The first conception is most closely associated with exchange theorists, notably Homans (1975), and some symbolic interactionists, but most recently has been given a strong defense by Collins (1981). Looking at Collins's defense in particular, I will argue that this conception leads to a methodological individualist approach to sociology that is ultimately unable

Source: Journal for the Theory of Social Behaviour, 19, 2, 1989, pp. 195–211.

to explain a wide range of macrosocial phenomena such as deindustrialization, power and economic crisis. The second conception represents the view of the so-called Structural Sociologists —theorists like Blau (1970; 1977), Mayhew (1980) and Turner (1984). It fosters a holistic approach to sociology that, I argue, cannot achieve its own stated goals. In contrast with all of the other conceptions, the fourth does not conceptualize social structure in terms of organizational properties of social systems but rather in terms of shared rules. It is traditionally associated with ethnomethodologists, some symbolic interactions, and other sociologists who employ a linguistic model to conceptualize social structure. Recently, it has been most forcibly defended by Giddens (1979; 1981; 1984) with whom it is now distinctively associated. I shall argue that because this conception, like the first, ends up reducing the organizational features of society to an epiphenomenon of human behavior, it too proves unable to account for the range of phenomena we expect social structure to explain. The third conception interprets social structure as a causal mechanism constituted by relationships among social positions that accounts for social phenomena in terms of tendencies, strains and forces inherent in the nexus of those relationships. Most closely associated with the more traditional variants of the Marxian tradition, it also has adherents among symbolic interactionists and network theorists.

The four conceptions of social structure

Structure as patterns of aggregate behavior that are stable over time

Two of the most prominent theorists to define social structure as stable patterns of aggregate behavior are George C. Homans and Randall Collins. "As used by sociologists," says Homans (1975: 53), " 'structure' seems to refer first to those aspects of social behavior that the investigator considers relatively enduring or persistent." Similarly, Collins (1981) defines social structure as "micro-repetition in the physical world."

> From a microviewpoint, what is the "social structure"? In microtranslation, it refers to people's repeated behavior in particular places, using particular physical objects, and communicating by using many of the same symbolic expressions repeatedly with certain other people.
>
> (Collins 1981: 995)

By microtranslation, Collins means the translation of all macrophenomena into microphenomena. "A microtranslation strategy reveals the empirical realities of social structures as patterns of repetitive micro-interaction" (Collins 1981: 985). Collins goes on to say that "strictly speaking, there is no such thing as a 'state', an 'economy', a 'culture', a 'social class'. There are only collections of individual people acting in particular kinds of microsituations – collections which are characterized thus by a kind of shorthand" (Collins 1981: 988). According to Collins, "The 'state' exists by virtue of there being courtrooms where judges repeatedly sit, headquarters from which police leave to ride in the same squad cars, barracks where troops are repeatedly housed and assembly halls where congresses of politicians repeatedly gather" (Collins 1981: 995).

Homans and Collins both advocate a reductionist approach to sociology, one that attempts to explain phenomena from the bottom up. Homans, of course, is well-known for his advocacy of methodological individualism. Collins does not go quite that far, but he too believes that "the dynamics as well as the inertia in any causal explanation of social structure must be microsituational" (Collins 1981: 990). In particular, Collins believes that all social phenomena, even the most macro, are built up by an ever expanding complex of conversational encounters, which he calls "interaction ritual chains." Like Homans, Collins disbelieves in the objective existence of collective entities:

> Social patterns, institutions, and organizations are only abstractions from the behavior of individuals and summaries of the distribution of different microbehaviors in time and space. These abstractions and summaries do not *do* anything; if they seem to indicate a continuous reality it is because the individuals that make them up repeat their microbehaviors many times, and if the 'structures' change it is because the individuals who enact them change their microbehaviors.
>
> (Collins 1981: 989)[1]

On this view, structure is defined in behavioral terms: In fact, structure is conceived as a form of behavior – stable or repeated behavior. Once structure is defined behaviorally, it becomes relatively easy to build the macro level up from the micro level. Microstructure consists of a few people repeating their behavior and macrostructure consists of a lot of people repeating their behavior. It also makes perfect sense why in the view of Homans and Collins the explanatory dynamic in social explanation must be at the micro level. Collins is certainly correct that if social structure is just an abstraction, social structure cannot be much of an independent variable; abstractions do not exhibit causal forces. Consequently, macrosocial structure is largely epiphenomenal. For that matter, microstructure is also epiphenomenal for the same reason. Since it is just an abstraction with no independent effects, it is not clear that structure is a very useful concept at all on this view.

Structure as lawlike regularities among social facts

The idea of social structure as lawlike regularities among social facts is traditionally associated with Durkheim and more recently with the school that has come to be called Structural Sociology (see, for example, Blau 1977; Mayhew 1980; Turner 1984). According to this view, social facts or group properties are related to each other by a pattern of lawlike regularities, which together constitute social structure. It follows that the job of the sociologist is to uncover those regularities through empirical observation and thereby describe social structure.

This conception of social structure leads to an approach to the discipline that is quantitative, positivist and sociologically holist. The approach tends to be quantitative because the regularities governing the behavior of social facts are generally construed to be relationships of what Durkheim called "concomitant variations." This means that quantitative variations in one social fact are related to quantitative variations in other social facts. The approach tends to be positivist in its assumption that the regularities are simply out there to be found without the aid of theory and in its strong affinity with the positivist covering law model of explanation. According to the covering law model, scientific explanation consists of subsumption under a law. For example, if there were a law specifying that if event A occurs, then event B must occur, then event B could be explained as a logical deduction from this law and the prior occurrence of event A. Of course, for the covering law model to work, phenomena actually need to be governed by such deterministic laws or at minimum by somewhat looser laws that at least specify invariant probabilities that the B event will occur (Porpora 1983; 1987).

Finally, this conception of social structure leads to a sociologically holist approach because it treats the behavior of social facts as a domain of phenomena that is completely autonomous of the psychological level. To see this, suppose there were a statistical law specifying that if group size increases by a particular amount, then there will be a 40 percent probability that group division of labor will increase by a particular amount. If such a law actually existed and if a group's size increased by the specified amount, then we could logically deduce that there is a 40 percent probability that the group's division of labor will increase by the specified amount *without knowing anything that is going on at the level of the individual actor*. If such a law existed, it would just make no difference to the science of sociology what was happening with the individual members of the group.

Because this conception of social structure rigidly divorces sociology from psychology, it represents social structure as something entirely devoid of the influence of human agency.[2] On this sociological holist view, social structure operates mechanically and naturalistically over the heads of individual actors.

Social structure as systems of human relations among social positions

The conception of social structure as systems of human relationships among social positions is most characteristically associated with the Marxian tradition. The systems referred to are characteristically modes of production while the social positions referred to are class positions. The human relationships are class and intraclass relations such as domination, competition and exploitation.

Clearly, this is hardly the only interpretation of Marx's conception of social structure, but it is a common and rather traditional one. I shall not attempt to show exegetically that it is the most faithful reading of Marx because my interest is more in the viability of this particular conception of social structure than in how closely it corresponds to Marx's original texts. This conception of social structure is not even limited to the Marxian tradition. Among others, some symbolic interactionists and network theorists adhere to it as well. Patriarchies and racial modes of exclusion can also be viewed as systems of relationships among social positions, although here the social positions will be defined in terms of gender and race rather than class. On the micro level too, the structure of units such as the family can be viewed as a system of relationships – those linking the husband/father, wife/mother, and children, all of which are social positions.

Just as the second conception of social structure we considered is closely tied to the positivist philosophy of science, there is a strong affinity between the concept of structure as a system of human relationships and the post-positivist philosophy of science advocated by the so-called realists (Benton 1981; Bhaskar 1975; 1979; Harré and Madden 1975; Isaac 1988; Manicas 1987 and Secord 1983; Outhwaite 1987). According to the realists, the world is a complex composite of entities, each having its own causal properties, i.e., tendencies, forces, and capabilities. These causal properties in turn are a function of each entity's internal structure. For example, by virtue of its internal structure, a table is causally capable of exerting a force upward that counteracts the force of gravity on objects placed on it. Similarly, because of our own more complex internal structure, we humans are causally capable of intervening in the world in a purposive way (Outhwaite 1987: 22).

It follows on the realist view that science has two tasks: to explain the causal properties of each entity in terms of its internal structure and to explain the occurrence of particular events in terms of conjunctures of the causal properties of various interacting mechanisms. Neither of these tasks involves the lawlike correlations among events that are so integral to the positivist covering law model of explanation. The first task does not even relate events but rather generating mechanisms and consequent causal properties. The second task explains events in terms of the operation of such causal properties, but since it is assumed that any causal mechanism can be counteracted by others, there is no expectation that events themselves will be invariably related to each other.

A system of relationships among social positions may itself constitute just the sort of causal mechanism that the realist philosophers have in mind. Capitalism, according to a Marxian analysis, is a case in point. According to the Marxian perspective, the internal structure of capitalism causally generates certain deleterious tendencies, some of which eventually alter the very nature of the system. For example, the competitive relationship among capitalists leads to a decline in their number that ultimately results in a concentration of wealth and the transformation of capitalism from a competitive to a monopoly phase. It is also the competitive pressure of capitalist relations that leads to the overaccumulation of productive potential and consequent crises of underconsumption. And it is the conflict of interests built into the relationship between capitalist and proletariat that produces the fundamental class struggle in the system. In a realist manner, Marxian analysis thus attempts to explain the tendential properties of capitalism in terms of capitalism's internal structure.

In contrast with the previous conception of social structure, this one is not a version of sociological holism. It does not portray social structure as something that operates over the heads of human actors. Instead, social structure is a nexus of connections among them, causally affecting their actions and in turn causally affected by them. The causal effects of the structure on individuals are manifested in certain structured interests, resources, powers, constraints and predicaments that are built into each position by the web of relationships. These comprise the material circumstances in which people must act and which motivate them to act in certain ways. As they do so, they alter the relationships that bind them in both intended and unintended ways.

Although this conception assumes that people are motivated to act on the interests structurally built into their social positions, the assumption is not a deterministic one. Interests always represent presumptive motives for acting, but actors may fail to recognize their interests, and even when they do recognize them, they may choose to act against them in favor of other considerations. However, since when actors fail to act in their interests they incur some cost, it is expected that actors generally will act in conformity with their interests. Even here, that does not necessarily mean that interests determine specific actions. Actors frequently respond to their structured interests in creative ways that in principle cannot be predicted in advance.

However they act, individuals affect the structural relationships that bind them in intended and unintended ways. Thus, according to this conception, there is a dialectical causal path that leads from structure to interests to motives to action and finally back to structure. The structural relationships and the various, often conflicting interests they generate are both the material conditions motivating action and the intended and unintended consequences of such action. This sounds very much like Giddens's well-known concept of the duality of structure. The crucial difference is in what Giddens means by structure. What Giddens means by structure are cultural rather than material conditions, and as we shall see in the discussion section, neither interests nor indeed any structured motive other than rule-following plays much role in Giddens's account.

Social structure as rules and resources

The conception of social structure as rules and resources is now distinctly associated with Anthony Giddens, who elaborates his meaning of structure as follows:

> Structures can be analysed as rules and resources, which can be treated as 'sets' in so far as transformations and mediations can be identified between the reproduced properties of social systems.
>
> (Giddens 1981: 26)

> A distinction is made between *structure* and *system*. Social systems are composed of patterns of relationships between actors or collectivities reproduced across time and space. Social systems are hence constituted of *situated practices*. Structures exist in time-space only as moments recursively involved in the production of social systems. Structures have only a virtual existence.
>
> (Giddens 1981: 26)

The distinction between Giddens's conception of social structure and the one we just examined in the previous section is clearly drawn in the second passage cited above. According to the third conception, social structure consists of those patterns of relationships that Giddens refers to as social systems. For Giddens, such patterns of relationships do not themselves constitute social structure. Rather, for Giddens, structure consists of the rules and resources associated with those relationships.

According to Giddens, rules and resources "structure" (i.e., generate and reproduce) the systemic patterns of relationships we see. He says, for example, that " 'structure' [i.e., rules and resources] refers to 'structural property', or more exactly to 'structuring property'," that reproduces the social system (Giddens 1979: 64). Thus, the difference between the third conception of social structure and Giddens's is that for the third, structure refers to the actual organization of society – the distribution of income, the division of labor, etc., – whereas for Giddens, structure refers to an organizing principle behind the actual organization, namely rules and resources.

According to the third conception, the constitutive relationships of social organization themselves have causal properties. The poor, for example, are constrained by the (relational) distribution of jobs in society or opportunity structure. In contrast, Giddens dismisses this conception of structure as naive (Giddens 1984: 16). He says that "Such conceptions are closely connected to the dualism of subject and social object: 'structure' here appears as 'external' to human action, as a source of constraint on the free initiative of the independently constituted subject" (Giddens 1984: 16). Instead, Giddens interprets social relationships in the same manner as Collins, that is as abstractions from our repetitive or routinized behavior (Giddens 1981: 26; 1984: xxiii, xxxi, 17). Thus, like Collins, Giddens denies that social relationships themselves have any independent causal properties. Of course, unlike Collins, Giddens does not tilt toward methodological individualism: he recognizes social mechanisms beyond the individual that generate and reproduce the relationships, namely rules, norms, ideology, and symbolic orders. In this regard as well, Giddens is something of a realist: for him, the rules, norms, etc., are all real causal mechanisms operating in the social world.

What Giddens does not embrace is materialism. The practical difference between Giddens's conception of structure and the third relates to the causal significance of objective, social relationships and more fundamentally to the analytical priority of those relationships vis-à-vis intersubjective rules, norms, ideologies, and symbolic orders. At bottom, this is a difference between a materialist and an idealist approach to sociology. As we have seen, Giddens characterizes the third conception as portraying structure as something external to the agent, and I think that this assessment is correct. On the same construal, rules, norms, ideology and symbolic orders are all internal to the collectivity of agents as cultural constructs that are intersubjectively shared. Thus, on Giddens's own rendering, we are talking about the difference between a concept of social structure as an objective reality and a concept of structure as an intersubjective reality.

To put this point another way, the rules, norms, etc. that Giddens considers to be structure all depend for their existence on their at least tacit acknowledgement by the participating agents. In this sense, they are not objective or material but cultural. Certain relationships, on the other hand, such as the relationship of people to job opportunities can exist across differences in norms or rules, regardless of whether or not any of the participating actors realizes that they are embedded in them (Benton 1981: 17). They thus represent objective, material circumstances external to the participating agents.

To give primacy to these material circumstances is not to embrace a reductive materialism in which human action is merely a deterministic reflection of material circumstances or in which human actors are mere "carriers of structure". The trick is to develop a nonreductive materialism that gives primacy to the material without embracing determinism. That is what the third conception of social structure attempts to do. The trick is easy enough to accomplish once we abandon the positivist understanding of causality as involving deterministic laws. We can then speak of the causal force that people's material circumstances exert on their behavior without making any deterministic claims about the ways in which that behavior is connected to those circumstances. We can admit the mediating role of ideology, norms, rules and symbolic orders while still maintaining an underlying connection between material circumstances and behavior.

For all of Giddens's talk about the *duality of structure* and *structuration*, Giddens does not offer us a framework resolving the tension between the material (or objective) and the ideal (or subjective) realms. He does not offer us even a nonreductive materialism. The duality of structure and structuration both refer to "the mutual dependence of structure and agency" (Giddens 1979: 69), to structure as both the cause and effect of human action (Giddens 1981: 27). If by structure Giddens meant something objective and material, the duality of structure and structuration would indeed reconcile the material and the ideal in a satisfactory way. However, as we have seen, by structure Giddens is essentially referring to rules, which belong as much to the subjective realm as agency. Thus, the duality of structure and structuration mediate only among different elements of the subjective realm and do not touch base with material circumstances.[3] It is largely for this reason that many of Giddens's critics have accused him of subjectivism (Callinicos 1985; Johnson *et al.* 1986; Turner 1986).

Discussion

I will begin the discussion with the second conception of social structure because I do not want to devote much space to it. I have criticized this position extensively elsewhere (Porpora 1983; 1987), and space prevents me from repeating myself. Here, I will simply sketch the argument that I think is decisive against it.

The search for lawlike connections among social facts capable of supporting explanations conforming to the covering law model is futile because as even the proponents of this enterprise concede (Blau 1970: 335–336; Mayhew 1980: 363), connections among social facts are mediated by intervening processes involving individual actors. The problem is that the behavior of individual actors does not conform to laws, not even to statistical laws. Thus, the relationships between the social facts connected by those intervening processes on the individual level cannot be lawlike either.

Consider, for example, the putative relationship between size and the division of labor that Structural Sociologists spend so much time on. Again, the Structural Sociologists concede that the relationship between these two variables is mediated by intervening processes involving individuals; the structural sociologists simply choose not to look at these intervening processes. However, given this concession, in order for there to be a lawlike relationship linking size and differentiation, size would have to affect individuals in some lawlike way, and the individuals so affected would have to respond in lawlike ways relating to differentiation. But since individual human behavior is not governed by such laws – not even statistical laws, the mediating processes involving individuals will not connect size and differentiation in a lawlike way either.

In the absence of such lawlike regularities, the covering law model of explanation is inapplicable, and all the search for laws yields is a set of statistical generalizations. Since such statistical generalizations do not meet the criteria of the covering law model that the Structural Sociologists themselves want to employ, it is not clear that these generalizations have any explanatory status at all. Instead, in order to really explain the relationship between size and differentiation in any particular case, the entire causal process linking the two will have to be examined, including the intervening part of the process involving individuals. Once we recognize this, we see that the whole enterprise of sociological holism – explaining social facts entirely in terms of social facts with no reference to individual behavior – cannot but fail.

The first conception of social structure we considered, the conception of social structure as stable patterns of aggregate behavior, is also rather weak. As we have seen, it reduces social structure to an epiphenomenon of individual human behavior. It may not be immediately apparent that this is a mistake. After all, in his important book, *The Credential Society*, Collins (1979) manages to make a major contribution to our understanding of stratification apparently without reference to social structure. Instead, Collins explains how elite social positions come to be monopolized by various subcultures comprised of common conversational styles, topics and assumptions. Following Bourdieu, Collins refers to the ability to fit into such subcultures as cultural capital. Depending on the group, such cultural capital can be acquired through either informal socialization or through formal organizations specifically designed for that purpose such as preparatory schools for the wealthy or professional schools for physicians, lawyers and managers. According to Collins, it is the gatekeeping control that various subcultures exercise over key positions that makes the pattern of stratification what it is.

Yet, however great Collins's contribution is to our understanding of stratification, we still need to ask whether he provides for a full account of it. Does he even identify the most fundamental element? I would submit that the answer to both questions is no. In fact, the very power of Collins's account is predicated on the existence of a prior system of social relationships. To see this consider two questions: First, why is the cultural capital of some groups such as organizational elites more advantageous than that of others such as common laborers? And second, how are the groups with the more advantageous cultural capital able to exercise their gatekeeping control? The answer to the first question is wealth and power while the answer to the second question is simply power. The question then is whether power is more properly construed as a behavior pattern or as a dispositional property inherent in a social position that is itself defined in relation to other social positions. If the latter view is more accurate, as I believe, then, once established, relationships are in an explanatory sense more fundamental than behaviors, and so the necessity becomes apparent for a more robust conception of social structure than Collins provides.

Collins believes that power and even social positions are mere abstractions of behavioral patterns (Collins 1979: 53, 59). Thus, according to Collins, power is simply an abstraction from the type of behavioral pattern that ensues when the more powerful interact with the less powerful. This, however, is a major mistake. It doesn't explain why in formal organizations, for example, the boss exhibits the behavior pattern of the powerful and the subordinate the behavior pattern of the less powerful. Why isn't it the other way around? The answer to that obviously is that the boss by virtue of his or her social position has certain prerogatives over the life of the person in the social position of subordinate. Those prerogatives include the abilities to fire, to promote, and to determine the pay and workload of the subordinate. The first point is that these abilities are not themselves behaviors but dispositional properties built into the social position of boss. Although these abilities never actually may be manifested, they are what explain the behavior pattern we see. The second point is that these abilities are dispositional properties of a social position (the boss) that only exists in relation to other social positions (the subordinates). In short, the power that explains whatever behavior patterns we observe is rooted in social relationships. It is for this reason that I say that the relationships are analytically prior to the behavior. (See Isaac 1988 for a more thorough critique of the behavioral approach to power along the same lines.)

Once we see that Collins's theoretical conception of social structure cannot even fully support his own contribution to our understanding of stratification, it becomes further apparent that it cannot account for all sorts of other social phenomena we expect a strong conception of social structure to explain. For example, a focus on behavior patterns and in particular on the face-to-face behavior patterns – the interaction ritual chains – that Collins stresses, cannot explain capital flight overseas, corporate insensitivity to the environment, or the capitalist push toward technological innovation. The explanation for all that resides in the competitive system of relationships among capitalists that characterize capitalism.

Collins might argue that the relationship of competition is only an abstraction from the competitive behavior of the capitalists, which is the only thing we see, but this again would be a mistake. In the first place, even if this were true, it would not be an abstraction from face-to-face behaviors of the capitalists. The capitalists often compete with rivals they never meet. In the second place, we do not actually see people competing in the economy;

we see them going to the factory or office, operating machines, pushing papers or closing deals. We know these people are competing because we realize as they do that the various business organizations are locked in a zero-sum game in which one's gain is another's loss. It is this zero-sum nature of the collective pursuit, again a relational property, that explains whatever competitive behavior patterns we observe – not the other way around. Again we observe the analytical priority of relationships to behavior.

The force of Collins's position comes from a certain nominalism. Collins does not believe in the objective existence of collective entities like nations, classes or relationships; he believes that these are only abstractions from aggregate patterns of behavior. As he says, quite legitimately, none of these things exists except insofar as they are instantiated by particular people behaving a certain way. In saying this, Collins evidently wants to avoid the problems with collective entities associated with structural functionalism. Again, that is a legitimate concern, but the logical problem with structural functionalism was not the positing of collective entities but the attribution of an illicit teleology to those entities that is properly ascribed only to agents like human beings (Agassi 1960; Turner & Maryanski 1979).

Collins's mistake is his nominalist assumption that only particulars are real. Following Collins's argument, we could say that human beings are only abstractions; in reality human beings are only billions of individual cells interacting with each other. Of course, we could continue to make this reductive argument until we arrive at elementary particles. At that point, however, a surprise awaits the reductionist. The findings of modern physics are clearly that at the level of rock bottom reality, relationships are more real than particulars (Barbour 1966; Davies 1984). As one physicist puts it, "An elementary particle is not an independently existing unanalysable entity. It is, in essence, a set of relationships that reach outward to other things" (H. P. Stapp; cited in Davies 1984: 49). The point is that if even physicists have come to recognize the objective existence of relationships, there is no reason for sociologists not to do so where warranted as well. As I have tried to argue, it is warranted.

Finally, let us turn our attention to Giddens's notion of structure as rules and resources. Here, it must be conceded that rules and relationships go together. In fact, to use Giddens's terminology, we might even say they are recursively related. Rules establish social positions that are related by differences in power. People in those social positions then use whatever power they have to change the rules in intended and unintended ways. This recursive process predates all individual actors and probably goes back to the origins of our species. As Bhaskar (1979) notes, human actors do not so much create society as recreate it in each generation. However, although rules and relationships go together, they are different. The question is which has analytical priority, rules or relationships. Giddens gives analytical priority to rules and in fact denies that the relationships of a social system have any causal properties independent of the rule-following activity of human actors. In the remainder of this section, I will argue that relationships do have such independent causal properties and, moreover, that such relationships, *once established*, are analytically prior to the *subsequent* rule-following behavior of actors.

The simplest place to consider the causal properties of relationships among social positions is the culture of poverty debate. At issue in that debate was why the poor remain poor. On one side were the culture of poverty theorists who attributed the persistence of poverty to cultural factors, to the resocialization of each new generation of poor people into rules and norms and ways of thinking that perpetuate their poverty. On the other side of the debate were those who attributed the persistence of poverty to the objective circumstances of the social position the poor find themselves in. One feature of those objective circumstances is the absence of the cultural capital to which Collins has called our attention. This essentially involves a reference to the distribution of resources, which Giddens also acknowledges. However, another feature of the objective circumstances of the poor relates to the distribution of jobs or social positions in society. Specifically, the poor stay poor partly because they do not have access to good jobs or even to jobs that although perhaps not good are stepping stones to better jobs. In theoretical terms, what we are talking about here are relational properties of a social system – the relationships of social positions (jobs) to each other and to space. We are talking, moreover, of the causal effects of those relationships on the life chances of the poor. Ultimately, we are talking of those relationships as precisely the sort of external constraint on action, the existence of which, as we have seen, Giddens wishes to deny. Giddens of course talks quite a bit about the distribution of systemic relationships over space, but, significantly, he talks about them largely as effect and not as cause. The causal role of objective relationships has no place in Giddens's core concepts of the duality of structure or structuration. Thus, to whatever extent there is merit in the objectivist position in the culture of poverty debate, Giddens's silence on the causal properties of objective relationships is a serious lacuna in his theory.

That lucuna is present as well in Giddens's treatment of domination. According to Giddens (1979: 93–94), domination is based on rules of authorization and allocation. By authorization, he means "capabilities which generate command over persons," and by allocation, he means "capabilities which generate command over objects" (Giddens 1979: 100). The question is who or what possesses these capabilities. It is not individuals qua individuals that possess these capabilities but rather individuals as incumbents of social positions. In other words, these capabilities are attached to social positions. They are in a sense the causal properties of those social positions.

It is not clear whether Giddens would deny the last point. Indeed, in some places, he seems to accept it (Giddens 1979: 117). However, if Giddens does accept that qua capabilities or resources, causal properties are deposited in social positions, then, since social positions only exist in relation to each other, this is tantamount to accepting an independent causal influence of systemic relationships on behavior, which is something that Giddens apparently does want to deny. (Benton 1981: 17 makes a similar point in relation to Bhaskar.)

The major thrust of Giddens's structuration theory, however, is that such social positions are just an abstraction from the rule-following behavior of actors. Giddens suggests that domination resides in the interactive behavior and that this behavior reconstitutes the domination by its reaffirmation of the rules through which it occurs. The problem is that rules make their entrance at two points in time, which Giddens conflates. For example, the positions of boss and subordinate in an organization are certainly established by powerful actors at one point in time by formal, constitutive rules. Those rules give the boss the capabilities of firing, promoting and otherwise affecting the well-being of the subordinate. The rules thereby create a relationship between the position of boss and the position of subordinate that grants certain causal powers to the boss that allow the boss to dominate the subordinate. At another point in time, the positions of boss and subordinate are filled by actual incumbents.

If we now want to analyze the interaction of the incumbents of these positions, the question is which is analytically prior, the established relationship into which they both have entered or the rule-like, routinized manner of the interaction they subsequently establish. It seems clear that the relationship and the causal powers it affords the boss are what predominantly determine the character of the subsequent interaction. Much of that interaction is not even rule-like. The rules don't usually tell the subordinate that he or she has to endure the angry outbursts of the boss or always stay at work long after quitting time just as the boss does. It is the subordinate's recognition of the causal powers inherent in the position of boss that makes him or her act that way. Of course, such behavior can become rule-like and routine and thus reaffirm the authority of the boss, making it easier for him or her to dominate the subordinate. But even here what is being reproduced or reconstituted by the emergent rules is not the underlying power relationship itself; that is secured by the original, formal, constitutive rules that established the relationship in the first place.

We thus have to distinguish three things: the original constitutive rules that establish relationships of domination, those relationships themselves, and the tacit, informal rules that emerge when people enter those relationships and begin interacting. Because Giddens (1979: 66–67) conflates the first order of rules with the second, he obscures both the intermediary, causal role of relationships in his treatment of domination and the analytical priority of such relationships to the subsequent rule-like behavior of actors that emerges when they are placed in those relationships.

Among the causal powers that are deposited in social positions are interests. Interests are built into a social position by the relationship of that position to other positions in the system. To return to an earlier example, capitalists have an interest in maximizing profit because they are in a competitive, zero-sum relationship with all others occupying the position of capitalist. Here again, as something built into a social position by a web or relationship, interests confront the actor as an external force. Interests are a force that expresses itself in actors' motives and, through motives, in their actions. In other words, actors are motivated to act in their interests, which are a function of their social position. Again, this doesn't mean that actors always with necessity act in their interests, but if they don't they are likely to suffer. A capitalist who shows no concern to maximize profit is liable to cease being a capitalist.

It is hard to know how Giddens can accommodate this point while denying the causal influence of systemic relationships. It is not even clear that Giddens would want to accommodate it. He speaks of structure as constraining or enabling, but never of it motivating. Giddens's actors do not seem to be motivated to do much beyond follow the routines that reproduce the system. The problem is that many systems, like capitalism, never reproduce themselves exactly; they are ever changing as a result of the consequences of actors' actions. Consequently, actors in those systems are routinely responding in nonroutine, nonrule-like ways to altered circumstances. What motivates them to respond in the ways they do? Giddens's concept of structuration and the duality of structure do not answer this question.

Conclusion

Because of the difficulty in articulating what social structure means, one major objective of this paper was simply to identify clearly some of the most prominent alternative conceptions. A second major objective was to comparatively evaluate them. Here, I argued that the conception of social structure as patterns of aggregate behavior is too weak because it reduces structure to an epiphenomenon of human behavior and consequently ignores the independent causal forces inherent in structural systems. The conception of structure as a system of lawlike regularities among social facts is strong but untenable because there is no prospect of finding sufficiently strong regularities to play a role in the covering law model of explanation to which this conception is closely tied.

My argument with Giddens's conception of structure as rules and resources is essentially that what it identifies is cultural structuring rather than social structuring. By this, I mean that it refers to the structuring of our behavior by culture as opposed to social relations.[4] I am prepared to admit that culture structures and shapes our behavior in the ways that Giddens describes. I do not want to confuse this with what I consider to be the more fundamental structuring of our behavior by social relations, the occurrence of which Giddens apparently does want to deny. The prospect of such confusion is very real since as Giddens (1979: 64) himself admits, it is as social relations that structure ordinarily has been understood in Anglo-American sociology. The whole culture of poverty debate, for example, counterposed structure, understood as social relations, to culture in explaining the persistence of poverty. That debate cannot even be conceptualized in terms of Giddens's understanding of structure, and even here I am forced to use other terms such as social relations to explain what I mean.

The way Giddens has shifted the meaning of structure goes largely unnoticed. I think that is unfortunate because as I have tried to argue, the arrangement of social relationships in the world, however they came to be in the first place, is now analytically prior to rules, norms and ideology in explaining our current predicament. I still believe that the term structure should be reserved for that referent.

Notes

1 Collins (1988) has recently softened this position somewhat, but he still maintains that relationships are abstractions. As he puts it, "I see no ultimate objection to attributing as much reality-status as Meinong's Golden Mountain to the Parsonian value-system or the nation-state . . . Idealizations, illusions and ideologies can play a part, but mainly as things to be explained, not as the ultimate explanations" (Collins 1988: 242). According to Collins, the ultimate source of sociological explanation is still the co-present interaction of individuals.

2 By agency, I mean human purposiveness and all that that entails such as wants, beliefs, desires, emotions, etc. Similarly, when I speak of the psychological level of analysis, I am referring to the level of individual actors and the mental states that properly are only attributable to them.

3 On the micro level, Giddens does sometimes refer to material circumstances such as the physical properties of the body and of location. Although important, such considerations represent only a slight nod in the materialist direction, and when Giddens turns his attention to the macro level, material circumstances play virtually no role in his analysis.

4 I owe this distinction between cultural and social conceptions of structure to Kyriakos Kontopoulos of Temple University.

References

Agassi, J. (1960). Methodological Individualism. *British Journal for the Philosophy of Science* 10: 135–46.

Barbour, I. G. (1966). *Issues in Science and Religion*. New York: Harper & Row.

Benton, T. (1981). Some Comments on Roy Bhaskar's 'The Possibility of Naturalism'. *Radical Philosophy* 27: 13–21.

Bhaskar, R. (1975). *A Realist Theory of Science*. Leeds. Leeds Books.

—— (1979). *The Possibility of Naturalism*, Atlantic Highlands, NJ: Humanities Press.

Blau, P. (1970). Comment [on Homans] in Robert Borger and Frank Cioffi (eds.), *Explanation in the Behavioral Sciences*. Cambridge: Cambridge University Press.

—— (1977). *Inequality and Heterogeneity: A Primitive Theory of Social Structure.* New York: The Free Press.

Callinicos, A. (1985). Anthony Giddens: A Contemporary Critique. *Theory and Society* 14: 133–166.

Collins, R. (1979). *The Credential Society: An Historical Sociology of Education and Stratification.* New York: Academic Press.

—— (1981). On the Microfoundations of Macrosociology. *American Journal of Sociology* 86: 984–1014.

—— (1988). The Micro Contribution to Macro Sociology. *Sociological Theory* 6: 242–253.

Davies, P. (1984). *Superforce: The Search for a Grand Unified Theory of Nature.* New York: Simon and Schuster.

Giddens, A. (1979). *Central Problems in Social Theory: Action, Structure and Contradictions in Social Analysis.* Berkeley: University of California Press.

—— (1981). *A Contemporary Critique of Historical Materialism.* Berkeley: University of California Press.

—— (1984). *The Constitution of Society.* Berkeley: University of California Press.

Harre, R. & Madden, E. (1975). *Causal Powers.* Totowa, NJ: Rowman & Littlefield.

Homans, G. C. (1975). What Do We Mean by Social 'Structure?' in Peter Blau (ed.), *Approaches to the Study of Social Structure.* New York: The Free Press.

Isaac, J. (1987). *Power and Marxist Theory: A Realist View.* Ithaca: Cornell University Press.

Johnson, T., Dandeker, C. & Ashworth, C. (1984). *The Structure of Social Theory: Strategies, Dilemmas and Projects.* New York: St. Martins.

Manicas, P. T. (1987). *A History & Philosophy of the Social Sciences.* New York: Basil Blackwell.

—— and Secord, P. F. (1983). Implications for Psychology of the New Philosophy of Science. *American Psychologist* 38: 399–413.

Mayhew, B. (1980). Structuralism versus Individualism: Part I. Shadowboxing in the Dark. *Social Forces* 59: 335–375.

Outhwaite, W. (1987). *New Philosophies of Social Science: Realism, Hermeneutics and Critical Theory.* New York: St. Martins.

Porpora, D. (1983). On the Prospects for a Nomothetic Theory of Social Structure. *Journal for the Theory of Social Behaviour* 13: 243–264.

—— (1987). *The Concept of Social Structure.* Westport, Ct.: Greenwood Press.

Turner, J. H. (1986). A theory of Structuration. *American Journal of Sociology* 4: 969–977.

—— (1984). *Social Stratification: A Theoretical Analysis.* New York: Columbia University Press.

—— & Maryanski, A. (1979). *Functionalism.* Reading, Mass.: Benjamin/Cummings.

14

REALISM AND MORPHOGENESIS

Margaret Archer

Social theory has to be useful and usable: it is not an end in itself. The vexatious fact of society has to be tackled *in* theory and *for* practice. These two tasks cannot be separated, for were practical utility to be the sole criterion we would commit ourselves to instrumentalism – to working with theoretically ungrounded rules of thumb. Conversely, a purely theoretical taming of the vexing beast may give a warm inner glow of ontological rectitude but is cold comfort to practical social analysts. They want a user-friendly tool kit and although it cannot come pocket-sized with an easy reference manual, customer services have every right to complain when handed an unwieldy device without any instructions on the assumption that if they handle it sufficiently this will somehow sensitize them to something.

Yet, because social theorists have fought shy of 'emergence' we are very short indeed of concrete exemplars, that is of ways of approaching the vexatious fact of society which are based four-square upon the acknowledgement of its emergent properties. Instead, there is a glaring absence of bold social theories which uncompromisingly make 'emergence' their central tenet. With the exception of Lockwood's[1] seminal though incomplete attempt to beat a pathway, others have laid a few more paving stones before losing their nerve and heading back for shelter in either the Individualist or the Holist camps. The former was the case with Buckley, who having launched the notion of morphogenetic/morphostatic processes of structural development then withdrew their ontological underpinnings, by construing emergent properties as heuristic devices: 'the "structure" is an abstract construct, not something distinct from the ongoing interactive process but rather a temporary, accommodative representation of it at any one time'.[2]

Conversely, Blau,[3] after painstakingly working on the derivation of complex social properties from simpler forms of exchange, seems to have become absorbed by the holistic impact of the former on the latter rather than

Source: Realist Social Theory: The Morphogenetic Approach, chap. 5, pp. 135–161 (referred to in the text as RST).

remaining exercised by their interplay. Full-blooded emergentist theories are hard to find because their prototypes failed to negotiate a passage between Individualism and Holism without coming to grief on one or the other.

Forewarned that the signposts reading 'reductionism' and 'reification' are roads to hell paved with bad conceptualizations, no doubt central conflation promises ontological security to more and more theorists. Yet theirs is a very pharisaical self-satisfaction. They expect thanks for not being guilty of grasping at atomism, or unjustly privileging society or the individual, or of whoring with social facts. They congratulate themselves on their theoretical abstemiousness in dieting only on areductionism and on the tithes of hard syncretic endeavour it has taken to consolidate their position. Then they compare themselves favourably with those of us who freely confess that theory is in a mess, that we can point to few worthwhile offerings – but believe the only thing to do is to admit it, confront it, and hope to do something about it.

Consequently, Bhaskar's work is of considerable interest since his ontological realism, premissed explicitly upon emergence, is used to develop the framework of a social theory which seems set fair to navigate a passage between Individualism and Holism. Although a 'realist metatheory is however clearly compatible with a wide variety of theoretical and methodological approaches'[4] and Bhaskar's philosophical realism is therefore a general platform, capable of underpinning various social theories (though incompatible with any form of downwards or upwards conflationism because their epiphenomenalism nullifies the stratified nature of social reality), his Transformational Model of Social Action (TMSA) can claim to be a social theory in its own right. Of course it is incomplete (taking on the philosophical underlabouring doesn't mean finishing the job for us), but this very incompleteness leaves room for exploring whether it can be complemented and supplemented by the morphogenetic/static approach. (Henceforth this is referred to as M/M.)

Although the answer will be in the affirmative, there are certain qualifications to be made, for this is what the whole business of clambering on theoretical shoulders is all about. Moreover there are some crucial clarifications and disassociations which also have to be established. In particular it is undeniable that many commentators (and, at times and with caveats, Bhaskar himself) have noted affinities between TMSA and central conflation in the form of Giddens' structuration theory. Thus before being able to build upon the affinities between TMSA and the morphogenetic approach, because of their common grounding in realism it is necessary to provide a convincing demonstration that Bhaskar's model contains basic assumptions which prevent it from being swept into the central conflation camp. Specifically, these concern emergence itself; fundamental to realism but fundamentally unacceptable to central conflationists. Certainly, there was a moment when the siren call of mutual constitution proved strong, indeed there are passages of dalliance with the sirens, but the emergentist groundings of TMSA were too robust for the spell to last. Ulysses made his getaway and might not have paused at all had there been other obvious ports of sociological call at the time. Equally, had there been no elective affinity between Emergentists and Elisionists, based on their common rejection of the terms of the Holist/Individualist debate, there would not have been the inclination to think that the enemy of one's enemy must be a friend. Thus some ground clearing is needed to identify where the positive affinities lie between three social theories which are equally negative about the terms in which the old debate was conducted.

Morphogenesis, structuration and the transformational model of social action

To begin with, it seems as though the objective and approach of the TMSA and M/M approaches are very close indeed. In *The Possibility of Naturalism*, Bhaskar drafts what can be called a 6-point Charter, which becomes embodied in his TMSA.

> I argue that societies are irreducible to people and . . . sketch a model of their connection. (1)
>
> I argue that social forms are a necessary condition for any intentional act, (2)
>
> that their *pre-existence* establishes their *autonomy* as possible objects of investigation and that (3)
>
> their *causal power* establishes their reality (4)
>
> The pre-existence of social forms will be seen to entail a transformational model of social activity . . . (5)
>
> the causal power of social forms is mediated through human agency (6)[5] (my notations)

Point (1), which talks of the need for a model which *connects* structure and agency resonates well with the aim of the M/M approach which is to link the two rather than to sink the differences between them. Nevertheless, it is far from decisive. After all, structuration theory does not argue that societies are reducible to people; there are structural properties even if these are held to require human instantiation and the concept of 'modalities' is advanced to account for their interconnection. Fifteen: all to analytical dualism and the duality of structure. Point 2, sees structuration edging ahead since these structural properties are the very medium of social action, whereas M/M has serious reservations about social forms being a necessary condition for *any* intentional act, seeing the break with nature as too great and arguing that natural interaction can supply the necessary and sufficient conditions for intentionality. This point has already been defended in the last chapter [of RST] and the reader must adjudicate, but in any case it leaves the score at 30 : 15 to structuration.

Point (3), insisting upon the *pre-existence* and *autonomy* of social forms (and both are crucial) marks a real turn of the tide. Temporality is integral to the M/M approach and contained in its first axiom 'that structure necessarily predates the action(s) which transform it'. Because of this there is always a Phase 1 in any sociological enquiry where it

> *is* assumed that some features of social structure and culture are strategically important and enduring and that they provide limits within which particular social situations can occur. On this assumption the action approach can help to explain the nature of the situations and how they affect conduct. It does not explain the social structure and culture as such, except by lending itself to a developmental enquiry which must start from some previous point at which structural and cultural elements are treated as given.[6]

Autonomy is also temporal (and temporary) in the joint senses that such structural properties were neither the creation of contemporary actors nor are ontologically reducible to 'material existents' (raw resources) and dependent upon current acts of human instantiation (rule governed) for all their current effects. These effects do produce a 'visible pattern', the well-known detectable regularities in human interaction which are never a matter of social hydraulics in the M/M approach. Yet this is very different from Giddens's assertion that 'social systems only exist through their continuous structuration in the course of time'.[7] Pre-existence and autonomy denote *discontinuities* in the structuring/restructuring process which can only be grasped by making analytical distinctions between the 'before' (Phase 1), the 'during' (Phase 2) and the 'after' (Phase 3), none of which is to deny the necessary continuity of human activity for the endurance of all things social.

Here Bhaskar is equally uncompromising about the need for examining a 'before': 'society pre-exists the individual'.[8] The church-goer or language user finds their beliefs or language *ready made at birth*, so 'people do not create society. For it always pre-exists them . . . Social structure . . . is always *already made*'. Consequently, Bhaskar's own comment upon Giddens is that he himself is 'inclined to give structures (conceived as transfactually efficacious) a stronger ontological grounding and to place more emphasis on the pre-existence of social forms'.[9] Because the 'relations into which people enter pre-exist the individuals who enter into them, and whose activity reproduces or transforms them; so they are themselves structures'.[10] They are structures by virtue of being emergent properties which are irreducible to the doings of contemporary actors, yet derive from the historical actions which generated them, thus creating the context for current agency. This brings the score to 30 : all.

Now, it follows for Bhaskar that if this is the case, then what I term central conflation 'must be corrected in a fundamental way'[11] and the other forms of conflation rejected. The three models which Bhaskar criticizes correspond respectively to what I have called upwards, downwards and central conflation. The critique of the three is identical. Thus 'on Model I there are actions but no conditions; on Model II conditions but no actions; on Model III no distinction between the two'.[12] The distinction is indispensable, not just because of their pre-existence and autonomy but because relational properties have causal powers (Point 4), though not ones which work in a naturalistic manner (on which more later, especially in chapter 7 [of RST], for this is where M/M has much to add). If prior emergent properties really condition subsequent interaction, then their reality cannot be withdrawn by reducing them, as Giddens does to 'memory traces' which falls back onto the 'personalization' strategy of Individualism. This is a case of the 'desperate incorporation' of the vexingly social into seemingly more tractable individual terms; as Gellner[13] caricatured it, 'Algy met a bear, the bear was bulgy, the bulge was Algy . . . the individual may consume what Durkheim and others have called social facts, but he will bulge most uncomfortably, and Algy will still be there . . . I suspect that actual investigators will often, though perhaps not always, prefer to have Algy outside the bear.' Uncomfortably mutually constituted as they now are, there is no question of examining their interplay or talking about their independent causal powers. Conditions and actions have to be examinable separately in order *to* talk about conditioned action. The real literacy levels in Castro's example (chapter 3 [of RST]) exert their effects even were there complete Cuban amnesia about their origins or the nature of this distribution. Morphogenesis is now leading 40 : 30.

Thus in *making* this temporal distinction, Bhaskar employs the image of a sculptor at work fashioning a product out of existing materials using the tools available. The M/M approach would merely add that some materials are more resistant than others, that tools vary in their adequacy and that the sociological identification of such differences is indispensable. What this is indispensable to is the key question, 'when are we going to get transformation rather than reproduction, or vice versa'?

Morphogenesis and morphostasis are very close indeed to the notions of transformation and reproduction, and all four terms only make sense as processes which come 'after' something which existed 'before' them. Thus for social structure 'it is no longer true to say that human *agents* create it. Rather we must say; they *reproduce* or *transform* it. That is to say, if society is already made, then any concrete human praxis . . . can only modify it: and the totality of such acts *sustain or change it*.'[14] Again Bhaskar is driven to part company with Giddens because of the latter's restricted use of the present tense alone. Thus,

> it is because the social structure is always *given*, from the perspective of intentional human agency, that I prefer to talk of reproduction and transformation rather than of structuration as Giddens does (though I believe our conceptions are very close). For me 'structuration' still retains voluntaristic connotations – social practice is always, so to speak, *restructuration*.[15]

In my own terms, morphogenesis is always a transformation of morphostasis. Thus Bhaskar's fifth point, namely, that the 'pre-existence of social forms will be seen to entail a *transformational* model of social activity', also seems to represent game point. Since the TMSA has a 'before' (pre-existing social forms), a 'during' (the process of transformation itself) and an 'after' (the transformed, since social structures are only relatively enduring), the same goes to Morphogenesis and is clinched because TMSA must also see its last phase as being the start of a new cycle. As Bhaskar notes, emergence implies 'a reconstruction of the historical processes of their formation out of 'simpler' things'.[16] Logically it follows that we can also theorize about the ongoing emergence of more complex things provided we see these as spaced out over time, clearly differentiate between antecedence and consequence in this succession, and above all retain the demarcation between pre-existing conditions and current actions.

The sting is in the tail, in the very last clause. The M/M approach insists upon the need to sustain an analytical distinction between structure and agency if a transformational model is to prove workable, that is to do the work which practising social analysts need it to do. The reason why this is not game, set and a rather dreary match to morphogenesis is that Bhaskar displays some qualms about adopting the analytical dualism between the two upon which the workability of his TMSA depends. The vexatiously unique character of the social makes many of Giddens's ways of grasping it particularly appealing. This is the seductiveness of central conflation and it signals the start of another game.

The siren call of inseparability

The peculiarity of all things social is that they are activity dependent. Without human activity nothing in society could have its genesis, continuation, or undergo change. On this we can all agree: unlike nature, social reality is not self-subsistent. This is its ontological oddity and what makes it peculiarly vexatious to tackle. However the problem becomes less vexing if we concentrate steadily on the question 'specifically whose activities are responsible for what and when?' In the past debate and in the present vacillations we are examining, it seems that the root of confusion lies in an over precipitous and quite unnecessary leap from the truistic proposition 'No people: no society' to the highly questionable assertion, 'this society; because of these people here present'. The leap has its attractions when we think in the most general terms about the historical panorama of 'the societal', for how could this have kept going from age to age without the continuous sustaining activities of succeeding generations of actors and how, in any particular age, can its on-going be divorced from the myriad of meanings and praxes without whose interweaving there would be no social fabric? The attraction does depend, however, upon the powerful imagery of the 'seamless web', an endless bale of material unrolling through time, without break or cut; a tissue which at any point in time can only be grasped in its totality, for it has no distinct parts since each is woven into the rest, so at most it has a pattern – albeit a changing one which is always the product of the weaving and inseparable from the woven.

Powerful images are rarely dimmed by counter-arguments, this is the wrong medicine for the bedazzled, so we have to deal (initially) in their own currency. Let us counterpoise a variant image in the same terms; society as a garment handed down through the human family, showing the wear and tear accumulated on the way, the patching and over-patching, the letting out and taking in done for different purposes, the refurbishing performed at different times, until the current garment now contains precious little of the original material. It has been completely refashioned (which brings us back to Bhaskar's sculptor) until perhaps the original only figures as 'something old' in a new wedding outfit. Why does this help? Because this image points up disjunctions, the ability to inspect different parts, the purposes and times at which they were introduced, by whom, and how these were treated by the next recipient. This is precisely how I propose treating social structures and the relations between them and human activities. Giddens remains rivetted by the first image and Bhaskar too is still impressed. What is wrong with it is what it fosters in theorization.

To start with we all endorse the obvious; 'No people; no society'. Furthermore, those we are considering would also concur that 'there is an ontological hiatus between society and people',[17] the properties possessed by the former may be very different from those possessed by the latter, upon whose activities the first depend. Agreement might just stretch as far as Bhaskar's statement that 'People and society are not . . . related dialectically. They do not constitute two moments of the same process. Rather they refer to radically different things.'[18] However, it is at this point that Giddens makes the leap to 'this society because of these people here present'. Structural properties only become real (as opposed to having a virtual material existence) when instantiated by actors, instantiation therefore becoming dependent upon current activities which, in turn, depend upon the knowledgeability of contemporary agents about what they are doing. Bhaskar is tempted to make the same leap and for the same underlying reason, namely that in society we are not dealing with a self-subsistent reality. Dwelling upon this he advances three propositions about its distinctive nature, which if true would indeed land him on the side of conflationism. The first two which point to the activity-dependence and concept-dependence of social structure are indeed very close to Giddens' stance on society's constitution in the activities of highly knowledgeable human agents, as Outhwaite has noted.[19] I want to argue that the first two propositions do not work, that Bhaskar has recognized this and that his proposition three (the effects of social structures are only operative through human activity) eventually persuades him not to jump at all.

Proposition 1, is that social structures, 'unlike natural mechanisms . . . only exist in virtue of the activities they govern, and cannot be identified independently of them'.[20] As Benton[21] has argued persuasively, if the operative word is 'govern', then the statement cannot be upheld. On Bhaskar's own argument, power for example, may exist unexercised thus governing nothing at all at the present time. Benton however, left a loophole for activity-dependence, through allowing for those activities necessary to sustain the *potential* for governance. Thus, in the case of a State, its full coercive power may remain unexercised but actions such as the (current) raising of taxes and armies may well be necessary for it to retain its potential power of coercion. Bhaskar accepts the criticism and grasps the loophole. Thus to him

> a structure of power may be reproduced without being exercised and exercised in the absence of any observable conflict . . . so long as it is sustained by human practice – the practices which reproduce or potentially transform it. In this sense the thesis of activity-dependence of social structures must be affirmed. Social structures exist materially and are carried or transported from one time-space location to another only or in virtue of human praxis.[22]

This could indeed have been written by Giddens and to be fair, it works for some aspects of social structure. The really crucial point is that it does not work for all. If we think of a demographic structure, this might appear activity-dependent – it goes on being structured the way it is if people literally go on reproducing and not reproducing in a particular pattern. Yet suppose all activities were harnessed to transforming it, the (top-heavy or whatever) structure would not disappear for several generations. Whilst it endures, whose activities are sustaining it? Those who constitute it just by being alive? Certainly, but this is simply the 'no-people: no demography' truism, for it was not *their* intention to structure it that way nor the unintended consequence of *their* actions, nor the intentionality of contemporary agents for we have presumed they all seek its transformation. *Here the activity-dependence of such structures can be affirmed in only one acceptable way: by reference to the activities of the long dead.* This demographic structure is not due to the people here present in anything other than the truistic sense. We are dealing with a relatively enduring emergent property, (proportional relations between age cohorts are internal and necessary to a top heavy demographic structure) which temporarily proves resistant to concerted activities to transform it.

How much of a maverick is this example? Not one at all, for there are at least three classes of properties which work in identical fashion. To begin with, the same argument can be used of many other levels and distributions (such as capital), though not all (such as eye colour). Secondly, and especially where emergent properties are those involving human relations with nature (from dust-bowl effects and green-house effects, through the consequences of extinction of species and exhaustion of minerals, to pollution and puncturing the ozone layer), there seems to be a growing fund of properties *upon which* the future *of* human activity depends, which may be irreversible in the present yet some of which require no continued reproduction, for past activities have made them permanent or chronic features of contemporary life. It is unnecessary to be bright Red or Green to acknowledge that our unfriendly relations with nature have consequences which are visited on the heads of subsequent generations, some of which they strive not to reproduce and others which they are incapable of transforming. Instead they suffer if they must and circumvent if they can – but both activities are constrained by properties and circumstances which are not of their making.

In case the above examples look as though they have been extracted from close to the point where Giddens freely grants them the status of 'material existents', or where others might object that the property which is not activity dependent in the present consists in physical laws which were triggered by past actions, we can point to another huge area replete with properties immune from such criticisms. If we think of culture then all knowledge was certainly activity dependent for its genesis and elaboration. Nevertheless, once recorded (chiselled into runes or gathering dust in the British Museum), it constitutes knowledge without a current knowing subject. It is knowledge because it retains the dispositional character to be understood, though it persists unrecognized, sustaining potential powers (of contradiction and complementarity with other cultural items) which remain unexercised. Ontologically it exists and if the theory it states is true, if the technique it describes works, or if the belief it articulates is justifiable, these remain the case quite independently of current actors knowing it, using it or believing it. We know that they are real by virtue of their releasable effects, because the old recipe, if workable, will still work if tried a hundred years later when someone rediscovers it and has the motive to try it. In this case they activate it which is very different from saying that they instantiate it, for the item in question does not *become* real, true or useful simply because someone tries it out. The significance of a Cultural System which exists (is existentially independent of knowledge about it) yet has crucial causal relations with Socio-Cultural level, which is indeed activity dependent, will be explored much further in chapter 7 [of RST]. Emergent cultural properties have been introduced at this point merely as another large category of the social which is ontologically independent from the activities of those people here present.

Thus, where emergent properties are concerned, the preceding arguments show that it is an *empirical question* whether their activity-dependence is *present tense or past tense.* Each and every instance of the latter makes the leap to 'this society because of these people here present' entirely unjustified.

Bhaskar's second thesis about the distinctive oddity of social structures is that 'they do not exist independently of the conceptions that the agents have of what they are doing in their activities'.[23] Again this is very close to Giddens' assertions about actors being very knowledgeable indeed about their social doings, that little goes on behind their backs, and that society depends upon their skilled performances. Bhaskar's own thesis is open to three interpretations. Firstly is he asserting that social structures only exist because agents have *some* conception of what they are doing? As Benton rightly points out this has no bite whatsoever: 'it seems to me hard to sustain the concept of an agent at all without the notion of conceptualization of activity, so that insofar as human agents are a necessary condition for the existence of social structure (and this is hardly disputable) then the thesis is sustained'.[24] It is, but what is sustained here is simply the truistic 'no people; no society'. Secondly then, is the thesis of concept-dependence that the existence of social structures depends upon agents having the *particular* conceptions they do of what they are doing? Whilst a few relational properties are of this kind – friendship, loyalty, and commitment, many other structural relations are sustained by law or coercion, censorship or ideological manipulation, and sanctioning processes which maintain the relational property precisely by overriding the diversity (and conflicting nature) of agents' concepts of what they are doing – or inducing mystificatory ones. This Bhaskar concedes and has to if he is genuinely declaring war upon empirical realism and the privilege it gives to the experiential. To begin with he accepts that 'the *generative* role of agents' skills and wants, and of agents' . . . beliefs and meanings must be recognised without lapsing into an interpretative fundamentalism by conferring *discursive* and/or *incorrigible* status on them'.[25] This in itself neither distances him from Giddens (who talks of degrees of 'discursive penetration' and of corrigible knowledge) nor does much for his conviction that agents' particular conceptions may be systematically distorted by ideology. Since agents' conceptions may be wrong, *inter alia* because of ideological distortions, then in consistency Bhaskar has to grant that 'the *conditions* for the phenomena (namely social activities as conceptualized in experience) exist *intransitively* and may therefore exist independently of their appropriate conceptualization'.[26] The introduction of 'conditions that exist intransitively' marks the break with Giddens, for important things are now indeed going on behind our backs. As Bhaskar writes, 'of such relations the agents involved may or may not be aware'.[27] Indeed his whole emancipatory programme depends on the claim that they do at T^1, but need not at T^2. Thus when 'types of explanation succeed in identifying *real*, but hitherto *unrecognised*, conditions and patterns of determination they immediately augment our knowledge',[28] and with it our freedom. All of this has severed the entente cordiale with Giddens' 'highly knowledgeable agent', without however entailing a full retraction of the concept-dependence thesis.

For a final possibility remains. Bhaskar allows that structures may exist independently of their *appropriate* conceptualization, but could still reply that they depend upon being *inappropriately* conceptualised. In other words, the thesis may specify a causal relationship between agents' misconceptions and the endurance of social structures, implying of course that changes in the former would contribute to changes in the latter. Examples are not hard to find (like the rise and decline of the fur trade or ideology and ideological demystification) but to universalize this proposition, quite apart from its conspiratorial overtones, is to swallow a story about the functional necessity of every inappropriate concept and of the fundamental *a prioristic* coherence of concepts and reality. Again there are no grounds for demonstrating this as an *a priori* truth; the matter seems to be one for empirical investigation, particularly since we can find evidence of large conceptual shifts (feminism) which existing structures have withstood largely unchanged. And what this points to in turn is the indispensability of theorizing about them and then investigating *whose* conceptual shifts are responsible for *which* structural changes, *when*, *where* and under *what* conditions.

In short, none of the arguments about the concept-dependence of social structures justifies the leap to 'this society because of these people here present and the concepts they hold'. On the contrary many social structures seem resilient in the face of profound conceptual disagreements between agents about their doings and their shifting concepts of what structures are like. Again, we return to restate that the concept-dependence of such structures can be affirmed in only one acceptable way: by reference to the concepts (ideas, beliefs, intentions, the compromises and concessions plus unintended consequences) of the long dead. These continue to feature in present structures, despite strenuous efforts of current actors to change them, as with racism and sexism.

Bhaskar's third thesis about the ontological peculiarity of society is that social structures are only present in and through their effects, that is only in and through the activities of human beings. Once again the drift towards Giddens is pronounced and threatens to impale the TMSA on the 'simultaneity model' for which Layder correctly takes structuration theory to task. For how 'can objective structures be both outside and determinative of interaction, whilst at the same time being the internally generated outcome of such interactions? This is what the simultaneity model asks us to accept'.[29] Benton too is quick to pounce, for at this point, the very existence of emergent properties is at stake, the danger being that they are simply going to disappear, being incorporated into 'other people' in typical Individualist fashion. Quite rightly, he insists that the only protection against this is if structural conditions and human activities are kept separate, namely if we adhere strictly to analytical dualism rather than succumbing to the duality of structure. Thus to sustain the existence of emergent properties 'it is necessary to distinguish between those activities of agents which are exercises of their own intrinsic powers, and those activities which are really powers which reside in social structures, but operate through the activities of human agents'. The difficulty is, though, 'if any person "A" is the agent of an activity "a", then "A" must be the possessor of the power of which "a" is the exercise. If this is accepted then it follows that, at best, we can distinguish only between powers of agents possessed in virtue of their intrinsic natures, and powers of agents possessed in virtue of their relational properties.' This is of course as far as structuration theory would go, given Giddens' mistrust of emergence. To Benton, this spells the collapse of the TMSA programme. Bhaskar's 'conception of social structures does not, after all, sustain them as autonomous possessors of causal powers, or, therefore, as *sui generis* realities. Roy Bhaskar is, it seems, committed to a variant form of individualism in social theory.'[30] Benton admits to being both sceptical of his conclusion and intrigued to see where it breaks down.

It does, though a little more work has to be done than is contained in Bhaskar's riposte. It is insufficient to state that social structures are only efficacious in and through the activities of human beings (as a condition for avoiding reification) for all descriptive individualists would assent to this. Yet the effects of emergent properties are not those of 'other people' and reification is not involved in saying so. Bhaskar most certainly would not wish to slide into the 'personalization' strategy of Individualists and he is explicit that in talking about structures he has switched the focus from *people* to *relations* (including those with positions, nature and social products such as machines and firms). Still this is not quite conclusive, for as we saw [earlier in RST] Watkins was perfectly happy to bundle the 'beliefs, resources and inter-relations of individuals' into his charter for Methodological Individualism in which 'the ultimate constituents of the social world are individual people'.[31] It is only in the final phrase of this exchange that Bhaskar gets off the hook. 'What remains of "individualism", he writes 'is a residual truth: that nothing happens in society save in or in virtue of something human beings do *or have done*'[32] (my italics).

This unaccentuated 'or have done' needs to be given its full force. If the argument did hang on 'something people do', then there would be commitment to 'this society because of those people here present', no escaping reductionism, and no evading Benton's conclusion. The addition, 'or have done' avoids all three for it lets in *past actions* and full force can be given to Auguste Comte's insight that the majority of actors are the dead. That force is the force of emergence, namely that it is now perfectly possible to talk about emergent properties and the results (or the results of the results) of past actions, which pre-date all current actions of contemporary agents and yet condition them – in the form of enablements or constraints which are not dependent upon current activities nor influential because of their contemporary conceptualization (be it correctly, incorrectly, or not at all). Reification does not threaten. It is affirmed that social structures are only efficacious through the activities of human beings, but in the only acceptable manner, by allowing that these are the effects of *past actions*, often by long dead people, which survive them (and this temporal escape is precisely what makes them *sui generis*). Thus they continue to exert their effects upon subsequent actors and their activities, as autonomous possessors of causal powers. How they carry over and how they exert their effects is just what the M/M approach attempts to theorize. Endorsement of analytical dualism in relation to structure and agency (distinguishing pre-conditions from present activities) is now not only permissible, it is essential to the TMSA programme.

If the siren call of central conflation had continued, Benton had pointed to the ineluctable conclusion. In the end it was resisted and there is a world of difference between Giddens' insistence that 'structure has no existence independent of the knowledge that agents have about what they do in their day-to-day activity'[33] and Bhaskar's statement that 'the mark of intransitive objects of knowledge then becomes that they exist and act independently of the knowledge of which they are the objects'[34] and his affirmation that social structures are such intransitive objects. With the assertion in *Reclaiming Reality*, one to which no central conflationists could ever put their name, that 'society may thus be conceived as an articulated ensemble of such *relatively independent and enduring structures*'[35] (my italics) we can now move on to a discussion of the *interplay* between these structures and human agents in a manner which is closed to the central conflationist who denies this possibility by rendering them mutually constitutive.

Separability: the interplay between structure and agency

This final set proves rather easy going as central conflation steadily fades as a threat to TMSA which plants itself firmly on its backline of Emergentism to make strong and decisive returns. The outcome is a necessary one because if Bhaskar holds fast to the ontological role he has assigned to emergent properties then he can really have no truck with the 'duality of structure', as conceived of in structuration theory. It seems *logically* inescapable that if the 'powers', 'tendencies', 'transfactuality' and 'generative mechanisms' inhering in social structures can exist unexercised (or unrecognized), in open systems like society, then there *must* be a disjunction between them and the everyday phenomenal experiences of actors. This Bhaskar asserts forcefully in his repudiation of empirical realism and the privilege it accords to the experiential. However, it follows from the fact that the two often or usually are 'out of synch' with one another that analytical dualism then becomes a logical necessity when Bhaskar moves from his general consideration of realism to advance the TMSA as a contribution to social theory. Because the emergent properties of structures and the actual experiences of agents are not synchronized (due to the very nature of society as an open system), then there will always be the inescapable need for a two-part account. Part 1 seeks to disengage the properties (their 'powers' etc.) *per se* of social structure: part 2 conceptualizes the experiential, namely that which is accessible to actors at any given time *in* its incompleteness and distortion and replete with its blind spots of ignorance. Thus the two accounts will not be the same, but written from different standpoints, for one will include elements which the other lacks and vice versa.

Thus, Bhaskar writes that he 'wants to distinguish sharply, then between the genesis of human actions, lying in the reasons and plans of human beings, on the one hand; and the structures governing the reproduction and transformation of social activities, on the other; and hence between the domains of the psychological and social sciences'.[36] The need for this distinction and the two accounts which it calls for are entirely alien to Elisionism. Unfortunately the phraseology in which this is expressed has to be read carefully, for parts of the formulation are only too redolent of structuration theory.

This is the case with the following statement: 'Society is the ever-present *condition* and continually reproduced *outcome* of human agency: this is the duality of structure. And human agency is both work (generically conceived), that is (normally conscious) *production*, and (normally unconscious) *reproduction* of the conditions of production, including society: this is the duality of praxis.'[37] Although the first sentence sounds as if it comes straight from structuration theory we established in the last section that something very different from 'simultaneity' is meant by Bhaskar, and that therefore 'condition' should actually be read to mean 'pre-condition' and 'outcome' to imply that which post-dates given actions. (This of course is identical with the two basic theorems of the M/M approach.) However, Giddens means one thing and one alone: that structural properties require 'instantiation' by present agents to *be* efficacious and that 'outcomes' are part and parcel of the selfsame and simultaneous process – in what is a unitary account. On the contrary, Bhaskar underscores the need for two accounts in the above quotation, one which deals with the 'duality of structure' (though to him spread out over time, as a 'tensed' process, rather than compacted in the present) *and another*, dealing with the 'duality of praxis' (where 'production' and 'reproduction' are again spaced in time and may well involve different agents altogether). This need for *separate accounts* of 'structure' and 'praxis' firmly separates the TMSA from structuration. For in the latter the two can *only* be separated by the artificial bracketing exercise, which recommits structuration to simultaneity because the *epoché* confines us to the same *époque* and prevents exploration of the interplay between structure and agency over time. In contradistinction Bhaskar's 'two accounts' entail a commitment to analytical dualism and issue in the need to investigate their interplay (in a third account), an interplay whose exploration is firmly blocked in structuration theory.

In fact a little reflection shows that, realism itself is *predicated* upon analytical dualism. This is underscored when it quits the realm of abstract ontology and enters the domain of practical social theorizing. At any given T^1, *both* accounts are required, since at any point in time, what Lockwood distinguished as 'system integration' may be at variance with 'social integration' – and explaining the outcome at T^2 involves examining their interplay. The admission of two accounts, *contra* central conflation, always implies the need for a third which combines them. This is what sets analytical dualism apart from any of the triple versions of conflation whose common fallacy is always to issue in one-dimensional accounts; crude epiphenomenal reductionism in the upwards and downward versions, more sophisticated but still 'compacted' in the central version since only an artificial bracketing exercise can separate them, not in reality but purely for analytical convenience dependent upon one's interests.

Once Bhaskar has differentiated in his TMSA between the need to *retain* 'No people: no social structures' (in order to avoid reification) and the need to *reject* 'these structures, because of these people here present' (in order to avoid the slide into Individualism), then the widening of the time frame to include the emergent and aggregate consequences of past actions and past agents, actually makes analytical dualism a methodological necessity to the TMSA itself.

Human activity is seen as 'consisting in the transformation by efficient (intentional) agency of pre-given material (natural and social) causes'.[38] Although there is one sense in which social forms have to be *drawn upon* (to Bhaskar for the very framing of intentions), there is another sense, which is entirely alien to conflationary theorizing, in which these *pre-existing* properties *impinge* upon contemporary actors and cannot be subsumed under voluntaristic concepts like 'instantiation'. The prior emergence of relational properties impinge willy nilly on current actors and their situations, implying no compliance, complicity or consent from the latter. This relational conception of structures, explicitly incorporating time past as well as time present, then

> allows one to focus on the *distribution* of the structural conditions of action, and in particular . . . differential allocations of: (a) productive resources (of all kinds, including for example cognitive ones) to persons (and groups) and (b) persons (and groups) to functions and roles (for example in the division of labour). In doing so, it allows one to situate the possibility of different (and antagonistic) interests, of

> conflict *within* society, and hence of interest-motivated transformation in society structure.[39]

In this we have a clear statement that the actors here present are not responsible for creating the distributions, roles and associated interests with which they live. Equally important is the crucial recognition that the *pre-structuring* of actors' contexts and interests is what shapes the pressures for transformation by some and for stable reproduction by others, in the present. Theories of change are not defied by infinite social complexity, reproduction is anchored in vested interest and not mere routinization, and transformation is not an undifferentiated potential of every moment, it is rooted in determinate conflicts between identifiable groups who find themselves in particular positions with particular interests to advance or defend.

The foundations of analytical dualism have now been laid down, yet to complete the TMSA as a social *theory*, the 'third account' of the *interplay* between social structures and human agents is now required. Bhaskar recognizes this, namely that mediating concepts are called for to explain *how* structure actually does impinge upon agency (who and where) and *how* agents in turn react back to reproduce or transform structure (giving rise to morphogenesis or morphostasis in my terms). In the following description of these 'mediators', it should be noted that what a large distance now separates them from Giddens' free-floating 'modalities' (i.e. the 'interpretative scheme', 'facility', or 'norm', that is stocks of knowledge, power and conventions, which are universally available rather than being *differentially distributed* and *concretely located*). By contrast, Bhaskar claims that 'we need a system of *mediating concepts*, encompassing both aspects of the duality of praxis, designating the "slots", as it were, in the social structure into which active agents must slip in order to reproduce it; that is a system of concepts designating the *"point of contact" between human agency and social structure.* Such a point, linking action to structure, must *both* endure and be immediately occupied by individuals'[40] (my italics). These types of *linkages* are concrete ('slots'), specifically located ('points of contact'), and are differentially distributed (not all can 'slip' into the same 'slot'). Conceived of as relationships, they satisfy the requirement of temporal continuity and are irreducibly emergent since they include but do not reduce to the 'interactions' between the individuals who occupy or engage in them.

Their precise designation overlaps with that employed in the M/M approach, though it might prove slightly too restrictive for the latter. Thus, Bhaskar claims that it 'is clear that the mediating system we need is that of *positions* (places, functions, rules, duties, rights) occupied (filled, assumed, enacted etc.) by individuals, and of the *practices* (activities etc.) in which, in virtue of their occupancy of these positions (and vice versa), they engage. I shall call this mediating system the position-practice system'.[41] Now 'position' is an ambiguous concept. If it means 'position as the passive aspect of role', which is a fairly common usage, then it is too narrow for my purposes. Agents certainly do have an important 'point of contact' with structure through the roles they occupy/assume, but it is *not the only one.* If, on the other hand, 'position' conveys its more everyday meaning ('the position in which they find themselves'), that is problematic (or felicitous) *situations* or *contexts* which are not tightly associated with specific normative expectations – therefore making it otiose to call them 'roles' (as for example, with the 'underprivileged', or 'believers' or those 'holding theory x') then the overlap would be complete. The latter meaning seems acceptable to Bhaskar from the quotation above and given that his own usage often embraces it. For example, when discussing the experiential lifeworld at T^2, he comments that this is 'dependent upon the ontological and social *contexts* within which the significant experience occurs'.[42] Although this does not seem to be a bone of contention between us, it is raised here because in M/M approach a great deal hangs upon *not confining* all the problems which agents confront in the structures they inherit from the past to roles (and thus *not limiting* morphogenetic potential to those exigencies confronted in them or *confining* interests to those vested in roles). As far as interplay itself is concerned, the M/M approach will have much more to add about the *way* in which structures impinge upon agents at the 'points of contact'.

A final and major source of agreement with the TMSA deserves highlighting. From the M/M perspective, the structural conditioning of action (by constraints or enablements) is *never* a matter of 'hydraulic pressures' – which is why it is preferable to speak of 'mediators' linking them rather than 'mechanisms' connecting them, for there is nothing mechanical about the processes involved (and none of the concomitant denial of human subjectivity). The same goes for the TMSA, since to Bhaskar, intentionality is what demarcates agency from structure. Hence, 'intentional human behaviour is caused, and . . . it is always caused by reasons, and . . . it is only because it is caused by reasons that it is properly characterized as intentional'.[43] The M/M approach reflects the same conviction and therefore actually conceptualizes the conditional effects of structure upon action in terms of the former supplying *reasons* for different courses of action to those who are differently positioned. Exactly how it does so, by shaping the situations in which people find themselves, will be explored in chapter 7 [of RST]. It is raised here merely to show the general congruence of the two approaches.

Picturing transformation and morphogenesis

We have talked about two accounts of 'structure', of 'interaction' and of a third account of the 'mediating processes' linking the two. These now need picturing in a form which sets these linkages out in a way which is quite different from the simple upwards and downwards or sideways arrows, distinctive of *any* diagrammatic representation of conflationary theorizing. The main difference, of course, is that while conflationary theorists *may* assign importance to the passage of time, they entirely fail to acknowledge the intrinsic *historicity* of the process. Time instead, is a medium through which things happen rather as air is to breathing-beings. But at any moment in time, the assumptions of epiphenomenalism or mutual constitution mean that the process can be depicted in exactly the same way. The reverse is the case for non-conflationists for whom the process itself is strung out over time (and each moment does *not* conform to the same eternal diagram but to a specific phase on a historical flow chart). Both analytically and in practical analysis, different phases are disengaged, not as mere aspects of a unitary process, but as parts of a temporal sequence. Moreover, since structures are held to be only relatively enduring and transformation/morphogenesis characterizes the final phase, then the model also indicates subsequent cycles of the ongoing process.

Thus any one cycle which happens to rivet our attention, because of its substantive interest, is also recognised to be preceded by anterior cycles and followed by posterior ones – whether these are reproductive or transformatory, morphostatic or morphogenetic. Necessarily action is continuous ('no people: no society') but because of their actions over time, structures are discontinuous (only relatively enduring) and once they are changed, then subsequent activities are conditioned and shaped quite differently (this society is not exclusively the product of those here present any more than future society is solely what our heirs produce). How specific analytical cycles are carved out historically depends upon the problem in hand: what follows are generic diagrams whose contents the investigator would supply. Having argued that there is considerable congruence between the TMSA and the M/M approach, this will finally be clinched if, and only if, they picture the process in a manner quite distinct from conflationary theorists, and through generic diagrams which closely resemble one another. Both it will be argued are indeed the case, though to sustain this argument it is necessary to pinpoint important developments and refinements in Bhaskar's picturing.

In the earlier *Possibility of Naturalism* (1979) he supplied what can be called his preliminary model of the society/person connection. In many ways it is too fundamentalist. As can be seen in Figure 1, (i) although it contains a 'before' and an 'after' it lacks real historicity: despite the break in the middle,

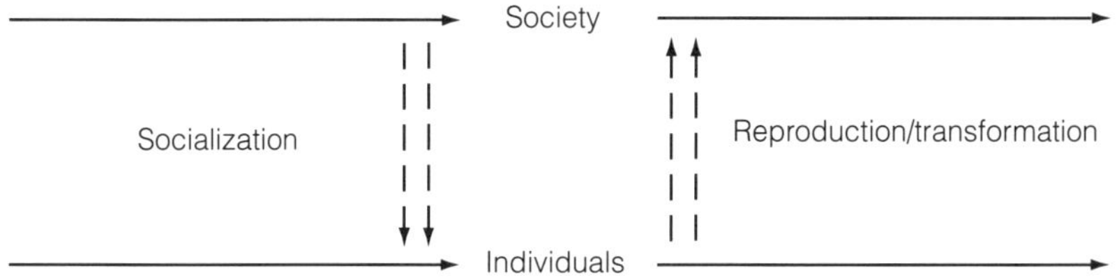

Figure 1 Bhaskar's model of the society/person connection.

it could be well construed as a heuristic device which represents each and any moment, not a determinate phase in an historical process: (ii) in several ways it is 'overpersonalized'; structural influences appear to work *exclusively via socialization* and seem to exert their influence directly upon (all) *individuals*: (iii) the 'before' and 'after' are unconnected by interaction and unmediated by the 'relations of production'. In short, (i), (ii) and (iii), respectively point to the down-playing of historicity, emergence and mediation.

Now, although the existence of *two-way* arrows sets this model at variance to both upwards and downwards conflation, the features which are repressed in this representation (historicity, emergence and mediation) are exactly those which it has been argued, firmly separate the TMSA from central conflation. Were this the end of the story, then this model could readily be appropriated by central conflationists and it is perhaps largely responsible for the affinities which some have noted with structuration theory.

However, ten years later, Bhaskar elaborated on this fundamentalist model and did so by inserting precisely those features which were repressed in the above. In *Reclaiming Reality* (1989) crucial revisions are introduced into Figure 2; (a) the prior *emergence* and current influence of structural properties at points 1 and 2, as the unintended consequences of past actions and unacknowledged conditions of contemporary activities, are now explicitly introduced: (b) their influence is to limit actors' understanding of their social world which is compounded, at 3 and 4, by limitations in self understanding, thus rendering the *necessary production process* (which is now introduced) the *mediated* product of agents who are far from highly knowledgeable about why they find themselves in the relations they do and why they do whatever they then do in those situations: (c) the *temporal* phasing of the process is now prominent, the diagram is now a sequence through time – 1 is the explicit outcome of an antecedent cycle and 1′ signals the start of a new and different posterior cycle (if transformation ensues). If reproduction is the outcome, then we are in for a structural replay in the next cycle but not necessarily an action replay.

Given these three refinements, the model now superimposes neatly onto the basic morphogenetic/morphostatic diagram. Superimposition seems fully justified by some of Bhaskar's comments which explicitly distance TMSA

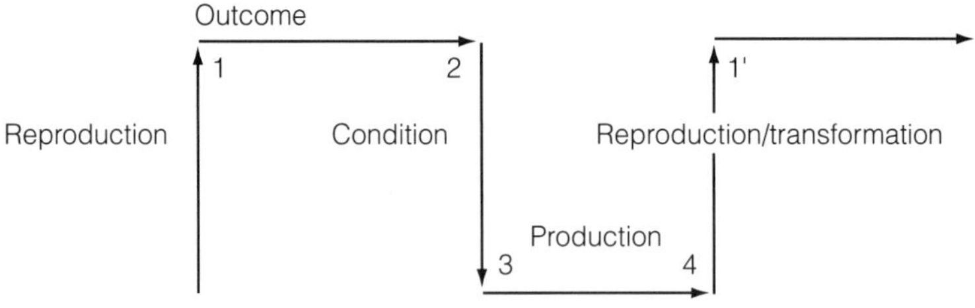

Figure 2 Bhaskar's refined transformational model of structure and praxis.

from central conflation and structuration theory in particular. (1) Because of emergence, he insists upon the influence of *prior* structures on *subsequent* interaction which transforms them, and now represents this *historically* rather than *sub specie aeternitartis*, as in the first diagram. (2) He remarks that he 'inclined to give structures (conceived as transfactually efficacious) a stronger ontological grounding and to place more emphasis on the pre-existence of social forms' than is Giddens, but now also stresses that 'theory need not be static, but can depict, in abstract fashion, flows, cycles and movements . . . tendentially applicable to concrete historical situations'.[44] In fact, *temporality* is not an option but a necessity, for as he states 'social structures are to be *earthed* in space and *situated* in time and space/time is to be seen/scene as *a flow*'.[45] (3) Thus it is justifiable to introduce the flow explicitly as historicity *but also* to break it up into phases for he maintains that the TMSA 'generates' a clear criterion of historically significant events, namely those that 'initiate or constitute ruptures, mutations or generally transformations of social forms'.[46] (4) Finally, his refined diagram now contains *mediating* processes, that is it deals with relations between positioned praxes which are not reducible to interpersonal interaction between their occupants/encumbents. Similarly in the M/M approach, interaction is held to emanate from those in positions/situations which are not of their making yet which condition much of what they can make of them.

The basic morphogenetic/static diagram is presented in Figure 3. Its basic theorems, which constitute analytical dualism are (i) that structure necessarily pre-dates the action(s) which transform it (Bhaskar as we have seen agrees but adds weight to the analytical découpage when he emphasizes that 'the games of the life-world (Lebenswelt) are always initiated, conditioned and closed outside the life world itself'[47]), and; (ii) that structural elaboration necessarily post-dates those actions which have transformed it (to Bhaskar structures are only relatively enduring and whether they do last or become transformed is the product of positioned praxis not voluntaristic interaction).

With minor alterations the TMSA and M/M diagrams now readily combine as in Figure 4, with Bhaskar's notations entered above the lines and my own corresponding ones below them in brackets.

Since all the lines in Figure 4 are in fact continuous, the dualism is

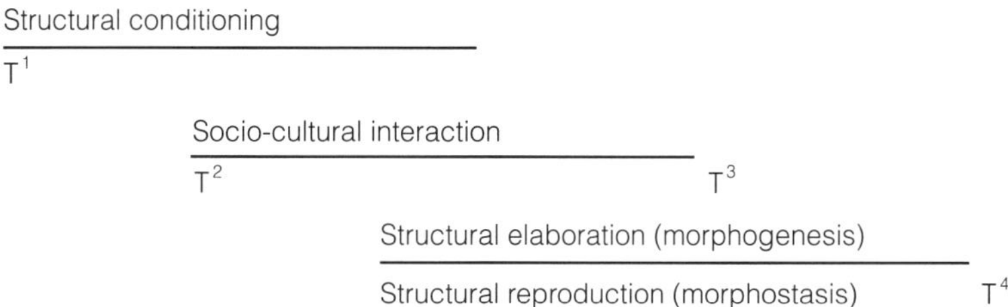

Figure 3 The basic morphogenetic/static cycle with its three phases.

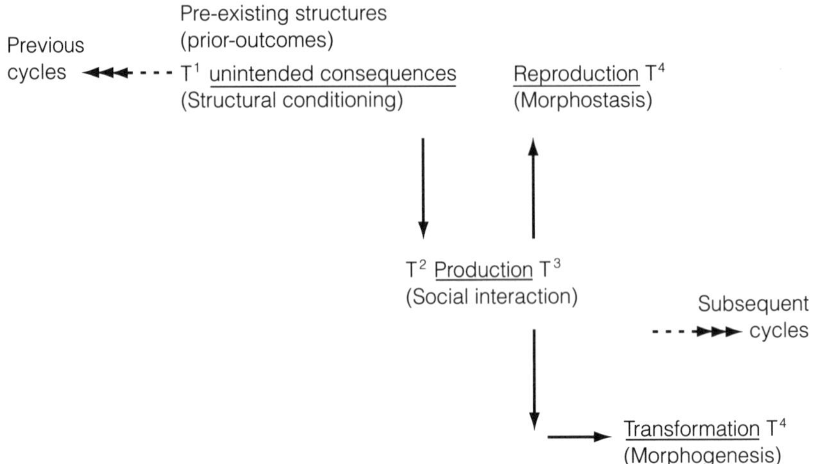

Figure 4 Superimposing the Transformational Model of Social Action and the morphogenetic/static cycle.

analytical rather than philosophical, a theoretical necessity for unravelling and explaining the processes involved in the *structuring* of society and the specific forms of *re-structuring* to take place – *over time.* The projection of all horizontal lines forwards and backwards connects up with anterior and posterior cycles of the historical *structuring process.* This is equally generic to both the TMSA and the M/M approach, and accounts for the possibility of their co-picturing. However, I retain a preference for my own graphics for the simple but important reason that my T^2 and T^3 period (where prior structures are gradually transformed and new ones slowly elaborated) shows diagrammatically that there is no period when society is *un-structured.* In a purely visual sense, Bhaskar's T^2–$T^{1\prime}$ (contrary to his intention) *could* convey that structural properties are suspended for this interval, whilst they undergo 'production'.

I have been arguing that *analytical* dualism is a matter of theoretical necessity if we are to obtain purchase on those processes which are accountable for determinate social changes – that is if we are to advance usable social theories for working investigators (for whom a social ontology which asserts *tout court* that the potential for reproduction or transformation inheres in each act at every moment is a white elephant). As Bhaskar maintains, the TMSA 'can sustain a genuine concept of *change*, and hence of *history*'.[48] The same claim is made for the M/M approach, and is one I hope to have demonstrated substantively in the *Social Origins of Educational Systems* (1979).[49] There is agreement that this is something which upwards, downwards and central conflationary theories cannot do. Indeed, in the latter, change remains 'something of a mystery'[50] for Bhaskar. It does indeed, and what has been examined earlier are the reasons why it must for those who uphold the 'duality of structure'. Thus structuration theory bows out at this point with Giddens' anticlimatic statement that there is 'little point in looking for an overall theory of stability and change in social systems, since the conditions of social reproduction vary so widely between different types of society'.[51] Consequently his social ontology hands the practitioner a 'sensitization' device; the TMSA and M/M approaches try to provide tool kits, and whilst tools presume that practitioners have to do considerable (substantive) *work* with them, they are also designed to be worked with and to be of practical use on the job.

Given this objective, it is important to emphasize that the compatibility established between the TMSA and the M/M approaches are anchored in realism itself. Just as Individualism and Holism represented social ontologies whose commitments to what constitutes the social world then issued in programmatic injunctions about how it should be studied and explained (that is Methodological Individualism and Methodological Holism as conflationary programmes working in opposite directions), so the realist social ontology also enjoins a Methodological Realism which embodies its commitments to depth, stratification and emergence as definitional of social reality. Thus the burden of this chapter has been to demonstrate that given these fundamental tenets of realism, they can only be respected and reflected by a Methodological Realism which approaches structure and agency through 'analytical dualism' – in order to be able to explore the linkages between these separate strata with their own autonomous, irreducible, emergent properties and which consequently repudiates any form of conflation (be it upwards, downwards or central) in social theorizing.

Certainly Outhwaite[52] is correct that this means social realism is compatible with a wide range of social theories, but I believe this breadth is a matter of substantive rather than formal complementarities. In other words, whilst it is perfectly possible to have fierce realist debates about the relative *substantive importance* of different structures and generative mechanisms (of the marxist versus anti-marxist variety), nevertheless in *formal terms*, such antagonists would also be co-protagonists of Methodological Realism. This is because formally, realism itself is committed to an explanatory framework which acknowledges and incorporates (a) *pre-existent structures* as generative mechanisms, (b) their *interplay* with other objects possessing causal powers and liabilities proper to them in what is a stratified social world, and (c) non-predictable but none the less explicable *outcomes* arising from interactions between the above, which take place in the open system that is society. In substantive terms, disagreements can flourish about which structures, what types of interplay and what outcomes should be prioritized and how they ought to be analyzed, but without any discord over the nature and format of explanation itself. Therefore, since the M/M approach makes no substantive judgements either, it is not surprising to find that its generic diagram, founded foursquare upon 'analytical dualism', also superimposes directly onto the basic explanatory framework as pictured in the only full-length book to date which is devoted to Methodological Realism. By introducing the common headings, 'Structure', 'Interplay', and 'Outcome', the similarities with Andrew Sayer's[53] figure (here Figure 5), entitled the 'Structures of causal explanation' are clearly marked – as they should be if the arguments which have been advanced in this chapter, namely, that 'analytical dualism' is intrinsic to social realism, are sustained.

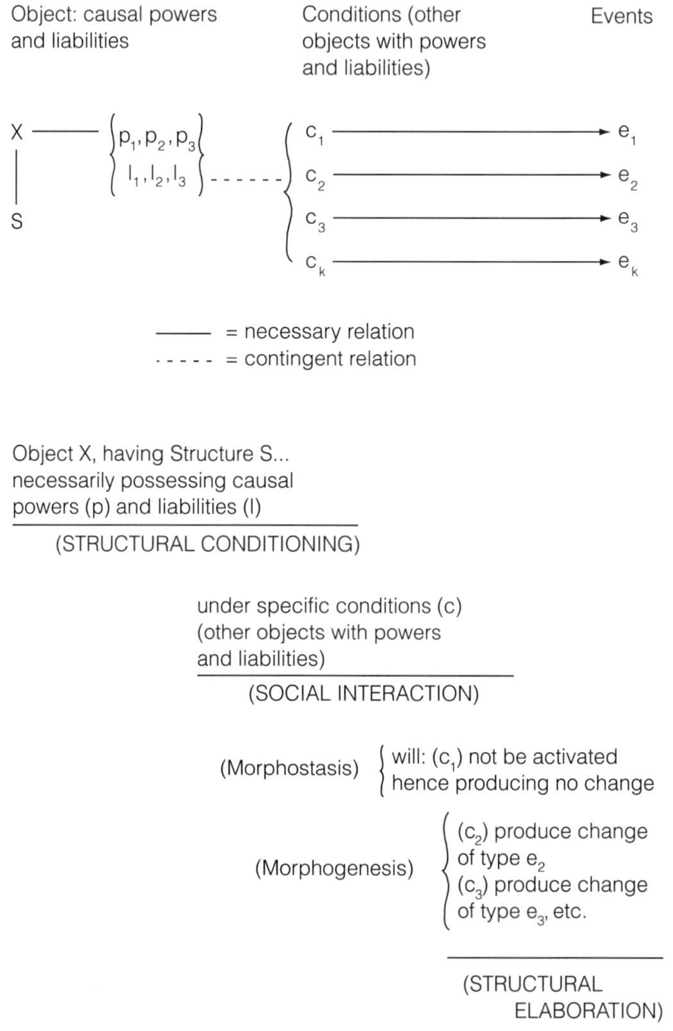

Figure 5 Co-picturing Methodological Realism and the morphogenetic/static approach.

The TMSA is the generous under-labouring of a philosopher who has actually dug beyond disciplinary bounds: the M/M approach is produced by a working sociologist, recognizing the obligation to go deeper into precision tooling to supply a social theory which is pre-eminently usable. Thus the M/M approach seeks to go further than providing 'a clear criterion of historically significant events': it attempts not merely to identify but also to unpack. Thus there is yet more fine-grained work to be done on the conceptualization of structural conditioning, on the specification of *how* structural influences are transmitted (as reasons not hydraulics) to particular agents in determinate positions and situations (the who, the when and the where), and on the strategic combinations which result in morphogenesis *rather than* morphostasis (which outcome).

This is precisely what the next chapter [of RST] sets out to do, although it will take the following three to complete the exercise by dealing with the tripartite phases making up the morphogenetic cycle. This undertaking appears to have Bhaskar's recent blessing, given that he endorses the need to think of the flow of social reality as 'differentiated into analytically discrete moments' and as being 'rhythmically processual and phasic to the core – a feature which distinguishes it from structuration, or more generally any 'central conflation' theory'.[54] This constitutes an important methodological gloss on his earlier statement that, 'it is, I suggest, in the (explanation of the) differentiation and stratification, production and reproduction, mutation and transformation, continual remoulding and incessant shifting, of the relatively enduring relations presupposed by particular social forms and structures that sociology's 'distinctive theoretical interest lies'.[55] So it does, and my main concern goes beyond producing an acceptable social ontology for it seeks to present a workable social theory. Yet the latter has to be predicated upon the former (or the slippage into instrumentalism is fatal). This is precisely the reason for the present chapter, namely to demonstrate how an Emergentist ontology necessarily entails analytical dualism, especially if it is to generate a workable methodology – for the practical analysis of vexatious society.

Notes

1 David Lockwood, 'Social integration and system integration', in G. K. Zollschan and H. W. Hirsch (eds.), *Explorations in Social Change*, Houghton Mifflin, Boston, 1964.
2 Walter Buckley, *Sociology and Modern Systems Theory*, Prentice Hall, New Jersey, 1967.
3 Peter Blau, *Exchange and Power in Social Life*, Wiley, New York, 1964.
4 William Outhwaite, 'Realism, naturalism and social behaviour', *Journal for the Theory of Social Behaviour*, 1990, 20: 4, p. 366.
5 Roy Bhaskar, *The Possibility of Naturalism*, Harvester Wheatsheaf, Hemel Hempstead, 1989, pp. 25–6.
6 Percy S. Cohen, *Modern Social Theory*, Heinemann, London, 1968, p. 93.

7 Anthony Giddens, *Central Problems in Social Theory*, Macmillan, London, 1979, p. 217.
8 Roy Bhaskar, *Reclaiming Reality*, Verso, London, 1989, p. 77.
9 Roy Bhaskar, 'Beef, structure and place: notes from a critical naturalist perspective', *Journal for the Theory of Social Behaviour*, 1983, 13, p. 85.
10 Bhaskar, *Reclaiming Reality*, p. 4.
11 Bhaskar, *Reclaiming Reality*, p. 76.
12 Bhaskar, *Reclaiming Reality*, p. 77.
13 Ernest Gellner, 'Explanations in history', in John O'Neill (ed.), *Modes of Individualism and Collectivism*, Heinemann, London, 1973, p. 262.
14 Bhaskar, *Naturalism*, pp. 33–4
15 Bhaskar, 'Beef', p. 85.
16 Bhaskar, *Reclaiming Reality*, p. 80.
17 Bhaskar, *Naturalism*, p. 37.
18 Bhaskar, *Reclaiming Reality*, p. 76.
19 William Outhwaite, 'Agency and structure', in J. Clarke, C. Modgil and S. Modgil (eds.), *Anthony Giddens: Consensus and Controversy*, Falmer, Basingstoke, 1990, p. 70.
20 Bhaskar, *Reclaiming Reality*, p. 78.
21 Ted Benton, 'Realism and social science: some comments on Roy Bhaskar's *The Possibility of Naturalism*', *Radical Philosophy*, 1981, 27, p. 17.
22 Bhaskar, *Naturalism*, p. 174.
23 Bhaskar, *Reclaiming Reality*, p. 78.
24 Benton, 'Realism', p. 17.
25 Bhaskar, *Reclaiming Reality*, p. 98.
26 Bhaskar, *Naturalism*, p. 51.
27 Bhaskar, *Naturalism*, p. 26.
28 Bhaskar, *Reclaiming Reality*, p. 91.
29 Derek Layder, *Structure, Interaction and Social Theory*, Routledge and Kegan Paul, London, 1981, p. 73.
30 Benton, 'Realism', p. 17.
31 J. W. N. Watkins, 'Methodological individualism and social tendencies', in May Brodbeck (ed.), *Readings in the Philosophy of the Social Sciences*, Macmillan, New York, 1971, pp. 270–1.
32 Bhaskar, *Naturalism*, p. 174.
33 Anthony Giddens, *The Constitution of Society: Outline of the Theory of Structuration*, Polity, Cambridge, 1984, p. 26.
34 Bhaskar, *Naturalism*, p. 14.
35 Bhaskar, *Naturalism*, p. 78.
36 Bhaskar, *Reclaiming Reality*, pp. 79–80.
37 Bhaskar, *Reclaiming Reality*, p. 92.
38 Bhaskar, *Reclaiming Reality*, p. 92.
39 Bhaskar, *Naturalism*, p. 41.
40 Bhaskar, *Naturalism*, p. 40.
41 Bhaskar, *Naturalism*, p. 41.
42 Bhaskar, *Reclaiming Reality*, p. 97.
43 Bhaskar, *Naturalism*, p. 90.
44 Bhaskar, 'Beef', p. 85.
45 Bhaskar, 'Beef', p. 93.
46 Bhaskar, *Reclaiming Reality*, p. 77.
47 Bhaskar, *Reclaiming Reality*, p. 95.
48 Bhaskar, *Reclaiming Reality*, p. 77.
49 Sage, London and Beverly Hills, 1979.

50 Bhaskar, *Reclaiming Reality*, p. 77.
51 Giddens, *Social Theory*, p. 215.
52 William Outhwaite, 'Realism, naturalism and social behaviour', *Journal for the Study of Social Behaviour*, 1990, 20: 4, p. 366.
53 Andrew Sayer, *Method in Social Science: A Realist Approach*, Routledge, London, 1992.
54 Roy Bhaskar, *Dialectic: The Pulse of Freedom*, Verso, London, 1993, p. 160
55 Bhaskar, *Naturalism*, p. 41.

Part III

THE THEORY OF EXPLANATORY CRITIQUES

15

INTRODUCTION

Explanatory critiques

Roy Bhaskar and Andrew Collier

Until recently it was generally taken for granted that there was a fallacy involved in arguing from an "is" to an "ought", or from a fact to a value, or from an indicative to an imperative. The certainty that prevailed about this was marked by the use of the term "Hume's Law" for the impossibility of making such a move, and "the naturalistic fallacy" for attempts to do so. One of us (Andrew) remembers being told as an undergraduate in the 1960s, that Hume's Law was one of the few things in philosophy that was agreed to have been proved.

But even then, people were beginning to challenge this dogma. Searle argued that from the fact that I have promised to do something it follows that I have an obligation (other things being equal) to do it ["How to Derive 'Ought' from 'Is'", *Philosophical Review* 73, 1964]. It came to be widely argued that ethics necessarily had something to do with "human flourishing", a view associated with Philippa Foot and Elizabeth Anscombe. Senses of "good" for which there are clear factual criteria (a good friend cannot be one who tells malicious lies about you, a good trade unionist cannot be one who crosses the picket line) were once more recognised as morally significant (as they had earlier been by Bradley and Hegelian ethics generally). But although these developments took away the obviousness of "Hume's Law", it was always possible if often implausible, to claim that all fact-to-value arguments involved covert shifting between distinct factual and evaluative senses of some word or phrase. A further step was taken when Roy Edgley pointed out that factual statements could undoubtedly criticise something, since they criticised all those other factual statements that they contradicted [see his article "Reason as Dialectic" in *Radical Philosophy* 15, 1976, reprinted below. Compare his book *Reason in Theory and Practice*, Hutchinson, London, 1969]. This was the beginning of the end for Hume's Law. But Edgley did not spell out in any detail the way that factual statements could criticise wider social institutions, which are not themselves statements. However he did say:

> social science, in criticising other, ideological social theories and ideas as deeply contradictory, and so contradicting them, at the same time criticises as contradictory, and so contradicts, the society in whose structure those inconsistent and conceptually muddled theories and ideas are realised.
>
> ("Reason as Dialectic", p. 7)

This is I think the first explicit statement of the theory of explanatory critiques in a nutshell, but it was left to Roy Bhaskar to work this insight into a theory, and give this sort of criticism a name: *explanatory critique.*

While many social scientists accepted and still accept "Hume's Law", it was clear enough that they and their readers acted as if their factual or explanatory theories had practical, moral or political implications. People who were convinced by the theories of Freud drew the conclusion that infantile sexuality should not be suppressed and that children should be told the truth about sex and biological reproduction. Marx's *Capital* does not prescribe any new values, it describes and explains capitalist economies, yet it is a landmark in the history of socialist advocacy. In fact practically all explanatory theories about human life and society generate moral or political programmes, but Marx and Freud, with their fellow "master of suspicion" Nietzsche, do so in a special way, which gave rise to that title. They explain ideas that we have and live by, in ways that throw doubt on their truth. They do not *replace* the question of the truth of an idea by the question of its causal origin – a procedure which has its place for certain purposes, but would have no great practical import. Rather, they pose the questions of the causation and function of an idea together with that of its truth or falsehood, in such a way that the causal accounts show why we tend to have certain kinds of false belief. For instance, a true account of oppression in a society would subvert that society, so it is not surprising that there should be mechanisms in oppressive societies for hiding the oppression from the oppressed, and very often from the oppressors too.

This "suspicion" of the truthfulness of ideas on the ground of an account of their origin is continuous with a familiar sort of argument at the everyday, pre-theoretical level: "they would say that, wouldn't they?" But in Marx's analysis of ideology, Nietzsche's analysis of the genealogy of morals and Freud's analysis of repression and rationalisation, this suspicion becomes a theoretical tool with far-reaching uses.

One aim of critical realism has been to produce a theory of science and social science which does justice to the practice of these disciplines, in place of theories, often held by the scientists themselves, that do not. While the critical potential of social science has often been noticed, it has also often been treated as an error, a departure from the ideal of a neutral, value-free science. Marx for instance has been accused of "smuggling" the "evaluative" concept of exploitation into what was supposed to be a work of objective social science (*Capital*). Some Marxists, such as the Austrian economist Rudolf Hilferding, have thought that Marxism had to be analysed into two logically distinct theories – the explanatory theory of *Capital* which, as objectively true, could have helped any politician whatever their politics, and a humanist value system which was the source of Marx's socialist views. Other critical social scientists, wanting to preserve the critical potential of their work but accepting the fact/value divide, have thought it best to state their values openly at the outset, and then mingle facts and values freely in their work. But this is not what Marx or Freud did. (The issue here is not whether Marx's or Freud's conclusions are in fact true, which can only be decided empirically. It is what their practice of social science was, and how it is related logically to their practical aim, objective and proposals.)

Both Marx and Freud seemed very concerned to keep value judgements out of their premisses, yet both produce theories with practical implications. This is what offends those who accept Hume's Law: they feel that values must have been brought in surreptitiously at some point, just as a conjurer who pulls a rabbit out of a hat must have put it in there first. But if it can be shown that Marx and Freud's practice is logically kosher – that objective explanatory science need not be value-neutral – an exciting possibility arises: that an objective study can actually *discover* values that it did not assume beforehand.

The theory of explanatory critique makes it explicit how this can be done. The starting point is that a social science can study both ideas, and what those ideas are about. For instance, the study of a particular society and a particular time will include information about the class structure of that society at that time, and also about the ideas prevalent in that society, which will include ideas about its class structure. It may be that many people in that society believe that it is a classless society, when in fact it is not. After all, John Major claimed that Britain would soon be a classless society, while he presided over a government under which inequality rose to its highest level for a hundred years. Presumably he sincerely believed what he said, and perhaps some other people believed him too. Such beliefs may not be accidental. They may, for example, be caused directly or indirectly, in all or in part by just that class structure whose existence they are denying.

Such beliefs may also have effects on that class structure, for instance by preventing people from trying to alter it. In the strongest case, it may be that a social scientific study can show that a given society necessarily generates, and relies on for its own reproduction, certain false beliefs about itself. But that is something *wrong* with that society, which (other things being equal) ought to be put right.

At this point two objections might be raised. It might be said that the view that one ought to believe what is true is itself a value judgement. In one sense it is – it clearly has prescriptive force. But it is not an optional value judgement; it follows from the nature of the case. One does not even know what belief is if one does not know that you should believe what is true – that it makes no sense to say "that is true, but I do not believe it"; yet it is a perfectly objective fact that people have beliefs:

> that truth *is* a good (*ceteris paribus*) is not only a condition of moral discourse, it is a condition of any discourse at all. Commitment to truth and consistency apply to factual as much to value discourse; and so cannot be seized upon as a concealed (value) premise.
>
> (*The Possibility of Naturalism* p. 63, reprinted above)

So to be induced to believe something which is false does not just often *cause* other harm, it always *is* harm. Not of course by any means necessarily the worst harm that can befall a person, but harm nonetheless.

The second objection is that it is not always a bad thing overall to have false beliefs. It is best if an assassin has false beliefs about his victim's whereabouts. To take a more everyday case, it is usually wrong to tell a person with a jealous disposition the truth that their partner has slept with someone else. There is also information that the human race ought never to have acquired. For instance the knowledge obtained by the Nazi scientists who subjected prisoners to prolonged X-ray filming, discovering thereby information about human physiology which could not have been got in any other way, but also leading to the painful death of the innocent victims shortly after the experiment [see R.D. Laing, *Wisdom, Madness and Folly*, Macmillan, London 1985, p. 69]. And there is knowledge which can only be put to bad use, like the knowledge how to make an atomic bomb, or which will almost certainly be put to bad use, like the knowledge how to choose the sex of one's children. It is arguable that some scientific research programmes should be closed down because their results are almost certain to be misused (genetic engineering, for example). However, none of this proves that knowledge is not a good or false belief an evil; only that there are other goods and evils too; and that most things, including true or false belief, are only good or evil "other things being equal". Perhaps one reason why people so readily accept the view that facts cannot have practical implications is that, if a fact is true, it is true whatever else is true, whereas if a fact implies that something should be done, it almost never does so whatever else is the case.

Now let us return to our example of class structure. Someone might claim that the society in question was so much better than any feasible alternative that the false beliefs that oiled its wheels were a price well worth paying. Plato thought just that about his Republic: its citizens should believe a "noble lie" about the origins of classes to reconcile them to their inequality. The first point to note about this is that it doesn't affect the logical point that a valid argument from fact to value has been produced, since that only requires that false belief be a disvalue, not that it outweigh all other values.

The second point is this: for all that it is sometimes best to hide the truth, we quite rightly assume that, as a rule, people hide the truth in order to get away with wrongdoing. More generally that hidden truth helped to perpetuate wrongdoing or social ill, whether we have the results of conscious intentionality or not. The "noble lie" is not the worst thing about Plato's Republic, but it is a clue to the worst thing: the repression of most of its citizens. A free and equal society would not need lies. For this reason explanatory critiques of the sort just described have an important place in the politics of human emancipation. They expose not just false beliefs, but the false beliefs by which oppression and injustice are disguised, whether consciously or not, and perpetuated.

The theory of explanatory critiques is also very far-reaching philosophically. Once we have a single valid fact-to-value (or is-to-ought) argument, the claim that such arguments are necessarily fallacious falls, and the motive for resisting other sorts of fact-to-value argument is removed. Arguments from the conditions of human flourishing (one might add: not only *human* flourishing) come into their own.

This opens up the possibility of extending realism into the realm of values and morality, finding an "intransitive dimension" underlying moral thought and moral change, parallel to – and perhaps in tandem with – that dimension which underlies scientific thought and scientific change; a moral realism, too, which is naturalistic in the sense that it does not look for real values in a Platonic world of ideas or a Kantian world of noumena, but in the real world which we all inhabit. Recent developments in critical realism have given two leads to be followed up about what that morality might be: one, echoing Kant and Hegel though without their idealism, suggesting that the project of universal emancipation may be implicit in every free action; the other, echoing in a different key the medieval idea that being as being is good and evil is a privation of being, suggesting that all ills may be thought of as absences. But these ideas belong to the dialectical stage of critical realist thought, and so are outside the scope of the present section. We think it may help to see what is at issue in the following passages, though, if one keeps in mind the possibility that the grounding of values in facts may not just be sometimes possible, but that it may be that any rational value judgement *must* have factual grounding. If this is so, then any evaluative argument which starts from values alone – or rather which does not start from facts – must be seen as radically incomplete.

We now pass to an introductory discussion of the six texts printed in this section.

Reason as Dialectic: Science, Social Science and Socialist Science (Roy Edgley)

This paper from *Radical Philosophy* 15 (1976) does not start from an explicitly critical realist account of science, but from two positions shared indeed by critical realists but uncontentious among all but the most extreme relativist philosophies of science – namely that science gives us knowledge of what it is about, and that two contradictory statements cannot both be true. However it does give an account of how a purely descriptive and explanatory theory can be critical of its object, three years before the publication of *The Possibility of Naturalism*. Starting from the question whether the claim that you cannot argue from facts to values vitiates Marx's notion of scientific socialism, Roy Edgley points out that a scientific theory is necessarily critical of theories inconsistent with it and that to show up a contradiction in a theory is to criticise it. But since societies include theories, that means that a theory about a society can be a criticism of that society. He links this with the Marxian notion of reason as dialectical, that is, as exposing discrepancies between appearance and reality, themselves to be explained in terms of contradictions and conflicts in the underlying or deeper reality.

Scientific Realism and Human Emancipation, 2.5–2.7 (Roy Bhaskar)

Although there is a brief account of explanatory critiques in the passage in *The Possibility of Naturalism* from which the above quote is taken, the full account of them (previewed in Roy Bhaskar's article "Scientific Explanation and Human Emancipation" in *Radical Philosophy* 26, 1980) occurs in these sections quoted below. The first of these sections ("Facts and Values: Theory and Practice") opens with an argument which fights on two fronts. On the one hand, Roy Bhaskar is defending the critical potential of the knowledge given by social science; and on the other, he is arguing that such knowledge never occurs in a vacuum or autonomously or unaffected by non-cognitive factors. It always occurs in the context of a social structure and an already ongoing set of desires and practices. The "rationalism in politics" that Oakeshott and other conservatives criticise in the Enlightenment and its heirs is a real error, and consists in ignoring this second point. But that conservatism itself errs in ignoring the former: that culturally dependent and late in time as the coming of theoretical knowledge is, it can criticise and transform the practices amongst which it emerges, and thereby also the structures in which they are embedded. It is possible to defend the emancipatory effects of reason in politics without being a "rationalist in politics" (and as in politics, so in morality).

The situating of factual theories in the midst of practices (which necessarily involve values) is necessary to avoid "rationalism in politics", or utopianism in the bad sense given to that word by Marx and Engels. But it could risk trivialising the claim that factual theories entail values, by conceding that they have a value input too. No adherent of Hume's Law would be surprised or offended by this, and no social scientist would be able to claim that their theory had new evaluative implications. This trivialising is avoided by the claim that whereas at the causal level the relation between values and factual theories is symmetrical (values motivate theories which motivate values and so on), at the logical level the relation is one-way (factual theories entail values but values do not entail factual theories). This is expressed by the alternating double and single arrows in diagrams 1 and 2 (pp. 412–13 [173 of SRHE]).

The passage from pp. 415–17 below [176–180 in SRHE], together with the later sections on levels IV and V, is the classic critical realist statement of the theory of explanatory critiques. The argument is essentially that already outlined in this introduction. Four abbreviations used but not explained within this passage should be noted. IA = intrinsic aspect, the normative, action-guiding or future-oriented aspects of any cognitive process or product, the sense in which Bhaskar wants to uphold judgmental rationality (see *Scientific Realism and Human Emancipation* pp. 16 ff. passim); EA = extrinsic, geo-historically caused aspects of any cognitive process or product, the sense in which Bhaskar is also committed to the causal explicability (and potential efficacy) of all ideas (see p. 532 of this volume for an explanation); TMSA = transformational model of social activity (see p. 207 of this volume for an explanation); and CP – *ceteris paribus* ("other things being equal").

In sections 2.6 and 2.7 of SRHE (pp. 418–43 below) explanatory critiques are situated in relation to the other ways in which theory can transform practice, and this is further spelt out with reference in particular to Marx (level V) and an egalitarian model of psychotherapy or consciousness-raising, called "depth inquiry" (level VI). There is a short commentary on these levels of practical rationality in "Explanation and Emancipation" (pp. 459–61 below [*Critical Realism* pp. 188–190]).

One warning to the reader: there are a number of diagrams and formal schemas in this excerpt. Some readers find these wonderfully illuminating and able to fix the argument in their minds; others find themselves spending much time deciphering them, only to discover that what they say is said in a less formal and therefore more accurate way in the text. If you are one of the first kind of reader, you will no doubt welcome these schemas; but if you are one of the second (as Andrew is) do not be put off. A careful reading of the verbal text will tell you all you need to know.

Explanation and Emancipation (*Critical Realism*, chapter 6) (Andrew Collier)

This chapter was written partly as an introductory commentary on Roy Bhaskar's text, partly as a defence of his theory of explanatory critiques, and partly as an exploration of the potential of that theory for politics and ethics. On one issue (the extent to which prior values can legitimately influence theory, generating a degree of relativism) it is critical of Roy's account. The first of its four sections outlines the crucial argument about explanatory critiques of structures which give rise to falsehoods, refuting "Hume's Law". The second discusses analogous arguments based on human needs rather than cognitive truth or falsehood. It goes on to draw parallels with Spinoza's ethics and Freud's psychoanalysis. These can be read as consisting in explanatory critiques of our individual emotional make-ups, applied through self-knowledge (Spinoza) or by something like the depth inquiry discussed under level VI of practical rationality in the last excerpt (Freud). It concludes with comments on these seven levels.

The third section is a discussion of the relation between the Spinozistic "cognitive paradigm of ethics" which can arguably be founded on the theory of explanatory critiques, and the theory of human emancipation as something by no means purely cognitive; for while knowledge of one's deception or self-deception can undeceive one and is to that extent liberating, knowledge of one's oppression may initially just make one more unhappy and discontented, though that knowledge and any ensuing (additional) discontent is a necessary (not a sufficient) condition for one's eventual self-emancipation from that oppression.

In the final section of this chapter, the question of the relation of critical realism to politics is raised. Critical realism is committed to human emancipation, but that is a very general phrase. How does it cash out? It is clear that there is some sort of connection between critical realism and socialist politics (at least a biographical one in the case of both authors of this introduction, and many other critical realists). Yet philosophical positions hardly ever *entail* political positions or *vice versa*, and this case is no exception. All the same, there may be some relation: critical realism shows the fallacy of several of the classical arguments against socialism; and it supports the *possibility* of a form of socialism which is neither a market economy nor a command economy nor a mix of the two, but a genuine extension of pluralistic democracy into economic life.

Neutrality in the Social Sciences (Hugh Lacey)

This is a paper from a position close to if not within critical realism, which defends some reservations about the idea that explanatory critiques can give us a theoretical basis for human emancipation.

It starts by making some useful distinctions between different ways in which one can be committed to beliefs, theories and values. The reservation about explanatory critiques as emancipatory is twofold. First, he draws attention to another way in which values can motivate the acceptance or rejection of theories. It is based on Rudner's claim that to be committed to a theory is to hold that the cognitive grounds for it are so strong that we need not worry about the harmfulness of acting on it were it to turn out to be false. This seems to refer to a practical rather than a theoretical commitment. It is clear that when the consequences that acting on a particular theory would have, if it turned out to be false, are horrendous enough, one ought not to act on that theory even if it is almost certainly true. We might be 99.9 per cent certain that a particular experiment will not lead to the destruction of all life on Earth, but if there is a 0.1 per cent chance that it will, we ought not to do it. On the other hand it might be quite reasonable to act as if a theory with a 55 per cent chance of being true were true if the harmful consequences of this action were it false are trivial. This sort of practical reasoning has long been known to gamblers, and its philosophical reflection goes back to Pascal, though it might be argued that, despite Pascal, it would be rational to believe the 99.9 per cent probable theory, though not to act on it. Nevertheless this problem about commitment to dangerous theories does raise serious issues when combined with the second point.

The second point concerns the extent to which the *ceteris paribus* ("other things being equal") clause saps explanatory critiques of their emancipatory potential. There is no disagreement here either about the ability of explanatory critiques to yield value judgements other things being equal, or about their inability to yield unconditional value judgements. The point is how far these value judgements can take us if they are only "other things being equal", since other things never are equal. If an explanatory critique of market economies finds them wanting, that may be a *prima facie* case for abolishing them; but if any attempt to do so would inevitably lead to Stalinism, then the case against abolishing them might still be overwhelming. Unless of course it were the case, say, that an unavoidable consequence of retaining market economies were the destruction of life by an ecological disaster. Whether any of these depressing possibilities is true is of course an empirical question. Philosophical argument on this matter can only point us to the need for empirical inquiry, unless of course it leads to the sceptical conclusion that since we can never foresee which other things will not be equal, we can never know what it is best to do. Hugh Lacey sees a way out in focusing on movements such as co-operative groups of impoverished people for collective self-help, which have the potential for ameliorative action with foreseeable, because local and limited, consequences, and without the large-scale projects of structural change which the term "human emancipation" suggests. How far such movements can go towards the elimination of the evils that they seek to remedy is of course an empirical question. Lacey's political point seems to be to challenge the sharp critical realist distinction between "amelioration of states of affairs" and "transformation of structures", somewhat in the spirit of Popper's critique of social engineering.

Addressing the Cultural System (*Culture and Agency*, chapter 5) (Margaret Archer)

This chapter returns to the premisses of Roy Edgley's paper to defend a thesis which is essential to all explanatory critiques: that the ideas integral to a society can be logically contradictory, and that to show that they are is to criticise them and so to criticise that society. For some forms of relativism the rule against contradiction is just a local principle of some societies, with no purchase on those that do not accept it; for others, the question whether the ideas prevalent in a society contradict each other does not even arise, since ideas are studied only in their causal relations, not their logical relations. Margaret Archer presents a lucid case for preserving two distinct studies of two analytically distinguishable aspects of any society: the logical relations ("the Cultural System") and causal relations ("the Socio-Cultural level"). The claim that one should understand ideas in their context, for instance, could mean the logical context of other ideas which might support or conflict with them, or their causal context. The main theme of this chapter is that these levels should not be conflated. Margaret Archer also shows that a number of the examples used by relativists do not support relativist conclusions about logic.

Conclusion, *Crime, Reason and History* (Alan Norrie)

After the various discussions of explanatory critiques, we come with this text to a contemporary instance of explanatory critique. Since this chapter is the conclusion of a full length book, Alan Norrie has supplied brief accounts of the arguments in the various chapters referred to in the text, so that the reader can judge for him- or herself the strength of the critique. The claim is that the legal system includes justifications for its various practices (for example punishment) in terms which are ultimately contradictory or incoherent. These terms are various instances of an ideology which he calls "juridical individualism". The contradictions within this juridical ideology reflect contradictions between its assumption of unconditioned individual responsibility and the reality of crime as caused by particular social institutions and conditions. So that Norrie's arguments, if valid, are an indictment at once of explicit juridical theories, implicit ideology and the society in which these things arise as, in some measure, a smokescreen to obscure social realities.

A.C.
R.B.
February 1998

16

REASON AS DIALECTIC

Science, social science and socialist science

Roy Edgley

The current crisis, social and intellectual

The current crisis in world affairs, in particular the economic and social crisis in those countries that dominate world affairs, the advanced industrial states of Europe and America, is reflected in an intellectual crisis, especially in those countries. As they move into the so-called 'post-industrial' phase, into 'technological society', their dominant form of theoretical knowledge, scientific knowledge, increasingly becomes a crucial economic resource, a factor of production; and the intellectual crisis reveals itself as a radical uncertainty about the nature and status of science. Europe invented modern science, and just as, during the centuries of European imperialism, Europe sought to dominate the rest of the world, so Europe's dominant form of knowledge, science, has been involved in the imperial conquest of other cultures. Thus the conflict between the advanced industrial states and the Third World, a conflict that is an essential component of the current world crisis, is reflected intellectually in a conflict between science and other forms of thought – for example, between European *medical* science and such apparently unscientific forms of medicine as acupuncture.

As social institutions designed for the production and distribution of theoretical knowledge, the universities are of course deeply involved in the crisis, and it is not surprising that they have been centres of ferment in the last decade or so. They are the social points at which the intellectual aspect of the crisis has its most explicit theoretical expression. Anthropologists have become hypersensitive about applying their own concepts of science and rationality to what used to be called 'primitive' cultures and belief systems. Psychologists and psychiatrists discuss and re-draw the distinction between sanity and madness. And at the most abstract level, philosophers – well,

Source: Radical Philosophy, 15, 1976, pp. 2–7.

many English-speaking philosophers, I suppose, continue to do logic, philosophy of logic, and epistemology as if they inhabited the ivory tower of timeless Platonic forms, the Third World of Popper rather than of Che. But even ivory towers cannot be completely insulated, and the general philosophical preoccupation with the distinction between reason and unreason has taken specific forms that relate more explicitly to the social situation. In particular, in English philosophy two new sub-disciplines, not distinguished and named before, have emerged as growing points within and between the old philosophical specialisms, and both in that historical fact and in their own content have reflected intellectually the general social crisis. I am referring to the philosophy of science within the general field of epistemology, and to the philosophy of the social sciences which has developed between the philosophy of science and the old sub-discipline of political philosophy. The chief preoccupation of these two new sub-disciplines has become the distinction between science and ideology.

In both fields one can trace in the analytical tradition a more or less gradual relaxation of the constraints thought to be implicit in the idea of science and reason. In the philosophy of science Popper sought to replace inductivism and verificationism with the less stringent requirement of falsificationism; Kuhn argued that even that was too stringent for revolutionary science; and Feyerabend has argued that all science is or ought to be revolutionary science, and in his article and book *Against Method*, as the title indicates, claims that the only rule of method in the acquisition of knowledge is 'Anything Goes'. In a rather different way, the philosophy of the social sciences has similarly helped to soften up the idea of rationality: as a practising social scientist with an unusual degree of philosophical self-understanding, Chomsky has attacked behaviourist constraints imposed in the cause of scientificity; and Popper's doctrine of the unity of science, implying that in methodology and logical structure the social sciences are indistinguishable from the natural sciences, has been opposed by the idea that the social sciences have their own special logic and methodology. In some writers – Winch, for instance – this methodology involves the claim that societies under investigation may legitimately employ canons of rationality quite different from, but not inferior to, its own. We seem to be presented with a choice between equally unacceptable alternatives: on the one hand, an empiricism that is unable to account for much of the historical phenomenon of science; and on the other hand, a relativism that makes radical criticism impossible, and in doing so seems to be self-refuting.

Marxism as scientific socialism

The place of Marxism in this discussion is distinctive and instructive. Its failure to fit the dominant empiricist model in the philosophy of science is even more striking than the failure of other, more generally accepted, theories and phases of modern science: within the European conception of science it is a genuine peculiarity. Yet Winch's relativism does not obviously save it, even as relativistically rational. Marxism is, after all, a European product, conceived explicitly as heir to the great tradition of natural science that Europe invented: it is not a form of thought characteristic of a foreign society, defining a conception of rationality necessarily alien to our language and culture, and therefore apparently uncriticizable from our European point of view. On the contrary, to the extent that Marxism characterizes other cultures, it does so as one of those cultural exports that Europe's imperial capitalism did not, so to speak, bargain for, and which it now faces as an alien threat.

Endogenous to Europe, then, Marxism has been typically criticized by European intellectuals within the analytical tradition, especially philosophers of science and of social science, as unscientific, as muddled about the nature of science and its own relation to it: those with an explicit demarcation criterion, such as Popper, have put it firmly in its place as pseudoscience. But this general difficulty of appreciating Marxism's claim to be a science is not peculiar to analytical philosophers and those scientists whose understanding of science has been articulated and shaped by analytical philosophy. It is not even peculiar to non-Marxists in general. Within Marxism itself, many have deeply felt and wrestled with it. There is in fact one specific form of the problem that is common to Marxist and non-Marxist discussions – a form posed by Marxism's self-description as 'scientific socialism'. Marxism presents itself as both social science and political movement, as both scientific theory and revolutionary practice: as something concerned not only to understand the world but also to change it. Discussions within Marxism about whether the socialism is distinguishable from the science, and if so how these two elements are related, reveal that certain conceptions of science and reason are deeply entrenched as common property on both sides of the divide between Marxists and non-Marxists.

These common conceptions involve a family of shared ideas about the distinction between fact and value, theory and practice, description and prescription, science and morality. Contemporary English-speaking discussion of these ideas has a characteristic parochialism, and seems to suggest that apart from anticipations by Hume ('is' and 'ought') and perhaps Mill (science as indicative and art as imperative), their history belongs to 20th-century analytical philosophy, from Moore's 'naturalist fallacy' through the emotivism of Ayer and Stevenson to Hare. But it is clear that the European mainland shared much of this thinking and made its own contribution to the history of the distinctions as they developed under the impact of science and capitalism from the 17th-century onwards. Kant, Comte, Weber and Poincaré, as well as Mach and the Vienna Circle, all struggled to digest philosophically the phenomenon of science, and in the process distinguished it logically and epistemologically from value, or practice, or morality. Here, for instance, is Poincaré making the point in a way familiar to contemporary English philosophers:

> It is not possible to have a scientific ethic, but it is no more possible to have an immoral science. And the reason is simple; it is, how shall I put it? for purely grammatical reasons. If the premises of a syllogism are both in the indicative, the conclusion will equally be in the indicative. In order for the conclusion to be put in the imperative, it would be necessary for at least one of the premises to be in the imperative. Now, the principles of science, the postulates of geometry, are and can only be in the indicative; experimental truths are also in this same mode, and at the foundations of science there is not, cannot be, anything else. Moreover the most subtle dialectician can juggle with these principles as he wishes, combine them, pile them up one on the other; all that he can derive from them will be in the indicative. He will never obtain a proposition which says: do this, or do not do that; that is to say a proposition which confirms or contradicts ethics.
>
> ('Morality and science', 1913)

Given such a general climate of opinion, Marxism seems to be faced with some difficult choices: as social science it cannot be socialism, and as socialism it cannot be social science; the two elements might be conjoined, but not logically connected or unified. 'Value-free' science can, of course, have a practical application as technology, but technology can only specify means to ends and must therefore be supplemented with a choice of ends or objectives that cannot be settled scientifically. This is roughly the view of the Austro-Marxist Rudolf Hilferding, in his book *Finance Capital*, and of most of the orthodox Marxism of the Second International. In his neo-Kantian version of Marxism in his lecture on 'Kant and Marx' (1904), Karl Vorlander identifies the values of Marxism as ethical: 'Socialism cannot free itself from ethics historically or logically, neither on the theoretical level nor in fact.' But *ethical* socialism is Utopian, and in practice reformist rather than revolutionary, liberal and social-democratic rather than Marxist; and it is well known that Marx himself was contemptuous of morality and treated it theoretically as essentially ideological. Under these constraints *scientific* socialism came to be represented, predominantly in the Third International and in Stalinism, as a theory specifying laws of inevitable social change. Between this and the alternative of ethical socialism, Marxism as a programme of revolutionary action was effectively squeezed out of the picture of coherent possibilities.

This ideological emasculation no doubt reveals the almost inexhaustible capacity of the status quo to protect itself under threat. But is that emasculation avoidable from a rational point of view? I want to make some suggestions to that end: suggestions that are both fairly simple and very general because they re-theorize (by developing arguments originally put forward in my *Reason in Theory and Practice*, London 1969) the overall structural relations between the relevant basic and very general categories. From this perspective the conception of science from which the emasculation results is itself ideological, in fact a crucial part of the European ideology out of which Marxism developed as a radical innovation and critique. As ideology, this conception reflects important, but relatively superficial, aspects of science, aspects that mask and contradict its deeper nature and potential. Historically speaking, it is this embryonic reality within the womb of European science that Hegel and Marx, heirs and critics of the Enlightenment, develop and deliver as social science. As such, the Marxist conception of science is both continuous with, and radically different from, the prevailing conception. The question of the scientificity or otherwise of Marxism cannot therefore be answered by noting its failure to conform to Enlightenment standards of science articulated by Hume and Kant and developed by their modern followers. On the contrary, the question is whether Marxism embodies a different conception that supersedes its rivals.

Science and reason as dialectic

The conception of science and reason that Marxism explicitly offers in distinguishing itself from the Enlightenment is: dialectic. It is this Hegelian inheritance that is contrasted with the 'metaphysical' conception of science shaped in 'the mechanical philosophy'. Mechanistic science is allowed to have both a necessary historical role and a continuing validity in certain areas of investigation. But dialectic, it is claimed, is essential for the 'historical' sciences. Moreover, to focus on the present topic, Marxists have frequently claimed that this conception of science as dialectic is required to solve the problems set by the idea of scientific socialism. The deformations of both ethical socialism and Stalinism involve mechanistic conceptions of science.

It is this view that I want to explore and give support to. But first it should be noted that there is an easy way out which in fact settles nothing. A dialectical conception, it might be said, is a view that conceives of opposites as in unity: scientific socialism is such a unity, since it unites fact and value, theory and practice, science and political revolution. That, of course, only sets the problem. It doesn't solve it. The problem precisely is how to conceive of science in such a way that value and practice can be seen as involved in it.

I shall now try to outline a solution of this problem in terms of the idea of contradiction, which is central to dialectic. The idea of contradiction is also, of course, central to analytical philosophy. But on this matter the two traditions face each other with blank incomprehension. For both, contradiction is a concept, or rather a category, of logic; and it is in the philosophy of logic of each tradition that the differing conceptions of science have their roots.

Roughly and briefly, the Hegelian view is that reality is in a constant process of change, and that this temporal, historical process is due to the contradictions within the essence of things. These contradictions oppose each other, and change is the resolution of that opposition and the replacement of those contradictions by others on a higher plane, so that change through resolution continues. Now Hegel was, of course, an idealist, and though analytical philosophers claim to see some truth in the claim that *ideas* can be contradictory, the Marxist dialectic is materialist, not idealist, and from the analytical point of view the doctrine that there are contradictions in material reality seems nothing short of outrageous. In such a context, the concept of contradiction, it seems, must lose its specifically logical content and cease to be a category of logic: it can only mean something like 'conflict' or 'opposition between forces'. Marx himself sometimes speaks of 'collisions' rather than 'contradictions'; and many Marxist writers, when discussing dialectic, seem satisfied with this evacuation of the specifically logical content of the idea of contradiction, or at least fail to take up the point seriously, as if they have no understanding of the basic position from which the objection is made.

The analytical view: dialectic not logic

We can see the analytical side of this lack of comprehension starkly represented in Popper's critique of the idea of dialectical logic in his 'What is Dialectic?'[1] Popper claims that dialectic is most plausible as an empirical theory about the temporal or historical development of thought. But under that interpretation, it precisely cannot be logic, and this for three general reasons that can be identified in Popper's argument and its background of modern philosophy of logic:

(1) There are no contradictions in reality. Popper approvingly quotes the words of the mathematical logician Hilbert: 'The thought that facts or events might mutually contradict each other appears to me as the very paradigm of thoughtlessness.' Now, it might be supposed that this doctrine is true of material reality and thus undermines the Marxist dialectic, dialectical materialism. But, it might be argued, it could be taken to be true of the whole of reality only if the common philosophical contrast between thought and reality misled us into believing that thought itself is not a part of reality; but, of course, thought is a part of reality, and in that part there can be contradictions. However, to the extent that it is admitted that there can be contradictions in thought, the concession is heavily qualified. For the argument that there can be no contradictions in reality seems to apply in some sense to any part of reality, thought included. The argument is that if the proposition 'p' contradicts the proposition 'q', the proposition 'p' & 'q' must be false, i.e. nothing in reality can correspond to it. In other words, if the proposition 'p' contradicts the proposition 'q', it is logically impossible that

both *p* and *q*: there can be no state of affairs corresponding to a contradiction.

(2) As this argument presupposes, logical relations are truth-value relations between propositions. In the paper 'What is Dialectic?' Popper speaks of sentences, but whatever the word used they are denizens of what Popper now refers to as the Third World.

(3) Logical relations are atemporal, not chronological relations. Logic, unlike dialectic, is not concerned with temporal or historical change, with processes. In particular it is not concerned with the origins of processes or with genetic or causal explanations of them. It is not developmental (or any other kind of) psychology, or history, or sociology.

These three doctrines are the basis of the philosophy of logic characteristic of twentieth-century analytical philosophy, and constitute a central part of the self-reflective theorizing involved in the development of the special discipline of modern logic, and with it the logic and methodology of science, between Frege and Popper.

An analytical model of science

With this in mind, I want now to reconstruct a simple but influential model of science incorporating these ideas, and show how it relates both to our original question of science, values and action, and to the connected question of dialectic. The relevant aspects of the model are articulated in Wittgenstein's *Tractatus*. The logic and methodology of science represents science as a body of propositions between which hold certain truth-relations (including, perhaps, probability-relations). The basic notion of truth is essentially concerned with the relation of a proposition of the reality it is about, the relation of a proposition to its subject-matter – to what, in view of the tradition, we had better call its object. It is often said that the aims of science are to describe, explain, and predict. In the philosophy of science these aims are represented in the claim that scientific theories are descriptive, explanatory and predictive. But it is essential to ask: descriptive, explanatory and predictive *of what*? The answer is that these categories of description, explanation and prediction characterize ways in which scientific theories relate to their object; or perhaps better, as in Popper's account (with description replaced by testing) these three characterize aspects of the single way in which scientific theories relate to their object. At any event, scientific theories are propositions that describe, explain and predict the reality they are about. Guided by the central importance of this distinction and relation between theory and reality, or what a different tradition would have called subject and object, we realize that if a theory is self-contradictory it is logically impossible for reality to be truthfully described by it. There can be no contradictions in reality.

Science as practical: technology

It seems to be a consequence of the structure of this model that in being descriptive, explanatory and predictive of reality, scientific theories cannot be evaluative or practical, cannot have any evaluative or practical implications. Yet is this really the case? One vitally important kind of evaluative and practical implication is commonly attributed to science conceived in this way – namely technological implications. Indeed, it might be said that once science is conceived in this way, technology is its only possible evaluative and practical role, so that as a paradigm of rationality in theory, science constitutes for practice the paradigm of technological rationality. For example, Ohm's Law in theory of electricity says that in any electrical circuit the voltage, current and resistance stand in a constant relationship, that is, with a given voltage and a higher resistance the current flow will be lower. From this there seems to follow a technological implication that can be characterized in a variety of such general ways as that it tells us: what to do in order to do something else; or, how to do a certain thing; or, by what means or in what way we can do something. In this example, Ohm's Law seems to imply that in order to lower the current flow in a circuit with a constant voltage, we must or may or ought to increase the resistance. It is this piece of technological know-how that is embodied in the electrical device known as a rheostat, a variable resistance that can be wired into a circuit, e.g. in a wireless receiver, to enable us to control the current flow in the instrument. In general, it is by virtue of this sort of implication that scientific knowledge, in Bacon's aphorism, is power; that science gives us mastery or control over nature, making us, in Descartes's words, 'masters and possessors of nature'. This is certainly at least a part of what was in Marx's mind when he urged the crucial role of science in man's relation to Nature and society: at present they dominate and master us, but with the knowledge science gives us, we enter a cosmic struggle in which we can ultimately realize the ancient Faustian dream without its awful penalty; we can turn the tables on Nature and society, liberate ourselves by mastering them, and so move from the realm of necessity to that of freedom, in which at last we make our own history.

These dramatic possibilities, long dreamed of by the great visionaries of the scientific revolution, seem at this very moment to be starting their conversion into reality. As advanced industrial societies move into the so-called post-industrial stage, into technological society, their essential structure is changing to bring about this unity of theory and practice, the systematic application of scientific knowledge to the problems of production through technology. That being so, it is of some interest to note that philosophers, especially analytical philosophers, have devoted so little time and effort to investigating and clarifying the concept of technology, by which scientific theory seems to come into such close logical relation to practice. It is this idea, of course, that Hume is seeking to characterize in his famous aphorism 'Reason is and ought only to be the slave of the passions'; Kant considered it in his account of 'hypothetical imperatives'; Sidgwick says some things to the point in *The Methods of Ethics*; and in *The Language of Morals* Hare developed a theory that has since been sporadically examined and criticized by others. Significantly, all these contributions have been made by ethics; though this is clearly an area of important overlap between ethics and the philosophy of science, the latter has on the whole steadfastly ignored the problems of technology, apparently conceiving itself, perhaps with unconscious but understandable elitism, as the philosophy of 'pure' science rather than the philosophy of science both 'pure' and 'applied'. As far as our present topic is concerned, the chief problem in this area of technology is precisely whether, and if so how, scientific theory, or more generally factual, empirical or descriptive propositions, can have evaluative and practical implications: for instance, how, if at all, Ohm's Law can imply a technical imperative or value judgment containing the word 'ought' or one of its family, e.g. that in order to increase the current in a circuit with a constant voltage, one must or may or ought to lower the resistance.

I shall not pursue this problem here,[2] but simply record my view that technological statements, though not moral judgments, are genuinely prescriptive, practical, or evaluative, and really do follow from empirical statements of fact and scientific theories; and therefore, that technology represents a crucial breach, from within science itself so to speak, of the supposed logical barrier between fact and value, between theory and practice. But what kind of practice is legitimated by the idea of technological rationality? The first thing to note is that technology is not simply the use of knowledge for some practical purpose, as if knowledge were here just a means to some practical end: the idea of technology is not just the idea that knowledge is practically useful. For instance, the knowledge that a diplomat is homosexual may be used to blackmail him. In this sense, the knowledge is a means to an end external to its content; whereas in technology it is the content of the knowledge that represents theoretically the real relation of those states of affairs that a practical point of view represents as means to ends. As we have seen, among the categories involved in this idea are those of power, control and domination; and just as it is essential in characterizing science as descriptive, explanatory and predictive to ask 'Descriptive, explanative and predictive *of what?*', so it is essential here to ask 'Power, control and domination *over what?*' The answer is, of course, the same in both cases. What a scientific theory, as technology, gives us power, control or domination over is what it is descriptive, explanatory or predictive of: that reality, or part of it, that constitutes its subject-matter or object. As a theory of or about electricity, Ohm's Law in its technological applications enables us to control electrical phenomena. We could say that in technology the power relation has the same object as the theory whose application it is. More generally, if we can talk of scientific knowledge as a relation between subject and object, between a knowing subject and what he has knowledge about, we can say that the power relation has the same terms as the knowledge relation: the subject with the knowledge also has the power, and the object he has knowledge about is what his knowledge gives him power or control over. This is one of the main reasons why the *human* sciences, if conceived according to the doctrine of the unity of science in the model of the natural sciences, can seem to be oppressive rather than liberating in their practical applications. Unlike the natural sciences, which as technology give power to human subjects over non-human nature, the object of the human sciences is or essentially involves people, and it is over people that these sciences as technology give power. If in these sciences subject and object were identical, this technology would constitute (one kind of) self-control. When subject and object in the human sciences are different, or thought of as different, as in our society or the technocratic society some sociologists foresee for the post-industrial phase, the human sciences as technology constitute the power of some people over others: in B. F. Skinner's honest but menacing designation, the behavioural sciences, for instance, yield a 'technology of behaviour control'.

Science as critical practice

Even if it is the case, then, that the idea of technology helps to bring fact and value, theory and practice, into some kind of unity, it is far from obvious that this is the kind of unity envisaged by Marx's conception of science as dialectical. Indeed, this kind of unity, characteristic of technocratic society, seems to be involved in an essentially non-dialectical conception of scientific theory as purely descriptive, explanatory and predictive of its object. It is because the relation of theory to object is conceived as purely descriptive, explanatory and predictive that the practical relation of subject to that object is a relation of power, the object of the theory being conceived in that theory's practical implications as under the control of the subject. One important thing missing from this model of scientific theory – if it is compared with Marx's conception of social science – is the idea of *criticism*. Marx's social science is socialist science by being, as science, a critique of its object, capitalist society.

Now, the simple model of science already outlined contains not only the embryonic idea of technology but also the implicit notion of criticism. The notion is implicit rather than explicit because the model represents only the relation of a single scientific theory to reality, its object. But if we enrich the model with a second theory about the same object, and consider the relation not of theory to object but of theory to theory, the possibility arises of a relation between the two theories that is a relation at once of contradiction and of criticism. Given two theories about the same subject-matter, one can contradict the other and implicitly criticize it as wrong, as mistaken. This notion of wrongness or mistakenness, whether of action or theory, is evaluative, as criticism or appraisal in general is evaluative. It is not technologically evaluative. Nor is it *morally* evaluative. The familiar and widespread tendency to identify values with *moral* values, and to regard reason as value-free, is simply a fundamental part of the prevailing ideology of science.

Popper himself sees criticism, as well as description, explanation and prediction, as crucial to science; and he therefore sees science as in some sense essentially evaluative. But at vital points in his account he reveals how his Third World conception of logic, specifically his anti-psychologism in the philosophy of logic, misleads him. One central part of Popper's argument in 'What is Dialectic?' concerns 'the dialectical saying that the thesis "produces" its antithesis'. Actually, he objects, 'it is only our critical attitude which produces the antithesis, and where such an attitude is lacking – which often enough is the case – no antithesis will be produced. Similarly, we have to be careful not to think that it is the "struggle" between a thesis and its antithesis which "produces" a synthesis. The struggle is one of minds.' And later: 'The only "force" which propels the dialectic development is, therefore, our determination not to accept, or to put up with, the contradiction between the thesis and the antithesis. It is not a mysterious force inside these two ideas, not a mysterious tension between them which promotes development – it is purely our decision, our resolution, not to admit contradictions.' What is at least strongly suggested here is that the notion of contradiction, in being a category of logic, is not itself evaluative or critical, and does not imply criticism. To characterize something as contradictory, Popper seems to say, is one thing, a logical thing; to criticize it is another, logically independent, thing, a matter of psychological attitude and decision rather than of logic.

I have argued elsewhere that the connection here is, on the contrary, internal and conceptual; that to characterize something as a contradiction, where that concept is a category of logic, *is*, at least by implication, to criticize it; and moreover that to criticize a theory is to criticize the actual or possible acceptance of that theory by some actual or possible subject. It is in fact difficult to make much sense of Popper's notion of criticism, given his view that what one criticizes are *theories*, and his Third World doctrine of knowledge without a knowing subject, i.e. of theory without a theorizing subject. What would be the *point* of criticizing a theory, if not to criticize its actual or possible *acceptance*? Contrary to the Platonic conception of logic that has characterized the subject from Frege to Popper, logical categories are themselves implicitly critical; and in their use as characterizations of theories or propositions, they criticize or appraise those theories by criticizing or appraising their acceptance by actual or possible subjects. The connection between logic and the faculty of reason cannot be just contingent.

It follows from this – or is perhaps a presupposition of it, but in any case is true – that people, as well as propositions, can contradict themselves, i.e. that people can hold contradictory views. The critical point of characterising a theory in terms of the logical category of contradiction therefore implies or presupposes that in this sense there can be contradictions in reality. To say 'Smith contradicted himself' is to make a statement about Smith that is itself non-contradictory and at once empirical, logical and evaluative, i.e. critical; it could not be critical if there could not in this sense be contradictions in reality. The contradictory thing said by Smith does, of course, putatively describe something that is logically impossible; but his asserting and believing it is logically possible, though logically impermissible.

In this way, science in general must be critical and evaluative. But as has already been suggested, the evaluative nature of scientific theories in relation to other theories and views cannot be understood Platonically, simply in terms of logical implications between descriptive propositions and value-judgements. Just as, in construing these value-judgements as criticism, we imply that (in the sense outlined) *what* is criticized, e.g. a contradiction, can have a real existence in some subject's thoughts and attitudes, so the criticism itself is empirically instantiated as: opposition – opposition to what is being criticized. Indeed, criticism is an activity or practice, the activity or practice of opposing, and without that activity there could be no such thing as science. Science understood philosophically, i.e. Platonically, as a logical structure of theories would be impossible and unintelligible without the idea of scientific activity, theoretical practice, including the practice of criticism; and with it the understanding of an argument not abstractly, as a set of propositions distinguishable into premises and conclusion – with some logical relation between them – but concretely as the activity of arguing. Science essentially involves arguing against people's theories and views, that is, critically opposing them: or, as we sometimes say, *attacking* them. The representation of science simply as an attempt to understand the world forgets that its point in so doing is also to change that part of it which consists of misunderstanding. 'The real is partly irrational: change it': that is the imperative of science.

Social science as criticism of its object

Now, however true all this might be, it will no doubt be objected that it is irrelevant. For all these claims about the critical nature of scientific activity fail to come to grips with the essential feature of the Marxist conception of science as dialectic. Of course, it will be said, science involves criticism, but the object of that criticism, *what* is criticized, is always some other theory: the critical relation is always between theories; it is horizontal, so to speak, never vertical, never a relation between a theory and *its* object, the reality it is about. In relation to its *object*, a scientific theory is always descriptive, explanatory and predictive, never critical. For example, the cosmological theory that the universe is expanding may by implication be critical of the theory that the universe is stable, but it is not critical of its object, i.e. of the universe itself and of its size from one moment to another.

I am willing to concede this, as a point about *natural* science; provided that the criticism of theories is understood as having, even in natural science, a *social* target in the acceptance of those theories by possible subjects, including social institutions (e.g. the Church as a target of Copernican criticism). But Marx's theory of capitalism is *social* science, and although it is sometimes held by Marxists that all science is or should be dialectical, it seems indubitable that in Marxism dialectic is primarily and essentially intended to characterize *social* science. If we claim that all science, including natural science, is or should be dialectical, we must also recognize some crucial differences in what we might call degree of dialecticity between natural and social sciences. If we hold that the natural sciences are dialectical, this means: (a) that the reality investigated by natural science has an underlying core ('essence') that differs radically from (conflicts with) its phenomenal appearance; (b) that this underlying core is constituted essentially by conflicting forces; and (c) that the natural sciences develop historically through theory-change centrally involving determinate contradiction between theories, such that new theories both negate and preserve the old.

But in the social sciences there are further vital dimensions to the dialectic, involving the logical category of contradiction both at the level of the object and in the relation, the interaction, between theory and object. For the object of social science is or essentially involves people in society; people are peculiar as objects of science in being also subjects with their own theories, views and ideas, scientific and otherwise, about their activities, about their social practices and institutions. These theories, views and ideas stand in much closer logical relation to those social practices and institutions than do theories, views and ideas about the natural world to their object; and in particular, the logical relation of contradiction, at least in its form as inconsistency, can be instantiated not only between people's thoughts but also between their actions and practices. Marx says that people's ideas about their social practices and institutions *reflect* the society in which they live. Society is itself a human product, and its production and reproduction have to be seen partly in terms of the ideas that constitute the self-understanding of the members of that society. More specifically, these ideas reflect and are instantiated in the surface features of the social structure, and thus form an ideology that obscures the underlying realities of that structure. Scientific critique of this ideology reveals that its appearance as consistent contradicts its own deeper nature; under examination it is revealed as confused and self-contradictory, and even in that it 'reflects', though it does not assert, the confused and self-contradictory nature of the underlying social reality. In this way social science, in criticizing other, ideological social theories and ideas as deeply contradictory, and so contradicting them, at the same time criticizes as contradictory, and so contradicts, the society in whose structure those inconsistent and conceptually muddled theories and ideas are realized. Marx's critique of what he calls 'the system of bourgeois economy' attacks at one and the same time both the theories and concepts of political economy and capitalism itself.

It may be thought that this brief account fails to recognize that the Marxist dialectic is materialist, not idealist. My reply is that as a theory of society, Marx's materialism asserts that what is basic in society is the economy – that part of the structure concerned essentially with the production of material goods and thus the satisfaction of material needs. That this 'material base' of social activities is inseparably interwoven with ideas is evident from the section of *Capital* on 'The Fetishism of Commodities'.

Thus the critical practice constituting Marxist social science involves practical opposition to the basic self-contradictions of capitalist society, its aim (and thus prediction) being the supersession of those contradictions. In two crucial ways, Marx's critique is not a moral or ethical critique, and its practice is not moral practice, at least as those notions have often been understood. First, its criticism is not of personal immoralities but of society's structural irrationalities. Second, it is not doctrinaire in supposing that the changes required can necessarily be effected by ideas alone, i.e. by the theoretical practice of reasoning with and exhorting people. Whatever morality is, in both ways Marxism is not morality *as distinct from* science: its central values are (and need only to be) those of reason, i.e. dialectic.

To conclude self-reflectively: if that is the role of science, what place is left for philosophy? Coupled with the descriptivist conception of science has been a view of philosophy as itself analytical and descriptive: philosophy can (in the end) only describe the structure of (scientific and other) language, and must leave everything as it is. But in this paper I have been doing philosophy: my aim has been also to show by example that just as science in general can and must be critical, and at an epistemologically basic level critical of existing concepts, and just as social science in particular can and must be critical of its object, society, so philosophy can and must be part of that same general project of social criticism, distinguished if at all only by the fundamentality of its target, the basic categories instantiated in society, in terms of which reality, including the social reality of science itself, is currently understood and shaped. I have criticized a dominant conception of science, and therefore a powerful tendency in the current social practice of science and the emerging technological society in which that conception and practice have a central role.

Notes

1 *Mind*, 1940; reprinted in *Conjectures and Refutations*, London 1963.
2 See my 'Reason in Theory and Practice', op. cit., chap. 4.11.

17

FACTS AND VALUES

Theory and practice

Roy Bhaskar

> Science is meaningless because it gives no answer to our question, the only question important to us, "what shall we do and how shall we live?"[1]

I now intend to show that the human sciences are necessarily non-neutral; that they are intrinsically critical (both of beliefs and their objects) and self-critical; that accounts of social reality are not only value-impregnated but value-impregnating, not only practically-imbued but practically-imbuing; and that in particular they both causally motivate and logically entail evaluative and practical judgements *ceteris paribus.* I will not be so concerned with the way in which factual and theoretical judgements are predisposed by value and practical commitments. This is partly because these connections have been better recognised,[2] but more because I want to address myself to an historic aspiration: the hope that the human sciences might yet come to be in a position to cast some light on the question 'which really interests us', of what to do and say, feel and think.

On the thesis advocated here, social science is non-neutral in a double respect: it always consists in a *practical intervention* in social life and it sometimes *logically entails* value and practical judgements. In particular the possibility of a scientific *critique* of lay (and proto-scientific) ideas, grounded in explanatory practices based on recognition of the epistemic significance of these ideas, affords to the human sciences an essential emancipatory impulse. Such a *conatus* does not license an unmediated transition from factual appraisals to practical imperatives in particular situations. But mediated by the explanatory power of theory and subject to the operation of various *ceteris paribus* clauses, we do nevertheless pass securely from statements of fact to practice. Appreciation of the emancipatory dynamic of explanatory theory dissolves the rigid dichotomies – between fact and value, theory and practice,

Source: Scientific Realism and Human Emancipation, London: Verso, 1986, chap. 2, sections 5, 6 and 7, pp. 169–211

explanation and emancipation, science and critique – structuring traditional normative discourse.

Besides the positivist and irrationalist creeds of the neutrality and impotence of social science, together with their sundry (e.g. hermeneutical; historicist) displacements, I will also be objecting to a rationalistic intellectualism or *theoreticism* which conceives social science as immediately efficacious in practice. This view, which comes in traditional-authoritarian, utilitarian-technocratic (including reformist socialist, e.g. Fabian) and Stalinist variants, is often coupled with, or indeed founded on, a barely disguised contempt for the cognitive worth of the actors' point of view.[3] In opposition to it, I want to insist that social science always only happens in a context which is at once always understood, preconceptualised, and codetermined by non-cognitive factors too. So that, on this stance, social theory appears, at its best, in the form of *conditioned critique.* As critique, it presupposes and engages with those preconceptualisations; as conditioned, it is subject in its genesis, reception and effect, to extra-scientific, extra-cognitive and non-ideational, as well as scientific, cognitive and ideational, determinations (whose critical understanding is itself part of the business of theory). This is of course an implication of historical *materialism.* To understand critique as conditioned by agencies outside itself is not to impugn its explanatory power (or normative force), merely to be realistic – that is, self-reflexively scientific (descriptively and explanatorily adequate) – about its practical impact.

On the position advanced here, knowledge, although necessary, is insufficient for freedom. For to be free is: (1) to know one's real interests; (2) to possess both (a) the ability and the resources, i.e. generically the power, and (b) the opportunity to act in (or towards) them; and (3) to be disposed to do so. An interest is anything conducive to the achievement of agents' wants, needs and/or purposes; and a need is anything (contingently or absolutely) necessary to the survival or well-being of an agent, whether the agent currently possesses it or not. Satisfaction of a need, in contrast to the fulfilment of a want or purpose, cannot ever *per se* make an individual or group worse off. Notice that freedom can be no more the simple recognition of, than escape from, necessity. Engels and Sartre must be adjudged equally wrong insofar as circumstances, capacities, wants (and/or needs) etc. contain non-cognitive components. It is salutary to remember that there is a logical gap between 'knowing' and 'doing' which can only be bridged by 'being able and wanting to do in suitable circumstances'. It is my contention that that special qualitative kind of becoming free or liberation which is *emancipation*, and which consists in the *transformation*, in self-emancipation by the agents concerned, *from an unwanted and unneeded to a wanted and needed source of determination*, is both causally presaged and logically entailed by explanatory theory, but that it can only be effected in *practice.* Emancipation, as so defined, depends upon the transformation of structures, not the alteration or amelioration of states of affairs. In this special sense an emancipatory politics or practice is necessarily both grounded in scientific theory and revolutionary in objective or intent.

Although I argue that social science sometimes entails, often informs and always affects values and actions, I am far from holding that either can be wholly determined by or analytically reduced to social science. Social science cannot determine or uniquely ground values, because there are other good things in life besides explanatory knowledge; and it cannot determine, or on its own rationally inform, action, because this is always a matter of will, desire, sentiment, capacities, facilities and opportunities as well as beliefs.

Moreover, to resolve the jaded dichotomies by elucidating the rational connections between the terms customarily dichotomously opposed, in no way gainsays the categorial differentiation of the poles. Here again, as before, on an integrative pluralistic approach, we must think the unity of distinctions within (and as) connections.

I am taking it for granted that human beings are characterised by a biological basis, by the capacity for intentional agency and for the reflexive awareness and organisation of such agency and by a thoroughly social existence. What is normally meant by 'consciousness' refers to those aspects of our praxis in which we are (progressively) (i) sentient, (ii) aware, (iii) attentive, (iv) reflexively self-aware, attentive and articulate and (v) occupied in planned (controlled, deliberate, integrated), reasonable (intelligent, well-grounded, responsible) collective, coordinated or mutual activity. Although Turing-based and more generally computational models can capture some features of human intelligence, they cannot do justice to either the biological or the social dimensions of our praxis, in which all the other features of our conscious (and unconscious) life and agency are marinated.[4] For insofar as we are machines, we are *sentient* ones, related by homologies to other animals (and not merely analogies with man-made machines). Moreover, our characteristically human powers (such as speech) are both ontogenetically rooted in the maturation of an organism and phylogenetically steeped in the (biological) history of an evolving species. Our sense of self and agency are pervaded with affect, and when we attach significance and meaning to the world of objects, others and ourselves we do so, from our ontic standpoint, as feeling organisms. Second, if we are sentient machines, we are also *mobilising* ones, situated *ab initio* in a pre-formed, potentially public social world. And in our transformative causal agency, mobilising pre-existing structures, we endow the world with consequences, realising (or not) our purposes in it, and conferring meaning upon it, including the physical and cultural products of our agency (such as Turing machines), reproducing or transforming those structures in the course of our agency.[5] Human consciousness, understood as an aspect of human praxis, is an irreducibly bio-social product in a psychological mode.

Science informs values and actions which in turn motivate science, so one is in effect dealing with fact-value and theory-practice helices here. These helices can be rationally developing precisely to the extent that there is a sense in which facts and theories non-trivially entail values and practices but not vice-versa. To simplify matters I will consider in the first place only relations involving practical judgements rather than actions (the connections between the two will be considered shortly).

The asymmetry between the F → V and T → P relationships, on the one hand, and the V → F and P → T relationships, on the other, stems from the consideration that whereas factual and theoretical considerations not only predispose and motivate, but, in favourable epistemic circumstances (to be spelt out in a moment) and subject to the operation of various *ceteris paribus* clauses, logically entail value and practical judgements; value and practical commitments, while they may (and in general will) predispose and sometimes motivate, do not (non-trivially) entail factual and theoretical judgements.[6] It is just these asymmetries which make the helices potentially rational ones: that is progressively developing spirals, rather than merely self-confirming, and so self-destroying, more or less rapidly vanishing circles. The helices can be set out as in Diagrams 1 and 2 below, where the double lines indicate relations of entailment and causal influence (inclination, etc.) and the single lines causal influence only.

The scientistic denial of the value-impregnation of factual discourse, involving the reification of propositional contents, shares with the positivistic denial of its converse, viz. the value-impregnating character of factual discourse, a naive extentionalist theory of meaning (whether in physicalist, sensationalist or Platonist guise). Moreover, it shares with the theoreticist conception of the unmediated efficacy of theoretical discourse a neglect of the non-cognitive bases of action, spawning a voluntarism of theoretical praxis; while the converse 'practicist' error (of anti-intellectualist irrationalism)

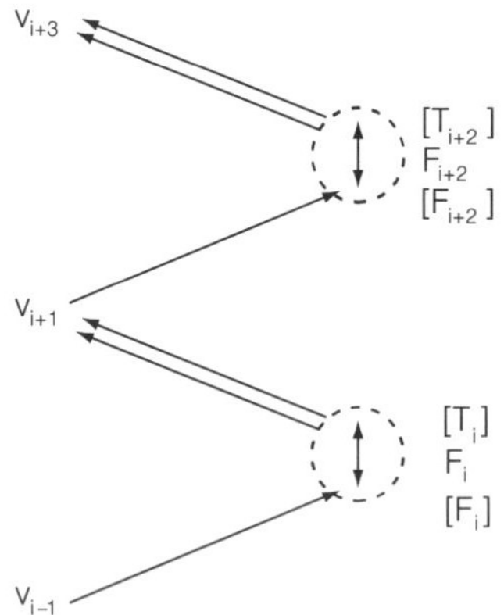

Diagram 1 Fact/value helix

N.B. F, V stand for fact-theory complexes ans values respectively; [F], [T] stand for factual and theoretical components within fact-theory complexes.

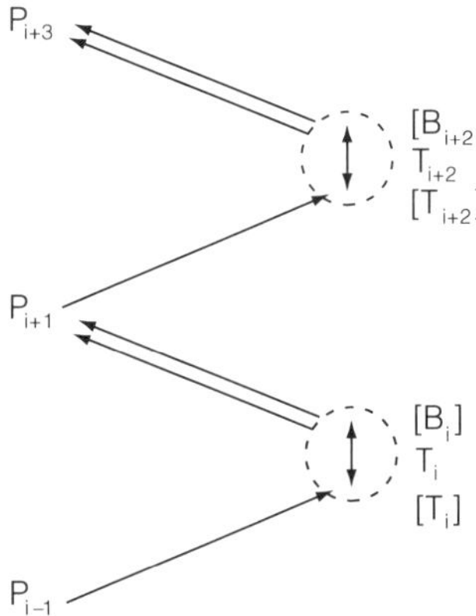

Diagram 2 Theory/practice helix

N.B.T, P stand for theory-belief complexes and practices (and actions) respectively. {T} {B} stand for theoretical and other (e.g. evaluative) components within theory-belief complexes.

ignores the cognitive bases of action. There are hyper-naturalist and hyper-rationalist analogues of theoreticism and scienticism respectively. Theoreticism, as defined above, leads naturally to the denial that practice (to the extent that it is not merely a redescription of theory) plays any rôle in the generation or development of theory. Similarly ethical hyper-naturalism tends to the denial of any causal impact of values on the process of theory. These errors can be tabulated as below, where the treble arrows indicate unmediated efficacy or direct expression.

Table 1

F	$\nrightarrow$	V	positivism (and displacements)
V	$\nrightarrow$	F	scienticism
F	$\Rrightarrow$	V	ethical hyper-naturalism ($\longrightarrow$ V $\nrightarrow$ P)
V	$\Rrightarrow$	F	ethically based epistemological idealism[7]
T	$\nrightarrow$	P	irrationalism
P	$\nrightarrow$	T	hyper-rationalism
T	$\Rrightarrow$	P	theoreticism ($\longrightarrow$ P $\nrightarrow$ T)
P	$\Rrightarrow$	T	ultrapositivism (or ultra-pragmatism)

Once the value-implications of theory, and the rational assessability of wants (in virtue of their grounding in beliefs) is established, then Diagram 2.9 on p.128 {of SRHE} can be modified as in Diagram 3 below. The bases of action may be classified into five broad types: cognitive, conative, affective, dynamic and circumstantial.[8] The *dynamic* bases of action[9] comprise the *powers* necessary to perform an action in appropriate (normal or specified) circumstances. These powers may be subdivided into two general kinds: the *competences*, including practical capacities, skills and abilities of various sorts;

and the *facilities*, including political, economic, normative (moral, legal, etc.) resources and more generally possibilities. Competences constitute the *intrinsic*, facilities the *extrinsic* dynamic bases of action. It is plain that an agent may possess a competence without the corresponding facility and vice-versa. The five bases of actions are only analytically separable. Thus there are cognitive competences, facilities to acquire competences, etc.; and in general for any category of agent and act the bases will be causally connected and often internally related. All the bases of action have structural conditions and effects, and each basis is in general necessary for any action, so that in particular the intrinsic/extrinsic contrast cannot be identified with the praxis/structure distinction. The circumstantial basis of action is a holdall, which includes structures not directly implicated in the action and the whole welter of material and social conditions and contingencies that comprise an agent's 'context'. It is the dynamic basis of action, and the coincidence of competences and facilities in human transformative agency, that lies at the heart of the transformational conception of social activity espoused here.

As already intimated in §2, inasmuch as theoretical and practical explanations (of the patterns recapitulated in §1), succeed in identifying real, but hitherto unrecognised conditions and patterns of determination, they immediately augment our knowledge – of the objective and subjective conditions and the effects and forms of praxis. And hence, *ceteris paribus*, they augment both the rationality of our actions and the degree, or possibility, of our freedom (on the definition enlisted above). But there is a significant asymmetry between the extrinsic dynamic and circumstantial bases of action and the others. Any beneficial effect of knowledge on action, e.g. in the direction of enhanced rationality or greater freedom, at these levels presupposes mutual or collective effort; and as in general each base is necessary for any action, such effort is a condition for the realisation or implementation of *any* scientifically inspired change. In short, the benefit of any scientific enlightenment depends upon a *politics.* Politics may itself be conceived most abstractly as any practice oriented to the transformation of the conditions of human action; more concretely, as practices oriented to or conducted in the context of struggles and conflicts over the development, nature and distribution of the facilities (and circumstances) of human action; more starkly, as practices oriented to the transformation of the structured sets of social relations within which particular social structures operate and particular social activities occur. Insofar as emancipation depends upon the transformation of structures, and such structures are general (extensive), a *self*-emancipatory politics, oriented to that transformation of unwanted and unnecessary sources of determination, will of course need to be a *mass* (extensive) one. But such a politics *need* not be necessary for the transformation of particular or local constraints or for constraints stemming from the subjective (psychological) conditions, or (poiesological) forms or (praxiological) effects as distinct from the objective (social-structural) conditions of action.[10]

My core argument is simple. It turns on the condition that the subject-matter of the human sciences comprehends both social objects (including beliefs) and beliefs about those objects. Philosophers have been prone to ignore the internal relations connecting them: empiricists by objectivising beliefs (naturalising them or otherwise undermining their epistemic significance, scouting the IA of consciousness, in the terms introduced in 1.3); idealists by bracketing objects (in one way or another extracting the belief from the historical context of its formation, denying the EA of consciousness). These relations, which may or may not be intra-cognitive – depending upon whether the first order object is itself a belief – are *both* causal and epistemic. In the ontological or intransitive dimension of some particular belief (or epistemic$_2$) we are concerned with relations of causal *generation;* in the epistemological or transitive dimension with relations of representative adequacy (truth) and *critique.* But it is the causal relation of generation which grounds the epistemological programme of critique.

Let a belief P, which has some object O, have a source (causal explanation) S. I am going to contend that if we possess:

(i) adequate grounds for supposing P is false; and
(ii) adequate grounds for supposing that S co-explains P, then we may, and must, pass immediately to
(iii) a negative evaluation of S (CP); and
(iv) a positive evaluation of action rationally directed at the removal of S (CP).

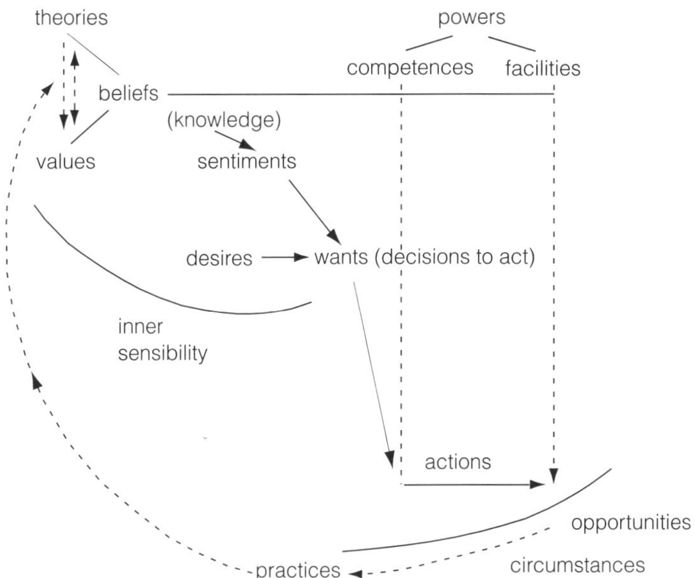

Diagram 3 The five bases of action and practices, values and theories

That is, inasmuch as we can explain, i.e. show the (perhaps contingent) necessity for some determinate false consciousness, or perhaps just some determinate consciousness under the determinable 'false', then the inferences to a negative evaluation of its sources and a positive evaluation of action oriented towards their dissolution are, *ceteris paribus*, mandatory. Of course such action can only be rationally justified to the extent that there are grounds for supposing the source dissoluble (or sufficiently transformable). The notion of false consciousness employed here simply involves in the first instance that of disjuncture, mismatch or lack of correspondence (representative adequacy) between belief and object. But, as I shall presently show, this general pattern of argument may be readily extended to accommodate more interestingly specific forms of false consciousness, and indeed more generally of defective or unfulfilling being. However it should be made plain that the T.M.S.A. does not *per se* licence the supposition of a society without some false consciousness or, more generally, socially remediable ills.

In principle this pattern of inference applies equally to beliefs about *natural*, as well as social, objects, on the condition (and to the extent) that the relevant *source* of false consciousness, S, is itself a social, or at least socialisable, object, i.e. an object amenable to social control (or influence). But then S cannot be the same as O and will not, at least insofar as it is praxis-independent (e.g. the speed of light, the specific gravity of mercury), be internally related to O; and neither S nor P can, at least in the praxis-independent case, be causal conditions for the genesis or persistence of O (or some causal condition or effect of O), as in the cases of psychological rationalisation and ideological mystification, where S, P and O are typically causally interrelated.[11] Only in the cases of beliefs about social objects can the illusory (or more generally defective) character of consciousness be a condition of what it is about. However, given that beliefs about nature are social objects, *all* the modalities of false consciousness may apply to our understanding *of*, as distinct from *in*, science.

I shall call (i) the *critical* and (ii) the *explanatory* condition. Of course even if the critical condition alone is satisfied, then we also pass immediately to a negative evaluation of P (CP), and of actions based on or informed by P (CP). But I want to distinguish this kind of '*criticism*' which, although it formally violates and so refutes 'Hume's law',[12] remains silent on the causes of error, from an '*explanatory critique*'. Criticism, in Marx's words, 'knows how to judge and condemn the present, but not how to comprehend it'.[13] The essence of Marx's objection to criticism may, I think, be stated thus: it employs value (and especially, although not necessarily, moral) terms in the absence of any kind of causal grounding. At its best, i.e. if elaborated in naturalistic (i.e. non-intuitionist or -emotivist) form, it can furnish objective grounds for belief and action which, if true, extend our freedom. But criticism says nothing *about*, although it may of course (intentionally or unwittingly) causally affect, the (causal) conditions of action, the springs of belief and behaviour, the sources of determination. And so it cannot illuminate the topic of the transformation of the sources of determination from unnecessary to rationally wanted ones. Only a discourse in which the explanatory as well as the critical condition is satisfied, can be intrinsically emancipatory.

'Depth-explanations' may be undertaken at each of the levels corresponding to the four kinds of limits on actors' knowledge identified earlier (see Diagram 2.7 on p. 126 above), corresponding to the subjective and objective conditions of action, and its effects and forms in both the dimensions of interactions between agents and transactions with nature. Templates of these types are provided by the Freudian theory of rationalisation; the Marxian theory of ideology; phenomenological and ecological studies of the mechanisms of interactional and natural-transactional counterfinality; and developmental and structural studies of the mechanisms of operational-instrumental-technical and communicative-presentational-moral competences (e.g. in the work of Piaget, Chomsky, Habermas and Goffman).

The fine structure of most of these explanatory species is considerably more complicated than that depicted in the bare form of an explanatory critique. Moreover many, perhaps most, of the significant depth-theorists at the praxiological and poiesiological levels have both disclaimed any critical intentions and formulated universalistic theories – with questions of facilities, blockages and structural change marginalised. Despite this, I think it can be shown that, shifting the marginalia into more central loci, transitions from facts to value and theory to practice can be effected in essentially the same way as in the Marxian and Freudian paradigms. I cannot attempt to demonstrate this here. Instead I want to focus on the logical structure of an explanatory critique. The possibility of such a critique constitutes the kernel of the emancipatory potential of the human sciences; and the possibility of the effectivity of such a critique in human history comprises perhaps the only chance of non-barbaric, i.e. civilised, survival for the human species. But to illustrate the possibilities here fully, I want to develop the argument on a series of levels, which may be regarded as so many ratchets of historical reason.

REASON AND THE DIALECTIC OF HUMAN EMANCIPATION

> *The world has long since dreamed of something of which it needs only to become conscious for it to possess in reality. . . To obtain forgiveness for its sins mankind need only declare them for what they are.*[14]

Seven levels of rationality may be identified as follows:

Level	Rationality	Reason	
Level I:	Technical rationality	Instrumental reason	
Level II:	Contextually-situated instrumental rationality		
Level III:	Practical rationality	Critical reason	practical = criticism
Level IV:	Explanatory critical rationality		explanatory = critique
Level V:	Depth-Explanatory-Critical rationality	Emancipatory reason	
Level VI:	Depth rationality		
Level VII:	Historical rationality	Historical reason	

Instrumental v. critical reason

At the first two levels, no attempt is made to question the logical heterogeneity (and impenetrability) of facts and values. Despite this, the human sciences may still have (so to speak, contingently) emancipatory implications in virtue of (i) their use as sheer technique and (ii) their effects, in the context of the existence of relations of domination, exploitation and oppression.

Level I: technical rationality

Patently, the human sciences may be used, like any other sciences, to achieve more or less consciously formulated and justified ends, which may of course be adjudged either (and more or less) good or bad. In particular, explanatory theories may be used, in conjunction with statements of particular initial conditions, to generate technical imperatives akin to 'put antifreeze in the radiator (if you want to avoid it bursting in winter) CP'. If such imperatives ever appear to depart from the ends-means schema, this is only because they implicitly presuppose a context of human purposes in the domain of their intended applications. This is the only kind of rationality positivism knows.

Level II: contextually-situated instrumental rationality

The human sciences, even at the rung of instrumental reason, are not symmetrically beneficial to the parties involved in relations of domination, etc. For, in the first place, explanatory knowledge increases the range of real (non-utopian) human possibilities, which may of course also mean decreasing the range of imagined ones, by showing certain of these to be purely imaginary.

But CP this will tilt the balance of (in a broad sense) political argument, discussion, vision and choice against the status quo. This is quite consistent with the existence of only a simple external connection between knowledge and politics.

Secondly, even on an instrumental interpretation, explanatory knowledge appears as a necessary condition for rational self-emancipation – whether what the agent seeks emancipation from be the oppression of individuals, groups, classes; of practices, institutions, organisations; of relations, structures and systems; of material situations, ideational complexes, interactive networks; or of remediable lacks, incapacities and unfulfilments – acting as unnecessary, positively or negatively, by their presence or absence (or by their commissions or omissions), compulsions or constraints on action. Hence the oppressed, dominated, exploited, repressed, denied have an *interest* in knowledge which their oppressors lack, in the straightforward sense that it facilitates the achievement of their wants and the satisfaction of their needs. And their oppressors, or more generally the oppressing agency, inasmuch as their (or its) interests are antagonistic to the oppressed,[15] possess an interest in the ignorance of the oppressed (and perhaps even in their own ignorance of the nature, or the fact of their oppressing). Thus the human sciences, and at a remove philosophy, cannot be regarded as *equally* 'a potential instrument of domination' or of 'the expansion of the rational autonomy of action'.[16] The human sciences are not neutral in their consequences in a non-neutral (unjust, asymmetrical) world. And it is just this which explains their liability to periodic or sustained attack by established and oppressive powers.

Level III: intra-discursive (non-explanatory) critical or practical rationality

The point has been well made[17] that any science depends upon intra-discursive criticism, i.e. criticism of other actually or possibly believed (and therefore potentially efficacious) theories, hypotheses etc. Acceptance of some theory T entails CP a series of negative evaluations: on theories incompatible with it, on beliefs such theories underpin, on actions sustained or informed by them. Although 'X is false' does not just *mean* 'don't believe (act on) X', it certainly CP entails it. Conversely 'X is true' entails 'act on X (in appropriate circumstances) CP'. It is just this that makes applied science, and indeed any rational or even intentional (speech or other) action possible. (*That* there is a link between beliefs and actions is transcendentally necessary; what this link is, is a topic for the various sciences). It is only if one were to deny any ontological connection between beliefs and actions, or theory and practice that one could plausibly suppose that a change in theoretical judgements does not entail a change in practical judgements CP. But denying such a connection makes practical discourse practically otiose. Again this point is consistent with a contingent relationship between a science and its subject-matter; and it applies, quite indifferently, at the level of intra-discursive critical rationality, in all sciences alike. All the sciences, then, irrespective of their subject-matter, are intrinsically critical, and so evaluative.

Mutatis mutandis this point applies to all discourse at what might be called the level of practical rationality. A truth claim typically involves both a prescriptive or imperative ('act on X') and a descriptive or evidential ('X is grounded, warranted, justified') component or dimension. What distinguishes truth claims in science from those in ordinary life is not their logical structure, but the nature of their evidential requirements, which incorporate various logical, empirical, inter- and intra-theoretical controls; the object or referent of the truth claim, which is characteristically a causal structure or explanatory mechanism; the persons (and communities) to which the claim is made and presented for redemption and ratification; and the sorts of uses to which the claim, if it is both validated and true, can be put.

Level IV: explanatory critical rationality

All the sciences make judgements of truth or falsity on beliefs about their object domains. But the human sciences, in virtue of the distinctive feature of their domain, that it includes, *inter alia*, beliefs about social objects, also make (or at least entail) judgements of truth or falsity on (aspects of) that domain. And such belief/object correspondence, or lack of it, appears immediately as a legitimate object of social scientific explanation. To recapitulate the central argument: if we have a consistent set of theories T that (i) shows some belief P about an object O to be false, and (ii) explains why that, or perhaps some such false (illusory, inadequate, misleading), belief is believed (or held), then the inferences to (iii) a negative evaluation of the object (e.g. system of social relations) accounting for the falsity of the belief (i.e. mismatch in reality between the belief P and what it is about O) and (iv) a positive evaluation of action rationally directed at removing (disconnecting or transforming) that object, i.e. the source(s) of false consciousness, appears mandatory CP. This could be represented, informally, in the inference scheme below as:

I.S.1 (i) T > P. (ii) T exp 1(P) → (iii) -V(S → I(P) → (iv) $V\varphi_{-s}$ and we certainly seem to have derived value conclusions (CP) from purely factual premises.

Now for some possible objections.

1. It might be objected that 'P is false' is not value-neutral. But if it is not value-neutral, as is indicated by the prescriptive component involved in truth claims, then the value-judgement 'P is false' can be derived from premises concerning the lack of correspondence or mismatch of object and belief (in the object domain). Moreover, as assuming that such judgements are intrinsic to any factual discourse, we are nevertheless able to infer from them, together with explanatory premises, conclusions of a type which are *not* intrinsic to *every* factual discourse (viz. those specified in (iii) and (iv)), we do have a transition here that goes against the grain of Hume's law, however it is supposed to be interpreted or applied. On the other hand, if 'P is false' is value-neutral, then the inferences to 'P ought not to be believed (CP)' and 'Don't believe (act upon) P (CP)' certainly seems inescapable.

2. The suggestion that science itself presupposes or embodies commitment to certain values such as objectivity, openness, integrity, honesty, veracity, responsibility, consistency, coherence, comprehensibility, explanatory power, etc. should certainly be welcomed – suggesting as it does that the class of the 'value-neutral' is as empty as that of Austin's original 'constatives'.[18] But it does nothing either to salvage Hume's law or to invalidate inference types (iii) and (iv). These turn on the special feature of the sciences of belief that commitment to truth and explanatory power entail the search for theories which will often possess value-implications that cannot be regarded as conditions of, or as already implicit as anticipations in the organisation of, scientific activity in general.

3. It might be maintained that, although inference type (iii) is valid, (iv) is faulty, so that no commitment to any sort of action is entailed by the critical explanatory theory. But this is not so. For one can reason straight away to action directed at removing the sources of false consciousness, provided of course that one has good grounds for supposing that it would do so, that no ill (or sufficiently overriding ill) effects would be forthcoming, and that there is no better course of action which would achieve the same end. Naturally the

inference scheme, as a philosophical reconstruction, does not determine what such practical-critical-revolutionary action is: that is the task of substantive theory. Of course the injunction 'remove (annul, defuse, disconnect, dissolve, transform) sources of false consciousness (CP)' does not specify *what* the sources are, any more than 'lying is wrong' tells us which statements are lies.

Behind this objection, however, lie two considerations of some moment. First, the kind of theory underpinning (iv) may be different from the explanatory theory at (ii) informing (iii). Diagnosis is not therapy. We may know that something is causing a problem without knowing how to get rid of or change it. Secondly, an explanatory critique of this type does not in general specify how we are to act after the source of mystification (false consciousness) is removed. It focuses on action which 'frees' us to act, by eliminating or disconnecting a source of mystification acting as an unwanted source of (co-)determination, replacing that source with another wanted (or perhaps just less unwanted) one, so permitting (absolute or relative) liberation from one stream of constraints or compulsions inherited from, as the causalities (and casualties) of, the past. But it does not tell us what to do, if and when (and to the extent that) we are free. Thus emancipated action may (and perhaps must) have a different logical form from emancipatory action.

4. Granting this, it is clear that there is still a gap, or rather two gaps, between the positive evaluation of a course of action at step (iv), in what I shall now discriminate as a practical (evaluative) judgement, and that course of action. The first gap is that punctuated by the *ceteris paribus* clause. Spanning this gap takes us to what I shall call a concrete axiological judgement (CAJ), prescribing what is to be done in the particular circumstances which actually prevail. The second gap is that which holds between such a judgement and the prescribed action. This gap has endeared itself to generations of philosophers under the rubric of the problem of *akrasia* or 'weakness of the will'. Crossing it transports us into the realm of practice proper. Can these gaps be bridged? It should be remembered that some, perhaps implicit, CAJ is always present (and so formed) and some action or other is always performed; so that, unless we are to ascribe a mysterious spontaneity at these levels, the question is never *whether* but *how* the gaps are bridged, and in particular whether they can be rationally crossed from the side of theory – i.e. whether general judgements can be applied to particular situations and particular judgements translated or enacted into practice.

There is nothing special to evaluative or practical discourse about the need for a CP clause: all statements which possess or presuppose an ontic or assertoric content of any generality require it in the context of their actual or possible applications in open systems. The multiplicity and plurality of causes and the transfactuality of laws all disclose evaluative counterparts. For just as what happens in open systems is determined by a multiplicity of causes, what is to be done in them will be determined by a multiplicity of evaluative, theoretical, dynamic and conjunctural (circumstantial) considerations. Further, just as the same mechanism may be exercised in the generation of a plurality of events and the same (kind of) event may in general be codetermined by a plurality of mechanisms, so the same value or goal may be manifest in a plurality of acts and the same act may satisfy (*inter alia*) a plurality of possible values. Moreover the virtue or rationale of an end or possibility is no more undermined by the applicability in some particular situation of countervailing, modifying or reinforcing values and rights than gravity is undermined by the existence of double-decker buses or multistorey houses. The fact that exactly and only what is to be done can rarely, if ever, be uniquely deduced from general maxims, which accounts for the barrenness of universalisability even as a purely formal criterion (or test) of morality or conduct, stems from these features of action-situations:

1 their ineradicable *openness*, which vitiates deducibility in particular instances or actualities in the sphere of practical (as of theoretical) reason;
2 their *diversity*, under the dense (thick) and highly specified (and differentiated) descriptions under which we must and do normally act;
3 their *historicity*, which vitiates the universality of norms, placing them under the sign of an actual or possible scope restriction.

The kinds of action situations of normative concern to us rarely, if ever, repeat themselves;[19] but it does not follow from this that the same underlying or generative causes are not present at work in them. What follows from the collapse of any *normative actualism*, such as Kantian prescriptivism, utilitarianism or natural law theory, is not the subjective e.g. expressive, pragmatic, spontaneous or intuitive, character of normative discourse (as e.g. in emotivist, existentialist or intuitionist ethics), but the historically specific *or* mediated character of norms, understood tendentially as transfactually applicable (within the restrictions imposed upon their range or realisation by their historically transient or mediated nature). A transcendental realist ontology requires, it will be seen, as much readjustment in ethics as in epistemology. In the particular case at hand the warrant for the transfactual applicability of the content of the practical judgement, (iv), in some particular concrete axiological judgement, (v), is given by our grounds: (a) for the existence, in the domain of the CAJ's application, of the transfactually efficacious, mystifying structural source of determination, S, specified in the explanatory theory at (ii); and (b) for the feasibility of the emancipatory strategy commended in (iv). This at once justifies the CP clause at (iv) and sanctions the CAJ at (v).

But how do we pass from (v), the CAJ, to (vi), action? The CAJ, as so far specified, is grounded in purely factual considerations, including the agent's assessment of her or his own powers (capacities and facilities). The agent is to be conceived as always already acting, but for any transformation in her praxis, all the bases of action must be satisfied (or allayed); so that even if we suppose that the CAJ is sincerely held (cognitively instantiated), there can still be no guarantee, or even strong presumption (at least at this stage of the argument), that the agent will in fact act in the self-prescribed way. All that can be said is that: if the CAJ is sincerely held and can attach itself to any necessary additional affect and/or desire, so as to find expression in a want; and if the agent can muster the appropriate powers and the circumstances are as described or presupposed in the CAJ; then the action *must* occur. If this does not happen we will naturally look for conflicting wants, changed circumstances etc. The CAJ licenses only the supposition of a predisposition (if a want is a disposition), or (metaphorically) an inclination, orientation, charge, pressure, force or bent in the direction of the action. Theory cannot affect the transition from theory to practice. Only practice itself can do that. It is in this sense that the explanatory critique is always *conditioned* critique.

Our schema thus allows for the following notionally distinct stages: (i) theoretical critique (satisfaction of the critical condition); (ii) explanatory critique (satisfaction of the explanatory condition); (iii) value judgement; (iv) practical judgement; (v) concrete axiological judgement; (vi) transformation in agent's praxis; (vii) emancipatory action, i.e. praxis oriented to emancipation; (viii) transformative praxis, consisting or culminating in the dissolution or progressive transformation of structural sources of determination (emancipating action); (ix) emancipated (free) action.

An inference scheme analogous to ISI applies in the case of the natural sciences. For inasmuch as they are concerned in their own substantive critical discussions not just to isolate and criticise, but to comprehend and causally explain, illusory or inadequate beliefs about the natural world, then they too – assuming the second-order standpoint of the intermediate sciences (in the terminology of § 1) of the natural sociology (or social psychology) of belief – may come to explain false consciousness of nature, at least partially in terms of human causes (e.g. faulty instruments, inadequate funds, superstition, the power of the church, state, party or corporations, etc.). This could be represented by

$$I.S.1' \text{ (i) } T > P. \text{(ii) } T \exp 1(P_n) \rightarrow \text{(iii) } - V\,(S_s \rightarrow 1(P_n)) \rightarrow \text{(iv) } V\varphi_{-S_s}$$ [20]

It is of some interest to dwell on this standpoint. Natural science is here conceived as a resultant, product or vector of both natural and cultural (or more generally social) determinants, so that beliefs about nature appear as akin to a mixed or B-type determination (on human actions, etc.) in the sense introduced in § 1. This can be represented in a simple parallelogram of forces, as in Diagram 4. In Diagram 5 such a parallelogram is used, more specifically, to depict the effect of experience in a theoretically pre-formed context,[21] and more especially to illustrate the way in which experimentation may select within a theoretically defined range (as argued in 1.4). In Diagram 6 the parallelogram is used, more broadly in a topological transform of

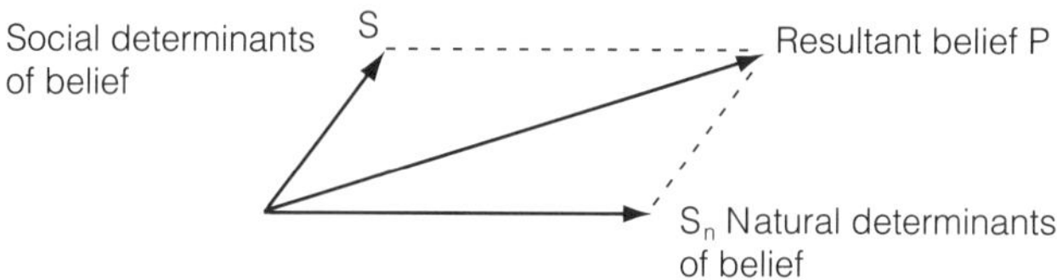

Diagram 4

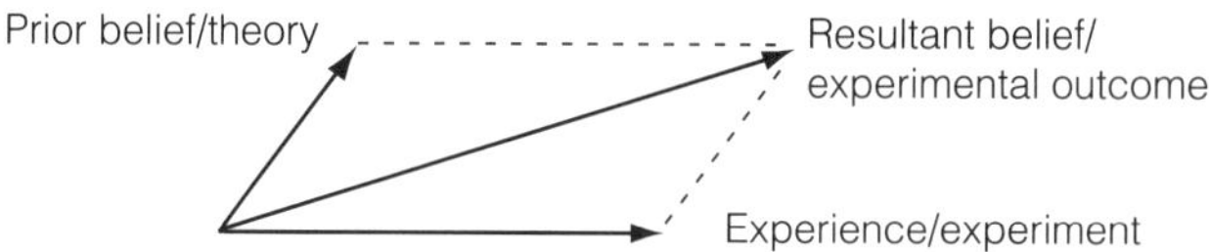

Diagram 5

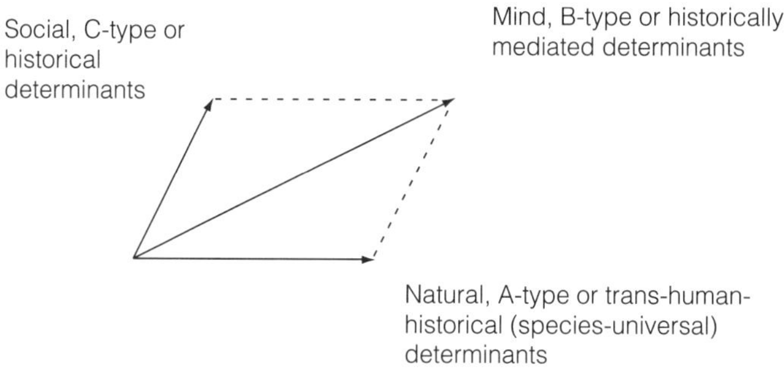

Diagram 6
(N.B. These interpretations are distinct)

Diagram 2.4 on p. 116 above [of SHRE], to represent the formation of mind or B-type modes generally, and to represent the historical mediation of trans-human-historical or species-general determinants. (These two interpretations of 6 are distinct: many natural determinations are in their determining form not trans-human-historical.)

In virtue of their explanatory charter, the human sciences must make judgements of truth and falsity and these, in the context of explanatory theories, entail value judgements of type (iii) and (iv), so that inasmuch as they are in a position to give well-grounded explanations of false consciousness, then, the human sciences *must* and the natural sciences *may* (mediately, via the natural sociology of belief) come to form judgements on the causes, as well as the contents, of consciousness. *Mutatis mutandis*, similar considerations apply to judgements of rationality, coherence, consistency etc. Thus I.S.1 can be generalised in the cognitive direction represented in I.S.2 below, where X (P) stands for the contradictory character of some determinate set of beliefs viz.

I.S.2 $T > P. T \exp X(P) \rightarrow -V(S \rightarrow X(P)) \rightarrow V\varphi_{-s}$

But the human sciences are not only concerned to explain '*cognitive* ills': their *explananda* are not exhausted by beliefs. Their manifest takes in the explanation of such '*practical* ills' as ill-health, misery, repression, including the socio-economic ills of oppression, brutality, war, exploitation, poverty, waste, etc. and the psycho-social ills of pathological violence, neurotic compulsion, boredom, hysteria, etc.; and, in between such ills and the cognitive ones, the '*communicative* ills' of deception (including self-deception), distortion, etc. Together they comprise such generic ills as frustrated needs, ('unwanted') subjection, unused resources, or underdeveloped powers (competences and facilities), unfulfilled possibilities and thwarted intra-subjective, inter-subjective and collective intentionality (amounting to '*irrationalities*'), plus gross inequalities in the distribution of powers and liabilities between agents (classes, groups, etc.) (constituting '*injustices*').

This immediately indicates two further lines of development. First, I.S.1 can be straightaway generalised to deal with the explanation of non-cognitive ills, with a corresponding deduction of evaluative and practical judgements, as in I.S.3 and I.S.3′ below, where I-H stands for ill-health and S-D for systematic self-deception:

I.S.3 $T \exp. \text{I-H}. -V(\text{I-H}) \rightarrow -V(S \rightarrow \text{I-H}) \rightarrow V\varphi_{-s}$
I.S.3′ $T \exp. \text{S-D}. -V(\text{S-D}) \rightarrow -V(S \rightarrow \text{S-D}) \rightarrow V\varphi_{-s}$

Clearly ill-health and systematic self-deception may constitute unwanted sources of determination, and insofar as they can be dissolved or replaced by a less unwanted source, so that they are *ipso facto* unnecessary, such a pattern of argument may directly inform emancipatory strategies. However, it will be immediately obvious that these deductions, despite their evident epistemic and practical weight, are no longer from purely factual premises or from what is immediately or self-evidently constitutive of purely factual discourse; and so they do not formally refute Hume's law. It is precisely on this rock that most previous attempts at its refutation, including Searle's attempted derivation of an 'ought' from the notoriously tenuous institution of 'promising',[22] have foundered.

But further reflection shows another possibility here: namely that there are *non-cognitive* conditions, such as a degree of good health and the absence of marked asymmetries in political, economic and the other modalities of power, for discourse (including factual discourse) in general to be possible. If this is correct, then a formal derivation of an 'ought' can proceed as in

I.S.4 $T > P.\ T\ \text{exp.I-H.}\ T\ \text{exp.}\ (\text{I-H} \rightarrow I(P)) \rightarrow -V(S \rightarrow \text{I-H}) \rightarrow V\varphi_{-s}$;
and
I.S.4′ $T > P.\ T\ \text{exp.S-D.}\ T\ \text{exp.}\ (\text{S-D} \rightarrow I(P)) \rightarrow -V(S \rightarrow \text{S-D}) \rightarrow V\varphi_{-s}$.

What this highlights is that *practical* or effective (including here communicative) *freedom*, and in particular freedom sufficient to enable the agent to activate or summon all five orders of consciousness specified on p. 171, may well be a condition for engagement in any explanatory-emancipatory discourse. But emancipation from specific constraints (whether psycho-social or social in form or origin) may be a prior condition for such practical freedom. Clearly this situates the possibility of various kinds of vicious circle (leading to historical and biographical or compound stasis or regression), in which the entrapped lack the means to understand the means of their entrapment and so cannot find or consciously employ the means for escape or release from it. Equally it grounds the possibility of various virtuous historical circles, on which emancipation from a specific constraint or compulsion and enhanced practical freedom conduces to an explanatory-emancipatory discourse. Here the historical limits and transformational tendencies of structural sources of determination checking the satisfaction of needs or the realisation of possibilities are identified, informing strategies and practices, in turn empirically and practically facilitating the development of theory, in the helical way indicated in Diagram 2.

Is there a sense in which IS1 and IS2 are *epistemically* prior to their non-cognitive generalisations? Yes, inasmuch as empirically controlled retroduction to explanatory structures always occurs in the context of, and typically (in science) assumes the form of, criticism of beliefs (consciousness) – scientific, proto-scientific, ideological, lay and practical. But this does not mean that such beliefs and/or the structures which explain them are necessarily causally prior or most important in the subject-matter under study; or that their study must take precedence in the organisation of scientific work, once that subject-matter has been thoroughly hermeneutically permeated and, if and when necessary, its consciousness of itself critically explained; or that an explanatory critique of consciousness is not itself historically conditioned and limited by factors external to the society from which it arises, such as the existence of practical (and communicative) freedoms from various orders of constraint and compulsion, as exemplified in IS4 and IS4′.

Let me summarise the argument to this stage. On the view advanced here the critical rôle of the human sciences in human history is not an optional extra: it is *intrinsic* to their explanatory function – for this depends indispensably on the identification and description, and proceeds naturally to the explanation, of ideas. If the critical condition in an explanatory critique of consciousness expresses the intrinsic aspect (IA) of any science of consciousness, the explanatory condition expresses the extrinsic aspect (EA) of such a science. To reject the former, objectivistically, is characteristic of empiricism:

it ignores the relation between beliefs and their objects (P and O). To reject the latter, subjectivistically, is typical of idealism: it ignores the relation between beliefs and their causes (P and S). An explanatory critique unites both aspects. If what lies behind the failure to sustain practical rationality at Level III is the (implicit or explicit) denial of an ontological connection between beliefs and actions, theory and practice; the basis of the failure to sustain explanatory critical rationality at Level IV is the failure to recognise the possibility of an explanatory link between the truth value of a belief and its causal genesis, reception and effect. If criticism without explanation is impotent, explanation without criticism will often just be simply false. Although the explanatory critique of consciousness has a certain epistemic priority, the paradigm may be readily extended to other facets of social being, including inter alia those which are effective conditions for explanatory-critical science. The human sciences appear then as necessarily subversive and auto-subversive, in a stratified and changing social world.

Emancipatory reason

Level V: Depth-explanatory critical rationality

The most thoroughly explored applications of IS1 and IS2 involve the phenomena of psychologial *rationalisation* and *ideological mystification.* These phenomena are characterised by two distinctive features:
(1) a doubling of necessity between misrepresentation P and source S so that the, or some such, misrepresentation is not only causally necessitated by, but causally necessary for, the persistence or modulation, reproduction or limited (non-essential) transformation of its source; and
(2) an internal relationship between source S and object O, so that the misrepresented object O is either the same as, or at least causally (and essentially) dependent on, the source of the misrepresentation S.

Thus in the simple depth-psychological model considered in § 4 we had

(5) $s \rightarrow p[-s].sp[-s] \rightarrow \psi$; or more simply
(5)′ $s \rightarrow p \rightarrow \psi$

where the agent N misdescribed the real (i.e the causally efficacious) reason, s, for ψ by p; where p was itself a contingently necessary releasing condition for ψ; and where p was itself generated, in context, by s. To explain this, we now posit a structure S such that ψ is (perhaps contingently) necessary for its persistence or modulation as in

(6) $S \rightarrow (s \rightarrow p[-s].sp[-s] \rightarrow \psi) \rightarrow S'$ or, more simply
(6)′ $S \rightarrow (s \rightarrow p \rightarrow \psi) \rightarrow S'$

Given $s \neq p$, i.e. p [-s], the evaluative and practical deductions proceed as in IS1.

This paradigm may be extended to include the self-mystification of forms of social life or systems of social relations in ideologies. Thus, the contradictions which mystify Colletti[23] turn simply on the necessary coexistence in social reality of an object and a (categorially) false presentation of it, where it is the inner (or essential) structure of the object which generates the categorially false presentation (or appearance). (7) is isomorphic with (5):

(7) $E \rightarrow A[-E]. EA[-E] \rightarrow P$, or more simply
(7)′ $E \rightarrow A \rightarrow P$; and (8) is isomorphic with (6):
(8) $R \rightarrow (E \rightarrow A[-E]. EA[-E] \rightarrow P) \rightarrow R'$ or, more simply
(8)′ $R \rightarrow (E \rightarrow A \rightarrow P) \rightarrow R'$

where E = essence, A = appearances, P = practices and R, R′ = the modulated reproduction of some system of social relations (such as the capitalist mode of production).

The sense in which the misrepresentation A is not only necessitated by, but necessary for E, invites comparison with the populational and consequence explanatory frameworks discussed in § 3. The basic form of a consequence explanatory framework was, it will be remembered, given by $d.(a \rightarrow b) \rightarrow a$.[24] Can this capture the sense in which A is necessary for E? Provided that we understand this quasi-adaptive necessity, in terms of the T.M.S.A., as the necessity of appearances for practices which reproduce (or modulate) a mode of production essentially characterised by certain relations, the $A \rightarrow E$ link can be represented by the following survival matrix, illustrating the case of *eliminative generation:*

(9) (i) $K_e A_{tl}, \ldots\ldots\ldots K_e A_{tn}$
(ii) $K_{e\text{-}Atl}, \ldots\ldots\ldots\ldots \text{-}K_e A_{tn}$

This quasi-adaptive or 'functional' relation can then be represented as $(K_e A_{tl} \rightarrow P_{etl}) \rightarrow K_e A_{tn}$

But to capture the $E \rightarrow A$ link, the *productive generation* (or preventive selection) of the quasi-adaptive (reproductive) property, we need a matrix of, in populational terms, a more Lamarckian kind:

(10) (i) $K_e\text{-}A_{tl} \ldots . K_e A_{tn}$
(ii) $K_e\text{-}A_{tl} \ldots . \text{-}K_e\text{-}A_{tn}$

The appearance-generative relation can then be represented by $K_{etl} \rightarrow (P_{atn} \rightarrow K_{atn})$, yielding a population characterised at t_n by $K_e A_{tn}$, i.e. by the presence of the 'functional' property (appearance). If we rationalise times, and combine the quasi-Lamarckian and quasi-Darwinian moments, we obtain the following pattern:

(11) $K_{etl} \rightarrow (K_e A_{ti} \rightarrow P_{eti}) \rightarrow K_e A_{tn}$;

or, more fully,

$$(11)' \quad K_eA_{tl} \rightarrow K_{eti} \rightarrow (K_eA_{tj} \rightarrow P_{etj}) \rightarrow K_e\, A_{tn},$$

which render the substance of $(E \rightarrow A \rightarrow P) \rightarrow R'$ and $R \rightarrow (E \rightarrow A \rightarrow P) \rightarrow R'$ respectively in (8).

Can anything be said here about whether there are any general conditions on the internal structure, E, of a quasi-self-reproducing system, T, which generates and contains within itself (i.e. T) a functionally necessary misrepresentation (A) of itself? It seems plausible to suppose that E must possess at least sufficient internal differentiation to justify attributing to it a '*Spaltung*' or *split*; and that if T is to be capable of endogenous (essential) transformation, rather than merely modulated reproduction, the split must constitute, or be constituted by, *antagonistic* (opposed) *tendencies.* But apart from the Colletti style contradiction built into the notion of the system's misrepresentation of itself, it seems *a priori* unlikely that what the human sciences may empirically discover about the various structural sources of its consciousness will justify the application of a single unified category of 'contradiction' to those structures. Instead, one might conjecture a galaxy of concepts of contradiction clustered around the core notion of the axiological indeterminacy generated by the logical archetype (together with the evaluative connotations this secretes). The specific concepts of contradiction would then achieve their individuation in the constraints they impose upon such indeterminacy, and in their theorisation of its form. Note however that in the relationship between a feature of social life and its systematic misrepresentation (most generally, in ideologies) there does seem to be a species of contradiction which has analogies with, but is non-identical to, that between a notion and its dialectical supersession in Hegel. And it can be plausibly maintained that the possibility of such an essence/appearance contradiction which, once it both exists and has been discovered, is susceptible to a purely analytic description, is a condition of any human science (or mode of self-reflection).

Perhaps the most justly famous depth-explanation, that in Marx's *Capital*, has the logical structure of a triple critique: of theories, of the practical consciousness such theories reflect or rationalise and of the conditions explaining such consciousness, viz.

$$\text{I.S.12:} \quad T > P_d \,.\, T \exp (S \rightarrow (A \rightarrow P_d)) \rightarrow \text{-}V(S \rightarrow (A \rightarrow P_d)) \rightarrow V\varphi_{-s},$$

where P_d stands for theoretical and discursive consciousness and A is proxy for practical consciousness, in a reproductive scheme which would look something like

(13) $R \rightarrow ((E \rightarrow A[-E]).(E.A[-E] \rightarrow P_d[-A[-E]]). E.A[-E]. P_d[-A[-E]] \rightarrow P) \rightarrow R'$

at least as an initial simplification. (Characteristically, the relations between theoretical and practical consciousness will be much more complex, and there is a sense in which any adequate symbolic representation needs a way of tying practical consciousness more closely to practice, which in turn requires more modulated differentiation.) But in Marx and the Marxian tradition generally, the criticised (discursive and practical) consciousness is regarded not just as false but as ideological – where ideology is counterposed to science. In addition to the *critical* and *explanatory* conditions one thus finds a further set of *categorial* conditions. Here beliefs are typically criticised for their *unscientificity simpliciter* (as in the critique of vulgar economy) and/or for their incapacity to sustain the irreducible *specificity*, the *sui generis* reality, of the subject-matter of the domain (as in the critique of classical political economy). Thus in reification, fetishism, hypostatisation, voluntaristic conventionalism, organicism etc. social life is presented, in one way or another, in an a-social (and so de-historicised) mode – a condition rooted, for Marx, in the alienation and atomisation characteristic of capitalism as a specific form of class society. For example, on Marx's analysis, the wage form collapses a power (labour power) to its exercise (labour), the domain of the real to the actual, while the value form fetishistically represents social relations in the guise of natural qualities. The critique of these gross categorial errors can be represented as

I.S.14 $T > P. T \text{ exp } -S_c (1(P)) \rightarrow -V(S \rightarrow -S_c (1(P))) \rightarrow V\varphi_{-s}$
I.S.15 $T > P. T \text{ exp } -S_o (1(P)) \rightarrow -V(S \rightarrow -S_o (1(P))) \rightarrow V\varphi_{-s}$

P once more stands for consciousness generally; $-S_c$ and $-S_o$ stand for the unscientific and desocialising character of the forms in question; and the double bracketing reminds us that we are dealing with categorially illusory forms, not merely illusory beliefs.

Marxian critique of consciousness differs from *Baconian* critique of illusion in that it does not merely pinpoint obstacles in the way of cognitive experience, but isolates forms which structure and inebriate experience. But it differs from *Kantian* critique in that it understands these forms as objective systems of constraints, historically produced, reproduced and potentially transformable, which explanatory theory may show to be either (1) quite simply false, in not being properly or validly applicable to experience at all – in a first-order critique of consciousness, as e.g. in the case of the wage form; or (2) true but systematically self-misunderstood or -misrepresenting, in being validly applicable to experience but only *within* certain historical limits, contrary to the form's own self-presentation – in a second-order critique of consciousness, as in the case of the value form. It is analogous to *Hegelian* critique in that it sees reflection on the conditions of possible knowledge as at once reflection on a system of humanly produced constraints, but it differs from it, in that the medium of this reflection is explanatory theory, the form of the constraints are transcendentally real and historically defined, and the agency of their dissolution is transformative (e.g. class) praxis rather than speculative experience. It anticipates too the great insight of *Nietzschean* 'critique' that 'among the conditions of life might be error'[25] but locates the source of error in structural causes, neither fated nor fixed.

The characteristic mistake indicated in a second-order critique, the self-dishistoricisation, especially detemporalisation or eternalisation, of a social form can be regarded as a cognitive error analogous to that pinpointed in IS2, as in

$$\text{I.S.2}' \quad T > P.T \text{ exp } \text{-}t(P) \rightarrow \text{-}V(S \rightarrow \text{-}t(P)) \rightarrow V\varphi_{-s}$$

where -t stands for detemporalisation, with the categorial nature of the error brought out in

$$\text{I.S.16:} \quad T > P.\ T \text{ exp } \text{-}t(P) \rightarrow \text{-}V(S \rightarrow \text{-}S_o(\text{-}t(P))) \rightarrow V\varphi_{-s}; \text{ or as in}$$

$$\text{I.S.17:} \quad T > P.\ T \text{ exp } \text{-}S_o((F(t_1 \ldots t_i)T(t_i \ldots t_j)F(t_j \ldots t_n))\ (P)) \rightarrow \text{-}V(S \rightarrow \text{-}S_0((F(t_1 \ldots t_j)T(t_i \ldots tj)F(tj \ldots tn))\ (P))) \rightarrow V\varphi_{-s}$$

What, finally, are we to make of Engels's celebrated rebuke to Lafargue: 'Marx rejected the political, social and economic ideal you attribute to him. A man of science has no ideals, he elaborates scientific results and if he is also politically committed he struggles for them to be put into practice. But if he has ideals, he cannot be a man of science, since he would then be biased from the start'.[26] While interests both predispose and motivate analyses and their acceptance/rejection in the human sciences, so that Engels's scientistic repudiation of the $V \rightarrow F$ connection is disingenuous, it remains the case that no value judgements other than those already bound up in the assessment of the cognitive power of Marx's theory are necessary for the derivation of a negative evaluation of the capitalist mode of production (CP) and a positive evaluation of action rationally oriented towards its transformation (CP). Thus the political commitment that Engels attributed to Marx as, so to speak, a contingent extra, can (on the assumption that Marx's depth explanation is correct) be logically grounded in his scientific practice alone. Of course the theories now required to confirm, extend, develop or refute Marx's own analyses can only be consequent upon engagement in investigations of comparable scope and penetration.

DEPTH, RATIONALITY AND CHANGE

From the beginning we are unlogical and therefore unjust beings and we can know this: this is one of the greatest and most insoluble disharmonies of existence.[27]

Clear paradigms exist in the human sciences of IS1-4, most notably in the traditions inaugurated by Marx and Freud, but also in some of the work of the theorists of the day-to-day lived world of social interactions with one another and material transactions with nature (e.g. in the understanding of such phenomena as counterfinality). But is there a sense in which the *application* of these inference schemes, and hence of the type of explanatory critique they presuppose, is transcendentally necessary? That is, is there a respect in which these schemes are not only, as I have shown, necessary for the explanatory projects of the human sciences, but necessary for the unbounded projects and conduct of everyday life? And if there is, how are these types of project interconnected?

Level VI: Depth-rationality

To set the scene, imagine two interlocutors X and Y. Let us suppose that one of them, Y, experiences some frustration in her life. The other, X, can be thought of, if one likes, as a proxy for 'social science'. Y's frustration may be associated with a belief Q which she cannot get rid of (e.g. an obsession) or some circumstance C (e.g. of unemployment) which seriously constrains her. Let us suppose X surmises the existence of a structural source of determination S inducing Q or C. What is to be done? Consider three possibilities here: (i) Y continues to suffer under Q or C; (ii) some non-discursive and/or external procedure or event (e.g. force, medication; or a coup d'état) removes Q or C so that, under heavy sedation, she no longer believes Q or she now works, under conditions of forced labour, in the arms industry, as the new regime prepares for an expansionist war; or (iii) X and Y jointly institute an enquiry into the conditions producing or inducing Q or C with a view to identifying the responsible causes and taking, or helping to take, appropriate remedial action.

Which of these possibilities is to be preferred? Adoption of solution (i), i.e. stoic acceptance of irrationality, is a counsel of despair. Moreover it cannot be generalised to the first person case of doubt (or more generally choice) without vicious axiological regress. Solution (ii) can be ruled out on the grounds that it is not emancipatory, in that it does not replace an unwanted with a wanted source of determination but merely counteracts or replaces the effects of one unwanted source of determination with another [or in the second case, perhaps, one unwanted form of expression of the same source of determination with another unwanted expression of it] . This has the corollary that inasmuch as the original source of determination is not defused, even if it is successfully counteracted, it may continue to exert a latent power. Moreover it can also be argued that the externally imposed end-state does not constitute, but merely simulates, the originally desired end state (Y wanted not merely to be free not to think Q but to be free to think -Q (not Q), R, S and T etc.).

The alternative (iii) of a depth enquiry (D-I) is possible where reason fails but has not yet exhausted its resources; and it is practicable, where Y's beliefs and actions are generated or underpinned (positively compelled or negatively constrained) by un- or incompletely-known (or unacknowledged) processes, and where Y seeks to understand them in order to undermine, abrogate or transform them. A D-I may be defined generally as any co-operative enquiry, which includes the frustrated agent(s) concerned, into the structure of some presumed set of mechanisms, constituting for that agent an unwanted source of determination, with a view to initiating, preserving or restoring the agent's wellbeing, including her capacity to think, speak, feel and act rationally.

Four points must be immediately noted about this definition. What constitutes an agent's wellbeing cannot be stipulated *a priori*, but must itself be discovered, in relation to the agent's antecedent notion of her wellbeing in the course of the explanatory critique and emancipatory practice such a D-I presupposes. And what is rational cannot be laid down in advance but must likewise be determined, in relation to our pre-existing ideas of rationality (comprising its nominal essences, so to speak), in the context of the D-I itself. That said, it is important to avoid the presumption that rationality is (i) a universal or monolithic concept, (ii) exclusively epistemic or cognitive in character,[28] (iii) primarily applicable to statements rather than actions, projects (practices) etc., (iv) equivalent or analogous to consistency in argument. The rationality of a (line of) historical action is not the rationality of a pattern of formal argument. But while the latter always depends upon the former, logical consistency is never sufficient and frequently violated in rational transformative praxis (e.g. in the diachronic development of science). Secondly, although the concept of a DI has been introduced as an ideographic, practically-oriented *application* of some or other determinate explanatory critique, the *theory* at the heart of the critique itself depends crucially for its own development and empirical confirmation on such investigations (whether on living or historically reconstructed materials). Accordingly the links between theory and practice, and pure and applied research, though not eliding their distinctions, are bound to be much tighter than in the natural sciences (as is indicated by the internal limits on naturalism discussed in § 2 and exemplified in the helix of Diagram 2). Thirdly, corresponding to the different types of inference scheme outlined in § 6 above, there will be different forms of DI. These must not, however, be hypostatised. For the explanation of cognitive ills will in general make reference to practical and communicative ills, and vice versa; poor facilities may induce competential ills and affective malaises, etc. We are here in the world of interdependence and internal relations, as well as of depth, diversity and historical change. Finally, consider the desire for emancipation which motivates the DI. If and when historically transformable and unnecessary sources of the determination of ills are identified, an emancipatory drive can neither be posited *a priori* nor predicted in historicist fashion. It cannot be posited *a priori* for, although it is a necessary truth that people act on their wants, it is not a necessary truth – but on the contrary plainly false – that they always act on their interests and needs. And it cannot be predicted in historicist manner, not because of some special cussedness on the part of people's desires, but because historicism is, as a species of actualism, false in the social and natural world alike. However the desire for emancipation from specific, and more or less systematically interrelated, sets of compulsions and constraints, understood as a socially produced social object, will be a critical topic for meta-investigations, which must then be reflexively incorporated into the substantive theory of the practice from or for which emancipation is sought. Thus once such a meta-DI, investigating the emancipatory drive, has been iteratively incorporated into the explanatory diagnostic theory of the malevolent structure, it may then inform the strategic emancipatory theory of the transformative practice. At the same time, these theories may reciprocally modify and enhance the emancipatory drive.

The structure of a simplified D-I may be elucidated as follows:

(1) Y wants to, but is unable to perform an act, or a systematic class of acts, ψ, where a relatively general and grounded view of human nature, shared by X, suggests that ψ should be possible. The status of this presupposition will be discussed shortly. This inability is experienced by Y as the frustration of a need or the unfulfilment of an objective possibility.

(2) Scientific realism suggests that there is, or may be, a mechanism M preventing ψ, either by constraining, blocking or by compelling not ψ.

(3) General explanatory theory T investigates the structure of blocking/compelling mechanisms in the domain in question under the control of empirical data and researches.

(4) The application of T to Y depends upon the agent Y, as well as the

scientific investigator X. For it is Y's interpretations, actions and determinations that are at issue. Subjectivity in the human sciences is not an obstacle: it is an essential part of the data. But ontological authorship does not automatically transmute to epistemological authority. The Y-dependence of the D-I means that Y must have a really efficacious interest in disengaging M or at least in a class of acts, which may now be expanding, of the ψ type which M prevents. And that coinvestigator X must not have an interest 'in the distortion of M-descriptions or their application with respect to ψ or to Y. Concretely this raises the question of the costs of emancipation for Y, and of the conditions under which it may be a second-best solution for Y; and it presupposes, on the part of X, the willingness to learn (in the general spirit of Marx's Third Thesis on Feuerbach) and the continual development both of T and of X's own self-understanding.

(5) At a deeper level the success of the detailed investigation of the way in which M works so as to prevent Y's ψ'ing depends upon an internal differentiation within the experience of Y, at least insofar as Y's own practices are interwoven into its effectivity (implying rejection of the empiricist/utilitarian notion of emancipation as the alteration of the external circumstances of effectively autonomised individuals).

Moreover it should be reiterated that cognitive emancipation depends in general upon non-cognitive conditions; and that cognitive emancipation is necessary but insufficient for full, human emancipation (as shown by the example of the slave who knows only too well that he is a slave but still remains one). In fact *dissonance*, not liberation (or the rational elaboration of an emancipatory strategy), may be the immediate result of enlightenment. And such dissonance may lead either towards practical-critical-transformative-revolutionary action or alternatively to despair. Moreover, constraints upon cognitive emancipation itself are imposed by the imbrication of ideologies into the practical contours fixed by the material imperatives in social life (in historical materialism), by the preformation of ideational contents (in psychoanalysis) and by the projects of others (in social phenomenology). Hence emancipation can no more be conceived as an internal relationship within thought (the idealist error) than as an external relationship of 'educators', 'therapists' or 'intellectuals' to the 'ignorant', 'sick' or 'oppressed' (the typical empiricist mistake).

(6) The object of the D-I is emancipation, but we must allow the possibility that the D-I will reveal the ψ-preventing mechanism to be unchangeable (under the current and/or foreseeable, including all co-produceable, sets of circumstances under which Y lives) and/or the view of human nature which grounded the presumption in favour of its changeability to be radically flawed. And we must allow the possibility that the initial want for ψ is not a 'happy' one, in that though Y wants it, it may not 'suit' her, i.e. be in accord with what the D-I shows to be or consist in (or to be fulfilling of, or to move towards) her nature; so that, though she wants it, she not only does not need

it, but has a positive need not to ψ. In the D-I, or rather in the theory-practice helix it initiates, wants and prescriptions are themselves transformed. Note further that although it is not possible for Y to continue to want something that is knowingly not in her nature,[29] her socialised nature is in itself in continuous transformation (so that nothing of empirical import follows from this analytic truth); and, more importantly, that there can be no *a priori* guarantee that it is only in human nature or a particular agent's nature to do what is conducive to her survival, flourishing, happiness, well-being *even* if she knows what this is: only an historical experience, incorporating the D-I, can disclose Thanatos or Kali or manicheanism to be myths. It is the possibility of needs/wants conflicts that I had in mind in defining emancipation in § 5 as the transformation from an unwanted and unneeded source of determination to a wanted and needed one. Certain forms of labour may be (either always or at least under all conceivable historical circumstances) both unwanted and constraining, but nevertheless needed. Conversely, unless a source of determination is unwanted, the emancipation is not self-emancipation and is unaccompanied by any experience of enhanced well-being or possibility by the agents concerned.

Emancipation itself may be conceived either (i) as the process of the changing of one source or order or mode of determination S_1 into another S_2; or (ii) as the act of switching from S_1 to S_2, both S_1 and S_2 perduring, but S_1 in a de-activated state.

Now, I want to propose that the possibility of a D-I is a transcendental condition of any human science, and hence at a remove of any science or philosophy and of every rational practice or act of self-understanding at all. If the fundamental norm of theoretical discourse is descriptive or representative adequacy or truth, that of practical discourse is the fulfillment, realisation or satisfaction of human wants, needs and purposes. If there are real grounds (causes) for belief and action, then it is possible we are mistaken about them, and if we fail in truth we may also fail in satisfaction. There are three possible responses to this: we can deny it, and revert to a form of *fundamentalism* – this is the path of classical philosophy; we can shrug our shoulders with a '*tant pis*' and carry on with the ordinary business of living – this is the homely way of *commonsense*; or we can seek to identify the causes of our truth – and satisfaction – failures – this is the royal road to *science.* On this road, the question which interests us is no longer merely the simple one of the causes of belief and action, it is the question of the causes of these causes: it thus presupposes an ontological *stratification* within the constitution of our theoretical and practical agency which classical philosophy and commonsense join hands in denying. To enquire into the causes of error is the same thing as to enquire into the possibility of rationalisation, self-deception, deception of others, counterfinality and systemic (ideological) mystification; and to enquire into the conditions of these cognitive-communicative malaises immediately raises the question of the conditions of practical ones – from ill-health to brutal oppression. And to enquire into the causes of practical failures – from the frustrated projects of individuals to the missing, misidentifying or misunderstanding of historical opportunities of eliminating ills or realising goods – is at the same time to enquire into the conditions of possibility of impossible relations and the conditions of impossibility of possible ones; and to enquire into the conditions of the dehiscence of needs and possibilities, of the conditions of frustrated needs and unfulfilled possibilities of satisfying them, immediately raises the question of the mechanisms of cognitive – communicative smokescreening at work. To stress, the explanatory critical discourse is not about whether we may be said to act or choose or believe or know, it is about the structural sources of the options from which we, in our everyday practices, more or less freely, choose. This is a question which can only be taken up by the depth human sciences (at their various – e.g. historical, phenomenological, psychodynamical – levels). In the human sciences the problem of error, oppression, etc. must thus be fused – in the explanatory-critical D-I – with the problem of the causes of error, oppression, etc. as part of the programme, paramorphic (but non-identical) to that of Kepler, Galileo and Newton, of the investigation of the shifting deep structures, moving like continental plates, producing, in myriad forms, the turbulences and routines of our historical experience, the manifest phenomenology of everyday social life.

I stated above that the D-I is prompted or informed, at the initial stage, by a view about human nature, which will be refined, revised or refuted (or perhaps confirmed and consolidated) in the D-I itself. It is this view which forms the characteristically ethical ingredient associated with the D-I, or more generally explanatory critique (cf. Diagram 1 on p. 173 above). Such an anthropology need not, and, on the transformational view, should not, be an a-historical one. But some anthropology is the condition of any moral discourse at all. As ontology stands to epistemology, so anthropology stands to ethics; indeed one could say that anthropology just is the ontology of ethics. But just as a theory about the nature of the world is implicit in any cognitive claim, a theory about the nature of (wo)men is implicit in any moral one. (And it is easy to identify analogues of the epistemic and ontic fallacies here. Extreme examples are provided by Kantian formalist prescriptivism and Benthamite naturalistic utilitarianism respectively.) To say that 'X is good for an agent (or agents) N', or that 'N ought to φ' is to say that the nature of N is such that A or φ'ing promotes or realises or fulfils N's (species, class, group, individual) nature – conduces, in some more or less vital way, to N's survival or flourishing – as that nature essentially is and/or has been biologically and historically (psycho-socially) formed. Notice that this is not to say that N necessarily wants 'A' or 'φ' – it is just this which gives moral dialogue its characteristic normative bite. Moreover this leaves open the question of the universality of the nature that is presupposed in moral discourse. Now it seems grossly implausible to suppose that human beings do not, qua human beings, share characteristics (such as purely physical ones!) which differentiate them as members of the same species from members of different species: there is a scientifically impeccable ground for this assumption, viz. in their common genetic constitution. At the same time, this 'common nature' is never expressed in anything but thoroughly socialised, more or less historically specific and very highly differentiated forms. We cannot identify a common nature under psycho-socially meaningful descriptions. There is the further consideration that the transformational view espoused here suggests that essential forms of a psycho-social kind, considered as real because causally efficacious, are the products of prior transformations and/or in the process of contemporary transformation and/or subject to the possibility of future transformation, although it should be noted that the T.M.S.A. does not assert the nonexistence of summative social universals. I suggest that the most plausible resolution of these three desiderata lies in the supposition that any particular agent N* possesses a 'nature'[30] which can be componentialised into at least: (i) a common human nature, grounded in genetic structure and manifested in certain species-wide capacities (e.g. language-use); (ii) an historically specific nature, of a quite highly differentiated kind, whose development was initiated at the time and place of birth, deriving from class, gender, occupational positions, experience, etc., shared in common with other agents subject to the same general determinations; (iii) a more or less unique individuality. (i) never manifests itself in anything but a historically mediated form, although it is *not* itself human-historical in constitution (cf. the analogue of B-type determinations depicted in Diagram 6 on p. 191 above); just as a person's individuality ((iii) above) is only ever expressed in some or other socially *classifiable* ways. What (i) licenses is the supposition of the existence of universal powers (and liabilities), certainly needs and very probably wants (and so interests). Now it is of the first importance to appreciate that it is not an argument against the universal existence of a power or need (or basic ground in nature) that it can only be exercised or realised where certain historically specific circumstances are present (any more than it is an argument against the existence of a magnet's power to attract iron filings when there are none about). Neither is it an argument against the existence of a power or need that its existence can only become articulated and recognised under definite historical conditions. If moral discourse is, as I have suggested, grounded in historical anthropology and this is componentialised in the manner just proposed, then we can allow that it makes sense to ascribe the *existence* of rights (and goods) for all human beings *qua* human beings, in virtue of their possession of a common (although always historically mediated) nature, ultimately grounded in their biological unity as a species, composed in particular of common powers and needs [albeit manifest in a myriad variety of historically different ways], even though these rights (and goods) can only come to be formulated as demands, recognised as legitimate and exercised as rights under very definite historical conditions. To collapse a right to the historical conditions of its recognition, realisation or exercise is to commit some ethical form (as distinct from analogy) of the epistemic fallacy, grounded in the actualist collapse of anthropology.[31]

Now if the emancipation is to be *of* the human species, or some proper subset of it, the powers of the emancipated community must already exist (although perhaps only as powers to acquire or develop powers) in an unactualised form. (It should never be forgotten that the world is not just the totality of what is actually the case, but includes what might or could be, grounded in the structural properties of things, as well.) The key questions for substantive theory then become: what are the historical conditions for the actualisation of these powers (competences and facilities)?; what are the transformative tendencies at work?; whence come the historical agencies for change? etc. Such questions, which transport us to Level VII of historical rationality as such, cannot be answered outside the context of some specific theory.

But can anything be said about the conditions of possibility of emancipatory practices in general? For emancipation to be possible, the following conditions must be satisfied. First, *reasons must be causes*, or discourse is ontologically redundant (and scientifically inexplicable). But the potentially emancipatory discourse, given the T.M.S.A. and the general conception of an open world, can only codetermine action in an already pre-structured, practical and collective context. Second, *values must be immanent* (as latent or partially manifested tendencies) in the practices in which we engage, or normative discourse is utopian and idle. I think that Marx, in conceiving socialism as anticipated in the revolutionary practice of the proletariat, grasped this. And it is on this feature that Habermas's deduction of speech-constitutive universals also turns.[32] But if there is a sense in which the ideal community, founded on principles of truth, freedom and justice, is already present as a prefiguration in every speech-interaction, might one not be tempted to suppose that equality, liberty and fraternity are present in every transaction or material exchange; or that respect and mutual recognition are contained in the most casual reciprocated glance? It is an error to suppose that ethics must have a linguistic foundation; just as it is an error to suppose that it is autonomous from science or history. Third, *critique must be internal to* (and conditioned by) *its objects*, or else it will lack both epistemic grounding and causal force. But it follows from this that it is part of the very process it describes, and so subject to the same possibilities of unreflected determination and historical supersession it situates. Hence continuing self-reflexive auto-critique is the *sine qua non* of any critical explanatory theory.

Fourth, at the emancipatory moment, there must be a *coincidence of subjective needs*, experienced as affective and effective drives, informed by vision, imagination, daring and explanatory theory, on the one hand, *and of objective possibilities*, already at or close to their historical conditions of realisation, as the articulated and achievable goals of groups, rather than merely the abstract properties of structures: a dynamic coincidence of competences and facilities in a conjunctural combination of cognitive, conative, affective conditions and circumstantial context. Finally, for emancipation to be possible, *knowable emergent laws must operate.* Such laws, which will of course be consistent with physical laws, will be set in the framework of explanatory theories elucidating the structures of cognitive and non-cognitive oppression and the possibility of their transformation by men and women. Emancipation depends upon the untruth of reductionist materialism and spiritualistic idealism alike. On reductionism – if the physical process level is L_p, and the level at which emancipation is sought is L_e, then either L_p completely determines L_e, and no qualitative change is possible; or qualitative change is possible, and the laws of L_p are violated. On idealism – either emancipation is entirely intrinsic to thought, in which case it is unconditioned and bondage and irrationality become inexplicable; or, if it is conditioned, it cannot be intrinsic to thought. Emergence is a condition of explanation, which in turn is a condition of emancipation. The possibility of emergence is not of course the reason why an emergent powers theory, if it is, is true. It is rather that if human beings, and social forms in general, are emergent from but conditioned by nature, then there is at least the possibility that, provided 'we do not anticipate the world with our dogmas but instead attempt to observe the new world through the critique of the old',[33] the human sciences could still be of some benefit to the greater majority of humankind.

Notes

1 L. Tolstoy, quoted in M. Weber, 'Science as a Vocation'. *From Max Weber: Essays in Sociology*, New York 1946, p. 143.

2 See e.g. C. Taylor, 'Neutrality in Political Science', *The Philosophy of Social Explanation*, ed. A. Ryan, Oxford 1973.

3 See e.g. from the Fabian camp, 'we have little faith in the "average sensual man", we do not believe he can do much more than describe his grievances, we do not think he can prescribe his remedies', B. Webb, *Our Partnership*, entry for 24th December 1894, London 1948.

4 Cf. ed. P. Secord, *Explaining Social Behaviour*, London 1982.

5 Cf. Marx: 'A spider conducts operations which resemble those of a beaver, and a bee would put many a human architect to shame by the construction of its honeycomb cells. But what distinguishes the worst architect from the best of bees is that the architect wills a cell in his mind before he constructs it in wax. At the end of every labour process, a result emerges which had already been conceived by the worker at the beginning, hence already existed ideally. Man not only affects a change of form in the materials of nature; he also realises [*verwirklicht*] his own purpose in those materials', *Capital Vol. 1*, Harmondsworth 1976, p. 284.

6 If 'ought' implies 'can', the non-trivial implication of a power is a presupposition, not an entailment, of the ought-statement – an implication which depends on a theory (i.e. factual knowledge) of the agent and his or her circumstances. (Cf. N. Cooper, *The Diversity of Moral Thinking*, Oxford 1981, p. 181.)

7 E.g. of a subjectivist, pragmatist, emotivist, existentialist – or a quasi-objectivist (e.g. Platonist or intuitionist) – sort.
8 I here include the volitional under the conative basis of action. But it is arguable that the will, comprising the unity of a well-functioning ego, should be accorded a distinct place.
9 Cf. G.H. Wright, *An Essay on Modal Logic*, Amsterdam 1951. Neglect of the dynamic bases of action amounts to forgetting the historicity of the agent and her *Umwelt*; and by assuming the existence of competences and facilities, it obscures the politics of their development, acquisition and distribution.
10 It is of course plausible to conjecture systematic relations between the zones analytically differentiated in Diagram 2.7 on p. 126 above, especially in view of the intrinsically social content of the objects of the psychological groups of sciences. In which event it is plausible to suppose that while an emancipatory practice in the other dimensions will not take the form of a mass politics (but that of an individual one – say speech-therapy) they may presuppose such a politics as a historically facilitating (or enabling) condition.
11 Weak quasi-natural analogues of these explanatory-critical modes, where the proximate source of mystification S' is an artefact or naturalised social object or alternatively a socialised natural object, as in some forms of primitive fetishism, are usually subject both to B-type mediation, i.e. they are mixed modes in the sense of § 1, and deeper forms of explanation on which S' is socio-theoretically redescribed. It is not the physical properties of shoes which explains the shoe fetishist's fetishism, but the meaning shoes have in his or her life, which once understood, shows the shoe as a (condensed) code for something else, some specific socio-somatic configuration.
12 See R. Hare, *Freedom and Reason*, Oxford 1963, p.109. This attribution has been (in my opinion unconvincingly) disputed – see e.g. A. McIntyre, 'Hume on "ought" and "is"', *Against the Self-Images of the Age*, London 1971. The vexed passage in Hume is at *A Treatise of Human Nature*, ed. L.A. Selby-Bigge, Oxford 1965, III. 6.1, p. 468–70.
13 *Capital Vol. I*, p. 639 n.
14 'Marx to Ruge', September 1843, *Early Writings*, Harmondsworth 1975, p. 209.
15 This depends on the balance of what they stand to lose and to gain if they forego their oppressing.
16 A. Giddens, *New Rules of Sociological Method*, London 1976, p. 159.
17 R. Edgley, 'Marx's Revolutionary Science', *Issues in Marxist Philosophy, Vol. III*, eds. J. Mepham and D.H. Ruben, Brighton 1979.
18 See J. Austin, 'Performative-Constative', *Philosophy and Ordinary Language*, ed. C. Caton, Urbana 1963.
19 When they do it is usually either under conditions of historical stasis or neurotic (or quasi-neurotic) compulsion, both profoundly historical configurations; so that the repetition itself becomes the particular action situation requiring explanation and change. But if the surface structure of the moral world has more of the aspect of Bergsonian continuous novelty than Nietzschean eternal recurrence, it is important to remember that this surface has a historical, relatively enduring, depth to it – precisely the object of explanatory social science and emancipatory political action.
20 The case referred to in § 5 (p. 179 above) where a praxis-dependent natural object acts as a source of false consciousness can be represented as:

$$\text{ISI* (i) } T \rightarrow P. \text{ (ii) } T \text{ exp } 1(P_n) \rightarrow \text{(iii) - } V(S_n\psi \rightarrow 1(P_n) \rightarrow \text{(iv) } V\varphi_{-sn}\psi$$

Where a socially irremediable natural object causes systematic false consciousness it is possible to imagine a *deploring* stage (iii) without a stage (iv). Whether this is or would be a rational, as distinct from a likely, attitude is another matter.

21 Cf. D. Bloor, *Knowledge and Social Imagery*, London 1976, chapter 2.

22 See J.R. Searle, *Speech Acts*, Cambridge 1969, chapter 9.

23 L. Colletti, Marxism and Dialectic, *New Left Review 93*, 1975.

24 I have altered the notation from that used in § 3, p. 146, viz. D.(A → B) → A, to avoid confusion with the examples under substantive discussion here.

25 F. Nietzsche, *The Gay Science*, New York 1974, p. 121.

26 F. Engels to P. Lafargue, 11 August 1884, *Correspondence Engels-Lafargue*, Paris, p. 235.

27 F. Nietzsche, *Werke in drei Bönden*, Munich 1954, Vol. I, p. 471.

28 Remember that the epistemic priority of critique of inadequate consciousness does not carry over into their sociological priority over critiques of defective or unhappy being generally. If we tacitly work with a cognitive conception of rationality, then we must accept the paradox that it is not rational to be fully rational because there are non-cognitive bases and aspects of and determinants upon [optimally-rational, as indeed all] action. Cf. H. Meynell who remarks: 'It is not intelligent or reasonable, after all, to treat men as though they were beings wholly determined by intelligence and reason, and not at all affected by emotion or physical desire [as well]', *Marx, Freud and Morals*, London 1981, p. 182.

29 If this appears to happen, we will expect that the agent's nature has been incompletely or wrongly specified; or alternatively that it has changed.

30 It should be unnecessary, but is nevertheless perhaps advisable, to make it explicit that the concept of a nature here, and human nature in general, is not to be hypostatised. It functions purely syncategorematically, acting as a placeholder for, and awaiting filling by, substantive scientific descriptions.

31 A good example of this error is provided by McIntyre's criticism of A. Gewirth's *Reason and Morality*, (Chicago 1977) in *Against Virtue*, London 1981, pp. 64–65, when McIntyre equates the existence of a right with the intelligibility of the making of a claim to it, which is patently always highly specific and local in character.

32 J. Habermas, 'Towards a Theory of Communicative Competence', *Enquiry 13*, (1970).

33 'Marx to Ruge', September 1843, *Early Writings*, p. 207.

18

EXPLANATION AND EMANCIPATION

Andrew Collier

> Schopenhauer . . . would have sickened, become a *pessimist* (which he was not, much as he would have liked to be) had he been deprived of his enemies: of Hegel, of woman, of sensuality, of the human will to survival.
>
> (Nietzsche, *The Genealogy of Morals*, p. 241)

Whether or not Schopenhauer was a pessimist personally, Schopenhauer's philosophy, which entails that the only emancipation from misery is extinction, and that the moon is to be preferred to the earth since there is no life on it, is, by *almost* general consent, the epitome of pessimism. But Bryan Magee, early in his book on Schopenhauer, says:

> Even professional philosophers tend to see him in this light, as is evidenced by the title of Frederick Copleston's book *Arthur Schopenhauer: Philosopher of Pessimism*. Yet this is odd, because it is an elementary point in logic that no truth claim can entail a value-judgement. If a valid argument has a value-judgement anywhere in its conclusions this can only mean that the same value-judgement was already to be found somewhere in the premisses: you cannot derive an 'is bad' from an 'is'. No general philosophy – no ontology, epistemology or logic – can entail pessimistic conclusions. Professional philosophers ought always to have known, without having to read Schopenhauer to discover it, that in this sense his pessimism is logically independent of his philosophy; and so it is.
>
> (*The Philosophy of Schopenhauer*, p. 13).

I thought it worth quoting this at length because it shows how an intelligent and fairly representative modern philosopher could be so convinced of this

Source: *Critical Realism*, London: Verso, 1994, chap. 6, pp. 169–204.

dogma that you can't argue from a fact to a value as to be led to say ridiculous things by it.

For this reason, I want to start this chapter by plunging (almost) straight in to an argument of Roy Bhaskar's which seems to me to make a clear and irreparable breach in the Hadrian's wall which modern philosophy has built to keep those nasty Pictish facts from marauding within the boundaries of the empire of value. Once this breach is made, the invasion can be extended in all sorts of directions.

But one preliminary point needs to be made. The arguments from facts to values are more like evidential or scientific than deductive arguments – unsurprisingly, for values exist in open systems, and value-judgements are normic, always (or almost always) holding *other things being equal*. Introducing a previously unrecognized premiss may vitiate a validly derived conclusion from a true premiss. In deductive reasoning, if P implies Q, then P and R implies Q (e.g. if 'the sheep's in the meadow' implies 'the sheep isn't in the fold', then 'the sheep's in the meadow, the cow's in the corn' implies 'the sheep isn't in the fold'). But in evidential reasoning, 'he was seen running from the scene of the murder with a smoking gun' may imply 'he probably did the murder'; but add 'his gun could not have fired the bullet that killed the victim', and the conclusion no longer follows. It has often been pointed out that moral reasoning is more like the latter: 'taking money from that Coca-Cola machine would be theft' may imply 'you shouldn't take money from that Coca-Cola machine' – but combine it with 'it is the only way to get coins to phone the President and stop a nuclear war', and the case is altered (I allude to the film *Dr Strangelove*). Bhaskar takes this into account by including a *ceteris paribus* ('other things being equal') clause in the conclusion of all his fact-to-value inferences.

Explanatory critiques in social science

In this section, then, I want to concentrate on a single argument that establishes the credentials of explanatory critiques as breaching the fact/value divide.[1] In Bhaskar's texts, this argument is embedded in a general account of fact – value relations (in PN), or of the ways in which theory can affect practice (in SRHE). But I focus on the central argument, on the principle that if we can first storm the castle, these lower terraces can easily be taken. To this end I state the case in my own words, and conclude by quoting the passage where Roy Bhaskar sums it up most lucidly.

Social science, like any science, presents ideas, claimed to be *true* of the object studied, i.e. of society. Unlike the objects of natural sciences, the object it studies, society (or any concrete society), includes ideas. For society can only exist insofar as human agents act, reproducing and transforming the social structure. And human agents act in accordance with ideas. Even though ideas may be causally secondary to economics (at least in the dimension of 'vertical explanation'), and history may be the history of class struggles, as Marx claimed, there can nevertheless be no understanding of the English Civil War and Commonwealth without understanding Puritanism, or of modern Iran without understanding Shi'ite Islam, or of American foreign policy without understanding B movie westerns. So an account of the ideas prevailing in a society will be an essential part of a social-scientific account of that society.

Now many of the most significant ideas in any society will be ideas *about* features of that society. For instance, in Britain in the 1980s, a large number of people believed that unemployment was the result of the fecklessness of the unemployed. Any account of social attitudes, political behaviour, etc. in that period would need to mention that fact. But it would also need to mention the *real* causes of unemployment in the structure of British financial institutions, the world market, government policy, etc. Hence the explanations that were part of the social-scientific study, and the explanations that were part of the society studied, would contradict. If the social science had got it right, then the people it described who had the opposite explanation must have got it wrong. Hence the social science criticizes (part of) its object. There can be no equivalent of this in the natural sciences. Black holes may be unpleasant things to contemplate, but that is no criticism of them. They exist – or don't – and there's an end of it.

Further, the social scientist will not be content with noting the existence of a false belief in the fecklessness of the unemployed; he or she will want to explain it. And whether the explanation is something subtle and socially pervasive, like the atomistic nature of social relations in a commercial society, or something crude and contingent, like lying press-lords, the criticism of the belief will rub off on to its cause. To say that some institution causes false beliefs is to criticize it. Given that (other things being equal) it is better to believe what is true than what is false, it is also better (other things being equal) that institutions that cause false beliefs should be replaced by, or transformed into, those that cause true ones.

Further still, particular institutions and false beliefs about them may be in a *functional* relation, such that the false beliefs serve to preserve the institutions that they are about. Where institutions oppress a substantial number of people, they will only be stable if protected by such false beliefs. In such cases, to propound the truth is not just to criticize, but to undermine the institution.

Hence, the production of explanations of social institutions is not only, as a general rule, a precondition of criticizing and changing them; sometimes, it *is* criticizing them, and beginning the work of their subversion. One classic example of this kind of explanatory critique to which Bhaskar refers is provided by Marx's account of the wage form. Wage-labour only occurs where the workers do not possess the means of labour (tools, workplace, raw materials), and therefore have to sell their power to work to someone who does. This initial separation of means of labour from worker is not given by nature, but the result of history. It perpetuates itself, since the product of the worker's labour belongs to the owner of the means of labour, and only a portion of it is paid to the worker – in general, too small a portion for the worker to be able to acquire the means of labour.

However, because the worker's pay takes the form of the price of the labour-power he or she has sold, it appears as if 'exchange is no robbery', and, while pay levels may be the subject of negotiation, some wage level or other would be 'fair'. Wage-labour spontaneously generates this ideology of 'wages as payment for labour', which, however, is *false*, in that (a) what is actually paid for is labour-power, (b) labour-power can only be a commodity when *labour* is not possible for the worker without such an exchange, since he or she is deprived of the means of labour, and (c) only a portion of the product of labour goes to the worker – and the surplus accruing to the owner ensures that the worker's deprivation of the means of labour is perpetuated.

In this case, not only does the institution of wage-labour *cause* false beliefs about itself, it also *protects itself* from the wrath of the workers by this illusion. To expose it is to criticize the wage system (i.e. capitalism), and to spread this word is to stir up dissent from capitalism, which of course is just what Marx intended.

Another sort of case – slightly less clear-cut as an instance of fact-to-value argument, but very important for social science and its political implications – is that in which the causally efficacious institutions or distinctions in society are not the emotively charged ones. Lévi-Strauss reports that Bororo villages are arranged in circles and divided between two moieties, the Cera, who live in the northern half, and the Tugaré, who live in the southern. The men of each moiety must marry into the other one, funerals must be conducted by someone from the other moiety than that of the deceased, and elaborate mythological and ritual distinctions are associated with this division. Cutting across it is the division between the 'upstream' (eastern) and 'downstream' (western) halves of the village. And within each moiety, there are different clans, each with their traditional functions. All these distinctions are highly charged, and regulate the cultural and sacred life of the village. They give the villagers a self-understanding based on symmetry, complementarity, fraternity. Yet cutting across all these three charged distinctions, there is the division into three unequal endogamous groups, upper, middle and lower.

> Three societies which, without realizing it, will remain for ever separated and isolated, each imprisoned in a kind of pride which is concealed even from itself by a smokescreen of institutions, so that each is the unconscious victim of devices, the purpose of which it can no longer discover.
>
> (*Tristes Tropiques*, pp. 319–20)

And as the Bororo are, so are we Europeans, with our 'Europe of fatherlands' and our national prejudices, trailing a bloody history, and obscuring even more effectively than the wage form the class lines along which our interests really divide.

The dissonance between causal power and emotive chargedness of institutions does not of course involve a formal contradiction between two beliefs; so it is possible for someone, without formal inconsistency, to recognize, for instance, that Britain is only nominally a monarchy, yet to get excited about royalty. However, this is a phenomenon very close to *displacement* in the psychoanalytic sense, which I shall discuss in two sections' time as susceptible to explanatory critique.

The hardened fact/value dichotomist might respond: the argument jumps from fact to value when it introduces the assumption that it is best to believe what is true. However the questions 'what should I believe about x' and 'what is true about x' are not logically independent questions. In fact they are equivalent, in the sense that the answer to one is necessarily the answer to the other. It simply doesn't make sense to say 'that is true, but I shouldn't believe it' or 'I should believe that, though it is not true'.

This may seem to prove too much. For it looks as if it implies that true belief is always better than false belief, and it was only intended to prove this *other things being equal*. It is better that a would-be murderer should have *false* beliefs about his victim's whereabouts.

But the absolute character of the inference from 'it is true' to 'I should believe it' applies only in the first person case. I cannot separate the question of something's truth from the question whether I should believe it, but someone else, who has reason to believe that I might misuse the knowledge to do evil, or even just be deeply hurt by it, may judge that it would be better if I had false beliefs on a subject. (The relation between the tight argument from 'it is true' to 'I ought to believe it' and the looser argument from 'it is true' to 'he or she ought to believe it other things being equal' looks tricky. Deductions do not change validity according to who makes them. But the point is that since to believe something is to hold it true, 'I ought to believe it' can have no other grounds than 'it is true' has; 'he or she ought to believe it' can. I should note that this form of the argument is mine rather than Bhaskar's.)

As I have given this account of explanatory critiques in my own words, I shall now conclude it with a longish quote from Roy Bhaskar which sums it up lucidly:

> If, then, one is in possession of a theory which explains why false consciousness is necessary, then one can pass immediately, without the addition of any extraneous value judgements, to a negative evaluation of the object (generative structure, system of social relations or whatever) that makes that consciousness necessary (and, *ceteris pari-*

> *bus*, to a positive evaluation of action rationally directed at the removal of the sources of false consciousness). Might it not be objected, however, that the fact/value distinction only breaks down in this way because one is committed to the prior valuation that truth is a good, so that one is not deriving a value judgement from entirely factual (natural) premises? But that truth *is* a good (*ceteris paribus*) is not only a condition of moral discourse, it is a condition of any discourse at all. Commitment to truth and consistency apply to factual as much as to value discourse; and so cannot be seized upon as a concealed (value) premise to rescue the autonomy of values from factual discourse, without destroying the distinction between the two, the distinction that it is the point of the objection to uphold.
>
> (PN, p. 63)

I have lifted this argument about explanatory critiques out of its context for the sake of clarity. Now it has to be said that the section in which this passage occurs is supposed to defend arguments *both* from facts to values and *from values to facts*. Indeed, he starts by saying that it is 'now often conceded that the facts are in some sense tainted by, or contingent upon, our values' (p. 55). He intends first to support this view, then to show, more contentiously, that some fact-to-value arguments can *also* be valid.

But this raises a doubt as to whether he may not be cutting off the branch he is sitting on. For if facts are already valuey, it is no great matter that they entail values. If we can argue from values to facts and then back to values again, the conclusions of the whole argument will be of the same evaluative nature as the premisses, which will not surprise anyone. In this case it will be quite plausible to argue that the intervening, supposedly factual stages are a bit valuey. Either the fact/value gap has not been bridged, since the whole argument is valuey, or it has not just been bridged, but the distinction abolished altogether, which is not what Bhaskar is claiming. Let us consider his argument.

He discusses value-to-fact arguments under the following heads:

(a) from the standpoint of the subject of investigation
  (i) concerning the selection of problems,
  (ii) concerning the conclusions,
  (iii) concerning the standards of inquiry;
(b) from the standpoint of the object of investigation;
(c) from the standpoint of the relation between subject and object.

I shall argue that his argument is inconclusive since (as we shall see) under (a) (i) and (ii) he argues *against* those kinds of value-to-fact argument; under (a) (iii) he subsumes this value-to-fact argument under *relativism*, and then defends one, very restricted form of relativism, while refuting the more general kind; however, the kind of relativism he defends is not the kind that licenses value-to-fact arguments. Under (b) he does defend value-to-fact arguments – but in a way that only works on the assumption that there are *no* valid fact-to-value arguments. There is no separate discussion of (c); instead, he goes on to defend fact-to-value arguments, in the manner summed up in the last quote above.

My reason for criticizing Roy Bhaskar's argument now, rather than sticking to paraphrase and exposition and leaving criticism till afterwards, as elsewhere in the book, is that this criticism defends the radical and far-reaching nature of his fact-to-value argument, against concessions that would tend to weaken it.

(a) (i) It is sometimes argued that, in the social sciences, the complexity of the subject-matter forces us to be selective, and the selection is value-determined; Bhaskar argues that such complexity is equally to be found in natural sciences, and is selected from on *practical* criteria only in the *applied* sciences, whether natural or social. In pure sciences, principles of selection are not imposed but discovered. 'Thus while it is practical interests which determine which out of the infinite number of possible compounds of carbon are studied, it is theoretical interests which motivate the identification of its electronic structure' (PN, p. 56). The evaluative selection argument confuses the natural/social distinction with the pure/applied distinction. So *this* case for value to fact arguments doesn't work.

(a) (ii) A stronger case is argued on the basis of '*interference* between the subject's interest in the object and its knowledge of it' (PN, p. 56). If human interests were bound up with geometric theories, said Hobbes, we would fight wars about them. In the case of social-scientific theories, they are and we do. But if we are *conscious* of such interference, we can correct it; if we are not, it is no use stating our evaluative premisses, since we will be misled about them. Hence explicit evaluative premisses for social science are either unnecessary or misleading. 'Interference' remains as a problem to be overcome, but not as a source of acceptable premisses.

(a) (iii) This view 'posits a relativity in the methodological norms secreted by different conceptual schemes or paradigms, together with a value-dependence of such conceptual schemes of the sort already discussed under (ii)'. Bhaskar does not say why he treats this view more favourably than (ii). On the surface, it would seem that in this case, too, we could correct the interference of interests if we were conscious of it, while unconscious interference would be a problem to be overcome. But his strategy is to describe it as a special case of relativism, and to criticize anti-relativist arguments for confusing '*epistemic relativity*, which asserts that all beliefs are socially produced', with '*judgemental relativism*, which asserts that all beliefs (statements) are equally valid, in the sense that there can be no (rational) grounds for preferring one to another' (PN, p. 57). (It may be useful for the present argument to substitute 'cognitive' for 'rational' in the last sentence, since the value-to-fact relativist typically claims that there are moral or political, but not cognitive, reasons for preferring one theory.)

It seems to me that Bhaskar has misread the polemical situation here. Those who are called or call themselves relativists generally hold that epistemic relativity does imply judgemental relativism. Once these are distinguished, as Bhaskar does, the characteristic position of relativists is undermined. The epistemic relativity which Bhaskar accepts is widely held by anti-relativists. And this epistemic relativity is of no help at all to those who want to argue from values to facts.

I conclude that none of the arguments from the nature of the *subject* to value-to-fact inference work.

(b) The issue here is whether some features of the object studied in social science require that it use evaluative language. That values are among the objects studied does not by itself require their description to be couched in valuey language, as Bhaskar rightly notes; a student of canine behaviour does not have to bark. But certain features of the object may require such language, Bhaskar claims. Now of course if the argument which I have already set out (though in PN it comes after) succeeds in showing that we can argue from facts to values, some social-scientific language will indeed be value-laden. But it will be so not in advance of or in addition to but just *by virtue of* being descriptive and explanatory. In this case, there is no question of *bringing* values to the discourse, and hence no real value-to-fact inference.

It seems to me that both the example and the general argument which Bhaskar gives to show the need for evaluative language are really cases of fact-to-value, not value-to-fact argument. Thus he cites Isaiah Berlin's example, that of the following four true statements about what happened in Nazi Germany: 'the country was depopulated', 'millions of people died', 'millions of people were killed', 'millions of people were massacred' – the fourth is both the most evaluative and the most precise and accurate; it gives more of the truth than the others. That is so, but the evaluative force arises entirely out of the factual content. It is not that by bringing values into the discourse one makes it a fuller statement of the truth, but that by making a fuller statement of the truth one implies more values.

At the theoretical level, the argument is that there is an irreducible, but corrigible, hermeneutic moment in social science; that one cannot get started without understanding the *meaning* that actions had for their agents, that institutions have for their participants, etc. But these meanings may be systematic delusions. To understand the Bolsheviks' actions at the time of 'War Communism', one has to understand that they thought they were initiating a rapid transition to a fully communist society; but one must also understand that, in fact, they were irreparably destroying the worker–peasant alliance on which the prospect of socialism in Russia depended, and transforming themselves into a self-perpetuating elite. By incorporating both understandings into one's account, one inevitably *criticizes* their self-understanding and consequent actions – and hence becomes evaluative. What is this but an explanatory critique? The problem here is that Bhaskar has not at this stage introduced the notion of an explanatory critique as a way of arguing from facts to values; hence he is producing good arguments against people who insist that social sciences must have no evaluative *conclusions*; and treating these arguments as if they showed that social sciences may have evaluative *premisses*.

Bhaskar does not discuss (c) separately, but goes on to discuss fact-to-value arguments instead. If my assessment of his arguments is correct, he has found no real place for value-to-fact arguments – and so has not undermined the far-reaching consequences of his notion of explanatory critiques for ethics and politics. Why was he so keen to find defensible value-to-fact arguments?

He wants to take his distance from two mistaken views, each of which he sometimes calls 'scientism'. The first is the idea that a theory could, so to speak, create values where none had been before. Theories can have practical consequences, but only because we are all already valuing various things, as an inevitable part of living. His argument about the value of truth does not deny that truth is a value for us, but claims that it is a value that is presupposed by all our doings as cognitive beings. Non-cognitive explanatory critiques – to which I shall come shortly – likewise depend on our having values – needs, wants, desires, emotions – which may indeed be radically *transformed* by the work of theory, but can in no way be created by it *ex nihilo*. It is doubtful whether anyone ever thought it could; the Fabian example he quotes[2] is a telling instance of the Webbs' elitist arrogance, but does not fit the description since an evaluative input is assumed (the masses can describe their grievances, though not prescribe their remedies). But at least Bhaskar is forestalling a possible misreading of his own work by criticizing this view.

The second mistaken view from which Bhaskar is taking his distance is that which denies the legitimacy of sociological studies of science, and the political struggles over science that may arise from them. While we cannot understand science without understanding that it is an attempt to deepen our knowledge of its intransitive object, the scientific community is also a social group subject to similar constraints and pressures to other such groups. This may affect its findings. At worst, there are cases of deliberate falsification, as in some studies of supposed racial determinants of intelligence, or in Soviet biology in the Lysenko period. Even when this is absent, it is possible to find what you want to find, and easier still to miss what you don't want to find. And even assuming all the results of a research project are objectively true, the area chosen for investigation may be determined by contentious ideological assumptions or practical interests. Thus it is likely that drug companies have concentrated on artificially synthesized drugs to the detriment of research into those occurring naturally in plants; and it is certain that military might and commercial profit are the chief determinants of which secrets of nature get uncovered. In a world where science was funded with a view to satisfying human needs and conserving planetary resources, quite different discoveries might be made – neither more nor less objective than the findings of modern science, but useful for different purposes. (I am certainly not belittling intellectual curiosity as a legitimate motive for science – but its economic efficacy is minimal.) Hence social studies of science may be of value in alerting us to likely sources of error; in well-established experimental sciences, this is a marginal role, but in the human sciences it is very significant. And such studies may inform political struggles over allocation of resources, and over the applications of science.

But these points do not mean that we can argue from values to facts. Research is motivated, but it is not the motivating values that determine its factual findings (or if it is, they are placed under suspicion of being 'false facts'); here, Bhaskar's formalization of the issues is less than helpful; he sets out to defend both 'F→V' and 'V→F' arguments, but the arrows do not mean the same in the two cases. As he says himself (using 'F' for facts, 'V' for values, 'T' for theory, 'P' for practice):

> the asymmetry between the F→V and T→P relationships, on the one hand, and the V→F and P→T relationships, on the other, stems from the consideration that whereas factual and theoretical considerations not only predispose and motivate, but, in favourable epistemic circumstances . . . and subject to the operation of various *ceteris paribus* clauses, logically entail value and practical judgements; value and practical commitments, while they may (and in general will) predispose and sometimes motivate, do not (non-trivially) entail factual and theoretical judgements.
>
> (SRHE, p. 173)

But this is to accept what he had rejected in PN (pp. 54–5), that 'no factual proposition can be derived from any value judgement', and 'any factual conclusion depends upon premises containing at least . . . one factual proposition'.

My exposition of Bhaskar's account of cognitive explanatory critiques in social science, and my defence of their status as unilateral fact-to-value arguments, is now complete. In the following section I discuss some approximations to and extensions of explanatory critique, with wider implications for social science, politics and ethics.

Other kinds of explanatory critique

Now that the fortress of non-naturalism (the doctrine that facts can't imply values) has been taken, it is possible to extend the notion of explanatory critique, and thus to begin to develop a naturalistic theory of practical reason in general. In this section, I shall discuss three ways in which this can be done.

(A) There are other and worse ills than cognitive error and inconsistency; social sciences can also uncover them. Roy Bhaskar writes of extending the pattern of argument 'to accommodate more interestingly specific forms of false consciousness, and indeed more generally of *defective or unfulfilling being*' (SRHE, p. 178, my italics). Social sciences may generate values and motivate practices by exposing these phenomena too.

(B) Explanatory critiques based on knowledge (not necessarily scientific knowledge) of human emotions have sometimes been presented as the basis for a practice of personal emancipation – without the concept of an explanatory critique being explicitly formulated – notably in the ethics of Spinoza and in Freudian psychoanalysis. An explicit theory of explanatory critiques such as Bhaskar's can throw light on these projects, and perhaps form the groundwork of a naturalistic moral philosophy. As Bhaskar puts it: 'A transcendental realist ontology requires, it will be seen, as much readjustment in ethics as in epistemology' (SRHE, p. 187).

(C) Having loosed the stranglehold of non-naturalism, it may be possible to construct a general theory of practical reason in all its varieties, showing the differences as well as the similarities of familiar kinds of practical reasoning to that involved in explanatory critiques. Bhaskar lists seven levels of rationality and discusses them (SRHE, pp. 181ff).

In these ways, it can be shown that Tolstoy's remark quoted at the head of the chapter on facts and values (SRHE, p. 169) is mistaken:

> Science is meaningless because it gives no answer to our question, the only question important to us, 'what shall we do and how shall we live?'

Bhaskar shows how science, and more generally knowledge, *can* help us with this question, and thus resumes the great tradition of philosophy exemplified by Socrates and Spinoza, which endeavours to be at once logical and scientific in method, and (if I may be allowed the word) existential in content.

(A) 'But the human sciences are not only concerned to explain "*cognitive* ills"', says Roy Bhaskar, and goes on to list numerous others under the categories practical ills, communicative ills, irrationalities and injustices (SRHE, p. 191). Insofar as these all involve some avoidable frustrations of human needs, one can draw a parallel with the explanatory critiques already discussed: social science does not only bring into view beliefs, their falsehood and their causal relations with the social structure; it also reveals human needs, their frustration, and the relation of those needs and that frustration to the social structure. This aspect of social science is also critical of its object. For while there is no formal contradiction involved in admitting that something is a human need but denying that it should (other things being equal) be satisfied, such a position can be said, in a looser way, not to *make sense*. One could here appeal to an (inverted) use of G.E. Moore's famous argument against naturalism in ethics. Moore claims that any definition of 'good' must be mistaken, since it always *makes sense* to say (for instance, to a utilitarian) 'I know this action will promote the greatest utility, but is it good?' It seems to me that, once it is conceded that, for example, children have a basic need to play (will have wretched childhoods and become inhibited and miserable adults, lacking in skills and social skills if they are prevented from playing), then it makes no sense to ask 'but *ought* children be allowed to play?' – unless on the basis of some exceptional 'other thing' that is not equal (e.g. 'in the present famine, we will all starve if the children don't spend all their time helping to get food').

Social sciences, then, generate practical emancipatory projects by showing there to be (a) a need, (b) some obstacle preventing its satisfaction, and (c) some means of removing this obstacle. This is not a matter of mere technical imperatives, coming into play only *if* you want the projected good; given that a social science can tell us not only about the means of satisfaction but also about the need itself, it may ground *assertoric imperatives*, i.e. *since* you need this, remove that obstacle thus.

As in the case of cognitive explanatory critiques, there may be a functional as well as a causal relation between the frustrated need and the frustrating institution. The frustration of the need may be not only *generated by* some social institution, but also *necessary for the reproduction of* that institution. So the exploitation of frustrated needs is not always a mere epiphenomenon of the frustration (like commercial pornography for the sexually frustrated); for instance, the frustrated need of workers for possession of the means of their labour is the essential foundation of the system (capitalism) that perpetuates that frustration, since it is what drives them to sell their power to work to a capitalist. Thus there is an exact parallel with the cognitive explanatory critique, with frustrated need replacing false belief.

A few words are required here about the Marxian notion of 'contradictions of capitalism'. It is clear that Marx's intention in using this concept is to provide an explanatory critique of capitalism; his claim to be a 'scientific socialist' largely means that his case for socialism consists entirely in an explanatory account of capitalism – and this explanation is a critique because it unearths contradictions in capitalism.

Some of these contradictions are cognitive, as we have seen – involving 'contradictions' in the logical as well as the dialectical sense. But there are also what may appear at first to be two other kinds: (1) contradictions between the requirements of capitalism and those of human needs – e.g. 'alienation', exchange-value/use-value contradictions, exploitation; and (2) internal contradictions, causing capitalism to malfunction, in its own terms: for example, the falling rate of profit, overproduction crises. In fact I think that all contradictions have both aspects, since (i) (a) the needs with which capitalism contradicts are not abstract human needs in general, but the historically complexified needs of people in capitalist societies, and (b) capitalism presupposes for its own functioning these needs which it frustrates. In both these ways, the needs are *internally* related to capitalism, though this does not mean that they are wholly constituted by it. Furthermore, (ii) internal malfunctions (a) are arguably only possible given that people are not infinitely malleable, since their needs are rooted in biology, and hence have a 'coefficient of adversity' to full incorporation into the functionality of the system; (b) are only objections to the system given their adverse effects on human needs. I wouldn't worry at all about a stock market crash if it didn't lead to unemployment, etc.

Hence, accounts of the contradictions of capitalism are a subset (probably the most important subset) of need-based explanatory critiques. And the *cognitive* contradictions of capitalism are essential to that system precisely because they obscure the need-based ones. It should be added that Bhaskar regards it as unlikely that a unified notion of contradiction can be arrived at (SRHE, p. 197); rather, a number of kinds of non-cognitive contradiction may be 'clustered around' the notion of logical contradiction from which they derive their name, united perhaps by a sort of 'family resemblance'.

(B) Spinoza's ethics is noteworthy as being, on the one hand, a system of ontology and psychology motivated entirely by moral concerns, and, on the other, a system of morality entirely in the indicative; Spinoza does not say 'we ought to . . .' but 'the free person/one who is led by reason will . . .'. This is made possible by the following triad of doctrines: (a) that an emotion can only be overcome by another emotion; (b) that emotions are not simply data, which cannot be criticized – they involve beliefs, which may be more or less adequate, and the emotion consequently more or less rational; and (c) that we are free to the extent that we have rational emotions, based on adequate ideas. This we achieve not by an 'act of will', taking sides with existing rational emotions against existing irrational ones, but by a work of reason transforming irrational into rational ones, by substituting adequate for inadequate ideas.

This may be restated in these terms: the work of personal liberation is a work of transforming one's emotions by means of explanatory critiques of them. As one comes to understand one's emotions better, one can eliminate contradictions and misconceptions from them. This understanding is never achieved by pure 'introspection', for our emotions are what they are because of our interaction with the world. The increase of self-understanding is equivalent to the increase of our powers both to act on the world, and to be affected by it through the senses.

For Spinoza, the explanatory critique, if genuinely seen to be true, of itself transforms the emotion; for once we see the beliefs involved in an emotion to be ill-founded or inconsistent, those beliefs are necessarily changed, and the emotion thereby transformed. Here at least, explanation *is* emancipation;

however, the production of the explanation is a process that also occurs under a non-cognitive description: an increase in interactive powers.

If Spinoza's idea of the work of moral thinking is that of explanatory self-critique, his case against rival moral outlooks is also a sort of explanatory critique. For he regards, for instance, the kind of moral blame which assigns ultimate responsibility to agents as of a piece with vindictive emotions, and to be undermined along with them by an understanding of human motivation.

Roy Bhaskar does not explicitly draw parallels between his theory of explanatory critiques and Spinoza's approach to moral questions, but I believe Spinoza provides the best historical paradigm for that 'readjustment' of ethics that transcendental realist ontology requires, and I think that the possibility of a neo-Spinozist ethics opened up by critical naturalism is a fruitful and exciting one. And Bhaskar *does* refer, as an example of explanatory critique, to another project of personal self-emancipation the similarity of which to Spinoza's has often been noted: psychoanalysis. Freud himself wrote 'I readily admit my dependence on Spinoza's doctrine', and though he 'did not seek philosophical legitimation', he 'never claimed priority' (letter to Dr Lothar Bickel, 28.6.1931, quoted in Hessing, ed., *Speculum Spinozanum*, p. 63).

Let us consider a long passage in which Freud explains to his patient the Rat-man how psychoanalytic treatment works. If the passage lacks the finished look of some of Freud's accounts, since it is an informal exposition in response to the Rat-man's questions, it has the advantage of being at once a concrete piece of therapeutic work with a concrete symptom, and an explicit application of Freud's general theory of our mental structure. The mismatched emotion which sets off the discussion was the Rat-man's self-reproach at not having been present at the moment of his father's death – a reproach so intense that it made him unable to work.

> When there is a *mésalliance*, I began, between an affect and its ideational content (in this instance, between the intensity of the self-reproach and the occasion for it), a layman will say that the affect is too great for the occasion – that it is exaggerated – and that consequently the inference following from the self-reproach (the inference, that is, that the patient is a criminal) is false. On the contrary, the physician says: 'No. The affect is justified. The sense of guilt cannot in itself be further criticized. But it belongs to another content, which is unknown (*unconscious*), and which requires to be looked for. The known ideational content has only got into its actual position owing to a mistaken association. We are not used to feeling strong affects without their having any ideational content, and therefore, if the content is missing, we seize as a substitute upon another content which is in some way or other suitable, much as our police,

> when they cannot catch the right murderer, arrest a wrong one instead. Moreover, this fact of there being a mistaken association is the only way of accounting for the powerlessness of logical processes in combating the tormenting idea.' I concluded by admitting that this new way of looking at the matter gave immediate rise to some hard problems; for how could he admit that his self-reproach of being a criminal towards his father was justified, when he must know that as a matter of fact he had never committed any crime against him?
>
> At the next sitting the patient showed great interest in what I had said, but ventured, so he told me, to bring forward a few doubts. – How, he asked, could the information that the self-reproach, the sense of guilt, was justified have a therapeutic effect? – I explained that it was not the information that had this effect, but the discovery of the unknown content to which the self-reproach was really attached. – Yes, he said, that was the precise point to which his question had been directed. – I then made some short observations upon *the psychological differences between the conscious and the unconscious*, and upon the fact that everything conscious was subject to a process of wearing-away, while what was unconscious was relatively unchangeable; and I illustrated my remarks by pointing to the antiques standing about in my room. They were, in fact, I said, only objects found in a tomb, and their burial had been their preservation: the destruction of Pompeii was only beginning now that it had been dug up. – Was there any guarantee, he next inquired, of what one's attitude would be towards what was discovered? One man, he thought, would no doubt behave in such a way as to get the better of his self-reproach, but another would not. – No, I said, it followed from the nature of the circumstances that in every case the affect would for the most part be overcome during the progress of the work itself. Every effort was made to preserve Pompeii, whereas people were anxious to be rid of tormenting ideas like his.
>
> ('A Case of Obsessional Neurosis', pp. 313–15).

Let us take this point by point. (1) We start with an inappropriately intense emotion. It is recognizedly irrational, since the affect (the feeling of self-reproach – hereafter 'F') is recognized to be stronger than warranted by the idea to which it is attached (of his absence from his father's deathbed – hereafter 'Y'). (2) Freud postulates another idea, X, which is the *real* cause and object of F, since something must explain it, and Y does not. (3) X, since it is unknown yet effective, must be repressed; thereby F, dissociated from it, was *displaced* on to Y. (4) In reply to the question 'how will the discovery of X (to which *ex hypothesi* F was appropriate) help get rid of F?', Freud answers that only the unconsciousness of X enabled it to persist unaltered. Once conscious, it would be subject to 'wearing-away'. Freud goes on to identify the unconscious with the infantile, preserved by repression. X turns out to be an infantile wish that his father would die. Once the infantile wish is brought into adult consciousness, it loses its terrors; the original emotion Y + F has disappeared, and the infantile residue X + F can be coped with when brought into the context of an adult's sense of reality and proportion.

This constitutes a kind of explanatory critique in which the emotion Y+F is (a) characterized as mismatched, (b) explained as a displacement of X + F, (c) replaced by abreaction of X + F, which is then (d) weathered away by the 'daylight' of reason.

It is worth mentioning that, along with the often discussed assumptions that there are mental causes and unconscious ideas, there is here the interesting assumption that ideas and feelings can be mismatched, and underlying this an ideal of rationality as the alignment of the relation of mental phenomena to their causes with their relation to their objects. When it is revealed that the object of an emotion or belief is not its cause, rectification is in order. In this respect, Freud is a card-carrying Spinozist. But in two ways his account is less 'cognitivist' than Spinoza's. First, in that for Freud the mere *knowledge* of the true origins of the mismatched emotion in repression and displacement will not by itself undo these processes; unless that knowledge has so to speak come up from the unconscious, complete with its attendant feelings, assent to it will merely be a 'second registration' of the knowledge, not an abreaction capable of effecting a cure. Second, in that the emotional tie with the analyst, 'transference', is one effective element in the process of bringing unconscious ideas into the light of day, which can often succeed where pure Spinozist reflection would fail.

(C) In the section 'Reason and the Dialectic of Human Emancipation' (SRHE, pp. 180–211), Bhaskar lists and discusses seven levels of practical rationality. The fourth is explanatory critical rationality of the sort already discussed. The fifth and sixth strike me as being special cases of it rather than distinct levels: under level V, 'depth-explanatory critical rationality', he discusses Marx's account of ideology, with its characteristic elements of theoretical ideology (the rival explanatory account) which reflects and rationalizes the practical consciousness which is itself a mystifying reflection of the social reality of which it is a necessary element. The passage on level VI, 'depth-rationality', is an account of a possible kind of depth inquiry undertaken by two people with a view to understanding and remedying some frustration to which one of them is subject. This looks built to accommodate psychoanalysis, though the account is generalized to include the case where the frustrating agency is an external circumstance rather than a neurotic symptom. The open-ended nature of this quest, with its possibilities of discovery and disillusion, is brought out. These two levels are grouped together as emancipatory reason, presumably because both set out to explain with the explicit intention of thereby helping the work of emancipation. Level VII, 'historical rationality', is concerned with questions about the unactualized powers and transformative tendencies already present, which may generate the possibility of human emancipation. It is mentioned only to say that these questions can only be answered in the context of some theory (presumably a theory of history as the progressive realization of human potential, after the manner of Kant, Hegel or Marx).

I now turn to the 'lower' levels, for even these familiar forms of practical reason foreshadow the critical and emancipatory reason that has been our concern so far. The first is technical rationality – the only sort of practical rationality known to positivistic 'neutral science': instances of this concern means to some external end. Bhaskar says that they only seem to do more than this if they implicitly suppose human purposes. It may be noted in passing, though, that if human sciences provide an *explicit* account of such purposes, they may transform technical into assertoric imperatives by supplying an extra (factual) premiss, and are then on their way to the level of non-cognitive explanatory critiques. However, Bhaskar makes a different point about the potential of instrumental rationality, which takes us to level II: 'explanatory knowledge increases the range of real (non-utopian) human possibilities, which may of course also mean decreasing the range of imagined ones, by showing certain of these to be purely imaginary' (SRHE, pp. 181–2). Such knowledge is empowering to a movement of the oppressed. Of course, it may also be empowering to the oppressors, but not unambiguously so, for the latter have an interest in obscuring the real range of available possibilities from the oppressed, hiding possibilities of a better life that depend on transformed structures, and holding out unreal possibilities of a better life within existing structures. This is not necessarily a cynical dodge: the oppressors may equally obscure the unwanted possibilities from themselves. But all this means that even purely instrumental knowledge (including, it might be added, some supplied by the *natural* sciences) is not necessarily neutral. As Althusser put it: 'true ideas always serve the people; false ideas always serve the enemies of the people' (*Lenin and Philosophy*, p. 24).

Finally, there is level III, intra-discursive critical or practical rationality: every theory implies criticism of incompatible theories and the practices based on them. 'X is false' entails 'don't believe X', and, other things being equal, 'don't act on X'. This point, which is the first condition of explanatory critiques proper, also has some practical import even in the absence of an explanation of the disproved or contested beliefs.

All seven of these levels share a common structure, in that they are ways in which an already existing and ongoing practice is transformed by a theory which supplements or contradicts some of the ideas implicit in the practice. None of them can create a practice out of nothing, but all of them can transform practices in ways that could not have occurred without them. The 'primacy of practice' holds, historically and ontologically. But it does not imply that theory is redundant or epiphenomenal or merely explicative or neutral as to ends.

A non-cognitive model of emancipation; a cognitive model of ethics?

It is clear that Roy Bhaskar is anxious to avoid the misreading of his theory of human emancipation which, on the basis of the prominence given to explanatory knowledge in that theory, would take it as a purely cognitive process. There are of course special cases where it is. When it is *just* a set of false beliefs that enslaves, their replacement by true beliefs *is* liberation. But the vast bulk of human bondage, misery and oppression is not like that. The extension of explanatory critique from cognitive error to unsatisfied needs makes it clear that false belief is not the only chain that binds us, and it is massively outweighed by others in terms of urgent human problems. Peasants who grow food they cannot afford to eat, unemployed workers, homeless families, bullied wives, tortured prisoners, may all know exactly what would make them free, but lack the power to get it. And Roy Bhaskar has something to say about the nature of emancipation, based on his conception of the way we interact with the structured world outside us.

But first it should be said: (1) that though the oppressed *may* understand their oppression quite well, they may not. In the example from Marx, workers who take wages to be payment for work done may or may not perceive their wages as unjust, and would most likely welcome a rise, but will not recognize their systematic exploitation, rectifiable only by a change of social structure. They will not undertake political action to take over the means of production so long as they see the existing system as only accidentally exploitive. Their cognitive deception is the first line of defence against their social emancipation. Hence cognitive enlightenment is a necessary, though not a sufficient, condition of their emancipation.

(2) It should also be said: that workers who *have* seen through the wage form to the relations of exploitation that lie behind it are so far unfree, that they have an uphill struggle ahead, and may be less 'happy' in a superficial sense than the forelock-touching Tory Working Man; '*dissonance*, not liberation . . . may be the immediate result of enlightenment' (SRHE, pp. 204–5).

Yet to a degree they are already more emancipated. No one with any self-respect would prefer to be a contented dupe than a clearsighted dissenter. But it remains true that the main part of the work of emancipation is not cognitive, but consists in toil and trouble, conflict, changes in power relations, the breaking up of some social structures and the building up of others.

The etymology of the word 'emancipation', almost always favoured by Roy Bhaskar over its near-synonym 'liberation', emphasizes more than the latter the idea that it is always *from* some previous bondage that one is emancipated. Hence it is distinguished from simple *empowering*, which may also, of course, be the result of (applied) new knowledge.

Bhaskar characterizes emancipation in the following way:

> It is my contention that that special qualititative kind of becoming free or liberation which is *emancipation*, and which consists in the *transformation*, in self-emancipation by the agents concerned, *from an unwanted and unneeded to a wanted and needed source of determination*, is both causally presaged and logically entailed by explanatory theory, but that it can only be effected in *practice.* Emancipation, as so defined, depends upon the transformation of structures, not the alteration or amelioration of states of affairs. In this special sense an emancipatory politics or practice is necessarily both grounded in scientific theory and revolutionary in objective or intent.
>
> (SRHE, p. 171)

There are a number of points to ponder here.

1. The italicized phrase 'from an unwanted and unneeded to a wanted and needed source of determination' encapsulates a theory of what freedom is. It is 'no more the simple recognition [of], than escape from, necessity' (SRHE, pp. 170–1). That is to say (taking the points in reverse order), freedom cannot mean that we escape the causal order of the world, not only because of the intrinsic incredibility of such a notion, but because (a) an uncaused action could no more be *my* action than something that happened to me without my will would be. My actions are those that I – my character, opinions, desires – cause. Certainly, as has often been pointed out, an action has reasons, not just causes – otherwise it would not be an action. But those reasons must *also* be the causes of the action; for if they are not, then either that 'action' is uncaused, i.e. an accident, and therefore not an action, or it is caused by something other than the reasons for it, in which case the 'reasons' are mere rationalizations, and the 'action' once again a mere happening, that we mistakenly think we cause. We are free only if our reasons have effects – and what has effects is a cause. (b) If we are either to know or to act upon the world – and neither is possible without the other – we must both be affected by the world through our senses, and affect the world through our bodily movements. To do either, we must be no disembodied spirits, but made of the same stuff as the world about us, subject to the same causal laws.

So freedom must be 'in-gear' rather than 'out-of-gear' freedom; it is not a matter of disengaging ourselves from the world so that it gets no grip upon us – for by the same token, we would get no grip on it. We do not escape from necessity in that what we do we do in ways governed by causal laws.

If we *could* disengage ourselves *mentally* from the causal nexus (for it hardly makes sense to think we could disengage ourselves physically), we would actually not be *escaping from* necessity, but rather simply recognizing it – the former of the notions Bhaskar dismisses. Such recognition of necessity would no more be freedom than the prisoner who 'comes quietly' is freer (though he may be less bruised) than the one who resists arrest. However, it is worth mentioning in passing that Engels, to whom Bhaskar attributes this conception of freedom, meant something else by this phrase 'recognition of necessity'. He did not mean accepting being dragged along willy nilly; the image is rather of the yachtsman, whose knowledge and skill enable him to sail near the wind, while the person who does not know how to use the force of the wind will be driven in whatever direction it happens to be blowing. 'Necessity' here, as for Bhaskar, stands for the necessary tendencies of things, not some inevitable fate.

2. The idea of a 'wanted and needed source of determination' is so strikingly discordant with 'out-of-gear' concepts of freedom that it warrants comment. The adherent of 'out-of-gear' freedom may see this idea as just as inadequate as the 'coming quietly' idea of freedom. To extend the metaphor: you get arrested by a decent cop instead of by a real pig. But this rests on the misunderstanding of causation as a kind of compulsion by an outside agency. In special cases, indeed, a causal mechanism may be an alien force, conquerable or not. But among the 'sources of determination' are the laws of our own being, and of the environment which makes it possible for us to be. To take an everyday example, I have not chosen the fact that tea refreshes me, while coffee sets off a slight allergic reaction. But given this fact, I am freer if I can find somewhere that serves tea than I am if I can only get coffee. While this is not an instance of emancipation, the following may be. (a) (At the personal level) if I am cured by psychoanalysis of a disabling obsession or inhibition, I am no less necessitated to act without it afterwards than to act in accordance with it before. Yet I am surely freer. (b) (At the micro-social level) if I am part of a strife-torn household that makes daily life a nightmare for me, I am less free than as part of a loving one, and may emancipate myself by getting out of the former into the latter; yet each will involve its own kind of constraints (and corresponding enablements). (c) (At the macro-social level) different kinds of society are governed by different kinds of laws. I don't only mean legislative enactments (though of course that is also true), but social mechanisms generating different possibilities and tendencies. The future of the area where I live may be determined by market forces, or by plans made by a neighbourhood meeting. In the latter case I can participate in determining my future environment, and live in some confidence that it will not become uninhabitable. Of course, I lose the possibility of speculating on the property market. But in both cases, there is a generative social mechanism determining what happens – and in both cases, that mechanism works only through the actions of human agents. And of course, in both cases, there are material constraints: build a house upon subsiding subsoil, and it will crack.

Yet the transition from market forces to neighbourhood meeting would clearly be experienced by most people as an emancipation.

It should be evident that emancipation into such 'in-gear' freedom can't be achieved either by pure cognitive enlightenment or any other purely 'inner' or 'mental' change. It 'can only be effected in *practice*', i.e. it requires hard work, transforming recalcitrant structures, with the technical and social means at our disposal, into other, more congenial structures. This brings us to the third point.

3. There is an important distinction between 'amelioration of states of affairs' and 'transformation of structures'. There can of course be freedom-enhancing ameliorations of states of affairs. I would like a holiday in Greece next year, but can't afford it; if I had a rise in salary, I could afford it, and so that amelioration of my state of affairs would to a degree increase my freedom. Furthermore, it might take practical activity to achieve this, whether collective (trade union militancy) or individual (getting promotion). But it would be absurd to call this 'emancipation'. This term implies that there are objectively existing, effective, relatively enduring, but alterable structures constraining one's possibilities: political tyranny, class exploitation, apartheid, patriarchy, bureaucracy, press monopolies, the property market, and so on. Emancipation involves transforming them; and the whole depth-realist theory indicates that there is a real hiatus between reforms at the level of the actual, retaining existing structures (e.g. pay claims, tax reforms, electoral reform, a bill of rights) and structural changes (e.g. the socialization – or privatization – of the economy, the transfer of political power from one class to another, the break up of the nation-state). There is a hiatus in the sense that one will never change structures by the cumulative effect of reforms in accordance with those structures: tax reforms will not abolish class privileges, and so on.

I should say here that, though I have given examples that I consider plausible, realist philosophy cannot as such tell us which changes are structural, which not; only empirical social-scientific inquiry can do that. And there are disagreements about this issue. For example, I have heard it said that the replacement of patrilineal by matrilineal inheritance of surnames would have deep structural effects, though I myself doubt whether any linguistic reforms will even ameliorate states of affairs, let alone transform structures – more likely they will preserve them by obscuring the fact that nothing has changed.

Nevertheless, there is a certain kind of reformist politics which does presuppose that whatever social transformations are required can be made without at any stage implementing 'structural reforms'. In the ironic words of Leon Rosselson's song, 'We'll change the country bit by bit/ So nobody will notice it/ Then ever after, never fear/ We'll sing The Red Flag once a year'. Depth realism, by contrast, draws attention to the same facts as Tawney's remark that you can peel an onion leaf by leaf, but you can't skin a live tiger claw by claw. If some changes can only come gradually, there are others that can only come all of a sudden. Hence, 'emancipatory politics or practice is necessarily . . . revolutionary in objective and intent'. 'Revolution' here refers to the necessarily deep and sudden changes; it does not necessarily imply violence (except in the sense of the ancient distinction between natural and violent motion), though no one but a pacifist or a Hobbesian can doubt that violent revolutions are sometimes necessary. But it is clear that this notion of structural transformation sits easier with Marxist than with Fabian politics.

One reservation needs to be made here though. There is a certain kind of Marxist politics which sees emancipation as an all-or-nothing thing; it is assumed that nothing short of socialism is any sort of emancipation worth having, while the achievement of international socialism would emancipate all and completely, so that thereafter only ameliorations of states of affairs would be required. Bhaskar's definition of emancipation cannot be tied to any such all-or-nothing conception. One can transform *some* of the many unwanted and constraining structures, without transforming them all; and this can still be distinguished from mere amelioration of states of affairs. We have many instances of such partial emancipations: the great bourgeois revolutions which emancipated Europe from feudalism, but delivered it over to capitalism; the national liberations of the twentieth century, which ousted colonial rule, yet often replaced it by military regimes or corrupt bureaucracies; the overthrow of fascism, which everywhere replaced it either by bourgeois democracy or bureaucratic 'state socialism'; the political emancipation of Eastern Europe in 1989–90, which has for the most part led to economic and social developments which are the opposite of emancipatory. As yet we have *no* instance of 'total emancipation', and it would be utopian to predict its possibility. Most likely, emancipation will always occur as a multiplicity of partial emancipations. This does not preclude the possibility that some repressive mechanisms may be explained in terms of other, more basic ones: imperialism, and modern forms of sexism, may be explained in terms of capitalism, for example. But this is a substantive issue for social science, and cannot be resolved by philosophy. At most, Bhaskar's theory may suggest a framework into which we can fit the Marxist notion that the economic structures are 'determinant in the last instance', though not necessarily 'dominant', should concrete research justify it. I mean the notion that generative mechanisms are stratified, so that, on the one hand, they *conjointly* determine events, in no fixed proportion; yet on the other, one of these mechanisms may be rooted in, emergent from, and explained by another.

4. In the passage quoted from SRHE, p. 171, Bhaskar also says that emancipatory politics is necessarily 'grounded in scientific theory'. Why should this be? The argument so far has shown such grounding to be possible, rather than necessary. But if emancipatory politics means transforming structures, it must be based on knowledge of those structures. It is such knowledge that transforms the will to ameliorate states of affairs – which is

after all the necessary *motive* of emancipatory politics – into the project of transforming those structures which generate the unwanted states of affairs. Social evils may stare one in the face, but social structures don't. One can see people sleeping on the streets, and listen to their complaints; but one has to do research to understand the market mechanisms which cause this tragedy, and how they can be changed. William Morris is reported to have said that he didn't need Marx's *Capital* to tell him that the rich robbed the poor; if he nevertheless read his copy of *Capital* until it fell apart, perhaps that was because the *mechanisms by which* the rich rob the poor need to be analysed and understood if we are to abolish them.

If it is clear by now that Bhaskar's conception of human emancipation is not a cognitive one, I think it is also becoming clear that his paradigm of practical reasoning – of ethics – *is* a cognitive one. For while 'there are other good things in life apart from explanatory knowledge' (SRHE, p. 171), and most of ethics will be talking about those good things, not *about* explanatory knowledge, its kind of talking will be describing and explaining, not simply prescribing or evaluating. We talk most usefully about values when we do so by talking about facts. Unless people had values already, no amount of 'edifying discourses' could induce them, but given that people unavoidably have values, the way to change those values for the better is by increasing knowledge, both descriptive (e.g. what it is like to be a forest-dweller turned out of one's home and livelihood by a rancher), and explanatory (e.g. how come ranchers have the motive and the power to turn the forest-dwellers out?). Bhaskar has not elaborated this idea of a cognitive paradigm of ethics, which, so far as personal ethics is concerned, might look very like Spinoza's. But the possibility of such an ethics is implicit in his thought.

Some of the essential points of Roy Bhaskar's view of emancipation are summed up in his list of five conditions of the possibility of emancipatory practices (SRHE, pp. 210–11).

> First, *reasons must be causes*, or discourse is ontologically redundant (and scientifically inexplicable).

As we have seen, our reasons for acting must have real effects through our action, co-determining events in the open systems of the world with divers other causes which pre-exist them and operate alongside them.

> Second, *values must be immanent* (as latent or partially manifested tendencies) in the practices in which we engage, or normative discourse is utopian and idle.

This precludes the 'theoreticism' or 'scientism' criticized above, according to which theory can conjure values out of its own hat, where none existed before. We are all engaged in practices prior to the initiation of theory, and all practices necessarily involve and secrete values; the initial motive both for theory and for the transformations of practices that it effects must lie in those values. This also precludes the Platonist or Kantian location of values in an ideal or noumenal world distinct from the world in which we live, along with 'Cheshire Kantian' views such as emotivism or prescriptivism. And at the political level, it precludes the utopian project of basing programmes on how people might be in the future, rather than on what they need now.

> Third, *critique must be internal to* (and conditioned by) *its objects*, or else it will lack both epistemic grounding and causal force.

That is to say, *if it is to have emancipatory effects*, an explanatory critique must be part of the society of which it is a critique. An explanatory critique of the institutions of ancient Babylon will hardly be emancipatory in modern England, or even modern Iraq; a Martian sociologist could report back on the state of the modern world without it having any effect on the world at all. And if the critique must be made from within, it is subject to all the same pressures that distorted the ideas that are the object of its critique. Hence it must always be ready for *self*-critique, and consequent self-revision. The point about 'epistemic grounding' is more contentious, and extraneous to the issue of emancipation. It suggests that the explanatory critique of Babylon by a modern or Earth by a Martian are not just ineffective, but impossible.

> Fourth, at the emancipatory moment, there must be a *coincidence of subjective needs . . . and . . . objective possibilities*, already at or close to their historical conditions of realization, as the articulated and achievable goals of groups, rather than merely the abstract properties of structures.

This specifies one of the non-cognitive, or only partly cognitive, conditions of emancipation. People must actually *feel* the need for change – and for just that change that is a real emancipatory potentiality of the time. Only then can an emancipatory programme that is at once realistic and popular – and hence actualizable – be projected.

> Finally, for emancipation to be possible, *knowable emergent laws must operate.*

This is perhaps the most surprising claim, for it amounts to saying that idealist and reductive materialist philosophies are incompatible with human emancipation, in that, if they were true, that emancipation would not be a possibility. Let us take reductive materialism first.

Suppose that, while everything is governed by physical laws, there are no laws at the level of social existence, i.e. that there are no irreducibly social mechanisms; what would be physically possible would be socially possible, and the only way to apply knowledge in transforming social institutions would be by redescribing them as physical entities, explaining them physically and acting upon their physical structure. But (a) for most examples one can think of, such a manner of transforming social structures is inconceivable; (b) even if possible, it would presuppose a prior identification of the entities to be transformed under a social description, and a decision to transform them because of what they are under that description – without the aid of any explanatory theory of them under that description; (c) such a transformative practice, even if possible, would be systematically indifferent to the *social* properties of the entities affected by the transformation process, and hence manipulative rather than self-emancipatory.

For the most part, the political effect of denying emergent social laws is to uncritically use pre-scientific theories full of unexamined assumptions about social causality, and at the same time assume that anything that is physically possible is socially possible. Thus the crucial fact that some physically possible and humanly desirable outcomes (e.g. the bringing together of unused resources, unemployed workers and unmet needs) may be impossible within a given social structure (e.g. a market economy) is obscured.

Idealism is, on the one hand, theoretically, unable to explain the constraints which make emancipation necessary, and, on the other, practically, destined to preserve real constraints from which we could have emancipated ourselves, by proclaiming an emancipation entirely internal to 'the mind' or 'discourse'. In times of difficulty for liberation movements, there will always occur a secession of erstwhile partisans of emancipation into such movements for 'inner' liberation, and this was noticeably the case in the 1980s. It is for this reason both that realist philosophy has been very much against the stream in 'radical' circles in this period, and that it has itself been a major political intervention as an antidote to this 'retreat to the inner citadel'.

Philosophy and socialism

While Roy Bhaskar makes no secret of his socialist beliefs, his account of human emancipation is in very general terms, not specifically socialist ones. The question has often been posed, what is the relation between 'critical realism' and socialist politics? In this section I try to answer this question. The first thing to say is that the relation is not one of entailment. It is perfectly logically possible to combine such a realism with right-wing or middle-of-the-road politics. Indeed, no philosophical position – according to the conception of philosophy in question – entails any specific political position. Political positions, if rational, are arrived at by means of explanatory critiques of the societies they pertain to; these are the work of empirical social sciences. Marx was right to think that the grounds for socialist politics were in the 'critical analysis of capitalist production'. Whether or not the content of his politics was correct depends on whether that analysis was correct. This is a substantive social-scientific issue, which cannot be resolved by philosophical argument.

However, there are two ways in which the realism and the socialism are linked. First, there are a number of arguments commonly used for certain non-socialist positions, or for versions of socialism which hope to avoid confrontation with and transformation of existing structures, which arguments are undermined by transcendental realism. We have already seen two of them: the gradualist argument that states of affairs can be ameliorated in all requisite ways without transforming any structures; and the idealist 'radicalism' which seeks to liberate the world by changing the colour of our discursive spectacles. I will mention one more here: certain sections of the political right, sometimes called the 'libertarian right', also claim to be working for human emancipation. There is another kind of rightism, which appeals not to liberty but to law and order, the national interest, traditional values, and so on. Since this kind of rightism – which may very well be realist – does not use the language of emancipation, I do not need to discuss it here. The 'libertarian right', however, would find it very difficult to make a plausible claim to be on the side of emancipation without presupposing a specific theory of human nature and social structure: that people are autonomous individuals, and society exists only by virtue of their voluntary or compelled relations (i.e. relations that are in each case the expression of *someone's* will, so that one person's unfreedom always results from another's bullying). Now the transformational model of social activity refutes this position, while taking into account the facts that lend it plausibility vis-à-vis holistic conceptions. It thus leaves the libertarian rightist without any ontological ground to stand on; an alternative defence of libertarian rightism would have to be found if that position were to remain in the field, and it is difficult to imagine what such a defence might be.

In addition to these refutations of alternative political positions, there is another relation between Bhaskar's philosophy and a certain kind of socialist politics. I am referring to the *homology* which exists between the transcendental realist world-view and a certain political model. I am mindful of the fact that homologies can be misleading, and we do well to treat them warily. Some homologies have been very important in the history of ideas, yet of no philosophical importance; the fact that one set of ideas is homologous with another, *true*, set of ideas is no evidence for the truth of the former set. For instance there is a homology between Newton's atomist mechanics and the 'abstract individualist' conception of society; yet Newton's mechanics was an excellent scientific theory, which enabled much new knowledge to be discovered, even though it finally turned out to be inadequate, and in some respects was even contradictory; abstract individualism, on the other hand, has generated nothing but intellectually infertile and humanly destructive errors. Moreover, Newton's justified prestige has lent credence to these errors.

However, in the present case, I shall suggest that, while there is certainly a homology, there may be more than that in the offing. But first, the homology: according to transcendental realism, there are hierarchies of structures in the world, e.g. molecules are composed of atoms, cells of molecules, organisms of cells, societies of people – and in no case are these 'wholes' reducible to their parts, or the parts to their wholes. There are irreducible mechanisms existing at each level, which could not for the most part be predicted from knowledge of the higher- or lower-level mechanisms. This view contrasts with a number of one-level ontologies, which claim either that parts are mere aspects of some whole, so that ultimately there is only the Absolute, of which everything is an aspect; or that wholes are mere collections of parts, understood only when broken down into their components, which alone are ultimately real; or that some intermediate level of entity (e.g. 'selves') are the only reality, their parts being mere aspects, and the larger entities which they make up being mere collections. The common assumption of these three ontologies – that there must be one and only one ultimately real level – is homologous with a common assumption in political philosophy, namely the idea of *sovereignty.*

It is assumed by many writers – Hobbes and Rousseau, Hegel, but also modern political commentators discussing such issues as Britain's place in Europe, or home rule for Scotland and Wales – that there must be sovereignty at some one political level, and that if, for instance, it is located in the nation-state, neither smaller local units nor international organizations can have any but a derivative and retractable power. Likewise, in debates about the politics of economics (public versus private ownership, centralization versus de-centralization, market versus planning, etc.) it tends to be assumed that there must be one level of *units*: that while the 'firm' may be a multinational corporation, a government department or a backyard workshop, there must be some one level at which power is located, outside which there are relations of the market, and inside which there are relations of management. This assumption sets the agenda for debates about possible variants of socialism: it generates the dilemma 'either a command economy, or market relations between separate co-operatives'.

Yet it is no more obvious that such managemental monism is necessary than that some one-level ontology must be true. Even the corporate structure of monopoly capitalism includes relatively autonomous subsidiaries, and models such as guild socialism, though untried, are not obviously impracticable. There may be an alternative to market and command economies alike, in genuinely multi-levelled democratic structures, with real powers located at each level, adequate to deal with the problems of that level.

Likewise with regard to political structures: federal systems in which powers are really located at more than one level (not just devolved from one level to another) have long existed. In other words, even now 'sovereignty' is not in reality absolute. If it is necessary for world peace and ecologically sound planning that, on the one hand, international agencies with real powers be set up and that, on the other, units much smaller than most nation-states (in United Kingdom terms, cities and counties) take over wide fiscal, legislative and economic planning responsibilities, then the illusion of sovereignty as an absolute is a pernicious one.

The homology between such multi-levelled structures of economic and political power, and Bhaskar's conception of a real plurality of causal mechanisms, scientific strata, enduring structures, must be obvious. Is it more than a homology? If we understand political and economic agencies not as mere repositories of legal legitimacy but as enduring structured entities (government departments, firms, trade unions, political movements, armies), with real powers and tendencies generated by their internal structures and their places in wider structures, then it is plausible to suggest that multi-levelled social organization is an *instance* of multi-levelled causal power. The myth of sovereignty – of the nation-state or of the economic firm – may (over and above its obvious apologetic function on behalf of nation-states and firms) be no more than an instance of the same epistemic 'idol' (in Bacon's sense) as the discredited one-level metaphysical systems: Hobbes's particles, Leibniz's monads, phenomenalism's sense-data, Bradley's Absolute. And the vision of a pyramid of democratic loci of political and economic power, from the street and shopfloor meeting to the planetary plan, may have no inherent impracticability – only the uphill task of overturning the vested interests that oppose it.

Notes

1 I am not claiming that Roy Bhaskar is the only philosopher to have shown how we can argue from facts to values. On the one hand, his arguments vindicate the practice of many philosophers before Hume and Kant who argued validly from facts to values without having to defend this against anti-naturalist critics – as indeed non-philosophers do all the time. On the other hand, there have been a number of defences of fact-to-value argument in recent philosophy; most, I think, rely on some notion of specifically moral facts, and hence are not really naturalistic. One, however, anticipates some of Bhaskar's arguments: Roy Edgley, in his book *Reason in Theory and Practice* and his article 'Science, Social Science and Socialist Science: Reason as Dialectic'.

I concentrate on Bhaskar's version of the argument because of the purpose of this book; I also think it is the fullest and most fruitful version.

2 we have little faith in the 'average sensual man', we do not believe he can do much more than describe his grievances, we do not think he can prescribe his remedies.

(B. Webb, *Our Partnership*, entry for 24 December 1894, quoted in SHRE, p. 170n)

References

Althusser, L. (1970) *Lenin and Philosophy*, NLB, London.
Bhaskar, R. (1986) SRHE (*Scientific Realism and Human Emancipation*), Verso, London.
Bhaskar, R. (1989) PN (*The Possibility of Naturalism*) 2nd edition, Harvester Wheatsheaf, Hemel Hempstead.
Freud, S. (1969) 'A Case of Obessional Neurosis', in *Collected Papers, vol. 3*, Hogarth Press, London.
Hessing, S. (1977) *Speculum Spinozanum*, Routledge, London.
Lévi-Strauss, C. (1976) *Tristes Tropiques*, Penguin, Harmondsworth.
Magee, B. (1987) *The Philosophy of Schopenhauer*, Oxford University Press, Oxford.
Moore, G.E. (1959) *Principia Ethica*, Cambridge University Press, Cambridge.
Nietzsche, F. (1969) *Genealogy of Morals and Ecce Homo*, Vintage Books, New York.

19

NEUTRALITY IN THE SOCIAL SCIENCES

On Bhaskar's argument for an essential emancipatory impulse in social science

Hugh Lacey

> Let a belief P, which has some object O, have a source (causal explanation) S. I am going to contend that if we possess: (i) adequate grounds for supposing P to be false; and (ii) adequate grounds for supposing that S co-explains P, then we may, and must, pass immediately to (iii) a negative evaluation of S (CP [i.e., *ceteris paribus*]); and (iv) a positive evaluation of action rationally directed at the removal of S (CP).
>
> (Bhaskar, 1986, p. 177)

> If one is in the possession of a theory that explains why false consciousness is necessary, then one can pass immediately, without the addition of any extraneous value judgment, to a negative evaluation on the object that makes such consciousness necessary and to a positive evaluation on action rationally directed at removing it.
>
> (Bhaskar, 1991, pp. 155–156)

1 Introduction

In several writings, Bhaskar (1979; 1986; 1991; 1993) has put forward a short, sharp argument that not only are the social sciences not neutral, but also that they contain an "essential emancipatory impulse" (1986, p. 169). I aim only to evaluate this argument, not to attempt an overall assessment of Bhaskar's valuable contributions to the philosophy of the social sciences.

I find Bhaskar's argument, summarized in the quotations above, original, ambitious, enticing, suggestive and rich in implications; but also difficult to

Source: Journal for the Theory of Social Behaviour, 27, 2/3, 1997, pp. 213–41.

interpret. In large part this is due to the abstractness and abruptness of its presentation; it does not (e.g.) unfold by way of a critical reflection on actual practices and theories of the social sciences. But also in part it is due to genuine ambiguities. In order to expound the argument, so as to make it open to critical assessment, I find it necessary to engage in some extended preliminary clarifications (with substantive implications extending well beyond the limits of this paper), and to introduce some terminology of my own.

1.1 Characteristics of the social sciences

Clearly Bhaskar does not discern an emancipatory impulse in most of the practices that usually are called "social sciences" in contemporary universities. I will call them "*social sciences*". For him, they are not properly considered "sciences" (but perhaps "ideology", Bhaskar, 1986, p. 198), since he holds that genuine sciences comprehend phenomena in relationship to the underlying structure and law from which they are generated (Bhaskar, 1978), so that a social science would not consider social phenomena in abstraction from the social structures which are among their causes. Genuine sciences also involve a mode of conducting investigation which is systematic and empirically-grounded, so that a scientific theory is properly accepted if and only if it manifests the *cognitive values* (which I will abbreviate as *cv*) to a high degree according to the most rigorous available standards.

The *social sciences* represent, in large measure, a body of understanding (systematic and empirically-grounded, to be sure) whose import derives from its role in the practices driven by the predominant and ascendent values of our time, and whose explanatory (and, where applicable, its anticipatory and predictive) compass is limited to the phenomena that are "significant" for these practices and to an articulation of the social (and natural) world suited to further their maintenance and expansion. They represent a mode of understanding that reflects the "common sense" linked to these values, that lacks the conceptual resources to define systemic negativities (sufferings with systemic causes), that often identifies current ascendent tendencies and manifested social regularities as laws of human nature, that generally does not identify the structural conditions of action (and belief) and so exaggerates the (causal) significance (and thence entitlements) of individual achievement, and that often assumes that the only viable possibilities for the future are those that can be realized within the prevailing structures. This assumption may appear to be empirically confirmed, as the social forces informed by it prevent (or narrow the social space for) the unfolding of alternative possibilities; but in fact it remains part of the "untested consciousness" of this mode of understanding.

As I interpret Bhaskar, a minimally adequate social science must be conducted within a framework that enables the empirical investigation of the assumptions of the *social science* mode of understanding, a framework that (in principle) would enable the formulation of theories that could either agree or disagree with them. Since they are assumptions "about the social world", they should not be immune to the outcomes of empirical inquiry. Such a framework will not accept, as a condition of inquiry, the untested consciousness of the *social science* mode of inquiry, *and* it will include resources sufficient to investigate the causes of the persistence and social efficacy of the various items of untested consciousness.

Elaborating a little (and perhaps expanding somewhat) what Bhaskar intends, the framework of a minimally adequate social science will include (among others) the following features: (1) Social structures are identified and their generative powers investigated in detail; they are treated as variables, both dependent and (relatively) independent, i.e., as historically caused and as having a variety of effects, with (in principle) no features of their generative mechanisms treated as immune in causal analysis and to being considered variables that are potentially related to phenomena both desired and undesired by the privileged and the powerful within the structures. (2) Empirically identified regularities and tendencies are treated as objects for theoretical investigation in order to discern how they are generated from underlying law and structure, what the generative mechanisms are and, thus, what are their historical boundary conditions. (3) It recognizes that the *real* is not exhausted by the *actual*, but includes also the *possible*. There are novel possibilities which, given the constraints of the actual, can only be realized on a small scale in marginal spaces within actual structures, and which need structural change for full blossoming. These include, but are not limited to, possibilities of emancipation. Theoretical and research resources for exploring such possibilities will be developed, so that claims about future possibilities can move beyond the level of untested consciousness—beyond an acceptance of the inevitability of the *status quo* as defined by actual relations of power, and beyond a value-driven voluntarism. Encapsulating the possibilities latent in the actual accompanies the explanation of actual phenomena as the objective of theory in social science. (4) It contains conceptual resources to articulate the complex interaction of the personal and the structural. It investigates the structural conditions of agency, and the necessity of agency in the reproduction and transformation of social structures. (5) All social phenomena, including the prevalence of beliefs among the members of a social group, are open to social explanation. Such beliefs may be investigated in terms of their structural (partial) causes; and, in general, beliefs are treated as objects open to both causal explanation, and critical and empirical inquiry concerning their truth value. (6) It investigates social negativities with sufficient conceptual resources to allow for the possibility that they have structural causes, systemically linked with the "positive" features of the structures. Since its primary object is the underlying generative mechanisms, rather than observable regularities and tendencies, it attends comprehensively to the phenomena (including negativities) generated by the mechanisms, and thus to the relations among the phenomena. Conversely, in order to gain access to the underlying mechanisms, it does not limit empirical investigation principally to the "positive" features. (7) It investigates negativities, as they are articulated and concretely experienced by those who suffer them themselves. Thus, the investigation requires not only the relevant conceptual resources, but also the appropriate moral sensibility to be able to engage in a dialogue of equals with those who are suffering. (8) Connected with the previous condition, many of the categories used in social science theories will be value-impregnated, and so imply relationships to human wants, needs and interests and their satisfaction or frustration. This is necessary for both descriptive adequacy and maximum explanatory power. In the natural sciences, it may serve explanatory interests to describe phenomena in terms that abstract from their relations with human lived experience and practical life; in the human sciences, to attempt to do so is to abstract from human agency, and so to misidentify the object of inquiry. (9) It is reflexive. As a social practice, it is subject to explanation in its own terms.

Bhaskar denies the title "social *science*" to any mode of inquiry that lacks features like these. His ground seems to be that a science should adopt certain *cv* (cognitive values): especially *explanatory power*, including *capability to identify the limits of applicability of rival theories and the conditions under which they are considered acceptable by their opponents*; *capability to identify novel possibilities*, which is more important than the often hailed predictive power, which generally can be manifested in social inquiry only under conditions of significant constraint; and *empirical adequacy*, which is interpreted to capture the force of (7) above, and which is not relevantly present when theory is constrained by untested consciousness. Antecedently to research activity and outcomes, I interpret him as maintaining, the *cv* prioritize engaging in research with the features described. "Science" does not include untested consciousness.

1.2 Neutrality and impartiality

Neutrality is one of the sub-theses of the view that the sciences are value free. The others are what I call *impartiality* and *autonomy* (Lacey, 1997a; in progress).

Impartiality is a thesis about the grounds on which scientific judgments, those about which theories are to be accepted and rejected, are based. It may be summarized in general terms as: properly made theory choice rests solely upon the empirical data and on whether the theory manifests the *cv* to a high degree—or to a higher degree than do rival theories—(according to the highest standards of evaluation) with respect to the data, regardless of how the theory may accord with or serve the interests of any value (or other "extraneous") perspective. (*Autonomy*, a thesis about the conduct of scientific practice, will not be discussed.)

In this paper, I will consider two thesis of *neutrality* (both of which concern accepting or believing theories; there are other theses of neutrality that concern the application of theories, Lacey, 1997a; in progress):

1 A scientific theory does not logically imply any value judgment; or, accepting (believing) a theory does not commit one rationally to holding or not holding any particular value judgments.
2 Accepting a scientific theory neither supports nor undermines the holding of any value perspective; the judgment that a theory is soundly accepted has no consequences (positive or negative) concerning the value perspective one adopts.

Bhaskar's critique of neutrality concerns the first thesis. I will consider the second in § 3.

2 Preliminaries

2.1 Beliefs

Beliefs are propositional attitudes that play causal roles (together with desires, intentions, having goals, etc) in generating actions. When we refer to a "belief", the fundamental expression is "X (an agent) believes that p". A belief is always a belief of an agent, and it may be shared among agents. A belief is true if and only if its propositional content is true. Thus, the critical evaluation of a belief that p is identical with the cognitive assessment of p. An agent's beliefs come in networks of logical and evidential relations; so that X may "justify" the belief that p, by pointing to further beliefs (that q, that r, etc) and their logical or evidential relations with p. The causal role of beliefs is represented in "practical syllogisms" (not in lawlike schemata), in which an agent's actions are represented as following (rationally) from her having certain goals (desires) and beliefs (Donagan, 1987; Lacey, 1996; Lacey & Schwartz, 1986). An agent's (X's) beliefs, themselves, have causes, which may, or may not, *include* her assessments of evidence, and other explicitly cognitive or rational factors.

I distinguish: X *has* the belief that p if that belief plays a causal role in her behavior, i.e., if it is among the beliefs that appear in practical syllogisms that explain her actions. X *holds* the belief that p—"B_x(p)"—if she reflectively endorses that p; and she can defend p from criticisms to her own satisfaction by pointing to its place in a network of evidential and logical relations. X *holds the consolidated* belief that p—"B_x(p)"—if she judges that p belongs to the class of rationally acceptable beliefs, those that (methodologically) require no further investigation. A belief *informs an action* (an action is performed on the *basis* of a belief) if the belief is among those of the practical syllogism that explains the action; it *informs one's activity* if it regularly informs one's actions and/or it is among the presuppositions that play a role in the articulation and justification of the value perspective (§2.2) within which the objectives of one's actions are evaluated.

An informal ideal of rationality includes that there be an identity between the beliefs one has and those one holds; or at least that if X holds the belief that p, then it would be irrational for X to act in ways that were informed by ¬p. But it is not, in all situations, part of the ideal that there be an identity between the beliefs one holds and one's consolidated beliefs, partly because in many of the contexts in which we must act consolidated beliefs are not available, and partly because genuinely creative activity (and activity driven by our deepest hopes) will be informed by beliefs with tenuous degrees of confirmation. Presumably, however, when one holds consolidated beliefs, and they are relevant given the context and immediate objectives of action, one's actions should be informed by them; and the ideal includes, *ceteris paribus* (which I will abbreviate as *cp*), the desirability of expanding the stock of consolidated beliefs that one holds. Inferences, like the one expressing part of the informal ideal of rationality are called by Bhaskar (1986, p. 183) "transcendentally necessary" for practical rationality; I call them "*general conditions on rationality.*"

I said above: if X holds the belief that p, then it is irrational for X to act on the basis of ¬p. X's holding p involves X's making a negative valuation (irrationality) on actions of hers that are informed by ¬p. But if X also make a negative valuation of Y acting on the basis of ¬p, it will not necessarily be the judgment that Y is acting irrationally. For if Y holds ¬p, then it would be irrational for him to act on the basis of p. The negative value judgment would be made on other grounds, such as the belief that Y's acting on the basis of ¬p would have harmful consequences. If X holds the considered belief that p, things are different. Now X seems committed to holding that it would somehow be desirable if everyone held the belief that p, and to making a negative value judgment on the actions of anyone (and thus Y) that are informed by ¬p. (Cf. Bhaskar, 1986, p. 179). Again, the negative judgment cannot be that the actions are irrational (at least in Y's case). Rather, I think it presupposes, as all reasoning reflected in the practical syllogism does, that action based on false beliefs cannot attain (*cp*) the agent's intended objectives. The negative judgment is either that such actions have undesirable or unforeseeable (and thus potentially undesirable) consequences, or that they reflect diminished freedom in the agent.

2.2 *Values, value judgments and value perspectives*

Much of the grammar of values parallels that of beliefs, though it is more complicated and sometimes obscured by the greater amount of contestation surrounding values. For details and argument about all the themes of this section see Lacey & Schwartz (1996).

A *value* v, is of an agent or agents; and when we refer to a "value", the fundamental expression is:

[V] X values that φ be characterized by v.

There are various kinds of values (which may overlap in various ways): when φ = myself, we have my personal values; φ = persons in general or relations and interactions between persons, moral values; φ = an institution, institutional values; φ = society, social values; φ = works of art, aesthetic values; φ = scientific theories or systematic bodies of beliefs, cognitive values; etc. *Cv* (cognitive values), thus, are the criteria of a "good" scientific theory, a theory worthy of rational belief. I leave it open here what is the list of *cv* though (end of § 1.1) I indicated what are the important ones for Bhaskar. In referring to them as "cognitive" values, I do not imply that other kinds of value judgments should be understood as not involving an essential cognitive (rational, discursive, argumentative) element.[1] When I use "value" without a qualifier, I mean value that is not a *cv*.

We also say that "X values **v**". I will call **v** an *object for value* for X. Usually "X values **v**" fills in for an expression like "X values that φ be characterized by a certain type of relationship with **v**". Each object of value is associated with a specific relationship or relationships (Anderson, 1994).

Values have both desire (want, goal) and belief dimensions. More explicitly, I suggest that [V] implies:

[D] It is a fundamental, constant and long-standing desire of X that φ be (become) characterized by v; and (and perhaps because)

[B] X believes that being characterized by v is partly constitutive of a "good" ("worthily desired") φ.

Regarding [D], X subordinates her other objectives (pertaining to actions and interactions involving φ) to v (*cp*), or *values* the immediate objectives of action in virtue of their contribution to its realization. Values, thus, serve to explain the immediate objectives of X's actions that are cited in the relevant practical syllogisms, so that sufficiently expanded practical syllogisms will eventually come to include reference to her values. Regarding [B], depending on the φ in question different considerations will come into play. When φ = human person, the values involved concern the characteristics of a fulfilled, flourishing, meaningful, or well lived human life; and they concern the relations among persons that foster (and partly constitute) fulfilled lives, and that do not rest on conditions that produce diminished lives. When φ = myself, the values include characteristics that are partly constitutive of my personal (individual) identity. When φ = society, the values involve characteristics of social structures and organization that contribute to human well being. No matter what φ may be, I suggest that contribution to human well being is always the "bottom line" of value discourse.

I distinguish between "having", "holding" and "adopting" values. An agent has a set of values which includes items corresponding to various φ. X *has* a value v to the extent that it is *manifested in* her *behavior*, i.e., that reference to v partially explains the immediate objectives of her actions. Manifestation is a matter of degree (reflecting tensions between the desire and belief dimensions of values). Where X's life displays behavior constantly, consistently and recurrently manifesting v, I will say that v is *woven into the life* of X. X also *articulates* her values *in words*. There usually is a "gap" between the values manifested in X's behavior and those articulated by her. (Similarly with beliefs.) I will also say that v is *embodied in society* to the extent (like with manifestation, a matter of degree) that society, in its normal functioning nurtures institutions that offer roles into which v is woven, encourages behavior that manifests it and reinforces its articulation. Where X articulates a v that is not highly embodied in society, (*cp*) we would expect that it would be highly manifested in her behavior only with difficulty.

X *holds* the value v, if she reflectively endorses v (in articulation), and commits herself (accepts the obligation) to diminish progressively the gap between the manifestation and articulation of v in her life. That commitment, of course, will be empty unless it is possible to diminish that gap. I suggested above that this possibility is partly connected with the degree of v's embodiment in society. To be genuine, then, the commitment needs to be accompanied by investigation of the causes of the gap, and efforts to remove them, and—in the light of the suggestion—this may involve action towards social change, towards producing a society in which different social values are manifested (see Lacey & Schwartz, 1996, for the idea of manifestation of social values). Investigation of this kind confirms that there are links that can partly be explained causally between (e.g.) the personal and social values X has and holds. One holds values in clusters that, in part, are linked causally. I will call such a cluster {v} a *value perspective*.

X *adopts* {v}—"A_x{v}"—if X holds each v in {v}; if X can defend the possibility, given the constraints of prevailing material and social conditions, of {v} being more fully manifested consistently, constantly and coherently in a person's behavior, and more fully embodied in society; and if X can offer reasons for each of the beliefs that the relevant φ's having v is worthily desired. Those reasons will, at least in part, appeal to a view of human nature (cf. Bhaskar, 1986, pp. 207–210), a view of what constitutes human well being and of what lies within human potential. Adopting a value perspective, thus, has "presuppositions"—beliefs that an agent holds about what is possible, and about human nature. (I will also say that X adopts each item of her adopted valued perspective.)

So far, I have spoken of X's values as characteristics that X desires φ [herself, persons, society, etc} to have, and that X believes are worthily desired of φ. We also speak of X making *value judgments*. There are *at least* three kinds of value judgments. The *first* is the judgement that v is a value, or, more precisely, the judgment that v is worthily desired of φ. Note that sometimes v = (the absence of u). I will refer to u as a "negative value".

When we refer to negative value judgments, we need to distinguish "¬(u is a value)" and "the absence of u is a value". I use V(x) to symbolize the judgment that **x** is an object of value. To value ¬**x** is to value some x′ where x′ and **x** are incompatible. The *second* is the judgment that v_1 is subordinate to v_2. I will regard judgments of these two kinds as available to be included in {v}, since they have the same kinds of presuppositions as values—so that here (depending on the context) v can indicate a value or a value judgment. When X makes a value judgment in either of these senses, I will assume that it is included in X's adopted value perspective. The *third* is judgment about (evaluation of) the degree of manifestation (or embodiment) of v in φ, or about comparisons of the degrees of manifestation of v in φ_1 and in φ_2, or in φ at times t_1 and t_2.[2] Holding values presupposes the ability to make such judgments.

2.3 *Accepting and rejecting theories*

The notion of "to *accept* a theory (T)" has various uses. I (Lacey, in progress) distinguish the following: a) to entertain T provisionally; b) to commit to a research agenda framed by T; c) to endorse that T is better confirmed than available rivals; d) *to hold the consolidated belief that* T; to endorse that T is properly placed in the stock of knowledge or of rationally acceptable beliefs, or of items that (according to available methodological canons) require no further investigation; e) *to adopt* T; to apply T in one's practical projects; or, more generally, to use T to inform one's actions (as a source of beliefs about means to ends and about the attainability of ends; and as a constraint upon the presuppositions of one's value perspective).

2.31 *Consolidated belief and adoption*

Clearly, one will not adopt T (of some domain D), whether or not it is held among one's consolidated beliefs, unless one holds that actions informed by T will contribute towards the fuller manifestation of one's values. Thus, one may hold T among one's consolidated beliefs, yet not apply it. Applying T may not serve one's interests; T may only provide understanding of domains of no interest from one's value perspective; or one may hold that applying T would have undesirable side-effects. The move from consolidated belief to adoption, therefore, explicitly involves value judgments.

Is holding the consolidated belief that T a stance entered into without depending on value (as distinct from *cv*) judgments? Think of those consolidated beliefs that constitute the most deeply entrenched items of scientific knowledge, those of which we claim [pragmatic] certitude, though not [epistemic] certainty, those concerning which within the scientific community there reigns consensus that further research is not required; where, according to the consensus, further research (including that which currently lies outside of our reach, e.g., because we lack relevant technology or the social conditions to support it) would not lead to a change of judgment about T, other than at the levels of refinements and standards of accuracy—presumably because it would just be to replicate what has already been replicated many times over.

When we hold the consolidated belief that T (of D), we judge, according to *impartiality* (§ 1.2):

> (i) T manifests all the *cv* to a very high degree, with respect to an appropriate class (E) of empirical data drawn from observations of phenomena of D, according to the highest recognized standards of evaluation of the degrees of manifestation of the *cv*.

In accordance with *impartiality*, judgments of consolidated belief rest solely on the available empirical data and assessments by the scientific community of the degrees of manifestation of the *cv* in rival theories with respect to these data with values playing no role.

2.32 Standards for evaluating the degree of manifestation of cognitive values

What are the *standards* according to which we "measure" the degree of manifestation of the *cv*? Without elaboration, I suggest that they include interpretations of the following (Lacey, in progress): (a) The items of E have been reliably obtained (replicated? replicable?), and empirical generalizations obtained from them reflect reliable inductive and statistical analysis. (b) E includes items pertinent to putting T into critical confrontation with competitors, and to clearly defining the bounds of the domains of which T is soundly accepted. (c) E contains items that are *representative of* the possible data that could be obtained by observing (often after constructing) *characteristic phenomena* of the domains of which T is accepted. (Note that these three standards apply specifically to empirical adequacy.) (d) T has been tested against a "sufficient" and "appropriate" array of rivals. (e) The degree of manifestation of the cognitive values in T (of D) compares favorably with their manifestation in the most soundly entrenched theories. (f) Criticisms (especially those that make explicit what would count as more adequate manifestation), that T does not manifest the *cv* sufficiently to warrant being placed in the stock of scientific knowledge, have been adequately responded to according to the consensus of the scientific community. (g) The community of scientists is adequately constituted to warrant deference to consensus arrived at in it.

2.33 Rudner's argument

In a famous article, Rudner (1953) argued that when we accept T we are committed to the judgment (which I paraphrase into my terminology):

> (ii) T manifests the *cv* to a sufficiently high degree (of D) so that the legitimacy of its being used to inform our actions is not to be challenged on the ground that consequences of moral significance (or, consequences undesired from one's value perspective) might follow from so acting if T were to turn out to be false (of D).

We might put it: we need sufficient certitude to compensate for our necessary lack of certainty, but gaining that certitude is implicated in the value judgment that the undesirable consequences of acting on the basis of T, should T be false, do not warrant (pending further investigation) withholding action on the basis of T.

Could we have good reasons to affirm (i) but deny (ii)? If so, what type of reasons? It would have to be that the *cv* were not sufficiently manifested in T (of D). But, by hypothesis, T manifests the *cv* to a very high degree according to the highest recognized standards of evaluation—so much so that the scientific community concurs that further investigation is not required (§ 2.31). So, the denial of (ii) would involve questioning the adequacy of the recognized standards of evaluation, or of their customary interpretations. Items (c), (d), and (g) on the list of standards (§ 2.32) would be likely foci for such questioning. Was T adequately tested against data that are representative of characteristic phenomena of the domain in which applications of T would have implications, in particular the ones that would be risky should T be false? Was T tested adequately against rival theories which, should they be true, would involve fewer such risks if used to inform our actions? Is the community of scientists adequately constituted to warrant deference to consensus in it?

In principle, these questions can always be raised because: the domains of testing (especially experimental) and application do not coincide; theory is underdetermined by the data; and the criteria of what constitutes scientific competence may implicitly be tied to particular values. I am interested in the questions here, however, only insofar as they lend themselves to answers in practice—i.e., when the alleged characteristic phenomena are specified, a rival theory outlined, or evidence presented that the composition of the scientific community makes it prone to "bias"; when they point to inquiry potentially relevant to answering the questions.

Questioning the standards in this way implies that there are not adequate grounds to affirm the consolidated belief that T (at least of the domains relevant for action on the basis of it). Thus, the same ground that serves to deny (ii) also serves to deny (i). Then, *cp*, affirming (i) implies affirming (ii). As Rudner says: "The scientist *qua* scientist makes value judgments". Holding the consolidated belief that T (of D) implies the judgment that all the testing *relevant for affirming (ii)* has been conducted, so that it involves making both the judgments (i) and (ii). On my interpretation of Rudner's argument, the key link between (i) and (ii) is provided by the standards for "measuring" the degree of manifestation of the *cv* in a theory. A value judgment appropriately, and essentially, is involved in assessing these standards. Thus, a value perspective may lead one to push for higher standards (or, more accurately, more rigorous interpretations of available standards); and differences in value perspectives—and thus different judgments regarding (ii)—may lead to different standards being deployed, and thus different judgments regarding (i) being made. (I develop the argument further, and respond to objections to it, in Lacey, in progress).

3 Neutrality: discussion of the second thesis of neutrality

The first thesis of neutrality (§ 1.2) states that accepting a theory does not commit one rationally to holding any particular value judgments. I will consider it to be qualified by "except those value judgments that may be derived from general conditions on rationality" (§ 2.1). Some say that it follows from the general thesis that fact does not entail value (what Bhaskar calls "Hume's Law"); others from the thesis (proposed, e.g., in emotivist metaethical theory) that value judgments are not open to cognitive or rational assessment. But, in the natural sciences, it holds (if it holds; see Lacey, forthcoming), not for these reasons, but in virtue of the character of scientific theories, namely that theories represent objects in terms of quantity and law, in terms of being generated from underlying structure, process and law, abstracted from relations with lived experience and practical activity; that theories do not represent objects with value predicates. Then, the languages of theory and value judgments are simply incommensurable.

In my statement of the second thesis of neutrality I interpret "accept" in the sense of "hold the consolidated belief" (sense (d), § 2.3). At first sight it might appear that it follows from the first thesis, that accepting a theory has no *consequences* concerning the value *perspective* one adopts follows from the claim that accepting it has no *logical implications* concerning value *judgments*. But it does only if one accepts that value judgments are not open to cognitive assessment, not if we consider (as in § 2.2) a value perspective to consist of an integrated complex of values and value judgments (moral, personal, social, etc) rendered coherent by various presuppositions, among the most important of which are conceptions of human nature and views about what is possible. It is in virtue of having this kind of structure that there may be critical (rational) discussion about a value perspective.

A scientific theory offers understanding of a domain of phenomena; not only explanations of actual phenomena, but also encapsulations of the possibilities they allow. (Here, I reflect Bhaskar's: real = actual + possible.) Thus a theory may imply to be impossible (possible) what a value perspective presupposes to be possible (impossible), or it may contradict a posit of a conception of human nature. Theories may be inconsistent with the presuppositions involved in adopting value perspectives. Suppose that T is inconsistent with the presuppositions of adopting a value perspective {v}. Then, accepting T implies rejecting these presuppositions, which (in turn) will lead to the rejection of {v}, unless adopting {v} can be newly rendered coherent under different presuppositions. In this sense, accepting T undermines or is incompatible with adopting {v}; though, as reflected in the qualification in the previous sentence, T remains formally consistent with the value judgments contained in {v}. Provided that T has been accepted in accordance with *impartiality*, values from rival perspectives have played no cognitive (as distinct from perhaps a causal) role in undermining the adopting of {v}.

For the sake of comparison with the logic of Bhaskar's argument, I will try to get at the logic in play here more clearly by representing it in the following schema [where "→" indicates "entails"; "--→" indicates "presupposes"; and "p" represents the content of a belief that is a presupposition of X's adopting {v}; remember also that B indicates holding a belief, *B* holding a consolidated belief, and A adopting a value perspective]:

$B_x(\mathrm{T})$
$B_x(\mathrm{T} \rightarrow \neg \mathrm{p})$
Therefore, *cp*, $B_x(\neg \mathrm{p})$
$\mathrm{A}_x(\{\mathrm{v}\}) \dashrightarrow \mathrm{B}_x(\mathrm{p})$
Therefore, *cp*, $\neg \mathrm{A}_x(\{\mathrm{v}\})$
Therefore, *cp*, $\mathrm{A}_x(\neg\{\mathrm{v}\})$.

Some comments on the three inferences:

In the first place, this schema captures well the way in which accepting a scientific theory and holding a value perspective can be incompatible. It is a practical incompatibility, not an inconsistency drawn within a theory. It concerns relations between the cognitive and practical stances of an agent, and is not properly described as drawing a value judgment from a consolidated belief in a theory. The key premise for the second inference precludes this description obtaining.[3]

Secondly, the *cp* may not obtain in different ways in the three cases. Regarding the *first* inference, it would not obtain (apparently) only if X had "lapsed" in rationality.[4] Regarding the *second* inference there are conditions that rationally make a difference: if X can rearticulate her value perspective grounding it in different beliefs (that are consistent with all theories that she accepts), then the conclusion does not follow.

Regarding the *third* inference, remember (§ 2.2) that to adopt ¬{v} is to adopt some {v′}, where {v} and {v′} are incompatible. The conclusion follows provided that X has identified an alternative {v′} and come to accept its presuppositions. Otherwise X may simply remain in a crisis of values. There is no rational guarantee that such a crisis can always be surpassed. Here, the *cp* obscures a condition that cannot normally be counted on to obtain even with the passage of time; but the inference indicates an impetus—deeply rooted in the "logic" of the discourse of values—to find ways to move from not holding a value perspective to holding one incompatible with it. I said above that the inference under consideration is not properly described as inferring a value judgment from the consolidated belief that T. But (Rudner's argument) if X holds the consolidated belief that T, it follows that X endorses the value judgment: "The possibility that T might turn out to be false and, if so, have morally undesirable consequences, is not a ground for claiming that one ought not act on the basis of T". That this is the case counts against the possibility that somehow a value perspective incompatible with {v} is covertly shaping the argument and making it compelling. For, as laid out in my interpretation of Rudner's argument, once we read from the schema the potential incompatibility between accepting T and holding {v}, we cannot reach a consolidated belief about T until questioning, deriving from {v}, concerning the standards of evaluation in play has been thoroughly explored and exhausted. The way in which the scientist *qua* scientist makes value judgments serves to minimize the likelihood that values will covertly sway the case towards T. This is not meant to suggest that another value perspective {v′} may not be an important (causal) factor in the generation and consolidation of T, and where that is the case we might expect that {v′} would be readily available to become held (and so the third inference made), once the second inference were made.

4 Bhaskar's argument: critique of the first thesis of neutrality

Bhaskar maintains that theories in the social sciences, under certain conditions, (I) do not satisfy the first thesis of neutrality; moreover, that (II) they favor the interests of emancipation. The summary statement of his argument is contained in the quotation presented at the beginning of the paper. I offer a reconstruction of it.[5]

Concerning (I), I interpret Bhaskar to maintain that, under the specified conditions, holding a consolidated belief in a theory implies (*cp*) adopting particular value judgements. His argument concerns a theory (T) with two features: (i) it implies that a certain proposition p is false; and (ii) it explains that among a group of people [X] the belief that p is widely held—it explains $B_{[X]}(p)$; more fully, T implies (represents, posits) that c is a co-cause of $B_{[X]}(p)$ where c is an identified social object.[6] When the scientist (S) holds the consolidated belief that T, the argument goes, he is compelled rationally, *cp*, (iii) to adopt a negative valuation of c—to adopt $V(\neg c)$.

Concerning (II), if S also accepts a theory or consistent set of theories (T′), where T′ may or may not be identical to T (1986, p. 185), which implies that the practices ($P_{[Y]}$) or activities of a certain group [Y] will (may) contribute causally to remove c, then he is compelled rationally, *cp*, (iv) to value these practices positively—to adopt $V(P_{[Y]})$.[7]

The argument can be represented in the following schema:

$B_S(T)$
$B_S(T \rightarrow \neg p)$ . . . (i) in paragraph above.
Therefore, $B_S(\neg p)$
B_S (T→ [c is a co-cause of $B_{[X]}(p)$] . . . (ii)
Therefore B_S[c is a co-cause of $B_{[X]}(p)$]
(I) Therefore, *cp*, A_S [$V(\neg c)$] . . . (iii)—denial of neutrality
$B_S(T')$
$B_S(T' \rightarrow$ [it is possible to remove c]
$B_S(T' \rightarrow$ [$P_{[Y]}$ will (may) contribute to remove c]
(II) Therefore, *cp*, A_S[$V(P_{[Y]})$] . . . (iv)—partiality to emancipation

4.1 *Evaluating inference (I)—the denial of neutrality*

Now I will offer some comments towards understanding and evaluating the argument, first concentrating on (I). Note that I have reconstructed it so that, as in my critique (§ 3) of the second thesis of *neutrality*, it concerns cognitive and practical attitudes of an agent. Conclusions about value judgments are not drawn within a theory.

4.11 *Value-impregnated terms in theories of the social sciences*

The argument (beginning of § 3) that the natural sciences are neutral (first thesis)—that theories represent objects in abstraction from their relations with lived experience and practical activity—does not apply to the social sciences, for to abstract social objects in such a way would be to deny their reality as social objects. For Bhaskar, *within* T we may describe social objects in terms of their contribution to satisfying human wants, needs and interests, and to enhancing and diminishing human lives; so that the language of T contains value-impregnated terms, as does the language used to describe the items of which T is intended to be empirically adequate. Suppose that empirically we observe that vast numbers of people are suffering profoundly in a certain society, and that, in T, we conclude that c is largely responsible for this suffering. Then, *cp*, adopting $V(\neg c)$ (or at least $\neg V(c)$) follows from accepting T; just as, in Bhaskar's example (Bhaskar, 1986, p. 75), from "In Germany under Nazi rule, millions of people were massacred", a negative valuation of Nazi rule follows. In each case, given that one accepts the description of the social object, it would be unintelligible not to adopt the respective value judgment.

In cases like these, that the theoretical (and descriptive) categories are value-impregnated underlies the inferences. But that they are value-impregnated indicates that T was constructed in a framework that presupposes commitment to certain values. Then, it might be argued, adopting certain value judgments does not really follow (*cp*) from the acceptance of T alone, but from accepting T together with the value judgments presupposed in the construction of T (so that the first thesis of *neutrality* has not been refuted). Bhaskar correctly points out that the fact that the categories of T are value-impregnated does not imply that it does not manifest the *cv* better than do rival theories.

Nevertheless, he intends that his argument not draw upon theoretical categories being value-impregnated as, according to him, Taylor's (1985) argument for denying the neutrality of the social sciences does; so that the key premises in the argument involve only the consolidated belief that T, together with the entailed beliefs that p is false and that c co-causes (among [X]) the belief that p. Only the falsity of p, not that "belief in p is detrimental to the achievement of human goals and the satisfaction of human wants" is intended to play a role in the argument (Bhaskar, 1979, p. 82). "False" and "cause" are not impregnated with the values of any particular perspective.

4.12 Mediation by general conditions on rationality

The inference (I) clearly is mediated by some general condition(s) on rationality (§ 2.1). Bhaskar says:

> . . . to criticize a belief as false is *ipso facto* not only to criticize any action or practice informed or sustained by that belief, but also anything that necessitates it
>
> (Bhaskar, 1979, p. 80).

The negative valuation of c follows (*cp*), according to Bhaskar, directly from the belief that it is the cause of a false belief, not *because of* the mediation of a prior negative valuation of holding the false belief (or of the actions informed by it), although *at the same time* a negative valuation of holding the false belief can also be made. Making the negative valuations of c and of holding the belief that p are, to some extent independent. Thus, e.g., c may be more negatively valued than B(p)—or, after considering the *cp* conditions c, but not B(p), may be negatively valued, or *vice versa*. While this is a subtle point, I think that it is essential to Bhaskar's intended argument.[8]

I am not convinced that such a direct movement (*cp*) from the consolidated belief that ¬p to a negative valuation of a co-cause of holding the belief that p, is a general condition on rationality. Consider the case where S's negative valuation of $B_{[X]}$(p), on the above-stated ground, is more than compensated for by positive valuations (including of rationality) of particular actions of members of [X] based in part upon p. In this case, does the negative valuation of c still stand? If not (as I am inclined to think), that is because the movement from consolidated belief that ¬p to negative valuation of a co-cause of B(p) is mediated by a negative valuation of B(p). This suggests that the argument would be rendered better by inserting the following steps immediately before (I) in the schema:

> $B_S(\neg p) \rightarrow cp$, B_S (anyone's acting on the basis of B(p) will be detrimental to the achievement of their—and others'—goals and the satisfaction of their needs)
> Therefore, cp, $A_S[V\neg(B_{[X]}(p))]$ . . . (iiia).

But Bhaskar explicitly rejects this insertion. I leave the matter for further discussion.

4.13 When the ceteris paribus *condition does not obtain*

Under what conditions, leaving to the side the possibility of lapsed rationality (Note 4), might the *cp* not obtain? *One* has already been suggested in the previous paragraph, but on the assumption that (iiia) mediates the inference to (iii). In that case the *cp* in (iiia) might not obtain because positive valuations of actions based on B(p) outweigh the negative valuation derived from the falsity of p.

A *second* would be that c also co-causes phenomena which are so positively valued as to outweigh the negative valuation. Among other things it is the business of T to articulate the full range of effects of c, and in general—I assume—among those effects are others which warrant valuation, positive or negative, and some represented in value-impregnated categories, from which (*cp*) other value judgments about c, with the same status as (iii), may follow. This raises the possibility that the *cp* involved in (iii) may rarely obtain. In those cases where it does not obtain, one's consolidated theoretical beliefs would have impact on the value judgments one adopts only by way of a complex judgment of "weighing and compounding" the various particular judgments that follow (*cp*—where the "other things" that are equal, relevant to each of the particular judgments, are different) from T. This complex judgment, itself a value judgment, clearly does not follow (*cp*) from T, though it draws essentially upon T,[9] which, we might say, represents phenomena in ways that make apparent that they have to be considered in our value deliberations.

A *third* condition would be that p is of little moment or relatively isolated in the agents' networks of beliefs. This suggests that a value judgment about the significance of activity informed by B(p) is implicit in the argument.

A *fourth* follows from the suggestion that (iii) follows from the premises *via* the intermediary of:

> $\neg A_S[V(c)]$ . . . (iiib).

Thus, that adopting a negative valuation of c follows (*cp*) from withholding a positive valuation of c. To adopt a negative valuation of c is to adopt a positive valuation of some c′, where c and c′ are incompatible (§ 2.2). S might not be able to make the move from (iiib) to (iii) because neither T nor any other theory (e.g., T′, in (II)) that he accepts provides support for the belief that a relevant c′ is possible which will not have equally undesirable effects as c, including with respect to the beliefs widely held under c′. (More on this point below.)

4.14 The relevance of Rudner's argument

The argument under consideration assumes that S holds the consolidated belief that T. Thus (Rudner's condition) T manifests the *cv* to a sufficiently high degree, according to the highest recognized standards, that the moral consequences of acting on the basis of T, should it turn out that T be false, do not warrant withholding on activity informed by T—and so, do not warrant withholding on, e.g., adopting a negative valuation of c. Remember (§ 2.2) that the adoption of a value involves its manifestation in behavior as well as its articulation in words, so that adopting V(¬c) implies engaging in *action* (praxis) informed by some V(c′).[10]

Bhaskar considers his argument to apply to certain theories in the social sciences, as distinct from the *social sciences* (§ 1.1). He is particularly interested in instances where c designates social structures and p a belief that is among the presuppositions of a value perspective that is deeply embodied in c. E.g., c might designate the economic, political and social structures of neoliberalism (briefly: the system which prioritizes free trade, private control of capital, a reduced role for government, and which deeply embodies individualist values—see Note 12), and p the belief that, for the foreseeable future, there are no significant realizable possibilities outside of these structures.

It is not clear to me that Rudner's condition can be satisfied in connection with theories of this type. Adopting a negative valuation of c (in this example) clearly runs against powerful viewpoints and interests. From their value perspective, acting on the basis of T threatens highly negative moral consequences, perhaps the destruction of all the value they perceive as having been constructed within c.

Has T (and perhaps also T′) been evaluated against high enough standards? The question is pertinent since the consequences of acting to remove (transform) c would be in the future, and so are not available for direct empirical investigation *now*. Indeed, the point of acting to change c is to attempt to bring about hitherto unrealized possibilities. So, it cannot be said that T has been tested concerning the domains where the risky consequences might occur, not willfully or inadvertently, but because the domains do not yet exist; and, if they are to come to exist, that will be a consequence of a praxis informed by T. The opponent correctly points out that being tested against data from such a future domain {or, from an actual one that is sufficiently like it} is a relevant standard against which to measure the degree of manifestations of the *cv*. He might add: especially in view of the historical record that displays numerous cases where action to remove prevailing structures produced (unintentionally) seriously negative consequences, what makes the current proposed praxis different from these historical cases? I will call this the "conservative argument".

A DILEMMA

The conservative argument raises an important issue, by pointing to a *dilemma* confronting S (the social scientist who wishes to hold the consolidated judgment that T), and those who wish to engage in legitimated praxes to change c. *On the one hand*, the legitimacy of a praxis (informed by T or T′) to change c presupposes (among other things) that one has a consolidated belief that T. *On the other hand*, the decisive (contested) evidence for T can only be obtained if the praxis is actually enacted. If, in order to act legitimately, we must first have the decisive evidence, we will never act; *and* if we do not act we will not gain access to the decisive evidence. Waiting for the outcome of more research before acting will not change the situation. The conservative argument does not propose waiting, pending identified investigation that might produce agreement. It is an argument not to act for the sake of change. But, if we do not act, then (it follows from T) the negatively valued phenomena linked with c will remain in place or might even be exacerbated. We cannot evade the dialectic of social change and gaining social knowledge.

If one chooses to act, one makes the value judgment that the negative value manifested under c is greater (probably) than what would be generated by the praxis entered into to change c; and that the positive value generated by the latter would be greater than that manifested under c—thus the risk of acting on the basis of T, even though should it be false there would be negative consequences, is worth taking. I think that the move from (iiib) to (iii) also requires this value judgment, but it is implicit in holding the consolidated belief that T. Since the conservative argument does not propose any further research to do now, its denial of the consolidated belief that T also rests on a value judgment.[11]

Can the dilemma introduced above be avoided, or its impact rendered less significant? In the natural sciences too the dilemma can arise. In a way, that provides the context for Rudner's argument. Generally, however, in the natural sciences its impact is greatly diminished because of the methodological role of *experiment*. Experiment enables us to explore certain hitherto unrealized possibilities of nature, the conditions of their realization, and some of the consequences of their realizations in relatively contained, "safe" spaces.

Laboratory phenomena often constitute "mini-representations" of what we desire to construct in our social and natural environments, and are sufficiently representative so that through investigating them, many of the value related questions can be settled. Thus, e.g., while the legitimacy of introducing a technological practice may presuppose holding the consolidated belief that *t*, we do not first have to introduce the practice fully developed to obtain virtually decisive evidence in support of *t*; often experiment suffices for all practical purposes to this end. Experiment can have this kind of role when we have reason to believe that the same generative mechanisms are in play in the related laboratory and socially constructed and/or natural phenomena, and when we can control relevant variables of these mechanisms. In the social sciences, since social structures are among the generative mechanisms, since we cannot submit them to experimental control, and since behavior produced in closed spaces is not characteristic human behavior, experiment cannot play a comparable role.

COUNTERING THE DILEMMA

Can we identify actually occurring social phenomena that might be able to play a role logically and methodologically parallel to that played by experiment concerning the natural sciences and their technological applications? Within certain limits I think that we can. To illustrate this, let p be "There are no significant viable possibilities, in the foreseeable future, for the more widespread achievement of human wants and for the satisfaction of human needs outside of neoliberal structures". One might add "and thus the only values that can be manifested in human lives to any significant extent are those deeply embodied in these structures and their supporting institutions". What sort of empirical data might directly offer some support to ¬p, especially to "There *are* hitherto unrealized possibilities . . . "? My focus will be upon historically novel possibilities.[12]

I suggest that relevant evidence may be found by observing the practices of groups on the margins of the predominant structures. I have in mind especially groups of impoverished people, who profoundly experience sufferings that have (in large part) structural causes. These are people for whom belief in p implies little hope (except for some individuals) of a life in which their wants are achieved and their needs satisfied, so that among them we might find anticipatory attempts at organized action that manifests values (e.g., cooperation, participation, work as internal to human flourishing, valuing local culture and knowledge, and solidarity) different from those embodied in the mainstream, and thus activity which, if successful, would serve to support ¬p. The margins might provide sources for novel possibilities, and small-scale realizations of them. (Obviously, they also provide a context for the realization of undesirable possibilities.) Having identified alternative positive possibilities, the question then arises of the conditions for their maintenance and growth. Those conditions would (eventually) involve collaboration with other groups like them and with sectors of mainstream institutions (including religious, university, civic, governmental—even business), especially with those whose articulated values are in tension with the dominant embodied values.

Clearly, with growth, there would be modification of the dominant structures, but it would be—as it were—tested "step by step" in an unfolding process of development in which there is an "organic" unity between means and ends, and between ameliorative action and praxis for social transformation. My ideas here have been greatly influenced by thinking characteristic of the "popular movement" (often referred to as "new social movements" in sociological and anthropological writings) in Latin America. (See Lacey, 1995, for development of this, and references.) Note that local cooperative action with immediate ameliorative goals, e.g., to provide employment, may simultaneously deepen the manifestation of cooperative values, and test empirically the structural sources of unsatisfied needs. Such action, and research on its possibilities,[13] does not *presuppose* that considerable amelioration is not possible within the structures, perhaps under suitable reforms.

The dilemma introduced above cannot be fully removed. It is the generality of its formulation that makes it intractable. It can be mitigated considerably in the context of research on the groups identified above. Consider praxes whose objects are (a) simultaneously to meet the basic needs of a group and to consolidate alternative values manifested among its members, and (b) to enable the spread of these values to other groups. The only consolidated belief that their legitimacy requires is that there are actually groups manifesting such values, and their spread is possible under specified conditions. While it is true that the evidence for this belief can only be decisively obtained if the praxes are enacted, the enactment is step by step and so it and its morally relevant consequences are subject to investigation at each step. At any step, the risk pointed to in the conservative argument is small. Thus, if the belief is said not to have been tested against high enough standards, what further research needs to be done can be defined and carried out without large-scale social transformation being required. If that research further consolidates the belief, the Rudner conditions has been satisfied as decisively as it can be satisfied.[14]

BHASKAR'S INFERENCE AND THE PARTICULAR CO-CAUSES INVOLVED

Let us now return directly to Bhaskar's inference (I) to adopting a negative valuation of c. Concerning the particular case of p that I have been considering, there are numerous co-causes of the belief that p being widely held, which—with appropriate theoretical elaboration—may *include* the current dominant social structures and the way in which they embody individualist values, the projection of class interests, specific micro-mechanisms for the inculcation of ideology, the social decline of institutions that articulate alternatives, and the belief that alternatives will be suppressed.

Now, I have suggested that the decisive evidence for the falsity of p (if it is false) would come from the investigation of the anticipatory possibilities already realized to some extent in marginal, disadvantaged groups. One of the co-causes of the belief that p, then, would be either the absence of this investigation, or the lack of acquaintance with its results. These, in turn, would (in part) be effects of the absence of relations of communication and mutual engagement between researchers and these groups, itself an effect (in part) of class divisions.

Clearly, the co-causes are numerous and various and exhibit layers of immediacy; and the strength of the evidence supporting our judgments that "c is a co-cause of the belief that p" will vary with the instantiation of "c". In the case under discussion, the same research that empirically supports that $\neg$p also provides evidence for (e.g.) the absence of prior investigation and of relations of communication and mutual engagement being among the co-causes of the belief that p. In other cases, the evidence is indirect, identical with the evidence for T, and obtaining only in virtue of the two propositions being entailed by T.

I have already indicated that, when c designates a dominant social structure, Bhaskar's inference (I) is not sound (in view of the Rudner condition), except perhaps (and contrary to Bhaskar's intentions) under the presupposition of a strong (and contentious) value judgment. In the present case, I think that the inference is sound (subject to the qualifications made above in §4.13). The key difference is that, in this case, different value judgments need not lead to differences regarding the consolidated beliefs that $\neg$p and that c is a co-cause of the widespread belief that p, (in part) because any T whose cognitive evaluation they depend upon need not be widely encompassing. Where the co-causes are relatively immediate, the passage from (iiib) to (iii), *cp*, is likely to be quite direct, because the very conditions that make the research possible (Notes 13; 14) are likely to involve S already having adopted V(c′), for some c′ (where c′ is incompatible with c), e.g., c′ = (mutual engagement with one of the groups in question).

4.15 Are relevant consolidated beliefs available?

So far I have conducted the discussion on the assumption that T manifests the *cv* to a high degree, according to currently accepted standards, and that it does so better than any competing theory (including available theories Σ of the *social sciences*). Under this assumption, reserve about whether T constitutes a consolidated belief derives exclusively from the Rudner condition.

As Bhaskar has characterized the social sciences, they address issues that the *social sciences* do not; in particular they investigate the *social sciences*—the conditions for belief in their theories, the historical and structural limits of their application, their role in legitimating current structures, etc.[15] This seems to be the basis for his claim that an appropriately developed T, which has Σ among its objects of purview, has greater explanatory power than Σ.

It is not clear to me that this is sufficient basis for the claim, and especially for the more general claim that T manifests all the relevant *cv* more highly than does Σ. From the fact that T can identify the limits of application of Σ, it does not follow that T can encapsulate (except parasitically upon the development of Σ) all the possibilities that are encapsulated in Σ. With the aid of Σ, but not of T, we may be able to explore the possibilities not yet realized within the current structures—and, given that social structures are maintained, reformed and transformed in the course of intentional action of numerous agents, and that all social structures leave some spaces relatively unaffected, it seems implausible that within T we would be able to articulate in any detail the extent of the possibilities that might be realized within the realm that Σ is exploring.

Of course, T and Σ are in conflict regarding (e.g.) p. But their domains, and the possibilities they may encapsulate, may only *overlap*; that of Σ may not be included in that of T. Then, acceptance of T or of Σ may, for all practical purposes, amount to a matter of interest in different domains of possibilities—not greater explanatory power, but explanatory power (and capability to encapsulate possibilities) *in the domain of interest*. In that case, values would be presupposed in making the consolidated judgment that T.

4.2 Evaluating inference (II)—valuing emancipatory practices

Now, let us consider inference (II).

Bhaskar introduces the two inferences to support his contention that not only do the social sciences (like the *social sciences*) fail to be neutral, but also (unlike the *social sciences*) they serve the interest of emancipation. It is this contention that drew me to make a detailed examination of the inferences. Space does not permit me to analyze "emancipation" in detail here. Consider:

> It is my contention that the special qualitative kind of becoming free or liberation which is *emancipation*, and which consists in the *transformation*, in self-emancipation by the agents concerned, *from an unwanted and unneeded to a wanted and needed source of determination*, is both causally presaged and logically entailed by explanatory theory, but that it can only be effected in *practice*. Emancipation, as so defined, depends upon the transformation of structures, not the alteration or amelioration of states of affairs
>
> (Bhaskar, 1986, p. 171).

Emancipation involves self-emancipation but, given the sources of determination (and the characteristics of human nature itself), emancipation cannot be gained by individual agents alone. Emancipation requires solidarity; its degree of manifestation in society will be greater as the manifestation of solidarity is greater, and as the range of agents representing anticipations of emancipation increases. In my terminology, emancipated agents adopt their own values (§ 2.2) in the light of soundly held beliefs both about human nature and about what is possible; and being emancipated is essentially linked with the emancipation of other agents. But there are structural obstacles to agents becoming emancipated. Structural transformation is necessary for emancipation; but the practices aiming for structural transformation, if they are to produce emancipation, must produce self-emancipation.

False beliefs (certainly those pertaining to the presuppositions of an agent's value perspective, such as p) are overwhelming barriers to emancipation. By hypothesis, they have structural co-causes c. The fullness of manifestation of emancipation thus requires the transformation of c, (though lesser degrees of its manifestation do not). But it does not follow that any practice of any group, directed towards removing c, will further the interest of emancipation. Some such practices, obviously, may deepen oppression. Hence, the *cp* in (iv). Even if (iv) does follow *cp* it does not follow that T′ (or T) serves the interests of emancipation, or that the valuing of a practice that may serve to remove c derives from the value of emancipation.

In line with my discussion of the *cp* in (iii), however, this points to a factor which is too significant and omnipresent to be absorbed into a *cp* clause. We cannot be confident that (iv) follows, *cp*, unless T′ also implies "$P_{[Y]}$ may contribute to further the manifestation of emancipation". That is an important conclusion, but it involves an additional premise which uses value-laden categories.

The additional premise also draws explicit attention to the relationship between [X] and [Y]. The groups must largely be distinct, since the members of [Y], acting to remove c, presumably will not believe that p. And [Y] cannot be identical with [S], the group of social scientists and members of non-oppressed classes linked with them, for emancipation must be self-emancipation (cf. Bhaskar, 1993, pp. 258–270).[16] [Y], like [X], must be largely composed of members of the oppressed classes; and it can include members of [S] who act in solidarity and cooperation with them. To be emancipatory, the practices of [Y] must have the trajectory of including more of the members of [X]. This does not require that c *first* be transformed.

While c is a co-cause of a social phenomenon, viz. the widespread belief that p among members of the oppressed classes, the causes of an individual agent's belief that p (though linked with c in ways that are well worth discussing) are different. An agent X may come rationally to believe that ¬p on the basis of observation of or participation in a marginal group of the kind discussed above, or in the practices of a largely marginalized or suppressed tradition, or numerous other ways. This grounds the possibility of emancipatory practices. The intended trajectory of the practices of these marginalized groups—always more inclusive and varied—involves *simultaneously* testing the limits of actual structures *and* shaping the form of institutions that could be the basis of new social structures. *Simultaneously* it is ameliorative *and* directed to transforming social structures; for it is activity aiming to meet the needs and satisfy the wants of its practitioners *now*, while creating conditions for their expansion and consolidation. The values that are intended to be embodied in the alternative social structures are being formed, and tested for viability, in small-scale (and expanding) representations of what is hoped will become society-wide. In this way participation in the practices of emancipation is itself an anticipatory expression of emancipation. There is a dialectical unity between means and ends. I suggest that only practices in which this dialectical unity is present can properly be called emancipatory.

From the perspective of adopting this value of emancipation, we see that in general Bhaskar's inference (II) does not hold, except in the particular case where the additional premise is deployed.

5 Conclusion

The promise of Bhaskar's argument is that there is a quick rational move from coming to accept theories in the social sciences to adopting value judgments partial to emancipation. Moreover, Bhaskar maintains, the proposed quick move depends neither on the mediation of value judgments nor of value-impregnated theoretical terms. I have argued, however, that any sound moves from theory to value judgments are mediated in the way that Bhaskar hoped to avoid; and perhaps more importantly, that—in view of considerations drawn from Rudner's condition—it is doubtful that Bhaskar's argument (even when modified to acknowledge the mediations) is applicable to theories in the social sciences in which social structures are posited to play key causal roles. But his argument (modified in this way) does appear to apply for theoretical analyses developed within the "logic of the popular movement". None of my criticisms, of course, query Bhaskar's more general view of the relevance, and necessity, of social theory for emancipatory practices.

Notes

1 My statement of *impartiality* (§ 1.2) presupposes a *distinction* between *cv* and other kinds of values, but not necessarily a *separation* in the course of making the various kinds of value judgments. My views on *cv*, and their relationship with the views of other philosophers are discussed elsewhere (Lacey, 1997b; in progress).

2 The negative value judgments at the end of § 2.1 involve a combination of the first and third types. Action is negatively valued *because* (in one case) it reflects a

negative value (irrationality) being too highly manifested in X's behavior, and (in another case) because the values (freedom, "producing desired consequences") have diminished manifestations in Y's behavior. Clearly the latter judgment encapsulates a number of unstated negative value judgments. The value judgment, deployed below in Rudner's argument (§ 2.33), involves the interplay of all three types, though in a more complicated way. It balances the low probability of gaining very high negative value consequences against the high probability of gaining certain high value consequences.

3 "Adopts" is not a simple descriptive predicate (§ 2.2); it also carries the force of "reflectively endorses", of commitment or obligation, and of being rationally grounded. The conclusion does not follow if an agent only holds or has a set of values, for then the set of values does not have the presuppositions, and so the key premise is not applicable. Also, if "B_X" in the first two premises were replaced by "B_X", then we would only be able to conclude (*cp*) "either $\neg A_X(\{v\})$ or $\neg B_X(T)$".

4 There are no conditions in which a rational agent can affirm: "If these conditions obtain, I will be rationally justified in holding the first two beliefs, but not the third." X "lapses in rationality" when she fails to bring the two beliefs to attention simultaneously, of if she forgets one of them, or has not attended to the inference pattern among the propositional contents of the beliefs, or is unaware that it constituted a valid pattern, etc.

In connection with the second and third inferences also, the *cp* may not obtain because of lapses of rationality; and also where agents are insufficiently articulate about their values, where there is self-deception, weakness of will and voluntarism. In all these situations failure to make the inferences is subject to causal explanation, but not rational justification.

5 I do not include here the close reading of Bhaskar's texts from which I draw my interpretations. (I am well aware that I have not done justice to all the subtle and penetrating details that abound in Bhaskar's discussions, and that my focus on his one succinct argument may obscure how much I agree with Bhaskar.) When he uses expressions like "explain a belief" and "explain the falsity of a belief", I take them to mean: "explain that an agent or the members of a group hold the belief" and "explain that agents hold the belief in question, where the belief is false". I also take it that "explain an illusion" and "explain false consciousness" should be treated in the same way as "explain the falsity of a belief". The terms, "illusion" and "false consciousness" perhaps are descriptions used when we think that certain specific kinds of explanations can be found.

6 "p" represents "R(o)"—that a particular social object (o) has a property or set of relations (R). The particular case, $o = c$, has special interest in discussions of ideology. Examples given of c are systems of social relations and generative structures (1979, p. 81; 1986, p. 184). "$B_{[X]}(p)$" is symbolism which I introduce in order to avoid potential ambiguities in the argument. "[X]" represents a social group, whose behavior and beliefs are explained and whose possibilities of action are encapsulated in T. "S" will represent the community of social scientists who accept T. So "B_S" refers to the beliefs held by the social scientists, and $B_{[X]}$ to those of the group being investigated. The case where S is included in [X] can be of special interest.

7 Bhaskar does not raise clearly the question of who the agents of [Y] are, and how they might be related either to S or to the agents in [X]. This will be relevant to the discussion of the soundness of the inference, and to the issue of emancipatory consequences.

8 Recall (end of § 2.1) that if S holds the consolidated belief that $\neg p$, then S negatively values B(p) (and actions informed by p), but one must distinguish the

cases $B_S(p)$ and $B_X(p)$, where $S \neq X$. The negative valuation of $B_S(p)$ rests upon the irrationality of S acting on the basis of p; of $B_X(p)$ on the basis (I suggest) of the judgment that, *cp*, X's acting on the basis of p is likely to have consequences "detrimental to the achievements of X's goals and the satisfaction of X's (and others') wants". Since, in the argument, S is not a member of [X], it is only by directly moving (*cp*) to the negative valuation of c, that one can avoid the inference resting on the role of value-impregnated terms.

9 The same conclusion is drawn whether we consider Bhaskar's argument, or my version with the insertions. Note that, like Bhaskar, I do not think that matters of falsity generally override other valuations. The point made here is reinforced when we note that the same argument can be made of all of the co-causes of $B_{[X]}(p)$. But the argument suggests no ranking of these valuations, or of them in comparison with other valuations that may also follow (*cp*) from T, or of other valuations to which one may be committed. The fine structure of explanations of beliefs being held might throw some clearer light on these matters. Especially on points like this it would be helpful if the abstract argument had been supplemented by critical analysis of examples.

10 Adopting $V(\neg c)$ implies *some* action towards the transformation of c in the direction of c′ (as understood in the previous paragraph); though not necessarily *any* such action. In this context, inference (I) concerns *some*; (II) *any*.

In some passages (e.g., Bhaskar, 1986, p. 188) where he proposes that there are a number of conceptually distinct stages that follow conclusion (iv) and eventuate in emancipated action, Bhaskar appears not to accept that adopting $V(\neg c)$ implies engaging in action informed by some $V(c')$. But he does not offer an explicit account of making value judgments. My interpretation and critique of his argument deploys my own account (§2.2), which I use because it enables me to provide a sympathetic reconstruction of the argument.

11 Bhaskar offered his argument as a way to avoid this conclusion (Bhaskar, 1979, p. 79). So I am reluctant to leave the matter here—where opponents remain just trading opinions about future possibilities, effectively identifying what is possible with what is desirable from their respective value perspectives.

The opponent of S (call him S′) who proposes the conservative argument is left accepting Σ (a loosely connected set of theories of *social science*). S′, but not S, thinks the Rudner condition is satisfied of Σ, with value judgments (closely related to those referred to in the text) accounting for the difference. But there is not complete symmetry between S and S′. S′ declines to accept T solely by appeal to the Rudner condition not being satisfied. S rejects Σ, not simply by appeal to the Rudner condition, but by placing at least some of the items of its "untested consciousness" into a context where further investigation of them is opened up. T provides explanations of some phenomena that are left unexplained in Σ. See §4.15 for further discussion.

12 Here I pick a proposition about which there is virtual unanimity today in *social science* and across the political spectrum that is competing "realistically" for public office, one broadly endorsed among all the competing versions (neoliberal, neoconservative, social democratic, etc) of what capitalist structures and their supporting institutions should be like today. If it is true, the possibilities of emancipation are severely limited, and so it would represent a great tragedy. Social science, which may be able to inform the interests of emancipation, therefore needs to throw light on this proposition. With the demise of the Soviet empire, it seems to have been widely taken for granted that relevant possibilities cannot be realized under "socialist" structures. If "socialist structures" are those in which such values are solidarity, equality and work as a fulfilling activity are

embodied, the end of the Soviet empire provides no relevant evidence, since its structures (like capitalist ones) were structures of domination.

Usually p is accompanied by something like p′. "Within capitalist structures and their supporting institutions, there are continually expanding opportunities—eventually, in principle open to everyone—for individuals to achieve their wants and satisfy their needs, provided that they take the appropriate individual initiatives".

I do not want to suggest that p has no basis in empirical inquiry (and similarly p′). *Social science* engages in comparative inquiry of phenomena framed by actual social structures. It may well be represented in Σ (theories of *social science*) that other structures ("socialist", bureaucratic authoritarian, traditional, etc.) do not permit comparable ranges of possibilities—genuinely expressive of human nature—to be viable. I will not contest such representations here, except to note that often the inference is made from "in capitalist structures, quantitatively more actual wants can be achieved" to "the class of wants that can be achieved in capitalist structures includes those that can be achieved in other structures"; and that the contestants are not committed to offer a global alternative to capitalism—a series of local proposals, each responsive to culturally shaped wants, needs and interests, may be more appropriate. This last point is important, since *social science* may recognize no global competitors to capitalism today. If there are alternative possibilities, perhaps actually they can only be realized locally—and perhaps any widespread alternative will be constructed from the variety of local programs in a way that respects and nurtures ongoing local variety. (A view like this seems to be present in Bhaskar (1993), pp. 266–268.)

Within Σ, explanations of p may be offered in terms of the proposal that the values (individualist) embodied in capitalist structures are especially in tune with human nature and, thus, that people really want these structures and what can be aspired to in them; or in terms of the absence of competing global institutions or of "institutional inertia"; or (in some neoconservative versions) in terms of the preparedness of the agents of these structures to use their virtual monopoly of power to suppress any budding alternatives. In a recent "op-ed" article ("Depois do dilúvio neoliberal", *O Estado de São Paulo*. September 30, 1996) the Portuguese sociologist, Boaventura de Sousa Santos, links the grip that p appears to have on the contemporary imagination to the fact that neoliberalism has gained control of "the five strategically most important resources . . . : technology, information and the means of communication, the financial markets, natural resources, and the arms of mass destruction".

Among its proponents, p tends to function in a complex rhetoric combining layers of fact (theory), value and threat, often operating in alternating sequences, with the context of discussion determining which layer comes to the fore. The more that the fact and value layers are contested, the more the threat layer becomes apparent, for p is crucial for the legitimation of the dominance and ascendancy of capitalist structures. I think that it is in this context that we can begin to explain the extraordinary cruelty used against those who were trying to demonstrate ¬p (without proposing a global alternative) through a liberating praxis in the recent struggles in Central America (Lacey, 1991; Chomsky, 1985).

13 There are important questions about the conditions necessary for engaging in research on alternative possibilities, e.g., concerning the relationships that must be established between the participants in the groups and the researcher. Observation, adequate to discern the values of the group, which should recognize "the cognitive worth of the actors' point of view" (Bhaskar, 1986, p. 170) may require active engagement with its practices and thus adopting its values. Thus,

engagement in the research may already be part of the process of growth involving the collaboration of sectors of other institutions, and so involve the partial transformation of these institutions. I cannot address these questions here. Cf. Bhaskar (1986), pp. 201–211.

14 A "personalized" variant of the conservative argument might be raised in connection with research that involves mutual engagement with marginalized groups. One of the conditions of the research—of being able to observe the reality of the marginalized, disadvantaged group—is to engage mutually with the members of the group, an activity that requires manifestation of a value, that those who affirm p may take not to be possible of manifestation. So, to enter into the research presupposes that ¬p. Of course, to object in principle to the attempt to enter into it is to presuppose that p. This highlights that certain realities may only be able to be recognized and investigated by those who adopt certain values. I do not think that this affects the logic of the current discussion, but it may dim the practical force of the argument. It also raises methodological problems that can have deep implications, within the institutions (e.g., universities) that foster research, concerning their priorities.

15 *Social science* may also consider belief in T to be among its objects of inquiry—in social psychology (e.g.) it may investigate family, genetic, and various social influences on the development of "deviant beliefs" and their associated behaviors. Σ may investigate phenomena that, from the perspective of T, need to be characterized in view of their location within a larger context.

16 It seems to me that, *cp*, $A_S[V(P_{[S]})]$ does not follow from Bhaskar's premises. Generally, the practices directed by intellectuals and their allies aiming towards changing social structures do not produce new structures in which emancipation is evident. These practices often also display disregard for the lives and well-being of those who are being organized for the sake of their emancipation. The *cp* does not always obtain. Then, the success of [S] in removing c should not be identified with the achievement of emancipation; though it might be the removal of a barrier to emancipation. Emancipation must be self-emancipation, and so it will be well manifested only within structures that have been constructed in the course of practices expressing the (developing) values of the oppressed themselves in solidarity with their allies (cf. Lacey, 1995). This point might be contrasted with Bhaskar's distinction between "emancipatory" and "emancipated" action (Bhaskar, 1986, p. 186).

References

Anderson, E. S. (1994). *Values in ethics and economics*. Cambridge: Harvard University Press.

Bhaskar, R. (1978). *A realist theory of science*. Atlantic Highlands, NJ: Humanities Press.

Bhaskar, R. (1979). "Social science as critique: facts, values and theories", in *The Possibility of naturalism: a philosophical critique of the contemporary human sciences*. Atlantic Highlands, NJ: Humanities Press.

Bhaskar, R. (1986). "Facts and values: theory and practice"; "Reason and the dialectic of human emancipation", in *Scientific realism and human emancipation*. London: Verso.

Bhaskar, R. (1991). "Social theory and moral philosophy", in *Philosophy and the idea of freedom*. Oxford: Blackwell.

Bhaskar, R. (1993). "Social science, explanatory critique, emancipatory axiology", in *Dialectic: the pulse of freedom*. London: Verso.

Chomsky, N. (1985). *Turning the tide: U.S. Intervention in Central America and the struggle for peace*. Boston: South End Press.

Donegan, A. (1987). *Choice: the essential element in human action*. London: Routledge & Kegan Paul.

Lacey, H. (1991). "Understanding conflicts between North and South", in M. Dascal (ed.), *Cultural relativism and philosophy: North and Latin American perspectives*. Leiden: E. J. Brill.

Lacey, H. (1995). "The legacy of El Salvador's murdered Jesuits". *Journal of Peace and Justice Studies*, **6**, 113–126.

Lacey, H. (1996). "Behaviorisms: theoretical and teleological". *Behavior and Philosophy*, **23**, 61–78.

Lacey, H. (1997a). "The dialectic of science and advanced technology: an alternative?" *Democracy and Nature* (in press).

Lacey, H. (1997b). "The constitutive values of science". *Principia 1* (in press).

Lacey, H. (forthcoming). "Scientific understanding and the control of nature". *Science and Education*.

Lacey, H. (in progress). *Values and scientific understanding: is science value free?* (provisional title).

Lacey, H. & Schwartz, B. (1986). "Behaviorism, intentionality and socio-historical structure". *Behaviorism*, **14**, 193–210.

Lacey, H. & Schwartz, B. (1996). "The formation and transformation of values", in W. O'Donohue & R. Kitchener (eds.), *The philosophy of psychology*. London: Sage.

Rudner, R. (1953). "The scientist *qua* scientist makes value judgments". *Philosophy of Science*, **20**, 1–6.

Taylor, C. (1985). "Neutrality in political science", in *Philosophical Papers*, vol. 2. Cambridge: Cambridge University Press.

20

ADDRESSING THE CULTURAL SYSTEM

Margaret Archer

This chapter is devoted to the argument that a dualistic approach to cultural analysis can deliver the theoretical goods which conflationism failed to produce. Eventually I hope to show that the advantages of approaching the structural domain by distinguishing analytically between System and social integration also accrue in the cultural realm, yielding similar improvements in the explanation of stability and change. The whole enterprise thus looks towards a promising land where the theoretical unification of structural and cultural analysis might be accomplished.

This promise was one which none of the theorists already examined ever under-valued. It was the golden apple which the downwards and upwards conflationists thought they could grab by their familiar tactic of rendering one the virtual epiphenomenon of the other and which the central conflationists thought they could graft by their usual strategy of elision. But in theoretical development there are never easy pickings: like those who borrowed the mechanical analogy, the organic analogy or even the cybernetic analogy, the conflationists are punters with their 'formula' for breaking the bank. Thus my hope for unification is just that – not an expectation – and my procedure is correspondingly different. It is not an argument *by analogy* with a particularly fruitful form of structural analysis; it merely starts by making an analogous analytical distinction. The elements so distinguished then have to be conceptualized in their own terms and a set of theoretical propositions formulated about their interconnections. Succeeding chapters thus grope towards a reconceptualization of the cultural domain, utilizing analytical dualism, but until this has been completed it is impossible to determine whether the resulting propositions will parallel those advanced by Lockwood in the structural realm.

To approach the Cultural System (CS) from a dualistic perspective means

Source: Culture and Agency, Cambridge: Cambridge University Press, 1988, chap. 5, pp. 103–42.

talking about characteristics proper to it but distinct from the Socio-Cultural (S-C) level. Of course almost every word in that sentence is contentious. First, 'what is a Cultural System'? At this stage complex definitions with intricate subdivisions (for example, language, knowledge, beliefs, theories, semiotic patterns, conceptual schemes, signification systems, socio-symbolics and so forth) serve no point. At this point it is only necessary to know what kind of animal we are dealing with in order to make clear how we propose handling it.

To get off the ground it is sufficient to say that a Cultural System is held to be roughly co-terminous with what Popper called Third World Knowledge. At any given time a Cultural System is constituted by the corpus of existing intelligibilia – by all things capable of being grasped, deciphered, understood or known by someone. (The inclusion of components depends on this dispositional capacity alone, and not on whether contemporary social actors are willing or able to grasp, know or understand them, which are matters of Socio-Cultural contingency.) By definition the cultural intelligibilia form a system, for all items must be expressed in a common language (or be translatable in principle) since this is a precondition of their being intelligible. In other words they have at least one characteristic shared with at least one other component (language) which is also the precondition of them being a system.[1]

It follows that if Cultural Systems are defined in this way, then there is ultimately only one such System *at any time*.[2] For at any particular point in time, if an intelligible exists someone may come across it in a sense quite akin to (or actually involving) geographical or archeological discovery. By corollary, the use of Cultural Systems in the plural strictly refers to different time periods, such that the System at T_2 compared with T_1 is different because of the growth of knowledge, elaboration of beliefs, accumulation of literature and so forth.[3] Obviously this answer to the question 'one System or many?' will have to be strenuously defended against those who maintain that people of different cultures live in different worlds and who go on to deny the possibility of successful translation between them.

Equally it will be necessary to defend the existence of invariant logical principles for describing the 'characteristics proper to a Cultural System'. If analytical dualism is to be sustained, let alone prove fruitful, then we need to be able to ascribe properties to Systemic relations themselves and in such a way that they do not collapse into the judgements of social actors. Otherwise Systemic properties would not remain 'distinct from the Socio-Cultural level'.

The procedure adopted again takes off from a Popperian springboard, namely his distinction between subjective mental experiences, on the one hand, and objective ideas on the other. That the ideas of, say, Buddha agree with those of, say, Schopenhauer is to say nothing about the subjective mental experiences of the two people – it is a *logical* statement: to say that the ideas of Schopenhauer were influenced by those of Buddha is to assert something about subjective mental experience – it is a *causal* statement. 'So we have actually these two different worlds, the world of *thought-processes*, and the world of the *products* of thought-processes. While the former may stand in *causal* relationships, the latter stand in *logical* relationships'.[4] The precise formulation of the above should be underlined: causal relationships are contingent (they 'may' pertain) whereas logical relationships *do* obtain. In other words, items in society's 'propositional register' *have to stand in some logical relationship* to one another. This is the case even if the relation between propositions[5] is one of independence: for this is logical independence ascribed in conformity with the same principles of logic.

Thus the Cultural System is composed of entia which stand in logical relations to one another – the most important of which are those of consistency or contradiction between items since *both* are vital elements in an adequate theory of cultural stability and change. Obviously no version of the Myth of Cultural Integration addressed logical relationships separately precisely because each elided the CS and the S-C levels.

Conflationists always talk about logical and causal connections simultaneously and judge the pair to make a coherent whole. The approach adopted here challenges all three elements which contribute to that judgement – that the Cultural System is free from logical contradiction; that the Socio-Cultural level exists in causal harmony; and that relations between the two are universally integrative. On the contrary, by distinguishing logical relations (pertaining to the CS level) from causal ones (pertaining to the S-C level) I want to make the interface between them an area of intensive exploration and theorization, the results of which should say much about the *conditions* of integration, without taking this state to be a foregone conclusion in the cultural realm. Cultural integration is demythologized by rendering it contingent upon the particular pattern of interconnections *at* the two different levels and *between* the two different levels.

The approach to cultural analysis which will be developed throughout Part II can thus be summarized in the following propositions:

(i) There are logical relationships between components of the Cultural System (CS).
(ii) There are causal influences exerted by the CS on the Socio-Cultural (S-C) level.
(iii) There are causal relationships between groups and individuals at the S-C level.
(iv) There is elaboration of the CS due to the S-C level modifying current logical relationships and introducing new ones.

Taken together they sketch in a morphogenetic cycle of Cultural Conditioning→Cultural Interaction→Cultural Elaboration. Cycles are continuous:

the end-product of (iv) then constitutes the new (i) and begins another cycle of cultural change. Separating out the propositions in this way is prompted by the adoption of analytical dualism: its profitability must be judged by the explanation of cultural dynamics which results from it.

This chapter will concentrate exclusively upon proposition (i). To recap: A dualistic approach is being advocated for cultural analysis, such that only logical relationships pertain to the Cultural System and only causal ones obtain within Socio-Cultural interaction. The following discussion concentrates upon the CS level and its logical characteristics alone. Here *the prime concern is to establish the existence of objective contradictions and complementarities within a Cultural System, independent of any reference to the S-C level.* This is crucial given the working hypothesis that these Systemic features exert important influences *on* the Socio-Cultural level (point (ii) above) and, through it, on cultural dynamics in general. However, if exploring the effects of CS properties, like contradiction and consistency, appears profitable for explaining cultural stability and change, then it is necessary to conceptualize them in a particular way. It must be possible to talk about their existence cross-culturally, that is in formal rather than substantive terms. For if formal properties are inextricable from parochial contents, it will remain impossible to test the social significance of these Systemic features. Even if an effect was associated with the presence of a contradiction in a certain society, there would be no way of establishing whether the result derived from the particularistic contents of the inconsistency rather than being consequential upon contradiction itself. Since the aim is to advance more audacious hypotheses about the general (and neglected) effects of logical relations between CS components, these themselves will constitute the major concepts at this level.

Using the concept of 'contradiction' as the touchstone for discussion of CS properties, it is as well to clarify three claims about their status which are made here, but have proved extremely contentious in other quarters: (1) Ontologically it is maintained that there are objective relations of contradiction whose existence is not dependent on people's awareness of them; (2) epistemologically it is claimed that these can be known by reference to invariant logical principles the applicability of which is not relative to time or place; (3) methodologically it is argued that the problems involved in their cross-cultural identification are not intractable. Each claim will be spelled out briefly and in relation to the opposition that it has attracted. In every case these objections are so fundamental that were they to be sustained our four-point project for reconceptualizing cultural dynamics would have to be abandoned, having foundered on its first proposition.

(1) As an emergent entity the Cultural System has an objective existence and autonomous relations amongst its components (theories, beliefs, values, arguments, or more strictly between the propositional formulations of them)

in the sense that these are independent of anyone's claim to know, to believe, to assert or to assent to them. At any moment the CS is the product of historical Socio-Cultural interaction, but having emerged (emergence being a continuous process) then *qua* product, it has properties of its own. Like structure, culture is man-made but escapes its makers to act back upon them. The CS contains constraints (like the things that can and cannot be said in a particular natural language), it embodies new possibilities (such as technical applications undreamed of in the pure theory on which they are based), and it introduces new problems through the relationships between the emergent entities themselves (the clash of theories), between these and the physical environment (mastery and ruin), between these and human actors (proud makers and brave openers of a Pandora's box).

Consequently contradictions exist independently of people noticing them or caring about them – indeed since there are an infinite number of situations upon which any theory may bear, it might well contain logical contradictions of which no one is aware. (Similarly, the relationship between a problem and a solution, which is an example of a compatibility, is ultimately divorced from whether anyone *does* understand it, though not from the capacity of someone *to do so*. Thus a soufflé recipe might not have been used by anybody living, but it would still work for the cook who eventually tried it.)[6]

The fundamental objection to this view comes from those who deny the very existence of Systemic (CS) properties like contradictions. What some of us present as such are held instead to be entirely derivative from the Socio-Cultural level, inadmissibly dissociated from it and only knowable through it. Winch provides a basic statement of this objection in his formula that the 'logical relations between propositions. . . depend on social relations between men'.[7] (This is of course a philosophical version of upward conflation, taking the typical S-C→CS form, and depending here on the elision of 'meaning' with 'use'.) Hence to Winch 'what is real and what is unreal shows itself *in* the sense that language has . . . we could not in fact distinguish the real from the unreal without understanding the way this distinction operates in the language'.[8] Therefore the last thing that we can do is to stand outside any community and aside from its linguistic conventions and then 'legislate about what is real for them or what counts as a contradiction in their beliefs'.[9] Thus Winch begins to pull the ontological rug from under the Cultural System, making it collapse into the Socio-Cultural realm. Later, more trenchant relativists seek to complete the process.

By now a repertoire of responses to this fundamental objection has been well rehearsed. To begin with, critics have regularly pointed out that although there is undoubtedly plenty of variation in the social relations between men, no one has provided a convincing demonstration that logical relations are capable of the same variability. Next, the use theory of meaning on which philosophical conflationism depends has attracted considerable criticism and the final indignity of being stood on its head – that is, the counter-claim that often the usage of concepts depends upon exploiting their lack of meaning, double meaning or ambiguous meanings.[10] In other words the intelligibilia are not always or even usually the dependent variable as the S-C→CS formula assumes *a prioristically*. Finally, anyone who repudiates the use theory of meaning cannot then allow meanings to be relocated in some other use context (like the works of the 'metaphorical' interpreter or the mystificatory practices of the dominant group), for the original objection would (re)apply. Thus if meaning can be separated from use, rather than just from the use of certain people, then meanings have to be granted ontological status. Such arguments provide support in *principle* for the approach adopted here which claims this status for *Systemic* contradictions and complementarities. However, they themselves have not been proof against comeback, as will be examined in the next section.

(2) Epistemologically it is assumed here that the question 'what counts as a contradiction?' can be answered by reference to the same criteria everywhere, namely those of formal logic:

> Internal consistency is probably the most important and evident of these. The numerous 'laws' of mathematics and logic may be viewed as various elaborations on this most central rule of the symbolic world. We refer here not to a psychological need for consistency on the part of the person or persons who hold symbolic statements . . . but to the relationship among the symbols themselves which can be characterized and rearranged, drawing on the laws of consistency intrinsic to the symbolic world.[11]

Providing that the identity of the components can be established (that is, neither is too vague for us to know what *p* stands for) then the principle or law of contradiction asserts that nothing can be both *p* and *not-p*. Whether a particular relationship between CS items is found to be contradictory, consistent or independent in no way rests on claims made about it on the part of any group (for example the 'certainty' of a community of believers or the theoretical prejudgements of a body of investigators).

This notion of an invariant logical principle, which is universally serviceable for identifying cultural contradictions, came up against the basic objection that what *counts* locally as being contradictory is fundamentally relative. This arose partly from encounters with extremely 'alien' beliefs the very obscurity and peculiarity of which fuelled the idea that 'intelligibility takes many and varied forms.'[12] From this it has been argued that the same logical criteria cannot be used universally to identify contradiction and consistency, because there are varieties of logic ('different mentalities' are a variant of this). Broadly this objection makes contradiction a matter of local convention. So the objection runs, the 'criteria of logic' advanced here are not 'a direct gift of God, but arise out of, and are only intelligible in the context of, ways of living or modes of social life as such. For instance, science is one such mode and religion is another; and each has criteria of intelligibility peculiar to itself.'[13] Hence *within* science or religion, beliefs can be logical or illogical, as understood from inside that form of life, but because standards of logic vary with the context there is no question of making such judgements across the two domains. Consequently the cross-cultural designation of contradictions is not on because our logical terms of reference are ethno-centric.

Again a series of ripostes have been marshalled to undercut this objection. Basically these insist upon the necessary universality of logical principles and deny that they can be construed as matters of local linguistic convention. The first reason for this concerns their indispensability to alien thought itself and is summarized in Lukes's argument that were the concept of negation and the laws of identity and non-contradiction not operative in S's language then how could 'they even be credited with the possibility of inferring, arguing or even thinking? If, for example, they were unable to see that the truth of p excludes the truth of its denial, how could they even communicate truths to one another and reason from them to other truths?'[14]

The related line of defence stresses the necessary invariance of logic if any outsider is ever to grasp what is being asserted in alien thought and speech. Here Hollis has developed his well-known argument about the need for a 'bridgehead' of logic plus low-level perceptual beliefs in order to get translation going. A fundamental condition of identifying the most everyday belief is to find the local word for 'no', for only if we can establish to what they will assent and from what they dissent can we make the great leap to agreeing that the cow is indeed in the corn. A language has a word for negation only if those who speak it hold the truth of a statement to entail the falsity of a denial of that statement – that is if its speakers share the same formal principles. But if it is essential to suppose that they do for identifying their most mundane beliefs, then the same argument holds for grasping their more and most exotic ones. 'If the natives reason logically at all, then they reason as we do.'[15]

Such arguments provide support *in principle* for the cross-cultural conceptualization of contradictions through the use of invariant logical principles. Winch, to whom most of these replies were addressed, half concedes their force when admitting that 'the possibilities of our grasping other forms of rationality different from ours in an alien culture . . . are limited by certain formal requirements centring around the demand for consistency'.[16] However, the relativist camp, far from being concessionary, has made a new and forceful case for the social co-variance of alternative logics which will require further examination.

(3) Undoubtedly there are methodological problems involved in the cross-cultural identification of Systemic properties like contradiction; the question is whether these are manageable or intractable. Obviously in advocating analytical dualism I shall be arguing for manageability (and putting forward management methods). What is worrying are the methodological reservations

of thinkers like Gellner and Lukes who, having made so much of the running against relativism, then see practical difficulties in escaping from local context – dependence. Basically they consider the Cultural System to be so firmly embedded in its Socio-Cultural context that although the two levels may be accepted as analytically distinct, this is a theoretical abstraction and they cannot, or cannot usefully, be studied dualistically. The generic problem is that CS intelligibilia are considered to become vague, denuded and open to misconstruction if prised out of their local S-C setting. Generalizations based on formal similarities tend to be avoided because of the danger of substantive distortion involved. Consequently cross-cultural comparisons are severely limited though not entirely precluded.

Thus the procedure I am advocating faces some hefty opposition from those who argue respectively that Cultural Systems, first, have no independent existence to study; second, are socially relative and only understandable in their own terms; and, third, cannot in practice be examined separately from the S-C level. Although these objections are in descending order of antagonism to the position adopted here, they really represent an ascending order of difficulties to be confronted. In other words, despite the intransigent hostility of 'philosophical conflationism', I believe it can be defused by reference to the same manifest deficiencies which completely flaw its sociological equivalents. Conversely, methodological reservations based on the 'contextual-dependence' of Systemic properties cannot readily be brushed aside. These require a sustained argument that the problems involved in studying the CS in analytical separation from the S-C are solvable; that the profitability of solving them and then proceeding to theorize dualistically are much greater than was thought. Hence the next two sections are concerned with establishing, first, the legitimacy and, second, the viability of analysing the Cultural System as distinct from the Socio-Cultural level.

Resisting the revival of relativism

The revival of relativism by Bloor and Barnes[17] constitutes an imperialistic 'strong programme' which stakes an explanatory claim for the sociology of knowledge to the entire cultural domain. As with some forms of imperialism, its first task is to boot out the present inhabitants and the candidates for immediate extradition are those philosophers who have misled generations into believing that the truth, rationality, success or progressiveness of knowledge (colloquially known as TRASP)[18] had quite a lot to do with people holding it. The strong programme is therefore the anti-TRASP charter. War is declared on the latter in order to defend the fundamental principle of *symmetrical* explanation, namely that the 'same types of cause would explain, say, true and false beliefs'.[19] What is strong, therefore, about this programme is that it asserts the *social* character and *social* causation of *all* knowledge. Nothing about beliefs themselves plays any part in accounting for why they are held (or not) and this includes their relational properties like consistency or contradiction.[20] It advocates a total relativism – totally hostile to the present undertaking.

If this is so, if all beliefs are relative, then it follows that those held at different times and places are incommensurable. They have no common measure in terms of percepts, concepts, truth, reason or logic, for these are all matters of local idiomatic evaluation. 'The words "true" and "false" provide the idiom in which . . . evaluations are expressed, and the words "rational" and "irrational" will have a similar function . . . The crucial point is that the relativist accepts that his preferences and evaluations are as context-bound as those of the tribes T1 and T2. Similarly he accepts that none of the justifications of his preferences can be formulated in absolute or context-independent terms.'[21] There are *no* such terms. Consequently two components (propositions) from two different contexts can never be said to stand in a contradictory or complementary relationship to one another; nor can consistency within one cultural context be assessed from the standpoint of another. According to this programme we can really only talk about local preference for the non-contradictory – in local terms. To do otherwise, as in this work, entails two propositions which are firmly rejected by the strong programme:

1 It implies the existence of some non-conventional and trans-contextual criterion by reference to which contradiction or consistency could be assigned to the relationship between CS items. The law of contradiction is used as that criterion in the present work, precisely because of the invariance of this logical principle. However, its universality is categorically denied from within the 'strong programme' and is indeed incompatible with thorough-going relativism.
2 It implies the ability to ascribe beliefs to social groups across time and space successfully. Both the necessity and the possibility of determinate translation are thus assumed, for they are preconditions of employing logical principles to attribute contradiction or consistency amongst or between alien beliefs. Translatability, however, is also strenuously repudiated by upholders of the 'strong programme': anything more than rough translation for rude purposes is inconsistent with relativism itself.

In order to justify my mode of addressing the Cultural System I have therefore to uphold the following two propositions against the arguments of radical relativism – first, the invariance of the law of contradiction; and, second, the possibility of successful translation.

The invariance of the law of contradiction

Obviously I believe that Mannheim kept his head rather than losing his nerve[22] when acknowledging that the universality of mathematics and logic was such that neither could be explained by reference to anything about the specific cultures in which they were adopted. In view of this, he quite rightly forewent a thorough-going sociology of knowledge. However, my particular concern is to restore certain logical principles to where Mannheim left them, thus retaining their serviceability in the attribution of properties like 'contradiction', 'consistency' and 'independence' to CS items located anywhere in time or space.

Bloor has provided a detailed attempt to demonstrate that 'mathematics is within the scope of the strong programme, and consequently that all beliefs whatever are within its scope'.[23] With Barnes identical arguments were later extended to logic, re-emphasizing the view 'that logical necessity is a species of moral obligation'.[24] The basic argument consists in denying any invariable principles within mathematics and it is held to be equally applicable to logic: instead both disciplines are socially co-variant.

Bloor gains elbow-room for socially caused variations in mathematical thinking by noting (*contra* J. S. Mill) that maths is not a direct 'abstraction' from physical reality because any concrete situation (like pebble sorting) can be 'abstracted' in any number of ways. He then insists (*contra* Frege) that the gap between the amorphous physical situation and its 'characteristic' ordering is filled not by *universal* ideas but by a variety of social conventions which renders these patterns of ordering 'characteristic' to a given society in exactly the same way as traditional patterns of rugweaving[25] and therefore equally variable between societies.[26]

The onus is thus on protagonists of the strong programme who conceive of mathematical necessity and, by extension, logical necessity, as social institutions, to supply us with convincing examples of 'alternative mathematics' and 'alternative logics'. Alternatives would be ones in which practitioners share a consensus on something we deem erroneous and where they engage in forms of reasoning which 'would have to violate our sense of logical and cognitive propriety'.[27] The problem with their examples, in both fields, is that these are intended to illustrate *variability*, which they always fail to sustain, while simultaneously these cases display brute *regularities*, which they never can explain.

Historically the fund of mathematical variation does not begin to match the range of socio-cultural variability, yet the former should parallel the latter if indeed it is socially determined – the original objection (p. 108) retains its force. Indeed, Freudenthal's detailed dissection[28] of the examples offered shows that rather than facing the prospect of returning empty-handed, the concept of an 'alternative' is elasticated in advance[29] and stretches well outside the realm of mathematical necessity to encircle various conventional differences which have no bearing on it.

One instance of this, particularly relevant to the law of contradiction, is Bloor's discussion of early Greek number theory since he concludes that this illustrates the relativistic status of the whole notion of contradiction. It is considered an 'alternative' because, as the generator of all numbers, 'one' was not regarded as a number itself – consequently resulting in claims about the oddness and evenness of numbers which today would be regarded as false. From this it is concluded that in the Greek classification '(d)ifferent things will therefore count as violations of order and coherence, *and so different things will count as confusions or contradiction*' (my emphasis).[30] But this only follows if the example constitutes a genuine alternative, which it does not. The question at stake here is one of *definitions* and their 'otherness' can readily be accepted as a matter of community consensus the local negotiation of which involves all sorts of non-mathematical considerations. What he is advancing are the different elements that can figure in arguments over the adoption of definitions and not alternative conceptions of the validity of mathematical proofs, entailing a reasoning which repudiates 'our' deductive logic but was deemed valid by the Greeks.[31]

Secondly, if we consider proofs themselves, then Bloor's concern to highlight stylistic variations in reaching conclusions only serves to obscure their common core: while he expatiates on the variability of methods used, he ignores the stunning *regularity* of the solutions produced by them. For instance, because Diophantus provided specific algebraic solutions rather than general methods of solution, his is hailed as a form of mathematical thinking that is as different from ours 'as the morality or religion of another culture is different to our morality or religion'.[32] Yet Diophantian solutions entail no violations of logic whatsoever and involve no error. Bloor ignores the latter point by 'not recognizing the simple fact that Diophantus's solutions to his problems, however he may have produced them, and although not general, are *correct*: the numbers cited satisfy the posed conditions'. On his account 'the occurrence of the same results within "alternative mathematics" – e.g. Diophantus's and ours – that are all "about" different societies, should appear as nothing short of a miracle'.[33]

In brief, since neither of these examples falls within the realm of mathematical necessity (which imposes no particular definitions as mandatory and no set style in which problems must be tackled), they cannot be construed as alternative conceptions of it. Consequently the original corollary to variability, namely that different things will count as contradictions to those like the early Greeks who were credited with an 'alternative mathematics', has not been sustained either.

Thus it becomes crucial whether Bloor's later work with Barnes is any more successful in breaking down either of the main barriers restraining relativism. In other words, can they deal with the apparent absence of a fund of 'alternative logics' which their strong programme requires, and with the presence of stubborn regularities in the principles of logic which seem to deny co-variance with social differences?

As a matter of fact, they claim, people do violate supposedly universal principles (like the law of contradiction) all the time. And these actions therefore withhold universality, compelling necessity or even practical utility from this rule of logic. Thus Barnes and Bloor invite us to '(c)onsider all the familiar locutions we find of pragmatic value in informal speech which appear to do violence to formal logical rules'.[34] By implication logical variations are everyday occurrences, so thick on the ground that there is no need to appeal to obscure systems of formal logic, invented by academic logicians, as their source of 'alternatives'.

The examples specifically adduced in supposed violation of the law of contradiction are the following locutions: 'Yes and no'; 'It was, and yet it wasn't', 'The whole was greater than its parts'; and 'There is some truth in that statement'.[35] These instances, presented as the tip of an iceberg on which the law of contradiction breaks up daily, must be genuine cases where two propositions, p and not-p are simultaneously asserted to be true. Spurious instances of apparent contradictions have always been easy to generate by simply failing to specify crucial elements like time and place (when supplied, propositions like 'the sun is shining' and 'the sun is not shining' are not contradictories). As everyday locutions, all of those above are verbal shorthand, each of them is incomplete and therefore none of them is fully propositional. Barnes and Bloor argue that their occurrence in discourse is only intelligible in terms of contingent local determinants, as relativism demands, for as deviations from the rules of logic they cannot be explicated by reference to supposedly universal rules. On the contrary, inspection of the four instances cited shows that 'local contingency' or 'context-specificity' boil down to no more than the specification of omissions, mentioned above, as necessary *before* the universal rule can be applied at all *and* prior to knowing *whether* it is applicable.

The first two exemplars, 'Yes and no' and 'It was, and yet it wasn't', obviously had the appeal of (apparently) reproducing the classical form of a logical contradiction – the assertion of p and not-p. However, both are incomplete because they are shorthand responses in a dialogue which has been suppressed. Ask speakers to transcribe their replies into longhand and they may well supply their own specification, thus obviating any violation of the logical rule. Consider the following three questions which could have elicited either locution:

Q1 'Was a letter expected from your lawyer?'
Q2 'Is he an architect?'
Q3 'Was the show a success?'

Now allow the respondent the use of longhand and the contradictories can disappear:

R1 'Yes, my lawyer's letter was expected in the near future, but no I didn't expect it to get here by today.'

R2 'He is a qualified architect, but not a practising one.'
R3 'It was a very successful production but a commercial disaster.'

It is not only valid but essential to have shorthand locutions transcribed, for only by examining the longhand version *can it be known whether a rule like the law of non-contradiction is applicable to them*. Often people will use formulae like 'Yes and no' or 'It was, and yet it wasn't' to express their inability, unwillingness or unreadiness to advance a propositional statement at all. They are other ways of saying 'I'm not sure' and clearly when a locution expresses nothing but uncertainty it cannot count as an instance of contradiction between two propositions, which is what violation of the law entails.

The last instance, 'There is some truth in that statement' could be applied to 'The whole was greater than its parts', and raises the old problem that we often do talk of propositions being sometimes true and sometimes false whereas the very definition of a proposition excludes this possibility. Traditionally this difficulty is removed by recognizing that if a proposition like 'The whole is greater than its parts' asserts that this is *universally* the case, then the existence of any exception to it serves to prove that it is false – *not* contradictory. However, to produce an exception we have to complete the proposition by specifying what kind of whole we are talking about – for example, a book is not of greater length than the sum of its pages – a completion showing the falsity of the *universal* proposition. Nevertheless it is true that the volume of frozen water is greater than that of melted ice. Thus when it is said that a statement is sometimes true and sometimes false, what is meant is that expressions like 'the whole' may be completed in some ways which express true propositions and in other ways which express false ones. To say ' there is some truth in that statement' is to volunteer to complete it in both of these ways!

Once again the strong programme confronts its dual difficulty – the absence of common-or-garden variability and the indubitable presence of regularity. On the one hand Barnes and Bloor do concede the general unacceptability of contradictions across the 'alternatives' examined and acknowledge the 'widespread acceptance of deductive inference forms and the avoidance of inconsistency'.[36] Immediately, however, they ask what *causes* people to avoid inconsistency and never whether anything regularly happens when they are *confronted* by contradictions, as one would expect from a trenchant version of upwards conflationism.[37] Thus biology is wheeled in to take care of these obtrusive regularities, working in tandem with sociology[38] which explains the variations. The social element is still considered vital because 'no account of our biologically-based reasoning propensities will justify a unique system of logical conventions'.[39] On the other hand, the varieties of logical system now appealed to are the various forms of non-standard logic developed in specialized academic contexts and not everyday abrogations of the law of contradiction. Moreover, these instances like intuitionist logic in the foundations of mathematics, proposals for three-valued logic in quantum physics and the four-valued logic of De Morgan implication, fail to impress a firm partisan of the strong programme, such as Mary Hesse, as *alternatives*. She freely admits that 'the possibility of different basic logics is not by itself very cogent, because it may be said that the examples we know of are all parasitic on standard logic.'[40]

Consequently Hesse supplements the programme with her own argument against any logical principle being a necessary condition of a belief system, without however significantly strengthening the relativists' case against the universality of the law of contradiction. Basically she asks how can the rationalist account for cases 'where we *have* found sign systems unintelligible (as in many anthropological and theological examples where the criteria of identity, for example, of men with birds, three persons in one, etc., do not answer to our criteria)',[41] but which we have eventually come to understand? So the argument goes, here are instances of contradictory beliefs which according to the rationalist should be unintelligible, yet we can come to understand them, but without resort to the rules which rationalists claim are indispensable to intelligibility, that is, utilizing the yes/no distinction. I shall argue that the two examples like the Brazilian Bororo's assertion that they are red macaws or the Trinitarian doctrine, do nothing to support her view that our understanding of these cases does not conform in obvious ways to the application of propositional logic or indeed, in the case of metaphors compares with the non-propositional use of language in poetry, that is an advocacy of artistic hermeneutics. On the contrary, the extent to which we can achieve an understanding of either belief is precisely the degree to which they remain obedient to the law of contradiction.[42]

Crocker's re-investigation of the Bororo[43] found that the male statement 'we are red macaws' hinged on the facts that these birds are kept as pets by Bororo women and that men are dependent on women, given matrilineal descent and uxorilocal residence. The statement is thus an ironic comment upon the masculine condition,[44] the understanding of which involved no extension of 'our language in unpredictable ways'[45] for we say much the same in English with the words 'hen-pecked'.

More generally, a claim to have rendered any metaphor or simile intelligible always depends upon 'cashing it in'[46] propositionally. It means identifying at least one aspect of something which is consistent with something otherwise unlike it. Hence the explication of poetry is *not* non-propositional – Burns asserts the truth of his love sharing attractive properties with the rose but also, we can feel confident, the falsity of her 'being prone to black spot' or 'benefitting from mulching'.

Trinitarian doctrine has a vast propositional history and unlike Hesse I maintain that it is only *publicly* understandable through it and not beyond it. The desperate struggles within the early Church (Doceticism or Gnosticism versus Arianism or Sabellianism)[47] are perfectly comprehensible as attempts to advance consistent doctrine which avoided the *perceived contradiction* of asserting 'three persons in one'. Precisely because the Bishops of the first centuries were clear about the logical rules of intelligibility, they were equally aware that each of the above propositional interpretations, though logically consistent, had unacceptable implications (for example, the Gnostic christological doctrine reduced the second person to a phantasm *because* of its consistency – 'if he suffered he was not God; and if he was God he did not suffer'). Thus rather than accept any of the doctrines mentioned, the Councils took their stand on a semi-propositional belief, namely a mystery whose 'meaning (i.e. the proper propositional interpretation) is beyond human grasp'.[48]

So, what sense can be made of Hesse's claim that we can extend our understanding and give intelligibility to that which the faithful themselves deem a mystery? Certainly not through treating the Trinity to any metaphorical or symbolist interpretation, for such were formally repudiated from the Creed of Nicea onwards. Just possibly (though most improbably in this case) an outsider may occasionally come up with a propositional interpretation previously unthought of but acceptable to 'the natives'. But when this is so, it is a point in favour of logical invariance.

Thus I am arguing that *public* understandability of Trinitarian doctrine is exactly co-extensive with the law of non-contradiction being upheld within it and lapses with its suspension. We can all comprehend the doctrine 'before' it is deemed mysterious, but when faith sets in there is no means of comprehension for the outsider other than by becoming of the faith and sharing its mysteries. We can all comprehend 'afterwards', that is when the authority of the Apostolic church becomes the basis of the belief. For then the rules of contradiction and consistency came back into play, to identify heterodoxy and define orthodoxy[49] and these applications of authoritative doctrine are matters again generally understandable. Public intelligibility, then, is a thread which breaks with the suspension of the law of contradiction. The suggestion that faith is penetrable is, of course, true because it can be embraced, but this does not advance Hesse's case. Since it is nonsense to claim that one professes more than one faith, it is even more nonsensical to predicate an extension of our understanding upon this state of affairs.

Nevertheless Hesse considers that she still has a decisive argument in hand against the proponents of invariance, namely that all they 'could possibly prove would be a purely formal similarity of logical structure between belief systems. If language is to convey information, then it does necessarily follow that it contains at least some binary distinction corresponding to yes/no, agreement/disagreement, true/false, that is, it contains elementary "bits" of information. But this says nothing whatever about the *content* of formal logical principles.'[50] But my foregoing argument requires nothing more than the acceptance of this purely *formal* similarity of logical structure between belief systems. For *substantive* cross-cultural differences may also be superficial;

their mere existence provides no direct evidence for relativism. On the other hand, their *formal* similarities may give considerable theoretical purchase on the major question of whether there is any connection between the incidence of consistency or contradiction among CS items and patterns of cultural stability and change.

In her above conclusion Hesse believes that she has only given away something 'empty'.[51] Similarly, advocates of the strong programme doubtless believe that their major weapon remains in reserve. They, too, could indeed – again courtesy of biology – allow the invariance of the law of contradiction feeling secure that the last thing I could do is employ it as a tool in comparative cultural analysis. For its use is predicated upon the ability to ascribe beliefs to social groups across time and space which depends upon their translatability. Since the relativist denies the possibility of successfully ascribing beliefs through translation, he could grant me my universal rule safe in the conviction that I will only be able to use it locally. There is no harm in handing out a tool box, or benefit in receiving one, if the raw materials are then withheld.

The necessity of translation

Successful translation is a precondition of employing logical principles to attribute contradiction or consistency amongst alien beliefs or between those and our own. Unless we can feel confident in the beliefs we ascribe cross-culturally, nothing can be said about their relations. This confidence rests on the conviction that it is possible to produce adequate translations of the alien beliefs. Yet it is considered misplaced by founders of the strong programme, who are well aware that 'an anti-relativist argument' could 'be based simply upon the possibility of successful translation'.[52] For it is a necessary condition of a translation being correct that it matches sentences between languages with regard to truth-conditions, but for relativists of course this condition can never be met since what is true for the Nuer is not true for us. Thus as Newton-Smith puts it economically, 'the possibility of translation entails the falsehood of relativism. By contraposition, the truth of relativism entails the impossibility of translation.'[53]

The standard rationalist approach to translation, as formulated by Hollis, depends on the establishment of a bridgehead between two languages, that is 'a set of utterances definitive of the standard meanings of words'.[54] The investigator has to assume that 'he and the native share the same perceptions and make the same empirical judgements in simple situations', such as the cow being in the corn. These simple perceptual situations serve to anchor communication and to get translation going by allowing the researcher to identify standard meanings for everyday native terms, uncomplicated by cultural variables. Each of these key assumptions is denied in the strong programme, which seeks to blow up the pass between one language and another.

Thus to Barnes and Bloor, 'learning even the most elementary of terms is a slow process that involves the acquisition from the culture of specific *conventions*. This makes apparently simple empirical words no different from others that are perhaps more obviously culturally influenced. There are no privileged occasions for the use of terms – no "simple perceptual situations" – which provide the researcher with "standard meanings" uncomplicated by cultural variables. In short, there is no bridgehead in Hollis's sense.'

Hence, advocates of the strong programme conclude 'perfect translation cannot exist: there can only be translation acceptable for practical purposes, as judged by contingent local standards'.[55] Were the common-sense protest made that the bridgehead serves perfectly well for getting over the channel and into agreement with any French farmer that 'the cow is in the cowshed'/ 'la vache est dans l'étable', this kind of relativist could respond *either* by questioning the perfection of the translation *or* by stressing conventions shared by the speakers.

In the first case he could insist that these two sentences were only *pragmatic* equivalents by underlining the lack of precise equivalence between, perhaps, 'cowshed' and 'l'étable', or 'byre' and 'vacherie'. However, this reply does not carry any particular force in relation to *translation* since these terms show regional variations of equal magnitude within the 'same' language (English 'cowshed', Scottish 'byre' and American 'cowhouse'). This fact does not perturb Hollis's argument which is about the 'conditions of the possibility of language in general'[56] – so what is true for two languages applies equally to one. But it does raise problems for the strong programme, for it carries relativism beyond the endorsement of 'many worlds', each with its own truths, towards an infinite regress of decreasingly small worlds, also incapable of exchanging truths.[57]

Alternatively, the relativist might suggest that the Common Market is really very parochial: an Englishman, a Scotsman and a Frenchman are all locals (joking cousins) but the strong programme acquires its teeth when it has something on which to cut them, such as really alien concepts couched in thoroughly foreign conventions. This seems to be the preferred line of attack since Barnes and Bloor maintain that 'the bridgehead argument fails as soon as it is measured against the realities of . . . anthropological practice'.[58] How?

They cite the case of Bulmer's work among the Karam of New Guinea where 'he found that many of the instances of what we would call "bird" were referred to as "yakt". He also found that instances of bats were included amongst the "yakt", while instances of cassowaries were scrupulously denied admittance to the taxon.'[59] These discoveries are taken to mean that the anthropologist had acquired the local culture of specific conventions. In other words, what Bulmer was doing was not the impossible act of translating: instead he was learning Karam conventions until he could pick out 'yakt' as well as they did.

Quite the reverse; the anthropologist had made standard use of the bridgehead in his fieldwork and without it could not have come up with the above translation, which is a quite different achievement from becoming a Karam amongst Karam. Bulmer started by going into the field through his first language (for as we will see a little later, he could not do otherwise), sensibly selected a simple perceptual object, 'bird', and soon established a rough correspondence between it and 'yakt'. He could then pin-point where the two terms did not overlap by proceeding just as Hollis suggests – pointing to a cassowary, saying 'yakt' and receiving a dissent sign, pointing to a bat, saying 'yakt' and commanding assent from the natives. All of which is *only* possible through the use of ostension and correction *in* 'simple perceptual situations'.[60]

The fact that there was imperfect equivalence between the two terms did *not* rule out use of the bridgehead, for there were enough of 'our' birds which were also 'yakt' to get the translation going and take it beyond the point sufficient for 'practical purposes', cropping up in the field, to a specification of the non-overlapping areas between the two classificatory terms. From there the anthropologist could move on to a task – open to the translator but not to the Karam amongst Karam – of trying to explain why there is cross-cultural variation in a classification. Note that Bulmer's paper which the relativists chose to use is entitled '*Why* is the cassowary not a bird?'.[61] Classifications in our own language change (whales were fish; whales are mammals), but changes in them are not matters of *mere* convention, there are always theoretical reasons for them. Far from the bridgehead argument being 'a plea for a single pure observation language' as the relativists claim,[62] it is the translator who takes Hesse's 'theory-dependence' of descriptive predicates[63] seriously, for only through translation can the theories be explicated and an account of why different ones are held by different language groups be offered; the relativist merely lives with the theory, monolinguistically. He is finally shown up as the real parochial pragmatist. But the possibility of addressing these crucial *comparative* questions, as of translation itself, depends on the existence of a bridgehead – its roughness and readiness are quite immaterial.[64]

Not only will the bridgehead be rough and ready, it will also be floating rather than fixed. We advance with it in crab-like fashion, prepared to accept that the seemingly obvious truths we impute to aliens, in order to make sense of their behaviour, will undergo endless correction in the light of the evidential consequences of making such assumptions. The bridgehead is made and remade plank by plank – but which planks we change and which assumptions we alter is prompted by the resultant translations now making better sense than did their predecessors based on assumptions just discarded. Success in predicting the words and actions of those being translated confirms that the bridgehead can carry our weight. This is an empirical procedure validated by an empirical criterion.[65]

Indeed, one of the most persuasive forms of substantiation is supremely empirical, namely that we have not yet failed. No anthropologist has yet come home to report the aliens 'incomprehensible' and the supply of tribes is drying up. Yet it remains conceivable that one day we may fail, if not on this earth, at least with extra-terrestrials. Quite rightly this is of no great concern, for the unknown is the unknown and its relationship with *any* theory is identical – simply unknown. Moreover, the appeal to life on other planets performs no critical knife-work. Take for instance, Hesse's argument, intended to buttress the strong programme; to the effect that all cognitive terminology is 'relative to some set or sets of cultural norms' and that these 'might even *be as wide as biological humankind*, but if so, they would *still not* be rendered absolute or transcendentally *necessary in themselves*' (my emphasis).[66] This is completely off-target because the rationalist case is expressly and ineluctably predicated upon some version of the 'principle of Humanity'.[67] Rationalism is indeed earth-bound but this does not mean that it has feet of clay – even were it unable to translate standard inter-galactic. (Either the latter would remain incomprehensible or its translation would rely on the generalizability of some 'principle of intelligent life,' from or to humanity, which thus demonstrated its necessity.)

Translation is necessary to my undertaking because without it beliefs cannot be ascribed to people of other places and times, in which case nothing can be said about the formal logical relations between these beliefs. Yet relativists also want to assert things about alien beliefs – very different things like their relationship to local conditions and conventions, but assertions nevertheless – so why is translation not equally necessary to them? How can theories be identified as alternatives or indeed be known to be incommensurable if translating them is an impossibility? Their answer consists in circumventing the entire translation enterprise and making a direct assault on alien language and culture. As a strategy it could be called 'become as a child' or 'go native'. I shall argue that there are insuperable difficulties preventing the fulfilment of either injunction and that even if these could be spirited away it would not answer the above requirements and obviate the necessity for translation.

Before doing either, however, it is important to stress that quite regardless of whether my arguments prove convincing, their strategy *cannot* be a complete alternative to translation for it can only be attempted with other living people. Of its nature it deals only with the contemporary, with inserting oneself into some current alien context in order to assert its difference. By its nature it cannot then dispose of the necessity of translation when attempting to ascribe beliefs to the majority of cultural agents – for these are the dead. Furthermore although the strategy is doomed to incompleteness from the outset this does not make protagonists of the strong programme feel bound, in consistency, to eschew pronouncements on the mathematical thought of ancient Greeks, Enlightenment and Romanticism in eighteenth-century Europe, the politics of Second Empire France and so forth. However great the combined linguistic skills of these relativist authors, they could not have been exercised in discourse with the long dead.[68]

However let us now turn (1) to the strategy, (2) to its defects, and (3) to the reassertion of the necessity of translation.

(1) Hollis had defended the necessity of translation and developed his method of getting it going because where alien beliefs are concerned 'there is no more direct attack on meaning available'.[69] Barnes and Bloor question his premiss and seek a substitute for his procedure. To them

> the fact is that translation is *not* the most direct attack on meaning that is available. It was not available, nor did it play any part at all, in the first and major attack that any of us made upon meaning when we acquired language in childhood. First-language acquisition is not a translation process, and nothing that is absent here can be a necessary ingredient in subsequent learning. To understand an alien culture the anthropologist can proceed in the way that native speakers do. Any difficulties in achieving this stance will be pragmatic rather than a *priori*.[70]

Problems now arise because the fact that nothing which is absent in first-language learning can be a necessary ingredient of learning a second one may be a true statement (though it is neither obvious nor testable), but it is then allowed to obfuscate the undoubted truth that the presence of a first language is an ingredient, willy nilly, in subsequent language learning. This leads to difficulties which are indeed *a prioristic* and not just pragmatic.

(2) As language speakers we simply are unable to become as pre-linguistic children. One's mother-tongue cannot be cast aside, as your shoes can be left at the mosque door. Since all knowledge is conceptually formed (and therefore linguistically enshrined) then acquisition of a second language will inescapably be filtered through the first. Pragmatically, as anyone learning a foreign language knows, the ability to think in it comes fairly late on, *after* one has become proficient enough to stop translating-in-one's-head! Theoretically the idea of becoming like the pre-linguistic child is uncomfortably close to the mythological being whom Gellner dubbed the 'Pure Visitor', creatures capable of divesting themselves of their conceptual clothing[71] and surveying the cultural horizon from a decontaminated vantage point. Since linguistic strip-tease is not on, then it is an impossibility to 'go native' as the strategy recommends. It follows that, *a priori*, there is no alinguistic *entrée* accessible to existing language speakers.

Second, even were we to suspend these points for the purpose of argument, it is also the case that given the premisses of the strong programme, there could be no 'return of the native'. For without the possibility of translation there is no way in which the investigator of alien beliefs who had gone through the business of 'becoming as a child' could then report back what the natives did believe. In other words, not only is there no *entrée*, there would also be no *exit*.

Anthropology would then become a curious study indeed. The role of its professors would reduce to saying: 'If you want to understand the X, then go and live with them for five years as I did and then we will talk about the X in the X's language, replete with its conventions, reasons, truths, that is we will then talk together as natives.' It would remain impossible to ascribe beliefs to the natives and communicate these to others – and things get curiouser yet. For if one tries to imagine this capacity to move from one linguistic skin to another, stating and believing one thing in one language and something incompatible in another, then if translation is indeed an impossibility, one could not know that one was doing this oneself. In short, on the strong programme, *nothing relational* can be either privately known or publicly communicated about alien beliefs.

(3) Hence we come full-circle back to the necessity of translation. For as Newton-Smith argues 'if translation lapses so does the ascription of beliefs and the explanation of behaviour in action terms'.[72] It becomes impossible to describe the behaviour of aliens as constituting particular actions or to explain it by reference to the beliefs and desires producing them. Translation cannot be set 'aside as something problematic for a relativist while going on to talk about beliefs and actions as if these notions would remain unproblematic'.[73] If we cannot ascribe beliefs the end-result is that sociology has *no* role to play in explaining action. This must be handed over to behaviourism, materialism or indeed biology – in short, anything which excludes reference to the determinate beliefs of human subjects. Thus the strong programme ends up as the vanishing programme.

The problem of contextual dependence

However it is admittedly the case that some of those whose work has been drawn on to criticize the conflationists and the relativists also draw back from the notion of advancing formal cross-cultural propositions about the existence, inter-play and effects of contradiction and consistency. The reason for this is because, without retracting anything about the objectivity or knowability of contradictions, generalizations are resisted because the *methodological identification of a contradiction is held to be context-dependent*. Stated crudely, they are saying there is nothing much wrong with my enterprise except that it cannot be done. So the next question is whether contextual dependence does indeed constitute a total road-block? By an irony which is sweet, if it works, I will argue that this is only the case if the Cultural System and Socio-Cultural levels are not kept analytically distinct – the vindication of my position depends on sticking to it.

The crux of this problem is *how* methodologically one can 'assert the existence of a contradiction'. It arises from the simple and uncontestable fact that two cultural items (at the CS level) may appear contradictory in isolation but may not be so if considered in context. One reason why unease flares about projects like my own is that if evoking the context can remove the contradiction and yet the context itself is socially specific, how can anyone advance cross-contextual propositions? In other words, contextual dependence threatens to drive a different wedge, but still a wedge, between 'asserting the existence of a contradiction' (universally) and 'what counts as a contradiction' (locally). The problem unfolds as follows:

(i) Some contextual reference is needed precisely because cultural components are interrelated with one another. Usually their interlacement with others has to be addressed in the very process of identifying them and this is necessarily prior to saying anything about the nature of interconnections with yet other components. Thus for instance, the religious notion of 'salvation' is only identifiable in the context of related concepts like 'sin', 'redemption', 'grace' etc. Consequently, for any two cultural items under consideration, we have to take into account the respective contexts of both and *also* the context *against which* they are judged to be contradictory or consistent. Too much local context and there ends up being so little in common that comparability goes out of the window.

(ii) Gellner is undoubtedly right that the difficulty of letting the context in, as one must, is the absence of flood gates. For there is nothing in the context itself which dictates just how much of it is relevant to any proposition, concept or unit, or which regulates how we should select from it. The problem is that how much is taken in can be decisive for our judgements: too little contextual reference and many pairs of items appear absurdly contradictory (just as ripping two statements out of context in a book and then juxtaposing them can be used by a reviewer to make any author look ridiculous). Conversely, too much contextual charity and almost anything can be freed from the charge of inconsistency. The problem thus is that we need to make reference to the context but appear to lack rules specifying what can properly be let in and what can justifiably be kept out. In Gellner's words '(c)ontextual interpretation is in some respects like the invocation of *ad hoc* additional hypotheses in science: it is inevitable, proper, often very valuable, and at the same time dangerous and liable to disastrous abuse. It is probably impossible in either case to draw up general rules for delimiting the legitimate and the illegitimate uses of it.'[74]

(iii) Finally, the death-trap opens up. Without rules delineating which part of the context may be taken into account, then everything can be rendered consistent simply by invoking the convenient part or enough of it. Consequently contradictions make their exit, the social role of

> inconsistency disappears and with it much of our understanding of cultural change which 'may occur through the replacement of an inconsistent doctrine or ethic by a better one, or through a more consistent application of either. It equally blinds us to the possibility of, for instance, social control through the employment of absurd, ambiguous, inconsistent or unintelligible doctrines.'[75] Certainly in specific cases it may be possible to *argue* that the over-charitable interpreter, committed to absolving the concepts he is examining from the charge of logical incoherence, is either misdescribing the social context or manipulating the context in order to make sense of the beliefs.

Sometimes, as Gellner illustrates, to make sense of the concept is to make manifest nonsense of the society, the functioning of which may indeed depend upon the use of incoherent 'bobility' type concepts. At other times it may be possible to show that the context wheeled in to make sense of beliefs actually makes a mockery of them. Take a case where social explanations are adduced to remove inconsistencies in beliefs: contradictions in Zande accounts of witchcraft. Some maintain these can be disposed of by placing them in the context of their social effects (ritual statements are 'about' the power structure of Zande society). But, as Hollis argues, since a bewitched Zande does *not* simply believe that he has offended a higher authority, he believes he is the victim of witchcraft, this use of context implies that believers do not know what their beliefs are about and that what they think they believe is misguided.[76]

The problem with contextual charity is partly that cases of mismanagement are not always so blatant as the above. Overcharitability may *not* be detectable through the mangling of social practice or the misconstruction of beliefs, for the above is as much an instance of bad sociology as it is an illustration of the point in question. A good but charitable sociologist may get away with murder but he will not leave incriminating evidence behind. And if he does not, then on what can he be indicted? For, more profoundly, the problem is that in the absence of rules governing appeal to the context there *is* no dividing line between excessive benevolence and legitimate reference. This is the ultimate death-trap: anything can be rendered consistent provided only that it is well done. The expulsion of contradiction from sociology merely depends on a high quality manipulation of context; and since charity and quality are not mutually exclusive, the flood gates stand ajar.

I want to suggest that this problem basically arises from the failure to maintain a working distinction between the logical and the causal, and that it is capable of solution. These arguments will be explored by returning to Gellner's paper on 'Concepts and society', in which he battles with the problem of too much contextual charity, seeks laudably to rescue the notion of cultural contradictions, but in the end cannot yield up a cast-iron restraint for over-benevolence which would prevent inconsistencies from being plausibly explained away. It seems to me that the reason why he cannot erect an effective flood wall is that, like the theorists taken to task, he too does not differentiate analytically between properties of the Cultural System and those belonging to the Socio-Cultural level.

(1) Gellner begins with the perfectly valid point that 'concepts and beliefs do not exist in isolation, in texts or in individual minds, but in the life of men and societies'.[77] However, this fact does not itself enjoin us to analyse cultural items in any particular way. It contains no methodological injunction either

(i) proscribing their examination 'in isolation' from life (CS level), or
(ii) insisting that they be examined at their nexus with social life (CS + S-C levels).

(2) However, Gellner seems to think that it does, or at least that there are good reasons for abjuring (i) and pursuing (ii). Thus he talks of avoiding (i) because of the 'unrealistic literal-minded scholasticism' of 'textual' (that is, CS) analysis, in contrast with 'the unfortunate need to *interpret* just what the concepts in question meant to the participants', which implies endorsing (ii) (that is, the CS + S-C approach).[78] This need apparently arises from the fact that texts and sayings may be broad, vague and fragmentary with ill-defined logical implications for conduct. Its corollary is taken to be that we therefore must interpret the meanings they have for people since these are the key to their conduct. I cannot contest what Gellner says about many 'texts' but I do challenge his implicit contrast with 'meanings'. It simply cannot be assumed that because some or many 'texts' are vague that meanings *must* be more precise. They can be vague too. Nor is 'precision' the preserve of the Socio-Cultural level; a geometry text is just the opposite of being broad, vague or fragmentary and has the clearest implications for conducting geometrical exercises, but its meaning to the average schoolboy is probably the messiest hodge-podge. It is therefore at the very least a matter of *methodological choice* to eschew the analysis of 'texts', procedure (i); and not a question of *methodological necessity* to plunge into the interpretation of 'meanings', procedure (ii). However, Gellner does dispense with (i) and proceeds with (ii).

(3) In then interpreting what concepts meant to participants Gellner invokes *two different aspects of context* in elucidating their concepts and beliefs. These are the social context as:

– other ideas (CS logical relations)
– other people (S-C causal relations)

This of course is an inevitable corollary of adopting procedure (ii) which deals with both CS + S-C levels for this makes the two kinds of context pertinent.

In turn I want to make three points against this methodological procedure: that it is *unnecessary* to Gellner himself for the arguments he wants to advance about the existence of contradictions; that it *impoverishes* the sociological examination of the role played by contradictions; and, most seriously of all, that this is what *prevents him from firmly closing the door on over-charitable contextual interpretation*. First, then, in so far as Gellner is seeking to show the existence of conceptual contradictions (in opposition to the charitable contextualists who always end up asserting the consistency of beliefs), I consider procedure (ii) unnecessary, for the demonstration of the contradictions in question only depends on contextual reference to *other ideas*. Thus, for example, the Berber concept of *igurramen*, people blessed with prosperity and capable of conferring this on others by supernatural means, attributes a clutch of characteristics to its possessors 'including magical powers, and great generosity, prosperity, a consider-the-lilies attitude, pacifism and so forth'.[79] Clearly contradiction exists here, but purely because these properties are *logically* incompatible with one another. As Gellner comments 'an *agurram* who was extremely generous in a consider-the-lilies spirit would soon be impoverished and, as such, fail by another crucial test, that of prosperity'.[80] Equally it is merely a logical corollary that those credited with the full clutch of characteristics *cannot* possess all of them if they are to get by. Here a consultation of the 'texts' is not unrealistic scholasticism; it is all that is necessary to demonstrate 'contradiction'. In other words, this can be done exclusively at the Cultural System level. It is true that Gellner is interested in some other related questions, such as the divergence between concept and reality in relation to *agurram*-hood being essential for the working of the social system, but this would seem to depend upon precisely the CS/S-C distinction that I am advocating. For the 'reality' of being an *agurram* is a matter of causal relations with other people and these effects therefore can be analysed at the Socio-Cultural level.

Secondly, it follows that this treatment of the cultural context is one which *impoverishes* the problems that can be addressed (that is, the *relation* between Gellner's own above two concerns – the existence and the effects of contradiction). By including in the context what it *means in practical life* to be an *agurram* (bearer of a social role replete with logical contradictions) is in fact methodologically to run together the concept and reality – that is the co-existence of inconsistent demands and the entirely different question of how people live with them. Thus Gellner writes that 'fieldwork observation of *igurramen* and the social context in which they operate has convinced me that, whilst indeed *igurramen* must entertain lavishly and with an air of insouciance, they *must* also at least balance their income from donations from pilgrims with the outgoings from entertaining them, for a poor *agurram* is a no-good *agurram*'.[81] But by making the (S-C) need to cope part of the context of *agurram*-hood (they *must* balance their books), this contextual imperative removes some extremely interesting Socio-Cultural questions. It prevents the examination of *how*, by what strategies, ploys and financial chicanery the successful *agurram* manages to balance his accounts, and by doing or not doing *what* the no-good *agurram* fails.

In essence we do not want to lose the problem of how the same inconsistency is coped with by different sets of people, for this denudes understanding of Socio-Cultural mechanisms and machinations. But this is lost if strategic action is mixed up with logical relations as part of the bundle called 'context' (that is, logical relations–problem situation–practical solutions). This bundle is indeed its 'meaning to participants', but we should unpack it. Certainly when a contradiction is detected it becomes a key task to explain how it is possible that this inconsistency does not appear as such or is made tolerable in daily life. This is a vital issue but its detection and exploration depend on maintaining analytical dualism in one's methodological approach. Furthermore, as is always the case, interplay between the levels gets lost too. For example, it appears an intriguing question how the (S-C) failure of an *agurram* to cope is squared with his supposed (CS) selection by God and also how many no-good *igurramen* (S-C) it takes for divine providence to be queried (CS)?

Thirdly, and most important of all, I think that what stops him from shutting the floodgates on overwhelming charity really and effectively is this attempt to distinguish what people 'really mean' (by reference to a conjoint CS/S-C context) from what they 'textually' say they mean. What Gellner himself is 'anxious to argue is that contextual interpretation, which offers an account of what assertions "really mean" in opposition to what they seem to mean in isolation, does not by itself clinch matters. I cannot arrive at determinate answers (concerning "what they mean") without doing a number of things which may in fact pre-judge the question: without delimiting just which context is to be taken into consideration, without crediting the people concerned with consistency . . . or without assumptions concerning what they can mean.'[82] Yet having argued this he also argues for a fuller use of the contextual method of interpretation, fuller in the sense that it allows for the possibility that what people mean may sometimes be absurd. But in the absence of rules governing contextual invocation what protection does this offer against the above charitable deficiencies? Only, ultimately to Gellner, the maintenance of a 'vivid sense of the possibility that the interpreted statement may contain absurdity'.[83] But if, as seems likely, charity atrophies this 'vivid sense', what then? Merely an irresolvable haggle over interpretation between the universally benevolent and those who have kept a certain acerbity – when this happens we are all of us in the pit. For if there are no rules about what parts of the context it is legitimate to invoke there is no court of appeal against improper usage.

A suggested solution to the problem of contextual dependence

What the last few pages were concerned to establish was basically that it is only possible to have a workable concept of 'cultural contradiction' if the distinction between the Cultural System and the Socio-Cultural level is maintained sociologically and sustained methodologically. Gellner, it seems, did come to hold a very similar sociological distinction indeed, for later on he writes that: 'Despite these difficulties inherent in using the notion of a "system of belief" instead of the individual or group credited with holding it – difficulties for which there may be no formal solution – I nevertheless think it essential that the great Dividing Line be drawn in some such terms.'[84] My suggestion is that the problem of drawing the dividing line is made out to be worse than it is because Gellner's *méfiance* of 'texts'[85] rules out a practicable *method* for using analytical dualism.

In 'Concepts and society' this resulted from the first step – rejecting 'textual' analysis in isolation from life in favour of interpreting 'meanings' in social life. For 'meanings' invoke both levels (CS + S-C) and therefore the context of interpretation also involves both levels. The rest of the problem stems from that: from the mixing of the logical and the causal. Logical contradictions become confused with and concealed by social strategies for coping with them when they are treated as a bundle – social explanations can be trundled in to dispel seeming logical inconsistencies and there is no effective way of shoving them out.

Put even more succinctly the 'problem' of contextual-dependence arose from trying to do too much at once. It stemmed from attempting to deal with the Cultural System and Socio-Cultural life simultaneously *because* they *are* intertwined. Instead I suggest that the death-trap can be skirted by proceeding more slowly. Specifically this involves examining the Cultural System first, in isolation from social life, before addressing the Socio-Cultural level and then the relations between them. By doing this, by separating 'sayings' and 'meanings' in Gellner's terms, it does seem that we can solve the problem posed by contextual-dependence, namely what part of the context can be legitimately brought in and what portion justifiably kept out. The difficulty which Gellner was left with was due to the absence of any such general rules; but in this he gives us the hint that the way out of the difficulty is to find a rule.

My next step is thus to adduce such a rule. But I must make it crystal clear that this only applies to the Cultural System level and only works if this level is rigidly, though only analytically, separated from Socio-Cultural life. Quite simply, if the Cultural System (CS) is held to be constituted of nothing but objective items, 'texts' and the *logical relations* between them, then the only part of the context which is relevant to them, because of their dependence on it, are the '*other ideas*' to which they are related. In sum, if we clearly distinguish between the two cultural levels, the Systemic and the

Socio-Cultural, then we can also differentiate between the aspects of context – 'other ideas' and 'other people' – on which the former and latter depend respectively. Schematically this can be represented as shown in Table 1, the key point being that the logical and the causal are systematically separated.

Resistance might be expected from others who maintain that the two levels are so inextricably intertwined, because of the constant interchange between them, that their separation is not on even as a matter of methodological convenience. That this view is ill-founded can be shown by a side-glance at those insisting most strongly on the tightest bonding between 'sayings' and 'meanings', that is, proponents of the 'family resemblance' approach to human categorization who insist on the continuous role of natural-language speakers (S-C) in defining what 'spread of resemblances' is carved out by a particular word, concept or idea (CS). Their reaction should presumably be along the following lines: the constituents of 'texts', indeed one of their most basic, namely words themselves, are constantly changed through usage – by the erosion of old and the accumulation of new attributes picked out by them. Thus words (regarded as CS entities here) are subject to ceaseless grinding at their margins by (S-C) use and this incessantly dissects the world in new ways and hence continuously inscribes these changed meanings on the CS register. Since the latter is never free from (S-C) buffeting, it would therefore be artificially frozen by any methodological attempt to examine it separately.

However, none of this actually precludes the analytical separation of levels which is fundamental to the rule I am seeking to advance, provided that two features of the process they describe are fully recognized by those who approach lexical categorization in this way. The first involves acceptance of the accumulating body of evidence that categories do have 'core features', for example, 'focal colours', 'natural prototypes', 'best examples' or 'basic-level objects',[86] which have now been investigated in relation to a wide range of taxonomies. The implication of this work is the existence of anchorages constraining the potential 'spread of resemblances' to movements akin to a boat on its mooring, rather than the volatile lexical dissections suggested, for example, by the original Whorfian hypothesis.[87]

The second concerns the equally important point that changes in the 'spread of resemblances' named by a particular word not only 'revolve' around core attributes but also 'evolve' over time. Consequently it is only necessary to insist upon the temporality of our analytical separation (word X

Table 1

Cultural level	*Context on which dependent*	*Relations between them*
Cultural System	Other ideas	Logical
Socio-Cultural	Other people	Causal

covers Y attributes at T_1), for any incompatibility to disappear, since our methodological procedure in no way denies changes through usage – it only stresses that they take time. In general the continuousness of a process must *not* be confused with the instantaneous registration of its effects (for confusion itself, resistance or thresholds may be involved) and this is especially so since speakers often disagree over changes of usage.

Indeed, though this is not our main concern, we are now well on the way towards a micro-morphogenetic framework for analysing interplay at the lexical level. Thus 'one influence on how attributes will be defined by humans is clearly the category system already existent in the culture at a given time'.[88] This would constitute the CS conditioning which confronted natural-language speakers, whose subsequent S-C disagreements about word usages could then result at T_2 in a new 'spread of resemblances', provided that these lexical changes did not tug too hard at their moorings, that is did not negate the co-occurrence of attributes in the perceived world.

In sum, the macroscopic effrontery of our proposal to separate textual ideas (CS) from people's meanings (S-C) turns out to be of utility to the micro-concerns of those whose first reaction was to flinch away from it. However, let us now return to the main issue, namely the question of generating a rule to regulate contextual-reference, which does indeed depend upon separating the two aspects of any ideational context – the CS and the S-C.

When 'asserting the existence of a contradiction' (CS) the rule which is invoked is that *only* reference to 'other ideas' upon which the items in question logically depend, or to which they can be shown to be logically related may be admitted to dispel the contradiction which appears when the said items are taken in isolation. Thus a contradiction exists if two CS items are logically inconsistent with one another and this inconsistency cannot be removed (reduced to an apparent contradiction) by elucidating their logical connection to another/other CS item(s). A simple example is the apparent contradiction between the proposition that water boils at 100°C and the observation that it does not do so at the top of a mountain or the bottom of a valley, which is resolved by showing that both are logically related to two contextual items, temperature and pressure. Then the first proposition is rewritten as 'water boils at 100°C, standard temperature and pressure', and this specification of the law then embodies the observations which appeared to contradict it.

To be more precise, the rule entails that not all 'other ideas', but propositions alone are relevant when 'asserting the existence of a contradiction'. For contradiction or consistency can only be attributed to propositions, that is to sets of statements which are either true or false (though with metaphysical propositions like 'there is a God', we may never be able to prove that it is one or the other, only that it cannot be both). *Propositions, as opposed to sentences or utterances or many of our thoughts, cannot be ambiguous, that is true in some interpretations and false in others. Thus where the attribution of contradictions is concerned, the only pertinent part of the cultural context is the propositional itself.* [89]

Clearly, however, we want this part to be as big as possible, because it is the pool from which items are drawn to resolve apparent contradictions and therefore the undesirable effect of settling for a smaller reservoir is that other 'societies' will be made out to be (i) more prone to inconsistency than they are, and, (ii) than we are – since we all know our own pools best. Thus one methodological objection to adopting our rule is that by limiting reference to the CS context of 'other ideas', and propositional ones at that, we have automatically and artificially reduced the type and number of items which can legitimately be consulted – because many of them do not come in the form of propositions. In short, a critic might say that our rule produces a job specification for a small pool which will boost inconsistencies and give a boost to ethno-centricism.

I agree that much of the time 'other ideas' are not presented and packaged to meet the logician's requirements (that is, scientific texts and religious creeds probably are exceptional). More usually we do confront them as sentences, utterances and recorded fragments but in fact the last thing that our rule enjoins is that they should be sent packing immediately because they are not fully propositional (that is they are capable of being interpreted in several ways and therefore appear to assert several things at once, or one of several things without it being clear which). On the contrary, the methodological injunction associated with our rule is 'make the fullest possible reference to the admissible context in an attempt to complete propositions'. Although this context remains firmly restricted to 'other ideas', it is recognized that any approach leading to errors (i) and (ii) above is both self-vitiating and socially vicious and therefore the rule is completely resistant to decontextualization.[90]

Ironically the same cannot be said for many who would oppose our rule, and particularly those adept at extricating intelligibility from the oddest sayings. For these are the arch-decontextualisers – absorbed in displaying their own cryptographic virtuosity (despite the odds) rather than demonstrating the common sense of others (despite oddities of expression). Witness here the common abuse of anthropology by certain philosophers who perversely pluck an enigmatic saying from an exotic text and then speculate freely on what the natives could conceivably have been getting at. Here we should note that the context evoked to disclose intelligibility is the philosophers' own and not the natives', for the procedure is to make the armchair creak under the pressure of speculation rather than to get out of it and consult every available text of native sayings, or if need be, go into the field and ask if the locals can supply contextual clarification (that is, more sayings). Indeed this is the main attraction of using anthropology – full reference to the complete ideational context is often ruled out because it is impossibly expensive to track down or, even better, is irretrievably lost. (Thus the prizes go to speculative ingenuity which 'shows' that all native talk about contents of cooking pots is really the statement of cosmological recipes, or better still that cosmologies are actually about raw carrots.) But puzzles can always be invented by decontextualization from the 'other ideas' which give them sense (see note 44), and to many of 'us' most statements in modern science seem just as enigmatic because their ideational context is unfamiliar. Yet in that area, fullest reference to the 'other ideas' available at the time is what makes sense of (false) assertions about the existence of 'phlogiston' or the 'embryo as homunculus', *not* their transposition into a modern context where the only way of saving their perpetrators from the charge of inanity is to foist some meaning on them which cannot be disavowed from the grave.

In sum, the fullest possible application should be made to the CS context in order to rescue intelligibility from ambiguity and to obtain the highest warranted ratio of propositions to utterances. Methodologically this may mean asking the subjects to supply contextual clarification by amplifying on previous sayings or commenting on existing texts. Where the subjects are not extant this implies an even closer scrutiny of texts with the same aim in view – an explication of what else they knew and what other information was available to them – for this was the only material from which they could fabricate both true and false propositions and therefore from which contradictions and consistencies could arise.

Exactly the same is the case for subjects' *own* sayings about their Socio-Cultural environment which are as admissible as contextual referents as any 'other ideas' about anything else (and can be used in the same way to complete one another). The fact that what was known to them or what they could find out about their social environment might (and this is not at all self-evident) more obviously have been manipulated by 'other people' than what they could know about their physical environment is of no concern in the assertion of a contradiction. For all propositions are based on restricted material and all restrictions were caused by something, but the logical relations which ensue between them are emergent properties and thus irreducible to the biological, geographical or Socio-Cultural causation involved. We are dealing with the *results* of limited knowledge and it is therefore the fact of the limitation which counts, not its source.

Thus the methodological injunction remains – 'incorporate from the ideational context only that which is needful to complete propositions or to demonstrate that a given "saying" is non-propositional'. If this is successfully performed for two items, then, assuming the adequacy of translation and the invariance of logic, it becomes possible to characterize the relations between them as contradictory or consistent. In the process we must thus expect to encounter some items, which although meaningful to (certain) subjects, are not of propositional status. These have been the main source of the great interpretative debate between the 'intellectualists' and the 'symbolists'[91] which is of relevance here in so far as both sides have assumed that they are indeed dealing with native propositions, but what is being asserted as true or false is a matter for theoretical determination by the investigator. (This is yet another instance where 'sayings' and 'meanings' are compacted, with the familiar unhelpful consequences.)

Instead I would follow those who have maintained that we confront a difficult methodological problem rather than a choice between theoretical alternatives. In this connection Sperber has argued very persuasively that people hold their *factual* beliefs (which are true or false) quite differently from their *representational* beliefs (which do not pretend to propositional status). Neglect of this distinction is a systematic methodological deficiency:

> Most accounts of beliefs are written as if the utterances of so-called informants should all be taken on the same level, irrespective of whether they are produced in answer to the ethnographer's queries, during ordinary social intercourse, on ritual occasions, in judicial proceedings, etc. All native utterances get distilled together; their quintessence is then displayed as an homogeneous world-view where, indeed, no epistemological differentiation of beliefs occurs. This, however, is a fact of ethnography, not of culture.[92]

Lukes also presses his argument to the same conclusion. The problems of how beliefs are held and should be interpreted involve methodological difficulties but this does not render them matters for theoretical arbitration. Instead these questions 'are susceptible to empirical investigation. And if no given piece of evidence is decisive between alternative interpretations, some crucial mass of it will not fail to be so.'[93] Methodologically, then, it is not easy to get at the propositional uncluttered by a mass of Socio-Cultural overlay belonging both to those investigated and imported by investigators as part of their theoretical baggage. But this only makes the process of disentanglement, which is a necessary precondition for using our rule, a matter of methodological ingenuity not of theoretical intractability. In the process one will have learned a good deal about 'meanings' as well as 'sayings', about the S-C as well as the CS, but an approach based upon analytical dualism enjoins that the two should be kept separate in order to examine their interplay. Two implications of following this rule are worth drawing out in conclusion.

First, it involves always taking what people say/write seriously and doing this *even* when we are sure that they mean something different. To anticipate an obvious objection, I do agree that there are *certain circumstances* in which we can know unequivocally that public 'sayings' and private 'meanings' are at variance with one another, for example, formal speeches in Parliament, the writings of those living under dictatorships, or some of the things we say to our children. In all these cases the speaker/writer can tell us (and give good reason) why what they said or wrote was not what, or exactly what, they meant. Nevertheless the distinction is worth maintaining because here the 'sayings' tell us a good deal about their interconnections with the rest of the Cultural System – about what is logically entailed by parliamentary procedure (which is a completely different question from why people subscribe to it); what the logical consequences are of doing something unlawful (which again is entirely distinct from the acceptability of the laws in question); or about the logical restrictions on communication – we tell a four-year-old that it rains 'because the clouds open' since the child is incapable of grasping all the links in a full account of precipitation. Correspondingly our 'meanings' in these circumstances indicate a good deal about our Socio-Cultural attitudes towards the Cultural System – whether we feel bound to it or constrained by it, or, in the last case, of how we live with it and transmit it to others. Once again the vital interplay between them would be lost if 'sayings' and 'meanings' were run together or (when possible) if the valid meaning were substituted for the public 'text'.

Secondly, following this rule, two items are contradictory if no other CS item can reduce them to an apparent contradiction. And the implication is that this remains the case whether or not the population involved is aware of the inconsistency. An objective contradiction remains just that at the level of the Cultural System, even if it never troubles anyone in his Socio-Cultural life. Thus Gellner's *igurramen* must themselves be aware of the contradictory requirements of their roles, even if other Berbers are not, but this awareness is not what makes *agurram*-hood inconsistent. Equally, Evans-Pritchard's account of witchcraft among the Azande, which he holds to involve logical contradictions, continues to embody these (if his account is correct), despite the twenty-two Socio-Cultural reasons he advances to explain why this incoherence never bothers them and is not in fact recognized by them.[94] This points to a very important category of cases where the objective Systemic contradiction (CS) has no (S-C) meaning and would therefore be missed by those who rejected 'sayings' in favour of 'meanings', but which may still be socially influential, since we do not have to be aware of all the things that impinge upon us or may come to do so.

What this rule proscribes is any appeal to the social environment in which contradictions manifest themselves and are lived out in one way or another – in unawareness, by strategic coping, or direct confrontation, etc. Considered as a *context*, the Socio-Cultural level can do *absolutely nothing* to resolve a logical contradiction (by showing it to be only apparent). Another way of putting this is that *contextually* contradictions at the CS level are *not dependent* on any of the goings on at the S-C level, since logical relations are independent of causal ones at T_1 (though not vice versa – a very important asymmetry as will be seen later). Again let us be crystal clear what is being asserted: I am not claiming that the two levels are independent of one another; the whole point of analytical dualism is to be able to investigate the relations between them. Obviously the S-C level crucially effects the CS level – after all, the latter originates from the former, from ideas, beliefs, 'texts' dreamed up by people and people continue to form theories, formulate novel creeds and write new texts, which become part of the CS level and may indeed transform it at T_2. But all this concerns the interplay over time of the two levels. Analytically, at any given point in time, the items populating the CS realm have escaped their creators and have logical relationships among one another which are totally independent, at that time, of what the population notices, knows, feels, or believes about them. At future time what people do about them *may* be highly significant for the CS universe, but only if the things done in turn enter the CS register (as a new theory superseding an old one, a new ethic replacing a previous one and so forth) in which case they, in turn, escape their progenitors and immediately assume logical relations amongst themselves and with prior ideas. The crucial point therefore is that analytically, for the time being, that is at any given T_1, Cultural System relations are not context-dependent upon Socio-Cultural relations.

Consequently in 'asserting the existence of a contradiction', we never need to and never should descend from the logical to the causal level, for of all the interesting bearings that Socio-Cultural interaction has upon the Cultural System, the ability of the former to arbitrate on the logical status of the latter is not one of them.

Those who attempt to treat the Socio-Cultural level as the context of the Cultural System can learn nothing more about existing logical relations from existing causal ones. Instead, all they do is to blur the issue because in fact they are embarking on a separate enterprise, that of understanding or explaining. They enter the realm of trying to understand the meaning of X and Y to participants, of attempting to explain how a population can hold X and Y simultaneously, or why other people consider X and Y antipathetic. These are vital questions (which will be addressed when we examine the Socio-Cultural level), but they are quite distinct from whether X and Y are in contradiction according to the canons of logic. What they are in fact about is how people live with logical contradiction or logical consistency in their Cultural system. Yet this is precisely what we want to explore; to make it part of our tools of identification is to rob us of our topic.

Notes

1 Mary Hesse holds that this is a 'positivist point in the sense that it presupposes that there can be no language unless we (now, or perhaps at some future time) understand it as a language' in which beliefs are expressed (*Revolutions and Reconstructions in the Philosophy of Science*, Harvester, Brighton, 1980, p. 37). On the contrary I would argue that the untranslatable *could* constitute a different Cultural System but since it was nothing more than the emission of sounds (marks or smells etc.) it *could* equally be a literary spoof or a deliberate randomization of sounds. Even given her gesticulating Martians and strong circumstantial evidence for their using language, if we failed to establish consistent signs for 'yes'

and 'no' then we could never *know* that they had either language or beliefs – but the relativist would be in exactly the same position.

2 Cultural Systems are open ones and in principle actors can penetrate any part of them, though in practice there may be both physical, social and intellectual barriers preventing some or all of them from doing so. At times, for example, attempts are made at the Socio-Cultural level to make the Cultural System operate as a closed one. Ironically there is no better evidence of the openness of the System to its social environment than efforts to manipulate it in this way: ultimately the failure of all such attempts from Edicts of Seclusion, stringent censorship, to Top Security measures show that, because of their intrinsic ease of transfer, ideas are generically incapable of closure. Equally, at times physical obstacles like uncrossable mountains or unnavigable oceans have appeared to shut one part of the cultural universe off from another. But even under these circumstances, since we cannot predict future discoveries, then at any given T_1 penetration is not simply a principle for it may be accomplished at any moment. Historically (and that also means to the best of our historical ability) it could well be maintained that at least two different 'societies' S1 and S2 (tribes or islanders for example) possessed cultures which had emerged autonomously and operated in isolation with no knowledge of the other *prior* to T_1. (The possibility of the discovery of S1 by S2 or vice versa at T^1 remains open of course.) If such isolation can be established there appears to be no objection to someone asserting the plurality of Cultural Systems as a temporary empirical fact, provided that this state of affairs is accepted to be time-bounded and is not assumed to have been universal for or almost synonymous with primitive societies (many of which had extensive contacts).

3 The use of T_1, T_2 etc does not imply linear cultural development through time. Certainly a strong case can be made for this in relation to scientific knowledge over the last four centuries, but allowance must also be made for periods of cultural stagnation (i.e. T_1 lasts for centuries) and of cultural regression (i.e. the CS at T_2 is impoverished compared with T_1).

4 Karl R. Popper, *Objective Knowledge*, Oxford, Clarendon, 1972, pp. 298–9.

5 It might immediately be objected that all that is intelligible is not propositional – the usual contenders being either desires, questions or commands. There, however, intelligibility rests upon assumptions, which involve propositions, that certain states of affairs do obtain. Other contenders are concrete objects, artefacts or events. Here the relevant proposition is the relation asserted to hold between them or their parts, since sense experience alone never yields knowledge without a reflective analysis, entailing language, of what we are experiencing. For knowledge is knowledge of propositions and can only be known by discriminating between abstract features which are aspects of the concrete situation or object.

6 'The student of the history of ideas will find that ideas have a kind of life (this is a metaphor, of course); that they can be misunderstood, rejected, and forgotten; that they can reassert themselves, and come to life again. Without metaphor, however, we can say that they are not identical with any man's thought, or belief; that they can exist even if universally misunderstood, and rejected.' Popper, *Objective Knowledge*, p. 300.

7 Peter Winch, *The Idea of a Social Science*, Routledge & Kegan Paul, London, 1958, p. 126.

8 Peter Winch, 'Understanding a primitive society', in Bryan R. Wilson (ed.), *Rationality*, Oxford, Blackwell, 1979, p. 82.

9 Steven Lukes, 'Some problems about rationality', in Wilson (ed.), *Rationality*, p. 204.

10 'One might sum up all this by saying that nothing is more false than the claim that, for a given assertion, *its use is its meaning*. On the contrary, its use may depend on its lack of meaning, its ambiguity, its possession of wholly different and incompatible meanings in different contexts, *and* on the fact that, at the same time, it as it were emits the impression of possessing a consistent meaning throughout – on retaining, for instance, the aura of a justification valid only in one context when used in quite another.' Ernest Gellner, 'Concepts and society', ibid., p. 45.

11 Amitai Etzioni, *The Active Society*, New York, Free Press, 1968, pp. 26–7.

12 Winch, *The Idea of a Social Science*, p. 102.

13 Ibid., pp. 100–1.

14 Lukes, 'Some problems about rationality', p. 209–10.

15 'What, then, is special about Identity, Contradiction and Inference? The answer is, I believe, that these notions set the conditions for the existence not only of a particular kind of logical reasoning but also of any kind whatever . . . They express, rather requirements for something's being a system of logical reasoning at all. To look for alternatives is like looking for a novel means of transport which is novel not only in that it has no engine but also that it does not convey bodies from one place to another.' Martin Hollis, 'Reason and ritual', in Wilson (ed.), *Rationality*, pp. 231–2.

16 Winch, 'Understanding a primitive society', p. 100. Immediately, however, he resists the implication of having accepted general logical criteria by adding that 'these formal requirements tell us nothing about what in particular is to *count* as consistency'. This seems to be an innocuous statement that it is the contents of propositions rather than their logical relations which are socially variable.

17 The main works to which reference is made are: David Bloor, *Knowledge and Social Imagery*, London, Routledge & Kegan Paul, 1976; Barry Barnes, *Interests and the Growth of Knowledge*, London, Routledge & Kegan Paul, 1977; David Bloor, 'Polyhedra and the abominations of Leviticus', *The British Journal for the History of Science*, vol. 11, no. 39, 1978; 'The strengths of the strong programme', *Phil. Soc. Sci.*, 11, 1981; Barry Barnes, 'On the "hows" and "whys" of cultural change', *Social Studies of Science*, vol. 11, 1981; Barry Barnes and David Bloor, 'Relativism, rationalism and the sociology of knowledge', in Martin Hollis and Steven Lukes (eds.), *Rationality and Relativism*, Oxford, Blackwell, 1982; David Bloor, *Wittgenstein: A Social Theory of Knowledge*, Macmillan, London, 1983.

18 H. M. Collins, 'What is TRASP?: the radical programme as a methodological imperative', *Phil. Soc. Sci.*, 11, 1981. Instead of TRASP, 'the tenet of symmetry implies that we must treat the natural world as though it in no way constrains what is believed to be' (p. 218). That the strong programme is incompatible with a realist ontology is a conclusion hard to avoid – at least on most interpretations of it.

19 Bloor, *Knowledge and Social Imagery*, p. 5. This principle opposes 'conventional' philosophical approaches for their supposedly 'teleological' character, i.e. for the assumption that the truth or reasonableness of a belief was itself sufficient to explain its adoption. Simultaneously this wrongly absolved the philosopher of any need to advance causes for such beliefs and equally wrongly condemned the sociologist to reserve his causal explanations for cases of error.

20 For a general criticism of this position see Larry Laudan, 'The pseudo-science of science', *Phil. Soc. Sci.*, 11, 1981. Bloor's reply 'The strengths of the strong programme' is in the same issue.

21 Barnes and Bloor, 'Relativism, rationalism and the sociology of knowledge', p. 27.

22 Bloor writes of Mannheim: 'Despite his determination to set up causal and symmetrical canons of explanation, his nerve failed him when it came to such apparently autonomous subjects as mathematics and natural science', *Knowledge and Social Imagery*, p. 8.
23 Erik Millstone, 'A framework for the sociology of knowledge', *Social Studies of Science*, vol. 8, 1978, p. 117.
24 Bloor, *Knowledge and the Social Imagery*, p. 141.
25 Ibid., pp. 88f.
26 Thus by driving the social element through the gap between physical reality and the mathematical principles imposed on it, 'Bloor has opened the way to the idea – indispensible for his entire project – of socially determined "variations in mathematical thinking". Each such variant, then, constitutes – in parallel to the Kuhnian "paradigm" in natural science – an "alternative mathematics", and the relation of these variants to one another is analogous to that which (in Kuhn's account) exists between different paradigms.' Gad Freudenthal, 'How strong is Dr Bloor's "strong programme"?', *Studies in History and Philosophy of Science*, vol. 10, 1979, p. 72.
27 Bloor, *Knowledge and Social Imagery*, pp. 95–6.
28 Freudenthal, 'How strong is Dr Bloor's "strong programme"?' pp. 73f. He concludes that Bloor's theoretical affirmations about an alternative mathematics and 'above all his claim that logical necessity is a social phenomenon – are not tenable and, moreover, that the allegedly confirming case-studies do not, in fact, bear upon them' (p. 82).
29 Bloor purports to 'offer illustrations of 4 types of variation in mathematical thought each of which can be traced back to social causes'. However, his delineation of the examples to come represents a departure from his original specification of an alternative, i.e. alien consensus on something we deem erroneous and which entails violation of our notions of logical propriety. The four instances are '(i) variation in the broad cognitive style of mathematics; (ii) variation in the framework of associations, relationships, uses, analogies, and the metaphysical implications attributed to mathematics; (iii) variations in the meanings attached to computations and symbolic manipulations; (iv) variation in rigour and the type of reasoning which is held to prove a conclusion'. *Knowledge and Social Imagery*, p. 97.
30 Ibid., p. 98.
31 Exactly the same argument can be used against Bloor's most extended example, the polyhedron as a negotiated mathematical concept. Indeed since much of his argument deals with the fact that for a given set of definitions of what constitutes polyhedra a theorem may be shown not to hold, then the notion of mathematical validity is shared by the negotiators rather than being the subject of negotiation. See Bloor, 'Polyhedra and the abominations of Leviticus'.
32 Bloor, *Knowledge and Social Imagery*, p. 103.
33 Freudenthal, 'How strong is Dr Bloor's "strong programme"?', p. 77.
34 Barnes and Bloor, 'Relativism, rationalism and the sociology of knowledge,' p. 41 n.
35 Ibid., pp. 41–2n.
36 Ibid., p. 43.
37 The following are typical avowals of upwards conflationism: 'When Durkheim and Mauss said that the classification of things reproduces the classification of men, they were nearer to the truth than their critics have allowed', Bloor, 'The strengths of the strong programme', p. 212; 'People, it is agreed, are not under the control of their discourse or their own verbal artefacts: the relationship

is the other way round', Barnes, 'On the "hows" and "whys" of cultural change', p. 481.

38 'At whatever point it is found necessary, the explanation of credibility may swing from social to biological causes', Barnes and Bloor, 'Relativism, rationalism and the sociology of knowledge', p. 44.

39 Ibid.

40 Mary Hesse, *Revolutions and Reconstructions in the Philosophy of Science*, Brighton, Harvester, 1980, p. 38.

41 Ibid., pp. 37–8.

42 Obviously I am not arguing that only the propositional is intelligible and even where *beliefs* or *theories* are concerned, I fully accept Sperber's argument for the incidence of 'pre-propositional' ideas in many societies and areas of discourse. The point is however that if and when such pre-propositional terms are completed, then their completion is in conformity with, and not in abrogation of, the principle of contradiction whose invariance is defended here. See Dan Sperber, 'Apparently irrational beliefs', in Hollis and Lukes (eds.), *Rationality and Relativism.*

43 J. C. Crocker, 'My brother the parrot', in J. D. Sapir and J. C. Crocker (eds.), *The Social Use of Metaphor: Essays on the Anthropology of Rhetoric*, Philadelphia, University of Pennsylvania Press, 1977.

44 As Sperber comments: 'So, the enigmatic subject-matter of so many learned discussions turns out to be but an indirect form of expression well within the bounds of commonsense rationality. No doubt, many other puzzling cases around the world could be handled in similar fashion'. Dan Sperber, 'Apparently irrational beliefs', in Hollis and Lukes (eds.), *Rationality and Relativism*, p. 153. Doubtless too we can 'invent' puzzles by treating doctrines like Trinitarianism as if we had just come across an isolated hymn containing the strange assertion: 'Firmly I believe and truly God is three and God is one.'

45 Hesse, *Revolutions and Reconstructions in the Philosophy of Science*, p. 38.

46 '(C)laims to have identified the metaphorical uses of words and gestures must be rationally justified. This involves cashing the metaphors and therefore the notion of "metaphorical use" never has any explanatory force.' Martin Hollis, 'Reason and ritual', in Wilson (ed.), *Rationality*, p. 238.

47 Henry Bettenson (ed.), *Documents of the Christian Church*, Oxford University Press, 1967. See section IV, 'The person and work of Christ'.

48 Sperber, 'Apparently irrational beliefs', p. 175.

49 The key statement about Apostolic succession, advanced by St Iranaeus and used by the Catholic Church against its doctrinal rebels ever since, is that 'with this church, because of its position of leadership and authority, must needs agree every church, that is, the faithful everywhere' p. 69. This basing of belief on authority is remarkably clear in the original Creed of Nicea (AD 325), where after the profession of articles of faith are specially listed seven propositions which 'the Catholic and Apostolic Church anathematizes', Bettenson (ed.), *Documents of the Christian Church*, p. 25.

50 Hesse, *Revolutions and Reconstructions in the Philosophy of Science*, p. 38.

51 Ibid., p. 39.

52 Barnes and Bloor, 'Relativism, rationalism and the sociology of knowledge', p. 39.

53 W. Newton-Smith, 'Relativism and the possibility of interpretation', in Hollis and Lukes (eds.), *Rationality and Relativism*, p. 114.

54 Hollis, 'Reason and ritual', p. 238.

55 Barnes and Bloor, 'Relativism, rationalism and the sociology of knowledge', p. 38.

56 'What is here true of two languages applies equally to one.' Hollis, 'Reason and ritual', p. 230.

57 This is the implication of their conceptual relativism. 'One clear implication arises from the character of concepts as arrays of judgements of sameness. Every such array, being the product of a unique sequence of judgements, is itself unique. No array in one culture can be unproblematically set into an identity with an array from another culture', Barnes and Bloor, 'Relativism, rationalism and the sociology of knowledge', p. 39. But what is a culture to them? Clearly not 'all English language speakers', nor anything so big as a nation – a region then? a community? a locality? a family? or a small group of like-minded thinkers?

58 Ibid., p. 36.

59 Ibid., p. 38.

60 Note the relativists' ambivalence *vis à vis* the notion of a 'simple perceptual situation'. On the one hand they wish to deny them to any rationalist translator in the field, but on the other hand they are quintessential to Barnes' and Bloor's account of language learning, either by the young native or by the mature anthropologist (see pp. 122–6). Their account of learning concepts through processes of ostension and correction, leading the similarities and differences between 'birds' and 'aeroplanes' to be arranged and judged in a particular way is in fact perfectly compatible with Hollis's procedure *for* establishing the bridgehead. Indeed if the latter is not on, neither is language learning on this account.

61 R. Bulmer, 'Why is the cassowary not a bird?', *Man*, n.s., 2, 1967.

62 Barnes and Bloor, 'Relativism, rationalism and the sociology of knowledge', pp. 39–40.

63 Mary Hesse, *The Structure of Scientific Inference*, London, Macmillan, 1974, pp. 16f.

64 Thus Lukes appears to be completely correct that 'the considerations advanced by Barnes and Bloor – that classifications are "socially sustained" and patterns of knowledge "institutionalised", that language learning involves the acquisition from the culture of specific conventions, that concepts seen as arrays of judgements of sameness may not coincide across cultures, and that the "facts" are "theory-laden" and have different imports to different scientists depending on their theoretical frameworks – all of this argues at best for conceptual and perhaps perceptual relativism.' Lukes, 'Relativism in its place', in Hollis and Lukes (eds.), *Rationality and Relativism*, p. 266. Evidential support can be adduced against perceptual relativism (e.g. colour discrimination appears to be universal rather than linguistically determined. See B. Berlin and P. Kay, *Basic Color Terms*, Berkeley, University of California Press, 1969) and against conceptual relativism (since variations can be given a non-relativistic explanation). And, once let down by linguistic determinism in areas like basic colour terminology or geometric forms (where the human perceptual system appears to determine linguistic categories rather than the reverse), then their argument amounts to an assertion that the fact that something is round and red plays the same role in leading us to believe that it is and that it isn't. The absurdity of this conclusion undermines the equivalence postulate of the 'strong programme'. See also Eleanor Rosch, 'Human Categorization', in N. Warren (ed.), *Studies in Cross-Cultural Psychology*, vol. 1, 1977.

65 With one exception the whole bridgehead procedure is empirically grounded. The only *a priori* assumption made is that the very possibility of meaningful disagreement is entirely dependent on *some* foundation in agreement, which no state of affairs can falsify. 'But *what* that foundation is, what must be presupposed for the interpretation of beliefs and belief systems to proceed is in a sense an empirical matter, or at least revisable in the light of experience', Lukes, 'Relativism in its place', p. 272.

66 Hesse, *Revolutions and Reconstructions in the Philosophy of Science*, p. 56.
67 Lukes, 'Relativism in its place', pp. 264–74.
68 Moreover, inspection of references shows the use of translations to be common practice amongst members of the school. It might seem uncharitable to note that the bibliography of *Knowledge and Social Imagery* contains no item which is not in English, were it not for the fact that I find translation both unobjectionable and necessary. It is Bloor who has objected to it, yet for example he states that his illustrations of Diophantus's thought are 'taken from Heath's (1910) translation and commentary', *Knowledge and Social Imagery*, p. 99.
69 Martin Hollis, 'The limits of irrationality', in Wilson (ed.), *Rationality*, p. 214.
70 Barnes and Bloor, 'Relativism, rationalism and the sociology of knowledge', p. 37.
71 Ernest Gellner, *Thought and Change*, London, Weidenfeld & Nicolson, 1964, pp. 105–13.
72 Newton-Smith, 'Relativism and the possibility of interpretation', p. 114.
73 Ibid., p. 115.
74 Gellner, 'Concepts and society', p. 48.
75 Ibid., p. 43.
76 Cf. Hollis, 'Reason and rituals', p. 226.
77 Gellner, 'Concepts and society', p. 22.
78 Ibid., p. 19.
79 Ibid., p. 43.
80 Ibid., p. 44.
81 Ibid., p. 45.
82 Ibid., pp. 38–9.
83 Ibid., p. 48.
84 Ernest Gellner, 'The savage and the modern mind', in Robin Horton and Ruth Finnegan (eds.), *Modes of Thought*, London, Faber, 1973, p. 169.
85 This Gellner continues to demonstrate, in ibid. However, in the lead-up to the statement cited about the need for a Dividing Line, he accepts that 'There are two principal methods normally employed for identifying, isolating a "belief system": one uses the observer's own sense of coherence, and the other invokes written sources and documents. The possibility of bias or arbitrariness inherent in the first method is obvious. But the danger is clearly not absent from the second method either.' Ibid., p. 168. However, while in 'Concepts and society' Gellner had really plumped for the first method, this article represents a cautious shift to the second, which is what I am exploring here.
86 Eleanor Rosch, 'Universals and cultural specifics in human categorization', in R. Brislin, S. Bochner and W. Lonner (eds.), *Cross-Cultural Perspectives on Learning*, New York, Halstead Press, 1975. E. Rosch and C. B. Mervis, 'Family resemblances: studies in the internal structure of categories', *Cognitive Psychology*, vol. 7, 1975.
87 Eleanor Rosch, 'Linguistic relativity', in A. Silverstein (ed.), *Human Communication: Theoretical Perspectives*, New York, Halstead Press, 1974.
88 Eleanor Rosch, 'Principles of categorization', in E. Rosch and B. Lloyd (eds.), *Cognition and categorization*, Hillsdale, New Jersey, Erlbaum, 1978, p. 29.
89 Consequently for *this* purpose not only is the S-C context irrelevant, but so too are tracts of the CS itself because some of its constituents, like musical scores or paintings are not propositional and thus whatever their importance, these components cannot figure in contradictions.
90 Incidentally this rule solves the problem (at the CS level) of the context itself being socially specific and therefore precluding any cross-contextual generaliza-

tions. For if what is being dealt with is exclusively the presence or absence of logical connections, the specificity of their contents is immaterial. Moreover, since it is none of our business to pass judgements on contents we must therefore be prepared to declare that an alien belief system based on some metaphysical entity (let us call it 'Alpha'), the existence of which is not open to falsification, may be of a much higher logical consistency (i.e. a coherent 'Alpha theology') than that of a modern science-based Cultural System.

This is what Hollis has termed taking the stance of the 'unbelieving theologian'. Any religion may begin in revelation (unintelligible or perhaps incredible to the investigator) but its communication demands theology and it is no accident that every world religion has laboured for centuries on the consistency of the latter. Without this, how else could unbelievers find the logic of many theologians impeccable but still reject their premisses? Only because it is the contents of propositions which may take 'many and varied forms', but not the logical relations between them. Thus I trust that we have disposed of both the supposed difficulty of contextual specificity and the potential criticism that ethnocentricism lurks within the use of logical criteria to identify contradictions. On the contrary, logic, being universal, is also neutral. It is an empirical matter whether any particular modern Cultural System turns out to manifest fewer contradictions than medieval or primitive ones. Using logical criteria does not stack the cards in favour of either modernity or the primitive world.

91 Cf. E. Leach, 'Ritual' in *International Encyclopaedia of the Social Sciences*, vol. 13, New York, Macmillan, 1968; M. E. Spiro, 'Religion: problems of definition and explanation', in M. Banton (ed.), *Anthropological Approaches to the Study of Religion*, London, Tavistock, 1966; S. Turner, *Sociological Explanation as Translation*, Cambridge, Cambridge University Press, 1980; Robin Horton, 'Tradition and modernity revisited', in Hollis and Lukes (eds.), *Rationality and Relativism*; D. Sperber, *Rethinking Symbolism*, Cambridge, Cambridge University Press, 1975.

92 Sperber, 'Apparently irrational beliefs', in Hollis and Lukes (eds.), *Rationality and Relativism*, p. 165.

93 Lukes, 'Relativism in its place', p. 292.

94 Evans-Pritchard, *Witchcraft, Oracles and Magic Among the Azande*, Oxford, Oxford University Press, pp. 475–9.

21

THE PRAXIOLOGY OF LEGAL JUDGEMENT

Alan Norrie

> And this universal language (law) comes just at the right time to lend a new strength to the psychology of the masters: it allows it always to take other men as objects, to describe and condemn at one stroke. It is an adjectival psychology, it knows only how to endow its victims with epithets, it is ignorant of everything about the actions themselves, save the guilty category into which they are forced to fit.
>
> (Barthes, 1973, 45)

> When a science goes round in circles without managing to overcome its contradictions it is always because it is based on concepts, on a definition of its object, which have not been subjected to a sufficiently radical critique, one which is sufficiently well-informed philosophically.
>
> (Sève, 1975, 20)

1 The political nature of juridical individualism

[Established] principles of individual justice and rational legalism [. . .] underlie the orthodox theory and practice of criminal law, [but] at the same time [there is perpetual] ambivalence within that theory to them. [. . .] I suggest that the time ha[s] come to move beyond attempts to shore up or reconstruct the criminal law so as better to match principle to practice [or to resolve contradiction]. I propose [. . .] an historical approach to the principles of the criminal law, and identif[y] [a] link between the legal forms of social control that emerged in the early nineteenth century and the [contradictory] ideologies of the Enlightenment [that underlie and inform them].

The link [is] provided by the two Enlightenment-inspired philosophies of retributivism and utilitarianism, and the key to understanding the nature of the law lay in the contradictions at the heart of these two philosophies of punishment. These contradictions were historically generated in the modern

Source: *Crime, Reason and History*, London: Butterworths, 1993, pp. 221–60

period by the interplay between an abstract individualist ideology of just punishment and the reality of crime as a social and political phenomenon. First, crime was the product of the conditions in which the lower social orders lived and against which they struggled, but in philosophical ideology it was the product of a free individual for which punishment was deserved. Secondly, this abstract ideology represented the social world as consensual, whereas in reality it was racked by social and political conflict [. . .]

These conflicts within ideology underlay the tensions and contradictions within the criminal law. Liberal theorists like Hart have elaborated the retributive and utilitarian principles which inform that law. If those philosophical principles are fundamentally flawed, we should expect to see the results of this in the law itself. The central ideological figure within Enlightenment thought is the abstract juridical individual. [The following figure charts] the various ways in which this homuncular form operates within the criminal law, analysing the tensions and contradictions to which it gives rise.

(i) Psychological individualism

There are two main elements within the ideological form of the juridical individual. One is a psychological individualism, which operates in two ways in the criminal law. First, it screens out a range of possible excuses that stem from the context within which individuals operate. Within the philosophy of punishment, it was the abstract freedom of the individual which justified punishment retributively (Norrie, 1991), and it was the contradiction between the ideal image of the free individual and the social reality of poverty and need that undermined that theory, leading to its historical downfall. Enlightenment-derived ideology legitimates punishment on the basis of individual responsibility. But in order to do so, it must ensure that the individual be 'sealed off' from the social relations which give rise to action. Within the criminal law, it is necessary for the practice of attributing fault to individuals that this abstract form of individualism be maintained through a variety of doctrinal mechanisms. The criminal law operates with a form of psychological individualism, but this central ideological form involves a constant work of political closure to keep the social context at bay.

The second, related operation performed by this psychological individualism is the apparent depoliticisation and de-moralisation of both the philosophy of punishment and the criminal law. Neumann wrote that:

> The philosophical system appropriate to the *Rechtsstaat* is that of Enlightenment . . . [B]ut only because man was seen as universal man, as infinitely perfect being without individual features, . . . was . . . a pre-established harmony . . . between state and society . . . possible.
>
> (1987, 70)

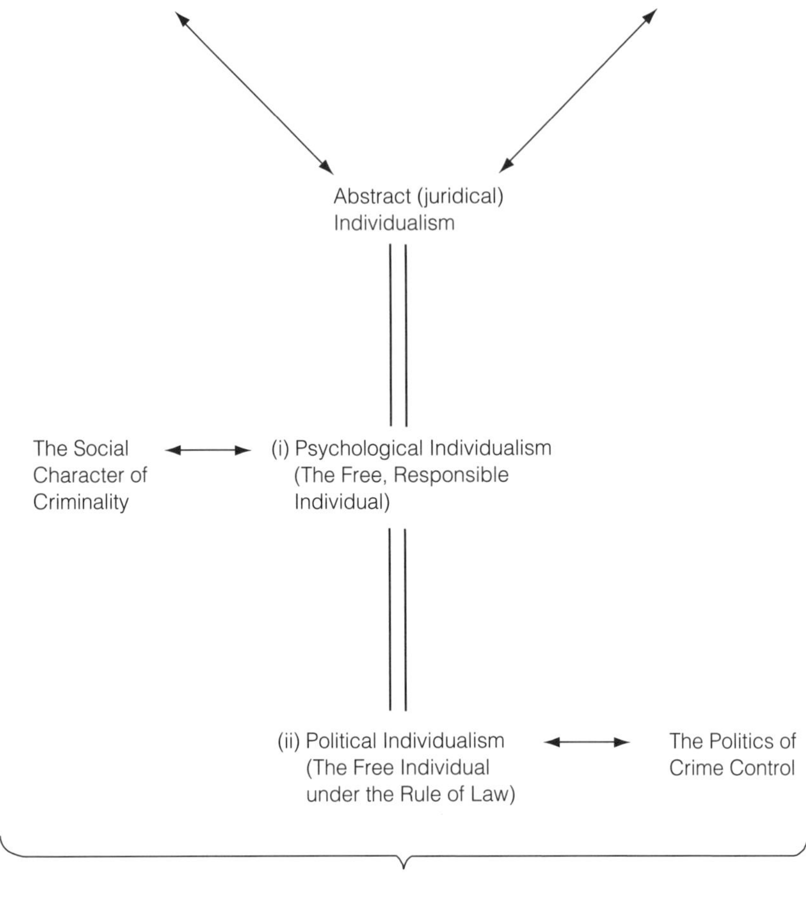

Liberal theory wishes to portray the criminal law as existing within a consensual world in which all individuals *qua* individuals come together under the law. This is central to the theory and practice of the criminal law, as well as to the philosophical legitimation of the criminal justice system as a whole. But in a society based upon deep social and political conflicts, this representation can only be maintained if the conflicts can, so far as possible, be excluded from the court of law. Harmony between state and society in the context of the criminal process can only be maintained if social conflicts are filtered out in advance. The concept of the abstract psychological individual contributes to this political goal by removing such conflicts from the courtroom.

Thus the psychological individual at the heart of the criminal law is a political and ideological construction which operates to seal off the question of individual culpability from issues concerning the relationship between individual agency and social context. It seeks to exclude a broad view of social relations which would locate individual actions within their determinative context, and to exclude moral and political counter-discourses from the law. The concept of the abstract psychological subject or citizen which the law fashions stands as a denial of the social, moral and political context within which individuals operate. Presenting the question of responsibility in an apolitical, amoral and asocial form, it performs a negative and repressive political task of closure and exclusion.

In considering the nature of law, it is important to understand that the political element in this construction of the legal individual is an active though indirect one. Abstract psychological individualism is presented as an ideal and apolitical representation of human agency, but it stands in opposition to the realities of concrete social individuality, which threaten to undermine the conviction process. The work of excluding those 'external' realities is practical and ongoing, and determines the evolving shape of legal doctrine. The abstract form of the law is used to police the borders of the conviction process (that is, the law) against contextual raiding parties. There is a constant political task of maintaining the abstract psychological boundaries of doctrine against corruptive invasion from the socially, morally and politically constituted 'other'.

(ii) Political individualism

The second main element within the law's abstract individualism, which is more directly political, stems from the Janus-faced character of the legal form (Norrie, 1991, 199–203). The abstract psychological individual performs a negative and repressive role in establishing an ideal subject or citizen to 'stand before' the judge and to justify the state's punitive repression of actual individuals. However, the juridical subject also plays a positive and affirmative role in that it 'stands up for' the individual against the state even if it is presented in an abstract and repressive form. The citizen in law stands as an ideal representative of the real person against any overweening power claimed by the state. The liberal theory of citizenship denies actual subjectivity, but still establishes an abstract form of individual right. It is upon a conception of political individualism that the categories of responsibility within the criminal law are based, and they therefore stand as a potential defence against state power. The abstract juridical individual has a dualistic character: judged against the actualities of human life, it functions to repress individuals; measured against the strength of state power, it can act to defend them.

Thus the legal forms of subjectivity within the criminal law stand as potentially important controls upon what the state can do to individuals who come before its courts. This is true both in relation to the forms of responsibility which must be satisfied in order to convict, and in relation to potential controls on the disposal of convicted persons at the sentencing stage. But precisely because the ideology of juridical individualism establishes this positive protection of the subject, it becomes the site of a second tension within legal doctrine. Here the conflict is between the nature of the criminal process as a mechanism of social control in a divided society, and its ideological representation as the embodiment of free and equal citizenship.

The reality of crime control is primarily one of 'us and them', of the control of the lowest social classes by a social and political elite drawn from the middle and upper middle classes. The ideological representation is one of a world of free and equal subjects under the rule of law. Thus criminal doctrine is elaborated in terms of a logic of subjective individual right, but this logical and principled elaboration of the rules is constantly put under threat by a more direct set of political demands reflecting perceived social control needs. This socio-political conflict within the law is often referred to in orthodox thinking as a tension between 'principle' and 'policy', but there is a danger in this mode of representation that 'policy' becomes seen as an unthreatening technical addendum to an otherwise apolitical legal system. It is not that what goes on under the name of 'policy' usually represents the political conspiracy of an elite; rather, this conflict within the criminal law is inherent in a society in which ideological forms of free and equal individualism coexist with a socially structured world of crime and punishment. Viewed in this light, the demands of 'policy' are seen as a more systemic and structured set of socio-political imperatives than its polite quasi-technical appellation suggests. As with its psychological individualism, so with its political individualism, the law's essential form is crucially mediated by political concerns.

In reviewing the character of juridical individualism in the criminal law, I wish to indicate and underline the political nature of the liberal legal enterprise not just at the 'obvious' level of the intersection between 'principle' and 'policy' around the concept of the legal subject, but also at the deeper level of the structuring of the legal subject around a psychological individualism that excludes social, moral and political conflict from legal discourse. Politics does not overlay a set of pre-existing apolitical concepts: it contributes to the construction of their deep structure, and it polices the boundaries of legal doctrine in accordance with them. It has to do this, for the law's abstract individualism is the site of a tension between narrower (more individualistic) and broader (more contextual) conceptions of individual agency. The work of policing the boundaries is an essentially political task, a matter of choice that is not determined (although it is deeply influenced) by pre-existing legal materials. Judges choose to open up or close down the concepts because the contradictory form of the abstract individual forces them to go one way or the other. They normally tend towards the narrower, more individualistic, options that are available to them for the practical reason that this strengthens the conviction process.

2 Juridical individualism in the criminal law

My starting point is a theory of legal ideology that sees criminal doctrine as shaped by particular historical conditions and as founded on conflicts which express themselves as tensions and contradictions within the law. Criminal law is an expression of a social and political practice, and it bears the marks of the conflicts within that practice. Because it is founded upon the political ideology of the juridical individual, criminal law is constructed upon the conflicts inherent in that ideology. My aim has been to explain the problems of logic within the law as structural problems that can be contained or managed but not resolved. More than just the product of bad lawyering, they are at the very heart of the liberal legal project. They cannot be resolved by the further elaboration of a rational principled account of the law because such an account is impossible. The project is unachievable because it is inherently flawed.

[One can] examine [. . .] the central elements in [criminal law of] *mens rea*, intention and recklessness, and [. . .] consider [in] the law of intention [. . .] the division within the law between intention and motive. With the notable exception of Hall (1960), criminal lawyers have accepted the centrality of the division between intention and motive as a datum of the legal enterprise. While intention is central, motive occupies a peripheral role, scratching an existence at the edges of doctrine. Yet motive remains central to human agency and to broader moral and political claims about the nature of fault. The reason why this 'much more advanced level of ethical criticism' (Hall, 1960, 83) is ignored is that motive introduces the questions of social need and right that would directly challenge the allocation of fault. The focus on intention excludes the motives of those living at the margins of society and those whose political values the existing order wishes to marginalise.

Yet motive does not go away because the law's psychological individualism tells it to, and it persists as a problem within legal doctrine. While generally excluded from the conviction process, it is admitted at the politically more 'safe' stage of sentencing, where its effects are controlled by the application of judicial discretion. It is true that admission of individual particularity at this latter stage threatens to undermine equality of treatment under the ideology of the rule of law. But the administration of such equality through formal legal categories at the conviction stage is so morally inadequate that it can only survive on the basis that individuality is allowed in through the back door of mitigation.

Furthermore, motive remains as a constant challenge to doctrine in 'dramatic' situations such as those associated with duress and necessity, and in circumstances in which the formal categories have not been tightly enough drawn to exclude disruption of the law. In relation to the former situations, the strategy is to establish certain exceptional excuses which operate above and beyond the 'normal' requirements of *mens rea*. These permit a measure of 'special' justice, while legitimating its denial in the majority of cases which do not directly fall within the special category. In relation to the latter, the law can either use the distinction between motive and intention to fend off 'political' challenges to an 'apolitical' system (*Chandler*, 1964), or seek to find some abstract formulation to neutralise the direct moral–political challenge of the disruptive or troublesome citizen (*Ghosh*, 1982).

These cases reveal a central element of legal practice, although one that is normally presented as peripheral. It is the political use of a depoliticised or demoralised individualism to exclude moral and political challenges to the order of things. From this starting point, the 'real' legal debate can take place, and it is here that the shifting terms of the law of direct and indirect intent become our focus. But even on doctrine's own terrain, there is no guarantee of a smooth development. Having drawn the line between abstract psychological individualism (intention) and social individuality (motive), legal debates find themselves impaled on the second conflict within juridical ideology between political individualism and socio-political power. This conflict emerges in the contradictions in the law of intention between narrower definitions reflecting subjectivist principle and broader accounts that rely on objective elements. The shifting positions on the *mens rea* of murder over the last thirty years can only be understood in terms of this conflict.

The subjectivist/objectivist split within criminal liability is the central focus of [any analysis of] the law of recklessness. The 'indefensible' character of the law in this area has been remarked upon by orthodox theorists (Smith and Hogan, 1988, 67). So, at the level of the conflict between individual right and socio-political power, the argument about contradiction within the criminal law is easily made. [There is], however, [. . .] a more fundamental [. . .] interconnection between the two contradictions at the heart of the law. I [would] argue [. . .] that the subjectivist and objectivist dichotomy in the law of recklessness is itself the product of a prior historical depoliticisation and de-moralisation that occurred in the nineteenth century. The terms in which the conflict between subjective right and objective liability are fought out are *already* the product of a prior historical 'resolution' of a conflict in legal ideology. The inadequacies of the law of recklessness are the product of this layering of the contradictions within the legal form.

It is because of this that philosophical attempts to reinstate a core of moral judgment within the law of recklessness founder. To succeed, they would have to confront the lack of consensus at the heart of the social order, and, as a consequence, to reverse almost two centuries of legal development. One important result of this historical–conceptual impasse is the unsatisfactory nature of *both* positions in the subjectivist/objectivist controversy. Neither side can capture the moral issues at the heart of fault because the necessary moral and political concepts have already been removed from the picture. The subjectivists' liberally minded insistence on a narrow definition of advertent recklessness both appears to be 'right' in terms of legal principle *and* to miss an important moral definition of fault. The problem for those taking an objectivist position is that they must conflate the deeper sense of individual moral fault that the subjectivist ignores with a form of liability that exceeds individual fault by virtue of a broad authoritarian standard of reasonableness in human conduct. The moral distinctions that would have to be made are impossible because of the fact–value split within criminal responsibility. But this is no 'mistake'. It is the product of a social and historical process that engineered the exclusion of moral and political issues from the field of individual responsibility in order to render criminal conviction more certain.

[One can also] compare [. . .] and contrast [. . .] general *mens rea* in relation to individual crime with strict and corporate criminal liability. [T]he problems associated with the social and legal control of corporations stem from the nexus between individualism and social class which lies at the heart of the general criminal law. The essential focus of the law is on harms associated with the lower social classes – 'street crime', committed by actual individuals. Corporate harm is accordingly doubly removed from the realm of 'normal' crime. As a matter of social and ideological construction, corporations are hard to perceive as criminals, and as a matter of legal practice, they are hard to capture within individualistic legal forms.

The effects of this double difference are seen in the areas of strict and corporate liability. With regard to the former, the ideological difficulty is to the fore, leading to a legal differentiation that cannot be substantiated. As Williams says, 'it is impossible to abstract any coherent principle on when this form of liability arises and when it does not' (1983, 934). The appeal to a formal distinction, which the law requires to make in order to legitimate itself as law, cannot obscure the real underlying socio-political differentiation. With regard to the latter, the use of an individualistic, anthropomorphic account of corporate responsibility serves only to obscure the socially organised nature of harm in a world where an increasingly naked profit motive drives the corporate organisation. The weakness of the [individualistic] 'head and hands' principle is in a political sense a strength because, in making conviction harder, it legitimates the view that corporate wrongdoing is indeed non-criminal. It also obscures the broader economic motives behind corporate harm by personalising and individualising blame in a way that reform proposals radically challenge. The problem for reformers is that in socialising fault, they threaten to indict the economic system as a whole and therefore to transcend and dissolve the realm of the criminal law as a distinct 'apolitical' entity.

[T]he role of abstract individualism [can also be seen] in the construction of the central elements of *actus reus*. With regard to acts, [a] central focus [is] upon the requirement that an act be voluntary. The double play around the central antitheses of the juridical individual observed in intention is repeated. On the one hand, judges and orthodox scholars must police the boundaries of the concept of involuntariness so as to ensure that a broad, contextualised conception of 'moral involuntariness' is excluded or limited. The safety valve of necessity and duress operates to maintain the strict general principles of individual responsibility based on a narrow physical conception of involuntariness. On the other hand, the requirement of physical involuntariness is itself subject to attack through a kind of 'super-individualism' which traces voluntariness back to a prior, morally culpable voluntary act, albeit one that cannot be directly tied to the actual *actus* required by a formally and technically proper criminal law.

This 'super-individualism' stands in the same relation to subjectivist principle in the law of voluntary acts as do the objectivist positions in the law of intention and recklessness, although it involves a different *modus operandi.* It is a way of overriding the established, principled stance in favour of a socio-political control objective, although this is couched paradoxically in the language of subjectivity. This is most clearly seen in the context of intoxication, a condition that has the double demerit from the law's point of view of both offering a potential excuse to the criminal actor through the denial of voluntariness (or intention) *and* of being a social phenomenon commonly linked with working-class crime.

The law of omissions performs a different function to the law of voluntary acts, but the crucial mediation is provided by the form of the juridical individual. Voluntariness locates responsibility in individual acts in isolation from their context, whereas the law of omissions is concerned with maintaining that isolation in relation to failures to act. The interconnectedness of social life raises the possibility of a broad conception of responsibility to prevent a wide range of structurally as well as individually induced harms: for example, the responsibility of the rich for the poor. The political aim of the criminal law of omissions is to establish a sphere of responsibility that does not encroach upon the 'normal' omissions of a society based upon economic *laisser faire.* The law of omissions draws on the key ideological form of the abstract individual who is only committed to the extent that he commits himself through his own prior act. A convenient nexus is established between individual economic and juridical activity, primarily through the ideology of contract or analogy with it. In the process, however, the law evolves so narrowly that even elementary duties of social help are excluded from the field of liability.

The political decision to formulate the law of involuntary acts and omissions narrowly through the use of an individualistic conception of duty can be contrasted with the different functional context provided by the law of supervening cause [in the law of causation]. The theoretical problem for the law is the same, though the solution is different. In a socially interconnected world, individuals are both the producers of causes and themselves located within causal chains. At what point is the law to draw the line that delimits the effects of one person's agency from those of another? The use of broad and vague concepts of voluntariness and coincidence as the breaks on causal sequences contrasts with the narrow conceptions of involuntariness in the law of acts and of causal connection in the law of omissions. This can be understood in terms of the different socio-political goals in the three areas. In the law of acts, the idea of moral involuntariness is excluded, whereas it is accepted in the law of supervening cause. In the latter area we are concerned not with the acts of the criminal, but with those of the victim or a third party. The effect of a broad conception of involuntariness in relation to acts would be exculpatory, because it would broaden the range of claims available to the accused. The effect in relation to supervening cause, however, is the reverse because a broad conception of involuntariness works against the claim that a new cause has intervened.

In both areas of the law, the basic premise is that of individual agency and responsibility, but the actual construction of the legal concepts is dependent upon a political choice between more and less contextual conceptions of the juridical individual. The endorsement of a more contextual account of the individual in the law of supervening cause confirms both the tension within the basic legal form, and the role of political considerations in 'fixing' the law's form in particular areas. Similarly, if we compare the idea of a coincidental supervening cause with the role of causation in the law of omissions, we note the broad and indeterminate character of the line drawn by the vague concept of coincidence in the former (where indeterminacy increases inculpation) and the narrow and determinate character of the line drawn in the latter by the precise concept of the duty to act (where precision increases exculpation). One can only understand these differences according to the functional context of increasing the likelihood of conviction in causation cases and decreasing it in situations of omission. The specific character of individual agency is shaped by the underlying socio-political agenda.

[Necessity/duress and insanity are] two of the most important general defences within the law, and [their logical problems are also generated by] the nature of legal individualism [. . .]. Necessity and duress [play an important] role [. . .] within the overall logic of the law of criminal responsibility. The important links between the existence of these defences and the law of intention and agency have already been discussed. They operate as a safety-valve for the law: a box into which are pigeonholed those situations in which it is hardest to separate intention and agency from context. Yet because these defences operate against the logical grain of the law's abstract individualism, they sit uncomfortably with the standard legal categories. They occasion theoretical concern amongst criminal lawyers, some of whom would like to 'rationalise' the law by dissolving the defences into a capacious residual discretion at the sentencing stage. These defences challenge the law's psychological individualism, and the social control functions which underlie it, by opening up the legal sphere in which matters of social and political context can be contested. At worst, they threaten to be a contextual Pandora's Box, the opening of which generates a social and political counter-logic to that of the law. For these reasons, the very existence of necessity and duress as defences to some or all offences remains a permanent point of contention within judicial discourse. They play upon the fault line generated by the law's decontextualised individualism and this accounts for their continually 'provisional' character within legal discourse.

[With regard to] the defences of insanity and diminished responsibility, [. . .] the particular nature of the phenomenon of madness means that the law's abstract individualism appears in the shape of a narrow rationalist test of insanity. The position is complicated by the conflictual yet cooperative relationship between lawyers and doctors. The medical approach opposes an individuated and concretely determined model of the mad person to the law's test of rational individualism. Psychiatry thus plays on the other pole in the opposition between psychological individualism and contextualised individuality. However, the psychiatric point of view only opposes legal individualism to a limited extent, for what is lacking also within the psychiatric understanding is a recognition of the broader social context of mad behaviour. It is the limited nature of the psychiatric critique of the law that is both the cause and the effect of the political alliance between the two professions, at the same time as it is the source of occasional dramatic disagreements between them. They oppose each other in the ways in which they construct individual conduct and responsibility, but they agree in seeing the problem as being one *of* individual conduct. It is this situation of alliance without underlying ideological agreement that explains both the practical success and theoretical inadequacy of the partial defence of diminished responsibility.

Finally [one can] move [. . .] from the substantive law that governs the process of conviction to the sphere of broad discretion that exists at the post-conviction stage. For most orthodox criminal law texts, sentencing is not a topic that attracts detailed consideration. At one level, this is understandable, for sentencing has a different function to conviction, and therefore assumes different forms. Yet to recognise the differences is not to deny the fundamental ideological continuity between the two stages, and there is also a danger of not seeing that the differences at the sentencing stage are *determined* by what occurs at the conviction stage that has preceded it. In examining the law of intention and agency, [one can see] how the problem of social context is either pigeonholed through the excuses, or postponed, finally to re-emerge as a relevant factor at the sentencing stage. The abstract individualism that governs the law is only possible on condition that a significant measure of discretion exists at the sentencing stage. Moral and political considerations have so far as possible been wrung out of the law, but they must find their place in the politically safe discretion of the judge once conviction is secured. A 'wise polity' must have the mechanisms strictly to control those forms of harm that endanger it, but must temper its legal 'justice' with individual 'mercy'. Individualism in the law and individuality in the sentence are organically linked elements in the criminal justice system.

Despite the differences, however, the same ideological forms which underlie conviction emerge once more at the sentencing stage, albeit in a less controlled form. It is the law's psychological individualism that underlies retributive sentencing principles, but these are undermined by individualising and contextualising ideologies of rehabilitation and dangerousness. Ideas of just deserts also embody the values of political individualism within the legal form, but these are undermined by the politics of punishment associated with a general utilitarian theory. Seen in this light, the indeterminacy of the sentencing stage is not just the product of the determinacy required at the conviction stage. It is also the result of the setting loose of the contradictions inherent within the historical and ideological project that is the criminal law. With the strict legal requirements of the conviction stage slackened off, those contradictions are given freer rein. The sentencing stage with its wide discretions can thus be seen as the culmination of a particular, historical form of social control. It can also be seen as confirmation [. . .] that the criminal law is founded on ideological principles that are in their essence contradictory, so that rationalistic readings of the law are bound to fail.

3 Criminal law as praxiology

I have sought to portray both the practical and real quality of the law and its ideological character. I have also sought to show the law's illogicality and the historical logic that underlies it. The key to the critique presented here is the idea of law as a particular, historical form of social practice that is based upon an ideological representation of human life through the idea of the abstract legal individual. It is this responsible individual that the law respects through the 'rational' application of legal rules. That the matter of responsibility is much more complex than legal individualism can allow, or that the deduction and application of legal rules must be much less rational than orthodox legal theory is prepared to recognise, does not mean that the system is impractical. On the contrary, despite the deep flaws in its self-understanding and representation, criminal law remains a crucial and powerful social practice. As such, it is vital for political and ideological reasons that the law maintain its self-image as a system based upon individual responsibility and justice. It is for this reason that it is important to understand the limits of individual justice, and the political functions that it performs.

The concept of law as an ideological practice is also important in terms of the way that we understand the theory of criminal law. There is a tendency to see the law's concepts as reflecting the way individuals 'really are', or the way life 'really is'. To a point, this is true: individuals are agents, they do form intentions, they do take risks, and so on. But this is not the whole story; indeed it is a dangerous half-truth that obscures the significance of the social, moral and political context of agency which alone makes proper judgment of conduct possible. The concept of the abstract psychological individual suppresses the synthesis of individual form and social content necessary to such judgment, but this is what it is *supposed* to do. In Barthes's words, the language of the law lends 'a new strength to the psychology of the masters' precisely because it can 'describe and condemn at one stroke' while remaining 'ignorant of everything about the [criminal] actions themselves'.

Similarly there is a deep conviction reflected in legal practice and scholarship that law really is in principle a system of logically derived rules. Legal cases do indeed seek to present their conclusions in a formally rational way. The point, however, is that their rationality is undercut because of the social and political fault lines on which the doctrinal categories are built. Lawyers, nonetheless, continue to argue as if rational justification is possible. As part of an historical and practical control process, there is every reason why they should do so. Law can only operate on the basis that it has a formal existence above and beyond 'local' issues of morality and politics (cf. Fish, 1993). But there is no need for a critical legal theory, seeking to get behind the legal forms and to relate them to their underlying historical and practical tasks, to take what is said at face value. Given the marked propensity of criminal law theory to 'go round in circles', there is every incentive to follow Sève's advice and to seek a deeper critique that can understand the underlying contradictions that operate as mental blocks in the way of theoretical progress. The problem with orthodox liberal, positivistic approaches to criminal law is that this is precisely what they fail to do.

Following Bhaskar (1979), I suggest that if we think of criminal law as a particular form of social and historical practice, we should consider its theory, which reflects and legitimates that practice, as a form of knowledge which can be described as a 'praxiology'. This term refers to any theoretical account of a form of social agency that, like law, is tied to, and limited in its level of understanding by, a set of possible practices and outcomes. The range of concepts available within a praxiology is governed by the set of social practices and outcomes that it represents, informs and legitimates. Because the practice of the criminal law operates with concepts of individualism and formal rationality, orthodox criminal law theory is also tied to these concepts, and cannot transcend them.[. . .]

The essence of a praxiology is that it takes the part represented by the practice to be the whole, and in so doing it both obscures the whole and, ultimately, misrepresents the practice. In the case of orthodox criminal law theory, by ignoring the relationship between the legal practice of conviction and punishment on the one hand and the social context of crime on the other, it is unable to see the broader picture and to get to the bottom of the conundrums of the criminal law itself. Praxiologies are condemned to repeat the problems that the practices to which they are attached give rise because they cannot get beyond them. Thus, for example, the old problems of individual versus social responsibility and of subjectivism versus objectivism remain unresolvable problems for criminal law theory because they stem from the historical practice of the criminal law. While a critique such as the present one cannot indicate how such problems would ultimately be resolved, it can indicate the basic historical foundations of the problem in the way that an 'internal' praxiological account cannot.

The praxiological explanation of juridical subjectivity takes the modern social fact of individualistically constituted legal responsibility as the basis for a descriptive and normative account of criminal liability, but it does so in a onesided way. Individually instantiated social agency is translated into individualistically constituted, desocialised responsibility. Recognition of the social dimension of individual agency transforms our knowledge, understanding and judgment of the implications of such agency. Legal knowledge, tied to the criminal law practice of punishing *individuals*, is founded upon a misrecognition that is necessary to the legitimacy of the criminal law. Similarly, representation of the legal process as in principle rational is necessary for the law's legitimacy, but entails a misrecognition of the role of political judgment within the legal categories. It is these misrecognitions which both constitute the basis for the continuing practical 'success' of criminal law theory, and prevent it from transcending the *idées fixes* which govern the social practice of the criminal law. It is the social and historical practice of the criminal law that establishes both the practical necessity and the intellectual impossibility of the orthodox, liberal, positivist tradition in criminal law scholarship.

Note

1 Bhaskar (1979, 37) defines a praxiology as: 'a normative theory of efficient action, generating a set of techniques for achieving given ends, rather than as an explanatory theory capable of casting light on actual empirical episodes.'

His examples are forms of knowledge such as neo-classical economic theory, rational and public choice theories in the social sciences, utilitarian and liberal theory in the political sciences. Many of these theories share much in common with orthodox liberal legal theory. They all seek to explain and guide action individualistically while bracketing off historically given social relations, or denying their importance for the understanding of how economic, political and social relations actually operate.

References

Barthes, R. (1973) *Mythologies*, St Albans: Paladin.
Bhaskar, R. (1979) *The Possibility of Naturalism*, Brighton: Harvester.

Fish, S. (1993) 'The Law Wishes to Have a Formal Existence', in A. Norrie, *Closure or Critique: Current Directions in Legal Theory*, Edinburgh: EUP.

Hall, J. (1960) *General Principles of Criminal Law* (2nd edn), Indianapolis: Bobbs-Merrill.

Neumann, F. (1987) *Social Democracy and the Rule of Law*, London: Allen and Unwin.

Norrie, A. (1991) *Law, Ideology and Punishment*, Dordrecht: Kluwer.

Sève, L. (1975) *Marxism and the Theory of Human Personality*, London: Lawrence & Wishart.

Smith, J. and Hogan, B. (1988) *Criminal Law* (6th edn), London: Butterworths.

Williams, G. (1983) *Textbook of Criminal Law* (2nd edn), London: Stevens.

Part IV

DIALECTIC AND DIALECTICAL CRITICAL REALISM

22

INTRODUCTION

Dialectic and dialectical critical realism

Roy Bhaskar and Alan Norrie

Prior to 1993, Roy Bhaskar was best known for his realist accounts of the natural and social sciences and, stemming from the latter, his concept of emancipatory critique. Less well known in this period was his interest in the concept of dialectic which was pursued in a number of brief articles concerned with the character of Marxist thought and the Hegel–Marx nexus. In his *Dialectic: The Pulse of Freedom* (hereafter *DPF*), Bhaskar combines these two interests to provide a new dialectical account of critical realism which would recognise the importance of the dialectical tradition in western thought up to Hegel, but which, on the basis of the established critical realist conceptual vocabulary, would reveal the limits of that tradition and move beyond them.

So doing, *DPF* would involve a qualitatively developed dialectical critical realism (hereafter DCR) that would radicalise earlier positions and cast a fresh light on the entire western approach to philosophy from Plato to Hegel and beyond. It would also underlabour further for the modern social (and natural) sciences and, in particular, provide a philosophical basis for Marxian social theory consistent with Marx's own underdeveloped methodological insights. Most ambitiously, it would also establish the groundwork for a new ethical theory which, building upon emancipatory critique, could resolve the problematic theory–practice dichotomy associated with radical forms of social science.

In the Preface to *DPF*, Bhaskar describes his work as involving 'a preservative generalisation and enrichment of critical realism that is a non-preservative sublation of Hegelian dialectic' (p. xiii). To Hegel's dialectics of identity, negativity and totality, Bhaskar will offer the four terms of non-identity, negativity, totality and transformative agency, and he adds that where he and Hegel share common terms, DCR will provide radically different interpretations of the concepts in question. The central task of *DPF* is to synthesise dialectical methods with existing critical realist concerns, *inter alia* associated with ideas of ontological depth and the differentiation of the ontic from the epistemic, and to push critical realism further into the fields of 'reference and truth, spatio-temporality, tense and process, the logic of dialectical universalisability and on to the plane of ethics'. There, a combination of moral realism and ethical naturalism opens up the possibility of moving from 'the form of judgements to the content of a freely flourishing society' (ibid.).

The dialecticisation of critical realism

This complex and profound development of critical realism involves a broad and multiform treatment of dialectic: in its historical and systematic forms; epistemically, as the logic of argument and the method of immanent critique; ontologically, as the dynamic of conflict and the mechanism of change; and normatively-practically, as the axiology of freedom. Central to dialectic is the concept of absence, for dialectic is defined as 'the absenting of constraints on absenting absences or ills (which may also be regarded as constraints)' (p. xiv) and this applies whether it be an epistemological matter of remedying an argument, an ontological matter of socio-historical change, or an ethical question of human freedom.

This standpoint contrasts with an entire tradition from Plato which has prioritised (and positivised) the positive, producing the characteristic error that Bhaskar calls *ontological monovalence*: the reliance on a 'purely positive, complementing a purely actual, notion of reality' (pp. 4–5). Argument, development and ethics are all marked by what they lack. There is a fundamental bipolarity of absence and presence, so that negativity is a condition of positive being; it is this essential relationship that is dialectic, a process that is 'the pulse of freedom' (p. 385).

The dialecticisation of critical realism[1] is in these terms itself a dialectical *process* that has four moments. The movement involves a theoretical development from a first moment (1M) to a second edge (2E) to a third level (3L) and on to a fourth dimension (4D). 1M primarily involves critical realist concepts that will be familiar to readers of Bhaskar's earlier work. Here concepts like structure, differentiation, change, alterity (for example epistemic/ontic non-identity within ontology), transfactual efficacy, emergence and systemic openness have already been developed, but they will be reworked and enhanced at 2E in the light of dialectical categories such as negativity, negation, becoming, contradiction, process, development and decline, mediation and reciprocity. 1M concepts might be seen as implicitly calling for (as explicitly lacking) the dialecticisation they receive at 2E. 1M concepts suffice 'for, e.g. an adequate account of science which abstracts from space, time and the process of change, which posits "principles of indifference"' (p. 8);[2] but which science can afford to abstract from the spatio-temporal or from change, and which 'principles of indifference' are ultimately adequate to an understanding of the social or the natural world? At 2E, the marriage of critical realism and dialectics opens up the prospect of an understanding of the way sciences must be if they are to be adequate to 'cosmology . . . human geo-history . . . personal biography, laborious or routinised work but also joyful or idle play' (pp. 8–9). 1M concepts taken to the 2E dialectical edge are opened up to the world of the concrete universal, the unity of being in its subjection to, and expression of, 'causality, space and time in tensed rhythmic spatialising process' (p. 392).

At 2E, however, a third level (3L) is already implicitly invoked. Thus, most simply, an absence or omission, say an incompleteness in a scientific theory, generates a contradiction (manifest, for example, in science in a band of significant anomalies or aporias), split or alienation, which can only be remedied by a resort to a greater totality, e.g., a fuller, deeper, wider or more complete scientific theory. The internal and intrinsic connectedness of phenomena deduced from the dialecticisation of 1M at 2E reveals the implicit need for totalising motifs which can theorise totality (totality as fundamentally open, not closed – see pp. 25, 273) and constellationality as well as (what turns out to be) their internal forms: connectivity, relationality, reflexivity, concrete universality, subjectivity and objectivity, autonomy-within-duality and hiatus. What is more, if we then recognise the pro-activity and the constitutionality of these internal forms within constellations, sub-totalities or totalities, as we must once we acknowledge the possibilities of knowledge and agency (subjectivity and agency within objectivity and duality), then 3L is also the level which produces new philosophical accounts of reason, rationality and phronesis (practical wisdom), and which then leads to the fourth dimension (4D) of 'the unity of theory and practice *in practice*' (p. 9).

The bipolarity of absence and presence

DPF is divided into four chapters, two shorter sandwiching two longer. Chapter 1 introduces the main themes and explores critically Hegel's dialectic, while Chapter 4 returns to some of the Hegelian dilemmas that result from the deployment of dialectics within an ontologically monovalent (*irrealist*) problematic. The latter also explores the philosophically underdeveloped basis for Marx's historical materialist use of dialectic. Chapters 2 and 3 concern themselves severally with the exploration of the moves to 2E and 3L from the dialecticisation of 1M, and the ethical and practical conclusions that result from the 3L to 4D development.

Chapter 2 begins with Absence, then moves to Emergence and Contradiction and thence, via further consideration of Hegelian dialectic and its relationship to Marx, to the development of DCR tropes concerning the nature of mediation, totality, relationality and the nature of what Bhaskar labels TINA formations. Space dictates a highly selective account of the argument, which will seek to focus on the specific development of DCR itself.

The two initial sections of Chapter 2 can be seen as standing for the essential bipolarity of the negative (Absence) and the positive (Emergence) that is entailed by placing absence at the heart of positivity. For DCR, 'non-being is a condition of possibility of being' (p. 46) and dialectic 'just is, in its essence, the process of *absenting absence*' (p. 43). Absenting processes are crucial to the onto-logic of *change*, while *argument* involves the epistemic absenting of mistake, and absenting absences which block needs is essential to axiological freedom. Importantly, if absence (negativity) is one pole of the positive, then the positive cannot be successfully positiv*ised*. Absence opens up the critique of the fixity of the subject in the traditional subject–predicate propositional form. Dialectic becomes the 'great 'loosener'', permitting empirical "open texture" . . . and structural fluidity and interconnectedness' (p. 44).

The positive bipolar of absence in critical realism is then presented through the concept of emergence. A 1M category already well known, for example, in the idea of 'synchronic emergent powers materialism', emergence involves the generation of new beings (entities, structures, totalities, concepts) 'out of pre-existing material from which they could have been neither induced or deduced' (p. 49). Emergence involves 'something new', a quantum leap: matter as creative or autopoietic. Taking emergence to 2E, Bhaskar now links new entities with their own causal powers to space-time as a 'relational property of the meshwork of material beings' (p. 53) and to the possibility of emergent spatio-temporalities with their own processual rhythmics. This gives rise to a 2E insistence that the here and now embody the presence of the outside and the past, so that 'emergent social things . . . not only presuppose . . . but also are *existentially constituted* by . . . or [perhaps just] merely contain . . . their geo-histories' (p. 54).

Contradiction and dialectical motifs

Holding absence or real negation and positivity together as a bipolar dual generates contradiction in argument, in history and in practice. The next four sections of Chapter 2 are concerned with the nature of dialectic and contradiction, the differentiation of Hegelian from critical realist dialectic via the underdeveloped insights of Marx, and the fundamental errors of irrealist dialectics from Aristotle to Kant and Hegel. Contradictions may be external, internal, formal-logical or dialectical. Dialectical contradictions involve 'connections between entities or aspects of a totality such that they are in principle *distinct* but *inseparable*', so that there is both existential presupposition *and* opposition. They establish tendential mutual exclusion at the nub of history, knowledge and the pursuit of freedom.

As regards knowledge, the idea of dialectic as the 'great loosener' suggests an important nexus between dialectical and analytical reasoning and dialectical and formal-logical contradiction. Formal-logical contradictions within analytical thinking may indicate the site of real dialectical contradictions, for the former are understood as 'real constituents of the *Lebenswelt*' (p. 58) that cannot be resolved, *pace* Hegel, through the logicising of being. To the contrary, DCR, with its emphasis on ontological depth and structural causation identifies the common ground in contradictory propositions, not sublating them, but situating them in structural and causal contexts and in the rhythmics of geo-history. This engenders a *dialectic of dialectical and analytical reasoning* in which dialectical reasoning 'overreaches' (rather than transcends) analytical reasoning. Logical contradictions may be the sign and the site of real contradictions in the world, to be located and explained, thereby pointing the way forward to the understandings – and the practices – required to overcome them.

By this point in the progression of Chapter 2, Bhaskar has now established the basic building blocks of the move from 1M to 2E. There then follows an important section which outlines a variety of dialectical motifs which can rest upon a realist understanding of absence, emergence and contradiction. Amongst these are *mediation*, the idea of an 'intermediary or means of some sort' (p. 113), which is central to the idea of the bipolarity of being and absence, and which is necessitated by the ideas of internal connection and particularity within totality. Linked with mediation is the idea of *duality*, described broadly as 'the combination of existential interdependence . . . and essential . . . distinction' (p. 115). Duality locates the specific within the general, agency within structure, freedom within the conditioned, and it is marked by two closely linked dialectical motifs: those of *hiatus-in-the-duality*, which defends autonomy against either reificatory or voluntaristic collapse, as well as locating the possibility of dislocation; and *perspectival shifts*, such as that required by the duality of agency and structure in sociological contexts. Similarly, *constellationality* signifies the necessary connectedness of things, such as the dialectical unity of dialectical and analytical reason described above: the former builds on the latter, overreaching but not transcending it, while the latter is at a loss without the former.

What, however, if, in either theory or practice, the dialectical overreach is denied and an analytical proposition 'turns its back' on a dialectical conclusion? The lack or absence that dialectic would have made good is suppressed and this suppression requires defence, supplementation or compromise. This is the realm of the ironically titled *TINA* ('There is no alternative') *syndrome.*[3] *TINA formations* are 'internally contradictory, more or less systemic, efficacious, syntonic . . . ensembles . . . displaying duplicity, equivocation, extreme plasticity . . . and rational indeterminacy (facilitating their ideological and manipulative use)' (p. 117).

Of course, TINA formations are only revealed as such insofar as their limits and obfuscations have been revealed through their systematic grounding as parts of more complex, structurally deep, contexts and understandings. Such understandings are no more than the 'drive to totality' (p. 123) endemic in scientific activity, and *totality* is the final dialectical concept to consider here. As we have already said, the 2E treatment of 1M concepts invokes a move beyond 2E and on to a third level occupied by totalising dialectical concepts. Totality is the key 3L concept just as absence plays that part at 2E. The domain of totality is that of 'intra-actively changing embedded ensembles, constituted by their geo-histories . . . and their contexts, in open potentially disjointed process' (p. 126). It involves, from the point of view of the whole, and thereby complementing absence's effect on the part, a 'break with our ordinary notions of identity, causality, space and time', requiring us to see things as they are '*existentially constituted*, and permeated, *by their relations with others*' (p. 125). In the ontic realm of totality, identity thought cannot be adequate and there is a need 'to conceptualise *entity relationism*', thus underlining the need once more for a move beyond analytical thinking about dialectical phenomena.

Dialecticising critical naturalism

The move from 1M through 2E to 3L now being made, Bhaskar is in a position towards the end of Chapter 2 to revisit the critical realism of *The Possibility of Naturalism* and to consider its relation to DCR. Critical realism was 'unwittingly . . . a perfect vehicle for, or at least exemplar of, social dialectics', but it itself needs to be dialecticised. So doing, Bhaskar deploys further important concepts for DCR including the explication of human nature as *four-planar social being*, or the 'social cube', and the significance of *power$_2$ relations* for society and philosophy. Social life qua totality is constituted by four dialectically interdependent planes: of material transactions with nature, inter-personal action, social relations, and intra-subjectivity. The social cube must be conceived in terms of depth and stratification and the elements of each plane are 'subject to multiple and conflicting determinations and mediations' (p. 160) in a totalising conception which dialecticises existing realist ideas such as the transformational model of social agency and the position-practice system.

This depiction of the multiplicity and structuring of human social being is aligned with the important theme of power$_2$, or *generalised master–slave-type relationships*. This links DCR to both Hegel's master–slave dialectic and Marx's analysis of wage slavery, ideology and the fetishism of commodities, but it is also generalisable to all socially structured power relations such as those of gender, race and age through which agents, groups or classes get their way 'against either . . . the overt wishes and/or . . . the real interests of others (grounded in their concrete singularities)' (p. 153). This is an important substantive argument about the nature of modern societies and the multi-form *constraints$_2$* to which they give rise. Sanctioned by DCR's realist social scientific grounding (see below), it explains what dialectical ethics and practice orient themselves to and against, as well as licensing modern critical phenomenological readings of, for example, 'the co-existence of Disneyfication/McDonaldisation, poverty and waste' (p. 162) in the 'New World Order'.

But more than this, DCR relates the existence of historical power$_2$ relations to the forms of western philosophy. This intrinsic philosophical significance is seen for example in Bhaskar's linking of analytical philosophy to the expression of an *ontology of stasis*, so that analytics unselfconsciously assume the role of 'normalisation of past changes and freedoms, and the denegation of present and future ones' (p. 177). Since a philosophy of ontological stasis is closely linked to the most fundamental philosophical errors which characterise western philosophy, such as ontological monovalence, DCR raises fundamental – appropriately dialectical and realist – questions about the relationship between power relations and knowledge in the 'Great Arch of Knowledge' tradition deriving from Plato and Aristotle. Master–slave relations, money, instrumental reasoning, reification, alienation may all be systematically connected to irrealism, actualism, monovalence, analytic and theory–practice split.

Ethics in dialectical critical realism

Critical realism is well known for its role as 'underlabourer' for the natural and social sciences, posing and answering transcendental questions about what the world and human beings must be like for science to be possible. At the same time, however, it has also had an ethical dimension which is rooted in the analysis of scientific practice, and seen in Bhaskar's analysis of emancipatory critique and its ability to traverse the fact–value gap (to derive ought from is). If Chapter 2 of *DPF* is concerned with the dialecticisation of underlabouring, Chapter 3 develops emancipatory critique to present DCR as an ethical system in its own right. 'My project,' says Bhaskar, 'is normative' (p. 279). Here at the level of 4D, *DPF* builds an ethics out of the positions established at 1M, 2E and 3L based upon: ontology; the nature of dialectic as the absenting of absence; explanatory critique; and dialectics of truth, desire and freedom. These lead to a moral theory that moves 'from primal scream to universal human flourishing' (p. 180), in which 'concrete singularity ['the free flourishing of each'] is the relational condition of concrete universality ['the free flourishing of all']', and where this ethical conclusion is concretised as 'an immanent and tendential possibility . . . necessitated by structural conditions', but one that is 'held in check by global discursively moralised power$_2$ relations' (p. 202).

The essential elements in DCR's ethical philosophy are concepts of ontology, alethic truth, dialectic and dialectical universalisability. Ontology has always played the major part in critical realism, and it is the foundation stone of Bhaskar's ethics. It grounds alethic truth, defined as 'dialectical reason and ground in theory and the absence of heterology [unreconciled otherness]; it is true to, for, in and of itself.' With regard to the epistemic, it 'furnishes the non-arbitrary principle of ontological stratification that powers the dialectic of scientific discovery'. With regard to the ethical, which unites what we know with what we are, and leads on from (and back into) both, 'the true = the moral good = freedom, in the sense of universal human emancipation' (pp. 219–220). It is the unifying ontic ground for the cognitive and normative aspects of human being, understood in four-planar form.

As ethical basis, alethia is centrally linked to dialectic. Bhaskar writes that 'at the outset', 'the most important thing to appreciate' is that any ill 'can be looked upon, or dialectically transposed, as an absence, and any absence can be viewed as a constraint' (p. 259), and this is tied to the alethic for in 'the moral realm, alethic truth, the good, is freedom, [which] depend[s] on the absenting of constraints on absenting ills' (p. 212). It is this grounding of the ethical in the ontological that distinguishes DCR from other contemporary philosophies. The *transfactual* character of moral truth means that Bhaskar's ethics depends on, for example, neither a (neo-Kantian) ideal speech situation *pace* Habermas, nor on a (neo-Contractarian) original position *pace* Rawls.

Dialectical universalisability

In turn, dialectic goes hand in hand with the idea of *dialectical universalisability*. This involves a characteristic form of argument in which a commitment to the negation of 'x' entails further commitment to the negation of those things that x itself entails. Thus the ontological starting point of the absenting of constraints on being entails a progressive commitment to the absenting of all such constraints. We have briefly seen such a move already in the epigrammatic move from primal scream to universal human flourishing. It is the basis for the argument that any truth statement 'can be seen to imply a commitment to the project of universal human emancipation, involving the abolition of the *totality of master–slave relations*' (p. 180); and the claim that the 'desire to overcome constraints (including $constraints_2$) on the satisfaction of desires, wants . . . and needs . . . implies a conatus . . . to knowledge of all four planes of the social tetrapolity at the hub of which I placed the social cube' (p. 180). The following summarises dialectical universalisability as the argument which drives to alethia:

> the real transformative negation of the ill presupposes universalisability to absenting agency in all dialectically similar circumstances. This presupposes in turn the absenting of all similar constraints. And by the inexorable logic of dialectical universalisability . . . this presupposes the absenting of all constraints as such, including $constraints_2$. . . . And this presupposes in its wake a society

> oriented to the free development and flourishing of each and all, and of each as a condition for all. . . . So the goal of universal human autonomy is implicit in every moral judgement.
>
> (pp. 263–4)

Emancipatory critique and axiological freedom

DCR involves both *moral realism* and *ethical naturalism*. Moral realism entails that morality is an 'objective real property' (p. 259), i.e. alethic, but a distinction has to be made between morality as practical, relational and explanatory-critical and as it actually exists within an already moralised world. The distinction is the basis for a *critical* moral realism that is not reducible to a sociology of ethics. Ethical naturalism entails that moral properties can be suitable objects of study for the social sciences, and the combination of realism and naturalism leads to the conclusion that the constitutive morality of a society can be shown to be essentially limited or false in its ethical claims. It is an appropriate function of a social science to be involved in examining beliefs about social objects, beliefs which it may show to be false. If the social sciences can also explain their falsity, then, subject to a *ceteris paribus* clause, 'one can move without further ado to a negative evaluation' of the belief and 'a positive evaluation of any action rationally designed to absent it' (p. 262).

Falsity entails ontic untruth and its identification involves an implicit criticism of any action based upon it, as well as, by extension, a commitment to do something about it. This positive and negative evaluation of action results from the conception of social science as *explanatory critique*. It leads immediately to practice, but also to a conception of *emancipatory axiology* because its fuller significance is that it 'can be [dialectically] *generalised* to cover the failure to satisfy other axiological needs, necessities and interests besides truths, including those which are necessary . . . for truth, such as basic health, education and ergonic efficiency' (p. 262).

Dialectics of truth, desire and freedom

Here we see a universalising move in the argument that is particularly apparent in the linked *dialectic of truth* that Bhaskar deploys alongside his conceptions of explanatory critique and emancipatory axiology. There are a number of ways in which any 'expressively veracious' (truth) judgement must be universalisable, but among these is the strong sense that it has to be 'oriented to the concrete singularity of the addressee . . . and universalisable to any other concrete singular so situated' (p. 178). It is important to see that this orientation to concrete singularity relies, in Kantian terms, on an 'assertoric' – there is no surreptitious categorical – imperative, on what an agent ought to do in her situation, but there is still a possible generalisation from the addressed agent to the addressor.

If the addressee experiences constraints on her needs, the addressor, through his orientation to her concrete singularity as expressed in his judgement, stands in her place, implying solidarity and commitment to the critical explanation of her situation. That in turn entails a location of her concrete singularity within a 'theory of human nature – (needs and interests) – in society – in nature' (p. 179). This dialectical generalisation then involves a further universalisation since any social ill discovered through solidarisation will be seen as a constraint on freedom, so that any truth judgement 'implies a commitment to universal human emancipation and a society in which the concrete singularity of each and all is realised' (ibid.).

This argument for 'assertorically imperatival sensitised solidarity' (p. 262) applies to buttress the argument from explanatory critique to emancipatory axiology, but both require further dialectical arguments concerning freedom and desire for their moral completion, for it is the dialectic of *desire to freedom* that ultimately drives, and demands, the search for truth. The starting point of this dialectic is the ontology of absence, the experience of it, and the desire to absent that experience. Absence is experienced as constraint, as 'unfulfilled needs, lacks, wants or, in the setting of primary polyadisation [i.e., the dependence of the human infant on other human beings] elemental desire' (p. 285). Desire involves the recognition of *difference* (between desirer and the desired), which entails *referential detachment* (the separation of the act of desiring from the desired object), which in turn entails the recognition of the intransitive world of causality, ontological stratification and alethic truth. These in turn involve the recognition of power_2 relations, the absences they create and the desire to absent those absences.

As can be seen from the above, desire is no abstract category, but involves specific relata such as the needs and lacks (the absences) it desires to absent. The specific desires at the core of DCR's moral realism concern the absenting of unfreedoms and various aspects of freedom require therefore to be identified and dialectically universalised. There are several degrees of freedom, ranging from the agentive (the capacity to do otherwise, analytic to the concept of action) to Berlin's negative and positive liberty (which Bhaskar treats as mutually entailing), to, more deeply, freedom as emancipation. The last means 'the transformation from unwanted, unneeded and oppressive to wanted, needed and liberating (including empowering) states of affairs, especially structures' (p. 282). These degrees of freedom are then dialectically universalisable to universal human emancipation, autonomy and well-being in the eudaimonistic society.

What flows from the ethics of DCR? A critical morality which is processual in its orientation, directed to the lived experience of those experiencing constraints, especially constraints_2. Emphasising the permanent experience of resistance to oppression, dialectic cannot itself be 'in the business of telling people . . . what to do'. It is best conceived as an 'inner urge that flows universally from the logic of elemental absence', manifesting itself wherever lack, need, want or desire are blocked. It is most especially experienced where $power_2$ relations hold sway. It can be conceived as ontic pulse, both real and moral, as 'the heartbeat of a positively generalised concept of freedom . . .' As such it is 'irrepressible' (p. 299).

Critical appraisal of *DPF*

Andrew Collier has been a foremost interpreter of Roy Bhaskar's work and his *Critical Realism* (1994) has assisted in disseminating it to a wider audience. His review of *DPF* together with his further critical thoughts on its ethics are presented here as a different point of entry into a complex work, which as Collier notes, 'joins battle . . . with the whole philosophical heritage'. Collier's criticisms of *DPF*'s ethics articulate a viewpoint that will probably not be unique, and it is important that the issues he raises are debated and clarified.

In his review of *DPF*, Collier takes the reader to its core with his discussion and general support for the importance of a doctrine of absence based upon causal as well as perceptual criteria for existence, and founded, *pace* Sartre, on a non-anthropocentric stance. Collier also makes the important point that *DPF* is 'political through and through', though it may be considered whether his admonition about those politics takes Bhaskar's quoted comment out of context.

If *DPF* is political through and through, so is it moral, and it is here that Collier raises important questions about what he sees as the Kantian nature of Bhaskar's principle of dialectical universalisability, 'defended through the notion that the non-universalising agent is involved in a theory/practice contradiction. . . .' (Review, p. 9). Such a universalising strategy is notoriously barren: why does the infant's primal scream demand autonomy rather than that the world should be full of noise? An act can be universalised under a number of different descriptions, giving rise to quite different moral maxims, as Collier argues with the example of the assassination of the Grand Duke in Sarajevo in 1914. And if speech acts are to be universalised, what counts out the exhortation of the fascist thug to victimise a racial minority ('Realism and Formalism', pp. 3, 4)? Collier gives a number of examples of 'this world' conduct which cannot be universalised without morally counter-intuitive and contradictory results.

This is not the place for a detailed consideration of Collier's claims, but it may help the reader to have some sense of how Bhaskar might respond. In his review of *DPF*, Collier writes of the need for a *materiale Wertethik* to supplement what he sees as *DPF*'s formalism, while in 'Realism and Formalism', he suggests that the universalisation of morals must 'in each case . . . be grounded in the nature of the case' (p. 10). Yet this is surely what Bhaskar himself argues in *DPF* through his insistence that the principle of dialectical universalisability is mediated through all the moments of the concrete (not abstract or purely formal, but dialectical and singularised) universal. This will include *inter alia* the dimensionalities of four-planar social being (*DPF*, p. 179), the specificity of $power_2$ relations and the uniqueness of the individual human being. In this, social science/knowledge plays a crucial role in terms of explaining the real location of agents in social and natural relations as the basis for assertoric statements as to what the agent ought to do. There is no question of universalising the speech act of the fascist thug so long as a valid social explanation exists as to the nature and consequences of fascism.

Similarly, Collier's example of the different moral evaluations attached to the different descriptions of the Archduke's assassination should be compared with Bhaskar's deployment (*Plato Etc.*, p. 110) of Isaiah Berlin's example of the most accurate social scientific explanation of the Holocaust as also being the most morally forthright and truthful ('the Jews were murdered'). As Bhaskar says there, 'the most adequate description of a phenomenon will be that entailed by the theory which *maximises explanatory power*' and such a criterion of adequacy can then provide a substantive basis for 'the dialectics of assertorically sensitised solidarity'.

Applying and developing DCR

In the same year that *DPF* was published, Alan Norrie, a legal theorist and criminal lawyer, published *Crime, Reason and History* (hereafter *CRH*). *CRH* acknowledges a debt to Bhaskar's pre-dialectical work through its critical realist use of the concept of *praxiology* as part of an explanatory critique (see Part III), but its main thrust was to treat the evolution of legal forms as systematically entailing contradictions that were ignored, evaded or suppressed by mainstream writers. There was also an insistence that suppressions in ideas and in practice reflected deeper suppressions in the historical evolution of modern society so that legal texts were at once historical and social expressions of power relations. This brief description indicates various possible connections between *CRH* and a dialectical critical realist social theory, and the two pieces included here are recent developments of a dialectical approach which draw on *DPF* in the areas of law, morality and social science. So doing there is an engagement with, and development of, the dialectical phenomenology of what Bhaskar terms *personalism*, 'perhaps the dominant moral ideology for $subjects_2$' (*DPF*, p. 265) in modern capitalist societies.

In 'The Limits of Justice', Norrie takes up the idea of the contradictory moral pull of legal ideas of justice on the modern consciousness. From one point of view, ideas of individual responsibility capture important aspects of what it means to be a human being; but at the same time, they decontextualise the individual and repress the social responsibility that underlies individuals' acts and undercuts their moral blame for wrongs done. This antinomy of justice/injustice is played out through three discussions which reflect on: the need for a critical realist standpoint in place of either liberalism or poststructuralism; the historico-logical splits in the criminal law around a central concept such as 'recklessness'; and the dialectical location of the responsible individual between social relations and individual subjectivity.

The essay speaks for itself, but it may be helpful to bring out some of the implicit and explicit connections with DCR. The argument's strategy is one of *immanent critique*, pushing at the limits of the liberal theory of justice to reveal what is suppressed, and then to locate those limits, with what lies beyond them, in the ontic context of emergent social history. So doing, the essay draws on *DPF*'s account of *dialectical connection* and *contradiction* as a means of 'overreaching' legal analytical reasoning. It portrays the law of recklessness as in effect a *TINA formation* historically rooted in *power*$_2$ *relations*; while the discussion of the 'sense of justice' effects a *perspectival switch* from the standpoint of structure to that of agents in a social community. While this section draws on Rom Harré's account of the primary and secondary structures of human being and social life, there are clear connections here with Bhaskar's broader, ontologically more inclusive, conception of *four-planar social being* and the sense of *entity relationism* to which it gives rise.

Norrie's concluding answer to the practical question 'what is to be done' about criminal justice reflects the sense of 'suspension' that a dialectical account entails. There are no simple answers, so that politically committed *phronesis* balances the available options. At the same time, the paper's reference to alternative moral and political forms of judgment to those of western law provides a sense of the moral limits of (absence within) such law, and the *pulse to freedom* that beats behind it.

'Between Structure and Difference' generalises the lesson from criminal law to a broader understanding of western liberal legality, what Boaventura de Sousa Santos calls the 'law of the citizenplace'. The paper steers a path between a view of law as autonomous, as in positivist, neo-Kantian and Weberian views and a poststructuralist view of it as the site of an existential violence in the place of a sublime ethicality. Engaging with de Sousa Santos's *Towards a New Commonsense*, it argues for a critical realist understanding of social structure and totality as the basis for a dialectical understanding of law's ability to differentiate itself while retaining its relational connectedness with social, political and economic structures.

Arguing that ideas of 'law' and 'legality', even if they are radicalised to include notions of 'interlaw' and 'interlegality', retain an uncritical understanding of liberal law, the paper argues that the key idea of the legal subject in the law of the citizenplace (Bhaskar's 'personalism' again) was in the same historical moment at once a site of freedom and emancipation *and* of suppression of alternative modes of social organisation. It is this dialectical positioning of law within *power*$_2$ *relations* that engenders a sense of its structuration in the moment that it proclaims its difference. This is another version of the dialectic of structure and agency and it generates an ('external') image of legal practice as structurally shaped but also as possessing its own ('internal') forms (what Norrie calls 'legal architectonics'). DCR ideas such as those of the *perspectival shift* and the *hiatus-in-the-duality* naturally complement this resolution of the longstanding problem of how a thing can both be itself and something else. In effect Norrie employs DCR to argue once more for law's *entity relationism*.

Notes

1 For the dialecticisation of a central critical naturalist conception, the transformational model of social action, see Chapter 2.9.

2 Unfortunately this was originally misprinted, in a typographical error, as 'principles of difference'.

3 The term was infamously coined by Margaret Thatcher when Prime Minister of the UK. The irony lies in the fact that there usually are alternatives, so that TINA statements are false closures enforced in an area of various possibilities, requiring various forms of supplementary and contradictory control to maintain them. A practical and literal illustration would be the closure of the British mining industry effected by the temporary establishment of a virtual police state – in the name of freedom.

23

CRITICAL REALISM AND DIALECTIC

Roy Bhaskar

§5 Prima facie objections to critical realism

There is one other preliminary matter that should be dealt with here before I turn to Hegelian dialectic. It may be contended that critical realism is, or began as, a philosophy of – and *for* – science, even if it is conceded that it is not a scientistic philosophy.[1] How then can I treat of theory generally, or by what right do I identify it as a subset of the domain of the real, or indeed envelop in my critique philosophies – including epistemologies – which do not purport to be about science? Let us consider the last objection first. There is an important grain of truth here. There is indeed a big difference between science and everyday knowledge, which the philosophical tradition has – at least in its post-Lockian period – tended to conflate or otherwise obscure, the significance of which I will bring out anon. But I think, and would like to show, that science provides a hidden 'analogical grammar'[2] for the metacritical analysis of philosophies – at any rate at 1M. (At 2E, 3L and 4D the wider social context is more important, though we should never underestimate the power buried in the human psyche-soma.) Correspondingly, transposing philosophical theses of an epistemological kind into their presuppositions about and implications for science can be extraordinarily illuminating. In particular it effects a *concretization* (itself a dialectical development) of these, which makes it easier to identify exactly what their insights, aporiai, tensions and effects are. A parallel recasting of ethical positions and arguments into social theoretic positions can be equally illuminating. To turn to the first objection now, it is the case that the transcendental arguments used to establish critical realism were in the first instance thrown up by existing reflections on (theories of) science, of which they constituted an immanent critique. But in C3 I intend also to derive (dialectical) transcendental realism both without recourse to science and by taking up the challenge of Heideggerian existential phenomenology. There I will consider

Source: *Dialectic: The Pulse of Freedom*, London: Verso, 1993, chapters 1.5–1.7, 2.1, 2.2 and 2.7.

science precisely as engaged concernful human activity with *Dasein* exploring its *Umwelt* with its equipment (language, pre-existing, yet not necessarily articulated, knowledge and tools), constituting a 'referential totality' ready-to-hand; that is, I will in effect treat science as an *existential* (employing categories). I will also consider the extent to which dialectical transcendental, more generally critical, realism can be generated by reflection on the presuppositions of the pathology of everyday life.

Finally, I should make it explicit that I do not see science as a supreme or overriding value, but only as one among others to be balanced (in a balance that cannot be wholly judged by science) in ergonic, emancipatory and eudaimonistic activity. Nor do I think the objects of science exhaust reality. On the contrary, they afford only a particular angle or slant on reality, picked out precisely for its explanatory scope and power. Moreover, alongside ethical naturalism I am committed to moral realism and I would also like to envisage an adjacent position in aesthetics, indeed viewing it as a branch of practical philosophy, the art of living well. A last word here. Starting with knowledge as a systematic phenomenon I reject that cognitive triumphalism, the roots of which lie in the epistemic fallacy, which identifies what is (and what is not) with what lies within the bounds of human cognitive competence. Reality is a potentially infinite totality, of which we know something but not how much. This is not the least of my differences with Hegel, who, although a more subtle exponent of cognitive triumphalism, Prometheanism or absolutism, nevertheless is a conduit directly connecting his older contemporary Pierre de Laplace to Lenin and thence diamat and the erstwhile command economies of the omniscient party states. But Hegel was a much more subtle exponent of cognitive triumphalism, as we shall in due course see.

§6 On the sources and general character of the Hegelian dialectic

There are two principal inflections of the dialectic in Hegel: (α) as a logical process of reason; and (*β*), more narrowly, as the dynamo of this process, the method, practice or experience of determinate negation. But to understand both one must go back to the roots of this most complex – and hotly contested – concept in ancient Greek thought. Here I will be dealing briefly with material that I will treat in C2 in thematic and historical detail.

(*α*) Derived from the Greek *dialectikē*, meaning roughly the art of conversation or discussion – more literally, reasoning by splitting into two – Aristotle credited Zeno of Elea with its invention, as deployed in his famous paradoxes – most notoriously, of motion. These were designed to vindicate the Eleatic cosmology by drawing intuitively unacceptable conclusions from its rejection. But the term was first generally applied in a recognizably philosophical context to Socrates' mode of argument, or *elenchus*, which was differentiated from the Sophistic *eristic*, the technique of disputation for the sake of rhetorical success, by the orientation of the Socratic dialogue towards the disinterested pursuit of truth. Plato himself regarded dialectic as the supreme philosophical method and the 'coping-stone' of the sciences – using it to designate both the definition of ideas by genus and species (founding logic) and their interconnection in the light of a single principle, the Form of the Good (instituting metaphysics). At one and the same time dialectic was the means of access and assent to the eternal – the universal-and-necessarily-certain – and such Forms or Ideas were the justification for the practice of dialectic. In this inaugural moment of the western philosophical tradition, fundamentalism, classical rationalist criteria for knowledge and dialectic were indissolubly linked. Aristotle's opinion of dialectic, which he systematized in his *Topics*, was considerably less exalted.[3] For the most part he regarded it as a mere propaedeutic to the syllogistic reasoning expounded in his *Analytics*, necessary to obtain the assent of one's interlocutors but, being based on merely probabalistic premisses, lacking the certainty of scientific knowledge. This last was, however, dependent on the supplementation of induction by *nous* or that intellectual intuition which allowed us to participate in the divine, i.e. knowledge as Plato had defined it (although Plato had not claimed to achieve it), the true starting points (*archai*) of science. There are places, however, where Aristotle took dialectic, as the method of working from received opinions (*endoxa*) through the discussion and progressive probative augmentation of conflicting views and aporiai, as an *alternative* way of arriving at *archai*.[4] If he had taken this course consistently, Aristotle, however, would never have satisfied Platonic criteria for knowledge (*epistēmē* rather than *doxa*), never have got beyond induction. The first great *achieved* identity theorist was already caught in a vice between Plato and Hume – a vice that was to determine the subsequent trajectory of western philosophy: *historical determination by rationalist epistemology, structural domination by empiricist ontology*.

The sense of conversational interplay and exchange, involving the assertion, contradiction, distinction and qualification of theses, was retained in the practice of medieval disputation. It was this sense that was probably most familiar to Kant, who also took over the Aristotelian conception of dialectic as relying on premisses which were in some measure inadequate as well as the analytical/dialectical contrast. For Kant, dialectic was that part of transcendental logic which showed the mutually contradictory or antinomic state into which the intellect fell when not harnessed to the data of experience. By a turn to transcendental subjectivity, Kant combined, or seemed to combine, the satisfaction of rationalist demands on knowledge with empiricist criteria for being – but only at the price of leaving things-in-themselves unknowable. Kantian dialectic showed the inherently *limited* nature of human cognitive and moral powers, the resulting inherent impossibilities, as well as the conditions of possibility of human (non-archetypal, non-holy) intelligence and will. For Kant this was enlightenment, but it entrained a systematically sundered world and a whole series of splits, between knowledge and thought, knowledge and faith, phenomena and noumena, the transcendental and the empirical, theory and (practical) reason, duty and inclination, this world and the next (splits which were also interiorized within each term separately), as well as those expressly articulated in the antinomies. These dichotomies were to be only weakly (albeit influentially) repaired in the teleologies of the *Critique of Judgement*.

This spread of connotations of dialectic includes, then, argument and conflict, disputation, struggle and split, dialogue and exchange, but also probative progress, enlightenment, demystification and the critique of illusion.

Hegel synthesized (α) this Eleatic idea of dialectic as *reason* with another ancient strand, (β) the Ionian idea of dialectic as *process* – in (γ) the notion of dialectic as the self-generating, self-differentiating and self-particularizing *process of reason*. This second (Ionian) idea typically assumed a dual form: in an *ascending dialectic*, the existence of a higher reality (e.g. the Forms or God) was demonstrated; and in a *descending dialectic*, its manifestation in the phenomenal world was explained. Prototypes of these two phases are the transcendent dialectic of matter of ancient scepticism, in which the impermanence of the sensate world, or the existence of error, or of evil, is taken as a ground for positing an unchanging or completely true, or perfectly good, realm – logically, of the forms, theologically of God; and the immanent dialectic of spiritual diremption of neo-Platonic and Christian eschatology from Plotinus and Eriugena to Silesius and Böhme, which sought to explain why a perfect and self-sufficient being (God) should disclose itself in the dependent and imperfect sphere of matter. Combination of the ascending and descending phases results in a quasi-spatio-temporal pattern of original unity, loss or division and return or reunification (graphically portrayed in Schiller's influential *Letters on the Aesthetic Education of Mankind*) or a quasi-logical pattern of hypostasis, actualization and redemption. Combination of the Eleatic and Ionian strands yields the Hegelian absolute – a logical process or *dialectic* which actualizes itself by *alienating*, or becoming other than, itself and which restores its self-unity by recognizing this alienation as nothing other than its own free expression or manifestation – a process that is recapitulated and completed in the Hegelian system itself.

The three principal keys to Hegel's philosophy – spiritual monism, realized idealism and immanent teleology – can now be cut. Together they form the pediment to it. The outcome of the first dialectical thread in Kant was a view of human beings as bifurcated, disengaged from nature and inherently limited in both cognitive and moral powers. Hegel's generation, as we shall see in C4, experienced the Kantian splits, dichotomies, disharmonies and fragmentations as calling for the restoration of what Charles Taylor has nicely called an 'expressive unity'[5] – lost since the idealized ancient Greek world – that is, in philosophical terms, for a monism – but one which, unlike

Spinoza's, paid due heed to diversity, which would be in effect a *unity-in-diversity*, and to the constitutive role of subjectivity; that is, one which preserved the legacy of Luther, Descartes and the Enlightenment formulated in the great Kantian call to 'have courage to use your own reason'[6] or radical autonomy from 'self-incurred tutelage',[7] and that was firmly predicated on the achievements of the critical philosophy. For Hegel the problem of elaborating a non-reductionist and subjective monism gradually became tantamount to the problem, posed by the ascending phase of the second dialectical thread, of developing a complete and self-consistent idealism. Such an idealism would, in fusing the finite in the infinite, retain no dualistic or non-rational residues, thereby finally realizing and vindicating the primordial Parmenidean postulate of the identity of being and thought *in* thought, underpinned by a progressivist view of history. Neither Fichte nor Schelling had been able to accomplish this. In Fichte, the non-ego or otherness of being, although originally posited by mind, remained as a permanent barrier to it; so that the principle of idealism became a mere *Sollen* or regulative ideal. Schelling, on the other hand, genuinely transcended dualism in his 'point of indifference' uniting man and nature, but less than fully rationally. For Schelling, this identity was achieved only in intuition, rather than conceptual thought, with the highest manifestation of spirit art rather than philosophy, so that the Parmenidean principle remained unrealized in thought. By contrast, in the Hegelian *Geistodyssey* of infinite, petrified (natural) and finite mind, the principle of idealism, the speculative understanding of reality as (absolute) spirit, is unfolded in the shape of an immanent teleology which shows, in response to the problem of the descending phase, how the world exists (and, at least in the human realm, develops) as a rational totality *precisely* so that (infinite) spirit can come to philosophical self-conciousness in the Hegelian system demonstrating this. Absolute idealism is the articulation and recognition of the identity of being in thought *for* thought.

In this logical process or dialectic the problem of reunification of opposites, transcendence of limitations and reconciliation of differences is carried out in the characteristic figure of what I shall call 'constellational identity'. In this dialectical inscape, which qualifies the monism of Hegelianism, the major, typically idealist, term (thought, the infinite, identity, reason, spirit, etc.) over-reaches, envelops and contains the minor, more 'materialist', term (being, the finite, difference, understanding, matter, etc.) in such a way as to preserve the distinctiveness of the minor term and to show that it, and a fortiori its distinctiveness, are teleologically necessary for the major one. The effect of the Hegelian perspective or *Ansicht* is, on Hegel's own account, 'more than a comfort, it reconciles, it transfigures the actual which seems unjust into the rational'.[8] 'To recognize reason as the rose in the cross of the present and thereby to enjoy the present, this is the rational insight which reconciles us to the actual, the reconciliation which philosophy affords.'[9]

'The dissonances of the world' thus appear, in his friend the poet Hölderlin's words in *Hyperion*, 'like the quarrel of lovers. Reconciliation is in the midst of strife, and everything that is separated finds itself again' – in the movement of self-restoring sameness or self-reinstating identity, which is the life of absolute spirit.

Hegel conducts four principal types of demonstration of this life:

1 the introductory educative dialectics of *The Phenomenology of Spirit* in the medium first of individual experience and then of collective culture;
2 the systematic ascending dialectic of the *Logics* in the abstract sphere of the categories;
3 the systematic descending dialectics of the philosophy of nature and spirit; and
4 the illustrative historical dialectics of Hegel's various lecture series, mainly in the realms of objective and absolute spirit.

(β) The motor of this process is dialectic more narrowly conceived. This is the second, essentially negative, moment in what Hegel calls 'actual thought', which drives the dialectics of (1)–(4) on. It is styled by Hegel as the 'grasping of opposites in their unity or of the positive in the negative'.[10] It is not the case, according to Hegel, that a concept merely excludes its opposite or that the negative of a term (or proposition) simply cancels it. If this were so then Aristotle's criticisms of Platonic *diairesis* and Kant's of pre-critical metaphysics would indeed entrain the anti-speculative implications they themselves drew. Rather, to the contrary, from the vantage point of reason, as distinct from the understanding, a genus always contains, explicitly or proleptically, its own differentiae; and, in a famous inversion of the Spinozan maxim '*omnis determinatio est negatio*', negation always leads to a new richer determination – this is *transformative negation* – so imparting to categories and forms of life an immanent dynamic and to their conflict an immanent resolution rather than a mutual nullification. Although the principle of the mutual exclusion of opposites, entailing rigid definitions and fixed polarities, is adequate for the finite objects grasped by common sense and the empirical sciences, the infinite totalities of reason (which, of course, constellationally embrace the former) require the dialectical principle of the identity of exclusive opposites. And Hegel's central logical claim is that the identity of opposites is not incompatible with their exclusion, *but rather depends upon it*. For it is the experience of what in non-dialectical terms would be a logical contradiction which at once indicates the need for an expansion of the universe of discourse or thought and at the same time yields a more comprehensive, richly differentiated or highly mediated conceptual form. It is *this* experience in which dialectic proper consists as the second member of a triad composed of the understanding, dialectic (or negative) and speculative (or positive) reason, representing the principles of identity, negativity and rational totality respectively. I will go into the fine structure of this dynamic shortly. On this interpretation, the dialectical fertility of contradictions depends upon their analytical unacceptability. (Hence any dialectical logic must incorporate an analytical one as a special – and vitally generative – case.) From the achieved vantage point of (positive) reason the mutual exclusivity of opposites passes over into the recognition of their reciprocal interdependence (mutual inclusion): they remain inseparable yet distinct moments in a richer, more total conceptual formation (which will in turn generate a new contradiction of its own). It is the constellational identity of understanding and reason within reason which fashions the continually recursively expanding kaleidoscopic tableaux of absolute idealism.

Dialectic, then, in this narrow sense, is a method – or better, experience – of *determinate negation* – which enables the dialectical commentator to observe the process by which the various categories, notions or forms of consciousness arise out of each other to form ever more inclusive totalities until the system of categories, notions or forms as a whole is completed. And in a still narrower sense – in which it is the second member of the understanding-dialectic-reason (U-D-R) triad – it is the truth, theory of or comment on (dc′ in the terminology introduced in §4 above) the experience or practice of the phase (notion, etc.) immediately preceding it, yielding or showing a contradiction – in effect a *theory/practice inconsistency* – which speculative reason (dr′) will resolve, only, of course, for the resolution in turn to be susceptible to a further dialectical probe. Now it is clear enough that if we stay at the level of the understanding we will not find or recognize contradictions in our concepts or experience – in general it takes an effort or quantum leap – in what we may call a *σ transform* – to find the contradiction(s), anomalies or inadequacies in our conceptualizations or experience – and another quantum leap – which we may call a *τ transform* – to resolve them. And Hegelian dialectic is just this method or practice of stretching our concepts to the limit, forcing from and pressing contradictions on them, contradictions which are not immediately obvious to the understanding (hence the need for the σ transform), and then resolving them, a resolution which is not immediately obvious either (hence the need for the τ transform). (This is one of the reasons why Hegelian dialectic is so difficult to *understand*; and a respect in which Hegel's talk about the self-development of the concept, as if it were automatic [understanding-like], is at the very least disingenuous.) From this perspective Kant's great merit is that he advances, at least in the case of the antinomies, to the level of dc′ (he makes the σ transform), but fails to take the further leap into speculative reason, fails to resolve them (to make the τ transform), so falling back as a (transcendental idealist) philosopher of the understanding. But in fact Hegel does not think that the U-D-R scheme exhausts the matter. I should hasten to add that the σ and τ transforms are my own gloss on Hegel. He thinks the understanding, which at one point he characterizes as an 'almighty power', is a great advance on the pre-reflective reasonableness of ordinary life which readily tolerates contradictions without finding anything problematic in them, so there is need for a transition from pre-reflective thought, what I shall call the *ρ transform*, to the understanding before we are in a position to engage in ordinary (non-speculative) science or philosophy. It was, of course, to this pre-reflective reasonableness that the later Wittgenstein was always trying, but never quite able, to return. Hegel also thinks that we have to 'return' to life, but after (dialectical and speculative) philosophy – in post-philosophical wisdom (in what I will call the *υ transform*). So we could schematize the whole process as in Figure 1.

For Hegel, then, truth is the whole, the whole is a process and this process is reason (dt′ as dp′ as dr′). Its result is reconciliation to life in (Hegelian) freedom. Error lies in one-sidedness, incompleteness and abstraction. Its symptom is the contradictions it generates and its remedy their incorporation into fuller, richer, more concrete, inclusive, englobing and highly mediated conceptual forms. In the course of this process, the famous principle of *dialectical sublation* (ds′) or *Aufhebung* is observed: as the dialectic unfolds, no partial insight is ever lost. In fact the Hegelian dialectic progresses in two basic modes: (*α*) by bringing out what is implicit, but not explicitly articulated, in some notion or social or conceptual form (what I will term 'teleonomic push'); or (*β*) by repairing some want, lack or inadequacy in it ('teleological pull'). Both are instances of *real negation* in my terms, but only (*α*) is consistent with a rigorously ex ante, *autogenetic* process/progress of a kind to which, however we interpret him epistemologically (on which in a moment), he is certainly in his dialectics committed. Both may, moreover, be said to involve some theory/practice inconsistency, at least insofar as the notion or form makes, implicitly or explicitly, some claim to completion or adequacy, as the category Being from which the *Logics* start may be said to do. Truth is, however, not only the whole but a norm against which the adequacy of any particular reality to its notion and its stage in the development of the notion or reality (i.e. the idea in its otherness and return to self-

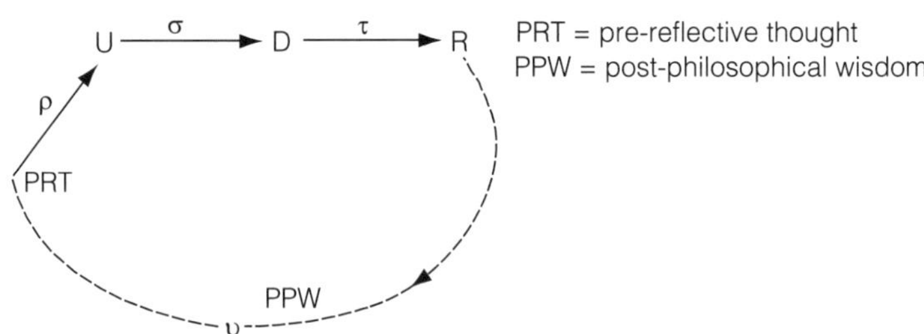

Figure 1 The logic of Hegel's dialectic

consciousness) can be assessed. 'Dialectical', then, in contrast to 'reflective' (or analytical) thought – the thought of the understanding – grasps concepts and forms of life in their systematic interconnections, not just their determinate differences, and considers each development as a product of a previous less developed phase, whose necessary truth or fulfilment it, in some sense and measure, is; so that there is always some tension, latent irony or incipient surprise between any form and what it is in the process of becoming. In short, Hegelian dialectic is the actualized entelechy of the present, comprehended (and so enjoyed) as the end of everything that has led up to it.

§7 On the immanent critique and limitations of the Hegelian dialectic

It is now possible to make some systematic connections between the Hegelian dialectic and the argument we have developed so far, and to comment further upon the former. I shall distinguish (α) Hegel's global dialectics, of the kind discussed in §6(α), from (β) his local dialectics, of the sort schematized by the U-D-R movement of thought and from, within this, the dialectical moment proper (γ). The general character of any U-D-R movement or transition is that of a preservative determinate negation. Now this has the very interesting property of representing a *non-arbitrary principle of stratification*, structuration or superstructure-formation, which I shall explore later. Suffice it to say now that, properly transposed and situated, it forms the kernel to the solution of an important class of philosophical problems (those turning on the absence of an analogue of dr′ or dg′ at 1M) as well as being an interesting ontological figure in its own right (forming, for instance, an analogue of real material emergence). Within any U-D-R movement, the dialectical moment proper (dc′) reports and speculative reason (dr′) remedies a *real negation* or absence in the base concept or form at, let us say, level L_1. The dialectical movement to the resolution at L_2 consists in a *transformative negation* of a determinate and preservative type (in consciousness or experience of that at L_1). But I have said in §3 above that all transformative negations are also real negations (though the converse is not the case). In virtue of what is *this* transformative negation a real negation? It absents the absence in L_1. (This is the sense in which determinate negation is the negation of the negation.) It does this by *dialectically bracketing* and retaining or incorporating the base concept, say e; the lack, inadequacy or internal incoherence within e, identified in D; *and* the tension, inconsistency or contradiction between e and what it is meant or trying to be (or implicitly is), identified in the probing comment, and a fortiori the theory/practice inconsistency between the base concept and its comment, in what is in effect a continually unfolding process within a permanent memory store. In this expanding warehouse of reason, each successive operation is in principle bracketed and retained.* Hegelian determinate negation constitutes, then, at once a transformation in the consciousness of the dialectical observer and an expansion of the existing conceptual field. Both are (in principle) additive and cumulative: nothing except absence itself is lost.

The Hegelian totality is constellationally closed, completed. Hegel's, like Aristotle's, is an achieved identity theory, but, unlike Aristotle's, it incorporates the sequence of stages (or conceptual shapes) leading up to it as moments within it and is in fact nothing but this movement of shapes including the finalizing consummating stage, the self-consciousness of spirit as (absolute) spirit in the Hegelian system itself. Speculative philosophy – and its social matrix, rational history – is constellationally finished, at an end. It is at a plateau. There remains a future, of course, but this can be grasped by the understanding – it does not require dialectic or speculative reason. This is the constellational identity of the future within the (Hegelian) present. Now, whatever Hegel says about the autogenetic development of the concept, it is clear as noonday that very few of Hegel's local dialectics take the (α) teleonomic push form, that is, satisfy the requirements of rigorous ex ante progress. It is the failure of concepts and forms to meet the requirement of the posited end – the absolute idea as absolute spirit – this lack and this teleology, that pulls the Hegelian dialectic forwards. It is generally only *retrospectively*, ex post, that a stage can be seen to be deficient. If Hegel's local, and by extension global, dialectics *did* satisfy the ex ante requirement, then the dialectical comment that issues from the σ transform (dc′) and the speculative reason issuing from the τ transform that resolves it (dr′) could both – and together – be said without qualification to constitute immanent critiques – dc′ of the base concept or form (at L_1) and dr′ of that and dc′. As it is, we have to qualify this, and to distinguish accordingly between (α') genuinely autosubversive (ex ante radical and so determinate transformative) *negations* and (β') merely retrospectively situatable (ex post) ones. (In the latter case the critique is really transcendent, not immanent.) And accordingly we might distinguish between good and bad radical negations. Of course, as the Hegelian totality is constellationally closed, all the contradictions, whether teleonomically or teleologically generated, are *internal ones* – and neglect of external contradictions and more generally constraints, has been a damaging feature of Marxian social theory in the Hegelian mould, one which the foil, say, of Aristotelian dialectics may help to correct. This question of the autogenesis of the dialectical movement is closely bound up with the *linearity*

* Negations do not nullify and contradictions do not spread within this system – because to say of something that it is false does not remove it (it has been said) and to say of a pair or more that they are contradictory is not itself contradictory (their contradictoriness is bracketed and negated at a higher level and in this simple way – which bears obvious analogies with the theory of types in standard logic – both the contradictions and their determinate negation are retained).

of the Hegelian dialectic. Once again Hegel's theory is at odds with his practice here. His dialectics are not in fact logically, as distinct from textually, linear: they job around all over the place, affecting an incessant variety of *perspectival switches* motivated by Hegel's desire not to just illustrate his dialectics but also to absorb and treat more and more phenomena dialectically in a continuing – and in principle open-ended – process of dialectical suction. Nor is there any reason in principle why dialectics of a Hegelian (or non-Hegelian) type should be linear. They could consist in recursively unfolding matrices, *Gestalten* or any of a variety of topological modes. Surface linearity does, however, seem imposed by the requirements of the textual, especially narrative, form – in what I have elsewhere called 'continuous series'.[11] (Derrida's use, and concept, of spacing is in fact a conscious attempt to overcome this.) These issues of autogeneticity and linearity are related to, but in principle distinct from, the epistemological status of Hegel's dialectics. There are three main interpretations: (a) that they are, or purport to be, totally self-generative and autonomous, dependent on no external subject-matter – the realization of the dream of intellectual intuition from Aristotle to Fichte in a *hyperintuitive*[12] and parthenogenetic process, including – in the transition from Logic to Nature, i.e. in the alienation of the absolute idea – a moment heterocosmic with the creation of the world by God; (b) that they are, or purport to be, the dialectical treatment of various subject-matters, most notably those treated by previous philosophers, which Hegel has thoroughly (and perhaps totally) assimilated and critiqued and is now dialectically expounding – this is the *transformative* or re-appropriative interpretation, most notably formulated as a critique of Hegel's own self-understanding (or representation) of his practice by Trendelenburg; (c) that they are simple phenomenological *descriptions* of a dialectic in the real or at least of the notion as conceptually understood reality – an interpretation that obviously fits the *Phenomenology* and the historical lecture series best and which has been most persuasively and influentially argued by Kojève.[13] I shall return to these issues later.

Corresponding to the distinction just made between good and bad radical negations (and immanent versus transcendent critiques), I want to distinguish between good and bad totalities. *Good totalities* are, though this is not their only characteristic, open; *bad totalities* are, whether constellationally or otherwise, closed. Now this is the exact opposite of Hegel's point of view. For him an open totality would conjure up the spectre of an infinite regress – it would be a 'bad infinite'. But why should an open totality involve an infinite regress? An infinite regress implies *more of the same*, that significant changes (and even the principles of change) might not change, which is just what the concept of an open totality denies. Later I will show that totalities in general are and must be open. But for the moment let us stick with Hegel. Even if it is admitted that there is some kind of inadequacy or lack in an open totality (tautologically, a lack of completion), there is no inadequacy or lack in the *thought* of an open totality, which is what is at stake here. This thought can even, and perhaps must, be constellationally contained within the present (itself an indefinite boundary zone between past and future). Of course, Hegel's realized idealism, his principle of identity, will not allow him to accept this; there must be no mismatch – rather an identity – between totality and the thought of totality. But if truth consists in totality and the conformity of an object to its notion, it is clear that the concept of an open totality must be more true (complete and adequate) than the concept of a closed totality, because it is more comprehensive, englobing and contains the latter as a special case.

As I have described it, the real work of the dialectic is done by the σ transform which identifies the anomaly or lack in e (at L_1) and the τ transform which remedies it at L_2. I shall show in §9 how this U-D-R process can illuminate the epistemological dialectic in science, just as the non-arbitrary principle of stratification (logically) or superstructure-formation (spatio-temporally) involved in Hegelian preservative dialectical sublation illustrates analogous principles in nature and society. I shall also be arguing in C2.6 that although Hegel's global and crucial local dialectics fail, dialectical arguments are a perfectly proper species of transcendental argument belonging to the wider genus of retroductive (ascending) – explanatory (descending) argumentation in science. Dialectical arguments (and, for instance, the ontological necessities [and contingencies] they can establish) are no more the privilege of absolute idealism than transcendental arguments are the prerogative of Kant. I shall further argue that in the theory/practice inconsistency which the dialectical moment proper (dc′) reports he has identified the most basic form of critique (in philosophy, science and everyday life): immanent critique. Unfortunately, locally and globally theory/practice inconsistency (which I shall sometimes abbreviate to T/P inc.) or incoherence is always for Hegel resolved in thought, in theory. The practice therefore remains. Transformative negation is confined to thought. There is no 4D in Hegel, rather the transfiguration of actuality in the post-philosophical reconciliation or υ transform. Once again Hegel is untrue to his theory of truth. If reality is out of kilter with the notion of it, it is reality which should be adjusted, not its truth. The unity (or coherence) of theory and practice must be achieved in practice. Otherwise the result is not autonomy, but heteronomy and the reappearance of a Kant-like rift. Even the thought of the unity of theory and practice (in theory or practice) must be achieved in practice. Hypostatizing thought not only detotalizes the reality, it also detotalizes the *thought* of reality. Here once more the Hegelian totality is revealed as incomplete. This amounts, of course, to an immanent critique of Hegel: his totality is incomplete, his theory inconsistent with his practice and the master concept which drives his dialectics on (for the most part teleologically) – lack or absence (in my terms, real negation) – is not preserved within his system. Positivity and self(-identity), the very characteristics of the understanding, are always restored at the end of reason. Hegelian dialectic is un-Hegelianly-dialectical.

It is also a special case. Within the σ and τ transforms – as at the actual or notional moment D which mediates them – we have moments of *indeterminate* and *underdeterminate negation*. (The same applies mutatis mutandis in the case of the ρ and υ transforms.) Linear radical negation – the production of an outcome as a result of a self-negating process alone – is clearly untypical: as we move in the *Logics* from simple to more complex categories (and the same holds true in Hegel's other textual dialectics), more and more determinations are brought in – and we shall see later that Hegel's doctrine of the speculative proposition, for example, can be heuristically fruitful in social science – but these determinations are always still internal or radical ones, or at the very best constellationally internal. More generally, it is clear that real transformative negations in geo-history are very rarely of the (even essentially) preservative, i.e. additive (superimpository), type. Indeed, insofar as every notional or social form – including those occurring in the universality of thought – is finite (i.e. insofar as the premisses of Hegel's dialectic of determinate being or 'matter' is true), all space-time beings are 'vanishing mediators'.[14] However, in an Hegelian *Aufhebung*, is not error (partiality, one-sidedness) lost? Hegel will perhaps want to say that the erroneous has been retained as a partial aspect of the truth, but either the error has been cancelled in the coming-to-be or fruition of the end or nothing has been cancelled and *Aufgehoben* loses its threefold meaning – to annul, preserve and sublimate – and the whole Hegelian project is without point or rationale, for, at the very least, a lack of reconciliation to actuality must be lost. In fact in any genuine (materialist) *Aufhebung* it is clear that something has to be lost, even if it is only time ([neg]entropy). On the other hand, it is equally obvious that processes occur in geo-history which are not, at least with respect to some determinate characteristic and within some determinate space-time band, negating but purely accretory, cumulative engrossments or developments. Generally one cannot say a priori whether the geo-historical outcome or result (dr^0) of a process of a Hegelian-dialectical type will

(a) consist of the resolution of the contradiction, inadequacy or lack (dr†);
(b) consist in a rational or reasonable resolution of it (dr');
(c) consist in a rational resolution which conforms to the Hegelian form of radical preservative determinate negation (dr'') – a form which, in its concrete employment, only makes sense if one is prepared to distinguish between essential, significant or valuable characteristics and those which are not
(d) and affords us reconciliation to life (dr'''), let alone
(e) encourages mutual recognition in a free society (dr'''').

Waiving this last for the moment, we can say that Hegelian dialectic identifies what is patently a limiting and special case of a more general schema which can be written as

$$dr^0 \geq dr^\dagger \geq dr' \geq dr'' \geq dr'''.$$

Any general theory of dialectic will have to be able to situate the conditions of possibility and limits of non-resolutary results, non-reasonable resolutions, non-radical-preservative-determinate-negational reasons, and non-reconciliatory radical preservative determinate negations.

[. . .]

DIALECTIC

The logic of absence – arguments, themes, perspectives, configurations

§1 Absence

In C1.3 I argued that real negation > transformative negation > radical negation of a determinate, indeterminate, fuzzy, duplicitous and a mélange of other genres. In C1.6 I claimed that it is real negation or the *absent*, whether in the guise of the inexplicit (as in the case of teleonomic push) or the merely incomplete (teleological pull), that drives the Hegelian dialectic on, and that will drive the dialectic past him. Incidentally the epistemological dialectic sketched in C1.9 can function as the Hegelian dialectic normally operates, by simply overcoming incompleteness – e.g. by augmenting generality or depth without prior anomaly.[15] However, the more typical case here will be that where an inconsistency, caused by a relevant conceptual or empirical lacuna, generates the move to further completeness – in a Gödelian dialectic of:

absence → inconsistency → greater completeness

in principle without end.

Real negation is most simply first considered as the *presence* in some more or less determinate region of space-time (comprising, as a relational property of the system of material things, an objective referential grid) *of an absence* at some specific level or context of being of some more or less determinate entity, thing, power, event, aspect or relation, etc. Consider as a paradigm a stapler missing from a desk drawer, or a tool from a workbench. I want to focus here for ease of exposition on simple determinate non-being within a determinate locale, which, relative to any possible indexicalized observer on any possible world-line, is existentially intransitive, whether or not the absence is positively identified, or even identifiable. But the argument may be easily extended to deal with less determinate kinds. Thus the region may be not only as large or small as is naturally possible but indefinite and/or open. And the entity may be, if it is present, hidden and perhaps necessarily unobservable to creatures like us, whether prosthetically aided or not. The absence may be deep or superficial, real but not actual. The region may be totally empty, constitute a level-specific void or just not contain x. x may be never anywhere (as in simple non-existence), sometimes somewhere else (as in finite or limited existence) or just spatio-temporally distant (as in the 'duality of absence' and, we can add, 'presence', mentioned in C1.3). The absent thus includes, but is not exhausted by, the past and outside. And it may be more or less systematically (e.g. causally) connected to the presence or absence of other determinate beings. At the boundary of the space-time region it may be difficult to say whether x is present or absent or neither or both (or both neither and/or both); and, if 'present' and 'absent' are treated as contraries, we are once more confronted with the spectre of rejecting the principle of non-contradiction or excluded middle or both. Note that the possibility of action/passion at-a-distance and/or across (possibly level-specific) voids – in effect, non-substantial process – provides another ground for regarding real negation (absence) as the more basic category than transformative negation (change). I will postpone treating complications that derive from the fourfold polysemy of real negation, noted in C1.3, viz. (a) as simple absence (our focus here), including nothing; (b) as simple absenting, e.g. through divergent distanciation or substantial or non-substantial process (with or without transformation), (c) as process-in-product, e.g. as in the existential constitution of the nature of an absence by its geo-history; and (d) as product-in-process, e.g. in the iterable or non-iterable exercise of its causal powers. Similarly for those that derive from the phenomena of emergent and/or divergent (or possibly convergent) spatio-temporalities of causally efficacious absent things.

Someone may ask 'what is being negated in real negation?' In the case where x has been absent*ed* from a domain of being, whether by transformation and/or by distanciation, the propriety of this way of speaking may perhaps be granted. But where x is altogether absent from being, as in never anywhere existence, if the reader wishes to substitute 'non-being' for 'real negation' I have no objection. For it is my intention to maintain in this section (1) that we can refer to non-being, (2) that non-being exists, and that (3) not only must it be conceded that non-being has ontological priority over being within zero-level being, (4) but, further, non-being has ontological *priority* over being. In short, negativity wins. My aim in vindicating negativity in what may seem a prima facie paradoxical way is to foreground the contingency – both epistemological and ontological – of existential, not least human existential, questions which the tradition of ontological monovalence screens. I shall contend that this exercise is necessary for that emancipation of dialectic for (the dialectic of) emancipation that is the aim of this work.

My first objective is to argue, against Plato and Frege, that reference does not presuppose existence; more specifically, that it does not presuppose either factual existence or positive factual existence. I want to differentiate within the class of ontics – understood as the intransitive objects of specific epistemic inquiries – positive existences or presences, which I shall dub 'onts', from negative existences or absences, which I shall nominate 'de-onts'. Next I am going to identify the ontic content, i.e., if you like, the referential force, weight or charge of a proposition with what Hare has called its 'phrastic', and to make modified use of his further terminology of 'neustics' and 'tropics'.[16] As I shall employ his triptych, tropics – initially introduced to register mood – demarcate domains of discourse, e.g. to distinguish the fictional, I, and the factual, F; neustics convey attitudes such as acceptance, rejection or indecision, written as √, x and / respectively; while phrastics express the ontic content of a proposition, the state of affairs it describes or is about, which may be positive or negative, represented as (e) and (-e). A (positive or negative) affirmative factual claim typically occurs at the moment at which (in what I will characterize in C3.2 as the dialectic of truth) '*referential detachment*' – informally the ontological detachment of the referent from the (inter-subjective/social) referential act (reference), initially justified by the axiological need to refer to something other than ourselves – becomes legitimate and necessary. The argument for referential detachment is the argument for existential intransitivity and, in science, is the ground for the argument for the stratified, differentiated and changing ontology which critical realism has hitherto deployed. And to speak of the 'ontic content' of a proposition is merely to indicate the ontic or referential aspect of the 'referential–expressive' duality of function which is a necessary component, or so I shall argue, of an adequate theory of truth. But I should also hereby give notice that I will be working with a much more general notion of 'referent' and 'reference' than the ontologically extensionalist mainstream countenances. On my position, one can refer not only to existent (or nonexistent) things, but also to such things characterized in particular ways. Thus we can refer to laws, powers and tendencies; to totalities, relations and aspects; to intensions, intentions and actions (or inactions); and to our discourse about all of them. To refer is just to pick something out for discussion and/or other action, and thus there are no more a priori limits on what we can designate than there are on what we can discuss. This does not abolish the distinction between the activities of reference and predication, but merely enables us to say (predicate) things about everything we normally do and necessarily must.

I have argued elsewhere that we can refer within, as well as (of course) to, fictional discourse. Typically this will presuppose an operation on a tropic. Thus the staging of *Macbeth* will convey the 'conversationally candid' implication, to invoke Grice's convenient expression, that Macbeth did not exist, and in referential and other acts in *Macbeth* we characteristically suspend our belief in that implication. Within the realm of factual discourse, the rejection of a proposition, say to the effect that caloric exists, depends upon an operation on a neustic, denying, in the transitive dimension, the existence, in the intransitive dimension, of caloric or whatever. Let us pass now to real negation. To assert that Pierre is not in the café or that the *Titanic* sank or that Fred's golf balls were lost or that Sara couldn't keep her date with Jemma or that Sophie missed her cue in the matinée presupposes a factual neustic in the transitive dimension, but the ontic content of the proposition – that which we reject or accept and what it is that, in (groundedly) accepting, we referentially detach from our speech acts – is now, unlike the case of caloric, negative. Real negation involves an operation on the phrastic (–e), and the negativity is now explicitly ontological. But patently I can refer to, as I can perceive (or be in a position to infer), Pierre's absence, just as readily as I can refer to the denial of caloric's existence or to Macbeth's fictionality. All three convey negative existential import. But, as I have set up the sequence, they do so in three different ways. The tropic fictional operator 'I' implies, but is not the same as, the neustic rejection of an existential proposition, which in turn implies, but is not the same as, phrastic de-ontification. There are at least three different modes in which things may be said not to be (and I want to assert the logical propriety of fictional and factual, I and F, acceptance and rejection, √ and x, and being and non-being ( ) and (–) operators) – although, of course, there is only one sense in which things are not. F√ (–e) gives the fine structure of the simple factual positive affirmation of Pierre's death.

Real negativity, understood most simply as absence, or, qua process, absenting, and a fortiori the critique of ontological monovalence, is vital to dialectic. Absenting processes are crucial to dialectic conceived as the logic of *change* – which is absenting. Absenting absences, which act as constraints on wants, needs or (more generally) well-being, is essential to dialectics interpreted as the logic of *freedom*. And the whole point of *argument*, on which dialectic has been most traditionally modelled, is to absent mistakes. The absence concerned may be transfactual or actual, in process or static, internally related in a totality or isolated, an inaction or not (cf. 1M–4D).* The dialectical comment (dc′) typically isolates an absence (which the resolution repairs), indicating a theory/practice inconsistency or irrelevance, and advis-

* Statements about transfactualities should not be confused with statements about negativities, although the classes intersect. The d_r/d_a distinction gets its force from the fact that a tendency (which may be positive or negative) may be exercised without being actualized in a (positive or negative) outcome. The d_r/d_+ distinction stems from the consideration that things, their causal powers, their processual and possibly mediated exercise and their results may be absent (negative) as well as present (positive). That said, it should be clear that the concept of a tendency absent from actuality presupposes the critique of ontological monovalence; and that absenting processes are, in open systems, all tendencies, so that the distinctions are interdependent. Indeed the elision of natural necessity, the epistemic fallacy and ontological monovalence I shall declaim as the unholy trinity of irrealism. (The pun is intentional: holes – voids – constitutive absences.)

ing against its dialectical (critical realist) universalizability.** In dialectical critical realism the category of absence is pivotal to 1M–4D links. Thus a 1M non-identity or alterity may generate a 2E absence causing a 3L alienating detotalization or split-off resulting in a fragmented impotent self – *or* to a transformed transformative totalizing praxis absenting the split, or, let us suppose, a reconstituted unity-in-diversity, diagrammatized in Figure 2. This is just one example of malign/benign 1M–4D links, in which 2E absence/absenting is the key mediation between 1M non-identity, 3L totality and 4D agency, which has as its prototype the absenting of absence manifest in the satisfaction of desire. More generally, dialectics depends upon the positive identification and transformative elimination of absences. Indeed, it just is, in its essence, the process of *absenting absence.* Moreover, I shall show in C4.2 how the key to the critical diagnosis and rational resolution of the problems of philosophy, generated by 1M destratification or homology, 3L detotalization, 4D de-agentification and 2E positivization, lies in the repair of the absence of the concepts of structure and heterology, concretion, relationality and totality, agentive agency and, above all, absence itself. Reference to absence is quintessential to non-idealistic dialectic. Hence my polemical reference in C1.3 to 'subject', as distinct from traditional predicative and propositional, negation. Later I will connect the concept of, if you like, referential negativity to developmental negation, the critique of the presupposition – which I shall call 'fixism' – of fixed subjects in the traditional subject-predicate propositional form (which presupposes the rigidity, and hence arbitrariness, of definitions), Fischer's notion of necessary as distinct from impossible contradiction (contradictio in *subjecto* rather than in *adjecto*), expressing the idea of a subject in process of formation and the possible uses of the Hegel-derivative 'speculative proposition' in social science.

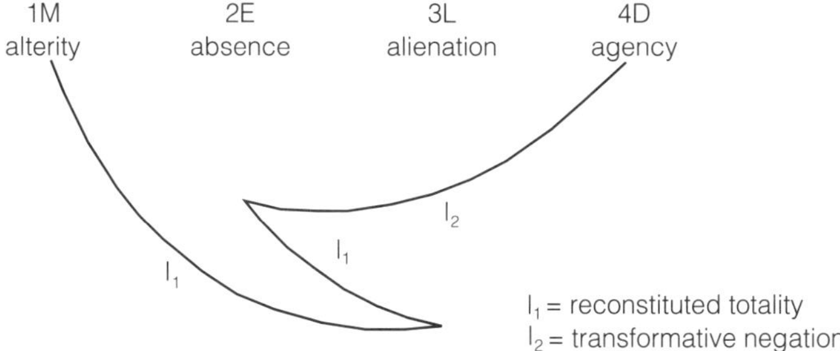

Figure 2

** For the moment this may be regarded as transfactual, processual-directional-developmental, concrete, agentive (agent-specific or actionable) and transformative – a formula I will later both explain and qualify.

An extreme case of absence is never anywhere existence. This can be expressed in the form of a non-existential proposition, e.g. in science. Popper holds such propositions to be unfalsifiable, and so 'unscientific'. Despite the fact that counter-examples abound in science (phlogiston, the aether, Vulcan), this is normally taken as gospel. However, in real science, individuals, particulars and universals are always already known under some more or less precise description, tied, when existential questions become pertinent within the specific context of inquiry, to definite demonstrative and recognitive criteria of existence – which they may simply fail to satisfy. Moreover, fallibilism itself depends upon the idea of identifying and remedying mistakes. This entails at the very least (leaving aside the not necessarily trivial sense in which error may be said to consist in the lack of truth) registering the recognition of error in the speech act of denial, which is absentive, and upon comprehending error as paradigmatically *dependent* upon absence; and its correction the repair, that is, the absenting, of the absence. Dialectic is at the heart of every learning process. Furthermore, it is easy to see that in any world in which human agency is to be possible, the human agent must be able to bring about a state of affairs which would not otherwise have prevailed (unless it was over-determined). Sophia acts, and so absents. That is, to put the matter in (anti-)Kantian terms (and so as to show the quiescence and de-agentification implicit in transcendental idealism), the human agent must be able to effect the source of the 'given'. So ontic change (and hence absence) must occur in a world containing human agency. Hence epistemic change must be possible and necessary too. Moreover, both meta-epistemic change (to accommodate change in change about beliefs) and conceptual change (to enable change in definitions) must be possible and necessary also. We begin to envisage dialectic as the great 'loosener', permitting empirical 'open-texture', in the manner of Waismann, and structural fluidity and interconnectedness, in a Marxian-Bakhtinian fashion, alike (and their distinction to boot). Again, unless Sophia sees herself necessarily *acting and so absenting*, she cannot reflexively situate (and hence detotalizes) herself. That is to say, she in practice alienates and reifies, and hence *absents* herself and/or her agency, in a way for which she cannot consistently account. Not to admit absence to our ontology (in that very admission) is to commit *performative contradiction*, the basic form of theory/practice and reflexive inconsistency, and self-referential paradox.

To this it might be argued that there cannot be a complete parity at the transcendental level between the positive and the negative. Fictional disclosure is dependent upon a matrix of factual discourse, in which neustic crosses are cradled by axiologically necessary ticks, in which in turn absences are only identifiable via the network of positive material things. To this objection there are a number of ripostes. First, the identification of a positive existent is a human act. So it involves the absenting of a pre-existent state of affairs, be it only a state of existential doubt. This may be taken as a transcendental deduction of the category of absence, and a transcendental refutation and immanent critique of ontological monovalence. Second, the material world operates as a referential grid for the identification of positive and negative existents, onts and de-onts, only in virtue of their mutual exclusion relations, that is to say, in virtue of their differences in space and changes in time. Only in a state of eternal all-pervasive token monism would the category of absence not be necessary for the deduction of coherent concepts of space and time (which would be really redundant). Such a monism would make all becoming, including acts of identification, impossible. In any event we know it to be false. More important is to note the connection between causality and absence. All causal determination, and hence change, is transformative negation or absenting. All causes are in space-time and effects are negations. Later I shall make much of the point that causality must be grasped as intrinsically tensed spatio-temporalizing process. For the moment we need only record that there is no substance without causality, no material system without its changes. This can also be regarded as a transcendental refutation of monovalence and token monism (which must detotalize the monist). The identification of positive existents depends upon a changing (and therefore at least ontologically bivalent) world.

At this point, having registered the connections between space and difference and time and change, I want to digress slightly to comment upon the difference between change and difference. Both categories are essential (and presuppose absence). But (a) change cannot be analysed in terms of difference, as the analytic tradition from the late Plato has been wont to do, any more than (b) difference can be analysed in terms of change, the converse fallacy of the dialectical tradition from at least Plotinus.

(a) Change cannot be analysed in terms of difference because it presupposes the idea of a continuing thing in a tensed process. If the ontologically monovalent tradition dates from the Parmenidean 'one', mediated by the Platonic exegesis of negation as difference, it is completed by the Kantian error of supposing that one can always replace statements about negativities or their derivatives by ones employing purely positive predicates. But Pierre's absence from the café does not *mean* the same as Genet sitting in his place or Pierre's playing football instead of meeting Sartre. (b) Difference cannot be analysed in terms of change because it includes the idea of two or more non-identical tokens, which cannot be necessarily reduced to a unitary origin (which would have to be the single unique origin of everything to yield the required result). More to the immediate point, to allow at least two (and by an extension of this argument, an indefinite number of) non-identicals is transcendentally necessary for our discourse to achieve referential detachment, that is, to be able to talk about something other than itself or even to talk *about* itself at all. Intransitivity is as transcendentally irreducible as I will later argue tense to be. Of course none of this is to deny that differentiating changes and changing differences occur. (In the meantime the reader should be forewarned that in this chapter [and indeed throughout this book], I will be conducting a side polemic against monism, reductionism and fundamentalism, including the ideas of unique beginnings, rock bottoms and fixed foundations, all of which smack of anthropic cognitive triumphalism, which I will connect to centrism and endism as endemic to irrealist dialectics as well as the bulk of analytics.)

My third response to the objection claiming ontological priority for the positive is to argue that a world without voids (absences), that is, a 'non-clumpy' material object world, in which, as on the classical Cartesian-Newtonian paradigm, action is by continuous contiguous impact – in its canonical atomistic form, of condensely compacting particles (a conception which Newton never eschewed*) – would be a world in which nothing could move or occur, as it presupposes an impossible conjunction of atomicity, rigidity and immediacy. That is to say, in effect, non-atomicity (and hence constitutive absence) and/or action-at-a-distance (and hence across voids) are transcendentally necessary features of an intelligible material object world.**[17] Transmission of energy, like information in inter-personal communication, is possible only by (substantial or non-substantial) travel across, at the very least, level-specific gaps. This being granted takes me to my fourth argument against the ontological dominance of the positive. If a totally positive material object world – a packed world without absences – is impossible, there is no a priori reason to exclude the opposite – namely a total void, literally nothing. Negativity is constitutively essential to positivity, but the converse does not follow. Leave aside the Heideggerian question of why there is something rather than nothing. There could have been nothing rather than something. Of course this is a counterfactual. Beings exist. But by transcendental argument, non-being is constitutively essential to being. Non-being is a condition of possibility of being. No non-being is a sufficient condition of impossibility of being. But there is no logical incoherence in totally no being. Dialectical arguments establish the conditions of possibility (dr′) of the conditions of impossibility (dc′) of some initially established result or posit. Now, employing a strategy of 'dialectical detachment' from our initial premiss – positive existence – in the metacritical end-game, we can argue that not only is a total void possible, but if there was a *unique* beginning to everything it could only be from nothing by an act of

* The Michelson–Morley experiment was designed to determine the velocity of the aether relative to the earth.

** This has a philosophical social analogue in what Lovejoy, thinking especially of Leibniz but equally applicable to Hegel, has called 'the principle of plenitude',[18] but which could perhaps be more aptly labelled 'the principle of repletion'. Its inapplicability to a world dominated by scarcity (more precisely the combination of scarcity and waste), characterized by enormous inequities and subject to absolute ecological constraints should not need remarking.

radical autogenesis. So that *if* there was an originating Absolute, nothing would be its schema or form, constituted at the moment of initiation by the spontaneous disposition to become something other than itself. Similarly, if there was a unique ending to everything it would involve a collapse to actualized nothingness, absolutely nothing. In sum, complete positivity is impossible, but sheer indeterminate negativity is not.*

Within the world as we know it, non-being is at least on a par with being. Outwith it the negative has ontological primacy. Let us linger within the everyday world. Let me also concede the force of the point that, while the converse is equally the case, without positive being we could not know negative being; and even, recognizing the counterfactuality of the hypothesis explored in the previous paragraph, conceive of non-being as contained within a base or zero-level being. Why, it might be enquired, do I want to talk of non-being in referring to such prosaic facts as Jemma not keeping her date with Jacques? To say that Jemma or Pierre or the rain or food or self-esteem or the aether *is not* (is lacking) in some determinate context of discourse is to designate a real absence at some level, perspective, aspect, context and/or region of space-time. 'Is' and 'real' discharge the burden of ontology; 'not' and 'absent' denote negativity. To admit that real absence exists and real absentings occur is tantamount to conceding that non-beings, i.e. de-onts, are, happen, etc. We thus have the theorem: ontology > ontics > de-onts. In §6 I shall argue that it is inconceivable that 'ontology' does not refer and in C4 I shall examine the origins of the dogma of ontological monovalence and its generative role in the aporiai of irrealist philosophy in its analytical, hitherto dialectical and post-Nietzschean forms. Its effects include, as I have already suggested, the deproblematization of existential questions (as the 1M denial of natural necessity deproblematizes essential ones), securing the transmission of a pre-posited positivity from knowledge to being,

* It is customarily presupposed in cosmological discussion (a) that our cosmos is unique (so to speak, synchronically, diachronically, laterally and transcategorially); therefore (b) that its beginning was *the* unique beginning of everything – and in particular of matter, energy, space and time, the concepts of which therefore cannot be employed for or outside it; (c) that the cause of its beginning cannot be considered without antinomy or vicious regress; or (d) insofar as it can be it must be of a monadic-fissuring type, rather than as is characteristically the case in known intra-cosmic geneses, viz. beginnings of a dyadic/polyadic-fusing kind[19] (e.g. as involving an asymmetric compression of pre-existent forces); and finally (e), worst of all, that if there was a unified theory capable of explaining the physical development of the cosmos, perhaps after the earliest moments of time, this would ipso facto yield a 'GTOE' – Grand Theory of Everything.[20] These assumptions bear the heavy imprint of philosophical anthropocentrism, monism, verificationism, actualism, reductionism and cognitive triumphalism. (b) goes against the Lucretian dictum 'nil . . . fieri de nihilo' and the Hobbesian maxim that 'nothing taketh a beginning from itself'. Particular or absolutist monistic ontification is illicit. In respect of (c), note a polyadic-fissuring genesis of a Schillerian dialectic would give it a minimum five-term structure, without allowing for indeterminate or subsequent multiple negation.

dogmatically reinforcing the former as hypostatized ideas or reified facts, disguising the human agency involved and absenting (and alienating) scientists and laypersons alike from their products. The transmission of positivity from knowledge to being, covered by the epistemic fallacy and then reflected back in its ontic dual, takes place at a posited or hypothesized point of subject–object identity, abolishing intransitivity in what is in effect a point of categorial duplicity, which is actualistically generalized into eidetic eternity. Eliminating absence, most sharply experienced in contradiction and remedied by greater completeness or totality, eliminates change and error alike. Monovalence is the ideology of categorial (including epistemological) stasis. Once more, precisely the same result is achieved by the absenting of alterity, and thus the difference between change and error too. The epistemic fallacy, ontological monovalence and the actualist collapse of natural necessity (and possibility) are of a piece: the unholy trinity of irrealism.

Conversely, welcoming negativity and later totality and agency alongside 1M non-identity, depth and transfactuality to our ontology situates some very interesting possibilities. What is present from one perspective, at one level, in some region may be absent from, at or in another. Presences and absences may be recursively embedded and systematically intermingled in all sorts of fascinating ways. They may stretch forward temporally, spread outwards spatially, spiral inwards conceptually, mediate, switch or transfigure each other relationally, perspectivally or configurationally, structurally sediment, abstract, concretize, contradict and coalesce themselves. Once we specifically thematize causal efficacy, emergence, tensed spatializing process, totality and sui generis social forms, all sorts of topologies become possible: hidden depths, tangled loops, inverted hierarchies, mediatized, virtual and hyperrealities; holes-within-wholes (and vice versa), binds and blocks, intra- as well as inter-action; juxtaposed, elongated, congealed, overlapping, intersecting, condensed spatio-temporalities; intertwined, dislocated and punctured processes. We shall explore some of these in due course. As it is, consider the crucial impact that the symptomatic silence, the telling pause, the vacuum, the hiatus or the generative separation possess. Or remember the effects of the non-occurrences, the undone or left alone – the letter that didn't arrive, the failed exam, the missed plane, the monsoon that didn't occur, the deforestation of the Amazonian jungle, the holes in the ozone layer, the collapse of 'actually existing socialism', the spaces in the text, the absent authors and readers it presupposes, both the too empty and the too full. Absences, immediately or on reflection, all.* There are intervals, voids and pauses, desire, lack and need within being; and such absences and their tendential and actual absenting are, or so I

* The 'too full' reveals, in the human world, an absence of continence, balance or justice: the jewel of wisdom in the Aristotelian doctrine of the 'mean'.

am arguing, transcendentally and dialectically necessary for any intelligible being at all.

§2 Emergence

The official motive force of the Hegelian dialectic is, as we have seen, the contradiction that leads to the expansion of the universe of discourse or conceptual field by the positive identification and elimination of absences, including its former incompleteness in some relevant respect. But before I come to contradiction, I want briefly to broach the topic of emergence. This is a 1M category of non-identity but is (a) specifically ontological while (b) falling within the generic Hegelianesque class of stratificational dialectics. In emergence, generally, new beings (entities, structures, totalities, concepts) are generated out of pre-existing material from which they could have been neither induced nor deduced. There is a quantum leap, or nodal line, of (one feels like saying) the materialized imagination – or even, with Hegel, reason – akin to that occurring in the σ or τ transforms of the rudimentary epistemological dialectic of C1.9. This is matter as creative, as autopoietic. It seems, if it can be vindicated, to yield a genuine ontological analogue of Hegelian preservative determinate negation. It consists in the formation of one or other of two types of superstructure (only the first of which has generally been noted in the Marxist canon), namely, by the superimposition (Model A) or intraposition (Model B) of the emergent level *on* or *within* the pre-existing one – *superstructuration* or *intrastructuration* respectively. There is no reason why the two models should not be used in complementary fashion, say in the concept of the *intrinsic superstructure.* These do not exhaust the formal possibilities, especially once one allows extraneous, contra-punctual and transvoid action, emergent and divergent (and generally detached) spatio-temporalities and disembedding mechanisms, including the disembedding of time from space (as in an aeroplane flight) and the disembedding of space from time (as in telephone reception). But they are the most obvious ones. Emergence presupposes the rejection of the ancient antagonism of (normally physicalistic) reductionism and (typical spiritualistic) dualism alike, neither of which can sustain a concept of *agentive agency*, presupposing *intentional* materially embodied and efficacious *causality;* and both of which posit the non-phenomenality of intentionality. It acknowledges irreducible real novelty, while rejecting a transcendent cause for it – what Hegel, with medieval Christendom and Kant (especially) in mind, will pejoratively refer to as a 'beyond' or *Jenseits.*

However, before I praise emergence, I must bury Hegelian versions of it. In the real world, whether we are dealing with conceptual, social (concept-dependent, but not -exhaustive) or entirely natural (extra-conceptual) terrain, ontological dialectical processes are not generally the product of radical negation alone, let alone that of the linear kind to which Hegel leans. For our world is an open-systemic entropic totality, in which results (dr^0 in the symbolism of C1.7) are neither autogenetically produced nor even constellationally closed, but the provisional outcome of a heterogeneous multiplicity of changing mechanisms, agencies and circumstances. Moreover, in real emergence the processes are generally non-teleologically causal, only socio-spherically conceptual; and the higher level (ultimately, in Hegel, absolute spirit or, to borrow Charles Taylor's felicitous expression, 'cosmic Geist'[21]) does not posit, but is rather formed from, the lower level.[22] Furthermore, whether the outcome is, macroscopically, a new type of *structure*, or, microscopically, merely a token, or a *structuratum*, to employ Andrew Collier's useful distinction,*[23] it normally remains heteronomously conditioned and controlled by the lower-order one – onto or into which it has been super- or intraposed. Again, real emergence has an inverse that does not figure in the entelechy of the Hegelian scheme, viz. *disemergence*, the decay, demise or disjoint detachment of the higher-order level. Further, emergence may involve a substantial degree of non-preservative, rather than simply additive, superstructuration. And the result may be internally complex and differentiated, consisting in a 'laminated' system,[24] whose internal elements are necessarily 'bonded' in a multiplicity of structures (perhaps composed of their own structural hierarchies and sub-totalities). Such systems may be decentred, asymmetrically weighted, and contextually variable, as in the case of the Dennettian-Joycean self, composing an internal pluriverse (to purloin Della Volpe's redolent term[25]), populated by a plurality of narratives, in internal discordance and even palpable contradiction.[26]

Indeed emergence, which I treat in C3 as an example of the dialectic of the real and the actual, establishes distinct domains of difference qua alterity – real determinate *other-being*. Such domains have to be understood in their own terms before (α) any scientistic synchronic or (β) historicist diachronic explanatory reduction can be contemplated. Thus (α) chemical phenomena had first to be classified, described and explained in a dialectic of sui generis chemical principles before any explanatory reduction to physics became feasible,[27] while (β) the tradition of neo-Platonic-eschatological-Hegelian-vulgar Marxist thought has been plagued by assumptions of originarity, uni-linear directionality and teleological necessity of an empirically and conceptually untenable kind. It is best to take specific cases in this neck of the philosophical woods. To comprehend human agency as a causally and taxonomic-

* The concept of a structuratum, is, however, homonymous, between an ontological instance of a structure *or* a concrete individual or singular, which will normally be the condensate of, or of the effects of, a multiplicity of disjoint, and even contradictory, structures or of their ways of acting (generative mechanisms or causal powers). It will characteristically remain heteronomously conditioned, dependent upon and influenced by the levels out of which it has emerged, even where it is causally efficacious on them, as clearly society is on nature and agency on inanimate and animate matter alike.

ally irreducible mode of matter is not to posit a distinct substance 'mind' endowed with reasons for acting apart from the causal network, but to credit intentional embodied agency with distinct (emergent) causal powers from the biological matter out of which agents were formed, on which they are capable of reacting back (and must, precisely as materially embodied causally efficacious agents, do so, if they are to act at all), but from which, in an open-systemic totality in which events are not determined before they are caused,[28] neither such beings nor the transformations and havoc they would wreak on the rest of nature could have been predicted ex ante. On such a *synchronic emergent causal powers materialism*, reasons (that are acted on) just are causes. Against dualism, we can say that it is in virtue of our complex biological constitution that human agents have the powers we do; while denying, against reductionism, that a power can be reduced to its material basis or condition of possibility any more than the acceleration of a car is the same as its engine. Contemporary reductionist materialisms both face insoluble aporiai and sneak dualism (of a disembodied linguistified neo-Kantian kind) in by the back door.[29] For instance, the very statement of eliminative materialism appears inconsistent with its project – a self-eliminating act. At the time of its utterance such a statement transforms the material world, yielding a performative contradiction or theory/practice inconsistency again. And in a non-solipsistic (or non-token-monist) world, central state materialism cannot account for the understanding of meaning which mediates two or more neuro-physiologically distinct states in inter-subjective transactions, whether they consist in buying a bunch of bananas or enunciating central state materialism itself.

This is just as well. For accepting the causal efficacy of reasons enables us to make sense of the programme of experimental science. For in an experiment scientists co-determine an empirical result which, but for their intentional causal agency, would not have occurred; yet which at the same time potentially affords us epistemic access to the real, transfactually efficacious, but normally empirically counterfactual[30] *causal structures of the world*.[31] (Transfactual thus underpins counterfactual truth.) This furnishes us with a transcendental deduction of emergence, at least for the human realm, which at the same time functions as an immanent critique of scientistic reductionist materialism. But it is furthermore of philosophical significance in two respects. First, insofar as it is inconsistent with the ontological actualism, regularity determinism and spatio-temporary block universalism (which I shall henceforth shorten to blockism) with which reductionism has normally been associated. Thus, for instance, determinism, as it is normally understood, viz. in the Humean-Laplacean manner, such that knowledge is possible so that 'the future is present to our eyes', can be seen to rest on a naïve actualist ontology of laws (the antinomies of which will in due course be fully exposed), and is posited on supposing that because an event at time t_k was *caused* (say, at t_j) to happen, it was *bound* (e.g. at t_i) to happen before it is caused – a confusion of ontological determination with epistemological predeterminism, unwarranted in an *open system* constituted by irreducible alterities – other-beings, as important to the critique of irrealist dialectics as non-beings are to irrealism generally.* Second, it is significant in that it links 1M causally efficacious determination to 2E transformative negation (and the critique of actualism to that of monovalence). In a moment I am going to connect causal efficacy with what I am going to call a '*rhythmic*' defined as a tensed process in space-time. And just as causal powers are processes-entified-in-products, we could say causality is transformative negation in processual (rhythmic) determination. It could be asked why are the pivotal concepts of change and agency being neglected? They are not. For agency is intentional causality and consists in efficacious absenting. Nor is 3L being left out of the picture. For an absenting alienation, absented alienation, splitting detotalization or split-off can exercise a causal effect, and in §7 I shall systematically discuss the intra-active and mediating holistic causality typical of a totality.

In a multi-determined, multi-levelled, multi-linear, multi-relational, multi-angular, multi-perspectival, multiply determined and open pluriverse, emergence situates the widespread phenomena of dual, multiple, complex and open control. Thus typically, in our zone of being, higher-order agencies set the boundary conditions for the operation of lower-order laws. Thus in contemporary capitalist society it is economic considerations which explain when, where and how the physical principles engaged in engineering are put to use (or held in abeyance). This principle also offers keys to the unravelling of the old Marxian conundrum of the 'superstructures'. On Model A we can readily say that it is the relations of production which determine the boundary conditions for the operation and development of the forces of production, and similarly for the relationship between polity and economy. On Model B, in which we envisage the superstructure as intrastructure, that is, formed within the base level, we can argue that it is the latter which provides the framework principles for, or conditions of possibility of, the 'higher' level which may complexify, be supervenient on or relatively autonomous from the base level or, one could say, the totality or whole in which it is interiorized. Thus, deploying Model B, the politics of the new world disorder or the spread of postmodernist culture can be seen as occurring within the context of global capitalist commodification, both figuratively and literally – and, as already remarked, there is no reason why these models should not be deployed concurrently.

* To those reductionists – tendentially type monists – who would deny the phenomena of emergence, contemporary ecological findings come as an awesome warning. For they show the extent to which industrialized humanity has been intervening in (increasingly socialized) nature, and will suffer from its recoil.

Emergence entails both stratification and change. So far I have concentrated on emergent entities and causal powers. But if, as I have already argued, all changes are spatio-temporal and space-time is a relational property of the meshwork of material beings, this opens up the phenomena of *emergent spatio-temporalities.* There are two paradigms here, both instantiated in reality: (α) they could be relata of a new (emergent) system of material things and/or (β) they could be new (emergent) relata of a pre-existing system of material things. In either event they establish new 'rhythmics', where a rhythmic is just the spatio-temporal efficacy of the process. (In a Wittgensteinian family circle, process can then be regarded as spatialized tensing, the mode of becoming [as absenting] or [plain] absenting of effects.) A rhythmic may be transfactual or actual, positive or negative (i.e. an inefficacy), intra-active or inter-active, agentive or not (corresponding to 1M–4D). If a substance is paradigmatically a thing, a rhythmic may be substantial or non-substantial (where the non-substantial is aligned under the class of non-being-mediated). If it is non-substantial, then the causal rhythmic of a process must, and even if it is substantial it may (cf. [β] above), be reckoned to be a sui generis causal power of space-time itself. Space-time thus takes on, potentially, a fivefold character as: (a) a reference grid, (b) a measure, (c) a set of prima facie mutual exclusion relations, (d) a potentially emergent (cf. [α]) property, perhaps with causal powers of its own, and (e) a generally entropic process. Eventually I will want to tie space, time and causality very closely, around the theorem of the reality and irreducibility of (always potentially spatializing) tense and the potential and typical spatio-temporality (and hence processuality) of all causal efficacy in the definition of process as the mode of absenting which is the becoming and begoing of effects.

In the meantime, for those who doubt the propriety of such a close linkage (and emphasis on spatio-temporal process), just ponder the extent to which emergent social things (people, institutions, traditions) not only presuppose (that is to say, are dependent on) but also are *existentially constituted* by (as a crucial part of their essence) or merely *contain* (as part of their proprium or accident, to drop into scholastic vocabulary for a moment) *their geo-histories* (and, qua empowered, possibilities for their spatialized futures). In the same way I will argue, when I come to totality and holistic causality, that emergent social things are existentially constituted by or contain their *relations*, connections and interdependencies with other social (and natural) things.[32] This is 3L territory. For the moment I want to stick with 2E spatio-temporalities. Constitutive geo-history displayed in contemporary rhythmics or in the processual exercise of accumulated causal powers and liabilities is only one of several ways in which in §8 I will consider the phenomena of the presence of the past (and outside). But just ponder the extent to which although we may live *for* the future, we live, quite literally, *in* the past.[33] Generally the phenomenon of emergent spatio-temporalities situates the possibilities of overlapping, intersecting, condensing, elongated, divergent, convergent and even contradictory rhythmics (causal processes) and, by extension, space-time measures (overthrowing, inter alia, the idea of a unitary set of exclusion relations).

In exemplication of this phenomenon let me dwell on intersecting and overlapping spaces and times – see Figure 3. The last case in the figure shows how discrepant spatio-temporalities can often, but not always, be coordinated either by reference to some explanatory significant loco-periodization or, as here, by reference to a zero-level or base space-time, established by some conventionally agreed (not necessarily physically basic) dating and locating system. As a final example consider the amazing and putatively contradictory juxtaposition or condensation of differentially sedimented rhythmics one can find in a city like Los Angeles[34] or New Delhi, where temples, mosques, traditions, religious rites, weddings, inter-caste conflict, electric cables, motor cars, television sets, rickshaws, scavengers and disposable cans coalesce in a locale.

Indeed specifically *conceptual emergence*, e.g. as in the σ and τ transforms of the epistemological dialectic sketched in C1.9, generally depends upon the exploitation of the past or exterior cognitive resources (once again, Bachelard's 'scientific loans') constituting so much conceptual bricolage. But it may also be effected by means of a perspectival switch, the formation of a new *Gestalt*, level or order of coherence *without* any additional input.[35] Emergence is, of course, also necessary for the intelligibility of the actual working of the Hegelian dialectic, which operates merely by filling in, or absenting the absence of, what is from a higher-order perspective a level-specific void. And although in the end Hegel cannot sustain it, this, as Marx famously remarked but insufficiently explained, does give the basic form or essence of many, if not all, dialectics. Emergent entities are, of course, as already remarked, one kind of totality, constituted by the internal relationality of their aspects. This raises the question of the limits or boundaries of an emergent totality. Is it, for instance, an organism, upon whose 'internal teleology' so much of the plausibility of Hegelian ontology intuitively rests; or is it rather the organism in its *Umwelt* or environment constituted at least in part by the various 'affordances' the environment offers for the organism in question?[36] In general one can resolve the problem of the individuation and

Intersecting spaces :	Pavements used for sleeping; sofa-beds; table/desks
Intersecting times :	the Queen's speech written by the Prime Minister's press officer (with advice from an advertising firm) opening Parliament in the House of Lords
Overlapping spaces :	residencies, offices and factories within the same locale
Overlapping times :	constitutional procedure ———————— (c. 1690–1990)
	political power ———————— ----- (c. 1790–1990, continuing)
	economic process ———— ----- (c. 1890–1990, continuing)
	'fashion' - (c. 1990)
	1690 1790 1890 1990

Figure 3

articulation of an emergent entity and its various aspects only by reference to the explanatory power of the theory which a particular *découpage* permits. This, in turn, will depend to a degree upon our explanatory purposes. However, this does not subjectivize explanation in science (or everyday existence), for what I will call the '*reality principle*' (invoking its Freudian ancestry) imposes its own stratification on science and lay life. Dialectical critical realism sees totalities within totalities (but studded with blocks, partitions and distance) recursively. But they are by no means all, or normally, of the Hegelian, pervasively internally relational, let alone centrist, expressivist and teleological kind. Rather they are punctuated by alterities, shot through with spaces, criss-crossed by traces and connected by all manner of negative, external and contingent as well as positive, internal and necessary determinations and relationships, the exact form of which it is up to science to fathom. Similarly, as we all now see, not all dialectical connections are contradictory and not all dialectical contradictions are or depend upon logical contradictions in the way I have argued Hegel's paradigmatically do.

§3 Contradiction I: Hegel and Marx

In C1.9 I isolated the motive force that logical contradiction plays in Hegelian dialectic (at least in theory) in heralding the expansion of the existing conceptual field. But by juxtaposing Marx to Hegel I want to show that logical contradiction is not the same as dialectical contradiction, although the two classes intersect. Moreover, by no means all dialectics depend upon contradiction, and even less violate the logical norms of identity and non-contradiction. First I want to examine contradiction in its widest compass.

The concept of contradiction may be used as a metaphor (like that of force in physics) for any kind of dissonance, strain or tension. However, it first assumes a clear meaning in the case of human action, which may then be extended to goal-oriented action, and thence, by a further move, to any action at all. Here it specifies a situation which permits the satisfaction of one end or more generally result only at the expense of another: that is, a *bind* or constraint. An *internal contradiction* is then a *double-bind* or self-constraint (which may be multiplied to form a knot). In this case a system, agent or structure, S, is *blocked* from performing with one system, rule or principle, R, because it is performing with another, R′; or, a course of action, T, generates a countervailing, inhibiting, undermining, overriding or otherwise opposed course of action, T′. R′ and T′ are radically negating of R and T respectively. As the Hegelian and Marxian traditions have a propensity for internal as distinct from external contradictions, it is worth pointing out that external constraints (not generated by a common causal ground [dg′]) may nevertheless hold between structures which are internally related, i.e. existentially presuppose one another.

External contradictions – constraints – would appear to be pervasive –

indeed, exemplified by the laws and constraints of nature (such as the speed of light), to be established by the mere fact of determinate spatio-temporal being. But, of course, it does not follow from the condition that every being is constrained, that every particular constraint on a being is absolute or necessary. This should go without saying. Only a blanket actualism would deny it. How about internal contradictions? Their possibility is directly situated by the phenomena of emergent entities (which is why I interposed my discussion of §2), internally related grounded ensembles and totalities generally. However, leaving this aside, it could be argued that for the very fact of change to be possible, even if the source is exogenous, there must be a degree of internal '*complicity*' within the thing to the change: that is, in that it must, in virtue of its nature, be '*liable*' to the change, so as not to be impervious to its source, and so must possess a counter-conative tendency in respect of the condition changed, which may be more or less essential to the thing's identity. (By definition in such a case – of change, not demise – it must also possess a conative one.) Only unchanging, ultimately eternal, things would lack such a tendency, and such things would seem to have to be or contain everywhere everywhen – a Spinozan monism or Leibnizian monadism. In any case this establishes the most basic kind of *existential contradiction*: finitude. Spatio-temporal location may seem an external constraint, but insofar as it is the fate – condition of being – of such things to perish, i.e. to be limited in extent, it must be reckoned an internal contradiction, even though their extent and duration be entirely contingent. When we turn to human life, existential contradiction may assume the mantle of standing oppositions between mind and body, fact and fancy, desire and desired, power and need, Eros and Thanatos, master and slave, self-determination and subjugation.

Formal logical contradiction is a type of internal contradiction, whose consequence for the subject, unless the terms are redescribed and/or the discursive domain is expanded (as happens in Hegelian dialectic), is *axiological indeterminacy:* 'A and –A' leaves the course of action (including belief) indeterminate, or, at least if relevance, contextual, spatio-temporal and normic constraints are imposed, underdetermined; and so subverts the intentionality, and, ceteris paribus, the rationality, of any praxis that would be founded on, or informed by, it. Such axiological indeterminacy in the intrinsic, intentional or normative aspect of social life is quite consistent with a determinate intransitive result, especially if the agent must act – that is to say, if what I have elsewhere described as the 'axiological imperative'[37] applies – for consistency and coherence are not the only generative or causal factors at work in social life (this is the constellational identity of the intrinsic within the extrinsic[38] or, loosely, the rational within the causal). To suppose that they are is to make the epistemic fallacy of logicizing being, into which Hegel falls. The inverse, Kantian, mistake is to extrude thought from, detotalizing, being. Against this, it is important to understand that when logical contradictions are committed, they are real constituents of the

Lebenswelt. Moreover, they may be consistently described and explained, as the intransitive objects of some epistemic inquiry (say into the state of secondary school mathematics in Essex in 1992). What could be more symptomatic of partial, monovalent (and, if I may say so, complacent) thought than to deny the occurrence of logical contradictions in (social) reality?

Dialectical contradictions are, like logical contradictions, also a type of internal contradiction. They may best be introduced as a species of the more general category of *dialectical connections*. These are connections between entities or aspects of a totality such that they are in principle *distinct* but *inseparable*, in the sense that they are synchronically or conjuncturally internally related,[39] i.e. both (some, all) or one existentially presuppose the other(s). Here we are in the domain of what I have elsewhere called *intra*- rather than *interaction*,[40] which may take the form of existential *constitution* (cf. p. 54 above), *permeation* (presence within, i.e. 'containment') or just *connection* (causal efficacy) – either in virtue of spatio-temporal contiguity or across a level-specific void. The connection may be absolute, epochal, structurally periodic, conjunctural or momentary. Dialectical connections, including contradictions, may hold between absences and absentings as well as positive instances and processes, and the causal connections and existential dependencies may be transfactual or actual. Real dialectical contradictions possess all these features of dialectical connections. But their elements are also *opposed*, in the sense that (at least) one of their aspects negates (at least) one of the other's, or their common ground or the whole, and perhaps vice versa, so that they are *tendentially mutually exclusive*, and potentially or actually tendentially transformative. Are dialectical contradictions necessarily radical in my terms? This depends upon the – ideally, real – definition of the contradictions. If what is negated is the ground of the negation or the totality then they are necessarily radical; if not, not. The case where one of the poles of a contradiction is the ground itself corresponds to the dyadic mode of the Hegelian dialectic, as the negation is then not only necessarily radical but also linear. But any number of aspects of a totality may be so related (as in the polyadic case of the Hegelian dialectic). Such a radically negating ensemble is thus multi-linear. Both Hegel and Marx were biased towards internal, radical and linear negation – a fact partly explained by the narrative presentational form, or sequential flow or 'continuous series' of the nineteenth-century expository text (as a comparison between *Capital* and Marx's notes and letters bears out).

Dialectical contradictions are not per se logical contradictions. But logical contradictions can also be dialectical contradictions *insofar as they are grounded in a common mistake*, whether the mistake is isolated or not. (The importance of this for the metacritical dialectics of discursively formulated or practically expressed philosophical ideologies will become clear in C4.) Dialectical and logical contradictions, as two species of internal contradiction, intersect but are not coterminous. However, we can describe the logical contradiction as dialectical only when the mistaken ground is isolated, and can do so coherently (without at least a degree of axiological indeterminacy) only when its contradictoriness is removed – which is precisely, on my exegesis, what Hegel intends to do, and sometimes succeeds (brilliantly) in doing.

Dialectical contradictions may be more or less antagonistic, in the sense of expressing or representing or even constituting the opposed interests of (or between) agents or collectivities; and, if antagonistic, they may be partial or latent or rhythmically dislocated, and manifest to a greater or lesser extent in conflict, which in turn can be covert or overt, transfactual or actual, as well as being conducted in a variety of different modes. Of course there are contingent (and within the contingent what should really be distinguished as a distinct class, the accidental) in addition to necessary, and external besides internal, contradictions, thus one has

[1] connections ≥ necessary connections ≥ dialectical connections ≥ dialectical contradictions;

[2] constraints ≥ internal contradictions ≥ dialectical contradictions ≥ logical dialectical contradictions;

and

[3] dialectical contradictions ≥ antagonisms ≥ conflicts ≥ overt struggles;

while of course

[4] real negation ≥ transformative negation ≥ radical negation ≥ linear negation.

[3] is not supposed to rule out non-dialectical, e.g. purely external or contingent, conflicts. On the other hand, it is a mistake to think of conflicts as 'more' empirical than contradictions. The contradiction between contending parties in the law courts may be palpably visible, while deep conflict may never show itself in experience. Hence all the relevant concepts possess a 1M real/actual and 2E real/present contrast. Suppose one distinguishes power$_1$, as the transformative capacity analytic to the concept of agency, from (the transfactual or actual) power$_2$ relations expressed in structures of domination, exploitation, subjugation and control, which I will thematize as *generalized master–slave* (-type) *relations*. The poles of such antagonistic dialectical contradictions, exemplified by the famous contradictions between capitalist and worker or the looker and looked at or master and slave itself, are typically differentially causally charged. One should note, however, that this is seldom completely one-sided and always potentially reversible – as in Foucauldian counter-conduct or strategic reversal. (Power$_1$ includes power$_2$ of course.) In

such cases one may talk of a dominant and subordinate pole; and more generally of the primary and secondary (etc.) aspects of a contradiction or contradictions in a totality. Indeed unless, more generally, there were *structural asymmetries* in a multi-angular pluriversal context, it would be difficult to conceive, against inertial drag, causes of change, let alone of directionality, in geo-history. The grounds, structures or mechanisms which generate real dialectical contradictions may themselves form recursively (geo-historically variable componential), hierarchical, power$_2$-dominated, complexes or totalities. Furthermore, any of the figures I have just discussed may induce secondary, tertiary or multiply proliferating elaborations or connections of dialectical or non-dialectical kinds.

In the social world all the figures, from constraint to conflict, will be concept- or meaning-dependent. It is important to stress that this holds for formal logical contradictions too. These are entirely dependent upon (normally tacit) semantic and contextual considerations. We only assume 'A' and '–A' are contradictory because we take for granted that the successive occurrences of the grapheme 'A' are tokens of the same type. But a sceptic could easily deny this, asking what semiotic, hermeneutic or other considerations have prevented the nature of A from changing, and in many cases be right to do so.

'Materialist' dialectical contradictions of the type defined above, such as those identified by Marx in his systematic dialectics, *describe (dialectical), but do not suffer from (logical), contradictions*. The mechanism is not in general teleological, but even when it is, its teleology presupposes causality (a lesser form for Hegel). The practical resolution of the contradiction here is the non-preservative transformative negation of the ground, which is the problem, not the solution. This involves what I am going to call '*transformed transformative totalizing transformist praxis*' ($d\varphi'$) in the struggle, presaged upon Marx's analysis of the dialectic processes (dp') of capitalism, for a sublation (ds'), traditionally known as 'socialism', of the replaced social form. Of course Marx's analysis may *contain* logical contradictions – as a line from Böhm-Bawerk to Roemer has contended – but then it is just straightforwardly faulty, a faultiness which may in turn be dialectically explained. The co-presence of absence and presence, that is, the combination of actual absences and real presences (tendential, transfactual) of opposites (at different levels), i.e. of negative sub-contraries and positive contraries, enables the traditional table of oppositions to be satisfied simultaneously prior to, rather than in the switch occurring in, the resolution. Moreover, Marx's dialectical contradictions cannot be said to constitute an identity, but at most a grounded *unity*, of opposites.[41] (One might be tempted to contrast here the Kantian independence, Hegelian identity and Marxian unity of opposites.) Marx's concern is with the *dialectical explanation* and *practical transformation* of capitalism, not with the transfigurative redescription of, and reconciliation to, *Das Bestehende* (the actually existing state of affairs).

None of this is to deny that Marx's systematic ontological and programmatic relational dialectics of the capitalist mode of production presupposes a critical epistemological dialectic of an Hegelian C1.9 kind: that is, an immanent critique of the pre-existing political economy of his day, involving the identification of contradictions, and more generally aporiai, anomalies and absences (such as that of the distinction between labour and labour-power, an absence readily explained by the commodification of the latter), entailing the characterisic nodal (dc′) and resolutionary (dr′) transforms of a process which, insofar as it inaugurated a research programme, it would be surprising if it did not require further development and deepening.[42] But in terms of C1.8, D_3 – ideology-critique – is now distinguished from D_1 – the ideology or self-understanding of the form or practice in question. This becomes part of Marx's explanandum, as in the case of his identification and description of commodity fetishism. Moreover, once a research programme has been initiated, dialectical detachment from the latter can occur, so that the ongoing metacritique of capitalism, identifying new defence mechanisms and causal tendencies and explaining them, need not be entirely immanent (radically negating in character*). However, to be effective, a radical relational dialectic, dependent upon the causal efficacy and conditioning** of ideas, presupposes a hermeneutic which takes agents to the point where immanent critique, registering theory–practice inconsistencies (cf. D_2), is possible. In any event, there is now an internal rift within the conceptual realm, comprising a conflict of reasons, mobilized around what I am going to call *hermeneutic hegemonic/counter-hegemonic struggles* in the context of generalized master–slave $power_2$ relations.

Let us accentuate the philosophical contrast between Hegel and Marx by elaborating the way the logical contradictions of Hegelian dialectic differ, as species of internal contradiction, from the real dialectical contradictions of materialist analysis and critique. The driving force (in principle) of Hegelian dialectic is the transition, paradigmatically of the elements (e) and (–e), from positive contraries simultaneously present and actual (thereby continually violating the principle of non-contradiction, as Hegel both does and says he does) into negative sub-contraries now simultaneously actual and absent, but retained as negative presences in a cumulative memory store, as the dialectical reader's consciousness or the path of history moves on to a new level of speculative reason. At this stage they are now retrospectively redescribed as moments of a transcending totality. Contradiction has cancelled itself. And they are now, in what we could call Hegel's *analytic reinstatement*, restored to

* Thus to use the terminology I introduced in SRHE, pp. 25–6, one can say MC_2 (explanatory critique) > MC_1 (the identification of an absence corresponding to real negation) > immanent critique.

** It is important to remember this is an axiom of materialist thought, itself bearing Hegelian credentials (according to which objective spirit formed the humus out of which absolute spirit grew).

their positive self-identity. No longer contradictory, they now illustrate what I have just adumbrated as 'dialectical connection'. *Hegelian dialectic, when it is contradictory, is logically contradictory but not dialectically determinate; conversely, when it has become dialectically determinate, there is nothing contradictory about it at all.* That is to say, when the elements are contradictory, they are not per se dialectical; but, when they are dialectical, they are no longer opposed. Hegelian dialectic is the continual transition from the one state, 'understanding', to the other, 'speculative reason'; it *is* this transition and everything is always in it. But it is never simultaneously dialectical *and* contradictory. The materialist dialectic is. It involves a simultaneity of grounded (transfactual) presence and (actual) absence, of practical (existential) inclusion and mutual (tendentially transformative) exclusion. It is this which makes it genuinely dialectically contradictory in a stratified ontology that pre-exists the discourse that describes it.

There is no need, however, to deny Hegel the accolade of articulating dialectical contradictions if we reject, as I shall argue we should, a punctualist view of time. We can then say that what Hegel achieves, i.e. the co-presence of absence and presence, within an (actualist) extended temporal stretch in the mode of succession in time, Marx accomplishes instantaneously within a (transfactually) extended structural depth, in the mode of ontological stratification. Breaking free from both actualism and spatio-temporal punctualism allows for a vastly expanded table or matrix of opposition, as illustrated in Figure 4.

Allowing for the embedding of presence and absence, past and present, inside and outside, essence and appearance, transfactual and actual, in a combination of ontological stratification and internally tensed distanciated space-time (or set of such rhythmics) situates the possibility of a new, genuinely multi-dimensional and dynamic logic. Adding the possibilities permitted by 3L intra-active totalizing relationality, enabling the embedding of, for

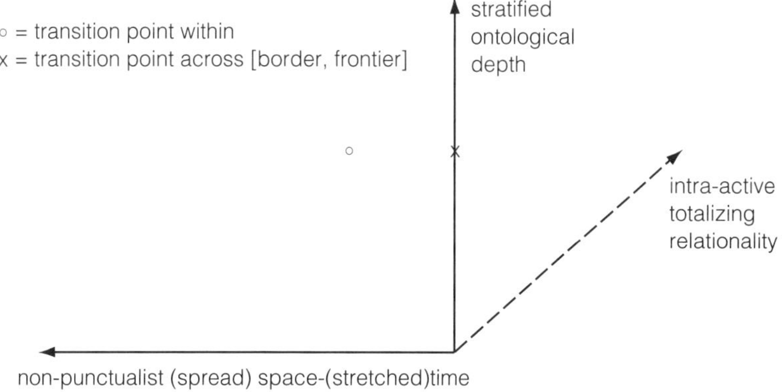

Figure 4

example, containment and separation and 4D transformative praxis, enabling the embedding of, for example, agency and power, spreads the canvas even wider. However, reverting to my main point here, and simplifying, while Hegel describes the contradictions of the sundered world at the dawn of the age of modernity (which Kant prefigures) in a non-contradictory and reconciliatory way, Marx attempts to explain the contradictions of that world (giving it a real definition as capitalist) in order eventually to change it. This could be summed up by the formulae:

[5] HD = Logical contradiction → dialectical connection → transfigurative redescription [→ analytic reinstatement].

[6] MD = Dialectical connection → dialectical contradiction → transformist praxis → practical resolution.

Now to complicate matters. Hegel is a deeply ambiguous figure. He is both – Hegel Mark I – the first practitioner of a new socio-geohistoricist mode of thought and expressly interested in change (before 1806), and – Hegel Mark II – the last great metaphysician who (almost) succeeds in realizing the traditional goals of philosophy within an immanent metaphysics of experience (after 1800) and increasingly fearful of change. (Note the discrepant times.) Of Hegel Mark II we could echo Marx on Proudhon: 'Although there has been history . . . there is no longer any.'[43] Indeed this is a potent motif of the philosophical tradition – one which could be provisionally and partially identified as the *normally unconscious and characteristically aporetic normalization of past, and denegation of present and future, change*. Of course Hegel does not believe that the geo-historical process has totally stopped. Hence he refers to Russia and America as lands of the future. But these belong to what I will call the '*demi-actual*'. The future is *demi-present: constellationally closed*. Like Rorty, he believes the 'last conceptual revolution has occurred'[44] – and for Hegel the concept spelled *Begriff* just is 'conceptually understood reality'. It is important to appreciate that Hegel 'Mark I' and 'Mark II' correspond to or designate moments of real history (not just phases of his intellectual career). But this does not prevent Hegel Mark II presenting brilliant diagnoses of real, including non-logical, dialectical contradictions, as witnessed by his remarkable analyses of the contradictions of civil society which he never sublates. Moreover, we have already noticed the normic nature of Hegel's real dialectical practice (see C1.8 – p. 30 above). So Hegel moves closer to Marx. But Marx also steps nearer to Hegel. For his analysis of the capitalist mode of production does not remain at the level of the Hegelian 'understanding' but takes the form of a critique of political economy, engaging σ and τ transforms of the latter, identifying conceptualized forms (value, commodity, money) as diagnostic clues to the inner workings of his intransitive object of inquiry. So a fairer representation of the true nature of Hegel's and Marx's

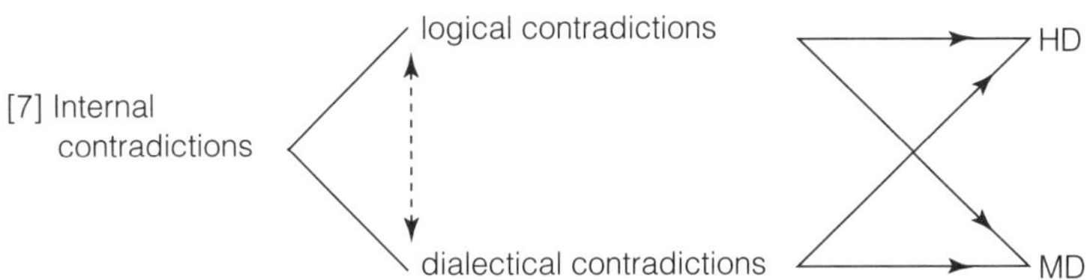

Figure 5

real dialectical practice might be as suggested by the schema in Figure 5. It should perhaps be stressed here what is implicit in [5] and [6] above, viz. that the sequential orders of the Marxian and Hegelian dialectics typically differ, viz.:

[8] HD: Logical contradiction – transition – dialectical connection – reconciliatory theoretical result.

[9] MD: Dialectical connection – dialectical contradiction – dialectic praxis – transformative negation – resolutionary practical result.

Hegel's resolution is in theory. Marx's is in practice. But this must not be misunderstood. The resolution of all contradictions, including logical contradictions, is practical both in the sense (a) that they consist in the transformative negation of the pre-existing (contradictory) state of affairs and (b) that, qua actions, they are moments of social practices (e.g. typesetting, mathematics). The further senses in which there are differences at stake between Hegel and Marx depend (c) upon some social schematization or theory – a practice, of course – differentiating, for instance, manual from mental labour and/or (d) the different orientations of theoretical and practical reason – with the former concerned to adjust our beliefs to the world and the latter to adjust the world to our will. Following Hegel we can distinguish theoretical reason (dr_t'), practical reason (dr_p') and absolute reason, that is, their unity, coherence or consistency (dr_a'), which is to be achieved for dialectical critical realism in the Cartesian product of senses (a) and (d), viz. practically oriented transformative negation ($d\varphi'$), rather than recapitulative redescription – a concept which, in the end, Hegel cannot sustain, in virtue of his constellational closure of dialectical praxis and reason alike.

Theory/practice inconsistency, which is entailed by, though it does not entail, a dialectical comment (dc′), is of special interest for a number of reasons. First, because of its immediately *auto-subversive*, self-deconstructive, performative and radically negational *character*. Second, when set in the context of hermeneutic-hegemonic struggles over $power_2$ or the practical *transfinity* of generalized master–slave relations, because of its significance as a form of immanent (and so necessarily non-arbitrary or ad hominem) critique, insofar as it turns on an agent or community rejecting in its practice what it affirms in its theory and/or expressing in its practice what it denies in its theory. Third, because a cumulative series of theory/practice inconsistencies, in which each phase brings out, precisely, as the *scotoma* or blind spot of the previous phase, the point of its greatest ex ante strength as in fact its greatest weakness (the dc_k' as the dr_j' of the dc_i' [of the $dr_i'_{-1}$]) constitutes what may be called an *Achilles' Heel critique* (as in the sequential parthogenetic process of Hegelian dialectic phenomenology), which is of the greatest moment in the history of philosophy and science alike.* Fourth, because insofar as a theory or practice violates an *axiological necessity*, it immediately generates a most interesting kind of *compromise form*, to be explicated in §7. Fifth, because it shows the subject involved to be internally riven, alienated and/or *untrue to itself*. Sixth, because of its *lack of dialectical universalizability*, again to be treated subsequently.

I now want to insist on the practical nature of all theory and the quasi-propositionality of all practice, insofar as it is dependent upon, but not exhausted by, its conceptual, and thus belief-expressive aspects ('actions speak louder than words').** This immediately generates the theorem of *the duality of theory and practice*, in that by means of a transcendental perspectival switch, each can be seen under the aspect of the other. Consequences of this are that a theory or practice may be immediately, or more normally mediately, theory/practice inconsistent; and that theory/theory inconsistencies or logical contradictions proper may be seen under the aspect of theory/practice or practice/practice contradictions, which I will call *quasi-logical contradictions* and *axiological inconsistencies*. Moreover, it follows from the quasi-propositionality of practice that practical or theory/practice inconsistencies will yield at least axiological underdetermination; and from the practical character of theory that insofar as theory/theory contradictions violate axiological necessities they will entrain the compromise form referred to in the previous paragraph, which may be provisionally regarded as necessitated by what I earlier called the reality principle. Note that this does not abolish either (α) the intransitivity of, or (β) the characteristic difference in orientation or 'direction of fit' (sense [d] above) between, theory and practice – generating the important dialectical figure of the non-identity, alterity or *hiatus-in-the-duality* – or (γ) their respective locations in some social schematism (sense [c]). It follows from this that, even if dialectical connections, as defined above, are regarded as necessary for a configuration to be said to be 'dialectical',

1 there is no a priori reason why all dialectics should be social, and hence conceptualized;

* So we can extend the theorem on p. 62 above: $MC_2 > MC_1 >$ immanent critique > AH critique.

** Of course the best conceptualization will often be a hotly contested matter, especially in the context of $power_2$ relations.

2 neither is there any reason why all social dialectics should involve contradictions, whether dialectical, logical or both;
3 there is no necessary reason for believing that all dialectical contradictions involve quasi-logical contradictions or axiological inconsistencies, although there are good grounds for supposing that they will be frequently ideologically mediated by such;
4 only a sub-class of dialectical contradictions involve logical contradictions;
5 all these types may be described and potentially explained (in the intrinsic aspect of science) without contradiction; and finally
6 only epistemological dialectics necessarily breach, at certain critical moments, the formal principles of identity and non-contradiction.

In short most, if not all, dialectics are consistent with adherence to the norms of formal logic (as illustrated in Figures 6 and 7). This result will be qualified subsequently by consideration of the interconnection between epistemological and other dialectics and the effects of the illicit epistemo-logicization of reality in §10 but it is important to insist on it now. Dialectical critical realism will situate, but not just negate, 'logic'.*

Insofar as theory is practical, it will depend (analytically) upon some prior piece of practical reasoning, e.g. about the efficacy of the practice in arriving at an adequate description of the world. But this depends upon theory, which incorporates theoretical and practical reasoning alike. And insofar as practice is quasi-propositional, it will depend (analytically) upon some anterior theoretical reasoning, e.g. about the nature of the world that the practice is designed to change. But this depends upon practice, which also encompasses both theoretical and practical reasoning. And so we have the lemma of the *duality of theoretical and practical reasoning*, mediated by the transformative character of theory and the conceptuality of practice. Once again this does not annul their distinction. The upshot of theory is belief about the world; that of practice, action on it. That theory will express our will and depend upon our wants, and practices will express our (concrete axiological[45]) judgements and depend upon our beliefs. Figure 7 is designed to illustrate this. (These two aspects, expression or manifestation and dependency, are different. In the former case theory manifests, qua practice, the upshot of practical reason; and practice manifests, qua quasi-propositional, the outcome of theoretical reason. In the latter case, theory merely existentially presupposes, but is not also, the practical reason upon which it depends; and similarly for practice.)

* This is perhaps the point to remark that in characterizing dialectic as the 'logic of absence' in the title of this chapter, I am exploiting a more generic sense of 'logic' than that captured by commitment to the principles of identity and non-contradiction – the sense employed in this passage.

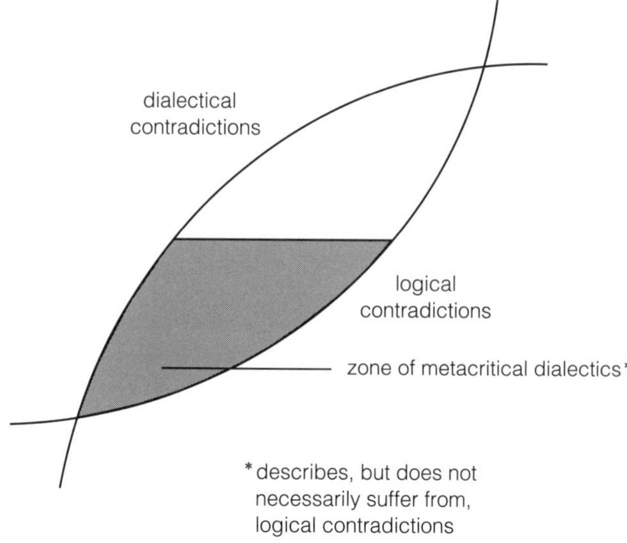

Figure 6 Dialectical and logical contradictions intersect but are not coterminous

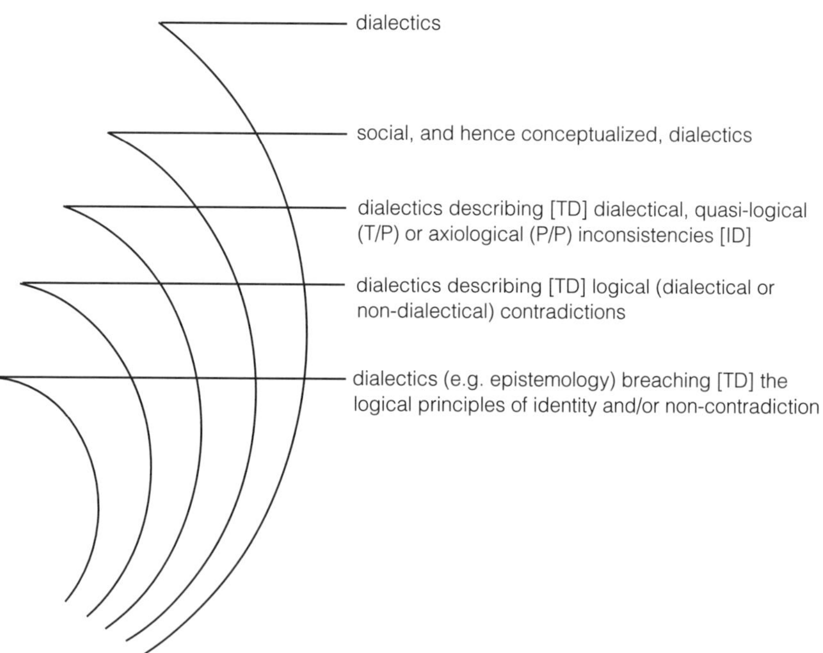

Figure 7 Most dialectics are consistent with formal logic

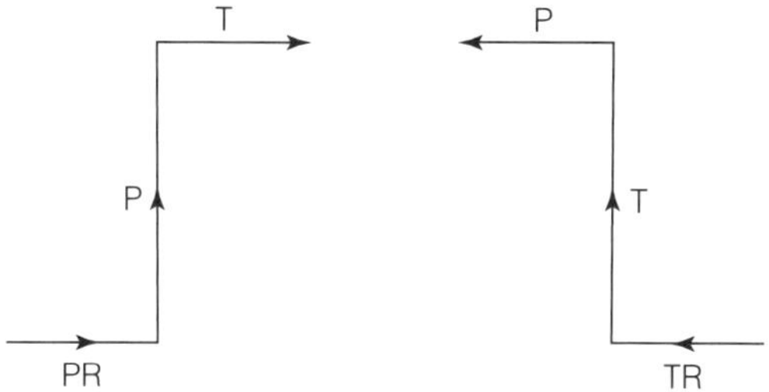

Figure 8 Theory, practice and reason

In the Marxist tradition dialectical contradiction has been most frequently characterized in contrast to either (α) exclusive or so-called 'real' opposition or conflict (Kantian *Realrepugnanz*[46]) on the grounds that their terms mutually presuppose each other, so that they comprise an (existentially) inclusive (as well as tendentially exclusive) opposition; and/or (β) formal logical opposition on the basis that their relations are *meaning*-(or content-)dependent, not purely formal, so that the negation of A does not lead to its annulment, but to its transformative replacement by a new, richer form B. Associated with the first contrast is the theme of the 'unity of opposites', the trademark of Marxist ontological dialectics from Engels on. At the level of social theory this motif most often reduces to internal relationality of antagonists in a structure of domination (with conflicting, mutually exclusive, interests – ultimately one in the preservation, the other in the abolition, of that structure). Associated with the second contrast is the conception of immanent critique as central to the project of radical negation, which is the hallmark of Marxist relational dialectics from Lukács on, with the emphasis on the causal efficacy (as distinct from mere material-infrastructural conditioning) of ideas. In both traditions dialectical contradictions are held to be characteristically 'concrete', in comparison with their 'abstract' analytic contrasts, a distinction I examine in §7.

In Marx's works the terms 'contradiction' (*Widerspruch*), 'antagonism' (*Gegensatz*) and 'conflict' (*Konflikt*), which I have differentiated above, are often used interchangeably. But if some conceptual consistency is imposed, it can be said that in Marx's mature economic writings the concept of contradiction is deployed to denote inter alia: (a) *logical inconsistencies* or other intra-discursive theoretical anomalies, which are related to or can be perhaps reduced to the concept of logical contradiction; (b) extra-discursive (although, of course, generally conceptually mediated) *non-dialectical oppositions*, e.g. supply and demand as comprising forces of relatively independent origins interacting in such a way that their effects tend to cancel one another in notional, momentary or enduring equilibria, which approximate to the Kantian *Realrepugnanz*; (c) *structural* or synchronic or local-period-ized *dialectical contradictions* intrinsic to a particular social form; (d) *geo-historically specific dialectical contradictions* that bring into being a social form and/or crises in the course of its development which are then resolved in the process of transformation which they help to cause. Contradictions of type (d) involve forces of non-independent origins operating so that a force F itself tends to produce or is itself the product of conditions stemming from a ground, namely social form S which simultaneously or subsequently produces a countervailing force F′, tending to frustrate, subvert, overcome or otherwise transform F and/or the social form that grounds it, that is, to radically negate them. Such geo-historically specific contradictions are exemplified by those which arise between the relations and forces of production, and particularly between the increasingly socialized nature of the relations and the definitionally private character of the forces. These rhythmic contradictions are grounded for Marx in structural ones of type (c), such as between wage-labour and capital or between the use value and the exchange value of the commodity, which provide ab initio the formal conditions of their possibility. Such (c)-type contradictions are then in turn geo-historically explained (so that we have a meta-ontological dialectic of [c] and [d] types) in terms of (e) an original *generative separation*, split or alienation of the immediate producers from the means and materials of their production. This generates an alienation from their labour and from the planes of their material transactions with nature, their social interactions with each other, the network of social relations in which they produce, and ultimately themselves. The prototype of dialectical generative separation is the Hegelian '*Beautiful Soul*' alienated from her community, but it is given a specific dialectical meaning in Marx. (c) – (e) contradictions are all real dialectical ones.

The identification of (a)s, corresponding to the moment of dc′ in the critique of political economy, is of course a part of the real (non-preservative) transformative negation of it, at the level of dr_t'; (b)s are simple external contradictions, although it is always possible that a more totalizing analysis at what I have called the 'intensive' and 'extensive' margins of inquiry[47] (and will rehearse in §7) may always reveal them to be internally related. In respect of the thematization of the concept within Marxism it should be noted that dialectical contradictions of types (c)–(e) both constitute real inclusive oppositions, in that their terms existentially presuppose one another (cf. α), and are systematically and intrinsically related to mystifying forms of appearance, such as the value or wage forms (cf. β). These dialectical contradictions neither violate the principle of non-contradiction – for, as already stressed, they may be *consistently described*; nor are they scientifically absurd in any fashion – for the notion of a real *inverted*, or otherwise mystifying, conception of a real object, perhaps the result of the ensemble or ground containing the very phenomena mystified, may be readily accommodated within a critical realist stratified, non-monovalent, totalizing ontology of the sort to which Marx is committed in his mature work, though never able fully to develop. Yet there is a long line of criticism in Marxist, as well as non-Marxist, thought (which begins with Bernstein and reaches its apogee with Colletti) which claims that the notion of dialectical contradictions in reality is incompatible with one or more of formal logic, coherent discourse, scientific practice or materialism. This is not so. For dialectical, as other species of, contradictions, whether simply within being (cf. α') or between being and thought within being (cf. β'), may be straightforwardly consistently described and scientifically explained. It is only if logical, which may sometimes also be dialectical, contradictions are *committed*, as distinct from described, that the norm of non-contradiction is infringed, and provided logic is included within reality, not detotalized, exteriorized, split off or hypostatized (in Platonic-Cartesian-Kantian manner), its fetishistic or otherwise categorically mystifying character betrays no absurdity in the critical discourse in contrast to the conceptualized reality described. It is thus quite incorrect to argue, as Colletti does,[48] that any scientifically legitimate concept of contradiction must reduce to Kantian *Realrepugnanz* or non-dialectical, merely external, opposition. This is the legacy of Colletti's Humean-Kantian empirical realism. Hegel's conceptual realist gloss merely embellishes it and, as we shall see, leaves its structure intact. In particular lacking the concepts of non-logical natural necessity, non-self-cancelling contradiction and an open totality, real negativity and (post-Hegelian Mark II) transformative change disappear from Hegel's own theoretical horizons. Hegel loses not absence, but the concept of absence, and with that the essence of the dialectic itself.

§7 Dialectical motifs: Tina formations, mediation, concrete universality, etc.

In this section I discuss some characteristic dialectical mechanisms and manoeuvres, tropes and themes, several of which have already been floated. In §§1 and 6 above I mentioned '*heterology*'. This can mean one or more of the following: (1) not true of, or applicable to, itself (in which case its contrary is autology); (2) not the same as itself (where the contrary is homology); and (3) not true for and/or to itself (which is in part the contrary of autonomy, and which I shall sometimes specify as 'alterology'). Its primary sense is (1), which can be exemplified by the fact that the word 'cheese' is not itself a cheese, whereas the word 'word' is a word. In Hegelian dialectic 'A' is necessarily also 'not A', and as such other than itself and generator of a determinate outcome, 'B'. It is by means of heterology in senses (1) and (2) that the forwards or ex ante movement of the dialectic unfolds, with the dialectical comment (dc′) in particular explicating what is true of, but not present in, some base concept or form. Only in the self-realization of the absolute idea in absolute spirit do we reach a plane which is not heterological. And in the translucent ex post or retrospective light – the analytic reinstatement in dialectical connection – it casts, each form building up to it can be seen as, after all, *true of, for and to itself*, as such, as contained within and *mediated* by absolute spirit, auto[U]-hetero[D]-auto[R]-logical (in the terms of C1.6). (This is the constellational identity of identity and difference within identity for the sake of identity.)

This brings us naturally to the key dialectical notion of mediation. Hegel might have remarked that all determination is mediation. Indeed Hegelians often use 'to mediate' as synonymous with 'to negate', and 'self-mediation' with 'self-negation'. Only the beginning of a local dialectic is unmediated or immediate. This does not mean that the posited element is arbitrary, because it itself can be seen as mediated by the Hegelian systemic circle. (Wherever we begin, we will achieve the whole, although for presentational and quasi-transcendental reasons, Hegel usually begins with the intuitively simplest element in some regional domain, e.g. Being in the *Logics*.) Although it has philosophical antecedents in the Aristotelian doctrine of the mean, its most usual philosophical employment is to specify an *intermediary* or means of some sort. Thus Marx conceives labour to be the primary mediator between humanity and nature, with various 2nd, 3rd. . . nth order mediations produced on or within (§2 models A and B respectively) the generative separation wrought by capitalism, including private property and the state.[49] Mediation can connote both indirectness and hierarchy. The former is exemplified by the sense of mediation as a medium, and specifically as involving (a) spatio-temporal stretching or distanciation; (b) communicative mediatization (the press, TV, etc.); and (c) postmodernist virtualization or hyperrealization (as readily accommodatable as the figure of inversion within a stratified and non-detotalizing ontology). The latter is more characteristic of Hegel-derivative dialectics, and here the crucial figure is that of the *concrete universal*, which I shall discuss in some detail below. Typically the concrete universal manifests or individualizes itself via one or more particular differentiations in some (what I will call) *concrete singular*. Hegel identifies each of these terms as necessary moments of the notion and each can be seen to mediate the other two. (I give advance notice that I will object to the Hegelian account of the concrete universal, arguing for a conceptualization of it which is both more nuanced and complex.) Indeed, any aspect, (temporalized) moment or (spatialized) determination of a totality may be said to mediate any others and/or the whole. *Process*, as the mode of spatio-temporalizing structure, can be seen as a mediator, e.g. in the social world between structure and agency, or more generally between transfactual efficacy and eventual effect, or within the tensed tri-unity of causality, space and time. *Most generally, if A achieves, secures or eventuates in C (either in whole or in part) via or by means of B, then B may be said to mediate their relation.* It is in this sense that I will argue, for instance, that the past mediates the transition to the future, rhythmics mediate causality, social relations mediate individual agency and philosophy is mediated by the deep analogical grammars of lapsed science and contemporary society.

'*Alienation*', which will also be the subject of detailed scrutiny later, means *being something other than*, (having been) separated, split, torn or estranged from oneself, or *what is essential* and intrinsic *to one's nature* or identity. What is *intrinsic* to oneself need not be internal to, in the sense of physically inside, one – as in the case of a person's kindness or a magnet's field;[50] and what is still essentially one's own at one level (e.g. one's humanity) may be alienated at another (e.g. by being subjugated to gross indignity). To be alienated is to lose part of one's autonomy. Also conceptually tied to 'heterology' is *alterity*. Thus language use, for instance, establishes a relation of sheer other-being, alterity or existential intransitivity, to what it is about. I have argued this cannot be diachronically reduced to an originary (or end) – the dialectical temptation – or synchronically eliminated in the elision of the referent – the converse mistake. Recognition of irreducible alterity, non-identity or difference is essential to any future socialist dialectics which would avoid the sinking back into a simple undifferentiated expressive unity, the most elementary stage of the Schillerian schema, that was part of the fate of the erstwhile 'actually existing socialist states'.

'Constellationality' (although also to be found in Adorno) is my term of art. I have referred to both '*constellational identity*', which is essentially a figure of *containment* (in the sense of being a part of), and '*constellational unity*', which is essentially a figure of *connection* (in the sense of being bound together); and I have used it in both materialist non-pejorative and idealist pejorative ways. Thus one can write, within a materialist context, of the constellational identity of being and thought in the sense that thought is both (a) within being, but (b) over-reached by being, as (c) an emergent product of being. And one can write of the constellational unity of dialectical and analytical reason, meaning that they are bound together as essential and interdependent aspects of the transitive dialectical process of science. Hegel's principle of the identity of identity and difference makes it difficult for him to sustain the difference between identity and unity. And the concept is almost always used by him in a teleological context as a figure of closure: principally of (α) the closure of being within his system – hence the non-actual, non-rationalized *demi-actual existent*; or (β) the closure of the future within the present, as described by absolute idealism – hence the *demi-present future*. This is Hegel's great metaphysical ceteris paribus escape or λ clause (as I have called it elsewhere),[51] which is in effect a *weak actualism*[52] and its blockist analogue, weak blockism, of which (α) and (β) are indeed forms, conveniently detotalizing what Hegel cannot 'explain'. Moreover, it is the principle of the constellational identity of opposites, of science within philosophy and of the future within the present, etc., that generates the centrism, triumphalism and endism that I taxed him for in §5 and which directly link to the three members of the unholy trinity, viz. the epistemic fallacy, the primal squeeze and ontological monovalence dissected in §6.

The theme of constellationality is affiliated to, but not the same as that of, *duality*. Duality normally connotes *the combination of existential interdependence* (or, even sometimes at some ontological level and/or from some perspective, identity) and *essential* (and therefore conceptual) *distinction* (including, at the limit, autonomy). It may be exemplified by the duality of absence and presence in spatio-temporal mediation, of theory or practice in absolute reason, or of structure and agency in social practice – where the figure of the *hiatus-in-the-duality* makes possible such important phenomena as dislocation, as well as preventing voluntaristic or reificatory collapse, of the dualities. Closely related to dualities are *perspectival switches*. Such switches may be realistically *grounded*, viz. in terms of some intransitive feature of the object under study, or given a neo-Kantian or Nietzschean interpretation, viz. in terms of the subject's epistemic or evaluative interests or her will-to-power (or caprice). A perspectival switch may be said to be *transcendental*, insofar as a switch constitutes a necessary condition of that from which it is switched, where the latter may be seen to be transcendentally significant in the sense specified in the previous section. Examples are dyadic tacit/explicit structure of knowledge as analysed by Polanyi[53] or perception as construed by Merleau-Ponty. There are two types of *dialectical* perspectival switches: (a) those which are the results of a relevant valid dialectical argument, as elaborated in §6; and (b) those which may be said to constitute a '*reflection*'. This term can be introduced by noting that in Hegel each phase of the dialectical process can be regarded as a compounded product or boxed focus, consisting in the cumulative results of successive U-D-R sequences. Now Hegel's practice is not in fact conceptually uniformly linear and there is no reason in principle why any term in an organic totality should not be reflected into any other, including compounds of such. In fact, *perspectival fluidity and multi-facetedness* is an essential requirement for any concrete (and, a fortiori, totalizing) inquiry, particularly in the socio-sphere. It should go without saying that Hegelian dialectic purports to be the constellationally completed reflection on reflection.

The consequential heterological outcome of the ex ante or forward movement of some local Hegelian dialectic is, as I have noted, a theory/practice inconsistency. But what happens, more generally, if a transcendental or dialectical necessity, established (let us suppose) by sound argumentation, is contravened? To contravene such a necessity, in some theory or practice, is, insofar as the necessity pertains to the world in which we must act, to contravene an *axiological* (or practical) *necessity* too. I am going to call such necessities, after the watchword for Mrs Thatcher's commitment to an antiquated monetarism (and to remind us of the fallibility of our claims to knowledge of them), a *TINA* ('there is no alternative') *necessity* imposing *TINA* imperatives. Theories and practices which violate such necessities, if they are to survive and be applicable to the world in which we must – in virtue of the axiological imperative – act: (a) require some *defence mechanism*, safety net or security system, which may well, in systematically related ensembles, (b) necessitate supporting or reinforcing *connections*, in the shape of duals, complements and the like elsewhere; and (c) need to assume the cloak of some conjugated *compromise formation* in a world where axiological necessities press about them. Such mechanisms, connections and formations are Tina ones and the whole complex comprises the '*Tina syndrome*'. All transcendental and/or dialectical necessities, insofar as they potentially implicate our speech action, can be seen by a valid perspectival switch as axiological necessities too.

Thus consider subject–object identity theory, whether of a hylomorphic, (Hegelian) phenomenological or phenomenalist kind. This will appear explicitly anthropo*centric* from a metacritically realist dialectical perspective. Now such a theory, insofar as it is to be applicable to the transcendentally – axiologically – necessary real world of (relatively or absolutely) independently existing and spatio-temporally causally efficacious things, at the very least, will have to covertly graft onto or transmute itself into an anthropo*morphic* correspondence theory, adopting some amalgamation of them or shuttling between the two positions: a typical Tina compromise. However, for general knowledge to be possible (without which particular knowledge is useless), given such an anthropic base, an actualism, postulating the invariant invariance – or constant conjunctivitis – of the subjectively defined particulars, will be required: a typical Tina connection. Moreover, an empirical (or conceptual) realist actualism, to be applicable to the normal normic open-systemic world, where constant conjunctions rarely obtain outside the laboratory and a few other (e.g. astronomically) locally-temporally closed contexts, will need to invoke a ceteris paribus clause inconsistent with itself (for the generalization cannot be both actual and universal) to survive: a typical Tina defence mechanism – or metaphysical λ safety net; but also, of course, a *performative contradiction* – or theory/practice inconsistency. Metacritically, then, the denegation or violation of an axiological necessity must deploy itself as an auto-subversive, radically negating, internally split, axiologically inconsistent Tina compromise formation, necessarily presupposing what it (explicitly or implicitly) denies. In general, then, *Tina formations* are internally contradictory, more or less systemic, efficacious, syntonic (and, as I shall argue, regressive) ensembles, only demonstrable as such, of course, insofar as they have been transcendentally or otherwise refuted, displaying duplicity, equivocation, extreme plasticity and pliability and rational indeterminacy (facilitating their ideological and manipulative use). Moreover, they generate a characteristic range of paradoxes and effects, including the scotomatic ('Stoicism'), schizoid ('Scepticism') and introjective or projective duplicative, replicative or fragmentary forms ('the Unhappy Consciousness'), so well analysed by Hegel in the justly celebrated chapter on 'Self-consciousness' in the *Phenomenology*. We have already observed another instance of a Tina formation in the tacit duplicity of the dialectical antagonists of subjective empiricism and objective idealism in §6. Insofar as Hegel is aware of his tacit reliance on empirical data (that is, insofar as he wants to avoid *reflexive inconsistency*, another name for performative contradiction) this dialectic must take Hegel back in the direction of Kant: to epistemological heteronomy.[54] Conversely Kantian ethical autonomy – the categorical imperative is the prototype of Hegelian autogenetics – is liable to an exactly parallel charge from Hegel.[55]

The invocation of a Tina λ clause can appear as a 2E inconsistency or contradiction, a 3L split or detotalization, but it can also assume the mantle of a straight 4D auto-deconstruction or the 1M non-identity of a theory besides, and requiring something other than, itself. In this respect it is akin to Derridean 'supplementarity', as comprising at once addition and substitution, and to the other members of what Gasché has described as the 'infrastructural chain'.[56] Together these may be regarded as so many metacritical or dialectical comments – a notion I will generalize to that of the *dialectical remark* (drk†) – on the hierarchies of traditional philosophy. But Derrida's models are too closely tied to the practice of hierarchical inversion, chiasmus and erasure. The more general concept of a Tina formation is required for the analysis of the effects of the violation of any axiological necessity, although the way it manifests itself, on any particular occasion, in a multiply determined, contradictory, agentive and internally and externally related world, will be both contingent and variable.

Tina formations are occasionally, although not always, repressed. They thus inevitably raise questions about ideology, $power_2$ formations, hegemony and resistance. A classic instance, admirably analysed by Alasdair MacIntyre on a number of occasions,[57] is that of 'Diderot's Syndrome'. Diderot asked, in *Le Neveu de Rameau*, what happened when an axiological necessity, such as the sexual impulse – or, one might say, the need for food, recognition, de-alienation or autonomy – is denied overt expression. Freud's life work, from his commencement of the (soon to be abandoned) cathartic method,[58] was, of course, a quest for an answer to Diderot's question. Marxists and Nietzscheans ask it too. More to the immediate point, so does Hegel. Indeed to say that some conceptual or social form is at once both false and necessary (which we have seen in §6 is a distinguishing feature of dialectical argument), incoherent yet indispensable, (for Hegel, logically) contradictory but dialectically essential is just to say that it is a Tina compromise formation. Indeed the Hegelian dialectic may be regarded as a progressive compounding of Tina compromise upon Tina compromise, until in the self-realization of the absolute idea and the final overcoming of its self-compromise, in the absolute spirit of absolute idealism we achieve, at once, absolute clarity and absolute compromise. But in the backwards or retrospective reconciliation that this Palladian vantage point affords, negativity is undone, contradiction is cancelled, the implicit explicit, the absent present, plenitudinous positivity restored and actuality rationalized, and we are offered ex post, as the left

Hegelians alleged, another sort of compromise: constellationally conciliatory comprise with the prevailing order of things, rationally transfigured under the configuration of the absolute idea.

Notice that both (a) the Tina compromise form, embodying theory/practice inconsistency,* performative contradiction or reflexive inconsistency, which the dialectical comment registers, and (b) the vicious regress inherent in the self-predicative and self-referential paradoxes and the Fichtean endless task issue in (α) axiological indeterminacy – in Wittgenstein's terms 'we do not know how to go on [and/or, as in (b), when to stop]' – and (β) the lack of progressive (e.g. informational) import, characteristic of degenerating programmes, practices, systems and pathologies generally. And the rational non-valent/Socratic response to both depends upon the explicit recognition and elimination of absences (e.g. of some relevant incompleteness) which Hegel, in his analytic reinstatement in dialectical connection, forecloses. For in closing a potentially, necessarily and actually open totality, and so shutting out the possibility of further essential progress, Hegel performs two self-deconstructive acts. First, he commits himself to that very Fichtean vicious regress which Hegelians know as the 'bad infinite'.[59] What could be more wearisome than merely replicating the status quo (constellationally/essentially or otherwise)? Second, because in overcoming it, he commits himself to the auto-subversion in the injunctive paradox intrinsic to it. We cannot just bring about what already is (although we can attempt to do so) – at the Plateau-nic incessantly revolving turntable that would constitute the constellational closure of geo-history.[60] The transformational character of praxis will ensure that we are always also transforming the structures that we are in the very process of reproducing. In announcing the constellational closure of history, Hegel re-opened the floodgates of tensed geo-historical processes, most notably through the mediation of Marxism. His injunctive paradox is an ethical displacement of the problem of induction, homologous in form with the paradoxes I have already noted (in C1.9). The (1M) resolution of all these turns on the conception of ontological stratification (and alethic truth) and on an open epistemic and practical totality.

If ideology is most generally conceived, as I shall argue in §9 below, as generated and reproduced and/or transformed at the intersection of power, discursive and normative social, material, inter- and intra-subjective relations, then a narrower concept of it, encapsulating the pejorative connotations of the term, would see the *ideological intersect* of what I have called the 'social cube'[61] as embodying categorial error, of which paradox is just a surface form.[62] The narrower concept may be exemplified by the view of war as a game or women as inferior to men or Marx's justly famous analyses of the value and wage forms.[63] Ideologies, in this narrower sense, necessarily

* The split in Hegel between theoretical and practical reason is epitomized by Hegel's *unreciprocated* recognition of Napoleon at Jena.

constitute Tina formations and, as such, are liable to explanatory critique (a concept I will resume in C3.7). But insofar as they are causally efficacious, the social relations and interests underpinning them (and thus also the ideologies themselves) will not bend to explanatory critique alone. Rather this will depend on a type of agency to which I have already alluded: *transformed* (autoplastic [cf. 1M non-identity]), *transformative* (alloplastic [cf. 2E negativity]), *totalizing* (all-inclusive and auto-reflexive [cf. 3L]) and *transformist* (oriented to structural change, informed by explanatory critique, concrete utopianism and participatory – animating/activating research) praxis (ideally comprising dr$_a'$ in dφ at 4D). This will involve the intertwining of politics of at least four types: *life* (including e.g. health, career) *politics*, whose subjects are concrete singular agents, and whose ethical counterpart will be a consequentially derived virtue theory; *movement* (e.g. feminist, green) *politics*, motivated by the aspirations of differential collectivities and oriented to the extension of freedoms qua rights; *representative politics*, expressing the needs and interests of different communities but whose bottom line will be the preservation of existing freedoms qua rights; and *participatory-emancipatory politics*, coordinated by a concern with fundamental structural change in a rhythmic to eudaimonia, understood as universal human flourishing. Each itself depends on ergonically efficient ego-emancipatory existential security systems, grounded in relations of fiduciariness, care, solidarity and trust, oriented to reflexively monitored transformation, in the context of hermeneutic hegemonic/counter-hegemonic struggles over discursively moralized (ideologically constituted) power$_2$, i.e. generalized master–slave, relations. The eventual dialectic, the grounds and directionality of which I will attempt to vindicate in the next chapter, will depend upon the sequence: *e*rgonic efficiency → *e*mpowerment → *e*mancipation → *e*udaimonia. A eudaimonistic pluriverse would consist in a plurality of processes in which heterology was minimized to a level in which it could be said that each was *true to, of and for themselves and each other and the trans-specific contexts* which they both contain and are contained by. (See Figure 9.)

There are two more major concepts to discuss: totality, including concrete universality; and levels. In respect of my section-unifying concept of heterology, they are, in a certain sense, polar opposites for whereas levels make

Figure 9 Dialectic of the 7 E's and 6 T's

heterology, e.g. in the form of depth, possible, totality seeks to exclude heterology and to embrace all in a unity (albeit of differentiated aspects).

Totality ignites a principal point of difference between transcendental and absolute idealism, which deposits a source of tension within a materialist framework. The Hegelian dialectic is a concrete totality, generated by contradiction, in a process of continual *Aufhebung*, that is, of preservative superstructuration which, when it is achieved, as Hegel claims it is in his system, constellationally closes both being and knowledge, united by the principle of identity, alike. By contrast the Kantian dialectic is a comment (cf. dc′) on the limits of finite human intelligence[64] to the effect that it is incapable of *knowing* the infinite totalities of reason, and that the (perhaps eternally challenging) desire to do so plunges it into an intrinsically antinomic mire. This is dialectic as *limit* (dl′). Now suppose Hegel had claimed merely that we know the world and that it is in part contradictory (and perhaps that it must be so, even if only for us to be able to know it). Suppose, moreover, that Kant, for his part, had maintained that we do not know all of the world (or at the very most know that we do so) and that human powers are at least potentially limited. Then their respective positions would have been negotiably compatible, and indeed arguably acceptable. If, further, neither had fallen sway to the conceptual realist aspiration and thought to ground the conditioned in terms of the unconditioned, but they had been content, instead, merely to ground the more in terms of the less conditioned; and at the same time they had rejected an empirical realist account of embodied, finite being (which Hegel, no less than Kant, accepts) – then their positions would have approximated those of critical realism. (It is, as I have already urged, the squeeze on natural necessity, ontological stratification and scientific theory between metaphysics [the sovereign of necessity] and experience [the clerk of contingency] that accounts for the antinomial dialectical duplicity of conceptual and empirical realism.) Let us speculate further that Kant had self-reflexively attempted to situate the critical philosophy in the context of his day (as Hegel did for absolute idealism). Then he could have contemplated the possibility of dialectical limits of the applicability of categories in virtue of the relativity of the geo-historical specificity of the objects to which they applied (as Marx was later to do) *and* trumped Hegel in virtue of the latter's constellational closure and fear of an open totality. Kant could have gone on to strengthen his hand by pointing out that, as inescapably finite, limited, embodied space-time voyagers, we are necessarily restricted to some local present, to some or other particular position on our epistemic-ethical-axiological world-lines, from which, in analogy to a light-cone, some but not other possibilities are open and some but not other positions visible to us. Thus transitive relativity – but meta-reflexively situated in the context of a common cosmos, punctuated by absence and alterity, from which we clumpily, chaotically and stochastically emerged to come to know, transcendentally and scientifically, the intransitive reality of a 'growing-knowers'' philosophically Copernican-Darwinian world.*

If, to continue the fable, Kant had rejected the second analogy and, with it, empirical realism tout court, he could then have discarded the presuppositions of the third antinomy and treated human beings as causally efficacious agents, with degrees of freedom (as Hegel correctly appreciated), in a world that is not determined before it is caused, so that if S_1 causes S_2 at $s - t_i$ and S_2 causes S_3 at $s - t_j$ it does not follow that S_3 is determined at $s - t_i$. Suppose, moreover, Kant's attention now swung to the practical sphere. He could have noted how the greater proportion of *women* (which has to be italicized, given his misogyny) and men had powers that could be, but were not, realized and needs similarly unsatisfied, despite the plenitude of possible resources; and he could have begun to seek the specific socio-geo-historical causes of this condition (as Marx was to do). Kant could then have conceived a practical totality, neither as a transcendent *Jenseits* nor as a Fichtean endless task, but as unachieved but realizable – in an open world, shaped and conditioned but dependent ultimately upon rational agency – informed by the supreme ethical virtue of wisdom – in a dialectic of truth and freedom that I will articulate in C3. In this way he could have played a part in forging that chain of identities-in-difference (or, if you prefer, non-equivalent equivalences) that unite the marginalized majority, and proleptically, under appropriately transformed descriptions, the entirety, of the human race. But then, of course, Kant would have been a dialectical critical realist.

The drive to totality in science is given by the need to maximize explanatory power. But it is up to science to discover to what extent a subject-matter is internally related and hence in the domain of the 'intra-active'. We can define three basic kinds of intra-action: (1) *existential constitution*, in which event, one element or aspect (moment, determination, relation, etc.), e_2, is essential and intrinsic to (in the sense explained earlier, in which it is not necessarily a physical part of) another, e_1; (2) intra-*permeation*, when e_2 is present within, although not essential to the nature of, e_1, the sense in which e_1 may be said to *contain* e_2; and (3) intra-*connection*, the sense in which one element, e_2, is causally efficacious on an element internally related to it, e_1. This raises a number of issues. It may be questioned whether permeation is really a case of internal relationality if the permeating element is not essential to the permeated one. But an element may be necessary to the existence of another (under the appropriate descriptions) without being essential to its nature. Do the other modes not depend on intra-connection? Sympathetic as I am to the force of this objection, there is no reason why a *possible* connection should not bind elements. (3) is tantamount to dialectical connection and we have already noted that dialectical connections may or may not be dialectic-

* This should not be taken as an endorsement of neo-Darwinist ideology, particularly in the light of current research.[65]

ally contradictory. More generally, all the basic modes of intra-activity may be reciprocal or non-reciprocal, transfactual or actual, positive or negative, polyadic or dyadic, and agentive or non-agentive. Can a transcendental deduction be given for totality (the key 3L concept) as has been done for real negation or absence (the principal 2E category in C1.3)?

This seems relatively easy for social life. Consider once more our paradigmatic book (with transcendentally necessary spaces, or level-specific voids, in it) in the library, whether it is 'in' (present) or 'out' (absent). There is an obvious sense in which the book, if recently published, existentially presupposes all, or at least many, of the others, and the spatio-temporal traditions which nurtured it (and may indeed be said to have conditioned, permeated or rhythmically generated it). That is to say, it would have been impossible without the others. Or consider the text itself. It is an internally related totality. As are the elements of a language, or the ebb and flow of a conversation, the sequential 'habitus' of a routine, the systemic interdependencies of the global monetary system, a play, a sculpture, or an experimental project oriented to the demediation of nature. Or consider simply a musical tune, melody, beat or rhythm. Or reflect on the semantic structure of a sentence, bound in a complex of paradigmatic and syntagmatic relations (and metaphoric and metonymic presuppositions). Or on its physical structure – for instance, the location of the spaces and punctuation marks within it. Not to treat such entities as totalities is to violate norms of descriptive and hermeneutic adequacy. In particular, insofar as any or more of the above are transcendentally necessary conditions of science, as reflection will easily show that they are, as good a deduction of totality as transcendental realism demands has been found. (Later I shall consider how one might set about a deduction both of science and of transcendental realism without recourse to science.)

So totalities must exist for social life to be possible. But what of nature? First, it might be entered that unless there were internal, and specifically dialectical, contradictions (which presuppose internal relations), there would be no internal (radically negating) tendencies to change either for individual things or for their types (including natural kinds) or, more drastically, for the world as a whole, so that the emergence of, for example, science would have been impossible. If my first argument turns on the transcendental necessity of ontological change, my second turns on that of the transcendental necessity for taxonomy in science. Thus it could be argued that unless some explanatorily significant things had properties which were existentially essential to them, that is, such that they were not just necessarily connected, but internally related, to them, scientific classification, which depends upon the possibility of real (as distinct from merely nominal) definitions, would be impossible. Internal relationality, and so the conceptual possibility of the analytic a posteriori, is bound to the Leibnizian level of the identification of natural kinds, as natural necessity is tied to the demonstration of explanatory adequacy in the dialectic of explanatory and taxonomic knowledge in science. To revert to the model illustrated in Figure 2.12 on p. 110 above, when scientists have gone so far that they can deduce the reason S_j for the phenomena S_i that their concerns are for the reason for that reason – along the epistemological dialectic to S_k – they make it definitional of the structural entities of S_j that they possess the explanatory essential properties that they do.[66] Without them, the activity of classification, in an open-systemic world (in which events are normally 'conjunctures' and things are usually 'compounds' or 'condensates'), would become as arbitrary as that of explanation. For if classification is justified only on the basis of superficial resemblance rather than real identity of structure, then there is no rationale for the stratification of science. This depends upon grasping suitably groomed structurata as tokens of real structures, whose intransitive existence and transfactual efficacy is a condition not only of science, but also of life. Resemblance, like regularity, theory generates insuperable paradoxes, as we shall note in due course. In what follows I will focus, however, on the social realm, where the concept of totality is so patently at home.

To grasp totality is to break with our ordinary notions of identity, causality, space and time, justified by the 'analogical grammar' of the classical mechanistic corpuscularian world view that I have criticized elsewhere.[67] It is to see things *existentially constituted*, and permeated, *by their relations with others*; and to see our ordinary notion of identity as an *abstraction* not only from their existentially constitutive processes of formation (geo-histories), but also from their existentially constitutive inter-activity (internal relatedness). It is to see the causality of a upon b affected by the causality of c upon d. Emergent totalities generate emergent spatio-temporalities. Not only do we get overlapping spatio-temporalities (whether or not, the [non-]entities concerned are of the same or different kinds) but as the intrinsic is not co-extensive with the internal we also have real problems of identity and individuation. When is a thing no longer a thing but something else? When has the nature, and so the explanation for the behaviour, of a (relative) continuant changed? This may be due to either diachronic change (transition points), synchronic boundaries (borders), and/or changing constitutive intra-activity. Aporiai for philosophy, but real problems of individuation, definition, scope and articulation for science. I am going to argue for spatio-temporal, social and moral (real) relationism; in the domain of totality we need to conceptualize *entity relationism*.

How does one research a totality? Starting from any one element, one must in general investigate two margins of inquiry. At the *intensive margin* we will find more and more elements and/or the whole – and in principle their relations – 'reflections' (see p. 116) – contained, condensed, packed into, implicated in and causally efficacious on the initial element, in any number of modes; for instance, either by their presence or by their absence or both. (Thus 'tomato' and 'sandwich' are co-present even when unuttered [and so actually absent], in their paradigmatic and syntagmatic relations, with an utterance of 'cucumber'.) Similarly totalizing at the *extensive margin*, we will discover the initial element reflected, in different ways, into other elements of the totality and/or the whole. And the same applies to the whole itself. A wide variety of constitutive, permeative and causal relations may occur at the intra-active frontier of an aspect or totality. We must continually remember not to confuse the intrinsic and the (material object) internal, that permeation may show that non-corpuscularian fluidity revealed by physical fields and that, in defiance of the Cartesian-Newtonian paradigm of action, intra-active (organic) causality may be effected across a void, i.e. comprise action at a distance.* Reflections of whatever type (and in particular their nth order relations) may be exteriorized at the extensive margin and the saturated result re-interiorized or vice versa, and so on recursively. Compounding results of successive reflections may comprise totalities of their own. It is important here to discriminate between (α) *totalities simpliciter* (including allegedly 'complete' ones); (β) *sub-totalities*, which possess discontinuities, hiatuses, spaces, binds, barriers, boundaries and blocks between totalities; and (γ) *partial totalities*, which may also contain external, contingent or no connections between the elements of such sub-totalities. In the social world we are almost always concerned with partial totalities. However, once we introduce such 1M–4D motifs as stratification, intra-position, constitutive geo-histories, emergent rhythmics, multiple binds, reflexivity, openness and transformative agency in a materialist framework shot through by all manner, angle, level and kind of determination (on which more in a moment), the theoretical possibilities increase exponentially, approximating a Hegelian 'bad infinite' – a conclusion Hegel was able to avoid only by the arbitrary devices of constellational closure and generally unilinear presentation. That the exponential does not in practice materialize is due to the finite, limited and conditioned character of real partial totalities; and the requirement imposed by science that it is only after an a posteriori subject-specific inquiry that a totality, such as a mode of production, can be described, or the real definition of an object such as a crystal be furnished. However, thinking of totalities as intra-actively changing embedded ensembles, constituted by their geo-histories (and/or their traces) and their contexts, in open potentially disjointed process, subject to multiple perspectival switches, and in structured open systemic flux, enables us to appreciate both the flickering, chameleon-like appearance of social being and the reason why narratives must be continually rewritten and social landscapes remapped.

I now want to develop a concept of holistic causality and illustrate how it

* This may make it difficult to say whether a potential causal effect should be attributed to locations within the void, or even, given the conceptual connections between identity, causality, space and time, whether it is wholly intelligible to talk of individuating specific locations within it.

might be used in a dialectic of de-alienation. We already know that causality presupposes structural possibility, transfactual efficacy, possessual exercise, the possibility of mediation and the likelihood of multiple determination of results. It may take milder forms than the rather bold 'determination', such as conditioning, limiting, selecting, shaping, blocking, influencing, etc.; and it may stimulate, release, nurture, enable, sustain, entrain, displace, condense, coalesce, bind, in addition to the poietic 'generate' or 'produce'. But let me subsume this variety under the generic 'determination'. I will then say that *holistic causality* is at work when a *complex 'coheres'* in such a way that:

(α) the totality, i.e. the form or structure of the combination, causally determines the elements; and
(β) the form or structure of the elements causally codetermine each other, and so causally (α') determine or (β') codetermine the whole.

Case (β') applies where the totality is emergent (i.e. has emergent causal powers as a totality) and/or constitutes the ground of the elements. Several caveats must be immediately sounded. Remember we are dealing with partial totalities; so that my concept of holistic causality necessarily cannot be expressive or centred in the way that Hegel's totality is, although it is quite consistent with a gamut of species of domination. Moreover, one particular element within the totality, rather than the totality itself, may constitute the ground of the totality, which will in general be asymmetrically weighted and involve various degrees of attachment and detachment ('relative autonomy') of its elements. Alternatively, the totality may be grounded in a deeper structure (or totality) in which the holistic causality at work in this instance merely mediates the relationship between the super-ground and the elements of the totality. In either event, the totality is itself *structured*, and so may contain or be contained by dialectically contradictory (and more or less antagonistic) or, on the other hand, mutually reinforcing or supporting (e.g. Tina-connective), relationships. The efficacy of the elements and/or the totality may depend upon dual, multiple, joint or contextual action. Super- or intra-structures may be formed on or within it. The totality, at least partially constituted by its geo-historical formation and context, is in open process, intrinsically and extrinsically, so that its form, elements and effects will be continuously *configurationally changing.* These changes or determinations must be understood as transformative negations or absentings, rhythmically exercised, holistically explained and subject to or mediated by intentional causal agency in the social world. So that here we may talk of the constitutional unity and, to neologize developmentally, 'fluidity' of the concept of '[causal] determination' as transfactual efficacy, transformative negation, tensed (spatializing) process, holistic causality and intentional absenting or agency.

A rudimentary dialectic may illustrate some of the relationships at stake.

A generative separation, creating an alterity, may entrain an absence, or transformative negation, rhythmically exercised in virtue of the causal powers of the entities involved. Suppose N is an agent alienated from something essential and intrinsic, but now absented from and extrinsic to her. A happy retotalization occurs as a result of her (and let us suppose, collective) embodied intentional causal agency. And we have a dialectic of de-alienation in which N is reunited with a part of herself, now no longer divided and perhaps aware for the first time of the fact of how essential (transfactually real, although not actually experienced) the estranged aspect of the totality of her being was to her identity, and so, by difference, constitutive of her new sense of self-identity.

I now want to turn to the closely connected theme of the *concrete universal*, already mentioned when discussing mediation above. It is not essential to a concrete universal, as I shall develop the concept, that it, or its components, comprise totalities (although it is so for the restricted notion that Hegel deploys). What does it mean to call something 'concrete'? We can get two purchases on this. First, it really makes sense only in contrast to its co-relative – '*abstract*'. Secondly, insofar as it has a positive meaning of its own, its nearest synonym might be 'well-rounded', in the sense of balanced, appropriate and complete for the purposes at hand. Actualities or their descriptions may be concrete (so that the term has a characteristic intransitive/transitive bivalency), as may my experience. *But the concrete ≠ the actual ≠ the empirical.* If *Capital* is regarded as an adequate description of the capitalist mode of production, the intransitive object of its theoretical result may well be said to be *capital in-concretion*,[68] which will be transfactually applicable wherever the concept of capital is, but the results of which will be codetermined (a) by the residue of other economic modes, (b) by intra-structural mechanisms and intransitive objects only specifiable at a level of generality, detail and/or extension with which Marx did not attempt to engage (including much not set out in his famous 'six brochures' and much else not traditionally included in the Marxian superstructure or base, e.g. the reproduction of labour-power, the ecosphere, gender, ethnicity, the unconscious) and (c) by the other moments of the concrete universal I am about to describe – besides the *pan-concrete* totality (of totalities) that was the ultimate intransitive object of Marx's work. Capital-in-concretion is in turn not equivalent to Althusser's 'concrete-in-thought'. Nor is it the same as the 'synthesis of many determinations' to which Marx refers in his Introduction to the *Grundrisse*, which articulates the logic of the (more or less concrete) *conjuncture.* Nor again is it the same as Hegel's famous example of a rose in his *Introductory Lectures* as 'the unity of different determinations' where he describes the multiplicity of aspects of, in my terms, a *concrete singular.*

The main differences between Hegel and dialectical critical realism turn on the (a) *separability*, (b) *multiple determination* and (c) *spatio-temporalization* of the concrete universal. The minimum formula necessary for the concrete universal (CU) is a *multiple quadruplicity.* Thus once the idea of process, conceived as the mode of spatio-temporalizing structural effects, is combined with the Hegelian emphasis on specificity or particularity (which may itself be more or less structurally sedimented and/or spatio-temporally localized), in addition to the moments of universality and singularity, then it is clear that the CU must reveal itself as a *quadruplicity.* Now, leaving aside for the moment the multiplicity of aspects of a totality, in open systems in any particular concrete instance, a multiplicity of mechanisms, specific differentiae, rhythmic processes and episodic events may all be at work as components of the concrete (whatever the focus of one's interest), so that the CU must be conceived at the very least as a *multiplicity of quadruplicities* or multiple quadruplicity.

For Hegel the concrete universal was constituted typically by a universal, a specific or particular and an individual or singular element; and these elements were inseparable, i.e. could not exist without each other. We can, of course, immediately ask Hegel (and even more pertinently, the British Hegelians) whether the CU is supposed to refer to something real or merely, in neo-Kantian fashion, imaginary; and, if the former, whether the universal is ultimately logico-divine (and therefore possessually space-time transcendent) or material (and so in space-time). Hegel's answer would be to reject the question. For him the real is ideal and the infinite is embodied. And his project is to establish this. So let us not pursue this point; but take up more concrete (less abstract) points of difference with Hegel. First, *separability.* In an experiment, otherwise efficacious determinants on causal outcomes are isolated out or otherwise controlled. This is *demediation:* the instantiation of a universal law in a singular, although of course normally replicable, instance or sequence. Second, let us take the missing term in Hegel. We have seen that once the Plateau-nic end is achieved, because everything is always stable, everything is always changing. The constellational closure of space-time is accompanied by the elimination of (post-Hegelian) structural change and thus of the concepts of periodicity and locality, as indispensable to socio-geohistoricity, where differential rhythmics or processes have to be related in an explanatory hierarchy of structural levels or modes articulated around transitions at the explanatorily most basic (or otherwise interesting) level or its rhythmic (and in relation to which other changes can be ordinated). A similar argument – from deep structural change – furnishes a minimal defence of some synchronic/diachronic distinction as necessary for explanatory social science. Third, Hegel's irrealism does not allow him the possibility of what I have called '*referential detachment*', i.e. the ontological dislocation of referent from the act of reference, which in turn cannot be, in virtue of his commitment to the categorially duplicitous principle of subject–object (transitive–intransitive) identity, clearly differentiated from sense. Hence the genuine indexicality of sense of a word like 'I' becomes the impossibility of *referential indexicality* (and thence token-reflexivity) of a concrete singular, without which tensing, dating and locating (and hence any science, or even discourse, let alone geo-history) would become impossible. Finally, structures, including unknown ones, constituting sheer *unactualized possibilities* (which may embrace the dispositional identities of physical fields or agentive selves) or their *transfactual efficacy* in open systems manifest universalities without singularities – a situation which Hegel's actualism cannot permit.

But at this juncture we come head on to the multiple quadruplicity of the/a/some CU. In general in open systems we will be dealing with a constellation of mechanisms, mediations or differentiae and components of a conjuncture. Open systems characteristically make determination not only non-linear but also non-radical. The mediations may be mechanisms themselves or more or less idiographic contexts, episodes or objects (e.g. uniquely laminated structurata). Thus process was described earlier as the mode of spatio-temporalizing structure. However, there may be a number of such modes or rhythmics for any such structure; and in principle the same applies to the levels of specific mediation and concrete singularity. (Events or social singulars such as persons may have more than one rhythmic.) This gives us four modes of *illicit abstraction*, viz. destratification, deprocessualization, demediation and desingularization. But even this is too simple, taking into account 2E–4D desiderata. Elements at any one of the four levels of the CU may be totally or partially bound into totalities, and there may be internal relations between the levels. Next 2E. Elements, whether internally related or not, may be efficacious as either absent or present, and if internally related, they may be dialectically contradictory or not, but this does not add a further difficulty of principle. Finally 4D. Human agency implicates a network of social relations, inter-personal action, intra- or inter-actions, material transactions with nature and inter-subjectivity that not only further complicates the CU but also requires investigative techniques sui generis as well as displaying an emancipatory conatus of its own, as I aim to show. Corresponding to 1M–4D requirements we have *another* set of four modes of illicit abstraction: destratification (again), denegativization, detotalization and de-agentification. Figure 10 illustrates multiple determination in the case of events. Figure 11 shows a case of the binding of structures in a totality

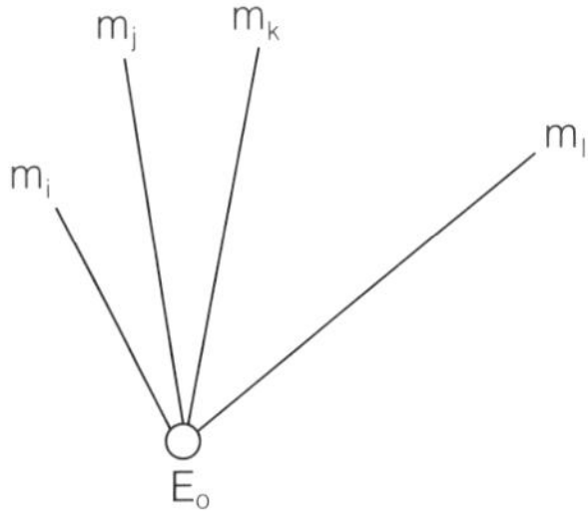

Figure 10 Multiple determination in open systems

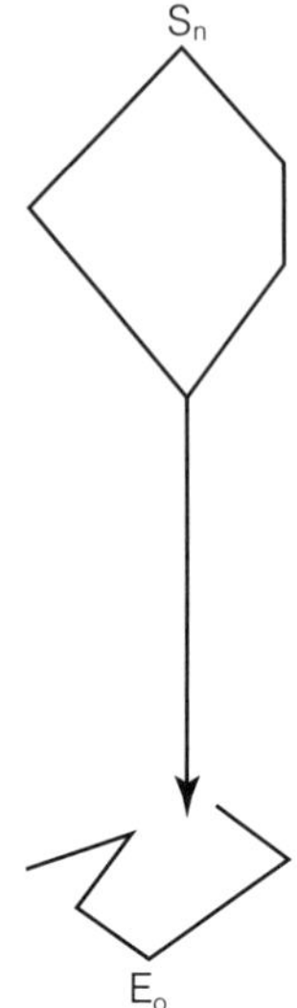

Figure 11 Totality of structures co-influencing a bound conjuncture of events

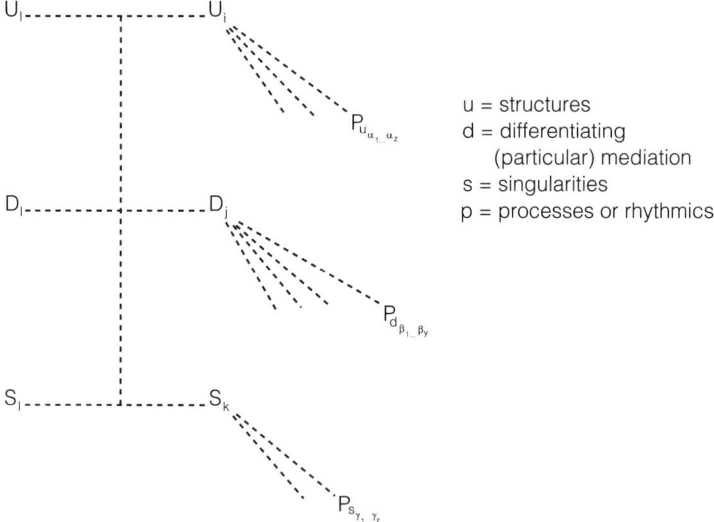

Figure 12 The concrete universal as a multiple quadruplicity

codetermining a similarly based conjunctural context. Figure 12 depicts the basic concept of a CU as a multiple quadruplicity. But increasingly throughout this book I will be thematizing *concrete singularity* as the key to the realm of freedom, including the abolition of human heterology. As for the problems of individuation and articulation which I have left open, there is no resolution for them other than to allow this to be determined in the specific case by the theory or set of theories which maximizes explanatory power. Of course this will depend in part on one's explanatory objectives. This does not, however, subjectivize explanation. For there are clear principles of depth (stratification) and completeness (totality) which allow us to decide whether one theoretical, and, a fortiori, applied, explanation is better than another.

This allows me to move on to the final theme of this section – that of *levels.* If totality permits 'within-ness', levels allow 'about-ness'. We have already witnessed it in the guise of ontological stratification providing both (*α*) the key to the 1M resolution of a whole class of philosophical problems of which the Platonic self-predicative ('Third Man') paradox and the problem of induction are the best known, and (*β*) the basic principle of theoretical explanation in science around which the *DREI(C)* model revolves. (*α*) resolves the problems of what I shall call, borrowing a term from Peter Manicas,[69] 'the transdictive complex', where transdiction for me connotes both the vertical or structural depth and horizontal or transfactually efficacious aspects of 1M transcendental realism. The basic principle behind the resolution of this problem-field turns around the concepts of ontological stratification and, as we shall see in C3, alethic truth, and the corresponding avoidance of vicious regress or cumulative homology, i.e. explaining something in terms of itself, rather than a new level of structure (or degree of completion or totality).

Is there a basic schema of *applied* scientific explanation? There is; and it is applicable in the fields of theoretical and practical reasoning alike. Like the theoretical model it has its primary progressive and secondary regressive moments. The first step in the explanation of some concrete phenomenon, say a conjunctural episode, composed, in the fashion of partial totalities, of both external and internally related elements, will be to *r*esolve it into its components. The next step will be to *r*edescribe these components in theoretically significant terms, so that the transfactually efficacious principles of theoretical science can be brought to bear on them. Then, employing those principles, taking into account the particular mediations and the operative geo-historical processes in the case at hand, to *r*etrodict back to possible antecedent causes. Next, comes the *e*limination of what will always constitute a plurality of possible causes in open systems, until one has *i*dentified a full enough set (which may comprise a totality) of causes for a concrete applied explanation to have been said to have been provided, given one's explanatory objectives. There will almost always then follow a regressive movement in which the initial phenomenon is redescribed in the light of its causes. Hence we have the *RRREI(C)* model of applied scientific explanation, with the 'C' standing for correction. However, unlike theoretical explanation in at least many of the natural sciences, viz. from explanatory significant structures to their higher-order structural explanation, applied explanations of concrete singulars, like changes in a particular structuratum, are a much messier affair. In a dialectical pluriverse an event e at a level L is as likely to be (multiply) explained by elements at the same and lower-order levels in addition to higher-order (deeper) ones, and/or even laterally, diagonally, tangentially by elements not locatable in the categorial or generic order at all. Failure to distinguish theoretical and applied explanations, and to discriminate levels of abstraction, as well as topic, scope and perspective, have bedevilled disputes within Marxology in particular. In the first place we have here an intransitive object which is changing so that geo-historically specific theories, e.g. for contemporary 'consumer capitalism', are necessary. Second, one has to consider seriously whether a theory explicating the social presuppositions of capitalism and, allegedly, not just the contradictions and crises tendencies that flow from its deep structure but also its fundamental processual dynamic, should even attempt to explain relative prices (so that the 'transformation problem' may embody something akin to a fundamental category mistake). There is more than a hint of actualism here.

Alongside the 'pure' models of theoretical and applied scientific explanation, one can differentiate *intermediate*, *regional*, *local-periodized* and *idiographic* studies exemplified by work on ecology, party politics, Fordism and biography respectively. Ontological extensionalism would disconnect and decompartmentalize phenomena. Despite my warnings about actualism and my stress on the complexity and differentiation of our world, dialectics will always strive to cut across disciplinary boundaries, as phenomena in a mishmash world do, and to *totalize*, to draw together the intrinsically connected into an internally concrete (= well-rounded) whole.

Level-specific concepts, such as stratification, emergence, embedding, recursion, reflexivity, the dialectical comment (dc′), dialectical reason (dr′), are essential to the dialectics we have been investigating hitherto. It is therefore especially important to see that the concrete universal, and totality generally, do not negate, but depend upon them – just as the reverse is true. It is incompleteness (insufficient totality) in the shape of absence that must drive our dialectic on to consider non- and extra-Hegelian dialectics in the next section, before in §9 we turn to transformative agency itself as our paradigm.

[. . .]

Notes

1 Cf. PON2, p. 64 and RR, p. 182.
2 G. Buchdahl, *Metaphysics and the Philosophy of Science*, Oxford 1969, p. 3.
3 Cf. J. Evans, *Aristotle's Concept of Dialectic*, Cambridge 1977.
4 See, e.g., Topics 1, 2, 101e, 3b.
5 *Hegel*, Cambridge 1975, CI and passim.
6 *Kant on History*, ed. L. W. Beck, New York 1963, p. 3.

7 Ibid.
8 *Die Vernunft in oder Geschichte*, ed. J. Hofmeister, Hamburg 1933, pp. 77–88.
9 *The Philosophy of Right*, Oxford 1952, p. 12.
10 *Science of Logic*, London 1969, p. 56.
11 RTS2, p. 123.
12 See M. Rosen, *Hegel's Dialectic and Its Criticism*, Cambridge 1982, pp. 73ff.
13 See especially *Introduction to the Reading of Hegel*, New York 1969.
14 To borrow a phrase from S.Žižek, *For They Know Not What They Do*, London 1992.
15 Cf. RR, p. 32.
16 See R. Hare, 'Meaning and Speech Acts', *Philosophical Review* (1970), pp. 19ff.
17 Cf. RTS2, p. 87.
18 Cf. A. Lovejoy, *The Great Chain of Being*, Cambridge, Mass. 1936.
19 Cf. J. Shotter, *Knowing of the Third Kind*, Utrecht 1990.
20 Cf. F. Pirani, 'Cosmology in Crisis', *New Left Review*, 191 (1992).
21 *Hegel*, Cambridge 1975, CIII.
22 Cf. M. Bunge, *Method, Model and Matter*, Dordrecht 1973, C9.
23 See *Scientific Realism and Social Thought*, Hemel Hempstead 1989.
24 See ibid.
25 G. Della Volpe, *Logic as a Positive Science*, London 1980.
26 D. Dennett, *Consciousness Explained*, Harmondsworth 1991.
27 Cf. RTS2, C2.5, PON2, C3.3, and SRHE, C3.1.
28 Cf. RTS2, p. 107.
29 Cf. my entry on 'Materialism', in *Dictionary of Twentieth-Century Social Thought*, eds W. Outhwaite and T. Bottomore, Oxford 1992, and PIF Part 2 respectively.
30 From which Nancy Cartwright's *How the Laws of Physics Lie*, Oxford 1983, derives its actualist title.
31 Cf. RTS2, C1.3.
32 For a similar point, see B. Ollmann, *Dialectical Investigations*, London 1993, C1.
33 For a specific social interpretation of what I am treating as a generic phenomenon, see Arno J. Mayer, *The Persistence of the Old Regime*, London 1981.
34 Cf. M. Davis, *City of Quartz*, London 1991, and E. Soja, *Postmodern Geographies*, London 1989, C8–9.
35 Cf. M. Polanyi, *The Tacit Dimension*, London 1967.
36 Cf. J.J. Gibson, *The Senses Considered as Perceptual Systems*, London 1966.
37 PON2, p. 92 applies.
38 Cf. SRHE, pp. 26 and passim.
39 PON2, p. 42.
40 SRHE, p. 110.
41 Cf. M. Godelier, 'System, Structure and Contradiction in *Capital*', in R. Blackburn, ed., *Ideology in Social Science*, Glasgow 1972.
42 Cf. in this connection the important work of R. Kanth, *Capitalism and Social Theory*, New York 1992, R. Albritton, *A Japanese Approach to Political Economy* (forthcoming) and A. Shamsavari, *Dialectic and Social Theory*, London 1991.
43 *The Poverty of Philosophy*, Collected Works, Vol. IV, London 1976, p. 192.
44 *Contingency, Irony and Solidarity*, Cambridge 1989.
45 SRHE, p. 185.
46 *Critique of Pure Reason*, trans. N. Kemp Smith, London 1967, b. 329–36/a. 273–80.
47 SRHE, p. 113.
48 'Marxism and the Dialectic', *New Left Review*, 93 (1975).
49 On private property as a second-order mediation, see C.J. Arthur, *Dialectics of Labour*, Oxford 1984, and I. Mészáros, *Marx's Theory of Alienation*, London 1970.
50 Cf. RTS2, pp. 76–7.

51 Cf. SRHE, p. 274.
52 RTS2, C2.4.
53 Cf. my entry on 'Tacit Knowledge', *Dictionary of the History of Science*, eds B. Bynum and R. Porter, London 1981.
54 Cf. W.H. Walsh, 'Subjective and Objective Idealism', in D. Heinrich, ed., *Kant oder Hegel?* Stuttgart 1983.
55 Cf. W.H. Walsh, *Hegelian Ethics*, London 1969.
56 See R. Gasché, *The Tain of the Mirror*, Cambridge, Mass. 1986. A good introduction to supplementarity is contained in C. Norris, *Derrida*, Harmondsworth 1987. See also J. Llewelyn, *Derrida on the Threshold of Sense*, London 1987, and G. Spivak's 'Introduction' to *Of Grammatology*, where the concept of supplementarity is most systematically developed in regard to Rousseau's writings on 'Writing'.
57 See, for example, *After Virtue*, London 1981.
58 See D. Will, 'Psychoanalysis as a Human Science', *British Journal of Medical Psychology*, 93 (1980).
59 See for an exposition I. Soll, *Hegel's Metaphysics*, Chicago 1964, C4.
60 For an excellent exposition, see C. Taylor, *Hegel*, Cambridge 1975, CXIV.
61 SRHE, C2.2.
62 See my review of Terry Eagleton's *Ideology: An Introduction*, London 1991, in *Philosophical Books*, 33 (1), 1992.
63 Cf. N. Geras, 'Marx and the Critique of Political Economy', in R. Blackburn, ed., *Ideology in Social Science*, Glasgow 1972.
64 For expository convenience I consider only pure reason, but its extension to practical and aesthetic reason is simple. Cf. C4.3.
65 Cf. especially G. Webster, 'The Relation of Natural Forms', in M.-W. and P. Saunders, eds, *Beyond Neo-Darwinism*, London 1984, and B. Goodwin et al., eds., *Dynamic Structures in Biology*, Edinburgh 1989.
66 For a more detailed account, see RTS2, C3.
67 RTS2, p. 83.
68 I owe this term to T. Smith, *The Logic of Marx's Capital*, New York 1991.
69 *A History and Philosophy of the Social Sciences*, Oxford 1987, p. 10. He himself attributes the term to Maurice Mandelbaum.

24

DIALECTICAL CRITICAL REALISM AND ETHICS

Roy Bhaskar

§1 Ontology

In C2.6 I differentiated two senses of 'ontology': the sense in which everything is within being and the sense in which we might want to demarcate specifically ontological as opposed to, for instance, epistemological, relational or ethical dialectics. I defended ontological arguments and contended that it was inconceivable that the term 'ontology' not refer. I contrasted three compatible uses to which the concept might be put: (1) to distinguish *philosophical* from *scientific ontologies* (the latter consisting in the specific ontics of determinate transitive epistemic inquiries); or as a unified concept either (2) picking out different orders of abstraction, levels of inquiry, domains of extension, perspectival angles, etc. or (3) designating some characteristically dialectical mechanism or manoeuvre, such as contradiction or emergence, master–slave relations or constellationality, and applying it across disciplinary boundaries. I have also argued in previous publications that philosophical ontology in sense (1) need not be dogmatic and transcendent, but may be immanent and conditional, taking as its subject-matter just that world investigated by science (presupposed or acted on by other social practices) yet from the standpoint of what can be established about it by transcendental argument. This counters the traditional Humean-Kantian objection to ontology, but leaves the necessity of the conclusions contingent upon the acceptability of the premisses. Hegel claims to get round this in an immanent self-entailing/validating phenomenological circle. In this chapter I shall explore how one can establish transcendental arguments both (a) for, as distinct from, science and (b) for transcendental realism (or, more generally, for dialectical critical realism) without recourse to science, so tying the metacritical knot without Hegelian metaphysical rope.

Source: Dialectic: The Pulse of Freedom, London: Verso, 1993, chapters 3.1, 3.2, 3.7 and 3.10.

I have also argued that any theory of knowledge presupposes an ontology in the sense of an account of what the world must be like, for knowledge, under the descriptions given it by the theory, to be possible. Thus Hume, Kant, Mill, Nietzsche and Rorty all presuppose an empirical realist theory of causal laws, on which empirical regularities are at least necessary, if not sufficient, for them. For example, it is Rorty's failure to thematize ontology – epigrammatized by his inane remark that he wishes Heidegger had never used the word 'being'[1] – that is responsible for the antinomies of agency, which duplicate those of Kant, that spoil his work.[2] Failure to be explicit in one's ontology merely results in the passive secretion of an *implicit* one. From the critical realist perspective, the *epistemic fallacy*, enshrined in the dogma that statements about being can and will always be analysed as or explicated in terms of statements about our knowledge of being, is a multi-consequential disaster. In the first place, as just indicated, it merely masks the generation of an implicit ontology – in the dominant modern form, a Humean one of atomistic events and closed systems; and a fortiori of an implicit realism (here, empirical realism); and, insofar as critical realism (which not only problematizes ontology but also gives it a radically different content) isolates axiological/transcendental/dialectical necessities, in a triple series of *Tina compromises.* Ontology – and realism – are *inexorable.* The crucial questions in philosophy are *not whether, but which.* Second, it conceals a deep-seated anthropocentric/anthropomorphic bias in irrealist philosophies and western thought generally – the *anthropic fallacy* – the exegesis of being in terms of human being. Thus, being is explicated, in both the conceptual realism of rationalism and the empirical realism of empiricism, in terms of an attribute of *human* being. Even Heidegger does not escape the charge of anthropism. For in *Being and Time* being is always mediated by *Dasein* or human being; and, in his later works, he rethematizes ontology in terms of its human traces from the pre-Socratics to the contemporary age of nihilism and technology. In other words, Heidegger does not so much redefine or overcome as evade 'the scandal of philosophy'.* Third, it co-exists symbiotically with an esoteric naturalization of knowledge – e.g., in the Humean case, with the reification of facts and fetishism of their conjunctions; that is to say, with the compulsive determination of knowledge of being by being. This is the reciprocal, equilibrating *ontic fallacy.* Fourth, transposed to the social domain and set in a hermeneutic, semiotic or otherwise linguistified key, the collapse of the intransitive dimension or the denegation of ontology takes the

* This is, 'not that their proof has yet to be accepted, but that such proofs are expected and attempted again and again'.[3] Compare Bertrand Russell at about the same time: 'if you are willing to believe that nothing exists except what you directly experience, no other person can prove you wrong, and probably no valid arguments against your view exist.'[4] I shall shortly give such a proof.

form of the analysis of being as our discourse about being – the *linguistic fallacy.* Indeed this, or some displacement of it, is the guise which the epistemic fallacy now customarily wears in each of (a) ordinary language, linguistic – or just plain analytic – philosophy, (b) Marxist philosophy and (c) poststructuralist and, more expansively, postmodernist thought. In this chapter I am going to (α) longitudinally, theoretically deepen and (β) laterally, topically enrich the ontology of critical realism which I am dialecticizing. At (α), already committed to a stratified, differentiated and changing world (in contrast to the flat, uniform depthlessness of empirical realism), critical realism is developed to encompass the categories of negativity and totality. As this chapter proceeds we shall move through the four moments or levels of dialectical critical realism outlined in C1.4, displaying the concepts, implications, resolutions, critiques, explanations and dialectics most characteristic of each level in turn. The dialectical critical realist dialectic is a four-term one in contrast to Hegel's three-term dialectic, but the structures of the two terms nominally shared with Hegel are very different. At *1M* (prime moment) the categories are of *non-identity* (in opposition to Hegelian identity). At *2E* (second edge) they are those of *negativity*; at *3L* (third level) *totality*; and at *4D* (fourth dimension) *transformative agency.* The critiques here take the forms at 1M of ontological actualism, at 2E of ontological monovalence, at 3L of ontological extensionalism and at 4D of ontological de-agentification. Laterally, at (β), already committed to an entity (perceptual), causal (explanatory) and predicative (taxonomic) realism, dialectical critical realism is broadened to embrace a spatio-temporal, moral and alethic (truth) realism. The effect of not making these extensions would be to *detotalize* being. Thus moral irrealism literally *devalues* social life.

Hitherto the most significant theses of critical realism, if we leave aside its extension onto the social terrain, have turned on relations of non-identity. Thus both (a) the distinction between the *intransitive and transitive dimensions*, which makes ontology possible and necessary again, and (b) the distinction between the domains of *the real and the actual*, which situates ontological stratification and transfactuality (and the corresponding analysis of laws as the tendencies of deep structures) posit distinctions or *non-identities within a constellational identity.* The motif of non-identity connects to a familiar poststructuralist refrain, and encompasses (c) the *critique of centrism.* The chief centrism which 1M dialectical critical realism identifies is that at work in the anthropic fallacy. This is the common unifying bias in (a) and (b), viz. the tying of being and knowledge alike to the realms of subjectivity and actuality (nowhere more transparent than in Hegel's doctrine of Essence, the supposedly most realist book of the *Logics*), and which has as its prima facie paradoxical condition and result the 4D de-agentifying reification of facts and their conjunctions. From (a) flow the issues we have just rehearsed of the quadruple ineluctability of ontology, realism, critical realism and dialectical critical realism; and of the duplicities and equivocations, pliabilities and compromise formations, manifest as absences, splits, reifications, theory/practice inconsistencies and susceptibility to dialectical comment and explanatory metacritique$_2$ implicit in subject–object identity theory and its necessary duals. The concept that blocks subject–object identity is *alterity*, particularly in the form of referential detachment; the concept that it masks is *absence*. (b), like (a), is susceptible to immanent critique, transcendental refutation, metacritical diagnostic and proto-explanatory analysis. The overall critique at 1M turns on the non-identities at stake in the relationships described by $d_r > d_a > d_e$ (which links [a], [b] and [c]) where d_r includes the causal (transfactual) as well as the existential (structural) aspects of depth realism). The arch criminal here is anthropic actualism or generalized subject–object identity theory. All this will be systematically articulated in §4 after discussion of its emergence and derivability in §3 and the dialectic of scientific discovery and truth it entails in §2. In this block the outstanding questions of (i) dialectical or developmental consistency and the nature of (dialectical critical realist) (ii) theory/practice consistency and (iii) universalizability are clarified – the last two of which link directly to the concepts of the dialectical comment and heteronomy, dialectical reason and autonomy (a practico-theoretical bridge concept) and the unity or coherence of theory and practice in practice (dr_a' in $d\varphi$).

2E is the abode of absence – and, most generally, negativity, the dialectical category par excellence. Indeed it can be viewed as implicated in all the other moments, categories and dialectics and 'a simple dialectical presentation' would proceed from it as we shall see in §11, rather than the more topical route followed in the bulk of this chapter. Many of the principal issues have already been mooted in the preceding chapters. The cardinal points turn on appreciating that absence exists, causes effect absentings (changes – that is to say, changes *are* absentings), ills can always be seen as absences, which act as constraints, and that (empowered) praxis can always be seen as potentially absenting (causally efficacious) agency, which can remove remediable ills. In the course of this chapter these aphoristic mottos are presented in a dialectic of negativity, which terminates in a state of the good (emancipated, eudaimonistic/free flourishing) society. Some brief points, resuming earlier themes. (a) *The critique of ontological monovalence* and the related assertion of the reality (in nature as well as society) of non-existents, inefficacies, omissions, voids, etc.; the relatively humdrum formula of 'non-being (or inaction) within zero-level being (or agency)' (which in the social world dislocates structure from agency) to the more daring arguments for the ontological priority of the negative; the progressively more exclusive concepts of real, transformative, radical and linear negation with multiple process/product, real/actual, ontological/epistemological ambiguities; the essentiality of contradiction – from external constraints to overt (for example, hermeneutic hegemonic/counter-hegemonic) struggles over power$_2$ or master–slave-type relations – for change; the mutual implication of causal determination and transformative negation, and the minimal definition of dialectic as absenting absence. (b) *The reassertion of the geo-historicity of being*, of tense and place as irreducible and spatio-temporality as real, of the tri-unity of space, time and causality in tensed spatializing process, of emergent, divergent, possibly convergent, causally efficacious spatio-temporalities and rhythmics, of the constitutive presence of the past and outside. (c) *The unity of the 'two' senses of negativity*, the intertwining of the notions of absences and ills, which will transport us from the notion of social science as explanatory critique through emancipatory axiology to the radical implications of the dialectic of freedom to be sketched in §10 – understood as absenting constraints (especially $constraints_2$) on absenting absences or more generally remediable ills (which act as constraints). At this point we are able to substantiate our maximal definition of dialectic as the progressive, though contingent and non-linear, development of freedom; and the transitions from form to content, centre to periphery and figure to ground become explicit.

3L is the home of totality. The chief sin here is *ontological extensionalism.* This functions to *disconnect*, as monovalence operates to *deny change in*, *being*, and anthropo-actualism *necessity* in it (squashing structure and eliding difference). Ontological extensionalism is manifest in, for example, the hypostatization of thought, but most generally in and as *alienation*, detotalization, disintegration, repression and split-off. The materialist prototype of alienation stems from the generative separation which is the condition of possibility of a *fivefold* alienation of the immediate producer/reproducer/transformer from (a) their product and (b) the four planes of social life – in virtue of their alienation from their labour. These four planes are of course (i) material transactions with nature (and material objects generally), (ii) intra-/interpersonal relations, (iii) the network of social relations in which the former are embedded, involving power, discursive and normative dimensions and their ideological intersect, and (iv) the domain of an agent's own subjectivity. Totality depends upon internal relationality, and to the extent that a subject-matter shows it, we have to think it under the aspects of *intra-activity*, including *existential constitution* of an element by another, permeation (or containment) and connectedness (or causality). The topics of mediation, margins of inquiry, perspective and concretion – both qua *concrete universality* ↔ *concrete singularity*, conceived as multiple quadruplicity, and qua the constitutive role of creative fantasy in the *concrete utopianism* that yields at once hope and possibility to the totalizing depth praxis – have already been broached. At 3L we have dialectics of unity and diversity, of intrinsic and extrinsic, of part and whole, of centrification and peripheralization, within *partial totalities* in complex and dislocated open process, substantively under the configuration of global commodification. The internal aspect of totality is *reflexivity*, a world geo-historical phenomenon, which we have seen deployed in the concept of a meta-reflexively totalizing situation in the context of a stratified distanciated self, defined ultimately by the dispositional identity of a person with their changing causal powers. Ethical dialectics fall under totality and dialectical critical realism's dialectic of desire to freedom, in which the totalizing logic of dialectical universalizability plays a crucial role, is mediated not only by the reality principle (which we can now call alethia) but also by the virtue of practical wisdom or *phronesis*.

4D is the zone of transformative agency. This may be omitted *three* times in a philosophy. First, in the lack of a concept of *embodied intentional causal agency*. This may take the form either of a physicalistic reductionism or a spiritualistic dualism – the former entailing de-agentification, the latter disembodiment – or *both*. Second, in the *reification* of facts, where 'reification' means the attribution of a purely thing-like characteristic to human beings, their products and/or relations, and in the *fetishism* of conjunctions, where 'fetishism' means the attribution of animistic (ultimately, anthropomorphic) magical powers to things, attendant upon empirical realism. Third, in the logic of *commodification*, which makes in reality the 1M category mistake of reducing powers to their exercise, reifying labour-power and fetishizing its product. (In this way a scientific worker may come to be doubly alienated – from her product in reality, and from the thought that it is her product.) Crucial here to the avoidance of the first error is an *emergent powers materialism*, in which reasons are, and good reasons may be, causes. 4D is the site of dialectics of *reversal*. And in a dialectic of consciousness and self-consciousness in reason in §7, or that of material interest which will take the agent via instrumental reason from critical to depth totalizing explanatory critical rationality in §10, I make out a case for imparting a certain, if highly contingent, *directionality* to geo-history, presaging a society in which the free flourishing of each is the condition of the free flourishing of all. In any event here the critiques of cognitive and political triumphalism, finalism and endism, i.e. of the constellational closure of the future, are resumed and it is shown how these and the injunctive paradox intrinsic to right-wing Hegelianism and indeed arguably conservatism generally, viz. to reproduce the status quo, are auto-subversive. Agency, whether in the shape of mowing a lawn or in what I shall call the transformed transformative *trustworthy* totalizing transformist *transitional* praxis which would unite the interests of the human race-in-nature, is a species-specific ineliminable *fact*. It is worth bearing in mind, in the context of the world historical problem of agency for the radical libertarian left, that even inaction makes a difference.

Let me turn now, rather more briefly, to the lateral extensions to the ontology of critical realism. There is nothing at all anthropocentric about the reality of space, time, tense and process. I defend the irreducibility of MacTaggart's A series (past, present, future) to his B series (earlier than, simultaneous with, later than), that is, to be more specific, the *reality of tense* and the *irreducibility of space-time* on any world-line both for the transitive observer and for the intransitively observed. In C2 I stressed the tri-unity of space, time and causality in tensed (spatializing) process, understood as the mode of becoming of effects. But what exactly is the reality of the tenses? *The reality of the past* is that of the *existentially intransitively caused and determinate* (where caused means produced, determined and it is the case that a thing can be determinate even if not determinable); that of the *present*, of the (indefinitely extendable), indeterminate *moment of becoming*; and that of the *future*, that of the more or less *shaped* (conditioned, circumscribed, grounded) *mode of possibility of becoming* (under some set of descriptions) and hence becoming in due course existentially intransitively determined and determinate. My immediate antagonists here comprise an uneasy alliance of ego-present centrism or indexicalism (on which only the present exists), blockism (on which all times co-exist), punctualism and closure.

A transitive-relational/intransitive distinction plays a key role in morality too. Morality specifies an action-guiding relationship to the systems of intra- and inter-subjective, social and social–natural relations. But, though in this respect it is analogous to tense, it *is* (α) anthropic or social-relation dependent and (β) lies on the transitive-relational side of the divide. Because of (β) we must distinguish (a) *descriptive, redescriptive* and *explanatory critical morality* (in the transitive-relational dimension) from (b) the *actually existing*, constitutive or participants' *morality* or moralities (in the intransitive dimension), which sustains the *irreducibility of 'ought' to 'is'*, i.e. the possibility of criticism and a fortiori critique. As a moral realist I hold that there is an objective morality. But how can it be known? This is where ethical naturalism comes in. It lies in the *transition from fact to value* (and theory to practice). So there is an ethical alethia, ultimately grounded in conceptions of human nature, in the context of developing four-planar social being, with the moral consciousness of the species in principle *open.* Just because we can get, through explanatory critique, from fact to value, the first-person activating character of moral judgements poses no problem for dialectical critical realism's moral realism. Secondly, the anti-naturalistic fallacy often functions merely to screen the generation of an implicit emotivist or descriptivist morality reflecting the status quo ante of actually existing morality – it de-moralizes (in the transitive dimension) by reflecting the morality of an actually existing already moralized world (in the intransitive dimension). Here we have dialectics of practical problem-resolution, consciousness-change and emancipation. *Universalizability* serves as both (1) a test of consistency and (2) a criterion of truth. But the so-called 'communitarians' are right to insist on the epistemic *relativity* of moral judgements (in the transitive dimension) and the *diversity* of actually existing moralities (in the intransitive dimension). Dialectical critical realism holds, however, that epistemic relativity is quite consistent with judgemental rationality, here, in the practico-ethical realm, as in the realm of the descriptive-explanatory work of science (including the description and explanation of actually existing moralities).

My alethic realism consists in the *truth of things* not propositions, and is satisfied just as that moment when *referential detachment* of an explanans in an explanatory process becomes legitimate and necessary in the dialectic of science. Briefly, an adequate analysis of truth will show it to comprise a *tetrapolity*, involving four components or moments: (α) *normative-fiduciary*, in the communicative sub-dimension of the social cube, (β) adequating, in the transitive dimension, (γ) *expressive-referential*, in an ontic-epistemic duality, and finally (δ) *alethic*, in the intransitive dimension. Recognition of the alethic moment – truth as dr′ or dg′ – in a genuinely ontological employment, resolves, as we shall see briefly in §4 and more fully in C4.2, a host of philosophical problems – in fact, almost all those standard aporiai which depend on homology or vicious regress. *In the moral realm, alethic truth, the good, is freedom*, depending on the absenting of constraints on absenting ills.

I have talked about two kinds of ontological extensions in the ontology of dialectical critical realism, (α) longitudinal and (β) lateral. But there is a need for a third kind – (γ) scalar. Most (implicit) ontologies are *simplistic.* Hegel might just as well have defined dialectic as seeing the *complex* in the simple, as seeing the positive in the negative. Indeed this is part of the meaning of 'concretion'. We have seen in C2 the prominence that dialectical critical realism gives to notions such as recursion, embedding, intermingling, the hiatus, constellationality, perspective (and perspectival switches), reflections (in the sense of C2.7) both within and between different categories and categorial groups and/or levels. Thus we have to think of social beings as constituted by the presence of others and of their formation; and of at least four distinct types of tendency; of phenomena such as natural absences, empty selves, hidden depths (cf. C2.8), of the penetration of philosophy by science and society, of the presence within the absence of the future, of the whole in the heap, the void at the heart of being.

But it might be objected at this point, what exactly is the argument for ontology, not in the philosophy of science (which may indeed meet the criteria dialectical critical realism describes) but in general? The argument for *ontology* is just the argument for *existential intransitivity*, which is just the argument for *referential detachment.* Realism in the sense that involves existential intransitivity is a presupposition of *discourse* which must be *about* something other than itself, of *praxis* which must be *with* something other than itself* or of *desire* which must be *for* something alterior to itself. To someone who doubts whether referential detachment exists just ask them to repeat and/or clarify what they have said, and then ask them what it is that they have repeated or clarified. It must be a referentially detached (social) entity. Any creature capable of differentiation must be capable of referential detachment. This does not immediately establish the case for alethic truth. For that we must have a creature capable of dividing the world into essential and non-essential attributes, and of appreciating that the former do not always manifest themselves in actuality. With the *first referential detachment* of

* Cf. the critique of foundationalism I have elaborated elsewhere.[5]

structure and the transfactual efficacy it affords, we get the first taste of *alethic truth*, the dialectical reason or ground for things. And now we are doing science, from a position in which the primordial activities of referential detachment and the necessity for ontology may be readily forgotten. But also, insofar as differentiation is itself a causal act and causation is absenting, we are on the terrain of dialectic, upon which 1M non-identity and transfactuality can thus retrospectively be seen to depend.

It will be recalled from the *Phenomenology of Mind* that the Stoic (be s/he Aurelius or Epictetus) is indifferent to reality, the Sceptic denies its existence in theory but affirms it in practice (and so is guilty of theory/practice inconsistency), while the Unhappy Consciousness makes it explicit in the introjection or projective postulation of another world. After the demise of positivism in the wake of the double blow of relativity theory and quantum mechanics, philosophy found itself in a double bind. In failing to thematize (or at least reproblematize) ontology and so to articulate a new one – which could accommodate transitive and intransitive change and stratification alike – it tended to transmute along the transitive dimension into a variety of forms, which I will treat in logical, not necessarily chronological, order. First came a sociological conventionalism, exemplified by writers such as Bachelard and Kuhn, like Stoicism indifferent to reality yet at the same time aware of the context of master–slave or oppressive $power_2$ relations at work. Thus the scientific neophyte was pictured as accepting on purely 'positive' grounds (in the early Hegelian usage, that is to say, acceptance on the basis of authority) the craft of her trade. Meanwhile there would be sporadic outbursts of internecine warfare as new ways of thinking and probing things were vaunted, which resembles nothing so much as the section of the *Phenomenology* entitled 'the spiritual kingdom of the beasts, or the affair itself'. This stoic indifference to reality gave rise to a post-structuralist collapse to scepticism, in which Derrida can write 'there is nothing outside the text'[6] and probably neither mean, definitely not believe and certainly not act on it, entailing palpable theory/practice inconsistency. The duplicity implicit in post-structuralism then became explicit in the unhappy consciousness of a pragmatist like Rorty, who considers that there is a reality (even if only in the guise of incoming causal impacts) but forbids us to talk about it. This convoluted introjection gives way to the explicit Dadaist contradiction of Feyerabend who sees no reason for imposing any constraints on the 'doubles' of the real world we can make. But on close inspection all these beautiful souls of 1967 turn out to be still at work in the struggle for symbolic capital, money and power.* The history of post-positivist philosophy thus mimics certain famous dialectical topographies.

* The life-and-death struggle is a continuing theme of Hegel and cannot be reduced to the chapter on 'Self-consciousness'. It is explicit in the dialectics of nobility, wealth and war. In the same way the struggle for recognition to which the life-and-death struggle is

The self-referential paradoxes and theory/practice inconsistencies attendant upon the denial of referential attachment = existential transitivity = ontology are so patent that it might seem that the difficult task is not to give a transformed transformative response to the Heideggerian 'scandal of philosophy', but how to begin to explain irrealism. For that is the *real* scandal of philosophy. I postpone attempting to unravel it until C4.

§2 The dialectic of truth

'Truth' seems at once (a) the simplest and (b) the most difficult of concepts. (a) Saying 'true' to a proposition is to give one's assent to it – this is its primary function, whereby redundancy and performative theories derive their plausibility. But one is thereby committed to a claim *about* the world, roughly to the effect that that is how things are, from which correspondence theories since the time of Aristotle have drawn their currency. This claim carries the normative force 'trust me – act on it', whence pragmatic theories gain their footing. At the same time this claim, if challenged, needs to be *grounded*, a requirement that seems to point in the direction of coherence theories. So a truth judgement will typically carry or imply a fourfold dimensionality, possessing (i) *expressively veracious*, (ii) *descriptive*, (iii) *evidential* and (iv) *imperatival-fiduciary* aspects. This four-dimensionality is intrinsic to the judgement form as such, and is not limited to truth judgements. Each aspect is universalizable, albeit in different ways, and aspects may be loosely attached to the concrete universal and the social cube (as mentioned in C2.10). To these matters I will return. For the moment it is sufficient to appreciate that it is in virtue of its basic *world-reporting* meaning (its descriptive 'this is how things are in the world' component) that truth-talk satisfies a *transcendental-axiological need*, acting as a steering mechanism for language-users to find their way about the world.

(b) But 'truth' is at the same time the most difficult of concepts in which, as I will briefly indicate, there is hardly an extant theory without some flaw but in which it is equally hard not to recognize some truth or power. Moreover, it has ramifications for theories of meaning and reference (which I will address), perception, causality, agency, experiment, communication (and thus also philosophical sociology and ontology generally, which will also be pursued in the course of this chapter). In respect of the familiar distinction between meaning and criteria of truth, although the latter must be (α) universalizable in *form,* (β) their *contents* may well be as *variable* as the

---

indissolubly linked is a continuing refrain in Hegel. Moreover, I think the metaphor can be taken quasi-literally in referring to scientific and philosophical social systems, in addition to politics and life generally.

contexts in which truth claims are made. Thus in particle physics repeatable registration of tracks on a monitor brings out both these aspects.

After a short comment on some of the aporiai of recent truth theories – and a slightly more detailed look at the concept in the Marxian canon – I proceed to give my own stratified theory of the meaning of truth and then show it at work in the dialectic of scientific discovery. I then pass on to the implications of what I have already in §1 prefiguratively nominated the 'truth tetrapolity' before an excursus into questions of dialectical, T/P consistency and universalizability returns me to issues of meaning, reference and criteriology in the sciences.

The most important historical theories of truth this century, outside the Marxist camp, have been the correspondence, coherence, pragmatic, redundancy, performative, consensus and Hegelian theories of truth. Correspondence theories had their heyday during the mid-century supremacy of logical positivism, although they were also supported by some critics, such as Austin, of the latter. The basic objection to the most influential correspondence theories – the early Wittgenstein's picture theory, Tarski's semantic theory and Popper's theory of increasing verisimilitude or truth-likeness in the development of science – applies to all alike: there seems no 'Archimedean' standpoint from which a comparison of the competing items can be made. Together with a rejection of immediate knowledge, and of the reification of facts (the realization that facts are established results, made, not apprehended[7]), the recognition that matching is a metaphor (that a transitive theory is not *like* what it is about) and that semantic theories are homologous (say the same thing – albeit at different levels), it seems correspondence theories must be abandoned, especially when they act as the non-compacted component of subject–object identity = duplicity theories. That said, it has to be recognized that there is an inherent TD/ID bipolarity or ambivalence in concepts like 'facts' and 'truth', which cannot be completely gainsaid in an adequate truth theory.

Coherence theories seem most plausible as an account of the criteriology rather than meaning of truth. Hegelian theories may be regarded as a special case of them in which it is the conformity of an object to its notion (ultimately the whole, closed totality), rather than vice versa, that defines truth. But, whether in Hegelian dialectical or more analytical declensions, coherence theories seem to presuppose something like a correspondence-theoretic account of 'correctness'. However, if the world were regarded as a text it could be argued that there could be no better account of correspondence than coherence.

The two main influential species of pragmatism derive ultimately from (1) Peirce, James and Dewey and (2) Nietzschean perspectivism. (1), which has been recently popularized by Rorty and seems currently to be accepted by Putnam and possibly Davidson, maintains that the only workable concept of truth is warranted assertability (and dovetails neatly with constructivist and intuitionist theories of mathematics). It is vulnerable to the objection that a proposition may be warrantedly assertable but false. (2) For the Nietzschean tradition which informs post-structuralism, truth is 'a mobile army of metaphors', ultimately an expression of the will-to-power, which must be thought, as both necessary and impossible, 'under erasure' (cf. C2.8). It is hard to see this position, whether in its Derridean or Foucauldian guises, as anything other than palimpsesting itself out of existence, self-erasing.

The other theories must be handled even more briefly. The redundancy theory, initially formulated by Ramsey, seems either to smuggle in truth by the back door or to deny the axiological necessity of the truth predicate. Performative theories of the kind advocated by Strawson, Hare and Searle seem more satisfactory in this respect, but they in turn underplay the extent to which the use of the truth predicate needs to be grounded, a requirement stressed by Kripke. Consensus theories are subject to the dilemma that if given a strict interpretation, twenty million Frenchmen can be wrong; or, if given an ideal-typical formulation, that they do not explicate our existing concept of truth.

Slightly longer on the Marxian tradition. In the writings of its founders (a) 'truth' normally *means* 'correspondence with reality', usually interpreted under the metaphor of reflection or some kindred notion, while (b) the *criterion* for evaluating truth claims normally is, or depends upon, human practice. 'Reflection' enters Marxist epistemology at two levels. Marx talks of both (1) the immediate form and (2) the inner or underlying essence of objects being '*reflected*'. But while what is involved at (1) is an explanatory postulate or methodological starting point, at (2) it is a norm of descriptive or scientific adequacy. Thus whereas at (1) Marx criticizes vulgar economy for merely reflecting 'the direct form of manifestation of essential relations',[8] his concern at (2) is precisely with the production of an adequate representation or 'reflection' – a *task* which involves theoretical work and conceptual transformation, not a single passive reproduction of reality. Note that a 'reflection', as normally understood, is both (α) *of* something which exists independently of it (in the ID) and (β) *produced* in accordance with certain principles of projection or representative convention (in the TD). However, if (α) is not to become epistemically otiose (as, for example, in Althusser) there must be some *constraints* on the representative process generated by the real object itself (in the way in which an experimental outcome depends upon the structure under investigation).

Marx and Engels talk of 'images' and 'copies', and Lenin of 'photographs', as well as reflections. These metaphors readily encouraged collapse of case (2) to case (1), of the cognitive to the causal functions of the metaphor, of Marx's deep correspondence theory to the simple reflection theory of dialectical materialism. In reaction to the latter, western Marxism typically comprehended truth as the practical expression of a subject rather than a theoretically adequate representation of an object, whether in coherentist (as Lukács), pragmatist (as in Korsch) or consensualist (as in Gramsci) form. If the generic weakness of 'reflectionist' (objective empiricist) Marxist theories of truth is neglect of the socially produced and geo-historic structure of truth judgements, that of epistemically idealist western Marxist theories is neglect of the independent existence and transfactual efficacy of the objects of such judgements. What is needed clearly is a theory which neither elides the referent nor neglects the socially produced character of judgements about it.[9] It is to the development of such a theory that I turn now.

An adequate theory of truth must take account of the fact that there are four basic concepts of it, or components in its analysis:

(α) truth as *normative-fiduciary*, truth in the 'trust me – act on it' sense, in the communicative sub-dimension of the social cube;
(β) truth as *adequating*, as 'warrantedly assertable', as epistemological, as relative in the transitive dimension;
(γ) truth as *referential-expressive*, as a bipolar ontic-epistemic dual, and in this sense as absolute; and
(δ) truth as *alethic*, as the truth of or reason for *things* and phenomena, *not propositions*, as genuinely ontological, and in this sense as objective in the intransitive dimension.

I have already labelled these moments as the 'truth tetrapolity'.

Some comments on the tetrapolity. It is best illustrated by being situated in the context of a rudimentary dialectic of truth, which can then be filled out. A group of scientists are (a) subjectively empirically certain about the reason S_j for some well-attested phenomena, S_i. They succeed in convincing their colleagues about the (b) inter-subjective facthood of S_j, so that it becomes referentially detached at t_2 as (c) the reason for S_i or the objective truth of S_i, while the new wave of scientists is at the same time heading the search for the reason S_k for S_j in the next round of scientific discovery (which will produce the alethia of S_j). So we go from *subjective certainty* → *inter-subjective facthood* → *alethic truth.* The key moment occurs at (γ)–(δ) in the dialectic of $S_i \rightarrow S_j \rightarrow S_k$, when scientists are no longer concerned with verifying statements about S_j, accept its bipolar facthood and regard themselves in the DREI(C) moment of the logic of scientific discovery as having identified the reason(s) for S_j, referentially detached them and moved onwards in the direction of S_k. Typically at this moment the scientists will have the best possible (Lockian/Leibnizian) grounds for the attribution of natural necessity to, and the truth of the propositions designating, the phenomena of S_i. (α)–(δ) may also be regarded as expressing degrees of groundedness. Thus the axiological imperative in social life means that we may sometimes have to act on propositions that are not even warrantedly assertable (β). Note that on (γ) truth is still ontogenetic, tied to language use; but at (δ) we are concerned with the truth, ground, reason or purpose of things, not propositions. Of course, such alethic truths must still be expressed in language and are subject to correction in the regressive moments of the dialectic of scientific discovery. But this does not alter the fact that it is a fundamentally different, though dialectically interconnected, concept at stake. Epistemological relativism at (β) (in the TD) is, of course, consistent with judgemental rationalism (in the IA) and ontological realism (in the ID), but the concept of the transitive dimension should be metacritically extended to incorporate the whole material and cultural infra-/intra-/superstructure of society. It is the being-expressive bipolar concept at (γ) which accounts for philosophical intuitions about the difference between 'truth' and 'warranted assertability', but the point of (judgement of) correct identification and referential detachment is marked primarily by the change in the direction of scientific inquiry rather than perceptual and/or causal revelation of the truths of S_j, which are (alethically) of S_i. Notice that truth at (δ) is praxis-dependent (2E), totalizing (3L), in the sense that it is oriented to maximizing explanatory power, and contextualized (4D) by the dialectic of the science concerned, as well as, of course, expressing ontological stratification (1M).

The dialectic of truth can be articulated in two obvious ways:

1 by being situated in the context of gradations of natural necessity – with 'D' describing the Humean, 'R' the Kantian, 'I' first Lockian (synthetic *a posteriori*) and then Leibnizian (analytic *a posteriori*) moments of knowledge of natural necessity in the dialectic of explanatory and taxonomic knowledge I have already rehearsed (DREI(C));
2 by superimposing this dialectical transcendental realist model on the Hegelian epistemological dialectic first elaborated in C1.9, as illustrated in Figure 1 below.

Alethia, as we shall see, is the resolution of the standard textbook 1M problems of philosophy. It is dialectical reason and ground in theory and the absence of heterology; it is true to, for, in and of itself. It furnishes the non-arbitrary principle of ontological stratification that powers the dialectic of scientific discovery. Transposed to the ethical domain, the true = the moral good = freedom, in the sense of universal human emancipation, as will be shown in §§7–11. For the moment we have to return to more quotidian matters.

We are concerned with three distinct phenomena:

(α) *dialectical*, or, as I have sometimes called it, *developmental consistency* in a process;
(β) *theory/practice consistency* in a praxis in some process;
(γ) *dialectical universalizability.*

(α) may be social, as in the case of a progressive research programme (where one's criterion may be, for instance, optimization of the rate of scientific advance measured on some scale), or natural, as in the case of the maturation of a caterpillar into a butterfly or an acorn into an oak (where, if one wants to

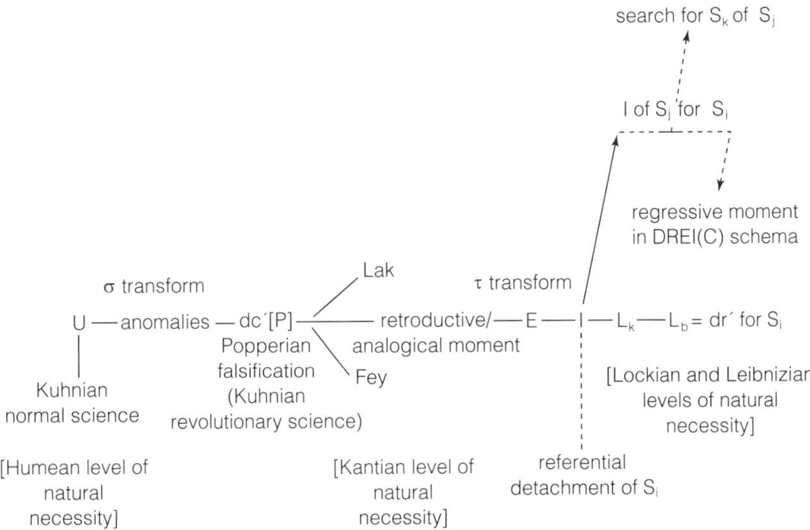

P, Lak and Fey stand for the Popperian, Lakatosian and Feyerabendian moments in science
L_k and L_b refer to Lockian and Leibnizian levels of natural necessity respectively
cf. also Figure 2.12 at p.110

Figure 1 The epistemological dialectic of science

impose a criterion, it may be beauty, or normalicity of development or whatever). The point about consistency here is that no general formula for it can be given: criteria are necessarily *intrinsic* to the process concerned. There may be a Lockian Hour in science (and perhaps philosophy) but then there may not be, as is readily verifiable from reading a range of novels of different genres. Normally one would be talking here, as in the case of the more tractable (α) and (β), about a *process-in-product-in-process.*

Two metatheorems may be immediately stated:

I. Universalizability is both (a) a test for consistency and (b) a criterion for truth in the fields of theoretical and practical reason alike.

II. End-states, which should be universalizable, are not always realizable by agents (e.g. one can't get from x to everywhere and one can't go to y from just anywhere). However, in general it is plausible to suppose that one can progress towards them, or mitigate regress away from them. [P]

(β) T/P consistency on the part of an agent N should

1 be practical,
2 satisfy P (and, if possible, prefigure the end-state or at least be as far as possible consistent with it),

3 be grounded in an explanatory theory or set of theories of
   (a) the current situation,
   (b) the desired end-state, and
   (c) the transition from (a) to (b).

(γ) Both an agent's praxis and its groundings (3) should be universalizable in the senses that they be

1 transfactual,
2 concrete – satisfying all the moments of the concrete universal (including, of course, concrete singularity),
3 actionable, in the sense of agent-specific, and
4 transformative, in the sense that it is oriented to change (in the direction of the postulated end-state [P]).

(δ) All the aspects of the judgement form – in theoretical and practical reasoning alike – are universalizable – although in different ways:

(a) expressive veracity: 'if I had to act in these circumstances, this is what I would act on';
(b) fiduciariness: 'in exactly your circumstances, this is the best thing to do';
(c) descriptive: 'in exactly the same circumstances, the same result would ensue';
(d) evidential: 'in exactly the same circumstances, the reasons would be the same'.

(c) and (d) are merely implications of the principle of sufficient reason (which I have elsewhere called ubiquity determinism). We need not quarrel with this, save to note that if a normic (transfactual) and concrete interpretation is not given of the 'same circumstances' they fail. Fiduciariness carries with it the 'conversationally candid' implication of expressive veracity, so (b) might be said to imply (a), as (d) might be said to imply (c). Note that the four moments of the judgement form are internally related. And that in the ethical sphere, taking into account the concrete singularity of the particular agent entails that the imperatival aspect be only, in Kantian terms, 'assertoric' (i.e. in accordance with the agent's wants, in a potential dialectic of wants, needs and interests) rather than (personalistically) categorical or (technologistically) hypothetical. This is also presupposed by the criterion of actionability. It is worth mentioning too that the judgement form through its fiduciary-imperatival and descriptive-plus-evidential aspects has a *theoretico-practical duality* built into it. Theoretical reason, which merely says the world is so-and-so, still implies a commitment to act on it. And so by a perspectival switch it informs practice. This is important because the expressively veracious aspect stipulates, and through its implication of fiduciariness presupposes, not only (1) that if the agent addressor A was placed in a situation of the agent addressee this is how she would act, but also (2) that she shows *solidarity* with B in degrees running from minimal advice as in (1) through forms of moral and material assistance (including speech and writing, of course) to (3) empowerment and (4) engaging in a totalizing depth praxis designed to bring about the desired state of affairs – that is, either, in the case of practical reason, in accordance with some grounded end-state or -process; or, in the case of theoretical reason, in accordance with the descriptive implications of saying how the world is so. So every speech act must be regarded as making an *axiological commitment.* Moreover, given that to say how the world is is implicitly to advise agents to act on that basis, not to assist or empower them when it is in one's capacity to do so is to be guilty of T/P inconsistency ceteris paribus. That is, in the context of a balanced life, bearing in mind that amour de soi is the basis of altruism (only the empowered can empower) and that A's object is not to substitute her action for that of B but rather to solidarize with it.

(ε) Less importantly, the descriptive component and the expressively veracious and fiduciary components of the judgement form can be loosely associated with the levels of particular mediations and concrete singularity in the concrete universal; and the expressively veracious and fiduciary moments as representing respectively the plane of the stratification of the personality and the plane of interpersonal transactions in our four-planar theory of social being.

The significance of these results will become clear in the dialectic of freedom. But for the moment it is sufficient to note the alignment of dialectical reason, alethia, T/P consistency, dialectical universalizability, non-heterology in an expanded sense of being true to, for and of oneself and each other and autonomy; and that of susceptibility to dialectical comment, T/P inconsistency, immanent critique, Tina formation, heterology and non-autonomy, absence, detotalization and split.

It is incumbent upon me to say something about the concepts of meaning and reference, traditionally associated with that of truth. The centrepiece of any adequate theory of meaning must be the semiotic triangle (see Figure 2). If the traditional nominalist error has been to elide the signified, the customary post-modernist stance has been to elide the referent. If it is the signifier that transmits the locutionary force in the communicative sub-dimension of the social cube, and the detachable referent which enables us to talk *about* something (including what we are currently saying), it is the role of the signified, that may be bound in layers of differentially sedimented semantic stratification, which enables the conceptual distanciation, exploiting perhaps the slightest of analogies, metaphors and metonymies, which plays such a creative role in the paramorphic model-building essential to science. Each of signifier, in the communicative sub-dimension, signified, in the transitive dimension generally, and referent, in the intransitive dimension, may (a) be caught up in eddies of their own and (b) have attached to them, e.g. through

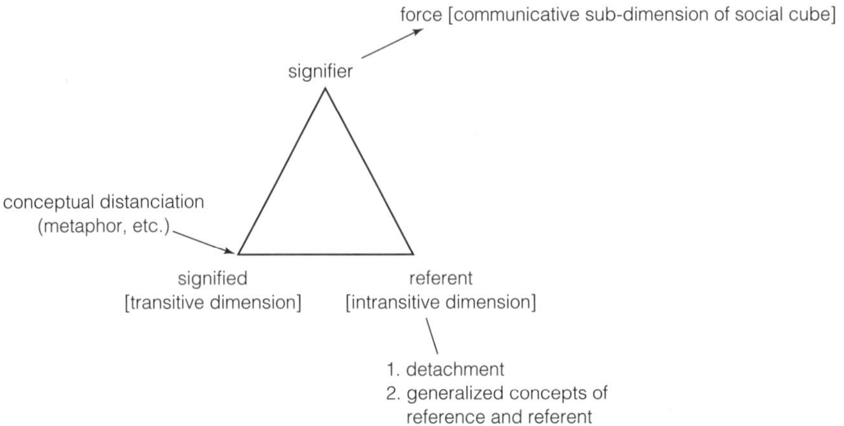

Figure 2 The semiotic triangle

paradigmatic and syntagmatic, structured and differentiated relations, multiple other semiotic triangles enfolding on the element which must be thought under the aspects of (c) geo-historical process-in-product(-in-process) and (d) intra-activity. Together (c) and (d) explain the acuity of the notion of the trace structure of the signifier. Each may, moreover, act as a proxy for, or simply as, an other, and they are typically internally related which explains the poverty of a purely extensionalist analysis of language use. Identity here is constituted through difference and change.

The most important ingredients in an adequate dialectical critical realist account of reference are already caught in Figure 2, viz. (i) the notion of referential detachment and (ii) the generalized concept of the referent with which I am working. Once one breaks from atomistic-punctualist-monovalent-extensionalist justificationalism one can treat of *any* significant chunk of reality (irrespective of whether this makes it easy to handle logically); and to treat of it non-anthropically one must be capable of non-anthropically detaching the referent from the human act which picks it out, which is also to detach oneself from the referent. Problems about the status of the referent – is it real or imaginary, transfactual or actual, positive or negative, in relation or a self-subsistent entity, an aspect or a totality, social-relation-dependent or not? – then become much more tractable.

Finally a word on the criteriology of the sciences. Practical reason is, or depends upon, an applied science. But both the natural and social sciences may be pure or applied; so there is no unique way to carve up the sciences. All we can say is that in the ethical realm we will typically be dealing with a complex of applied social sciences in which the third 'R' – signifying 'retrodiction' – depends upon the multiple application of law-like tendency statements with prior DREI(C) retroductive-analogical theoretical credentials.

[. . .]

§7 Social science, explanatory critique, emancipatory axiology

In C2.9 I argued for a position in the philosophy of the social sciences that I characterize as 'dialectical critical naturalism'. Dialectical critical naturalism posits a series of ontological, epistemological, relational and critical differences between the social sciences and the experimental sciences of nature which mediate and transcend the dichotomy between hypernaturalistic positivism and dualist or syncretic hermeneutics which has split the social sciences since the hermeneutics of Schleiermacher was taken up by Dilthey.[10] In particular it argues (i) that the necessary conceptuality of the subject-matter of social science does not exhaust, and may indeed mask or distort, it in a manner which a critical social science can expose; and (ii) that the existence of unacknowledged conditions, unconscious motivation, tacit skills and unintended consequences afford to the social sciences a putative enlightening role for lay actors. Its transformational model of social activity avoids the twin errors of reification and voluntarism in a dislocated duality of structure and agency, while the relational conception of social life evades the pitfalls of individualism and collectivism alike. A four-planar conception of developing human nature in society, embedded in non-human but partially socialized nature, is composed of the stratification of the personality, material transactions with the physical world, inter-/intra-personal relations and social relations sui generis defining the position-practice system in virtue of which more or less structurally sedimented institutions are causally efficacious (ultimately via past or present human agency which is intentional under some description). The 'social cube' has power, normative and discursive sub-dimensions, which intersect in ideology. Ideology in a strong sense embodies categorial error, but is, at any rate in its broad sense, the site of hermeneutical alongside other struggles over $power_2$ relations of exploitation, domination and control. These relations are in principle subject to tactical or strategic reversal and may be the object of conjunctural suspension or structural abolition.

In §1 I briefly described the way in which dialectical critical realism (which comprises naturalism as a special theory of the social sciences) is committed to a combination of (α) *moral realism* and (β) *ethical naturalism*, which I shall now detail. Its moral realism contends that morality is an objective real property, but the first present (and universalizable) action-guiding character of moral claims and judgements entails that a distinction has to be made between (a) the real transitive-relational moral property, which connotes a position on a set of intra-subjective, inter-subjective, social and social–natural relations; and (b) the intransitive morality of an always already moralized (or a-moralized) world. The distinction between (a) and (b) allows my moral realism to be critical and to sustain the irreducibility of ethics to descriptive sociology. In particular it would be useful to differentiate *descriptive*, *redescriptive* and *explanatory critical morality* in the transitive (more properly relational, because morality is practical, designating an *action-guiding* relation on or to something) and *actually existing morality* or moralities in the intransitive dimension, and, inter alia, to characterize, taken in combination with (ß) my ethical naturalism, the *constitutive morality* of a society as *false* and to demonstrate it, in the manner of an explanatory critical dialectical argument, as a *false* (or limited) *necessity* (cf. C2.6). For my ethical naturalism implies that moral propositions can be *known*; and, in particular, social-scientifically vindicated; so that, contrary to Moore's supposed naturalistic fallacy, there is no unbridgeable gulf between fact and value, or theory and practice. I am going to argue against the conventionally accepted base assumption of [1] the evaluative *neutrality* of social science, not only through the easy demonstration of the evaluative character of its discourse but also through the prima facie more difficult demonstration of the scientific legitimation of values, for [2] the conception of social science as *explanatory critique* and thence to [3] the idea of social science as *emancipatory axiology* and ultimately [4] to a notion of it as *dialectic.* The naturalistic transformation from 'is' to 'ought' – which is not only compatible with, but also *grounds*, the moral realist *irreducibility* of 'ought' to 'is' – that is to say, the transition from *fact to value*, presages the transitions between and dialectics of *theory and practice, form and content, centre to periphery, figure to ground, desire to freedom*, and to the sensitized solidarity of the totalizing depth praxis and the dialectics of de-alienation and emancipation.

Conceptually, the most important thing to appreciate at the outset is that any ill (and indeed, ceteris paribus, any object of practical reasoning) can be looked upon, or dialectically transposed, as an absence, and any absence can be viewed as a constraint. Such constraints include constraints$_2$ and inequities. Such ills may be seen as moral untruths. Thus we have the metatheorem: *ills* → *absences* → *constraints* (including *inequities*) → (moral) *falsehoods* → (and, if categorially absurd, I shall write them as 'ideologically†' so). From the standpoint of practical reason inasmuch as they are (i) *unwanted*, (ii) *unnecessary* and (iii) *remediable* or removable, they should be transformatively negated, i.e. *absented.* I shall negatively generalize the concept of constraint, so that there is an *equivocity* of *freedom from* and *freedom to* (and Isaiah Berlin's celebrated distinction appears as two poles of ultimately the one concept). The root conception of freedom with which I shall be working is that of autonomy in the sense of self-determination. Rational autonomy will then incorporate cognitive, empowered and dispositional or motivational aspects. Reason as such may constellationally embrace the disposition to reason, but if the reason concerned is cognitive, then empirically they are distinct items. Conversely human beings may indeed desire to be free, as such and in general, but lack the concrete power and/or knowledge to achieve particular freedoms, say the right to suffrage, literacy or health care. Thus as criteria for rational agency one must

(α) possess the knowledge to act on one's own real interests (the cognitive requirement);
(β) be able to access the skill, resources and opportunities to do so (the empowered component); and
(γ) be disposed to so act (the dispositional or motivational condition).

Of course the 'knowledge' referred to in (α) may be tacit competence, knowledge how rather than propositional knowledge that, practical not discursive.

There are some other matters to clear up before I commence my deduction of [1]–[4]. Moral reasoning is a species of practical reasoning, characterized, inter alia, by the fact that it is (non-uniquely) dialectically, and so specifically transfactually, concretely and actionably, 'binding' and universalizable in form, and that its ultimate object is flourishing human beings-in-nature. Practical reasoning may arise from a failure to satisfy some desire, want or interest. It logically presupposes both a *negative* (proto-)*critique* and a *positive* (proto-)*theory* of how to remedy the situation – an aspect of the duality of theory and critique. To be slightly pedantic for a moment, what is required is clearly to *d*iagnose the problem, *e*xplain it and then take appropriate *a*ction to absent it. This is the *DEA model of practical* problem-resolution or *reasoning*. It is important to note that when applied in the sphere of moral reason this has to satisfy a *prefigurative condition* or moment, which stipulates (1) that the action concerned, and the process more generally, do not undermine the end or objective and be as far as possible consistent with it and (2) that, insofar as it is possible, it in some way expresses or embodies the principles or values of the end-state or -process. The DEA model may depend on the exploitation of the RRREI(C) model of applied social scientific explanation, which itself depends on the iterated applications of the DREI(C) model of pure scientific explanation. All this will involve the meta-ethical virtue of *phronesis* or practical wisdom, a virtue that the good applied scientist typically has. Suppose one's objective in a DEA context is normative change, then a simplified praxis would turn on the *d*escription *e*xplanation and *t*ransformation of actually existing morality (the *DET model* of *normative change*), as part of a *totalizing depth praxis* incorporating, inter alia, a posteriori participatory research inquiry (including a detailed and specific analysis, for the conjunctural situation will in general be novel and unique), explanatory critique and concrete utopianism (I will sometimes refer to the conjunct just as the explanatory critical theory†) leading into a theory and practice of transition, including the sensitized solidarity to which I have already referred. There is one final preliminary. I want to differentiate (1) instrumental (including technical), (2) critical, (3) explanatory critical, (4) depth explanatory critical, (5) totalizing depth explanatory critical and (6) dialectical rationality, appended by (7) geo-historical directionality.

It is pretty obvious that social scientific discourse is in fact evaluative, as is the principal reason for it, the value-saturated character of what social scientific discourse is about, so I will not discuss this side of the equation any further here.[11] The value-implicational, rather than the value-impregnated, character of social science is much more interesting. Charles Taylor, John Searle, A.N. Prior, Philippa Foot, Elizabeth Anscombe and many others have all tried to refute 'Hume's law' stipulating 'no ought from an is'. Valuable though their attempts have been, which I have discussed elsewhere,[12] a morally irrevocable refutation of Hume's law has to be from processes that are constitutive of purely factual discourse. Now the subject-matter of social science is composed not just by social objects but by beliefs about social objects, and if such beliefs are false (a judgement which is within the remit of social science), and one can *explain* the *falsity*, then, subject to a ceteris paribus clause, in virtue of the openness of the social world and the multiplicity of determinations therein, one can move without further ado to a negative evaluation of the explanans and a positive evaluation of any action rationally designed to absent it. This is the heart of the missing transcendental deduction of facts from values. It turns on discovering the *alethic truth of falsity*, and thus, as should not surprise us, on both 1M ontological stratification and 2E ontological bi-/poly-valency. Actually there are even simpler transitions, which I shall go into shortly, but they do not possess comparable diagnostic value and the immanent critical force of the argument form just advanced. Thus, at level 2 of critical rationality, to criticize a belief is implicitly to criticize any action based on or informed by it. But in this case the dialectical ground (dg′) for the criticism and the dialectical reason (dr′) for its falsity is not brought out. Similar considerations apply at the level of purely technical reason. Notice that even at the level of instrumental rationality in the context of $power_2$ relations social science – at least at the degree of alethic truth – is not neutral in its implications for the oppressor and the oppressed. The oppressed have a direct material interest in knowledge of these relations that the oppressors do not. Is this why there is a constant tendency for those in power in times of (or in revenge for) crisis to repeat the sin against Socrates and education generally? The real importance of the explanatory critical derivation of values from facts and practices from theories[13] is that it can be *generalized* to cover the failure to satisfy other axiological needs, necessities and interests besides truths, including those which are necessary conditions for truth, such as basic health, education and ergonic efficiency.

But an even simpler argument is to hand. For a nominally descriptive statement has, in virtue of the fourfold character of the judgement form discussed in §2, the assertorically sensitized normative fiduciary implication 'act on the basis of it'. It will be remembered that the four internally related components of the judgement form are comprised by (a) expressively veracious, (b) descriptive, (c) evidential and (d) normative-fiduciary aspects. However, the argument I employed in §2 for assertorically imperatival sensitized solidarity applies with equal force here. This immediately takes us into a conception of social science as not only non-neutral (against [1]) and as implying explanatory critique [2], but as *emancipatory axiology* [3]. This is through what I will denominate as the '*ethical tetrapolity*', which may be expressed as follows:

> [axiological commitment implicit in the expressively veracious moral judgement] → (1) fiduciariness → (2) content of the explanatory critical theory† complex ↔ (3) totalizing depth praxis of emancipatory axiology → (4) freedom qua universal human emancipation.

The transition from form to content is a logical extension of the transition from fact to value. It may be regarded as spelling out the substance that the fiduciary remark implies, prefiguring a society based on a normative order of trust, just as the totalizing logic of the depth praxis follows from the dialectical universalizability of the (especially the imperatival and evidential) components of the judgement form.

What is the content at (2) which *trust* presupposes? It is the positive *naturalistically* grounded four-planar theory of the desired end-state or -process which encompasses (as the positive to the negative moment) the explanatory critique in the strict sense, which itself must be ultimately naturalistically grounded in a four-planar theory of changing and changeable human nature-in-nature. This latter may be suggested as an exercise in concrete utopianism, postulating an *alternative* to the actually existing state of affairs, incorporating unacknowledged and even hitherto unimagined possibilities for the satisfaction of wanted needs and wanted possibilities for development, grounded in sustainably potentially disposable resources in the context of a different social order. There is no gulf, but a two-way flow, between (2) and (3), which will incorporate a theory and practice of *transition* to a proximate or ultimate objective. As each moment of the judgement form is universalizable in the ways made explicit in §2, i.e. is transfactual, concrete (qua quadruple so as to include rhythmics, mediations and singularities), actionable and transformative, the logic of the ethical tetrapolity will be inexorably totalizing, finding identity through difference and unity in diversity. This is the moment of the dialectic of mutual recognition of, and action in accordance with, shared *contra-central* interests in the fragmented *periphery*, the dialectical perspectival switch from the systemically mediatized (even virtualized) reality of the *figure* to its unseen but dialectical *grounds* (e.g. from capital to the generative separation that sustains it).

So far I have not shown how the ethical tetrapolity encompasses step (4), the goal of universal human emancipation. This I will now rectify. We have the theorem of the dialectical equivalence, or at least transmutability, of ills, absences, constraints, inequities and falsities. Insofar as an ill is unwanted, unneeded and remedial, the spatio-temporal-causal-absenting or real transformative negation of the ill presupposes universalizability to absenting agency in all dialectically similar circumstances. This presupposes in turn the absenting of all similar constraints. And by the inexorable logic of dialectical universalizability, insofar as all constraints are similar *in virtue of their being constraints*, i.e. qua constraints, this presupposes the absenting of all constraints as such, including $constraints_2$ (i.e. the abolition of all master–slave-type relations) and other inequities. And this presupposes in its wake a society oriented to the free development and flourishing of each and all, and of each as a condition for all, that is to say, universal human autonomy as flourishing, the dr_p', the free = the good = the moral alethic society. So the goal of universal human autonomy is implicit in every moral judgement. But, as by a valid transcendental perspectival switch, theoretical can be seen under the aspect of practical reason (cf. C2.3), the objective of the eudaimonistic society is contained in every expressively veracious assertoric utterance. Furthermore, in virtue of the quasi-propositional character of every act, it is arguably implicit in every intentional deed. But as the logic is totalizing, and every absence can be seen as a constraint, this goal of universal human autonomy can be regarded as implicit in an infant's primal scream. This argument, however, supplies us with only the *formal* criterion of freedom qua universal human flourishing. The *substantive* criteria have once more to be fleshed out by a *naturalistically grounded* four-planar theory of the possibilities of social being in nature in the direction indicated by the formal criteria. That is to say, by a concretely utopian exercise in social science conceived now as absenting constraints on absenting absences or ills (cf. C2.10); that is, as *dialectic* or the *axiology of freedom* [4]. The formal desiderata are characterized by an orientation to the criterion of *concrete singularity* – truly the key to the realm of freedom of each and all, and of each as a condition of all, by absolute reason, autonomy and the absence of heterology, that is, each agent is true of, to, in and for herself and every other. As I stressed in C2.10, it requires no Rawlsian veil of ignorance or Habermasian ideal speech situation to justify it. As a check on the validity of the formal criteria one can ask are there any others, which are not contained or sublated by it, which are sincerely universally universalizable? Its converse is marked by susceptibility to immanent critique, dc′, T/P inconsistency, heterology, alienation, inequity and oppressive $power_2$ relations. Alethically it would be a normative Tina compromise form. This indeed is our existential now.

Now for some comments on the substance of the ethical tetrapolity. First on steps (2) ↔ (3). This raises, predictably enough, a number of problems. How are the subjects, whom I will call '$subjects_2$', who are committed to actually existing morality while occupying subaltern poles of discursively moralized $power_2$ relations, to be brought into this dialectic, which I have hitherto described essentially as one of social science? We may sketch a typical *dialectic of morality* thus:

descriptive morality → immanent critique (T/P inconsistency, dc′) → redescriptive morality → hermeneutic and material counter-

> hegemonic struggle → metacritique (MC_1) → explanatory critical morality (dg′, dr′, MC_2) → totalizing depth praxis (incorporating a self-reflexive monitoring process and the prefigurative and thus means/ends consistency condition) → emancipatory axiology.

Personalism, perhaps the dominant moral ideology for $subjects_2$, is characterized by the attribution of responsibility to the isolated individual in an abstract, desocialized, deprocessualized, unmediated way, with blame, reinforced by punishment (rather than the failure to satisfy needs), as the sanction for default. But emotivism, decisionism, prescriptivism, descriptivism, sociological reductionism, nihilism, all – like personalism – trade on the assumption that values cannot be naturalistically grounded, based on the assumption that no transition from fact to value (and a fortiori from form to content) is possible. But through the theoretico-practical duality of the judgement form, it is the easiest thing in the world to pass from fact to value, and as *rational causal/absenting agents* we do it all the time. However, any such dialectic of morality as I have described will presuppose both a subjective dialectic of desire → wants → interests → emancipatorily oriented purposes; and an objective dialectic in which the constraints upon action are perceived as dependent on the reality of social, including screened $power_2$, relations and hence their transformative negation as dependent upon collective and ultimately totalizing agency. Totalizing praxis requires a vast stretching of the *moral imagination.* In considering this it should be borne in mind that only the empowered individual can assist or effectively solidarize with the powerless, so that amour de soi, rather than amour propre, is the true fount of all 'altruism', and that it is enlightening not egoistic for the individual to acknowledge her real self-interests. Here one might envisage the following dialectic (of 7 E's):

> self-*e*steem ↔ mutual *e*steem (where the intra-dependence of action itself reflects both the fiduciary nature of the social bond and the reality of oppressive social relations) ↔ *e*xistential security ↔ *e*rgonic efficiency ↔ (individual → collective → totalizing) *e*mpowerment ↔ universal *e*mancipation ↔ *e*udaimonia.

The success of the immediate goals of the totalizing depth praxis will depend to a large extent on whether the emancipatory agents are capable of latching on to immanent emergent or partially manifest tendential processes (including cultural ones) and stretch them in the desired direction. Insofar as fiduciariness or trustworthiness both underpins esteem in the dialectic of the '7 E's' and is both an initiating moment in and an essential condition for the success of the totalizing depth praxis, we must add a fifth 'T' to our formula of the TTTTφ of C2. But this is the politics of *transition* and so we can add a sixth alliterative 'T' to characterize the politics of the totalizing depth praxis as:

*t*ransformed *t*ransformative (marking the coincidence of autoplastic and alloplastic change, subjective needs and objective possibilities) *t*rustworthy *t*otalizing *t*ransformist (committed to deep structural change) *t*ransitional praxis.

Any dialectic of liberation from ills (qua absence) is committed to the possibility of changing four-planar human nature, so that we must regard the *moral evolution of the species as open.* A beneficent objective dialectic, relating the strengths of virtue theory, deontology and consequentialism, which may be called the 'ethical circle', and which should be understood as inserted in the context of the transformational model of social activity advanced in C2.9, is depicted in Figure 3; and a related topology of the four kinds of politics I discussed in C2 is illustrated in Figure 4 in the figure of the concrete universal, with the rhythmic component of the quadruplicity represented by

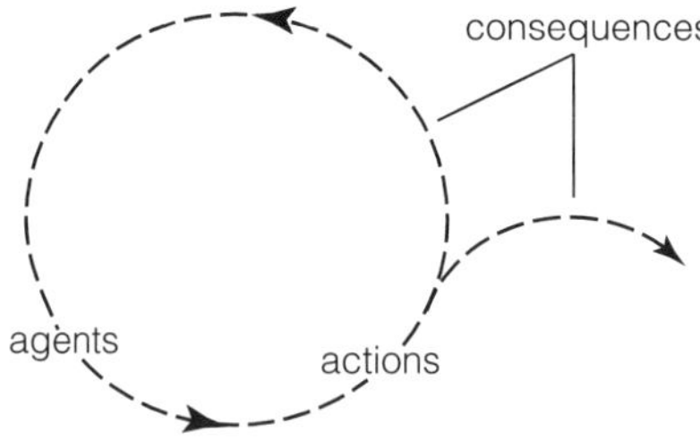

Figure 3 The ethical circle

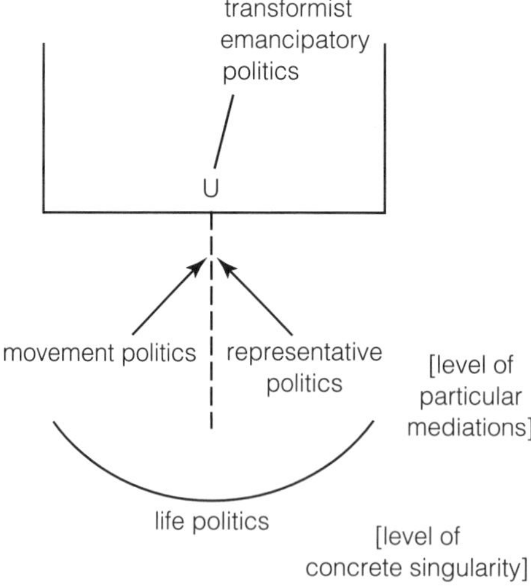

Figure 4 Four types of politics and the concrete universal

movement politics. Finally the *practical* character of the knowledge required should be re-emphasized.

The orientation of the free society to concrete singularity is represented in Figure 5. Is it possible to second-guess the substantive criteria? Clearly it is posited on a massive change in four-planar human nature. The totality of master–slave-type relations would be done away with, including the end of the generative separation of the immediate producer and the fivefold alienations which result from it. For to be alienated is to be separated from oneself or something essential to one's nature or being. One can envisage a vast extension of (reciprocally, thence universally, recognized) rights, which are precisely freedoms; and a greatly extended constitutional democracy, including as much local autonomy and participatory democracy (precisely collective self-government) as would be consistent with the rational regulation of the massive redistribution, transformation and limitation of resource use dictated by considerations of equity and ecology alike. Considerations of size are pertinent here. For participatory democracy, or just participation-in-democracy, suggests decentralization and local autonomy, while global constraints and inequities point to circuitous decision-making routes. At the global level one might consider a Council of the Peoples and a Council of the States or Regions. The normative order would be based on trust, solidarity and care, if not indeed love. If so, economic arrangements might be structured around a minimal viable standard of living in exchange for caring duties without the compulsion to work, in the sense of selling one's labour-power. But the dispositional or motivational aspects of free rational autonomy, including its agonistic and expressive ingredients,* would be given free rein in a socialized market[14] with a bias to empowering the tacit knowledge of the immediate producers and collective enterprises organized on a

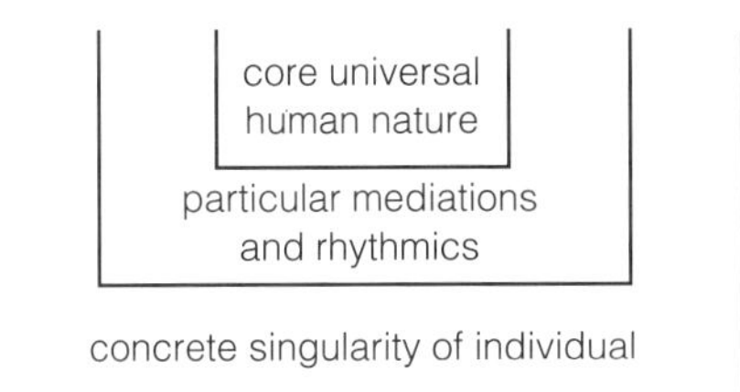

Figure 5 The concrete singularity of the human agent

* It is neglect of this component of singular freedom, together with a planning apparatus expressing productive relations only consistent with an economically basic level of technology, inscribed sociologically within an undifferentiated expressive unity, which, in the context of global intradependence, especially in the form of the constitutive intrinsic outside, and the presence of the past, especially in the form of constitutive geo-historical process, accounts for the economic and civil kenosis of the erstwhile actually existing socialist states.

cooperative basis. As transitional slogans one might venture 'from each in accordance with their wants, abilities and needs' (since people may possess different needs to work) and 'to each according to their essential needs and innovative enterprise'. Global, regional and local informed democracy (which may well incorporate a syndicalist component as representative of particular mediating and/or disadvantaged groups) would ensure the rights of future (and differential) generations and other species were taken into account and decide upon such issues as the rate of depletion of scarce resources and feasible population growth. Education in a creative flourishing of the arts and sciences would be at a premium in such a society. Indeed this would in essence consist in a continually *reflexive learning process*, appropriate to a transitional dialectical rhythmic to a goal which, as in a Fichtean (but not endless) progress, may only ever be asymptotically approached.

Even with this reservation, one has to step back a little. What about phenomena like 'moral distance' despite global intradependence, the presence of the past, the inequities induced by the failure of expectations, the genuine psychopath, the virtualization of actuality, totally contradictory conceptions of efficiency grounded in different objective functions? One has to ask whether there is not any constraint on the lack of constraints or limit to the principle of dialectical universalizability? First a principle of *balance* (cf. Aristotle) would place a limit (cf. Kant) on an emergent (cf. Marx) totality (cf. Hegel) that does not apply, or applies only in special cases, to the constituents of a totality in the way in which I will elaborate further in §§8–10 and C4.2. Second, it should be remembered that I am to an extent second-guessing what naturalistic substantive social science might discover about the unrealized possibilities of four-planar social being. (Even so, whatever this comes up with, progress in the direction of the formal criterion will be in general possible, even if it consists in halting [further] regression away from it.) Third, four-planar social being is always everywhere changing, and changeable. Process in open totalities entails that all politics are transitional, and that all causally efficacious transformative praxis is continually negating the status quo.

In §10, after further exploring the realms of totality and agency, I will return to the dialectic of desire, mediated by the axiological necessities I initially called the reality principle but which we can now know as alethically attainable truth and practical wisdom, to freedom, in the sense of universal human autonomy as flourishing. But it is worth making three concluding points here. First, one needs only a *conatus* to knowledge to get the dialectic of freedom going. Agent N desires x but is constrained. Ceteris paribus, N wishes to remove the constraint on x and hence to know how to absent the absence of x. That is to say, the intrinsic releasing conditions for knowledge of the generative mechanism which will overcome the constraint on x are satisfied and then, by the logic of dialectical universalizability, to all similar constraints, and thence to all constraints qua constraints, corresponding, in Hegel's phrase, to the knowledge that man, as such, is free. Second, to the extent that the constraints on knowledge, or more generally on any other of the aspects of rational autonomy, are social, as they necessarily are in the case of constraints_2 on subjects_2, then only knowledge about constantly developing four-planar human nature, including, of course, social relations and hence the social sciences in sensitized solidarity with the tacit know-how of the subjects_2, can rationally inform emancipatory praxis. It is material interest in the form of the reality principle that will drive the dialectic of freedom on. Third, if a case can be made out for saying that natural science and technology can satisfy material desires in the epoch of consumer capitalism, it can equally be argued that looking at the contemporary phase from the standpoint of the forces of production, three phenomena stand out:

(a) a drastic reduction in necessary labour time;
(b) new, information-based ('post-Fordist') technologies requiring a socially aware workforce with implications for knowledge about the character of the relations of production, i.e. for social science;
(c) the developing globalization of commodity production, which increasingly makes transformative tendencies radically negational (auto-subversive) in character.

This suggests the possibility of a dialectic of globalizing self-consciousness which may presage movement in the direction of a totalizing depth praxis partially offsetting the dialectical lag of transformative agency behind social structures, with endemic crisis tendencies, so that the extrinsic enabling conditions for change are satisfied too. If this were so, the unity of theory and practice would be satisfied in practice and geo-historical directionality (level 7 on p. 261 above) would catch up with dialectical rationality (dr_a' in $d\varphi$). And we would be on the way to universal human autonomy.

[. . .]

§10 The dialectic of desire to freedom

The dialectic of desire to freedom is at once a dialectic of desire and a dialectic of freedom. In this section I will be resuming some earlier themes, especially those elaborated in §§2 and 7, tracing several dialectical pathways to the eudaimonistic society and exploring some of the implications of my argument. I should make it explicit at the outset that here I am, in a sense, engaging in an exercise of metacritical (metatheoretical) concrete utopianism; that this is not a historicist enterprise of anticipating the trajectory of a future which has yet to be caused, but rather depends in part upon us; instead I am attempting to articulate the tendential_b (see C2.4) *rational directionality of geo-history.* Our 'vehicular thrownness' establishes the explanatory primacy (in the EA) of the political over the ethical, while the extended argument of this chapter from absence to referential detachment to the logic of scientific discovery and alethic truth, entailing, when consistently pursued, the conception of social science as emancipatory axiology, suggests the normative primacy (in the IA) of the ethical over the political. (This is the constellational unity [and fluidity] of the ethical and [into] the political within the political.) My project is normative. I shall be making much use of the logic of dialectical universalizability. But, because we are in transitional rhythmics or processes, this logic must be embedded within a developmental *dialectic of the logic and practice of dialectical universalizability* incorporating *a dialectic of dialectical universalizability and immanent critique.* Because we are inhabitants of a dialectical pluriverse, characterized by complex, plural, contradictory, differentiated, disjoint but also coalescing and condensing development and antagonistic struggles over discursively moralized $power_2$ relations, subject to regression, entropy and roll-back, we cannot expect the *dialectic of real geo-historical processes*, from which the logic of totality, i.e. of dialectical universalizability, starts and to which it always returns, to be anything but a messy affair. This logic is a spatio-temporally, multiply and unevenly distanciated developmental process, in which so long as dialectical universalizability is not seen as a *transfactual, processually oriented, concretized, transformatively directional norm, subject to the constraint of actionability* in a world in which agents act on their perceived interests (including their perceptions of the interests of others), it is often going to seem to be falsified. But norms, although they can be broached and discarded, cannot be falsified by the irrationality of actual geo-history. They can be falsified, but only by the provision of a better, nobler, norm more fitting to the needs and propensities of developing four-planar socialized humanity. Pluralism, diversity, is intrinsic to the logic of totality, but as we are dealing with a dialectic encompassing immanent critique in counter-hegemonic struggle, inconsistency too must be conceded a value in its own right. It is a dialectic, not an analytic, of dialectical universalizability that I am about.

I will be arguing that just as the concept of *constraint* must be *negatively generalized* to include unwanted and unnecessary, and so remediable, ills qua absences and hence that to constrain such a constraint is to liberate, the concept of *freedom* must be *positively generalized* (and substantialized) so as to encompass not just such obvious items as rights, equities and (participation-in-)democracies, but needs and possibilities, such as possibilities for self-development and self-realization. In the dialectic of dialectical universalizability and immanent critique, the former may be related to the positive, the latter to the negative generalization. My orientation here is, as always, to concrete singularity and the goal of a society in which the free flourishing of each concretely singular agent is a condition of the free flourishing of all.

I start with some metatheorems, say something about the pivotal concept of autonomy, before delineating various conceptions of freedom and rehearsing the character of the judgement form, T/P consistency and dialectical universalizability. We know (1) that a reason can be a cause, and to cause is to negate is to absent (transfactually, rhythmically, potentially holistically and possibly intentionally); (2) that ills which are unnecessary and unwanted (conditions that I will take as presupposed for expository convenience) can be considered as absences, and so constraints, but also as falsehoods to concretely singularized human nature; (3) that dialectic is, in the human world, most basically, the absenting of constraints (including the $constraints_2$ on $subjects_2$ which derive from exploitative or oppressive $power_2$ relations, and the inequities that flow from them); and (4) that by a negative transcendental perspectival switch, to constrain is to contradict is to absent; and finally (5) that the moral truth or alethia, the good, is dialectically universal freedom.

The most basic meaning of autonomy is self-determination. 'Complete autonomy' would imply the absence not of causes, but of prior or external ones (e.g. subjugation). Of course, the world in which we act is always going to be constrained by (a) natural laws and ecological limits, (b) the nature of globalized and temporally distanciated four-planar social being, (c) one's values, projects and rationality in attempting to accomplish them, including, for instance, the balance of the four types of politics in one's life. Autonomy presupposes freedom of choice (and hence a degree of axiological underdetermination).* But freedom of choice does not imply the absence of grounds for choice (as in complete axiological indeterminacy). And, in one sense of 'free', one will be free just to the extent that one possesses the power, knowledge and disposition to act in one's real interests, e.g. wanted needs, or development or flourishing, including one's wants *for* others. However, this is perhaps better looked at as a *criterion for rational agency* (a departure from my earlier usage). And one can then say if one uses one's *autonomy* both *rationally* and *wisely* (i.e. in accordance with the virtue of phronesis, including its connection with the criteria of mean, balance, totality, health and wholeness) then one will be able to, or tend to be able to, realize one's ideas in practice. Hence the connection between autonomy, functioning as a theoretico-practical dual concept potentially linking truth to freedom, and the unity – or, better, coherence – of theory and practice in practice, i.e. absolute reason. The concept can be extended or its presuppositions explicated, in many directions. Thus nothing which was reified, i.e. like labour-power treated as a commodity, could be said to be truly autonomous. Self-determination is normally a necessary condition for self-realization, and if one's self includes one's potentialities, then one can reasonably be said to be alienated from them. And only a self which, in solidarity, has emancipated itself can be said to have become self-determining, i.e. autonomous. This is

* It was a disastrous mistake of Hegel's to identify freedom and necessity – the sign of his actualism and acceptance of authority, i.e. of his 'positivity', and his equation of freedom with fate.

at once a prefigurative ('presence of the future') condition on emancipation and a process-in-product ('presence of the past') condition for autonomy. It is the same requirement that makes the imperatival aspect of the judgement form, in Kant's terms, an assertorically imperatival one. This presupposes that the addressee of the judgement wants advice and discussion and the same applies at the level of more material forms of solidarity. This is also an implication of both the concrete singularity and the actionability or agent-specificity implicit in dialectical universalizability.

Now to the even broader concept of freedom. At its root level, to be free is to be without, i.e. to have no/absent, constraints in some respect, and liberation is the absenting of the respects (concrete constraints). To be free *from* constraints on x is to be free to *do* x. Hence the equivocity of Berlin's alleged contrast. But we can distinguish various degrees of freedom, which may be fruitfully compared with the various levels of rationality I set out in §7:

1 (a) agentive freedom, viz. the capacity to do otherwise which is analytic to the concept of action;
  (b) formal legal freedom, which neither implies nor is implied by (1a);
2 (a) negative freedom from, which, I have just argued, is tantamount to
  (b) positive freedom to (a disempowerment, for instance, can be seen as a constraint).
3 Emancipation from specific constraints, where emancipation is defined as the transformation from unwanted, unneeded and oppressive to wanted, needed and liberating (including empowering) states of affairs, especially structures. Clearly this can be universal, collective or individual. By this point one will have become interested in criteria for rational agency and be susceptible to the logic of dialectical universalizability.

At what point in the ethical tetrapolity does the logic of dialectical universalizability bite? At the transition between the ground of the fiduciary remark and the remoralization of the world that is the object of the explanatory critical theory which both informs and is informed by the totalizing depth praxis I discussed in §7. Thus take the simple judgement 'smoking harms health': we can postulate the transition → the harming of health as such is wrong → absence of health is an ill → ills such as that, which function as a constraint on life, are wrong → all such constraints should be absented → all constraints, as such, should be absented. What makes a dialectic of such (dialectical) universalizability necessary? My ethical naturalism implies that an epistemological dialectic will be necessary for the transition to the realm of freedom, which paradigmatically violates norms of purely analytical consistency. In addition T/P inconsistency is characteristic of all formative/learning/maturation/developmental processes. Note that the fact that my moral realism, in the context of developing four-planar social being (or, as I shall sometimes say, 'human nature'*), makes substantive moral truth changing counts for, not against it; and provides another point of linkage with the 'communitarians'.

Let us, after this necessary digression, resume the progression of degrees of freedom. We now have the concept of

3′ universal human emancipation from (unnecessary) constraints as such.

The next level of freedom is

4 autonomy, in the sense of self-determination discussed above; and corresponding to it,
4′ rational autonomy; and
4″ universal human autonomy.

This must be conceptualized as in nature and, as such, subject to the rights of other species and over time, so that it extends to the rights of future generations. At this point the positive generalization or stretching of the concept of freedom mentioned earlier becomes possible. First to *needs*, whether absolute, in the sense of necessary for survival, or relative, in the sense of necessary in the context of geo-historically grounded possibilities. Thus freedom as:

5 wellbeing, with the emphasis on the absence of ills and the satisfaction of needs; and corresponding to it,
5′ universal wellbeing.

The next extension is to see the realization of concretely singularized *possibilities for development* (including the potential for possibilities of development), in the context of developing, and by a further level shift, the possibilities of further developing, four-planar social being as *rights*, and a fortiori as *grounded freedoms*, subject only to the requirement of totality, that it is consistent with the universally reciprocated recognition of such rights, i.e. that it does not transgress the concretely singularized grounded freedoms of others. We thus have freedom as

6 flourishing, with the emphasis on the presence of goods (benefits) and the realization of possibilities, which entails
7 universal human flourishing, or the eudaimonistic society.

By now, of course, de-alienation and the totality of structurally sedimented

* The first locution is better, because if an independent meaning can be put on human nature then it may function as a norm against which, for example, social institutions can be judged.

master–slave relations will have long been abolished and, in the context of the open moral evolution of humanity, the erstwhile power$_2$-holders and oppressors will see their interests under transformed descriptions. My task now is to show how this most (ontologically) negative philosophy can generate the most (ethically) positive results.

The simplest way of introducing the logic of consistency and universalizability is to register that you cannot say 'you ought to φ' and not φ in materially the same circumstances without committing a practical or performative contradiction, i.e. being guilty of T/P inconsistency. It is this simple principle, taken to the limit, that binds the trustworthiness of any sincere statement to T/P consistency, dialectical universalizability, dialectical reason, autology, autonomy and universal human autonomy; and, conversely, the lack of dialectical universalizability to T/P inconsistency, performative contradiction, reflexive inconsistency, susceptibility to dc′, heterology, heteronomy and Tina compromise. More fully, now, we know from the treatment of §2 that universalizability is both a test for consistency and a criterion of truth (an acceptable experimental result must be repeatable in principle); that T/P consistency is a matter of *praxis* (in a *process*), which should be *practical, progressive* (in the sense specified in p. 220) and *theoretically grounded*; and that both praxis and grounding should be universalizable in the sense that they be *transfactual, concrete, actionable* (agent-specific: ought presupposes, not implies, can) and *transformative*, i.e. oriented to the objective(s) of the praxis, which, in the field of practical reasoning, will be ultimately grounded in a theory of four-planar human nature. At this juncture two objections may be mooted. Will not the particularities of each concrete situation be so great and specific as to render nugatory the criterion of universalizability? No – for the onus is on the backslider to show that mediations and singularities of a situation are both (a) *relevant* to and (b) *significant* for the matter at issue. It is no objection to the payment of taxes to cite the fact that one is red-headed – *unless* such persons are systematically discriminated against on such grounds. How do I know a priori that the *substantive* naturalistic criteria will be in accordance with the *formal* criterion, viz. the free development of each as a condition for the free development of all, articulated in §2 and §7? On the argument of §2 one requires only that the process be *progressive* (or minimally regressive), which is obviously an issue for debate. Moreover, the non-actualist, non-historicist substantive theory will situate only *possibilities* for advance towards (or halting regress from) the desired direction.

In this book I have been articulating what is the ontology of absence. This is our starting point. It is not anthropic because absence is, I have argued, a necessary feature of the natural world, and one which, moreover, has ontological priority over presence (cf. C2.1 and C3.5). Nevertheless, in the ethical domain, which is (see §1) social-relation dependent, it is essential to commence from experienced or experiencable absences, which are unfulfilled needs, lacks, wants or, in the setting of primary polyadization, elemental desire (so that difference is ontologically prior to identity). Desire entails referential detachment, whence we proceed through causality and classification to ontological stratification and alethic truth. From absence also springs constraint qua contradiction, and via the contradictions within and between differentiated and stratified entities, we proceed to emergence and thence to totality inwardized as the reflexivity shown in agency. But reflexive agency is capable of judgement and so is subject to the dialectical universalizability of the judgement form. Sociality necessarily implies solidarity, with or in self-emancipation and an orientation to the totalizing depth praxis to universal human emancipation which will usher in the good society, oriented to concretely singularized universal human autonomy. This is the dialectic of desire from freedom, which we could nominate (1) the *dialectic of agency*, set off by the absence or lack implicit in desire.

Now in §7 I argued for the transition from fact to value and theory to practice, presaging the transition from fiduciary form to naturalistic content (and the dialectical perspectival switches from, for instance, the figure of capital to the ground of labour or from the media star to the dole queue, or from the centre of the Pentagon or the Tokyo Stock Exchange to the periphery of Somalia or the New York homeless) in two ways: (α) through the process of *explanatory critique*, which is familiar from my previous writings so I will not pursue it further here, and (β) through the *theoretico-practical duality* of the judgement form developed in §2. We can, however, proceed even more directly from (γ) the axiological commitment implicit in the expressive veracious judgement, whether in the domain of theoretical or practical (or other kinds of) reasoning, straight to the ethical tetrapolity I outlined in §7, and to the goal of universal human autonomy, without making the detour through the explicitly moral realm, viz. as follows:

> [I] [axiological commitment in the expressively veracious judgement (e.g. an assertoric utterance)] → (1) concretely singularized fiduciariness (→ solidarity) → (2) explanatory critical theory plus concrete utopianism plus theory of transition (in a theory–practice helix based on participatory research) ↔ (3) totalizing depth praxis, including, of course, the politics of transition → (4) universal human autonomy, (a) subject to the constraints imposed by (i) the needs and rights of future generations and other species (ii) and ecological limits and (iii) the principle of balance or the dialectical mean and the meta-ethical virtue of phronesis or practical wisdom; and (b) grounded in a conception of the open-ended moral evolution of the species, ideological struggle and the material dynamics of change.

The resulting normative order will be based on the multiple generalization of the TMSA, including the traditionally feminist virtues of care, sensitivity to the suffering of others (for to suffer is, as Marx remarked, what it is to be), solidarity and *trust*. It is worth mentioning here that it is the trustworthiness of the primary polyad which endows the infant with the existential security that at once silences its scream, nurtures its self-esteem and lays the basis for the amour de soi which underpins solidarity and altruism alike. The reality of the social bond, based on the primary existential of trust, both quenches desire and, in the process of development, transforms its object, in (2) *the dialectic of education of desire* to wants and only collectively attainable needs by the axiological necessities which comprise the reality principle, understood as the alethic truths of four-planar contemporary society.* The logic of desire and of interest point in the same direction.

The transition from form to content – and the context – of the eudaimonistic society – is implicit in every desire, assertoric remark or successful action. Let us look at some of the other ways at which we can arrive at the same result. We can resume with (3) the *dialectic of malaise.* A malaise is an ill and a constraint. Insofar as it is unwanted and unneeded, we are rationally impelled, ceteris paribus (a qualification which is always necessary in open systems, but which it would be tedious to repeat), to a commitment to absent it, and thus to an absenting practice. And thence into absenting all dialectically similar ills, and thus to absent all the causes of such constraints, including oppressive $power_2$ formations, and from there to absent all ills or constraints, and hence their explanatory critically identified causes, precisely insofar as, *in constituting ills or constraints, they are dialectically similar.* And from here it is, in theory, but a short hop to the free society, which satisfies or approximates or approaches the formal criterion of the free flourishing of each and all, as substantiated by a four-planar theory of human nature in society.

Second, from (4) the *dialectic of cognition*, we can begin from frustrated desire or the pathology of everyday life (see §3). Agents N desire x and are constrained from achieving it. They wish to remove this constraint. They therefore seek out its causes and acquire the practical knowledge to get rid of them. Again, by the logic of dialectical universalizability, they are committed to getting rid of all dialectically similar structures and hence to their causes and to the acquisition of the knowledge to absent them. Thence they are rationally committed to getting rid of all dialectically similar situations which act as constraints qua constraints. And thence once more to the flourishing society. Next from (5) the *dialectic of equity.* The principle of sufficient practical reason states that there must be a ground for differences. If there is no such ground then we are rationally impelled to remove them. This will almost inevitably initiate a drive to overthrow the totality of master–slave relations, and implant in their place a society based on a core equality

* Those with a taste for alliteration will note that it is a sixth T, trustworthiness, that underpins the dialectic of 7 E's in §7 and that I added before totalizing to the other 5 T's of transformist transitional politics. See Figure 9 on p. 121 above.

between human beings by virtue of their shared species nature with differentiations justified by the concrete specificities and singularities, needs and powers* of the particular individual. The dialectic of equity can also be used to develop and generalize Gewirth's argument for the recognition of freedom and wellbeing as universalizably necessary conditions for successful action,[16] say φ under a description, to an argument for the *realization* of the *potential* of all agents to perform dialectically similar acts; and from there to an argument for the *development* of all dialectically similar potentials; and from there it is but a short step to argue for the development of all *potentials qua potentials* and we are at Marx's definition of a socialist society as one 'in which the free development of each is the condition of the free development of all', i.e. the eudaimonistic society, which may be regarded as an extended explication of the principle of equity. Gewirth, for his part, does not see how far the logic of universalizability must take him. Next (6) the *dialectic of de-alienation.* Insofar as a person is separated from something essential to their needs, nature or healthy human functioning, no one who is not prepared to see themselves so alienated can fail to be committed to its restoration, insofar as they do not infringe the reciprocally recognized rights of others. This is a prima facie case for *socialism*, insofar as it rationally portends the sublation of the generative separation of the immediate producers from the means and materials of production and *their* rational regulation of their use.

The dialectic of de-alienation can be broadened, as anticipated in §5, into a (7) generic *dialectic of desire.* If the dialectic of desire involves the desire to be desired and this involves the desire to be recognized, then, again through the logic of dialectical universalizability insofar as this involves the capacity to enjoy rights and liberties, it entails the *real enjoyment* of equal and universally reciprocally recognized rights and liberties, including the right to de-alienation and the enjoyment of health, education, access to resources and other liberties. And by an extension and deepening of the argument it entails the right of all $subjects_2$ to be free of, and thus to the abolition of, the totality of master–slave relations, including internalized and intra-psychic ones, globally and inter-/intra-generationally and with due respect to the needs and rights of other species in the context of developing four-planar human nature. This dialectic rationally demands the satisfaction of the cognitive and empowering conditions for universal human autonomy, so that, in the first instance, if agents are so disposed, it must be included within level (4) of freedom, but then, in the next place, upon their coming to see their real interests, under the description of the free development of the concrete singularity of every other individual as a condition for their own free development. This takes us into (8) the *dialectics of transition*, and the two-way traffic between truth and freedom, form and content, on which I will comment

* The speculation that such matters are not subject to rational investigation is refuted by the work of Len Doyle and Ian Gough,[15] Maureen Ramsey and a flourishing research industry.

immediately below. The generic dialectic of desire ([7] above) can be motivated in part by (9) the *dialectic of desire for freedom.* This turns on the consideration that *human beings, by and large, want to be free, under some* (sets of) *description(s).* And the logic of dialectical universalizability will rationally motivate them to accept freedom for *all* in dialectically similar circumstances, and then ultimately freedom as such (as dialectically valued) irrespective of circumstance. This will clearly depend not only upon immanent critique as part of counter-hegemonic struggle but also upon the possibility of mutually reinforcing virtuous spirals and spreads among freedoms – powers and needs – such as might be involved in extending participation in democracy, generalizing and safeguarding universally recognized rights, implementing equities (implicit in dialectical universalizability), abolishing oppressive $power_2$, and ultimately the totality of such (again by the logic of universalizability) relations, radically concretely singularized local, regional, and necessarily global (see §7) autonomies (implicit in absolute reason – dr_a' in dφ) and socializing the market without the compulsion or lack of opportunity to work subject to the recognition of the duty to care implied by the right to flourish. Let us now consider (10) the *dialectic of universalizability* itself. The T/P consistent fiduciary remark implies solidarity, ranging from moral and material support through empowerment, in its aspect of freedom, to participation in the depth totalizing practice concerned. This may be implicated in a dialectic of social science from neutrality to explanatory critical rationality to emancipatory axiology to dialectic per se (the subject of the sequel to this book) and by transition from descriptive morality through immanent critique to redescriptive morality to formal omissive metacritique through counter-hegemonic struggle to explanatory critical morality and metacritique (MC_2, dg′, dr_p') through the totalizing depth praxis to emancipatory axiology.

One could add to these dialectics indefinitely. There is (11) a *generic dialectic of interests.* It is in N's real interest to φ, since it contributes to her flourishing or wellbeing or develops her potentialities. She is constrained from φ-ing by x. She seeks to absent x, and to unearth the causes of x, say an oppressive $power_2$ relation R, structuring an institutional complex. She is driven to solidarize with others oppressed by R, and logically to all oppressed by R. They engage in the totalizing depth inquiry and praxis necessary to overthrow R. The reality principle will probably show R to be systematically buttressed by, or interconnected with, a network of such relations and institutions. This will underpin the conatus to dialectical universalizability. The reality principle will also see to it that the transition between perceived interests and wants and perceptions (by agents) of their real interests, at the minimum, of wanted needs, occurs. From seeking to absent the causes of x, she will seek to absent the causes of all similar x's, i.e. frustrations on human flourishing for herself, and for everyone else so frustrated. From viewing the constraints on φ-ing as wrong, and as seeking to absent them, she will view all dialectically (transfactual, actionable, concretized) similar constraints as wrong and seek to absent them. And then she will processually orient herself against constraints qua constraints, that is, constraints as such, and to absenting the absence of a society based on the principle of concretely singularized universal human autonomy subject to the relational condition of totality, that it be a mediated unity predicated on diversity.

In principle, the logic of dialectical universalizability takes two forms – one (α) corresponding to the level of critical reason and the other (β) corresponding to the level of (totalizing depth) explanatory critical reason. But the first without the second is inefficacious and so considerations from the lowest level of reason, instrumental reason, will drive agents from (α) to (β). Their respective logics are as follows:

In case (α):	to absent an ill
	to absent all (dialectically) similar ills
	to absent all ills as such.
In case (β):	to absent an ill
	to seek out the causes for the ill.
Then either (i):	to absent it/them
	to absent the causes of all (dialectically) similar ills
	to absent all ill-producing causes as such
	to absent all ill-producing causes seen as constraints
	to absent the absence of universal human emancipation.
And/or (ii)	to seek out the causes of all (dialectically) similar ills
	to seek out the causes of all ills, seen as $constraints_2$ as such, and
	to absent them, i.e. set out on the path to the eudaimonistic society.

It is worth going into this in a bit more detail. Tautologically, people act in accordance with their perceived interests, and if their perceived interests are their real interests, instrumental reason alone will entail the passage from explanatory to (ultimately, totalizing depth) explanatory critical reason. It would seem that through what I will call the (12) *dialectic of material interests* agents will discover that altruism is in their purely egoistic interests. In §7 I argued the case for the rational necessity of the eudaimonistic society from the side of post-Fordist production, let us now approach it from the point of view of consumption in the age of consumer capitalism. To get from wants, which are frustrated, to wanted needs is to get from perceived to real interests, and from individual to collective agency (and thence to that totalizing agency prefiguring a unity-in-diversity). Agents only have to grasp the causal connection between a referentially detached frustration and a referentially detached systemic $power_2$ relation. This is the education that the reality of the social bond, both of social bondage and of the social solidarity between

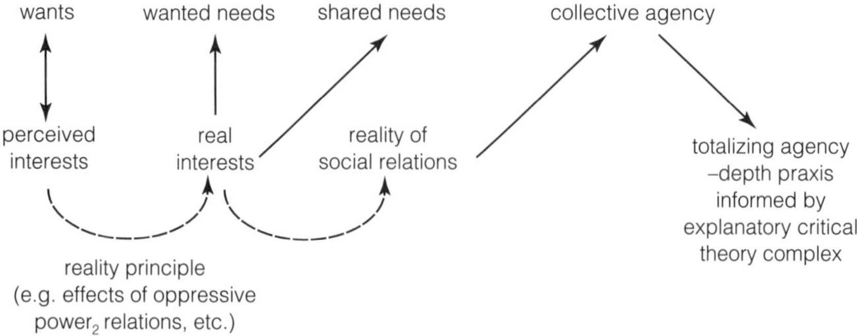

Figure 6 The dialectic of material interests

subjects$_2$, i.e. the reality principle, will impose on their own self-interests. (See Figure 6 below.) Failure to discover the alethia of the contours of their four-planar social circumstances will lead to the continued frustration of their own desires, while failure to act on it will lead at least to cognitive dissonance, T/P inconsistencies and *pathologies of praxis.* The reality principle will secure a dialectic from instrumental rationality via explanatory critical rationality to the eudaimonistic society. In this way it nicely complements the dialectic from consciousness via self-consciousness to reason articulated from the standpoint of production in §7. The naturalistic vision that wo/men as such are free, vastly extended from Hegel's conception of liberty, but that to win their freedom they must absent the constraints$_2$ on it, will inform the moral realism of all who are or side with subjects$_2$. The dialectic desire → wants → interests → knowledge → real interests → desired (wanted) needs → collective → totalizing agency is entailed by the most self-centred interest. But what of the possibility of the oppressors 'buying off' individuals? This cannot be generalized of course – the roulette wheel always wins. But it may work in particular cases. Are such agents to be written off as lost souls? They have sacrificed their rational autonomy, and perhaps lost their self-esteem. But they remain in essence free. And this is where the unity of immanent critique and dialectical universalizability in the dialectic of self and solidarity must balance sensitivity to concrete singularity and transfactuality with sensitivity to absence and actionability. This, too, is just one of the reasons why the dialectic of desire to freedom cannot predict, but only inform, the future.

The dialectic of desire to freedom is essentially a *dialectic of content from truth to freedom via wisdom.* In principle and in practice this is a two-way process. Freedom is as much a condition of truth as vice versa, and in the learning process which is the dialectic of theory and practice each mutually informs the other. But, for any degree of freedom, given only a commitment to moral realism, one augments it in a dialectic, initiated by desire through referential detachment to truth conceived as an axiological need, and alethically as expressing both the grounds (truth) of one's grounds and the requirements of the reality principle. In practical reason this last must always be supplemented by the *actionability* (or feasibility) principle. A social bond may be real, but if subjects can be persuaded neither, as Habermas would put it, by 'the force of the better argument', nor by the causal impact of that bond on what they take their real interests to be, directional action based on consciousness of that bond is impractical.

Suppose it is suggested that I have smuggled morality into the fiduciary nature of the expressively veracious remark. This does not matter a jot. Through the naturalistic, descriptive and evidential components of the judgement form, and the requirement that differences, changes and unchanges (i.e. the status quo) be grounded in a substantial theory of four-planar and concretely singularized developing human nature, the *form* of the moral judgement is explicated by the *content* of the explanatory critical† (= explanatory critical plus concrete utopian plus transitional) theory. Theoretical reason merely says that the world is so and entails a commitment to act on it. Practical reason says how we are to change the world in accordance with naturalistically grounded theory. The moral truth or moral alethia, the good, is universal human flourishing, and it, subject to the principles of prefiguration and actionability, absents or deconstrains all the constraints in its way. The logic of my argument entails that both needs (the negative generalization) and resources and opportunities for the development of potentialities (the positive generalization) are rights, subject to reciprocal and universal recognition and democratically adjudicated global constraints. But what of rational agency itself? It is in a person's real interest to flourish, and to come to acquire the disposition, knowledge and power to do so. And it is in a person's interest simpliciter to come to know what their real interests are, unless overriding circumstances prevail. Why the exit clause? From the standpoint of concrete singularity implicit in my moral realism an agent has to treat herself as an emergent totality. A different principle applies to emergent totalities, including internally related collectivities of agents, from their constituent moments, aspects or parts. The world is an open system in process, in which in particular circumstances, all sorts of contingencies may arise and, in certain circumstances, justify backsliding. A principle for emergent totalities could justify this, and indeed argue that a virtuous existence *requires* the breaking of actualistically formulated or geo-historically specific rules. (The same position could be arrived at by the application of the principle of actionability.) This can be generalized. Totalities are not aggregates. So we can apply, at any place-time-context, *a principle of fold-back*, which is at once a recognition of the character of a non-centrist-expressivist-triumphalist-endist process, and an application of the principle of actionability* and of the doctrine of the Aristotelian mean (which I have already invoked in §7), specifying only optimal progress (which may be negative) in the direction to which the logic of dialectical universalizability flows, putting a constraint on the constraining of constraints, which may on occasion be a necessary condition for any moral or social progress at all.**

The same principle for emergent totalities should make it explicit that morality is not exhaustive – it is only part of the art of 'living well' – with space – literally, a room of one's own; time – literally again (cf. Marx on the shortening of necessary labour time, i.e. of the working day, as a prerequisite for the realm of freedom) – for the cultivation and enjoyment of aesthetic, more generally hedonistic, private and public pleasures. Conceptions of the good society have almost always over-socialized man (sic). As the logic of dialectical universalizability has the causal efficacy of a normative conatus – a tendential drive – it is important to recognize the constraints placed on it by the principle of actionability, which will reflexively incorporate principles of prefigurationality. Moral realism and axiological and spatio-temporal constraints will see to it that the ungrounded discriminations shown in love, friendship, particular concerns, are not undermined. Neither will the phenomenon of 'moral distance'. But it is this very same phenomenon, conceived as *moral distanciation* or the stretching of the moral imagination that the logic of dialectical universalizability requires, that enables its extension to include the rights of unborn generations, other species, the ecosphere and possibilities such as the violation of life, or even possibilities of life, elsewhere in the cosmos by space travel.

Freedom, like truth, satisfies all the moments of dialectical critical realism. It is stratified at 1M (in being composed of levels and degrees, informed by ontologically stratified alethic truth); a geo-historical process of absenting constraints, especially constraints$_2$ on the absenting of ills or the presencing of possibilities at 2E (thus the moment of concrete utopianism, which identifies 'the positive in the negative', must always be grounded in real possibilities-in-process); inexorably totalizing at 3L in virtue of its form and content and in the transition from form to content (including the excluded, empowering the powerless, rendering visible the unseen and explanatorily

* This is perhaps the place to stress the non-actualist character of actionability. Actionability implies that a thing can be done, not that it will. It is also worth pointing out that the moral realism I am articulating, entailing the irreducibility of 'ought' to 'is', is in no way hypostatizing. For moral truth, as social-relation dependent, is of course constellationally contained within being.

** This may be in a dialectic of constellational progress → transition → entrenchment, on which one could bring to bear the dialectic of nodal/switch/connector (totalizing) points and measure relations. However, even for successful entrenchment, it may be necessary to constantly counterpose to the presence of the past a vision of a more *pleasurable* future, to sociological individualism, the transfactuality of global intradependence, etc. etc.

critiquing the conditions of injustice, animating at both margins of inquiry in every intra-action, fundamentally constitutive power$_2$ relations included); and irreducibly agentive at 4D, neither disembodying nor de-agentifying (reifying) concretely singular human beings and oriented to the totalizing collective self-absenting of their ills. This last remark raises two issues. First, the dialectic of self and solidarity foreshadowed by the assertoric and fiduciary components of the imperatival moment of the judgement form. The slave who knows her slavery must come to know and articulate and achieve her humanity before she can become free. The eudaimonistic society must satisfy the criteria for rational agency, subject to the principle for emergent totalities, for universal human autonomy to be effective. But the greater danger is surely not that of unwanted solidarity in the individualism of consumer capitalism. Although I have argued that the reality principle will tend to undermine this individualism, it is here in particular that immanent critique must be remorselessly practised arm in arm with the logic of universalizability. However, in a world at once increasingly homogeneous and increasingly inequitous, transformative tendencies will become exponentially radicalized (i.e. radically negative) and activity become increasingly intra-activity. Eudaimonia, necessarily universalizing, will prove even more impossible in one country than socialism was.

In this section we have been tracing through the implications of the theoretico-practical duality of the judgement form, and/or that of the explanatory critical† grounds entailed by the practical fiduciary remark (which, by a valid perspectival switch, applies equally to every expressively veracious assertoric sentence). Both can be derived, via the chain from the absence implicit in elemental desire through referential detachment and acknowledgement of the reality principle to ontological stratification and alethic truth. And both point, via the logic of dialectical universalizability, to the eudaimonistic society. The dialectic

> [II] absence (2E) – primal scream – desire – referential detachment (1M) – alethic truth – assertoric judgement – dialectical universalizability (3L) – universal human emancipation (4D) – eudaimonistic society-in-process

is concordant with Marx's goal of a (in my terms, concretely singularized) 'association in which the free development of each is the condition for the free development of all'. But how consistent is it with the other basic principles – as distinct from actually existing practices – of socialism? In §7 I have already partially answered this question, suggesting distributive principles along the lines of 'from each according to their concretely singularized wants, abilities and needs and, at a minimum threshold, from what they would expect to receive from others ceteris paribus, i.e. unless exceptional circumstances prevail', where this is to be understood as the right to be subject to universally reciprocated and recognized rights and, 'to each according to their essential needs, wanted possibilities and social virtues (e.g. creative enterprise, willingness to participate in necessary but undesirable or arduous tasks) and, at a minimum threshold, what makes it unnecessary to sell their labour-power'. This would certainly satisfy Marx's distinction between the realm of necessity and the realm of freedom, in which the development of human energy became 'an end-in-itself' including the possibility of a state of affairs in which labour became 'life's prime want' provided labour is taken in the generalized sense of C2.9. Before commenting further on this I want to make some elementary points about a eudaimonistic society.

First, autonomy leaves the world axiologically underdetermined. There must be a field of unconstrained choice, save for respect for global constraints and universal rights. Second, such a society would be an open process. Geohistory would not have come to an end (nor does it make much sense to say that it would start then). Contradictions would exist, of necessity. Difficult decisions would have to be taken, democratically – at a plurality of spatial and organizational levels and spheres of interest – by sometimes circuitous decision-making routes. There would be competing conceptions of the details of the eudaimonistic society, grounded in competing theories of four-planar social being, almost inevitably represented by competing parties. Diversity and pluralism would flourish. Under such conditions one can invert and transform the Hegelian triad as follows:

(α) *Universal civic duty* – unless exceptional circumstances prevent an agent from performing any such duty, conceived precisely as the right to be subject to universal rights and participate in globalized democracy.

(β) *Social virtue* – in which innovation, initiative, enterprise, participation in (participatory, representative, syndicalist and other forms of) democracy, and/or in a socialized market, would be rewarded. It is to be hoped that increasingly these rewards would be internal to the practices concerned, but if this proved not to be the case, then the rewards would be material ones.

(γ) *Individual self-realization* – not (at least, not necessarily) in the family but exactly how the socialized, singularized individual pleases – the domain of unquestioned choice.

The importance of the second realm of social virtue (corresponding to Hegel's 'civil society') is, in part, that it provides a forum for the *expressive* and *agonistic* aspects of human behaviour (cf. C2.9) and the *tacit knowledge* of the immediate producers (as distinct from the bureaucratic knowledge of corporations and planning bodies). It cannot be gleaned from Marx's writings whether he appreciated the need for a mediating realm, but it seems unlikely that he did. Ironically, most indebted to the oppositional realm of Essence epistemologically, he paid scant regard to it programmatically. Is this because he underestimated the presence of the past in humanity – of dead labour in living labour? The presence of the past would also receive its due in the shape of the commitment to *constitutionality*, seen precisely as a resource for the future. (γ) corresponds, of course, to the domain of what I have been calling life politics. A balanced life would be a unity-in-diversity, in which (γ) could not be appropriately captured by the concept of 'leisure'. Universal civic duty, (α), would be coordinated around maximum possible free choice of activity in partial totalities based on a normative order informed by the values of trust, solidarity, sensitivity to suffering, nurturing and care. Each of these realms would be in the interest of all. Thus, at (β), everyone would benefit from a greater efficiency of resource use in which currently external (dis)economies were internalized. A final point to stress here. Such a society would still be in transition: emancipatory/transformist, as well as movement, politics would carry on, with the evolution of the moral consciousness of the species as open as the arts, sciences and technologies. (Cf. Figure 7.)

I have been arguing for a combination of moral realism and ethical naturalism. Moral realism is manifest in the fiduciary aspect of the logic of dialectical universalizability and is grounded in the fact that I cannot help but take a position in an already moralized world. This position will comprise a relational dialectic. Ethical naturalism is manifest in the alethic aspect of the logic of dialectical universalizability and is grounded negatively in the aporiai of other positions (e.g. the endless regress of decisionism, where values must inevitably be grounded in facts, as they will be so explained) and positively in the fact that I have shown how moral propositions (e.g. 'lack of access to educational resources is wrong' or 'capitalism is based on a categorial error' or 'the inter- and intra-national distribution of resources is characterized by growth in inequities') can be known, i.e. true and adequately justified. Substantially the position developed here is a consequentialism (with universal human autonomy oriented to concrete singularity as perhaps a Fichtean task only ever asymptotically approachable) – with, at the deontological level of the ethical circle I described in §7, a hugely expanded conception of universally recognized and concretely singularized rights to include, inter alia, needs and potentialities for development, on the basis of a positive generalization of the concept of freedom, subject only to 'trumping' by a catastrophe clause; and, at the level of virtue theory, a radically transformed table of virtues, grounded in solidarity, reflecting the reality of social intradependence, and nurtured by care and sensitivity to sufferings, enjoyments and needs of others and nature (so that the ecological would be among the virtues). In the eudaimonistic society every concretely singular individual would be true to, of, in and for herself and every other.

One final comment. There is a difference between emancipatory and emancipated action, as there is a difference between the liberation of oneself and the removal of a constraint from the outside (this is not to denigrate the

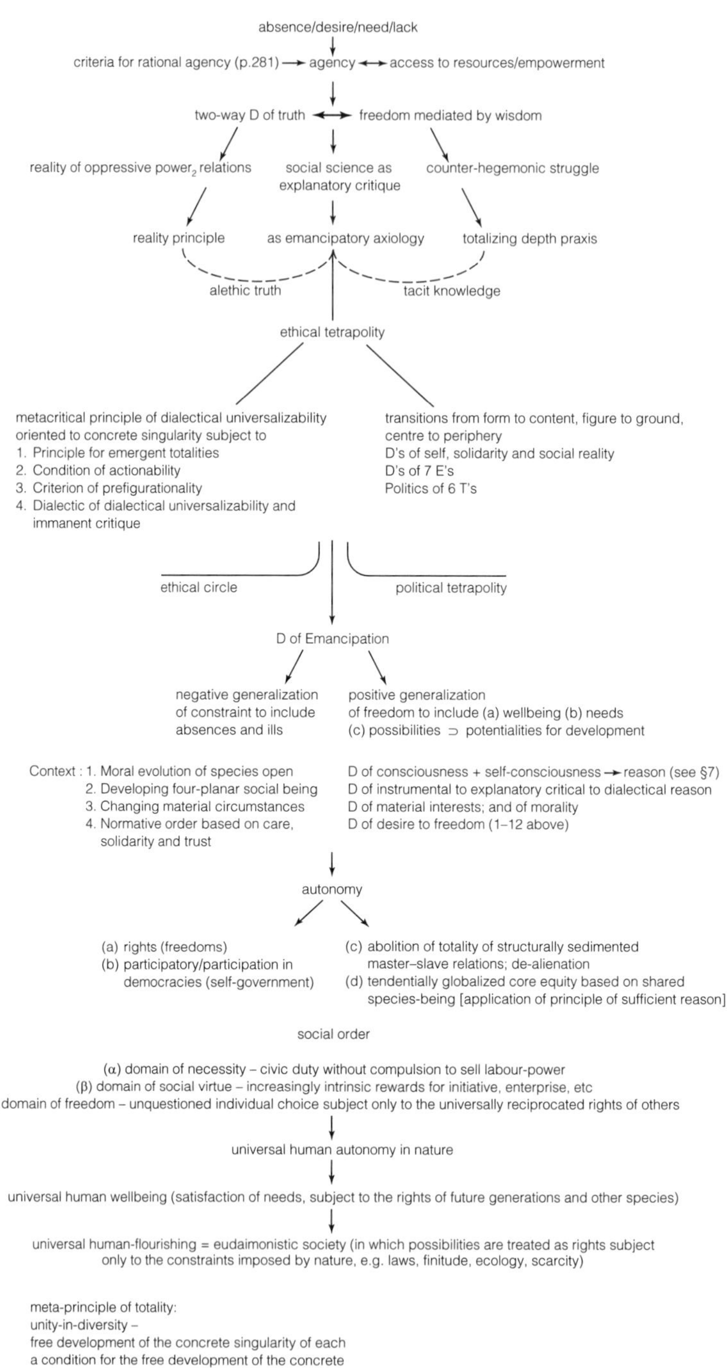

absence/desire/need/lack
criteria for rational agency (p.281) → agency ↔ access to resources/empowerment
two-way D of truth ↔ freedom mediated by wisdom
reality of oppressive power$_2$ relations
social science as explanatory critique
counter-hegemonic struggle
reality principle
as emancipatory axiology
totalizing depth praxis
alethic truth
tacit knowledge
ethical tetrapolity
metacritical principle of dialectical universalizability oriented to concrete singularity subject to
1. Principle for emergent totalities
2. Condition of actionability
3. Criterion of prefigurationality
4. Dialectic of dialectical universalizability and immanent critique
transitions from form to content, figure to ground, centre to periphery
D's of self, solidarity and social reality
D's of 7 E's
Politics of 6 T's
ethical circle
political tetrapolity
D of Emancipation
negative generalization of constraint to include absences and ills
positive generalization of freedom to include (a) wellbeing (b) needs (c) possibilities ⊃ potentialities for development
Context : 1. Moral evolution of species open
2. Developing four-planar social being
3. Changing material circumstances
4. Normative order based on care, solidarity and trust
D of consciousness + self-consciousness → reason (see §7)
D of instrumental to explanatory critical to dialectical reason
D of material interests; and of morality
D of desire to freedom (1–12 above)
autonomy
(a) rights (freedoms)
(b) participatory/participation in democracies (self-government)
(c) abolition of totality of structurally sedimented master–slave relations; de-alienation
(d) tendentially globalized core equity based on shared species-being [application of principle of sufficient reason]
social order
(α) domain of necessity – civic duty without compulsion to sell labour-power
(β) domain of social virtue – increasingly intrinsic rewards for initiative, enterprise, etc
(γ) domain of freedom – unquestioned individual choice subject only to the universally reciprocated rights of others
universal human autonomy in nature
universal human wellbeing (satisfaction of needs, subject to the rights of future generations and other species)
universal human-flourishing = eudaimonistic society (in which possibilities are treated as rights subject only to the constraints imposed by nature, e.g. laws, finitude, ecology, scarcity)
meta-principle of totality:
unity-in-diversity –
free development of the concrete singularity of each a condition for the free development of the concrete singularity of all

Figure 7 Implications of the dialectic of freedom

value of the latter, merely to remind the reader that the former task still remains). The concrete utopian imagination is not a prescription for the future. The eudaimonistic society would be an open one in which it would be up to the totality of concretely singularized individuals to decide what to do with their freedoms. Dialectic is the process of absenting constraints on absenting absences (ills, constraints, untruths, etc.). It is not in the business of telling people, in commandist (Stalinist) or elitist (Social Democratic) fashion what to do. Rather it is better conceived as an inner urge that flows universally from the logic of elemental absence (lack, need, want or desire). It manifests itself wherever $power_2$ relations hold sway. It is the heartbeat of a positively generalized concept of freedom as flourishing and as autonomy and as reason. It is irrepressible.

Notes

1 'Pragmatism Without Method', in P. Kurtz, ed., *Sidney Hook: Philosopher of Democracy and Humanism*, Buffalo, New York 1983, p. 263.
2 PIF, Part 2.
3 *Being and Time*, Oxford 1963, p. 249 (originally published 1927).
4 'On Vagueness', *Australian Journal of Psychology and Philosophy*, 1 (1923).
5 SRHE, pp. 161–2.
6 *Of Grammatology*, p. 168.
7 Cf. SRHE, C3.6.
8 Letter to Engels, 27 June 1867.
9 For more detail on Marxian theories of truth, see my entry on 'Truth' in *A Dictionary of Marxist Thought*, eds T. Bottomore et al., 2nd edn, Oxford 1992.
10 See my entry on 'Naturalism', in *Dictionary of Twentieth-Century Social Thought*, eds W. Outhwaite and T. Bottomore, Oxford 1992.
11 But cf. PON2, C2.6, and PIF, Appendix 2.
12 PIF, pp. 154–5.
13 Cf. SRHE, C2.5–7.
14 Cf. D. Elson, 'Market Socialism or Socialization of the Market?', *New Left Review*, 182 (1989).
15 *A Theory of Human Needs*, London 1991.
16 See A. Gewirth, *Reason as Morality*, Chicago 1979. For a clear exposition and defence of Gewirth's argument, see D. Beyleveld, *The Dialectical Necessity of Morality*, Chicago 1991.

25

THE POWER OF NEGATIVE THINKING

Andrew Collier

Roy Bhaskar's previous writings have belonged to definite regions of philosophy – for the most part the philosophy of science and social science. But their implications have been much wider. They have been one of the various twentieth century attempts to undo the damage done by Descartes and his successors, and in my view the most successful attempt. *Dialectic* leaves this guerrilla struggle in the marginal zones and joins battle in open country with the whole philosophical heritage. To change the metaphor, it stakes out the whole philosophical ground and claims it for a new, dialectical critical realist, ontology. And this is such a huge task that, even in over 400 pages, there is no space to do more than stake out the ground; the work of planting and watering the crops remains ahead.

Dialectical critical realism is divided into four groups of themes (things tend to come in fours in this book, capping Hegel's dialectical triads):

> 1M (first moment) concerned with non-identity, stratification, multiplicity, depth;
> 2E (second edge) concerned with absence and negativity – the theme foregrounded in the book, and so also here;
> 3L (third level) concerned with totality, reflexivity, internal relations;
> 4D (fourth dimension) concerned with transformative agency, human emancipation.

As against these themes, Roy identifies four tendencies in the ontology of modern philosophy which act "as a block on the development of the social sciences and projects of human emancipation" (p. 2) : it is "anthropomorphizing, actualizing, monovalent and detotalizing". Three of these are familiar

Source: Radical Philosophy, 69, January–February 1995, pp. 36–9.

errors against which Roy's earlier work has been directed: "anthropomorphizing" – the epistemic fallacy, which takes theories about what we can know to settle questions about what there is; "actualizing" – the reduction of powers to their exercise, denying any enduring structures underlying the flux of events; "detotalizing" – the assumption that we have best explained something when we have reduced it to its atomic components; and "monovalent" (this is the newcomer) – the doctrine that there is only being, not non-being. Bhaskar's dialectic, "the logic of absence" as it is called in the subtitle to chapter 2, aims to overcome this error.

I have remarked elsewhere that the time-honoured metaphor of nutcracking needs to be slightly altered to catch what Marx did to Hegel's dialectic: the kernel was broken into bits, which Marx retrieved, but which could not be put together again. Roy's earlier account of dialectic is similar: there are various kinds of contradiction, not logically connected, but linked by a family resemblance – a resemblance to logical contradiction; yet they are not, or not only, logical contradictions. A large part of Roy's task in this book is the collection, listing and classification of various dialectical nut-pieces: internal relations, wholes, contradictions, and above all, real absences and absentings. It is this inventory-nature of the book which gives it its characteristic style, quite unlike the tightly argued and fully exemplified texts of Roy's earlier works. Roy himself writes of exploring a "conceptual labyrinth". In relation to the classical (Hegel/Marx) dialectic, the central case (largest nut-piece) seems to be that in which one structure necessarily generates two conflicting tendencies. An example might be Marx's claim that mechanised industry tends to produce both an ossified division of labour and a need for mobility of labour and fluidity of skills (*Capital* vol. 1, pp. 617–18). But the pervasive feature of Roy's own account of dialectic – Ariadne's thread that may hopefully lead us through the labyrinth – is the concept of real absence, and the verb "to absent". I shall therefore discuss this concept at some length.

Absences

Given Roy's claim that we use causal as well as perceptual criteria for existence – e.g. that we don't doubt that magnetic fields exist, though we can't see them, since they have effects – it should not surprise us that absences can be real: the absence of vitamin C in a person's diet causes scurvy. It should be noted in passing, though, that this presupposes that vitamin C is part of our necessary diet. Otherwise the graffito "reality is an illusion caused by lack of alcohol" would not be a joke.

Absences have already been theorised in modern philosophy by Sartre, and Roy takes up his example, which as he notes uses perceptual criteria for absence: Pierre's absence from the café, in the first chapter of *Being and Nothingness*. But for Sartre, there are only absences because there are people ("for-itselfs"). It is because Sartre is expecting to meet Pierre there that the café reveals itself as the ground organised around the figure "Pierre's absence". This is not the case with the judgement "Wellington is not in this café" which he may make to amuse himself (*Being and Nothingness* p. 10). Yet the two facts are equally objective, that Pierre is, say, sleeping off a hangover in another part of Paris, and that Wellington has been safely entombed in Westminster Abbey since 1852. These can be described without reference to absences. Hence, according to Sartre, without us the world is a "plenitude of being", and if we project negative concepts into it we are being anthropomorphic. We say that a storm destroys a building because we use buildings and not rubble, but the rubble has just as much being as the building.

Roy is defending the non-anthropocentricity of absences. Obviously it isn't enough to say that after all Pierre *really isn't* there, because neither is Wellington, and so on. The notion of absence, so generalised, would be trivialised. There is another argument that Roy does use, which I don't think works either: that there must be empty space between material particles, otherwise motion would be impossible. In the first place, this strikes me as *a priori* science: the idea of the ubiquity of matter, as taught by Descartes and Spinoza, is doubtless *false*, but only empirical science can show that it is. And secondly because Sartre would reply: empty space is not nothing, it is the real gap between material particles, and hence part of the plenitude of the in-itself.

Nevertheless I think that Roy is right and Sartre wrong. To avoid artifacts, let us take the example of a tree destroyed by a bush fire. Granted that there remain ash, smoke and so on, the tree as a structured organic entity has been destroyed. If we accept the reality of emergent strata of nature (as I think we must on the grounds of Roy's arguments in earlier books), we must accept the reality of destruction, independently of us. Likewise with the effects of drought (absence of rain) on soil and plant life and so on. This notion of real absentings links up with two important, and I think true, doctrines of medieval philosophy which Roy also retrieves: (1) that logical negation and real negation are distinct: one can assert the reality of an absence; absence is not a mere projection of the negative form of judgement; and (2) "*ills* . . . can always be seen as *absences*" (p. 238). I take it that (2) refers to real absences, for of course *anything* can be seen as an absence if this is just a shadow of negative judgement – e.g. sight can be seen as the absence of blindness and so on. But Augustine, Aquinas and co. wanted to insist that there was a sense in which blindness is (asymmetrically) the absence of sight, and that something similar can be said of all ills. This opens up the possibility of a value-realism which is based in the nature of being: just the sort of realism that we need in order to theorise environmental ethics.

Because of the importance which I attach to this idea of real absences, I am a little worried about the way that absences and absentings proliferate in Roy's book. I am worried that the concept might be trivialised, and its use in axiology undermined. There are two sources of this worry: (a) every action (indeed every causing) comes to be seen as an absenting – baking a potato absents a raw potato, eating it absents hunger, and so on. But of course baking the potato makes present a baked potato, eating it makes present a full stomach. The real distinction between absenting and making present, and hence between absence and presence, is replaced by a formal one, with no axiological potential.

(b) My second worry is that Roy over-reacts to ontological monovalence by giving non-being priority over being. There might (logically) not have been anything – true enough, so far as logical possibility goes: "complete positivity is impossible, but sheer indeterminate negativity is not". I am not convinced that complete positivity is *logically* impossible. Nothing (excuse the pun) hangs on this. But there does seem to be some non-scientific cosmology in the offing: "if there was a *unique* beginning to everything it could only be from nothing by an act of radical autogenesis" (p. 46). Whatever the arguments for and against the Big Bang and/or creation by God, both seem more intelligible than such autogenesis of being from nothing – and Roy presents no arguments against either. I take it he actually rejects autogenesis too, and favours a pluralistic account of the origin of the universe as we know it. But Roy has in the past (whatever some critics have said to the contrary) always been careful to avoid legislating in advance for the sciences, and there is no reason to backpedal on this now.

When we come to particular negativities, absences or "de-onts" as Roy calls them (rather confusingly, since the prefix "de" signifies, not negativity, but removal of what was previously present, and that is not intended here), they surely can only be individuated by reference to "onts", positive beings. A hole needs a rim and sides, and these must be "onts"; an ont must indeed be limited, but this may be by other onts. Or consider the difference between various silences: the embarrassed silence after an unintelligible paper, the angry silence after a lovers' quarrel, John Cage's musical composition *4 Minutes and 33 Seconds of Silence*, a Quaker Meeting, the reticence of a resolute Heideggerian hero. They are immensely different in their effects, but their different *structures* can only lie in the different ways they are framed by onts. All this suggests to me that while de-onts exist, some of the ways in which they depend on onts are one-way dependencies. I stress that these criticisms are all aimed against overstretching and so weakening the theory of absences, by way of "bending the stick", and not against the claim that absences have real effects, and so are themselves real, or that they exist in the natural as well as the human world.

The underlying reality or "alethic truth" of dialectic is for Roy the "absenting of constraints on the absenting of absences"; this is more straightforward than it sounds. If someone hasn't got a job, that is an absence; getting one would be absenting the absence; government policy may be a constraint (i.e. an imposed constraint) on that absenting; getting a different government might absent that constraint. Despite its technical vocabulary and dense foliage, this book is political through and through, and I think the most profitable way to read it, for anyone with the leisure to do this, would be to go through working out political examples for all the abstractly specified bits of dialectic of which it is such a storehouse.

Moral realism

Now I come to the explicitly moral and political parts of the book. Roy's aim is to present a naturalistic version of moral realism: he has already shown in his accounts of explanatory critiques how values can be derived from facts; his account in relation to science of the (possible) rationality of judgements within the relativity of our knowledge at any given time, which in turn exists within an objectively real world, provides a model for an account of the objective reality of values while recognising the relativity of any particular moral code. An immense amount of work needs to be done to fill out this promising sketch for moral realism. The clue that Roy provides us itself requires a lot of analysis of examples and rebuttal of possible objections before we have a realist ethics. This clue is surprisingly Kantian, though it also has resonances of the ancient and medieval idea that since all action explicitly aims at some good, it must implicitly aim at the Good itself. Sartre's idea that free action should take freedom as its goal, and Habermas's idea of an ideal community implicit in communication, are also echoed. The Kantian aspect is the principle of universalisability, defended through the notion that the non-universalising agent is involved in a theory/practice contradiction or heterologicality – e.g. the parent who tells a child "if you tell lies your nose will grow long like Pinocchio's". This is supplemented by the idea that since every action aims at absenting some constraint, the agent is committed by universalisability to freedom in general. Hence "as logic is totalizing, and every absence can be seen as a constraint, this goal of human autonomy can be regarded as implicit in an infant's primal scream" (p. 264). One might be facetious and ask why the maxim extracted from the scream by universalisation should not be "everything in the universe should make as much noise as possible". More seriously it might be asked whether freedom in general can be affirmed – whether it is not the case that one freedom is always incompatible with some other: not just with someone else's freedom, but with other possible freedoms of the same agent; to be free in one respect is always to be constrained in another. I do not mean to say that Roy's moral realism should be rejected – it is an attractive proposal and I would like to see it developed. But it is limited by its formality, and needs to be supplemented by a "*materiale Wertethik*", in Scheler's phrase: a substantive theory of objective worth.

Politics, power and the social cube

Finally to the explicit politics of *Dialectic*. Roy distinguishes power, "the transformative capacity intrinsic in the concept of action as such" (p. 402), i.e. *pouvoir*, to be able; and power$_2$, "the capacity to get one's way against either the overt wishes and/or the real interests of others in virtue of structures of exploitation, domination, subjugation and control, i.e. generalized master-slave type relations." (p. 402). This is a useful distinction, given the liberal and Nietzschean tendency to subsume the first kind under the second, transforming slogans like "knowledge is power" from a commendation to a condemnation of knowledge. And in terms of it, the aim of Roy's libertarian socialist politics can be summed up as "the abolition of power$_2$".

But there is a real danger here of backtracking on all we should have learnt from Marx. Roy accuses Marx of remaining "fixated on the wage-labour/capital relation at the expense of the totality of master-slave relations (most obviously those of nationality, ethnicity, gender, religious affiliation, sexual orientation, age, health and bodily disabilities generally)" (p. 333). But if it is just a question of denouncing oppression, we don't need Marx – Abiezer Coppe did it far more trenchantly back in 1649. What Marx gave us was an explanatory theory of the mechanisms generating oppression, according to which the wage-labour/capital relation explains some of the others.

Another way of putting this would be in terms of Roy's valuable notion of the "social cube", according to which social being is four-planar, the four planes being

> "[a] = plane of material transactions with nature
> [b] = plane of inter-/intra-subjective [personal] relations
> [c] = plane of social relations
> [d] = plane of subjectivity of the agent"
>
> (p. 160).

Now most people on the left would argue that personal oppression is structurally rooted, i.e. power$_2$ at [b] is rooted in/explained by structures at [c]. Central to Marx is the further claim that [c] is rooted in/explained by [a]. These points could be expressed in the concepts of Roy's *Dialectic* as: *the explanatory structure (or even alethic truth) of power$_2$ is inequality of power$_1$ at plane* [*a*]. If this explanatory hypothesis is false, it may be criticised at the level of substantive social science. But I hope it will not simply be lost behind talk of generalised master-slave relations.

These comments are all intended in a constructive spirit. After all, *Dialectic* is the most systematic work so far by the best philosopher of our generation. It merits long and careful thought, and development in relation to concrete examples.

Finally, I would like to repeat in public one plea to Roy: to give us his marvellous ideas in shorter and less self-embedded sentences, using words not symbols, and where possible words with Anglo-Saxon rather than Greek or Latin roots; and with that I wish Roy the absence of $constraints_2$ on concretely singularized merriment this Christmas, and a eudaimonistic New Year.

26

REALISM AND FORMALISM IN ETHICS

Andrew Collier

Critical realism has implications for ethics as well as for ontology. I shall start by listing four ways in which Roy Bhaskar's work lays the foundations for a realist ethics – foundations on which I hope to build in a forthcoming book. The kind of ethics involved can be called a naturalistic theory of values as existing independently of our value judgements. But there is also another strand in Bhaskar's writing on ethics of which I am more critical, and the rest of this paper will be devoted to its criticism.

First, then, to the four points which I accept as foundations for a realist ethics:

1 The position defended by Bhaskar is a version of naturalism: values are inherent in facts about the world. Roy Bhaskar has done more than any other recent philosopher to rehabilitate naturalism after several generations of philosophers (with a few dissenting voices) have taught us to treat it as "the naturalistic fallacy". Moreover his refutation of the "naturalistic fallacy" fallacy i.e. his vindication of naturalism is based on explanatory critique, which is a form of argument central to the case which needs to be made for a realist ethics.
2 Bhaskar's non-anthropocentric ontology makes a non-anthropocentric value theory a live option (for if being were relative to us, morality could hardly fail to be so), and suggests it by way of homology, though it does not entail it.
3 The account of scientific change as making sense only on the assumption of a reality independent of us, of which scientific discovery deepens our knowledge, suggests that an analogous argument could be propounded about moral change. Bhaskar explicitly commits himself to this possibility: "morality, like knowledge, has an intransitive object" (*Plato Etcetera*, p. 151) – i.e. there is something that moral discourse is about, which exists independently of us and can be discovered by us.

4 Finally, Roy Bhaskar's idea (which runs through his *Dialectic*) that all ills can be seen as absences, echoes the Augustinian principle that being as being is good and evil is a negation or privation of being. It is this that I shall develop elsewhere as the core of a realist theory of values.

But in *Dialectic* and *Plato Etcetera* Roy Bhaskar propounds another account of morality, which has several features of Kant's, including some of its drawbacks.

His claims are (1) (after Habermas) that every speech act appeals for trust from the other, and implicit in this is an ideal of human solidarity; and (2) (after Kant) that every action, even every desire, implies a claim for freedom from constraint, and hence (by universalisability) commits one to an ideal of universal freedom. Thus "the goal of universal human flourishing is implicit in every practical deed and every fiduciary remark" (*Plato Etcetera* 148), and one must "speak (or just act) and be committed to the project of universal human emancipation, or be committed to Cratylan silence" (p. 153) – and presumably to inaction.

I shall first look at the straightforwardly Kantian side of this, and argue that it shares Kant's formalism. Bhaskar may not wish to deny this – he calls it a formal criterion for the good (*Plato Etcetera* p. 147), leaving substantive criteria to be derived from explanatory critiques – but I think he wants to get much more out of the formal principle than it will sustain. I shall look at two means by which he tries to fortify the Kantian principle, namely his statement (which I endorse, so far as it goes) that "the principle of sufficient practical reason states there must be grounds for differences" (*Plato Etcetera* p. 148) and the notion of performative contradiction (alias heterologicality alias theory/practice inconsistency).

Second, I shall look at the claim that *freedom* or *emancipation* is implicit in human action. And third, I shall ask whether the goal of universal emancipation in the sense used here is a possible one.

Roy Bhaskar's claim is that we are logically bound to universalise the mutuality implicit in our speech acts and the will to freedom implicit in our acts generally. (Given the brevity of Roy Bhaskar's use of the former argument, I hope my brief reply will be excused. If I were replying to Habermas, a fuller account would be necessary). Initially it might seem as if the speech act claim does not require the additional principle of universalisability since mutuality is already implicit in the speech act. But it is easy to see that this is not so. If one fascist thug says to another, "there are some blacks, let's go and beat them up", the mutuality is present, but extends only to fellow fascist thugs. Much of the mutuality of ordinary conversation is of this kind, if less brutal. What is shared in it is solidarity against "them", contempt for "their" idiocies and foibles. Among people who abstain from this sort of gossip, polite conversation is quite difficult to make at all (I have noticed this among Quakers). So the universalisation principle is required to transform limited solidarity into universal solidarity. However not all speech implies solidarity even against "them". Whole language games are devoted to putting people down, to their face as well as behind their back, and some people use language for little else. Do statements like "I hate you!" or "you're dead!" imply mutuality? Only to the extent that they use a common understanding of the meaning of words. They are acts of hostility in a common medium, just as acts of physical violence take place in the common medium of our materiality. You cannot (verbally) insult a person without a shared language anymore than one can beat up a ghost, in the lack of a shared materiality. But there is no more to it than that. So the argument from speech like the argument from action presupposes the introduction of a universalisability principle.

The problem with the universalisability principle has long been recognised: its formality. It leaves unanswered the question: which features of the action should be universalised, or: under what description should the act be universalised. The act of shooting the Archduke at Sarajevo in 1914 can be described as an act of pulling a trigger (neutral), killing a man (wrong), tyrannicide (right), starting a war (wrong), initiating the emancipation of European nations from imperial domination (right) and so on. Many harmless actions can quite naturally be described in forms in which they are non-universalisable, e.g. catching the 8:17 bus from Shirley to Southampton University. Everybody could not do that – it only takes 76 seated and 8 standing. Of course Kant wanted to universalise not acts under any description, but the maxims of acts. So in this case it might be "in order to get to work when it's raining, use the most convenient form of public transport", which is perfectly universalisable. But rationalisation being what it is, people tend to provide maxims for their actions which are universalisable, out of the many that they might choose. Then all sorts of objectionable actions pass the test. E.g. if a man murders his father who is about to disinherit him he may do it on the maxim "take the necessary steps to secure your rightful inheritance". In order to make the universalisability principle look plausible, one has to presuppose that the description under which the act will be universalised is the relevant one. But the universalisability principle cannot itself provide criteria of relevance. In the absence of them, it is viciously formal. And this question of the right description of the act is a serious one. Consider the war crimes that have rationalised themselves as "defoliation" or "population adjustment". Suppose someone says that the right description of the act is the fullest one. In choosing between a set of descriptions, this may be a good principle, but of course one cannot prescribe infinite filling out of the description, and any description can always be made fuller in many ways, many of which are irrelevant to the morality of the act. The description needs to be full *enough*; when is it full enough? The universalisability principle can never tell you; only a substantive theory about what has worth can tell you. Incidentally, this point about different descriptions shows up the inadequacy of the distinction between consequentialism and intrinsicalism as views about the morality of actions. Every definition of an action includes some consequences – the only question is: how many?

The principle of sufficient practical reason as formulated by Bhaskar looks less formal, but it actually still needs the same supplementation before it can yield any moral results. If A is treated worse than B because she is a woman and B is a man, we still need the premiss "differences in sex are irrelevant to the matter in question" before it will follow that the different treatment is unjust. This is not to say that this principle of sufficient practical reason is useless: it does put the onus on the defender of inequality to show relevant differences. But it does not by itself rule out the possibility that they might succeed in doing so in a way that meets the formal requirements even in cases where the resultant inequality is unacceptable. The question of which generalisation to make is as necessary in ethics as in science or in politics: still water or a standing stone equally exemplify Galilean and pre-Galilean inertia; a worker exploited by a Jewish capitalist may generalise to "all Jews are exploiters" or to "all capitalists are exploiters", and it is terribly important politically that they do the latter, and reject the former generalisation. Bhaskar has said in his *Dialectic* that universal human emancipation is implicit in a child's primal scream, but who knows whether the child would universalise to "all should be free" or "all should yell"?

Kant thought that an immoral act committed its agent to some sort of contradiction. Bhaskar has something to say about what sort this might be, i.e. a performative contradiction. An example would be a parent telling a child lies about what will happen to them if they tell lies – "your tongue will drop out", or whatever. The action contradicts what it recommends. But there are two problems with Bhaskar's use of this notion. First, he ties it in with "prefigurative politics" in a way that suggests that many right actions would be examples of performative contradictions. Thus he says that the struggle for a good society should be "subject to the side constraint that it be prefigurationally achieved". I wonder whether Roy Bhaskar would find a performative contradiction in smacking a child for hitting another child or imprisoning a man for kidnapping, or expropriating the expropriators (liberals, of course, might object to all these things, but then what is a liberal but one who believes in the inalienable right of the fairly powerful to rob and bully the less powerful without interference from the more powerful); or what about Engels living and supporting Marx on the proceeds of exploitation so that they could work for an end to exploitation, or revolutionaries in a civil war (or indeed the allies in World War II) killing people so as to bring about a society in which life is respected. I see no inconsistency in these things any more than in a surgical operation, where the means – cutting someone open – does not prefigure the cure in any way, but does cause it. This is not a plea for "the end justifying the means" if that is read as saying that some ends will justify any means whatsoever. It is a plea for evaluating the means along with the end and considering the various means–end packages with a view to getting enough information about the good and evils involved to decide between them.

The other problem is that most immoral actions involve no performative contradiction at all. A burglar may hope that he won't be burgled, but unless he indulges in moral indignation against someone who burgles his house, his theory is not inconsistent with his practice. It may be said that Roy Bhaskar's point refers to human emancipation rather than to morality as such, but I think he is talking in such general terms that emancipation is meant to include all goods. "In seeking to satisfy my desire, I am logically committed to the satisfaction of all dialectically similar desires" (*Plato Etcetera* p. 141). What sort of commitment is this? "I want my desires satisfied" certainly does not logically entail "I want your desires satisfied". If I am a nasty piece of work, my desire may be precisely that your desires remain unsatisfied. Even if I am averagely endowed with egoism, I am likely to have some desires that contingently conflict with someone else's. And there is no hypocrisy involved in seeking to satisfy my desires at the cost of yours. A person who seeks special privileges for themselves at the expense of other people is guilty of selfishness, not of hypocrisy.

My accusation of formalism might be parried by Bhaskar by saying that I am taking his universalism to be abstract universalism like Kant's, whereas what he had in mind was a Hegelian concrete universal. I would reply that for this concept to apply, there would have to be some more or less universal reality mediating the particular desire and the universal project of emancipation. What I mean can be illustrated by reference to an example from Mill and one from Sartre. When Mill says that since everyone desires their own happiness the happiness of all is an end for all, he is guilty of the fallacy of composition. But if "all" referred not merely to the sum of people but to a really constituted collective, there would be no fallacy.

The difference between the sort of context in which universalisability applies and the sort in which it does not is also well illustrated by Sartre's two examples, both of which he thinks generate universalisability, one plausibly and the other most implausibly.

> If I am a worker, for instance, I may choose to join a Christian rather than a Communist trade union. And if, by that membership, I choose to signify that resignation is, after all, the attitude that best becomes a man, that man's kingdom is not upon this earth, I do not commit myself alone to that view. Resignation is my will for everyone, and my action is, in consequence, a commitment on behalf of all mankind. Or if, to take a more personal case, I decide to marry and to have children, even though this decision proceeds simply from my situation, from my passion or my desire, I am thereby committing not only myself, but humanity as a whole, to the practice of

> monogamy. I am thus responsible for myself and for all men, and I am creating a certain image of man as I would have him to be.
> (*Existentialism and Humanism*, pp. 29–30).

In the first case, leaving aside Sartre's dubious reconstruction of the Christian trade unionist's motives, universalisability clearly does apply: a Christian believes that God's will is valid for all humankind, and so wants others to obey the same will; a Communist wants the Communist political project to succeed, and so must want others to commit themselves to the same project. But in the second case, where there is no mediating term between the individual choice and the choice for all, the choice is in no way for all. In choosing marriage for oneself one does not, unless one is a bigot or an egotist, enjoin marriage upon a homosexual or a monk. This illustrates that the universalisability of the first case is not implicit in the nature of action, but in the nature of the case in question.

This is not to say that there is no place for universalisation in morals, but in each case it must be grounded in the nature of the case – in being, not in logic. This becomes even clearer if we ask what the scope of universalisation is. For Kant, universalisation founds duties to rational beings, but we have duties to non-rational beings too. And those duties are necessarily different from duties to rational beings. Even if I talk to the trees, as the song says, it is presumably not immoral to lie to them. All duties are universal, but some are more universal than others.

Now to the claim that freedom or emancipation is implicit in action as such, or indeed in desire as such. The move seems to be: to desire or will something is to desire or will that that desire or will be successful or unimpeded. At this point the principle of universalisability takes over, and we are said to be committed to a general unimpededness of human desiring and willing.

But in the first place, it is not at all clear that to will to x is necessarily also to have a second order will to be unimpeded in xing. One may even have a second order will to be impeded in xing, either because one does not at some level approve of one's desire to x, or because one has a Nietzschean love of encountering obstacles that are hard to overcome. There are different cases in which one wishes to x and in which one wishes to be free to x. I wish to be free to emigrate, but I don't wish to emigrate. The Pilgrim Fathers wished to be free to worship in a Puritan manner because they valued Puritan worship, but not because they valued freedom, as is shown by their persecution of other forms of worship in New England. This persecution was intolerant, but not hypocritical: they had never said that freedom to worship was valuable in itself. A public-spirited motorist may want to park on a double yellow line, but not want to be free to park on that spot. The devotee of sexual bondage may want precisely that their desires be satisfied unfreely. In short there are no logical links between wanting to do something and valuing the freedom to do that thing. There are often very intelligible causal links, but that is another matter.

So far I have argued that neither freedom nor universality are necessarily willed in any case of willing or desiring. I now want to argue that the goal of universal freedom in all respects is inherently unrealisable. The easiest part of this is arguing that some people's freedom is incompatible with others' – that freedom for the pikes is death to the minnows and vice versa. This is also the easiest point to reply to: it can be said that human emancipation does not mean total freedom for everyone, but rather *the same* freedom for everyone, and hence no freedom to invade the liberties of others. However to slogan "the same freedom for everyone" reproduces at the political level the formality of the universalisability principle: there are many different contents to this Kantian "just society". The freedom of all to sell their (unequal) wares would be one; free access of all to the necessities of life would be another, incompatible with it. We have to decide not just *whose* freedom but *which* freedoms. Different freedoms are available in our society of "mobile privatisation" from those available in a society with public space and public transport; the freedoms of the market society are not those of the society of self-managing communities. We have to choose our freedoms and therewith our concomitant unfreedoms. That is surely one of the implications of Roy Bhaskar's admirably realistic characterisation of emancipation as replacing unwanted constraints by wanted and needed ones. If I want to go for country walks, and if I further want to be free to do so, then I want landowners and forest managers to be constrained not to fence off the footpaths across their land. If I want to be free to live in an unpolluted city, I want motorists to be constrained not to use their cars so much, and so on. And of course the same person may want these constraints and be constrained by them.

So the slogan, popular in Eastern Europe at the time of the anti-Communist revolutions there, that "freedom is indivisible", cannot be accepted. So far from being indivisible, freedom is inherently divided. Lenin says somewhere that freedom is a very valuable commodity that needs to be rationed very carefully. For freedom is $power_1$ in Bhaskar's terms – *pouvoir*, being able; and $power_2$ (domination) is based on inequalities in $power_1$. Human emancipation consists in the prioritisation and rationing of freedoms, not their indiscriminate affirmation.

I conclude then that a human desire or action does not in every case imply a commitment to freedom; that commitment to one's own freedom does not by itself commit one to universal emancipation; and that if universal emancipation means the freedom of all in all ways, it is not a coherent goal. The transition from individual desire to universal emancipation breaks down at three points. To determine which freedoms are desirable, we must turn not to formal considerations, but to considerations of what has intrinsic worth.

27

THE LIMITS OF JUSTICE

Finding fault in the criminal law

Alan Norrie

Introduction: challenging the 'penal equation'

Crime is a serious social problem to which society does not have a serious answer. Loud voices say that if our stock responses fail, we need more of the same. It should be easier to detect and convict criminals, punishments should be harsher. The resulting calls for 'law and order,' with emphasis on the latter, endorse what we may call the 'penal equation.' This is the simple formula, 'crime plus responsibility equals punishment,' that has informed our social control practices for two hundred years. The rationale for this equation is that crime requires punishment as retribution and deterrence, and criminal justice qualifies individuals as deserving of the state's legitimate sanctions. It is this sense of justice, responsibility and desert, justifying social control through criminal punishment, that is the focus of this paper.

Criminal justice fixes a badge of responsibility to the individual's lapel, and thereby justifies retribution and deterrence. Yet retribution appears to evoke backward-looking ideas of revenge, while deterrence, *pace* the present Home Secretary, hardly seems to work.[1] Over the past hundred years, reformers have sought to move the system from these tired rationales. Recently, calls for reparation, reconciliation and mediation, as well as for increased use of diversion, non-custodial penalties and forms of intermediate treatment indicate the need, perceived by professionals throughout the system, for changes which can break the iron grip of the 'penal equation.' Legal justice is contrasted with reintegrative approaches,[2] with what can broadly be termed 'relational justice.'[3] Yet, as Sir Louis Blom Cooper has noted, such developments remain peripheral and for that reason sustain the mainstream. Mitigating its worst features, they 'positively acknowledge the centrality of the courts and prisons as the instrument to be deployed.'[4]

So what is to be done in terms of challenging this equation? Is it possible

Source: Modern Law Review, 59, 1996, pp. 540–56.

to move beyond it? Were we to do so, would there be loss as well as gain? It is easier to acknowledge the problems associated with the penal equation than to solve them. As Michel Foucault noted,[5] the history of penal reform is as old as the penal system and we should be aware of the pitfalls of grand designs. Blom Cooper calls for a new 'theoretical underpinning' and a new, radical alternative to the criminal justice system, but he does not actually provide one.[6] While sympathetic to the call for a new theoretical approach, my argument will be that a *direct linkage* between theory and reform may be problematic. That is not, however, to argue that theory does not illuminate the problems of the criminal justice system, or that practice is not enhanced by it. What is needed, I shall argue, is a theoretical approach that can encapsulate an *ambivalence* in our assessment of the legal conception of justice, one that can explain its weaknesses, but also its strengths. It is important neither to reject totally nor to accept uncritically the conception of justice established within and by criminal law, and this necessitates a theoretical position which can take us beyond those approaches which make rejection or uncritical acceptance the two alternative choices available to us.

The approach will be to find a theoretical route beyond criminal law and justice, but to go 'beyond the law' by going 'through' it. So doing, we achieve a more complex and sophisticated picture of what is at stake in the 'penal equation.' It is one thing, as criminological thought from Italian positivism,[7] to Barbara Wootton,[8] and now Blom Cooper has done, to dismiss legal ideas of retribution and deterrence as outdated, inefficient and unenlightened. It is another to engage with law to show *through that engagement* the limits, but also the strengths, of legal forms as forms of justice. It is important to stress the double-sided character of law. A strict legal approach contributes to the failure of criminal justice to reflect society's moral (retribution) and practical (deterrence) needs, but we must also recognise the positive side of law. In particular, we should recognise the strong liberal, and in its own terms progressive, current of thinking which extols the virtues of law and, to some extent, punishment. This approach to criminal justice was most influentially expressed by H.L.A. Hart in the 1950s and 1960s.[9] It underpins the work of criminal law writers like Glanville Williams, Smith and Hogan,[10] and Andrew Ashworth.[11] It insists that it is a moral strength of the criminal justice system that it is law based. This is true at the procedural level, at which civil liberties issues are contested,[12] but also in the substantive law as concerns responsibility and punishment. Liberal theory argues that we ought to punish only those who act freely, either in terms of their capacity or control over their actions. Law respects autonomy and personhood, and this is a value in itself.

The ambivalence evoked by these ideas stems from the ease with which one can criticise them. What does it mean to be a free or autonomous criminal given that processed crime is clearly linked statistically (and always has been) with particular socio-economic backgrounds? Here we encounter the flaw in 'justice model' thinking: the problem of how to achieve 'just deserts in an unjust society.'[13] Still, we should not discard lightly the libertarian dimension to liberal thought. This is apparent if we reflect on the practical resonance that responsibility and freedom have in modern society. Consider the complaints of prisoners undergoing discretionary, indefinite sentences about the special additional punishment and the injustice of not knowing when they may be released: a point recently illustrated in Lord Donaldson's comments on the case of Myra Hindley.[14] Consider too the ways the law's categories of responsibility seemingly reflect the moral feelings of many who come before it. For example, in the case of homicide by a battered wife, it is important to many that the accused achieve what they see as the more just, while arguably still inadequate, verdict of voluntary manslaughter through provocation. The alternative of diminished responsibility, in pathologising the woman, does not reflect the moral truth of the accused's position and is therefore experienced as unjust.[15]

We should recognise a paradox: that the 'penal equation' in some ways reflects serious moral distinctions, but at the same time provides a weak basis for a morally sound, or effective, system of social control. We may agree with Stan Cohen, who some years ago described the legal concepts of guilt and justice as old concepts needed by a new criminology, but we need to reflect both on the resonance of such an argument and the Janus-like character of law to which it gives rise. The legal approach, Cohen also wrote, makes us 'forget that by the time many offenders get to this wonderful justice system the damage has already been done.' It is obvious, he says, 'to anyone who has spent five minutes in a court or prison that it would be blatantly unjust to return' to an undiluted legal approach.[16] From one side, the 'penal equation' is part of the problem, from another part of the solution. The picture is ambiguous. Any adequate theoretical underpinning, even more so practical reforms, must acknowledge our ambivalence about criminal justice.

In the following section, I seek to locate this ambivalence and ambiguity by considering the theoretical perspectives within which legal justice is currently understood. Moving from the liberal approach, which essentially endorses the legal conception of justice, to the deconstructive approach, which essentially rejects it (while still seemingly wishing to hold on to it), I begin to outline a critical realist approach which would seek a standpoint beyond a more simple endorsement or rejection. Thereafter, I seek to show the inadequacy of the legal conception of justice with regard to a central concept of criminal responsibility (recklessness) and to explain this inadequacy in critical realist terms. Then, in a third section, I seek to develop the argument by contrasting a legal conception of responsibility with a conception based upon realist psychology. From these arguments, I then conclude in relation to the limited but significant overlap between a legal conception of justice and one derived from a critical realist standpoint. It is this overlap that leads to the ambivalence and ambiguity surrounding legal justice.

Theoretical questions about justice

Liberalism and justice

If we are going to confront criminal law and justice, we need first to consider the traditions within which they are understood. Our starting point has to be liberalism, for the theory of punishment and criminal justice is founded on it. Since I have already discussed this (above p. 541, and see below, p. 546), I will deal with it briefly here. While generalisations always do violence, there is an identifiable core to liberalism which involves its conception of the individual as an abstract, universal, subject endowed with rational action, autonomy and self-determination.[17] The individual is a unified, centred being who acts as the basis for legitimating the state, law and punishment. He gives consent to the state[18] or recognises its rational necessity.[19] He participates in its law as a rational legal subject. Punishment unifies political legitimacy and legal sanction. The rational subject receives 'just deserts' from the state through law. The 'penal equation' — crime plus responsibility equals punishment — is founded on liberal bedrock.

Poststructuralism and justice

This liberal subject has been subjected to sustained critique from a variety of perspectives. The poststructuralist approach, influential in recent years, stresses instability and disunity within the individual subject. It points to what is excluded by the construction of the liberal individual and it affirms the moral value of difference over universality.[20] To the rational will of liberalism, it opposes human needs and sentiments associated with 'the body.' To abstract reason, it opposes embodied being and particularity. It emphasises singularity, an ethics of the contingent, over generality. Most importantly, it calls into question the idea of the individual as a unified, centred being, insisting on the fragmented character of subjectivity. I am not one but several persons and my central identity is a construction denying the difference within me. In order to be a unified subject, I must repress this otherness.[21]

This critique has important consequences in terms of showing how a theory of liberal law, which purports to include, excludes. A theory of what all individuals have in common, liberalism excludes difference: of gender, race, class and community. It does so in favour of a single, only apparently neutral, standard that is in fact gendered (male), classed and aged (middle), and raced (white). But there is, I would suggest, a danger of overkill. Liberalism as a locus of exclusion may be a fair argument, but does it lead one to exclude in turn the positive political and legal effects of liberalism? A system based on individual rights, on reason and universality surely has some advantages. If the desired answer is 'no,' as seems to be the case among poststructuralists who, for example, want to argue for rights, then the question that must be faced is, why not? On grounds simply of 'strategy,' which appears a weak basis, or on solid theoretical grounds which concern the interplay between legal, personal and social identity, however these may be conceived in post-structuralist terms? Notwithstanding attempts to come to terms with this question, there seems to be an unresolved theoretical and methodological issue for poststructuralism. In seeking a critical standpoint in what lies 'beyond,' poststructuralism ultimately has a problem in coming to terms with the forms of the social world as they are. Either it insists on the deconstruction of existing forms of subjectivity and reason (including those of the law), and therefore that the criteria for progressive political and moral change exist beyond 'what is,' in a *necessarily* inchoate 'other;' or it illicitly returns to what exists, for example, legal rights, seeing this as strategically necessary for moral and political practice in the meantime. The latter approach is illegitimate in terms of the method of deconstruction, but cries out to be implemented in the face of real, pressing injustice.[22]

These sceptical comments notwithstanding, it is important to hold on to the poststructuralist emphasis on the partiality, the exclusivity and the incompleteness of law and legal justice, and the difference that it masks, in order to probe the paradox and the ambiguity of legal justice I have described. But we need other theoretical terms with which to understand the Janus-like character of law described above.

Critical realism and justice

My approach is through the critical realist work of Roy Bhaskar and others in the philosophy of social science,[23] and Rom Harré in social psychology.[24] Bhaskar's starting point is the social and historical (constructed) character of forms of knowledge, but he holds on to the idea that social and historical processes are real and emergent.[25] Human beings live in society and history, by and through norms, forms and relations that are structured and shaped, including those of the law. Recognising that we are part of an emergent social and historical world, we can hold on to the insights of poststructuralism concerning difference and exclusion without positing an abstract ethical 'beyond.' There is no metaphysical 'other,' but there is real emergent history and developing social structure, and these generate actual difference, conflict, change, sometimes crisis. Difference, 'something new,' emerges in real time, space and history. New perspectives and critical standpoints, new ways of looking at old phenomena, including the phenomena of law and justice, are produced in this process of emerging change and difference.

A crucial aspect, which Bhaskar has recently developed, concerns the use of a dialectical approach.[26] The essence of such an approach is given in the ideas of dialectical connection and contradiction within a social totality. Dialectical connection exists:

> between entities or aspects of a totality such that they are in principle *distinct* but *inseparable*, in the sense that they are synchronically or conjuncturally *internally* related, ie both . . . or one existentially presuppose the other.[27]

Dialectical contradiction also refers to situations where elements existentially presuppose each other, but in this case they are also in conflict. Elements are in dialectical contradiction where one premise cannot be satisfied save at the expense of another to which it is internally related. In this situation, 'a system, agent or structure, S, is blocked from performing with one system, rule or principle, R, because it is performing with another, R^1.'[28] We can use this sense of dialectical connection and contradiction to locate the problems of difference, exclusion and partiality poststructuralism identifies, without being drawn onto a metaphysical plane, if we recognise that these problems are the effects of social and historical conflicts, and contradictions which penetrate and constitute the forms through which we live. If the world is contradictory, then we need to understand phenomena like law, legal justice and subjectivity in their contradictory aspects. Theory must be able to identify and explain the different, opposing and exclusionary propositions that a social and historical phenomenon generates. Thus, a theory that claims that both 'p' and 'not-p' are true may offend against a system of formal logic, but may more truly capture the different aspects of the object of investigation. What kind of theory can hold together, for example, the arguments, which are both held to be true, that law promotes and obstructs equal opportunities?[29] Holding the different and contradictory propositions concerning a phenomenon together as a way of understanding its totality involves thinking dialectically.

The approach to legal justice adopted here is not based on what lies in a metaphysical sense 'beyond,' but on the contrasts that we identify between the claims of legal justice and other moral and political claims that emerge historically within social structures. Our critical faculties exist on the same historical terrain as the social forms through which we live. Living in the here and now, thinking dialectically about the forms of justice that emerge within society, explains both our satisfactions and dissatisfactions with legal justice. Law is constituted by, and constitutes, social practices. As social beings in historical time and place, formed by a multitude of historical and contradictory experiences, we bear witness to the moral and political values in law, but also in other forms of justice that abut, complement and negate legal forms. We can compare and contrast legal justice with, for example, relational justice, so-called 'popular justice,' 'substantive justice,' as well as forms of justice in other contexts like the family or the workplace. There is also important scope for comparative and anthropological dimensions, looking at forms of justice in societies different from our own.[30] These provide the real critical standpoints from which to examine the law.

There is one further concluding point to be made concerning the significance of development and change in society. As our experience emerges in a historical period that throws up new ideas of the world, so we come to re-evaluate our old judgments. Moreover, in a world in which many of the old certainties and securities are disappearing, we revisit legal justice and what it can deliver with a different eye to that which seemed appropriate earlier. While we remain sceptical and ambivalent about legal justice, we recognise the role its forms play in recording and resisting various forms of tyranny. It is important to be able to say these things today and the same will be true, probably truer, tomorrow. The question is whether we can develop a theoretical method, adequate to our changing experience, for questions of law.

With these comments about legal justice, and the relationship between legal and other forms of justice, we can now move to a more concrete analysis of one example of justice in the criminal law.

Justice and criminal law

The liberal subject lies at the core of the 'penal equation' and therefore at the core of the criminal law. It is expressed, for example, in Ashworth's central idea of individual autonomy and choice as the basis for desert and punishment. From these premises is born the dominant subjective approach to criminal law and the 'general' 'positive fault requirements' of intention, foresight, knowledge and belief.[31] Criminal responsibility should be based upon a concept of guilt, which means on actual mental states, hence the term 'subjective.' Yet even a defender of the liberal model must recognise its limitations. Ashworth comments 'how individualistic, even atomistic, are the assumptions implicit in the liberal theory which underlies the subjective principles.'[32] Liberal theories of subjective right and justice need to be supplemented by premises of a more social or communitarian kind, and this would be true, for example, in the law of recklessness. Yet the development of these additional premises is not synthesised with the existing subjectivist categories. Rather, they are grafted on, producing an area of law in which there is substantial incoherence.

A problem in the law of recklessness

In the law of recklessness there are two competing and conflicting approaches, based upon actual foresight (the subjective approach) or foreseeability (the objective approach) of a criminal risk. The distinction may be explained by thinking of someone lighting a fire in a haystack to keep warm at night.[33] If the haystack is burned down, there may be a charge of criminal damage, but responsibility could be based on whether the person actually foresaw the risk of burning the haystack (the subjective approach), or whether it would have been foreseeable to a reasonable onlooker (the objective approach), even if the person involved did not foresee it. The subjective approach says that there must be foresight in fairness to the accused; the objective approach that people ought to come up to a general standard of behaviour in fairness to the rest of society.

The objectivist case of *Caldwell*[34] prompted apoplexy in criminal law scholars.[35] What was regarded as an established bastion of 'subjectivism,' the law of criminal damage, had been hijacked by the judiciary. The old *Cunningham* requirement of actual foresight of a risk was supplemented by a new test of foreseeability to a reasonable person (see the later case of *Elliott* v *C (a minor)*[36]). Pouring scorn on subjectivism, Lord Diplock proposed in *Caldwell* a double test including subjective and objective variants. An accused was reckless if:

> (1) he does an act which in fact creates an obvious risk that property will be destroyed, and (2) when he does the act he either has not given any thought to the possibility of there being any such risk or has recognised that there was some risk involved and has none the less gone on to do it.[37]

What evoked the criticisms? At one level it was the practical inconsistencies of the law. Smith and Hogan gave the example of the unthinking D who points an air rifle at V and pulls the trigger. The pellet breaks V's glasses and destroys his eye. D is responsible for the broken glasses because a foreseeability test works in criminal damage cases, but not for the destruction of the eye because a foresight test operates for offences against the person. If the person dies in a year and a day, however, D will be guilty of manslaughter, where again an objective foreseeability test operates. Because of inconsistency, Smith and Hogan castigate the law as 'indefensible.'[38]

The nature of the problem

Williams takes a more theoretical approach revealing the underlying definitional problems.[39] His argument is that the two parts of the Diplock formulation are inherently contradictory. On a subjective test, all that would be required is foresight of *some* risk, while part (1) of the test purports to state that the risk must be 'obvious'. Furthermore, the jumbling of approaches means that the person who foresees a risk, but then rules it out in his own mind, falls foul of neither the subjective nor the objective criteria. This is the so-called *Shimmen* loophole.[40] A would-be karate expert boasted of his ability to aim a kick a fraction of an inch away from a plate glass window. He smashed the window and was charged with criminal damage. He claimed that he had calculated and ruled out the risk, so could not be said to have given no thought to it, while having ruled out the risk in his mind meant that he could not be said to have recognised the risk and taken it.

Unfortunately, he was caught because he said that he had eliminated 'as much risk as possible,' suggesting he recognised that there was still some risk that he had foreseen and taken. He would not have been caught, however, had he slightly changed his story, and that story been believed. It was surely not the judges' intention in *Caldwell* to establish a loophole for a defendant such as Shimmen.

In short, the law of recklessness is inconsistent and contradictory. It oscillates between subjective and objective approaches. According to followers of the subjective view, the judges manipulated the law in order to make convictions easier, and in the process betrayed liberal principles of justice. Yet the underlying problem is not the 'perfidy of the judges,' but the inadequacy of the moral categories, subjectivist *and* objectivist, for judging criminal responsibility. On the one hand, as Antony Duff has argued,[41] subjectivism does not go far enough. While it is appropriate to see awareness of risk as one basis for responsibility, subjectivism cannot recognise the recklessness of he who does not foresee, but is 'practically indifferent' or callous, an attitude of what one might call 'cruel' indifference that is not tied only to matters of foresight or foreseeability. Callousness may be manifested in the *failure* to foresee the risk to which conduct gives rise, so subjectivism is too narrow. On the other hand, objectivism is too broad. While it catches the unthinkingly callous or indifferent person that subjectivism misses, it fails to separate the callous from the stupid or merely thoughtless. It also fails to recognise the special significance of subjective awareness as one form of responsibility.

Thus, the problem of inconsistency and contradiction is not the result of judges failing to make up their minds between different approaches, but of the inadequacy of each approach standing by itself. This leads to the desire to combine them, but combining them does not work either. Rather than complementing each other, they only expose their different defects, producing in the process the anomaly of *Shimmen*. They are Siamese twins of judgment, symbiotically linked, yet unable to coexist. Consistency, the hope for a rational rule of law, founders on the rocks of the raw juridical materials, the competing subjectivist and objectivist approaches to recklessness. It is not wrecked by simple judicial inconstancy. This conclusion, however, only leads to further questions. Why the contradictions? What is so fundamentally awry with the law's categories? Are the judges looking for something that they cannot find in the law, which then threatens to subvert it?

The problem's social and historical roots

There is a clue in the older subjectivist case of *Cunningham* which relied on Kenny's turn of the century definition of 'malice.' This old legal term, still used in serious offences against the person, denoted subjective awareness of a risk in so far as it concerned recklessness. Kenny argued, however, that this subjective meaning of malice had to be distinguished from an older *moral* form of recklessness. He wrote that 'in any statutory definition of a crime, "malice" must be taken not in the old vague sense of "wickedness" in general.'[42] That 'old vague sense' of wickedness had been discussed by early modern criminal lawyers in relation to the doctrine of implied malice in the law of murder. Foster described malice as 'a heart regardless of social duty and fatally bent upon mischief,' as the manifestation of a 'wicked, depraved and malignant spirit.' These full-blooded moral terms are not, it seems to me, a million miles away from Duff's callously reckless — practically indifferent — individual that the criminal law ought to recognise but does not. In pre-modern times, lawyers recognised the need for what one might call *morally substantive* accounts of criminal responsibility. By the time Kenny wrote, however, at the turn of the century, such an approach was described as 'vague.' What lay behind this change?

A crucial pivot was the work of the Victorian Criminal Law Commissioners who reduced the old moral approach to malice to a question of *wilfulness* and, therefore, to a matter of subjective knowledge. Wilfulness became the bridge between *moral substance* and *mental form*:

> It is the *wilful exposure* of life to peril that constitutes the crime . . . Where the offender does an act with manifest danger to life wilfully, *that is, with knowledge of the consequences*, he may properly be said to have the *mens mala* or heart bent upon mischief.[43]

The Criminal Law Commissioners also argued that the old morally substantive approach led to 'danger of error and uncertainty in its application.' What should be seen as a matter of fact, and therefore relatively uncontentious, became a 'matter of law' and 'involved in doubt.'[44] Translating the old morally substantive conception of recklessness into a question of subjective knowledge was a way of avoiding contention and uncertainty, but it also led to the contradictions in the modern law. Neither subjectivism nor objectivism could reflect the morally substantive aspects that are part of our social judgments of recklessness and which are caught, for example, by Duff's formulation of practical indifference. In reaching beyond subjectivism, I think the judges are, in part subconsciously, looking for legal categories to reflect moral judgments of responsibility they think the law should embody,[45] but the route is barred by the process of factualisation and demoralisation that went into the making of the modern criminal law. In *Caldwell*, they took refuge in an objectivist doctrine that mirrored the subjectivism they rejected. Neither approach, however, could reach the moral parts that only a substantive morality might reach, because both were designed to close the door upon a moral dimension of recklessness. Moral arguments that were too much at large would be too contentious and political. They would threaten the routine working of a legal code in a time, as today, of disagreement as to what constituted right and wrong in general, and moral recklessness in particular.

The apparently 'factual' mentalistic approach seemed to counter this subversion, but it barred the door to morally substantive conceptions of recklessness. It gave the law categories of judgment, but categories which were forever damned in their ability wholly to reflect underlying moral judgments.

Employing legal categories of subjective and objective recklessness to reflect social and moral judgments of responsibility and justice is always, therefore, a question of fighting with one hand tied behind one's back. Criminal law categories of fault, like recklessness, are presented in liberal theory as informed by a broader moral philosophical conception of responsibility, and they are. But they are also *doppelgänger*, pale shadows of a moral and political substance that is excluded in the interest of the positivisation of law and depoliticisation of the courtroom. The so-called vagueness of the old approach resulted because old style moral malice was left at large in the community, and was open to the conflicts and gradations of moral judgment that exist there. The foresightful, autonomous individual was linked to a moral process of judgment, because foresight *is* relevant to judgments of wrongdoing, but it was also a way of *excluding* such judgments taken more broadly, because they might disrupt the working of the law, the working of legal justice, and therefore the 'penal equation.'

Relating this to the theory of the previous section, we can understand the subjectivist/objectivist controversy in the law of recklessness dialectically. Subjectivism and objectivism both necessitate and contradict each other as forms of legal justice emergent within a particular historical context. These historical forms can be critically compared with other views on, or forms of, justice generated by modern social relations but excluded from the law.[46] There is an historical limit to legal justice which stems from its development out of an engagement with the underlying social and political contradictions present in modern English society, and which the liberal conception of subjective justice (and, equally, its objective twin) sought to exclude. In post-structuralist terms, there is an 'other' beyond subjectivism and objectivism, but it is the other of real history and emergent social perceptions, and does not pertain to a metaphysical 'beyond.'

Yet it must be remembered that a limited conception of justice is still a conception of justice, so that there is an overlap between the legal conception and broader conceptions glimpsed 'through a glass darkly' by the law and lawyers. It is this overlap that we will eventually consider once we have moved to develop further a dialectical sense of what justice and responsibility mean.

The sense of justice

We began with a dilemma concerning the 'penal equation.' On the one hand, the liberal model of justice is a source of dissatisfaction. We keep convicting and punishing so-called 'responsible individuals,' but the attempt to deter just seems to lead to the need for more deterrence and we question the value of the retributive justice the penal equation delivers. On the other hand, we recognise the practical ways in which the liberal model resonates with individual moral experience. People hold on to a system that still reflects a sense of justice and this is not a matter of simple 'false consciousness.' This ambivalence is also carried into the heart of criminal law. There, in the example of recklessness, we have a legal subject with foresight, a concept that is reflected in its mirror, the objectivist law in *Caldwell*. This legal subject/object partially expresses and reflects issues of judgment, but also misses those central aspects of justice that may be described as morally substantive.

The 'internal' and the 'external'

We are left with a view of liberal legal justice that stresses its paradoxical form. Can we hold on to these ambiguities without appearing plain contradictory? In postmodern terms, we could perhaps simply accept the dilemma, recognising that only a sense of what is strategic can tell us how to view law. The limits of discourse, the finitude of meaning, the need for a supplement, all force us to embrace the conflict. Becoming playful or pragmatic, we acknowledge the way things are 'in a postmodern world.' In critical realist terms, by contrast, we can draw upon an historical and dialectical understanding of liberal law which holds together its contradictory aspects as expressions of a particular social and historical totality. In previous work,[47] I portrayed law as sited on an edge between abstract, general attitudes of individual subjectivity (the person as rational, intentional, foresightful, voluntary) and representations of human agency as contextualised (crime as a product of socially and historically generated moral conditions). This contradictory location has its provenance in the Enlightenment representation of a world of free individuals coming together in civil society. But crime is a social problem generated in ways that can be statistically correlated. It can be located differentially in different socio-economic groups. This social context is refocused through law into a matter of individual responsibility, justice and deterrence. Each act of crime is relocated from the social sphere, where crime is produced, to the individual criminal agent, who is left, in less than splendid isolation, to 'carry the can.' It is the consequences of this translation, which is also a repression, a refusal to see the individual as always-already social, that lie behind the dilemmas of legal justice and criminal law. What is suppressed always returns, and I traced the dilemmas produced as they surfaced and resurfaced across the terrain of criminal law's 'general part.'

This argument has an 'external' historical and sociological form that I still maintain, but I now want to develop it to include an 'internal point of view.' We need to understand the social and political functions that legal individualism fulfils, but we also need, as I have indicated, to understand the resonances of the legal individualist conception of justice, reflected, for example, in the struggles of prisoners to have the penal equation restored, or battered women to have their story acknowledged in and through legal categories. An 'external,' historical and structural approach is insufficient to understand the ambivalence we feel towards the legal conception of justice. Questions of judgment and justice are not just politico-historical effects of a particular social structure, they pose real existential questions for individuals and communities.[48] There is an issue of moral agency 'inside' the historical and structural questions as to how criminal law works, or does not work. The split between individual and social context is not only a structural decoupling in law and society, it is also present phenomenally for individuals as they negotiate the moral effects of their actions.

Selfhood and society

In short, after the historical and sociological critique of the inadequacies of criminal law and the penal equation, there remains a liberal, in effect Kantian, question to be asked: what does criminal *justice* mean for the individual?[49] But it cannot be answered in a Kantian way, for that would take us back into the false unity of the liberal subject. We need to explain how it is that our categories of judgment give rise to ambiguity and paradox. One way to do this is to draw upon the 'new psychology' of Rom Harré,[50] a founder of modern critical realism. Harré's approach can be introduced by a quotation which focuses on the ambiguity present in the psychological experience of personhood. This concerns a sense, stated at its strongest in what follows, of both being and not being in control of ourselves and our actions:

> On the one hand we feel we know all the facts that impinge upon us, and we seem to be in control of the actions we perform. We experience ourselves in one sense as being all-knowing and all-controlling. But at the same time life does not go as we want, and we do not understand why. Perhaps our conscious mind is not after all the strategic controller of the system, but just the middle manager of the mind, . . . subject to more compelling and longer patterns of authority.[51]

Harré is describing here the balance of personhood between a sense of self as autonomous, and the pervasive pull and push of social relations which create and undermine that sense. A more common way of experiencing this feeling may be in less black and white terms than Harré employs here, but the ambivalence we often feel as to how much we are in control of our lives hinges on the polarity Harré describes. In his account, the individual self is a project wrought out of social difference. Social and normative 'conversations' constitute the 'primary structure' of human life, since society always exists before the individual, who is delivered into, and develops a sense of being out of, a relationship to the social. Nonetheless, individual, personal being is a real phenomenon, for persons operate within a society that requires them to act as individual selves. The self is then a 'secondary' but necessary structure generated by, but differentiated from, the 'primary' social structure. Social relations are reproduced because persons exist both as role-playing individual agents and, more fundamentally, as selves. They are created out of a language, in some ways peculiar to modern societies, of individual biography, identity and capacity for action. This language creates the sense of being a self 'behind' the social roles that individuals perform, although, in Harré's account, the ability to be 'one's self' is intimately linked to, and generalised from, the ability to perform individual social roles.

Individual selfhood is real but inherently, dialectically, linked to the primary social structure through the playing of roles. The self is ambiguously sited between a sense of itself as autonomous and its location in social relations which produce and maintain it. This is illustrated, for example, in the uncomfortable sense that, while we feel in control of what we say or do, we sometimes appear only to speak the parts bequeathed to us by history and context. Thus, the child who vows never to speak to his children as his parents spoke to him is surprised to find as a parent the very same words coming out of his mouth. The self is always in relation, which amounts to saying that selfhood *is* a relation, at the same time as it understands itself as autonomous. Being a person involves being in relation to others in time and space, *and* denial of that relation. The denial is an existential presupposition stemming from the dualistic character of selfhood, for the act of denial (of sociality) is also an act of (individual) self-constitution. Mastering a language of selfhood, we become selves, although not without a sense of ambiguity. We feel in control but, every so often, realise we are not.

Selfhood, society and justice

This ambiguity translates into moral judgments of wrongdoing and a sense of justice. In ordinary moral life, we may follow a two-phase approach in which at first we are angry and seek to blame, and then later proceed to judge the person more 'in the round,' taking their circumstances and overall situation into account. We interpret what was done as part of a person's history which disposed them to actions of certain kinds regardless of their will. We 'explain' what they have done and, so doing, come to excuse them. In morally judging crime, we do something similar. Even in the most demonised cases like those of Rosemary West or Myra Hindley, we come to wonder how they could have done what they did. We do not do this in order to deny the sense of wrong in their acts, but we are led to wonder about their ultimate responsibility for them, no matter what the law's judgment may be. We also come to see the refusal to understand by those who unthinkingly condemn as itself a failure of human being.[52] Thus, our initial reaction of anger and condemnation is followed by a sense that the criminal was also a victim. So doing, we move from the sense of the individual as an autonomous agent (the law's view) to that of the person as a constructed social phenomenon.

But then, there is a further stage that is particularly significant and remarkable with regard to serious crimes. After the initial sense of anger and condemnation, and the second stage of contextual interpretation, we go back to the question of responsibility in a more considered way. How many are really satisfied, for example, with the sense that can be drawn from Myra Hindley's recent essay,[53] that the person who committed her crimes was 'another person' from the Hindley of today? There remains a sense of moral reckoning that corresponds to neither the immediate sense of responsibility (the sense employed by the law) nor the diffuse, contextualising approach to which I have also referred. It is a floating sense of what doing justice means, one that is hard to pin down. It operates in the space between what a person did and the ways in which that person was herself created, a dialectical space between conflicting alternatives, but a sense that is part of our lives as moral individuals and agents.[54]

Part of this sense involves living with and coming to terms with events in our pasts, even those that are long past. This deeper sense of responsibility is, accordingly, particularly seen in the case of serious crimes committed many years ago by someone such as Myra Hindley, and also in the current interest in prosecuting former Nazi war criminals. The past may be 'another country,' occupied by 'other people,' yet the sense of injustice that a denial of past responsibility evokes or the sense of justice that demands the trial of serious crimes done long ago is linked, I suggest, to the complexity in understanding what individual life is as both a socio-historical and a personal phenomenon. This sense of the need to come to terms with the past and to acknowledge responsibility is a more complex phenomenon than that of individual responsibility within the liberal theory of criminal justice, but it clearly shares common aspects at a superficial level. Both involve a focus upon the individual, but the sense in which I am interested more deeply interrogates the sense of what it means to be a person.

It is this sense of conscious agency and selfhood as real, yet ambiguous and double-sided, that I take from Harré, but we need to add significantly to it if we are to understand the working of a concept of justice with regard to the bulk of ordinary crime. Most crime mercifully lacks the horror of child killing or wartime atrocity, and therefore does not attract the broad and consensual condemnation that the latter does. Many forms of crime, most notably crimes against property, occupy a contested social space in which conflicting views of right and wrong coexist. Here, the 'normative conversations' in Harré's 'primary structure' are contradictory and competing. They give rise to different views of what is acceptable in social conduct and individual actions concerning, for example, the possibility of law-breaking.

Social consensus about wrongdoing may historically be possible, but it is always a produced, contingent and variable phenomenon, rather than inevitable in a society based upon deep-seated structural tensions.[55] This has a major impact on the sense of justice in a community and its individual members, and presents a fundamental challenge to any consensual interpretation of Harré's account of the relationship between selfhood and the social. The social conflicts within Harré's primary structure inform persons and their conduct, and are part of the raw material of selfhood. Because social and economic life is inegalitarian and conflictual, the actions of individuals are coloured by inequalities and conflicting moral standpoints. Thus we act as selves, as agents, as persons in control, but also as people located in structures that are in themselves inherently conflictual, and this adds a further layer of complexity into our explanations of the dualism, the contradictions, the paradoxes in our judgments of criminal wrongdoing.

Just deserts from one side is social injustice from another. There are always two sides to the question of criminal responsibility. The problem for law, for criminal justice, for the penal equation, is that it is one-sided in its treatment of people being in control. There is a double exclusion here: of the social conditions of selfhood and the structural conflicts which inform those conditions. Selfhood is real, but doubly conflicted — existentially and in terms of its location within the historical conditions of modern society. The penal equation does its work, but only by ignoring the moral import of these conflicts on our sense of justice.

Conclusion

But what could the criminal justice system make of this? This paper has developed some of the ideas which underlie an ambivalent attitude to the 'penal equation,' including some alternatives to it, which can be grouped under the umbrella of 'relational justice.' Whether it be mediation, reparation, reconciliation or diversion, non-custodial or intermediate treatment, there have been a number of attempts to break the 'penal equation' in favour of more 'relational' forms of justice. If we compare relational with criminal justice, the former might be seen as more appropriate in the light of the arguments advanced here. Relational justice involves a sense of the particularity of human life, a sense of social engagement, and a sense of responsibility that is contextualised both in terms of looking to the wrongdoer's past acts and their provenance, and to his relationship with a community that includes his victim. It returns the individual to the normative conversations out of which his agency emerged, offering the prospect of a reconciliation and a new beginning.[56]

Criminal justice, by contrast, remains stuck with a backward-looking and desocialising view of the role of punishment, particularly in so far as it relies on imprisonment. It also has a static conception of individual responsibility, in which the individual is indubitably in control, save in very tightly circumscribed exceptional situations. That sense of control is not an illusion. It is part of human agency, but it is partial. In a situation like provocation, we see this as battered women push to recognise a contextually sensitive account of how they act when they are provoked. The aim in developing the defence is to push against its abstract boundaries and make it recognise the moral and political context in which provoked women act. The law is being pushed beyond its abstract conception towards an approach which sees the nature and meaning of 'being in control' as more complex and ambivalent, but the movement is small and faltering.

Because the sense of being in control involves ambiguity, not simple illusion, the law still touches the subjective understanding of being a person. In situations involving the relationship between the individual and the state, this is extremely important. Laws which confine the liberty of the subject are precisely rules concerning the amount of control that the person has over his life *vis-à-vis* the police or the prison authorities. There is an irreducible existential basis to the demand for rights, because such a demand is a demand for control of oneself and one's conditions of life. This is not a matter of what is strategic, but a moral demand based upon the sense of being a person, even if we know that that sense is a more ambiguous one than liberal political theory allows. This is why law touches those who resist the discretionary powers of state officials, such as the Home Secretary, with regard to life sentences.

Can we move from these theoretical views directly to the kind of radical reform of the criminal justice system advocated by Blom Cooper?[57] An ambivalent view leads to caution. Liberal law gives us a conception of a rights-bearing subject at a price. The subject enjoys formal rights, to the extent that he does, in a trade-off. Formal rights exist within existing social and political arrangements. They allow subjects to speak, but in strictly limited terms. There is a political closure that relational forms of justice would begin to set loose, and it is this that I think condemns relational justice to operate in the margins of the social control system and to act only to ameliorate the main engine of social control, criminal justice and the criminal law.

But is this necessarily undesirable? In one way it is. Relational justice is less alienating, more morally expressive and developmental. Against this, criminal justice does in principle operate a system of rights, reflecting the idea of being in control of one's actions. If we were to move to a more relational approach, one that went behind the idea of the subject in control, would we not also be in danger of losing the defences relating to individual subjectivity that law in principle embodies? Nor is relational justice in any sense 'politically innocent.' Relational justice is itself an historical and social practice, a form of control in a society in which structural inequality has a profound effect on the criminal justice system. Moving beyond a formal system, it is potentially more invasive than law. If one likes the politics, one may accept the invasion, but there is a political choice to be made with its own consequences.

The picture of reform that emerges is a nuanced one. If radical changes are sought, we need to ask what their consequences will be in the light of a broad understanding of how law operates. We need a radical theory, one that can get to the roots of law. Such a theory must come to terms with the ambivalences that we experience in thinking about the penal equation. Holding in mind the overall relationship between legal justice and the structural social injustice within which the equation operates, such a theory must criticise the absences and failures, but also recognise the positive aspects of liberal legality. There are political choices to be made. It may push for recognition of the needs of disadvantaged groups where they are barred by the law's decontextualising: this is the import of the battered women and provocation debate. But it must be conscious that this is a political task and that, in the absence of the possibility of progressive change in the broader society, liberal legality itself involves a progressive agenda: this is the import of the juridical critique of arbitrary discretion in life sentences.

The upshot of this conclusion is to argue for a necessary but uneasy relationship between theory and practice. They operate at different, irreducible levels. Theory does not lead immediately to systematic practical conclusions, but that does not mean that it is irrelevant to practice or that it cannot illuminate it. In truth, practice can never escape theory. It is only a question of how adequate and explicit theory is. The argument of this paper has been that a contradictory and ambiguous phenomenon like law needs a theory sufficiently sophisticated to capture contradiction and ambiguity within legal forms without simply surrendering to it. Such a theory would treat law dialectically, in its 'external' structural aspect, as a contradictory social phenomenon which both reflects and refracts modern historical conditions, and in its 'internal' experiential aspect, as a set of categories with some purchase on the ways in which moral and political agents live their lives under such conditions.

Notes

1 Norrie, *Crime, Reason and History* (London: Butterworths, 1993) ch 10, esp pp 198–205. I argue there that retributive and deterrence theory have a common root in the individualism of Enlightenment ideology, and this accounts *mutatis mutandis* for the different problems both experience. My focus in this paper is on criminal law and justice, so the discussion will primarily relate to questions that are usually seen as being in their essence retributive.

2 Braithwaite, *Crime, Shame and Reintegration* (Cambridge: Cambridge University Press, 1989).

3 Burnside and Baker, *Relational Justice* (Winchester: Waterside Press, 1994). For a good summary of the contrasts and similarities between retributive and

reparative ideas, see Zedner, 'Reparation and Retribution: Are They Irreconcilable?' (1994) 57 MLR 228.

4 Blom Cooper, 'Social Control and Criminal Justice: An Unresponsive Alliance,' paper presented at the British Society of Criminology Conference 1995, 11.

5 Foucault, *Discipline and Punish* (Harmondsworth: Penguin, 1977).

6 Blom Cooper's only real proposal is for a return to the bipartisan political consensus on criminal justice issues which existed in the 1970s.

7 Ferri, *The Positive School of Criminology* (Chicago: Kerr, 1901).

8 Wootton, *Crime and the Criminal Law* (London: Stevens, 1963)

9 Hart, *Punishment and Responsibility* (Oxford: Clarendon, 1968).

10 Williams, *Criminal Law: The General Part* (London: Stevens, 1961); *Textbook of Criminal Law* (London: Stevens, 1983); Smith and Hogan, *Criminal Law* (London: Butterworths, 1992).

11 Ashworth, *Principles of Criminal Law* (Oxford: Oxford University Press, 1991).

12 Ashworth, *The Criminal Process* (Oxford: Oxford University Press, 1994); Sanders and Young, *Criminal Justice* (London: Butterworths, 1994).

13 American Friends Service Committee, *Struggle for Justice* (New York: Hill and Wang, 1971); Ashworth, 'Criminal Justice and Deserved Sentences' [1989] CLR 340; Murphy, *Retribution, Justice and Therapy* (Dordrecht: Reidel, 1979); Norrie, *op cit* n 1, pp 207–209; Norrie, *Law, Ideology and Punishment* (Dordrecht: Kluwer, 1991) chs 3, 9. In the latter, I argue for the historical continuity and intrinsic quality of this problem for liberal retributive theory.

14 *The Guardian*, 19 January 1996.

15 O'Donovan, 'Defences for Battered Women Who Kill' (1991) 18 JLS 219; McColgan, 'In Defence of Battered Women Who Kill' (1993) 13 OJLS 508; Horder, *Provocation and Responsibility* (Oxford: Oxford University Press, 1992).

16 Cohen, 'Guilt, Justice and Tolerance: Some Old Concepts for a New Criminology' in Downes and Rock (eds), *Deviant Interpretations* (Oxford: Martin Robertson, 1979) pp 35–41.

17 Norrie, *op cit* n 13.

18 In the contractarian tradition: Hobbes, *Leviathan* (Harmondsworth: Penguin, 1968); Beccaria, *Of Crimes and Punishments* (Oxford: Oxford University Press, 1964). See Norrie, *op cit* n 13, ch 2.

19 In the German idealist tradition: Kant, *The Metaphysical Elements of Justice* (Indianapolis: Bobbs Merrill, 1965); Hegel, *The Philosophy of Right* (Oxford: Oxford University Press, 1952). See Norrie, *op cit* n 13, chs 3–4.

20 Derrida, 'Force of Law: The "Mystical Foundation of Authority"' (1991) 11 Cardozo L Rev 919; Douzinas and Warrington, *Justice Miscarried: Ethics, Aesthetics and the Law* (Brighton: Harvester Wheatsheaf, 1995); Goodrich, *Oedipus Lex* (California: University of California Press, 1995).

21 Barron, 'The Illusions of the "I": Citizenship and the Politics of Identity' in Norrie (ed), *Closure or Critique: New Directions in Legal Theory* (Edinburgh: Edinburgh University Press, 1993).

22 Norrie, 'Closure and Critique: Antinomy in Modern Legal Theory' in Norrie, *op cit* n 21. Compare Cornell, *The Philosophy of the Limit* (London: Routledge, 1992), with Douzinas and Warrington, *op cit* n 20, ch 5, and the latter with the 'practical application' of a Levinasian approach in Lyotard, 'The Other's Rights' in Shute and Hurley (eds), *On Human Rights* (New York: Basic Books, 1993). The last mentioned piece appears indistinguishable from a liberal natural law approach.

23 Bhaskar, *A Realist Theory of Science* (Leeds: Leeds Books, 1975); *The Possibility of Naturalism* (Brighton: Harvester, 1979); *Reclaiming Reality* (London: Verso, 1989); Collier, *Critical Realism* (London: Verso, 1994); Outhwaite, *New Phil-*

osophies of Social Science (London: Macmillan, 1987). What follows is a necessarily limited and selective account of the realist argument.

24 Harré, *Personal Being* (Oxford: Blackwell, 1983); Harré, Clarke and de Carlo, *Motives and Mechanisms* (London: Methuen, 1985). Harré's work is considered below, pp 552–554.

25 Central to Bhaskar's argument is a strong distinction between epistemology and ontology. He is both an epistemological relativist and an ontological realist. His argument against much constructivist thinking is that it collapses these two domains, endorsing what he sees as a widespread 'epistemic fallacy' in Western thinking. See, for example, his discussion of the work of Rorty: Bhaskar, *Philosophy and the Idea of Freedom* (Oxford: Blackwell, 1991).

26 Bhaskar, *Dialectic: The Pulse of Freedom* (London: Verso, 1993). I develop what follows somewhat further with regard to law in Norrie, 'From Law to Popular Justice: Beyond Antinomialism' (1996) 5 *Social and Legal Studies*, pp. 383–404.

27 Bhaskar, *ibid* p 58.

28 *ibid* p 56.

29 Lacey, 'Closure and Critique in Feminist Jurisprudence: Transcending the Dichotomy or a Foot in Both Camps?' in Norrie, *op cit* n 21.

30 Abel, *The Politics of Informal Justice* (London: Academic Press, 1982); de Sousa Santos, *Special Issue on Popular Justice* (1992) 1 *Social and Legal Studies*; Merry and Milner, *The Possibility of Popular Justice* (Ann Arbor: University of Michigan Press, 1995). Discussion of such alternatives still requires substantial conceptual clarification: Norrie, *op cit* n 26.

31 *op cit* n 11, ch 5. This section draws on and develops the, in some ways more complete, argument in Norrie, *op cit* n 1, ch 4.

32 *op cit* n 11, p 132.

33 *Stephenson* [1979] QB 695.

34 [1981] 1 All ER 961.

35 Williams, 'Recklessness Redefined' (1981) 40 Cambridge LJ 252; Smith, 'Law Reform Proposals and the Courts' in Dennis (ed), *Criminal Law and Justice* (London: Sweet & Maxwell, 1987).

36 [1983] 2 All ER 1005.

37 *Caldwell* [1981] 1 All ER 961, 967.

38 Smith and Hogan, *Criminal Law* (London: Butterworths, 1988) p 67.

39 Williams, 'The Unresolved Problems of Recklessness' (1988) *Legal Studies* 74.

40 *Shimmen* (1986) 84 Cr App R 7. See also *Reid* [1992] 3 All ER 673.

41 Duff, *Intention, Agency and Criminal Liability* (Oxford: Blackwell, 1990) ch 7. My argument, however, is that there are fundamental social and political reasons which block the practical juridical development of Duff's position. See below pp 549–550, and Norrie, *op cit* n 1, pp 77–83.

42 Kenny, *Outlines of Criminal Law* (Cambridge: Cambridge University Press, 16th ed, 1902) p 186, cited in *Cunningham* [1957] 2 All ER 412.

43 *Fourth Report* (1839) XIX Parliamentary Papers, xxiv (emphasis added).

44 *Seventh Report* (1843) XIX Parliamentary Papers, 24.

45 The formulation of recklessness in cases like *Stone and Dobinson* [1977] 2 All ER 341 and *Satnam and Kewal* (1984) 78 Cr App R 149 can only be understood in terms of an imprecise reaching beyond the subjective and objective concepts available within the law towards a morally substantive approach. See Norrie, *op cit* n 1, pp 70–71.

46 It is significant that it was the issue of reckless rape that was instrumental in promoting a more critical perspective on the existing forms of recklessness. This resulted in large part from an emerging feminist consciousness in the 1970s that

the existing forms of recklessness did not reflect what many women regarded as acceptable sexual conduct. A similarly critical, and potentially innovative, reflection on the law's justice is being developed out of the experience of women who have endured domestic violence in the law of provocation.

47 Norrie, *op cit* n 1.

48 cf Norrie, 'Legal and Moral Judgment in the General Part' in McVeigh, Rush and Young (eds), *Criminal Legal Doctrine* (Aldershot: Dartmouth, 1997).

49 I develop this argument further in Norrie, '"Simulacra of Morality"? Beyond the Ideal/Actual Antinomies of Criminal Justice' in Duff (ed), *Philosophy and the Criminal Law* (New York: Cambridge University Press, 1998).

50 *op cit*, n 24.

51 Harré *et al.*, *op cit*, n 24, pp 24–5.

52 One must distinguish the reaction of families of homicide victims from the knee-jerk reaction of those who follow the tabloid press, although it seems to me that families are often not helped to live with their loss by the views of the latter.

53 *The Guardian*, 18 December 1995.

54 To say this is not to argue against Myra Hindley's parole, an issue once again in the news. Determination of her case should rest on existing agreed legal rules and criteria, according to which it seems she should now by rights be released.

55 Reiner, *The Politics of the Police* (Hemel Hempstead: Harvester Wheatsheaf, 2nd ed, 1992).

56 Although this may be highly constrained in practice by the political context within which relational forms of justice are introduced: Dignan, 'Reintegration through Reparation: A Way Forward for Restorative Justice?' (paper delivered at Fulbright Colloquium on Penal Theory and Penal Practice, University of Stirling, September 1992). The problem here relates to the danger from the criminal justice system's point of view that an emphasis on relationality would open up the moral and political issues of justice that are closed off by the abstract individualism of the penal equation.

57 *op cit* n 4.

28

BETWEEN STRUCTURE AND DIFFERENCE[1]

Law's relationality

Alan Norrie

In recent times, the critical impact of the sociology of law has been diminished as a consequence of the rise in popularity of poststructuralist analyses of law. Such analyses sometimes claim a more fundamental radicalism that they see as lacking in the treatment of law as a sociological phenomenon (Derrida 1990). They see themselves as insisting on a continuous deconstruction that would go beyond law's social and historical underpinnings to a deeper, never fixed, moment of proto-being and negativity in the confrontation with an unknown and unknowable 'other'. While helpfully challenging the false certainties that attend traditional ways of understanding law, ultimately this confrontation with alterity seems a blind alley. What is regarded as a virtue becomes a vice since deconstruction provides no position from which critique can be launched, no point or points from which it can measure and be measured. 'Otherness' becomes a black hole which sucks in critique without return, leaving its bearer either with existential pain or alternatively to resort to an unlicensed endorsement of what exists, a pragmatics of law and politics (Norrie 1996a).

The most damaging consequence of poststructuralism is that it relocates critical thinking on the terrain of the directly ethical, that is as a matter of unmediated moral choice. It fails to provide a point of purchase on what is socially and historically given, and therefore on what is socially and politically possible. As a biproduct of this unmediated ethicality, poststructuralism fails to provide a theoretical basis for an understanding of what is good as well as bad in a phenomenon such as law. The bipolar insistence on justice/injustice that stems from a 'messianic' concept of what an ultimate justice would entail leads to an inability to analyse in a nuanced way the *limits of*

Source: The Emergence of Law Through Economy, Politics and Culture, 1997, vol. 1, chap. 2, Oñati: International Institute for the Sociology of Law.

justice in the here and now. It is only if law is analysed as a social and historical phenomenon that such an analysis can be undertaken, because it is in the emergence of law from structure and history that we observe the moral and political positives and negatives that emerge from and attach to it (Norrie 1996a, 1996b).

In the wake of the poststructuralist attack, the sociology of law has soldiered on with important developments from classical positions (Hunt 1993; Cotterrell 1995), or with positions which draw on newer work. Hunt and Wickham (1994) have sketched a theory of law as governance after Foucault, and Teubner (1987; 1988) has developed the systems approach of Luhmann to provide an account of law as autopoietic. Yet this newer work has hardly yielded significant critical gains for the sociology of law. On the contrary, Hunt and Wickham premise their Foucaultian account on a modified version of Weber's definition of law, which they charitably describe as 'sociological', but which in reality represents no advance on nineteenth century legal positivism.[2] Similarly, autopoietic theory's insistence on the normatively closed character of the legal subsystem and its incommensurability with other subsystems suggests an *a priori* shutting off of law from its social and historical roots. What may be a social aspect of law's practice, its desire to see itself as formal (Fish 1993), becomes a theoretical premise of this sociology of law. While this approach may yield insights into the blindness of legal practice, it does so at the expense of instating a fundamentally unsociological premise at its heart (Norrie 1993b; 1997).

If poststructuralism has sought to reduce questions of law's social specificity, newer sociological approaches have responded by reintroducing conceptions of law that give it the same kind of autonomy as nineteenth century positivist and neo-Kantian (Norrie 1993b) theories. The need is to move beyond this particular Scylla and Charybdis to a position that is *neither sociologically reductive nor juridically essentialist.* This involves an approach that can combine a sense of law's specificity in particular social and historical periods with an insistence at the same time on its social relationality. Law is what it is, as it were, but it is also at the same time what it is not: it is a specific form (this is its 'difference' in my title) of historically constituted sociality (a creation of 'structured' social relations, again, in my title).

This seems no more than a conundrum: how can something both 'be' and 'not be' at the same time? To understand this sense of being-and-not-being, it is necessary to adopt a non-positivistic, non-analytical, *dialectical* sense of what terms such as 'being' and 'identity' mean. Now the idea of dialectic has been oft used and abused, and I do not wish here to explore its different possible meanings. In history and sociology, however, it may be employed to indicate the idea of a contemporaneous emergence of contradictory tendencies, and the idea of contradiction is central to what I wish to say here (see also Norrie 1996a; 1996b). But such an idea is underpinned *philosophically* by a view of how it is possible for a phenomenon to be at one and the same time posited and negated, and this entails a radical rethinking of notions such as those of being or identity. As Roy Bhaskar has put it, thinking dialectically involves

> break[ing] with our ordinary notions of identity . . . . It is to see things *existentially constituted*, and permeated, *by their relations with others*; and to see our ordinary notion of identity as an *abstraction* not only from their existentially constitutive processes of formation (geo-histories), but also from their existentially constitutive inter-activity (internal relatedness).
>
> (Bhaskar, 1993, 125)

Law, I will argue, must be understood as being existentially constituted by its relations with the society of which it is a part, such that a sense of its identity (as all too readily provided by positivist and neo-Kantian definitions) apart from those relations is, in the strongest of senses, inconceivable. Such an approach, I shall argue, is a key to reviving a theoretical basis for the sociology of law by permitting a sense of law's specificity in particular historical-relational contexts. This conception would refuse any dichotomisation of legal projects into either the 'internal' (the doctrinal) or the 'external' (the sociological and historical).[3]

In referring to work in the sociology of law, I have thus far failed to mention what is perhaps the most important recent contribution, the *magnum opus* of Boaventura de Sousa Santos. This is a monumental achievement in the sociology of law, and the motor of this paper is provided by a dialogue with certain of its central themes. The strength of this work is its recognition of the need to locate the analysis of different forms of law in a plurality of historical and structural sites. De Sousa Santos's aim is to provide an understanding of the *plurality* of legal forms which is the basis for a critique of the dominant positivist-analytical tradition in western legal theory. While sharing this basic vision, I will develop my argument by proposing two things against de Sousa Santos. First, I will contend that he fails to establish fully his critique of the positivist-analytical tradition because he is unable to grasp law's specificity (its *differentia specifica*) as a contradictory social form. He ultimately falls back into that tradition. This argument relates to de Sousa Santos's treatment of the form of law central to modernity, the law of what he terms the citizenplace, which will be the main focus of this paper. Second, I will argue that his account of the structures that 'secrete' law is too pluralistic for his own argument, but more importantly, it is inadequate for an understanding of law's structural creation. The scope of this paper is thus in one way much less ambitious than de Sousa Santos's immense project, but it tackles what I see as flaws at its core, at least the first of which drags it back onto the terrain of an old and bankrupt problematic from the point of view of the sociology of law.

I begin with a brief discussion of the appropriate relationship between a positivist-analytical conception of law and the sort of critical conception that I believe the sociology of law should seek to establish. This leads me into a discussion of de Sousa Santos's work. From there, I move to consider questions of the specificity of modern law (the law of the 'citizenplace'), and then to the relationship between the 'structuration'[4] of law and its specificity. I conclude briefly by describing laws, in the terminology of Roy Bhaskar (1993: 404), as 'uniquely laminated structurata' entailing their own internal/external relational modes of being.

For a sociological critique of positivist-analytical approaches

A primary problem for the sociology of law is to establish, from the point of view of a social science, its legal object of study, the definition of what it is to investigate. From one, in my view incorrect, standpoint, there is no problem. The sociology of law can simply take up from where orthodox positivist science of law has left off. It can use definitions that have been analytically deduced from the nature of legal practice, and proceed to build a sociological approach on this positivist foundation. The sociology of law thus benefits from the pre-existing development of positivist legal science, and serves indeed to supplement it. This is essentially the starting point, for example, of the Weberian approach and its derivatives mentioned above.

From a second point of view, it is a problem for the sociology of law that it develops in the footsteps of positivist science. The positivist theory of law is not an innocent creation which can be unproblematically supplemented by sociological analysis. On the contrary, positivist definitions are part of the *explanandum* for the sociology of law, and the historical fact that the sociology of law follows the positivist science of law is both a problem and a challenge. The problem is that one cannot simply take such a *committed* analysis for granted, while the challenge is to take positivism seriously as a social phenomenon in itself without endorsing it. That *in nuce* is the mistake of autopoietic theory. The theory of legal positivism/analytics must be analysed sociologically in the same way as any more immediately embedded or practical manifestation of law.

Some years ago, Neil MacCormick (1976) challenged the sociology of law to be serious about the definition of law. In response to a sociological paper which had declined to produce such a definition, MacCormick cogently argued that it was impossible for any science to embark upon an analysis of its declared object of study without at least some working definition of what that object of study was. Since legal positivism maintained a wealth of such definitions, this was the basis for a fruitful collaboration between sociology of law and legal positivism. While MacCormick acknowledged that legal positivism was an incomplete science, because it ignored the nature of law as a social institution, so too was the sociology of law unless it collaborated with legal positivism in establishing the definition of its object of study, law. The scene was set for collaboration between the two approaches to the nature of law.

Things, however, cannot be so easy. MacCormick's basic point about sociology of law's need for a working definition of its object of study is well taken, but there is a real problem in moving from that to the adoption of a positivist definition of law. Such definitions are *socially produced understandings of a social practice*, reflecting and rationalising the taken for granted world of those within the practice itself (Cotterrell 1983). They are what Roy Bhaskar (1979) has termed 'praxiologies', by which he means a theoretical account of a form of social agency which is tied to, and limited in its understanding by, the social practices it represents, informs and legitimates. In my own work on the criminal law, I have argued for such an understanding (Norrie 1993a). Seemingly adequate at the level of a particular practice (i.e. apparently adequate from the point of view of practitioners), praxiological knowledge of law may be inadequate at the level of social scientific analysis in exactly the same way as, for example, the religious knowledge of a priest would be to a sociologist of religion, or that of a cargo cult follower to an anthropologist. Praxiologies take the part represented by the practices they reflect to be the whole, and in so doing they may both ultimately obscure the whole and misrepresent the part. To give this parts/whole metaphor the three dimensionality it requires, one can say that law and legal practice constitute phenomena within a *structured social totality*. Analysed from the standpoint of totality, the particular self-understanding of the lawyer may prove both inadequate and misleading. It follows that it may require reconceptualisation from the point of view of a more totalising form of knowledge, such as that represented by social science.

Two illustrations of the pertinence of this argument may be given with regard to the sociology of law. The first concerns the question of legal plurality, cogently argued for by de Sousa Santos (1995). What are sociologists of law to make of forms of social control which fail to embody positivist tenets of law, and therefore fail to be described as 'legal', but which in context perform functions that might otherwise qualify as law? If we draw our definitions from the positivist-analytical tradition, we may foreclose our analysis of what law is by privileging one conceptualisation while denying others. Many social scientists have appreciated this point in their examination of so-called 'alternative modes of dispute resolution', or forms of popular justice. Yet, interestingly, it can be argued that despite the 'good intentions' of social scientists, their work has often been seriously flawed by their inability to move beyond traditional definitions of law derived from the positivist-analytical tradition.

Thus the legal pluralist literature often becomes embroiled in the debate about 'informalism', a debate which owes its provenance to the pre-existence of a concept of 'legal formalism' (Norrie 1996b). The latter concept is of course a product of the neo-Kantian philosophy of law associated with Kelsen and introduced into the sociology of law by Weber (Norrie 1993a). It is central to the 'practical' (i.e. praxiological) understanding of western law, but for that reason highly misleading as the basis for a definition of alternatives to such law. Such alternatives are better seen as 'differently formed' rather than 'informal'. They involve differently organised combinations ('architectonics') of form/content relations which are socio-politically shaped within particular historical contexts. In this they are no different from western forms of law and should be understood as such.

Following de Sousa Santos, one could argue for a plural conception of law, in which he identifies six different kinds of law relating to the six different structural sites that he identifies in capitalist societies: the *householdplace*, the *workplace*, the *marketplace*, the *communityplace*, the *citizenplace* and the *world-place*. His argument is that in capitalist societies, five of these structural sites are ignored in favour of the prioritisation of one, the 'citizenplace', and that this is achieved in part through the formulations of positivist legal theory which reflect and embody the one site while ignoring the others. A critical sociology of law therefore needs to look beyond the knowledge form that is prioritised within capitalist societies, the positive law of the citizenplace, if it is to adequately represent the plural phenomena of law. To this, I would only add that there is also a need to identify clearly the *differentia specifica* of law in these different contexts, a point which comes out of my second concern. This focuses down on the adequacy of traditional conceptions of law not to the legal field as a whole, i.e. across the six structural places, but to the coverage of that realm of law which the positivist-analytical tradition purports to describe: the law of the citizenplace in de Sousa Santos's term. The problem here concerns the ahistorical and non-relational quality of the positivist definition. The question I will pose in the next section, however, is whether de Sousa Santos provides us with a better method than that of positivist-analytical science.

The 'internal' and the 'external' in de Sousa Santos's critique

According to de Sousa Santos, whom I follow initially, but then depart from, the citizenplace 'is the set of social relations that constitute the "public sphere" and, in particular, the relations of production of the vertical political obligation between citizens and the state' (1995: 421). In the countries of the capitalist core, it is a place of democratic freedoms and legal guarantees, but these are limited in two ways. First, they are limited according to a broader conception of emancipation which de Sousa Santos identifies in the Enlightenment philosophy of Rousseau, for whom emancipation involves social equality as well as individual freedom, and the delegitimation of differences based on private property (1995: 71). The creation of the citizenplace 'allowed for the shifting of the global emancipatory promises of modernity to the promise of state democratisation', a much narrower approach. Second, the development of state democratisation, including the creation of state (positive) law, operated as an occlusory screen behind which despotic forms of social power could operate unhindered. From the time of the nineteenth century constitutional state

> *a more or less democratic state power* could *coexist* with more or less despotic forms of social power without the democratic nature of the political system being thereby questioned. Similarly, *the more or less democratic law of the state* could *coexist* with more or less despotic forms of nonstate law without the democratic nature of the official legal system being thereby questioned.
>
> (1995: 97, emphasis added)

Here de Sousa Santos rightly reveals the problematic character of a positivism that would prioritise one form of law and decontextualise it from its historical and relational context. We cannot understand the character of modern law unless we understand its relationship with other forms of power and social regulation and its emergence within a particular historical period. But I would want to propose an objection to de Sousa Santos's formulation, because it does not go far enough into the problem of modern law. His critique remains an *external* one, criticising modern law not *in itself*, but in its links with other forms of law and power. This is seen in the formulation I have just quoted (see where emphasis is added), where the problem of democratic law is portrayed as lying in its coexistence with other forms of power, not as something that is *intrinsic to it*. Consider also this formulation of the relationship between the positive law of the citizenplace and alternative forms of law and power:

> Capitalist societies are less democratic, *not because the law of the citizenplace is less than democratic*, but rather because this form of law, no matter how democratic, must *coexist* with five other forms of law that are more despotic, and operate in constellation with them.
>
> (1995: 450, emphasis added)

The problem for the 'not . . . less than democratic' law of the citizenplace is that it must always act in constellation with other forms of law. This means that its 'not . . . less than democratic' character is forever dragged down by its association with other more despotic forms with which it is forced to coexist. This leads de Sousa Santos into two types of formulation. In one, the law of the citizenplace is held up and contrasted with other types of law as the sphere of 'empowerment of civil society vis-à-vis the state' (1995: 98), while hiding the play of despotism elsewhere in the constellated social totality. This is in effect the old Weberian form-versus-substance antinomy given leftist clothing. It does little more than reflect the self-understanding of the lawyer of the citizenplace as regards her own practice of affirming civil and political rights (1995: 98). It rationalises a liberal legal politics and therefore is sociologically uncritical as regards law. In the other formulation, which is more critical, de Sousa Santos insists on the *constellatory* character of all legal practice, that is that law is always a *combination* of practices derived from the different structural sites. It is always, he says, more proper to speak of *inter*law and *inter*legality rather than of law and legality to indicate this constellatory legal miscegenation (1995: 464).

But this second formulation, though more aware of the difficulties of understanding law as a contradictory social form, retains the initial problem of *externality*. The idea of the intermixing of types of law is already on the basis of a conceptualisation of law that permits it a certain integrity. Concepts of 'law' and 'legality' are conceptually established prior to the admission of the problems of 'interlaw' and 'interlegality'. It seems to me that the legal positivist could say, with for example MacCormick (above), that de Sousa Santos has shown the need for broader legal formulations, but that he has not fundamentally undermined the positivist-analytical approach. The problem lies outside the law the positivist has chosen to examine. Perhaps s/he gives that law a false priority, perhaps s/he ignores its occlusive effects, perhaps s/he does not see the invasion of other legal forms, but broadening and opening out one's analysis does not require abandoning the initial starting point in a positivist-analytical conception. Indeed, it might be argued that de Sousa Santos ultimately supports the positivist analysis by revealing the historical importance of positive law, so long as one bears in mind the importance of other forms too. The sociology of law needs a more radical critique of the character of modern positive law if we are to avoid this rejoinder. We need a critique that penetrates the law of the citizenplace (and *mutatis mutandis* the law of the other structural sites, though I do not deal with those here), not one that only *juxtaposes*, even critically, such law(s) with each other.

A dialectical critique of law's specificity

I propose that we start with a critique of the concept of law *within* the citizenplace to show its dialectical relationality. My quest is for a relational critique of law and legality that explores the contradictions that *constitute* such concepts, before ever they are constellated with other social forms. I suggest a twofold line of attack. The first concerns the quest for a specific characterisation of the nature of law, a *differentia specifica*, of legal form in the citizenplace.[5] The second concerns a theoretical method for locating legal form(s) within structural contexts. These lines of attack are ultimately two sides of the same coin: the comprehension of law as a historically specific structuratum. Both start from a critique of de Sousa Santos's position. The first, on the *differentia* of legal form in the citizenplace, is dealt with in this section, the second, on structuration, in the following section.

One weakness of de Sousa Santos's work concerns his failure to recognise the critique of legal form and legal individualism associated with Marxism, especially with Pashukanis, and also with certain varieties of modern critical legal studies. There is a serious gap in his work when he writes that Marx 'tended to reduce politics and law to state action' (1995: 413), maintaining that he failed to see that '"economic relations" were not only social, but also distinctively political and legal relations in their structural constitution' (1995: 413, see also 450). He cites in support of this argument the work of Poulantzas from the school of French structural Marxism, concerning whom his criticism is valid. He fails, however, to recall those sections of the *Grundrisse* and *Capital* in which Marx wrote of the contrast between the spheres of exchange and production, and the interplay between legal, political and ideological images and practices derived from, and assisting in the constitution of, these spheres. In particular, Marx wrote of the sphere of exchange as generating and necessitating the modern conception of the juridical individual. Pashukanis developed these comments into a theory of law and Marxism, which, while terse and introductory, said sufficient to establish the importance of these ideas and this approach for thinking about law and modernity. Much of what de Sousa Santos says, for example, about the 'second phase' of modern legal development (1995: 76–82), the phase of the increased social role of the state, was already anticipated in passages in Pashukanis's work (e.g. Pashukanis 1978: 129–130).

This tradition is relatively well known within the sociology of law, though relatively neglected in recent years (but see Cotterrell 1995; 1996). It reappears in different, and, in my view, less critical guise in the communitarian/critical legal studies literature of the 1970s and 1980s, where once again an emphasis was placed on the abstract individualism of the classical liberal theory of law. Now, de Sousa Santos acknowledges (compare 1995: 77, 98) that individual rights are central to the law of the citizenplace, and therefore to the conception of modern law as a sphere of formal rational activity. Yet his critique of modern law remains curiously blind to the *problems* of individualism at its core. The superficial logic of modern law, in its nineteenth century first phase, was a logic of individual freedom and obligation, and of citizens' rights. The problem for legal formalism was that this individualist logic was tied to particular social and political (normative) contents, and therefore developed out of and within a sphere of contested social and political issues.

The juridical individual represented in liberal discourse was a site of freedom and emancipation as de Sousa Santos notes. It also entailed, however, as the postcolonial literature reminds us (Fitzpatrick 1996), a *suppression* of alternative political and ideological views *in the name of individual freedom.*

And, as Freud reminds us in another context, what is suppressed always returns to disrupt, so that the work of lawyers became not the value free deduction of what was logically entailed from neutral premises, or the application of validly deduced rules to the determination of particular factual situations. Rather, lawyering became artificial 'boundary maintenance work', in which rules were constructed, developed and repaired in order to uphold a particular conception of social and political life against alternatives. Thus, taking my examples from the criminal law (Norrie 1993a; 1996b), a formal rational deduction of the rules of responsibility was constantly challenged by the fact that a central contradiction existed between a conception of the individual as a free responsible agent in himself, and a conception of criminal activity as socially generated and reflecting different moral and political values. Abstract legal categories, such as those of *mens rea* and *actus reus*, were means of constituting a responsible 'free' individual subject, but this subject was established on the site of socio-political conflict. The contradiction between abstract individualism and social conflict represents the historical crucible of legal doctrine, and is introjected within that doctrine. Law constantly wrestles with this contradiction, disrupting its positive-analytical logic. The construction of a historically constituted subject *qua* legal individual, the specific phenomenal form of the law of the citizenplace in its 'first phase', involved a socio-political intervention within a history of conflicting social relations, and that history left its indelible mark on law.[6]

A more radical critique of law in the citizenplace would start from the unstable and contradictory core that is constituted by the socio-political (il)logic of the juridical individual. Such instability renders positive legal science's quest for logical purity chimerical. Liberal lawyers and legal theorists in the positivist-analytical tradition construct a mythical sense of their practice as internally coherent. This is precisely the image of law that a sociological critique must problematise. The abstract juridical individual at the core of this problem in both liberal political and legal positivist theory, which are the twin embodiments of the theory of the citizenplace, is the central concept in an approach which upholds the possibility of logic and coherence, of formal rationality. To turn this around, legal formalism, the possibility of a formal and rationally deduced legal code, is based upon legal form, the form of the juridical individual. The problem is that this essential legal form is the site of intrinsic conflict. It is constructed out of denial, it is the place of a suppression, where irreconcilable socio-political forces meet. Accordingly, any logic constructed on its basis will be a logic which also embodies denial, suppression and conflict. The law of the citizenplace, before ever it confronts alternative places of law, is already a site of confrontation. Abstract individualism in legal theory is its embodiment and failed displacement. Before we talk of interlaw or interlegality, the mixing of different kinds of law, we should talk of law's dialectical relationality, meaning the internal/external conflictual structure of the classical legal form of the citizenplace.

If we interrogate law in this way, what are the implications? Law's 'molecular' structure, by which I mean its contradictory combinations of form and content, means that it is incomprehensible conceptually unless it is located dialectically within a social context. Law's specificity is, in other words, the specificity that a particular history *genetically engineers*. The conflictual character of social relations are expressed in and through law, even if traditional legal theorists spend all their time denying that this is the case through the explanation of law as a formal rational institution. The starting point for the sociology of law must therefore be the connection between what law claims that it is, but is not, an internally regulated, self-reflexive, formally rational system, and what law claims that it is not, but is, an engaged and contradictory practice inseparable from the social and historical forces which operate by and through it. The law 'wishes to have a formal existence' (Fish 1993), but in order to do so, it must deny its inability to stand by itself, that is its *syncategorematic* character. Legal places are social places, and law's contradictory inheritances and existences are to be read *symptomatically*, in terms of the contradictory social structures that they instantiate.

The structural context of law's relationality

This approach raises important questions not just about law, but about the relationship between law and social structure, and about how we are to understand the articulation between and within social structures. Here too I want to challenge de Sousa Santos's account. As we have seen, he operates with a conception of legal plurality, where law is spread across six different structured places: the householdplace, the marketplace, the workplace, the communityplace, the citizenplace and the worldplace. These six structural places generate different forms of agency: gender and generation, consumership, class activity, ethnicity, nationality and religion, citizenship and nationstatecraft. What is the relationship between structures? For de Sousa Santos, it is an open one in which no primacy can be given to one kind of structural determination over another:

> In abstract, none of the structural places separately establishes more or more important limits than the other. The six structural places taken together as constellations of social actions establish the horizon of determination, the outer structural limits of social life in capitalist societies. Within the structural limits there is a sea of contingency.
> (1995: 442)

This is a plea for a pluralist conception of structure in which 'concrete social action, agency is always a constellation of some or all the different forms of agency' (1995: 442) engendered by the different structural places. In this conception of a 'plurality of partial structures', 'social fields are played out in open-ended contingency and indeterminate social relations, insusceptible . . . of being explained by causal primacies . . .' (1995: 443), and 'assessments of relative importance even among "important causes" are unsustainable' (1995: 445). The analytical focus therefore 'turns to the identification and enumeration of important factors (the six structural places) rather than to their rankings' (1995: 445) because 'no asymmetries, hierarchies or primacies can be established in general . . .' (1995: 446).

This raises fundamental theoretical issues to which I must allude, but which cannot be attended to in the depth they require. Ultimately, one is forced back to questions in the philosophy of science concerning the status of knowledge about real causal structures that underpin the phenomenal forms of social experience. De Sousa Santos establishes a position against such realism in the first chapter of his work, which he then invokes in favour of his structural pluralism argument later. There, he writes that our increasing awareness of 'the bankruptcy of realist epistemology' makes us realise that 'facts and theories simply represent different perspectives and different degrees of vision within the same epistemological field' (1995: 444). From this point of view, any emphasis on causal analysis is likely to be misplaced because such analysis can 'only signal theoretical preferences in intelligible ways'.

From my own point of view, I think he overstates here, as he does in his first chapter, the nature of the crisis of scientific knowledge and realist forms of knowledge. While he is correct to challenge what he describes as 'realist *epistemology*' from a constructivist standpoint, he ignores the important school of realist thought that distinguishes between questions of epistemology and questions of *ontology* (Bhaskar 1979). While the produced character of all scientific knowledge, natural and social, reveals the essential problem in establishing epistemological forms of realism, it is still possible to maintain a distinction between the ways that knowledge is produced and the character of the world which knowledge seeks to represent and explain. This is one central point, for example, in the work of Roy Bhaskar, for whom de Sousa Santos's position would be a perfect example of what he calls 'the epistemic fallacy', that is the reduction of questions about the world to questions as to what we can know about it. This distinction is relevant *mutatis mutandis* to both the 'natural' and the 'social' world (Bhaskar 1979; 1993).

While not wishing to pursue this point further here, it is important to signal the philosophical backdrop to a less sceptical approach to questions of structure and causality. At one level, de Sousa Santos is absolutely right in arguing that action (which includes legal action) is 'always a constellation of some or all the different forms of agency' made possible by the constellation of structures. Indeed, all that I would query at one level is the use of the words 'some or' in this formulation, since the interconnections between structures are omnipresent and their information of agency is therefore complete, even where it is not apparent on the surface of social life. Yet I do not see the necessity of moving from this observation of the plurality of structures to the need to discard a conception of 'structural depth' which would enable us to understand the *articulation* of structures (their *structured* constellation) in a less plural way. Indeed, it seems to me that this is required by de Sousa Santos's own practice, no matter what his theory may say. There is a contradiction in his position when he writes, consistently with his overall argument but inconsistently with his proclaimed pluralism, that

> The development of *capitalist* societies and the *capitalist* world system as a whole are grounded on . . . constellations [of the six structural places], and not on any one of the structural places individually.
>
> (1995: 446, emphasis added)

If the conclusion from the observation of a plurality of structures is a structural pluralism, why refer to the overall development as being one of *capitalist* societies? Why consistently use this concept over, say a concept based on gender, nationality or citizenship as the organising concept in his argument? Could any other have been used, or is it not the case that de Sousa Santos sees these other concepts as important, but given their specific *modus operandi* by their location within capitalism? This certainly seems to be the case in relation to the citizenplace, with regard to which he writes that

> As *capitalism* became the exclusive development model of modern societies, most social relations could not possibly be governed according to the radical democratic claims of modernity. Indeed . . ., *in some social fields, capitalism would necessarily generate* despotic social relations . . . .
>
> (1995: 446, emphasis added)

One might provocatively suggest, following the title of his book, that 'common sense' has prevailed over theoretical protocol here, for such views appear to undermine his own pluralistic conception of structural determination.

In sum, it is important to hold onto de Sousa Santos's conception of the constellatory character of legal forms produced across a variety of structural spaces, but it is necessary to understand, first, the ways in which structural conflict inheres *within* those different forms, rather than being seen as the meshing of different legalities which enjoy a certain completeness in themselves, were it not for the existence of others. The conflicts of law are more endogenous than the formulation of interlaw and interlegality permits. Second, the relationship between legal forms and social structures is central, because it is the conflicts within and between structures and the relations they enable that generates the relationality which pervades legal forms. However, the acknowledgement of this point then necessitates serious thought about the articulation of structures, and here it seems that de Sousa Santos's formulation of an open equivalent articulation of structures can not reflect his own totalising conception of modern society as 'capitalist'. In place of such an approach, I think we need a more complex conception of the ways in which structures are themselves structured or articulated. We should conceive of law's social crucible as, in Bhaskar's description, 'an articulated ensemble of . . . relatively independent and enduring generative structures; that is, as a complex totality subject to change both in its components and their interrelations' (1979, 48).

Law between structure and difference

Such an articulated ensemble of structures constitutes a social totality, within which a concept of the dialectical relationality of social forms helps us understand the ways in which a phenomenon such as law maintains a practical sense of its self (a positivist self image), which is at the same time inaccurate, incomplete and misleading. I raised this point at the beginning through my discussion of a praxiological conception of law, and have now furnished the bones of a theoretical methodology to locate it. I now want to conclude by making two points about relationality, structure and law. The first point gives a theoretical underpinning to what has been said. As I argued at the beginning, the aim of grasping law as the product of relations within and between structures in a social totality is to see law as '*existentially constituted*, and permeated, *by {its} relations with others*' (Bhaskar 1993: 125). This involves a notion of identity that is entirely different from that available to positivist and analytical traditions of jurisprudence. It is also different from any sociological approach to law which draws on positive-analytical protocols.

This is a key theoretical point which links with the conception of dialectics that, drawing on Bhaskar (1993), I have outlined here and elsewhere (Norrie 1996b). From this point of view, a second point about law can be made. Law can be seen as the embodiment of complexly articulated structures. Bhaskar describes one such phenomenon as a 'structuratum', meaning

> a concrete individual or singular, which will normally be the condensate of, or of the effects of, a multiplicity of disjoint, and even contradictory, structures or of their ways of acting . . . . [A structuratum] will characteristically remain heteronomously conditioned, dependent upon and influenced by the levels out of which it has emerged, even where it is causally efficacious on them . . . .
>
> (1993, 50)

Such a conception is entirely appropriate to the understanding of law. Forms of laws, located in articulated sets of social structures, expressing the relations within and between those structures, and therefore thoroughly imbued with a relationality that orthodox theories seek to deny, can be seen, in the plural, as 'uniquely laminated structurata' (1993, 404). Such an idea, however, constitutes only one side of the story. It clearly needs to be filled out to give a sense of the internal relations within particular legal fields (or structurata). It provides a shaping context and set of conditions for talking about legal systems in different times and places, but it does not do away with the need to chart the character of the internal relations which contexts and conditions generate, and the ways in which in turn such internal relations express and mediate their structural locations. Elsewhere I have used the idea of *legal architectonics* to encapsulate the sense of internal relations that are at the same time historically and structurally 'laminated' (Norrie 1996b). Such architectonics are of course variable depending upon their different structural contexts. It is this internal/external location of law that allows us to compare and contrast different forms of regulation. It is precisely the use of orthodox positivist-analytical protocols for understanding law that have in the past obstructed this comparative project. As indicated above, I have argued this elsewhere with regard to the treatment of 'popular justice' as necessarily inferior to western-style 'formal' law (Norrie 1996b).

I conclude by returning to my starting point, the relationship between law as a reflexive, self-proclaimedly self-referential, science and law as an object of analysis for social science. The conception of law's relationality, linked to the idea of its contradictory structuration, provides the basis for a social and historical approach to legal analysis which treats the traditional positivist-analytical ideas of legal science as theoretically impossible. Hence, if these ideas enjoyed considerable acclaim in the nineteenth century, and no doubt still do today, then we must look elsewhere for reasons for this than in terms of the cogency of the ideas that sustain them. Where could we look? This paper has already suggested an answer: to their historical and social provenance, and thence to the practices within a particular society that they uphold, as well as those they suppress. A positivist-analytical conception of law is upheld by the social practices that it underpins, which in turn arise from the social structures that provide the spaces for such practices. The aim of the sociology of law should be to understand the relationality between legal practices, social practices and social structures. Since all three are interlinked elements within a contradictory historical totality, a grasp of this fact vindicates the sociology of law and counsels against even a thinking acceptance of positivist-analytical protocols. Such a methodology also points the way to a critical sociological understanding of law that, drawing on dialectics, avoids the 'devil' of substantiating a positivist-analytical conception of legal autonomy and the 'deep blue sea' of a reductionist or nihilistic approach.

Notes

1 Paper presented at Oñati International Institute for the Sociology of Law, Summer Course, on 'The Emergence of Law Through Economy, Politics and Culture', 1–5 July 1996.

2 The Weberian starting point is as follows (Hunt and Wickham 1994: 99): 'An order will be called law if it is externally guaranteed by the probability that coercion (physical or psychological), to bring about conformity or avenge violation, will be applied by a staff of people holding themselves specially ready for that purpose.' For a more fruitful engagement with Foucault, see Fitzpatrick (1992).

3 For 'practical' attempts to break down such a distinction in the context of the philosophy of punishment, see Norrie 1991, and in the context of criminal law doctrine, see Norrie 1993a. The latter work is more self-conscious about what it is doing.

4 For one well-known concept of structuration, see Giddens (1979). For a critique of Giddens from a critical realist position, see Archer (1996).

5 Singular here because I am concentrating on the law of the citizenplace, and the central form of that law, the law of its first, individualist, phase in de Sousa Santos's terms. These forms retain greater significance than his 'crisis of modernity' thesis allows in my view.

6 On the basis of this first contradiction, a second emerged in legal thinking, between 'the individual' and 'the state'. Such a division is of course better known to lawyers. In the criminal law, it takes the form of a contradiction between a logic of individual responsibility and a logic of state control (between 'law' and 'public policy'). (But it must be remembered that it is the form of expression at the level of legal experience of deeper conflicts that generated a 'legal individual' who would stand 'against' a 'state'). Put together, these two contradictions generate a situation in which the logic of the law, the logic of individual right, is constantly disrupted and unstable, so that claims to formal rationality are seriously undermined.

Bibliography

Archer, M (1995) *Realist Social Theory: the Morphogenetic Approach* (Cambridge, Cambridge University Press)

Bhaskar, R (1979) *The Possibility of Naturalism* (Brighton, Harvester)

Bhaskar, R (1993) *Dialectic: the Pulse of Freedom* (London: Verso)

Cotterrell, R (1983) 'English Conceptions of the Role of Theory in Legal Analysis' *Modern Law Review* 46, 81

Cotterrell, R (1995) *Law's Community* (Oxford, Oxford University Press)

Cotterrell, R (1996) 'The Rule of Law in Transition: Revisiting Franz Neumann's Sociology of Legality' *Social and Legal Studies* 451–470

Derrida, J (1990) 'Force of the Law: the Mystical Foundation of Authority' *Cardozo Law Review* 11, 919

De Sousa Santos, B (1995) *Toward a New Common Sense* (New York, Routledge)

Fish, S (1993) 'The Law Wishes to have a Formal Existence' in A Norrie (ed) *Closure and Critique: New Directions in Legal Theory* (Edinburgh, Edinburgh University Press)

Fitzpatrick, P (1992) *The Mythology of Modern Law* (London, Routledge)

Fitzpatrick, P (1996) (ed) *Law and Postcolonialism*, *Social and Legal Studies* Special Issue, 5(3)

Giddens, A (1979) *Central Problems in Social Theory* (London, MacMillan)
Hunt, A (1993) *Explorations in Law and Society* (London, Routledge)
Hunt, A and G Wickham *Foucault and Law* (London, Pluto)
MacCormick, D N (1976) 'Challenging Sociological Definitions' *British Journal of Law and Society* 3, 88
Norrie, A (1991) *Law, Ideology and Punishment* (Dordrecht, Kluwer)
Norrie, A (1993a) *Crime, Reason and History* (London, Butterworth)
Norrie, A (1993b) 'Closure and Critique: Antinomy in Modern Legal Theory' in A Norrie (ed) *Closure and Critique: New Directions in Legal Theory* (Edinburgh, Edinburgh University Press)
Norrie, A (1996a) 'The Limits of Justice: Finding Fault in the Criminal Law' *Modern Law Review* 59, 540–556
Norrie, A (1996b) 'From Law to Popular Justice: Beyond Antinomialism' *Social and Legal Studies* 5 (3)
Norrie, A (1997) 'Critical Legal Studies' in D N MacCormick and B Brown (eds) *The Philosophy of Law* (*Routledge Encyclopaedia of Philosophy*) (London, Routledge)
Pashukanis, E (1978) *General Theory of Law and Marxism* (London, Ink Links)
Teubner, G (1987) '"Juridification": Concepts, Aspects, Limits, Solutions' in G Teubner (ed) *Juridification of Social Spheres* (Berlin, de Gruyter)
Teubner, G (1988) (ed) *Autopoietic Law: a New Approach to Law and Society* (Berlin, de Gruyter)

INDEX